Short-Term Financial Management

Short-Term Financial Management

SECOND EDITION

TERRY S. MANESS

Baylor University

JOHN T. ZIETLOW

Mount Vernon Nazarene College

SOUTH-WESTERN
™
THOMSON LEARNING

Australia • Canada • Mexico • Singapore • Spain

United Kingdom • United States

SOUTH-WESTERN
THOMSON LEARNING ™

Finance Editor: Mike Reynolds
Development Editor: Elizabeth Thomson
Editorial Assistant: Lauren Feldman
Marketing Manager: Charlie Stutesman
Project Manager, Editorial Production: Barrett Lackey
Permissions Editor: Linda Blundell
Production Service: Graphic World Publishing Services
Photo Researcher: Marcy Lunetta
Copy Editor: Graphic World Publishing Services
Cover Image: Graphic World Publishing Services
Cover Printer: R.R. Donnelley Willard TLM
Compositor: Graphic World Publishing Services
Printer: R.R. Donnelley Willard TLM

COPYRIGHT © 2002 Thomson Learning, Inc.
Thomson Learning™ is a trademark used herein
under license.

ALL RIGHTS RESERVED. No part of this work
covered by the copyright hereon may be reproduced
or used in any form or by any means—graphic,
electronic, or mechanical, including but not limited to
photocopying, recording, taping, Web distribution,
information networks, or information storage and
retrieval systems—without the written permission of
the publisher.

Printed in the United States of America
1 2 3 4 5 6 7 05 04 03 02

For more information about our products,
contact us at:

**Thomson Learning
Academic Resource Center
1-800-423-0563**

For permission to use material from this text,
contact us by:
Phone: 1-800-730-2214
Fax: 1-800-730-2215
Web: http://www.thomsonrights.com

ISBN: 0-03-031513-1
Library of Congress Catalog Card Number:
2001088998

Asia
Thomson Learning
60 Albert Street, #15-01
Albert Complex
Singapore 189969

Australia
Nelson Thomson Learning
102 Dodds Street
South Melbourne, Victoria 3205
Australia

Canada
Nelson Thomson Learning
1120 Birchmount Road
Toronto, Ontario M1K 5G4
Canada

Europe/Middle East/Africa
Thomson Learning
Berkshire House
168-173 High Holborn
London WC1 V7AA
United Kingdom

Latin America
Thomson Learning
Seneca, 53
Colonia Polanco
11560 Mexico D.F.
Mexico

Spain
Paraninfo Thomson Learning
Calle/Magallanes, 25
28015 Madrid, Spain

Short-Term Financial Management

SECOND EDITION

TERRY S. MANESS

Baylor University

JOHN T. ZIETLOW

Mount Vernon Nazarene College

SOUTH-WESTERN

THOMSON LEARNING

Australia • Canada • Mexico • Singapore • Spain
United Kingdom • United States

SOUTH-WESTERN
TM
THOMSON LEARNING

Finance Editor: Mike Reynolds
Development Editor: Elizabeth Thomson
Editorial Assistant: Lauren Feldman
Marketing Manager: Charlie Stutesman
Project Manager, Editorial Production: Barrett Lackey
Permissions Editor: Linda Blundell
Production Service: Graphic World Publishing Services
Photo Researcher: Marcy Lunetta
Copy Editor: Graphic World Publishing Services
Cover Image: Graphic World Publishing Services
Cover Printer: R.R. Donnelley Willard TLM
Compositor: Graphic World Publishing Services
Printer: R.R. Donnelley Willard TLM

COPYRIGHT © 2002 Thomson Learning, Inc.
Thomson Learning™ is a trademark used herein
under license.

ALL RIGHTS RESERVED. No part of this work
covered by the copyright hereon may be reproduced
or used in any form or by any means—graphic,
electronic, or mechanical, including but not limited to
photocopying, recording, taping, Web distribution,
information networks, or information storage and
retrieval systems—without the written permission of
the publisher.

Printed in the United States of America
1 2 3 4 5 6 7 05 04 03 02

For more information about our products,
contact us at:

**Thomson Learning
Academic Resource Center
1-800-423-0563**

For permission to use material from this text,
contact us by:
Phone: 1-800-730-2214
Fax: 1-800-730-2215
Web: http://www.thomsonrights.com

Asia
Thomson Learning
60 Albert Street, #15-01
Albert Complex
Singapore 189969

Australia
Nelson Thomson Learning
102 Dodds Street
South Melbourne, Victoria 3205
Australia

Canada
Nelson Thomson Learning
1120 Birchmount Road
Toronto, Ontario M1K 5G4
Canada

Europe/Middle East/Africa
Thomson Learning
Berkshire House
168-173 High Holborn
London WC1 V7AA
United Kingdom

Latin America
Thomson Learning
Seneca, 53
Colonia Polanco
11560 Mexico D.F.
Mexico

Spain
Paraninfo Thomson Learning
Calle/Magallanes, 25
28015 Madrid, Spain

ISBN: 0-03-031513-1
Library of Congress Catalog Card Number:
2001088998

This book is dedicated to

My wife Nancy, son David,
and daughter Amy

T.S.M

My wife Kathy, and
daughters Julie and Christy

J.T.Z.

PREFACE

As we continue to teach and learn more about the area of short-term financial management, we are more convinced than ever about the importance of this area of financial management for our students. These feelings are confirmed by the increasing number of business schools offering course work in this area, by continued discussions with corporate practitioners, and by surveys indicating the amount of time that financial managers spend in this area. We also note, as many adopters have reminded us, that most finance students will do mostly short-term finance assignments when they go to work.

Over the years we have taught short-term financial management as a separate course or as a topic within other finance courses and have found that both undergraduate and MBA interest in this subject continues to grow. Numerous colleges and universities, including our own, have split the upper-level financial management curriculum into two courses, one of which is titled Working Capital Management, Short-Term Financial Management, Advanced Finance, Topics in Finance, or Financial Management II. Topics covered in these courses typically include all or many of the following topics: liquidity analysis; inventory, credit, and payables management; cash collection, concentration, and disbursement systems; cash forecasting; short-term investing, borrowing, and risk management; and finally, treasury information systems. We strongly believe that many important corporate decisions relate specifically to these short-term topics and that many of these topics are likely to grow in importance in the twenty-first century. Already, as one widely publicized study found, financial managers spend more than one-half of each day managing current assets and liabilities.

Although several other fine textbooks address the topic of short-term finance, we have not found them to be completely adequate across the board. Most courses currently require additional coverage of treasury and working capital management. Several key topics that need to be addressed more thoroughly include: bank selection and relationship management, credit management, short-term investing and borrowing, and treasury management information systems. Several texts include spotty coverage of the core cash management topics, and in our view, none have adequately utilized the cash flow timeline as an integrating focus. Others fail to incorporate shareholder value maximization as an overriding decision criterion. Finally, we have found that the books were either written at too high a level, making them difficult to use in an upper-level undergraduate course or MBA-level course, or oriented too much toward practitioners. Practical aspects are important, as is an analytical approach to the subject.

Coverage

This textbook is appropriate for upper-level undergraduate finance courses in financial management, intermediate financial management, short-term financial management, working capital management, treasury management, and cash management. It is also addressed to MBA-level financial management and short-term financial management courses, and we have included several cases and appendices that are especially attractive to upper-level undergraduate and MBA courses. Students should have completed an introductory corporate finance course as a prerequisite. It also serves as an excellent supplemental source for practitioners and students preparing to take the Certified Cash Manager (CCM) exam.

We have titled the book *Short-Term Financial Management* for two reasons. First, although we cover most of the topics of treasury management, we do not address long-term financing and pension issues that are part of that field. Second, we include current liability management, bank relationship management, and risk management issues, implying that much more than working capital management or cash management is included here. Nevertheless, we are confident that treasury department practitioners and those preparing for the CCM exam will find the material they need within our presentation. We both hold the CCM credential and continue to stay alert to new developments in the treasury management field.

We believe that the following strengths characterize our book:

Broader and better-integrated coverage of treasury and working capital management. Not only are core cash management concepts covered with adequate detail, but the text also uses valuation and the cash flow timeline as integrating themes. In-depth coverage is provided for credit management, bank selection and relationship management, and interest rate risk management. Furthermore, we provide coverage of inventory management, treasury management, information systems, and international treasury management. Two chapters on short-term investments and one chapter each on cash forecasting and short-term borrowing fill out the topical coverage.

Reader interest is captured by using a lucid writing style with a decision-making emphasis including numerous real-world examples and management decision dilemmas, which are solved later in the chapter. Text-integrating cases help the student put seemingly unrelated topics together. We also provide a special chapter on short-term financial modeling in order that interrelationships in cash, inventory, credit, payables, investments, and borrowing will be driven home. Reader interest and retention is also aided by chapter-beginning objectives. Survey evidence of state-of-the-art financial management practices is included throughout the text, along with footnote or end-of-chapter citations for readers wishing to review the empirical findings in greater detail. New to this edition, we also offer web sites at the end of each chapter that may be used to supplement chapter material or as a basis for web-based homework assignments.

Up-to-date presentations with the most recent developments in treasury management, banking deregulation, globalization of financial services delivery, and electronic ordering and payment. The reader will also find carefully incorporated sections on recent developments, such as electronic commerce (EC) and international cash management. We offer integrated sections in almost every chapter focusing on the international aspects of that topic, and for those desiring more, we have included an entire chapter on international cash management with a heavy focus on managing foreign exchange risk.

Cohesive organization is used throughout the text. Part I includes an introduction to working capital management and material on liquidity analysis and valuation concepts. Part II focuses on working capital management including credit and receivables, inventory, payables, and accruals. We provide thorough coverage of the payment system in Part III, which provides the infrastructure for developing cash collection, concentration, and disbursement systems. Part IV includes two chapters focusing on cash forecasting and financial modeling. Part V provides coverage of the short-term financial market environment along with the development of short-term investment and borrowing strategies. This part also includes a chapter on managing multinational cash flows. Part VI concludes with discussions of financial risk management, electronic data interchange, and treasury management information systems.

Problem-solving skill enhancement is provided through the numerous end-of-chapter questions and problems as well as the cases. The questions enable students to test their understanding of chapter concepts and relationships, and the problems require students to demonstrate understanding of each chapter's decision-making approach. All formulas are illustrated with an example to assist students in how to apply the formulas.

End-of-text appendix on the basic time value of money calculations. This assists those students who may not have received a strong presentation on time value computations, or who may have forgotten how to make the computations.

Changes to This Edition

Although the basic text coverage did not change appreciably from our previously published textbook, the following items highlight the major changes found in this edition:

"Useful Web Sites" are included at the end of each chapter.

Many new research findings have been added to the sections on inventory management, credit management, collections, cash position, disbursements, and electronic commerce.

A new section on Economic Value Added performance measures has been added to the valuation chapter.

A new section on Key Account Management systems has been added to the accounts receivable management chapter.

A greater emphasis on check fraud and payment method fraud protection has been added to the disbursements chapter.

Material on payment methods, global payment and banking systems, inventory management, electronic commerce and regulation has been updated and beefed up.

Two new integrative cases replace old cases: One is on cash forecasting (including daily and monthly cash forecasts) and the other on valuation analysis.

Numerous Focus on Practice boxes have been added in areas such as credit management, disbursements, and cash forecasting.

Statistical forecasting tools have been moved from the body of the cash forecasting chapter to a separate appendix.

End-of-chapter questions and problems have been streamlined in several chapters and problems reordered or changed in several chapters.

Important pedagogical items such as chapter objectives that begin each chapter, the financial dilemma vignettes highlighting the key issue in the chapter, Focus on Practice boxes that present actual business practices related to the material discussed in the chapters, and integrative cases were maintained in this edition.

Course Supplements

The course supplements have been designed to provide flexibility to instructors teaching the course at either the upper-level undergraduate or MBA level. Emphasis can be placed where the instructor wishes and can be varied depending on the background of the students. The following supplements are available:

Instructor's Manual Authored by Joe Walker, University of Alabama at Birmingham. A revamped and very complete instructor's manual is available and includes notes regarding the best approach for undergraduate or MBA-level coverage, solutions for all questions and problems, and numerous transparency masters. We also include an array of test questions, authored by William Ogden, University of Wisconsin at Eau Claire. The test bank includes both objective and essay, for those professors wishing to use them.

Spreadsheet Solutions Diskette All adopters will be provided with a diskette that is compatible with Microsoft Excel and other spreadsheet software capable of reading Excel files. The diskette contains worksheets for all end-of-chapter problems, financial spreadsheet solutions, and models for cases. The instructor may provide copies of these spreadsheets for student use, or they can be loaded on the host institution's network for more convenient student access.

PowerPoint Slides All adopters will be provided a diskette that contains lecture notes in the form of Microsoft PowerPoint slides.

Acknowledgments and Credits

Many people made significant and helpful contributions to this book. Without the classroom experience, guidance, and practical advice of these individuals, this book could not have been written. We welcome any constructive criticism any reader might have in order to further improve the presentation.

We were blessed with the assistance of an excellent group of reviewers who helped guide the development of the first edition of this text (with West Publishing) as well as the first South-Western edition. We very much appreciate their helpful assistance and ideas for improved presentation, and wish to continue to acknowledge the following individuals for their valuable input:

Edgar Norton	Fairleigh Dickinson University
David J. Wright	Notre Dame University
William Beranek	University of Georgia
James B. Kehr	Miami University of Ohio
Frederick W. Siegel	University of Louisville
Alan W. Frankle	Boise State University
Stephen Dukas	Kansas State University
Yong H. Kim	University of Cincinnati
Robert J. Sweeney	Wright State University
Michael D. Carpenter	University of Kentucky
Erika W. Gilbert	Illinois State University
David A. Burnie	Western Michigan University
Joseph E. Finnerty	University of Illinois
C. Steven Cole	University of North Texas
Gabriel Ramirez	SUNY-Binghamton

Brian Belt	University of Missouri at Kansas City
Steven A. Carvell	Cornell University
Richard Edelman	The American University
Joseph Finnerty	University of Illinois at Urbana-Champaign
D. J. Masson	The Resource Alliance
Graham R. Mitenko	University of Nebraska at Omaha
Donald A. Nast	Florida State University
Luc Soenen	California Polytechnic University
John D. Stowe	University of Missouri
Preston Gilson	Fort Hays State University
Waldemar M. Goulet	Wright State University
Bernie J. Grablowsky	United Property Associates
Daniel L. Schneid	Central Michigan University
James A. Gentry	University of Illinois
Erika W. Gilbert	Illinois State University
Duncan J. Kretovich	Portland State University
Surendra K. Mansinghka	San Francisco State University
Michael D. Sherman	University of Toledo
Antoinette C. Tessmer	University of Illinois at Urbana-Champaign
Alan Wong	Indiana University Southeast
Paul Ruggeri	Siena College
Josee St. Pierre	Universite du Quebec a Trois-Rivieres.

To aid in the development of this second edition, South-Western obtained the assistance of the following professors. We very much appreciate their helpful suggestions and ideas.

Jerry James	Indiana University
Brian Belt	University of Missouri, Kansas City
Edgar Norton	Illinois State University
Joseph Finnerty	University of Illinois, Urbana-Champaign

We are especially indebted to the following treasury management and bank personnel who provided the cutting-edge information we believe sets our book apart: D.J. Masson, Kevin Kilmer, Mark Gould, Bob Gray, Everett Likens, J.R. Lawhead, Bob Wiese, Eric Pierce, Karen Thor, Kathy Carr, Coleen Knerr, Mike Wright, Jeff Love, Dennis Aron, William Kiesel, Davis Smith, and Maryann Kriner.

The following individuals provided invaluable assistance in assembling background materials and providing clerical assistance: Denise Hess, Mary Peters, Heather Bell, and Molly Bixel of Mount Vernon Nazarene College and Shea Elkins of Mississippi College. The support of each of our institutions was also instrumental in allowing time for writing this edition.

We would like to thank the staff at South-Western for the editorial and production support that helped us complete the revision process.

Finally, we appreciate the two professors who introduced us to a lifelong love of cash and treasury management: Ken Burns of University of Memphis and Ned Hill at Brigham Young University (formally at Indiana University).

Terry S. Maness
John T. Zietlow

BRIEF CONTENTS

PART I   INTRODUCTION TO LIQUIDITY   1
Chapter 1   The Role of Working Capital   2
Chapter 2   Analysis of Solvency, Liquidity, and Financial Flexibility   22
Chapter 3   Valuation   48

PART II   MANAGEMENT OF WORKING CAPITAL   89
Chapter 4   Inventory Management   90
Chapter 5   Accounts Receivable Management   116
Chapter 6   Credit Policy and Collections   170
Chapter 7   Managing Payables and Accruals   210

PART III   CORPORATE CASH MANAGEMENT   227
Chapter 8   The Payment System and Financial Institution Relationships   228
Chapter 9   Cash Collection Systems   288
Chapter 10   Cash Concentration   312
Chapter 11   Cash Disbursement Systems   338

PART IV   FORECASTING AND PLANNING   379
Chapter 12   Cash Forecasting   380
Chapter 13   Short-Term Financial Planning   422

PART V   SHORT-TERM INVESTMENT AND FINANCING   445
Chapter 14   The Money Market   446
Chapter 15   Short-Term Investment Management   494
Chapter 16   Short-Term Financing   530
Chapter 17   Managing Multinational Cash Flows   554

PART VI   SPECIAL TOPICS   569
Chapter 18   Managing Financial Risk with Futures, Options, and Swaps   570
Chapter 19   Treasury Management Information   604

CONTENTS

PART I Introduction to Liquidity 1

Chapter 1 THE ROLE OF WORKING CAPITAL 2

Financial Dilemma *How Does Profit Differ from Cash Flow?* 3

Introducing the Cash Flow Timeline 4

The Relationship Between Profit and Cash Flow 7

Financial Dilemma *REVISITED* 10

Managing the Cash Cycle 13

How Much Working Capital Is Enough? 15

Summary 17

Chapter 2 ANALYSIS OF SOLVENCY, LIQUIDITY, AND FINANCIAL FLEXIBILITY 22

Financial Dilemma *What Happened?* 23

Solvency Measures 24

What Is Liquidity? 29

The Statement of Cash Flows 30

Liquidity Measures 32

How Much Liquidity Is Enough? 36

Financial Flexibility 38

Financial Dilemma *REVISITED* 41

Summary 41

FOCUSED CASE: Just for Feet, Inc. 46

Chapter 3 VALUATION 48

Financial Dilemma *Evaluating the Financial Impact of a Change in Credit Terms* 50

Two Approaches to Financial Decision Making 50

NPV Calculations 56

Basic Valuation Model 58

Financial Dilemma *REVISITED* 61

Choosing the Discount Rate 67

Capital Allocation Decision Making in Practice 71

Summary 72

Appendix 3A *Advanced Present Value Analysis* 80

INTEGRATIVE CASE—Part 1: Bernard's New York Deli 86

PART II   Management of Working Capital   89

Chapter 4   INVENTORY MANAGEMENT   90
Financial Dilemma   *Can Placing Fewer Orders Save Money?*   91
The Concept of Inventory   92
Basics of Managing the Average Inventory Balance   94
Inventory Management and the Cash Flow Timeline   100
Financial Dilemma *REVISITED*   102
Monitoring the Inventory Balance   103
Reducing the Size of the Inventory Investment   105
Summary   109
FOCUSED CASE: Fletcher Company   113

Chapter 5   ACCOUNTS RECEIVABLE MANAGEMENT   116
Financial Dilemma   *How Can I Make Sense of the Changing World of Receivables Management?*   117
Trade Credit and Shareholder Value   118
Financial Dilemma *REVISITED*   118
Managing the Credit Function   123
Establishing a Credit Policy   127
Receivables, Collections, and Electronic Data Interchange   153
Summary   154
FOCUSED CASE: Y Guess Jeans   162

Chapter 6   CREDIT POLICY AND COLLECTIONS   170
Financial Dilemma   *How Should We Monitor Customers' Financial Positions?*   171
Evaluating Changes in Credit Policy: The Cash Flow Timeline   172
Monitoring Collections   183
Financial Dilemma *REVISITED*   190
Collection Procedures   191
Evaluating the Credit Department   193
International Credit Management   196
Summary   198
FOCUSED CASE: Kimball International, Inc.   204
Appendix 6A   *Sophisticated Receivables Monitoring Techniques*   206

Chapter 7   MANAGING PAYABLES AND ACCURALS   210
Financial Dilemma   *Why Pay Early?*   211
Spontaneous Sources of Financing   212
Accounts Payable   212

Financial Dilemma *REVISITED* 215

Accruals 222

Summary 222

INTEGRATIVE CASE—Part 2: Smyth Appliance, Inc. 225

PART III Corporate Cash Management   227

Chapter 8 THE PAYMENT SYSTEM AND FINANCIAL INSTITUTION RELATIONSHIPS 228

Financial Dilemma   *Should We Get on the Electronic Payments Bandwagon?* 229

Value of Float   230

US Payment System   232

Concept of Float   245

Paper-Based Payments   246

Electronic-Based Payments   250

Financial Dilemma *REVISITED*   257

International Payment Systems   258

Managing the Bank Relationship   260

Services Provided by Banks   261

Bank Selection and Relationship Management   265

Managing Bank Relationships   266

Nonbank Providers of Services   274

Financial System Trends   275

Summary   277

Appendix 8A   *Checklist for Bank Evaluation   284*

Appendix 8B   *Optimizing the Banking Network   286*

Chapter 9 CASH COLLECTION SYSTEMS   288

Financial Dilemma   *How Can a Firm Accelerate Its Cash Collections?*   289

The Cash Flow Timeline and Cash Collection   290

The Cost of Float   291

Types of Collection Systems   291

The Lockbox Location Study   296

Financial Dilemma *REVISITED*   297

The Lockbox Model   298

Lockbox Bank Selection   301

A Lockbox Study Case Example   301

Summary   303

Appendix 9A   A *Linear Programming Formulation of the Lockbox Model   308*

Chapter 10   **CASH CONCENTRATION**   **312**

Financial Dilemma   *How to Consolidate Collected Balances*   313

The Basic Structure of a Cash Concentration System   314

Cash Concentration and the Cash Flow Timeline   317

Cash Transfer Scheduling   318

Financial Dilemma *REVISITED*   320

E.F. Hutton: A System That Lost Control   326

Cash Concentration: The Canadian Experience   328

FOCUSED CASE: Gold Star Laundry and Drycleaners, Inc.   **334**

Appendix 10A   *A Linear Programming Cash Transfer Model*   336

Chapter 11   **CASH DISBURSEMENT SYSTEMS**   **338**

Financial Dilemma   *Is It Time to Go Electronic with Payments and Payment Information?*   339

Disbursement Policy   340

Cash Disbursement and the Cash Flow Timeline   341

Disbursement Systems   347

Global Disbursement Strategies   358

Optimizing the Disbursement System   361

Financial Dilemma *REVISITED*   362

Summary   368

FOCUSED CASE: Structuring a Payment Decision   **375**

INTEGRATIVE CASE—Part 3: Harker Telecommunications, Inc.   **376**

PART IV   Forecasting and Planning   379

Chapter 12   **CASH FORECASTING**   **380**

Financial Dilemma   *Which Cash Balance Should We Forecast?*   382

The Cash Forecasting Process   382

Forecasting Monthly Cash Flows   383

Forecasting Daily Cash Flows   397

Financial Dilemma *REVISITED*   397

Summary   402

Appendix 12A   *Measuring Forecast Errors*   406

Appendix 12B   *Statistical Forecasting Tools*   411

Chapter 13   **SHORT-TERM FINANCIAL PLANNING**   **422**

Financial Dilemma   *What Does the Future Hold?*   423

Types of Models   424

The Modeling Process   424

A Simple Percent-of-Sales Forecasting Model   425

Basics of Building a Financial Model   427

A Short-Run Financial Planning Model   428

Model Logic   428

Understanding the Model   431

Financial Dilemma *REVISITED*   432

Optimizing the Financial Plan   435

Summary   437

FOCUSED CASE: Jones Salvage and Recycling, Inc. (Case A)   439

INTEGRATIVE CASE—Part 4: Toy World, Inc.   440

PART V   Short-Term Investment and Financing   445

Chapter 14   **THE MONEY MARKET   446**

Financial Dilemma   *Selecting an Investing Maturity*   448

Nature of the Money Market   448

Money Market Instruments   452

Money Market Calculations   469

Yield and Risk Analysis   474

Financial Dilemma *REVISITED*   478

Summary   486

Chapter 15   **SHORT-TERM INVESTMENT MANAGEMENT   494**

Financial Dilemma   *Evaluating Interest Rate Risk*   495

Short-Term Investment Policy   496

Cash and Securities Allocation Decision   498

Investment Decision-Making Process   501

Assembling the Portfolio   506

Financial Dilemma *REVISITED*   513

Summary   516

Appendix 15A *Cash Management Models*   521

Chapter 16   **SHORT-TERM FINANCING   530**

Financial Dilemma   *When is Prime not Prime?*   531

Financing and the Cash Flow Timeline   532

Financing Strategies   532

Short-Term Financing Alternatives   534

The Effective Cost of Short-Term Financing   543

Financial Dilemma *REVISITED*   544

Summary   545

FOCUSED CASE: Jones Salvage and Recycling, Inc. (B)   549

Appendix 16A   *The Effective Cost of Credit Lines*   550

Chapter 17   MANAGING MULTINATIONAL CASH FLOWS   554

Financial Dilemma   *What Can Be Done About Uncertain Currency Exchange Rates?*   555

Exchange Rates   556

Factors Affecting Exchange Rates   558

Foreign Exchange Exposure   559

Managing Foreign Exchange Exposure   560

Financial Dilemma *REVISITED*   562

Features of Non-US Banking Systems   563

Summary   564

INTEGRATIVE CASE—Part 5: Jones Salvage and Recycling, Inc. (C)   567

PART VI   Special Topics   569

Chapter 18   MANAGING FINANCIAL RISK WITH FUTURES, OPTIONS, AND SWAPS   570

Financial Dilemma   *What Can Be Done About Uncertain Interest Rates?*   571

Hedging Compared with Speculating   572

Hedging with Financial Futures   572

Financial Dilemma *REVISITED*   579

Hedging with Options   581

Hedging with Swaps   587

Financial Dilemma   *What Can Be Done About Uncertain Currency Exchange Rates?*   591

Financial Dilemma *REVISITED*   592

Other Hedging Instruments   593

Regulatory Issues   595

Summary   596

Chapter 19   TREASURY INFORMATION MANAGEMENT   604

Key Information Flows   606

Electronic Data Interchange   607

E-Commerce and the Internet   613

Auditing the STFM Information System   615

Summary   619

INTEGRATIVE CASE—Part 6: General Motors—Europe: The Regional Treasury Center International Finance   621

Appendix 19A—Time Value of Money   623
Glossary   G1
Index   I1

PART I
Introduction to Liquidity

Chapter 1   The Role of Working Capital
Chapter 2   Analysis of Solvency, Liquidity, and
             Financial Flexibility
Chapter 3   Valuation

Part 1 introduces the concept of liquidity. In Chapter 1, the management of the various working capital accounts such as inventory, receivables, payables, and accruals is linked to the impact each area has on cash flow and how these areas cause cash flow and profit to diverge. This chapter also introduces the key pedagogical tool used throughout the text, the cash flow timeline diagram, which is in each chapter to link the current decision-making area to the overall cash flow timeline. Chapter 2 introduces the reader to measurement issues of liquidity. Many traditional liquidity indicators are shown to measure other aspects of the firm such as solvency rather than liquidity. The chapter differentiates between solvency measures, liquidity measures, and financial flexibility measures. Part 1 concludes with a chapter focused on the valuation of cash flows. Strategic financial decisions such as capital budgeting and tactical financial decisions such as working capital management must consider the value impact of changing the pattern and amount of cash flows.

CHAPTER 1

The Role of Working Capital

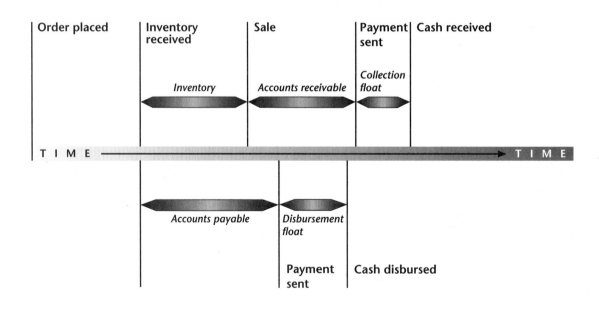

OBJECTIVES

After studying this chapter, you should be able to:

- View a firm as a system of cash flows as represented by a timeline.
- Understand how depreciation charges and working capital flows create a disparity between profit and cash flow.
- Appreciate the basic issues involved in managing working capital.

It is obvious that an unprofitable firm will experience financial difficulties that can lead to bankruptcy. It is less obvious how seemingly profitable firms may also experience financial strains that may lead to bankruptcy. This will be the case if operating cash flows are not managed properly. If too many resources are tied up in inventory or if accounts receivable are not collected in a timely fashion, then even a profitable company may not be able to pay its bills. A successful firm manages its operations from a profit and cash flow perspective.

In this chapter, we discuss the role that working capital plays in management of the operations of a firm. We begin by presenting the firm as a system of cash flows and discuss how operating activities impact cash flow and the various accounts that make up the financial statements of the firm. We clarify how the different working capital accounts depicted on the balance sheet create a disparity between profit and cash flow. A cash flow timeline structure is introduced that is the main pedagogical tool used throughout the textbook.

We then conclude with an introductory discussion focusing on the management aspects of the various working capital accounts, followed by a discussion on the appropriate or optimal level of working capital.

FINANCIAL DILEMMA

How Does Profit Differ from Cash Flow?

Sports Junction, Inc., a retail sporting goods corporation, just hired a new treasurer. The prime selling season is just beginning, and the company's management is looking forward to a record level of sales. The company is very profitable with a gross profit margin of 40 percent. Customers pay on time, averaging 30 days. The company doesn't use trade credit and pays for all inventory when purchased. The company's policy is to keep one month's sales on hand in inventory. Although the company is profitable, the new treasurer is wondering if the investment in inventory and receivables, during a brisk period of business, may eventually cause cash flow problems.

INTRODUCING THE CASH FLOW TIMELINE

Manufacturers purchase raw materials for production purposes, and retailers purchase inventory from wholesalers to satisfy their customers' demands. The inventory is converted into accounts receivable as customers make purchases on credit. Receivables are then collected by customers remitting payment to the company. Cash is received when the payment medium, such as a check, is collected through the banking system. Delay in collecting payment on the check on behalf of the seller is known as **collection float.**

The initial purchase of inventory creates an accounts payable owed to suppliers. The actual disbursement of cash occurs when the payment medium used to pay for the purchase, such as a check, is collected by the banking system. Delay created in the collection of payment on behalf of the supplier is referred to as **disbursement float.** The relationships between these various working capital accounts, along with collection and disbursement delays, are depicted on a timeline shown in Exhibit 1-1.

The cash flow timeline diagram relates the various working capital accounts on a time dimension scale. Indeed, it is this time dimension on which working capital management must focus. The longer that resources remain idle in inventory, receivables, or in collection float, the more value is lost. The longer that resources can be conserved through reasonable delay of cash payment of payables and accruals, the more value is gained. A significant difference between the date that cash is received and cash is paid, referred to as the **cash conversion period,** creates a financing problem for the firm. In general, firms must pay for resources received, such as inventory, before cash is received from its manufacturing and selling process. The shorter this cash conversion period, the more efficient the working capital policies and the less value lost due to working capital management activities.

We will develop a numerical example using the simple case of a firm just beginning operations to fully understand the intricacies of managing the cash flow timeline as represented in Exhibit 1-1. By working through the numbers in this example, we will learn how the various balance sheet and income statement items relate to the operations

EXHIBIT 1-1
A Cash Flow Timeline Diagram

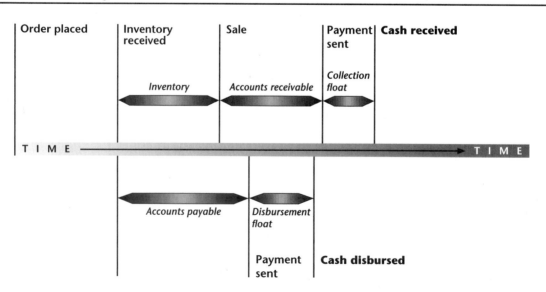

of the firm. In addition, we will be able to better understand the very important relationship between profit and cash flow.

Consider the initial balance sheet for the newly formed company San Juan Anglers, Inc. Assuming that the owners put in $500 and borrow $500 from a bank, the accounts on the balance sheet will have the following balances:

BALANCE SHEET: JUNE 1

Cash	$1,000	Debt	$ 500
		Equity	500
Total	$1,000	Total	$1,000

The next day, the owner spends a portion of the initial funds to purchase operating facilities ($600) and an initial supply of inventory ($300). In purchasing the inventory, the firm's suppliers allow it to purchase the goods on credit ($300). The firm does not have any initial cash outlay for inventory. The total payment is due, say, in 45 days or by July 15.

BALANCE SHEET: JUNE 2

Cash	$ 400	Accounts payable	$ 300
Inventory	300	Debt	500
Fixed Assets	600	Equity	500
Total	$1,300	Total	$1,300

Notice how total assets increased by $300, the dollar amount of the inventory purchased. This purchase is funded, not out of cash (cash only dropped to $400, reflecting the purchase of the fixed assets), but out of suppliers' funds. This transaction is evidenced by the creation of the liability account, accounts payable, in the amount of the inventory purchase, $300.

When the firm begins to produce and sell its products, it begins to generate operating expenses such as salaries, utilities, advertising, and depreciation of its fixed assets. When it sells its products on credit, accounts receivable are generated giving its customers, say, 2 months to pay for their purchases. The firm's balance sheet as of the last day of the month, June 30, and the income statement for the month of June are shown below. The balance sheet shows the $200 of operating expenses listed on the income statement (salaries, advertising, utilities, etc.) as an accrued operating expense. This practice is caused by charging off these expenses on the income statement even though they have not yet been paid in cash. The firm intends to pay these expenses on the first day of July.

BALANCE SHEET: JUNE 30

Cash	$ 325	Accounts payable	$ 300
Accounts receivable	700	Operations accruals	200
Inventory	0	Debt	500
Fixed assets	600	Common stock	500
(Accumulated depr.)	(100)	Retained earnings	25
Total	$1,525	Total	$1,525

INCOME STATEMENT: JUNE 1–JUNE 30

Sales	$700
Cost of goods sold	300
Gross profit	400

Operating expenses:	
Salaries, advertising, etc.	200
Depreciation	100
Operating profit	100
Interest	50
Taxes	25
Net profit	25
Dividends	0
Addition to retained earnings	25

The balance sheet as of July 1 is shown below. Note how operating accruals are zero, and the cash balance has been reduced by $200. The changes in these balance sheet accounts reflect the cash payment for the accrued expenses.

BALANCE SHEET: JULY 1

Cash	$125	Accounts payable	$300
Accounts receivable	700	Operating accruals	0
Inventory	0	Debt	500
Fixed assets	600	Common stock	500
(Accumulated depr.)	(100)	Retained earnings	25
Total	$1,325	Total	$1,325

Move forward to July 15. Consider the situation in which no new business transactions occurred during July. The firm owes its suppliers $300 for the inventory purchased during June. The new balance sheet below reflects the payment of this debt. Note that the reduction of accounts payable by $300 reflects the payment made, and the cash balance is likewise reduced by the $300 payment. The resulting cash balance is negative ($175). In actual practice, this would result in some problems for the firm. It is spending cash it doesn't have. But how can the firm be short of cash when the income statement reported a profit? The answer is that management paid cash for most, if not all of the expenses, but has yet to collect any cash from sales.

BALANCE SHEET: JULY 15

Cash	($175)	Accounts payable	$0
Accounts receivable	700	Operating accruals	0
Inventory	0	Debt	500
Fixed assets	600	Common stock	500
(Accumulated depr.)	(100)	Retained earnings	25
Total	$1,025	Total	$1,025

Finally, assume that all the firm's customers pay for their June purchases by July 31. The following balance sheet reflects the cash receipts of $700 and the corresponding reduction of accounts receivable by $700. The firm completes its first cash cycle with a profit of $25 reflected in the retained earnings account and a cash balance of $525, $125 more than it had in cash on June 1, following its purchase of fixed assets.

BALANCE SHEET: JULY 31

Cash	($525)	Accounts payable	$0
Accounts receivable	0	Operating accruals	0
Inventory	0	Debt	500
Fixed assets	600	Common stock	500
(Accumulated depr.)	(100)	Retained earnings	25
Total	$1,025	Total	$1,025

THE RELATIONSHIP BETWEEN PROFIT AND CASH FLOW

The example in the previous section should have raised two questions: First, why did the firm end up with $125 extra in its cash balance if it only earned a profit of $25? Second, why did the firm run out of cash during its operating cycle?

The first question can be addressed by recognizing that some of the firm's expenses result in a cash disbursement while others do not. For example, wages and utility expenses result in actual cash disbursements to employees and to the utility companies, respectively. In contrast, depreciation is simply an accounting entry to record the utilization of capital or fixed assets. Depreciation expense is not paid to anyone. Thus while the $100 depreciation expense charged on the income statement reduces profit, it does not reduce cash flow.

The second question can be explained by the existence of receivables, payables, and accruals. Receivables represent the dollar amount of sales that have yet to be collected. Thus the $700 of receivables on the balance sheet reflects $700 of sales that remain uncollected from customers. The customers actually pay for the goods on July 31. Payables reflect the resources the firm has the use of but has not yet paid for. Recall, the firm purchased $300 of inventory on June 2 that it could then sell, but payment for the goods was not required until 45 days later or on July 15. By July 15, the firm has had to pay $200 (paid on June 30) for operating expenses and $300 for its inventory purchases, but it had yet to receive any cash receipts from sales. While its operations were profitable as shown by its income statement, the firm still experienced a cash flow problem due to the difference in timing of cash disbursements and cash receipts.

From this discussion we see that there are two basic aspects of managing the operations of the firm. First, the firm must manage a cost structure so that it can generate a profit. As discussed, after the accrued expenses and payables were finally paid and receivables collected, cash flow equals net income plus depreciation expense. Second, the firm must manage its accruals, payables, receivables, and inventory (usually referred to as the working capital accounts) so that an adequate amount of liquidity is maintained and its interim cash flow position does not force the firm into bankruptcy or unplanned financial distress. Until all the accruals, payables, and receivables had worked themselves through their complete cycle, the firm experienced a wide range of cash from a deficit of $575 to a surplus of $125.

As shown in Exhibit 1-2, changes in the receivables, inventory, payables, and accrual accounts on the balance sheet as well as the depreciation expense account on the income statement can be used to adjust the income statement to reflect the true operating cash flow position of the firm. To arrive at cash receipts from sales, subtract an increase in the accounts receivable balance, or add a decrease in accounts receivable. A shorthand way to express this type of adjustment is to subtract the change in the accounts receivable balance (where the change can either be positive, an increase, or negative, a decrease) from sales revenue. Cash disbursed for cost of goods sold is calculated by subtracting the change in accounts payable and adding the change in the inventory account from the income statement item cost of goods sold. Cash operating expenses are calculated by subtracting the change in operating expense accruals and depreciation expense from operating expenses on the income statement. Although, in our example, interest and taxes are assumed to be paid in cash, both of these income statement items could also be adjusted by their respective accrual accounts and the deferred tax account if these accounts exist on the balance sheet. Cash flow from operations is then calculated by subtracting all cash operating expenses from cash receipts as shown in Exhibit 1-2.

EXHIBIT 1-2

Adjustments to Convert the Accrual Based Income Statement to a Cash Basis

Income Statement Account	Adjustment Account	Cash Flow Account
Sales	− Change in accounts receivable	= Cash collected from customers
Cost of goods sold	− Change in accounts payable + Change in inventory	= Cash paid to suppliers
Operating expenses	− Change in operating accruals − Depreciation	= Cash paid for operating expenses
Interest	− Change in accrued interest	= Cash paid to creditors
Taxes	− Change in accrued taxes − Change in deferred taxes	= Cash paid for taxes

Cash flow from operations:

Cash collected from customers

Minus cash paid to suppliers

Minus cash paid for operations

Minus cash paid to creditors

Minus cash paid for taxes

Equals cash flow from operations

EXHIBIT 1-3

June 1–June 30

Income Statement Account	Adjustment Account	Cash Flow Account
Sales $700	− Change in accounts receivable $700	= Cash collected from customers $0
Cost of goods sold $300	− Change in accounts payable $300 + Change in inventory $0	= Cash paid to suppliers $0
Operating expenses $300	− Change in operating accruals $200 − Depreciation $100	= Cash paid for operating expenses $0
Interest $50	− Change in accrued interest $0	= Cash paid to creditors $50
Taxes $25	− Change in accrued taxes $0 − Change in deferred taxes $0	= Cash paid for taxes $25
Net Profit $25		Cash Profit ($75)

Exhibits 1-3, 1-4, and 1-5 show how the June income statement is adjusted as the various expenses are paid and as customers pay off the accounts receivable. Exhibit 1-3 shows the difference between profit and cash flow on June 30. Cash flow is a deficit of $75 because no sales have been collected, and the only expenses paid are interest and taxes. Exhibit 1-4 shows a deficit cash flow of $575 by July 15. At this point, suppliers

EXHIBIT 1-4
June 1–July 15

Income Statement Account	Adjustment Account	Cash Flow Account
Sales $700	− Change in accounts receivable $700	= Cash collected from customers $0
Cost of goods sold $300	− Change in accounts payable $0 + Change in inventory $0	= Cash paid to suppliers $300
Operating expenses $300	− Change in operating accruals $0 − Depreciation $100	= Cash paid for operating expenses $200
Interest $50	− Change in accrued interest $0	= Cash paid to creditors $50
Taxes $25	− Change in accrued taxes $0 − Change in deferred taxes $0	= Cash paid for taxes $25
Net Profit $25		Cash Profit ($575)

EXHIBIT 1-5
June 1–July 31

Income Statement Account	Adjustment Account	Cash Flow Account
Sales $700	− Change in accounts receivable $0	= Cash collected from customers $700
Cost of goods sold $300	− Change in accounts payable $0 + Change in inventory $0	= Cash paid to suppliers $300
Operating expenses $300	− Change in operating accruals $0 − Depreciation $100	= Cash paid for operating expenses $200
Interest $50	− Change in accrued interest $0	= Cash paid to creditors $50
Taxes $25	− Change in accrued taxes $0 − Change in deferred taxes $0	= Cash paid for taxes $25
Net Profit $25		Cash Profit $125

have been paid $300, operating expenses of $200 have been paid, and the $75 of interest and taxes has also been paid. Still, no cash receipts have been collected to offset these cash disbursements. Finally, Exhibit 1-5 shows a cash flow of $125 reflecting the cash collections of $700 from customers offsetting the $575 of cash disbursements.

FINANCIAL DILEMMA REVISITED

Before turning to the next section, which explores the management of a firm's working capital accounts, let's see if what we have learned can be applied to the dilemma facing the newly hired treasurer of Sports Junction, Inc., the sporting goods corporation introduced at the beginning of the chapter. First, she had the staff gather historical balance sheet data for the month of January and make income projections for the months of February, March, and April.

BALANCE SHEET, JANUARY

Assets		Liabilities and Net Worth	
Cash	$70,000	Payables	$ 0
Receivables	$50,000	Common Stock	$150,000
Inventory	$30,000	Retained earnings	$ 0
Total Assets	$150,000	Total Liabilities/Net Worth	$150,000

PROJECTED INCOME STATEMENT	FEBRUARY	MARCH	APRIL
Sales	$50,000	$100,000	$150,000
Cost of sales	30,000	60,000	90,000
Gross profit	20,000	40,000	60,000
Fixed costs	10,000	10,000	10,000
Net profit	10,000	30,000	50,000

The staff used the following purchasing schedule and cash budget to help forecast the income statement and balance sheet. The purchasing schedule is developed from the basic accounting relationship that ending inventory (EI) is equal to beginning inventory (BI) plus purchases (PUR) less cost of goods sold (COGS) shown in equation 1-1:

$$EI = BI + PUR - COGS \qquad (1\text{-}1)$$

Management's policy is to maintain ending inventory, for any given month, equal to that month's cost of goods sold. A purchasing schedule can be developed by taking equation 1-1 and solving it for the dollar amount of purchases as shown in equation 1-2:

$$PUR = EI - BI + COGS \qquad (1\text{-}2)$$

For example, management's desired ending inventory for February is $30,000, based on February's estimated COGS of $30,000. February's beginning inventory is equal to $30,000, which is January's ending inventory. Plugging these values in for the variables shown in equation 1-2 results in the projected dollar amount of purchases required to maintain the targeted ending inventory levels. The purchasing schedule for the 3 projected months is shown below.

PURCHASING SCHEDULE	FEBRUARY	MARCH	APRIL
Desired ending inventory	$30,000	$60,000	$ 90,000
Less: Beginning inventory	30,000	30,000	60,000
Plus: Cost of goods sold	30,000	60,000	90,000
Equal: Purchases	$30,000	$90,000	$120,000

The company's receivables are outstanding an average of 1 month, so collections in 1 month are equal to the previous month's credit sales. Purchases are paid for in the month the purchase is made. These policies result in the following cash budget for the projected 3 months. In the cash budget, net cash flow is equal to cash collections, line 2, less cash disbursements, lines 5 and 6.

CASH BUDGET	FEBRUARY	MARCH	APRIL
1. Credit sales	$50,000	$100,000	$150,000
2. Cash collections	50,000	50,000	100,000
3. Purchases	30,000	90,000	120,000
4. Cash disbursed for:			
5. Purchases	30,000	90,000	120,000
6. Fixed costs	10,000	10,000	10,000
7. Net cash flow (2-5-6)	10,000	(50,000)	(30,000)
8. Plus: Beginning cash	70,000	80,000	30,000
9. Equals: Ending cash	80,000	30,000	0

The projected balance sheet follows from the income statement and the cash budget. Cash is taken directly from the last line of the cash budget. Receivables equal last month's receivables balance plus credit sales for the new month less cash receipts from receivables. Inventory is taken from the top line of the purchasing schedule. Accounts payable equal zero because the firm pays for all purchases with cash. Common stock is assumed to remain constant, and retained earnings grow by the amount of net profit retained each month.

PROJECTED BALANCE SHEET	FEBRUARY	MARCH	APRIL
Assets			
Cash	$ 80,000	$ 30,000	$ 0
Accounts receivable	50,000	100,000	150,000
Inventory	30,000	60,000	90,000
Liabilities and Net Worth			
Accounts payable	0	0	0
Common stock	150,000	150,000	150,000
Retained earnings	10,000	40,000	90,000

The treasurer does indeed have a dilemma. Her company is expected to earn a very reasonable rate of profit in the next 3 months, as evidenced by the income statement, but will run out of cash by the end of April. Cash is being drained by the ever-increasing investment in receivables and inventory. This simply emphasizes the importance of managing the working capital relationships to ensure that an adequate level of liquidity is maintained. The relationship between the income statement and the cash flow statement is shown below.

FEBRUARY

Income Statement Account	Adjustment Account	Cash Flow Account
Sales $50,000	− Change in accounts receivable $0	= Cash collected from customers $50,000
Cost of goods sold $30,000	− Change in accounts payable $0 + Change in inventory $0	= Cash paid to suppliers $30,000
Gross margin $20,000		Gross cash margin $20,000

Income Statement Account	Adjustment Account	Cash Flow Account
Operating expenses $10,000	− Change in operating accruals $0	
	− Depreciation $0	= Cash paid for operating expenses $10,000
Operating profit $10,000		Operating cash margin $10,000

MARCH

Income Statement Account	Adjustment Account	Cash Flow Account
Sales $100,000	− Change in accounts receivable $50,000	= Cash collected from customers $50,000
Cost of goods sold $60,000	− Change in accounts payable $0	
	+ Change in inventory $30,000	= Cash paid to suppliers $90,000
Gross margin $40,000		Gross cash margin ($40,000)
Operating expenses $10,000	− Change in operating accruals $0	
	− Depreciation $0	= Cash paid for operating expenses $10,000
Operating profit $30,000		Operating cash margin ($50,000)

APRIL

Income Statement Account	Adjustment Account	Cash Flow Account
Sales $150,000	− Change in accounts receivable $50,000	= Cash collected from customers $100,000
Cost of goods sold $90,000	− Change in accounts payable $0	
	+ Change in inventory $30,000	= Cash paid to suppliers $120,000
Gross margin $60,000		Gross cash margin ($20,000)
Operating expenses $10,000	− Change in operating accruals $0	
	− Depreciation $0	= Cash paid for operating expenses $10,000
Operating profit $50,000		Operating cash margin ($30,000)

The adjustments to the income statement clearly show that the growth in receivables and inventory are soaking up cash flow resources. During growth periods, firms with mismatched working capital accounts (in which resources are held in inventory and receivables longer than in payables), such as Sports Junction, Inc., can expect to experience cash flow problems. Growth causes a greater spontaneous investment in working capital accounts, which slows down the flow of cash. This dilemma could be resolved by slowing down the outflow of cash, such as finding suppliers offering longer payment terms. Other alternatives would be to reduce the investment in inventory by developing better supply channels or collecting outstanding receivables more quickly. Finally, if these are not feasible alternatives, the treasurer needs to establish a credit facility at a local bank so that funds could readily be borrowed during upswings in the firm's seasonal business cycle and the borrowings paid down on the back side of the seasonal cycle.

The next chapter will present ways to analyze the cash flow timeline, and Chapter 3 will discuss how to value the cash flows using basic time value of money techniques. Let's briefly discuss the role that working capital plays in the management of a firm's operations and consider why working capital is needed and how much is enough.

MANAGING THE CASH CYCLE

Even profitable firms can experience cash flow difficulties due to timing differences of cash receipts and cash disbursements. The **cash cycle** refers to the continual flow of resources through the various working capital accounts such as cash, accounts receivables, inventory, payables, and accruals. Expansion of the working capital asset accounts absorbs resources while expansion of working capital liability accounts provides resources. This continual transformation of resources over the production cycle results in periods of cash flow surpluses and deficits. The manner in which these working capital accounts are managed can ameliorate or accentuate cash flow difficulties.

It seems apparent that over the past decade, measures of working capital, such as the current ratio and working capital as a percentage of sales, have been trending downward. Companies ranging from Dell Computer and General Electric to Quaker Oats and Campbell Soup are moving in the direction of zero net working capital. Reducing net working capital yields two benefits. First, reductions in net working capital flow straight to cash flow. Second, the journey leading to reduced net working capital leads to a permanent increase in earnings. Working capital costs money, therefore, less of it increases earnings.

Managing Receivables

Accounts receivable is created when customers purchase goods on credit. This credit must be properly managed to generate a timely receipt of cash. First, the financial manager must decide which customers should be allowed to buy on credit. A general framework for this kind of analysis is the five Cs of credit. The financial manager must ascertain the customer's Character, Capacity to pay, Collateral, and Capital. After these aspects have been analyzed, the credit decision must be put in context of current business Conditions.

Second, the financial manager must decide on a set of credit terms to offer. Typical terms might be net 30 days, or 2/10, net 30. The first set of terms simply instructs the customer to pay the invoice amount 30 days from the invoice date. The second set of terms allows for a 2 percent discount if paid within 10 days from the invoice date, otherwise the invoice amount is due in 30 days. Obviously, the longer the allowed period to pay, the longer the customer will take to pay, which stretches out the receipt of cash. In most cases, a firm cannot set its credit terms independently. The terms offered must be competitive with terms offered by other firms in the industry.

Once credit is given, the outstanding balance must be monitored to ensure that outstanding credit balances are not growing faster than sales. The company should have a well-developed set of procedures to follow when a customer's account becomes past due. Immediate attention to past-due accounts is necessary and will increase the odds of collection. Chapters 5 and 6 provide discussion and decision models related to the management of receivables.

Finally, once the customer remits payment, management must create an effective collection system to reduce **collection float,** the time that is spent converting the payment medium into cash. Chapter 9 will focus on a variety of collection systems that can effectively manage collection float.

Managing Inventory

In general, inventory balances act as shock absorbers between the production process and an uncertain consumer demand, between two production processes that are interdependent, or between the supplier and the production process. The more inventory stored, the less concern there is about product shortages at the retail level or about shutting down a production line due to a shortage of work-in-process or raw material inventory that feeds it.

However, increases in inventory balances absorb financial resources, so it is imperative that inventory balances are managed to reduce financial requirements without excessively increasing stock-out risk. Excess inventory, while costly, does not impinge on sales. Inventory stock-outs potentially are more costly because they create lost sales.

There have been many advances in the area of inventory management. Perhaps the most noteworthy is the **just-in-time** system popularized by the Japanese and more recently a system known as **demand flow,** which builds on just-in-time management concepts but is broader. These inventory management systems are designed to reduce the levels of inventory kept at the manufacturing site while still meeting production demands by redesigning the operations process and by shifting inventory burdens to suppliers. Chapter 4 will focus on the cash flow implications of managing inventory.

Managing Payables

The vast majority of purchases made by one corporation from another are done on credit. In making the purchase decision, the buying firm should seek to purchase using the most favorable or longest terms possible. Then payment should be made at the latest date possible so that payment arrives when due and not before. Payables should be viewed as interest-free financing and should be used until the last date possible. The manager should seriously consider the pros and cons of taking a cash discount if offered. Although taking a cash discount speeds up the disbursal of cash, the reduction in the amount paid may be more advantageous to the purchaser than foregoing the cash discount and paying at the end of the credit terms. Managerial issues of managing payables are discussed in Chapter 7.

Once payment is initiated, management must have an effective disbursement system to efficiently control the actual outflow of cash. Chapter 11 will discuss how to design an effective disbursement system.

A well-managed cash cycle results from aggressively monitoring the receivables balance, from reducing idle inventory, stretching payables to the last day possible given the terms of purchase, and implementation of an effective cash collection and disbursement system. An excessively long cash cycle adds financing pressure on the firm and can generate liquidity crises.

The Cash Cycle and Electronic Commerce

Electronic commerce is revolutionizing the way that the various components of the cash cycle are being managed. Initially, individual companies developed proprietary systems to conduct electronic commerce that in many ways slowed the growth of the potential for electronic commerce. The advent of the Internet changed the rules of the game.

The Internet is supporting an explosion in the development of systems with the ability to impact all aspects of the cash cycle including product catalog and product ordering (sales), credit checking, product delivery, invoicing, and finally payment. Although the investment in the needed technology is large, and many issues (such as security) still remain, the ultimate cost savings and the increase in the efficiency of the cash cycle are significant. The following chapters will highlight specific applications of electronic commerce to the various components of the cash cycle, and Chapter 19 will provide an overview and a strategic look at the potential for electronic commerce and its impact on the cash cycle.

HOW MUCH WORKING CAPITAL IS ENOUGH?

The growing debate over the role of working capital focuses on why working capital exists and what is the appropriate level of working capital. One extreme point of view is that the optimal level of net working capital is zero. This point of view sees working capital as an idle resource providing little or no value. Value is created by the fixed assets of the firm that produces the product, demanded by consumers, from raw materials. Thus the production process creates something that did not exist before. Inventory and receivables are assets representing that same product but are created primarily in getting that product to the ultimate consumer. How much of their assets should firms commit to this working capital management phase?[1] The following discussion will examine each of the working capital areas and look at why each may exist.

Inventory

As we have seen, inventory is created by inefficiencies between the production cycle and the selling function. The greater the delays and waste in the production process, the greater the need for inventory. Inventory is generally viewed as a type of shock absorber providing a cushion for work-in-process inventory between two contingent production processes or between production of finished goods and the selling function. Work-in-process inventory could be eliminated with increased efficiencies in the production process. This increased efficiency would also reduce the need for finished goods inventory but may not completely eliminate it due to forecasting uncertainties.

Trade Credit: Receivables and Accounts Payable

Trade credit can be viewed as existing because of inefficiencies in the financing market. After all, why should a manufacturing firm that produces the product also provide the short-term financing for the purchase of the product when a well-developed financial

---

[1]A rough estimate is that in the United States working capital includes 40% to 50% of total assets.

FOCUS ON PRACTICE

HOW MANAGEMENT OF WORKING CAPITAL IS CHANGING Historically, because accounts such as inventory and receivables are assets, the more of them on the balance sheet, the better. After all, can a firm operate without working capital? However, today more and more firms appear to be setting a level of zero or very low net working capital as an operating goal. Exhibit 1-6 shows the trend of working capital requirements as a percent of sales for four well-known computer companies including Dell, Compaq, Apple, and Gateway from 1990 to 1998. The working capital requirements level is defined as the sum of receivables and inventory less accounts payable. As you can see, the trend is distinctly down with many of the companies actually experiencing a near-zero working capital requirements level for the more recent part of the period.[2]

[2]For additional discussion see: Tully, Shawn. 1994. Raiding a company's hidden cash. *Fortune* August 22: 82–89.

EXHIBIT 1-6
Working Capital Requirements as a Percent of Sales

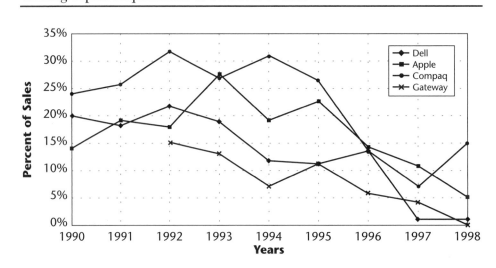

market exists that could be used to reduce the need for this activity on the part of non-financial firms. Why can't the customer make purchases with cash or financing obtained through traditional financial market channels such as commercial paper or bank lines of credit? If trade credit were eliminated, about half of a firm's working capital could be eliminated, thus improving the return on assets of all businesses.

It would seem that many parties share in the responsibility for reducing resources tied up in trade credit. The Federal Reserve and banking system must continue to take steps to encourage the use of electronic forms of payment over the traditional paper-based system. Although tremendous strides have been taken during the 1980s and 1990s, much remains to be done. On the manufacturing side, as production processes become more efficient and just-in-time inventory techniques applied universally, delays that create the need for inventory can be eliminated, reducing the need for extended credit terms.

Short-Term Investments

Why do firms hold funds in short-term investments? Firms may wish to hold funds in short-term investments as a financial cushion during a downturn in a business cycle. Having a liquidity reserve relieves the firm from having to obtain financing during times of need. The cushion could then be replenished as the firm's financial condition improves. Some view the excessive costs of bankruptcy necessitating the creation of a liquidity pool as a defense against bankruptcy. For example, Chrysler Corporation in the mid-1990's had a cushion of approximately $5 billion in short-term investments with annual free cash flow, defined as earnings plus depreciation and amortization minus dividends and capital spending, running between $1.5 and $2.5 billion annually. Why should the company maintain such a large liquidity reserve when its operations are generating such healthy cash flows? During the most recent recession, Chrysler used about $4 billion in liquidity, so management thinks that a sizable liquid reserve is appropriate. In addition, Chrysler indicates that it has significant expenses in the near future replacing antiquated capital equipment and new capital spending targeted at new product lines.

Like Chrysler, Ford Motor Company also maintained a large cash balance. Its holdings of cash and short-term investments approached $24 billion in 2000, nearly half of the company's market value. In April of 2000, recognizing that this level of cash was more than required for prudent management, Ford announced a recapitalization plan that is expected to return approximately $10 billion of this balance back to the shareholders.

At the other extreme, the CFO of Bell Atlantic Corporation declared that the appropriate level of cash for a firm to hold is zero.[3] Firms that maintain low cash balances by design must rely on the credit markets to provide them liquidity; a strategy that works great in a perfect world but runs the risk of liquidity crises when credit gets tight.

There may also be managerial motives for holding large liquidity reserves. Having a pool of ready resources that can be deployed for discretionary investment purposes enhances managerial power and prestige. The 1980s witnessed a new constraint on this type of activity in the form of the corporate raider. The existence of excessive free cash flow or large pools of liquid resources instigated many corporate raids.

Thus it would seem that reductions in resources in cash and short-term investments could be accomplished through increased efficiencies in the financial markets, legal environment, and institutional structures.

SUMMARY

There are two critical aspects to managing the cash cycle of a firm. First, the firm must operate at a profitable level. All firms incur certain levels of overhead or fixed costs. The firm must operate at a level such that the relationship between the fixed and variable costs result in operating profits.

Second, a profitable firm may still run into financial difficulties if operating cash flow is not managed properly. A profitable firm may still not be able to pay its bills if too many resources are tied up in inventory or if credit sales are not collected in a timely manner. A successful firm is one whose operations are managed from both a profit as well as a cash flow perspective.

Useful Web Sites

Association for Financial Professionals: www.afponline.org

CFO Magazine: www.cfonet.com

A great Web site for treasury management information: www.gtnews.com

Treasury and Risk Magazine: www.treasuryandrisk.com

---

[3]Mintz, S.L. 2000. Lean green machines. *CFOnet* July:1.

Questions

1. Discuss the sequence of resource conversions generally referred to as the cash cycle.
2. What causes cash flow and net profit to diverge? When will they be the same?
3. Discuss the two basic aspects of managing the operations of the firm.
4. What role do the five Cs of credit play in managing the receivables area?
5. How does collection float impact the cash cycle? Give an example.
6. How do inventory balances act as shock absorbers?
7. How does disbursement float impact the cash cycle? Give an example.
8. When the date that cash is disbursed comes before the date that cash is received on the cash flow timeline, what are some of the options available to the financial manager as to funding the disbursements?
9. Why do firms have working capital?
10. How can a profitable firm go bankrupt?

Problems

1. For each part below, calculate the amount of cash received by a company from its customers using the following data:

	BEGINNING RECEIVABLES	ENDING RECEIVABLES	SALES
a.	$0	$1,000	$5,000
b.	$700	$2,000	$10,000
c.	$2,000	$900	$15,000

2. For each part below, first calculate the dollar amount of purchases and then using that result, calculate the dollar amount of cash paid to suppliers using the following data:

	BEGINNING ACCOUNTS PAYABLE	ENDING ACCOUNTS PAYABLE	BEGINNING INVENTORY	ENDING INVENTORY	COST OF GOODS SOLD
a.	$0	$1,000	$0	$1,500	$5,000
b.	$0	$1,000	$500	$2,000	$7,000
c.	$500	$200	$1,000	$600	$5,000

3. Given the following balance sheets and income statement for Rockwall Enterprises, Inc.:
   a. Develop a cash flow statement.
   b. Discuss why the cash position of the company is different from the profit of the company. Specifically, note that net profit was $425, but the cash account stayed the same.

ROCKWALL ENTERPRISES, INC.
BALANCE SHEET: 12/31/01
(000s)

Cash	$ 500	Accounts payable	$ 200
Accounts receivable	750	Operating accruals	300
Inventory	400	Debt	1,000
Fixed assets	1,000	Common stock	500
(Accumulated depr.)	(400)	Retained earnings	250
Total	$2,250	Total	$2,250

ROCKWALL ENTERPRISES, INC.
BALANCE SHEET: 12/31/02
(000s)

Cash	$ 500	Accounts payable	$ 950
Accounts receivable	2,000	Operating accruals	275
Inventory	600	Debt	1,000
Fixed assets	1,000	Common stock	500
(Accumulated depr.)	(700)	Retained earnings	675
Total	$3,400	Total	$3,400

ROCKWALL ENTERPRISES, INC.
INCOME STATEMENT:
1/01/98–12/31/98

Sales	$9,000
Cost of goods sold	4,500
Gross profit	4,500
Operating expenses:	
Salaries, Advertising, etc.	3,500
Depreciation	300
Operating profit	700
Interest	100
Taxes	175
Net profit	425
Dividends	0
Addition to retained earnings	425

4. Given the following balance sheets and income statement for Landmark International, Inc.:
   a. Develop a cash flow statement.
   b. Explain why the cash balance increased by $350 when the company generated a net profit of $405.

LANDMARK INTERNATIONAL, INC.
BALANCE SHEET: 12/31/01
(000s)

Cash	$ 200	Accounts payable	$ 200
Accounts receivable	800	Operating accruals	300
Inventory	250	Debt	750
Fixed assets	1,000	Common stock	400
(Accumulated depr.)	(400)	Retained earnings	200
Total	$1,850	Total	$1,850

LANDMARK INTERNATIONAL, INC.
BALANCE SHEET: 12/31/02
(000s)

Cash	$ 550	Accounts payable	$ 250
Accounts receivable	700	Operating accruals	150
Inventory	150	Debt	395
Fixed assets	1,000	Common stock	400
(Accumulated depr.)	(600)	Retained earnings	605
Total	$1,800	Total	$1,800

LANDMARK INTERNATIONAL, INC.
INCOME STATEMENT:
1/1/02–12/31/02

Sales	$4,500
Cost of goods sold	2,200
Gross profit	2,300

Operating expenses:	
Salaries, Advertising, etc.	1,300
Depreciation	200
Operating profit	800
Interest	75
Taxes	320
Net profit	405
Dividends	0
Addition to retained earnings	405

5. Given the following balance sheets and income statement for Brothers, Inc.:
   a. Develop a cash flow statement.
   b. Why is the company able to make a profit while its cash account went to a deficit position?

BROTHERS, INC.
BALANCE SHEET: 12/31/01
(000s)

Cash	$1,000	Accounts payable	$1,250
Accounts receivable	1,500	Operating accruals	450
Inventory	1,750	Accrued interest	0
		Deferred taxes	0
		Debt	2,750
Fixed assets	3,000	Common stock	1,000
(Accumulated depr.)	(800)	Retained earnings	1,000
Total	$6,450	Total	$6,450

BROTHERS, INC.
BALANCE SHEET: 12/31/02
(000s)

Cash	($100)	Accounts payable	$800
Accounts receivable	1,850	Operating accruals	500
Inventory	2,100	Accrued interest	50
		Deferred taxes	100
		Debt	2,000
Fixed assets	3,500	Common stock	1,000
(Accumulated depr.)	(900)	Retained earnings	2,000
Total	$6,450	Total	$6,450

BROTHERS, INC.
INCOME STATEMENT:
1/1/02–12/31/02

Sales	$9,000
Cost of goods sold	4,000
Gross profit	5,000
Operating expenses:	
Salaries, Advertising, etc.	2,900
Depreciation	100
Operating profit	2,000
Interest	200
Taxes	800
Net profit	1,000
Dividends	0
Addition to retained earnings	1,000

References

Richard H. Gamble. 1996. Working capital: Key to cash flow that treasury rarely manages. *Corporate Cash Flow* 17(4):20–26.

John J. Goetz. 1995. Ten ways to conserve working capital. *Journal of Working Capital Management.* Fall:27–31.

L. C. Heath. 1989. Is working capital really working? *Journal of Accountancy* August:55–62.

Chang Soo Kim, David C. Mauer, and Ann E. Sherman. 1998. The determinants of corporate liquidity: Theory and evidence. *Journal of Financial and Quantitative Analysis* 33(3):335–359.

Raghuram G. Rajan and Stewart Myers. 1998. The paradox of liquidity. *Quarterly Journal of Economics* August:733–771.

Cecilia Wagner Ricci and Gail Morrison. 1996. International working capital practices of the *Fortune 200. Financial Practice and Education* 6(2):7–20.

George Schilling. 1996. Working capital's role in maintaining corporate liquidity. *TMA Journal* 16(5):4–7.

Hyun Han Shin and Luc Soenen. 1998. Efficiency of working capital management and corporate profitability. *Financial Practice and Education* 8(2):37–45.

K. V. Smith. 1973. State of the art of working capital management. *Financial Management* Autumn 2(3):50–55.

Bernell K. Stone. 1998. Liquidity assessment and the formulation of corporate liquidity policy. In *Readings in Short-Term Financial Management.* 3d ed. St. Paul, MN: West Publishing Company, pp 32–41.

Shawn Tully. 1994. Raiding a company's hidden cash. *Fortune* 130(4):82–89.

CHAPTER 2

Analysis of Solvency, Liquidity, and Financial Flexibility

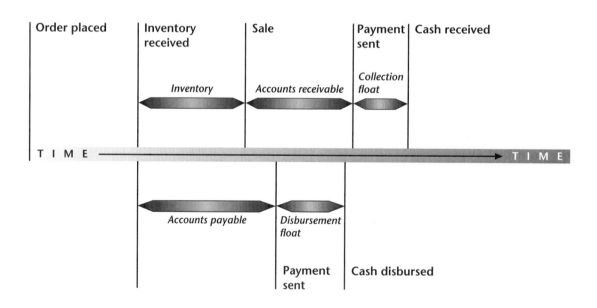

OBJECTIVES

After studying this chapter, you should be able to:

- Differentiate between solvency and liquidity ratios.
- Conduct a liquidity analysis of a company's financial position.
- Assess a firm's financial flexibility position.

Chapter 1 identified the importance that working capital management plays in impacting the operating cash flow of the company. Once the firm's working capital management policies have been determined, it is then important to monitor the impact that these policies have on the **solvency, liquidity,** and **financial flexibility** of the firm. A firm is solvent when its assets exceed its total liabilities. It is liquid when it can pay its bills on time without undue cost. Finally, it has financial flexibility when its financial policies, including financial leverage, dividend policy, profitability, and asset efficiency, are consistent with its projected growth in sales.

FINANCIAL DILEMMA

What Happened?

In 1993, things looked pretty bleak for Dell Computer Corporation. The company was growing too fast, inventories were ballooning, cash reserves were low, and receivables were growing faster than revenue growth rates. The company posted a loss for the most recent fiscal year, and the company was under attack by securities analysts for its speculative use of derivatives. Dell's stock price plummeted from $49 to $16 per share. However, the company's new CFO, Tom Meredith, saw an opportunity to turn the company around by bringing the "Golden Triangle," formed by the three key variables of growth, profitability, and liquidity, back into balance.[1]

---

[1]Stephen Barr. 1998. The best of 1998: Thomas Meredith. *CFO Magazine* September:42–43.

Exhibit 2-1 presents 5 years of balance sheet data and 5 years of profit and loss statements for Dell Computer Corporation. We will use these financial statements to demonstrate the calculation and interpretation of the solvency, liquidity, and financial flexibility ratios that will be presented.

SOLVENCY MEASURES

Although the ratios presented in this section are generally referred to as liquidity ratios, they really measure the solvency of the firm. As previously discussed, a firm is considered solvent when its assets exceed its liabilities. The solvency ratios presented in this section are based on balance sheet accounts and measure the relationship between

EXHIBIT 2-1
Balance Sheets and Income Statements for Dell Computer Corporation

	Dell Computer Corporation Annual Balance Sheet ($Millions)				
ASSETS	1995	1996	1997	1998	1999
Cash & Equivalents	$527.25	$646.00	$1,352.00	$1,844.00	$3,181.00
Net Receivables	537.97	726.00	903.00	1,486.00	2,481.00
Inventories	292.93	429.00	251.00	233.00	273.00
Prepaid Expenses	0.00	0.00	0.00	0.00	0.00
Other Current Assets	112.22	156.00	241.00	349.00	404.00
Total Current Assets	$1,470.36	$1,957.00	$2,747.00	$3,912.00	$6,339.00
Gross Plant, Property & Equipment	207.85	292.00	374.00	509.00	775.00
Accumulated Depreciation	90.87	113.00	139.00	167.00	252.00
Net Plant, Property & Equipment	116.98	179.00	235.00	342.00	523.00
Other Assets	6.66	12.00	11.00	14.00	15.00
TOTAL ASSETS	$1,594.00	$2,148.00	$2,993.00	$4,268.00	$6,877.00
LIABILITIES					
Long-Term Debt Due In 1 Year	$0.40	$1.00	$0.00	$0.00	$0.00
Notes Payable	0.00	59.00	27.00	146.00	0.00
Accounts Payable	447.07	466.00	1,040.00	1,643.00	2,397.00
Taxes Payable	24.94	0.00	0.00	0.00	0.00
Accrued Expenses	256.95	0.00	224.00	375.00	355.00
Other Current Liabilities	22.05	413.00	367.00	533.00	943.00
Total Current Liabilities	$751.41	$939.00	$1,658.00	$2,697.00	$3,695.00
Long-Term Debt	113.43	113.00	18.00	17.00	512.00
Other Liabilities	77.43	123.00	232.00	261.00	349.00
EQUITY					
Preferred Stock	0.01	0.00	279.00	0.00	0.00
Common Stock	0.40	0.93	1.73	3.22	12.72
Capital Surplus	356.77	435.07	193.27	743.78	1,768.29
Retained Earnings	294.56	537.00	611.00	546.00	540.00
TOTAL EQUITY	$651.74	$973.00	$1,085.00	$1,293.00	$2,321.00
TOTAL LIABILITIES & EQUITY	$1,594.00	$2,148.00	$2,993.00	$4,268.00	$6,877.00

EXHIBIT 2-1 continued

Dell Computer Corporation
Annual Income Statements
($Millions)

	1995	1996	1997	1998	1999
Sales	$3,475.34	$5,296.00	$7,759.00	$12,327.00	$18,243.00
Cost of Goods Sold	2,704.15	4,191.00	6,046.00	9,538.00	14,034.00
Gross Profit	771.19	1,105.00	1,713.00	2,789.00	4,209.00
Selling, General, & Administrative Expense	488.79	690.00	952.00	1,406.00	2,060.00
Operating Income Before Deprec.	282.40	415.00	761.00	1,383.00	2,149.00
Depreciation, Depletion, & Amortization	33.14	38.00	47.00	67.00	103.00
Operating Profit	249.26	377.00	714.00	1,316.00	2,046.00
Interest Expense	12.20	15.00	7.00	3.00	26.00
Non-Operating Income/Expense	24.06	21.00	40.00	55.00	64.00
Pretax Income	213.00	383.00	747.00	1,368.00	2,084.00
Total Income Taxes	63.82	111.00	216.00	424.00	624.00
Income Before Extraordinary Items & Discontinued Operations	149.18	272.00	531.00	944.00	1,460.00
Preferred Dividends	8.75	12.00	0.00	0.00	0.00
Available for Common	140.43	260.00	531.00	944.00	1,460.00
Extraordinary Items	0.00	0.00	−13.00	0.00	0.00
Adjusted Net Income	$140.43	$260.00	$518.00	$944.00	$1,460.00

current assets and current liabilities. In some respects, these solvency ratios demonstrate the degree to which current liabilities are covered in the event of liquidation.

Current Ratio

One of the first financial ratios ever developed was the ratio of current assets to current liabilities, commonly referred to as the **current ratio.** This ratio's origin can be traced back to the early 1900s. Although it has always been viewed as a liquidity measure, its approach to liquidity ignores the "going concern" aspect of the firm. It indicates the degree of coverage that short-term creditors would have if current assets were liquidated to pay off the current liabilities. Liquidating current assets to pay off current maturing liabilities would obviously disrupt the operating cycle of the firm and is clearly not an option unless the firm is being liquidated.

The calculation of the 1999 current ratio for Dell is shown below. Dell had $1.72 of current assets for every dollar of current liabilities.

$$\text{Current ratio} = \frac{\text{Current assets}}{\text{Current liabilities}}$$

$$\text{Current ratio} = \frac{\$6,339}{\$3,695} = 1.72$$

The 5-year trend for this ratio is shown below. Although there does not appear to be a trend for this ratio, it was lower in 1999 than it was at the beginning of the analysis period in 1995. It did appear, however, to be at a reasonable level because Dell had $1.72 of current assets covering a dollar of current liabilities. This would be perceived as adequate cushion by most creditors of computer retail operations such as Dell.

	1995	1996	1997	1998	1999
Current ratio	1.96	2.08	1.66	1.45	1.72

Quick Ratio

A variation of the current ratio is the **quick ratio,** also referred to as the **acid-test ratio.** The only difference here is that the quick ratio ignores inventory in the numerator on the basis that inventory is the current asset that is the furthest removed from cash.

$$Quick\ ratio = \frac{Current\ assets - Inventories}{Current\ liabilities}$$

$$Quick\ ratio = \frac{\$6,339 - \$273}{\$3,695} = 1.64$$

The 5-year trend for this ratio is shown below. Like the current ratio, Dell's quick ratio demonstrates little trend but ended the 5-year period at a slightly higher value than the level it started at 5 years earlier and did end the period at its 5-year high. This ratio indicates that in 1999 Dell had about $1.64 of cash, receivables, and other current assets exclusive of inventories covering a dollar of current liabilities. On the surface this would appear to be a reasonable level of coverage for the short-term creditors.

	1995	1996	1997	1998	1999
Quick ratio	1.57	1.63	1.51	1.36	1.64

Net Working Capital

Another common solvency measure is **net working capital.** Net working capital is the difference between current assets and current liabilities. This measure reports the dollar amount of long-term funds used to finance current assets if net working capital is positive or reports the dollar amount of current liabilities financing fixed or long-term assets if net working capital is negative. It is generally agreed that the greater the current assets relative to the level of current liabilities, the more solvent the company. Dell's 1999 net working capital calculation follows:

Net working capital = Current assets − Current liabilities

Net working capital = $6,339 − $3,695
= $2,644

The 5-year trend for net working capital is shown below. The level of net working capital generally increased each of the last 5 years (1995–1999) and has more than tripled since 1995.

(Millions of dollars)	1995	1996	1997	1998	1999
Net working capital	$719	$1,018	$1,089	$1,215	$2,644

One problem with net working capital is that it is an absolute measure rather than a relative measure. Generally, when the dollar amount of net working capital is larger, the firm's assets are also larger.

external financing sources), and the availability of credit lines. We will study the concept of financial flexibility in more detail later in the chapter.

It is interesting to study management's attitude and perception of liquidity. Campbell, Johnson, and Savoie surveyed the Fortune 1000 companies with a resulting 30% response rate. The purpose of the survey was to summarize management's perceptions of the importance of various factors on the internal monitoring of liquidity. They found that the traditional monitoring of accounts receivable and inventory, as well as short-term cash flow projections and good bank relationships, are viewed as extremely valuable tools in the management and planning of corporate liquidity. Perhaps the most important finding of this study is that a traditional method of analyzing financial statements—ratio analysis—is considered a weak tool for monitoring liquidity. It may be safe to say that it is not ratio analysis itself that is a weak tool but rather that ratios had yet to be developed that are effective at measuring the liquidity aspect of a business operation.

To properly measure and monitor liquidity, the standards and approaches used in the past must be discarded and a new framework must be developed. Ludeman[5] was one of the first proponents of developing a new perspective on liquidity analysis. He suggested that liquidity analysis should include the following:

- Amount and trend of internal cash flow.
- The aggregate lines of credit and degree of line usage.
- The attractiveness to investors of the firm's commercial paper, long-term bonds, and common equity.
- Overall expertise of management.

From this discussion, it should be obvious that liquidity is a complex issue, and the analysis of liquidity should consider the firm's ability to generate the necessary levels of operating cash flow and the availability of a stock of liquid resources.

THE STATEMENT OF CASH FLOWS

Exhibit 2-3 presents the Statement of Cash Flows for Dell Computer Corporation for 5 years.

Purpose of the Cash Flow Statement

The primary purpose of this cash flow statement is to provide information on the cash receipts and cash disbursements of a business operation during a specified time, which gets at the heart of measuring liquidity. The statement presents cash flow data organized into three areas including operations, investing, and financing. Those who use financial information, such as investors, creditors, and financial analysts, will find the cash flow data more helpful in assessing future cash flows, determining the relationship between net income and cash flow, and evaluating the ability of a firm to pay dividends, service its debt, and finance growth from internal operations.

Statement Structure

The statement of cash flow is divided into the three categories of operating activities, investing activities, and financing activities. Cash flow information grouped by activity is

---

[5]"Corporate Liquidity in Perspective" (full citation in end-of-chapter references).

A Variation on Net Working Capital

Shulman and Cox[2] refined the concept of net working capital by adding new interpretations to various working capital relationships. First, they observed that the traditional definition of net working capital (NWC) (i.e. current assets minus current liabilities) was not reflective of its real impact on liquidity. They offered an alternative interpretation that equated NWC to the difference between permanent capital (long-term liabilities and net worth) and net fixed assets. From this perspective, the dollar amount of positive net working capital measures that portion of current assets financed with permanent funds. In such a case, management is using long-term funds to finance current assets, which is a relatively safe strategy. A negative level of net working capital indicates that a portion of current liabilities are financing net fixed assets, which is a relatively risky strategy.

However, even with these interpretations, Shulman and Cox thought that net working capital was not a very useful measure because it combined in one measure operating strategies (strategies involving receivables, inventory, and payables) and financing strategies (strategies involving short-term investments and short-term debt). So to refine their analysis they created two new definitions. First, they defined **working capital requirements** (WCR) as the difference between current operating assets (such as receivables, inventory, prepaids, and other current assets) and current operating liabilities (such as accounts payable, operating accruals, and other current liabilities). These accounts represent spontaneous uses and sources of funds over the firm's operating cycle.

They then defined **net liquid balance** (NLB) as the difference between current financial assets, such as cash and marketable securities, and current discretionary or nonspontaneous financial liabilities, such as notes payable and current maturing debt. Students should note the relationship between WCR, NLB, and NWC, specifically, $NWC = WCR + NLB$. Exhibit 2-2 may help the reader visualize the connection between these three balance sheet measures.

NET LIQUID BALANCE. NLB serves as a measure of liquidity rather than solvency as proposed by Shulman and Cox. To see how NLB measures liquidity, remember the interpretation of a positive level of NWC: the dollar amount of current assets financed by permanent capital. Over the operating cycle of the firm, the dollar amount of positive working capital requirements, which is a component of NWC, will expand as sales expand (increasing receivables and inventory) and contract as sales contract (selling off of inventory and collection of receivables). During the upswing, the expanding dollar amount of WCR must either be financed by drawing down the NLB, adding to permanent capital by acquiring new long-term debt or equity financing, or both. Therefore, the more positive the net liquid balance, the greater the amount of liquid resources the firm has to finance its working capital requirements. If the increase in WCR is seasonal, then drawing down the net liquid balance is appropriate. However, if the increase in WCR is permanent because of a new higher level of operations, then the increase in WCR should be financed with a permanent source of funds to maintain the firm's level of liquidity. Dell's 1999 level of net liquid balance follows:

$$\text{Net liquid balance} = \text{Cash and equivalents} - \text{Notes payable and Current maturities of long term debt or leases}$$

$$\text{Net liquid balance} = \$3{,}181 - (\$0)$$
$$= \$3{,}181$$

---

[2]"An Integrative Approach to Working Capital Management" (full citation in end-of-chapter references).

EXHIBIT 2-2
The Relationship Between Net Working Capital, Net Liquid Balance, and Working Capital Requirements

Net Working Capital = NWC = CA − CL

Current Assets	Current Liabilities
Cash	
Marketable securities	Accounts payable
Accounts receivable	Notes payable
Inventory	Current maturities
Prepaids & other CA	Accruals & other CL

Working Capital Requirements = WCR = A/R + INV + Prepaids & Other CA − A/P − Accruals & other CL

Current Assets	Current Liabilities
Cash	
Marketable securities	Accounts payable
Accounts receivable	Notes payable
Inventory	Current maturities
Prepaids & other CA	Accruals & other CL

Net Liquid Balance = Cash + MKT SEC − N/P − CMLTD

Current Assets	Current Liabilities
Cash	
Marketable securities	Accounts payable
Accounts receivable	Notes payable
Inventory	Current maturities
Prepaids & other CA	Accruals & other CL

NWC = WCR + NLB

The 5-year trend for Dell's net liquid balance is shown below. This liquidity measure has demonstrated a consistently increasing value from $527 million in 1995 to $3.181 billion in 1999. Dell has significantly increased its stock of cash and cash equivalents relative to its use of short-term debt.

(Millions of dollars)	1995	1996	1997	1998	1999
Net liquid balance	$527	$586	$1,325	$1,698	$3,181

The absolute dollar NLB balance may be used as a measure of a firm's liquidity. If the measure is negative, it indicates a dependence on outside financing and is indicative of the minimum borrowing line required. Although a negative NLB does not by itself suggest that the firm is going to default on its debt obligations, it does imply that the firm has reduced financial flexibility.

WORKING CAPITAL REQUIREMENTS. Using working capital requirements as an index of working capital needs, Hawawini, Viallet, and Vora[3] performed a comparison of the working capital policies across industries. The WCR approach is useful because the traditional net working capital figure includes accounts that are not directly related to the operating cycle.

---
[3]"Industrial Influence on Corporate Working Capital Decisions" (full citation in end-of-chapter references).

For example, the cash account, the marketable securities account, and the notes payable balance should be viewed as balances that result from internal financial decisions or policies, not balances resulting from the cash cycle of the firm. They should therefore be excluded from consideration. This approach is consistent with the decomposition of net working capital into net liquid balance and working capital requirements developed by Shulman and Cox discussed earlier.

The authors then standardized working capital requirements by dividing it by sales, developing a **working capital requirements to sales (S) ratio** (WCR/S). They found that this ratio was statistically different across industry categories, indicating that industries have significantly different working capital needs. If all other factors are constant, the greater this ratio, the greater reliance a company will have on external funds given a change in sales. Thus the larger the WCR/S ratio, the less financial flexibility and less liquidity the firm will have because its operating cycle will require significant investment of funds. In those cases in which WCR is negative, the firm's cash cycle becomes a permanent source of financing, and the positive impact on liquidity will be significant. The 1999 ratio value for Dell, with WCR in the numerator and sales in the denominator, was:

$$\text{WCR/S} = \frac{(\$2,481 + \$273 + \$404) - (\$2,397 + \$355 + \$943)}{\$18,243}$$

$$= \frac{(\$537)}{\$18,243} = -.029$$

The 5-year trend for the working capital requirements to sales ratio is shown below. This ratio generally dropped over the 5-year period and was at a negative level in the last 3 years. This indicates that the firm has more funds available in payables and accruals than it requires for its receivables and inventory needs.

	1995	1996	1997	1998	1999
WCR/S	.055	.082	−.030	−.039	−.029

WHAT IS LIQUIDITY?

Liquidity has three basic ingredients: time, amount, and cost. The first essential ingredient of liquidity is the time it takes to convert an asset into cash or the time it takes to pay a current liability. Simply put, the quicker an asset can be converted into cash, the more liquid it is. A second ingredient of liquidity is amount. Does a firm have enough liquid resources to cover its financial obligations coming due? Finally, cost is the third ingredient. An asset is thought to be liquid if it can be quickly converted into cash with little cost. In summary, a firm is considered to be liquid if it has enough financial resources to cover its financial obligations in a timely manner with minimal cost. This approach to liquidity analysis takes a flow (of resources) as well as a stock (of resources) perspective and is very short-run in nature, relating to the firm's cash cycle as discussed in Chapter 1.

Liquidity may also be viewed as the ability of the firm to augment its future cash flows to cover any unforeseen needs or to take advantage of any unforeseen opportunities. Campbell, Johnson, and Savoie[4] referred to this concept of liquidity as financial flexibility. This viewpoint is much broader and would consider such things as the firm's "stability of earnings, its relative debt/equity position (which may affect its access

---
[4]"Cash Flow, Liquidity, and Financial Flexibility" (full citation in end-of-chapter references).

EXHIBIT 2-3

Dell Computer Corporation
Annual Statement of Cash Flows
($Millions)

	1995	1996	1997	1998	1999
INDIRECT OPERATING ACTIVITIES					
Income Before Extraordinary Items	$149.18	$272.00	$531.00	$944.00	$1,460.00
Depreciation and Amortization	33.14	38.00	47.00	67.00	103.00
Extraordinary Items, Discontinued					
Operations	0.00	0.00	−13.00	0.00	0.00
Funds from Operations—Other	24.69	10.00	29.00	24.00	455.00
Receivables—Decrease (Increase)	−116.62	−184.00	−200.00	−638.00	−598.00
Inventory—Decrease (Increase)	−72.08	−138.00	177.00	16.00	−41.00
Accts Pay & Accrued Liabs—					
Increase (Decrease)	202.43	0.00	0.00	0.00	0.00
Other Assets and Liabilities—					
Net Change	22.64	177.00	791.00	1,179.00	1,057.00
Operating Activities—Net Cash Flow	$243.38	$175.00	$1,362.00	$1,592.00	$2,436.00
INVESTING ACTIVITIES					
Short-Term Investments—Change	−180.86	−103.00	−647.00	−288.00	−1,118.00
Capital Expenditures	63.69	101.00	114.00	187.00	296.00
Investing Activities—Net Cash Flow	−$244.55	−$204.00	−$761.00	−$475.00	−$1,414.00
FINANCING ACTIVITIES					
Sales of Common and Preferred Stock	35.00	48.00	57.00	88.00	212.00
Purchase of Common and					
Preferred Stock	0.00	0.00	495.00	1,023.00	1,518.00
Cash Dividends	8.75	13.00	0.00	0.00	0.00
Long-Term Debt—Issuance	13.43	0.00	0.00	0.00	494.00
Long-Term Debt—Reduction	0.70	1.00	95.00	0.00	0.00
Financing Activities—Other	0.00	0.00	0.00	37.00	0.00
Financing Activities—Net Cash Flow	$38.98	$34.00	−$533.00	−$898.00	−$812.00
Exchange Rate Effect	1.78	7.00	−8.00	−14.00	−10.00
Cash and Equivalents—Change	$39.60	$12.00	$60.00	$205.00	$200.00

valuable to internal management and the external analyst because it matches inflows and outflows within each activity and makes it easier to identify related transactions within each category.

The **Financial Accounting Standards Board (FASB) Statement 95** provides a set of guidelines to help classify cash receipts and disbursements according to type of activity. Using these guidelines, **operating activities** is a residual category encompassing everything that is not classified as **investing activities** or **financing activities.** Exhibit 2-4 presents the general guidelines for the suggested classification scheme. The purpose of this classification scheme is to combine transactions with similar characteristics and to separate transactions with dissimilar characteristics. Grouping activities in this way enables analysts to identify significant relationships within each category and evaluate an entity's ability to meet its financial obligations. At the bottom of the statement, the net increase (decrease) in cash and cash equivalents is equal to cash flow from operations plus net cash flow from investing activities plus net cash provided from financing activities, plus any change in value from exchange rates.

EXHIBIT 2-4
Classification Scheme for Identifying Cash Flow Activities

OPERATING ACTIVITIES
Inflows of Cash
  Receipts from customers for the sale of goods
  Receipts from customers for the provision of services
  Interest receipts on loans
  Dividend receipts on equity securities

Outflows of Cash
  Payments to suppliers
  Payments to employees
  Payments of interest to lenders
  Payments to government

INVESTING ACTIVITIES
Inflows of Cash
  Receipts from loans
  Receipts from the sale of loans to another entity
  Receipts from the sale of debt or equity securities of other business entities, other than
    cash equivalents
  Receipts from the sale of property, plant and equipment, and other productive assets

Outflows of Cash
  Loans made to other business entities
  Loans purchased from other business entities
  Payments to acquire debt or equity securities of other business entities, other than
    cash equivalents
  Payments to acquire property, plant, equipment, and other assets

FINANCING ACTIVITIES
Inflows of Cash
  Proceeds from the issuance of equity securities
  Proceeds from the issuance of debt

Outflows of Cash
  Payments of dividends or other distributions to shareholders
  Payments to repurchase stock of the entity
  Payments of debt principal

LIQUIDITY MEASURES

Liquidity tied up in the current assets of a firm is continuously changing form within the total category of current assets. Indeed, this must be the case if the firm's current assets are truly liquid. For example, funds are originally invested in inventory. After a period of time, the inventory is sold. If the sale is a cash sale, the transaction is reflected in an increase in the firm's cash balance. Similarly, a credit sale results in an increase in the receivables balance. The eventual collection of accounts receivable results in an increase in the cash balance. During this cycle, various payments must be made to employees, suppliers, creditors, and the government. Funds owed to these groups are reflected in accounts payable and accruals. As funds become owed, these accounts increase, and as payments are made, these accounts decrease. There have been many measures designed to analyze the component parts of the cash cycle. The following sections present several of the more notable measures.

Cash Flow From Operations

One of the most direct flow measures of liquidity is cash flow from operations. Until FASB Statement 95, this number was not generally available from a firm's financial reports but could be estimated by taking reported profit after tax and adjusting for changes in the working capital accounts and adding back depreciation, amortization, and long-term deferrals.

In 1980, Largay and Stickney reported that the then-recent bankruptcy of W.T. Grant, a nationwide chain of department stores, should have been anticipated because the corporation had been running a deficit cash flow from operation for 8 of its last 10 years of corporate life.[6] This meant that every day the company's stores' doors were open, more cash went out the doors than came in the doors. Although this can certainly happen for short periods, and indeed is characteristic of firms going through a start-up or high growth period, it certainly can't be a long-term trend as in the Grant case. Over a long period, a company must generate a positive flow of cash from operations. A positive operating cash flow provides resources to invest in fixed assets or use to service creditors' and owners' invested funds. A deficit operating cash flow forces the firm to delay investment in fixed assets or to obtain external funds. In 1999, the 5-year trend for operating cash flow for Dell Computer Corporation was very strong. The company's cash flow generally grew each year.

(Millions of dollars)	1995	1996	1997	1998	1999
Cash flow from operations	$243.4	$175.0	$1,362.0	$1,592.0	$2,436.0

Cash Conversion Period

Richards and Laughlin developed a concept, referred to as the **cash conversion period,** as a useful framework for the analysis of the cash cycle.[7] Their approach, measuring liquidity from the perspective of a "going-concern," is contrasted with the traditional liquidation value approach using the standard accrual-based solvency measures such as the current ratio. Their flow approach to liquidity analysis actually blends operating balance sheet accounts with the related income statement items at a firm's given level of operations. Calculation of the cash conversion period relies on three accrual-based measures of activity, specifically:

- days inventory held (DIH)
- days sales outstanding (DSO)
- days payables outstanding (DPO)

that focus on the cash cycle of the firm as shown in Exhibit 2-5.

The first step is to estimate the efficiency of inventory management as measured by the average time an inventory item is in stock before it is sold. This is referred to as days cost of goods sold in inventory, or simply **days inventory held** (DIH). Conceptually, the ratio measures the number of days between the receipt of an item until it is actually sold to a customer, or the average number of days inventory sits idle. It is calculated by dividing ending inventory (or an average inventory balance may be used) by average daily cost of goods sold. The calculation of Dell's 1999 days inventory held is:

---

[6]"Cash Flow Ratio Analysis and the W.T. Grant Company Bankruptcy" (full citation in end-of-chapter references).

[7]"A Cash Conversion Cycle Approach to Liquidity Analysis" (full citation in end-of-chapter references).

EXHIBIT 2-5
The Cash Conversion Period

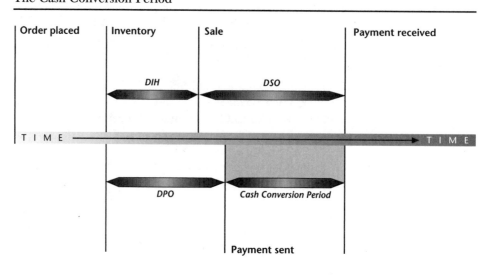

$$\text{Days inventory held} = \frac{\text{Inventory}}{\text{Cost of Sales}/365}$$

$$\text{Days inventory held} = \frac{\$273}{\$14,034/365} = 7 \text{ days}$$

The second step is to measure the efficiency of the credit and collections aspect of an operation by calculating the average collection period or **days sales outstanding** (DSO). This ratio is a measure of the average number of days that it takes for customers to pay for merchandise. The DSO is calculated by dividing end-of-period receivables (or an average of beginning and ending receivables may be used) by average daily sales. Dell's 1999 DSO is calculated using data from Exhibit 2-1.

$$\text{Days sales outstanding} = \frac{\text{Receivables}}{\text{Sales}/365}$$

$$\text{Days sales outstanding} = \frac{\$2,481}{\$18,243/365} = 50 \text{ days}$$

The third component in the analysis is an estimate of the efficiency of the accounts payable management as measured by **days payable outstanding** (DPO). Days payable outstanding is the time between the day that inventories are received and the day when payments are made for those inventories. This ratio can be calculated by dividing the ending accounts payable balance (or an average payables balance may be used) by average daily cost of goods sold.[8] The calculation for Dell's 1999 days payable outstanding measure is shown below:

---

[8]Instead of using cost of goods sold, purchases can be used. Purchases can be estimated using the accounting relationship, ending inventory equals beginning inventory plus purchases less cost of goods sold. Although the use of purchases is really more correct, we use cost of goods sold in this chapter because this approach tends to be used when calculating industry averages for benchmarking purposes.

$$\text{Days payable outstanding} = \frac{\text{Payables}}{\text{Cost of goods sold}/365}$$

$$\text{Days payable outstanding} = \frac{\$2,397}{\$14,034/365} = 62 \text{ days}$$

The cash conversion period is calculated by adding days sales outstanding to days inventory held (a concept referred to as the **operating cycle**) and then subtracting days payable outstanding.

$$\begin{aligned}
\text{Operating cycle} &= \text{Days sales outstanding} + \text{Days inventory held} \\
&= 50 + 7 \\
&= 57
\end{aligned}$$

$$\begin{aligned}
\text{Cash conversion period} &= \text{Operating cycle} - \text{Days payables outstanding} \\
&= 57 - 62 \\
&= -5 \text{ days}
\end{aligned}$$

The 5-year trend for Dell's cash conversion period is shown below.

(DAYS)	1995	1996	1997	1998	1999
DIH	40	37	15	9	7
DSO	57	50	42	44	50
Operating cycle	97	87	57	53	57
DPO	60	41	63	63	62
Cash conversion period	37	46	−6	−10	−5

Dell's cash conversion period declined dramatically from the range of approximately 40 days to a negative range of 5 to 10 days over the 5-year period with the majority of the change resulting from improved inventory management. The analyst must be careful in the interpretation of changes in the length of the cash conversion period. For example, the cash conversion period can be reduced even if the operating cycle expands by stretching payables by a greater number of days than the operating cycle expands. This is clearly not a signal of increased liquidity. Thus any changes in the length of the cash cycle must be analyzed according to its cause.

To review the cash conversion period concept, refer back to Exhibit 2-5. The cash conversion period is a measure of the time between the firm's payment for inventories and its customers' payment for finished products. Note that this measure does ignore the collection and disbursement float associated with the payment medium.

The concept of the cash conversion period provides useful information for the manager with the responsibility of managing and forecasting cash requirements. In practice, it becomes a measure of the time over which the financial manager must arrange for a credit line or other nonspontaneous financing. The greater the cash conversion period, the greater the financial strain and the less liquid the firm. A long cash conversion period can absorb a significant amount of liquidity during a period of growing sales and therefore must be managed very carefully.

Quicker turnover of the various current asset accounts, including accounts receivable and inventory, tends to indicate increased efficiency and enhanced cash flow. The analyst must determine the reason for the increased asset turnover to determine whether efficiency has changed or whether management policies have changed. Slower turnover in the liability accounts, including accounts payable and accruals, will also improve the cash cycle. Again, the analyst must make sure that the slower turnover is not affecting relations with suppliers.

In the case of Dell, the new CFO, Tom Meredith, identified the cash conversion period as a key performance indicator and spent his first couple of years focusing Dell's employees on how they could influence this metric. As a result, Dell continued to grow rapidly but no longer at the expense of liquidity and profitability. Meredith's new performance metrics, of which the cash conversion period was one, helped the company hone its direct-sales operations and build-to-order strategy, generate a multi-billion dollar portfolio of cash resources, and become one of Wall Street's top performers.

HOW MUCH LIQUIDITY IS ENOUGH?

So far we have discussed solvency from a balance or stock perspective and liquidity from a flow perspective. In reality, liquidity is a function of both a flow of cash resources that can be used to cover currently due obligations and a stock of resources that can be drawn down if the current cash flow is not sufficient. This section presents two measures that account for the combination of the stock of liquid assets and the flow of cash through the cash cycle. These two measures focus management's attention on the appropriate level of liquidity that should be maintained.

Current Liquidity Index

Fraser developed a type of liquidity flow index by combining cash assets (cash plus marketable securities) and cash flow from operations in the numerator divided by current liabilities.[9] Such a ratio, when it decreases over time, signals potential liquidity problems. We modified her ratio slightly and call the modified liquidity measure the **current liquidity index.** The interpretation remains the same. Dell's 1999 current liquidity index was:

$$\text{Liquidity Index}_t = \frac{\text{Cash assets}_{t-1} + \text{Cash flow from operations}_t}{\text{Notes payable}_{t-1} + \text{Current maturing debt}_{t-1}}$$

$$\text{CLI}_{1999} = \frac{\text{Cash assets}_{1998} + \text{Cash flow from operations}_{1999}}{\text{Notes payable}_{1998} + \text{Current maturing debt}_{1998}}$$

$$\text{CLI} = \frac{\$1,844 + \$2,436}{\$146 + \$0} = 29.32$$

The figures for cash assets, notes payable, and current maturing debt were taken from the 1998 balance sheet (see Exhibit 2-1), and the figure for cash flow from operations was taken from the 1999 statement of cash flows (see Exhibit 2-3).

The 4-year trend for the current liquidity index is shown below. Dell's current maturing obligations are more than adequately covered by the combination of its initial stock of liquid assets and its operating cash flow. Although there was a significant drop in the value of the current liquidity index from 1996 through 1999, Dell's maturing debt obligations were more than adequately covered by the firm's cash resources. For example, in 1999, Dell still had $29.32 of cash resources to cover each dollar of currently due debt.

	1996	1997	1998	1999
Current liquidity index	1,755.62	33.47	85.00	29.32

[9]"Cash Flow from Operations and Liquidity Analysis" (full citation in end-of-chapter references).

Lambda

Emery developed a liquidity measure from a function of the likelihood that a firm will exhaust its liquid reserve.[10] The measure consists of three parts. First, firms rely on a stock of liquid resources. These are resources that can be quickly converted into cash without impairing the operations of the firm. Examples of such liquid resources include cash, marketable securities, and lines of credit. The second component of the liquidity measure is the level of cash flow from operations expected over the planning horizon. The final component is a measure of the variability of the expected cash flow. These three components taken together form a liquidity index Emery refers to as **lambda,** as shown below:

$$\text{Lambda} = \frac{\begin{array}{c}\text{Initial liquid} \\ \text{reserve}\end{array} + \begin{array}{c}\text{Total anticipated net cash} \\ \text{flow during the analysis horizon}\end{array}}{\begin{array}{c}\text{Uncertainty about the net cash flow} \\ \text{during the analysis horizon}\end{array}}$$

The denominator of the above ratio is the standard deviation of the distribution of the firm's expected net cash flow from operations. It can be approximated by finding the range of the distribution and dividing it by 6 (i.e., optimistic cash flow minus pessimistic cash flow divided by 6). If future cash flows are expected to be similar to past cash flows, then historical data can be used to assess the future cash flow.

Lambda can be used like a z value from the standard normal distribution table. For example, a lambda of 3 means that there is only about one chance in a thousand that cash needs will exceed available cash resources, whereas a lambda of 1.65 signals a 5 percent chance of running out of cash. Exhibit 2-6 presents a table of lambda values from 1.645 to 3.291 and their associated probability values. Thus the lambda value gives an approximation of the probability of a firm running into a liquidity problem.

This measure represents the first attempt at incorporating information about the distribution of cash flow into a liquidity measure. It is very appealing because a firm with a relatively low liquid balance and a moderate level of cash flows may be just as liquid as a firm with a large liquid reserve and above average positive cash flows if the cash

EXHIBIT 2-6
Lambda Values and Their Related Probability Values

Lambda	Probability in Left Tail	Lambda	Probability in Left Tail
1.645	5.00%	2.108	1.75%
1.670	4.75%	2.170	1.50%
1.695	4.50%	2.241	1.25%
1.722	4.25%	2.326	1.00%
1.751	4.00%	2.432	0.75%
1.780	3.75%	2.576	0.50%
1.812	3.50%	2.808	0.25%
1.845	3.25%	2.879	0.20%
1.881	3.00%	2.969	0.15%
1.919	2.75%	3.090	0.10%
1.960	2.50%	3.291	0.05%
2.004	2.25%	>3.291	<0.05%
2.053	2.00%		

---

[10]"Measuring Short-Term Liquidity" (full citation in end-of-chapter references).

flows of the firm with the low liquid reserves are much more certain. In other words, liquid reserves are only needed to meet unforeseen circumstances that come about when there is a high degree of uncertainty regarding future cash flow. If the future is relatively stable, then there is less need for a significant level of liquid reserves.

FOCUS ON PRACTICE

Fitch Investors Service, Inc., a New York based credit-rating agency, recently unveiled a new cash-flow based rating system.[11] The rating system compares net free cash flow, defined as earnings available to pay debt after interest costs, taxes, and capital expenditures have been considered, to the average amount of debt maturing over the next 5 years and is thought to provide a useful early warning system for corporate bond investors. A high rating indicates the company should have continuing liquidity while a low rating would generally indicate that the company may have to raise additional financing.

[11]Investors have a new tool for judging issuers' health: Cash-flow adequacy. *Wall Street Journal,* January 10, 1994.

FINANCIAL FLEXIBILITY

Although not yet discussed, the role of sales growth is important because cash flow can be adversely affected by the growth rate of the company even though the company may be very profitable. For example, rapid growth puts a strain on the liquidity of those companies with large working capital requirements per dollar of sales. Management's response to that type of liquidity problem should be different than liquidity problems resulting from a lack of profitability or some other reason. Firms with a large market share in a slow growth industry tend to have very strong cash flows (such companies are often referred to as cash cows), while firms with a small market share in a rapid growth industry tend to have very poor operating cash flows.

Determining the rate of sales growth that is compatible with a firm's established financial policies is a key element in understanding financial flexibility. The concept of sustainable growth developed by Robert C. Higgins provides a framework to test whether a firm's growth objectives are contributing to its liquidity problems.[12]

Analysis of financial flexibility starts with the premise that there is a certain sales growth rate, referred to as the **sustainable growth rate,** that can be supported by the firm's current financial policies including asset turnover, net profit margin, dividend payout, and debt-to-equity ratio, without having to issue new external equity. Firms with growth rates that exceed this level will experience difficulties adhering to their target financial policies.

As a company experiences a growth in sales, it must finance the purchase of additional assets to support the higher level of sales. If a firm is not generating sufficient cash flow from operations to support the addition of new debt consistent with its debt-to-equity ratio so that new assets can be acquired, then the firm's target financial policies must be altered. Firms that grow faster than the sustainable rate must support that growth through cash generated from investing or financing activities (i.e., selling fixed assets, acquiring new debt in excess of the desired debt ratio, or selling additional equity

---

[12]"How Much Growth Can a Firm Afford?" (in end-of-chapter references).

shares). Firms growing at rates below the sustainable rate will have surplus cash to build an asset base, pay off debt, or possibly increase the dividend payout.

A firm's future growth potential depends on its total asset base. In other words, total assets must increase more or less proportionately with sales, or the firm's long-term ability to grow will be diminished. In addition, creditors often impose external restrictions on an operation in the form of financial covenants in loan contracts, and shareholders place a high value on the payment of dividends. These restrictions will dictate certain target values for various ratios (e.g., sales-to-total assets, debt-to-equity, and dividends-to-earnings).

When policy dictates certain values for these three ratios, sales growth is an interdependent variable in the operating system. If the firm has the ability to grow at a rate faster than its sustainable growth rate and management desires to achieve that higher rate of growth, then management should formulate a new set of financial policies that will allow the sustainable growth rate to approach the desired growth rate.

Following Higgins' approach, sustainable growth can be estimated by equating annual sources of capital to annual uses. First, define the following parameters:

S = Prior year sales.
gS = Change in sales during the planning year where g is the growth rate for sales and S is defined above.
A/S = Target ratio of total assets-to-total sales.
m = Projected after-tax profit margin.
d = Target dividend payout ratio (i.e., ratio of dividends-to-earnings).
D/E = target debt-to-equity ratio.

If sales are to increase by gS, then assets must grow proportionately to keep A/S constant. In other words, sales growth of gS will require an addition to the asset base of gS(A/S), which represents a use of capital.

Sources of capital originate from the liability and equity side of the balance sheet. Additions to retained earnings equal net profit minus dividends paid. This is depicted by the expression:

$$m \times (S + gS) \times (1 - d)$$

As equity increases by this amount, liabilities can increase proportionately and still maintain a constant value for D/E. The expression for the increase in liabilities is:

$$m \times (S + gS) \times (1 - d)(D/E)$$

Total uses must equal total sources, equating the two results in the following expression:

$$gS \times (A/S) = m \times (S + gS) \times (1-d) + m \times (S + gS) \times (1-d)(D/E).$$

The growth rate for sales (g) that satisfies the above equality is defined as the sustainable growth rate and presented below.

$$g = \frac{m \times (1-d) \times [1 + D/E]}{A/S - \{m \times (1-d) \times [1 + D/E]\}}$$

The critical operating variable in the equation is the addition to retained earnings, the major spontaneous source of cash in this framework. To support the growth objectives of the firm, it could be argued that new external equity could be issued if earnings retention is not sufficient to maintain the desired debt-to-equity mix. However, this ignores the nonspontaneous aspect of new equity issues and that conditions in equity

HOW LONG CAN A FIRM SURVIVE WITHOUT PROFIT OR CASH FLOW?[13]   What could be wrong with having an impressive customer base, $1 billion in cash, and expanding sales? After hitting a peak of 106 11/16 on December 10, 1999 and trending downward until mid-June 2000, Amazon.com, Inc.'s stock price settled into a trading range between the mid-40s and mid-50s.

The company's balance sheet negatives could be easily overlooked. Why? Because management was willing to go into the red to build up a dominant position in e-commerce, and as triple-digit growth rates and expansion into new product lines led to far heftier sales, Amazon would eventually cross over into profitability.

However, in June of 2000 it became evident that debt analysts and equity analysts were looking at the company through very different lenses. Debt analyst Ravi Suria, with Lehman Brothers, released a very negative report on the company's deteriorating credit situation. He in essence questioned the business model on which Amazon and most e-tailers are based. He argued that the excessive debt and poor inventory management at Amazon will make the company's operating cash flow worse the more it grows. However, the company's founder, Jeffrey P. Bezos, was quick to counter, saying the company will have positive operating cash flow over the last three-quarters of 2000 and is on the road to profitability. He did concede however that inventory control could be improved.

Because the company had some significant inventory missteps during the 1999 Christmas season, its cash flow nose-dived from a positive $31.5 million to a negative $320.5 million during the first quarter following the all-important Christmas season. By adding product lines such

continued

markets may not be conducive to new issues when funds are needed. The sustainable growth rate for Dell using end-of-year 1998 data is calculated below. We used 1998 data to calculate a sustainable growth rate for 1999 sales. Actual 1999 sales grew 47.99 percent versus a calculated sustainable growth of 270.49 percent.

$$g = \frac{.0765 \times (1-0.0) \times (1 + 2.3008)}{.3462 - [.0765 \times (1-0.0) \times (1 + 2.3008)]}$$

$$= \frac{.2525}{.0937} = 270.49\%$$

Dell grew at a slower pace than its sustainable growth, allowing the firm to use some of its excess financial resources to pay down its debt so that its debt-to-equity ratio fell from 2.30 in 1998 to 1.96 in 1999.

The 4-year trend for Dell's sustainable growth rate is shown below. Dell's strategies contributed to an increasing degree of financial flexibility as its asset-to-sales ratio fell (resulting from improved working capital management), and its profit margin improved. As a result, the firm was able to grow at annual revenue growth rates exceeding 45 percent from 1995 through 1999 without straining the firm's financial resources.

(PERCENT)	1996	1997	1998	1999
Sustainable growth	27.46	36.47	95.85	270.49
Actual growth	52.39	46.51	58.87	47.99

FOCUS ON PRACTICE

as electronics and toys, and building distribution centers all over the country, the job of policing its inventories became much more difficult. Amazon's ability to turn over its inventory declined since the end of 1998, falling from 8.5 times to just 2.9 times for the first quarter of 2000. In fact, inventory has been growing faster than sales.

On the positive side, operating losses fell from 26 percent of sales in the fourth quarter of 1999 to 17 percent in the first quarter of 2000 and should drop to a single-digit rate by the end of 2000 with a company-wide positive operating profit by the end of 2001.

Equity analysts have generally sided with Bezos and believe the debt analysts focused too heavily on the 1 year of Amazon's greatest expansion and then projected those costs forward. For Amazon, the costs came up front, but now, they argue, the company will exploit its ability to handle a far higher volume. Suria's critics claim he was looking at these one-time capital costs, assuming that Amazon would have to keep spending at those levels. However, now that the distribution centers are built, the company can work to make them more efficient. In fact, as Amazon's sales grow, some analysts estimate that it will require no more than one third of the investment of a brick-and-mortar retailer for the same amount of sales.

Who is right? Perhaps only time can tell.

[13]Adapted from: Can Amazon Make It? *Business Week* July 10, 2000:38–43.

FINANCIAL DILEMMA REVISITED

So what have we learned from Dell's experience? When management brings the three key variables of growth, profitability, and liquidity into harmony, the value created can be significant. Dell was able to sustain a strong growth rate without straining its resources because in part it restructured its working capital policies so that the operating cycle was able to not only become self-financing, it actually became a net supplier of funds for the firm. With the cash conversion period decreasing from 37 days in 1995 to a deficit of 5 days in 1999, cash flow from operations increased by a factor of 10 from $243 million in 1995 to $2.43 billion in 1999. Thus the firm was able to fund its growth with internally generated funds and did not have to rely to any large degree on outside funds.

SUMMARY

This chapter introduced the basic concepts of solvency, liquidity, and financial flexibility. All three concepts are valid, and all three are important. The issue for the manager, analyst, investor, or lender is to match the question being asked with the appropriate concept.

Solvency is an accounting concept comparing assets to liabilities. It is an appropriate measure addressing the degree of coverage of liabilities by assets in the event of liquidation.

Liquidity is more of a tactical concept related to the firm's ability to pay for its current obligations in a timely fashion with minimal cost. Payment can be made either through current period cash flow or by drawing down a stock of liquid resources. The question here addresses whether the firm has the cash resources to cover its debt service or other significant payment obligations on an on-going basis.

Financial flexibility, as measured by the sustainable growth rate, is a more strategic concept related to the firm's overall financial structure and whether its financial policies allow the firm enough flexibility to take advantage of unforeseen opportunities.

Useful Web Sites

Source for corporate financial statements: www.sec.gov/edgar.shtml

Questions

1. What is liquidity, and how does it differ from solvency?
2. How is liquidity related to financial flexibility?
3. How does the sustainable growth rate concept relate to the concept of financial flexibility?
4. How might a balance sheet measure of solvency be converted into a liquidity measure?
5. What new information is contributed by lambda that is not provided by the current liquidity index?
6. What useful information does the statement of cash flows provide?
7. Give your interpretation of a company's current ratio that has a value of 2.00? What is your interpretation of a company's current liquidity index value if it is 2.00? Does this help you understand the difference between solvency and liquidity?
8. In your own words, describe why the cash conversion period is listed as a measure of liquidity.
9. How are the current liquidity index and lambda like the flow measures of liquidity (such as cash conversion cycle and cash flow from operations) and the solvency ratios (such as current ratio)? How are they different?
10. Is it possible for a firm to have high (low) solvency ratios but low (high) flow measures of liquidity? Explain.
11. In your own words, what information does the rate of sustainable growth provide?

Problems

1. Compute the lambda value from the following financial data. To calculate the cash flow uncertainty number, use a range of 3 years of cash flow, find the difference between the high and low values, and divide by 6. Calculate lambda for 1993 using end-of-year 1993 cash assets, 1994 cash flow, and base uncertainty on the 3-year range of cash flow starting in 1991. Then calculate the value for lambda for each succeeding year, and discuss the appropriateness of the firm's management of its liquid resources.

YEAR	CASH FLOW	END OF YEAR CASH ASSETS
1991	100	
1992	90	
1993	80	50
1994	95	40
1995	100	20
1996	105	10
1997	130	15
1998	90	25
1999	75	30
2000	−25	40
2001	50	

The following financial data are to be used for problems 2 and 3.

	1998	1999	2000	2001	2002
Cash & Equivalents ^{CA}	$75	$75	$90	$100	$100
Accounts Receivable ^{CA}	300	400	600	550	500
Inventory	150	250	350	250	250
Gross Fixed Assets	600	700	800	800	800
(Accumulated Depr.)	(75)	(125)	(190)	(260)	(335)
Total Assets	$1,050	$1,300	$1,650	$1,440	$1,315
Accounts Payable CL	$125	$175	$250	$225	$200
Notes Payable CL	165	162	178	136	99
Accrued Operating Exp. CL	10	63	65	49	36
Current Maturities CL	50	98	100	40	40
Long-Term Debt	500	400	300	100	50
Shareholders Equity	200	402	757	890	890

	1998	1999	2000	2001	2002
Revenues	$1,500	$2,250	$3,000	$2,000	$1,500
Cost of Goods Sold	600	900	1,200	800	600
Operating Expenses	600	700	800	750	725
Depreciation	35	50	65	70	75
Interest	30	33	28	25	10
Taxes	94	285	420	142	36
Net Profit	141	282	487	213	54
Dividends	40	80	132	80	54

2. Using the information contained in the above financial statements, calculate the following ratios:
   a. Calculate the solvency ratios, current ratio, quick ratio, net working capital, and working capital requirements for each of the 5 years. Discuss and interpret the trends you see.
   b. Calculate cash flow from operations for 1999 through 2002, and interpret the 4-year trend.
   c. Calculate the cash conversion period for each of the 5 years, and interpret the trend.
   d. Assuming cash flow from operations to be the following:

1999	$250
2000	400
2001	425
2002	130

   calculate the current liquidity index, and interpret the 4-year trend.

    e. Compare and contrast your interpretation of the current ratio trend with your interpretation of the current liquidity index.

    f. What is your opinion of the firm's liquidity position and why?

3.   Calculate the sustainable growth rate for each year of the 4-year period 1999 through 2002, and compare it with the actual sales growth rate. Interpret and discuss disparities between the two growth rates.

The following financial data are to be used for problems 4 and 5.

	1998	1999	2000	2001	2002
Cash & Equivalents	$25	$75	$100	$50	$25
Accounts Receivable	450	700	1,200	2,000	3,000
Inventory	400	500	800	1,400	2,500
Gross Fixed Assets	1,000	1,000	1,500	1,500	2,500
(Accumulated Depr.)	(200)	(250)	(350)	(400)	(550)
Total Assets	$1,675	$2,025	$3,250	$4,550	$7,475
Accounts Payable	$100	$200	$400	$700	$1,226
Notes Payable	50	275	1,092	598	1,550
Accrued Operating Exp.	60	55	60	70	80
Current Maturities	50	50	50	50	200
Long-Term Debt	400	382	330	1,508	2,315
Shareholders Equity	1,015	1,063	1,318	1,624	2,104

	1998	1999	2000	2001	2002
Revenues	$1,500	$2,250	$3,750	$5,500	$9,000
Cost of Goods Sold	750	1,125	1,875	2,750	4,500
Operating Expenses	700	750	900	1,600	2,500
Depreciation	100	50	100	50	150
Interest	40	45	100	200	400
Taxes	(36)	112	310	360	580
Net Profit	(54)	168	465	540	870
Dividends	45	120	210	234	390

4.   Using the information contained in the above financial statements, calculate the following ratios:

    a. Calculate the solvency ratios, current ratio, quick ratio, net working capital, and working capital requirements for each of the 5 years. Discuss and interpret the trends you see.

    b. Calculate cash flow from operations for 1999 through 2002, and interpret the 4-year trend.

    c. Calculate the cash conversion period for each of the 5 years, and interpret the trend.

    d. Assuming cash flow from operations to be the following:

        1999 $40
        2000   −75
        2001   −550
        2002   −650

    calculate the current liquidity index, and interpret the 4-year trend.

    e. Compare and contrast your interpretation of the current ratio trend with your interpretation of the current liquidity index.

    f. What is your opinion of the firm's liquidity position and why?

5. Calculate the sustainable growth rate for each year of the 4-year period 1999 through 2002, and compare it with the actual sales growth rate. Interpret and discuss disparities between the two growth rates.

References

David R. Campbell, James M. Johnson, and Leonard M. Savioe. 1984. Cash flow, liquidity, and financial flexibility. *Financial Executive* 52(8):14–17.

Gary Emery. 1984. Measuring short-term liquidity. *Journal of Cash Management* 3(9):25–32.

Lynee M. Fraser. 1983. Cash flow from operations and liquidity analysis: A new financial ratio for commercial lending decisions. *The Journal of Commercial Bank Lending* 66(3):45–52.

Gabriel Hawawini; Claude Viallet; and Ashok Vora. 1986. Industrial influence on corporate working capital decisions. *Sloan Management Review* 27(4):15–24.

R. C. Higgins. 1997. How much growth can a firm afford? *Financial Management* 6(3):7–16.

J. A. Largay and C. P. Stickney. 1980. Cash flows, ratio analysis and the W.T. Grant Company bankruptcy. *Financial Analyst Journal* July/August:51–54.

K. W. Lemke. 1970. The evaluation of liquidity: An empirical study. *Journal of Accounting Research* Spring:47–77.

Douglas H. Ludeman. 1974. Corporate liquidity in perspective. *Financial Executive* 42(10):18–22.

Verlyn D. Richards and E.J. Laughlin. 1980. A cash conversion cycle approach to liquidity analysis. *Financial Management* 9(1):32–38.

Joel M. Shulman. and Raymond A.K. Cox. 1985. An integrative approach to working capital management. *Journal of Cash Management* 5(6):64–67.

Bernell K. Stone. 1988. Liquidity assessment and the formulation of corporate liquidity policy. In *Readings in short-term financial management.* 3d ed. St. Paul, MN: West Publishing Company, pp 32–41.

G. P. Tsetsekos. 1988. Liquidity balances and agency considerations. In *Readings in Short-Term Financial Management.* 3d ed. St. Paul, MN: West Publishing Company, pp 17–22.

FOCUSED CASE
Just for Feet, Inc.

Just For Feet, Inc. operates retail stores in the brand-name athletic and outdoor footwear and apparel market. Just For Feet was founded in 1977 with the opening of a small mall-based store, and opened its first superstore in Birmingham, Alabama, in 1988. As a result of the success and high sales volume generated by the larger store format, the Company has focused primarily on developing and refining its superstore concept. In addition to the prototype superstore, the Company operates high visibility, high profile "flagship" superstores in select markets, which provide added entertainment.

As of January 30, 1999, there were 120 Just For Feet superstores operating in 23 states and Puerto Rico. Of the 120 Company operated superstores, 23 superstores were opened in fiscal 1997 and 26 superstores were opened in fiscal 1998, along with 21 converted Sneaker Stadium superstores. The Company plans to open approximately 25 superstores each during fiscal 1999 and 2000.

As part of its long-term growth strategy, the Company entered the smaller specialty store market of the athletic and outdoor footwear and apparel industry in 1997 through the acquisitions of Athletic Attic and Imperial Sports, which are now operated

as the specialty store division of the Company. As of January 30, 1999, the Company operated 141 company-owned specialty stores in 18 states. The Company opened 51 new specialty stores in fiscal 1998 and plans to open approximately 60 new specialty stores in fiscal 1999 and approximately 50 to 100 in fiscal 2000.

The Company's financial statements are presented below. Assess the solvency, liquidity, and financial flexibility position of the company. Specifically address the following questions:

1. Why did the current ratio go up and the quick ratio go down?
2. Discuss the working capital cycle position of the Company.
3. Discuss the ability of the Company to pay its current obligations.
4. Compare and contrast the solvency position of the Company with its liquidity position.
5. Discuss the impact of the Company growing faster than its sustainable growth rate.
6. What conclusion might you draw about the liquidity management of the Company and its future?

BALANCE SHEET	JANUARY 30, 1999	JANUARY 31, 1998
ASSETS		
Current assets		
Cash and equivalents	$12,412	$82,490
Accounts receivable	$18,875	$15,840
Merchandise inventory	$399,901	$206,128
Other	$18,302	$6,709
Total	$449,490	$311,167
Property and equipment, net	$160,592	$94,529
Goodwill, net	$71,084	$36,106
Other	$8,230	$6,550
Total assets	$689,396	$448,352
LIABILITIES AND EQUITY		
Liabilities and net worth		
Current liabilities		
Short-term borrowings		$90,667
Accounts payable	$100,322	$51,162

Accrued expenses	$24,829	$9,292
Income taxes		$1,363
Deferred income taxes	$902	
Current maturities	$6,639	$3,222
Total current liabilities	$132,692	$155,706
Long-term obligations	$216,203	$16,646
Deferred lease rentals	$13,162	$7,212
Deferred income taxes	$1,633	$704
Total	$363,690	$180,268
Shareholders' equity		
Common stock	$3	$3
Paid-in capital	$249,590	$218,616
Retained earnings	$76,113	$49,465
Total shareholders' equity	$325,706	$269,084
Total liabilities and equity	$689,396	$448,352

STATEMENT OF EARNINGS	FISCAL 1998	FISCAL 1997
Net sales	$774,863	$478,638
Cost of sales	$452,330	$279,816
Gross profit	$322,533	$198,822
Franchise fees, royalties, etc.	$1,299	$1,101
Operating expenses:		
Store operating costs	$232,505	$139,659
Store opening costs	$13,669	$6,728
Amortization of intangibles	$2,072	$1,200
General and administrative	$24,341	$18,040
Total operating expenses	$272,587	$165,627
Operating income	$51,245	$34,296
Interest expense	($8,059)	($1,446)
Interest income	$143	$1,370
Earnings before income taxes	$43,329	$34,220
Provision for income tax	$16,681	$12,817
Net earnings	$26,648	$21,403
Shares outstanding	30,737	29,615
Diluted	31,852	30,410

STATEMENT OF CASH FLOWS	FISCAL 1998	FISCAL 1997
Net earnings	$26,648	$21,403
Adjustments to reconcile net earnings to net cash used by operating activities:		
Depreciation and amortization	$16,129	$8,783
Deferred income taxes	$12,100	$2,194
Deferred lease rentals	$2,655	$2,111
Change in assets and liabilities:		
Accounts receivable	($2,795)	($8,918)
Merchandise inventory	($170,169)	($56,616)
Other assets	($8,228)	($5,643)
Accounts payable	$34,638	$7,495
Accrued expenses	$7,133	$2,264
Income taxes	($181)	$543
Net cash used by operating activities	($82,070)	($26,384)
Net cash used for investing activities	($79,183)	($32,067)
Net cash provided by financing activities	$91,175	$2,156
Net (decrease) increase in cash and cash equivalents	($70,078)	($56,295)

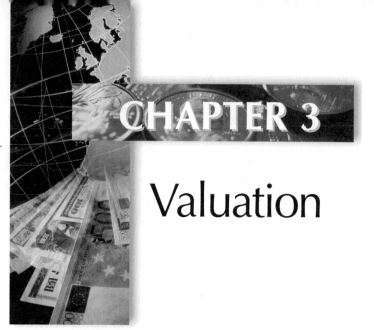

CHAPTER 3

Valuation

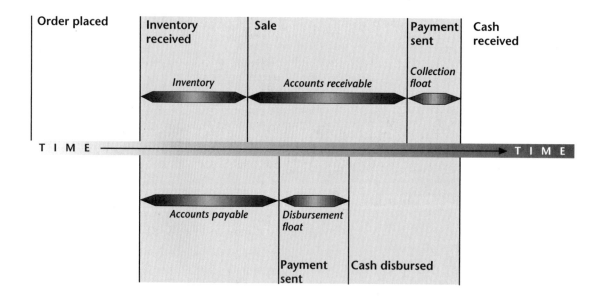

After studying this chapter, you should be able to:

- Use the cash flow timeline and discounting techniques to value future cash flows.
- Explain the importance of the time value of money for short-term financial decisions.
- Apply the net-present-value technique to select proposals that would enhance shareholder value.
- Explain how short-term financial decisions fit into the economic value added (EVA) framework.
- Recognize the difficulties involved in selecting an appropriate discount rate.

Capital budgeting is the process of generating, selecting, implementing, and controlling long-term investments in working capital and fixed assets. Because the primary objective of the publicly held company is to maximize shareholder wealth, this process should be carried out to appropriately balance risk and return within the context of the company's strategic plan. For consistency, multiyear working capital decisions should be made at the same time and in basically the same way as fixed asset decisions. Ongoing allocation of funds to inventories or receivables might be done in the context of an economic value added (EVA) framework, discussed later, or not reevaluated because the strategy of which they are part is projected to maximize shareholder wealth. Changes in working capital policy, however, should be subjected to capital budgeting evaluation using the net present value (NPV) method that is used for long-term capital asset selection.

The process of short-term financial decision making is often less complex than that of making long-term investment and financing decisions. Decisions whose financial impacts are limited to the present year's cash flow do not require extensive analysis because their desirability is only slightly affected by the time value of money. Although important, the tim-

ing of the associated cash flows is rarely the deciding factor in the "go/no-go" decision. Deciding which bank to use for a nonrenewable credit line would be an example of this type of decision. Many other decisions, such as permanent reductions of receivables or inventory, would change the firm's financial position for a period of years, however, and in those cases, the time value of money becomes vital.

In this chapter, we learn two approaches to short-term financial decision making, and we examine why a valuation approach is superior to the financial statement approach in cases in which the project's cash flows can be quantified. *Valuation* is the determination of the present dollar value of a series of cash flows. When deciding whether to adopt a policy, we take into account all cash flows and the time value of money. In Chapter 1, we focused on the unsynchronized nature of cash flows. In Chapter 2, we saw how this led to the maintenance of liquidity and some of the ways of measuring liquidity. In this chapter, we turn our attention to the dollar amounts that occur on the cash flow timeline and how they affect shareholder value.

Throughout this and the following chapters, we assume that the manager's objective is to *maximize shareholder value*, which simplifies to maximizing the common stock price. The implication for managers is that those policies and projects that should increase the company's stock price are to be favored. Short-term financial decisions have a significant affect on shareholder value, as we see in Exhibit 3-1. Inventory, payables, receivables, cash management, and short-term investing and borrowing decisions alter the firm's cash flows, cash conversion period, risk posture, net interest revenue, and information accuracy and timeliness. These, in turn, increase or decrease value.

The following hypothetical situation illustrates the types of issues that financial managers deal with, and it will help frame our suggested approach for determining the value effects of short-term financial decisions.

FINANCIAL DILEMMA
Evaluating the Financial Impact of a Change in Credit Terms

DigiView, a maker of digital video disk players, is thinking about changing its credit terms from "net 30" to "net 60," allowing 30 more days for consumer electronics retailers to pay for merchandise. DigiView believes the relaxing of terms would stimulate sales, particularly at the present time when many electronics retailers are facing intense competition and are financially strapped. The DigiView credit analyst is wondering how to evaluate the financial impact this alternative would have on the company.

TWO APPROACHES TO FINANCIAL DECISION MAKING

Two approaches may be used for making short-term financial decisions: the financial statement approach and the valuation approach. Their treatment of the advisability, timing, and risk of proposed decisions is contrasted. We then demonstrate how economic value–added systems attempt to incorporate aspects of both approaches.

Financial Statement Approach

The traditional approach to making working capital decisions, and the approach often taken in an introductory finance course, is to estimate the incremental revenue and expense effects of the proposal, then calculate the anticipated profit effect. If the effect is positive, the proposal would increase profits and it should be implemented. In the case of our financial dilemma, the DigiView manager would follow these steps:

1. Estimate the additional unit sales expected and multiply this by the profit contributed per unit.
2. Estimate the capital cost of the additional investment in receivables by subtracting the present average receivables balance from the balance expected under the new terms and then multiplying that difference by the annual cost of capital.
3. Determine the additional bad debt loss under the new terms.
4. Calculate the overall profit effect by subtracting the expenses from steps 2 and 3 from the revenue estimate made in step 1.

PROJECT ADVISABILITY IN THE FINANCIAL STATEMENT APPROACH.   The advisability of the project is based on the projected incremental profit: If the profit effect is positive,

EXHIBIT 3-1
Value Creation from Short-Term Financial Management Activities

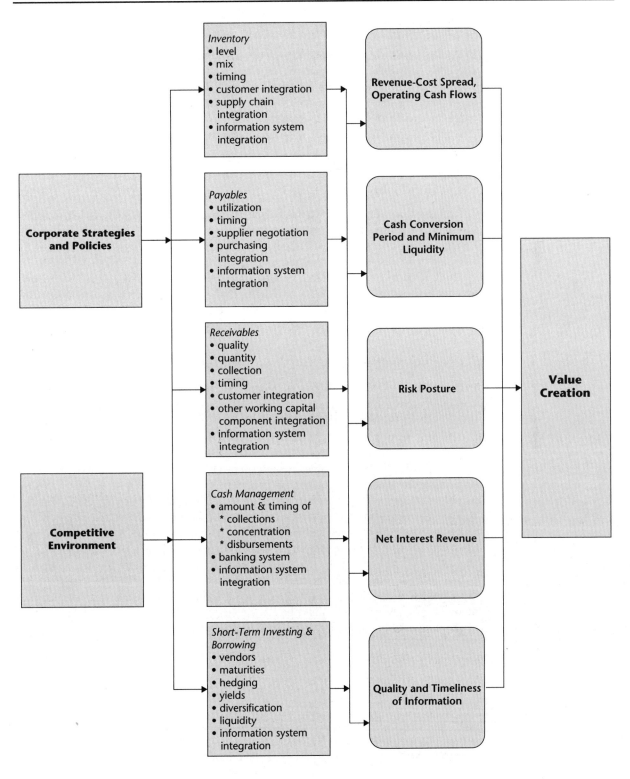

the analyst would recommend that the new credit terms be adopted.[1] The financial manager might slightly modify the traditional approach by dividing the profit effect by the change in receivables investment that was calculated in step 2. This modification would provide a rate of return on investment.

PROJECT TIMING CONSIDERATIONS IN THE FINANCIAL STATEMENT APPROACH. How does this approach account for the time value of money? It does so only indirectly, through the capital cost estimate made in step 2. How this occurs is not obvious. Let's say a company anticipates payment in 60 days on annual sales of $100 million, all of which are made on credit. Recognize that daily credit sales multiplied by the payment date gives the average accounts receivable balance:

Average receivables = ($100,000,000/365) × 60
Average receivables = $273,972.60 × 60
Average receivables = $16,438,356.16

Then this average receivables balance is multiplied by the annual cost of capital to estimate the financing cost of the ongoing investment. If that rate is 10 percent, the financing cost in this case is $1,643,836. This amount is then subtracted from the sales revenue (as part of the incremental profit calculation), giving $98,356,164 (= $100,000,000 − $1,643,836). We get almost the same result as if the entire sales amount is received in 60 days, and we discount the revenue for 60 days at a 10 percent discount rate. (Assuming daily compounding, the present value is $100 million less $1,630,176.90 or $98,369,823.10.) Some inaccuracy is introduced in the financial statement approach because the revenue and expense amounts are spread throughout the year.

PROJECT RISK TREATMENT IN THE FINANCIAL STATEMENT APPROACH. In the financial statement approach, the risk of short-term financial decisions is often overlooked. If the decision should have major balance sheet effects, the risk might be crudely measured by showing the resultant projected balance sheets. The analyst is interested in what effect a proposed course of action would have on the company's liquidity and cash position.

Approximate timing of financial effects can be seen through the use of pro forma, or projected, balance sheets. A more complete analysis might tie together projected income statements (based on the above incremental profit determination), projected balance sheets, and projected statements of cash flow. Proposal risk assessment is limited to whether the company's ability to pay near-term obligations would be impaired if the proposal were to be implemented. Traditional ratio analysis, using ratios such as the current ratio, quick (or acid test) ratio, inventory turnover ratio, average collection period, and the ratio of current assets to total assets, is conducted.[2] The analyst studies the changes in ratio values to establish when the financial effects might be most pronounced and how risky this might be for the company. *Risk* is implicitly defined as the effect of a project on liquidity or financial requirements.

---

[1] In equation form, using Δ to denote an incremental change, the evaluation of a change in credit policy would be: Δ profit = (Δ revenue − Δ operating expenses − Δ financing costs − Δ cost of bad debts).

If the analyst is careful to compute the incremental revenues and costs on a cash basis, this technique may provide the same accept/reject signals as present-value analysis according to Sachdeva and Gitman (see chapter references). We emphasize the present-value approach because it is more exact, its linkage to shareholder wealth maximization is widely accepted, and we can ensure consistency with the way in which long-life capital projects are evaluated.

[2] These and other liquidity measures are developed in Chapters 2 and 5.

APPLYING PRESENT-VALUE ANALYSIS TO SHORT-TERM FINANCIAL DECISIONS. Financial analysts are generally more comfortable applying NPV analysis to long-term capital projects than to short-term financial decisions. However, the criteria companies use in determining which projects merit NPV analysis indicate that even short-term financial decisions having multiyear impacts should be included. One company's criteria for whether to apply time value calculations when there might be some doubt regarding applicability are:[3]

Does the expenditure have long-run consequences?
Is the decision outside the ordinary course of business?
Does the unit proposing the investment put special emphasis on it?
Does the unit proposing the investment request top management deliberation?

Clearly, items 1 and 3 (and possibly 2 and 4) argue for NPV analysis of credit policy changes, inventory policy changes, information system investments, and banking relationship changes. Failure to subject these decisions to capital budgeting evaluation may result in misguided decisions, lowering profitability, and eroding shareholder wealth.

[3]Source: Richard J. Marshuetz. 1985. How Americans can allocate capital. *Harvard Business Review* January–February: 82–91.

ASSESSMENT OF THE FINANCIAL STATEMENT APPROACH. The financial statement approach, although popular, has two major shortcomings. First, it implicitly defines project riskiness as the project's effect on the company's liquidity. Although this may be valid for a struggling company, it is too limited for most companies. Ideally, risk analysis should encompass the variability of the project's cash flows and the effect of the proposal on the company's existing cash flow distribution. Second, this approach is flawed with respect to the evaluation of timing effects. Cash flows may occur any time within a month or quarter, and quarterly or annual pro forma statements may not capture the true liquidity strain of a proposed course of action. More importantly, the exact timing of cash inflows and outflows and the time value of money are overlooked. The analysis does not consider the preference for cash available today instead of at some point in the future. Cash available today has greater value because it can be invested to earn interest income or used to pay down short-term borrowings, thus reducing interest expense. The financial statement approach is appropriate for decisions whose financial impacts are limited to the present year's cash flow because their desirability is only slightly affected by the time value of money.

Valuation Approach

The second, and preferred, method of evaluating financial decisions is to calculate the **net present value** (NPV). This approach accounts for the exact timing of cash flows and their present values and results in making decisions that tie directly to maximizing shareholder wealth. The Focus on Practice box argues that NPV should be applied to many short-term financial decisions. When calculating the NPV of the proposed course of action, we net cash expenses against cash revenues, and we also account for the timing of cash inflows and outflows. A project with a positive NPV is considered acceptable for investment because its net cash flow more than covers the cost of capital needed to fund it; a negative NPV implies unacceptability. Computing the NPV involves four steps:

1. Determining the relevant cash flows.
2. Determining the timing of those cash flows.

3. Determining the appropriate discount rate.
4. Discounting the cash flows.

The decision criteria are:

If calculated NPV is positive, invest in the project.

If calculated NPV is zero, probably invest in the project.

If calculated NPV is negative, do not invest in the project.

Financial managers need to understand that money has a time value so they can determine the impact of short-term financial decisions on shareholder value. Specifically, it is necessary to incorporate the risk and timing of cash flows correctly when making financial decisions.

ASSESSMENT OF THE VALUATION APPROACH.   We have already seen that the financial statement approach is deficient in incorporating cash flow timing and risk. Only the valuation approach accurately represents the time value effect of cash flows and allows for an objective appraisal of cash flow risk. We therefore advocate its use. However, the valuation approach is difficult to implement in some cases, as shown in Exhibit 3-2. Financial managers have been able to address difficulties number 2 and 3 to a degree through the use of a planning framework known as "Economic Value Added," in which one gains an overall view of the company's financial position.

EXHIBIT 3-2
Practical Difficulties in Conducting NPV Analysis

1. The value of a proposal is directly tied to the difference of the present value of cash inflows and outflows. This implies that **valuation is predicated on the analyst's forecasting ability.** Although it is true that short-term projects with a "one-shot" payoff might be accurately evaluated, other projects have longer-term horizons (e.g., a permanent change in credit terms), and their cash flows are much more problematic. Furthermore, the very financial or product market inefficiencies that make short-term financial management valuable to the firm make the accurate projection of cash flows challenging. The degree of inefficiency and how long it might persist are exceedingly difficult to project.
2. Although the project's risk is captured in the discount rate, **the effect the project has on the corporation's overall business or financial risk is overlooked.** We assume, in other words, that the overall business and financial risk are unaffected by changes in working capital accounts.
3. **It is very difficult to value the effect of a project on the company's liquidity** because there is neither a theory of liquidity nor a "real-world" knowledge of what liquidity is worth. Yet, it is clear that liquidity is valuable, particularly in the case of companies that have a clear edge in this regard relative to their competitors. This difficulty exists whether we define liquidity as cash plus marketable securities or expand the definition to include short-term borrowing capacity (the latter, more inclusive definition is sometimes labeled the "liquid reserve").
4. Related to the valuation of liquidity, **we lack a well-developed understanding of the value of unused short-term debt capacity.** Especially perplexing is the value effect of a change in the maturity structure of debt, in which short-term debt is substituted for longer-term debt, or vice versa.
5. Finally, how does one handle the interactions between short-term changes to working capital accounts and long-term investment, financing, and dividend decisions? **Simultaneous effects on the magnitude of a corporation's cash flows and risk are difficult to pinpoint.**
6. Analysis of present value is not possible for some projects having permanent impacts, such as whether to upgrade the company's treasury information system. **Projects may not even have a quantifiable financial impact.**

Economic Value Added: An Attempt at Synthesis

Although we are oversimplifying, we may view the use of EVA models as an attempt to incorporate elements from both the financial statement approach and the valuation approach. Copeland, Koller, and Murrin, affiliated with management consultant McKinsey & Company, argue that value creation necessitates adopting a long-run viewpoint, managing all cash flows on both the income statement and balance sheet, and properly risk-adjusting cash flows from different time periods.[4]

Many companies are now linking major financial decisions to EVA. Essentially, this is net operating profit minus a charge for the opportunity cost of capital. It gives a one-period addition to value from a company's operations. Using EVA allows the financial manager to integrate both the revenues and costs of short-term decisions into the company's capital budgeting process for those companies that are not using NPV or that prefer to merge all decisions into one decision-making framework. Equation 3-1 gives the formula for calculating EVA, followed by an illustrative example.

$$\text{EVA} = \text{Operating Profit} - (\text{Cost of Capital})(\text{Capital Employed}) \qquad \text{(3-1)}$$

EXAMPLE OF EVA CALCULATION. Dwenger & Associates, a medical care practice, has a weighted-average cost of capital of 10 percent per year. It has used $30,000,000 of mostly long-term capital to run the practice, according to the most recent balance sheet. The most recent income statement shows the following:

Revenues	$40,000,000
−COGS	24,000,000
Gross profit	16,000,000
−Operating expenses	7,500,000
Operating profit	$8,500,000

The EVA for this period would be $5,500,000, calculated as follows:

$$\text{EVA} = \text{Operating Profit} - (\text{Cost of Capital})(\text{Capital Employed})$$
$$= \$8,500,000 - (0.10)(\$30,000,000)$$
$$= \$5,500,000$$

ADVANTAGE OF USING EVA. By emphasizing EVA as a planning framework throughout the organization, executives are gaining a better company-wide understanding of the importance of improved working capital management. The chief financial officer of one of the divisions at AT&T reports that EVA makes financial performance relevant to all company areas, from plant managers to payables clerks, as they see how their decisions and activities relate to EVA. Using a customized form of EVA, Valmont Industries, Inc. found that its best route to improvement in a French division was to reduce investment in receivables. Although division personnel had a culture-related objection to reducing credit to customers, top management was able to demonstrate through case study success stories what could be done. The cultural barrier was overcome, and downward spiraling EVA reversed as receivables were slashed.

CAUTION IN USING EVA. If not coupled with individual project NPV evaluation and future years' company-wide cash flow projections and risk analysis, EVA is justifiably criticized as a framework that focuses only on a single period and that does not properly

[4]See Tom Copeland; Tim Koller; and Jack Murrin. 1996. *Valuation: Measuring and managing the value of companies,* 2d ed. New York: John Wiley & Sons, p 22.

account for risk. McKinsey's "value-based management" framework joins EVA with "market value–added" (amount by which stock market capitalization increases in a period) and an emphasis on individual project discounted cash flow analysis to gain the benefit of both the financial statement approach and the valuation approach. The key issue for a company is not whether it uses EVA but whether it is conducted within a framework of NPV.

To calculate NPV, it is essential that the analyst understand the time value of money. Background information on time value concepts and calculations is provided in Appendix A at the end of the book. The following discussion applies a basic valuation model to short-term financial decision making.

NPV CALCULATIONS

The valuation approach to financial decision making requires that the analyst incorporate the time value of money and the riskiness of the cash flows. We begin our presentation with the time value of money and later add the complexity of risk analysis. The principles of valuation are carried out in financial management choices by calculating the NPV of each alternative and selecting the alternative with the highest NPV. To compute NPV, each cash inflow and outflow must be converted to its dollar value at a standard time. The time chosen is usually the present, which is labeled time period zero. Our calculations involve discounting all cash flows to the beginning of the timeline, then subtracting the present value of the outflows from the present value of the inflows.

Valuation: Simple Interest Case

We turn now to a simple way of finding the present value of short-term flows that typically show up on a corporation's cash flow timeline. Ignoring compounding, we can use a simple interest formula to "discount" the future cash flow(s) to approximate the present value effect of a financial decision. This formula assumes that interest is only added to or charged to the account at the end of the period, eliminating the possibility of earning "interest on interest."

SIMPLE INTEREST USING AN ANNUAL INTEREST RATE.   We begin our discounting calculation with an annual interest rate. The following example introduces the formula and illustrates its application.

EXAMPLE. Mary has a $5,000 tuition payment due in 6 months, and she is wondering how much she must invest today to have the necessary funds at the end of 6 months. She plans to invest in a 6-month certificate of deposit (CD), which pays the interest in a lump sum at maturity at an annual interest rate of 7.5 percent per year. Mary's bank is unique in that it will tailor the CD size to the investor's requirements.

SOLUTION. We use the symbol k to denote the interest rate on an annualized basis. Investors often use this annualized rate, sometimes called the nominal interest rate. Equation 3-2 is the simple interest formula that we can use to discount the future cash flow to determine its present dollar equivalent, PV:

$$PV = \frac{FV_n}{1 + (k \times n/365)}$$

(3-2)

In which:

FV_n = future value received in period n
k = the interest rate earned per year
n = number of time periods from now

Mary equates 6 months to 182.5 days, which is the value we will use for n. Substituting the other values from the problem, we find that the present value, or the amount Mary must invest today in the CD, is $4,819.28:

$$PV = \frac{\$5,000}{1 + \left(0.075 \times \dfrac{182.5}{365}\right)}$$
$$PV = \$4,819.28$$

SIMPLE INTEREST USING A DAILY INTEREST RATE. An even simpler formula can be used if the interest rate k has already been converted to a daily rate i. This formula (Equation 3-3) requires that the interest rate and the number of periods be stated in the same units, which in our example is days. We demonstrate the formula by returning to our example. If the 7.5 percent annual rate is expressed as daily interest rate (we use seven decimal places to avoid significant rounding errors, so we get 0.075/365 = 0.0002055), we can determine the present value with a simpler equation:

$$PV = \frac{FV}{1 + (i \times n)} \qquad \text{(3-3)}$$

Substituting the values for Mary's upcoming tuition payment into Equation 3-3, we determine the amount that must be invested today to be worth $5,000 in 6 months (182.5 days):

$$PV = \frac{\$5,000}{1 + (0.0002055 \times 182.5)}$$
$$PV = \$4,819.26$$

The result differs only very slightly from that found using an annual rate, because the daily interest rate has been rounded off.

Valuation: Compound Interest Case

Notice that the simple interest formulas overlook the fact that interest can be earned on freed-up funds. For example, consider an investment with a stated, or nominal, interest rate of 8 percent but with a maturity of 6 months. The **effective annual rate** that the investor earns on two subsequent 6-month investments (which would yield 8 percent divided by 2, or 4 percent, per 6-month period) cannot be determined by multiplying the 6-month rate by 2. The effective rate would be higher than 8 percent because in the final 6 months interest will be earned on the original principal invested and also on the interest earned during the first 6 months. Accordingly, a slightly more accurate evaluation of financial decisions incorporates this "compounding" of interest through time. Whenever the interest is compounded semiannually (as with the consecutive 6-month maturities), monthly, or daily, the effective annual rate will exceed the nominal rate.

COMPOUND INTEREST USING AN ANNUAL INTEREST RATE. We can see what happens when we account for "interest on interest" by redoing our earlier example. Continuing with Mary's investment decision, we first introduce Equation 3-4, which reflects daily compounding:

$$PV = \frac{FV}{[1 + k/365]^n} \qquad \text{(3-4)}$$

In which:

FV = future value
k = annual interest rate
n = number of days until amount is received

Substituting, we find that the present value is $4,815.99:

$$PV = \frac{\$5,000}{[1 + (0.075/365)]^{182.5}}$$
$$PV = \$4,815.99$$

The keystrokes for doing this calculation using a popular financial calculator are shown in a footnote.[5] Notice that Mary can start with slightly less today and still reach her target because of the interest on interest that her account is earning. Notice also that the present value using simple interest ($4,819.26) is almost identical to that found when accounting for compound interest ($4,815.99).

JUSTIFICATION FOR USING SIMPLE INTEREST.   Because the results are so similar, we use the simple interest formula for most of our calculations in the remainder of the book. Another justification for using simple interest is its widespread use in calculating money market yields and short-term borrowing rates. Furthermore, simple interest calculations are easily done on a standard 10-key calculator.[6] We use simple interest while cautioning that the result may differ markedly when the investment has two or more of these characteristics: (1) frequent compounding, in which interest is added to the account daily or continuously; (2) a substantial amount of principal invested; and (3) long time horizons.

Having established the desirability and mechanics of the valuation approach to decision making, we are now ready to apply our knowledge of discounting to short-term financial decisions.

BASIC VALUATION MODEL

Earlier, we suggested that businesses should make financial decisions that add value to the corporation. The NPV rule simply compares the benefits of a proposed project with the costs, including funding costs, and recommends implementation of those projects whose benefits at least offset the costs. Determining the NPV of a proposed course of action applies the valuation approach to financial decision making. After presenting the

---

[5]The keystrokes for doing this computation on a Hewlett-Packard 10-B financial calculator are as follows:
5000 [FV]
365 ■ P/YR
7.5 [I/YR]
182.5[N]
Press [PV] to get $4,815.99.

[6]For readers using this material to help prepare for the Certified Cash Manager examination, we note that only a basic nonfinancial calculator (on-screen, because the examination is now computer-based) is allowable.

NPV model, illustrating its use, and identifying some of its weaknesses, we will be equipped to resolve our chapter-opening financial dilemma.

We start by recognizing that NPV is the difference between the present value of all cash inflows (or cash receipts) and all cash outflows (cash disbursements) attributable to the proposal:

$NPV = (present\ value\ of\ all\ cash\ inflows - present\ value\ of\ all\ cash\ outflows)$.

Expressing all cash inflows with positive signs, all cash outflows with negative signs, and with n being an integer representing the period in which we will receive the final cash flow, we can express the NPV in symbol form:

$NPV = (CF_0 + PV\ of\ CF_1 + PV\ of\ CF_2 + \cdots + PV\ of\ CF_n)$.

Time period 0 represents the beginning of the cash flow stream, which generally is the time at which the initial outlay for the project is made. We calculate the NPV by discounting the actual cash flows, as shown in the general formula for annual future cash flows in Equation 3-5:

$$NPV = CF_0 + \frac{CF_1}{(1+k)^1} + \frac{CF_2}{(1+k)^2} + \cdots + \frac{CF_n}{(1+k)^n} \qquad \text{(3-5)}$$

When making the transition to daily interest, it is logical to use a daily compounding process to reflect the fact that firms will invest more in overnight investments or pay down daily credit line borrowing if funds are released from working capital investments. However, as previously noted, a simple interest formula can serve about as well for short-term financial decisions and is computationally much quicker. We can revise our simple interest formula (see Equation 3-3) for the NPV context quite easily. Allow N to be a counter for the number of cash flows occurring; n continues to be the number of periods (days) until the cash flow is received, and i represents the daily interest rate:

$$NPV = CF_0 + \frac{CF_1}{(1+i \times n_1)} + \frac{CF_2}{(1+i \times n_2)} + \frac{CF_n}{(1+i \times n_N)} \qquad \text{(3-6)}$$

Notice that Equation 3-6 is just an expanded version of our earlier simple interest formula (Equation 3-3), with the ability to handle more than one cash flow. Because of their simplicity, we will attempt to use one of the simple interest formulas whenever possible.

There is one other helpful simplification. Even though they are not "one-shot deals," many short-term financial decisions can be handled as if they were, to make accept-reject decisions. This means that Equation 3-3 can be applied even in some cases in which there is a series of cash flows, and the decision has multiyear financial effects. Evaluating the first sale occurring under new credit terms, for example, is sufficient to determine whether the new terms are beneficial to our company. In other cases, the more general formula in Equation 3-6 must be applied.

Applying the Model

The steps we follow in the remainder of the chapter in making decisions with the NPV model are listed below.

1. Lay out the relevant cash flows on a cash flow timeline.
2. Determine whether the cash flows can be represented by a single sum, meaning we ignore all cash flows except those linked to the first sale under the new policy and

discount with a simple interest formula (see Equation 3-3), or the cash flows must be handled as a "mixed stream" of differing dollar amounts (see Equation 3-6).

3. Select an appropriate discount rate, based on the riskiness of the proposal and what interest rate projects in that risk class must earn.

4. Discount future cash flows, subtract any initial outlays necessary for the project, and determine if the NPV is positive (accept), zero (probably accept), or negative (reject).

The calculated NPV, and the resulting accept-reject recommendation, depend greatly on the accuracy of the inputs—estimates of the relevant cash inflows, estimates of the relevant cash outflows (including the initial investment required, if any), and the choice of the discount rate. The next section deals with the cash flows, and in later sections we illustrate the discounting process and address the discount rate.

Cash Flow Estimation

There are three distinct types of cash flows to be considered in most financial decisions. First, the relevant cash inflows are the cash benefits arising from sources of cash increases. We must ask ourselves what would be the net increase from these cash-producing sources, being careful to include only those that change as a result of the proposed course of action. If we initiate a new product line or expand an existing line of business, the dollar amounts related to the new business are used as the cash inflows. When we are considering two alternative ways of doing something, however, we must be careful to compute the change in inflows based on the difference between the two alternatives.

Second, as we look at the cash outflows, we must again be careful to include only those cash flows affected by implementing the proposal. For example, **fixed costs** that do not increase with sales volume, unless changed by the proposal adoption, are ignored in computing the cash flows associated with a change in sales. Many working capital policy decisions affecting the company's sales level do not change such fixed costs as salaries, utility expenses, and insurance. The *relevant costs* to consider are those that would be altered by the decision. The decision will almost always alter total **variable costs,** which are those costs that are expected to vary with sales.

Third, the initial investment necessary to implement the proposal must be determined. This investment may include set-up costs, physical asset acquisition or disposition costs, permanent increases in the company's investment in cash balances necessary for additional transactions, and other cash outflows incurred at the time the project is initiated. At this point, we have completed the task of laying out the relevant cash flows.

Our discussion of relevant cash flows has been necessarily brief.[7] We discuss more complex NPV modeling in the appendix to this chapter, and we tailor the model to decisions on inventory policy (in Chapter 4) and accounts receivable policy (in Chapter 6). Before concluding our valuation section, we note in Exhibit 3-2 several practical difficulties that the financial analyst might face in applying the NPV model to short-term decisions.

Valuation Using the NPV Model

We are ready to return to our financial dilemma and consider how to frame DigiView's dilemma in the context of the cash flow timeline and our NPV model. Our approach will

---

[7]Expanded discussion of cash flow estimation is available in any managerial finance textbook. For example, see Chapter 14 of Scott Besley and Eugene F. Brigham. 2000. *Essentials of Managerial Finance.* 12th ed. Fort Worth, TX: Dryden, 2000 or Chapter 8 of Lawrence J. Gitman. 2001. *Principles of Managerial Finance.* 10th ed. Reading, MA: Addison Wesley Longman. Advanced material, including tax and inflation adjustments, is found in Chapters 8–10 of Neil Seitz and Mitch Ellison. *Capital Budgeting and Long-Term Financing Decisions.* 3rd ed. Fort Worth, TX: Dryden, 1999.

be to first draw a cash flow timeline and then calculate the daily NPVs of present and proposed credit policies to provide a recommendation to the company. The cash flow timeline is a helpful tool for visualizing the timing of a decision alternative's cash flows. We will show cash inflows as vertical bars above the horizontal axis and cash outflows as bars extending below that axis.

FINANCIAL DILEMMA REVISITED

The DigiView decision is a financial decision in which sales would change, and yet the consideration of one sales transaction provides all the necessary information to determine whether DigiView would benefit from the new terms.[8] We can ignore the cash outflows associated with each sale because neither their amount nor timing change. For simplicity, assume DigiView's sales are $36,500,000 per year. This implies daily sales of $100,000 (=$36,500,000÷365). For each day's sales, the cash flow timeline for DigiView's credit terms at present (net 30) would appear as shown in Exhibit 3-3.

Using Equation 3-2, we can determine the present value of one day's sales. We use a discount rate of 10 percent per year, assuming that this is DigiView's short-term borrowing rate.

$$PV = \frac{\$100,000}{1 + (0.10 \times (30/365))}$$
$$PV = \$99,184.78$$

For the proposed credit terms of net 60 days, we have only a minor modification of the cash flow timeline, as shown in Exhibit 3-4.

The present value of the proposed terms would be found using the same formula, Equation 3-2. We use the same discount rate, although a slightly higher rate might be considered because of the greater risk for partial, late, or nonpayment when extending the credit period.

EXHIBIT 3-3
DigiView Present Credit Terms Cash Flow Timeline

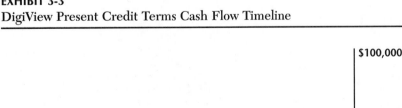

$100,000

D A Y S

0   30

---

[8]The value effect can be determined by evaluating one sale as long as two conditions are met: (1) the policy change does not change the growth rate of cash sales revenues or cash expenses, and (2) the policy change does not alter fixed costs subsequent to the time of the initial investment. The mathematical demonstration is given in Sartoris and Hill, 1983, cited in chapter references.

EXHIBIT 3-4
DigiView Proposed Credit Terms Cash Flow Timeline

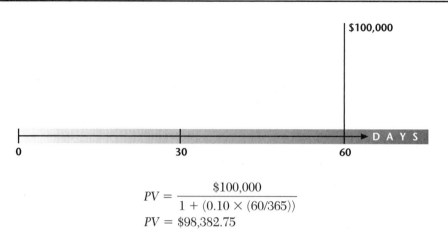

$$PV = \frac{\$100,000}{1 + (0.10 \times (60/365))}$$
$$PV = \$98,382.75$$

Note that if sales do not change at all with the proposed lengthening of credit terms, which is a very conservative assumption, DigiView would be losing $802.03 per day in present dollars ($98,382.75 versus the $99,184.78 formerly received). We could multiply this $802.03 difference by 365 to arrive at an approximate annual effect. In this case, the policy change would cause an annual value erosion of $292,740.95.[9] The proper analysis of the time value of money enables the analyst to make the value-enhancing short-term finance decision. Before making a final decision, the analyst would want to consider risk factors that could call into question the original projections. These risks could arise externally in the industry's environment, within the consumer electronics industry, or they may arise from some company-specific factor such as an interruption in production capability or material sourcing problem.

EXTENDED ANALYSIS.   Our analysis becomes more realistic if we allow for the positive effect on sales that we would expect to result from easier credit terms. The following table indicates the projected figures for our modified analysis.

EXTENDED NPV ANALYSIS OF
CREDIT PERIOD LENGTHENING

Variable	Projected Value
Initial investment	$0
Sales increase if terms eased	+3%
Cost of goods sold (inventory, labor, other related production costs)	65% of sales revenue
Payment terms—present (credit period for purchase and sale)	Net 30
Inventory Conversion Period Components:	
Inventory-to-production lag	30 days
Production-to-sale lag	10 days

---

[9]This approximation ignores the compounding to year-end of the intrayear daily flows. The NPV of the proposal, assuming the daily effects persist indefinitely and therefore constitute a perpetuity, would be $802.03/(0.10/365) = $2,927,409.50.

EXHIBIT 3-5
DigiView's Cash Flow Timeline, Present Credit Terms, Extended Analysis

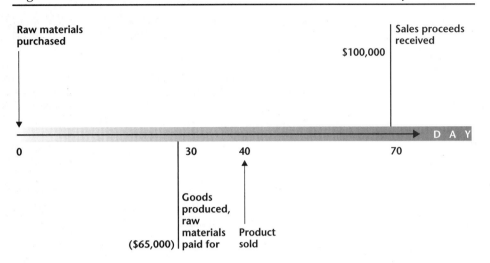

EXTENDED NPV ANALYSIS. Exhibit 3-5 shows the cash flow timeline for the extended analysis of the present 30-day credit period. Our calculations for the present credit period are based on the flows pictured. Then we assume the daily selling rate will increase by 3 percent under the 60-day terms (see previous table) and be even throughout the year.[10]

We compute the NPVs of the present terms and proposed terms and recommend the alternative with the largest NPV.

1. Present terms. First, we calculate the present value of the cash inflows. DigiView receives $100,000 in 70 days. The present value of the cash inflow would be:

$$PV_{cash\ inflow} = \frac{\$100,000}{1 + (0.10 \times (70/365))}$$

$$PV_{cash\ inflow} = \$98,118.28$$

We next calculate the present value of the cash outflows:

$$PV_{cash\ outflow} = \frac{\$65,000}{1 + (0.10 \times (30/365))}$$

$$PV_{cash\ outflow} = \$64,470.11$$

---

[10]If we were working with uneven or lumpy sales, we would have to first compound the intrayear flows to their year-end values. This step is necessary to use the formula for determining the present value of an annual perpetuity, which assumes a series of end-of-year cash flows. Illustrating with a day 70 cash flow, we would first calculate the year-end value of each of the cash flows (CF) using this formula:

$$\text{Future value (FV) at end of year } 1 = CF(1 + k)^{(365-70)/365}$$

After individually compounding all intrayear flows to year end, we would sum them, then insert the end-of-year sum into the annual perpetuity formula:

$$\text{Present value (PV) of annual perpetuity} = CF \text{ per year/discount rate}$$

The general approach to discounting perpetuities is covered in the appendix at the end of the chapter (see the Linke and Zumwalt article, listed in the chapter references, for more on using the intrayear compounding formula).

The **daily NPV** is then the difference between the present value of the daily inflows and the present value of the daily outflows:

$$Daily\ NPV = PV\ of\ inflows - PV\ of\ outflows$$
$$= \$98,118.28 - \$64,470.11$$
$$= \$33,648.17$$

We can calculate the NPV for the present credit period by using a perpetuity formula to turn the daily NPV into an aggregate NPV. The implicit assumption here is that the daily NPV would persist indefinitely. We provide a perpetuity present value formula in Equation 3-7.

$$NPV = \frac{Cash\ flow\ per\ period}{Interest\ rate\ per\ period} = \frac{CF}{i} \qquad (3\text{-}7)$$

We have seen that the daily NPV is $33,648.17. The daily interest rate would be 0.10/365 = 0.0002740. Substituting, we get an NPV for the present credit period of $122,803,540.15:

$$NPV = \frac{\$33,648.17}{0.0002740}$$
$$NPV = \$122,803,540.15$$

We now compare these results with the NPV of the proposed change in terms.

2. Proposed terms. Exhibit 3-6 shows the cash flows for the proposed credit terms, assuming that aggregate sales would increase by 3 percent. The new level of daily sales is thus $100,000 + (0.03 × $100,000) = $103,000. Note on the cash inflow timeline the extra 30 days related to the longer credit period (70 + 30 = 100 days). Because cost of goods sold is 65 percent of sales revenue, daily cost rises to 0.65 × $103,000 = $66,950.

We follow the same approach in arriving at the NPV of the proposed terms, by first calculating the present value of the stream of daily cash inflows and then that of the daily cash outflows:

EXHIBIT 3-6
DigiView's Cash Flow Timeline, Proposed Credit Terms, Assuming Sales Increase

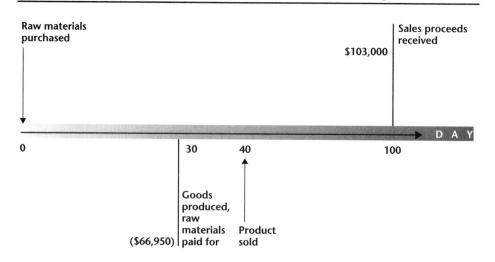

$$PV_{cash\ inflow} = \frac{\$103,000}{1 + (0.10 \times (100/365))}$$
$$PV_{cash\ inflow} = \$100,253.33$$

We next calculate the present value of the cash outflows, based on 65 percent of $103,000:

$$PV_{cash\ outflow} = \frac{\$66,950}{1 + (0.10 \times (30/365))}$$
$$PV_{cash\ outflow} = \$66,404.21$$

The *daily* NPV is then the difference between the present value of the daily inflows and the present value of the daily outflows:

$$Daily\ NPV = PV\ of\ inflows - PV\ of\ outflows$$
$$= \$100,253.33 - \$66,404.21$$
$$= \$33,849.12$$

We have seen that the daily NPV is $33,849.12. Dividing by the daily interest rate, we get an NPV for the proposed credit period of $123,536,934.31:

$$NPV = \frac{\$33,849.12}{0.0002740}$$
$$NPV = \$123,536,934.31$$

3. Decision rule. As with any mutually exclusive capital budgeting problem (only one alternative may be selected), the decision rule is to select the alternative with the highest NPV. Because the proposed terms give a higher NPV, the credit period extension is recommended. One caution is appropriate: If the analyst thinks that the cash flow effect will only last several years, an annuity formula should be used to estimate NPV instead of a perpetuity formula. (See *Annuity Discounting* in Appendix A at the end of the book.)
4. Risk factors. The key risk factor in this discussion is the amount and duration of the positive sales effect. The opportunity cost of funding, captured in the discount rate, is 10 percent. As noted earlier, this represents DigiView's short-term borrowing rate. This rate is linked to the business and financial risk before the change in credit terms. If that risk increases (decreases) as a result of the change in terms, the discount rate should be increased (decreased). In a later section, "Risk and the Discount Rate," we provide guidance on that adjustment.

   In practice, because that risk is hard to estimate, analysts could use sensitivity analysis as a decision aid. If sales increase only 2.5 percent, instead of 3 percent, would they still add value (have a higher NPV than the present terms)? If so, the analyst becomes more confident in the recommendation to adopt the new terms. Or, more formally, one could use simulation, in which probability distributions for revenues and expenses are combined in a quantitative model to determine a whole distribution of NPVs for a proposed financial change. The probability of having an NPV in excess of the present terms' NPV can be assessed. The reader may refer back to Exhibit 3-2 to review the difficulties in conducting NPV analysis.

Concluding Comments on Valuation

The NPV model, used in conjunction with the cash flow timeline, is a powerful method for evaluating the financial dimensions of project proposals. We summarize with three

EXHIBIT 3-7
Using the NPV Model for STFM Decision Making

Principle/Concept	Explanation	Implications and Cautions
1. Use simple interest, instead of having to utilize compound interest to discount future cash flows.	Time frame too short to cause major difference in investment desirability, so simple interest calculations usually adequate.	1. Calculations are easier, enabling those not trained in finance to make them. 2. Be cautious: multi-year cash flows and large dollar amounts argue for compound interest formulas and use of a financial calculator or computer spreadsheet.
2. Capture nonfinancial aspects of short-term finance decisions.	Along with an alternative's NPV, consider political/legal, ethical, and stakeholder ramifications before making a decision. Suppliers and customers are key stakeholders, because they are the company's depository and lending banks.	1. Get input from legal department, other areas such as purchasing, accounting, production, and marketing to bring various perspectives into decision. 2. Consider ethical dimensions of decisions. 3. Incorporate external stakeholder views, where possible.
3. Unlike long-term capital projects, most short-term decisions have no initial investment other than variable cost(s).	Make decisions by laying out operating cash outflows (from variable costs such as labor and materials) and operating cash inflows (from sale), then discounting future flows, and netting to get NPV.	1. Short-term financial decisions are typically simpler than long-term decisions. 2. At times there are fixed costs that must also be included at the time of the decision, or in a later period. 3. Fixed assets are sometimes necessitated by short-term decisions. This results in an initial investment amount. It also results in noncash depreciation charges, which affect future cash tax payments. A good example is when a manufacturer converts to a "just-in-time" inventory system.

pointers about using the NPV model in short-term financial decision making. First, we can often use a simple interest formula, which ignores compounding, to value short-term financial decisions. Second, we must remember that nonfinancial considerations at times predominate in working capital decisions. For example, the parts subsidiaries of domestic automakers have had to stock a large inventory of exhaust system parts as a result of a government regulation stipulating that specific levels of inventory be available for recent model-year cars and trucks. The impact on and reactions of stakeholder groups other than common stockholders must also be taken into account in decision making. Third, unless fixed assets or future-period fixed costs change because of the proposal, there will rarely be an initial investment to consider in the project evaluation.

We recap our discussion up to this point in Exhibit 3-7. Main points are summarized in that exhibit.

We have purposefully left a very important topic for the end: selection of the appropriate **discount rate.** This subject can quickly become complex, and we postpone until the chapter appendix some of the advanced considerations.

CHOOSING THE DISCOUNT RATE

In all of the calculations, a discount rate has been supplied. How do we determine the discount rate, k, used to determine the present values of cash flows? The appropriate discount rate is based on the riskiness of the cash flows. Conceptually, the rate chosen should reflect opportunity cost, or the interest rate one could earn on the next-best investment opportunity of equal risk. Asset risk ("stand-alone risk") is usually defined as the variability of the asset's cash flows for the company as a whole, whereas risk is a function of the variability of the average project undertaken. Risk heavily influences the required returns on the company's equity and debt securities. Correspondingly, the discount rate used for making long-lived capital budgeting decisions is the company's **weighted-average cost of capital,**[11] in which the funding sources generally included are long-term.

Discount Rate Selection and Project Lifespan

Three unique problems face the analyst trying to determine a discount rate for short-term decisions. First, corporations rarely raise funds specifically to finance the types of projects considered in short-term finance. This handicap is not present when making capital budgeting decisions, such as building a new plant or buying a major piece of machinery. The analyst is without the luxury of having market signals of funding cost such as those available for fixed-asset decisions. Second, the short time horizon of many decisions (other than those with multi-year effects) implies that we cannot use the long-term cost of funds and will, instead, have to tie the discount rate to a short-term interest rate. Third, risk should be incorporated into the discount rate, but how do we do it? The riskiness of many short-term projects is negligible, ambiguous, or both. For example, changing the number and location of collection points for mailed customer checks would not be very risky. As a banker making a loan to a corporation implementing a new collection system, what interest rate would you charge for the loan? What risk adjustment, if any, would you make to reflect the differential risk of this or other related short-term decisions? Or, as the financial analyst making the go or no-go recommendation on this proposal, what discount rate would you use? Finance theorists recommend choosing a discount rate that reflects the opportunity cost of deploying funds in this particular project, which in turn is determined by both the project's risk and lifespan. Further guidance is provided in the chapter appendix.

USE OF THE WEIGHTED AVERAGE COST OF CAPITAL.   Some might argue for using the company's weighted-average cost of capital as a discount rate for all short-term as well as long-term investment decisions. Typically calculated using only long-term funds, this benchmark works well for long-term decisions. The short-term financial context is more

---

[11]Calculation of the weighted-average cost of capital using actual company data is presented in George E. Pinches. 1992. *Essentials of financial management,* 4th ed. New York: HarperCollins.

complex. First, we noted earlier that current asset allocations are seldom, if ever, financed solely with long-term capital. This argues against simplistic use of the weighted-average cost of capital based only on long-term funding sources. Second, the average cost of short-term funds is very difficult to estimate. For example, how do we assign a cost on accruals or accounts payable financing? Even on bank borrowing, the bank may disguise its loan pricing by adjusting it upward or downward based on the volume of cash management or other nonlending services the company uses. The interest rate that a company pays may also be artificially high as a result of imperfect competition in the local lending market for companies of its size. To help resolve the dilemma of what rate to use, we will distinguish between one-shot and multiyear projects.

One-Shot Versus Enduring or Multiyear Projects

Other than the distinction between risky and risk-free projects, the most important guide to the appropriate discount rate is whether the decision involves a one-shot intrayear cash impact proposal or enduring multiyear effects.

ONE-SHOT PROJECTS. One-shot decisions, such as whether to take a cash discount on a one-time purchase, whether to enter into a 1-year contract with a treasury service provider, or which bank to use for a one-time working capital loan, are much like other operational purchasing decisions. When buying office supplies, you typically shop around until you find the best price. No calculating is done to compute the present value effect of these items. The corporate financial analyst will probably not do an NPV analysis of one-shot financial decisions either. Exceptions might occur when the dollar amounts are very large or when the flows occur at various points within the next year (especially when they are staggered toward year-end); two alternatives may be compared based on the NPVs. When money has a very high time value, such as in an economy experiencing hyperinflation, present value analysis is also warranted. Finally, whenever there are follow-on effects, such as the linkage of a loan with reduced rates on future buys of cash management or loan products, one should try to integrate these with NPV analysis, as demonstrated in the multiyear project approach that follows.

The appropriate discount rate for one-shot projects is usually the firm's short-term borrowing or investing interest rate. This follows the opportunity cost concept, in that investors can make approximately that interest rate if their funds are not used by the firm. Cash flows are going to be tied up (or freed up) for less than a year, and the rate of return that could be earned on those flows is a short-term rate. Note that this might entail using a discount rate in excess of the company's average capital cost when the organization is illiquid and borrowing at very high interest rates. Furthermore, if the proposal is more risky that the typical near-term project, a higher rate could be applied, such as that paid on short-term notes by speculative-grade ("junk") issuers. Examples of such projects might be those located in less-developed countries, in which there is a great deal of near-term uncertainty.

RECAP FOR ONE-SHOT PROJECTS. The upshot is that (1) one-shot projects may not be subjected to NPV analysis if the cash flows are not significant, and (2) the analyst may be forced to use considerable judgment in applying the opportunity cost concept when determining a discount rate. At the margin, if the company is consistently cash poor (illiquid) and must fund temporary outlays with borrowing, the borrowing rate may serve as the discount rate. If the company has excess cash, the investing rate may be used because dollars diverted to a project will come from the liquidation of investments. The foregone interest, then, is the true opportunity cost attributable to the project. Risk adjustment, as a result of project cash flows that are either less risky or more risky than the company's typical project, results in using a lower or higher discount rate than the short-term borrowing or investing rate.

MULTIYEAR PROJECTS.   When policies or projects have multiyear effects, it is important to conduct NPV analysis to maximize shareholder wealth. Short-term financial decisions, particularly those involving a payables, receivables, or inventory policy change, often have long-term cash flow effects. Thus they should compete for capital along with all other multiyear capital budgeting proposals. Assuming they have associated cash flows that are no more or less variable than those of capital projects normally undertaken, the weighted-average cost of capital should be used as the discount rate.

Risk and the Discount Rate

The general principle followed in financial decision making is "the greater the risk, the greater the required rate of return." Because bondholders and stockholders require compensation for risk in the form of higher required returns, the discount rate should be higher if the riskiness of the project's cash flows is greater. Generally, projects having greater variability in their anticipated cash flow distributions should have those flows discounted at a higher rate than projects characterized by less variability.

RISKLESS VERSUS RISKY PROJECTS.   Some short-term decisions are practically risk free, such as whether to take a cash discount on a one-time buy. We could use a short-term risk-free rate, generally the 3-month Treasury bill rate, to discount cash flows related to such decisions. For riskless projects with multiyear cash flows (e.g., switching from biweekly to monthly payroll disbursement system, establishing a lockbox network for collections, or implementing a new computerized treasury management information system leased at a contracted price), the Treasury bond rate could be used as the discount rate. Although some analysts would prefer to again use the Treasury bill rate, the Treasury bond rate can be thought of as a composite of a sequence of the present and future Treasury bill rates and therefore may be preferable.[12]

For decisions that affect the company's cash flows in a significant and unpredictable manner (e.g., a change in credit terms), we must include some type of risk premium to account for the greater risk. The simplest approach is to start with the cost of funds that are borrowed for short-term purposes. This cost might be the prime lending rate for some middle-sized companies, a certain amount above the prime rate for smaller companies, and a certain amount below the prime rate for larger companies. Companies with very large marketable securities portfolios would prefer to use the interest rate being earned on those securities because the opportunity loss when financing short-term projects is the interest given up when they sell off some of the investments. Depending on how risky the project is perceived to be, a risk premium might be added to that short-term rate. We now turn to a more formal discussion of the risk premium.

---

[12]A lucid and persuasive argument for discounting multiyear risk-free project cash flows with the Treasury bond rate to match holding period interest rates to the periods in which cash flows are received is found in Neil Seitz and Mitch Ellison. 1999. *Capital budgeting and long-term financing decisions.* 3rd ed. Fort Worth, TX: Dryden.

Project Life and the Risk-Adjusted Discount Rate

For decisions whose effects stretch beyond 1 year, it is essential that the analyst consider making a risk adjustment when determining the appropriate discount rate. The following equation models the discount rate as the sum of the risk-free rate of return investors can earn, a risk premium reflecting the risk of the company's typical projects, and an adjustment for whether a project possesses greater or lesser risk as compared with a normal project.[13]

$$k_{adj} = k_{rf} + k_{avg} + k_{\Delta} \qquad \text{(3-8)}$$

In which:

k_{adj} = risk-adjusted discount rate
k_{rf} = risk-free rate
k_{avg} = risk premium for company's typical project
k_{Δ} = risk adjustment for specific project

Notice that the sum of the second and third terms in Equation 3-8 ($k_{rf} + k_{avg}$) equates to the company's cost of capital. The fourth term, k_{Δ}, gives the modification to the cost of capital necessary to arrive at k_{adj}, a **risk-adjusted discount rate.** Furthermore, the project risk adjustment k_{Δ} will be positive if the project under consideration is riskier than the company's typical project, but negative if the project is less risky than those normally considered. There are two main approaches to determining the amount of risk adjustment, k_{Δ}. The analyst may either use the **capital asset pricing model** (CAPM) or the company's cost of capital as modified by subjective risk classes.

CAPITAL ASSET PRICING MODEL.   The CAPM is a mathematical representation of the relationship between risk and return, which gives the analyst an estimate for k_{adj}. This model is covered in Appendix 3A. We simply note here that for the analyst trying to pinpoint the effect of risk on a project's required rate of return, using the CAPM can provide an estimate of the necessary adjustment consistent with the shareholder's view of risk.

SUBJECTIVE RISK CLASS ADJUSTMENT.   Analysts uncomfortable with the assumptions underlying the CAPM, or who are unable to generate the necessary informational inputs for the model, might prefer to develop discount rates based on *risk classes*. Proposals having multiyear effects on the firm's cash flows would be assigned a higher discount rate if they have longer time horizons, or a very large range (or standard deviation) of cash flow outcomes. The riskier the project, the higher the discount rate, as Exhibit 3-8 illustrates.

Assigning discount rates based on risk classes is considered overly subjective by finance theorists, but it might be used by managers who have had difficulty in generating precise risk-adjusted discount rates.[14] Additionally, we should recognize that any

---

[13]This equation is adapted from one developed and discussed in John J. Clark; Thomas J. Hindelang; and Robert E. Pritchard. 1989. *Capital budgeting: Planning and control of capital expenditures.* 3d ed. Englewood Cliffs, NJ: Prentice-Hall, pp 219–222. Also, see that presentation for an example of how risk classes map into risk-adjusted discount rates.

[14]For a classic practitioner's perspective on why formal risk analysis has failed, see K. Larry Hastie. 1974. One businessman's view of capital budgeting. *Financial Management.* Winter: pp 36–44. Hastie makes a strong case for the use of sensitivity analysis, in which the key inputs are identified for further study. Their values can be varied up or down 5, 10, or 25 percent and the resulting NPV observed.

EXHIBIT 3-8
Risk Classes and Risk-Adjusted Discount Rates

Risk Class	Examples	Discount Rate
Low Risk	1. Change in lead concentration bank 2. Adoption of lockbox network 3. Automation of treasury information system	Significantly less than company's weighted-average cost of capital (k_Δ negative)
Moderate Risk	1. Change in cash discount 2. Switching to "just-in-time" inventory system	At or slightly less than weighted-average cost of capital (k_Δ negative but small)
High Risk	1. Shortening credit terms below industry standard 2. Decision to pay vendor invoices late	Above weighted-average cost of capital (k_Δ positive)

approach to project risk adjustment ignores the effect of a proposed project on the overall liquidity of the company—which might be the most attractive or unattractive aspect of the project. Accept/reject decisions should not be based solely on the outcome of an appraisal of project risk.

CAPITAL ALLOCATION DECISION MAKING IN PRACTICE

In this chapter we presented several approaches to short-term financial decision making and argued for a valuation approach that is consistent with "best practices" in capital budgeting. In this final section, we review recent studies of capital allocation decision making. Although not specifically addressed in many of the studies, anecdotal evidence suggests that the key driver for integrating working capital management into capital budgeting practices is the adoption of EVA or a similar framework such as cash flow return-on-investment (CFROI). The surveys we profile do not offer much evidence of working capital allocation inclusion in capital allocation practices, but they do provide evidence on degree of risk adjustment:

The Gilbert and Reichert (1995) study, especially valuable because of its scope and longitudinal insights, provides very useful insights into capital budgeting practices. Their survey of Fortune 500 corporate financial offices found that 85 percent of companies calculate NPV in their capital budgeting, and 91 percent calculate either NPV or IRR, another discounted cash flow evaluation technique. This was a marked increase from 1980 and 1985. Models for managing accounts receivable are used by 59 percent of the companies, and inventory management models by 60 percent of companies, but it is not clear whether allocations were considered alongside long-term projects with NPVs calculated.

Farragher, Kleiman, and Sahu (1999) conducted a mail survey of US-based companies included in the S&P Industrial Index. Like Gilbert and Reichert, they found that companies are using sophisticated capital evaluation tools, and they make strategic analysis a cornerstone of their capital investment process. Sixty-two percent of respondents indicated that corporate strategy was more important than individual project return/risk factors in searching for investment opportunities. Unfortunately, 15 percent do not evaluate working capital changes that might arise from capital projects. Slightly over one-half of respondents (55 percent) do require a quantitative risk assessment of forecasted investment *cash flows*, a significant increase from numbers reported in other, earlier studies. In most cases, this risk assessment was made with sensitivity analysis or scenarios (high-average-low outcomes), not with simulation models or capital market risk analysis (using CAPM). Even though risk factors are often nonquantifiable, about two thirds require a formal, written assessment of those factors. When moving to the final *capital project evaluation*, 47 percent of the companies require a quantitative risk-adjusted evaluation (the majority of those, about three in five, doing so with a risk-adjusted rate of return; the others adjusting the cash flows in a mostly subjective fashion). For the companies risk-adjusting the discount rate, a few more use the CAPM than do so intuitively.

In the manufacturing sector, Chadwell-Hatfield, Goitein, Horvath, and Webster (1996, 1997) found that companies use more than one evaluation technique for capital budgeting (and favor IRR and payback over NPV), and that sophisticated risk analysis is not emphasized even though managers appear to be concerned with risk. Undiversifiable (market) risk, as is captured in the CAPM, is not a significant factor in their capital budgeting analysis. Most companies operated with constraints on the total capital budget, turning down some attractive projects as a result (capital rationing). Of significance to our topic of relatively smaller working capital allocations, surveyed manufacturers often exempted projects with relatively low cost from formal financial analysis.

In a study of 232 small businesses with less than $5 million in sales and fewer than 1000 employees, Block (1997) indicated that nondiscounted techniques such as payback still dominated for evaluation, but that NPV and IRR usage as the primary evaluation technique had increased from 14 percent in 1983 to 28 percent in 1995. Almost 70 percent of firms specifically consider risk in doing their capital budgeting analysis, mostly by increasing the rate of return. For payback users, this means shortening the allowable payback period, and for NPV or IRR users, this implies using a higher discount or hurdle rate.

In none of these studies are we told whether cash holdings policy, credit policy, payables policy, or inventory policy decisions are subjected to NPV or other explicit capital budgeting analysis.[15] Clearly, the EVA methodology subjects operating-related cash flows and associated capital requirements to a similar evaluation. This brings continuity to company-wide resource allocation, as working capital must be scrutinized in the same way as all other capital requests. It also incorporates both the financial statement approach and the valuation approach that we presented at the beginning of the chapter.

SUMMARY

Short-term financial decisions offer the potential to create value for the firm. They do so by affecting the spread between revenues and expenses and altering operating cash flows, by changing the length of the cash conversion period, by changing the risk pos-

---

[15]A small sample survey by Visscher and Stansfield (1997), listed in the chapter references, found that most of 13 manufacturing plant controllers used payback to evaluate JIT conversion.

ture of the firm, by increasing or decreasing net interest revenue, and by changing the accuracy and timeliness of critical information.

Both the financial statement approach and the valuation approach offer insight into working capital management decisions. The financial statement approach is helpful for seeing the effect of proposed courses of action on the company's overall liquidity, but it suffers from a too-limited view of risk and ignores the time value of money. The valuation approach recommends computing the present value of cash flows to make appropriate decisions. The EVA models attempt to draw from both approaches to guide corporate financial policy-making and analysis. The NPV calculation is central to making value-maximizing financial decisions. The tools necessary to assess the time value of money for financial decision making were introduced and illustrated in this chapter. For most decisions, we can overlook the compounding of interest through time and can calculate value effects using a simple interest equation.

We also saw how companies could apply valuation tools to maximize the value of the cash flow timeline. We concluded the presentation by surveying several of the practical difficulties the analyst must overcome in arriving at value estimates. The key problem here is selecting the appropriate discount rate to use. If a working capital venture has a multiyear impact on cash flows, the company's weighted-average cost of long-term funds should be appropriate, as the project is competing with other capital projects for the firm's funds. For shorter-lived ventures, a different opportunity cost approach might be followed. In such cases, the company's short-term borrowing rate or short-term investing rate are the logical candidates. At times, the analyst may decide to average these rates or, if the policy decision involves more or less risk than the normal company project, develop a risk-class approach to discount rate determination.

Compared with capital budgeting and capital structure decisions, the time value of money is of less importance in short-term financial decision making. This is due partly to the low risk of most projects of this type and partly to their short lifespans. Some decisions regarding the management of cash and other working capital accounts do have lasting effects, however, necessitating our coverage of valuation theory and NPV. Financial managers wish to maximize the discounted net cash flows arising from financial decisions. They are aware that valuation concepts are sometimes inapplicable, perhaps because a project does not have identifiable cash inflows. Regardless, the choice of a discount rate is less critical in the short-term setting, and the decision on which is the "best" course of action from among several alternatives is therefore less sensitive to the discount rate chosen.

Surveys of capital allocation practices in U.S. firms indicate that formal models are used for receivables and inventory management by large firms, and that risk analysis is usually accomplished with risk-adjusted discount rates or sensitivity analysis. Although many firms do include working capital changes linked to capital projects, we remain unclear about how many firms conduct NPV analysis on strictly short-term financial decisions.

Useful Web Sites

Association for Financial Professionals: www.afponline.org

CFO Magazine: www.cfonet.com

Stern Stewart & Co.: www.eva.com/evaabout/whatis.shtml

Stern Stewart & Co.: www.eva.com/evaluation/overview.shtml

Global Treasury News: www.gtnews.com

Stern Stewart & Co.: www.sternstewart.com/cfo/home.shtml

Questions

1. Is the time value of money as important in short-term financial decisions as in capital project decisions? Why or why not?
2. Distinguish between the financial statement approach and the valuation approach to making short-term financial decisions. Which approach is superior for making short-term financial decisions? Why?
3. Use your understanding of long-term capital sources and the calculated cost of capital to indicate why economic value added would typically be different from net income.
4. When given data on daily sales, it would seem that an analyst would have to work with at least 365 days on a cash flow timeline to properly assess short-term financial policy decisions. Why is this generally not the case? When should you consider the actual cash flow pattern in its entirety?
5. In what circumstances does using a simple interest approximation formula result in the greatest inaccuracy compared with using a compound interest formula?
6. An investment offers a nominal rate of 7 percent per year. Would the annual effective rate be higher if interest is compounded daily or monthly? Explain, using illustrative calculations to support your answer.
7. What are the factors the financial analyst must assess in arriving at an appropriate discount rate for risky short-term decisions having multiyear effects?
8. Why is it difficult to determine the best discount rate to use in short-term decision making? Is it simpler than determining the discount rate for evaluating long-lived capital projects? Why or why not?
9. What effect, if any, does capital market efficiency have on a company's cost of capital? Does market efficiency necessarily characterize a company's short-term borrowing market?
10. Explain each term of the risk-adjusted discount rate equation (Equation 3-8), and how an analyst could arrive at the appropriate numerical value for that term.
11. Explain how the risk class of a potential venture can be used to determine a discount rate. To what risk class would you assign each of the following decision situations?
    a. Changing the credit terms you offer to your customers.
    b. Adopting a just-in-time inventory management system.
    c. "Stretching" payables 25 days beyond their due date.
    d. Initiating a hedging strategy for all receivables denominated in a foreign currency.
12. What are risk-adjusted discount rates? How might an analyst go about determining the specific amount of risk adjustment for a particular decision?

Problems

Note: When discounting or compounding, to ensure comparability and consistency use 31 days for 1 month, 182.5 days for 6 months, 273.75 days for 9 months, and 365 days for 1 year.

1. Kiernan Enterprises, a small manufacturer located in the eastern part of the United States, uses EVA as part of its performance measurement and evaluation

system. Below are data from its last two annual reports. The latter year, 2001, is Kiernan's most successful ever, a year in which the company improved its management of cash, inventory, and accounts receivable. The company was able to pay off its short-term debt entirely in 2001 as a result of the working capital management improvement.

a. Calculate the EVA for 2000 and 2001.

b. Suggest how improved working capital may increase EVA by increasing operating profit *and* reducing capital employed.

Kiernan Enterprises

SELECTED FINANCIAL DATA

REVENUE AND EXPENSE DATA:

	2000	2001
Revenues	$3,000,000	$4,500,000
Cost of Goods Sold	2,000,000	2,667,000
Gross Profit	1,000,000	1,333,000
Operating expenses	700,000	650,000
Operating profit (EBIT)	300,000	683,000

BALANCE SHEET DATA:

	2000	2001
Cost of Capital	8%	8%
Short-term and Long-term Capital Employed	$1,500,000	$1,350,000

2. Elizabeth anticipates receiving a check for $10,000 in 6 months. What is the present value of this amount if the interest rate Elizabeth could earn on short-term investments is 12 percent per year?

   a. Use the exact formula, with daily compounding of interest. (See note at the beginning of Problem Set.)

   b. Use the simple interest approximation formula.

   c. Comment on the difference between your results in parts *a* and *b*.

3. Julie needs to pay a $3,000 tuition bill 9 months from now. She has some money saved up that she could invest, but she is also considering a trip to Europe. She remembers reading something about how money grows over time, and she wonders if maybe she should just go ahead and invest some money today to pay the tuition bill.

   a. How much would Julie invest today to have $3,000 in 9 months if she can invest at a 10 percent annual rate? Use the simple interest approximation formula.

   b. Assuming Julie goes to Europe and waits 6 months to do her investing, how much would she need to invest then, again assuming a 10 percent annual rate and using the simple interest formula?

   c. Repeat *a* and *b* using the daily compound interest formula, and compare your results to the simple interest results. (See note at the beginning of Problem Set.)

4. "Pokey" Rice was hired as a financial analyst in global cash management for Anvaricorp, a Canadian-based multinational corporation. He has been assigned a collection float comparison analysis. He understands check float to be the total time elapsing between when the payor (check writer) mails the check and when Anvaricorp receives available (spendable) funds at its bank. Anvaricorp is trying to figure out the loss in value if it receives an Italian lira–denominated check, as opposed to a draft denominated in Canadian dollars. (A draft is a check-like payment instrument that must be approved by the payor or one of its agents

before it is honored.) The first step Pokey wishes to take in the analysis is to determine the difference in float between the alternative payment methods. He finds out that Anvaricorp receives average daily remittances of 100,000 lira from its Italian customers. The exchange rate is 2 lira per 1 Canadian dollar. Anvaricorp's weighted-average cost of capital, which it uses as a required rate of return on its investment decisions, is 12 percent per year. The number of mail days will be 8 calendar days in either case. On average, it would take 1.5 calendar days to process a draft before getting it deposited but 2.5 calendar days to process a lira-denominated check. After deposit, Anvaricorp does not get to spend the deposited amount until 2 days later for the draft or until 10 days later for the lira-denominated check (the check must be routed back to Italy and presented to the bank on which it was drawn). Assume that the latter amounts are also calendar days to simplify the analysis. Pokey is advised by the analyst who formerly did the analysis to use the following formula:

$$\begin{matrix} \text{Annual Interest} \\ \text{Gain/(Loss) of} \\ \text{Collections} \end{matrix} = \begin{matrix} \text{Difference in} \\ \text{Days of Float} \end{matrix} \times \begin{matrix} \text{Average Daily} \\ \text{Remittance} \\ \text{Amount} \end{matrix} \times \begin{matrix} \text{Weighted Average} \\ \text{Cost of Capital} \end{matrix}$$

    a. What is the annual interest gain or loss if Anvaricorp allows payment by lira-denominated checks instead of Canadian dollar drafts?

    b. Does the number calculated in part *a* really represent the difference in NPVs for the two payment methods? Explain.

5. The Texas International Chili Company figures it would experience an increase in NPV of $0.75 per day if it adopts new credit terms.

    a. If its annual opportunity cost of capital is 10 percent, what would be the total increase in shareholder value?

    b. Repeat part *a* with an opportunity cost of 12 percent. Comment on the reason you get different results, compared with *a*.

6. J. Walker Manufacturing Co. is financially distressed and must pay cash before delivery for its raw materials. It pays $40 per assembly at the time of order. The parts are received 30 days after the order. Five days after they are received, they are taken out of inventory and used in the manufacturing process. J. Walker incurs additional processing costs of $6.50 per assembly at the point in time when it manufactures its finished products. On average, it sells each finished assembly 95 days after manufacturing takes place.

    a. Draw a cash flow timeline of the events above, being careful to denote which flows are negative and which are positive.

    b. Figure out for how much J. Walker must sell each assembly to break even on a present value basis. Use a discount rate of 20 percent per year.

    c. Now assume that J. Walker decides to sell the finished goods for $48. How high could the discount rate be for J. Walker to still break even on a present value basis?

7. Medsco financial analyst Eddie Ogden estimates that the relevant up-front investment necessary to convert to and complete installation of a just-in-time inventory system is $50,000. Eddie figures that a risk-adjusted discount rate should be used. He looks in a financial newspaper and finds that the risk-free rate is 4 percent per year. The company's typical project carries a 3 percent risk premium above the risk-free rate. Eddie believes that this is a moderate-risk project, which generally implies a 1 percent reduction from the company's weighted average cost of capital to get a reasonable project discount rate. Eddie

does not believe that there will be any revenue effects of the change-over in systems. Assuming that the cost savings are a level perpetual stream:

a. How much must the annual cost savings be to make the investment a winner? Ignore any nonfinancial considerations.

b. Do you think Eddie's assumption that there will be no revenue effects is valid?

c. What nonfinancial considerations should Eddie take into account in evaluating this project?

d. Repeat all parts of the analysis, assuming now that the cost savings only occur for each of the next 5 years. Comment on the difference in your results, compared with the results you got in part *a*.

8. Jerome is the head of the accounts payable department at an Idaho-based manufacturer, Schooley & Company. He just read in a trade association publication that one of his competitors recently renegotiated longer credit terms with a vendor from whom his company also buys raw materials. Jerome wonders what increase in value his company would experience if he is able to successfully renegotiate his payable terms. Use the information below to help Jerome quantify the financial impact.

Present payment terms:	net 30
Renegotiated payment terms:	net 45
Purchases (once each 6 months):	$150,000
Annual opportunity cost of funds (nominal rate):	12% per year

a. What is the present value savings of one purchase made under the renegotiated terms?

b. Assuming the new terms become permanent, what is the value effect (NPV) of the new terms?

c. *Optional.* Jerome remembers that raw material costs have been going up at a 5 percent annual rate on the items purchased. Redo the analysis with this new assumption. (*Hint:* Use a formula used for valuing a constantly growing dividend stream, modified for the 6-month cash flow stream.)

9. Central Mississippi Devices has been selling switching equipment to computer companies on net-30 terms, in which payment is expected within 30 days of the invoice date. Concerned about deteriorating collection patterns, the credit manager has divided customers into two groups for examination purposes: prompt payors and laggards. Prompt payors (80 percent of Central's customers) pay, on average, in 35 days, versus a 72-day average for the laggards. The manager wonders if the credit terms should be modified to include a 2 percent cash discount on invoices paid within 10 days. The average invoice is the same for both groups, roughly $4,000. The manager expects 50 percent of the prompt payors to pay in exactly 10 days and the average on the other half to slip to 40 days. He thinks that 20 percent of the laggards will pay in 10 days, and the average on the others will slip to 80 days. Given these forecasts, he is not sure that the lost revenue from discount takers (who would then pay only 98 percent of the invoiced dollar amount) justifies the improved collection. The company's annual cost of capital is 11 percent per year.

a. Using NPV calculations, show the present value of the present collection experience.

b. Calculate the NPV of the proposed 2/10, net-30 terms.

c. Based on your net-present-value analysis, should Central Mississippi Devices adopt the cash discount?

d. What other factors should be taken into account before Central makes a switch, assuming such is justifiable on an NPV basis?

e. Sensitivity analysis involves varying the key assumptions, one at a time, and observing the effect on the key decision criterion—such as profits or NPV. In the NPV analysis above, how could sensitivity analysis be carried out? (If you have a financial spreadsheet available, conduct a sensitivity analysis that varies of the number of prompt payors who will pay in exactly 10 days, and report your findings.)

References

Gerald A. Achstatter. 1995. EVA: Performance gauge for the 1990s? *Investor's Business Daily* June 21:A4.

Anil Arya and John C. Fellingham, et al. 1998. Capital budgeting: Some exceptions to the net present value rule. *Issues in Accounting Education* August:499–508.

Stanley Block. 1997. Capital budgeting techniques used by small business firms in the 1990s. *Engineering Economist* Summer:289–302.

Patricia Chadwell-Hatfield; Bernard Goitein; Philip Horvath; and Allen Webster. 1996–1997. Financial criteria, capital budgeting techniques, and risk analysis of manufacturing firms. *Journal of Applied Business Research* Winter:95–104.

Aswath Damodaran. 1998. Value creation and enhancement: Back to the future. *Contemporary Finance Digest* Winter:5–51.

Ray Dillon and James E. Owers. 1997. EVA as a financial metric: Attributes, utilization, and relation to NPV. *Financial Practice and Education* Spring/Summer:32–40.

Avinach K. Dixit and Robert S. Pindyck. 1995. The options approach to capital investment. *Harvard Business Review* May/June:105–116.

Edward J. Farragher; Robert T. Kleiman; and Anandi P. Sahu. 1999. Current capital investment practices. *Engineering Economist* 44:137–150.

Erika Gilbert and Alan Reichert. 1995. The practice of financial management among large United States corporations. *Financial Practice & Education* Spring/Summer:16–23.

Roy E. Johnson. 1998. Scrap capital project evaluations. *CFO* May:14.

Yong H. Kim and Joseph C. Atkins. 1978. Evaluating investments in accounts receivable: A maximizing framework. *Journal of Finance* May:402–412.

Yong H. Kim and Kee H. Chung. 1990. An integrated evaluation of investment in inventory and credit: A cash flow approach. *Journal of Business Finance and Accounting* Summer:381–390.

Wilbur C. Lewellen; John J. McConnell; and Jonathan A. Scott. 1980. Capital market influences on trade credit. *Journal of Financial Research* Fall:105–113.

Charles M. Linke and J. Kenton Zumwalt. 1984. Estimation biases in discounted cash flow analyses of equity capital cost in rate regulation. *Financial Management* Autumn:15–21.

Timothy A. Luehrman. 1997. A general manager's guide to valuation. *Harvard Business Review* May/June:132–142.

Ann Monroe. 2000. Financials are king in evaluating an IT project. *Finance IT* January/February:21.

Kanwal S. Sachdeva and Lawrence J. Gitman. 1981. Accounts receivable decisions in a capital budgeting framework. *Financial Management* Winter:45–49.

William L. Sartoris and Ned C. Hill. 1983. A generalized cash flow approach to short-term financial decisions. *Journal of Finance* May:349–360.

William L. Sartoris and Ned C. Hill. 1981. Evaluating credit policy alternatives: A present value framework. *Journal of Financial Research* Spring:81–89.

Neil Seitz and Mitch Ellison. 1999. *Capital Budgeting and Long-Term Financing Decisions.* 3d ed. Ft. Worth: Dryden.

Sue L. Visscher and Timothy C. Stansfield. 1997. Illustrating capital budgeting complexities with JIT justification data. *Financial Practice and Education* Fall/Winter:29–34.

H. Joseph Wen; David D. Yen; and B. Lin. 1998. Methods for measuring information technology investment payoff. *Human Systems Management* 17:145–153.

Appendix 3A

Advanced Present Value Analysis

We cover three advanced topics in this appendix: the interaction between accounts receivables and inventories, valuation theory and short-term financial decisions, and risk adjustment in the valuation model. All these aspects make the decision-making process more realistic.

RECEIVABLES AND INVENTORY INTERACTIONS

Decisions that have an impact on a company's accounts receivable often affect its inventory position, and vice versa. The analyst is cautioned to consider the specific effect of each decision on all working capital accounts so as not to suboptimize. The danger is to maximize the value effect of one area but overlook value-reducing effects of that same decision on other areas. For example, more lenient credit terms may directly increase sales and profits but may lead to larger inventory positions, which will offset some of the profit increase. Inventory used currently in production gets captured in the cash flow timeline NPV analysis (where the associated cash outflow is shown), but there may be permanent 'cushion' amounts of inventory held as safety stock as well. Proper decision making requires that all effects of a decision be considered, including semivariable cost disbursements and side effects.[1] The wide availability of financial spreadsheets facilitates the more comprehensive analysis that we advocate.

VALUATION THEORY AND SHORT-TERM FINANCIAL DECISIONS

Imagine a company whose cash receipts and cash disbursements are perfectly synchronized and totally predictable (no forecast error)—one in which cash receipts provide just enough funds, at just the time needed, to pay employees, vendors, taxes, dividends, interest, principal repayments, lease payments, and all other bills. The company neither sells nor buys using trade credit, so it has no receivables or payables. It does not prepay, accrue, or defer any expense or revenue. It only purchases finished goods inventories and direct-ships them to customers so as not to have any inventories. You are surprised to see the balance sheet for our fictitious company:

CURRENT ASSETS		CURRENT LIABILITIES	
Cash	$0	Accounts payable	$0
Short-term investments	$0	Accrued expenses	$0
Inventories	$0	Notes payable	$0
Accounts receivable	$0	Current portion of long-term debt	$50
Prepaid expenses	$0		
Current Assets	$0	*Current Liabilities*	$50
Property, plant, & equipment	$1,000	Long-term debt	$450
		Equity	$500
Total Assets	$1,000	*Total Liabilities & Equity*	$1,000

You are probably thinking this is pretty far from reality, and you are right. Our exercise would be trivial except for one very sobering fact: this is exactly the type of world envisioned by the prevailing finance theories of valuation. These long-run theories posit that in a world of certainty, information symmetry, and perfect markets, required return (and value) can be linked to market risk (capital asset pricing model [CAPM]) or several risk factors (arbitrage pricing theory). There is no recognition of the uncertain, unsynchronized, uneven cash inflows and outflows that cause companies to hold cash and short-term investments as well as to contract for short-term credit lines. Market uncertainty and other imperfections causing companies to hold

---

[1]Even the pricing policy should be brought into short-term financial decisions, as noted in the Kim and Chung article listed in the Chapter 3 references. Their model is necessarily complex and beyond the scope of our presentation.

inventories or to offer and take advantage of trade credit are absent from these traditional valuation frameworks. The fact is that operating decisions, which implement capital projects through astute management of current assets and current liabilities, create value.

Gentry,[2] as developed further in Gentry and Lee,[3] has expanded the net present value (NPV) approach we used in Chapter 3 to include the large number of real variables that are continually changing. Gentry divides effects into a 4 x 4 matrix that classifies causal variables (henceforth termed drivers) as operational or other and as either influencing cash inflows or cash outflows. Some of the drivers making up the value creation process are:

	OPERATIONAL	OTHER

Cash Inflow Drivers	Sales patterns
	Collection patterns
	ST investment
	  returns
	Credit terms
		Short- or
		  long-term
		  borrowing
		Sale of stock
		Sale of fixed assets

Cash Outflow Drivers	Purchasing patterns
	Payment patterns
	Compensating
	  balances
	Delivery and
	  storage costs
		Capital
		  expenditures
		Share repurchase

Gentry and Lee then formulate the general NPV model, which we have modified slightly to allow for differential growth rates for cash inflows and cash outflows:

$$NPV = \frac{CI - CO}{1+r} + \frac{CI(1+g_I) - CO(1+g_O)}{(1+r)^2}$$
$$+ \cdots + \frac{CI(1+g_I)^n - CO(1+g_O)^n}{(1+r)^n}$$

In which: NPV = net present value

CI = cash inflows

CO = cash outflows

r = risk-adjusted cost of capital (discount rate)

g_I = growth rate of cash inflows

g_O = growth rate of cash outflows

[2]James A. Gentry. 1996. Short-run financial management. In Dennis E. Logue, *Handbook of Modern Finance*. Boston: Warren, Gorham, & LaMont, pp C3-1–C3-43.

[3]James A. Gentry and H.W. Lee. 1986. An integrated cash flow model of the firm. Faculty Working Paper 1314. Champaign, IL: College of Commerce and Business Administration, University of Illinois, December.

This model demonstrates the reality that value can be created (positive NPV) or destroyed (negative NPV) by changes in short-term financial policies, product demand, or production costs. Any policy or action that speeds up (affects the timing of) cash inflows or increases the amount (level) of those inflows will create value. Speeding up cash outflows or increasing the amount of outflows (e.g., absorbing a cost increase from a supplier) erodes value, all other things held equal. Gentry and Lee point out that the competitive position of a company influences its cash conversion period by determining its credit terms on the selling side (affecting receivables) as well as on the buying side (affecting payables).

This NPV model is attractive in that it incorporates the value-enhancing activities of cash managers, credit managers, purchasing agents, and others working on short-term financial decisions. However, Gentry and Lee note that NPV models do not explicitly include a financial market risk measure.[4] Thus it is conceivable that the risk-adjusted discount rate used in the NPV model is based on project (stand-alone) risk, not market risk (which the CAPM would identify as systematic or nondiversifiable risk measured by beta) as might be the case if one was doing a divisional cost of capital for long-term capital projects. The disparate treatment of short-run and long-run projects may be bothersome. The linkage between short-run financial decision making and long-run financial decision making is unclear at best and nonexistent at worst. We return to this concern in the concluding section ("CAPM-Based Discount Rates") after dealing with risk in general terms.

RISK CONSIDERATIONS

Short-term financial decisions also affect the business and financial risk of the organization. Business risk refers to the variability in operating revenues and costs and is linked to use of assets with fixed operating costs. To the extent a decision requires a permanent increase in investment in cash, receivables, or inventories, it results in higher fixed operating costs, which magnify the effect of any change in revenue on operating profit. Bank fees are a fixed cost of holding cash.

[4]Gentry (1990) indicates that yet-to-be-developed simulation, simultaneous equations, and control theory models will lay the groundwork for new theoretical linkages between short-term financial and long-run value-based decision making.

Inventory-related fixed costs include shrinkage as a result of theft or perishability and obsolescence as a result of technological advance or new product design. Receivables-related fixed costs include the computer hardware and the staffing cost for credit personnel that must be added to service new accounts. Financial risk is also affected by short-term decisions.

Financial risk is defined as the variability in "bottom-line earnings"—which could be net income or earnings per share. It is largely based on the amount of debt financing or leasing an organization takes on. Any investment in a current asset account must be financed, except in the rare instance in which another current asset account is reduced by an equal amount. The financing decision of interest here is what portion of the current asset increase is financed by short-term financing as opposed to long-term debt or lease financing or equity financing. Any change in debt financing, whether involving short-term or long-term debt, changes the financial risk posture of the organization. Within the debt category, short-term debt is considered more risky than long-term debt. There are two reasons for this:

- Long-term debt is usually "fixed rate," meaning the interest rate does not change from year to year, whereas every time short-term debt matures it is replaced at a different, possibly higher, interest rate.
- Continued availability of short-term financing is uncertain when the business's financial position or general economic conditions change. Banks or other short-term funds providers might be unwilling to continue to provide funds to the business (as is increasingly true with small business commercial lending in several areas of the country in the early twenty-first century).

The consequences of a large increase in the short-term interest rate paid or of being closed out of the short-term credit market are quite severe. Companies are often pushed into bankruptcy when they are denied access to their short-term borrowing facilities.

The risk effects that we are addressing here are important because they bear on the appropriate discount rate to be used for valuing financial decisions.

Discount Rate and Market Efficiency

The concept of opportunity cost is related to the investor's required rate of return for the company. Based on their perceptions of the average risk of the capital projects invested in by the firm, stock and bond investors collectively determine the return from the company's stock and bonds that would be necessary for them to provide capital to the firm. Thus the opportunity cost of investing in Ford stock is the return that would have been earned by investing in another stock of similar risk. When financial markets are efficient, meaning prices change freely and instantly in response to supply and demand and are not significantly affected by poor information or tax code barriers, a company's cost of capital should reflect the required rate of return, which should in turn reflect the riskiness of its typical capital projects. Efficiently priced securities give rise to an accurate cost of capital, which then becomes a hurdle rate against which the rates of return of long-lived capital projects can be compared; this also becomes a discount rate for determining the present value of future cash flows.

The CAPM can be used to determine the appropriate cost of equity or a decision-specific cost of capital to use in discounting cash flows. Although the exact relationship between business or financial risk and the discount rate is unknown, an increase in either one should increase the market risk, and hence the discount rate.

CAPM-BASED DISCOUNT RATES

The CAPM is a formulation of how common stock returns are determined. If a company is maximizing value, it is giving the highest possible returns to its common shareholders. If the stock market is "efficient," the CAPM says, the expected returns of any company's stock would be based on just one factor: systematic, or market-related, risk. As the market moves, so move the individual stocks making up the market, but to varying degrees. The degree of sensitivity to market movements is called *systematic risk*. Systematic risk is measured by beta.[5] The key point to observe is that CAPM can give us a required rate of

---

[5]An excellent source of basic information for anyone unfamiliar with beta or the CAPM is Lawrence J. Gitman. 2001. *Principles of managerial finance*. 10th ed. Reading, MA: Addison Wesley Longman. Advanced material may be found in Haim Levy and Marshall Sarnat. 1990. *Capital investment and financial decisions*. 4th ed. Englewood Cliffs, NJ: Prentice-Hall, pp 286–312; or in John J. Clark, Thomas J. Hindelang, and Robert E. Pritchard. 1989. *Capital budgeting: Planning and control of capital expenditures*. 3d ed. Englewood Cliffs, NJ: Prentice-Hall, pp 215–224, 269–319.

return for equity, which can then be combined with the cost of debt and the cost of preferred stock (if any) to derive the weighted-average cost of capital for the organization. The CAPM does this by modeling the equity rate of return as a function of systematic risk, or beta:

$$k_j = k_{rf} + \beta_j(k_m - k_{rf}) \tag{3-1A}$$

In which: k_j = required return for stock j

k_{rf} = risk-free rate of return

β_j = stock's systematic risk

k_m = required return on the market portfolio.

Expressed in words, the CAPM asserts that the required rate of return for security *j* is the expected risk-free rate plus a risk premium that is the product of beta and the overall "market risk premium." We use historical data or surveys to proxy for unobservable expectations for both the risk-free rate (k_{rf}) and the required return on the market (k_m). For example, if the most recent 3-month moving average of Treasury bond rates is 4 percent, the stock market return has averaged 10.5 percent per year over the past 60 years, and a company's beta (β_j) is found to be 1.5, then the required return would be

$$k_j = k_{rf} + \beta j(k_m - k_{rf})$$
$$k_j = 4\% + 1.5(10.5\% - 4\%)$$
$$k_j = 4\% + 9.75\%$$
$$k_j = 13.75\%$$

Beta estimates are available from some online services, major stock brokerage houses, the Standard & Poor's *Stock Record,* or the Value Line *Investment*

Survey. The difficult task is risk-adjusting beta to arrive at a new risk-adjusted required return on common equity. One approach is to set up risk classes, in which risky projects are simply assigned a higher required rate of return (and discount rate) or the CAPM beta is arbitrarily adjusted upward by several percentage points. Lower-risk projects would be assigned a rate lower than the company's cost of capital.

Instead of making such an adjustment, some analysts argue for a "project-specific" application of the CAPM. Here, the analyst determines an appropriate "asset" beta, in lieu of the standard beta calculated on the company's stock. The asset beta, ideally, would be the sensitivity of the project under review to stock market returns. How to determine such a beta is somewhat difficult for large capital projects and even more troublesome for short-term financial decisions.[6] Until finance theory more effectively addresses the relationship of liquidity to shareholder value, the CAPM will not enjoy widespread use for risk adjustment purposes.[7]

To summarize, finance theorists generally recommend using a company's weighted-average cost of capital to discount capital investment cash flows.

We concur that such an approach is advisable for evaluating most working capital policies having multi-year cash flows, in that these projects have a demonstrable value. We do not want to minimize the difficulty of arriving at an appropriate discount rate for such decisions, however. A risk-class approach, as was illustrated in Exhibit 3-8, might be optimal.

---

[6]With the increasing use of "project financing"of long-term capital projects, in which the company lines up financing for a specific project, this approach is quite attractive. The authors know of no instance in which this has been done to finance a change in inventories, receivables, or cash management systems, however.

[7]See James R. Morris. 1983. The role of cash balances in firm valuation. *Journal of Financial and Quantitative Analysis* December: 533–545 for an attempt at integrating short-term liquidity into the CAPM valuation theory. Morris noted that cash outflows resulting in cash position shortfalls force the firm to borrow, increasing the systematic risk of an end-of-period dividend payout.

INTEGRATIVE CASE—PART 1

Bernard's New York Deli
Steven M. Dawson
University of Hawaii

These deli-bucks are for cash flow what chicken soup is for a cold, thought Bernard Horowitz as he opened the package the printer had dropped off. Three months earlier he had moved his restaurant, Bernard's New York Deli, to a new location in the upscale Ward Centre shopping area. Faced with needing $30,000 to remodel and buy new equipment, a shortage of cash after the move, and the refusal of his bank to lend more, the deli-bucks were, he sensed, a brilliant inspiration. Customers could buy them for $8 each and after 90 days redeem them to pay for $10 worth of purchases. "Where else could people get 20 percent on their money in 90 days?" Bernard asked a reporter who had heard about them. If it all worked as planned, he would have the $30,000 cash, the remodeling would be financed, and he'd have a lot of customers coming back.

BACKGROUND

To build rapport and loyalty with customers, Bernard was advised by a friend in public relations to "tell them your story." He did so by preparing a brochure and placing it at the Deli's entrance. Customers who read it learned that Bernard Horowitz, namesake but not kin of the legendary pianist, had grown up in the Crown Heights neighborhood of Brooklyn. When he was a kid, he had often followed his nose into the kitchen where his mother chopped, mixed, kneaded, and roasted the family meals. Under her guidance Bernard had learned a thing or two which he'd later put to good use. Bernard's first job, at the age of 13, was as a part-time clerk behind the deli counter of the local food market. "An education like that you don't get in school," he observed later.

In 1974 Bernard went to Hawaii on vacation. Like so many others, before and since, he fell in love with the place. He returned home only to quit his job, pack his things, and move to Hawaii for good. It wasn't long before he was hired to manage Hawaii's first Burger King. Over the next 12 years, he had opened and managed several more and then became the Hawaii district manager. He had learned a lot about food, about managing people and restaurants, and about working for someone else.

In those days whenever he took a trip to the mainland, he had returned with a suitcase of deli food. "There was no other way to get stuff like that in Hawaii in those days," he recalled. Recognizing the need to "nosh," Hebrew for snack, he quit his job at Burger King, took out a second mortgage, and set to work. He used the New York City *Yellow Pages* to locate suppliers of everything from meats (Hebrew National) and gelfilte fish (Manischewitz) to soda (Dr. Brown's). In August 1986, "Bernard's New York Deli" opened in a tiny storefront near the University. There was room, barely, for table seating for 36 customers. He did take-out business, sold foods not available elsewhere, and acquired a following that craved New York deli specialties. Three years later he moved to suburban Kahala Mall. Room there was even smaller, just seating for 29, but the new location meant he could cater not only to the normal breakfast, lunch, and dinner clientele but also to the late-night movie crowd. "What more could a New Yorker want," Bernard recalled, "than the opportunity to work longer hours?"

A NEW YORK DELI IN HAWAII?

Hawaii, led by a diverse tourism industry, was a gourmet's delight. Residents and visitors pampered their

This case was prepared by Steven M. Dawson as a basis for classroom discussion rather than to illustrate either effective or ineffective handling of an administrative situation. Copyright © 1999 by the *Case Research Journal* and Steven M. Dawson, published by South-Western College Publishing.

For information regarding this and other CaseNet® cases, please visit CaseNet® on the World Wide Web at **casenet.thomson.com**.

You may wish to consult Chapter 12 if you are not familiar with the cash budgeting process.

palates with dishes whose origins evoked the far reaches of the Pacific Rim: kim chee from Korea and sateh from Thailand to local delicacies like poke and poi. In recent years a distinctive new Euro-Asian cuisine developed by Sam Choy, Alan Wong, and Roy Yamaguchi had put Hawaii prominently on the culinary map.

What had been missing in Hawaii for the two centuries since the arrival of Captain James Cook in 1778, and more than a millennium since its first settlement by Polynesian explorers, was a real, Jewish-style deli. It took a malihini, Hawaiian for "newcomer," from Brooklyn to see the opening. When Bernard opened his New York Deli, he brought more than just a "bite of the Big Apple." Most foods in a Jewish-style deli came to New York with immigrants a century ago from the far side of the next ocean, the Atlantic. By bringing a taste of New York, Bernard's actually brought Romania (pastrami), Italy (salami), Germany (sauerkraut and sausage), Ukraine (borscht), and the Baltic (pickled herring and lox).

ON THE MOVE, AGAIN

You can't keep a New Yorker away from the Big City for too long, and in January 1997, Bernard closed his suburban deli and moved to Ward Centre, an upscale shopping area located between Waikiki and the downtown business district. The new location had nearly four times the seating—55 seats inside and 66 outside on the lanai. Amused by having a lanai, an outdoor deck, for eating, Bernard wryly observed that not everything had to be like Brooklyn. Colorful pictures, Jewish sayings, street signs from New York, copies of the New York Times for sale, and an authentic deli food counter provided the ambience of a New York place-to-be for the action. Parking was ample, and business picked up quickly. Thanks to loyal customers and a feature story in the Sunday newspaper's restaurant section, opening day on January 3 was a big success, and revenues were all Bernard had hoped for. Sales for all of January were $110,000, followed by $100,000 and $105,000 in February and March. Bernard expected that with the existing table setup, sales would average about $95,000 a month.

Good as it was, it could be better. To take full advantage of the new location, the deli needed a little more equipment and a bit of remodeling to increase seating by another 50 customers. "This remodeling will really give us a boost," said Bernard, and he expected a 30 percent increase in sales. Based on the first three months at the new location, and his experience earlier, he expected monthly sales to be as follows:

	FORECAST		FORECAST
April	$90,000	November	$100,000
May	95,000	December	140,000
June	115,000	January	140,000
July	125,000	February	125,000
August	135,000	March	130,000
September	120,000	April	115,000
October	110,000	May	120,000

In June, sales would be 15 percent higher than without the remodeling, and starting in July the increase would be 30 percent.

The bigger-size restaurant at Ward Centre meant the action behind the counter could be as frenetic as in a New York eatery. It also meant Bernard had a bigger task of managing the finances. Long gone were the days when he had just three other employees beside himself. At Ward Centre, Bernard started with a staff of 30 servers, preparers, and cleanup people, and it would grow to 42 with the expansion.

The two big expenses in the restaurant were food and labor. Bernard priced items so that the food expenses were about 30 percent of revenues. He trained his wait staff to be careful about needlessly wasting food. One time he pointed to four unused butter slices left on a table. "Each costs us five cents and if this happens ten times a day, seven days a week, by the end of a year we've wasted over $700." Provide good service, we need repeat customers, but watch the waste was the message.

Employee labor costs were also about 30 percent of revenues and were of two kinds: those he paid directly as wages to employees, and those he paid elsewhere. Hawaii was a tough place to do business when you had high labor costs, thanks to a state government and business environment that a Forbes magazine article had called the "New Socialist Republic of Hawaii." With the last paychecks, Bernard had given all his workers two reports: first, the dollars he had paid them as wages and, second, the dollars he had to pay others for them. For a $1,000 monthly wage payment to an employee, he calculated he paid an additional $277.50 as follows:

$76.50	Employer social security withholding
6.50	State temporary disability insurance
61.00	State worker's compensation

115.00	Employer share of mandatory state medical insurance
14.50	State unemployment insurance
4.00	Federal unemployment tax

With three months at the new location and ten years of operating experience, Bernard had a comfortable feel for the relationship of revenues and expenses and did not expect a big change to occur after the remodeling was complete. "You need both more food and more employees when you have a bigger operation." Looking at the big picture and for the range of volume of business he expected to do, food and personnel costs would each be about 30 percent of revenues. Monthly rent at the Centre was $1,500 plus 6 percent of revenues. Other premise expenses, including security, insurance, and utilities, would run about $4,000 plus 6 percent of revenue. Kitchen, dining, and office expenses were 5.5 percent. Selling expenses, including advertising, the 4 percent state excise tax, 1.2 percent credit card charges, and printing, averaged 10.5 percent of revenues. Depreciation averaged $1,500 now and would rise to $2,000 a month in July when the expansion was done. It roughly equaled outlays for new or replacement equipment. Monthly payments on the bank loan were $3,210. All except the rent and food expenses were paid during the month incurred. Food generally had net 30-day terms with no discounts for early payment. Bernard didn't pay himself a regular salary. The Deli was organized as a Subchapter S corporation, and when surplus cash was available at the end of the month above the $5,000 he thought was a comfortable minimum, he took it out. "If my good wife didn't have a job, there'd be some really tough times."

The remodeling and expansion would cost about $30,000, and this was a problem. The move and startup had absorbed all the available funds. Cash was tight, just $3,000 at the start of April, and the outlook for getting more funds was discouraging. April and May usually were slow months for restaurants in Hawaii. Bernard believed it was a combination of the seasonal tourism slowdown and the preoccupation of customers with making tax payments. This meant internal funds would not supply the needed expansion capital and, to make it worse, near-term revenue projections wouldn't look good to the bank. Bernard already had a $160,000 bank loan at an interest rate of 10.75 percent. When he discussed increasing the loan, his loan officer replied, "Not at this time. You've

maxed out until we see how the new location goes." Bernard wasn't surprised. "The banks in Hawaii, just like the state authorities, are not pro small business."

DELI-BUCKS

Bernard's solution to the shortage of funds came from the gift certificates he'd sold at his very first location to help him get started. Why not use them again, but modified so they could fund the remodeling? Ordinary gift certificates could be redeemed right away and therefore would not fill the bill because the money was needed first for remodeling. The solution: deli-bucks. He'd sell deli-bucks with a 90-day delay before they could be redeemed and a one-year life from date of purchase. Ninety days didn't seem unreasonably long and that would give him time to get the remodeling done. Any longer and it might seem too long to customers. The one-year limit would keep the redemption from dragging out forever.

Customers obviously wouldn't see much sense in paying now instead of paying later. They needed an incentive and a discount would do it. Playing with the numbers, Bernard decided on selling $10 deli-bucks for $8. Ten dollars was a reasonable size for an order, putting out $8 was not a big outlay, and a 20 percent discount seemed enough to offer something of value to customers. With the 30 percent food cost, he felt he had a lot of room to maneuver in giving a discount for early purchase. Whether the deli-bucks were more costly than other sources of funds, such as the bank loan if it had been available, was a question Bernard didn't take time to consider. After all, customers would redeem the certificates for food, not cash. A bank loan in contrast would require a cash repayment. How soon after 90 days the certificates would be redeemed was tough to forecast. Based on his earlier experience with gift certificates, Bernard figured it would take him about three months to sell all the deli-bucks, with 50 percent being sold in April, the first month; 30 percent the second; and 20 percent the third. At this rate, cash collections would approximately match remodeling payments. In accounting terms the deli-buck receipts would be placed in a "precollected revenue" account, with the impact on rent, the state excise tax, and other expenses, except for credit card charges, occurring at redemption. Redemptions would begin in month four and would be at the rate of 50 percent the first eligible month, 10 percent the next, and then 5 percent per month for the remaining seven months of the year. The remaining 5 percent would probably be lost, forgotten, or even kept as souvenirs. For deli-bucks sold in April, 50 percent would thus be redeemed in July, 10 percent in August, and so on. Bernard guessed that 75 percent of the deli-bucks would be redeemed by regular customers and 20 percent by customers who would not otherwise have come to the restaurant. Furthermore, 45 percent of the deli-bucks would be redeemed by regular customers who increased their purchases by an average of $2. The deli-buck redemption expectations are already included in Bernard's forecast of revenues. Not having to pay for the first $10 would make it tempting to take an extra bagel home, to get a more expensive sandwich, or to splurge on dessert. He'd seen this happen earlier with the gift certificates.

Designing the deli-bucks was easy and a good opportunity to mix marketing with finance. Made to look like oversized currency, the certificates on one side had Bernard's picture, a fancy border with $10 signs in the corners, and the notation that the purchase cost was $8 and the value was $10 in food purchases with no redemption for cash. The other side had the logo for Bernard's New York Deli, a bright red apple with a bite taken out, more $10 signs, and the message "Pay now . . . eat later. These deli-bucks will be used to further our expansion and purchase additional equipment and more seating to make your experience more enjoyable. You will in turn receive a 20% discount on your future purchases." Each certificate had its own serial number so it could be tracked and to discourage counterfeiting.

After hearing about the deli-bucks, Joann Kapololu, manager of the Waikiki Beachcomber restaurant, praised Bernard's idea. "He obviously has a passion for what he does, and came up with something very creative. This brings dollars into his business, allows him to finance his dream, and the people who enjoy his food will be all over it."

The certificate package from the printer held enough of the deli-bucks to raise $30,000, and Bernard prepared an attractive poster to be placed near the restaurant entrance telling customers about them. The wait staff was briefed to respond favorably when customers asked about the certificates. All was ready.

PART II
Management of Working Capital

Chapter 4   Inventory Management
Chapter 5   Accounts Receivable Management
Chapter 6   Credit Policy and Collections
Chapter 7   Managing Payables and Accruals

The focus of Part 2 is on the management of the four major working capital accounts including inventory, receivables, payables and accruals. Proper management of these working capital accounts provides a profitable firm with a continual flow of cash and the necessary liquidity to achieve management's operating plan. Part 2 begins with Chapter 4, Inventory Management; the management of credit and receivables is discussed in Chapters 5 and 6. Finally, Chapter 7 studies the management of payables and accruals. As discussed in Part 1, the management of working capital involves the management of the transformation process of resources from the cash invested in inventory once payables and operating accruals are paid, through the operations or production process, followed by the selling process and, finally, the credit collections process. The management of this transformation process has a profound impact on the liquidity position of the firm.

CHAPTER 4

Inventory Management

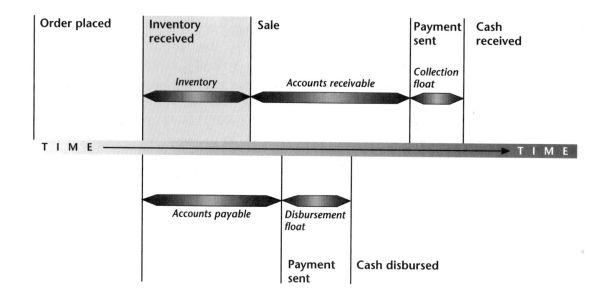

OBJECTIVES

After studying this chapter, you should be able to:

- Better understand the role that holding and ordering costs play in determining the appropriate inventory order quantity.
- Adjust the traditional economic order quantity (EOQ) model for quantity discounts.
- Appreciate how just-in-time concepts can be incorporated into the inventory order decision process.
- Assess the impact that different order quantities have on the timing and amount of cash flows related to the inventory purchase decision.
- Learn how to assess the actual behavior of inventory flows through the use of balance fraction measures rather than inventory turnover ratios.

The management of inventory plays an important role in the management of a firm's cash flow timeline. Keeping smaller inventory balances means less idle investment but requires many more orders of inventory, resulting in more disbursements of cash but each of a relatively small amount. However, keeping minimal inventory balances increases the likelihood of inventory shortages. As an alternative, keeping larger inventory balances means more idle investment in inventory. Fewer orders, each of a larger quantity, are placed that result in larger cash balances being disbursed but over longer intervals. This inventory strategy results in a lower probability of inventory shortages.

FINANCIAL DILEMMA

Can Placing Fewer Orders Save Money?

The treasurer of LUBE-RITE, Inc., a nationwide chain of lube centers, was just informed by the purchasing manager that one of the firm's suppliers of petroleum products has initiated a quantity discount program. Although the purchasing manager was excited about the prospects, the treasurer realized that the order quantity required to receive the discount would greatly increase the firm's investment in inventory. Larger orders would reduce ordering costs, but the larger quantities would increase the holding costs and opportunity costs of the inventory investment. She wondered if the trade-off in these costs was worth the quantity discount received.

Inventory is a difficult item to manage because it crosses so many lines of responsibility. The purchasing manager is responsible for supplies of raw material and would like to avoid shortages and to purchase in bulk to take advantage of quantity discounts. The production manager is responsible for uninterrupted production and wishes to keep enough raw materials and work-in-process inventory on hand to avoid disrupting the production process. The marketing manager is responsible for selling the product and therefore wishes to minimize the chances of running out of inventory. The financial manager is concerned about achieving an appropriate rate of return on invested capital. Funds invested in inventory are idle and do not earn a return. In fact, because of the inter-relatedness of these diverse areas, **supply chain management** has developed as a field in and of itself. Sometimes referred to as distribution or logistics, supply chain management, the process by which companies move materials and parts from suppliers through the production process and on to consumers, is now placed near the top of corporate strategic agendas. It is not uncommon to find companies cutting delivery time and reducing distribution costs, and at the same time increasing sales as they focus on the overall supply chain as a system rather than trying to manage the individual pieces of the logistics puzzle separately. A striking example of the impact of this kind of focus is the transformation of Apple Computer. It has become a model of manufacturing efficiency, reducing inventory levels from $2 billion in 1996 to under $20 million 3 years later.

This chapter does not attempt to teach you new inventory management techniques. Rather, the purpose of this chapter is to discuss the impact of inventory management on the cash cycle of the corporation. It will develop some basic techniques that can be used by the financial manager to effectively manage this important component of the cash cycle. Poor inventory management results in an illiquid corporation—one that must continually borrow to have enough operating cash on hand. Properly managed, the turnover of inventory releases cash in a timely manner, and this cash flow is then used to make payments on payables and other financial obligations as they come due and ultimately enhance the value of the firm.

THE CONCEPT OF INVENTORY

A major problem with managing inventory is that the demand for a corporation's product is to a degree uncertain. The supply of raw materials used in its production process is also somewhat uncertain. In addition, the corporation's production schedules contain some degree of uncertainty because of possible equipment breakdowns and labor difficulties.

Because of these possibilities, inventory acts as a shock absorber between product demand and product supply. If product demand is greater than expected, inventory can be depleted without losing sales until production can be stepped up enough to match the unexpected demand.

Three basic types of inventory must be managed: raw material inventory, work-in-process inventory, and finished goods inventory. Raw material inventory represents the initial input into the production process. For example, scrap metal or iron ore is used to make the metal necessary for the production of automobile frames and bodies, and chemicals represent the raw material necessary for the production of fertilizer. If a corporation such as Monsanto were to run out of the basic chemicals used in the production of fertilizer, that entire production process would have to be shut down.

FOCUS ON PRACTICE

A CLOSE SHAVE   Perhaps no stronger link can be made between working capital management and the value of the firm than that expressed recently by the treasury team at Gillette Company. The team has been telling Wall Street analysts that it would lift its depressed stock price through a restructuring and reorganization plan that includes a reduction of working capital by $1 billion over 18 months. Reduction in inventory is a major component of this restructuring plan because it will cut down on storage and financing costs as well as reduce the length of the production cycle. Analysts had been concerned about the rise in inventories and receivables at Gillette.[1]

[1]Jed Horowitz. 2000. Gillette shaves inventory costs. *Treasury and Risk Management* 10(3):14.

Work-in-process inventory represents items that are beyond the raw material stage but not yet at the completed product stage. For example, General Motors would consider an engine to be a part of its work-in-process inventory as it waits to be installed onto the frame of an automobile. The need for work-in-process inventory is obvious when the complexities of the typical production line are considered. For instance, assume that the production process of an automobile firm consists of two production lines: one to build the frame and body and the other to build the engine. The production line building the engine feeds into the production line building the car body. If work-in-process inventory (which consists of car engines) was not created, the two production lines would have to be perfectly synchronized at all times. Otherwise, the car body production line would be disrupted whenever the engine production line experienced any problems. With a stock of engines to draw on, the car body production line can continue to operate drawing down the work-in-process inventory of engines until the problems with the engine production line can be resolved.

To carry this example one step further, a finished goods inventory consists of completed automobiles. An inventory of finished goods must be maintained because of the uncertainty of the consumer demand for the corporation's product and the desire on the part of management not to run out of inventory for sale.

We should also mention a fourth type of inventory at this point: cash. The stock of cash held by a firm is a special type of inventory that uncouples the payment of bills from the collection of accounts receivable. The focus of this chapter is on the management of physical inventory, and Chapter 15 discusses the management of the stock, or inventory, of cash.

There are three basic motives for holding inventory. First, firms hold inventory in relation to the level of operating activity they expect in the near future. This is referred to as the **transaction motive.** For example, a grocery store receives periodic shipments of fresh produce in anticipation of customer demand over several days. Customers are not eager to take "rain checks" for items such as produce and meat; they will simply go to another store. A second motive is a **precautionary motive.** Our grocery store manager may order an additional quantity of goods as a cushion for an unexpected increase in demand. Of course, a precautionary balance of canned goods can be more easily managed than a precautionary balance of fresh fruit. The third motive for holding inventory is the **speculative motive.** Suppose the citrus orchards in Florida were devastated by a hard freeze. The grocery store manager might anticipate a future shortage of oranges and purchase a large quantity of frozen orange juice, hoping to have a competitive advantage in the future if a shortage of oranges does occur.

BASICS OF MANAGING THE AVERAGE INVENTORY BALANCE[2]

Stocking inventory requires a financial investment. From the viewpoint of a financial manager, the investment in inventory should be related to the demand for inventory, the cost of holding inventory, and the cost of ordering the inventory units. For example, the greater the consumer demand for the corporation's product, the greater the corporation's demand for raw materials, work-in-process, and finished goods inventory. If the cost of holding inventory increases, the financial manager will tend to stock less inventory. If the cost of ordering inventory items increases, the financial manager will tend to order more items per order and to place fewer orders. Given a demand for the inventory items, there is a trade-off between the cost of stocking inventory and the cost of holding inventory.

The Cost of Managing Inventory

Demand for inventory, holding costs, and ordering costs can be combined into an equation to compute the total cost of managing inventory. As Equations 4-1 and 4-2 show, the total cost of managing inventory has two components: the cost of ordering inventory and the cost of holding inventory.

Total cost = Total cost of ordering inventory + Total cost of holding inventory   (4-1)

Total cost = (Order cost per order × Number of orders) +
             (Holding cost per inventory item × Average inventory balance)   (4-2)

The first part of Equation 4-2 calculates the total cost of ordering inventory by multiplying the ordering cost per order times the number of orders placed. The number of orders placed is equal to the total number of inventory items demanded over the course of the planning period, such as a year, divided by the number of inventory units ordered with each order.

The second part of Equation 4-2 calculates the holding cost of the average inventory balance. This component of the total cost equation can be developed further if it is assumed that the corporation receives its ordered inventory items on the day its current inventory stock is exhausted and that the inventory items are used up at a constant rate. These two simplifications make the average inventory balance equal to the amount of inventory ordered and received plus the amount of ending inventory, which is zero, divided by 2.

To reduce the verbiage in the total cost equation, we use the following symbols and rewrite the total cost equation as shown in Equation 4-3:

Total inventory units demanded	T
Order quantity	Q
Fixed order cost per order	F
Holding cost per inventory unit[3]	H

$$\text{Total cost} = (F \times \frac{T}{Q}) + (H \times \frac{Q}{2})$$ (4-3)

---

[2]This section reviews the basic EOQ inventory management model. Those students familiar with this model may wish to skip or skim this section. For those less familiar with the EOQ model, this section provides a step-by-step development of the EOQ model.

[3]Holding cost per unit may include not only costs such as storage and insurance but also opportunity cost such as lost interest earnings on funds invested in inventory.

EXHIBIT 4-1
Trade-Off between Ordering Costs and Holding Costs

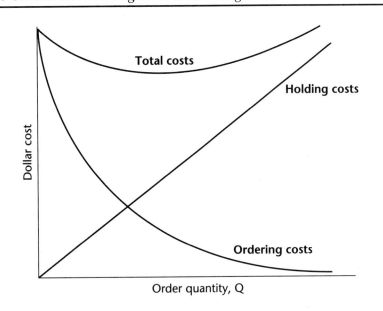

Careful inspection of Equation 4-3 shows the trade-off between ordering costs and holding costs, which presents an interesting challenge for the financial manager. Notice how a larger quantity ordered, Q, reduces the ordering costs (Q is in the denominator) by reducing the number of orders placed, while a larger quantity ordered results in a larger holding cost (Q is in the numerator) by increasing the size of the average inventory balance.

These relationships are graphed out in Exhibit 4-1. The number of inventory units ordered per order is on the horizontal axis, and dollar cost is on the vertical axis. As more units are ordered, the total ordering costs fall. This is because fewer orders are placed while holding costs increase because the average inventory balance gets larger. As the exhibit shows, the total cost curve, which is the sum of ordering costs and holding costs, first falls as units ordered increase, and then begins to increase. The optimal number of units to order is that order quantity that minimizes total costs.

The Optimal Quantity to Order

The goal of the financial manager is to choose that order quantity level that results in an optimal trade-off between ordering costs and holding costs so that the total cost of managing inventory is minimized. The order quantity that minimizes the total cost of managing inventory is generally referred to as the **economic order quantity** (EOQ).

This EQQ level can be derived by differentiating the total cost Equation 4-3 with respect to Q and setting the first derivative equal to zero to locate the minimum point on the total cost curve. The optimum inventory order quantity equation derived by doing this is shown in Equation 4-4.

$$EOQ = \frac{\sqrt{2 \times T \times F}}{H} \tag{4-4}$$

The EOQ is that quantity of inventory items that should be ordered each time an order is placed; it is the order quantity that minimizes the total cost of managing the corporation's inventory. The basic EOQ model, as represented by Equation 4-4, is based on some rather restrictive assumptions. First, this basic model requires a near-perfect forecast of inventory units demanded, T, and a constant rate of inventory usage. In addition, there must be a constant or fixed order cost, F, and a constant cost of holding each item of inventory. These assumptions are too restrictive for the model to be used in general. In a later section, we develop a way for the model to work in a more realistic setting. However, before we develop extensions of the basic model, we demonstrate how the basic model works.

An Example Using EOQ

Cory Manufacturing forecasts that its production process will require 500,000 tons of scrap metal over its planning period. Demand for Cory's products is not affected by seasonal variations and remains quite stable. Ordering costs amount to an average of $20 per order, which includes clerical and computer time, telephones, and mail. Holding costs per ton of scrap metal are estimated at $1.25. The costs are minimal given that the metal can be stored outside and management has never seen the need for insurance.

Given this information, we can calculate the EOQ for Cory Manufacturing.

$$EOQ = \frac{\sqrt{2 \times 500,000 \times \$20.00}}{\$1.25}$$

$$EOQ = 4,000 \text{ tons}$$

The optimal order size, that which minimizes total inventory costs, is 4,000 tons per order. Therefore, the financial manager should recommend that 4,000 tons of scrap be ordered with each order. The number of orders placed can be determined by dividing the total inventory units required (500,000) by the number of tons ordered with each order (4,000).

$$\text{Number of orders} = \frac{\text{Total inventory requirements}}{\text{Order size}} = \frac{500,000}{4,000} \tag{4-5}$$

$$\text{Number of orders} = 125$$

The number of orders that Cory must place over the production period is 125 orders. The average inventory balance can also be calculated. As discussed earlier, it is equal to the order quantity divided by 2, as shown below:

$$\text{Average inventory balance} = \frac{EOQ}{2} \tag{4-6}$$

$$\text{Average inventory balance} = 2,000 \text{ tons}$$

The inventory management problem is shown graphically in Exhibit 4-2. Ordered inventory arrives on the day that the inventory balance reaches zero. Therefore on that day the inventory balance is equal to the amount ordered, which is the economic order quantity. On the next day, the inventory balance begins to drop at a constant rate, as a result of the assumption of the constant rate of usage. This **usage rate** can be calculated by dividing the total inventory units required, T, by the number of days in the planning

EXHIBIT 4-2
Inventory Balance and the Reorder Point

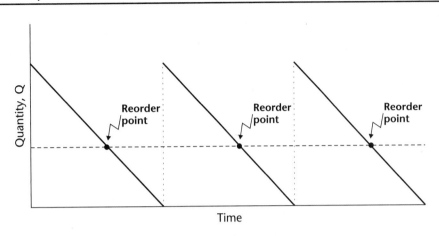

or production period. For this example, assume a production run that encompasses 375 working days. Equation 4-7 shows how to calculate the daily usage rate.

$$\text{Usage rate} = \frac{\text{Units of inventory required}}{\text{Number of days in the planning period}} \qquad (4\text{-}7)$$

$$\text{Usage rate} = \frac{500,000}{375}$$

$$\text{Usage rate} = 1,333 \text{ tons per day}$$

The daily usage rate is used to calculate the point at which Cory's management should place an order. The inventory level at which an order should be placed is called the **reorder point.** To calculate this inventory level, two items must be known. The first item is the daily usage rate that was calculated above. The second item is the number of days it takes to receive the shipment of inventory once the order is placed. In the past, Cory has experienced an average of 2 days delivery time. The calculation for the reorder point based on the usage rate and delivery time is shown in Equation 4-8.

$$\text{Reorder point} = \text{Daily Usage Rate} \times \text{Delivery Time} \qquad (4\text{-}8)$$
$$\text{Reorder point} = 1,333 \times 2$$
$$\text{Reorder point} = 2,666 \text{ tons}$$

When the inventory balance reaches 2,666 tons, management should place an order for 4,000 tons of scrap metal that is the economic order quantity. In 2 days, the inventory will be depleted (2 days at a daily usage rate of 1,333 tons per day), and Cory will receive its shipment of scrap metal before it begins operation on the next day.

What would happen to Cory's production process if the shipment was delayed or if the daily usage rate of inventory increased as a result of an unexpected demand for its products? The next section develops some extensions of the basic EOQ model.

Extensions of the Basic EOQ Model

At this point, there are two extensions of the basic EOQ model that need examination: the concept of safety stock and the impact of quantity discounts.

EXHIBIT 4-3
Showing How Safety Stock Can Be Incorporated into the EOQ Model

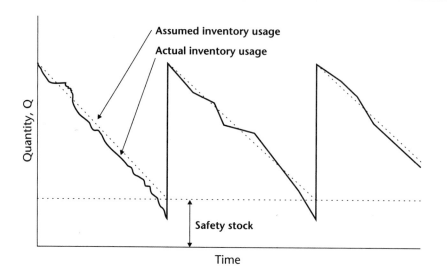

SAFETY STOCK CONSIDERATIONS.   Suppose that sales are not stable or that the production cycle or delivery time is uncertain. Under such conditions, extra inventory is warranted to guard against an inventory shortage. This extra inventory balance acts as insurance against running out of inventory and is often referred to as a **safety stock.**

Exhibit 4-3 demonstrates the importance of safety stock. The dashed line represents a constant rate of inventory usage, and the solid line represents actual usage. Note how a portion of the safety stock was used prior to receiving shipment of the inventory ordered.

A formal model for determining the optimal safety stock is not developed here, but there are two basic factors that affect the amount of safety stock needed. First, as previously mentioned, variability of demand, the production process, and delivery time will tend to increase the optimal size of the safety stock. The greater the uncertainty, the greater the need for the type of insurance provided by safety stocks. Second, high inventory carrying costs will tend to reduce the size of the safety stock holding stock-out costs constant. Obviously, however, stock-out costs are a function of the total inventory level held. Thus the financial manager must assess the variability of the demand and usage of inventory and analyze the trade-off between the costs of running out of inventory and the costs of holding a safety stock of inventory.

The presence of safety stock does not affect the calculation of *EOQ*, which is calculated ignoring the safety stock level. But it does affect the calculation of the average inventory balance and the reorder point. The average inventory balance becomes:

$$(EOQ/2) + (\text{Safety stock})$$

The reorder point becomes:

$$(\text{Daily usage rate}) \times (\text{Delivery time}) + (\text{Safety stock})$$

The desired safety stock is added to the previously determined average inventory balance to determine average inventory, and the desired safety stock is added to the original reorder point to determine the new reorder point.

EXHIBIT 4-4
Total and Component Inventory Costs Considering Quantity Discounts

QUANTITY	TOTAL COSTS	ORDER COST	HOLDING COSTS	PURCHASE COST
500	$270,313	$20,000	$ 313	$250,000
1,000	250,625	10,000	625	240,000
1,500	247,604	6,667	938	240,000
2,000	246,250	5,000	1,250	240,000
2,500	245,563	4,000	1,563	240,000
3,000	230,208	3,333	1,875	225,000
3,500	230,045	2,857	2,188	225,000
4,000	230,000	2,500	2,500	225,000
4,500	230,035	2,222	2,813	225,000
5,000	205,125	2,000	3,125	200,000
5,500	205,256	1,818	3,438	200,000
6,000	205,417	1,667	$3,750	200,000

The EOQ model is a useful financial management tool because it indicates the proper level of inventory to order based on the trade-off of the ordering costs and holding costs of inventory. Proper inventory control is necessary when the actual usage rate differs from that forecasted, so the order quantity can be adjusted to avoid inventory excesses or shortages.

ADJUSTING FOR QUANTITY DISCOUNTS. Often, a supplier will offer a discount for volume, which purchasers refer to as a **quantity discount.** The purchaser must decide whether the discount for purchasing a larger quantity justifies incurring the additional holding costs for storing the surplus inventory.

To account for the quantity discount opportunity, a third variable must be added to the total cost equation first developed as Equation 4-3. The additional variable is the dollar cost of inventory as shown below in Equation 4-9. The dollar cost of inventory for a given quantity is C', and the total volume of inventory required over the planning period is T. Note that C' is not a constant; rather, it is a function of Q, the volume of inventory purchased with each order.

$$\text{Total Cost} = (F \times (T/Q)) + (H \times (Q/2)) + (C' \times T) \tag{4-9}$$

To demonstrate the application of Equation 4-9, we continue with the example we have been working with and assume that our supplier offers the following quantity discounts.

QUANTITY (Q)	COST PER UNIT (C')
0-999 units	$.50
1,000–2,999 units	$.48
3,000–4,999 units	$.45
5,000–units	$.40

Exhibit 4-4 presents a table showing the total inventory cost and the component costs for a range of order quantities from 500 units to 6000 units. Notice that our original solution for the *EOQ* of 4000 units is far from optimal when quantity discounts are offered. Total cost is $246,250, with holding costs of $1,250 and ordering costs of $5,000. The optimal order quantity discount is 5000 units with a total cost of $205,125. Holding costs are $3,125, and ordering costs are $2,000.

EXHIBIT 4-5
Cash Flow Timeline for Inventory

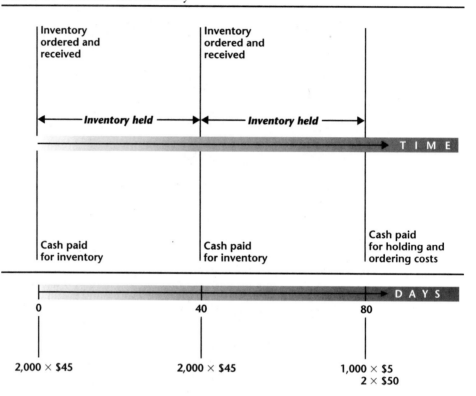

INVENTORY MANAGEMENT AND THE CASH FLOW TIMELINE

From the financial manager's point of view, inventory represents an idle investment of corporate resources. If the inventory is purchased with cash, there is an opportunity cost of the funds expended. If inventory is purchased on credit, then the firm incurs additional debt and interest expense, and its unused borrowing capacity is diminished.

Suppose a firm requires a total of 4000 units of inventory for a production run. Furthermore, assume that two orders for inventory are placed for 2000 units each. Inventory would be paid for with cash, and ordering and holding costs would be paid at the end of the production run. A cash flow timeline, shown in Exhibit 4-5, depicts these transactions.

The financial manager of the firm wants to make certain that this inventory order quantity minimizes the present value cost of managing the inventory process, while still meeting the needs of the production process. To calculate the present value of this inventory management policy, assume the following data:

Cost of capital, k:	10%
Inventory cost, C:	$45 per unit
Order costs, F:	$50 per order
Holding costs, H:	$5 per average inventory unit

Furthermore, assume that the inventory is consumed at a steady rate, and the production run period is 80 days. Thus the average daily usage rate of the inventory is 50 units per day = 4,000/80. Because two orders will be placed, each for 2000 units, and assuming that the orders are placed so that each inventory shipment arrives at the same time that the current inventory balance is used up, there are 40 days separating inventory arrivals. Therefore, the average inventory balance is 1000 units.

Calculating the present value cost of the current inventory policy is fairly straightforward. We use simple interest to account for the time value of money.

$$\text{PV Day 0 Cost} = 2000 \times \$45 \times \frac{1}{(1 + (0 \times (.10/365)))} = \$90,000.00$$

$$\text{PV Day 40 Cost} = 2000 \times \$45 \times \frac{1}{(1 + (40 \times (.10/365)))} = \$89,024.39$$

$$\text{PV Day 80 Cost} = (1000 \times \$5) \times \frac{1}{(1 + (80 \times (.10/365)))} +$$

$$(2 \times \$50) \times \frac{1}{(1 + (80 \times (.10/365)))} = \$4,990.62$$

$$\text{Total PV Cost} = \text{PV Day 0 Cost} + \text{PV Day 40 Cost} + \text{PV Day 80 Cost}$$
$$= \$90,000.00 + \$89,024.39 + \$4,990.62$$
$$\text{Total PV Cost} = \$184,015.01$$

What if smaller but more frequent orders were placed, resulting in more payments of a smaller size? The financial manager would pay less money up front for inventory and, therefore, would have a smaller opportunity cost for those funds. In addition, the inventory carrying costs would decline because less inventory is held. However, order costs would increase as a result of the increased number of orders placed. With the changing size and timing of the various cash flows, the only way to assess if a change in inventory policy will enhance shareholder wealth is to calculate the present value of the cash flows. The policy with the minimum present value cost should be the one that results in the greatest enhancement to shareholder wealth.

We can develop a general formulation to assess the cost of inventory management using a present-value timeline approach, as shown in Equation 4-10.

$$\text{Total Cost} = \frac{(F \times (T/Q)) + (H \times (Q/2))}{(1 + (i \times D))} \qquad \text{(4-10)}$$
$$+ \sum_{t=0}^{(T/Q)-1} \frac{(Q \times C)}{(1 + i \times (t \times (Q \times D/T)))}$$

In which:

T = Number of inventory units required

D = Number of days in the production period

Q = Inventory order quantity

C = Cost of each inventory unit

F = Fixed order cost per order

H = Holding cost per unit of inventory

i = Daily opportunity cost

To understand Equation 4-10, note that the first term in the equation is the present value of the ordering costs, $F \times (T/Q)$, and the holding costs, $H \times (Q/2)$, that are assumed to be paid at the end of the production period. The simple interest present value factor is $1/(1 + (i \times D))$. The second term is a summation of the present value of the cash flows to pay for each inventory lot purchase. The cost of each inventory lot purchase is $Q \times C$. The present value factor accounts for the timing of each purchase. The first purchase is at the beginning of the production period and $t = 0$. Thus the simple interest factor is $1/(1 + 0)$ or 1. The second purchase, $t = 1$, is on day $t \times (Q \times D/T)$. To understand this, first note that the daily usage rate of inventory is T/D. When Q is ordered, it takes Q/daily usage rate, or $Q/(T/D)$ days to use it up. This can be rewritten as $Q \times D/T$. Inventory purchases are made on day $t \times (Q \times D/T)$ for $t = 0,1,2,3,...(T/Q) - 1$.

FINANCIAL DILEMMA REVISITED

An example illustrates this equation. Returning to Lube-Rite's dilemma at the beginning of the chapter, we can now help the treasurer assess the value of the quantity discount offered through the use of the cash flow timeline formulation of the inventory decision. Assume the following values for the inventory decision variables prior to the discount offer.

$T = 1,000$

$D = 100$

$Q = 200$

$C = \$10$

$F = \$5$

$H = \$2.50$

$i = .15/365 = .00041$

Using these numbers yields the following values:

Total inventory holding costs = $250, $H \times (Q/2)$
Total ordering costs   = $25, $F \times (T/Q)$
Cost of each purchase lot   = $2,000, $C \times Q$

INVENTORY PURCHASE DAY $t \times (Q \times D/T)$	PRESENT VALUE FACTOR $1/(1 + i(t \times Q(D/T)))$	CASH FLOW	PRESENT VALUE HOLDING AND ORDERING COSTS	PRESENT VALUE OF PURCHASE COST
0	0	1.0000	$2,000		$2,000
1	20	.9918	2,000		1,983
2	40	.9838	2,000		1,967
3	60	.9759	2,000		1,951
4	80	.9682	2,000		1,936
	100	.9606	275	$264	
Total				$264	$9,837

Total Present Value Cost = $264 + $9,837
                         = $10,101

Now assume that the supplier is willing to discount the price per unit to $9.50 for purchase quantities of 500 units.

Total inventory holding costs = $625, $H \times (Q/2)$
Total ordering costs = $10, $F \times (T/Q)$
Cost of each purchase lot = $4,750, $C \times Q$

	INVENTORY PURCHASE DAY $t \times (Q \times D/T)$	PRESENT VALUE FACTOR $1/(1 + i(t \times QD/T))$	CASH FLOW	PRESENT VALUE HOLDING AND ORDERING COSTS	PRESENT VALUE OF PURCHASE COST
0	0	1.0000	$5,000		$4,750
1	50	.9799	5,000		4,654
	100	.9606	635	$610	
Total				$610	$9,404

Total Present Value Cost = $610 + $9,404 = $10,014

The present value cost of the inventory can be reduced from $10,101 to $10,014 by taking advantage of the quantity discount. In this case, the reduced cost of the inventory more than offset the additional holding costs and the larger initial payment for the inventory lot ordered.

This approach can be used to solve for the least cost order quantity, Q, in a similar fashion to the approach used by the quantity discount model. A simple solution is not possible because the present value factors for inventory costs, $Q \times C$, are functions of the quantity ordered, Q, which determines the timing of the purchases.

The traditional EOQ model is insensitive to the impact on present-value cost of the changes in the timing of cash flows resulting from different order quantities and different payment terms. In other words, if one supplier offered a combination of quantity discounts and payment terms different from another supplier, the basic EOQ model would not be able to adequately assess the differences between the present-value costs of the two options. Only the present-value timeline approach can accurately gauge the true cost differences between alternative inventory ordering strategies.

MONITORING THE INVENTORY BALANCE

Once an inventory policy has been established, the financial manager must constantly monitor the inventory balance to ensure that the firm is maintaining a proper investment in inventory. The financial manager should be concerned if the resulting investment in inventory is either greater than or less than that expected to result from the accepted policy. This section will present a variety of approaches that can be helpful in monitoring the firm's investment in inventory.

Inventory Control Systems

One of the most difficult areas of inventory management is inventory control. Consider a large department store chain and the thousands of inventory items that must be managed. It is now common that point-of-sale terminals linked to central computers are used as a means of controlling inventory. For example, today it is common for department stores, such as the Dillard's Department Stores, Inc. chain, based in Arkansas, to use electronic cash registers that are linked to a corporate central computer as a means of controlling its inventory. At the checkout counter, sales clerks scan relevant product data such as product code, number of items purchased, and the price, and the computer system keeps track of the inventory balance. Such a system lets management know exactly what is or is not selling and where. Inventory pileups or shortages can then be quickly averted.

Inventory Turnover Approach

The traditional approach to measuring a firm's investment in inventory is based on the firm's **inventory turnover ratio.** The inventory turnover ratio is found by dividing cost of goods sold (COGS) (although sometimes sales is used) over a given time such as a year, by the inventory balance held during that same time period. For example, suppose the annual cost of goods sold for Ureadem, Inc., a book publisher, was $100,000 and the year-end inventory balance was $18,000. The inventory turnover ratio is 5.55 = $100,000/$18,000.

A related inventory activity measure is **days inventory held.** This can be found by first calculating average daily cost of goods sold. Because we used annual cost of goods sold above, average daily cost of goods sold is found by dividing annual cost of goods sold by 365. Average daily cost of goods sold is $273.97 = $100,000/365. The number of days of inventory held is then found by dividing the inventory balance ($18,000) by average daily cost of goods sold ($273.97). The days inventory held is equal to 65.70 days = $18,000/$273.97. The greater this number, the greater the investment in inventory and the slower the inventory turnover.

Rather than monitoring the inventory balance using annual data, management must monitor the resources tied up in inventory over a shorter time, such as monthly, weekly, or daily. If inventory movement is slowing, the trend must be detected early enough to take corrective action. Suppose the financial manager collected the following data for the previous 6 months. The first two line items, cost of goods sold and ending inventory, are taken directly from the firm's monthly financial statements. The next two line items are based on calculations using the first two line items. Average daily COGS is calculated using the total dollar amount of cost of goods sold over an arbitrarily chosen time period, such as the just-completed quarter, divided by the number of days in the chosen period. In the following table, the chosen time period is the most recent quarter, and the number of days in a month is assumed to be 30. Thus average daily COGS for the quarter ending in March is $3.35 = (85 + 110 + 107)/90. Finally, average days COGS in inventory is calculated by dividing the ending inventory balance by the average daily COGS. The result is the average number of days of COGS held in the ending inventory balance.

	JAN	FEB	MAR	APR	MAY	JUNE
Cost of Goods Sold	85	110	107	93	73	68
Ending Inventory			68	55	42	44
Average Daily COGS (quarterly)			$3.35	$3.44	$3.03	$2.60
Average Days COGS in Inventory			20.3	15.9	13.8	16.9

From March through May, there is a decreasing number of days inventory held, which is a good sign. However, average days of COGS invested in inventory does jump up to 16.9 days in June, the second highest level for the 4-month period.

A Balance Fraction Approach

The following table shows the monthly dollar amount of purchases from January through June. In addition, the table shows the dollar amount of inventory left in each succeeding month after purchase. For example, in January, $100 of inventory was purchased. At the end of January, $50 of inventory remained in stock. Of the $100 of inventory purchased in January, $15 remained in stock at the end of February. The balance of the inventory purchased in January was sold in March. Summing up each column results in the dollar amount of total ending inventory for each month. The table clearly shows that ending inventory for each month consists of inventory items purchased over different periods.

For example, ending inventory for March consists of $50 of items purchased in March and $18 of items purchased in February.

MONTH OF PURCHASE	PURCHASE AMOUNT	JAN	FEB	MAR	APR	MAY	JUNE
January	$100	$50	$15				
February	$120		$60	$18			
March	$100			$50	$15		
April	$80				$40	$12	
May	$60					$30	$9
June	$70						$35
Total Inventory		NA	$75	$68	$55	$42	$44

To make this table useful for analysis purposes, we need to convert the dollar inventory balances to **balance fractions,** dollar inventory balance as a percent of inventory purchases. Let's follow an example to help demonstrate this concept. Look at the dollar figures for January in the table. In January, $100 of inventory was purchased. At the end of January, $50 of the January purchase remained as a balance. At the end of February, $15 of the January purchase remained as a balance. Thus 50 percent of January purchases remained as a balance ($50/$100) at the end of January, and 15 percent ($15/$100) remained as a balance at the end of February. The next table shows the balance fraction calculations for the rest of the months. Notice that the balance fractions are constant. There is a steady use of inventory resulting in 50 percent of a month's purchase remaining at the end of the purchase month and 15 percent remaining at the end of the month following the purchase month.

MONTH OF PURCHASE	PURCHASE AMOUNT	JAN	FEB	MAR	APR	MAY	JUNE
January	$100	50%	15%				
February	$120		50%	15%			
March	$100			50%	15%		
April	$ 80				50%	15%	
May	$ 60					50%	15%
June	$ 70						50%

We conclude from this analysis that inventory use has been stable, with no accumulation or depletion of inventory. This finding is in conflict with the conclusion drawn by the analysis based on the number of days inventory was held. This measure uses total inventory in the numerator. If sales or COGS are falling, then inventory will generally be lower as management adjusts its inventory purchasing to the new lower sales volume. In the denominator, if sales, or correspondingly COGS, are falling, the average daily cost of goods will be artificially high because the averaging period will include COGS from an earlier period. This is especially true the longer the averaging period. Thus the number of days COGS is held in inventory will generally fall as sales and purchases fall, not because of increased inventory usage but because of the sales and purchasing trend and the period chosen over which to calculate average daily COGS. The balance fraction method of monitoring inventory is not affected by sales and purchasing trends and is therefore a more accurate measure of inventory usage.

REDUCING THE SIZE OF THE INVENTORY INVESTMENT

In the past, inventory has been viewed as an asset. Like any other asset, the more of it that shows up on the balance sheet, the better. More recently, however, inventory has begun to be viewed as an expense and, therefore, as an item to reduce or even eliminate. Earlier, we talked about the shock-absorbing role that inventory plays in the production and sales areas. If this shock-absorbing role could be reduced, then the level of inventory could be reduced. This is the essence of the just-in-time inventory management system developed in Japan. The focus of the just-in-time method is on redesigning the production system, not reducing inventory, to streamline the ordering process and to eliminate waste and production errors, thereby improving the quality of the production process. Reduced investment in inventory typically comes as a result of this re-engineering process, as noted in the Focus on Practice box.

A just-in-time system demands a commitment to problem solving. With no inventory, inefficiencies and production flow design problems quickly surface. In the past, adding a greater stock of raw material or work-in-process inventory solved these problems. The just-in-time approach attacks the problem at its source, even to the extent of redesigning the production flow process.

Quality and loyalty is demanded throughout all stages of production if the just-in-time system is to work. Suppliers must be reliable and provide a high quality product or service. Employees must be efficient and dedicated to quality, and they must be willing to be cross-trained to perform a variety of functions and tasks.

Not all industries or firms are adaptable to this type of production process. Prime candidates are those firms that are large, with a major market share, and that have a relatively stable product demand or demand such that a master production plan can be developed and adhered to.

The just-in-time inventory system is one approach to managing the production flow. The more traditional approach has been to stock inventory. To determine which approach is best for management, an analyst must subjectively assess a given firm within a given culture. The just-in-time system has its own set of costs in terms of worker education and a significant investment in capital equipment, including a very sophisticated information system. For a given firm, incurring these costs may exceed the costs incurred under an alternative inventory system. Perhaps the most important aspect of the development of alternative production/inventory systems, such as the just-in-time system, is that it has caused us to change our inventory management philosophy from that of managing an asset to that of managing an expense or liability.

The inventory strategy followed by Toys "R" Us, a retail toy outlet based in Paramus, New Jersey, is in contrast to the just-in-time inventory system. Toys "R" Us uses inventory as a competitive advantage by offering the widest toy selection available on a year-round basis. In addition, they are able to offer prices at about 75 percent of department store prices because of their volume purchases. This winning combination of wide assortment and discount prices has fueled the company's growth. Thus while minimizing inventory stocks may be appropriate in some cases, stocking inventory may be appropriate in other situations. Inventory management decisions must correspond with competitive opportunities and the firm's strategic plan.

Technology allows management to design systems to more efficiently manage its operations, which ultimately impact the inventory area. Order costs are reduced with less costly and faster information systems. According to Stone, "firms that place orders, receive acknowledgments, make confirmations, and process shipping and delivering information through electronic data interchange transactions eliminate time delays, lower costs, and reduce errors."[4]

---

[4]"Just-In-Time: The Risk/Reward Trade-Off May Not Be What It Seems" (full citation in end-of-chapter references.

JUST-IN-TIME INVENTORY MANAGEMENT   Just-in-time (JIT) inventory management has literally become a household word. The concept has transformed inventory management from managing an asset to managing a process. Companies view inventory as an expense that can and should be reduced. JIT inventory management involves the development of sophisticated information systems that provide a forecast of inventory needs for the manufacturer and electronic communications between the manufacturer and its suppliers. Quality control is an essential element of JIT because one of the ingredients of a successful JIT system is reliability.

Major US companies from General Electric to Harley Davidson have endorsed the JIT concept. In the case of Harley Davidson, business has been reborn. Key benefits include:

- Significant reduction in plant size, which saves overhead as well as construction costs.
- Increased productivity through the use of electronic data interchange systems between manufacturer and supplier.
- Cost savings through less investment in inventory and lower financing costs—GE was able to trim inventory by 70 percent and Harley Davidson trimmed several million dollars from its work-in-process inventory investment.

Although it may seem that JIT inventory management invalidates the EOQ concept, the two systems are actually quite compatible. JIT inventory management actually maintains the same focus on ordering and holding costs but redefines the production process, substantially altering the relative magnitudes of the cost components used in calculating EOQ. As a result, inventory shipments may be received daily or hourly rather than weekly or even more sporadically. For example, a retailing company, The Gap, employed many of the concepts of JIT. The company boosted quality, strengthened ties with manufacturers, and redesigned its distribution system, enabling the company to supply its stores in New York City daily. This procedure ensures that the stores never run out of the hottest items.

Although many companies have successfully redesigned and integrated their operations on a domestic basis, the challenge remains to integrate on a global basis. For companies to compete effectively internationally, global integration of operations becomes a necessity. This means that a company manages its operations worldwide as a single entity to maximize competitive advantage in all of its markets on a global basis. One leader in global integration is Xerox. It standardized product development procedures for all markets rather than developing products for one market, and then it re-engineered those products for other markets worldwide, resulting in a dramatic savings in product development time. The company did not stop there. Next, Xerox standardized plant facility requirements worldwide to facilitate the comparison of product cost and inventory data. Finally, distribution centers were strategically located worldwide rather than by specific markets in isolation.[5]

As stated earlier, inventory management has evolved as a byproduct, with the main focus placed on redesigning the entire supply chain with increasing focus on quality and efficiency. One example of a company taking an aggressive approach to managing its supply chain is Wal-Mart, as discussed in the final Focus on Practice box. The company

---

[4]"Just-In-Time: The Risk/Reward Trade-Off May Not Be What It Seems" (full citation in end-of-chapter references).

[5]Robert E. Markland, Shawanee K. Vickery, and Robert A. Davis. *Operations management: Concepts in manufacturing and services* (full citation in end-of-chapter references), p 99.

FOCUS ON PRACTICE

SUPPLY CHAIN MANAGEMENT[6]   Wal-Mart, the world's largest retailer, has a goal of selling its merchandise so quickly that products are out of the store before it has to pay its suppliers. In fact, this strategy of quick inventory turnover is one reason Wal-Mart's profitability has grown faster than sales. To accomplish this, the company is building faster distribution centers and providing suppliers with more sales data on products so they can better match their production to Wal-Mart's peak selling seasons. The company also aggressively cut back on slow-moving inventory items. As a result, over 60 percent of Wal-Mart's inventory is sold before payments are made to suppliers. The goal is 100 percent.

A good example of Wal-Mart's distribution system is how it handles Proctor & Gamble products. At Wal-Mart's new distribution centers, products from Proctor & Gamble's trucks are unloaded directly onto trucks headed for Wal-Mart stores (the product is never put on warehouse shelves). Once a truck is full, it heads for the stores where it is on the store shelves in less than 4 hours and sold within 24 hours. Payment to Proctor & Gamble is generally made in 10 days.

[6]Emily Nelson. 1999. Wal-Mart may cut costs, boost earnings by changing merchandise handling. *Dow Jones Business News.*

has enhanced its profitability through inventory reduction by effectively redesigning its supply chain management system in alliance with its suppliers. Inventory reduction results when it becomes the cheaper alternative to the increasing costs associated with improving the efficiency of the supply chain process.

Sophisticated systems such as those used by Wal-Mart require a comprehensive information system. It is now common for information systems technology to play a critical role in the management of entire firm's supply chain and, therefore, the management of inventory. For example, an inventory planning system known as **material requirements planning** (MRP) focuses on the amount and timing of finished goods demanded and translates this into the derived demand for raw materials and sub-assemblies at various stages of production. Material requirements planning provides computer-based support for planning and control of operations from receipt of materials to shipment of orders. Users report significant improvement in their competitive and financial positions, customer service levels, and production scheduling. About half of the users were able to cut inventory levels, manufacturing costs, production lead times, and component shortages. With such a system, if a major customer defers an order by a month or so, the MRP system immediately readjusts materials purchases and related production schedules.

The evolution of resource requirements planning systems saw material requirements systems (now referred to as MRP I) merge into **manufacturing resource planning systems** (MRP II), a much broader and all-encompassing concept. Manufacturing resource planning systems are made up of a variety of functions that are linked together: business planning, sales and operations planning, production planning, master production scheduling, material requirements planning, capacity requirements planning, and the execution support systems for capacity and material. Output from these systems is then integrated with financial reports, such as the business plan, purchase commitment report, shipping budget, inventory projections in dollars, etc. And the evolution and sophistication of such systems continue today with MRP II systems evolving into systems referred to as **enterprise resources planning** (ERP). Enterprise resources planning systems are accounting-oriented information systems used for identifying and planning the enterprise-wide resources needed to take, make, ship, and account for customer orders. Enterprise resources planning systems consist of software modules that help manage the many different activities in different functional business areas. Vendors such as SAP, Oracle, and PeopleSoft are leaders in providing such software systems.[7]

SUMMARY

In this chapter we have seen that proper inventory management decisions, from the perspective of the financial manager, should be based on the cost of holding the inventory, the cost of ordering inventory, the opportunity cost of funds invested in inventory, and cost considerations based on quantity discounts. The final inventory decision should then take into consideration whether or not this minimum cost order quantity is workable within the inventory management system so that stock-outs are avoided.

Inventory is a major component in the supply chain of the firm and must also be viewed as a critical component in the cash flow cycle of a corporation. If improperly managed, inventory can be a major contributor to cash flow problems experienced by the organization. The level of inventory needed by an organization is a direct result of the design of its operation or production process. Therefore, monitoring the resulting inventory levels is important so that management can continually gauge the status of operations. We learned that some of the traditional inventory monitoring tools, such as inventory turnover and days inventory held, are biased by sales and production trends. A suggested improvement was to use a balance fraction approach.

There is anecdotal evidence that the growing success of just-in-time and supply chain management systems in the United States is impacting inventory management. Ratios such as inventory-to-sales, especially in the work-in-process and materials and supplies categories, have been falling steadily over the past decade.

Useful Web Sites

A great web site for articles and news on working capital management: Global Treasury News: www.gtnews.com
American Productivity and Quality Center: www.apqc.org
Industry Week Magazine: www.industryweek.com

Questions

1. What is inventory management primarily concerned with?
2. Why is inventory such a difficult item to manage?
3. Why is inventory needed? What role does it play?
4. What are the three different types of inventory and what role does each play?
5. What are the financial manager's concerns related to inventory management?
6. Explain what the EOQ solution represents.
7. How is risk handled by the EOQ model?
8. What are the three factors that affect the amount of safety stock needed? How does each factor differ from the other two?
9. Compare the EOQ solution to the present value timeline solution.
10. Discuss how the dollar amount of inventory can be reduced.
11. How can days COGS held in inventory be a misleading monitoring tool?

---

[7]Norman Gaither and Greg Frazier. 1999. *Production and operations management,* 8th ed. Cincinnati, OH: South-Western College Publishing, pp 417–418.

12. How is a balance fraction approach to inventory monitoring an improvement over the measure days COGS held in inventory?

Problems

1. Ardmore Farm and Seed has an inventory dilemma. They have been selling a brand of very popular insect spray for the past year. They have never really analyzed the costs incurred from ordering and holding the inventory, and they currently face a large stock of insecticide in the warehouse. They estimate that it costs $25 to place an order, and it costs $.25 per gallon to hold the spray. The annual requirements total 80,000 gallons for a 365 day year.
   a. Assuming that 10,000 gallons are ordered each time an order is placed, estimate the annual inventory costs.
   b. Calculate the EOQ.
   c. Given the EOQ calculated in part b, how many orders should be placed, and what is the average inventory balance?
   d. If it takes 7 days to receive an order from suppliers, at what inventory level should Ardmore place another order?

2. Lott Manufacturing, Inc. has been ordering parts for its production process in 10,000 units. Each order costs the firm $50.00 to place, and holding costs per unit average $3. Lott uses 200,000 units every 250 days.
   a. Calculate the EOQ.
   b. What is the difference in inventory costs between the EOQ and the current order quantity of 10,000 units?
   c. Given the EOQ calculated in part a, how many orders should be placed and what is the average inventory balance?
   d. If it takes 2 days to receive an order from suppliers, at what inventory level should Lott place another order?

3. Ardmore Farm and Seed (problem 1) was recently approached by its supplier with a new quantity discount program. The supplier offered the following quantity discounts:

Quantity	Cost Per Unit
0–4,999	$15.00
5,000–9,999	14.90
10,000–19,999	14.80
20,000+	14.70

Ardmore thought that these quantity discounts would give them a real competitive edge but realized that other costs would be affected, such as ordering costs and holding costs. What quantity should Ardmore order based on the quantity discounts offered?

4. Lott Manufacturing (problem 2) was recently approached by its supplier with a new quantity discount program. The supplier offered the following quantity discounts:

Quantity	Cost Per Unit
0–1,999	$5.00
2,000–3,999	$4.99
4,000–5,999	$4.98
6,000–7,999	$4.97
8,000–9,999	$4.96
10,000+	$4.95

What order quantity is optimal for Lott to place, considering the quantity discounts?

5. Ardmore Farm and Seed's (problems 1 and 3) new treasurer has suggested that the inventory decision should include consideration of the firm's opportunity cost of capital. The firm's cost of capital is currently estimated at 15 percent. Using the information contained in problems 1 and 3, estimate the optimal order quantity.

6. Lott Manufacturing's treasurer suggests that the true optimal order quantity should consider the firm's cost of capital, which is currently estimated at 20 percent. Using the information contained in problems 2 and 4, estimate the optimal order quantity.

7. Beverly Cosmetics is a cosmetic retailer. The company orders name-brand cosmetics wholesale and sells them at retail, generally through leased spaced in large malls. Beverly's management is trying to determine the optimal order quantity of one particular brand of perfume. The perfume wholesales for $10 per ounce and sells for $20.99 per ounce. Order costs are estimated at $75 per order, and holding costs are relatively small at only $.15 per ounce. Beverly's supplier offers quantity discounts of $.05 for order increments of 500 ounces. For example, the cost per ounce is $10 for order quantities of 1 to 499 ounces, $9.95 per ounce for order quantities of 500 to 999 ounces, etc. Beverly's annually sells about 50,000 ounces of the perfume each year (365 days). Beverly's cost of capital is 25 percent.
   a. What is the EOQ solution?
   b. What is the optimal order quantity ignoring the cost of capital?
   c. What is the optimal order considering the cost of capital?
   d. Compare the three answers and discuss whether or not they make sense to you.

8. A table of data is presented for cost of goods sold and ending inventory for the first 6 months of 2002 for EBCO, Inc.

	DEC	JAN	FEB	MAR	APR	MAY	JUNE
Cost of goods sold		100	150	225	200	125	90
Ending inventory		40	50	62	62	42	28

You may assume that each month has 30 days.
   a. Calculate the number of days of cost of goods sold held in inventory for March, April, May, and June, assuming quarterly cost of goods sold is used to calculate average daily cost of goods sold.
   b. Discuss your findings in part a. What is happening with the firm's investment in inventory?
   c. Below is a purchasing schedule and a schedule showing the dollar amount of those purchases remaining as an inventory balance for successive months. Calculate a balance fraction matrix, and discuss what it shows about the firm's management of its inventory balance.

		Ending Inventory Balances				
	PURCHASES	FEB	MAR	APR	MAY	JUNE
Feb	160	31	15			
Mar	237		47	23		
Apr	200			39	19	
May	105				23	11
June	76					17
End of Month Inventory		NA	62	62	42	28

   d. Explain the disparity between the conclusions reached in part b and part c. Which monitoring tool is more accurate?

9. A table of data is presented for cost of goods sold and ending inventory for the first 6 months of 2002 for Wynn Manufacturing, Inc.

	JAN	FEB	MAR	APR	MAY	JUNE
Cost of goods sold	1,000	1,500	2,100	2,700	3,500	4,800
Ending inventory	300	450	630	810	1,050	1,440

You may assume that each month has 30 days.

a. Calculate the number of days of cost of goods sold held in inventory for March, April, May, and June, assuming quarterly cost of goods sold is used to calculate average daily cost of goods sold.

b. Discuss your findings in part *a*. What is happening with the firm's investment in inventory?

c. Below is a purchasing schedule and a schedule showing the dollar amount of those purchases remaining as an inventory balance for successive months. Calculate a balance fraction matrix and discuss what it shows about the firm's management of its inventory balance.

		Ending Inventory Balances				
	PURCHASES	FEB	MAR	APR	MAY	JUNE
Feb	1,650	330	174			
Mar	2,280		456	234		
Apr	2,880			576	302	
May	3,740				748	402
June	5,190					1,038
End of Month Inventory		NA	630	810	1,050	1,440

d. Explain the disparity between the conclusions reached in part *b* and part *c*. Which monitoring tool is more accurate and why?

10. FLOAT-RITE, Inc. makes float tubes for fly-fishermen. The data display 3 months of sales, cost of goods sold, and ending inventory data. Calculate the days COGS held in inventory for August for three different averaging periods of 30 days, 60 days, and 90 days.

	JUNE	JULY	AUGUST
Sales	$50,000	$35,000	$20,000
Cost of goods sold	25,000	17,500	10,000
Ending inventory	7,000	5,000	3,000

References

Yong Kim, George C. Philippatos, and Kee H. Chung. 1986. Evaluating investment in inventory policy: A net present value framework. *The Engineering Economist* Winter:119–136.

Robert E. Markland, Shawnee K. Vickery; and Robert A. Davis. 1995. *Operations management: Concepts in manufacturing and services.* Minneapolis, MN: West.

Vinodrai K. Pandya, and J. Boyd. 1995. Appraisal of JIT using financial measures. *International Journal of Operations and Production Management* 15(9): 200–209.

A. Snyder. 1964. Principles of inventory management. *Financial Executive* 32(4):13–21.

Bernell K. Stone. 1995. Just-in-time: The risk/reward trade-off may not be what it seems. *Journal of Working Capital Management* Fall:32–36.

R. C. Walleigh. 1986. What's your excuse for not using JIT? *Harvard Business Review* March–April:38–54.

FOCUSED CASE
Fletcher Company

Background

Fletcher Company was originally founded by Eugene Fletcher some 50 years ago. The company recently celebrated its "Golden Anniversary" with the first-ever family reunion organized to coincide with the annual company picnic. Ira Fletcher, the son of the founder, serves as President and CEO for the firm. The company has been managed by various members of the extended family but over the last decade the company experienced such tremendous growth that a treasury function was recently created out of the controller's office and a Chief Financial Officer was hired from the outside, the first professional manager not part of the family.

The company has a very strong customer orientation and is very operations oriented. Jake Fletcher, one of Ira's two sons, heads up operations and is very proud of the fact that the company has never had to shut down its production lines because of inventory shortages or failed to meet customer demand. Jake's aunt is controller and has served in that position for 20 years. The company has a very good cost accounting system and the company continually receives praise from the outside auditors on the company's internal control systems that she has installed over the years.

Ira recently discovered that Fletcher's working capital requirements to sales ratio was seemingly out of line with the rest of the firms in the industry. A recent article in a trade publication indicated that Fletcher's WCR/S ratio averaged .10 over the last three years while the rest of the industry averaged .05[1] and for 2001 it was at an all time high of .115. Although Ira did not fully understand the significance of this measure, he was concerned that his

company's ratio was so far out of line from the industry performance.

OPERATIONS

Jake Fletcher, VP for Operations has instituted a very strong and reliable supplier network. Each crate of components has an invoice price of $8,000. Currently, Jake orders 750 crates at a time. The company's operations run at a relatively steady rate throughout the year and the company operates 7 days a week, 52 weeks each year.

CREDIT MANAGEMENT

Sue Fletcher, the youngest of the three Fletcher children, has served as corporate credit manager ever since she took over the position from her mother five years ago. Sue enjoys the credit area and particularly enjoys working with the company's customers. Although working with slow payers is a challenge, she receives a lot of satisfaction from the required negotiations and seeing the flow of payments come in from what originally seemed like impossible situations. She is a member of the National Association of Credit Management (NACM) and is actively involved in her local industry trade credit group. The company's days sales outstanding average 50 days and is only marginally higher than the industry average. Fletcher offers terms of net 45 days; although one or two of the larger firms in the industry offer terms of 1/10, net 30, most of the firms the size of Fletcher offer no discount and the net terms average about 45 days.

PAYABLES

The payables area is under the controller function and is run in a very efficient manner. The typical credit

---

[1]*Working capital requirements* is defined as the difference between the sum of accounts receivable, inventory, and other current assets and the sum of accounts payable and operating accruals. For more information on this ratio see Chapter 2. The resulting amount is a dollar amount. To standardize this measure, it is divided by annual sales to make comparisons between different companies.

terms received by Fletcher were 1/10, net 45. The company does not currently take the cash discount, fearing that paying cash 10 days after purchase would excessively strain the company's liquidity position given the relatively long operating cycle. The company has a policy of paying its bills when due and has followed the policy for the last several years, at least since the last major recession.

TREASURY

The newly hired CFO, John Cummings, previously served as treasurer at one of Fletcher's suppliers. John is a member of the local chapter of the Association for Financial Professionals (AFP) and received his Certified Cash Management (CCM) designation about five years ago. The treasury department he came from was well developed and had been instrumental in moving the company to incorporate economic value added (EVA) as a management philosophy and the company was very cash-flow focused. John's immediate project was to conduct a review of Fletcher's working capital policies and to determine their respective impacts on the Company's cash cycle. The Company seemingly stocked significant inventory as a result of ordering only five times per year. Because inventory figured so prominently in the calculation of the WCR/S ratio and the collections area seems to be managed consistent with industry practice, John decided to focus initial attention on the operations area and in particular to the area of inventory management. John determined that the after-tax cost of capital for Fletcher is 15 percent based on after-tax cost of debt and an equity cost based on the capital asset pricing model. The company's long-term borrowing rate has averaged about 10 percent and its short-term borrowing rate has been prime + 1 percent. Prime is currently 7.5 percent.

Data Collection

The CFO put together a small project team to study the operations area. He requested that the team calculate the annual cost of the company's current inventory policy. The team discovered that the company was placing five orders per year purchasing inventory in lots of 750 crates, which generated a rather significant average inventory balance. However, the operations manager reiterated that the company has never run out of materials and he reminded the team of the quantity discount that was received.

The inventory was stored in a rented warehouse owned by a local real estate developer. The annual warehouse rental was $120,000 and the annual insurance bill to cover the inventory was $5,000 for theft and fire coverage. In addition, it was estimated that annual costs involved in the current order processing system, including personnel time and communication costs, totaled $1,600. These costs were included in operating costs on the income statement.

John was wondering how the current system would compare with instituting a type of just-in-time inventory management. The project team, in exploring this approach found that the supplier was very willing to consider the change in strategy. To implement such a strategy, the supplier would require an accurate forecast of the units required well in advance, perhaps as much as 6 months in advance, to plan production. In addition, significant transportation planning would be needed to make the strategy successful to ensure against stockouts.

The plan would be to order 110 crates about every week and a half. While this was not a true just-in-time system, John felt that it was a reasonable compromise given the transportation issues that the project team uncovered in their analysis. The team computed that the order costs would increase about $50 per order from the current level as a result of implementing a forecasting system into the order processing system.

The company's financial statements are present below.

2001 PROFIT AND LOSS STATEMENT

Revenues	$50,000,000
Cost of goods sold	$30,000,000
Gross profit	$20,000,000
Operating expenses	$18,000,000
Depreciation	$650,000
Operating profit	$1,350,000
Interest	$550,000
Taxes	$200,000
Net income	$600,000
Dividends	$200,000

BALANCE SHEET
DECEMBER 31, 2001

Assets		Liabilities and Net Worth	
Cash	$500,000	Accounts payable	$4,100,000
Receivables	$6,850,000	Notes payable	$1,400,000
Inventory	$3,000,000	Mortgage	$5,000,000
Net fixed plant	$7,150,000	Equity:	
		Common stock	$2,000,000
		Retained earnings	$5,000,000
Total	$17,500,000		$17,500,000

REQUIRED

1. Compute the order cost per order and the operational holding cost per unit of inventory given the current ordering system.

2. Compute the annual cost of the current inventory management system including the cost of capital.
3. Compute the annual cost of the proposed system including the cost of capital.
4. What impact would the new system have on the company's WCR/S ratio? John also wondered what the new balance sheet might approximately look like if the new inventory management system was put in place?
5. How should the issues raised by Jake Fletcher be addressed? What are the risks that would be assumed if the "just-in-time" inventory system is adopted?
6. Which system do you recommend Fletcher adopt and why?

CHAPTER 5

Accounts Receivable Management

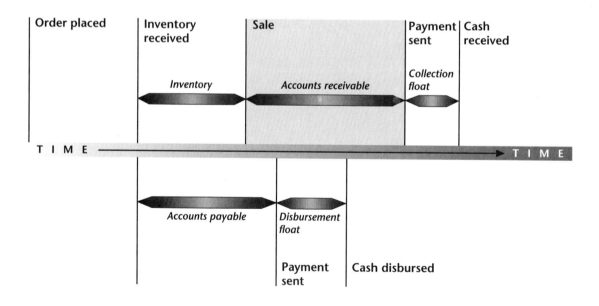

OBJECTIVES

After studying this chapter, you should be able to:

- Define credit policy and indicate its components.
- Describe the typical credit-granting sequence companies follow.
- Apply net present value analysis to credit extension decisions.
- Define credit scoring and explain its limitations.
- List the elements of a credit rating report.
- Describe how receivables management can benefit from electronic data interchange.

Michael Shane first learned about the business world by selling jeans and women's wigs. In a stroke of genius, he foresaw the emergence of a new market selling clones of brand-name personal computers (PCs)—and Leading Edge was born. At one point, Leading Edge had captured 6 percent of the market for PC clones. Shane suddenly sold out early, however, when the combination of tough competition, quality problems, and his poorly executed credit management strategy undercut the company's profitability. According to published reports, Shane's approach to doing business included forcing retailers to pay him as many as 4 weeks *before* receiving the computers, leading one analyst to suggest the company was universally hated by its dealers.

Shane's reversed credit policy (his company had a negative days sales outstanding) was made possible because of the customer demand spawned by the "Best Buy" rating accorded to Leading Edge machines by Consumer Reports. This unusual approach to accounts receivable management provided readily usable funds to fuel Leading Edge's rapid production and inventory expansion. In this chapter, we survey credit management, the essentials of credit policy, sources of credit analysis information, and the credit-granting decision. We show how net present value (NPV) analysis can be applied to a single credit extension decision, and how to refine that analysis to incorporate risk. Chapter 6 addresses the application of NPV analysis to overall credit policy, how to monitor accounts receivable, and collection procedures. The major managerial issue on which this chapter focuses is the credit-granting decision, as illustrated in the following Financial Dilemma.

FINANCIAL DILEMMA

How Can I Make Sense of the Changing World of Receivables Management?

Joe, assistant credit manager at a *Fortune 1000* company, just returned from the National Association of Credit Managers annual meeting, and is going through his notes. He opens up to some predictions made by credit executives about business credit practices in the future[1]:

- Credit will consist of fewer, but more highly educated and skilled individuals.
- Data will be received and deployed electronically via the Internet.
- Credit will be part of a seamless automated process from order generation through cash application.

---

[1] Rod Wheeland. 1997. The future of business credit. *Business Credit* July:53–54.

- Credit will have more analytical responsibilities including, but not limited to, portfolio analysis and capital forecasting.
- The majority of credit risk will not be outsourced to banks, credit insurers, and credit card companies.
- Credit will not become a sales/marketing function.

As Joe puts the report aside, some thoughts cross his mind for the first time: he wonders how valid these trends are, how credit can add value for shareholders, why it is done in the finance area, and how he can best prepare himself to be successful in the new environment.

TRADE CREDIT AND SHAREHOLDER VALUE

Trade credit arises when goods are sold under delayed payment terms. Selling goods on delayed terms has been traced back to the Roman Empire, when credit billing was relied on to reduce the obstacles faced in transferring money through unorganized trading areas.[2] The practice of selling goods to other companies without demanding cash payment is taken for granted today. Many companies have large investments in receivables. Great Dane Trailers, Inc., the largest US manufacturer of highway truck trailers, has $73 million invested in receivables (26 percent of total assets and 47 percent of current assets), as compared with $435,000 in cash and securities. Dun & Bradstreet (D&B) and Robert Morris Associates data covering 302 industries indicate that average receivables as a percentage of total assets hover around 25 percent. Receivables constitute a significant working capital investment for service companies and manufacturing companies.

When credit terms are offered, the seller is exchanging the title to the goods for the buyer's promise to pay on an agreed-on later date. **The financial manager can add value for the company's shareholders by properly influencing three areas: the company's aggregate investment in receivables, its credit terms, and its credit standards.** Exhibit 5-1 demonstrates that these decision areas are not the exclusive domain of the financial manager, but are influenced by the company's marketing strategy and the corresponding sales and market share objectives.

FINANCIAL DILEMMA REVISITED

As we consider Joe's question about how credit management adds value for the company, and the role of finance, we gain some insight from Exhibit 5-1. The diagram indicates the major issues addressed by the financial manager, each with a potential impact on share value. Overinvesting in receivables can be costly because the investment is typically financed by short-term borrowing and because it may signal acceptance of late-paying customers. If the credit terms (cash discount and period allowed for payment) are not competitive when compared with other sellers in the same industry or are misaligned with the product line profitability (e.g., long credit period on product having a slim profit margin), they can also diminish shareholder value. Setting the credit standard for customers incorrectly can erode shareholder value because of lost sales (when too

---

[2]For an excellent survey of the development of credit, see Chapter 1 of Christie and Bracuti, *Credit Executives Handbook* (cited in the end-of-chapter references). This section and several others are partly based on information found in that source.

EXHIBIT 5-1
The Influence of Receivables Management on Shareholder Value

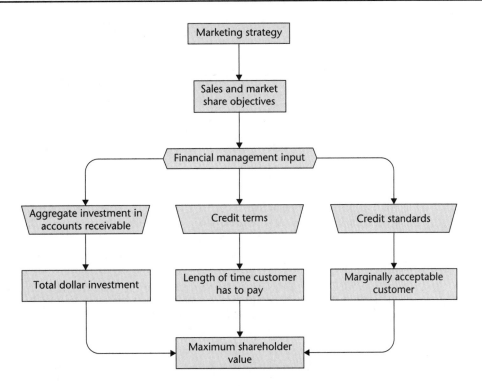

stringent) or uncollectible sales (when too lenient). Summarizing, the credit and collections function should control bad debts and outstanding receivables, maintain financial flexibility, optimize the mix of company assets, convert receivables to cash on a timely basis, analyze customer risk, and respond to customer needs.[3] Credit managers must accomplish this while holding down the cost of administering the function and ensuring the speed and accuracy of credit-related information. In a later section we cover some of the credit management trends of which Joe and other credit professionals should be aware.

Trade Credit Versus Bank Credit

The term *trade credit* generally applies to credit extended by manufacturers and whole-salers to their customers. As of early 2001, Federal Reserve Board statistics indicate that, for every dollar of short-term bank credit extended to businesses, $1.66 of trade credit is extended by suppliers, down slightly from a ratio of $1.78 to $1 in 1996.

Practitioners defend trade credit on two grounds: cost-efficiency and revenue. Although a business's customers could get the same funding from banks, often those bank loans come at a greater cost, with less efficiency, less speed. Some mistakenly see

---

[3]This summary is provided by and elaborated on by Rose Marie Bukics. 1995. Credit policy: Successful policy for the global marketplace. *Credit and Financial Management Review* 1:58–59.

EXHIBIT 5-2

Differences Between Trade Credit and Bank Credit

ATTRIBUTE	TRADE CREDIT	BANK CREDIT
Length of terms	Relatively short—usually 30, 60, or 90 days	Longer, and extended and repaid on a seasonal basis
Security	Usually unsecured, somewhat more lenient in extending credit	Higher standards for unsecured loans; otherwise secured
Amounts involved	Smaller, especially if customer buys from several sources	Large, especially for large companies or those dealing with a small number of banks
Resource transferred	Goods or services	Money
Extent of analysis	Extensive when size of transaction is large, involving large credit exposure	Bank's need for liquidity to meet deposit withdrawals necessitates in-depth analysis regarding safety and collectibility

trade credit as a "free lunch," because there is no explicit interest charge specified, but its cost is one of the costs of doing business and is built into the product's price.

Marketing and credit managers often advocate trade credit extension on two sales-related grounds: its convenience may trigger larger purchases, increasing the company's overall sales; and it builds goodwill and gives the supplier greater stability because of more consistent repeat sales. Some merchants argue that credit customers are more stable than cash customers and might become reliable repeat purchasers once they have been approved for a specific credit limit by the seller.

Other reasons trade credit might substitute for bank credit are linked to the fact that trade credit offered by businesses differs in some significant ways from the credit typically offered by banking institutions. Exhibit 5-2 illustrates some of the key differences. Note particularly the "security" and "resource transferred" contrasts.

Evaluating the Motives for Trade Credit

Formal studies of the rationale for the extension of trade credit go beyond the basic reasons previously cited. Four major motives have been identified[4]; we illustrate each motive with Ford's credit extension to car buyers:

- Financial motive. Sellers charge a higher price when selling on credit, generating a greater present-value profit based on the implicit interest rate charged; also, sellers raise capital at lower rates than their customers and have cost advantages vis-à-vis banks because of (1) the similarity of customers; (2) the information gathered in the selling process (size and frequency of orders, whether the cash discount is taken, timeliness of payments); (3) a lower probability of default (because the purchased goods are part of a product that is an integral part of the buyer's business, and the buyer needs to continue paying to maintain supply); and (4) a greater value of collateral to sellers than to banks in that they can rework and resell the product without much difficulty or expense. Ford has a much better understanding than banks of car buyer default probabilities and repossession resale value and has an established dealer network for resale of repossessions.
- Operating motive. Suppliers respond to variable and uncertain demand by the way in which they extend trade credit, instead of using more costly responses such as

---

[4]For more on this see the excellent reviews in Emery (1988), Long, and Ravid (1993), and Mian and Smith (1994), cited in the end-of-chapter references.

installing extra capacity, building or depleting inventories, or forcing customers to wait in line. Ford uses attractive lease terms and cut-rate financing (interest rates lower than the customer's bank rate) to stimulate sales if production exceeds sales and inventories are beginning to accumulate.[5]

- Contracting cost motive. Sales contracting costs between buyers and sellers are reduced for buyers because they can inspect the quantity and quality of goods before payment and reduce the payment if some goods are missing or defective; sellers have less employee or third-party theft because goods are less liquid than cash, and collection is not made at the time of delivery; the separation of the collection and delivery functions allows sellers to achieve efficiency gains that result from the specialization of labor. Furthermore, sellers gain valuable buyer creditworthiness information by observing whether credit buyers take cash discounts when offered. Ford recognizes that some buyers exercise their option to quit making payments when warranty-period repairs are unsatisfactory. Buying on credit provides "lemon insurance," and if no bank is involved, the resolution of customer dissatisfaction is more simple.
- Pricing motive. Sellers in certain industries are unable to alter their prices, perhaps because they are part of an oligopoly (and face a kinked demand curve or are part of a collusive agreement) or because of governmental regulation; unpublished variations in credit policy allow these sellers to charge varying amounts to their customers. Furthermore, normally credit-constrained buyers might be offered the same credit terms as more creditworthy buyers, in a sense lowering the effective price for them. When it does lower its prices through rebates, Ford often gives a choice of the price reduction or cut-rate financing. Customers can choose the best offer, based on their local financing options and present cash position.

Financial market or product market imperfections stand behind all these motives, which represent company responses to the imperfections. In each case, trade credit is considered more economical and efficient than other responses open to the companies. These motives are difficult to test in the real world, and it is very difficult to say which of these motives dominates as the rationale behind most trade credit. Studies by Long, Malitz, and Ravid (1993) and Deloof and Jegers (1996) provide strong support for the contracting cost motive. Trade credit gives customers time to inspect and determine the quality of merchandise. Moderate support is also provided for the operating motive. A recent, comprehensive study by Ng, Smith, and Smith (1999) finds no support for the operating motive, limited support for the pricing motive, and strong support for the contracting cost motive. They note that payment terms are market responses to the information problems plaguing business-to-business transactions.

Trends Affecting Trade Credit

The amount of trade credit outstanding may be trending downward in the United States because of three interrelated trends: adoption by some companies of a zero net-working capital objective, integration of receivables management with inventory management and enterprise resource planning (ERP) systems, and greater use of electronic commerce.

---

[5]Some economists contend that the spread of retail incentives and the aggressive way in which carmakers use them allow the auto industry to minimize the effects of interest rate increases—at least for a while, and while the increases are fairly small. See Bradshaw (1999), cited in the end-of-chapter references.

EXHIBIT 5-3
The Role of Credit Today

CORE FUNCTIONS (COMMON TO ALL COMPANIES)	EXPANDED FUNCTIONS (SOME COMPANIES)	EMERGING OPPORTUNITIES (FEW COMPANIES)
Develop credit policy	Customer visits	Inventory control
Collections	Purchasing/Vendor analysis	Product development
Credit analysis	Banking relationship	Accounts payable
Set credit terms	Analysis (beyond credit)	Working capital management
Management reporting	Billing/Invoicing	Management Information System (MIS) data warehouse
Accounts receivable	Develop credit-scoring model	Cash forecasting
Legal bankruptcy	Global risk management	Profit/Loss responsibilities
Cash application		

ZERO NET-WORKING CAPITAL OBJECTIVE. Because many companies are explicitly adopting a "zero net-working capital" goal or implicitly striving to reduce the order-to-cash cycle, the relative amount and duration of receivables may be expected to decline. Companies are more sensitive to the asset tie-up in receivables because of the use of economic value-added (EVA) metrics, as noted in Chapter 3. Reduced investment in receivables adds value by allowing investment in more profitable long-term assets and/or reductions in financing costs.

IMPROVED INTERNAL AND EXTERNAL CREDIT-RELATED INFORMATION. Internally, companies have integrated receivables management with inventory management and ERP systems. ERP systems, sometimes called enterprise systems, help corporate analysts see "the big picture." As an example, the SAP R/3 system has a financials module available that includes the accounts receivable and accounts payable functions, and a credit control feature that incorporates credit limits and an aging schedule (covered in Chapter 6). It also has a sales and distribution module that includes order transactions, providing information necessary for determining receivables balances. It appears that the role of the credit function is expanding (see Exhibit 5-3). Notice that billing and invoicing improvements, which cut down on disputes and delays that often stand behind late payments, as well as inventory control and working capital management, are being addressed by credit managers in some companies. Externally, expanded and readily accessible information has made it easier to assess creditworthiness and exposure to credit problems.

ELECTRONIC COMMERCE. Value increases come as the order-to-cash cycle shrinks as a result of electronic, automated procedures:

- Electronic ordering
- Electronic credit application and evaluation
- Electronic credit approval notification
- Electronic order fill instructions
- Electronic shipment documents, including advance shipping notices
- Electronic processing of shipments received information
- Electronic invoicing
- Electronic payment initiation and execution

And, to start the next cycle more quickly:

- Electronic cash application

FOCUS ON PRACTICE

INFORMATION TECHNOLOGY TRANSFORMS CREDIT DECISION MAKING Manual processing of credit decisions is becoming a thing of the past for many companies. A new Internet-based service offered by Fair, Isaac and Company, Inc. and Net Earnings allows small businesses to go to their bank's web site (assuming that bank has entered into a cobranding agreement with Fair, Isaac and Net Earnings), enter a business credit applicant's name and address, pay for the credit report by entering their own credit card numbers, and within one minute get a brief credit evaluation for $4.95 or detailed credit evaluation (including on-time and late payments and an overall risk rating) for $14.95. Because 71 percent of small-business computer users access the Internet and more than half of those Internet users regularly grant credit, this service should be popular.

Perhaps more impressive, a company called eCredit.com is offering businesses the ability to process entire credit and financing applications in seconds, rather than days. Useful for both online and traditional sales, eCredit has established a "Global Financing Network" that provides real-time credit and financing services for e-commerce by intelligently connecting businesses to financing partners and information sources worldwide. Credit and financing decisions can be completely automated. The founder, Dr. Venkat Srinivasan, believes that companies will increasingly outsource receivables to the point where receivables investment by nonfinancial companies will be very small.

"Net Earnings," www.pressfin062298.htm, accessed 10/6/99; http://www.ecredit.com/solution/realtime_credit.html *and* http://www.ecredit.com/solutions/index.html

The result is that financial markets are becoming more efficient, and some of the outstanding trade credit that is specifically linked to financial market inefficiency will be permanently eliminated. As noted in the Focus on Practice box, credit markets are becoming more efficient and effective as bank and nonbank service providers facilitate all phases of the cash-to-cash cycle.

MANAGING THE CREDIT FUNCTION

Credit administration involves establishing credit policy, as well as planning, organizing, directing, and controlling all aspects of the credit function. **Credit policy** includes credit standards, setting credit limits, the company's approach to credit investigation, credit terms, and the collection activity. In the remainder of this chapter and in Chapter 6, we investigate each of these dimensions of credit policy. We begin by defining the credit decision process. The **credit decision process** begins with marketing contact with potential customers and ends with the approval or disapproval of credit and setting the credit limit for approved customers. In between these points are credit investigation, contacts with the customer for information, finalizing written documents such as security agreements, establishment of the customer's credit file, and financial analysis. We return to the financial analysis aspects of credit extension in a later section of this chapter.

Overview of Credit Granting

We can gain a greater appreciation for the credit-granting process if we know the sequence of events initiated when a business makes a credit sale. The activity flowchart

EXHIBIT 5-4
The Credit-Granting Sequence

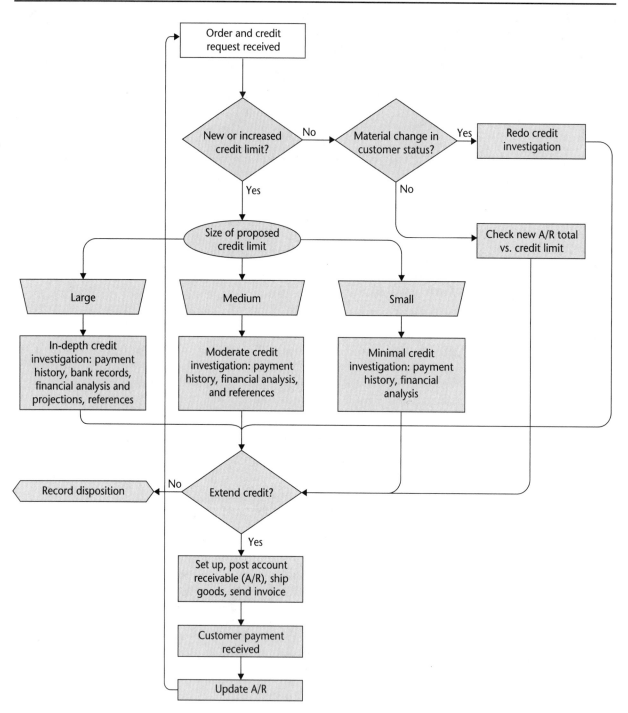

in Exhibit 5-4 shows a typical credit sequence. On receipt of orders from a new customer or from an existing customer with insufficient preapproved credit, the seller must determine whether to launch a credit investigation of the buyer. If it investigates, the seller might consult various information sources and tailor the depth of the investigation to the size of the account.[6] Assuming credit is approved, the credit department must also set a credit limit for a new customer, which is the maximum amount of outstanding purchases that the customer may have at any time. Items ordered are then shipped. For domestic customers, credit is granted "on open book," which involves sending an invoice and establishing an account receivable for this new customer. (A trade acceptance, which is a more formal credit agreement, is usually set up for foreign customers.[7]) When the buyer receives the goods or services, he or she inspects and checks the order and sets up an account payable to represent the amount owed. The buyer determines whether to pay within the cash discount period if that is part of the seller's credit terms.

If not, payment will probably be made near the end of the allotted credit period, typically 30 or 60 days. When the buyer remits payment, usually with a check, the seller wants to deposit that amount and credit the account receivable quickly—quick deposit means quicker availability of funds at the bank. Crediting the account, a process known as **cash application,** frees up that amount of the credit limit for additional orders from this customer—some of which might be backlogged awaiting credit approval. Of course, if the customer does not pay within the credit terms, the seller will send warning letters and follow other predetermined collection procedures, possibly involving an outside collection agency. As long as payments are received on a timely basis, the credit-granting process is a continuous flow of alternating orders and payments.

Analysis of a Single Credit Extension

Before detailing credit limits and credit terms, we demonstrate how to make proper credit-granting decisions. We assume that a complete credit analysis has already been conducted on each credit applicant. Our analysis is simplified because it shows the value effect of a one-time credit extension to a single customer. We use the valuation tools from Chapter 3 to model the credit-granting decision for an individual customer, and defer our discussion of overall credit policy to Chapter 6.

The definition of a **credit extension** is to allow a customer to defer payment. The acceptability of a single credit extension is evaluated by calculating the NPV of the potential credit sale. If the credit manager knew that the payment would be made, and exactly when, the NPV model (on a before-tax basis) would be simple. For a one-time credit extension, and assuming that the credit administration and collection expenses occur at the end of the credit period, we have the model shown as Equation 5-1:

$$NPV = \frac{S - EXP(S)}{1 + iCP} - VCR(S) \tag{5-1}$$

---

[6]When information cost is large relative to prospective account size and profitability, the manager can use a decision tree approach to credit investigation and granting, as demonstrated originally by Mehta and in more detail by Vander Weide and Maier (see citations in the end-of-chapter references). Stowe (see the end-of-chapter references) presents an integer programming model to make the joint decision of how much information to gather and whether credit should be approved. This work has been expanded in Scherr (1992; also 1996) in an appealing and logical fashion (see the end-of-chapter references). An elegant spreadsheet solution to this problem is in Ogden and Sundaram (see the end-of-chapter references).

[7]Acceptances and other international credit management differences are covered in more detail in Chapter 6.

In which: NPV = net present value of the credit sale

              VCR = variable cost ratio, per \$1 of sales

                S = dollar amount of the credit sale

            EXP = expenses for credit administration and collection, per \$1 of sales

                 i = daily interest rate

               CP = collection period for the sale

We begin with the present value of the sales revenue, then subtract the direct credit-related costs, and then subtract the variable costs (labor and raw material). What is left is the NPV of the credit sale. The discount rate, i, is the required return on capital, expressed as a daily rate ($k/365$). The annualized rate, k, is the opportunity cost of funds tied up in receivables; often, it is the company's weighted-average cost of capital.

The decision rules are then as follows:

If $NPV > 0$ Extend credit

If $NPV = 0$ Probably extend credit (marginally acceptable)

If $NPV < 0$ Do not extend credit

As an example, credit analyst Mike Grossman is considering a \$1,000 order from a new customer, which would be eligible for his company's standard 30-day credit terms. The company's weighted-average cost of capital is 13 percent. He assembles the following information:

$VCR = 0.70$

$S = \$1,000$

$EXP = 0.04$

$i = 0.13/365 = 0.0003562$

Substituting these values into equation 5-1, we compute the NPV of the proposed credit sale to be:

$$NPV = \frac{\$1,000 - 0.04(\$1,000)}{1 + (0.0003562 \times 30)} - 0.70(\$1,000)$$
$$= \$949.85 - \$700$$
$$= \$249.85$$

Because the NPV is positive, the credit sale will add to shareholder value and should be made. Once the sale is made, the focus shifts to processing customer payments and monitoring payment status of outstanding receivables.

Importance of Cash Application

Accuracy and speed are both important in crediting customers' accounts. Ideally, the credit and accounts receivable system is automated to better accomplish both of these objectives. The system should enable the credit manager to:

- Determine whether invoices are being paid according to terms of sale.
- Know the status of unshipped, previously approved orders.
- Determine the payment status and total exposure of any customer.
- Input to a centralized database updated data from remote locations.
- Route the order approval instructions quickly if a customer's economic or payment status changes.

One of the greatest advantages of an automated system is cash application: the ability of that system to credit outstanding customer invoices quickly and accurately. The open account system requires that each check or electronic payment received be carefully applied against the specific invoices being paid. Application of payments includes getting the necessary information, identifying the payor, applying the payment to invoice(s), and updating the permanent file and generating reports. Electronic commerce is advancing to the point at which more companies and their banks can send and receive electronic payments with remittance information attached. The latter information enables automatic updating of customer accounts without manual rekeying or visual inspection.

GATHERING INFORMATION. The source of information for applying payments might be punch cards returned with payments, a computer-generated printout of open items, or a listing of open items on a personal computer or microfilm/microfiche reader.

PAYOR IDENTIFICATION. A check's bottom line, called the magnetic ink character recognition (MICR) line, is one way of identifying the payor. The MICR line contains the check number, the bank's Federal Reserve transit routing number, the bank account number, and the amount of the check. Another way of identifying the payor is through an enclosed document called a **remittance advice,** which might be a prepunched card or tear-off section from the invoice, containing customer account number, date, and dollar amount. Sometimes, the customer simply includes a memo indicating what is being paid. Later in the chapter we cover EDI transmission of advices.

CASH APPLICATION. Companies using check MICR line data must have a cross-reference from the MICR numbers to the customer's account number. Companies using prepunched cards or tear-off invoice segments feed these into the appropriate optical scanning devices to read payment amounts into a computer. A preset routine, called an algorithm, checks amounts paid against outstanding amounts owed to apply the payment and credit the account accurately. If no match is made, the computerized report signals the need for manual processing by a receivables clerk.

We have completed our overview of management of the credit function. We turn our attention to the question of whether credit should be offered by a company and a deeper analysis of the major aspects of a credit policy.

ESTABLISHING A CREDIT POLICY

There are valid reasons for companies to offer credit in certain situations. We now consider whether it is in the best interests of a specific company to offer credit terms, and if so, what aspects of a credit policy have to be set. Our discussion includes credit standards, credit terms, the credit limit, and the use of expert systems to assist in these areas.

Should We Extend Credit?

To a large extent, a company follows the lead of other firms in its industry when deciding whether to sell on credit. What is less clear is the form and extent of the credit offer. Rather than give a checklist of factors to consider, we illustrate the complexity of the decision, as well as several of the interrelated factors, by viewing three separate decision situations in the following Focus on Practice box.

FOCUS ON PRACTICE

SHOULD A RETAILER OFFER AN IN-HOUSE CREDIT CARD? A retailer might choose to offer an in-house credit card, allow only the use of bank cards (e.g., MasterCard, Visa), or allow the use of either. Retailers' sour experience with their credit cards in recent years has pushed them away from reliance on in-house ("private label") credit cards.[8] The key tradeoff for department stores has been the additional sales stimulus of credit versus the "back office" cost of running the in-house credit department. A major uncertainty has been whether customers will buy more or less merchandise if allowed to use a bank card as opposed to the retailer's credit card. Specifically, is J.C. Penney's or Dillard's customer traffic increased and customer loyalty enhanced when many of the target customers possess their credit cards? Answers to such questions are difficult to pin-point without experimentation.

SHOULD RECEIVABLES BE SOLD TO A FACTOR? Credit department costs can be eliminated and cash advances received by selling receivables to a company specializing in such purchases. Called **factors**, these companies buy receivables from the firm at a discount from face value, possibly giving the selling firm a cash advance on the anticipated collections. Usually the receivables are bought on a nonrecourse basis, meaning that the factor now bears the risk of nonpayment. Mian and Smith find that economies of scale in credit-granting and credit-collection functions explain why small firms (especially those with sales below $5 million) commonly outsource credit to factors. Canterbury Belts, Inc., which sells to 6000 small specialty stores, estimates that it would have to hire between 12 and 15 people to do the credit processing presently done by its factor. Asselbergh finds, using a sample of Belgium firms, that less-liquid companies, those with longer collection periods, those with high capital spending needs, and those with unbalanced product portfolios (thus with higher business risk) tend to use factors.[9] Smith and Schnucker note that firm-specific investment by a seller in a trade relationship *lessens* the use of factoring, as the seller protects that investment by offering flexible payment terms to a financially troubled buyer, when a product line is customized (the factor can assess its value better than the buyer), and with geographically dispersed buyers and few repeat sales (resulting from the high information and monitoring cost for individual sellers in such cases).[10]

HOW SHOULD THE CREDIT ACTIVITY BE ORGANIZED? Manufacturers selling durable goods such as automobiles and farm machinery often decide to set their credit activity up as a captive finance subsidiary. This arrangement separates the financing arm of the company from the selling arm. Advocates claim this enhances efficiency and increases the overall debt capacity of the company. Were it a bank, the General Motors Acceptance Corporation would rank as one of the largest in the United States in total assets. Although company founder Henry Ford disdained financing cars, Ford Motor Credit Corporation extends so much credit that it now has the highest loan loss ratio of any finance subsidiary. Ford credit executives cite the increase in sales as the major advantage of the subsidiary arrangement, countered by the possibility of large loan losses in a recessionary environment, as the chief shortfall. Nationally, surveyed credit executives believe that the debt capacity of the total company (parent plus subsidiary) is higher when the credit area is separate, and generally argue that sales are higher as well.[11] Mian and Smith find evidence that large firms, especially those with rapidly growing receivables, are more likely to establish captive finance subsidiaries. They attribute this to economies of scale in assessing credit risk. They also document an increase in financial flexibility for companies establishing these subsidiaries.[12]

---

[8]1990. Retailers tiring of involvement with credit cards. *Investor's Business Daily* April 16:33.

[9]See Asselbergh, cited in the end-of-chapter references.

[10]See Smith and Schnucker, cited in the end-of-chapter references.

[11]For executives whose companies had established captive finance subsidiaries, there was uniform agreement regarding the increased debt capacity. For a matched group of companies that had not organized the credit function separately, however, the main reason cited for not doing so was "no real benefits derived" from setting up a subsidiary. See the Roberts and Viscione article cited in the end-of-chapter references for more on their survey conclusions.

[12]Mian and Smith (1992), cited in the end-of-chapter references.

These situations illustrate the practical and theoretical factors involved in the decision to offer credit. Market imperfections, mentioned earlier in the chapter, provide the main theoretical impetus for offering credit terms to potential customers.

Credit Policy Components

There are four major components of credit policy: credit standards, credit terms, the credit limit, and collection procedures. In this section, we briefly define these components; each is developed in greater detail in the following sections.

DEVELOPMENT OF CREDIT STANDARDS.   The profile of the minimally acceptable creditworthy customer defines the selling business's **credit standards.** Based on financial analysis and nonfinancial data, the credit analyst determines whether each credit applicant exceeds the credit standard and thus qualifies for credit. Credit extension for marginally acceptable customers may be for a much smaller dollar amount, for a short probationary period, or may need to be backed up by collateral or a bank's letter of credit, which guarantees the bank will pay invoices up to a predetermined dollar amount if the customer does not pay. The latter substitutes the creditworthiness of the bank for that of the customer buying on credit.

CREDIT TERMS.   The credit period, stipulating how long from the invoice date the customer has to pay, and the cash discount (if any) compose the seller's credit terms. A company's credit terms are usually very similar to that of other companies in its industry. A listing of different terms that are commonly offered is provided in our discussion of payables in Chapter 7.

CREDIT LIMIT.   If credit is extended, the dollar amount that cumulative credit purchases can reach for a given customer constitutes that customer's **credit limit.** The customer periodically pays for credit purchases, freeing up that amount of the credit limit for further orders. Four of five credit executives use credit limits for most of their customers.[13]

COLLECTION PROCEDURES.   Detailed statements regarding when and how the company will carry out collection of past-due accounts make up the company's **collection procedures.** These policies specify how long the company will wait past the due date to initiate collection efforts, the method(s) of contact with delinquent customers, and whether and at what point accounts will be referred to an outside collection agency.
Having established a basic understanding of credit policies, we are ready to launch into a deeper and more comprehensive discussion of the first three topics in the context of the manager's credit-granting decision. Collections are analyzed as part of Chapter 6.

The Credit-Granting Decision

Deciding whether and how much credit to give customers involves four distinct steps: development of credit standards, getting necessary information about customers,

---

[13]Besley and Osteryoung (1985); these findings were confirmed in Beranek and Scherr (1991) and Ricci (1999), who further finds that 39 percent of firms set credit limits for all of their customers (see the end-of-chapter references).

application of credit standards, and setting credit limits. Decisions should be consistent with the credit policy.

DEVELOPMENT OF CREDIT STANDARDS.   The standards that the customer must meet to be minimally acceptable for the extension of credit are usually based on the **five Cs of credit:** character, capital, capacity, conditions, and collateral. *Character*, thought to be the most important criterion, refers to moral uprightness, integrity, trustworthiness, and quality of management. Willingness to pay is tested when times are bad and there is pressure to compromise integrity. Past payment records and insights from a customer's existing suppliers are often all the information the credit analyst has on which to base an assessment. *Capital* refers to net worth, or the difference between total assets and total liabilities. It measures the cushion with which the business exists, or how much it has in assets over and above what is necessary to pay creditors. The seller should not place too much confidence in this figure, however, because in a liquidation assets are generally sold for less than the amount shown on the books. *Capacity* is the ability to repay debts when due, as measured by the company's ability to generate cash flows. This often includes a subjective analysis of the borrower's management and future outlook, both in normal and pessimistic economic conditions. Critical evaluation of the borrower's projected cash budget and most recent statement of cash flows is instrumental here. The general economy and industry environment, as well as the reason for the loan request, compose the *conditions*. Some of the specific issues that should be raised by the credit analyst involve economic analysis, as seen in Exhibit 5-5. The last consideration, and least important for the trade credit situation, is collateral. Assets pledged as security to back up a credit sale or loan are called *collateral*. The creditor holds claim to these assets in the event the borrower does not pay and the creditor must sell them to make up for amounts owed but not collected. Although it is rare to hold collateral on trade credit, receivables held on the books are often held as collateral for bank loans.

Although the five Cs provide a framework for developing credit standards and for credit investigation, this framework does not give any guidance as to the exact credit standards that maximize shareholder value. Furthermore, the framework does not specify how much information should be gathered, nor does it indicate when to reject applicants. Setting credit standards is one of the most difficult decisions a credit manager must make; trial and error or setting smaller credit limits for riskier applicants are two ways to resolve the inherent difficulty. Existing NPV modeling attempts are for a single order only, but estimates of default risk and payment timing may be expected to improve over time—meaning that future orders become relevant to the initial credit decision (Scherr, 1996).

After setting credit standards, the credit executive must determine a risk classification system and then link individual customer evaluations to the credit standards. This system has three components: a listing of risk classes, description of the types of customers that fit each class, and the credit policy for each class.

A customer that is large and that has an impeccable credit record will be assigned to the top rating class; a customer in a volatile industry but with good payment practices will be assigned to the second class; and a high-risk, financially weak customer will be assigned to the lowest class. Top-class customers are low risk and are allowed to order even large dollar amounts without credit approval, as long as the outstanding balance does not exceed the credit limit. Bottom-class customers, being high risk, are forced to obtain a payment guarantee (possibly through a bank letter of credit) or will not receive any credit and will be required to provide cash on delivery or even cash before delivery. For all classes except the lowest, credit approval might be automatic for small orders.

EXHIBIT 5-5
Useful Questions for Assessing Credit Conditions

1. At which stage of the business cycle—expansion, peak, recession, trough—are we? How does the customer relate to it?
2. Does the customer's business track the business cycle, or does it fluctuate so much as to move independently? Does it change direction before (lead) or after (lag) the business cycle?
3. What is the anticipated lifespan of the customer's industry cycle, and at what stage is it now? Is there serious overcapacity? Is industry activity tapering off?
4. Is the customer in a new product business that is subject to booms or busts?
5. What is the customer's main business, and how does it relate to the industry cycle?
6. Will the customer's industry function endure, or is the customer's role losing ground?
7. Are industry consolidations taking place?
8. What are the distinct risk characteristics of each of the customer's business segments? What must the customer do well to succeed?
9. At what stage of the business cycle is the customer most strongly affected? How is the customer's performance affected by those cyclical pressures?
10. What is the customer's historic ability to weather recession?

SOURCE: Adapted from P. Henry Mueller. 1978. What every lender should know about economics. *Journal of Commercial Bank Lending* December; reprinted in William W. Sihler, ed. 1981. *Classics in commercial bank lending.* Philadelphia: Robert Morris Associates, pp 47–56.

GATHERING NECESSARY INFORMATION. Available information should be gathered to help evaluate credit applicants up to the point at which the cost of additional information exceeds the decision-making benefit offered by having that information. Information sources include credit reporting agencies, credit interchange bureaus, bank letters, references from other suppliers, financial statements, and field data provided by sales representatives.

Credit reporting agencies, most notably D&B, are the major source of credit information. D&B is international in scope and has more than 300 offices worldwide. It provides computer (including e-mail), fax, mail, and telephone access to many of its products, including its "Business Information Reports." D&B maintains files on more than 12 million US firms; it also offers an investigation service that can provide credit managers with information on almost any company. An example of a Business Information Report is shown in Exhibit 5-5 and Exhibit 5-6. Particularly notice the "Payments Reported" section, which shows speed of payment (whether the customer took a discount and was prompt or slow with payment), the dollar amount of high credit extended, dollar amounts either presently owed or past due, selling terms, and the date of the last sale. The PAYDEX score of 67 is a payment index showing that only 67 percent (2/3) of its payments are made within credit terms. A score of 80 is considered very good, and scores above 85 are rare. Further explanation of the PAYDEX score is given on the last page of Exhibit 5-6. Also notice the "Banking" section, which can provide average balances, present balances, or both (stated in terms such as "middle five figures," which might be $60,000), size of bank credit line or loans outstanding, whether borrowing is secured or unsecured, and how these amounts will be repaid. By evaluating all the information in the Business Information Report, the credit manager can assess whether the customer is already overextended on bank credit, the degree of lateness in its payments to other sellers, and other significant legal or operating risks that might affect the ability of the customer to repay credit purchases.

When available in some reports, D&B also provides a useful credit rating. Exhibit 5-5 also illustrates the rating near the bottom of the page. The first part of the rating, the estimated financial strength, consists of a number and letter or two letters and is based on rateable net worth. The rating's second part—a number from 1 to 4—represents D&B's

EXHIBIT 5-6
Dun & Bradstreet Reports

DB

Business Information Report **DB**

SUBSCRIBER: 123-4567L
PREPARED FOR:

ANSWERING INQUIRY

DUNS: 00-007-7743	DATE PRINTED	SUMMARY
GORMAN MANUFACTURING CO. INC.	OCT 30, 199-	RATING 3A3
(SUBSIDIARY OF GORMAN		
HOLDING COMPANIES INC.,	COMMERCIAL PRINTING	
LOS ANGELES, CA)	SIC NO.	STARTED 1965
	2752	SALES F $13,007,229
492 KOLLER ST		WORTH F $2,125,499
AND BRANCH (ES) OR DIVISION (S)		EMPLOYS 105 (100 HERE)
SAN FRANCISCO CA 94110		HISTORY CLEAR
TEL: 415-555-0000		FINANCING SECURED
		FINANCIAL
CHIEF EXECUTIVE: LESLIE SMITH, PRES	CONDITION	FAIR

SPECIAL EVENTS
09/11/9-   On Sept 9, 199-, the subject experienced a fire due to an earthquake. According to Leslie Smith, President, damages amounted to $35,000, which was fully covered by their insurance company. The business was closed for two days while employees settled personal matters due to the earthquake.
03/17/9-   Subject moved from 400 KOLLER ST. to 492 KOLLER ST. on March 11, 199-.

° ° ° CUSTOMER SERVICE ° ° °

If you need any additional information, would like a credit recommendation, or have any questions regarding this report, please call our Customer Service Center at (800) 234-3867 from anywhere within the United States.

° ° ° SUMMARY ANALYSIS ° ° °

RATING SUMMARY . . . .
The "3A" portion of the Rating (Estimated Financial Strength) indicates that the company has a worth between $1 million and $10 million. The "3" on the right (Composite Credit Appraisal) indicates an overall "fair" credit appraisal. The "fair" credit appraisal was assigned because the company's overall payment record shows frequent slowness and because of D&B's "fair" assessment of the company's 12/31/9- fiscal financial statement.

Below is an overview of the company's D&B Rating(s) since 1-1-91:

RATING	DATE APPLIED
3A3	09/11/9-
	01/01/91

° ° ° PAYMENT SUMMARY ° ° °

This Payment Summary section reflects payment information in D&B's file as of October 29, 199-.

The PAYDEX for this company is 67.

This PAYDEX score indicates that payments to suppliers average 18 days beyond terms, weighted by dollar amounts. When dollar amounts are not considered, approximately 75% of the company's payments are within terms.

This report, provided under contract solely for use by subscriber as one factor in subscriber's credit, insurance, marketing or other business decisions, contains information compiled from sources D&B does not control and whose information, unless otherwise indicated in the report, has not been verified. In providing this report, D&B does not assume any part of the user's business risk, does not guarantee the accuracy, completeness or timeliness of the information and shall not be liable for any loss or injury resulting from reliance on this report. This report may not be reproduced in whole or part in any manner whatever. Copyright 1993 Dun & Bradstreet, Inc.

17G-115C-1

EXHIBIT 5-6
Dun & Bradstreet Reports

DB

Business Information Report

PAGE 2

Below is an overview of the company's dollar-weighted payments, segmented by its suppliers' primary industries:

| | TOTAL RCV'D | TOTAL DOLLAR AMOUNTS | LARGEST HIGH CREDIT | W/IN TERMS | DAYS SLOW | | | |
					<31	31-60	61-90	91+
	#	$	$	%	%	%	%	%
Total in D&B's file	24	785,150	250,000					
Top 10 Industries:								
1 Whol Printing Paper	8	747,500	250,000	64	18	18	–	–
2 Repair Service	2	7,500	7,500	–	100	–	–	–
3 Mfg Industrial Mach	2	2,000	1,000	50	50	–	–	–
4 Misc Services	2	750	500	33	67	–	–	–
5 Whol Non Durables	1	15,000	15,000	50	50	–	–	–
6 Air Courier Service	1	7,500	7,500	100	–	–	–	–
7 Mfg Service Ind Mach	1	2,500	2,500	50	50	–	–	–
8 Transportation Svcs	1	1,000	1,000	50	–	–	50	–
9 Mfg Photo Equipment	1	500	500	100	–	–	–	–
10 Mfg Plastic Products	1	100	100	100	–	–	–	–
11 Other Industries	1	100	100	100	–	–	–	–
Other Payment Categories:								
Cash experiences	2	450	250					
Paying record unknown	1	100	100					
Unfavorable comments	0	0	0					
Placed for collection:								
with D&B	0	0						
other	0	N/A						

The highest "Now Owes" in D&B's file is $250,000
The highest "Past Due" in D&B's file is $90,000

The total dollar amount from the 24 trade experiences listed is 6.0% of this company's annual sales as presented in the Summary. D&B considers the trade experiences to be representative of this company's payment habits.

PAYMENTS (Amounts may be rounded to nearest figure in prescribed ranges)

Antic	–	Anticipated	(Payments received prior to date of invoice)
Disc	–	Discounted	(Payments received within trade discount period)
Ppt	–	Prompt	(Payments received within terms granted)

REPORTED	PAYING RECORD	HIGH CREDIT	NOW OWES	PAST DUE	SELLING TERMS	LAST SALE WITHIN
03/9-	Ppt-Slow 90	1000	500	-0-	N30	1 Mo
02/9-	Ppt	250	100			4-5 Mos
	Ppt-Slow 30	2500	2500	1000		1 Mo
	Slow 30	500	500			2-3 Mos
	(005)	200				
	Slow 30-60	70000	70000	6500		1 Mo

This report, provided under contract solely for use by subscriber as one factor in subscriber's credit, insurance, marketing or other business decisions, contains information compiled from sources D&B does not control and whose information, unless otherwise indicated in the report, has not been verified. In providing this report, D&B does not assume any part of the user's business risk, does not guarantee the accuracy, completeness or timeliness of the information and shall not be liable for any loss or injury resulting from reliance on this report. This report may not be reproduced in whole or part in any manner whatever. Copyright 1993 Dun & Bradstreet, Inc.

(continued)

EXHIBIT 5-6 *(continued)*
Dun & Bradstreet Reports

DB   **Business Information Report**

PAGE 3

Date					Terms	
01/9-	Disc	2500	1000			1 Mo
	Disc-Ppt	25000	25000	0	2 to Prox	1 Mo
	Ppt-Slow 15	1000	500	250		1 Mo
	Ppt-Slow 30	15000	10000	5000		1 Mo
	Ppt-Slow 30	1000	0	0	N30	1 Mo
12/9-	Ppt	250000	250000	0		1 Mo
	Ppt	7500	250	0	N15	4-5 Mos
	(014)	250			Sales COD	1 Mo
	Ppt	500	0	0	N30	1 Mo
	Ppt	100	50	0	Regular terms	6-12 Mos
	Ppt-Slow 30	100000	100000	40000		1 Mo
	Ppt-Slow 30	70000	70000	50000	2 15 Prox	1 Mo
	Slow 30	7500	0	0		1 Mo
11/9-	Slow 30		0	0	N30	1 Mo
	Disc-Slow 30	30000	30000	7500		6-12 Mos
10/9-	Ppt	250	0	0		1 Mo
	Ppt-Slow 60	200000	200000	90000		6-12 Mos
09/9-	(024)	100	100		N30	1 Mo

°Payment experiences reflect how bills are met in relation to the terms granted. In some instances payment beyond terms can be the result of disputes over merchandise, skipped invoices, etc.
°Each experience shown represents a separate account reported by a supplier. Updated trade experiences replace those previously reported.

UPDATE
08/17/9-   On August 17, 199- KEVIN J. HUNT Sec-Treas stated for the six months ended June 30, 199- profits were up
         compared to same period last year.

FINANCE 09/11/9-		Fiscal Dec 31, 199-	Fiscal Dec 31, 199-		Fiscal Dec 31, 199-
	Curr Assets	4,643,821	4,825,611		5,425,125
	Curr Liabs	3,595,821	3,625,000		4,135,718
	Current Ratio	1.3	1.3		1.3
	Working Capital	1,048,000	1,200,611		1,289,407
	Other Assets	1,468,291	1,485,440		2,201,690
	Worth	1,879,451	1,912,112		2,125,499
	Sales	9,321,118	10,325,582		13,007,229
	Net Income	24,211	32,661		213,387

Fiscal statement dated Dec. 31, 199-:

			Accts Pay		2,125,114
	Cash	925,000	Notes Pay		450,000
Accts Rec	1,725,814		Bank Loan		1,100,000
Inventory	1,643,311		Other Curr Liabs		460,604
Other Curr Assets	1,131,000				------------
	------------		Curr Liabs		4,135,718
Curr Assets	5,425,125		L.T. Liab-Other		1,365,598
Fixt & Equip	1,667,918		Capital Stock		50,000
Other Assets	533,772		RETAINED EARNINGS		2,075,499
	------------				------------
Total Assets	7,626,815		Total		7,626,815

This report, provided under contract solely for use by subscriber as one factor in subscriber's credit, insurance, marketing or other business decisions, contains information compiled from sources D&B does not control and whose information, unless otherwise indicated in the report, has not been verified. In providing this report, D&B does not assume any part of the user's business risk, does not guarantee the accuracy, completeness or timeliness of the information and shall not be liable for any loss or injury resulting from reliance on this report. This report may not be reproduced in whole or part in any manner whatever. Copyright 1993 Dun & Bradstreet, Inc.

EXHIBIT 5-6
Dun & Bradstreet Reports

DB ▬▬▬▬▬▬

Business Information Report ◼

PAGE 4

From JAN 1, 199- to DEC 31, 199- sales $13,007,229; cost of goods sold $9,229,554. Gross profit $3,777,675; operating expenses $3,751,661. Operating incomes $26,014; extraordinary gain $187,373. Net incomes $213,387.

Submitted SEPT 11, 199- by Leslie Smith, President. Prepared from statement(s) by Accountant: Ashurst & Ashurst, PC. Prepared from books without audit.

— 0 —

Accounts receivable shown net less $12,586 allowance. Other current assets consist of prepaid expenses $64,471 and $1,066,529 of a loan from an affiliated concern. Other assets consist of deposits. Bank loans are due to bank at the prime interest rate, are secured by accounts receivable and inventory, and mature in 3 years. Notes payable are due on printing equipment in monthly installments of $27,500. Other current liabilities are accrued expenses and taxes. Long term debt consists of the long term portion of the equipment note.

On SEPT 11, 199- Leslie Smith, president, submitted the above figure(s).

Leslie Smith submitted the following interim figures dated June 30, 199-.

Cash	$1,011,812	Accts Pay	$1,932,118
Accts Rec	1,932,118	Owe Bank	1,100,000
Inventory	1,421,112	Notes Pay	350,000

Sales for 6 months were $7,325,001. Profits for 6 months were $103,782.

Projected annual sales are $14,000,000.

He also stated operating profits were below average due to heavy price competition in the industry, higher operating expenses, and decreased advertising budgets following the nationwide move towards cost containment.

PUBLIC FILINGS

The following data is for information purposes only and is not the official record. Certified copies can only be obtained from the official source.

° ° ° SUITS ° ° °

DOCKET NO:	12345		
SUIT AMOUNT:	$1,000	STATUS:	Pending
PLAINTIFF:	MAZZUCA & ASSOC.	DATE STATUS ATTAINED:	03/25/199-
DEFENDANT:	GORMAN MANUFACTURING CO. INC.	DATE FILED:	03/25/199-
		LATEST INFO RECEIVED:	03/31/199-
CAUSE:	Breach of contract		
WHERE FILED:	SAN FRANCISCO, CA		

° ° ° UCC FILING(S) ° ° °

COLLATERAL:	Accounts receivable - Inventory including proceeds and products		
FILING NO:	86188586	DATE FILED:	07/24/199-
TYPE:	Original	LATEST INFO RECEIVED:	10/04/199-
SEC. PARTY:	A.C. Paper, Palo Alto, CA	FILED WITH:	SECRETARY OF STATE/ UCC DIVISION, CA

This report, provided under contract solely for use by subscriber as one factor in subscriber's credit, insurance, marketing or other business decisions, contains information compiled from sources D&B does not control and whose information, unless otherwise indicated in the report, has not been verified. In providing this report, D&B does not assume any part of the user's business risk, does not guarantee the accuracy, completeness or timeliness of the information and shall not be liable for any loss or injury resulting from reliance on this report. This report may not be reproduced in whole or in part in any manner whatever. Copyright 1993 Dun & Bradstreet, Inc.

(continued)

EXHIBIT 5-6 *(continued)*
Dun & Bradstreet Reports

DB

Business Information Report

PAGE 5

BANKING
09/9-   Account(s) average high 6 figures. Account open over 10 years. Loans granted to low 7 figures on a secured basis. Now owing low 7 figures. Collateral consists of accounts receivable and inventory. Matures in 1 to 5 years. Borrowing account is satisfactory. Overall relations are satisfactory.

HISTORY
09/11/9-   LESLIE SMITH, PRES   KEVIN J. HUNT, SEC-TREAS
            DIRECTOR(S): THE OFFICER(S)
            BUSINESS TYPE: Corporation - Profit
                                          DATE INCORPORATED:
                                          05/21/1965
            AUTH SHARES - Common: 200   STATE OF INCORP: California
            PAR VALUE - COMMON: No Par Value

            Business started May 21, 1965 by Leslie Smith and Kevin J. Hunt. 100% of capital stock is owned by Parent Company.
            SMITH born 1926. Married. Graduated from the University of California, Los Angeles, in June 1947 with a BS degree in Business Management. 1947-65 general manager for Raymor Printing Co., San Francisco, CA. 1965 formed subject with Kevin J. Hunt.
            HUNT born 1925. Married. Graduated from Northwestern University, Evanston, IL. in June 1946. 1946-1965 controller for Raymor Printing Co., San Francisco, CA. 1965 formed subject with Leslie Smith.
            RELATED COMPANIES: Through the financial interest of Gorman Holding Company Inc., subject's parent company, the Gorman Manufacturing Co. Inc., is related to two other companies:
            1. Smith Lettershop Inc., San Diego, CA; commercial printing, started 1972.
            2. Gorman Suppliers Inc., Los Angeles, CA; commercial print, started 1980.
            Intercompany relations consist of loans.

OPERATION
09/11/9-   Subsidiary of Gorman Holding Company Inc., Los Angeles, CA, started 1965 which operates as a holding company for its subsidiaries. Parent company owns 100% of capital stock. Parent company has 2 other subsidiaries. Intercompany relations: consist of loans and advances.
            A consolidated financial statement of the parent company dated Dec. 31, 199- showed a worth of $4,125,112, with an overall fair financial condition.
            Commercial Printing specializing in advertising posters, catalogs, circulars and coupons.
            Net 30 days. Has 175 account(s). Sells to commercial concerns.
            Territory: United States.
            Nonseasonal.
            EMPLOYEES: 105 which includes officer(s). 100 employed here.
            FACILITIES: Rents 55,000 sq. ft. on first floor of one story cinder block building in good condition. Premises neat.
            LOCATION: Central business section on well traveled street.
            BRANCH(ES): Subject maintains a branch at 1073 Boyden Road, Los Angeles, CA.

This report, provided under contract solely for use by subscriber as one factor in subscriber's credit, insurance, marketing or other business decisions, contains information compiled from sources D&B does not control and whose information, unless otherwise indicated in the report, has not been verified. In providing this report, D&B does not assume any part of the user's business risk, does not guarantee the accuracy, completeness or timeliness of the information and shall not be liable for any loss or injury resulting from reliance on this report. This report may not be reproduced in whole or part in any manner whatever. Copyright 1993 Dun & Bradstreet, Inc.   RATED WITH PAYDEX VERSION

EXHIBIT 5-6
Dun & Bradstreet Reports

CALL 1-800-234-3867
Business information and analysis for your global credit,
marketing and purchasing decisions.

D&B Rating Key
The D&B Rating is a widely used tool that represents a firm's size and composite credit appraisal.

Rating Classification (Based on Worth from Interim or Fiscal Balance Sheet)				Composite Credit Appraisal			
				High	Good	Fair	Limited
5A	$50,000,000		and over	1	2	3	4
4A	10,000,000	to	49,999,999	1	2	3	4
3A	1,000,000	to	9,999,999	1	2	3	4
2A	750,000	to	999,999	1	2	3	4
1A	500,000	to	749,999	1	2	3	4
BA	300,000	to	499,999	1	2	3	4
BB	200,000	to	299,999	1	2	3	4
CB	125,000	to	199,999	1	2	3	4
CC	75,000	to	124,999	1	2	3	4
DC	50,000	to	74,999	1	2	3	4
DD	35,000	to	49,999	1	2	3	4
EE	20,000	to	34,999	1	2	3	4
FF	10,000	to	19,999	1	2	3	4
GG	5,000	to	9,999	1	2	3	4
HH	up to		4,999	1	2	3	4

Rating Classification (Based on Number of Employees)				Composite Credit Appraisal		
				Good	Fair	Limited
1R	10 employees		and over	2	3	4
2R	1	to	9	2	3	4

"--" (Absence of Rating)
A "--" symbol should not be interpreted as indicating that credit should be denied. It simply means that the information available to Dun & Bradstreet does not permit us to classify the company within our Rating key and that further inquiry should be made before reaching a credit decision.

Some reasons for using a "--" symbol include: deficit net worth; bankruptcy proceedings; lack of sufficient payment information; or incomplete history information.

DS (Duns Support)
Information available to Dun & Bradstreet does not permit us to classify the company within our Rating key. When contained in a Business Information Report, an investigation will automatically be performed within four business days, at no additional charge.

Key to Employee Range	
ER1	1,000 or more
ER2	500-999
ER3	100-499
ER4	50-99
ER5	20-49
ER6	10-19
ER7	5-9
ER8	1-4
ERN	Not available

Key to the D&B PAYDEX® Score	
PAYDEX	PAYMENT
100	Anticipate
90	Discount
80	Prompt
70	15 Days Beyond Terms
60	22 Days Beyond Terms
50	30 Days Beyond Terms
40	60 Days Beyond Terms
30	90 Days Beyond Terms
20	120 Days Beyond Terms
UN	Unavailable

ER (Employee Range)
Certain lines of business, primarily banks, insurance companies and government entities, do not lend themselves to classification under the D&B Rating System. Instead, we assign these types of businesses an Employee Range symbol based on the number of people employed. No other significance should be attached to this symbol.

For example, a Rating of "ER7" means there are between 5 and 9 employees in the company.

"ERN" should not be interpreted negatively. It simply means we don't have information indicating how many people are employed at this firm.

INV (Investigation Being Conducted)
When an "INV" appears, it means an investigation is being conducted on this business to get the most current details.

SOURCE: Copyright 1996 by Dun & Bradstreet, a company of The Dun & Bradstreet Corporation.

composite credit appraisal of the business. The latter score is helpful to the credit manager for account risk classification purposes. A rating of CB2, for example, suggests the company's estimated financial strength is between $125,000 and $199,999, with a "good" overall credit appraisal (see the last section of Exhibit 5-6 for a legend explaining these categories). The rating shown by Gorman Manufacturing Company at the beginning of the report is 3A3; the last 3 indicates a "fair" payment performance.

D&B also provides more than 100 products and services with different levels of analysis and content. For example, every 60 days it publishes the *Dun & Bradstreet Reference Book of American Business,* which includes summary information on more than 3 million businesses. It tells you a company's line of business, its location, and telephone number. And when available, it provides a company's estimated financial strength and composite credit appraisal.

Another major source of information is the network of **credit interchange bureaus.** These bureaus are departments of local credit associations that provide information in the form of "Business Credit Reports" and "Credit Interchange Reports." These credit associations are part of the National Association of Credit Management (NACM), and their reports are available only to NACM members. Major inputs to NACM reports include ledger experience information from NACM members' receivables files, bank information, and some public record information. Optionally, anyone accessing the NACM database can also request data from the Standard & Poor's (S&P) financial statement data on 6000 publicly held companies and key business facts on more than 30,000 publicly and privately held companies.

Trade associations also compile factual trade information from the companies in the association. A trade association is made up of companies in a single industry or in several closely related industries. For an annual fee, subscribers receive a report that summarizes financial data for companies in the association. The Financial Executives Division of the National Retail Merchants Association, for example, annually publishes the financial and operating results of department and specialty stores. Some of the data is split out for department stores versus specialty stores or for stores within a certain size bracket.

Finally, *banks* are a vital source of credit information. The credit executive can ask a bank officer at his or her bank to check with the customers' major banks to verify customer-supplied information and get loan payment and average deposit balance histories.[14] The customer may or may not be notified at the time it applies for credit that its bank will be consulted, but it is standard procedure to get the customer's permission first.

Ricci (1999) found that 79 percent of surveyed companies get information from D&B, and most companies get information from the potential buyer as part of their credit investigation.

Credit information is not always accurate or timely. The managerial questions asked in the following Focus on Practice box underscore some of the concerns credit executives share.[15]

APPLICATION OF CREDIT STANDARDS: CREDIT ANALYSIS.   Once the appropriate information has been gathered, a decision must be made about whether to extend credit to the applicant, and if so, how much to extend. Earlier in the chapter, we gave a general

---

[14]Banks are restricted in their provision of such information, however.

[15]Information used in these examples is mostly from 1990. To repair bad credit, advisors give clients someone else's data. *The Wall Street Journal* August 14:A1; and 1989. Dun's credit reports, vital tool of business, can be off the mark. *The Wall Street Journal* October 5:A1.

FOCUS ON PRACTICE

CAN I RELY ON CONSUMER CREDIT INFORMATION? "Credit doctors" in the Houston area used laptop computers and stolen access codes to find names of consumers with good credit records from credit bureau databases. They then sold this information (names, social security numbers, and loan histories) to clients with poor credit records, who used them to apply for credit. When payments were not made by the illegal users, the previously outstanding credit records were downgraded by the bureau. Purchases totaling $20 million were linked to fraudulent use of credit records in a 3-year period. Elsewhere, in 1997, a woman was awarded significant damages because one of the major consumer credit providers had false and libelous material on file—even though that information never resulted in a credit denial.

CAN I RELY ON CORPORATE CREDIT REPORTS? Controlling 90 percent of the commercial credit market, D&B data are vital as an input into many lending or credit-extension decisions. Perhaps because of the large number of reports that must be put together quickly, a significant minority of D&B corporate credit reports were found to be inaccurate or outdated, according to a report published in 1990. Some credit reporters working at D&B stated that they were responsible for as many as 20 reports per day. Courts have generally held that D&B is not liable for errors in reports. Much of the information is based on interviews with a company's top officials that are not checked for accuracy. Some information comes from bankruptcy court proceedings; the rest is estimated, especially when the company refuses to provide information. D&B, working to improve its performance, has instituted a computer system to monitor reporters' performance and, since 1986, has sent copies of its reports to the companies to cut down on errors.

EXHIBIT 5-7
Example of Corporate Credit Analysis

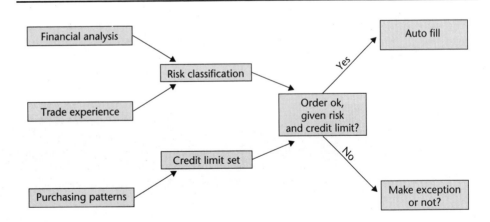

diagram for the credit-granting sequence. Exhibit 5-7 illustrates how one major corporation actually makes its credit decisions. It determines the applicant's risk classification based on financial analysis and trade experience. Although a customer's initial credit limit is based on this information, the customer's credit limit is periodically reset based on its purchasing patterns. When each new order is received, the risk classification and credit limit help determine approval. If approved, the order is automatically filled. If the risk classification and credit limit data indicate nonapproval, there is a manual override possibility to allow an exception to be made and the order to be filled anyway.

Credit executives consider both nonfinancial and financial factors to determine whether to extend credit and how much credit to extend. Nonfinancial analysis is primarily concerned with the *willingness* to pay and assesses the character of the applicant. Subjective analysis of the lending situation is also involved.

The other four Cs, capital, capacity, collateral, and conditions, are assessed primarily in financial ratio analysis and address the *ability* to pay. The seller may buy a third-party analysis, such as the D&B report in Exhibit 5-6, or do its own analysis. The objectives of a complete financial analysis are threefold[16]: assess the company's financial information, interpret comparative data regarding the company's competitors and economic conditions, and conduct financial market analysis to better understand the company's stock price patterns and valuation. The credit analyst is most interested in steps 1 and 2, although sometimes the best early warning of impending bankruptcy or credit rating downgrade is a drop in the company's stock or bond prices. A complete discussion of financial ratio analysis is beyond the scope of this book, but Exhibit 5-8 provides a summary of the major components that are analyzed, including many of the liquidity measures you learned about in Chapter 2.

The analyst would study both the trends in the company's ratios and how the ratios compare with those of key competitors or the industry average. The weaknesses of financial ratio analysis are:

- the noncomparability of data for companies using different accounting techniques
- the difficulty of deciding what the optimum value of a particular ratio should be
- the ambiguity of whether calculated ratios signal credit approval or nonapproval

Of these weaknesses, the latter is the most troublesome. A financial ratio analysis may reveal an applicant who looks good in certain areas but weak in others. Because financial ratio analysis looks only at one variable at a time (is univariate), it does not give a clear signal on whether to approve or reject such a customer. The best advice we can give for the beginning analyst is watch the trend and then ask probing questions. A *multivariate* model, which simultaneously accounts for several predictor variables, improves the credit analysis.

Credit scoring models weight variables depending on their helpfulness in discriminating between good and bad applicants, based on past payment histories. A "bad" applicant is one who would likely pay its bills in a severely delinquent manner, usually defined as more than 90 days past due. Scoring models are developed with the assistance of computerized statistical techniques such as multiple discriminant analysis. Years of past financial data and ordering and payment data for many customers are used to determine which financial or nonfinancial variables best predict whether a customer will pay its bills in a timely fashion. A very simple model might look like the following:[17]

$$Y = 0.000025(INCOME) + 0.50(PAYHIST) + 0.25(EMPLOYMT) \qquad \text{(5-2)}$$

In which: Y = the applicant's weighted score

$INCOME$ = the applicant's income for past year

$PAYHIST$ = the number assigned to represent the applicant's past payment habits, with 0 being poor, 0.5 okay, and 1 good

---

[16]For a good introduction to financial analysis, see Chapters 1–3 and Appendix I of Erich A. Helfert. 2000. *Techniques of financial analysis.* 10th ed. Boston: Irwin McGraw-Hill.

[17]The Equal Credit Opportunity Act, as implemented by the Federal Reserve Board's Regulation B, prohibits the use of information on race, gender, or marital status in scoring models, and age can only be used positively (for applicants 62 years and older).

$EMPLOYMT$ = the employment status, with 0 meaning unemployed, 0.5 meaning employed part-time, and 1 meaning employed full-time

If Michelle earned $25,000 last year, has a good payment history, and is employed full-time, her score is:

$$Y = (0.000025 \times \$25,000) + (0.50 \times 1) + (0.25 \times 1)$$
$$= 0.6250 + 0.50 + 0.25$$
$$= \underline{\underline{1.375}}$$

This calculated score is then compared with a cutoff score to determine whether Michelle should be extended credit. Assuming that experience has shown that most applicants with a score of at least 1.25 are good credit risks, Michelle will be extended credit. If her score was close to 1.25, judgment would be applied to determine whether she should be approved, and a score below that signals nonapproval.

A SAMPLE CREDIT SCORING MODEL.   A company selling to many small businesses might use the sample credit scoring model shown in Exhibit 5-9. Note the factors that might go into a typical credit score. In this model, the higher the final score, the better the chance of approval. Perhaps a minimum score of 100 would be necessary for an initial credit extension, and that might be limited to a small dollar amount such as $5,000. Recognize that the actual criteria, and how important each criterion is, varies from model to model and lender to lender.

At present, credit scoring is used primarily in consumer (as opposed to industrial) credit evaluation, in which there are a large number of applicants under review at any point in time. Although it saves time and is objective, it may not be very accurate; one study found that a scoring model performed no better than chance at predicting credit-worthiness.[18] In industrial credit evaluations, credit scoring models are best used as an initial screening device to separate out very good or very bad applicants, leaving the remainder for a trained credit analyst to decide. Another possibility is to use the model as a "second opinion," in which case the credit analyst uses the model as a check on his or her decisions. Recommendations for which the model and the credit analyst disagree can be studied further.

Scoring models have tended to focus almost exclusively on capacity and capital. By doing so, they overlook collateral, conditions, and character. Additionally, by focusing on risk, they also overlook expected return.[19] Finally, they do not allow exceptional strengths in one or two areas to offset a glaring deficiency on a variable that is weighted heavily in the scoring equation, even though you might logically expect that applicant to be a good credit risk.

In their 1988 Fortune 500 survey, Smith and Belt found that evaluation of the Cs of credit and credit scoring models were the most popular techniques used in the

---

[18]See the Winginton citation in the end-of-chapter references. Another model, developed with logistic regression, did slightly better than the discriminant analysis model but was still deemed too inaccurate to use by itself to make credit decisions. See the development of these issues in Reichert, Cho, and Wagner (cited in the end-of-chapter references).

[19]In response to these weaknesses, a conjoint analysis model has been developed to integrate all of these variables. Conjoint analysis is a multivariate statistical technique that allows the measurement of the joint (simultaneous) effect of two or more independent variables on the ranking of a dependent variable. In this case, the dependent variable is overall loan attractiveness. Although it holds promise, it is too early to tell if this application will be substantially better than present scoring models. For more on this application of conjoint analysis, see the article by Zinkham in the end-of-chapter references.

EXHIBIT 5-8
Key Financial Ratios for Credit Analysis

CATEGORY	FINANCIAL RATIO	FORMULA	INTERPRETATION	WARNING SIGNS
L I Q U I D I T Y	1. Current ratio	Current assets/Current liabilities	Higher is better, indicating increased ability to cover payables.	Watch out for values that are artificially inflated due to slow-moving, perishable, or obsolete inventory.
	2. Net working capital	Current assets − Current liabilities	Higher is better, indicating increased ability to cover payables.	Must evaluate in light of size of company; also watch out for values that are artificially inflated due to slow-moving, perishable, or obsolete inventory.
	3. Quick ratio	(Current assets − Inventory)/Current liabilities	Measures company's ability to pay current obligations with its most liquid assets. More conservative measure than #1 or #2; again higher is better, indicating increased ability to cover payables.	Flow concepts and receivable/payable synchronization must also be evaluated. Quick ratio still does not capture unsynchronized nature of receipts and disbursements (e.g., situation in which only CA are receivables, only CL are payables: if Q.R. = 1, you collect receivables in 60 days, but pay payables in 30 days, will be unable to meet payables).
	4. Cash flow to total debt	Net income + Depreciation expense / ST debt + LT debt or Net income + Depreciation expense / (Current liabilities–A/P − Accrued expenses) + LT debt	Higher is better, indicating ability to cover debt service (interest and principal repayments).	Low ratio often foreshadows bankruptcy. Company may be able to use large cash and securities position to offset temporary declines in cash flow.
	5. Cash flow from operations (CFFO)	Net income + Noncash charges + Change in operating current liabilities − Change in current assets (or just pull # from Statement of Cash Flows)	Larger amount is better. Gives flow concept of ability of company to generate cash from operations. Much better measure of additions to liquidity than earnings when company is capital intensive or growing rapidly.	Negative CFFO signals increasing inability to pay payables. Unhealthy firm must fund negative CFFO by selling off assets or issuing new liabilities, so compare investing and financing cash flows from SCF to give depth to analysis.

CATEGORY	FINANCIAL RATIO	FORMULA	INTERPRETATION	WARNING SIGNS
L I Q U I D I T Y	6. Cash cycle (CC) or Cash Conversion Period	CC = (Days inventory held + Days sales outstanding − Days payables outstanding) *or, equivalently,* CC = Inventory conversion period + Receivables conversion period − Payables deferral period	Shorter is better. Longer CC signals more of company's cash being tied up in operations. For any given balance sheet liquidity position, longer CC indicates that more of that liquidity is encumbered by operational working capital needs. Further, CC indicates dependence on outside financing.	Any unexpected lengthening of CC is bothersome. Determine source of deterioration (inventory conversion taking longer, collection experience deteriorating) to evaluate seriousness. Creditor may begin to stretch payables to compensate for longer operating cycle (OC = DIH + DSO).
	7. Cash turnover	CT = 365/CC	Higher is better. Measures how many "turns" company gets on cash tied up in operations. Views cash as inventory. More cash tied up in operations means more nonearning assets.	Watch for a slowdown over time.
	8. Net liquid balance	NLB = (Cash + ST investments) − (Notes payable + Current portion of LT debt)	Larger amount is better. Shows ability of nonspontaneous current assets to cover nonspontaneous (arranged) debts. Is unaffected by collectibility of receivables or salability of inventories. In effect, assumes operating cycle (A/R and inventories) is exactly matched by A/P, and prepaid expenses are exactly matched by accruals. Hypothetically, if CC = 0, how much residual liquidity does organization have? Offers credit analyst incisive supplement to CC. Gives insight into financial flexibility.	Watch for near-term principal repayments beyond one-year cutoff that separates CL from LT debts. This applies to revolving credit agreements, term loans, and bonds. Companies also may use leases in lieu of debt.
	9. Defensive interval or "Time to ruin"	$\dfrac{\text{Cash + ST investments}}{\text{Daily operating expenses}}$ = *where* Daily operating expenses = (COGS + Selling, general, & administrative expenses − Depreciation expense)/365	Higher is better, showing how long company can pay bills if it has a strike or other disruption of revenue stream, assuming it has lengthy DIH and DSO and has no ST borrowing capacity. When company has significant untapped short-term borrowing capacity, this measure is overly conservative. Also, the greater the proportion of ST debt as percentage of total financing, the less protection the cash value represents (interest and principal flows are not included in measure's formula).	Watch for deterioration in this number as a relative liquidity indicator. When labeled as "time to ruin," it provides an indicator of efficacy of hedging strategies used by the company. If company's hedges do not significantly increase "time to ruin," its hedging strategy is flawed. Latter consideration applies to creditors having significant commodity price exposure, foreign exchange transaction exposure, or interest rate exposure.

(continued)

EXHIBIT 5-8 (*continued*)
Key Financial Ratios for Credit Analysis

CATEGORY	FINANCIAL RATIO	FORMULA	INTERPRETATION	WARNING SIGNS
D E B T M A N A G E M E N T & C O V E R A G E	1. Times interest earned	$\dfrac{\text{EBIT}}{\text{Interest expense}}$ *or* $\dfrac{\text{Operating profit}}{\text{Interest expense}}$	Higher is better. How many times over could we pay interest expense from pool of funds available to pay it? If we take $1 - (1/\text{TIE})$, we get percentage reduction in operating profits that company could experience while yet allowing it to cover its interest payments. For example, if TIE is 4, company's operating profit could drop 75% $[=1 - (1/4)]$ before its ability to pay interest is impaired. Smaller values indicate reduced financial flexibility, increasing risk to other creditors (including trade creditors).	Provides an inaccurate indicator of ability to service debt. To a degree, it overstates that ability, in that accrual basis for EBIT recognizes revenue before cash is received and recognizes expenses after cash expenditures for labor and materials are made. Furthermore, lease payments, principal repayments, and preferred dividends are also financing-related cash outflows that must be covered, and these are not included in the formula. However, capital-intensive companies would see this ratio as understating cash generated and might add back depreciation and amortization to get a better picture of cash generated (yielding EBITDA). May wish to supplement with cash from operating activities (from Statement of Cash Flows) divided by interest expense or use a "fixed charges coverage ratio" to include sinking fund payments, lease payments, and preferred stock dividends in the denominator. Also, consider plans for new debt issues.
	2. Long-term debt to capital	$\dfrac{\text{Long-term debt}}{\text{Long-term debt} + \text{Equity}}$ *where* Long-term debt includes long-term notes and bonds, term loans, and capital lease obligations.	Lower is better. We are measuring percentage of long-term financing that is borrowed. More debt reduces financial flexibility and increases risk to other creditors including trade creditors.	This ratio does not account for ability of large operating cash flows to service debt. It is really measuring relative use of debt, and financial flexibility remaining (untapped borrowing capacity) more than drain on cash flow related to debt service. Short-term debt, operating leases, new/planned borrowing, and preferred stock dividends should be evaluated for more complete analysis.

CATEGORY	FINANCIAL RATIO	FORMULA	INTERPRETATION	WARNING SIGNS
C O N T.	3. Total liabilities to Total assets	$\dfrac{\text{Total liabilities}}{\text{Total assets}}$	Lower is better, for the same reasons indicated for #2. High values show proportionately greater use of borrowed money (less equity), which must be paid back with interest. This ratio is related to the "equity multiplier" that many companies use as a "ROE profit driver" in DuPont modeling: $$TL/TA = (1 - 1/EM)$$	Other than the fact that this ratio includes short-term debt, same concerns as for #2. Further comment is necessary because of linkage to ROE: if company's "operating return-on-assets" (EBIT/assets) exceeds interest rate on debt, it can effectively "lever up" ROE by using more debt. Increased profits and cash flows are offset, from trade creditors' vantage, by increased financial risk.
P E R F O R M A N C E	1. Return on equity (ROE)	$\dfrac{\text{Earnings available to shareholders}}{\text{Common equity}}$ *where* Earnings available = (Net income − Preferred stock dividends − Sinking fund payments − Amortization)	Higher is better, assuming it does not come with too much risk. This is a profit and performance scorecard for stockholders. It shows ability to generate profits, from stockholders' perspective.	Market value, economic value added, and realized shareholder returns are better performance metrics. Net income is not the same as cash flow. Risk may be high. Prospects for continued profits and cash flows more important from trade creditors' perspective.
	2. Profit margin on sales (or net profit margin)	$\dfrac{\text{Net income}}{\text{Revenues}}$	Higher is better. Measures ability to generate profits from each $1 of sales.	Same concerns as on #1.
	3. Return on total assets (ROA)	$\dfrac{\text{Net income}}{\text{Total assets}}$	Higher is better. Measures ability to generate profits from each $1 of assets. Decompose into $$NI/TA = NI/Sales \times Sales/TA$$ This shows us the two drivers for ROA: 1. Profit margin on sales (#2 above) 2. Total asset turnover, which shows us asset use efficiency. Turnover is diminished by overinvestment in fixed assets as well as working capital such as receivables and inventory.	Same concerns as #1.

EXHIBIT 5-9
Sample Credit Scoring Model

Here are some factors that might go into a typical credit score. The higher the final score, the better your chance of approval. Visit http://www.businessweek.com/smallbiz/content/may2000/fi000516.htm for more information.

CHARACTERISTICS	ATTRIBUTES WITH HYPOTHETICAL WEIGHTS			
Credit History of Principal(s) Data: Consumer Credit Report	Major Derog (bankruptcy, collections) −40 pts.	Minor Derog (minor delinquencies) −10 pts.	Satisfactory 15 pts.	No Record 0 pts.
Unused Credit Data: Consumer Credit Report	≥75% of Available 40 pts.	74%–33% of Available 30 pts.	<33% of Available 20 pts.	No Record 0 pts.
Credit History of Business Data: Business Credit Report	Major Derog −40 pts.	Minor Derog −10 pts.	Satisfactory 15 pts.	No Record 0 pts.
Industry Type Data: Federal SIC Code	Group A (manufacturing, with hard assets) 50 pts.	Group B 40 pts.	Group C 35 pts.	Group D (high risk, e.g., restaurant) 20 pts.
Available Liquid Assets of Business (e.g. bank balances) Data: Loan Application	<$6K 15 pts.	$6–$19K 20 pts.	$20–$49K 40 pts.	$50K & up 45 pts.
Net Worth of Principal(s) Data: Loan Application	<$50K 10 pts.	$50–$100K 20 pts.	$100–$250K 30 pts.	$250K & up 40 pts.

DATA: Fair Isaac Inc. and Business Week

credit-granting decision.[20] Some firms follow a sequential investigation process, in which more information is gathered only if the possible benefits of getting that information exceed the cost. Such an approach is strongly advocated because it allows marginal costs and benefits of information gathering to be equated, in theory determining the right amount of information gathering. Ricci (1999) found that the majority (55 percent) of the surveyed Business Week Global 1000 companies use more than one method, mostly ratio analysis and credit scoring, to decide how to grant credit. Just under 80 percent of the respondents use ratio analysis (at a minimum) in granting credit. She also found that most companies base the scope of the credit investigation on the size of the potential sale, rather than following a uniform or sequential investigation process.

EXPERT SYSTEMS.   Businesses are increasingly using rule-based computerized applications of artificial intelligence to credit decision making. The applications are very similar to the credit scoring models we discussed earlier. The credit-granting decision is one

[20]Smith and Belt (cited in the end-of-chapter references).

[21]Srinivasan and Kim (cited in the end-of-chapter references).

area in which pioneering work has been done.[21] The decision-making process of a veteran credit professional is mimicked by a computer in what is termed an expert system. The computerized database supporting this system might include complete customer information as well as a model to determine the appropriate credit limit (if any) for each potential customer. Advantages of the application of expert systems include increased productivity and lower costs of credit evaluation, higher quality of decisions by providing factual support without taking the decision out of the hands of the credit analyst, more consistent application of credit standards, reduced training costs when credit managers retire or leave the company, and use as a training tool to teach newly hired credit analysts how credit evaluation is done by the company. Here is an example of a credit extension decision rule from an expert system used in a consumer credit card decision model[22]:

> If gross income is equal to or greater than $20,000 and the applicant has not been delinquent and gross income per household member is equal to or greater than $12,000 and debt/income ratio is equal to or greater than 30 percent but less than 50 percent and personal property is equal to or greater than $50,000, then accept application (grant credit).

The expert system offers helpful guidance to the credit analyst, presumably leading to better decisions. Notice how the expert system allows a series of conditional rules to be combined to make the credit extension and credit limit decisions. The credit scoring models prescribed earlier in the chapter are limited to one-step decision making based on weighted averages of financial and nonfinancial data. Computer-aided decisions, particularly based on expert systems, offer the credit analyst significant information-processing capabilities. Human judgment is not replaced but enhanced.

Let's say that based on our assessment of a credit applicant, done with a subjective appraisal of the five Cs, financial ratio analysis, or a credit scoring model, we see this applicant as more risky than the typical applicant. How can we conduct risk analysis of the credit extension decision? We return to our credit extension example once again to demonstrate risk analysis.

RISK ANALYSIS.   Our earlier simple analysis of the NPV of a credit extension has implicitly made several key assumptions. First, we assumed that the customer would pay on the 30th day. In reality, the customer may pay early, on time, or late. Second, we have assumed a 100 percent certainty that the payment would be made on that date. The assumed certainty of that payment is unrealistic. Risk can be incorporated in the analysis by incorporating a probability distribution of payment dates. Third, we have assumed that the credit administration and collection expenses do not change regardless of when the customer pays.

Returning to our earlier credit extension decision, we can now make more realistic assumptions to illustrate the incorporation of uncertainty into the NPV analysis.[23] The question we address is, will the probabilities of late payment and need to refer delinquent accounts to a collection agency negate the positive NPV of the credit extension? Assume that the following collection experience mirrors customers such as the present applicant:

---

[22]Ehsan Nikbakht and Mohammed H.A. Tafti. 1989. Application of expert systems in evaluation of credit card borrowers. *Journal of Managerial Finance* 15:19–27.

[23]Risk analysis of this type was first developed in Friedland (see the end-of-chapter references).

PAYMENT TIMING	PROBABILITY
30 days or less	0.40
During 2nd month	0.40
3–4 months	0.15
After 4 months	0.05
	1.00

If we assume that payments are received evenly over these time periods, we can closely approximate actual cash inflows by substituting the midpoint of each time frame into the NPV analysis. We also need to know what the credit administration and collection expenses *(EXP)* are. Research of past company collection records reveals that variable costs incurred are approximately $40 per month, starting in the second month and extending no longer than through the fourth month. After the fourth month, the company gives up hope of ever collecting on its own, and refers the account to a collection agency. The collection agency is able to collect $800 on average (based on the fact that it collects nothing on some of the accounts and partial amounts from others), but legal and agency fees consume 25 percent of the amount initially collected. Consequently, on average the company comes out with an added cost of $200 on each referred $1,000 sale. The credit manager insists the company refer accounts for collection, however, to signal other accounts that the company is serious about its collections.

The data are shown in Exhibit 5-10. The net collection cash flow (column 5) is computed as ($1,000 − *EXP*) except for the referred accounts in the "more than 4

EXHIBIT 5-10

Credit Extension with Uncertain Collection Experience

BACKGROUND INFORMATION:

Terms:	net 30 days
Projected Invoice Amount:	$1,000
Variable Production Costs:	$700
Monthly Collection Agency Fee:	$40
Interest Rate (13% annual):	0.0003562

(1) COLLECTION PERIOD (*CP*, IN MONTHS)	(2) COLLECTION PERIOD MIDPOINT (MONTHS)	(3) PAYMENT PROBABILITY	(4) COLLECTION COSTS (*EXP*)	(5) COLLECTION CASH FLOW [$1,000 − (COL. 4)]	(6) PRESENT VALUE OF [P.V. OF (COL. 5) − (*VCR*)(*S*)]	(7) EXPECTED PRESENT VALUE (COL.3) × (COL. 6)
1 month or less	0.5	0.40	$ 0	$1,000	$294.69	$117.88
During 2nd month	1.5	0.40	$40	$960	$244.85	$97.94
3-4 months (2.5–3.5)	3	0.15	$80	$920	$191.42	$28.71
More than 4 months	—	0.05	$200 + $120	$480°	$(244.65)°°	$(12.23)

Expected NPV of Credit Extension:

$232.30

°Assuming it takes 1 month from the time of referral for the agency to collect.

°° The NPV is based on the 5-month delay, and is calculated as:

$$\$66.40 = \left[\frac{\$480}{1 + (0.0003562)(152)} \right] - \$700$$

months" row. For the referred accounts, the company collects $800 but pays the collection agency $200 in addition to the $120 of monthly collection costs it has already incurred (during the second, third, and fourth months). In column 6, the discounted value of the net collection cash flow is computed, and the variable production cost (which is not discounted because it takes place at time 0) is subtracted. Finally, in column 7, the expected present value of the credit sale is calculated. The payment probabilities from column 3 are multiplied by the present values from column 6 and then added. The expected present value of the credit extension, shown at the bottom of column 7, is $232.30. Although not as large as the NPV ($249.85) in the certainty analysis done earlier in this chapter, it is still positive, so the credit analyst should recommend that the sale be made. The credit analyst may want to modify the probabilities for new accounts with lower D&B ratings, worse financial ratios, or lower credit scoring values. Studying the payment histories of customers similar to the credit applicant proves helpful in this analysis.

ESTABLISHING CREDIT LIMITS.   Once the decision has been made to grant credit, the manager must determine the maximum credit balance allowable for the customer. Survey evidence provided by Besley and Osteryoung suggests the following are the major reasons companies impose credit limits and identifies "control risk exposure" as the primary reason[24]:

PRIMARY REASON FOR CREDIT LIMIT	NUMBER	PERCENTAGE
Control risk exposure	120	53.1
Customer financial position	63	27.9
Experience with customer	13	5.8
Other reasons	11	4.9

How high should the credit limit be? Traditional approaches to setting the credit limit include setting it equal to customer need, at 10 percent of customer net worth, at a percentage of high credit reported by other suppliers or banks (as shown earlier on the D & B Business Information Report), or by judgment (gut feeling). Evidence suggests that judgment is used predominantly (53 percent of surveyed firms), with ratio analysis (21 percent), and agency ratings (7.5 percent) the next most frequent. Beranek and Scherr surveyed practitioners and found that, for some or all buyers, about 30 percent of sellers believe that the probability of payment decreases with the amount of credit granted. This suggests that credit granting and credit limit setting are simultaneously determined in many cases. Improvement in decision quality and objectivity might be possible through the use of a formula approach; with the advent of computerized expert systems in credit management (covered at the end of this chapter), the trend is clearly in this direction.[25]

---

[24]Besley and Osteryoung also found that a few firms limited the total amount of credit extended to all customers because of a desire to avoid large debt exposure and because of other, more profitable, capital investment alternatives. The balancing of risk and return most often involves controlling individual account exposure.

[25]See Beranek and Scherr (1991; cited in the end-of-chapter references). Use of formulas to set credit lines was stimulated by the publication of "Credit Limits Established by Formula and Computer" by the Credit Research Foundation in 1970. See Wey (1983; cited in the end-of-chapter references) for arguments in favor of a formula-based model. Wey's model included nonfinancial, qualitative variables, applied to both wholesalers and manufacturers, and resulted in absolutely consistent risk classification and credit line recommendations.

CREDIT TERMS. Specification of when invoiced amounts are due and whether a cash discount can be taken for earlier payment are known as **credit terms.** The **credit period** is the time allowable for payment of the invoice amount. Determining whether a customer has adhered to the stated period is based on the seller's calculation of the actual payment period. Customer payment period usually starts with the invoice date, but in some industries the clock starts when the customer receives the goods. Sellers usually consider payment to have been made as of the date on which mailed payments are received at the assigned remittance address.[26] The length of the credit period varies by industry and according to product. Differences are linked to product characteristics as well as market structure and market condition; Exhibit 5-11 highlights some of the factors associated with observed credit terms. Credit terms are often set based on competitive conditions and are rarely challenged, being taken as "givens" to most sellers. Note, however, that sellers with large market shares or a "low price" market position have greater latitude to unilaterally change terms. Large customers may use market

EXHIBIT 5-11

Factors Affecting Credit Terms

FACTOR	INFLUENCE(S)
Market Share and Industry Structure	
Competition	1. Meet terms of competition. Less need to do so when the seller has a large market share or prices its output measurably lower than the competition 2. Offer longer terms in buyer's market
Product and Market Characteristics	
Operating cycle	Terms should match length of time for customer to process material, sell it, and collect funds from sale
Type of good	1. Raw material sold to manufacturers on shorter terms than intermediate or finished goods 2. Terms generally would not exceed sum of manufacturing time plus storage time
Perishability	1. Short shelf life is associated with rapid turnover and short selling terms 2. Canned goods and processed food products, with longer turnover period, have longer terms (can be stocked in larger quantities by the retailer)
Seasonality of demand	1. When demand is seasonal, longer terms are given during the off season, as compared with the active sales period 2. Supplier trades off financing costs related to these terms with the more even production this policy allows and the lower storage costs during the off-season
Consumer acceptance	More rapidly selling products accorded shorter terms because of rapid turnover
Cost and pricing	More expensive items, such as diamonds and jewelry, given 4 to 6-month terms; relatively inexpensive items, such as pharmaceuticals, have shorter terms
Customer type	Same product has different terms depending on whether customer is a retailer, wholesale jobber, or institutional buyer
Profitability	Higher profit margins allow for longer terms. Competition may force the seller to offer longer terms even though output prices are depressed, yielding negligible profits or even losses

SOURCE: Christie and Bracuti, pp. 386–388, cited in the chapter references.

[26]Almost 80 percent follow this procedure, according to survey findings in Ricci (1999; cited in end-of-chapter references).

power and low gross margins to unilaterally challenge and change the seller's terms to fit their preferences—lengthening the seller's credit period to the buyer's liking. Wal-Mart, K-Mart, and Sears have each pursued such a strategy in the 1990s.

Credit terms also include the **cash discount,** the percentage amount that can be subtracted from the invoice if the customer pays within the discount period. Terms of 1/10, net 30 allow a 1 percent cash discount for those paying within 10 days; otherwise, the face amount of the invoice is due in 30 days. Credit executives believe that payments on average are more prompt under 1/10, net 30 terms than under net 10 terms, which makes sense given the financial incentive to take the cash discount. Most companies do not allow customers to take unearned discounts, granting only a few days' grace beyond the stated discount period. That has not stopped many payors from trying, however! In that event, most companies also charge back the discount amount, whereas a minority return the customer's payment, indicating that it is an underpayment.

Do not confuse cash discounts with trade discounts. Companies will sometimes offer a trade discount, which is a price break given to customers for large quantity purchases, or simply because other suppliers offer these concessions. An example of the latter is the industry standard 8 percent trade discount that ladies' apparel makers offer to retailers, which amounts to a permanent price reduction—and illustrates how credit terms can substitute for price changes. Liz Claiborne, Inc., illustrates what happens when a company without sufficient market power attempts to unilaterally change the discount. Liz Claiborne increased the trade discount to 10 percent in 1990 in an attempt to gain competitive advantage but realized it was not generating sufficient additional sales to cover the 2 percent reduction in its gross margin and returned to the industry's 8 percent discount in late 1995. Trade discounts may be offered instead of or in addition to cash discounts.

In addition to giving an incentive to pay early, credit professionals must decide whether to use the "stick approach" for late payors. Past surveys have consistently found that many companies *do not* charge penalties for payments made beyond the credit period, even when the payment is 25 days late. Increasingly, however, interest charges are being made on late payments. US and UK surveys of credit executives indicate that most do not believe sales would increase much as a result of lengthening the credit period, and they seem to be more concerned about the affect of a change on the company's profits (perhaps because of changes in bad debt losses) than on sales. The most broad-based survey available, covering almost 400 retail, wholesale, service, and manufacturing businesses, found the following practices:

- Two-thirds of the companies offered credit but no cash discount; of these, most had net 10 (sometimes called "cash terms"), with the next most popular terms being net 30
- One-fourth of the companies offered credit terms with a cash discount; of these, 70 percent had 2/10, net 30 terms and 25 percent had 1/10, net 30 terms. The industry type had a major influence here; almost 80 percent of wholesalers offered their customers cash discounts, whereas only 36 percent of service firms offered cash discounts
- Utilization rates of offered cash discounts varied widely—one-fourth of the companies found that less than 20 percent of their customers took the cash discount, whereas another one-fourth of the companies found that more than 80 percent of their customers took the discount; 57 percent of the service firms stated that very few, if any, customers took the discount

- Four of five companies charged a service fee for late payments, usually 15 to 20 percent, and usually beginning with the net date; 30 percent of the companies both offered a cash discount and charged a service fee for late payment
- Almost one-half of firms surveyed indicated that they would offer special terms to assist in the promotion of new products[27]

Common credit terms of 2/10, net 30 allow the customer to pay $98 per $100 invoiced amount if the invoice is paid in 10 days. The main seller benefits include less short-term borrowing or more short-term investing as a result of the earlier receipt of cash and a possible increase in sales volume because the cash discount is equivalent to a price reduction. Should a seller offer a cash discount, and if so, how much? Analysis of the optimal cash discount has led to the following conclusions[28]:

1. The optimal cash discount depends on a product's variable cost—the lower a product's variable cost, the higher the feasible discount. There is some evidence that companies with lower gross margins are the most likely to reduce or eliminate their cash discount.
2. Logically, the cash discount offered should be based on the offering company's cost of funds; when the opportunity cost of funds changes, so should the cash discount.
3. Both the timing effect of the payments for discount takers and the effect for those not taking the discount must be considered when setting or changing the discount.
4. The size of the cash discount should be based on the product's price elasticity of demand or, in this context, how responsive sales are to changes in the cash discount.
5. The higher the rate of bad debt losses being experienced, the higher the optimal cash discount percentage.

Because the cost of *not* taking a cash discount is so high (see Chapter 7), it is surprising that customers do not automatically take the discount. Smith and Sell found that 51 percent of companies surveyed regarding their payment policies always take the cash discount, 40 percent sometimes take the discount, and the remaining 9 percent take the discounts even though they pay after the discount period. Credit executives would benefit from a more careful evaluation of their cash discounts. When evaluating the alleged sales-increasing effects of the cash discount, Frantz and Viscione[29] estimated that four of five firms would be more profitable if they eliminated their cash discounts. Other studies also found some practices that are inconsistent with profit or shareholder wealth maximization, noting that companies generally respond as follows:

- Change the cash discount if competitors do but do not change the cash discount when inflation, interest rates, or economic conditions change (contrary to 1, 2, and 5, listed previously)
- When having higher contribution margins, are not more prone to respond to competitive changes in discounts, but they should respond
- Do not think a 2-percent cash discount is equivalent to a 2-percent price cut, with the latter thought to have a greater impact on sales

---

[27]Hill, Wood, and Sorenson (cited in the end-of-chapter references).

[28]For more on cash discounts, see the Hill and Riener citation in the end-of-chapter references.

[29]"What Should You Do about Cash Discounts" (cited in the end-of-chapter references).

- When having relatively high levels of receivables on their books, are not more likely to assess a penalty fee for late payment, but such should be the case
- When having relatively high levels of receivables, should reevaluate credit policies more often, but in actuality there is no apparent relationship between the level of receivables and the frequency or recency of reevaluation

The most recent study addressing cash discounts finds a theoretical basis for observed practices. An empirical study by Ng, Smith, and Smith (1999) finds that cash discounts elicit information about buyer credit quality, in that not taking the discount signals higher risk of customer non-payment; terms are shorter when the buyer should be able to sell the merchandise quickly; terms are longer for international customers (who would need longer to inspect the goods and to arrange payment); and the discount is higher when product value is fast-changing (because of uncertain demand and resulting in doubtful collateral value).

Our survey of credit management and its relationship to value maximization is now complete. We turn now to two contemporary topics of great importance to the successful execution of credit strategy: the interface with collections and electronic data interchange (EDI), and the use of expert systems.

RECEIVABLES, COLLECTIONS, AND ELECTRONIC DATA INTERCHANGE

The usual distinction between receivables management and the cash collection function is blurring. Credit managers must take part in the structuring of sales terms to take advantage of the advances in EDI. When negotiating price, other factors such as credit terms, purchase volume, gross profit margins, and risk are intertwined. Furthermore, if credit approval is delayed, buyers using EDI purchase orders and just-in-time manufacturing can encounter serious problems. Companies are now able to ship products within 2 hours of receiving an order, and the seller must be able to handle electronically transmitted orders. Preferably, it can also issue electronic invoices, and be paid electronically, using a bank that is "EDI-capable" (can capture and report remittance detail as well as send and receive electronic payments) so that remittance information that can be automatically read by the seller's accounts receivable system may be bundled with the electronic Automated Clearing House (ACH) or wire payment.

One of the trends in receivables management is the use of data transmission to automate the cash application process. The lockbox bank or other lockbox provider captures the MICR line information on each customer's check. Other remittance information that the seller needs for posting payments to its receivables system is entered manually by the lockbox provider, and then an electronic data file is sent to the seller's computer by the provider. The posting of payments occurs in the evening; in the morning the seller's receivables staff deals with the exception items first by manually applying the items. Because the MICR information received from the bank uniquely identifies the payor, much of the receivables updating can take place automatically. The "hit rate," reflecting the items that automatically apply, may be as high as 95 percent when the seller modifies its billing system, enhances receivables software, and designs highly tailored data capture procedures with its bank or third-party lockbox provider. Ricci (1999) finds that a majority (55 percent) of surveyed Business Week Global 1000 companies did not yet have any of their receivables processes automated.

When its customers are not EDI/electronic funds transfer (EFT) capable, the seller may set up an ACH debit program. With the paying company's consent, the collecting company instructs its bank to collect funds from the paying company's bank, much like a check remittance. The seller (and to some extent, the buyer) avails itself of lower costs, improved cash flows, and certainty of payment. The reduction in lost checks and costs savings in accounts payable processing are advantages to the buyer.

The Internet is increasingly being used for all aspects of receivables management, including accessing applicant company data and D & B information.

SUMMARY

Investments in accounts receivable, particularly for manufacturing companies, represent a significant part of short-term financial management. This chapter offers the background concepts necessary for a proper understanding of a company's accounts receivable management. The key aspects of credit policy, credit standards, the credit-granting sequence, credit limits, and credit terms were detailed. We noted the key sources of information, particularly for corporate credit evaluation. The major tools now being used by businesses to analyze the risk of customer nonpayment—credit scoring, financial ratio analysis, and expert systems—also were profiled. Used in concert, these tools give the analyst clues regarding whether it is necessary to conduct risk analysis of credit extension and credit limit decisions, and if so, how much of a risk adjustment to make.

To recap, much of what we see practiced by credit managers is linked to what competitors are doing, and at times this conflicts with profitability or shareholder value maximization. Information can clearly offer a competitive advantage to the credit-granting firm. Greater use of credit scoring and expert system methods offer the potential to improve information processing efficiency and accuracy for the credit manager. Proper incorporation of the time value of money and proper use of net present-value techniques can ensure that cost, revenue, and payment likelihood estimates be used correctly to enhance shareholder value in credit-granting decisions.

In the next chapter, we look at an NPV decision-making model that might be used to improve decisions regarding the seller's overall credit policy. That chapter also discusses receivables monitoring and collection and benchmarks for credit performance evaluation.

Useful Web Sites

Center for Research in Electronic Commerce: http://cism.bus.utexas.edu/
Credit Research Foundation: www.crfonline.org
Dun & Bradstreet: www.dnb.com
ecredit.com: www.ecredit.com
eCFO: www.ecfonet.com
National Association of Credit Management: www.nacm.org
National Association of Credit Management: http://www.nacm.org/bcmag/bcmag-index.html
National Association of Credit Management: www.nacm.org/education/certification/certification html
National Association of Credit Management: http://www.nacm.org/usefulsites.shtml

Questions

1. What are the major arguments made by credit and marketing professionals for the extension of trade credit?
2. Is trade credit "free"? Explain.
3. List and explain the four major motives financial theorists have attributed to the extension of trade credit.

4. Regarding cash application:
   a. What is it?
   b. Why should a supplier ensure that cash application is rapid as well as accurate?
   c. Does rapid cash application on a given credit sale shorten the days' sales outstanding for that sale?
5. How do credit managers set credit limits for customers?
6. Why do you think character is considered to be the most important of the "five Cs"? How might it be assessed?
7. Summarize the major items offered on a D&B Business Information Report, indicating which one(s) you think is(are) most important for evaluating a new credit applicant.
8. Bank executives consider liquidity and debt ratios to be most important when evaluating a loan applicant. What ratios are they referring to, and why are these so important in bank credit and trade credit decisions?
9. What are credit scoring models? Why do companies that sell to a large number of customers use them?
10. A finance company that lends to "high risk" automobile buyers, finds the following variables important in classifying default probabilities: time at present residence, prior bankruptcy filing (yes or no), time in present job, monthly income, phone in name (yes or no), prior repossession of item purchased on credit (yes or no), and type of residence (e.g, apartment, rent house, own house). Listing each variable, suggest whether each variable increases ($+$) or decreases ($-$) anticipated default risk, and how you would evaluate the type of residence in assigning creditworthiness to applicants.
11. Summarize the survey findings regarding credit terms and cash discounts.
12. Why are credit departments in banks and major corporations implementing expert systems? In your answer, indicate what advantages and disadvantages companies that implement such systems might anticipate.

Problems

1. Associated Wet Goods, Inc., has derived the following consumer credit scoring model after years of data collecting and model testing:

$$Y = (0.25 \times EMPLOYMT) + (0.4 \times HOMEOWNER) + (0.3 \times CARDS)$$

In which: EMPLOYMT = 1 if employed full-time, 0.5 if employed part-time, and 0 if unemployed
   HOMEOWNER = 1 if homeowner, 0 otherwise
   CARDS = 1 if presently has 1 to 5 credit cards, 0 otherwise

Associated determines that a score of at least 0.65 indicates a very good credit risk, and it extends credit to these individuals.
   a. If Janice is employed part-time, is a homeowner, and has six credit cards at present, does the model indicate she should receive credit?
   b. Janice just got a full-time job. Should she be granted credit?
   c. Your boss mentions that he just returned from a trade association conference at which one of the speakers recommended that length of time at present residence (regardless of homeownership status) be included in credit scoring models. If the weight turns out to be 0.25, how do you think the variable would be coded (i.e., 0 stands for what, 1 stands for what, etc.)?

    d. Suggest other variables that Associated might have left out of the model, and explain how you would code them (i.e., 0, 1, 2 are assigned to what conditions?).

2. Refer back to Exhibit 5-9 to answer this question. A business credit applicant has the following profile:

Credit History	Minor delinquencies
Unused Credit	40 percent available
Credit History of Business	Satisfactory
Industry Type	C
Available Liquid Assets of Business	$11,500
Net Worth of Principal	$55,000

    If the cutoff score for extending credit is a score of at least 100 points, should this applicant receive credit?

3. Below is a modified cash flow timeline that includes "invoicing float," the credit period, and "collection float" on mailed payments. Use the following numbers to answer a through c below. Assume that the goods sold are already in inventory before the placement of the order.

Order & Invoice Preparation:	
Order entry and shipping	5 days
Invoice preparation & sending ("invoicing float")	3 days
Credit Period:	
Credit terms	30 days
Added delay (related to customer's payables policy)	2 days
Payment preparation	1 day
Payment Collection and Application:	
Mail, processing, availability delays ("collection float")	6 days
Cash application	0 days
Total delay from purchase communication to cash application:	___ days

    a. Noting that the total delay represents cash tied up from the seller's perspective, calculate the total delay from purchase communication to cash application.

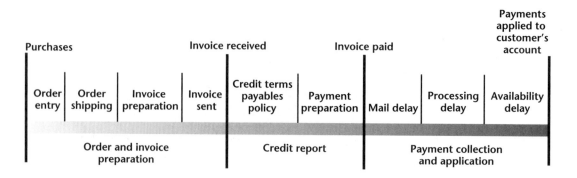

SOURCE: Copyright 1997 by the Treasury Management Association. All rights reserved. Used with permission of the Treasury Management Association.

    b. Why should the seller be concerned about the order and invoice preparation delays?

    c. What fraction of the total delay in your answer to part a is made up of the credit terms? Based on your answer, comment on the importance of managing all parts of the cash flow timeline.

4. A new credit applicant has assured you that he is creditworthy, pointing to 150% more cash on the balance sheet for the current year. Following are a balance sheet, income statement, and statement of cash flows for the customer's firm. Use this information to calculate the ratios provided in Exhibit 5-8. Using both balance sheets, calculate ratio values for both years for ratios consisting of both a balance sheet numerator and denominator. Comment on the trend of each of the balance sheet ratios. When necessary, assume the statement of cash-flow data will be the same in the coming year as it was in the sample year.

    a. Do all of the ratios support the customer's claim? Explain.

    b. Would you characterize the customer as more or less creditworthy in the current year, based on the trend of the majority of ratios calculated?

SAMPLE YEAR-END INCOME STATEMENT

Revenues	$16,000,000
Less: cost of goods sold	$9,200,000
Gross profit	$6,800,000
Less: operating expenses	$4,000,000
Less: depreciation	$200,000
Operating profit	$2,600,000
Less: interest expense	$300,000
Net profit before taxes	$2,300,000
Less: provision for income taxes	$450,000
Net income	$1,850,000
Earnings available for common shareholders	$1,850,000
Less: common stock dividends paid	$250,000
Addition to retained earnings	$1,600,000
Earnings per share (200,000 shares outstanding)	$8

SAMPLE BALANCE SHEETS
(CURRENT AND PRIOR YEAR)

ASSETS

	Current Year	Prior Year	Change
Cash	$2,500,000	$1,000,000	$1,500,000
Short-term investments	$1,300,000	$1,500,000	($200,000)
Accounts receivable	$1,700,000	$1,300,000	$400,000
Inventory	$2,600,000	$2,100,000	$500,000
Prepaid expenses	$900,000	$900,000	$0
Total current assets	$9,000,000	$6,800,000	$2,200,000
Property, plant, & equipment	$7,500,000	$6,800,000	$700,000
Total assets	**$16,500,000**	**$13,600,000**	**$2,900,000**

LIABILITIES AND OWNERS' EQUITY

	Current Year	Prior Year	Change
Accounts Payable	$1,600,000	$1,200,000	$400,000
Short-Term Notes Payable	$1,800,000	$1,300,000	$500,000
Total Current Liabilities	$3,400,000	$2,500,000	$900,000
Long-Term Debt	$3,900,000	$3,500,000	$400,000
Total Liabilities	$7,300,000	$6,000,000	$1,300,000
Common Stock at Par Value	$200,000	$200,000	$0
Paid-In Capital	$3,600,000	$3,600,000	$0
Retained Earnings	$5,400,000	$3,800,000	$1,600,000
Total Liabilities & Equity	**$16,500,000**	**$13,600,000**	**$2,900,000**

SAMPLE STATEMENT OF CASH FLOWS

Cash Flows from Operating Activities		
Net Income		$1,850,000
Adjustments to Reconcile Net Income to Net Cash		
Depreciation	$200,000	
Increase in Accounts Receivable	($400,000)	
Increase in Inventories	($500,000)	
Increase in Accounts Payables	$400,000	($300,000)
Net Cash Provided (Used) by Operating Activities		$1,550,000
Cash Flows from Investing Activities		
Capital Expenditures	($900,000)	
Decrease in Short-Term Investments	$200,000	
Net Cash Provided (Used) in Investing Activities		($700,000)
Cash Flows from Financing Activities		
Net Borrowing (Bank Line of Credit Agreement)	$500,000	
Proceeds from Issuance of Long-Term Debt	$400,000	
Dividends Paid	($250,000)	
Net Cash Provided (Used) by Financing Activities		$650,000
Net Increase (Decrease) in Cash		
Cash–Beginning of Year		$1,000,000
Cash–End of Year		$2,500,000
Net Cash Increase (Decrease)		$1,500,000

5. Karen Short wishes to apply NPV analysis to a newly received order. The company's credit terms are net 45 days. Its opportunity cost of funds is 12 percent. The order dollar amount is $30,000. She finds out from the cost accounting department that variable costs are approximately 65 percent of sales and that incremental credit administration and collection expenses approach 1 percent of sales.

    a. Assuming with perfect certainty that the customer will pay according to the credit terms, should Karen approve the order?

    b. Assume that further research indicates that payment probabilities and timing for accounts similar to the credit applicant are as follows:

PAYMENT TIMING	PROBABILITY
Within 45 days	0.50
45–60 days	0.30
60–90 days	0.15
More than 90 days	0.05

Assume that payments are received evenly within the above time brackets. The company's experience is that payment received after 90 days is obtained only after referral to a collection agency. The agency charges 30 percent of the dollar amount of the invoice. It collects, on average, 65 percent of the invoice amount, about 1 month after referral. Before the agency referral at day 90, and after the 45 days, the company incurs an additional $125 collection cost every 15 days. Based on the expected NPV of the revised situation, should Karen recommend credit extension?

References

Margereta Asselbergh. 1999. Factoring accounts receivable management: An integrated approach. Presented at the annual meeting of the Financial Management Association, Orlando, FL.

Moshe Ben-Horim and Haim Levy. 1983. Management of accounts receivable under inflation. *Financial Management* Spring:42–48.

William Beranek and Frederick C. Scherr. 1991. On the significance of trade credit limits. *Financial Practice and Education* Fall/Winter:39–44.

Scott Besley and Jerome S. Osteryoung. 1984. Accounts receivable management: The development of a general credit-granting algorithm for determining credit limits under funds constraints. Presented at the annual meeting of the Financial Management Association, Atlanta, GA.

Scott Besley and Jerome S. Osteryoung. 1985. Survey of current practices in establishing trade-credit limits. *The Financial Review* February:70–82.

Keith Bradshaw. 1999. Why higher interest rates haven't fazed automakers. *New York Times,* October 10, section 3, p 5.

George N. Christie and Albert E. Bracuti. 1986. *Credit executives handbook.* Lake Success, NY: Credit Research Foundation.

J. Chua. *A trade credit decision model with order size dependent credit risks.* Calgary: University of Calgary Working Paper.

Thomas E. Copeland and Nabil Khoury. 1981. A theory of credit extensions with default risk and systematic risk. *The Engineering Economist* 1(26):35–51.

Gregory E. Elliehausen and John D. Wolken. 1993. The demand for trade credit: An investigation of motives for trade credit use by small businesses. Washington, DC: Staff Studies 65, Board of Governors of the Federal Reserve System.

Gary W. Emery. 1984. A pure financial explanation for trade credit. *Journal of Financial and Quantitative Analysis* September:271–287.

Gary W. Emery. 1988. Positive theories of trade credit. In: Yong Kim (ed): *Advances in Working Capital Management*, vol. 1. Greenwich, CT: JAI Press, pp 115–130.

Gary W. Emery and N. Nayar. *Product quality and payment policy.* University of Oklahoma Working Paper.

Murray Frank and Vojislav Maksimovic. 1998. Trade credit, collateral, and adverse selection. University of British Columbia Working Paper.

F. Frantz and J.A. Viscione. 1976. What should you do about cash discounts. *Credit & Financial Management* May:30–36.

Seymour Friedland. 1966. *Economics of corporate finance.* Englewood Cliffs, NJ: Prentice-Hall.

Ned C. Hill and Kenneth D. Riener. 1979. Determining the cash discount in the firm's credit policy. *Financial Management* Spring:68–73.

Ned C. Hill, William L. Sartoris, and Daniel Ferguson. 1984. Corporate credit and payables policies. *Journal of Cash Management* July/August:56–63.

Yong H. Kim and Joseph C. Atkins. 1978. Evaluating investments in accounts receivable: A wealth maximizing framework. *Journal of Finance* May:403–412.

Joshua Levant and Ashwinpaul Sondhi. 1986. Finance subsidiaries: Their formation and consolidation. *Journal of Business Finance and Accounting* Spring:137–148.

Wilbur G. Lewellen, John J. McDonnell, and Jonathan A. Scott. 1980. Capital market influences on trade credit policies. *Journal of Financial Research* Fall:105–113.

Michael S. Long, Ileen B. Malitz, and S. Abraham Ravid. 1993. Trade credit, credit guarantees, and product marketability. *Financial Management* Winter:117–127.

Ileen Malitz. 1989. A re-examination of the wealth expropriation hypothesis: The case of captive finance subsidiaries. *Journal of Finance* September:1039–1047.

Dileep Mehta. 1968. The formulation of credit policy models. *Management Science* October:B30–B50.

Shehzad L. Mian and Clifford W. Smith, Jr. 1992. Accounts receivable management policy: Theory and evidence. *Journal of Finance* March:169–200.

Shehzad L. Mian and Clifford W. Smith, Jr. 1994. Extending Trade Credit and Financing Receivables. *Journal of Applied Corporate Finance* Spring:75–84.

Chee K. Ng, Janet Kiholm Smith, and Richard L. Smith. 1999. Evidence on the determinants of credit terms used in interfirm trade. *Journal of Finance* June:1109–1129.

Ehsan Nikbakht and Mohammed H.A. Tafti. 1989. Application of expert systems in evaluation of credit card borrowers. *Journal of Managerial Finance* 15:19–27.

William A. Ogden, Jr. and Srinivasan Sundaram. 1995. A spreadsheet solution for the optimal credit investigation/granting sequential decision. *The Credit and Financial Management Review* 1(1):14–17.

Mitchell A. Petersen and Raghuram G. Rajan. 1997. Trade credit: Theories and evidence. *Review of Financial Studies* 10:661–691.

Alan K. Reichert, Chien-Ching Cho, and George M. Wagner. 1981. *An examination of the conceptual issues involved in developing credit scoring models in the consumer lending field.* Federal Reserve Bank of Chicago Staff Memoranda, pp 81–83.

Cecilia Wagner Ricci. 1999. Receivables practices in American corporations. *Business Credit* April:32–35.

Gordon S. Roberts and Jerry A. Viscione. 1981. Captive finance subsidiaries: The manager's view. *Financial Management* Spring:36–42.

Frederick C. Scherr. 1992. Credit-granting decisions under risk. *Engineering Economist* Spring:245–262.

Frederick C. Scherr. 1996. Optimal trade credit limits. *Financial Management* Spring:71–85.

R. Schwartz. 1974. An economic model of trade credit. *Journal of Financial and Quantitative Analysis* September:643–657.

Arjit Sen. 1998. Seller financing of consumer durables. *Journal of Economics and Management Strategy* Fall:435–460.

Janet Kiholm Smith. 1987. Trade credit and informational asymmetry. *Journal of Finance* September:863–872.

Janet Kiholm Smith and Christjahn Schnucker. 1994. An empirical examination of organizational structure: The economics of the factoring decision. *Journal of Corporate Finance* March:119–138.

Keith V. Smith and Brian Belt. 1989. *Working capital management in practice: An update.* West Lafayette, IN: Purdue University, Krannert School of Management Working Paper 951, March.

Keith V. Smith and Shirley Blake Sell. Working capital management in practice. In: Keith V. Smith (ed): *Readings on the Management of Working Capital,* 2d ed. St. Paul, MN: West Publishing, pp 51–84.

Venkat Srinivasan and Yong H. Kim. 1987. Credit granting: A comparative analysis of classification procedures. *Journal of Finance* July:665–681.

———. 1988. Designing expert financial systems: A case study of corporate credit management. *Financial Management* Autumn:33–43.

John Stowe. 1985. An integer programming solution for the optimal credit investigation/credit granting sequence. *Financial Management* Summer:66–76.

James Vander Weide and Steven F. Maier. 1985. *Managing corporate liquidity: An introduction to working capital management.* New York: John Wiley & Sons.

Frank W. Wey. 1983. Establishing credit lines by formula. *Credit & Financial Management* May:24, 26.

John Winginton. 1980. A note on the comparison of logit and discriminant models of consumer credit behavior. *Journal of Financial and Quantitative Analysis* September:757–771.

F. Christian Zinkhan. 1990. A new approach for jointly evaluating the 'Six Cs' of loan analysis. *Akron Business and Economic Review* Spring:8–17.

FOCUSED CASE
Y. Guess Jeans

(Note: You may wish to consult the end-of-book Glossary and parts of Chapter 16 if you are unfamiliar with the bank lending terms that are included in this case.)

You are the credit analyst for Y. Guess Jeans. One of your major retail accounts, County Seat, has just asked for a credit limit increase of 20 percent. You presently are one of County Seat's largest suppliers of jeans and casual tops. At present, County Seat buys $2.5 million of merchandise per month from you.

Below are the financials that County Seat provides. Before you reach for the D&B report or check their payment history, you want to arrive at an independent appraisal based strictly on their financial ratios, financial statements, and supplemental information. Should the credit limit increase be approved? Provide guidance to the credit manager, indicating which indicators or financial ratios you see as most important in supporting your recommendation.

SUBMISSION TYPE:	10-Q www.sec.edgar.com
PERIOD OF REPORT:	19960803
FILED AS OF DATE:	1996/09/17
COMPANY DATA:	
COMPANY NAME:	COUNTY SEAT, INC
STANDARD INDUSTRIAL CLASSIFICATION:	RETAIL-DEPARTMENT STORES [5311]
FISCAL YEAR END:	01/29
FORM TYPE:	10-Q

As of September 17, 1996, 3,327,042 shares of Common Stock were outstanding.

Consolidated Financial Statements
COUNTY SEAT, INC. AND SUBSIDIARY
CONSOLIDATED BALANCE SHEETS
(Amounts in Thousands, Except Share Amounts)
(Unaudited)

	August 3, 1996	July 29, 1995	Memo: February 3, 1996
ASSETS			
Current Assets:			
Cash and cash equivalents	$10,603	$8,125	$8,166
Receivables	1,486	2,778	2,658
Merchandise inventories	132,580	143,474	110,744
Prepaid expenses	10,985	11,371	11,339
Deferred tax benefit	2,930	12,006	989
Total current assets	158,584	177,754	133,896
Property and equipment, at cost	119,425	117,466	120,277
Less—Accumulated depreciation and amortization	(65,943)	(52,128)	(61,674)
Property and equipment, net	53,482	65,338	58,603
Other Assets, net:			
Debt issuance costs	3,816	3,408	3,073
Deferred income taxes	2,111	6,455	2,486
Excess of purchase price over net assets acquired		75,215	
Other	814	1,408	1,303
Total other assets, net	6,741	86,486	6,862
Total assets	$218,807	$329,578	$199,361

(continued)

Consolidated Financial Statements—cont.
COUNTY SEAT, INC. AND SUBSIDIARY
CONSOLIDATED BALANCE SHEETS
(Amounts in Thousands, Except Share Amounts)
(Unaudited)

	August 3, 1996	July 29, 1995	Memo: February 3, 1996
LIABILITIES AND SHAREHOLDERS' EQUITY (DEFICIT)			
Current Liabilities:			
Borrowings under credit agreement	$ 81,800	$ 43,700	$ 27,000
Current maturities of long-term debt	26	29	25
Accounts payable	47,397	65,472	36,754
Accrued expenses	22,477	19,489	20,526
Accrued income taxes	1,348	1,962	1,111
Total current liabilities	153,048	130,652	85,416
Long-term debt	122,640	152,099	147,365
Other long-term liabilities	11,966	11,752	12,044
Commitments and contingencies			
Minority interest-redeemable preferred stock of Stores	48,521	40,389	44,319
Redeemable preferred stock of CSI	64,210	53,637	58,628
Shareholders' Equity (Deficit):			
Preferred stock: par value $.01 per share; 5,000,000 shares authorized; no shares issued and outstanding			
Common stock: par value $.01 per share; 50,000,000 shares authorized; 3,327,042, 3,327,042 and 3,327,042 shares issued and outstanding, respectively	33	33	33
Paid-in capital	22,193	22,193	22,193
Warrants	2,600	2,600	2,600
Common stock notes receivable	(5,139)	(4,973)	(4,982)
Accumulated deficit	(201,265)	(78,804)	(168,255)
Total shareholders' equity (deficit)	(181,578)	(58,951)	(148,411)
Total liabilities and equity	$218,807	$329,578	$199,361

COUNTY SEAT, INC. AND SUBSIDIARY
CONSOLIDATED STATEMENTS OF OPERATION
(Amounts in Thousands, Except Share Amounts)
(Unaudited)

	13 Weeks Ended		26 Weeks Ended	
	August 3, 1996	July 29, 1995	August 3, 1996	July 29, 1995
Net sales	$ 121,727	$ 130,110	$ 243,331	$ 254,299
Cost of sales, including buying and occupancy	90,283	95,123	185,812	190,061
Gross profit	31,444	34,987	57,519	64,238
Selling, general and administrative expenses	33,668	32,189	64,990	62,094
Depreciation and amortization	2,956	3,531	5,915	6,787
Loss from operations	(5,180)	(733)	(13,386)	(4,643)
Interest expense, net	5,742	5,865	11,098	11,638
Minority interest-dividends and accretion of redeemable preferred stock of Stores	2,143	3,022	4,202	4,715
Loss before income taxes and extraordinary items	(13,065)	(9,620)	(28,686)	(20,996)
Income taxes	4,095	(2,661)	(1,258)	(6,941)
Loss before extraordinary items	(17,160)	(6,959)	(27,428)	(14,055)
Extraordinary items, net of income tax benefit		9,997		9,997
Net Loss	(17,160)	(16,956)	(27,428)	(24,052)
Redeemable preferred stock dividends and accretion	(2,950)	(2,869)	(5,582)	(5,045)

COUNTY SEAT, INC. AND SUBSIDIARY—cont.
CONSOLIDATED STATEMENTS OF OPERATION
(Amounts in Thousands, Except Share Amounts)
(Unaudited)

	13 Weeks Ended		26 Weeks Ended	
	August 3, 1996	July 29, 1995	August 3, 1996	July 29, 1995
Net loss applicable to common shares	$ (20,110)	$ (19,825)	$ (33,010)	$ (29,097)
Per common share:				
Loss before extraordinary items	$ (6.04)	$ (2.95)	$ (9.92)	$ (5.74)
Extraordinary items		(3.01)		(3.01)
Net loss per common share	$ (6.04)	$ (5.96)	$ (9.92)	$ (8.75)
Weighted average shares outstanding	3,327,042	3,326,874	3,327,042	3,326,705

COUNTY SEAT, INC. AND SUBSIDIARY
CONSOLIDATED STATEMENTS OF CASH FLOWS
(Amounts in Thousands)
(Unaudited)

	26 Weeks Ended	
	August 3, 1996	July 29, 1995
Cash Flows from Operating Activities:		
Net loss	$(27,428)	$(24,052)
Adjustments to reconcile net loss to net cash used for operating activities:		
Extraordinary items		9,997
Depreciation and amortization	5,915	6,787
Amortization of debt issuance costs and discount	780	1,201
Minority interest-dividends and accretion of redeemable preferred stock of Stores	4,202	4,715
Rent expense in excess of cash outlays, net	53	189
Deferred tax benefit	(1,258)	(5,590)
Changes in operating assets and liabilities:		
Receivables	625	2,371
Merchandise inventories	(21,836)	(47,203)
Prepaid expenses	313	(1,236)
Accounts payable	11,211	25,358
Accrued expenses	2,746	(4,047)
Accrued income taxes	(70)	(1,865)
Other non-current assets and liabilities	15	(971)
Net cash used for operating activities	(24,732)	(34,346)
Cash Flows from Financing Activities:		
Borrowings under the Credit Agreement, net	29,800	73,700
Issuance of long-term debt		104,943
Debt and equity issuance costs and prepayment premiums	(1,257)	(6,781)
Principal payments on long-term debt and capital leases	(12)	(20)
Repayment of long-term debt		(150,795)
Issuance of common stock		104
Repayment of common stock notes receivable		160
Net cash provided by financing activities	28,531	21,311
Cash Flows from Investing Activities:		
Capital expenditures	(1,365)	(9,313)
Proceeds from disposal of property and equipment	3	14
Net cash used for investing activities	(1,362)	(9,299)
Net Increase (Decrease) in Cash and Cash Equivalents	2,437	(22,334)
Cash and Cash Equivalents:		
Beginning of period	8,166	30,459
End of period	$10,603	$ 8,125
Cash Paid During the Period For:		
Interest	$ 9,982	$ 13,570
Income taxes	$ 70	$ 514

ORGANIZATION AND NATURE OF BUSINESS

The accompanying interim consolidated financial statements represent those of County Seat, Inc. ("CSI") and its wholly-owned subsidiary, County Seat Stores, Inc. ("Stores") (together, "the Company" or "County Seat"). The activities of CSI consist principally of its investment in Stores.

The Company is the nation's largest specialty retailer selling both brand name and private-label jeans and jeanswear. The Company operated 740 stores in 48 states as of August 3, 1996. The Company's 681 County Seat stores, located almost exclusively in regional shopping malls, offer one-stop shopping for daily casual wear featuring a contemporary jeanswear look. The Company's wide selection of designer brands, including Girbaud, Guess?, Calvin Klein, Tommy Hilfiger, and popular national brands such as Levi's as well as its proprietary brands, County Seat, Nuovo and Ten Star makes County Seat a destination store for jeans. The Company operates 34 County Seat Outlet stores offering discount pricing on special purchase and clearance merchandise and 21 Levi's Outlet stores under license from Levi Strauss & Co. offering a full range of Levi's and Docker's off-price merchandise for both adults and children. The Company also operates four The Old Farmer's Almanac General Stores, a new retail concept selling products associated with American country living, under license from Yankee Publishing, Inc., the publisher of The Old Farmer's Almanac.

Credit Agreement

The Credit Agreement is funded through a syndicate of commercial lenders providing a senior secured reducing revolving credit facility to fund seasonal working capital requirements and the May 1995 redemption in full of all of the Company's then outstanding senior notes.

The Credit Agreement and the indenture for Stores' 12 percent Senior Subordinated Notes (the "Indenture") contain certain covenants which, among other things, limit the amount of debt of the Company, restrict the payment of interest on CSI's 9 percent Exchange Debentures, restrict the payment of cash dividends on Stores' Series A senior exchangeable preferred stock and the CSI Series A junior exchangeable preferred stock, limit expenditures for

property, equipment and rent under operating leases and require the Company to maintain certain financial ratios. The most restrictive financial covenants at August 3, 1996 for the Company included, as defined, a minimum current ratio (1.10 to 1.0); minimum interest coverage ratio (.90 to 1.0); minimum adjusted net worth, as defined ($30,000,000 including redeemable preferred stock); minimum EBITDA, as defined ($24,800,000) and minimum fixed charge coverage ratio (1.15 to 1.0). The Credit Agreement limits the level of capital expenditures to $4,000,000, $3,600,000, $5,000,000 and $5,000,000 in fiscal 1996, 1997, 1998 and 1999, respectively. The permitted capital expenditures will be increased if the Company generates defined excess cash flow levels.

Effective February 3, 1996, the Company amended the Credit Agreement to provide an increased borrowing commitment, secure borrowings with all assets of the Company, make certain financial covenants less restrictive and further limit capital expenditures. The Company incurred fees and expenses of approximately $1,300,000 in the first quarter of fiscal 1996 related to the amendment to the Credit Agreement, which will be amortized over its remaining term.

The Company has obtained an amendment effective August 3, 1996 and a discretionary waiver effective August 31, 1996 with respect to trailing 12-month EBITDA requirements under the Credit Agreement. The waiver will expire September 24, 1996, unless extended, and is revocable at the election of the requisite banks under the Credit Agreement. In the absence of a current amendment, it will likely be necessary for the Company to obtain amendments or waivers of covenants with respect to the remaining quarters of fiscal 1996 and thereafter. The Company is in the process of meeting with the members of its bank group to discuss additional changes to the Credit Agreement to modify its financial covenants and other terms. A semi-annual interest payment on the Company's 12 percent Senior Subordinated Notes is due October 1, 1996. In the absence of an amendment or extension of the waiver, the requisite banks will be permitted to prevent such payment. Failure to make such payment, whether or not prevented by the banks, will constitute a default under the Indenture after the 30-day grace period provided in the Indenture has expired. The Company has initiated discussions with certain holders of the 12 percent Senior Subordinated Notes with respect to a possible financial restructuring and is evaluating such other financial alternatives as may be necessary. In addition, if an appropriate amendment or waiver is not obtained, Stores will not be permitted to advance funds to permit CSI to make the interest payment due November 30, 1996, on CSI's 9 percent Exchange Debentures. No assurance can be given that satisfactory amendments, modifications or waivers to the terms of the Credit Agreement or the 12% Senior Subordinated Notes can be negotiated.

The commitment under the Credit Agreement provides for borrowings up to $135,000,000 including a $50,000,000 letter of credit facility. Availability under the Credit Agreement is limited to the lesser of certain percentages of eligible inventory or $135,000,000 through December 31, 1996. The commitment under the Credit Agreement will reduce to $125,000,000 on December 31, 1996. In addition, the commitment will be reduced if the Company generates defined excess cash-flow levels. The Credit Agreement matures on December 31, 1999. Availability is reduced by any amounts drawn under the facility as well as outstanding letters of credit. The Credit Agreement also requires that for a period of 30 consecutive days after each December 15 and before each February 15 of the following year, the Company must not have any aggregate borrowings (including Bankers Acceptances)

outstanding under the Credit Agreement, less cash on deposit, in excess of $50,000,000. The permitted aggregated borrowings during this 30-day period will be reduced if the Company generates defined excess cash flow levels. Borrowings under the facility are secured by the assets of Stores and guaranteed by CSI. CSI's guarantee is secured by a pledge of its primary asset, the outstanding common stock of Stores.

In connection with the amendment effective August 3, 1996, the interest rate on borrowings under the Credit Agreement has been increased by 0.5 percent. At the option of the Company, interest is payable on borrowings under the Credit Agreement at a prime rate plus 2.0 percent or a Eurodollar rate plus 3.0 percent. The Credit Agreement provides for a commitment fee during the period prior to maturity of 0.5 percent of the unutilized commitment under the Credit Agreement. Because of the revocable nature of the current waiver, all loans under the Credit Agreement were classified as a current liability as of August 3, 1996. Borrowings of $30,000,000 and $25,000,000 under the Credit Agreement were classified as long-term debt as of July 29, 1995 and February 3, 1996, respectively.

Loans, borrowing base, and letter of credit commitments under the Credit Agreement were as follows (dollars in thousands):

	26 Weeks Ended August 3 1996
At Period-End:	
Loans outstanding	$81,800
Borrowing base	$132,721
Available borrowing base	$10,078
Letter of credit commitments outstanding	$22,201
During the Period:	
Days loans were outstanding	182
Maximum loan borrowing	$91,000
Average loan borrowing	$66,490
Weighted average interest rate	8.22%

MANAGEMENT'S DISCUSSION AND ANALYSIS OF FINANCIAL CONDITION AND RESULTS OF OPERATIONS

Results of Operations

The following table sets forth the Company's operating results as a percentage of net sales for the periods indicated:

	13 Weeks Ended		26 Weeks Ended	
	August 3, 1996	July 29, 1995	August 3, 1996	July 29, 1995
Statement of Operations Data:				
Net sales	100.0%	100.0%	100.0%	100.0%
Cost of sales, including buying and occupancy	74.2	73.1	76.4	74.7
Gross profit	25.8	26.9	23.6	25.3
Selling, general and administrative expenses	27.7	24.7	26.7	24.4
Depreciation and amortization	2.4	2.8	2.4	2.7
Loss from operations	(4.3)	(0.6)	(5.5)	(1.8)
Interest expense, net	4.7	4.5	4.6	4.6
Minority interest-dividends and accretion of redeemable preferred stock of Stores	1.7	2.3	1.7	1.9
Loss before income taxes and extraordinary items	(10.7)	(7.4)	(11.8)	(8.3)
Income taxes	3.4	(2.1)	(0.5)	(2.7)
Loss before extraordinary items	(14.1)	(5.3)	(11.3)	(5.6)
Extraordinary items		7.7		3.9
Net Loss	(14.1)%	(13.0)%	(11.3)%	(9.5)%
Number of Stores:				
Openings	1	10	5	24
Closings	(5)	(4)	(10)	(5)
Net increase (decrease)	(4)	6	(5)	19
End of period	740	720	740	720

Net sales for the second quarter of fiscal 1996 were $121.7 million, $8.4 million or 6.5 percent below net sales of $130.1 million reported in the second quarter of fiscal 1995. A $13.1 million decrease in sales from comparable stores and a $1.8 million reduction in sales because of store closings were partially offset by a $6.5 million increase in net sales from new store locations. Comparable store sales in the second quarter of fiscal 1996 decreased 10.2 percent from the second quarter of fiscal 1995. Men's apparel and accessories contributed a decrease of 7.7 percent and women's apparel and accessories contributed a decrease of 2.5 percent to the comparable store sales

results. The Company defines comparable stores as stores that have reached their thirteenth full month of operations, excluding closed stores. Stores open less than 13 full months are defined as new stores.

Net sales for the first 6 months of fiscal 1996 were $243.3 million, $11.0 million or 4.3 percent below net sales of $254.3 million in the first 6 months of fiscal 1995. A $22.4 million decrease from comparable store sales and a $3.4 million reduction in sales because of store closings were partially offset by a $14.8 million increase in net sales from new store locations. Comparable store sales decreased 9 percent in the first 6 months of fiscal 1996 in comparison with the first 6 months of fiscal 1995. Men's apparel and accessories and women's apparel and accessories contributed decreases of 7.9 percent and 1.1 percent, respectively, to the comparable store sales results.

Selling, general and administrative expenses ("SG&A") increased 4.6 percent, in the second quarter of fiscal 1996 compared with the second quarter of fiscal 1995. For the first 6 months of fiscal 1996, SG&A was $2.9 million or 4.7 percent above the first 6 months of fiscal 1995. The increase was primarily caused by store operating expenses associated with new stores opened in fiscal 1996 and 1995. In the second quarter of fiscal 1996, the Company recorded expenses of $1.1 million to recognize deferred costs related to an executive severance agreement with Barry Parker, former chief executive officer of the Company. In the first 6 months of fiscal 1995, SG&A included a $1 million consulting fee related to the evaluation of the Company's financial structure. SG&A as a percentage of net sales increased to 27.7 percent in the second quarter of fiscal 1996 compared with 24.7 percent in the second quarter of fiscal 1995. For the first 6 months of fiscal 1996, SG&A as a percentage of net sales was 26.7 percent compared with 24.4 percent in the first 6 months of fiscal 1995. The increase in SG&A as a percentage of net sales was primarily a result of comparable stores reporting lower sales combined with approximately constant operating expenses.

Net interest expense decreased $0.2 million to $5.7 million in the second quarter of fiscal 1996 from $5.9 million the second quarter of fiscal 1995. Interest expense decreased $0.5 million to $11.1 million in the first 6 months of fiscal 1996 from $11.6 million in the first 6 months of fiscal 1995. The decrease for the first 6 months of fiscal 1996 was primarily a result of lower interest expense and issuance cost amortization of $1.9 million on the Senior Notes, reflecting the May 1995 redemption of the Senior Notes, partially offset by a $1.5 million increase in interest expense on borrowings under the Credit Agreement. Additional interest expense related to higher total debt outstanding was substantially offset by a lower net effective interest rate. Other net interest expense decreased by $0.1 million primarily because of lower discount and issuance cost amortization. The extraordinary charges in the second quarter of fiscal 1995 related to the redemption of the Senior Notes and the exchange of the then-outstanding 12 percent Senior Subordinated Notes for new 12 percent Senior Subordinated Notes.

Liquidity and Capital Resources: Financing and Operating Activities

Cash provided by operating activities is the primary source of liquidity and capital for the Company. After the impact of cash interest payments, cash used for operations for the 26 weeks ended August 3, 1996 and July 29, 1995 was $24.7 million and $34.3 million, respectively. The Company made cash interest payments of $10 million and $13.6 million in the 26 weeks ended August 3, 1996 and July 29, 1995, respectively. Because of the seasonal nature of the Company's business, positive net cash flow from operations is typically not generated through the first three quarters of the fiscal year. The decrease in cash used for operations in the 26 weeks ended August 3, 1996 compared with the 26 weeks ended July 29, 1995 was primarily a result of lower net spending on merchandise inventories, partially offset by reduced cash generated from operations. Additional liquidity to fund working capital activities is provided through borrowings under the Credit Agreement and open account trade terms from vendors. Although the Company has historically negotiated open trade terms with the majority of its domestic vendors, recent financial circumstances have caused the Company to rely more extensively on letters of credit for its domestic purchase terms. Trade terms are negotiated with each vendor and may be modified from time to time. County Seat is not dependent on factors to support the Company's purchases from its suppliers. County Seat generates cash on a daily basis by selling merchandise for cash or payments with national credit cards. County Seat does not offer its own credit card.

At August 3, 1996, the Company had cash borrowings outstanding of $81.8 million, $10.1 million available for borrowing under the Credit Agreement, banker's acceptances outstanding of $18.6 million, and outstanding commitments under the letter of credit facility of $22.2 million. Fluctuations in market interest rates affect the cost of the Company's borrowings under the Credit Agreement. The impact of fluctuations in market interest rates in the 26 weeks ended August 3, 1996, were not significant to the operating results of the Company. At August 3, 1996, borrowings under the Credit Agreement accrued interest at a rate of 8.6 percent.

CSI is a holding company, the primary asset of which is the common stock of Stores. Substantially all of CSI's operations are conducted through Stores, and

CSI depends on the cash flow of Stores to meet its payment obligations with respect to obligations under CSI's 9 percent Exchange Debentures. In the 26 weeks ended August 3, 1996, Stores paid dividends of $1.1 million to CSI to fund semi-annual interest payments on CSI's 9 percent Exchange Debentures. Remedies available to the holders of CSI's 9 percent Exchange Debentures for failure to make required interest payments include the right to accelerate such indebtedness. In the event of a failure to repay such defaulted indebtedness, the holders of the 9 percent Exchange Debentures could foreclose on the assets of CSI including the common stock of Stores, which would constitute an event of default under the Credit Agreement and the Indenture. No assurance can be given that the Company will have access to resources sufficient to repay defaulted indebtedness if so required.

CHAPTER 6

Credit Policy and Collections

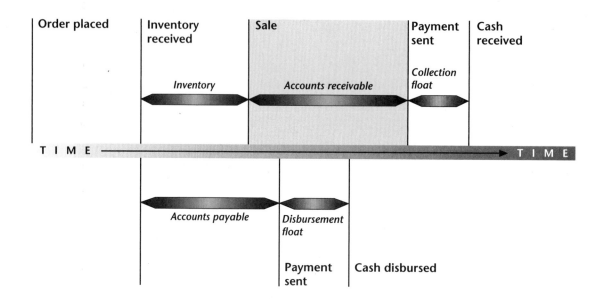

OBJECTIVES

After studying the chapter, you should be able to:

- Specify the advantages of using the net present value approach in evaluating credit policy alternatives.

- Calculate the net present value of proposed and existing credit policies, and select the best policy.

- Identify the three major traditional measures of collection patterns, calculate them, and indicate the conditions under which they give biased signals.

- Calculate and interpret uncollected balance percentages, and indicate why they are the preferred method for monitoring collection patterns.

- Describe present corporate credit policy practices.

- List and explain the major differences encountered when extending credit internationally.

The 1980s was a decade of financial restructuring, in which companies took on massive amounts of debt financing. Bankruptcies increased sharply in the early 1990s, and credit standards had to be revised to face the new realities. Suppliers found themselves facing new challenges regarding credit extension and receivables monitoring, as illustrated by the apparel industry in the accompanying financial dilemma.[1] In the new millennium, despite a very long boom phase for the economy, late payments and nonpayment are ongoing problems for corporations, and credit policy is as important as ever. Imax Corporation, the big-screen movie-system concern, has seen its revenues fall off and its debt downgraded to a "low junk" status in 2000 specifically as a result of difficulty collecting up-front lease payments from large theater companies that are either in or near bankruptcy. When we consider that nonfinancial companies have an estimated $1.65 trillion in trade receivables in the United States, the importance of a company's overall credit policy and collections becomes clear. In this chapter we continue the study of receivables management begun in Chapter 5, addressing how to make credit policy decisions that enhance shareholder value, monitor investments in accounts receivable, and manage the collections process.

FINANCIAL DILEMMA

How Should We Monitor Customers' Financial Positions?

The financial strength of US retailers has diminished so greatly that apparel manufacturers are faced with a new challenge. Relevant questions include how often to update information on this group of customers, and how best to organize the monitoring function. "Historically, suppliers would review credit monthly, but now it's being checked daily," noted one apparel industry consultant. Many apparel companies have responded to the need to be alerted rapidly to changes in their customers' financial status by establishing

---

[1]See 1990. Stores "Went from Bad to Worse" as Economy Deteriorated in 1990. *Investors Business Daily* December 27:21. Aggregate past-due statistics for the entire economy are provided later in the chapter.

credit departments for the first time. The added fixed costs of making these adjustments are believed to be more than compensated by quicker response times. Debt-laden customers are risky to do business with, and these suppliers have responded with decision making based on frequently updated and more accurate credit-related information.

In the previous chapter we developed strategies for assessing individual credit applicants. Our focus was on making individual credit extension "go/no-go" decisions that add to shareholder value. We now extend the analysis to the level of credit policy decisions affecting all customers, including using the net present value (NPV) model to evaluate credit policy changes. Our focus then turns to monitoring the receivables portfolio, and we provide means for assessing the efficiency of collections and the credit department. The chapter concludes with some of the complications that arise in conducting credit operations in foreign countries. Several advanced receivables monitoring techniques are presented in the chapter appendix.

EVALUATING CHANGES IN CREDIT POLICY: THE CASH FLOW TIMELINE

Credit management offers great potential for reducing the amount of cash tied up by a company's operations. The cash flow timeline is a convenient mechanism for viewing all of the cash flow effects of a change in credit policy, facilitating a capital budgeting valuation of those flows. The timeline includes days sales outstanding (DSO), which, as noted in Chapter 2, is one of the key components of a company's cash conversion period. Credit policies reducing DSO generally add value, but our framework illustrates that some policy changes add value even though they result in a higher DSO. See *Monitoring Receivables,* later in this chapter, for a review on calculating the DSO. We begin with survey evidence regarding what variables credit executives believe are important in making policy decisions, then we suggest two ways they can evaluate the effects of different policies. Finally, we conclude with several numerical examples.

Credit Policy Decision Variables

Financial managers may initiate a reevaluation of credit policy after conducting an internal receivables portfolio analysis (illustrated later in the chapter) or in response to a competitor's change in credit terms. When a company is thinking about lengthening its credit period or increasing its cash discount, what variables should it take into consideration? The Smith and Belt survey found that marketing and bad debt loss considerations predominated, with production capacity, inventory requirement, and degree of operating leverage (risk linked to asset-related fixed operating costs) being secondary considerations. Managers ranked the criteria variables they deemed important when evaluating credit terms changes (in descending order of importance): 1) effect on dollar profits, 2) sales effect, 3) receivables effect, and 4) return on investment effect. Because profits correlate closely with cash flows in short-term decisions, decisions that maximize profits tend to increase shareholder value. Risk considerations, although very important to investors, were not explicitly mentioned by the surveyed managers.[2]

---

[2]Smith and Belt, cited in chapter references.

Practicing credit executives believe they can estimate the effects of policy changes on profit, sales, and receivables levels. More than 84% of credit executives surveyed by Besley and Osteryoung[3] stated that they could adequately estimate default probability, delinquency probability, credit limits, opportunity cost of funds invested in receivables, and the company's overall cost of capital. The good news here is that either of the latter two variables might be used as a discount rate for discounting (valuing) cash flows, and the discount rate used can presumably be adjusted for risk. Thus managers are able to properly evaluate credit policy when making decisions about credit terms.

Incremental Profits Versus NPV

Scholars continue to debate whether the best overall criterion for evaluating credit policy changes is incremental profits, evaluated by using the financial statement approach, or NPV. The financial statement approach, sometimes termed a "heuristic approach," involves projecting condensed income statements for each alternative, then selecting the alternative with the highest profits. As we saw in Chapter 3, it typically involves three steps: determining the incremental receivables investment, the change in per-unit and total profits, and the change in bad debt expense. Although the financial statement approach often gives the same accept-or-reject signals as the NPV approach, it is not quite as accurate and does not indicate the anticipated value effect of a credit policy decision.[4] Furthermore, the NPV approach has been formulated so that, with the proper data, the analyst can determine the optimal credit period and the optimal cash discount. After developing the model, we apply it to changes in a company's credit standards, credit period, and cash discount.

NPV APPROACH.   We noted in our valuation presentation in Chapter 3 that the NPV approach is preferable for investment decisions because it is consistent with value maximization. Net present value is the difference between the present value of the cash inflows and the present value of the cash outflows. When choosing between several mutually exclusive credit policy alternatives, the decision rule is to select the credit policy that maximizes NPV. If no credit policy alternative gives a positive NPV, we do not offer credit to our customers, implying that we will sell to them on a cash basis only.[5] The NPV model can be used to make value-maximizing decisions, and we illustrate its use in connection with the cash flow timeline to evaluate several policy decisions facing the credit manager.

The model we use for evaluating credit policy decisions shows the change in NPV from adopting a new or proposed policy, and is adapted from the NPV model used in capital budgeting. The model is developed in several equations, beginning with the NPV of a newly proposed credit policy. We find the NPV of 1 day's sales under a newly proposed policy as:

[3]Besley and Osteryoung survey, cited in chapter references. Company size and industry apparently had very little effect on the accuracy of the estimation.

[4]The financial statement approach does not properly recognize the timing of account losses. Furthermore, it uses an overall cost of capital as a discount rate, which some believe is too high when computing the opportunity cost of the incremental investment in receivables.

[5]This presupposes that nonfinancial or nonquantifiable considerations do not override the recommendation based on the financial analysis. Also, there is another context in which a negative NPV project would be accepted: when considering several alternative means of performing a necessary function, and the only cash flows involved are outflows. These outflows represent costs, and the alternative with the highest NPV would still be selected, which in this situation would be the negative NPV value closest to zero. Selecting from among several EDI or receivables-monitoring software packages are examples of this type of decision context.

NPV average daily sales = PV of Sales to Discount-Takers + PV of Sales to Non-
Discount-Takers − Variable Operating Costs − Variable Credit & Collection Costs

You will find it much easier to work with this NPV formula if you break it into a separate step for each term of the equation. Step 1 involves computing the PV of the cash discount sales (if any), step 2 computes the PV of the nondiscount sales (customers paying full invoice amount at or after the standard credit period), step 3 calculates the variable operating, or noncredit, costs, and step 4 determines the PV of the credit administration and collection costs.

In symbols, the NPV of 1 day's sales under the new policy (Equation 6-1), is denoted by Z_N:

$$Z_N = \frac{[(1+g)S_E](1-d_N)p_N(1-b_N)}{(1+iDP_N)} + \frac{[(1+g)S_E](1-p_N)(1-b_N)}{(1+iCP_N)}$$
$$- VCR[(1+g)S_E] - \frac{EXP_N[(1+g)S_E]}{(1+iCP_N)}$$

(6-1)

In which: Z_N = NPV of new credit policy, 1 day's sales

$\quad g$ = percent growth of credit sales caused by new policy

$\quad S_E$ = existing credit sales under present policy, per day

$\quad d_N$ = cash discount offered in new policy

$\quad p_N$ = percent of credit customers expected to take new cash discount

$\quad b_N$ = bad debt loss percent under new policy

$\quad i$ = daily interest rate

$\quad DP_N$ = cash discount period under the new policy

$\quad CP_N$ = average collection period of paying customers under new policy

$\quad VCR$ = variable cost rate, per dollar of sales

$\quad EXP_N$ = variable collection/credit administration cost ratio under new policy

Notice that each term of the equation includes $(1 + g)S_E$, which is a shortcut means of getting the new sales level. Three symbols merit closer attention in Equation 6-1. First, i is the daily interest rate ($k/365$) at which the seller finances receivables or at which the seller invests monies freed up from a smaller receivables investment. The formula assumes interest is added to the account once a year, even though it is based on daily principal amounts (simple interest based on annual compounding). Second, there is no reason to assume that the ratio of noncredit variable costs to sales (VCR) would change under a new credit policy, so we do not attach an N subscript to VCR. Third, the value used for DP_N should be how long, on average, the cash discount takers actually take to pay. When evaluating a cash discount in a case in which the company has not previously offered a discount, the analyst may simply use the cash discount period instead of a historical pattern.

Unless a company is offering credit for the first time, the attractiveness of a new credit policy must be determined in reference to the existing credit policy. Again we solve for the daily NPV of the policy as follows:

NPV average daily sales = PV of Sales to Discount-Takers + PV of Sales to Non-
Discount-Takers − Variable Costs − Variable Credit & Collection Costs

We can change the subscripts in Equation 6-1 for each of the variables from N to E to denote the existing policy situation, and the NPV of 1 day's sales under the existing policy Z_E is found in Equation 6-2:

$$Z_E = \frac{S_E(1-d_E)p_E(1-b_E)}{1+iDP_E} + \frac{S_E(1-p_E)(1-b_E)}{(1+iCP_E)} - VCR(S_E) - \frac{EXP_E}{(1+iCP_E)} \qquad \text{(6-2)}$$

Z_E is the daily NPV of the existing credit policy. Although the VCR should take the same numerical value as in Equation 6-1, and S_E is obviously the same, all other variables will likely take on different values than those used in Equation 6-1. In many cases the discount rate i is kept the same, but if the proposed and present credit policies directly affect the likelihood of the estimated sales levels being achieved, the analyst might apply a different discount rate in Equations 6-1 and 6-2. As in Equation 6-1, if there is no discount policy under the existing credit policy, d_E and p_E are both zero; this makes the whole first term zero (PV of sales to discount takers) so it need not be considered.

To get the change in daily NPV when going from the existing to the new credit policy, simply take the difference between the daily net present values of the new and existing policies. In words, that is:

Daily NPV of Policy Change = NPV per day of New Policy

− NPV per day of Existing Policy

In symbols, we take the difference in NPVs of Equations 6-1 and 6-2, as shown in Equation 6-3:

$$\Delta NPV \ per \ day = \Delta Z = Z_N - Z_E \qquad \text{(6-3)}$$

Equation 6-3 gives us the change in daily NPV for a 1-day period, based on average daily sales. Because ΔZ reveals the change when going to the new credit policy, we recommend acceptance of the new policy when ΔZ is positive, indifference between the new and existing policies when ΔZ is zero, and rejection of the new policy when ΔZ is negative:

Decision Rule: If $\Delta Z > 0$, accept policy change

If $\Delta Z = 0$, indifferent about policy change

If $\Delta Z < 0$, reject policy change

Finally, we need a formula to convert a 1-day NPV effect, which is based on average daily sales, to the total effect on shareholder wealth resulting from the multiyear effect of the new policy. If the change has a permanent effect, Equation 6-4 results, which gives us a close approximation of the total NPV created by switching from the existing policy to the new policy[6]:

$$\Delta NPV = \frac{\Delta Z}{i} \qquad \text{(6-4)}$$

In words, Equation 6-4 tells us that the total NPV of a policy switch is the present value of all future daily NPVs.

Several comments should be made about the NPV model. First, the 1-day incremental to value, ΔZ, signals whether the alternative policy will be preferable. If it is positive, ΔNPV will be positive as well.[7] Second, because ΔZ constitutes a perpetuity of

---

[6]The NPV calculated from Equation 6-4 is not exact because of the simple interest formula used in the denominator of Equations 6-1 and 6-2. Except when there is a substantial dollar amount of daily sales or a very large change in daily NPVs, the approximation will be very close to the actual ΔNPV. We will compute the difference between the approximation and the actual ΔNPV when we evaluate the case of loosened credit standards, the first illustration of Equations 6-1 through 6-4.

[7]Recall from Chapter 3 that this property holds as long as there is no change in the growth rate of revenues or costs, or any fixed costs subsequent to the initial outlay necessary to implement the project.

daily NPVs, to arrive at its aggregated present value we divide it by a discount rate expressed in terms of the same period.[8] Dividing the 1-day value increment by the daily interest rate gives us the change in value for the company, NPV. Third, if given an annual interest rate, k, we can determine the daily rate assuming simple interest (annual compounding) by dividing k by 365. Although we are not compounding the calculated i on a daily basis in Equations 6-1 and 6-2, we can easily do so to get an exact value for Z.[9] By using an exact daily equivalent to the annual rate k, we gain a closer approximation to NPV in Equation 6-4, in which the value of i really matters. Fourth, there are several simplifying assumptions in this model.

ASSUMPTION 1.   All sales are credit sales. Notice that Equations 6-1 and 6-2 both address daily credit sales. For the value effect shown in Equation 6-4 to apply, the credit policy change cannot affect cash sales—meaning no existing customer can switch between paying at the point of purchase and waiting until the end of the credit period. Companies with only industrial sales may have negligible cash sales, but retailers clearly must consider switching effects when changing credit availability. Obviously, situations in which a company is considering offering credit terms for the first time, or for the first time to a group of formerly cash-paying customers, constitute a violation of the assumption; however, this violation can be handled very simply. Instead of using $(1 + g)S_E$ in each term of Equation 6-1, substitute $g(S_E)$, which represents the additional sales expected. Because Equation 6-2 is irrelevant in this situation, this revised Equation 6-1 gives the ΔZ needed to make the acceptance decision. Recapping, for companies offering credit for the first time, or when they only have information regarding the incremental sales that might arise from a policy change, they can replace $(1 + g)S_E$ with $g(S_E)$ in each term of Equation 6-1, and the revised Equation 6-1 gives us the change in value rising from 1 day's sales (and Equations 6.2 and 6.3 will be unnecessary). For customers that are normally sold to on "cash only" terms, ongoing sales are S_E and the incremental sales brought about by now selling on credit are gS_E—with the latter being the ones for which we are determining the value effect.[10]

ASSUMPTION 2.   The bad debt loss rate used for the proposed credit terms is the forecasted average of loss rates for new and existing customers and there is no difference in the loss rate for buyers taking the cash discount versus those paying at the end of the credit period. When forecasts of new customer sales are very uncertain, merging new and existing customer bad debt loss rates may cause a decision maker to choose a policy that would not be chosen were the risk made explicit. Regarding the second consideration, the loss rate for customers normally taking cash discounts may be lower in reality. This reflects discount-takers' superior financial position. Furthermore, if the seller can

---

[8]For a review of basic time value formulas, see the appendix at the end of the book.

[9]The interest rate if the company is getting paid daily interest on invested funds is different than the rate paid if the company is paying daily interest on borrowed funds. Equation 6-4 gives the correct change in NPV if Equations 6-1 and 6-2 are based on $(1+i)^{\text{no. of days}}$ instead of $(1+i \times \text{number of days})$. Using $n=30$ and $k=10\%$ $(0.10/365 = 0.00027397)$, divide by $(1 \times 0.00027397 \times 30) = 1.00821910$ using simple interest versus $(1+ .00027397)^{30} = 1.00825183$ using compound interest. On a \$1,000 future value, the difference in present values is only 3¢. Equation 6-4 then reflects the true value effect of the policy change's perpetuity of cash flows. Those uncomfortable with assuming that the cash flows really last "forever" should recognize that a very high percentage of the present value of the perpetual steam occurs in the first several years.

[10]Implicitly, we also assume the seller can replace the customers switching from cash to credit with new "cash only" customers without a significant change in any cost element. If that is unrealistic, another term must be added to account for the now-lower profitability from new "cash only" customers that replace switching customers in S_E, unless the only added costs are fixed costs, in which Equation 6-5 is used.

induce some slow payers who are financially strapped to pay early, the probability of not ever getting paid diminishes. Correspondingly, Equation 6-1 could be altered to use different values for b_N in the first two terms.

ASSUMPTION 3.   Other than the change in receivables investment, the new policy does not necessitate additional investment outlays for inventories or fixed assets, nor does it change the *VCR*. However, for a manufacturing firm, inventories increase spontaneously with sales. If sales are expected to increase because of the new policy, the company must operate below capacity to avert increased fixed assets. To see how to incorporate the financial effects of these outlays, we must distinguish between one-time permanent investments and ongoing fixed cost increases. Permanent investments in fixed assets or working capital items, such as inventory, that are caused by a proposed credit policy are subtracted from the calculated ΔNPV, in that they represent time 0 outflows. Ongoing periodic fixed costs related to these investments, such as warehousing fees or security and insurance expenses, must be discounted to their present value. To handle the increased fixed costs, we must calculate the difference between $PVFC_N$, the fixed costs under the new terms (on a present value basis), and $PVFC_E$, the fixed costs under existing terms. We see the net effect in Equation 6-5:

$$\Delta PVFC = (PVFC_N - PVFC_E) \tag{6-5}$$

We can then calculate a revised ΔZ, which we will call ΔZ^{l} in Equation 6-6:

$$\Delta Z' = \Delta Z - \Delta PVFC \tag{6-6}$$

The value effect for the company, $\Delta NPV'$ (Equation 6-7), would then be:

$$\Delta NPV' = \frac{\Delta Z'}{i} \tag{6-7}$$

Regarding the *VCR*, it is probably safe to assume that no change will occur unless the company is not receiving larger (smaller) quantity discounts as sales volume increases (decreases) as a result of the new credit policy.

ASSUMPTION 4.   The analyst is able to forecast each of the variables' future values with certainty. As was implied in Assumption 2, forecasts of sales for new customers or under a new credit policy should not have the same credibility as those for existing customers under the existing credit policy. This uncertainty, or the risk inherent in changing the credit policy, is never brought into the analysis. To do so requires assignment of probabilities, and the recommended alternative must recognize the decision maker's view of risk.

We may need to relax one or more of the first three assumptions as we consider several common credit policy decisions; uncertainty considerations are discussed briefly in a later section. We turn our attention to representative management decisions regarding credit standards, credit period, and a cash discount.

DECISION 1: LOOSENING CREDIT STANDARDS

Regents Manufacturing is considering loosening its credit standards, thereby extending credit to marginal customers it currently offers to sell to on a "cash only" basis. It presently has excess capacity, and therefore does not anticipate any change in fixed costs resulting from the higher sales triggered by the more lenient standards. Sharif Baskerville, a business school graduate recently hired by Regents, has determined that sales will increase by $10 million (sales are presently $100 million, and would increase

EXHIBIT 6-1
Regents Credit Easing Cash Flow Timeline

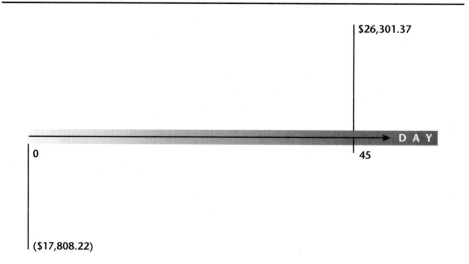

by 10 percent). The VCR as a percent of sales is 0.65. For the new customers, the bad debt loss rate will be 4 percent and the average collection period (or DSO) of paying customers will be 45 days (5 days longer than the DSO of present paying customers).[11] The company does not actively pursue the collection of late accounts, so the variable collection and credit administration expense will be negligible. The company's annual cost of capital is presently 15 percent. Regents does not offer a cash discount.

SOLUTION. Sharif begins by determining the daily interest rate, i, equivalent to the 15-percent annual rate. The daily rate, assuming annual compounding, will be:

$$i = 0.15/365 = \underline{0.0004110}$$

We can illustrate this situation on a cash flow timeline (see Exhibit 6-1), showing the present value of the additional sales on a daily basis.

Because Regents does not presently offer credit to these customers, Z_E is zero and ΔZ simplifies to Z_N. As noted in Assumption 1, Equation 6-1 gives the change in value for 1 day's sales, assuming Regents adopts the new credit standard. Sharif determines that the cost outflow for 1 day's sales is:

$$\text{Variable cost outflow} = -VCR(gS_E) = -0.65 \, (0.10 \times \$100 \text{ million}/365)$$
$$= \underline{-\$17,808.22}$$

Regents does not offer a cash discount, so the first term of Equation 6-1 is equal to zero and drops out. Sharif figures the cash inflow from the average daily sale, 45 days from now, using the numerator of the second term in Equation 6-1:

$$\text{Day 45 inflow} = [g(S_E)(1-p_N)(1-b_N)] = [(0.10 \times \$100 \text{ million}/365)(1-0)(1-0.04)]$$
$$= \underline{\$26,301.37}$$

The credit administration and collection expenses are negligible and do not need to be arrayed on the timeline. We arrive at the timeline shown in Exhibit 6-1.

---

[11]DSO should be based on an averaging technique or calculated based on a weighting technique, as we demonstrate later in the chapter.

Sharif substitutes the numbers into the NPV model (using Equation 6-1) to determine the change in value Regents shareholders can anticipate from loosening credit standards:

$$Z_N = \frac{((0.10\$100,000,000/365)(1-0)(1-0.04)}{[1+0.00004110(45)]} - 0.65\frac{(0.10)\$100,000,000}{365}$$

$$= \$25,823.76 - \$17,808.22$$
$$= \underline{\$8,015.54}$$

Because the 1-day change in NPV of the proposed relaxed credit standards is positive, Sharif recommends its adoption to the credit manager. The addition to shareholder value, given by the aggregate change in NPV (ΔNPV), is found using Equation 6-4[12]:

$$\Delta NPV = \frac{\$8,015.54}{0.0004110}$$

$$= \underline{\$19,502,530.41}$$

DECISION 2: LENGTHENING THE CREDIT PERIOD

Flying High Hang Gliders, Inc., is contemplating lengthening its credit period from the existing net 30 terms to net 60 terms. Reggie Miller, the credit analyst assigned to review the proposed credit change, has determined that the VCR ratio will be the same for existing and additional sales.[13] He estimates the additional sales to be $5 million. Reggie collects the following information from Flying High personnel:

Variable costs as a percent of sales:	70%
Existing sales:	$30 million
Bad debt loss rate now:	5%
Bad debt loss rate under 60-day terms:	6%
Days sales outstanding now:	45 days
Days sales outstanding under 60-day terms:	68 days
Credit & collection expenses now:	2% of sales
Credit & collection expenses under 60-day terms:	2.5% of sales
Opportunity cost of funds:	14%

SOLUTION. First, Reggie finds i, the daily equivalent to k:

$$i = 0.14/365 = \underline{0.0003836}.$$

[12]If the company receives interest on freed-up funds and pays daily interest on funds borrowed to support the receivables investment, the cash flow discounting should be modified slightly. Solve for the equivalent 45-day interest rate assuming daily compounding by taking $[(1+.15)^{45/365}] = 1.0173802$. Or, we could solve for the daily rate and then raise that rate to the 45th power: $[(1+0.15)^{1/365}-1] = 0.000382983$; $[(1+0.000382983)^{45}] = 1.0173802$. Substituting into Equation 6-1, $\$25,852.06$ is found as the value for the first term, and $\$8,043.84$ as ΔZ. Using Equation 6-4 and the rounded daily rate of 0.0003830, the aggregate value effect ΔNPV is:

$$\$8,043.84 / 0.0003830 = \$21,002,193.21.$$

Thus simple interest formulas understate the true daily and aggregate value effects if used when daily compounding applies.

[13]This is not to say that variable costs related to credit and collection will not change, however. The variable costs incurred when changing the credit policy are categorized as credit administration and collection expenses, which we have denoted EXP_N for credit sales under the new policy (in Equation 6-1) and EXP_E for credit sales under the existing policy (in Equation 6-2).

Next, he structures the information provided into the NPV model:

$VCR = 0.70$

$S_N = \$35 \text{ million}/365$

$S_E = \$30 \text{ million}/365$

$b_N = 0.06$

$b_E = 0.05$

$CP_N = 68 \text{ days}$

$CP_E = 45 \text{ days}$

$k = 14\%$

$EXP_N = 0.025$

$EXP_E = 0.02$

Third, he notes that the new sales level, shown as $(1 + g)S_E$ in the equations, is $35 million ($30 million + $5 million; g in this case is $5/$30, or 0.16667). CP_N will increase to 68 days, meaning on average paying customers will pay 8 days late. This compares to 15 days late under the present 30-day period. Because there is no cash discount in the present or proposed terms, we can drop the first term in Equations 6-1 and 6-2. Substituting the above values into Equation 6-1, Reggie finds Z_N:

$$Z_N = \frac{(\$35,000,000/365)(1-0)(1-0.06)}{1+0.0003836(68)} - 0.7\frac{\$35,000,000}{365} - \frac{0.025(\$35,000,000/365)}{1+0.0003836(68)}$$

$$= \$87,845.55 - \$67,123.29 - \$2,336.32$$

$$= \underline{\$18,385.95}$$

Reggie calculates Z_E in the same fashion, making the four necessary changes in the numerical inputs:

$$Z_E = \frac{(\$30,000,000/365)(1-0)(1-0.05)}{1+0.0003836(45)} - 0.7\frac{\$30,000,000}{365} - \frac{0.02(\$30,000,000/365)}{1+0.0003836(45)}$$

$$= \$76,757.21 - \$57,534.25 - \$1,615.94$$

$$= \underline{\$17,607.02}$$

The 1-day change in value, ΔZ, is then the difference between Z_N and Z_E, using Equation 6-3:

$$\Delta Z = \$18,385.95 - \$17,607.02 = \underline{\$778.93}$$

Because the 1-day value effect of $778.93 is positive, the financial analysis supports lengthening the credit period. Substituting ΔZ in Equation 6-4 determines the aggregate value added by the lengthened terms (ΔNPV), assuming the daily improvement persists indefinitely into the future:

$$\Delta NPV = \frac{\$778.03}{0.0003836}$$

$$= \underline{\$2,030,578.73}$$

Noting that the incremental *NPV* is large and positive, Reggie recommends adoption of the proposed change to net 60 terms because of the anticipated addition to shareholder value.

DECISION 3: OFFERING A CASH DISCOUNT

Siegel Apparel Mills is wondering whether to offer its customers, ladies wear retailers, a 2-percent cash discount if they pay within 10 days. At present it has net 30 terms. Top management has also asked what the optimal cash discount would be, should a cash discount be advisable. Rosa Kim is evaluating the proposed new terms of 2/10, net 30 versus the present net 30. Under the proposed terms she anticipates a 3-percent increase in sales volume and a 0.5% reduction in the bad debt loss rate, from 3 percent to 2.5 percent. She estimates that the percent of sales made to cash discount takers will be 40 percent, with the remaining 60 percent continuing to pay in 35 days (the present average collection period). She notes that Marvelous does not charge interest for late payments. Thus the collection period for nondiscount takers equals the existing collection period. Rosa decides that customers taking the discount will pay, on average, on the 10th day after the invoice date. Siegel's marketing activity has forecast sales for the upcoming year to be $20 million, assuming no change in the credit policy. The cost accounting department estimates the VCR to be 0.60 and the credit/collection cost to be 4 percent of sales. Rosa believes each of these variable cost elements will retain the same relationship to sales under the new terms. Marvelous presently has a 12-percent cost of capital.

SOLUTION. Rosa first determines the daily discount rate, i: $0.12/365 = 0.0003288$. Reminding herself that in her situation $CP_N = CPE$, Rosa calculates Z_N, Z_E and the incremental NPV of 1 day's sales, ΔZ. This is structured as the present value of the cash receipts from the discount takers plus the present value of the cash receipts of the nondiscount takers, less the variable costs and less the credit and collection costs.

$$Z_N = \frac{(1+0.03)(\$20,000,000/365)(1-0.02)(0.40)(1-0.025)}{1+0.0003288(10)}$$

$$+ \frac{(1+0.03)(\$20,000,000/365)(1-0.40)(1-0.025)}{1+0.0003288(35)}$$

$$- 0.60\frac{(1+0.03)\$20,000,000}{365} - \frac{0.04(1.03)(\$20,000,000/365)}{1+0.0003288(35)}$$

$$= \$21,500.05 + \$32,640.81 - \$33,863.02 - \$2,231.85$$

$$= \underline{\$18,045.99}$$

Rosa then computes Z_E, the NPV of the present terms, using Equation 6-2. The first term of Equation 6-2 is not relevant because there is no cash discount at present.

$$Z_E = \frac{(\$20,000,000/365)(1-0)(1-0.03)}{1+0.0003288(35)}$$

$$- 0.60\frac{\$20,000,000,000}{365} - \frac{0.04(\$20,000,000/365)}{1+0.0003288(35)}$$

$$= \$52,545.00 - \$32,876.71 - \$2,166.84$$

$$= \underline{\$17,502.44}$$

The 1-day incremental NPV, based on Equation 6-3, is then $543.55:

$$\Delta Z = \$18,045.99 - \$17,502.44 = \$543.55$$

The aggregate NPV for the perpetuity of 1-day value effects, assuming that the credit terms change has incremental effects that last indefinitely, is given by substituting into Equation 6-4:

$$\Delta NPV = \frac{\$543.55}{0.0003288} = \underline{\$1,653,132.60}$$

Because of the positive *NPV*, Rosa recommends the 2-percent cash discount. Management's second question is now pertinent: What cash discount t (if any) would be optimal, in the sense of having the maximum, positive *NPV*? If sales do not change and the proportion of customers taking the cash discount t bears a constant relationship to sales (e.g., 10 or 20 times the decimal equivalent of the discount), the optimal discount D for a 10-day discount period ($DP_N = 10$) is[14]:

$$D^\circ = \frac{[1-(1+i)^{(DP_N - CP_N)}]}{2} \tag{6-8}$$

Rosa recalls that the daily discount rate is 0.0003288. She plugs this value, along with the cash discount period and the normal credit period, into Equation 6-8:

$$D^\circ = \frac{[1-(1+0.0003288)^{(10-35)}]}{2}$$

$$= \frac{[1-(1+0.9918150)]}{2}$$

$$= \underline{0.0040925}$$

Because the calculated D° of roughly 0.4 percent rounds to zero, it appears to Rosa that Siegel would be better off *not* offering a cash discount, assuming sales do not change.[15]

Up to this point, we have worked only with projected data assumed to be known with certainty. This is tantamount to saying that there is no forecast error and that outside influences such as competitive reaction can be perfectly anticipated. Analysts choosing to introduce the variability of the inputs used in the *NPV* model might elect to risk-adjust the discount rate (i) used, but there is no obviously correct rate to use. Alternatively, they might evaluate credit policy decisions using the certainty equivalent version of the capital asset pricing model or the options pricing model.[16] At a minimum, analysts should conduct sensitivity analyses of the sales estimate, bad debt loss rate, and any other input variable that is uncertain.

Once the credit policy is in place, the credit management process focuses on monitoring and collections of credit sales. The next section develops the monitoring measures the manager can use and provides several measures for assessing credit department effectiveness and efficiency.

---

[14]Hill and Riener (see chapter references). This is a one-period model and does not ensure that the policy is optimal over a multiperiod horizon. See the Lee and Stowe citation in chapter references. Lee and Stowe developed a model that explains paradoxical observed discount practices, such as different discounts in the same product market. Behavior such as this may be rational, with asymmetric information about product quality communicated via the cash discount offered. See the discussion on trade credit theories in Chapter 5 for more on product quality and trade credit.

[15]Relative to the solution demonstrated, inflation increases the optimal cash discount slightly. Buyers are more prone to wait until the end of the credit period when inflation is significant, because they are repaying less in real (inflation-adjusted) terms. To keep the cash discount equivalent in real terms, terms of 2/10, net 30 established in a noninflationary era should be adjusted to 2.27 percent if inflation is 5 percent, 2.52 percent if inflation is 10 percent, and 2.99 percent if inflation is 20 percent. For 3/10, net 60 terms, the differences are even more dramatic: 3.66 percent with 5 percent inflation, 4.28 percent with 10 percent inflation, and 5.43 percent with 20 percent inflation. These results are shown in Ben-Horim and Levy (see chapter references).

[16]Both of these are implemented for a credit policy decision in Richard L. Meyer and Scott Besley. 1989. *A Normative View of the Credit Policy Decision.* Paper presentation at the Fifth Annual Symposium on Cash, Treasury, and Working Capital Management, Boston, MA, October.

FOCUS ON PRACTICE

SPEEDING COLLECTIONS DEEMED MOST IMPORTANT SHORT-TERM FINANCIAL MANAGEMENT ACTION[17]   Companies in the Fortune 1000 were asked by Smith and Belt to rank various short-term financial management practices as to which they consider to be most important. Based on a ranking of 1 being most important to 5 being least important, the results indicated that speeding collection of accounts receivable is the single most important action. Speeding collections was considered slightly more important than minimizing inventory investment, and moderately more important than minimizing bank balances or slowing disbursements for accounts payable. Only three respondents indicated "other" actions to be important. The tabulated results, including number of respondents selecting each action and their average ranking, are as follows:

ACTION	NUMBER OF RESPONSES	AVERAGE RANKING
Speed collection of receivables	96	1.73
Minimize investment in inventory	98	1.85
Minimize bank balances	83	2.75
Slow payment of payables	74	3.26
Other	3	3.00

[17]Smith and Belt survey, cited in chapter references.

MONITORING COLLECTIONS

The most carefully devised credit policy cannot keep a company's credit activity from becoming a problem area if the company does not diligently collect the receivables. Late payments require an increase in working capital for the seller and erode shareholder value because of the need to obtain financing from one of four sources (Chittenden and Bragg, 1997): increased debt, which leads to higher interest payments, reduced profits, and reduced borrowing capacity; increased equity, which dilutes and devalues existing investors' stakes if stockholder returns are unchanged; reduced capital investment in the future, limiting the seller's long-term business performance; or an increase in the length (and therefore the amount) of trade credit taken from suppliers. Cisco Systems, the world's largest networking equipment company, found this out in 2001 as some of its prime customers declared bankruptcy—reducing Cisco's sales and making a number of its "vendor financing" loans uncollectible. As noted in the Focus on Practice box, financial executives believe that accelerating collections is the single most important short-term financial management action a company can take. Delayed payments deny the seller the use of the money, result in increased collection costs, and increase the risk that payment will never occur. In this section we see how a company can monitor the receivables balance and the steps it can take to improve on collection of amounts due or past due.

Monitoring Receivables

Three traditional approaches to monitoring the receivables balance include DSO (also known as the average collection period) accounts receivable turnover, and the aging schedule. More recently, analysts have advocated the payments pattern approach, which shows uncollected balances based on the month in which the credit sales originated. We will discuss and illustrate each of these tools briefly.

The **days sales outstanding (DSO)** measure is computed by taking the latest period's accounts receivable balance and dividing it by daily credit sales. Daily credit sales, in turn, are computed by taking the period's sales and dividing by the number of days in the period—365, when computing DSO over a yearly period. The equation typically used for DSO is as follows:

$$DSO = \frac{Accounts\ receivable}{(Annual\ credit\ sales/365)}$$ (6-9)

The analyst then compares the DSO for the latest period to earlier periods, to the credit terms offered to customers, and possibly to a management target or an industry average. The Credit Research Foundation (CRF)[18] publishes a benchmark (for comparison purposes) calculation formula, basing the DSO_{CRF} calculation on the most recent 3 months:

$$DSO_{CRF} = \frac{(Average\ trade\ receivables\ balance\ for\ last\ 3\ months\text{-}ends \times 90)}{Credit\ sales\ for\ last\ 3\ months}$$ (6-10)

The DSO_{CRF} uses the last 3 months of data to "smooth" the data, or balance out an unusual receivables balance that might have occurred in one of the months.

However calculated, the computed *DSO* value is interpreted as the number of days of credit sales remaining uncollected, or how many days, on average, it takes for the company to collect credit sales. The latter interpretation suggests why this number is sometimes called the **average collection period.** If retailer C. J. Nickel's credit sales for January, February, and March were $100,000, $125,000, and $150,000, respectively, and the receivables balance at the end of March was $140,000, the calculation for DSO using Equation 6-9 would be as follows:

$$DSO = \frac{\$140,000}{(\$375,000/90)}$$

$$= 33.6\ days$$

Notice that we have simplified our calculation by assuming each month in the period has 30 days, giving us 90 days for the 3-month period, which is used in converting the period's sales to a daily rate.

In a planning framework, DSO can be used to determine the average receivables needed to support a forecasted sales level, as seen in Equation 6-11:

$$Average\ receivables = (Credit\ Sales/365) \times DSO$$ (6-11)

To illustrate, if credit sales are $100 million, and DSO is 33.6 days, average receivables are $9,205,479.36; this is found by taking $100 million divided by 365 and multiplying by the DSO:

$$\$9,205,479.36 = \$273,972.60 \times 33.6\ days$$

Accounts receivable turnover is simply DSO divided into the number of days in the calculation period, usually 365. If DSO calculated for the past year is 33.6 days, accounts receivable turnover is 365/33.6 = 10.86 times. Receivables turnover is interpreted as how many times a company's investment in accounts receivable "turned over" into sales during the period (on an annualized basis). A slightly different interpretation of the turnover is how many dollars of sales a dollar invested in receivables supports. In our

[18]The Credit Research Foundation represents a body of knowledge emphasizing the impact and contribution of the credit function on individual businesses and the national economy. Its forums, reports, surveys, and other material provide valuable information on new techniques and trends in credit, accounts receivable and customer administration and practices. Furthermore, they are a resource for information technology applications to support the credit, accounts receivable, and customer management functions.

illustration, each dollar invested in receivables supports almost $11 of sales. Similarly to DSO, as seen in Equation 6-11, this relationship can be used in a planning framework to determine the average receivables that are required to support a given level of sales:

$$Average\ receivables = Credit\ sales/Accounts\ receivable\ turnover \qquad \text{(6-12)}$$

Because it does not give any information not already available with DSO and does not tell us the average number of days customers are taking to pay, the analyst who already knows DSO need not calculate receivables turnover unless comparing to an external receivables turnover benchmark.

The **aging schedule** shows a percent breakdown of present receivables, with the categories shown typically as follows: current, 0–30 days past due, 31–60 days past due, 61–90 days past due, and over 90 days past due. In Exhibit 6-2, we show a spreadsheet a company might use to compute the percentage breakdown, followed by the aging schedule itself. The percentages shown at the bottom of the aging schedule are as a percentage of the receivables balance as of the date of the report. June's 46 percent is based on the $245,000 of credit sales made in June divided by the June 30 accounts receivable balance of $538,000 (shown on far right of the exhibit). Some companies develop multiple aging schedules, one of which shows account aging by risk class and another that shows aging by account size. Regardless of format, aging schedules are considered key pieces of information regarding collection efficiency by factors (companies that buy receivables from and then collect them for the original seller) and banks.

The uncollected receivable percentages (right column in the accounts receivable schedule) are based on the period-ending receivables balance, not the sales in the month the receivables originated. We see that $45,000 of January's credit sales remain uncollected as of June 30, constituting 8.36 percent of the June 30 receivables balance of $538,000. Also notice that all uncollected sales from February or months previous are lumped together in the aging schedule because they are 90 days or more overdue.

The three measures we have mentioned serve a twofold purpose. First, they can be compared to various standards that are based on the same period. Standards might include a key competitor's values, management targets, or the industry average. Second, each of the measures might be compared to the trend for that measure. Here the values for several previous periods are used to determine the historical trend to better assess the meaning of the current value.

Surveyed managers indicate a strong preference for using the aging schedule to monitor receivables, with the DSO nearly as popular, and accounts receivable turnover ranking far behind. Many credit departments use multiple measures: recent evidence points to fewer than one in four companies using only aging schedules, with 70% of companies using multiple monitoring methods.[19] Unfortunately, all three measures we have looked at share serious flaws. DSO and receivables turnover are sensitive to recent sales patterns and are reliable measures of a changing collection experience only if the credit sales patterns for current and preceding periods are identical. To depict the bias of DSO when sales are not constant, in Exhibit 6-3 we have constructed an example in which sales first increase then decrease, but the collection pattern is held constant: 60 percent of credit sales are collected in the month of sale, and the remaining 40% are collected the following month. Yet DSO first increases, then decreases, indicating a seemingly worsening, then improving, collection experience. Exhibit 6-3 graphically illustrates the biased signal given by DSO when sales are not constant. Rising sales produce a larger DSO, and declining sales produce a smaller DSO, even though no change has taken place in how

---

[19]Ricci, 1999; cited in chapter references.

EXHIBIT 6-2
Development of an Aging Schedule

Micro Toys, Inc., manufactures and sells miniature toy cars and trucks. It sells these on net 30 terms to toy retailers. Below (Panel A) are the last 6 months' sales and the Accounts Receivable balances at the end of June, the present (report) month. From this raw material, an aging schedule is developed (see below).

PANEL A: SPREADSHEET CONTAINING SALES AND ACCOUNTS RECEIVABLE DATA

ACCOUNTS RECEIVABLE SCHEDULE
MICRO TOYS, INC.
JUNE 30, 200X

Month	Credit Sales (000s)	Uncollected Amount (000s)	Uncollected as Percent of June 30 A/R° Amount
January	$275	$45	8.36%
February	$350	$50	9.29%
March	$400	$55	10.22%
April	$400	$65	12.08%
May	$450	$78	14.50%
June	$500	$245	45.54%
June 30 A/R Balance:		$538	100.00%

°A/R = Accounts receivable

From this schedule, the aging schedule can be developed (Panel B). Notice how the bottom row corresponds to the lower part of the rightmost column from Panel A:

PANEL B: AGING SCHEDULE

AGING SCHEDULE*
MICRO TOYS, INC.
JUNE 30, 200X

Age	Current	0–30 Days Overdue	31–60 Days Overdue	61–90 Days Overdue	Over 90 Days Overdue	
Month of sale	June	May	April	March	February and prior	Total
Accounts receivable (000s)	$245	$78	$65	$55	$95	$538
Percentage of June 30 A/R Balance	46%	15%	12%	10%	17%	100%

°For ease of calculation, all months are assumed to have 30 days.

rapidly credit sales are collected. The credit manager was signaled to take corrective action when there was no need to do so.

A further dilemma facing the analyst is the appropriate period from which to make the DSO or receivables turnover calculations. It turns out that the measures give quite different readings depending on whether they are figured from monthly, quarterly, or annual data.[20] The aging schedule is likewise plagued with sensitivity to the sales pattern,

---

[20]A weighted DSO that overcomes both biases has been recommended by Carpenter and Miller (cited in chapter references). Implementing this approach is based on determination of a standard receivables composition and a weighted DSO for every past month.

EXHIBIT 6-3
Bias in Days Sales Outstanding Induced by Sales Pattern

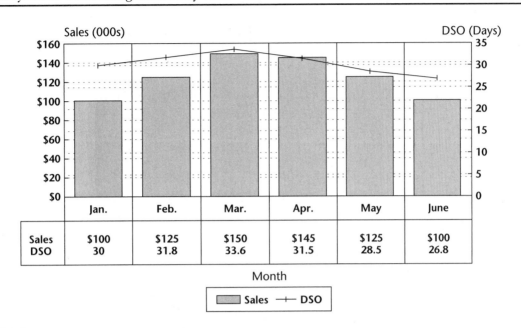

	Jan.	Feb.	Mar.	Apr.	May	June
Sales	$100	$125	$150	$145	$125	$100
DSO	30	31.8	33.6	31.5	28.5	26.8

Month

EXHIBIT 6-4
A Typical Accounts Receivable Portfolio Monitoring System

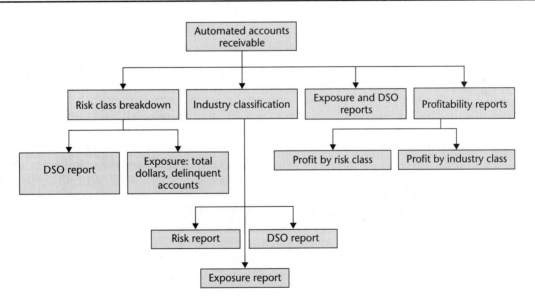

even when collection rates are stable. The higher the proportion of more recent sales, the heavier the weighting for collections of recent accounts, and the more favorable the aging schedule appears. The higher percentages reported in the current or slightly past due categories result from increasing sales, not from a better collection experience.

One company's receivables portfolio monitoring system, illustrated in Exhibit 6-4, shows the dollar amounts invested in receivables ("exposure"), DSO, and profitability by risk class and by industry. It exemplifies how the DSO and aging schedule measures

EXHIBIT 6-5
Uncollected Balances Schedule

Uncollected Balance Percentages
Micro Toys, Inc.
June 30, 200X

(1) MONTH	(2) CREDIT SALES (000s)	(3) AMOUNT UNCOLLECTED (000s)	(4) UNCOLLECTED BALANCE PERCENTAGE
January	$275	$ 45	16.36%
February	350	50	14.29%
March	400	55	13.75%
April	400	65	16.25%
May	450	78	17.33%
June	500	245	49.00%
June 30 accounts **receivable balance:**		**$538**	Payment index: **126.98**

might be integrated into an overall receivables analysis. It also enables a company to evaluate and revise its credit policies.[21] The goal is to achieve better-than-industry-standard credit losses as well as superior revenue generation, leading to higher earnings and cash flows, return-on-equity, and stock valuation. Later in the chapter, we show how companies use key account management systems and improvement initiatives to improve management of credit and the resulting receivables.

Uncollected Balance Percentages

The pitfalls of DSO, accounts receivable turnover, and the aging schedule have led to the development of an improved measure, in which the uncollected balances for each month are divided by the credit sales in the month when the receivables originated. Sometimes called the "payments pattern approach," the **uncollected balance percentages** accurately depict a company's collection experience, even when sales are changing. Exhibit 6-5 shows the earlier Micro Toys receivables example, but now the right column (column 4) shows uncollected monthly receivables computed as a percent of the credit sales in the month they originated. The uncollected balance percent is calculated by dividing the portion of the present receivables balance attributable to an earlier month's sales (column 3) by that month's sales (column 2). Given that January's credit sales were $275,000, 16.36 percent ($45,000/$275,000) of Micro's January credit sales remain uncollected as of June 30.

To conduct a trend analysis, the most recent uncollected balances percentages can be compared with the comparable month-earlier percentages. Once the July 31 report becomes available, we can see if the collection rate for credit sales made five months

---

[21]Space does not permit fuller treatment of credit portfolio management. A good basic introduction is in Knerr (cited in chapter references). Exciting developments on the linkage of portfolio management to shareholder value are profiled in "The Customer Value Imperative: Creating Shareholder Value through Consumer Credit Portfolio Management: An Industry Best Practices Report," a study conducted in 1999 by strategy consulting firm Oliver, Wyman & Company for the financial services association The Risk Management Association (RMA). Some companies use modern portfolio theory to find risk-diversifying opportunities in their consumer credit portfolios and commercial credit exposures. At the time of this writing, an executive summary of the report was available online at: http://www.rmahq.org/Ed_Opps/pubs/custval_execsum.html.

EXHIBIT 6-6
Using the Aging Schedule, DSO, and Uncollected Balance Percentages
to Evaluate Collection Efficiency

This is the situation Micro Toys faces 3 months after the original schedule.

Development of the Aging Schedule (steps 1 and 2)

1. ACCOUNTS RECEIVABLE SCHEDULE WITH AGING PERCENTAGES:

Panel A

Accounts Receivable Schedule
Micro Toys, Inc.
September 30, 200X

Month	Credit Sales ($000s)	Uncollected Amount ($000s)	Aging Percents: Uncollected As Percentage Of June 30 A/R Amount
April	$400	$65	15.47%
May	$450	$64	15.19%
June	$500	$69	16.25%
July	$450	$90	21.27%
August	$400	$80	18.91%
September	$350	$55	12.91%
September 30 A/R Balance:		**423**	**100%**

2. PASTE AGING PERCENTS INTO AGING SCHEDULE:*

Panel B

Age	Current	0–30 Days Overdue	31–60 Days Overdue	61–90 Days Overdue	More Than 90 Days Overdue	Total
Month of sale:	September	August	July	June	May and Prior	—
Accounts receivable ($000s)	$55	$80	$90	$69	$129	$423
Percentage of September 30 Accounts receivable balance	12.91%	18.91%	21.27%	16.25%	30.66%	100%

*For ease of calculation, assume each month has 30 days.

3. CALCULATE UNCOLLECTED BALANCE PERCENTAGES BY DIVIDING A MONTH'S UNCOLLECTED AMOUNT IN PANEL A BY CREDIT SALES FOR THAT MONTH:

Panel C

Month	Uncollected Balance Percentage
April	16.36%
May	14.29%
June	13.75%
July	20.00%
August	20.00%
September	15.60%

Panel D
DSO-6 months: (180 days)   **A/R / [(Sum of 6 months' credit sales)/180)]**

1. DSO as of June 30 (based on Exhibit 6-2):	*40.77 days*
2. DSO as if September 30 (based on above data):	*29.87 days*

earlier (February, in that case) have changed. If the percent uncollected is higher than the 16.36 percent seen in the June report, this signals a worsening collection experience.

Notice that an overall payment index can also be determined to check on the aggregate collection experience, shown at the bottom of column 4. In our illustration, the index stands at 126.98. If this number increases, we usually conclude that a greater percentage of previous months' sales remain uncollected. However, analysts must be careful interpreting this index when offsetting changes sum to the same total while masking a greatly altered collection pattern. As the most recent month is added to the analysis and the earliest month is dropped, offsetting changes in the uncollected balance percentages for the earliest month and most recent month produce the same index value, but obviously these should not be viewed identically by the credit manager.

Many companies use more than one collection efficiency measure, and analysts should be familiar with several approaches and their relative value. Using our earlier examples (Exhibits 6-2 and 6-5), with the same company's collection experience 3 months later, let's see how using all three measures either clarifies or muddies the analysis of collection efficiency (see Exhibit 6-6).

The aging schedule misidentifies the problem by making it appear that receivables 61+ days overdue is a serious issue, when such is not the case. However, it does accurately show the problem in the 0–30 and 31–60 days overdue categories. DSO misidentifies slightly worse collection experience with a signal of much better collection experience. Uncollected balance fractions show that the true picture is deterioration in the current month, which has spilled over into 1-month and 2-month late payments. The collection situation must be addressed immediately, but not in the "over 91 days overdue" category suggested by the aging schedule. In this situation, then, the uncollected balance fractions—and for near-term collections, the aging schedule—give insight for the collections analyst.

FINANCIAL DILEMMA REVISITED

Where does that leave the credit manager selling to an industry with a deteriorating financial condition, such as the apparel retailers we met in our first Financial Dilemma? Overall exposure to bad debt losses can be monitored with the uncollected balance percentages. A key account approach to individual customer monitoring, in which the payment patterns of the customers accounting for much of the company's sales are scrutinized, is a necessity. Using online credit agency data enables the credit manager to watch how the customers are paying other companies with which they do business. Even careful oversight cannot prevent all losses, however, as a consumer goods company realized when absorbing a $5 million loss subsequent to Macy's bankruptcy. Credit managers are in the difficult position of not wanting to jeopardize continued business with their best customers, yet wanting to avoid a large loss exposure. Effective collection practices help keep losses to a manageable level.

To summarize our discussion of receivables monitoring, we acknowledge the popularity of the DSO and aging schedule measures, but point out their unreliability when sales are changing. An improved measure, uncollected balance percentages, is recommended as a better approach to monitoring the collection experience. These percentages can be compared over time to reliably alert the credit manager to improving or deteriorating collections. Recent developments, which are more sophisticated than the above techniques, are profiled in the chapter appendix.

COLLECTION PROCEDURES

The collection procedures a company uses are triggered when the monitoring system shows an invoice is past due, or delinquent. The guiding principle behind collections is to collect the amount owed as close to the credit terms as possible, trying to preserve customer goodwill when doing so. Customers that are delinquent in payments may be experiencing temporary problems, in which case the seller often renegotiates the terms, stressing that the revised terms must be met. Partial payments are solicited where the full invoice cannot be paid. At some point, particularly when the outstanding invoices are very large, the seller will push for payment even at the risk of alienating the customer. The rationale is that a customer not intending to pay its legal obligations is not worth retaining.

Collection Effort

Normally, the initial contact with the customer is made within 10 days of delinquency. In the initial mailing, the seller often includes a statement of account, which is a listing of amounts sold to this customer recently, usually including the buyer's purchase order number(s). A copy of the unpaid invoice(s) may also be sent. A reminder letter may be followed up by phone or even personal contact, with referral to a collection agency and/or legal action as a last resort. Duplicates of either or both of these documents may be sent with follow-up mailings. The seller's sales force is kept informed about the situation and may be asked about any unusual circumstances or conditions affecting the late-paying customer.

The normal collection cycle lasts 2 or 3 months. Companies typically leave 10 to 15 days between their successive collection efforts. In the intermediate stages, the approach is to emphasize the need for cooperation and fairness and the importance of prompt payment on the part of the buyer for maintaining or improving its credit record. Attempts are made to formulate specific payment arrangements. In the final stages, a semifinal letter will be sent, warning of the possibility of involving external parties (collection agencies or lawyers) in the collection. The final letter might state that unless payment is received the account will be placed for collection in 10 days. Sometimes, having this letter signed by a senior officer in the company or the company's general attorney helps set the tone. If payment is still not received, documents pertaining to the account are sent to a collection agency or to the company's law firm. The customer is generally notified of this action and given a final opportunity to pay. The systematic follow-up throughout all collection stages communicates the seriousness of the customer's obligation as well as the importance of those obligations from the seller's viewpoint.

Union Corporation[22] is representative of the major collection agencies that creditors can turn to for help collecting delinquent accounts. It offers a two-phase collection service to more than 30,000 clients, including American Express.

- Phase I involves computer-generated collection letters, for a fee of $4.25 to $9.95 per account, depending on the number of accounts placed with Union.
- If Phase I is unsuccessful, Phase II may be pursued, in which commissioned collectors at 16 branch offices try to collect the account.

On average, clients retain Union for Phase I when accounts are 45 to 90 days past due. Phase II charges are on a contingency basis, meaning the client is charged in

---

[22]From 1990. Union Corp.'s Business Grows with Economic Uncertainty. *Investor's Business Daily,* August 3:32.

FOCUS ON PRACTICE

TEN WAYS TO GET PAID*

1. *Get it in writing.* Before starting the job, establish a fee agreement that explains finance charges, interest charges, hourly rates, and refundable or nonrefundable retainers.
2. *Bill immediately.* Bill right after work is completed, not at the end of the month. Send bills to a physical address, not a P.O. Box, and mark envelopes "Do Not Forward—Address Correction Requested."
3. *Charge interest.* Charging interest will prevent your bill from being put at the bottom of your customer's pile of unpaid bills, especially if yours is a service company and you cannot "repossess" already-delivered service.
4. *Offer a cash discount.*
5. *Work on retainer.* Get cash up front before doing service work, especially if this is your first work for the customer.
6. *Get references.*
7. *Establish a write-off policy.* For debt that is too difficult to collect, recognize that you may accept some level of bad debt.
8. *Follow up frequently.* Follow up more than once a month.
9. *Legalize your faxes.* Insert a clause such as "Fax is as original" to ensure it can serve as a legal document.
10. *Follow your billing procedure.* Be pleasant but firm, call and restate the terms at the first signs of delinquency, insisting on a firm payment plan and definite arrangements. In some cases accept a settlement less than payment in full to ensure getting some payment.

*From Robyn Nissim. 1996. Ten ways to get paid. *Entrepreneurial Edge* Summer:22–23.

proportion to the success Union has in collecting the past due bills. In total, Union collects $240 of the average $625 debt assigned to it, somewhat better than the industry average. The services of agencies such as Union are valuable because of the specialized expertise and information they possess, and the resulting lower operating cost. On many accounts, they are able to collect as much as 50–60 percent of the face value of invoices placed with them.

Collections pose special problems for smaller businesses, especially service firms. The Focus on Practice box provides some techniques that are helpful in such cases.

EVIDENCE ON COLLECTION PRACTICES   We noted in our credit policy presentation in Chapter 5 that many companies levy service charges for late payment. We survey here evidence that addresses several other collections-related questions. First, consider two related questions: Are companies more aggressive in their collection effort when their level of accounts receivable grow relatively large,[23] and do companies behave as if they understand the good will tradeoff when selecting their collection methods?[24] The answer to both of these questions is *yes*. One exception discovered when investigating the second question was that companies use techniques such as garnishment (creditors have amounts owed taken out of the delinquent payor's wages), which are very effective in collecting amounts owed, even though consumers dislike these techniques. State and national laws also have a clear impact on what remedies are used in collecting delinquent amounts.

---

[23]Importance is measured both by accounts receivable as a percent of total assets and by the DSO, and reported in Sartoris and Hill (1988), cited in chapter references.

[24]This hypothesis was studied by Richard L. Peterson, cited in chapter references.

Second, when asked the most effective means of collecting receivables, most companies replied that they use more than one method, most commonly letters and phone calls.

Legislation and Regulation

Many state and federal laws and regulations govern the extension of credit, the use and communication of credit information, and the procedures used in collection. The National Association of Credit Management annually publishes an extensive volume on this subject entitled *Credit Manual of Commercial Laws*. It includes general information on the legal aspects of security and collections, and state-by-state differences on topics such as contracts, secured transactions, truth-in-lending legislation, bankruptcy proceedings, collection agency requirements, and bad check laws. The manual's chapters on antitrust and trade regulation laws and legal phases of collections provide essential information for the credit administrator.

EVALUATING THE CREDIT DEPARTMENT

The credit manager is also concerned about the efficiency with which the credit department's operations are carried out. Briefly, a review of the departmental operations should include a study of staffing, employee performance, and expense ratios. Exhibit 6-7 illustrates the measures that might be tabulated. Ratio values for the company can be compared with its past years' experience as well as to the values for comparably-sized sellers in its industry. From 1960 through 1997 in the United States, percent current has been 81%, average (median) days delinquent has been 8.1 days, and the percent over 91 days past due has been 1.8 percent.[25] Trade associations are generally the best source of data on industry experience. Recent evidence points to the use of between two and four measures in management reporting of receivables positions, including DSO, aging schedules, uncollected balance percentages, and exception reports.[26] DSO and aging schedules were most prevalent.

The efficiency of collections is important, but so too is the efficiency of the credit department processes. Exhibit 6-8 provides some benchmarks of credit department efficiency from 1999. The top quartile performance is shown in the middle column, and the median performance in the right column. In the middle of the column you see overlap with our Exhibit 6-7 collection benchmarks. Companies are increasingly using electronic data interchange (EDI) to outsource their invoicing and/or receivables reconciliation to take advantage of expensive new technology, reduce staff time, improve customer service, and speed up exception handling. One approach to outsourcing involves providing your bank with a file of open (unpaid or partially paid) items. The bank keys the data necessary to post paid items to the company's system. The bank has access to company files to verify that the invoice numbers are correctly entered. It may also create and distribute paper or electronic invoices from company-provided billing files. As payments are received, banks update the company's customer records and send them an updated electronic file. Ideally, the "hit ratio" of automatically updated receivables records exceeds 90 percent. A second outsourcing approach, customized and typically more limited in scope,

---

[25]Ochs and Parkinson, cited in chapter references.

[26]Ricci, cited in chapter references.

EXHIBIT 6-7
Credit Management and Credit Department Benchmarks

CREDIT MANAGEMENT BENCHMARKS

Turnover
Days Sales Outstanding *(DSO)*
Best Possible DSO *(BP)*
Average Days Delinquent *(ADD)*   Benchmark Value: 8.1 days
Percent Current *(PC)*   Benchmark Value: 81%
Percent Over 91 Days Past Due *(Over 91)* Benchmark Value: 1.8%

Loss Control
Percent of Gross Bad Debt to Sales *(GBD)*
Percent of Net Bad Debt (net of recoveries) to Sales *(NBD)*

Cost
Credit Cost per Sales Dollar *($ Sales)*

Glossary:
Credit Sales refers to actual billings, and therefore includes freight, taxes, and containers.
Total Trade Receivables refers to all domestic accounts and notes, and includes past-due billings and accounts placed for collection.
Current Trade Receivables refers to the portion of domestic open accounts and notes not yet due.
Average Trade Receivables Beyond 91 Days refers to monthly average of trade receivables 91 days or more past due, aged on actual due date.
Collection Effectiveness Index is based on beginning quarterly A/R and end of quarter, A/R, and is calculated as follows:

$$CEI = \frac{\text{Beginning total receivables} + (\text{quarterly credit sales/3}) - \text{ending total receivables}}{\text{Beginning total receivables} + (\text{quarterly credit sales/3}) - \text{ending current receivables}} \times 100$$

$$\text{Days Sales Outstanding} = \frac{\text{Last three month ending total receivables balance}}{\text{Credit Sales for Quarter}} \times 30$$

$$\text{Best Possible DSO} = \frac{\text{Last three month ending current receivable balance}}{\text{Credit Sales for Quarter}} \times 30$$

$$\text{Percent over 91 days past due} = \frac{\text{Average Receivables over 91 days}}{\text{Average Total Receivables}}$$

SOURCES: Ronald K. Chung. 1995. Structural Reengineering of the Credit Process: Strategic Influence and Financial Control. *Credit and Financial Management Review* (1):5. Reprinted with permission. Benchmark data are based on overall data from domestic trade receivables in the United States from 1960 to 1997, as tracked by the Credit Research Foundation, and are mostly from manufacturers. It was published in Joyce R. Ochs and Kenneth L. Parkinson. 1998. Collections: What the Data Shows—A Conversation with CRF's Terry Callahan. *Business Credit* June:20–21.

entails services developed to fit the company's credit and receivables situation. The bank may go on-line with the company's receivables system to update the files (instead of merely transmitting a file and having the company do the update).

Improving efficiency and effectiveness in credit management is accomplished by reducing the investment in receivables, covered in the next section, and by integrating credit management with marketing and customer concerns, covered in the subsequent section.

Reducing the Investment in Receivables

The zero net working capital objective introduced in Chapter 1 and the Cash Conversion Period objective presented in Chapter 2 both strongly influence accounts receivable policy setting. Key to both objectives is a goal of reducing investment in receivables. Companies attempt to pare receivables to an optimal level by:

EXHIBIT 6-8
Credit Department Efficiency—Current Summary Statistics°

PERFORMANCE MEASURES	TOP 25%	OVERALL MEDIAN
Credit & Collection		
Gross Collection Effectiveness Index (CEI)	89.81	76.13
Gross Bad Debt to Sales (%)	0.0217%	0.0691%
Active Accounts per Employee	789	400
Cost per Employee:		
Without System Costs	$54,201	$71,313
System Costs Only	$8,000	$17,692
Cost per Sales Dollar:		
Without System Costs	$0.0005	$0.0009
System Costs Only	$0.0001	$0.0002
Days Sales Outstanding (DSO)	32.92	43.27
Best Possible DSO	24.24	31.11
Average Days Delinquent	3.44	8.70
Percent Current	89.53%	79.16%
Accounts Receivable		
Check Turnover per Cash Applier	32,631	18,360
Transaction Turnover per Cash Applier	246,667	126,000
Transaction Turnover Employee	150,000	77,633
Deduction Turnover per Cash Applicator and Deduction Specialist	4,418	2,500
Deductions as a percentage of Transactions	1.82%	4.23%
Cost per Transaction:		
Without System Costs	$0.2695	$0.5542
System Costs Only	$0.2071	$0.4646
Cost per Employee:		
Without System Costs	$32,826	$48,133
System Costs Only	$18,400	$32,000

°Accessed at http://www.nacm.org/crf/benchmark.html

1. Reducing invoicing float (the time elapsing between order shipment and invoicing);
2. Fine-tuning credit administration and credit policy, including credit standards, by reviewing the profit and bad-debt tradeoff periodically and considering the use of key account management systems (covered below);
3. Outsourcing and automating, which might address credit evaluation via credit scoring (Ricci's survey finds that few companies have automated this step, which motivates outsourcing of this activity), or factoring, which varies significantly by seller's industry and size (and can be done by banks, trade factoring firms, or intermediaries such as eCredit);
4. Reducing discrepancies and deductions, which represent disagreement between order and actual shipment made, possibly resulting from inaccurate or delayed order fulfillment (some practitioners have found that invoices that are "at issue" compose the primary reason for late payments);
5. Improving monitoring and collections, by using the benchmarks as standards of comparison, using multiple methods, and employing rapid and effective late-payor follow-up.

These methods generally reduce the time uncollected payments are outstanding and increase the quality (collectibility) of those amounts that are outstanding.

Organizational Integration of Credit Management: Key Account Management Systems

Continuously improving credit management to meet or exceed benchmark standards demands a holistic approach to credit, in which marketing and finance considerations are combined. Our opening discussion in Chapter 5 demonstrated that credit is an integral part of the marketing function as well as finance function. Our opening flowchart in that chapter (Exhibit 5-1) illustrates this connection by beginning with marketing strategy. Businesses have begun to see the need to improve all business processes— including credit standard-setting, credit evaluation, credit extension, and collections— which support their key customer accounts. These are large and/or growing customers that are important to the continued success of the seller.

As a seller's level of involvement with its customers increases from simple to complex, and the nature of its customer relationships evolve from "just transacting business" to collaborative, customer loyalty may be built by:

- A better understanding of the needs and wants of the key accounts
- Prioritizing accounts according to their potential value and the seller's available resources
- Making credit terms and policies an integral part of a well-designed sales and marketing offering.

Credit management benefits from and adds to a well-designed key account management system in much the same way that Materials Requirement Planning (MRP) influences inventory management. Objectives pursued with key accounts include market share, profit, sales growth, and DSO. To illustrate, Kodak's Office Imaging business unit seeks to drive shareholder satisfaction by committing to performance objectives in revenue, margin, and account objectives. Changes in the way receivables management is conducted will be triggered by advances in key account management sophistication and penetration.

INTERNATIONAL CREDIT MANAGEMENT

Our final topic is a brief survey of the international complications of credit management. The three major considerations are currency variations, the often arbitrary timing of customer payments, and the legal and economic environment. Currency variations are changes in the exchange rate at which the company can convert the cash from the receivable collection into the parent company's home currency. Mainly, the devaluation (reduced value of the foreign currency) that the domestic manager is concerned with arises from higher inflation rates and/or more rapid money supply growth in the foreign country. Customer payment timing is problematic because of different religious and cultural norms regarding the acceptability of late payment, the added complexity of international payment instructions, and the longer collection cycle inherent in most international transactions. Finally, the legal and economic environment creates problems caused by foreign exchange controls, country risk, widely varying credit laws, and poor customer credit history data. These three problem areas compound the level of difficulty in both credit policy decision making and monitoring and collections efforts.

Modifying Credit Policy Analysis

The added complexity of intentional credit management is evident whenever credit managers seek to alter the company's credit policy. For example, easing the credit policy—whether through a longer credit period or lower credit standard—is riskier for foreign sales because of the increased uncertainty about the dollar value of cash flows arising from foreign currency devaluation. Although an easing of credit standards or longer credit period should generate more sales, it also results in increased default risk and the possibility of the receivables deteriorating in dollar value as a result of foreign inflation and currency devaluation.[27] Part of this reduced value can be offset by an increase in the company's selling price because of the economy-wide inflation and the newly liberalized terms. Furthermore, regardless of the credit policy, the exporter may require a stronger assurance that payment will be received. Although the majority of sales made by US companies to established foreign companies are on open account, a significant portion of sales to new or less-established accounts use documentary collections or letters of credit, or those sales may have their receipts guaranteed by seller-purchased credit insurance offered by a third party.

Applying the credit policy is also more difficult. A company's in-house credit analyst may not be able to get a client D&B rating for many overseas clients, and bank credit information might also be less easily obtained. Although international credit decisions are more difficult, D&B can provide commercial credit information about many businesses worldwide. D&B's products and services draw on a global database of more than 60 million companies, and it gathers business information in 209 countries around the world. Some countries have cross-border data limitations that prohibit a US-based multinational company from transmitting creditworthiness and/or payment history data back to the United States.

Modifying Monitoring and Collections

In addition to the typical collection probability and timing estimates, credit managers must monitor currency exposure of foreign receivables. This refers to the vulnerability of the company to a decline in the value of the receivables at the time they are translated back into the parent company's home currency. Perhaps in conjunction with other treasury department personnel, they should develop a strategy for monitoring and possibly hedging (protecting the company against) the risk. The absolute size of the exposure of the receivables denominated in various currencies is a starting point. However, the potential for reducing that exposure should also be highlighted. One approach is to weight the dollar equivalent of each currency's exposure by dividing it by DSO or by the uncollected balance percentage index. The currencies with the highest quotients are then targeted for improved collection efforts.[28] Credit managers especially push for timely or even early payment (which is called "leading") when foreign currencies are expected to decline in value relative to the home currency. Repayment practices abroad often seem arbitrary to US-based managers, who observe payment patterns in the United States that are fairly stable except during recessions. Traditions regarding payment of amounts owed may be much different abroad.

---

[27]Shapiro (see chapter references) has developed a model to determine the expected marginal cost (in dollars) of extending one dollar's worth of credit by one period.

[28]For more on this approach, see the approach to managing foreign subsidiaries' receivables in Turner (cited in chapter references).

Finally, the legal and economic environments vary in foreign countries, constraining multinational managers in the control phase of credit management. Because receivables constitute part of the multinational's asset investment in a foreign country, credit managers should analyze the country's political risk. Risk factors range from the possibility of fund flows being blocked, to the entire operation being nationalized, with the company's remitted profits and asset investment being reduced or totally eliminated. Also, the legal remedies for late payment or nonpayment differ by country.

We conclude with two important observations about improving international credit management. First, the company should manage the entire cash flow timeline. Order-to-invoice delays in foreign subsidiaries have been a major problem area for US-based multinationals, according to a survey of treasurers conducted by Financial Executives Research Foundation.[29] Widely dispersed sales offices may mail billing information to a company's headquarters, greatly slowing the invoicing process. Computer hookups are a simple solution for such a problem. One food producer's West German subsidiary had a 6 to 10 day lag from order-to-invoice, which was cut to 1 or 2 days after computer terminals were installed at the warehouses. This saved the company an estimated 100,000 deutsche Marks per year in interest.

Second, and closely related to the first point, the entire credit evaluation, granting, monitoring, and collections process should be automated. A US paper manufacturer reduced its DSO from 100 to 72 days, and its bad debt loss rate from 1.2 percent to 0.4 percent of net sales by setting up a computer database of customer credit histories and by automatically generating invoices when orders are entered. An added advantage to an automated system is that the treasurer of a multinational company can net accounts payable and accounts receivable for each currency, arriving at a net exposure by currency.

SUMMARY

Our second credit management chapter developed the framework for applying the net present value model to credit policy decisions. This capital budgeting approach is recommended for valuing the impact of credit policy decisions because it properly incorporates cash flow timing and risk. The model is applied to changes in credit standards, the credit period, and the cash discount.

Once the credit policy is in place, the attention shifts to collecting receivables. This effort begins with proper monitoring of the receivables portfolio. Monitoring collection patterns is the credit manager's ongoing responsibility. The manager has several tools to aid in this oversight, including the aging schedule, DSO or the average collection period, accounts receivable turnover, and the uncollected balance percentages. Of these, the uncollected balance percentages are the only reliable and unbiased measure of customer payment patterns, because the other measures are biased by changing sales patterns and may be sensitive to the averaging period chosen for the calculations. Recent advances in monitoring are presented in the chapter appendix, Appendix 6A.

When the monitoring approach used (such as *DSO*) signals slowed collections, the credit manager initiates a series of contacts with the customer(s) involved. A form letter is often the first contact vehicle, followed by other letters, telephone calls, and initiation of outside collection efforts such as referral to collection agencies or litigation.

---

[29]Business International. 1988. *Automating Global Financial Management.* New York: John Wiley & Sons.

The chapter concluded with pointers on how to evaluate the efficiency of the credit department and some warnings regarding receivables management in the international arena. International considerations meriting special focus are foreign currency exposure; payment system particularities; and legal, cultural, and environmental differences.

Useful Web Sites

See Web sites referenced at the end of Chapter 5.
National Association of Credit Management: http://www.nacm.org/bcmag/bcarchives/bcarchives.html
Credit Research Foundation:
http://www.crfonline.org/surveys/benchmarking/benchmarking.shtml
Credit Research Foundation: http://www.crfonline.org/surveys/dso/dsoresults.html

Questions

1. What are the key variables for evaluating credit policy changes, according to credit managers? Are managers able to estimate the values for these variables adequately? Compare and contrast the incremental profit and NPV approaches to evaluating credit policy decisions.
2. List the assumptions of the NPV model. Are these assumptions valid when a company is considering extending its credit period from 30 to 90 days, if all its competitors retain a 30-day credit period?
3. What are the two major shortcomings of DSO and accounts receivable turnover? Which of these also plagues the aging schedule?
4. What is the relationship between DSO and total accounts receivable on a given company's balance sheet?
5. Why might it be argued that uncollected balance percentages are superior to other measures used to monitor customer payment patterns?
6. What collection monitoring measures do managers express a preference for in actual practice?
7. With the aging schedule, receivables amounts from past months are related to the present total accounts receivable balance. To what are the receivables amounts related when computing uncollected balance percentages? Why is this distinction important when evaluating collection efficiency?
8. Interpret the payment index shown at the bottom right of the uncollected balances schedule (see column 4 in Exhibit 6-5).
9. Why shouldn't a credit manager be overly aggressive when first contacting a customer who has just missed a payment due date?
10. What are the steps followed in the collection effort, along with their approximate timing?
11. What collection practices are actually used by businesses, according to evidence cited in the chapter?
12. What are the main differences faced by US credit managers when selling on credit abroad?

Problems

Note: Round calculations to the seventh decimal place when calculating daily interest rates. Use the simple interest rate unless otherwise specified.

1. Norton Wrench, a machine tool company, recently found out that one of its main competitors has tightened its credit standards. Norton's chief operating officer has asked you to make a recommendation to the executive policy committee on whether the company should tighten its standards. The marketing department estimates that annual sales will drop $20,000 from the present level of $275,000. The variable cost ratio is 0.7 and will not change, according to one of the cost accountants. Variable expenses related to collections and credit administration are projected at 1.25 percent of sales under the existing standards but 1.45 percent of sales under the proposed standards. The bad debt expense rate on both existing and incremental (lost) sales is estimated to be 7 percent. The DSO of 56 days is not expected to change and can be applied to any sales gained or lost due to a change in credit standards The company's annual cost of capital is 15 percent.
   a. Draw a cash flow timeline for 1 day's sales under the proposed standards.
   b. What is the value effect (ΔZ) of this decision on 1 day's sales?
   c. What is the overall value effect (ΔNPV)?
   d. Are there any nonfinancial considerations about which you believe the executive policy committee should be warned?

2. Gilbert Knitwear's president is convinced that the company must lengthen the credit period it offers to its customers, upscale menswear retail stores. She suggests to the credit executive that the stores have become less liquid and more indebted and need longer to pay their bills. As the analyst assigned to "run the numbers," you have determined that such a move will increase sales from $100 million to $105 million per year. The VCR is 0.65 and will not change, and the credit and collection expenses will increase from 2 percent to 2.5 percent under the proposal. DSO under the present 30-day terms is 42 days; under the proposed 45-day terms it will be 52 days, according to your best estimate. The bad debt loss rate is 4 percent, and it will not change for the additional sales. The company's annual cost of capital is 12 percent.
   a. Calculate the decision's 1-day change in value.
   b. Calculate the decision's NPV.
   c. Do you recommend lengthening the credit period?
   d. If the bad debt loss rate under the new credit terms is higher (8% versus 4%), does this change your recommendation?

3. A. Walton Book Publishers is trying to decide whether to offer a 3 percent cash discount for payments made within 10 days, making its new terms 3/10, net 30. On average, its paying customers currently pay in 40 days under its present terms of net 30. A sales analyst estimates that sales will stay the same. The existing bad debt loss rate is 3 percent; the rate under the new policy will be the same. It is estimated that 40 percent of A. Walton's paying customers will take the discount and pay on the tenth day, on average. The remaining paying customers will continue to pay in 40 days, on average. The company's annual cost of capital is 10 percent. Annual sales will remain unchanged at $250 million, and the variable cost ratio will continue to be 60 percent. The variable expenses for credit administration and collections will drop from 2 percent to 1 percent if the cash discount is implemented.
   a. What is the 1-day change in value related to the proposed terms?
   b. What is the change in daily net present value related to the proposed terms?
   c. Do you recommend that A. Walton initiate the cash discount?
   d. What is the optimal cash discount percent for A. Walton?

4. Rework the Flying High Hang Gliders, Inc., text example, assuming daily compounding instead of the simple interest stated in the text. (Hint: see footnotes 6 and 9 in the text.)
   a. How does the 1-day value effect change?
   b. How does NPV change?
   c. Comment on the reason for the differences in your answers as compared to the simple interest solutions shown in the text.
5. Rework the Siegel Apparel Mills text example, assuming daily compounding instead of the simple interest stated in the text. (Hint: see footnotes 6 and 9 in the text.)
   a. How does the 1-day value effect change?
   b. How does the decision's NPV change?
   c. Comment on the reason for the differences in your answers as compared to the simple interest solutions shown in the text.
6. You have been presented with the following accounts receivable information from Besley, Inc. Construct an aging schedule and calculate DSO and accounts receivable turnover for the 6-month period, using 180 days to calculate average daily credit sales.

   Besley, Inc., manufactures and sells wallboard for use in construction of modular homes. It sells on net 30 terms to contractors. Following are the last six months' sales and the accounts receivable balances at the end of June, the present (report) month.

ACCOUNTS RECEIVABLE SCHEDULE
BESLEY, INC.
JUNE 30, 2001

Month°	Credit Sales	Uncollected Amount
January	$ 75,000	$ 5,000
February	50,000	5,000
March	100,000	6,000
April	40,000	6,000
May	45,000	8,000
June	50,000	12,000
June 30 A/R Balance:		**$42,000**

°Assume all months have 30 days.

7. Calculate the uncollected balance percentages for the company in Problem 6. Discuss the insights you gain from this schedule relative to what you found in your analysis in Problem 6.
8. The following table gives the receivables data for Besley, Inc., (see problem 6) for the same 6 months, exactly 1 year later.

ACCOUNTS RECEIVABLE SCHEDULE
BESLEY, INC.
JUNE 30, 2002

Month°	Credit Sales	Uncollected Amount
January	$100,000	$10,000
February	90,000	10,000
March	80,000	12,000
April	200,000	12,000
May	100,000	16,000
June	150,000	24,000
June 30 A/R Balance:		**$84,000**

°Assume all months have 30 days.

Problem 8, continued:

For parts a-d (following),what conclusions do you draw based on your computations?

a. DSO

b. Accounts receivable turnover

c. The aging schedule

d. Uncollected balance percentages

e. Explain why your conclusions in part *d* might give a slightly different picture than those reached in parts *a-c*.

f. You have been informed that Besley's credit terms in both years were net 30. Are most of Besley's customers paying on time? Paying late?

g. What steps might Besley's credit personnel take to improve the success of their collection effort?

h. Compute the accounts receivable turnover Besley's should have experienced had all of its customers paid on the due date. How much of a reduction in outstanding total receivables would this have implied?

References

Moshe Ben-Horim and Haim Levy. 1983. Management of accounts receivable under inflation. *Financial Management* Spring:42–48.

Scott Besley and Jerome S. Osteryoung. 1985. Survey of current practices in establishing trade-credit limits. *The Financial Review* February:70–82.

Michael D. Carpenter and Jack E. Miller. 1979. A reliable framework for monitoring accounts receivable. *Financial Management* Winter:37–40.

Francis Chittenden and Richard Bragg. 1997. Trade Credit, Cash-flow and SMEs in the UK, Germany and France. *International Small Business Journal* 16(1):22–35.

Ginger Conlon, Lisa Napolitano, and Mike Pusateri, eds. 1997. *Unlocking profits: The strategic advantage of key account management.* Chicago: National Account Management Association.

Credit Research Foundation. 1999. *Credit professional's handbook: The technical reference manual for credit and customer financial managers.* Columbia, MD: Author.

Ned C. Hill and Kenneth D. Riener. 1979. Determining the cash discount in the firm's credit policy. *Financial Management* Spring:68–73.

Carl M. Hubbard and Fred H. Dorner. 2000. Analyzing credit policy adjustments. San Antonio, Texas. Trinity University, working paper.

Jeff Keller. 1995. Best practices in accounts receivable. *TMA Journal* January/February:34–37.

Sang-Hoon Kim and William Feist. 1995. Examination of the equivalent relationship between the two credit policy approaches: The opportunity cost and NPV approaches. *Financial Review* November:711–737.

Yong H. Kim and Joseph Atkins. 1978. Evaluating investments in accounts receivable: A wealth maximizing framework. *Journal of Finance* May:403–412.

Ruby Knerr. 1998. Gaining an understanding of your customers using portfolio analysis. *Business Credit* July-August:43–47.

Yul W. Lee and John D. Stowe. 1993. Product risk, asymmetric information, and trade credit. *Journal of Financial & Quantitative Analysis* June:285–299.

Joyce R. Ochs and Kenneth L. Parkinson. 1998. Collections: What the data shows. *Business Credit* June:20–21.

Rob Olsen. 1994. *Measures of performance: Credit collections and accounts receivable*. Columbia, MD: National Association of Credit Managers.

Richard L. Peterson. 1986. Collectors' use of collection remedies. *Journal of Financial Research* Spring:71–86.

Cecilia Wagner Ricci. 1999. A survey and analysis of accounts receivable practices in American corporations. *Financial Practice & Education* Fall/Winter:111–120.

R. Schwartz. 1974. An economic model of trade credit. *Journal of Financial and Quantitative Analysis* September:643–657.

Alan Shapiro. 1973. Optimal inventory and credit-granting strategies under inflation and devaluation. *Journal of Financial and Quantitative Analysis* January:37–46.

Michael D. Sherman and Brian Fisher. 1992. An Evaluation of the Statistic Accuracy of Monitoring Outstanding Accounts Receivable. *Proceedings of the 8th International Symposium on Cash, Treasury & Working Capital Management*, San Francisco, October 2.

Keith V. Smith and Brian Belt. 1989. "Working capital management in practice: An update. Krannert School of Management (Purdue University), Working Paper 951, March.

Charles R. Turner. 1981. Key to managing foreign subsidiaries' locally-generated trade receivables. *Credit and Financial Management* January:26–28.

FOCUSED CASE
Kimball International, Inc.

Kimball International, Inc., (NASDAQ symbol: KBALB) is a diversified furniture and electronics manufacturer that sells wood and metal office furniture, lodging furniture, and electronic assemblies (including computer keyboards and mouse pointing devices).° The Lodging Group (part of the "Furniture and Cabinets" segment) is experiencing dramatic growth in sales and income, increasing market share at the same time that the hospitality industry is continuing its refurbishing cycle. The assistant treasurer is considering increasing the company's investment in this high-growth area. He believes if the company changes its credit standards and credit period, it will add profitable sales. Along with the rest of the top management staff and the board of directors, he is concerned about the slowly growing or declining sales and/or market share in some of Kimball's segments (such as the original equipment manufacturers Cabinets and Furniture unit). Sales continued to grow at a moderate pace in the larger two of the company's three business segments—(Furniture and Cabinets, and Electronic Contract Assemblies), but sales in the company's smallest business segment—(Processed Wood Products and Other) declined from the prior year's first quarter. According to the company's 10-K annual report of its financial statements and operating results (as filed with the Securities and Exchange Commission, page 9):

> "Sales of Original Equipment Manufacturer (OEM) product lines, primarily television cabinets and stands, audio cabinets, and residential furniture, decreased in the three month period when compared with one year earlier. Lower sales volume of cabinets were caused by a major cabinet customer experiencing lower market demand for their products. Although certain other cabinet customers increased their volumes, this product line experienced an overall decline in sales volume. Production flexibil-

ity is inherent in the OEM supplier market and may cause short-term fluctuations in any given quarter. Volumes of contract residential furniture increased from the prior year. Some OEM production capacity was used for production of hospitality furniture during the quarter. OEM operating income declined from the prior year's level as a result of the decrease in sales volume and, to a lesser extent, an unfavorable sales mix toward lower margin products."

The assistant treasurer believes that the company's future is linked to marked growth in a few areas such as the Lodging Group. He has asked for your advice as the senior credit analyst in the credit department.

At present, the company holds roughly 25 percent of its $557 million asset base in the form of cash and marketable securities. Its present average credit period for paying customers of the Lodging Group is 54 days. The company extends 45 day terms to its customers. The bad debt losses on the Group's sales are a respectable 1.7 percent. Sales in the Lodging Group are $85 million, almost one-tenth of the company's $983 million sales. The variable costs for lodging furniture, excluding credit administration and collection costs, average 45 percent. The company's weighted average cost of capital is 10%. It presently has surplus funds invested at an average rate of 6.5 percent. Sales estimates under two independent proposals for changes in the credit policy are as follows:

Proposal A: Lengthen credit period to 60 days.

Proposal B: Ease up on credit standards.

Proposal C: Implement both Proposals A and B.

Other relevant aspects of the company's financial position were also provided to the credit analyst from the management discussion in the 10-K report (pp 10-11)

> Consolidated selling, general and administrative expense as a percent of sales increased 1.2 percentage points for the three month period (compared to the year earlier), primarily as a result of moderate additions to the Company's existing infrastructure supporting

---

°The company and its attributes are real, but the credit policy aspects are fictitious. Check with your instructor to see if he or she wishes to have you supplement the case data gathered from other print or electronic sources.

POLICY	SALES	BAD DEBT EXPENSE RATE (% OF REVENUE)	CREDIT ADMIN. & COLLEC. EXP. (% OF REVENUE)	LODGING GRP. PAYING CUSTOMERS' SALES COLLECTION PERIOD
Present	$85 million	1.7%	1%	54 days
Proposal A	$95 million	2.0%	1.1%	66 days
Proposal B	$100 million	2.3%	2%	63 days
Proposal C	$105 million	2.45%	3%	68 days

the higher sales volume, additions as the result of acquiring ELMO Semiconductor in the latter half of the prior fiscal year, and certain other costs that are variable with earnings.

Operating income for the first quarter of 1997 was $19,183,000, increasing 2.8 percentage points, as a percent of sales, when compared to the first quarter of 1996, primarily as a result of sales volume increases, the diminished effects of material price increases that were experienced in the prior year's first quarter, and manufacturing efficiency improvements, including benefits from quality and cost containment initiatives.

Investment income for the first quarter remained flat when compared to the same period in the previous year, as higher investment balances were offset by a lower effective yield. Other—net includes $3.8 million related to a loss on the sale of a foreign subsidiary in the current year, which is offset by a $3.8 million income tax benefit recorded in Taxes on Income. The remaining decrease in Other income or expense—net is primarily due to larger gains realized on the sale of assets in the prior year.

Taxes on Income includes a $3.8 million tax benefit relating to the sale of a foreign subsidiary in the current year's first quarter. This tax benefit was the result of a higher US tax basis in this subsidiary as a result of previously undeductible losses on the investment in this UK subsidiary. Excluding this tax benefit, the effective income tax rate decreased 1.3 percentage points in the 3 month period when compared with the prior year partly as a result of reduced European operating losses that provide no immediate tax benefit.

The company achieved net income of $13,521,000, or $0.65 per share for the first quarter of the 1997 fiscal year, a 61% increase over the prior year's first quarter net income of $8,418,000 or $0.40 per share.

LIQUIDITY AND CAPITAL RESOURCES
Cash, Cash Equivalents and Short-Term Investments totaled $140 million at September 30, 1996 as compared with $117 million one year earlier. Liquidity remained strong with working capital and the current ratio at $230 million and 2.7 to 1, respectively, at September 30, 1996, as compared with $204 million and 2.7 to 1, respectively, one year earlier.

Operating activities continued to generate positive cash flow, which amounted to $38 million for the 3 months ended September 30, 1996. Portions of the company's cash flow from operations were reinvested in the business to fund $9 million of capital investments for the future, primarily production equipment upgrades and improvements in the company's business information systems. Five million dollars was used for financing activities, primarily to pay dividends. Net cash flow, excluding purchases and maturities of short-term investments, amounted to a positive $26 million for the 3 month period ended September 30, 1996.

The company anticipates maintaining a strong liquidity position throughout the 1997 fiscal year with cash needs being met by cash flows provided by operations, available cash balances, and short-term investments on hand.

1. Which proposal, if any, should Kimball adopt? Defend your position based on the NPV effect and the present financial position of the company. Indicate why you chose the discount rate used in the analysis.
2. How does the financial position of the company strengthen or weaken the recommendation you made in part 1?
3. The assistant treasurer indicates to you that one of the Electronic Products senior managers thinks capital should be allocated to his unit instead of to the Lodging Group. How should the assistant treasurer respond to this concern? (You may use any business concept or approach to answer this, not limiting the answer to the credit policy proposals.)
4. What competitor reactions are likely if Kimball unilaterally makes one or both credit policy changes? How might this be incorporated into the present analysis?

Appendix 6A

Sophisticated Receivables Monitoring Techniques

Several different approaches have been developed or refined recently to better monitor (and forecast) collections. These are the decomposition method, the variance analysis model, the Markov chain approach, the lagged regression model, and the recursive regression model.

The **decomposition method** developed by Gentry and De La Garza[1] involves segregating the period-to-period changes in receivables into three effects: the collection effect, the sales effect, and the interaction effect. The interaction effect refers to the joint influence of sales and collections. The philosophy behind this method is very similar to that used in management accounting, in which budget variances are divided into price, volume, and mix categories. A notable difference is with what we are comparing recent experience; in this case, it is the last period's experience instead of budgeted amounts. The credit manager wishes to know the change in the controllable variable(s), which, in this case, is the collection effect and part of the interaction effect. Deterioration in the collection pattern signals corrective action. Although it takes time to construct the analysis schedule, this approach does help the analyst in determining when and how substantially the collection pattern has changed.

The **variance analysis model** builds on the decomposition model, and compares actual receivables performance to the budgeted amounts.[2] If the budget captures the unique conditions and sales levels a company is experiencing, or is so adjusted after the period is over ("flexible budgeting"), then the true reason(s) for changes in receivables levels can be discerned. The budgeted amount is calculated as expected sales multiplied by expected DSO.

Actual sales can be used instead of expected sales, once the period is over, to get a revised (or "flexible") budgeted amount. The model separates the collection experience variance (actual DSO minus budgeted DSO) from the sales effect variance (actual daily sales minus budgeted daily sales). If the collection experience variance is positive, or unfavorable, the analyst is prompted to determine the possible reasons and suggest some corrective actions the company might take. Additionally, the model separates the sales effect variance into its two components: the sales mix effect and the sales quantity effect. The sales mix effect is relevant because the company might sell different products with different credit terms, and the analyst should not fault the collection effort for the resultant increase in receivables.

Markov chain analysis is an elaborate means of identifying changes in the collection experience. It is related to the uncollected balance percentages presented earlier in the chapter, which are actually a simple application of Markov chains. This technique is applied by (1) identifying each possible payment stage at which an account might be (namely already paid, current, 1 month past due, 2 months past due, 3 months past due, or written off as bad debt); (2) specifying the "transition probabilities" for the average account, which is the probability it will move from one of the stages to any of the other stages; (3) using the results from stage 2 to estimate what the DSO, collection amount, and receivables amount should be; and (4) noting whether the actual experience mirrors what was expected from stage 3.

---

[1] James A. Gentry and J.M. De La Garza. 1985. Monitoring Accounts Receivable Revisited. *Financial Management* Winter: 28–38.

[2] A variance is defined as the actual dollar amount minus budgeted dollar amount. This technique was developed in George W. Gallinger and A. James Ifflander. 1986. Monitoring Accounts Receivable Using Variance Analysis. *Financial Management* Winter: 69–76.

Historical data or a forecasting technique such as exponential smoothing might be used to develop the stage 2 transition probabilities.[3]

A quick and relatively inexpensive way of determining a company's collection experience involves **lagged regression analysis.**[4] The amounts collected this period are model-determined percentages multiplied by sales made in this and previous months. The percentages are the regression coefficients b:

$$C_t = b_1 S_{t-1} + b_2 S_{t-2} + b_3 S_{t-3} + \cdots + b_i S_{t-i} + e_t \quad \text{(6A-1)}$$

In which: C_t = the amount collected during the present month, month t

S_t = the company's credit sales made in month t

b_t = the month t collection percentage of a given month's sales

i = the number of periods lagged

e_t = an error term to capture bad debt losses and unpredictable variations in collections.

The i subscripts for the collection percentages are a bit tricky. The percent of last month's sales being collected this month is represented by $i = 1$; when $i = 2$, we are referencing the sales from 2 months ago, and so on. In practice, the constant term one typically includes in a regression equation is omitted, which is equivalent to forcing the regression line through the origin. The error term picks up unpredictable influences, and to the degree that b terms sum to less than 100 percent, it would also incorporate the bad debt loss rate. Ignoring unpredictable influences and omitted variables, we have

an expression for computing the bad debt loss rate b as shown in Equation 6A-2:

$$b_E = 1 - (b_1 + b_2 + b_3 + \cdots + b_i) \quad \text{(6A-2)}$$

Equation 6A-3 is equivalent:

$$b_E = 1 - \sum_1^i b_i \quad \text{(6A-3)}$$

To implement the lagged regression approach, the analyst gathers the dollar amounts of monthly credit sales and collections for at least 3 years and inputs these to a statistical package or a financial spreadsheet. For example, in Excel select Tools, then select Data Analysis, and finally select Regression. (Make sure you have installed the data analysis add-in within Excel by selecting Tools / Add Ins / Analysis ToolPak before initiating the regression routine.) The computer calculates the b_i's, which are the percentages of each past month's sales that were collected during a particular month. These percentages can be monitored through time to see if they are changing. They can also be used to forecast cash collections in upcoming months. Using only 21 months of actual sales and collection data for one company, Shim and Siegel[5] fit the following equation:

$$C_t = 60.6\%(S_{t-1}) + 24.3\%(S_{t-2}) + 8.8\%(S_{t-3})$$

The r^2 for the model is 0.754, which indicates the goodness-of-fit was quite good. The t statistics for the first two b's were both 0.05 or less, and the third coefficient, b_3, was not significant at the 5 percent significance level. The latter was still judged acceptable, because such a small sample size was used to fit the regression equation. In practice, the analyst should use a larger sample. Finally, using either Equation 6A-2 or 6A-3, we find that the bad debt loss percentage b_E was = $[1 - (.606 + .243 + .088)]$ = .063, or 6.3%.[6] Another application of this model to a large department store chain found the goodness of fit (r^2) to increase significantly when including 4

[3]See Jarl G. Kallberg and Anthony Saunders. 1983. Markov Chain approaches to the payment behavior of retail credit customers. *Financial Management* Summer:5–14. See also Jarl G. Kallberg and Kenneth Parkinson. 1984. *Current asset management: Cash, credit, and inventory.* New York: John Wiley & Sons, pp 180–184, 190–192.

[4]This was suggested by B.K. Stone (1976; cited in chapter references); it was implemented by J.K. Shim in 1981. Estimating cash collection rates from credit sales: A lagged regression approach. *Financial Management* Winter:28–31.

[5]See J.K. Shim and Joel G. Siegel. 1988. *Handbook of financial analysis, forecasting, and modeling.* Englewood Cliffs, NJ: Prentice-Hall, pp 331–332.

[6]The Durbin-Watson statistic when testing for autocorrelation was 2.52, indicating a lack of autocorrelation. The standard error of the estimate for the equation was 11.63.

months of sales data in the model, as compared with only 1 month (r^2 increased to 0.5875 from 0.3805).[7]

A critique of the ordinary least squares (OLS) regression model just discussed does not aid the analyst in recognizing when there are significant changes in collection patterns, as opposed to minor and/or seasonal changes. Although a complete discussion is beyond our scope, we mention that the **recursive least squares (RLS) regression model** remedies this shortcoming. Essentially, this model allows the estimated collection fractions (the regression

coefficients) to change over time.[8] Although the OLS model considered above can be reestimated many times, such an approach is limited because pattern changes occurring during the model's estimation period contaminate the estimated fractions, and

---

[7]Kallberg and Parkinson, cited earlier, p 189.

[8]The only known application of this technique to receivables monitoring is in Michael J. Gombola and Douglas R. Kahl. *Identifying changes in receivables collection patterns.* Paper presentation at the Financial Management Association 1989 Annual Meeting, Boston, MA. Their model allows the collection fractions to vary over time, as opposed to the fixed coefficients OLS model presented earlier. The model is appealing because it is precisely the fact that collections fractions might change over time that interests the credit manager.

even after receiving the model results and realizing that the pattern has changed, the analyst cannot know when the change occurred. Even if the analyst could identify the timing of the pattern change, it would be necessary to wait a long time before having enough new data to refit a revised model. The RLS lagged regression model has a built-in method of updating an initial set of coefficient estimates, which, in this case, are the collection fractions. Errors observed in actual observations feed back into the model to enable an automatic adjustment of coefficients. Visual inspection of the coefficients on a computer printout enables the analyst to see when the collection experience changed.

The careful reader has perhaps noticed a common omission shared by all of the above techniques. Although each method helps to uncover changes in the collection experience, none tells us why the change occurred. Knowing whether to take corrective action certainly depends on the permanence of and reason(s) for the change. It is generally recommended that collection fractions be regressed on factors that might logically cause them to change. Factors suggested include the level of consumer confidence, buying power indices, the unemployment rate, current stage of the business cycle, health of the customers' industries, and many others. Results of this further regression modeling might help answer questions about permanence and aid in forecasting future collection patterns.

CHAPTER 7

Managing Payables and Accruals

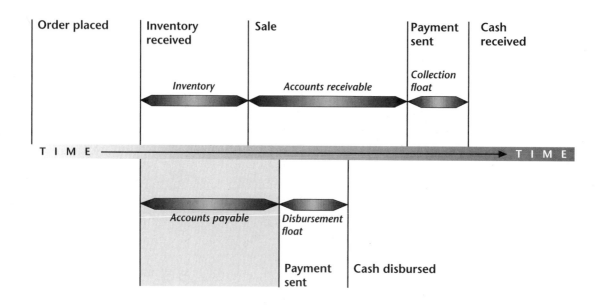

After studying this chapter, you should be able to:

- Apply time value of money principles to the payment of accounts payable.
- Decide when to take a cash discount for early payment and when to pay at the end of the credit period.
- Better understand the ethical issues involved in the payment decision.
- Better assess the status of the firm's accounts payables balance through the use of balance fractions rather than using more traditional but less accurate measures such as payables turnover ratios.

In early January, Macy's 20,000 suppliers got the bad news. They were informed that they would have to wait several more weeks to receive payment on the shipments they sent to R. H. Macy & Company prior to the Christmas holiday season. As January wore on, Macy's financial position deteriorated even more and by the end of January, Macy declared bankruptcy under Chapter 11. Macy, struggling under a heavy debt burden as a result of a leveraged buy-out during the late 1980s and a less-than-expected holiday shopping season, simply did not have the cash to pay the suppliers.

This chapter focuses on the third leg of the working capital cycle, the management of accounts payable and accrued operating expenses. As we have seen, a firm's working capital cycle begins with the purchase of inventory. This purchase generally initiates an accounts payable balance and the firm begins accruing expenses such as wages, salaries, and taxes. Inventory is then sold creating an accounts receivable balance. At some point, generally before the receivables are collected in cash, the payables and accruals are paid. These outflows are then "reimbursed" by the collection of the outstanding receivables. This cycle is continually replayed over and over again. However, in Macy's case, the cycle came to a halt as more cash was needed to pay creditors and suppliers than Macy was able to collect from sales.

Thus far in this text, we have discussed the management of inventory and receivables. We now turn our attention to the proper management of the payables and accruals generated by the operations of the firm. In this chapter, we discuss how payables and accruals represent sources of financing for the firm's investment in its working capital. We also discuss how to make proper financial decisions regarding the timing of payment for payables and accruals and some of the institutional aspects of structuring the information systems required for making such payments. The chapter concludes by discussing the importance of monitoring the payables balance so that payments are made in a time frame appropriate to the firm's policies regarding its payables.

FINANCIAL DILEMMA

Why Pay Early?

The financial manager of BBC, Inc., just received an invoice from a new supplier with the following terms 2/5, net 45. He understands that the terms allow him to take a 2 percent discount from the face amount of the invoice if paid by the 5th day after the invoice date. Otherwise, payment for the full invoice price is due on the 45th day from the invoice date. The financial manager is stumped because although the discount seems enticing, it forces him to make payment 40 days ahead of the actual due date.

SPONTANEOUS SOURCES OF FINANCING

A spontaneous source of financing occurs automatically as a result of operations. Two common spontaneous financing sources are payables and accruals.

An example helps to better explain how these spontaneous sources work. Suppose Ajax Chemical Company purchases a truckload of packaging materials from one of its suppliers. These materials are used to package its shipments of chemical products. When the delivery arrives at Ajax, an invoice is enclosed stating the terms of credit, but Ajax has the materials and can begin using them immediately without making payment of funds.

In this sense the supplier is extending credit to Ajax. Ajax can begin using the packaging materials to ship its products and only after the payables credit period is up does Ajax have to pay for its purchases. This allows Ajax to better match its receipt of cash from sales of its products with cash disbursements for its purchases.

ACCOUNTS PAYABLE

Accounts payable, also referred to as trade credit, is considered a spontaneous financing source because it is generated by the normal day-to-day operations of the firm. If there is demand for the firm's product, the firm will produce to satisfy that demand and in so doing must order materials and supplies for its production or service processes. If the materials and supplies are purchased on credit, a source of financing is created. Through the sale of the product, the corporation gains a resource that eventually generates a cash inflow enabling the spontaneously generated liability, the account payable, to be paid off.

Types of Purchase Terms

There are a multitude of purchase terms available. Chapter 5 presented a detailed discussion of credit terms, which are the same as purchase terms except from the perspective of the seller. This section does not reiterate the various credit terms available, except to highlight some of the more typical forms.

The exact terms depend on the product being purchased and the industry involved. For example, a gas station purchasing gasoline generally gets no longer than 10 days to pay for the purchase because the product is sold so quickly. Likewise perishable products generally carry short credit periods. On the other hand, the purchase of heavy industrial equipment may carry much longer credit periods. These products are more durable and can be reclaimed if payment is not made.

One common credit arrangement is an **open account.** Under this type of arrangement, once a customer has been approved for credit, the customer can make repeated purchases without applying for credit each time. When the goods are purchased, they are sent with payment due at a specified time after receipt of invoice. An example is net 30 days. In this case, the full amount of the invoice is due 30 days after the invoice date.

Another common set of credit terms involves offering a **cash discount** for early payment. An example is 2/10, net 30, which means that if payment is made 10 days after the invoice date, a 2 percent discount from purchase price can be taken. Otherwise, the full invoice price is due 30 days from the invoice date.

Not all credit terms are based on the invoice date. For example, some industries quote credit terms on a **prox** basis. Such terms allow payment on a specific date in the following month. For example, terms of 2/10, prox net 30 means payment is due on the

30th day of the following month or a cash discount of 2 percent can be taken if payment is received on the 10th day of the following month.

Other forms of credit purchases are seasonal dating and consignment. **Seasonal dating** is common in the toy industry and other seasonal businesses. Seasonal dating allows retail outlets to purchase inventory before the peak buying season and defer payment until after the peak season. For example, toy manufacturers allow retail outlets to purchase toys months before Christmas but pay for the inventory during January and February. The advantage to the manufacturer is to permit the production of the items over a longer time without excessive inventory buildup. An example of seasonal dating terms is 2/10, net 30, dating 90. In this case, the clock starts running 90 days after the invoice date. The purchaser can then take the cash discount if paid in 10 days with full payment due in 30 days after the 90-day period is up.

Consignment is an arrangement in which a retailer obtains an inventory item without obligation. That is, if the item is sold, payment is due. If the item is not sold, the retailer can simply return the item without penalty. An example of this type of an arrangement is the college textbook industry. Book publishers send their books to college bookstores only to have them returned if they are not sold.

Finally, a growing number of companies allow discounts if their customers permit the electronic debiting of their accounts. This type of payment system is discussed more fully in Chapters 8, 11, and 19.

The Cash Flow Time Line and Accounts Payable

A financial manager purchasing materials or services on credit gains an advantage by being able to use the goods or services to earn a profit without first having to pay for them. The time between receipt of the goods or services and the date on which cash payment is made constitutes **positive float.** The longer the payment delay, the better off the firm, as long as payment is not delayed past the credit period. If payment is not made within the prescribed credit period, suppliers often impose a penalty of 1 to 1.5 percent per month until payment is made. In addition, when a delinquent purchaser places another order, the order is not sent until overdue balances are paid. In general, financial managers should delay payment as long as possible while remaining within the stated credit period.

How long should the financial manager delay payment? The answer to this question can be put in the context of the cash flow timeline such as the one presented in Exhibit 7-1 showing the important payment decision dates.

EXHIBIT 7-1
Cash Flow Timeline for Disbursements

| Purchase Date | Cash Discount Date | Credit Period |

The financial manager has several payment options. First, payment can be made on the date of purchase. Second, payment can be made on or before the cash discount period. Third, payment can be made on or before the end of the credit period but after the cash discount period. Fourth, payment can be made after the credit period has expired.

How should the financial manager formulate the payment decision? We begin by listing some basic financial management principles related to the payment of accounts payable. We then develop a payment decision model to support these principles.

- A payable should never be paid until the last day of the discount period or at the end of the credit period and should never be paid early.
- A discount should be taken only when the effective interest rate implied by the discount rate and payable terms exceeds the opportunity cost of short-term funds over the same period.
- A payable should not be stretched past the credit period.

The payment decision model is relatively straight-forward and involves the following variables:

IP:	Dollar invoice price
DD:	Number of days that payment is delayed from date of purchase.
DP:	Discount period
CP:	Credit period
d :	Cash discount rate
k :	Annual opportunity rate
kb :	Annual borrowing rate
fee:	Annual fee and intangible cost of late payment.

These variables can now be arranged to arrive at the present value of delayed payment beyond the purchase date. The three net present value (NPV) models differ only by the assumed date of payment and the amount paid (either the invoice price or the invoice price less the cash discount). The first model, Equation 7-1, calculates the NPV assuming payment is made by the end of the discount period:

$$NPV = IP \times (1-d) / (1 + (DD \times (k/365))) \; (if \; DD \leq DP) \qquad \text{(7-1)}$$

In this equation, the NPV is equal to the present value of the discounted invoice price, assuming payment is made by the end of the discount period.

The second NPV model, Equation 7-2, assumes that payment is made after the discount period but no later than the end of the credit period:

$$NPV = IP / (1 + (DD \times (k/365))) \; (if \; DP < DD \leq CP) \qquad \text{(7-2)}$$

In Equation 7-2, the NPV is equal to the present value of the full invoice price, assuming payment is made after the discount period but no later than the end of the credit period.

The third NPV model, Equation 7-3, calculates the impact of paying after the credit period. Although ethical business practice dictates that payment should be made no later than the end of the credit period, a financial manager may be in such an illiquid situation that payment cannot be made at that time. In such a circumstance, it is important for the financial manager to estimate the cost of making the payment late. Although Equation 7-3 includes a late payment fee, which is an explicit cost of late payment, a cost that Equation

7-3 does not take into account is the lost goodwill of the supplier that occurs if stretching payments becomes typical behavior. Good business practice dictates that if payments are to be stretched, the financial manager should contact the credit manager at the supplying firm to work out a payment schedule.

$$NPV = IP \times (1 + (DD - CP) \times (fee/365)) / (1 + (DD \times (k/365))) \ (\ if\ DD > CP) \quad \text{(7-3)}$$

In Equation 7-3, the NPV calculation determines the present value of the invoice price plus the late payment fee.

Before entering numbers into the NPV model, let's discuss its logic. First, suppose that DD = 0, indicating that payment is made on the purchase date. In this case, the value of the cost of paying the payable is simply the discounted invoice price. Next, suppose that payment is made on the discount date. Then NPV is reduced because the same payment is made, but now it is made at a later date and the present value of a later payment is less than an equivalent payment made earlier. Next, suppose that payment is made at the end of the credit period. In this case, NPV is equal to the present value of the invoice price ignoring any discount. Whether this NPV is less than the NPV taking the discount depends on the relative sizes of the cash discount rate and the firm's investment opportunity rate. We explore this relationship later in this chapter. Finally, suppose that payment is made after the credit period. In this case, NPV is equal to the present value of the invoice price and late payment penalty.

Theoretically the cost of the lost goodwill should also be added to the numerator of the NPV expression. However, this can be difficult to assess. We reiterate that the financial manager should only stretch the payment of an invoice when the company's financial situation prevents payment from occurring within the credit period.

Using the NPV model, the financial manager should continue to delay payment for an additional day up to the end of the credit period as long as the NPV continues to fall. The objective is to pay on the day that minimizes the present value cost of the invoice.

FINANCIAL DILEMMA REVISITED

Recall the dilemma faced by the financial manager at BBC, Inc. The financial manager was faced with trying to decide whether it was worth taking a cash discount or keeping the funds invested and possibly even stretching the payable. Using the NPV model, the financial manager can arrive at the proper decision. Let's see what that decision should be.

The terms offered were 2/5, net 45. We may assume that the firm's investment rate is 10 percent, the cost of borrowing is 12 percent, the annualized late payment fee is 18 percent, and the invoice in question is for $10,000. Exhibit 7-2 shows the calculated value for NPV over various periods. From the NPV results, the obvious answer to BBC's dilemma is to take the discount and pay on the fifth day. This action minimizes the present value cost of making the payment. Payment on any other day incurs a higher present value cost for BBC.

The NPV model can be simplified when payment is either going to be made on the discount date or the credit period date. If these are the only two choices, the following simplified payables decision model can be developed. The cash discount should be taken and payment made at the end of the cash discount period if the relationship shown in Equation 7-4 is true.

$$IP \times (1-d) < IP / (1 + (CP - DP) \times (k/365)) \quad \text{(7-4)}$$

EXHIBIT 7-2
Calculated Value of NPV Assuming Ten Percent Investment Rate

DAYS DELAYED FROM INVOICE DATE	NPV
0	$9,800.00
1	9,797.32
2	9,794.63
3	9,791.95
4	9,789.27
5	9,786.59
10	9,972.68
15	9,959.07
20	9,945.50
25	9,931.97
30	9,918.48
35	9,905.02
40	9,891.60
45	9,878.21
46	9,880.41
47	9,882.61
48	9,884.80

Payment should be made at the end of the discount period if the discounted invoice price, IP $\times$ (1−d), is less than the present value of the full invoice price. Present value is calculated at the end of the cash discount period. This relationship can be simplified by solving for k as shown in Equation 7-5.

$$k < (d/(1-d)) \times (365/(CP-DP)) \tag{7-5}$$

Thus, if the firm's investment rate, k, is less than the annualized cash discount rate, it is better to take the cash discount and pay by the discount date. Delaying payment allows the paying firm to keep its funds invested at the annualized rate of k. If this rate is less than the annualized cash discount rate offered by the supplier, value can be enhanced by taking the cash discount. Otherwise, the funds should be invested and payment only made at the end of the credit period date. The difference between the invoice price and the discounted invoice price is in essence a finance charge for delaying payment from the discount date to the credit period date. If this charge is greater than what the firm can earn on its money by delaying payment, then it should take the discount.

What happens if the firm does not have the cash to pay the payables on the discount rate and therefore there is no opportunity to invest the funds? In this case, the firm needs to consider whether or not it is profitable to borrow the funds from a bank so that it can take the cash discount, assuming that funds to repay the bank will be available by the end of the credit period. In this case, as long as the annualized borrowing rate, k_b, is less than the annualized cash discount rate computed in Equation 7-5, it will be profitable to borrow the funds to pay the discounted invoice price on the discount date. This relationship is shown in Equation 7-6:

$$k_b < (d/(1-d)) \times (365/(CP-DP)) \tag{7-6}$$

Suppose that BBC's investment rate is 20 percent. Exhibit 7-3 displays the calculated values for NPV over the same period as that shown in Exhibit 7-2.

In this case the decision should be to forego the cash discount because the investment rate, k, of 20 percent exceeds the annualized cash discount rate, $(d/(1-d)) \times (365/(CP-DP))$, of 18.62%. In addition, because the investment rate exceeds the explicit

EXHIBIT 7-3
Calculated Value of NPV Assuming a Twenty Percent Investment Rate

DAYS DELAYED FROM INVOICE DATE	NPV
0	$9,800.00
1	9,794.63
2	9,789.27
3	9,783.92
4	9,778.57
5	9,773.22
10	9,945.50
15	9,918.48
20	9,891.60
25	9,864.86
30	9,838.27
35	9,811.83
40	9,785.52
45	9,759.36
46	9,758.95
47	9,758.55
48	9,758.14

penalty fee, the NPV expression decreases with each additional day of non-payment. Of course, this ignores any assessment of the implicit loss of goodwill with the supplier. The bottom line is that even if NPV declines past the credit period, the firm basically has agreed to a contract to pay no later than at the end of the credit period and payment should be made regardless of the financial consequences.

These numerical examples demonstrate the three principles of managing the payment of accounts payable presented earlier. Through the NPV model, we can verify that payment should not be made until at least the end of the discount period. Then, the

FOCUS ON PRACTICE

IS IT PAID, OR IS IT NOT PAID? One interesting problem in payment processing is the criteria for deciding when payment is made. Hill, Sartoris, and Ferguson, conducted a survey and discovered that there is an apparent divergence of opinion between payors and payees regarding the date payment is made.[1] Credit managers (payees) generally define date of payment as the day payment is received at the lockbox or collection location. Payables managers (payors), on the other hand, generally view payment as being made on the postmark date or day sent. Very few firms define payment date as the day they receive good or collected funds (i.e., cash in the bank). In most cases, a grace period is allowed that reduces the conflict over the divergence of opinion related to the date payment is made. This conflict may go away in the near future as more payments are made electronically. Recently the Financial Services Technology Consortium (FSTC) ushered in a new era of electronic payments with its e-check. E-checks can be issued on the day payment is due to the supplier and sent via e-mail message to allow posting in as little as a few hours. The good thing is that this allows the payor to have control of the funds until the last minute possible, yet still meet the supplier's terms.[2]

Finally, the survey asked if a suppliers charge a late payment fee when a customer pays 25 days late. Approximately 66 percent of the respondents indicated that they generally do not do so. Almost 25 percent of the respondents indicated that they would likely assess a late payment fee.

[1]See Ned Hill, William Sartoris, and Daniel Ferguson in chapter references.

[2]Linda Coven. 1999. The e-check cometh . . . as a replacement for paper checks. *Business Credit* 101(9):34–38.

discount should only be taken if the annualized discount rate implied by the credit terms exceeds either the investment rate or the borrowing rate. Finally, although the NPV model can easily calculate the impact of late payment, payment should only be stretched past the credit period if the firm is financially unable to make payment.

The late payment fee has both a tangible component and an intangible component. Many firms specify such a fee. This is a tangible cost of paying past the credit period. However, intangible costs include the ill will generated by consistently stretching payments past the credit period. This cost is difficult to measure but should be factored into the analysis so that the true cost of stretching can be assessed.

Ethics and the Payment Decision

Previously, we have suggested that a firm not stretch the payment beyond the end of the credit period. At times, it may appear that the NPV of stretching is a financially positive decision especially when the late payment fee is less than the firm's opportunity investment rate. However, when the credit terms were accepted, a contract to pay by a specific date was also accepted and good business practice dictates that contracts be honored.

Exhibit 7-4 presents three tiers of ethical standards by which to judge a company's actions. The lowest tier basically asks if the action is legal or is consistent with the intent of the law. The middle tier asks if you could explain to your parents what you do for a living, the business decisions you make, your business philosophy, and your rationale for your actions and decisions. The top tier requires a commitment to enhancing the well-being of the people you do business with, even if there is some cost to you.

EXHIBIT 7-4
Tiers of Ethical Standards[6]

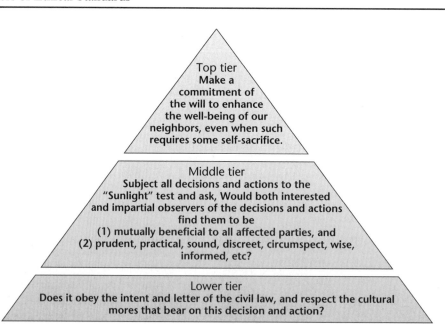

Top tier
Make a commitment of the will to enhance the well-being of our neighbors, even when such requires some self-sacrifice.

Middle tier
Subject all decisions and actions to the "Sunlight" test and ask, Would both interested and impartial observers of the decisions and actions find them to be (1) mutually beneficial to all affected parties, and (2) prudent, practical, sound, discreet, circumspect, wise, informed, etc?

Lower tier
Does it obey the intent and letter of the civil law, and respect the cultural mores that bear on this decision and action?

[6]SOURCE: Richard Chewning. Interested readers may also read Mary L. Woodell, 1991. Fraud? Imagine you're in the spotlight. *New York Times* November 24:F11. In this article, Woodell offers three tests to help you decide what is right. *The smell test:* Can you convince yourself it is right? *The what-would-your-parents-say test:* Could you explain your actions to your parents and retain their respect? *The deposition test:* Could you defend your actions in a televised trial shown nationwide?

Each tier, moving from the bottom to top, requires additional commitment on the part of the decision-maker to make those decisions that enhance the business relationship. At a minimum do what is legal according to the civil code, but always strive to make those decisions that build up relationships rather than tear them down.

Information Systems and Accounts Payable Management

To have an effective accounts payable system requires an organized information system. For example, when an invoice is received, it must first be validated. That is, does the invoice represent an order that was actually placed? Also, did the firm receive the goods, did the complete shipment arrive, and was it undamaged? Thus the invoice must be compared to the original purchase order. In addition, shipping documents and the receiving office documents must be checked to verify the receipt and condition of the shipment. Once verified, the invoice can be scheduled for payment. That is, a decision must be made as to the appropriate date to write and send the payment. Will the payment be made in time to take the discount, will the payment be scheduled to meet the credit period, or will payment be stretched and for how long? We have already discussed the decision-making process for this decision, but the point here is that the payment policy must be linked to the system involved in the actual scheduling of invoice payments.

This information system must be very efficient to take advantage of cash discounts, especially for discount periods less than 10 days. An inefficient information system simply causes the payor to miss many potentially lucrative cash discount opportunities.

Another facet of this information system is that once the payment of an invoice is scheduled, that information can be fed into the company's cash forecast system and the forecast of future cash disbursements updated automatically. This forecast linkage will be discussed more fully in Chapter 12.

The Internet is having a dramatic impact on the procurement and payment systems used by corporations today. Although consumers have been relatively slow in accepting electronic bill payment, the emergence of electronic marketplaces for industry groups is becoming an accepted method of doing business for a number of companies, as evidenced by the BuildNet, Inc., system discussed in this chapter's Focus on Practice box. The acceptance of such a practice has also expanded to the international marketplace.

FOCUS ON PRACTICE

ELECTRONIC MARKETPLACES   An example of an electronic marketplace is buildnet.com, a system that allows buyers and sellers in the building products and services industry to buy and sell electronically. For example, a builder can look ahead and see specific material and labor needs, each tagged with a "need-by" date. The bid requests, including product specifications and quantities, are automatically sent from the builder's computer through the Internet to his selected distributors. The distributor's computer, which is tied to internal real-time inventory and price updates, automatically responds to the builder with current and specific pricing, along with product availability. The builder's computer automatically accepts the prices within set tolerances and places an electronic order that includes the date required, delivery location, and billing method.

The distributor's computer accepts the order and creates a shipping slip. When delivered to the builder, products are checked against electronic purchase orders and signed for, often with a digital pen. With this authorization, the distributor generates and automatically sends an electronic invoice from the distributor's computer to the builder's computer. Payments are authorized and money changes hands, often as paperless bank-to-bank e-cash transactions.[3]

_____

[3]*The Buildnet E-business Initiative,* www.buildnet.com/ebusiness.htm.

Monitoring the Accounts Payable Balance

Once the firm's payment policy has been determined, it is important to monitor the execution of that policy on a routine basis. This section presents two ways to monitor the payment pattern and discuss the advantages and disadvantages of each. This material follows directly from the monitoring approaches discussed for inventory and receivables.

PAYABLES TURNOVER APPROACH.   The traditional approach to monitoring a firm's accounts payable balance is based on the firm's **payables turnover ratio.** The payables turnover ratio is found by dividing purchases (sometimes cost of goods sold is used) over a given period such as a year by the payables balance held during that same period.[4] For example, suppose that PAYRITE, Inc.'s total purchases for one year were $100,000, and the year-end balance in accounts payable was $18,000. The payables turnover ratio is 5.55 = $100,000/$18,000.

A related payables activity measure is the **number of days of payables outstanding (DPO).** This can be found by first calculating average daily purchases. Because we used annual purchases in the PAYRITE example earlier, average daily purchases is found by dividing annual purchases by 365. Average daily purchases is $273.97 = $100,000/365. DPO is then found by dividing the payables balance, $18,000, by average daily purchases, $273.97. The average DPO is equal to 65.70 days = $18,000/$273.97.[5] The greater this number, the slower the payables turnover and the longer the firm is taking to pay its suppliers.

Rather than monitoring the payables balance using annual data, the financial manager should monitor the resources provided by the payables area over a shorter time, such as monthly or even weekly. It is important for the financial manager to control payables so that appropriate cash discounts are not lost and that payables are paid by the desired time.

Suppose the financial manager collected the following data for the past 6 months. The dollar amount of monthly purchases is collected from the firm's purchasing records and the ending payables balance is based on the firm's monthly balance sheet data. Average daily purchases are calculated by summing the dollar amount of purchases over a predetermined time such as the most recent month or quarter. In this case, the most recent quarter is used. This sum is then divided by the number of days in the summation period, 90 days for a quarter based on a 360-day year. The result is the average daily purchases. The next line, Days Payables Outstanding, is calculated by dividing ending payables by the average daily purchases.

	JANUARY	FEBRUARY	MARCH	APRIL	MAY	JUNE
Purchases	100	120	100	80	60	70
Ending Payables			68	55	42	44
Average Daily Purchases(quarterly)			3.56	3.33	2.67	2.33
Days Payables Outstanding			19.1	16.5	15.7	18.9

From March through May, there is a decreasing DPO, which indicates that payments for outstanding payables are being paid more quickly. However, DPO does jump up to 18.9 days in June, the second highest level for the 4-month period.

---

[4]It is not uncommon to find average payables used in place of ending accounts payable balance. If the payables balance is growing or declining over the analysis period, average payables gives a better measure of accounts payable balance than does the ending payables balance.

[5]A short cut to finding this is to divide the number of days in a year, 365, by the payables turnover ratio. The equation 365/5.55555 results in the number of days of purchases outstanding, which is equal to 65.7 days.

A BALANCE FRACTION APPROACH. The following table shows the monthly dollar amount of purchases from January through June. In addition, the table shows the dollar amount of payables left in each succeeding month after purchase. For example, in January, $100 of inventory was purchased on credit. At the end of January, $50 of payables remained unpaid. Of the $100 of purchases in January, $15 remained unpaid at the end of February. The balance of the January purchases was paid in March.

Summing up each column results in the dollar amount of total ending accounts payable for each month. The table clearly shows that ending payables for each month consists of purchases over different periods. For example, ending payables for March consists of $50 of items purchased in March and $18 of items purchased in February.

MONTH OF PURCHASE	PURCHASE	OUTSTANDING PAYABLES					
		JANUARY	FEBRUARY	MARCH	APRIL	MAY	JUNE
January	$100	$50	$15				
February	$120		$60	$18			
March	$100			$50	$15		
April	$ 80				$40	$12	
May	$ 60					$30	$9
June	$ 70						$35
Total Payables		NA	$75	$68	$55	$42	$44

To make the above table useful for analysis purposes, we need to convert the dollar payables balances to **balance fractions,** dollar payables balance as a percent of purchases. Let's look at an example to help demonstrate this concept. Look at the dollar figures for January in the previous table. In January, $100 of inventory was purchased. At the end of January, $50 of the January purchase remained unpaid. At the end of February, $15 of the January purchases remained as a payables balance. Thus 50% of January purchases remained as unpaid ($50/$100) at the end of January and 15% ($15/$100) remained unpaid at the end of February. The following table shows the balance fraction calculations for the rest of the months. Notice that the balance fractions are constant. There is a steady pay down of outstanding payables resulting in 50% of a month's purchase remaining at the end of the purchase month and 15% remaining at the end of the month following the purchase month.

MONTH OF PURCHASE	PURCHASE	JANUARY	FEBRUARY	MARCH	APRIL	MAY	JUNE
January	$100	50%	15%				
February	$120		50%	15%			
March	$100			50%	15%		
April	$ 80				50%	15%	
May	$ 60					50%	15%
June	$ 70						50%

We can conclude from this analysis that payment practice has been stable with no variation in payment pattern of the firm's accounts payables. This finding is in conflict with the conclusion drawn by analysis based on DPO. DPO uses total payables in the numerator. If purchases are falling, then payables are generally lower. In the denominator, if purchases are falling, the average daily purchases are artificially high because the averaging period includes relatively higher purchases from an earlier period. Thus turnover generally falls as purchases fall, not necessarily because of a slower payment pattern, but because of the purchasing trend and the period chosen over which to calculate average daily purchases.

ACCRUALS

An **accrual** is an expense that has been incurred but has not yet been paid. There are basically two forms of accruals that provide a source of short-term financing for the firm: accrued wages and salaries, and accrued taxes. Accruals represent a source of financing because, for example, accrued wages represent a service performed by the firm's employees without an immediate payment for the services rendered. Likewise, the government provides financing to business firms because it requires quarterly payment for taxes. The fact that a firm is able to use these tax dollars for a full 3 months constitutes a source of financing.

A firm can increase its financing through accruals by paying its employees biweekly instead of weekly, or monthly instead of biweekly. However, the financial manager must take into consideration the reaction of its employees if it decides to change the frequency of wage or salary payments.

Accruals represent a spontaneous source of financing because as the business expands, the level of operations expands, as does the level of accrued wages and taxes. This source likewise decreases as the level of business activity declines.

SUMMARY

This chapter approached the determination of an accounts payable model from a present value perspective. We demonstrated that on the basis of time value of money considerations, a cash discount should be taken whenever the firm's investment rate is less than the annualized cash discount rate. In addition, the firm should borrow to take a cash discount when the borrowing rate is less than the annualized cash discount rate. If neither of these situations exist, then the firm should not pay until the end of the credit period. We also concluded that stretching payment past the credit period date should not be a normal business practice and should only happen when financial resources are not available to make a timely payment and the supplier has been prenotified.

The chapter concluded by presenting three payables monitoring tools. The balance fraction method is preferred over the payables turnover method and days payables outstanding since they are both influenced by seasonal purchasing trends.

Useful Web Sites

Online marketplace example: www.tradecard.com
Payables articles: www.treasury.pncbank.com/ProductPayables

Questions

1. What role do payables and accruals play in the working capital or cash cycle?
2. Explain how payables and accruals represent spontaneous sources of financing.
3. Why should firms offer cash discounts?
4. How long should accounts payable be held before payment is made?
5. What is the conceptual relationship between the firm's investment rate, the late payment penalty fee, and the discount rate in determining the appropriate date to make payment?
6. What are the tangible costs related to late payment and what are some of the intangible costs?

7. What is the role that information systems play in the payment process?
8. How does the balance fraction approach to monitoring payments improve accuracy of the monitoring information compared to the payables turnover approach?
9. How do accruals represent a source of financing?
10. How manageable are accruals? How does the management of accruals differ from the management of payables?

Problems

1. For the following set of terms, state whether you should take the cash discount or pay at the end of the credit term period assuming your investment rate is 15 percent.
   a. 1.5/20, net 50
   b. 1/5, net 60
   c. 5/10, net 45
   d. 2/10, net 30
2. You are currently reevaluating your payables policy. Your current suppliers offer terms of 1.5/10, net 40, with a late payment fee of 1.5 percent per month. A supplier wanting your business is willing to offer terms of 2.5/5, net 60 with no stated late payment fee. Your annual borrowing rate is 18 percent. Assume a 365-day year and an assumed $100,000 purchase.
   a. How long should you delay payment given the terms of your current suppliers? Prove your answer by relating the annualized cost of the discount to your investment or borrowing rate.
   b. How long should you delay payment given the terms of the competing supplier? Prove your answer by relating the annualized cost of the discount to your investment or borrowing rate.
   c. Based on an average invoice of $100,000, which supplier should you purchase from (i.e., which set of terms results in the minimum NPV cost)?
3. You are currently reevaluating your payables policy. Your current suppliers offer terms of 3/10, net 30 with a late payment fee of 1.5 percent per month. A supplier wanting your business is willing to offer terms of 1/5, net 60 with a late payment fee of 1.5 percent per month. Your annual borrowing rate is 16 percent. Assume a 365 day year. Base your analysis on an assumed $100,000 purchase.
   a. How long should you delay payment given the terms of your current suppliers? Prove your answer by relating the annualized cost of the discount to your investment or borrowing rate.
   b. How long should you delay payment given the terms of the competing supplier? Prove your answer by relating the annualized cost of the discount to your investment or borrowing rate.
   c. Based on an average invoice of $100,000, which supplier should you purchase from (i.e., which set of terms results in the minimum NPV cost)?
4. Collen Avenue Bakery purchases flour from a mill on a regular basis. The monthly purchase scheduling and ending payables is provided below.

	DEC	JAN	FEB	MAR	APR	MAY	JUNE
Purchases	25	45	80	120	100	90	50
Ending Payables		50	60	80	85	70	50

   a. Calculate the days payables outstanding for March, April, May, and June using quarterly purchases to calculate the average daily purchases.

b. What is your conclusion regarding the firm's payment behavior?

c. The following table shows the amount of payables remaining in successive months for purchases made during the January through June period of operations. Convert the table to a balance fraction matrix and discuss the firm's payment pattern as represented by the balance fraction table.

Account Payables Balances

	PURCHASES	JAN	FEB	MAR	APR	MAY	JUNE
Jan	45	20	22				
Feb	80		38	20			
Mar	120			60	30		
Apr	100				55	17	
May	90					53	15
Jne	50						35
		NA	60	80	85	70	50

d. What is your conclusion about the firm's payment pattern?

5. Wycliff Contractors, Inc., has the following monthly purchasing schedule and ending accounts payable.

	DEC	JAN	FEB	MAR	APR	MAY	JUNE
Purchases	400	375	350	325	400	500	650
Ending Payables		342	320	297	345	430	555

a. Calculate the days payables outstanding for March, April, May, and June using quarterly purchases to calculate the average daily purchases.

b. What is your conclusion regarding the firm's payment behavior?

c. The following table shows the amount of payables remaining in successive months for purchases made during the January through June period of operations. Convert the table to a balance fraction matrix and discuss the firm's payment pattern as represented by the balance fraction table.

Account Payables Balances

	PURCHASES	JAN	FEB	MAR	APR	MAY	JUNE
Jan	375	262	75				
Feb	350		245	70			
Mar	325			227	65		
Apr	400				280	80	
May	500					350	100
Jun	650						455
		NA	320	297	345	430	555

d. What is your conclusion about the firm's payment pattern?

References

James A. Gentry and Jesus M. De La Garza. 1990. Monitoring accounts payable. *The Financial Review* 25(4):559–576.

John F. Guilding. 1983. Redesigning accounts payable. *Management Accounting* September:42–46.

Ned Hill, William Sartoris, and Daniel Ferguson. 1984. Corporate credit and payables policies: Two surveys. *Journal of Cash Management* July–August:56–62.

INTEGRATIVE CASE—PART 2
Smyth Appliance, Inc.

Smyth Appliance, Inc., is a wholesale appliance store selling to contractors. The company has been in operation for more than 30 years and was started by Ted Smyth's grandfather. Ted is the company's chief financial officer (CFO). Ted has been with the company for 5 years, having come from a local bank as one of its lending officers. Five years ago, his father, then chief executive officer (CEO), died unexpectedly, and his brother Ralph took over as CEO, having been with the company since graduating from college. Ralph felt very comfortable with the operating and marketing/sales side of the business, but was very uncomfortable with the financial side of the business. Soon after he took over, he talked Ted into leaving the bank and joining the family business as its CFO.

The company historically has been very profitable, but has been experiencing increasing cash flow problems lately, partly as a result of the recession in the building industry. It seems as though more and more of Smyth's customers are delaying payment of their invoices.

This morning, Ralph has a sales forecast for the coming year on his desk as result of an intense executive meeting last week. The report includes an analysis of one of Smyth's product lines, kitchen units for manufactured housing. A kitchen unit consists of an oven, dishwasher, and refrigerator set. According to the report, Smyth can expect to sell 1800 kitchen units during the coming year, which is identical to the level of sales for the current year just ending. Sales are evenly distributed throughout the year.

Inventory Purchase and Payables

One of Smyth's suppliers is offering an aggressive price/quantity program on the kitchen unit. If Smyth orders 450 kitchen units at a time, the wholesale price that Smyth pays will drop 2 percent from the normal wholesale price of $700 per unit. Smyth currently places an order of 60 units 30 times a year. Smyth prices the kitchen unit at $1,050 to its customers. The best estimate is that placing an order costs about $150, including clerical time, follow-up, inquiries, paper, and computer and telephone expense. Storage or holding costs are estimated to run about $20 per unit, which includes insurance as well as charges for space allocation in the warehouse where space is leased to handle inventory.

In addition to the quantity discount program, the supplier also offers a different set of credit terms to those customers accepting the new quantity discount program. The new terms are justified given the cost savings to the supplier. The new credit terms will become net 60 days rather than the existing net 30 days. The supplier currently does not charge a late payment fee, but will do so under the new policy. A 28 percent annual fee will be charged (accruing interest on a simple interest basis daily) for payments received later than 60 days from invoice date. The supplier indicates that the late payment fee will be stringently applied. Under the old terms, Smyth had been paying 90 days past the invoice date with no late fee and continued good service. However, given the industry conditions, management at Smyth is aware that that they may not be able to expect the same kind of service given their past payment pattern. Net 30 days terms will remain for those customers not taking the cash discount, but they will begin to incur the same late payment fee.

Credit Terms and Accounts Receivables

Janet Sowell heads up the credit department for Smyth and has been in that position for almost 8 years. Smyth's credit policy is to sell to approved customers on the basis of net 60 days. Smyth's days sales outstanding (DSO) generally runs 90 days and Sowell has been reluctant to be too aggressive about collections, fearing loss of customers, especially in the current economic climate.

Sowell recently learned that several appliance wholesalers have started offering a 2 percent cash discount for payment within 10 days of the invoice date and net terms of 50 days. Her main concern is that if Smyth does not respond with a similar set of competitive terms, the company may begin to lose sales. In fact, she already has had several inquiries regarding a change in credit terms.

As she returns to her office from a meeting, she sees a phone message from Joe Moore, one of her better customers, on her desk asking her to return his call. Janet feels sure that he is inquiring about the possibility of a cash discount. She guesses that, based on the interest her current customers have shown in such a program thus far, about 30 percent will take the cash discount if offered. Those not taking the cash discount will still pay on average in 90 days. Sowell realizes that offering a cash discount of 2 percent reduces cash receipts, but she wonders how that will be offset by receiving the cash earlier, particularly because she sees the change in credit terms as only maintaining the current sales level. Janet is also aware of the discussion going on between the purchasing and inventory managers regarding the quantity discount program and wonders how that might affect her dilemma with the credit terms.

The Chief Financial Officer

In their weekly executives' meeting, Ted received all the information discussed above and is trying to sort it out. He wants to try to approach the problem by looking at the present-value impact of the decisions in the different areas. To calculate a present value, he will use a required rate of return of 20 percent and wants to evaluate the impact on cash flows for the kitchen unit product line over the coming year (a 360-day year). He figures that the best decision will be the one that increases the net present value (NPV) of the kitchen unit line's direct cash receipts net of direct disbursements.

REQUIRED

a. To start, calculate the EOQ using the basic EOQ equation in Chapter 4.
b. Now decide the optimum order quantity, assuming the firm's current situation (not considering the quantity discount program or change in receivables terms). Choose from order quantities of 10, 20, 30, 60, 100, or 120 units. Explain why this optimal

order quantity may be different from the EOQ answer found in part (a).
c. Ted realizes that it is imperative to match credit terms with Smyth's competitors, so all cases analyzed will consider the new credit terms. He decides to consider the four cases indicated below:
   CASE 1: New A/R terms
               Maintain old A/P, paying in 90 days with late fee
               Order the current quantity
   CASE 2: New A/R terms
               Maintain old A/P terms but pay in 30 days
               Order the current quantity
   CASE 3: New A/R terms
               New A/P terms, paying in 60 days
               Order the new higher quantity to receive discount
   CASE 4: New A/R terms
               New A/P terms, paying in 90 days rather than 60 days
               Order the new higher quantity to receive discount
To properly evaluate each case, Ted calculates the NPV based on a 360-day year.
d. As Ted is winding up his analysis of the four cases, he discovers that a competing supplier has offered a novel purchase plan. The supplier would like to set up a just-in-time-type inventory program with Smyth. Because Smyth's orders occur at a relatively constant rate throughout the year, the supplier suggests that if Smyth can provide a year-ahead estimate of inventory needs, the supplier can ship units on a daily basis, eliminating Smyth's need to accumulate inventory. In essence, the order quantity will be 5 units. The supplier estimates that ordering costs will be only $180 a year or about $.50 per order, and that inventory holding cost will be totally eliminated. The supplier also offers net 90 day credit terms with a 28 percent late fee (accruing daily).

Ted's main concern about this proposal is the risk of contracting for a year's volume of inventory, but he decides that this risk can be accounted for by adjusting the required rate of return up to about 25 percent. How does this alternative compare with the best of the four cases analyzed in part c? In addition to the NPV calculation, what additional factors should Ted consider before making his decision?

PART III
Corporate Cash Management

Chapter 8   **The Payment System and Financial Institution Relationships**

Chapter 9   **Cash Collection Systems**

Chapter 10   **Cash Concentration**

Chapter 11   **Cash Disbursement Systems**

Part III focuses on the heart of corporate short-term financial management: the efficient collection, movement, and disbursement of cash. Effective management of payables, inventories, and receivables frees up cash, but the ultimate benefit is predicated on the effectiveness of the company's cash management systems. In Part III, the costs and benefits of corporate cash management systems are presented to facilitate value-maximizing decision making. The context of cash management decisions is presented in Chapter 8. Chapter 8 introduces the US payment system and presents several differences found in foreign payment systems. It also details the company's relationship with its financial institutions and how best to manage that relationship. Chapter 9 develops several methods by which companies can efficiently collect cash. In Chapter 10, we indicate how to move the collected cash into one or more accounts to make investments, pay down borrowings, or cover disbursements. Finally, in Chapter 11 we build on the general payment system and bank information to show how to establish value-enhancing disbursement systems.

CHAPTER 8

The Payment System and Financial Institution Relationships

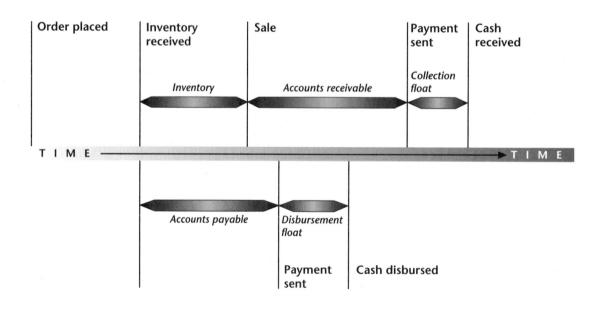

After studying this chapter, you should be able to:

- Explain the concept of float and calculate its value, indicating why it occurs in the US payment system.
- Specify and explain the roles of the two major components of the payment system.
- Describe the major paper-based and electronic-based payment systems.
- Describe how an automated clearing house transaction works, and how it fits in with electronic data interchange.
- Use an availability schedule to calculate availability on deposited checks.
- Explain the uses of an account analysis statement and balance requirements to compensate financial institutions for service fees.

Understanding the payment system is very important for the financial manager. Ninety percent of US corporate payments and 75 percent of corporate-to-corporate payments continue to be made by paper checks, but cash managers are increasing their use of electronic payment methods. Collecting and disbursing cash involves several decisions regarding the best payment system methods to use. These decisions can add value to the corporation, as the following financial dilemma illustrates.

FINANCIAL DILEMMA

Should We Get on the Electronic Payments Bandwagon?

Organizations have several alternatives for moving funds and paying bills. Checks can be written, or funds can be moved around electronically via electronic funds transfer systems. A related issue is how to handle available funds before paying bills. For Ann Richards, former treasurer of the state of Texas, this was the $1 billion question. By shifting from a paper-based system to a highly automated electronic funds transfer system, she was able to earn the state $1 billion in additional interest within 5 years. The 49

"Rapid Deposit" programs she initiated move an estimated $10 billion annually. Indicating how things were done before, Richards explains how the previous state treasurer carried a bond issue proceeds check for several hundred million dollars from New York to Austin in the pocket of his sports coat. "The former treasurer did not get mugged, but the people of Texas did," Richards declares, adding that the episode cost the state $20,000 in lost interest.

Cash managers wishing to emulate Richards' accomplishments are faced with several questions: Will the costs outweigh the benefits for our organization? Will parties we deal with be receptive to our new procedures? Does our present banking network allow for expedited and innovative payment methods?

Cash managers repeatedly have demonstrated that understanding the impact of payment mechanisms on the cash flow timeline can enhance profitability and shareholder value. This chapter develops the unifying concept of float, and also provides a background for later chapters on cash collection, concentration, and disbursement systems. We cover the banking system, paper-based and electronic payment systems, and the international payment system. US banking regulations that explain the popularity of several corporate cash management techniques are listed. We also note payment system trends and argue that despite rapid advances in electronic commerce, a cashless, checkless society is not in the foreseeable future. Finally, we show how to manage the corporate banking relationship. This is a lengthy chapter, but it is important that this material be understood because it explains the motivation for so many cash and working capital management techniques.

VALUE OF FLOAT

The single most important aspect of the US payment system when considering cash management is the existence of **float** on mailed checks. From the payor's perspective, float refers to the delay in value transfer from the time a check is written until it finally is charged to the payor's account. The cash manager can apply the valuation approach to calculating the value of float. Once again, we can use the cash flow timeline to illustrate a realistic situation and how to anchor the dates for our calculation appropriately.

We set up a cash flow timeline in the example that follows, illustrating changes in float and their value effect. We use a simple interest present value calculation for a company considering using newly available bar coding of ZIP codes, which leads to less mail time resulting from reduced Postal Service handling.

EXAMPLE. Crown Corporation collects $1,000,000 daily. It is presently considering investing in a machine that will both insert a bar code ZIP + 4 on outgoing envelopes and presort by destination. The Postal Service has already shown the cost savings for the machine in terms of reduced postage (about 3 cents per first-class item). Management wonders if there is a significant additional savings from the one-third day savings in mail float the Postal Service guarantees for companies using bar coding. Collection float at present is 3 days mail float, 2 days processing float, and 2 days availability float. Assume Crown's cost of capital is 10 percent per year.

The cash-flow timeline at present is graphed as follows:

How much value can be gained by Crown as a result of the reduced mail float? SOLUTION. The revised cash-flow timeline appears as follows:

Two approaches can be used to see the value effect of the reduced float: the first gives the present value of 1 day's collections, and the second uses that result to calculate the total effect.

Figure the PV of One Day's Collections under Both Mail Float Situations

The simple interest discounting formula presented in Chapter 3 (Equation 3-2) is reproduced here as Equation 8-1:

$$PV = \frac{CF}{1+(i \times n)} \tag{8-1}$$

Substituting for the present situation of a 7-day wait until cash is received gives us the present value of the collection float:

$$PV = \frac{\$1,000,000}{1+(0.10/365)(7)}$$

$$= \$998,085.86$$

The present collection float of 7 days leaves a present dollar value to the corporation of $998,085.86. To see if the present value will increase on adoption of the new terms, we make the same calculation for the proposal. Based on the anticipated collection float of 6.67 days, we have

$$PV = \frac{\$1,000,000}{1+(0.10/365)(6.67)}$$

$$= \$998,175.94$$

With the proposal, the collection float reduction to 6 2/3 days results in a present value of daily collections of $998,175.94. Thus Crown will gain about $90 = $998,175.94 − $998,085.86 *per day's* collections on a present value basis. This first calculation simply indicates the value effect of 1 day's transactions. To find the total value effect, assuming the savings will last into the indefinite future, we need to calculate the present value of a perpetuity of such flows.

Figure the Net Present Value (NPV) of a Perpetual Stream of Daily Collection

The procedure for determining the present value in total of a daily perpetuity is presented in the appendix at the end of the text and is reproduced here as Equation 8-2. In words, we take 1 day's cash flow and divide it by the daily interest rate.

$$PV = \frac{CF}{i} \tag{8-2}$$

Because we have the difference in daily cash flow ($90.077272) from the reduced mail float, we can get the present value of the reduced float bar coding and presorting proposal as follows:

$$PV = \frac{\$90.077272}{0.10/365}$$

$$= \$328,782.04$$

The system is worth \$328,782 to the company, on a present value basis. Notice that there is an implicit assumption that the difference in float is permanent. If we have reason to expect that 3 years from now float will drop to 6.67 days regardless of company preprocessing, we would discount the daily cash flow as a 3-year daily annuity.[1]

To determine if the proposal should be adopted, we must compare the present value of the benefits, roughly \$329,000, to the installed cost of the bar coding and presorting system. If the cost is less than \$329,000, the proposal will have a positive NPV and should be implemented. We present a more advanced present value analysis in our discussion of disbursement systems in Chapter 11, in which we compute the value effect of paying suppliers electronically instead of by check.

US PAYMENT SYSTEM

The two components of the US payment system are the banking system (which includes the Federal Reserve System) and the set of noncash payment mechanisms. This system is unique in that most other countries have only a handful of banks and use the postal system to assist in collecting and depositing payments. The US payment system is the backbone of the US banking and financial markets, which in turn facilitate the growth and stability of the US economy. In this section, we survey the major types of depository financial institutions, explain the payment responsibilities of the Federal Reserve System, and identify the means by which most payments are processed through the payment system.

Financial Institutions

The financial institutions that participate in the economy's payment process are commercial banks, savings and loans associations, mutual savings banks, and credit unions. All four of these depository institutions, which we simply refer to as banks, are involved in handling checks as well as electronic payments. Despite the well-publicized weakness of many commercial banks, they continue to dominate the banking industry. Roughly 9000 commercial banks continue to operate in the United States, compared with 1600 savings and loans associations, 400 stock or mutual savings banks, and 11,200 credit unions. Because so much of a company's cash management activity is linked to banks and banking regulation, the regulatory environment is a key component of the payment system. We subdivide our remaining discussion of financial institutions into product differences, geographic restrictions, and safety considerations.

PRODUCT DIFFERENCES.   Each type of financial institution has a slightly different thrust. Commercial banks are more oriented toward corporate services, savings and loans toward

---

[1]An approximation formula for the annual benefit of the days saved is Annual benefit = (Days saved) × (Daily cash flow) × (k) when k is the annual interest rate. The intuition here is that the product of the first two terms gives an amount that may be continuously invested over time. In our example, the annual interest benefit is \$33,333: \$33,333 = (0.3333 × \$1,000,000 × 0.10). This simplified formula ignores the compounded effect of daily savings throughout the period over which the total value effect is computed. If the effects of a proposal last only 1 year, this approximation will be fairly accurate.

EXHIBIT 8-1

Product Deregulation in the Depository Institutions Deregulation and Monetary Control Act

TYPE OF FINANCIAL INSTITUTION	NEW CONDITIONS
Commercial banks	Can now offer consumers, sole proprietorships, and nonprofit organizations 1. Negotiated order of withdrawal (NOW) accounts, which are interest-bearing checking accounts 2. Money market deposit accounts (MMDAs), accounts with a higher interest rate and a limit on the number of checks that could be written against them each month. These were meant to offer banks a competitive weapon to stem the deposit outflows to money market mutual funds. 3. SuperNOW accounts, with higher minimum balances than NOW accounts. The minimum balance differences were left to each bank's discretion beginning in the mid-1980s. **Note:** The MMDA and SuperNOW accounts were actually implemented subsequent to the Garn-St. Germain Depository Institutions Act of 1982.
Savings & loan associations	In addition to being able to offer NOW, SuperNOW, and MMDAs 1. Can lend up to 20% of total assets in consumer and commercial loans 2. Can issue credit cards 3. Can offer trust services (e.g., investment of funds left by an estate)
Mutual savings banks	In addition to the NOW, SuperNOW, and MMDAs 1. Can offer business accounts 2. Can lend up to 5% of total assets in commercial loans 3. Can offer trust services 4. Can issue credit cards
Credit unions	In addition to the NOW (in this instance, called "share draft" accounts), SuperNOW, and MMDAs 1. Can issue certificates of deposit (CDs) 2. Can offer student loans 3. Can offer safety deposit boxes 4. Can offer automated teller machines (ATMs) 5. Can issue credit cards 6. Can pay interest on business checking accounts (if the individual running the business already has an account), which any other type of depository institution cannot do

real estate development and mortgage finance, mutual savings banks toward mortgage finance, and credit unions toward consumer loan and deposit services. These institutions are becoming more like one another. The ability of savings and loans, mutual savings banks, and credit unions to operate more like commercial banks is a result of the passage of the **Depository Institution Deregulation and Monetary Control Act of 1980.** The major product-related provisions of that act are summarized in Exhibit 8-1.

Business firms (except sole proprietorships) are prohibited by law from receiving interest on bank checking accounts; this Federal Reserve **Regulation Q** provision limits firms to using demand deposit accounts for transactions and disqualifies them from holding negotiated order of withdrawal (NOW), SuperNOW, or money market deposit accounts (MMDA). At the time of this writing, banks are working to win passage of federal legislation repealing Regulation Q, with a likely three-year phase-in. One of the most important principles of cash management, that of minimizing idle cash balances, is premised on the opportunity cost of foregone interest linked to Regulation Q.

Businesses with deposit account balances large enough to justify the fixed monthly cost use daily transfers into "sweep accounts" to get paid overnight interest on deposit balances. Small businesses able to keep very small deposit balances, particularly those not requiring bank loans, may keep most of their transaction balances in money market mutual funds. Because these funds are not covered by deposit insurance, risk-averse cash managers use money funds investing exclusively in government securities. Small businesses would gain the most if Regulation Q is repealed and interest is paid on demand deposit balances.

Further alterations enacted as part of the **Garn-St. Germain Depository Institutions Act of 1982** allowed depository institutions to pay interest on MMDAs to compete with money market mutual funds and allowed savings and loan associations to lend to businesses. Although banks continue to set higher minimum balance requirements for SuperNOW accounts than for NOW accounts, in 1986 regulators removed interest rate distinctions between the accounts by eliminating the maximum NOW rate of $5\frac{1}{4}$ percent. In 1989, the **Financial Institutions Reform, Recovery, and Enforcement Act,** which was mainly addressed to failing savings and loans, further blurred the lines between depository institutions by allowing bank holding companies (the parent firm over several banks) to buy healthy saving and loan associations (S&Ls).

Nonbank institutions are also becoming players in the payment system. Brokerage firms, in particular, have either acquired banks or established **nonbank banks,** which accept deposits or make loans (but not both). These banks are used to consolidate and invest idle cash balances for the brokerage firm's customers. The **Competitive Equality Banking Act of 1987,** although allowing existing nonbank banks to continue to operate, prohibits the establishment of new nonbank banks. Small businesses, in particular, have benefited from the competitive Merrill Lynch "Working Capital Management Account" and lending and investing services offered by American Express. A Mentis Corporation study in 2000 found that nonbanks now have a larger small business market share of than banks.

The most recent legislation affecting the banking landscape is the **Financial Services Modernization Act of 1999** (also known as Gramm-Leach-Bliley). This law repeals the 1933 Glass-Steagall Act's prohibitions on bank-investment company affiliations:

- Banks may now affiliate with investment and insurance firms.
- A new organizational form, called a financial holding company, allows banking organizations to carry out new powers through nonbanking subsidiaries that are permitted to sell insurance and underwrite securities.
- Banks having a federal charter can conduct some of the insurance and securities activities through "financial subsidiaries."[2]

Furthermore, the nonbank banks, mostly set up as part of a "unitary thrift holding company" structure, were limited. Regulators were forbidden from approving any new applications received after May 4, 1999. The intended effect was to prevent Wal-Mart from taking on this charter, and thereby initiating large-scale consumer lending.

GEOGRAPHIC RESTRICTIONS.   Past regulatory limits on interstate branching are the major reason corporate cash management systems have included multiple banks.

---

[2]There is a real concern that the failure of a nonbanking firm controlled by a bank may now jeopardize the entire banking organization. For more on this and other issues related to the Financial Services Modernization Act of 1999, see the Federal Reserve Board of Minneapolis special issue of *The Region* (March 2000). At the time of this writing, it was available on-line at http://minneapolisfed.org/pubs/region/00-03/ index.html.

Interstate branching refers to the ability of a bank headquartered in one state to open branches in other states. If one bank can set up branches wherever it wished, there might not be a need for the cash manager to establish relationships with multiple banks for check clearing and cash concentration. Originally, limits on interstate branching were linked to fears of a concentration of financial power and a reduction of lending to businesses in small towns.

The **McFadden Act,** passed in 1927 and amended in 1933, limited bank branching by national banks to the same areas where state-chartered banks in that state were permitted to branch. This effectively prohibited interstate branching. Banks got around this limitation to some degree by setting up holding companies, which are controlling organizations owning 100 percent of the stock in separately chartered banks. The **Bank Holding Company Act of 1956** addressed this issue by prohibiting any further interstate acquisition by holding companies unless specifically allowed by state law in the state of the proposed acquisition. Because no state allowed these acquisitions at that time, only the very limited networks set up before 1956 existed until Maine passed an enabling law in 1978. As part of "regional compacts," most other states have since enabled bank holding companies from selected other states to acquire their banks, as long those states offer reciprocal privileges. The Garn-St. Germain Depository Institutions Act of 1982 allows interstate acquisitions of failed or failing banks or thrifts, primarily to reduce the costs of government bailouts of troubled institutions.

The mid-1990s experienced a final crumbling of the walls prohibiting interstate acquisitions and interstate branching. The key piece of legislation was the 1994 passage of the **Interstate Banking and Branching Efficiency Act** (IBBEA). Key provisions included:

- Allowing bank holding companies to acquire a bank located in any state beginning September 1995 (interstate banking).
- Allowing banks in one state to merge with banks in another state beginning June 1997, unless either of the two states had prohibited interstate mergers between the law's enactment and the end of May 1997.
- Allowing banks to establish new branches in states where they did not previously have a branch if the host state expressly passed a law permitting such branches (interstate branching).

With interstate branching allowed, corporations use far fewer banks, making it possible to do business with one large bank that has nationwide branches to both accept deposits and clear checks. Short-term financial management should become less costly and more efficient as deposits are granted immediate or next-day availability in almost all cases. Transfers, including account funding and concentration account transfers, will be greatly reduced because balances will be automatically pooled in a bank's bookkeeping system. We are already seeing these effects, shown in the following Focus on Practice.

SAFETY CONSIDERATIONS.   Bank safety is also important because banks play such a vital check-clearing role in the payments system. The mid-1990s have been very positive for banks: In 1992, the Federal Deposit Insurance Corporation (FDIC) had 1000 banks on its problem list, but by mid-year 1999 this number had declined to only 62 banks. These troubled banks pose special problems for their depositors. The FDIC only guarantees the first $100,000 of a depositor's money. The too-big-to-fail doctrine practiced before 1991 ensured that depositors with money in very large banks would be covered even above the $100,000 limit. However, under the **Federal Deposit Insurance**

WHAT EFFECT IS INTERSTATE BANKING AND BANK CONSOLIDATION HAVING IN THE UNITED STATES?
The Treasury Management Association (now called the Association for Financial Professionals) conducted a survey of 4000 members in early 1999, and received the following responses from 587 corporations:

- Bank consolidation, mostly resulting from mergers and acquisitions, resulted in increased delays in bank decision making, more errors in monthly bank statements and/or account analysis statements, and some operational disruption in corporate treasury departments. Almost half of the respondents saw banks as now less loyal to their business customers, and believed that their business relationship had diminished importance to their banks.
- Of the respondents, 314 found interstate banking advantageous, with half of these companies consolidating services within existing banks (primarily local depository services, cash concentration services, and balance reporting services) or moving services to other banks (67 respondents had discontinued relations with one or more banks because of those banks' inability to offer interstate banking capability). Of the 87 companies divulging their annual cost savings, three-fourths were saving $36,000 or less, but 23 respondents were saving an average of $247,200 annually. Primary benefits cited for interstate banking were mainly "fewer banks and services to monitor" and "improved collection and concentration," with some organizations seeing "reduced local account balances" as well.
- The most likely trends for the future, with the percentage of corporate respondents agreeing with the statement, are:
  - likely or very likely that bank services will become more commoditized (90%).
  - likely or very likely that monopolistic pricing will occur (80%), possibly as a result of specialization in certain service areas.
  - likely or very likely that there will be fewer sources of credit (80%).
  - likely or very likely that there will be faster convergence of technology standards (79%).

These findings are linked to the passage in 1994 of the Interstate Banking & Branching Efficiency Act, covered previously.

SOURCE: Phillips, Aaron L. 1999. Bank consolidation and interstate banking: Effect on treasury management. *TMA Journal* March–April:40–43.

Corporation Improvement Act of 1991, coverage of uninsured deposits is less certain. The FDIC must give acquirers of failed banks a choice of whether to bid for all the deposits or just the insured deposits. Acquirers have been prone to bid for the insured deposits, meaning uninsured depositors receive only part of their deposited funds back as assets and the remaining funds are liquidated by the FDIC. For example, in the closure of the First National Bank of the Panhandle (Panhandle, TX), there was a total exposure of about $752,000 in 102 accounts exceeding the $100,000 insured limit. Under federal law, these depositors and creditors holding deposit claims receive priority in payment from the subsequent sale of assets of the failed bank (over creditors holding nondeposit claims).

The FDIC continues to take over large banks when there is agreement among federal regulatory agencies that defaulting on uninsured deposits will pose a substantial risk to the payments system. International capital standards for banks, phased in during 1992 in the United States, further regulate bank soundness. Developed in 1988 by a committee of bank regulators from seven countries, the Basel standards require banks to have $3 of Tier 1 capital (common and perpetual preferred stock and minority interests, minus goodwill) for every $100 of total assets. Tier 1 plus Tier 2 capital (other preferred stock, mandatory convertible debt, and long-term subordinated debt) must be at least $8 for every $100 of risk-weighted assets. Risk weightings are 100 percent for business loans, 50 percent for home mortgages, and 0 percent for Treasury securities. Not surprisingly, banks have become more conservative in their business lending. One short-term finance implication is that cash management services may not be priced as attractively because the profit from gaining a company's short-term borrowing is not as great. In the early twenty-first century, there are concerns about the Basel standards and it appears based on a 2001 proposal, that they will be revised with implementation set for 2004.

Federal Reserve System

The Federal Reserve System (or the Fed) is the nation's central bank. As the "banker's bank," it:

- Acts as lender of last resort, lending money to banks through the "discount window."
- Is one of several bodies that supervises and regulates banks.
- Facilitates the payments mechanism.

The nationwide panic of 1907, which saw a breakdown in the nation's payment system and a full-scale run on banks, led to the passage of the **Federal Reserve Act** in 1913. We will further our understanding of the Federal Reserve System by discussing its organization, its functions, and its present and future involvement in the payment system.

EXHIBIT 8-2

Organization of the Federal Reserve System

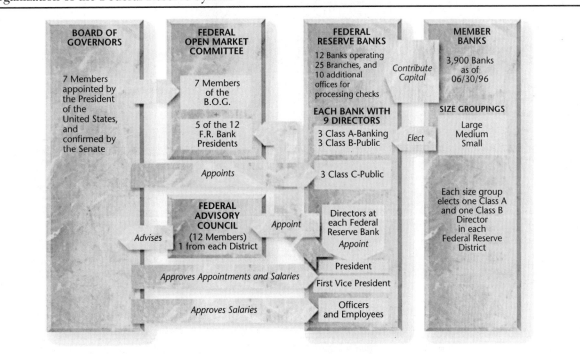

SOURCE: Board of Governors of the Federal Reserve System. Reprinted from *The Federal Reserve Today*, 13th ed, 1999, with permission of the Federal Reserve Bank of Richmond.

EXHIBIT 8-3
Boundaries of Federal Reserve Districts and Their Branch Territories

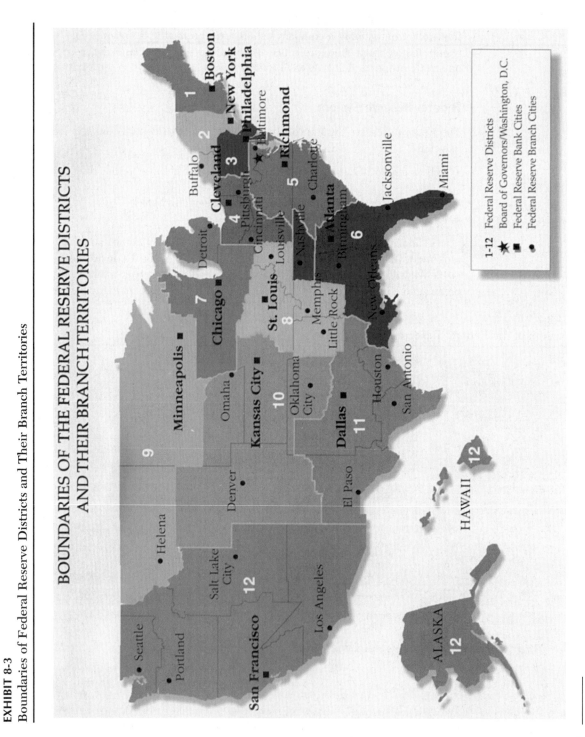

BOUNDARIES OF THE FEDERAL RESERVE DISTRICTS
AND THEIR BRANCH TERRITORIES

1-12 Federal Reserve Districts
★ Board of Governors/Washington, D.C.
■ Federal Reserve Bank Cities
● Federal Reserve Branch Cities

SOURCE: Board of Governors of the Federal Reserve System. Reprinted from *The Federal Reserve Today,* 13th ed, 1999, with permission of the Federal Reserve Bank of Richmond.

ORGANIZATION.   The Fed is made up of the Board of Governors, the Federal Open Market Committee, the Federal Advisory Council, Federal Reserve District Banks, and member banks (Exhibit 8-2).

The Fed is run by the seven-member Board of Governors, which is appointed by the President and confirmed by the US Senate. Terms of office for this federal government agency are 14 years, with one of the seven terms expiring every 2 years. The chairperson (Alan Greenspan, at the time of this writing) and vice-chairperson hold 4-year, renewable terms. The seven members of the Board of Governors also are members of the Federal Open Market Committee (FOMC), which makes most of the monetary policy for the US in its eight meetings per year. The FOMC forms monetary policy by buying and selling treasury securities (open market operations), which affects the reserve positions of banks, and, ultimately, the money supply. The Federal Advisory Council is made up of prominent commercial bankers, and meets at least four times per year with the Board of Governors.

The Fed, unlike the single central bank in most countries, is comprised of 12 district Federal Reserve Banks, with 25 regional branches spread across the country. There also are 11 regional check processing centers (RCPCs) set up to help clear checks. Together, the 12 district banks, most of the 25 regional branches, and 11 RCPCs give the Fed a network of 45 offices to clear checks. For example, in the seventh Fed district, checks are cleared through district offices in Chicago, Des Moines, Detroit, Indianapolis, Milwaukee, and Peoria. Exhibit 8-3 shows a map of the districts and branches. The Federal Reserve Banks are private organizations, with a corporate structure very similar to that of a commercial bank. Each Federal Reserve Bank issues stock and has a board of directors that elects the bank's officers and oversees the bank's operations. The buyers of that stock, and thus the true owners of the Fed, are the member commercial banks.

The Federal Reserve Banks differ from commercial banks in that their primary responsibility is to promote society's interest, not the interest of member bank stockholders who contribute the capital (refer to Exhibit 8-2). Furthermore, the Board of Governors supervises the district banks, limiting to some extent the powers and privileges of their stockholders.

The final component of the system is the group of Federal Reserve member banks, which presently number about 3400. Being a member of the Federal Reserve System has been a requirement of all national banks, and many state-chartered banks have joined voluntarily. Subsequent to the 1980 Monetary Control Act, membership has been much less important because all depository institutions may receive Fed payment services, must adhere to reserve requirements, and may now borrow from the Fed.[3]

INVOLVEMENT IN THE PAYMENT SYSTEM.   The Federal Reserve's official role in the payment system is "to promote the integrity and efficiency of the payments mechanism and to ensure the provision of payment services to all depository institutions on an equitable basis, and to do so in an atmosphere of competitive fairness."[4] The Fed's participation in the payment system includes:

- Putting into circulation new money printed by the US Treasury Department, and withdrawing damaged coins and worn bills.

---

[3]The Federal Reserve System requires depository institutions with check-like (transaction) accounts to keep a stipulated percentage of the dollar amount of these accounts on reserve as deposits with a Federal Reserve Bank (Fed Regulation D). The Fed's control over the amount of reserves deposited helps it to control the amount of money in circulation.

[4]Federal Reserve. 1990. The Federal Reserve in the Payments System. *Federal Reserve Bulletin* May:293.

- Processing approximately 16.5 billion checks a year, which consists of moving, sorting, and tabulating the checks, and debiting and crediting the proper depository institution's account.
- Supporting several private clearing systems by offering settlement services through its nationwide network of account relationships.
- Providing a nationwide electronic network for small-dollar electronic payments (automated clearing house [ACH]).
- Providing a way for depository institutions to quickly transfer large dollar amounts using wire transfers via "Fedwire," a nationwide wire transfer system.
- Regulating the availability schedules of banks, which indicate when checks or electronic deposits become available to the customer.

Before the establishment of the Federal Reserve System, banks settled checks drawn on each other exclusively at local clearinghouses. A **clearinghouse** is a central location where representatives of area banks meet, and each bank settles its balances with one institution (the clearinghouse) instead of with each other bank individually.

Until 1980, the Fed did not charge banks for its check processing. The Monetary Control Act mandated that the Fed begin charging for its services, partly to spur private-sector check clearing initiatives. Increasingly, banks are sending checks drawn on banks in another region to a large bank ("correspondent bank" at which the sending bank has an account) in that region, which processes the checks through its local clearinghouse; or directly to the bank on which the checks are drawn. In the past, almost all interregional checks would have been sent to the district Federal Reserve Bank. This circumvention of its check clearing system and the increased volume of electronic payments has reduced the Fed's role in US check processing.

MECHANICS OF CHECK CLEARING.   We can gain an understanding of the check clearing system by observing the life of a check. A check processed through the Federal Reserve System serves as our example. Consult Exhibit 8-4 as we follow a check through the clearing system.

EXHIBIT 8-4
Steps in Check Clearing

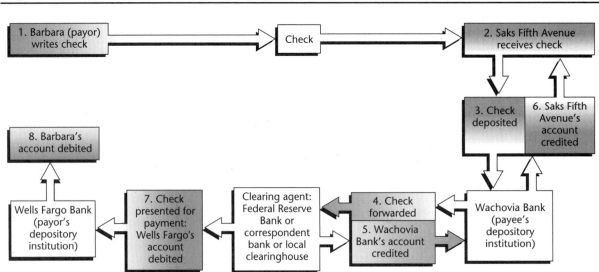

Barbara is on vacation in Atlanta, escaping the cold winter of Minneapolis. She buys a coat at Saks Fifth Avenue. She writes a check for the purchase amount (step 1). Saks receives the check in its processing area (step 2). That evening, Saks deposits her check at its bank, Wachovia Bank, along with many other checks Saks received that day (step 3). Referred to as the **collecting bank,** Wachovia first encodes the dollar amount in magnetic ink on the bottom right-hand side of the check, then batches this check with many others it has received that were written on banks outside the Atlanta area. It transports the checks to the Atlanta Federal Reserve Bank (step 4). The Atlanta Fed sorts this check and other unsorted checks it has received, according to the check's destination (the **drawee bank,** which in our example is the Wells Fargo Bank of Minneapolis). The Atlanta Fed settles accounts, crediting Wachovia Bank's reserve account according to a prearranged "availability schedule" (step 5). After settlement, checks drawn on banks in the Ninth District (Minnesota, North and South Dakota, part of Wisconsin) are grouped and sent to the Minneapolis Fed and Wachovia credits Saks' account (step 6). The Minneapolis Fed, in turn, returns Barbara's check to Wells Fargo and debits Wells Fargo's reserve account (step 7, called **presentment**). Wells Fargo then debits Barbara's checking account (step 8).

The clearing agent, often a Federal Reserve Bank, branch, or RCPC, uses the information printed at the bottom of the check to process the check. Known as the **magnetic ink character recognition (MICR)** line, this information can be read by scanning machines and indicates several items (see example in Exhibit 8-5).

1. The Federal Reserve Bank code (10) indicates which Federal Reserve district the check will be routed back to, if the Fed's check clearing system is used. Here, it signifies the Tenth District, for which the Kansas City Federal Reserve is the district bank.
2. The Federal Reserve office code indicates the Fed branch assigned to handling the drawee bank and, if followed by a second digit, what the availability

EXHIBIT 8-5
Sample Check

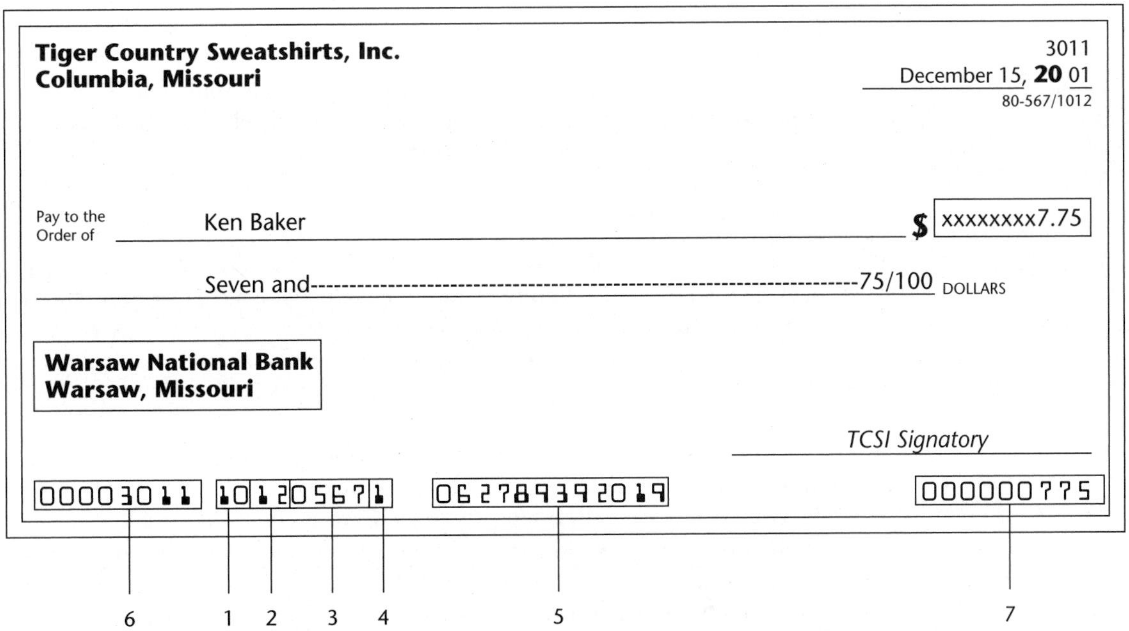

classification is for that bank (0 or 9 denote that same-day availability might be extended by the Fed to the bank of first deposit). (Notice that items 1 and 2 are combined in the denominator of the fraction included at the top right of the check underneath the date. This area is used for manual processing in the event the depositing bank does not have or cannot use automated check processing equipment.)

3. American Banker's Association (ABA) bank identification number specifies the exact bank on which the check was written, or drawn (known as the drawee bank). This number also appears in the numerator of the fraction at the top right of the check underneath the date; the 80 preceding it is a unique identifier for the state of Missouri.
4. A verification digit is used in conjunction with the other numbers to detect processing errors.
5. The account number of the payor, assigned by the drawee bank at the time the account is opened, appears near the middle of the MICR line.
6. The sequence number (also called an auxiliary on-us field) may appear at the far left or next to the account number and is usually the check number. It enables the drawee bank to sort cleared checks before returning the checks (or a sorted statement listing of them) to the payor.
7. The check's encoded amount appears on the far right of the MICR line, and indicates in dollars and cents the amount written or typed on the check by the payor. The bank at which the check is first deposited encodes it.

Items 1 through 4 make up the Federal Reserve District/American Banker's Association (FRD/ABA) bank ID number, which is often called the **transit routing number.** We discuss the use of this important number further in the later section on paper-based payments.

As many as two thirds of all interbank checks do not clear through the Federal Reserve System. As noted in Exhibit 8-4, the clearing agent may be a correspondent bank or a local clearinghouse. The bank of first deposit will select the clearing mechanism based on (1) the location of the drawee bank (which defines the options it has available for processing checks drawn on that bank), (2) the availability schedule associated with each of these options (which indicates when it will be given credit for the deposited amount), (3) the time of deposit, (4) the dollar amount of the check, and sometimes (5) the desires of the depositor. We now consider the various ways that a check might be cleared.

Clearing Mechanisms

There are numerous routes a check might follow as it clears from the receiving bank where it is first deposited back to the drawee bank on which it is written. Exhibit 8-6 shows us the options the receiving bank faces. After checks are coded, sorted, and verified ("proofed"), the bank must decide how best to route the check to get it cleared back to the drawee bank.

HOUSE/ON-US CHECKS.   For a check written **on-us,** meaning the payee deposits the check in the bank on which it is drawn, the bank simply credits the depositor's account and debits the payor's account. It later returns the checks, or possibly simply a record of all checks written during a period, to the payor. If the payee cashes the check, obviously the bank will not credit the payee's account. Approximately 30 to 35 percent of all checks are "on-us," and this percent will grow as banks merge and branch nationwide.

EXHIBIT 8-6
Bank Check Processing Flowchart

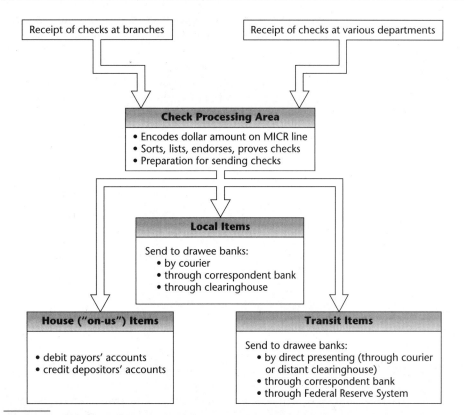

SOURCE: Copyright © 1994 by the American Bankers Association. Reprinted with permission. All rights reserved.

LOCAL ITEMS.   For a check written on other banks in the receiving bank's geographic area, the receiving bank might handle check clearing in one of three ways. First, it might send it by courier, with a group of other checks drawn on the same bank, to be swapped for checks drawn on itself that the other bank has received. This arrangement makes sense when many checks ordinarily flow between two banks in the same geographic area. It may seem unusual that banks would have accounts at other (competing) banks, but these correspondent accounts can be debited or credited in one transaction to efficiently clear many checks drawn on each. Second, the checks may be processed through a correspondent bank, which in turn may be engaged in large-volume check swapping with the major banks in a locality. Third, a local clearinghouse may be used. Each day, representatives from each bank that is a part of the clearinghouse meet to present checks to each other. The net value is debited or credited either to each bank's correspondent account or Federal Reserve account at the end of each business day.

TRANSIT ITEMS.   Checks drawn on banks that do not participate in a bank's local clearinghouse or exchange are called **transit items.** These are sometimes called "out-of-town" checks. Formerly, many of these were cleared by directly presenting hand-carried checks via courier, but the sorting and courier expense greatly reduced the practice except on large checks. Larger banks have started direct presenting more checks, with such arrangements often made with other large banks in reciprocal arrangements. The courier may present the checks to the drawee bank directly, or indirectly through the drawee bank's clearinghouse. The clearing bank must have a large volume of checks drawn on banks in the area to make membership in a remote clearinghouse pay off. Direct presenting might still be used when the dollar size is large enough to warrant gaining a day or two of speedier availability, the depositor is willing to pay for the extra expense (particularly air travel for the courier), or the local Fed cutoff for receipt of checks will be missed (and direct presenting will therefore get the check to the drawee bank much sooner). For example, on a $2 million check, a savings of 1 day of float, assuming the company's cost of capital is 10 percent, is approximated using Equation 8-3:

$$\text{Interest Earned} = \text{Amount per day} \times \text{Number of days} \times \text{Daily Interest Rate} \quad \text{(8-3)}$$
$$\text{Interest Earned} = \$2{,}000{,}000 \times 1 \text{ day} \times 0.10/365$$
$$= \$547.95$$

Effective January 1, 1994, the Fed amended Regulation CC to promote **same-day settlement** of directly presented checks. If a collecting bank presents checks to the place of business of a drawee bank before 8 A.M. local time, the paying bank must return the checks or pay the collecting bank by Fedwire by the close of business that day. The drawee bank can no longer charge the collecting bank a fee or force it to wait until the next business day to receive available funds. This has stimulated a resurgence in direct presenting, mentioned previously. Fed check processing volumes have fallen 12 percent as a result of same-day settlement.

The second alternative for clearing checks written on out-of-town banks is to send them to a correspondent bank located near the drawee bank. The main advantage of this arrangement is a later deposit deadline, or cutoff time, than would be offered by the nearest Fed office. This translates into quicker availability of the deposited funds, which the clearing bank generally passes on to the depositor.

The final possibility for handling transit items is to send them through the Federal Reserve System, which continues to process about 35% of all interbank US checks. Here there are two possibilities: send through the local Fed (the usual process), or bypass the local Fed and send them directly[5] to the Federal Reserve check-clearing office nearest the drawee bank. The last alternative is pursued when it means speedier availability and when the size of the check(s) justifies the added expense. One curiosity here is that the local Fed will allow the bank to piggyback the check(s) and accompanying listing (called a **cash letter**) with whatever checks that office is sending to the distant Fed office. This way the clearing bank can miss the local Fed's cutoff time but still meet the distant Fed's cutoff. The credit is still made to the bank's account at the local Fed, however.

The fact that the Fed grants the depositing bank credit according to a preset availability schedule but is not always able to present the check (debit the drawee bank) within that same period results in float. For a private bank, float refers to items taken on deposit but not yet collected. Float has made it profitable for depositors or banks to try to "beat the system," striving for quick availability on deposits and slowed presentment on checks written. For this reason, the availability schedule is an important document for the corporate cash manager, and we return to a fuller discussion later in this chapter. After gaining a deeper perspective on float and the Fed's attack on it, the remainder of this chapter discusses paper-based payments, electronic-based payments, the international payments system, and managing corporate banking relationships.

---

[5]Any routing that does not go through the Federal Reserve System facility nearest to the clearing bank might be labeled a "direct send."

CONCEPT OF FLOAT

The treasurer must first distinguish between collection float and disbursement float. **Collection float** refers to the elapsed time between when a customer writes a check and when the company is granted available or collected funds after depositing the check. **Disbursement float** is slightly different: it is the delay between the time when the company writes the check and the time when its bank charges the checking account for the amount of the check. On the same check, disbursement float may be slightly more because the Fed may grant the depositor's bank availability before it debits the drawee bank. Rarely, collection float is longer because the "hold" placed on the check by the depositor's bank (delay in availability) may exceed the time it actually takes to present the check to the drawee bank (which usually debits the drawee's checking account the same day). This is justified by the depositor's bank based on its concern about whether a given check might be returned ("bounces"), but Regulation CC places strict limits on hold periods, otherwise. We can gain a better appreciation for the management of collection or disbursement float if we break them down into their component parts.

Components of Float

There are three basic components to collection or disbursement float: mail float, processing float, and clearing float.

MAIL FLOAT.   The time that elapses from the point when the check is written until it is received by the payee is termed mail float. It may range from a day for local checks mailed out immediately to 10 days for a check sent to New York from Rome, Italy. Companies not having the time or clerical staff to monitor mail times can get the information in two other ways. First, the US Postal Service has published guidelines for delivery times on first-class mail and has contracted with Price Waterhouse to provide an outside measurement system to indicate success in meeting those targets. Additionally, consulting firm Phoenix-Hecht provides clients with mail times for many different "mailed from–mailed to" combinations.

Unfortunately, as part of its cost-cutting program, the Postal Service has taken somewhat longer for delivering nonlocal mail in recent years. It has improved service consistency, however, and is able to deliver according to its published schedule 85 to 95 percent of the time. Companies that invest in specialized machinery that make bar codes representing ZIP codes (in ZIP + 4 format) and presort outgoing mail can reduce Postal Service processing time by one third of a day.

PROCESSING FLOAT.   The time that transpires from the time the check is received at a post office box or company mailroom and when the check is deposited at the bank is termed **processing float.** Smaller companies, governments, and nonprofits have characteristically been the slowest in posting credits to the receivables file and transmitting the checks to the bank. Companies with a lockbox arrangement with a bank can eliminate much of this float. This is because bank personnel empty the post office box several times a day and begin processing the checks and crediting the company's bank account the same day, perhaps even after normal business hours.

CLEARING FLOAT.   Sometimes called "availability float," **clearing float** is the delay in availability incurred after deposit. The length of this component of float is linked to the bank's availability schedule in connection with the location of the payor's bank. When considered as part of disbursement float, it has a somewhat different meaning: The time lag is from the point when the payee deposits the check until the Fed or local clearing-house presents the check to the drawee (disbursing company's) bank, and the bank in turn debits the payor's checking account.

Part of the clearing float is then properly labeled **Fed float** (or holdover float), because the Fed may grant availability to the clearing bank before it presents the check to (and debits the account of) the payor's bank. Fed float has been greatly reduced since 1980, because the 1980 Monetary Control Act mandated that the Fed eliminate or charge for Fed float. The Fed processes checks more quickly and has become more consistent in its clearing times. The Fed has several methods it uses to reduce float.

- Check truncation. This involves expediting clearing by scanning the data on the check's MICR line and then processing only that data back to the payor's bank. This is called **electronic presentment,** and is primarily done with large checks. To illustrating, the 12th Federal District (San Francisco region) presented about 15 to 17 percent of its volume electronically in 2000.
- High-dollar group sort. This is a Fed service offering special expediting of large dollar amounts through the clearing system, with the Fed granting the depositing bank immediate (same-day) credit if it deposits the check early in the morning. The Fed targets any noncity drawee bank getting at least $10 million of daily presentments from outside its Fed district.[6]
- Interdistrict transportation system. This simply means the Fed redesigned its air transit routing modes and techniques to shorten delays and minimize systemwide float.
- Later presentments and deposit deadlines. The Fed initiated a second, mostly electronic, presentment of checks later in the morning to supplement its standard early morning presentment, and it also allowed banks to deposit checks as late as 2:30 A.M. (instead of at midnight) for some items processed through RCPCs. It charges an extra fee to banks using the later deposit deadline.

Float, a major reason to use checks when paying and to avoid collecting through checks, has become less of a factor in the US payment system because of these initiatives. Fed float has declined in the 1990s and early 2000s to a daily amount ranging from $600 to $800 million (from a 1980 amount of $10 billion) as a result of fewer paper checks being sent to the Federal Reserve; this reduces holdover float. More use of electronic payments, particularly direct-deposited payrolls, has speeded payments and reduced float. Some paying banks are opting to accept electronic presentments of checks drawn on them, which leads to faster debiting of those banks' reserve accounts, and again reduces Fed float. Now the Federal Reserve claims the ability to collect over 90 percent of the value of all checks deposited with it within 1 day after they are deposited in the collecting bank. Perhaps this reduction in check float will help spur greater use of electronic payments, which have no float, as disbursing companies have less incentive to use checks.

PAPER-BASED PAYMENTS

The three major paper-based payments mechanisms are checks, drafts, and depository transfer checks. Each of these clears through the same channels and, to a large degree, substitutes for each other. Except for small purchases, checks are by far the most popular means of payment: An estimated 68 billion checks were written in 2000, with a total

[6]An example listing, for the Federal Reserve's San Francisco listing, may be found at: http://www.frbsf.org/fiservices/feeschedules/hdpresnt.pdf

EXHIBIT 8-7

Growth of Payment Types in the United States

TYPE OF PAYMENT	(in trillions of dollars)				
	1980	1985	1990	1994	1998
Check	19.4	31.9	43.5	50.6	56.1
ACH	0.3	2.1	4.7	9.1	18.1
CHIPS and wires°	85.0	187.5	421.1	506.6	679.1
Total	104.7	221.5	469.3	566.3	753.3

°Wires are for funds transfers only (exclude Securities transfers).

SOURCE: 1980–1994 data adapted from Table 2, page 13, of Summers, Bruce J. and R. Alton Gilbert. 1996. Clearing and settlement of U.S. dollar payments: Back to the future? *Federal Reserve Bank of St. Louis Review* 78:3–27. Summers and Gilbert gathered these data from annual reports of the Board of Governors of the Federal Reserve System and the Bank for International Settlements. Check data for 1998 is estimated by the Green Sheet, Inc., 1998 ACH data is from NACHA, and 1998 CHIPS and wires data is from the Bank for International Settlements.

EXHIBIT 8-8

Consumer Retail Spending by Method

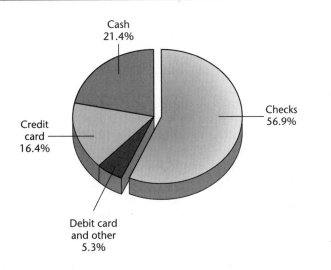

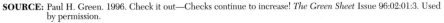

SOURCE: Paul H. Green. 1996. Check it out—Checks continue to increase! *The Green Sheet* Issue 96:02:01:3. Used by permission.

dollar amount of close to $70 trillion. Individuals write 55 percent of the checks, businesses 40 percent, and government 5 percent. Exhibit 8-7 shows the growth in the dollar value of interbank checks processed as well as the use of electronic payment mechanisms. Although the number of checks written continues to grow at about 2 percent per year, the dollar volume of those checks has increased less than ACH and large-value funds transfers done through Fedwire and the Clearing House Interbank Payment System (CHIPS). (These latter electronic payment systems are discussed later.)

Although we will not go into detail on coin and currency payments, we note that these cash payments remain important for consumer purchases.[7] To illustrate, 81 percent

[7]Coins are important for their use in vending machine purchases and produced by the US Mint as needed. Currency refers to paper bills issued by the Federal Reserve and is considered a liability of the issuing Federal Reserve district bank.

of people surveyed in the United States prefer to pay cash for restaurant dinners, compared with only 7 percent who prefer personal checks and 10 percent who prefer to use credit cards. This same survey found that the preferred method for paying home mortgages was by personal check (69 percent), with only 20 percent paying cash, and the remainder using electronic withdrawals or some other method.[8] Another recent study of consumer retail spending found that, on the whole, checks are much preferred to cash. Exhibit 8-8 shows the entire breakdown, which indicates that checks accounted for 57 percent of the dollar value of US retail purchases, whereas cash was a distant second at 21 percent (also notice that credit and debit cards together match cash usage). The preference for checks is even more pronounced for business-to-business transactions, although some large companies now require their suppliers to be paid electronically.

Checks

Some people think that the amount of money showing in their checking account balance is held in the bank's vault, but this is not the case. Your checking account balance is actually a computer entry, an electronic record representing how much the bank is committed to pay on the checks you write. Traditional, noninterest-bearing checking accounts are known as **demand deposit accounts.** Since early 1981, banks have offered checking with interest, or a NOW account, to individuals, sole proprietorships, and nonprofit organizations.[9] Either type of account obligates the bank on which the item is drawn to honor requests for withdrawals on demand. This simply means that the bank will pay the check when presented with it, unless the account balance is insufficient.

Only one of every 200 checks is not honored. Banks therefore assume that the drawee bank will honor deposited checks. They call the deposited checks **cash items** and give depositors immediate provisional credit for them. "Immediate" means the bank credits the depositor's account balance on the day the check is received, and "provisional" implies the bank can reverse the credit if the payor has insufficient funds or if for any other reason the check is not honored at the time the check is presented to his or her bank.

Does this mean the depositor gains available or spendable funds equal to the amount of the deposit? Not always. We need to distinguish between ledger balances and collected balances. The **ledger balance** reflects all credits and debits posted to an account as of a certain time, but this balance may not be entirely spendable. If a person deposits five checks before his or her bank's daily cutoff time, he or she may not be able to withdraw some or all of the amount of the total deposit. The **collected balance** (sometimes called the available balance) may be somewhat less than the ledger balance because of availability delays applied to the checks by the bank.[10] These "holds" placed on checks are spelled out in the bank's availability schedule, and holds greater than 1 or 2 business days apply primarily to consumer checking accounts. One bank's policy follows:

> A deposit made before closing time on a business day (except holidays) is credited to your account that day. We will make funds from your deposits available to you on the first business day after we receive your deposit. Depending on the type of check you deposit, funds

---

[8]From a survey conducted for the Payment Systems Education Association, reported in 1988. Cash Remains King *ABA Banking Journal* January: 123.

[9]NOW accounts are authorized by the Monetary Control Act of 1980.

[10]Some banks honor checks up to the ledger balance, even though technically they only have to pay checks summing to the available balance. The banks do this to preserve customer goodwill and may not have made the policy known to customers in the past. Under Regulation CC, banks are required to publish their availability schedules and abide by them, but they may offer different availability to various classes of customers.

may not be available until the fifth business day after the date of your deposit. However, the first $100 of your deposit will be available the first business day.

The Federal Reserve has dealt with a major concern of check depositors by shortening the maximum allowable hold period banks can place on checks. Effective September 1990, the Fed's **Regulation CC** stipulates that from the day of deposit local checks must be available within 2 business days and nonlocal checks within 5 days.[11] Regulation CC implemented the mandate of the **Expedited Funds Availability Act** of 1987, which required that shorter availability schedules be put in place. Banks still have the right to delay availability for a longer period when they believe the deposit will not be paid (the check will not be honored after being presented to the drawee bank), when more than a certain dollar amount is deposited in 1 day, when a check that was returned unpaid is redeposited, when the account has been repeatedly overdrawn, or when there is a computer or communications system malfunction. When checks do bounce, they are called **return items.** Although from the time of deposit checks only take 1 to 5 days to be presented to the drawee bank, returned checks may take 5 to 14 days to work back to the clearing (depositing) bank. This is because any endorsements are verified as the check works back to each bank that handled it.[12]

Drafts

A draft is a written order to make payment to a third party, in which the entity ordered to pay the draft is usually a bank. Any party holding a credit balance for the person writing the draft may have a draft drawn on it. For example, a store may draft on another store, or a bank may draw a draft on another bank. A draft is similar to a check: it is an order to pay and involves three parties. This distinguishes it from a note, which is a promise to pay involving only two parties. When drawn on a bank, the draft differs from a check because the payor's bank will pass it on to the payor for approval before the payor has to make funds available to pay the draft amount.

Drafts also differ from checks in three other ways. First, drafts are not necessarily drawn on a bank, whereas checks are. Second, drafts are not always payable on demand. **Sight drafts** are payable on demand, but **time drafts** are payable at some future date. Third, the purposes for which drafts are written are often different. Sight drafts often must have documentation attached to verify that conditions for payment (receipt, or "sight" of goods) have been met. Time drafts are usually dated after verification of a shipment of goods. These are commonly used in export sales because of uncertainty about the creditworthiness of the buyer and to give the buyer the time to inspect the shipment before taking title to the goods.

Three forms of the draft concept merit our attention. A common variety of draft called a **payable through draft** (PTD) gives the payor 24 hours to decide whether to honor or refuse payment after it has been presented to the payor's bank. They are used

[11]Local checks are those deposited in a bank located in the drawee bank's Federal Reserve check processing zone.

[12]To speed up check clearing, a group of 11 large banks have formed the Electronic Check Clearing House Organization (ECCHO). This enables the banks to process information from each other's checks using the electronic information from the MICR line, instead of waiting for the physical check to be presented. This notifies banks about a day earlier of incoming presentments, allowing banks to identify returned items more quickly. Return identification, in turn, aids banks trying to prevent check fraud: under the old system, bogus checks may be deposited and the funds withdrawn before the depositor's bank realizes the checks will not be honored.

for claim reimbursement by insurance companies, which use the 24-hour period to verify the signature and endorsements. A **government warrant** is essentially a PTD issued by a government agency. Finally, a **preauthorized draft** is initiated by the payee, who has been authorized to draw against the payor's account. Banks sometimes collect mortgage payments this way.

Drafts can cause special problems for the cash manager using them for payment:

- Drafts must be handled by the company (and usually by its bank as well), adding to the company's clerical workload.
- The extra processing time and the 24-hour delay results in a delay in funds availability to the payee, which may create ill will.
- The bank might impose an extra balance requirement (larger compensating balance) or processing fee for its part in handling the draft; this offsets some or all the benefit of the delay in debiting the payor's account.

Depository Transfer Checks

Unsigned checks used by firms to move funds from one account to another are called **depository transfer checks** (DTCs). They are often used to move (concentrate) monies collected in many different locations into a pooled account in a concentration bank, where the money can be invested as a single large amount. These DTCs may be paper or electronic. In the case of a paper DTC, a check is prepared by the concentration bank and is drawn on the company's checking account at a local or regional bank. A daily report showing each DTC is compiled by the concentration bank and sent to the company. In the case of **electronic depository transfers** (EDTs), the local or regional account is debited electronically and the funds are sent through an automated clearinghouse to the concentration bank account. The bank charge for an electronic transaction may be more expensive than a paper DTC, but the EDT provides quicker availability in the concentration account for the company. Compared with wire transfers, electronic DTCs are a slower but less expensive means of moving funds.

Future of Paper Payments

Some observers have labeled the check a dinosaur and foresee a checkless society in the near future. Yet check growth has continued at about 2% per year, and we believe the check will be with us for the foreseeable future. The increasing use of plastic debit cards, which allow consumers to pay grocery and other bills through an electronic charge to their bank accounts, is definitely slowing the growth in the number of checks written, as is the federal government's decision to no longer pay any of its bills by check (with the exception of some benefit transfers), effective in 1999. **Electronic check presentment,** in which paying banks have the option of converting scanned checks into electronic presentments at the Federal Reserve, is allowing checks to be debited more quickly. This reduces check float and speeds return item processing.

ELECTRONIC-BASED PAYMENTS

The delays in check collection and presentment have spurred the development of faster means of moving funds. These electronic funds transfer techniques transfer value in a paperless or electronic form. The three major methods are wire transfers, EDTs, and automated debit and credits. Wire transfers are conducted through the Federal Reserve's Fedwire system, and EDTs and automated debits and credits are processed through automated clearinghouses.

Wire Transfers

The best way to quickly move money from one place to another is with a wire transfer. A **wire transfer** is a bookkeeping entry that simultaneously debits the payor's account and credits the payee's account. The only thing that is "wired" is the encoded message requesting the transfer, which is sent via telephone lines. Value is transferred immediately, which is the distinguishing feature of wire transfers. Formerly, domestic wire transfers took place over Bankwire (a private network of banks) and Fedwire (the Federal Reserve's system), but Bankwire is now defunct.[13] **Fedwire** is a linked network of the 12 Federal Reserve district banks that transfers funds for banks (and by extension their customers) by debiting or crediting the banks' reserve accounts.

The number of wire transfers is small relative to other payment systems, but the dollar volume is very large compared to that of checks. The dollar volume continues to grow annually, with $1.5 trillion being transferred on most days. The Clearing House Interbank Payment System (CHIPS) also involves wire transfers, but is primarily an international payment system and is considered later in this chapter.

WIRE TRANSFER USES.   Companies and banks opt for wire transfers when they want to gain immediate access to large dollar amounts. Small dollar amounts are not transferred because the Fed charges banks for the service it provides. Banks pass the cost on to the customer in the form of a fee ($10 charged to the initiating party; $7 to $10 charged to the recipient) or require a higher balance in the company's noninterest-bearing checking account. When banks borrow overnight from customers (via repurchase agreements) or each other (via federal funds borrowing), the money must be transferred on one day and transferred back the next.[14] This necessitates rapid and efficient movement of funds, which at present can only be accomplished by wire transfers. Settlement is immediate and final for such transfers, meaning there is no availability delay and no worry about the transfer bouncing. Companies find wire transfers economical for moving large balances from several banks to a concentration bank, where the total amount can be used to pay down borrowings or invested in a higher-interest large-denomination investment. Municipalities such as the city of Philadelphia have eased cash flow crises by having the state wire transfer payments that routinely are made in support of city services. Wires are also commonly used in large real estate transactions and occasionally to collect disputed amounts.

MECHANICS OF WIRE TRANSFERS.   The steps involved in a wire transfer are diagrammed in Exhibit 8-9. The customer wanting to make payment (the originator) may contact his or her bank in one of several ways: telephone, specialized telex machine or facsimile machine, telegram, or personal computer (e-mail). Some type of account number or authorization code validates the identity of the originator to prevent fraud.

---

[13]Although not used much by businesses, Western Union offers wire transfers to customers. An individual conveys a payment order to a local Western Union office, which enters the message into its personal computer and conveys the order to another office in the vicinity of the payee. The receiving office picks up the message on its PC and issues a check to the order of the payee. The payee can then come by and pick up the check and take it to be cashed or deposited.

[14]Customers and lending banks view this as an overnight investment.

EXHIBIT 8-9
Diagram of a Wire Transfer

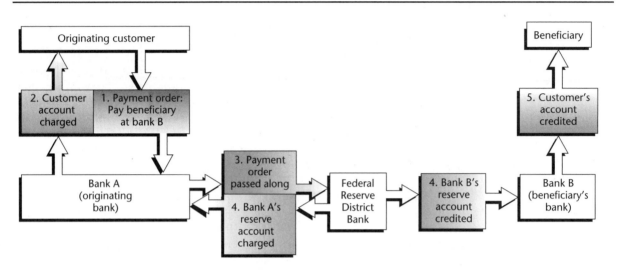

Formally, when the originating customer requests that money be paid to a beneficiary, this is called a payment order (step 1). The customer's bank (bank A) then deducts the amount of the requested payment from the customer's available balance (step 2). At this point, the customer's bank (originating bank) communicates the payment order to the Fedwire office at the nearest Federal Reserve district bank (step 3),[15] which then subtracts (debits) the amount of the transfer from the originating bank's balance at the Fed (reserve balance) and adds to (credits) the account of the beneficiary's bank (bank B; step 4). The Fed also notifies bank B of the transaction.[16] Bank B then credits the beneficiary's ledger and available balances and notifies the beneficiary by phone, in writing, or through a new balance report (step 5).

ADVANTAGES AND DISADVANTAGES OF WIRES.   Wire transfers have several advantages. They can be completed in a matter of minutes and are the best method for quickly moving large sums of money. They accomplish immediate final transfer of value without the worry of whether the check will bounce or the ACH will be reversed. When collecting a large sum of money from a customer of questionable creditworthiness, this finality is an appreciable advantage to the seller. However, because of the number of parties and necessary confirmations and other supportive tasks, they are also the most expensive on a per-transaction basis. The expense mounts when two entities within the same company are originator and beneficiary, respectively (as in the case of wiring money to concentrate into a larger balance), and the company must incur fees on both the sending and receiving ends.[17] As ACH transfers move toward same-day transaction, their lower cost will result in the displacement of many wire transfers.

[15]Small banks not connected to the Fedwire computer can instruct larger correspondent banks to initiate wire transfers on behalf of their customers, or initiate the transfers by telephoning or sending a message via a personal computer telephone hookup to the nearest Federal Reserve District bank.

[16]When Bank B is in a different Federal Reserve District than Bank A, the payment order information is communicated through the FedNet communication system to Bank B's Federal Reserve District Bank.

[17]When the entity being paid (beneficiary) initiates the wire transfer, as is the case when a company's headquarters initiates concentration of funds from several distant banks, the transaction is called a "wire drawdown."

Automated Clearing Houses

A fast and relatively inexpensive means of processing large numbers of routine transactions was developed in the early 1970s. Known as **automated clearing houses (ACH),** this system is composed of a loose network of associations spread across the country. The 34 ACH associations include more than 12,000 financial institutions and over 40,000 corporations. The associations provide information about ACH transactions, along with the benefits and costs. All transactions must be handled by an ACH operator. The Fed is the primary operator of the underlying value transfer system, directly or indirectly handling 90 percent of all ACH transactions, the others spread among three private sector operators. The most popular uses for entities conducting ACH transactions are the automatic (direct) deposit of paychecks and Social Security checks, explaining why the average ACH transaction amount is $3,300.

Electronic depository transfer checks (EDTs) are a common payment mechanism that uses the ACH system. Electronic depository transfer checks are not really checks but are paperless, unsigned payments (electronic debits) that transfer funds using the ACH system. They are often communicated via a personal computer and usually are accompanied by an electronic (paperless) message encoded in a specialized format. Electronic depository transfer checks require the payor's bank to produce a computer file of payees, which is sent to one of the ACH associations for availability to the payee either the next day or the day following. Next-day availability is desirable for transfers used in deposit concentration, so that monies can be invested more quickly. This rapid availability contrasts with paper DTCs, which may take several days to clear because they must travel through the mail.

Payors know at the time of order initiation exactly when they will have their accounts charged for the dollar amount of each transaction. Two complicating factors affect the timing of order initiation, however. First, not all banks are members of the ACH system. Thus a company wishing to pay all its employees through direct deposit will likely have to pay a few by means of checks. Second, not all banks have the systems that enable them to electronically transmit payment orders (and accompanying information) to the appropriate ACHs. Two private ACH operators, Arizona ACH and Visa, have already automated all financial institutions for which they provide service.

A final point to be made about the ACH system is the growing role of private institutions in ACH processing. The Fed presently directly processes about 80 percent of all ACH payments, but the three private operators (Visa, New York, and Arizona) have captured 20 percent of the market and are growing.

GROWTH OF ACH TRANSACTIONS.   Referring to Exhibit 8-7, it is evident that ACH volume is a fast-growing payment system. Growth in dollar volume is particularly impressive for 1985 through 1998, when volume was growing at roughly 18 percent per year. The annual number of ACH transfers in the United States grew from 850 million to almost 4 billion from 1989 to 1997, reflecting the fact that the number of companies using the ACH system grew from 100,000 to 750,000. Growth would have been even faster had potential users been offered more inducement to use the system. The company or individual paying through an ACH debit loses the advantage of disbursement float, the delay between the time the check is written and when funds are subtracted from the account. Unless there is some offsetting benefit such as a longer credit period before payment (the ACH debit) is initiated, the customer sees little reason to switch. State governments have started mandating ACH payment of taxes owed, choosing the stick approach over the carrot approach.

PURPOSE OF THE ACH SYSTEM.   The Fed is strongly encouraging greater use of electronic deposits and payments through the ACH system for two reasons. First, the payments are paperless, saving banks large amounts of money and back-office time. The ACH transactions save financial institutions an estimated 30 to 35 percent compared with checks. The second advantage is related: the recipient of the payment gains faster availability and can credit the payor more quickly than would be the case for checks. Automated clearing house processing is ideal for payroll deposits, insurance premium collections, and corporation-to-corporation payments. One survey found that 73 percent of large companies (sales in excess of $500 million annually) and 48 percent of middle market companies (sales from $100 million to $500 million) are using or plan to use an ACH service.[18] Public and nonprofit organizations, particularly governments, have found ACH collections attractive. Fundraising consultants are beginning to advocate automated collection of pledges.[19] The major disadvantage to using the ACH transactions is that the payor loses the customary float when writing checks, and payment terms may have to be renegotiated to induce payor participation.

MECHANICS OF ACH TRANSACTIONS.   Exhibit 8-10 illustrates the mechanics of an ACH transaction and identifies the players involved. Two clarifying comments aid in our understanding of the ACH. First, there is no physical clearinghouse, as would be the case with a local clearinghouse used in check swapping. Instead, the entries are debited and credited to the appropriate banks' accounts on the clearinghouse operator's computer. Second, all transactions eventually culminate in financial institution debits and credits at a Federal Reserve district bank. All but four of the ACH operators are housed in Federal Reserve facilities, which settle ACH transactions by debiting or crediting the appropriate banks' reserve accounts. Even for the three private operators who process ACH transactions (which are basically just information flows), settlement of the funds transfers still takes place at a Federal Reserve location. The net effect of all transfers involving a particular bank is handled by a debit (if the total is negative) or credit (if positive) to that bank's Federal Reserve account.[20]

Payroll processing illustrates the steps involved in an ACH transfer. Let's say Consolidated Freightliners (the originator) pays its employees monthly. It first prepares a computer file of electronic entries, which include the company's and employees' account numbers and bank transit routing numbers, as well as the dollar amount of the payments. It then sends the file electronically (via PC and telephone line) or manually (courier hand-carries a computer magnetic tape or diskette) to Consolidated's bank (the **originating depository financial institution** [ODFI]). The bank sorts out the on-us credits for employees having checking accounts at that bank and credits their accounts. If it has any, the bank then combines the other entries with those submitted by other companies and sends Consolidated's remaining entries on a computer tape to the local ACH. The ACH operator must first sort the transactions involving the banks in its area and then sends nonlocal transactions to other ACHs. The ACH then credits the employees' banks (called **receiving depository financial institutions** [RDFI]) according to

[18]Survey conducted by EDI Research, Inc., and reported in McEntee, Elliott C. and William B. Nelson. 1989. The ACH Network: Meeting corporate needs. *Journal of Cash Management* March/April:12–14.

[19]Organizations can get higher pledge amounts, guaranteed fulfillment of pledges, automatic pledge renewal, reduced solicitation costs, and more predictable cash inflows simply by having donors preauthorize automated debits to their checking accounts each month. For more on this see Beverly Kempf. 1990. Moving donors to EFT. *Fund Raising Management* 4(November):51–52, 62.

[20]Do not confuse ACH operators with the 34 regional ACH associations. ACH associations, like other trade associations, include banking and corporate participants in a geographic area that participate in ACH payments or collections.

whether Consolidated has selected 1-day (next day) or 2-day settlement.[21] The ODFI's account is likewise charged for the total amount of the payroll being processed through the ACH. Consolidated must be certain to have adequate funds in its checking account, because the bank will in turn debit Consolidated's account. The ACH then sends a tape to each RDFI bank, including all account numbers and dollar amounts of employees having accounts at that bank. The RDFI credits each employee's checking account appropriately. Consolidated's bank will provide it with periodic bank statements and/or daily deposit reports so that its treasurer can monitor the company's cash position.

Banks charge slightly less for a 2-day settlement cycle than for transactions processed on a 1-day cycle. In fact, different banks have different cutoff times by which originators must submit the computer file, and each bank may charge a different amount for the same ACH origination service.

SUMMARY OF ACH ADVANTAGES AND DISADVANTAGES.   Proponents claim numerous advantages for using the ACH system.

Advantages of ACH usage are the following:

1. Reduced costs for banking, reconciliation and cash application, and handling return items (the Federal Reserve charges $3 for handling a returned check but only 2 cents on a returned ACH transaction). EDS Corporation, which supplies check-processing services to small banks, estimates that moderately sized banks spend $13 million to $40 million per year to process checks. The per-item fees companies pay for ACH debits and credits range from 10 cents to 20 cents. Banks are able to process ACH debits for 5.7 cents per item, compared to 10.5 cents per check, and pass the savings on to companies. Banks much prefer to collect loan payments electronically, with an estimated savings of up to $4.11 per payment, by eliminating loan coupons and other processing costs.
2. Faster inflows because of the possibility of collecting insurance premiums and other payments through the ACH; check-related mail and processing delays are eliminated.
3. More reliability, resulting in better service to customers and employees because of the control over payment timing and the fact that fewer exception items must be dealt with.
4. Greater security, because checks can be tampered with and lost in the mail.
5. More accurate forecasting of funds availability, because of certainty as to when the transaction will take place.

Disadvantages for ACH usage offset the above advantages somewhat:

1. Disbursement float and control are reduced for the payor, which may lead to a renegotiation of all payment terms.
2. Up-front systems costs may be very high for the necessary investment in computer hardware and software, especially for a smaller bank or originator; recent movement toward PCs has reduced the hardware costs considerably.
3. Lack of uniform notification practices and payment formats has plagued the ACH industry. Some depository institutions are not timely in their notification of customers, and presently there are several different formats for transmission of payment data.

---

[21]More precisely, the ACH operator is netting all transactions affecting a bank for a given settlement day and then has the Federal Reserve account of the bank debited or credited for the amount of the net balance. For an ODFI, 1-day settlement implies that an ACH processed Friday results in a debit for the total dollar amount on Monday, assuming it is not a bank holiday.

EXHIBIT 8-10
Mechanics of ACH Transactions

Five entities participate in the ACH system. They are defined as:

1. *Originator.* The originator is the entity that agrees to initiate ACH entries into the payment system according to an arrangement with a receiver. The originator is usually a company directing a transfer of funds to or from a consumer's or another company's account. In the case of a customer-initiated entry, however, the originator may be an individual initiating funds transfer activity to or from his or her own account. The term "company" is intended to be representative of the originator of electronic ACH entries and does not imply exclusion of other types of organizations.
2. *Originating depository financial institution.* The originating depository financial institution (ODFI) is the institution that receives the payment instructions from originators and forwards the entries to the ACH operator. A DFI may participate in the ACH as an RDFI without being an ODFI; however, if a DFI chooses to originate ACH entries, it must also agree to act as an RDFI.
3. *Automated clearing house operator.* An automated clearing house (ACH) operator is the central clearing facility, operated by a Federal Reserve Bank (FRB) or a private organization, that receives entries from ODFIs, distributes the entries to appropriate RDFIs, and performs the settlement functions for the affected financial institutions.
4. *Receiving depository financial institution.* The RDFI is the DFI that receives ACH entries from the ACH operator and posts them to the accounts of the depositors (receivers).
5. *Receiver.* A receiver is a natural person or an organization that has authorized an originator to initiate an ACH entry to the receiver's account with the RDFI.

The flowchart depicts the system participants and their relationships.

System participants

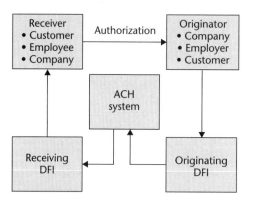

The ACH network supports a number of different payment applications. Unlike the wire transfer and check systems, the ACH is both a credit and a debit payment system. ACH credit transactions transfer funds from the originator to the receiver. ACH debit transactions, on the other hand, transfer funds (collect funds) from the receiver to the originator.

SOURCE: Adapted with permission from materials provided by the National Automated Clearing House Association (NACHA).

The relative advantage or disadvantage of using ACH depends on the application and the size of the company. Direct deposit and automated state tax payments are used by companies of all sizes, but other ACH uses vary significantly depending on company size. Notice in Exhibit 8-11 the results of the Phoenix-Hecht 1998 survey. The biggest change in the past several years has been the substantial increase in companies using the

EXHIBIT 8-11
ACH Service Usage by Company Size

SERVICE:	<$250M	$250M–$499M	$500M–$999M	$1B–$2.49B	$2.5+B	ALL RESPONDENTS
			SALES:			
Direct Deposit of Payroll	73.0%	74.9%	79.3%	84.8%	79.8%	75.4%
Automated State Tax Payments	70.3%	72.7%	80.8%	78.6%	80.3%	73.4%
ACH Debits for Cash Concentration	58.4%	65.4%	69.1%	79.5%	78.4%	64.5%
Corporate Trade Payments	38.2%	46.6%	52.7%	63.2%	70.6%	46.1%
Consumer Debits	15.4%	17.7%	18.5%	22.7%	25.4%	17.6%
Direct Deposit of Dividends/Pension	10.1%	11.8%	16.2%	20.5%	21.7%	12.8%

SOURCE: 1998. *Cash Management Monitor™: Report to Corporations.* Phoenix-Hecht, p 16.

ACH for state tax payments. Corporate trade payments are increasingly made electronically, but almost twice as many large companies (sales in excess of $2.5 billion) as smaller companies (sales less than $250 million) use electronic payments. It is also noteworthy that most companies now use ACH debits for concentrating their cash to a central bank account.

Use of ACH continues to grow, and recent developments such as weekend acceptance of tapes for Monday settlement and all-electronic transmittal and receipt of payment flows should increase use in the future.

FINANCIAL DILEMMA REVISITED

Should your company get on the electronic payments bandwagon? Unquestionably. Despite the expenditures to get up and running, the advantages far outweigh the costs. Furthermore, a large customer or supplier will soon force the issue for you because of their preferences for using electronic commerce applications, including financial EDI. The federal government has mandated that all of its vendors be paid electronically, and federal withholding taxes and some states' corporate taxes must be paid electronically by many businesses. Financial institutions and the regional or national ACH association provides much-needed help to guide your implementation process. A good illustration of how electronic payments can benefit a company is retailer use of "electronic checks." An estimated 25 million checks were converted to ACH debits by 25,000 retailers in 2000. When a consumer presents a check at the checkout, the merchant runs it through an electronic reader that captures the bank account number and routing information, along with the check number. The check is marked or stamped "Void" and handed back to the consumer. The consumer signs a receipt authorizing the electronic transaction, and keeps a copy for his or her records. The merchant initiates an ACH debit using the check information and transaction amount. The consumer gets a description of the transaction on his or her monthly statement.

Point-of-Sale Transactions Using Debit Cards

Increasingly, consumers are using debit cards to make purchases. The number of merchants accepting them exploded from only 50,000 in 1990 to several million today; two in three Americans now have at least one debit card. A **debit card** is very similar to a credit card, but the transaction is processed through an online hookup to local banks

(81 percent) or offline through the ACH system (19 percent) and the amount is immediately (or if ACH, within 2 business days) subtracted from the customer's checking account. By contrast, a credit card transaction is not a payment but is a loan from the credit card issuer.

The direct-debit point-of-sale (POS) program offered by one of the nation's largest regional automated teller machine networks, New York Cash Exchange (NYCE), illustrates this application of EFTs. The NYCE cardholders can use their ATM cards to pay for purchases at participating drug stores, home improvement centers, and grocery chains, and the funds will be electronically debited from their checking accounts. Customers get a receipt while in the checkout line, the transaction is processed back to the customer's bank, and the debit appears on the monthly bank statement. Retailers are charged a small fee per transaction, similar to the fee charged them for credit card transactions. Automated teller machines are being used in California to sell movie tickets, with the amount of purchase automatically debited from the purchaser's checking account.

Although some retailers issue their own debit cards, bank-issued ATM cards dominate the debit card field. In 1992, MasterCard and Visa both introduced debit cards that can be used nationwide at ATMs and retail establishments such as supermarkets, convenience stores, and gas stations. To gain some of the supermarket business for its debit cards, Visa USA cut its processing fee to 1 percent of each charge sale, versus the 1.25 percent nonsupermarket merchants must pay. Although the supermarkets must accept Visa credit cards to be eligible to accept the debit card, Visa officials reason that debit cards are more popular than credit cards with customers who are accustomed to paying by check or cash.

INTERNATIONAL PAYMENT SYSTEMS

Companies selling or purchasing goods abroad are aware of several important differences in foreign payment systems. A complete discussion of other countries' payment systems is beyond the scope of this text,[22] and we present only the basic aspects of international paper-based and electronic payment systems.

In one sense, doing business abroad is much simpler, because there are far fewer banks in each country. However, the customs and conventions of the different countries must be given attention. Cross-border check processing is especially problematic, taking from several days to several weeks for clearing. Several correspondent banks might be involved, which slows the process while adding to the expense. Banks also may charge a service fee for the transfer that varies with the amount involved; in the United States, a fixed charge applies regardless of dollar amount. Drafts also are used much more in international trade, a topic we return to in Chapter 9. Finally, many countries restrict data and/or currency outflows, complicating the task of the multinational corporation treasurer.

Paper-Based Payments

Checks are used in foreign countries but are not quite as popular. The major difference seen abroad is the prevalence of giro systems, particularly in Europe. The **giro system** is a centralized payment system, usually linked to the postal service, used primarily for

---

[22]Excellent surveys of various countries' payment and banking systems may be found in Back's book (see chapter references) and various issues of the *TMA Journal* (now called *AFP Exchange*).

retail payments. To use it, a company mails a bill to the customer with a stub attached to it that includes the seller's bank and account number. Called a **giro acceptance,** this computer-processable stub card is signed by the customer, who then takes it to the post office. The post office transmits what now amounts to a payment order to the customer's bank, which then debits the customer's account and arranges for this and other customers' payments to be credited to the seller's bank. The seller's bank then credits the seller's account and notifies the seller of the payment(s). The main advantage of the giro system is very little delay, or float, in a company's collections. The main disadvantage is that the seller is at the mercy of the buyer for payment initiation timing.

The use of checks is also reduced where postal systems are unreliable or consumers do not have checking accounts. In Latin America, for example, mail systems are too unreliable for sending checks, and fewer than 30 percent of households have checking accounts (compared to 90 percent in the United States). Until recently, check clearing occurred by arrangements between individual banks, because many central banks had no centralized check-clearing system, and in-country transportation was unreliable. Business-to-business payments were usually made by check, but these were either delivered or picked up by couriers, or deposited by the payor into the payee's account using a special deposit ticket. Consumers typically pay in person by cash or less frequently by check, either at a bank or the company's office. In Middle Eastern countries, central banks maintain control over the domestic clearing houses, and manual check clearing occurs in each country except Saudi Arabia. As a result, most corporate payments occur by check, which take from 1 to 3 business days to clear in the major cities and anywhere from 5 to 10 business days outside of the central clearing systems.

Value dating is another practice commonly used in foreign countries. Because banks abroad are allowed to (and do) pay interest on checking accounts, they must make up for the added interest expense by either charging fees for services rendered or engaging in value dating, which entails delaying the availability of deposited checks and retroactively advancing the debit date for cleared checks (the latter is called back-valuing). The number of days a customer loses is sometimes negotiable and may vary by customer type, bank, and country. When a company is subject to back-valuing by its banks, monitoring the company's bank balance becomes difficult and the company must do additional forecasting. Fortunately, banks in many countries offer automatic overdraft protection, so that the company is simply charged interest on overdrafted amounts as if it has taken out a small loan.

EFFECT OF THE EURO.   The single currency in Europe, the euro, and the single European market for financial services, are changing European cash management. First, large amounts can be transferred on a same-day basis with no value dating—enabling concentration and pooling of funds into a single currency. Second, the development of between-country transfers that are not value-dated is causing banks to begin dropping value dating on domestic payments. Third, the increased competition in banking services has lowered bank fees. Coincidentally, electronic balance reporting and payments initiation services are now being offered with Windows and Internet-based platforms. Cash management processes and receivables and payables management will continue to become more centralized and efficient.

Electronic Payments

Automated clearinghouse systems are not generally available abroad, because of the prevalence of the giro system. Exceptions are the United Kingdom, Canada, Brazil, and

Mexico. US companies can now initiate cross-border ACH payments to Canadian payees using a single computer-generated NACHA-formatted file. The added complexity here is the US dollar-to-Canadian dollar exchange rate calculation. Payments from Canadian companies can be received in a similar manner. Mexico introduced ACH via a bank-owned ACH operator, Cecoban, in the 1990s. Automated clearing house systems are being developed in Argentina, Chile, Colombia, and Panama. However, wire transfers are commonly used to transfer large dollar amounts internationally. We limit our discussion to CHIPS and SWIFT, the two international wire transfer mechanisms.

The **Clearing House Interbank Payment System** (CHIPS) was established in 1970 to handle interbank transactions needed to settle international transactions. The Clearing House Interbank Payment System is a private association of banks that operates through the New York Clearinghouse Association. Much of the flow of funds related to buying and selling dollar-denominated investments in major foreign financial centers (Eurodollar investments) is processed through CHIPS. Participating banks relay and receive payment messages over leased telephone lines to the CHIPS computer. The Clearing House Interbank Payment System settles roughly $175 billion daily.

Payments are not considered final until the end of the day, when each bank's position is determined by subtracting the total of all debits from the credits total. The net settlement sheet is then sent to the New York Federal Reserve, where banks with net credit positions receive a credit to their reserve account after the debits have been charged to banks with debit balances. The average wire transfer is for $2,500,000, and a bank may make many wire transfers during a day. Because the dollar amounts are so large, a participating bank may have a net debit position far in excess of the bank's reserve account balance, and the bank must transfer funds into the account by the end of the day. There is therefore some risk of settlement failure (in which the bank would not be able to make the necessary transfer), and the New York Clearinghouse has decided to implement immediate settlement (settlement finality) in the near future.

The **Society for Worldwide Interbank Financial Telecommunications** (SWIFT) is really just a communication network. Its services are used by parties in 189 countries, and over 6700 banks are connected to the network. It facilitates international payment orders because of a partly standardized message format and the ability to include additional payment messages with the payment order. At present, more than 1 billion messages are processed annually. Recent improvements, packaged as SWIFT II, include the ability to conduct interactive communications and a doubling of the number of characters the messages can include to 4000. The messages only cost 38 cents each, regardless of source or destination. Settlement of the orders is made through correspondent banks or CHIPS; in the latter case, it costs the payor about $12.

We can illustrate the workings of SWIFT by a simple example: Let's say a company in Australia wants to pay IBM for a computer. It instructs its Australian bank to wire money to IBM. The bank might then cable the message across SWIFT to a correspondent bank in New York, which debits the Australian bank's correspondent account for the amount of the transfer plus any fees. The US correspondent bank then pays IBM's bank, possibly working through yet another correspondent bank with which both of the banks have accounts.

MANAGING THE BANK RELATIONSHIP

Corporate treasurers are responsible for not only understanding the payment system but also for selecting the best bank(s) with which to conduct business and then maintaining good relationships with those banks. We survey the five major types of services that banks can provide, the key documents treasurers use to evaluate banks, and how banks charge for their service. We take an in-depth look at how treasurers select a bank or bank network for cash management and other services. We also introduce the major trends affecting banks' provision of corporate services.

The objective treasurers strive to achieve when managing the bank relationship is to ensure that all the company's banking services are provided reliably at a reasonable cost. Note that we did not say "at a *minimal* cost," because reliability of the corporate/bank relationship and adequate compensation of the company's banks take precedence over cost minimization. Value is created for a corporation by wise selection of banks, followed by careful monitoring of the banks, with new arrangements made when necessary.

The remainder of the chapter discusses the following: The first section provides background information regarding the major services banks offer to corporations, giving a logical starting point for treasurers determining banks with which to do business. The second section incorporates this information into a discussion of the bank selection process and principles regarding the management of the corporate/bank relationship. The chapter concludes with sections on banking system trends in the United States and abroad, including the increasing prominence of nonbank service providers, the ongoing unification of Europe's economic system, and the globalization of financial services provision.

SERVICES PROVIDED BY BANKS

Banks offer five major types of services that are of interest to the financial manager responsible for short-term financial management decisions.[23] The first three fall under the umbrella of "cash management" services: collections services (including the concentration of funds), payments services, and information services. The other two services are closely linked to the cash management services, as corporations that run short on cash need credit services, and corporations with excess cash use banks' investment services. Exhibit 8-12 summarizes the five banking services. We limit our present discussion to bank pricing and provision of cash management services; Chapters 9 and 10 cover collection and mobilization services, Chapter 11 covers payment services, Chapters 14 and 15 address investments, Chapter 16 discusses borrowing, and Chapter 19 covers information services.

To better understand this, we present the organization of the corporate services division in a typical bank. The treasury professional can understand the role and significance of cash management and related services when seeing the role and location of cash management in the typical bank's organizational structure. Throughout our discussion,

EXHIBIT 8-12
Major Banking Services

---

[23]Some "long-term" services we are not concerned with include leasing, investment banking, merger/acquisition counseling, and dividend-related services.

when we use the term **bank** we are referring to any financial institution that offers the particular service being discussed.

Banking Perspective on Corporate Services

Banks sometimes label services provided to corporate customers as "wholesale" services. Banks formerly used services such as cash management as a low-priced "loss leader" to gain a foothold with corporate clients, hoping to later add profitable lending arrangements. However, corporations increasingly shifted borrowing to nonbank sources in the 1980s and 1990s and bank loan profitability declined. During the same period, cash management services experienced a 19-percent growth, and both factors led to a repricing of cash management and related services. Three hundred banks presently offer cash management services, leading many observers to predict a shakeout and resultant exit by some of the banks. The growth rate has slowed to single digits, and the banks' offerings are so similar that some consider cash management services a commodity-type product. If so, the implication for banks is serious: more shopping around by corporate clients, leading to lower prices and less profitability.[24] The profitability of the overall relationship with the client, which encompasses all services a bank provides for the client, is the bank's proper focus.

ORGANIZATION OF CASH MANAGEMENT IN BANKS.   Organizationally, the cash management group is usually a separate department in the bank's corporate services division. Within the cash management group, there might be three distinct subgroups: sales, product development/management, and customer service.[25] The sales group generates income by selling cash management products to corporate clients, the product group develops new products and improves existing products, and the customer service group strives to quickly and accurately resolve client inquiries and complaints.

VALUE OF BANKS TO CORPORATE TREASURERS.   Corporate treasurers generally find banks' cash management officers very helpful as a place to obtain advice and information. However, this advice is most often oriented toward positioning the bank in the most favorable light. Conversely, bankers' major complaints regarding treasurers are that they are sometimes defensive, cover up ignorance of complex products, are unfair and tactless when having banks bid against one another, or overlook the fact that banks must make a profit on the total client relationship (and cannot accept thin margins on all services). Banks also expect to be informed as soon as possible of any adverse changes in the client's financial position and consider the treasurer to be the main source of information regarding the company and its banking needs. Many banks assign one individual to the overall client relationship; this involves overseeing all services provided to the client. Accounts (clients) that are large and profitable to the bank naturally have the best bank personnel assigned to them. With this banking environment context in mind, we now consider the five major corporate services provided by banks: collection, payment, information, lending, and investment.

---

[24]Quality of service should also become more important, and banks are devoting more attention to quality aspects such as speedy customer complaint handling.

[25]Many banks have a centralized customer service department, in which one customer service department not only handles cash management inquiries but also handles complaints and questions about all other services used by a client. Very technical questions are referred to product managers. In addition, a bank's operations area is the one actually doing the wire transfers and other transactions for the client.

EXHIBIT 8-13
Availability Schedule

Corporate Availability Schedule—Unencoded Deposits
Monday Through Thursday

ENDPOINT	ROUTING & TRANSIT NUMBER	FLOAT DAYS
Postal money order	0000-0020,0119,0800	1
Government checks	0000-0050,0051	1
Boston City	0110	1
Windsor Locks RCPC	0111,0118,0119,0211	2
Lewiston RCPC	0112	2
Boston RCPC	0113,0114,0115	2
Northwest New England RCPC	0116,0117	2
New York City	0210,0260,0280	1
Cranford RCPC	0212	2
Utica RCPC	0213	2
Jericho RCPC	0214,0219	2
New York Country	0215,0216	2
Buffalo City	0220	1
Buffalo RCPC	0223	2
Philadelphia City	0310,0360	1
Philadelphia RCPC	0311,0312,0313,0319	2
Cleveland City	0410	1
Cleveland RCPC	0412	2
Cincinnati City	0420	1
Cincinnati RCPC	0421,0422,0423	1
Pittsburgh City	0430	1
Pittsburgh RCPC	0432,0433,0434	2
Columbus City	0440	1
Columbus RCPC	0441,0442	2
Richmond City	0510	1
Richmond RCPC	0514	2
Charleston RCPC	0515	2
Charleston City	0519	1
Baltimore City	0520	1
Baltimore W/VA RCPC	0521,0522	2
Charlotte City	0530	1
Charlotte RCPC	0531	2
Columbia RCPC	0532	2
Columbia City	0539	1
Baltimore RCPC	0540,0550,0560,0570	2
Atlanta City	0610	1
Atlanta RCPC	0611,0612,0613	2
Birmingham City	0620	1
Birmingham RCPC	0621,0622	2
Jacksonville City	0630	1
Jacksonville RCPC	0631,0632	2
Nashville City	0640	1
Nashville RCPC	0641,0642	2
New Orleans City	0650	1
New Orleans RCPC	0651,0652,0653,0654,0655	2
Miami City	0660	1
Miami RCPC	0670	2
Chicago City	0710	1
Chicago RCPC	0711,0712,0719	1
Detroit City	0720	1
Detroit RCPC	0724	2
Des Moines City	0730	1
Des Moines RCPC	0739	1
Indianapolis City	0740	1

°All items drawn on any Federal Reserve Bank or Federal Home Loan Bank receive next-day availability.

°°State or local government checks and any cashier's, certified, or tellers checks (regardless of routing and transit number) receive next-day availability if a SPECIAL DEPOSIT TICKET is used. These tickets are available on request.

EXHIBIT 8-13 (continued)
Availability Schedule

FRIDAY

Deposits transacted during banking hours will receive Friday's ledger credit with availability calculated as follows:

Immediate Availability	On-us items only
Monday Availability (1 Business Day)	All Fed City and RCPC endpoints plus Kansas City and St. Louis endpoints
Tuesday Availability (2 Business Days)	All other Fed Country endpoints

New York Country 0215,0216	
Minneapolis Country	0911,0912,0913,0914,0915
Helena Country	0921
Denver Country	1021,1022,1023
Oklahoma City Country	1031
Omaha Country	1041
Dallas Country	1113
San Francisco Country	1214

Depository Services and the Availability Schedule

Standard check processing involves verifying the depositor's cash letter—which lists the checks and their amounts—and then encoding the dollar amount on the MICR line and sending the checks to a correspondent bank or the nearest Federal Reserve facility[26] to be cleared back to the bank on which the check was written. The depositor's ledger balance is credited, but the portion of the total deposit available as "good funds" ready to be spent varies according to the bank's availability schedule. Exhibit 8-13 illustrates part of the availability schedule offered by an Indianapolis bank. Notice that the first part of the schedule applies to checks deposited from Monday to Thursday and the second part for Friday deposits. It lists all checks that will receive 0 (same) day, or immediate availability, ordered by drawee bank transit routing number. The absolute latest ledger cutoff time—the time by which a company may deposit an unencoded check and get the stated availability is the closing time at a branch or headquarters—is usually 2:30 P.M., but for some branches it might be 7:30 P.M. (particularly on Friday). Saturday or Sunday deposits taken at branches are subject to Monday's cutoff. Checks must be deposited by the stated cutoff time to get the stated availability; otherwise, they are granted availability the next business day.

How quickly deposited amounts are made available by the clearing bank is related to the time of deposit, how distant the drawee bank is, whether it is in a Federal Reserve Bank city or a RCPC area, and whether it is in a check swapping agreement or local clearinghouse with either the clearing bank or one of the clearing bank's correspondents. This availability float time lag may not always coincide with the amount of time it takes the check to actually clear, but generally the two are closely linked.

Banks provide expedited check processing if the depositor is willing to perform extra tasks or pay the bank the extra charge involved. One task companies can perform to cut bank processing time and reduce service charges is to pre-encode checks before

---

[26]Major money center banks clear from 1 to 3 million checks daily in the New York City area alone.

deposit. This necessitates purchase of a MICR encoder, which is the machine used to imprint the check's dollar amount on the bottom right of the check. After endorsement, pre-encoded checks are bundled together, totaled, and sent to the bank. In addition to reduced per-check fees, the bank also offers a later cutoff time (e.g., 10 P.M.) for availability assignment. Even if the depositor does not perform extra tasks, the bank might offer a courier service to expedite collection of large-dollar checks.

BANK SELECTION AND RELATIONSHIP MANAGEMENT

The Bank Selection Process

The **bank selection process** involves assembling a system of banks to efficiently and effectively process all information and cash flows involving the corporation's short-term financial management. Except for very small organizations, corporations deal with more than one bank. Geographically widespread or large firms tend to use the largest number of banks, and particular industries exhibit varying usage of banks, although all groups are consolidating their banking systems toward use of fewer banks. Greenwich data show the typical US company uses seven banks for cash management services, with the larger companies averaging twelve banks and the smaller companies averaging only four. Multiple banks are also used abroad: Soenen and Aggarwal (1989) found half of all UK companies they surveyed had fifteen or more banking relationships each, and in the Netherlands and Belgium half of the companies dealt with five or more banks.

In the past, businesses chose banks primarily using a total **relationship approach,** in which credit and cash management services were both handled by the chosen bank. Increasingly, there is a decoupling or "unbundling" of services, popularizing the **transaction approach,** in which the treasurer selects the bank(s) that can best provide a specific service. Banks have developed sophisticated cost accounting and management control systems that enable them to identify profitability by product line and by customer, facilitating exact and competitive pricing of individual cash management services. Procedurally, larger firms often initiate requests for formal bids on cash management service offerings and prices, whereas smaller organizations generally shop around and then negotiate with a small number of select banks.

Selection Criteria

We now focus on selecting banks for cash management and related services, occasionally noting instances in which this process merges with aspects of selecting banks with which to borrow or invest. The literature on bank selection is extensive and very helpful in addressing practical considerations.[27] Because banks are so involved in the payments system, this is a crucial decision for the company. A comprehensive checklist for bank selection is reproduced in Appendix 8A. We highlight several of the major criteria companies use when first establishing which bank(s) to use for cash management and related services:

- Location
- Bank/Company Fit

---

[27]For the interested reader, a wealth of advice regarding bank selection including how to approach the competitive bidding process can be found in Nadler (1990), Rollins and Carfang (1989), Bierce and Ekedahl (1989), Cappello (1989), Ranking (1976), and Lordan (1973), located at the chapter references.

- Service Quality/Breadth (including development of nationwide branch network)
- Bank Creditworthiness
- Bank Specializations
- Price

More will be said about when and how to negotiate bank selection later in the chapter.

MANAGING BANK RELATIONSHIPS

Ideally, the corporation should monitor ongoing banking relations in reference to an established bank relationship policy. The **bank relationship policy** establishes the company's objectives, compensation, and review process for the banks it has a relationship with. The policy elements devised by E.F. Hutton subsequent to its legal problems linked to its overly aggressive banking posture are illustrative[28]:

- Defining bank relations (tiering): Rank banks in terms of importance to company, ranging from tier one banks used extensively in the past for credit and noncredit services to tier four banks, which are branches and some regional depository banks that typically do not provide credit services.
- Establishing compensation ranges: How banks in each tier should be compensated and a reasonable level of compensation.
- Establishing a method for adjusting target balances: Indicate how bank compensation is adjusted if a bank exceeds or falls below the target, with a goal of altering the bank's return on assets related to its business with the company.
- Defining relationship and communications responsibility: Specify who in the corporation is responsible for managing the overall relations with banks (usually the treasurer) and the frequency and form of company-bank communications;
- Defining compensation periods: How often the company will review compensation for each tier of banks, which is negotiated and confirmed with each bank, assisting in the overall objective of reaching a target compensation over a certain time.
- Defining payment methods: For credit services, this is normally in fees and interest charges; for non-credit services, payment might be in fees, compensating balances, or a combination of fees and balances.
- Defining compensation agreements and contracts: Here, the company's position is articulated as a first approach toward negotiating a written agreement or contract with each bank.
- Establishing an annual review process: Includes an overall rating of the bank, an estimate of the bank's past and projected income and expense on the company's account, potential new business with the banks, target compensation level reestablishment, and whether a bank will remain in the same tier, move to a new tier, or be terminated.

This approach's underpinning logic is to ensure that the bank maintains a satisfactory return-on-assets on the company's overall account. Prudent companies attempt to negotiate when differences of opinion occur with existing banks to preserve long-term relationships, rather than immediately switching banks. These relationships create value for the company in the form of predictability, speed, and flexibility of bank response to future company requests.

---

[28]For more on the Hutton approach, see the Beehler (1987) citation in the chapter references.

Account Analysis Statement

Banks provide corporate customers with an **account analysis statement,** which indicates the services used and the charges assessed to the company. The statement provides in-depth balance information, a 12-month balance history, a detailed listing and pricing of services used, and the degree to which the company's actual balances offset fees charged for the services used. The statement is valuable as a cash management tool because it helps company personnel identify whether excess balances are being held and to project balances necessary to avoid service charges. The charges are shown on a fee basis and a compensating balance basis by banks following the Treasury Management Association (TMA; now called the Association for Financial Professionals) standard presentation format, established in 1987 to facilitate bank comparisons. The availability schedule used may be negotiable in any case, because most banks have two or three different availability schedules (and possibly another one for pre-encoded checks).

Exhibit 8-14 illustrates the most important parts of the account analysis statement used by Bank One, Indianapolis, which conforms to the TMA (AFP) format. This particular statement summarizes the activity for three accounts for a client, with the net service charge (or credit) computed in the first schedule and individual services used shown in the second schedule. Near the top of the first schedule, starting with (E), is the average monthly ledger balance calculation (see the glossary at the end of Exhibit 8-14 for additional detail on each lettered item). The average float (G), representing checks deposited on which the bank has not yet collected funds, is subtracted from the average ledger balance (F) to arrive at average collected balance (H).[29] Simplifying the wording slightly, the relationship of collected to ledger balances is shown formally as Equation 8-4:

$$\text{Average collected balance} = \text{Average ledger balance} - \text{Float} \qquad \text{(8-4)}$$

Bank One distinguishes between collected[30] and available balances by adjusting the former by the Fed's reserve requirement—10 percent at the time of the schedule. Because the bank must hold reserves in nonearning assets (vault cash or deposits at the Federal Reserve), it does not count this part of the company's balances in the available balance. In the bottom of the left schedule (Q), we see the earnings credit rate (*ecr*) applied to balances held at the bank, which can be used to offset the service charges.

Recognizing that they are legally prohibited from paying a company interest on demand-deposit accounts, banks provide a bookkeeping credit to offset service charges incurred by the company. The *ecr* applied in the statement month was 5.66 percent. The *ecr* shown here is based on the 91-day Treasury bill rate. Banks' earnings credit rates are generally based on a prevailing money market rate (usually somewhat less than the 91-day Treasury bill rate from a recent auction) and a bank's business strategy, but typically are relatively low compared with the rates at which treasurers are able to invest surplus funds.

---

[29]The float, or average uncollected funds, calculation is a function of the bank's availability schedule and its cutoff times. A manager cannot assume that quicker availability implies higher collected balances because a bank may have an earlier cutoff time for assigning ledger credit to checks. Availability of funds on a check deposited at 3 P.M. at bank A, which has a 1 P.M. cutoff time and assigns 1-day availability, is the same as at bank B, which has a 4 P.M. cutoff time and 2-day availability. Deposits made after the cutoff time are not even granted ledger credit until the next business day. Furthermore, some banks base their availability schedules on actual check clearing times for each customer's checks, whereas others use averages based on past periods for the customer or a group of similar customers.

[30]Banks may also subtract from the average collected balance an amount necessary to compensate for loan services provided to the customer, if a lending relationship exists.

EXHIBIT 8-14

Account Analysis

BANK≣ONE.

RETURN ADDRESS
CITY, STATE, ZIP

A CONTACT: Account Officer or Banking Center Name
XYZ CORPORATION **B** FROM 07-01-199X
JOSEPH R. SMITH TO 07-31-199X
1234 MAIN STREET
CITY, STATE, ZIP PAGE 1
C GROUP NO. 001 00010-1234-6 GROUP ACCOUNT

ACCOUNT INCLUDED IN ANALYSIS

D DEPOSITS 001 01 00010-1234-6 001 01 00010-1234-7
001 01 00010-1234-8

E AVG POSITIVE LEDGER BALANCE	430,150.88
F AVG LEDGER BALANCE	430,150.88
G LESS AVERAGE FLOAT	175,942.16-
H AVG COLLECTED BALANCE	253,138.32
I AVG NEGATIVE COLLECTED BALANCE	1,070.40
J AVG POSITIVE COLLECTED BALANCE	254,208.72
K LESS RESERVE REQUIREMENT	25,420.97-
L AVG AVAILABLE BALANCE	228,787.85
M LESS BALANCE REQUIRED	137,604.72-
N NET AVAILABLE BALANCE	91,183.13
O RESERVE ADJUSTMENT COLLECTED	10,131.45
P NET COLLECTED BALANCE POSITION	101,314.58
Q EARNINGS CREDIT ALLOWANCE	1,099.81
RATE 5.66	
R TOTAL CHARGE FOR SERVICES	661.48-
S NET SERVICE CREDIT	438.33

BANK≣ONE.

RETURN ADDRESS
CITY, STATE, ZIP

A CONTACT: Account Officer or Banking Center Name
XYZ CORPORATION **B** FROM 07-01-199X
JOSEPH R. SMITH TO 07-31-199X
1234 MAIN STREET
CITY, STATE, ZIP PAGE 2
C GROUP NO. 001 00010-1234-6 GROUP ACCOUNT

SERVICES ANALYZED

SERVICE	NO. UNITS	UNIT PRICE	CHARGE FOR SERVICE	BALANCE REQUIRED
GENERAL ACCOUNTING SERVICES				
NEGATIVE COLLECTED BALANCE FEE	1,070	8.25	7.50	1,560.39
FDIC	74,498		12.10	2,517.10
ACCOUNT MAINTENANCE	1	13.000	13.00	2,704.33
CORPORATE CASH SERVICE	1	100.000	100.00	20,802.56
ZERO BALANCE ACCOUNT	2	20.000	40.00	8,321.00
DEPOSITORY SERVICES				
DEPOSITS	58	.300	17.40	3,619.65
DEPOSITED CHECKS: NON-LOCAL	348	.100	34.80	7,239.29
DEPOSITED CHECKS: LOCAL	27	.090	2.43	505.50
RETURN ITEMS	5	5.000	25.00	5,200.64
DISBURSEMENT SERVICES				
CHECKS PAID	1395	.150	209.25	43,529.15
STOP PAYMENTS	3	18.000	54.00	11,233.38
FUND TRANSFER SERVICES				
INCOMING WIRE TRANSFERS	2	8.000	16.00	3,328.40
RECONCILIATION SERVICES				
SERIAL SORT ITEMS	1	50.000	50.00	10,401.28
INFORMATION SERVICES				
MICROLINK FEES	1	80.000	80.00	16,642.05
D TOTAL CHARGE FOR SERVICES			661.48	137,604.72
				M

Illustrative purposes only—actual prices and rates may vary.

To see where the "Balance Required" (M) comes from, refer to the right panel of Exhibit 8-14 as a second schedule. Notice that the services used by the clients during the month, unit prices, and the resultant service charges are shown. In the rightmost column, labeled "Balance Required," the service charges are converted to the equivalent amount of demand-deposit balances. To do so, the *ecr* is first put on a monthly basis by dividing it by 365, then multiplying it by the number of days in the month (in this case, 31). Bank One converts each service charge line item to the equivalent balances necessary to cover those charges by applying Equation 8-5:

EXHIBIT 8-14 (continued)

A Bank One Relationship Manager, Account Officer, or Banking Center.

B Beginning/ending date.

C Group Account Number to which all accounts are tied.

D A listing of related accounts.

E The sum of the daily positive ledger balances for the month divided by the number of days in the month.

F The sum of the daily positive and negative ledger balances for the month divided by the number of days in the month. Balances for the last preceding business days are used for weekends and holidays.

G The difference between the average ledger balance and average collected balance for the month. Bank One assigns float item based on our published availability schedule.

H The sum of the daily positive and negative collected balances for the month divided by the number of days in the month.

I The sum of the daily negative collected balances for the month divided by the number of days in the month.

J The sum of the daily positive collected balances for the month divided by the number of days in the month.

K The portion of the positive balances Bank One must keep on deposit at the Federal Reserve. This amount, therefore, is not available to offset service charges.

L The sum of the average positive collected balances less reserve requirements, as defined by the Federal Reserve. (Less loan compensating balances, if applicable.)

M The total balances required for services rendered.

N The sum of average positive available balances less balances required for services.

O Reserves not used for deposit services are added back to the net available balance. For deficit balances, this is the additional reserves required to support deposit services.

P The collected balance position adjusted for credit commitments and other services used. These funds are available to your company to meet other corporate obligations. For deficit balances, this is the additional collected balances required to offset all service charges.

Q The dollar credit on the average positive available balances maintained. If there are negative balances at any time during the month, the applicable bank rate for short-term commercial borrowing will be assessed as a Negative Collected Balance Fee in the itemized services section of your Account Analysis Report.

R The total charge for services rendered.

S The amount remaining in dollars after service charges have been deducted from earnings credit allowance. If negative, this line will show the net charge for services.

SOURCE: Reprinted with permission of Bank One.

$$RCMP = \frac{SC}{\left(\dfrac{ecr}{365}\right)n} \qquad (8\text{-}5)$$

In which $RCMP$ = required compensating balances

SC = service charges for the month

ecr = earnings credit rate (annual)

n = number of days in month.

Equation 8-5 is modified slightly for banks not distinguishing between the average collected balance and the average available balance, with the adjustment being made in the denominator to reflect the required reserve ratio (rr). Because the required balances must cover required reserves as well as fees, it appears that the balances will be higher. In practice, banks adjusts the ecr upward to make the two approaches equivalent. Equation 8-6 gives the required compensating balances in light of the reserve ratio:

$$RCMP = \frac{SC}{(1-rr)\left(\dfrac{ecr}{365}\right)n} \qquad (8\text{-}6)$$

Given the company's total service charges owed of $661.48 for July, the "total charge for services" at the bottom of the second schedule (using Equation 8-5) indicates a required balance of $137,604.72:

$$\$137{,}604.72 = \frac{\$661.48}{\left(\dfrac{0.0566}{365}\right)31}$$

This represents how much in available balances the company must average during July to avoid paying fees for bank services rendered. Returning to the top schedule in Exhibit 8-14, we see \$137,604.72 inserted as the "Balance Required" (M).

The "Net available balance" (N) is then computed as the average available balance minus the balance required. At this point, Bank One recognizes that some of the balances the company held during the month were compensating balances required to support loans. These balances, not being transaction balances, are not subject to the Federal Reserve's required reserve ratio. Item (O) is therefore added back to the net available balance to arrive at the "Net collected balance position" (P) of \$101,314.58. This is the money the company actually can spend during the month, on average, in that it represents amounts above the compensating balance requirements.

But what if the company prefers to compensate the bank by paying a fee each month? The remainder of the schedule compares the earnings credit applied to the company's balances to the total service charges incurred. Be careful — the "Earnings credit allowance" computation (Q) below the net collected balance is found by multiplying the "Average available balance" of \$228,787.85 (L) by the monthly *ecr*. The company has "earned" \$1,099.81 based on its account balances (Q), versus the "Total charge for services" (see bottom of right schedule) of \$661.48 (R). The difference of \$438.33 (S) is a credit, which is often carried into future months to offset months when balances are inadequate to cover service charges. When the company has a net service shortfall, the amount might be directly debited to the customer's account or billed on an invoice to be paid within 30 days. If the company prefers to compensate the bank by holding larger balances, it may be given several months to make up for the shortfall. Settlement periods over which credits or shortfalls are cumulated might be quarterly, semiannual, or annual (calendar year). Charges are made on the cumulative shortfall at the period's end.

USES OF THE ACCOUNT ANALYSIS STATEMENT.   In addition to serving as an invoice for bank services rendered, the cash manager can use the account analysis to get an overall view of the company's balance levels and bank activity. Two impediments to interbank comparisons based on account analyses are the lack of uniform presentation formats (which is gradually changing) and the variety of cutoff times and availability schedules that compose banks' float calculations. Despite growing acceptance of the uniform account analysis format developed by the TMA, cash managers complain that many banks have been slow to adopt the voluntary standard. Consequently, cash managers are forced to either manually adjust different banks' statements to compare them or use third-party software that automatically reformats them to a uniform statement.

How Banks Charge for Services

Maximizing value from the company's banking relationships requires an understanding of how compensating balances work and the relative merits of paying for bank services by balances versus fees. We begin by illustrating the required compensating balance computation for cash management services.

CALCULATING COMPENSATING BALANCES.   Compensating balances are minimum or average deposit amounts required by banks as a means of charging for cash management or lending services. Banks formerly required customers to maintain a demand-deposit account balance of 10 percent of the credit line or loan principal amount, but competition has forced this figure lower. For large corporations, balances are not required, but show goodwill. When required on lending arrangements, companies must maintain the balances as well as pay interest on amounts borrowed.

As compensation for each cash management service, the bank computes the charges for a month's activity, then uses a formula to compute the equivalent amount of balances. The formula looks like Equation 8-5 or Equation 8-6. To illustrate, a company being charged $150 for direct sends during the month must have $150/0.004438356 = $33,796.30 in compensating balances, assuming a required reserve ratio of 10 percent and an *ecr* of 6 percent (using Equation 8-6):

$$Compensating\ Balances = \frac{\$150}{(1 - 0.10)\left(\frac{0.06}{365}\right)30}$$

$$= \frac{\$150}{0.004438356}$$

$$= \$33,796.30$$

At the time of this writing, most banks have no FDIC insurance premium assessed—in the Bank One schedule the FDIC charge that is shown ($12.10) is now zero. However, S&Ls and mutual savings banks do have assessments. Financial institutions that pass along assessments are either including a fee on the service charge schedule or are driving the compensating balance dollar amount even higher by further multiplying the denominator of the above formula by $(1 - \text{FDIC assessment rate})$.

Pros and Cons of Balances Versus Fees

Banks have generally favored compensating balances over fees as the method of remuneration for services performed, even though a recent survey indicated that just more than half of corporations are paying by fees. Bankers cite the following advantages of compensating balances:

- Compensating balances have the effect of increasing total deposits and assets, which are traditional benchmarks of a bank's success.
- Balances can be re-lent to another customer, which means that in the case of loan-encumbered balances some of the funds are actually lent twice—compensating balances required of borrower A are part of the loan made to borrower B.
- Balances form a cushion, so that a loan default is partly recouped by the bank.

Corporate cash managers generally prefer fees, although some balances might be kept in the bank anyway to meet transactions requirements and provide a liquid reserve that can be tapped quickly if needed. Demand deposits (except for nonprofit organizations) are noninterest-bearing accounts, which are ideally kept at a minimum unless the earnings credit rate is greater than the rate that can be earned on alternative investments available to the firm. This explains the first of several reasons cash managers favor fee-based compensation:

- The *ecr* is almost always less than the alternative investment rate.
- Lost interest related to the balances is not a tax-deductible expense, but fees charged by the bank are tax deductible.

- Fee-based compensation offers a tangible expense that can be easily monitored and budgeted.
- Fees are directly comparable between banks and are fixed for a year at a time,[31] whereas the *ecr* is a floating rate that is unpredictable.

A final consideration is the possibility of "double-counting" compensating balances. This can either occur when a bank counts the same balances as compensation for a loan and as compensation for cash management services or when the company has written a depository check for which it has been granted availability at the concentration bank, but has not had its checking account debited. Double-counting is uncommon at large and medium-sized banks because of their better processing systems, but it may occur at smaller banks. Taking advantage of double-counting without the bank(s) being aware of it is considered unethical by most cash managers—especially in the light of the way E.F. Hutton took advantage of its banks by initiating unnecessary lateral transfers to draw on uncollected balances.

Daylight Overdrafts and the Availability Schedule

Daylight overdrafts occur when a bank's Federal Reserve account book balance is negative during the day, possibly because it sends more funds via Fedwire than it receives, before final end-of-day settlements. Many of the overdrafts occur because of international funds transfers of government securities transactions.

Since 1986, a bank whose nonwire transactions add up to a net credit (excluding ACH transactions) receives that credit **retroactive to the opening of business.** This enables the bank to use the credit to offset any wire debits occurring throughout the day. When nonwire transactions add up to a net debit, that total does not have to be covered until the close of business, giving rise to large intraday or daylight overdrafts.

In the 1990s, the Federal Reserve changed the handling of such overdrafts, resulting in charges for banks' intraday use of funds. The changes involved charges for bank intraday overdrafts as well as institution of the following posting times:

1. Treasury and commercial ACH credits at the opening of business
2. ACH debits at 11 A.M., Eastern Time
3. Commercial check transactions and coin and currency deposits beginning at 11 A.M Eastern Time, and then hourly, with the amounts based on proportions of the deposits drawn on the various endpoints
4. Wire transfers and book-entry (securities) transfers continue to be posted, for overdraft measurement purposes, as they occur

This system makes available to collecting banks approximately half of the value of all check deposits by noon Eastern Time and roughly three fourths by 1 P.M.

These regulations reduce banks' daylight overdrafts, an implicit subsidy to paying banks, with several important cash management implications. First, funds are available in smaller amounts throughout each business day, instead of all at once. Cash managers have to be more careful to avoid intraday overdrafting of checking accounts if their bank charges for these overdrafts. Cash managers must also be careful to delay disbursing funds until check deposits and other nonwire credits are posted and made available. Third, because banks are charged a fee based on the size of their intraday overdraft, they may require account holders to fund check presentments before the Federal Reserve

---

[31]Most cash management contracts are based on 3-year bids, with a capped inflation adjustment allowable at the end of years 1 and 2.

EXHIBIT 8-15
Checklist for Cash Management Bank Selection

Prenegotiation Comparison Checklist

1. Is my existing service or relationship so substandard that I am unwilling to invest any more time in trying to improve it?
2. Has my current bank shown little or no interest in this aspect of our relationship?
3. Has my current bank recategorized our relationship in a way that means our importance has declined?
4. Has my current bank deemphasized products that are of particular importance to us, in a way that jeopardizes our future satisfaction?
5. Are we looking for an entirely new package of services, or trying to establish a new bank account structure?
6. Are these needs the result of an acquisition or major organizational change?
7. If my prices are *meaningfully* above market prices, am I satisfied that this is not the result of customization? Have I already approached my current bank about pricing improvements, to little or no benefit?
8. Have I already exhausted the capabilities or creativity of the bank(s) which have been investing in a true partnership relationship with us?

If you answer yes to any of questions 1–7, *and* yes to question 8, then you probably should bid out your services.

In bidding, the following checklist can help guide you to a complete decision:

1. Confirm that the bank fits your bank relationship philosophy.
2. Confirm that the features you want are already available—and that you know clearly which are still being considered, planned for, or are "in development."
3. Make sure you understand all financial components of the deal—all items you'll be charged for, contract terms, permissible price increases, volume discount levels, and penalties for non-performance (both yours and theirs).
4. Understand what implementation will entail, what resources the bank will commit, what resources you should expect to commit, and for what (if anything) you will be charged.
5. Know exactly who will service your account—from your calling rep to service and problem resolution people.
6. Ask what else the bank hopes to gain from this relationship over time.
7. Understand how your firm fits with the bank's strategic focus.

SOURCE: Cathryn R. Gregg, Treasury Strategies, Inc., 309 W. Washington St., Suite 1300, Chicago, Il 60606 (312) 443-0840.

fee is posted to the bank's reserve account. This has a disproportionate effect on larger banks, which tend to have sizable daylight overdrafts.

Financial managers are urged to carefully compare existing banks to new bidders to ensure the company is getting maximum value from its banking relationships. The true opportunity cost in terms of interest foregone (as a result of having to leave extra amounts in checking accounts to compensate banks) is not the Treasury bill rate but the overnight repurchase rate, the commercial paper rate, or the money market mutual fund rate offered by banks and brokers. In addition, there are many qualitative factors to examine, including how long the company has done business with its existing bank(s) and the other noncredit and credit services being provided by the bank(s). Exhibit 8-15 summarizes some of the factors to compare before negotiating a contract.

Optimizing the Banking Network

Recall the objective for bank relationship management with which we began this section of the chapter: to ensure that all the company's banking services are provided reliably at a reasonable cost. Potentially, if we assume some product differentiation and/or nonuniform pricing on the part of banks, there exists a banking system configuration (or several) that maximizes value for the company. Finding that optimum is elusive, given the role of qualitative criteria such as reliability that enter the objective function. Several theorists have attempted optimization through mathematical models: two of these are presented in Appendix 8B. We should take a systems view of overall bank relationship structure. Lending and cash management services often are tied together, even though some treasurers contend a "do-your-own" lockbox network is less expensive, even when taking loan considerations into account. Furthermore, banks aggressively sell their own and other institutions' securities, and treasurers generally find that the investment services are separable from other bank services. An exception is the sweep product, which is inextricably tied to the checking account balances the corporation holds.

NONBANK PROVIDERS OF SERVICES

Nonfinancial corporations are increasingly providing what were traditionally banking services. Service offerings are directed at other corporations and consumers and also the providing organization itself—in which the company, in effect, is making the service rather than buying it. Commercial and industrial conglomerates such as American Express, Ford, GE, Westinghouse, Sears, and J.C. Penney are leaders in acquiring financial institutions.

Much of the nonbank activity has taken place in lending. Banks traditionally provided most of the short-term and medium-term loans for businesses, but this has changed. Banks are no longer the dominant players in short-term funding that they once were: In 1997 there was $838 billion in commercial paper outstanding (including $188 billion issued by nonfinancial companies), compared to $814 billion in commercial and industrial loans made by banks.[32] Increasingly, banks are moving away from a direct finance role to a risk-sharing role, in which they guarantee the payment of corporations' commercial paper borrowings at maturity. Banks collect fees for providing the guarantee, and the issuer receives a better credit rating with a correspondingly lower interest rate. Almost one-half of all consumer and business loans are now originated by nonbank companies. An intriguing (if rare) example is the $50 million loan PepsiCo made to Marriott, at Marriott's request, reportedly to win a soda-fountain service contract. The nonbank penetration has pushed into nonlending services as well, however.

In the realm of information services, the primary nonbank providers are third-party vendors of balance reporting services. In the collections area, companies are progressively doing part of or all the lockbox work in-house or retaining a nonbank vendor. Consultants providing software to compare banks, mail time analyses, and bank rating services are primary examples of information service providers. Since 1974, payment and investment services have increasingly become the domain of money market mutual funds. From 1987 to early 2001, institutional (nonpersonal) assets held in these nonbank accounts grew from $84 billion to $785 billion, with almost $250 billion of that increase in the most recent 2 years. These accounts serve as interest-bearing payment vehicles, although the minimum check amount is typically $500. An interesting survey of bankers found that 79 percent believed money funds to be an important competitor to their money market deposit accounts, and 83 percent saw them as an important competitor to their CDs (Holmberg and Baker, 1996).

As geographic and product restrictions are lifted in this era of financial services deregulation, financial institutions may regain market share in some of the areas just mentioned or at least hold their own.

---

[32]Statistics based on Federal Reserve data.

FINANCIAL SYSTEM TRENDS

In this concluding section of the chapter, we profile general financial system trends, then delve into trends in the areas of imaging, information services, Internet banking, and international banking relationships.

We can identify two major trends that have an affect on the bank service areas. One tend is nationwide banking in the United States and the economic unification of Europe, both of which will be catalysts for an ongoing drift toward concentration in the industry and globalized banking. Another trend now unfolding that is related to nationwide banking is consolidation of banking networks. No longer will the company need to have multiple banks operating a collection and concentration network. Imagine a one-bank collection center, which can also pool and invest or pay down borrowings, instead of sending funds from various field banks to a different lead bank. In addition, this allows for greater pooling from various locations nationwide without the need to actually transfer funds, because the balances can be netted out within one bank's computer records. In the mid 1990s, one analyst projected that there would be ten banks with nationwide branches as early as the year 2000, but that proved to be far off the mark.

All of Europe stands to gain from the economic unification of Europe and the introduction of the common currency, the euro. We noted in our payment system section some of the effects. The full introduction of the euro in 2002 as the sole European legal tender should greatly reduce cash management inefficiencies and costs. There is an expectation that bank debt will drop from four-fifths of corporate borrowing (in France, Germany, and Italy) down to much lower levels, as a result of the pan-European credit market that develops. Bank mergers will also have major effects. Although the cultural, regulatory, legal, and organizational assimilation of merged banks takes time, economies of scale will be available in Europe and elsewhere. The Boston Consulting Group estimates the average cost of a wholesale cross-border transaction will drop from $47 to only 40 cents within 10 years; most of this will result from a lower foreign exchange charge. The European Union will further change the corporate banking landscape.

Imaging

An important trend affecting check routing, collections, and disbursements is **imaging.** Imaging is increasingly being used in two distinct applications: document imaging and check imaging. Document imaging is used for items such as invoices (particularly those processed by lockbox clerks) and loan applications. Check imaging is used for check truncation, as seen earlier in the chapter, as well as to avoid having to send batches of canceled checks back to customers. Instead, a computer image holding numerous miniaturized checks on each page is returned. The image of a questionable check may be inspected online before the paying bank decides to honor the check, as we discuss further in Chapter 11. Essentially, then, check imaging systems store images of the checks in the computer. These images can be compressed and printed out when needed. Proponents suggest that storing check images in computers can speed check processing in the following ways:

- Reduce check sorting by allowing for monthly checking account statements to be sent with a page or two of check images attached, instead of enclosing the physical checks.
- Eliminate encoding of documents such as internal debits, credits, and cash tickets.

- Electronically capture the data on adding machine tapes and other documents that accompany large deposits.
- Allow checks to be electronically "called up" on-screen to verify signatures, possibly comparing signatures on the checks with a digitized signature card (which may trigger "dishonoring" of fraudulent checks shortly after their presentment to the drawee bank).
- When there is a problem check, enable the clerk who is in charge of returning checks (to the bank of first deposit) to return an image instead.

Information Services

Banks offer corporate clients varied advisory services. Advisory services include all specialized and general financial management consulting that banks might provide to corporations. Several typical advisory services are:

- Lockbox studies: The bank uses a computerized model to study the pattern of mailed checks a company receives and advises the company on the best number and locations of lockboxes.
- Disbursement studies: Similar to lockbox studies, except the bank advises the client regarding controlled disbursement and zero balance accounts, the best locations of these accounts, and direct deposit.
- Financial management advice: Especially for smaller companies and nonprofits, banks may give advice about basics such as cash budgeting, pro forma statements, what cash management services might be cost-effective, and the types of bank lending for which the client might be eligible.
- International cash management studies: Included here are analyses of foreign countries' payment systems, economies, and the best approach to pooling cash and moving cash into or out of each country.
- Computerized treasury management information system hardware and software: In some cases, the bank will serve as a distributor under a license agreement with the developer of the computer system.

Banking on the Internet

The biggest development in the early 2000s is the explosion of what is variously called on-line banking, web-based banking, or Internet banking. Ernst & Young, in its 2000 Cash Management Services survey, discovered that 9 percent of all commercial users of electronic information reporting services received balance and transaction detail from their bank via the Internet (Forman and Shafer, 2000). That number was up from less than 1 percent 2 years earlier, and was expected to more than double in 2001. Many banks also reported either losing clients or being left out of new relationship consideration if they lacked a specific Internet ability. Corporate customers found that being able to access data anywhere they could access the Internet was a major advantage of on-line banking, with slow response time, scaled-down product offerings, and one-size-fits-all product offerings being the main disadvantages. In their survey of a cross-section of banks' Internet offerings, Ernst & Young found that 53 percent offer corporate clients balance and information reporting, 34 percent offer between-account transfers, 31 percent offer ACH transfers, 16 percent offer wire transfers, and 26 percent offer image delivery of checks and/or the associated payment documents. Most notable, more than 80 percent of banks plan to offer between-account, ACH, and wire transfer initiation functionality by the end of 2001.

International Aspects of Banking Relationships

All advising services remain strong, but the brightest aspect for banks is probably the international cash management services they provide. The combination of computerized treasury systems and international account balance inquiry and pooling capabilities is positioning some banks to gain market share by aggressively serving the needs of customers operating multinationally.

US financial executives anticipate worldwide emergence of financial super-markets, in which very large global "superbanks" compete aggressively against one another. However, anticipating the effect of global trends on US banks is more difficult. To provide US banks equal footing with banks operating in unregulated foreign markets, special organizational structures known as Edge Act branches and international banking facilities (IBF) have been established. Edge Act branches are branches outside the home state of the bank, which must limit their involvement to business abroad or financing foreign trade. The IBFs are not physical bank facilities but are a separate set of books kept by an existing bank. International banking facilities avoid reserve requirements, interest rate ceilings, and deposit insurance, enabling them to survive with much smaller margins. In recent years, the number and scope of Edge Act branches and IBFs have declined, mainly as a result of the foreign loan losses of large US banks. Large US banks continue to operate numerous branches abroad to service multinational customers. As is true for German and Japanese banks, less than 25 percent of US banks' assets and liabilities are foreign, as compared with more than 50 percent for Swiss banks and almost 50 percent for UK banks.

GLOBAL BANK CONSOLIDATION. To retain influence with increasingly relationship-driven corporate treasurers, banks are merging and expanding globally. Although 6 of the 10 largest banks are Japanese, 22 of the top 23 global banks, as rated by US corporate treasurers, are US and European banks—each with at least $170 billion in assets.[33] Many of these banks have a presence in 80 to 90 different countries, and Citigroup operates in 98 countries. Only one of these banks, agricultural lender Rabobank (Netherlands) has a AAA credit rating. In cash management, the technology-intensiveness has seen strong cash management banks invest more and get stronger. Large banks tend to see cash management as the area that cements corporate relations, and offers opportunities to cross-sell other bank services.

Because of the increasing reach of the global banks, US-based multinational corporations have been free to centralize European treasury operations, often selecting London or tax-haven locales such as Dublin Docks (Ireland), Belgium, or Holland to host their finance subsidiaries. The location of a US company's central treasury may be driven by tax treatment, exchange rate risks, or banking and other administrative costs. As an example, DuPont has been able to focus its 22-country European services with Bank of America, with Citicorp being its main service provider in all other areas of the world.

SUMMARY

We have presented the major aspects of the US and international payment systems in this chapter and identified the concept and value of float. The importance of understanding these foundational concepts is illustrated by the improvements made by the treasurer for

---

[33]Alexi Bayer. 1998. Banking's real world order. *Treasury & Risk Management* May/June:28–36.

the city of Seattle.[34] The treasurer set a goal of having all checks and currency invested on the day received and reducing mail float to 1 day. This meant eliminating office processing float (which had cost $250,000 in lost interest annually) and eliminating availability float—which, combined, totaled 5 days. Eliminating availability float implied clearing all checks through the bank the same day received. Although it took a year to change banking contracts, retrain staff members, and purchase bar coding and scanning equipment, the city largely was able to achieve its objectives. The city MICR encodes checks and deposits all on-us items at the various banks' check processing centers. It competitively bid the concentration bank contract and gained collected-funds status in one half day for checks other than on-us items. All told, the treasurer estimates the changes have reaped a present value benefit of $1.3 million per year for the city. Treasurers of all corporations, governments, and nonprofit organizations would be wise to emulate Seattle's example.

We developed the uniqueness of the US payment system as well as its major components. This system involves many more banks (which are smaller in size) than other countries. This patchwork is primarily related to the banking regulations, which focus on keeping banks from gaining too much economic power. As a result of past restrictions on interstate branching and bank acquisitions, companies must still work with several banks when paying or collecting funds from outside their local area. The $100,000 limit on bank deposit insurance has forced cash managers to limit deposit size and investment denominations when investing in bank-issued securities, although the too-big-to-fail doctrine has protected large bank depositors in the past. The recent change to US banking regulation to allow interstate banking and branching will make cash management less costly and more efficient.

The Federal Reserve System is a key player in the payment system because of its check clearing and regulatory roles. We noted the mechanics of check clearing and the importance of the check's MICR line. Paper-based payments include checks, drafts, and depository transfer checks. Check growth continues despite the regulatory push toward electronic payments. Electronic-based payments using wire transfers, EDTs, and automated debits and credits account for a large percentage of the dollar volume of today's payments. The ACH system is handling more payments and will continue to gain volume at the expense of checks. Popular uses to date include direct depositing of Social Security and employee payrolls.

We developed the banking aspects of the major cash management services used by corporations: depository services and information. Basic elements of these services have been defined and illustrated. Nonbank competition has been most noticeable for borrowing and investing services but promises to heighten in payments, collections (and concentration), and information. Companies are increasingly seeking to cut banking system costs by performing more of the banking services themselves. To a degree, this will be temporarily reversed by the market acceptance of *edi*, necessitating bank or third-party assistance for implementation.

Bank selection and relationship management are extremely important aspects of short-term financial management. We noted that the major factors related to bank selection are location, price, service quality and breadth, bank/company fit, bank creditworthiness, and bank specialties. The banking industry is undergoing major structural changes, partly as a result of continued deregulation of geographic restrictions and partly as a result of technology changes in the areas of imaging, network computing, and the use of the Internet. Furthermore, the increasing economic importance of the Pacific Basin, the Commonwealth of Independent States, Eastern Europe, China, and a newly

---

[34]See Lloyd F. Hara. 1987. Seattle's "no-float day." *Government Finance Review* December:7–10.

unified Europe will significantly affect the economies of scale available for banks competing globally.

Useful Web Sites

Association for Financial Professionals: www.afponline.org
Federal Reserve Board: http://www.federalreserve.gov/
Federal Reserve Board: http://www.federalreserve.gov/generalinfo/isb/
Federal Reserve Board: http://www.frbatlanta.org/publica/finan_update/index.html
Greenwich and Associates: www.greenwich.com
National Automated Clearing House Association: www.nacha.org
Phoenix-Hecht: www.phoenixhecht.com
Phoenix-Hecht: www.phoenixhecht.com/PDF/CorpMon2000.pdf

Questions

1. Why is there value in reducing float when a company collects payments made by check? Is the value of float reduction as great for the collecting firm when interest rates decline? Explain.
2. What are the two components of the US payment system? What sets it apart from other countries' payment systems?
3. Summarize briefly the major legislation regarding product offerings and geographic scope of depository institutions.
4. Why should businesses be aware of Federal Reserve Regulation Q?
5. What roles do the Federal Reserve System play in the payment system? How, specifically, does the Federal Reserve facilitate the payments mechanism?
6. Summarize the mechanics of check clearing. Summarize the various clearing mechanisms used and indicate when direct presenting might be used.
7. What information appears on a check's MICR line? Which, if any, of the items are helpful to a bank of first deposit as it considers various check clearing options?
8. Define each of the following types of float:
    a. collection float
    b. disbursement float
    c. mail float
    d. processing float
    e. clearing float
    f. Fed float
9. List and define briefly the means the Federal Reserve System has used to reduce Fed float. For a given check, what happens to the difference between the payee's collection float and the payor's disbursement float as Fed float is reduced? Does that difference disappear completely? Explain.
10. Name the three major paper-based payment mechanisms and explain each.
11. Why are coins and currency still used in the modern US economy? Specifically, why are they used instead of checks?
12. Distinguish between a demand deposit account and a NOW account. Which one do businesses use and why?

13. You just deposited a $1,000 check written on a bank in a neighboring state. Can the deposited funds be considered available funds? In your answer, distinguish between bank ledger balances and collected balances.
14. Summarize the check availability provisions of Regulation CC.
15. Do you think paper payments will disappear in the near future in the United States? Support your opinion.
16. List and define the three major electronic-based payments, giving the usage occasions, advantages, and disadvantages of each.
17. What objective are companies attempting to achieve when managing bank relations?
18. What is an availability schedule? Why should banks' availability schedules be compared by the cash manager, and what should the manager look for in making comparisons?
19. Futurists have long forecast a paperless US economy. Why have they been wrong? Include a discussion of corporate payment practices in your answer.
20. What does the popularity of the transaction approach to bank selection and relationship management imply about the competition among cash management banks? What are the pricing implications of this?
21. From a corporate risk perspective, what does the relationship approach to bank relations offer that the transaction approach does not?
22. Explain what an account analysis statement is and several of the uses it has for cash managers.
23. Define an earnings credit allowance; indicate how it is computed and how it compares with currently available yields on short-term investments. Why is its use so important for the company trying to decide whether to use fee-basis or compensating balances for bank service charge remuneration?
24. What are daylight overdrafts, and why might they be considered a bank credit service?

Problems

1. Phillips-Union 86 Corporation collects $105,000 per day. The cash manager has just been told of a new collection system using lockboxes that could reduce collection float from nine days to eight days by reducing mail and processing float a total of one day. Given the company's opportunity cost of funds of 12 percent and using simple interest formulas:
   a. Draw a cash flow timeline for one day's collection under the existing collection system. What is the present value of existing collections? Show your calculations for an average day's collections as well as in total for a perpetuity of daily collections.
   b. Draw a cash flow timeline for one day's collection under the proposed lockbox collection system. What is the present value of lockbox-based collections? Again, show the one-day and the total value effects.
   c. Ignoring bank fees to administer the lockbox system, would the cash manager recommend the new system?
   d. What will happen to the disbursement float for Phillips-Union's customers if the lockbox system is implemented?
2. Rework parts *a* and *b* of problem 1 using an opportunity cost of funds of 4 percent. Describe the effect on the difference between the two systems' present values, as compared with your findings in problem 1.

3. The capital budgeting approach to financial decision making requires comparing the present value of incremental cash inflows with the present value of incremental cash outflows. Given that the present value of the perpetuity of daily collection cash inflows has already been computed in parts *a* and *b* of each of the above problems, would you recommend adoption of the lockbox collection system if the only cash outflows were bank charges (an initial investment for Phillips-Union) of $104,750? (Hint: You must first compute the difference in the two perpetuities' cash flows to arrive at the incremental cash inflow.)
   a. Assume the opportunity cost of funds is 12 percent (as in problem 1).
   b. Assume the opportunity cost of funds is 4 percent (as in problem 2).
   c. What is the effect of the lower time value of money in part b on the present value of the project's net cash flows? (Hint: What is true of the value of day 2, day 3, and subsequent cash flows, in present dollar terms, when a lower discount rate is used?)

4. The Triton Corporation is trying to better manage its bank relationship. It requested and recently received via facsimile an account analysis statement for June. As happens with faxes, several of the line items are illegible, and the treasurer cannot get in touch with the bank liaison. Can you help complete the schedule? Assuming that the statement is done according to the TMA standard format (see Exhibit 8-14), the earnings credit rate is 4.00 percent, the reserve requirement is 10 percent, and Triton does not have any loan-related compensating balances. (Ignore the difference between negative and positive collected balances.)
   a. Fill in the missing line item labels and dollar amounts.
   b. Does Triton owe the bank the amount you have calculated for the net service credit/(debit), or can it carry this amount forward to offset future shortfalls?

Average ledger balance	$1,130,000
Less: _____	_____
Average collected balance	$890,000
Less: _____	_____
Less balance required	$525,000
Reserve adjustment collected	0
Total charge for services	$1,726.03
Net service credit/(debit)	_____

5. The following schedule has been developed as part of your bank's account analysis statement. Assuming no FDIC assessment, an earnings credit rate (already adjusted for the reserve requirement) of 4 percent, and 31 days in the month:
   a. Fill in the missing amounts in the Service Charge and Required Balance columns.
   b. Describe how the dollar amounts for "total charge for services" (listed at the bottom) will be used in the finalized account analysis statement sent out by the bank?

TYPE OF SERVICE	NUMBER OF UNITS	UNIT PRICE	SERVICE CHARGE	REQUIRED BALANCE
GENERAL ACCOUNT SERVICES				
Account maintenance	1	$15.00		
ZBA Master Account maintenance	1	$20.00		

(continued on next page)

DEPOSITORY SERVICES		
Deposits	47	$ 0.45
Deposited checks	1,000	$ 0.12
DISBURSEMENT SERVICES		
Regular checks paid	2,250	$ 0.15
RECONCILIATION SERVICES		
Full reconciliation surcharge	1	$45.00
Account reconciliation program checks paid (Note: represents last month)	2,100	$ 0.05
TOTAL CHARGE FOR SERVICES		

References

Philippa Back. 1998. *Corporate cash management.* 2nd ed. New York: Nichols.

Paul J. Beehler. 1987. Hutton's strategy for managing bank relationships. *Journal of Cash Management* January/February:16–20.

Andrea Bierce and Kathleen Ekedahl. 1989. The bank selection process. *Journal of Cash Management* July/August:13–15.

A. Barry Cappello. 1989. Finding a new bank. *Small Business Reports* 14(6):52–57.

Thomas F. Cargill. 1989. CAMEL ratings and the CD market. *Journal of Financial Services Research* 3:347–358.

Robert T. Clair and Paula K. Tucker. 1989. Interstate banking and the Federal Reserve: A historical perspective. *Federal Reserve Bank of Dallas Economic Review* November:1–20.

Jonathan D. Epstein. 2000. Banks close in on goal of interest-bearing accounts. *Treasury & Risk Management* November:7–8.

Federal Reserve. 1990. The Federal Reserve in the payments system. *Federal Reserve Bulletin* May:293–298.

Lawrence Forman and David L. Shafer. 2000. From doubt to adoption . . . Internet delivery of cash management services is changing the marketplace. *AFP Exchange* Fall:104–107.

Lyn Fritter and Robert W. Page. 1998. Evaluating your service provider. *TMA Journal* July/August:46–48, 50.

Chris Giodano. 1997. Teaming up for implementation success. *TMA Journal* September/October:9-10, 12–13.

Stevan R. Holmberg and H. Kent Baker. 1996. Commercial bank retail deposit strategy: The role of MMDAs. *Southern Business Review* 22(Fall):32–44.

John Holland. 1994. Bank lending relationships and the complex nature of bank-corporate relations. *Journal of Business Finance & Accounting* April:367–393.

Blair Houchens Miller. 1998. Are you profitable to your bank? Why you should care. *TMA Journal* July/August:28-30, 32–33.

George R. Juncker, Bruce J. Summers, and Florence M. Young. 1991. A primer on the settlement of payments in the United States. *Federal Reserve Bulletin* 77 November:847–858.

Sawaichiro Kamatam. 1990. Managing risk in Japanese interbank payment systems. *Federal Reserve Bank of San Francisco Economic Review* Fall:18–32.

Stephen M. Kearney. 1998. Managing bank relations at the U.S. Postal Service. *TMA Journal* November/December:64–67.

David Lordan. 1973. Criteria for a money mobilization bank. *The Banking Side of Corporate Cash Management* (Stonier Graduate School of Banking Research Study) Boston, MA: Financial Publishing Company, pp 51–61.

Steven F. Maier and Larry A. Marks. 1988. Applications and models: The three spires of excellence. *Journal of Cash Management* November/December:84, 86, 88.

Leslie N. Masonson. 1990. Everything you wanted to know about checks. *Management Accounting* July:26–29.

Dubos J. Masson. 2001. *Essentials of cash management.* 7th ed. Bethesda, MD: Association for Financial Professionals.

David L. Mengle. 1990. The case for interstate branch banking. *Federal Reserve Bank of Richmond Economic Review* 76 November/December:3–17.

Paul S. Nadler. 1990. Choosing a bank for the 90s. *Journal of Cash Management* September/October:50–51.

Aaron L. Phillips. 1998. Migration of corporate payments from check to electronic format: A report on the current status of payments. *Financial Management* Winter:92–105.

Aaron L. Phillips. 1999. Bank consolidation and interstate banking: Effect on treasury management. *TMA Journal* March-April:40–43.

Harley Ranking, Jr. 1976. Selecting a commercial bank. In *Treasurer's Handbook,* edited by J. Fred Weston and Maurice B. Goudzwaard. Homewood, IL: Dow-Jones Irwin, pp 577–593.

Cathy L. Rollins and Anthony J. Carfang. 1989. Negotiate a better deal with your cash management banks. *Corporate Cashflow* September:58.

Nancy L. Russell. 1999. Payment systems in the U.S. and Latin America: Contrasts and similarities. *TMA Journal* May/June:48, 50–51.

Warren D. Schlesinger, Fahri Unsal, and M. Raquibuz Zaman. 1987. Attributes of sound banking as perceived by small businesses: Results of a survey. *Journal of Small Business Management* October:47–53.

Susan Skerritt. 1998. What payment changes should we expect from the Euro? *TMA Journal* November/December:24, 26, 28.

Larry D. Wall. 1993. Too-big-to-fail after FDICIA. *Federal Reserve Bank of Atlanta Economic Review* January/February:1-14.

Note: Each issue of *Financial Update,* a newsletter published by the Federal Reserve Bank of Atlanta, includes articles on the latest regulatory developments and Federal Reserve System payment systems innovations. For information or to subscribe, write or call the Bank, or access the Web site:

> Public Information Department
> Federal Reserve Bank of Atlanta
> 104 Marietta St., N.W.
> Atlanta, GA 30303-2713
> PH: (404) 521-8788
> http://www.frbatlanta.org/publica/finan_update/index.html

Appendix 8A

Checklist for Bank Evaluation

Bank name
Address
Phone number
Bank contact: Name
Title/Dept.

I. Financial Strength
  Number of years in business
  Total assets
  Total commercial loans
  Ratio loans/assets
  Other loans:
      Real estate
      Consumer
      International
      Lease financing
      Asset based (e.g., factoring)
      Other
  Loan losses (past 5 years)
  Earnings history (past 5 years)
  Return on assets (past 5 years)
  Comments

II. Operations
  General reputation for service
  Data processing system:
      Type
      Date installed
  Rating of operations based on:
      Automation
      Number/experience of personnel
      Error correction system
      Quality controls
      Supervision
  Services available:
      Lockbox
      Wholesale/retail
  Preauthorized checks
  Special handling for checks
  Concentration account
  Wire transfer
      Federal Reserve wire
      International (e.g., SWIFT)

Operations (cont'd)
  Balance reporting
      Via telephone
      Via terminal
      Multibank
      Intraday
  Account reconciliation
      Full/partial
      Check storage
  Zero-balance disbursement account
      Method of funding (e.g., imprest balance,
      wire transfer, etc.)
  Direct deposit
  Payable through drafts
  Payroll services
  Overdraft privilege
  Remote disbursement
  Controlled disbursement
  Letters of credit
  Foreign exchange
      Forward contracts
  International branches
  Correspondent banks
      Domestic
      International
  Consulting
  Financial planning for executives
  Check cashing service for employees
  Credit investigations
  Investment services
      Bank's own instruments (e.g., commercial
      paper, banker's acceptances, etc.)
      Outside money market vehicles
      Money market fund
      Trust service
      Pension service
  Comments

III. Pricing
  Pricing for key services
  Method of compensation:
      Compensating balances

284

Pricing (cont'd)
>Fees
>Combination

Level of compensating balances for loans

Earnings allowance rate for compensating balances for services

Comments

IV. Credit

>Experience with type of financing required

>Line of credit available

>Makeup of bank's other commercial customers
>>Companies in our industry
>>Companies our size

>Comments

>Availability of:
>>Factoring
>>Mortgage financing

Long-term loans

Export financing

Inventory loans

Unsecured loans

Receivables financing

Special financing arrangements

Interest rate terms (e.g., 1.3 percent over prime)

Interest due dates

Conditions of default on loans

Credit insurance available

Comments

V. Bank/Company Fit

>Bank location

>Personal relationship with bank contact

>Access to bank executives

SOURCE: Copyright © 1986 Franklin Watts, Incorporated. Reprinted with permission of Grolier Publishing Company.

Appendix 8B

Optimizing the Banking Network

Several linear programming models have been developed to best allocate check activity, deposit activity, credit lines (including revolving credit agreements) and planned borrowing levels across a company's banking system.[1] The first attempt, called CASH/ALPHA, has been adapted by a number of companies. It takes as a given the credit-borrowing allocation across banks and specifies the following objective function (Equation 8B-1):

$$\min Z = \sum_{q=1}^{Q} CP_q + k \sum_{q=1}^{Q} (NCB_q - FLT_q) \quad \text{(8B-1)}$$

In which:

Z = the sum of total cash payments and the cost of total book balances

q = subscript denoting a particular bank

Q = total number of different banks being considered

CP = cash payments for tangible services

K = opportunity cost of balances (investment rate company could earn)

NCB = net collected balances

FLT = net float

The sum of total cash payments made to all banks is calculated in the first term of Equation 8B-1, and the cost of total book balances makes up the second term. There are five constraints to which the company must attend:

(1) $NCB \geq a(LOAN) + b(LINE)$
[compensating balance requirement]

(2) $CP + ecr(NCB) \geq SC$
[sum of fees and balance credits $ charges assessed]

(3) $CP \leq \alpha(SC)$
[bank's restriction on amount of charges payable by cash]

(4) $NCB \geq MAB$
[company's self-imposed minimum balance requirement]

(5) $LOAN \leq LINE$
[borrowing cannot exceed total credit line amount]

In which:

a = compensating balance rate on loans

b = compensating balance rate on credit line

$LOAN$ = level of the loan ($)

$LINE$ = level of the line ($)

ecr = earnings credit rate per dollar of net collected balances

α = fraction of service charges payable by cash

SC = total tangible service charges for given bank

MAB = minimum available balance to be maintained (company policy)

Notice in Equation 8B-1 that the level of tangible service charges and value of float vary with check and deposit activity levels. This model, and those like it, trade off float improvements with service charges. Modifications and improvements of this model have been developed by Stone; computationally they can be very cumbersome if the banking system includes numerous banks. Stone has developed two simplified "partial models," which do not guarantee optimization (in terms of cost minimization) but can be implemented in Excel.

Stone subsequently refined the above model to allow for compensation by noninterest-bearing time deposits and for annual settlement periods (surplus balances or shortfalls can be offset much later in the

---

[1]See Robert F. Calman, *Linear Programming and Cash Management/CASH ALPHA* (Cambridge, MA: MIT Press, 1986); Gerald A. Pogue, Russell B. Faucet, and Ralph N. Bussard, "Cash Management: A Systems Approach," *Industrial Management Review,* (Winter 1970): 55–74; and Bernell K. Stone, "Allocating Credit Lines, Planned Borrowing, and Tangible Services over a Company's Banking System," *Financial Management,* (Summer 1975): 65–78. Our presentation is primarily based on the latter source.

year). The revised model incorporates more bank compensation constraints, cash budgeting variables, and an expanded objective function. The revised objective function involves minimizing the sum of four costs:

Total cost = Short-term debt interest +
Credit commitment fees + Cash fees +
Opportunity cost of balances net of investment income

The model is more realistic, but Stone still calls it a modeling framework instead of an optimization model. Because compensation terms, fees, and borrowing and investment arrangements are subject to company/bank negotiations, the modeling framework serves primarily as a decision aid. It enables simulation of various cash budget scenarios and banking system design configurations, helping the corporate analyst determine when it would be most beneficial to renegotiate terms. Later, as actual cash flows and interest rates vary from the values used in the planning model, the analyst can rerun the model to optimally allocate bank debt. The analyst should be careful to factor in the quality of bank services, because the model focuses only on costs. Furthermore, the value-maximizing decisions require cash flows in the optimization equation to be discounted to their present values.

CHAPTER 9

Cash Collection Systems

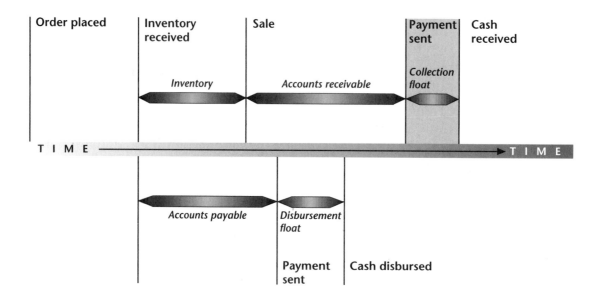

OBJECTIVES

After studying this chapter, you should be able to:

- Understand the various options that firms have to collect payments from customers.
- Differentiate between the various collection systems and choose the system best suited to the company's situation.
- Collect the basic data necessary for a lockbox study.
- Understand how a lockbox model works.

Once a firm has sold a product on credit, the financial manager's attention turns to receiving cash payment as soon as possible. The credit period offered by the seller is a key source of delay in receiving payment. However, there are important delays that occur even after the customer places the check in the mail. This chapter discusses the types of delays experienced from the time the payor remits payment until cash is received at the depositing bank. We then develop a model approach to designing a system to accelerate the receipt of cash.

FINANCIAL DILEMMA

How Can a Firm Accelerate Its Cash Collections?

Your firm continually experiences a shortage of cash. You offer the same credit terms as your competitors but they don't seem to be experiencing the same liquidity problems. As you survey your industry, you discover that all your competitors use a method to collect receivables that is different than yours. Your firm uses a very simple system. Invoices are sent with the orders and a remittance envelope is included. The corporate headquarters address is preprinted on the remittance envelope with the credit department's post office box number. Mail is delivered to the credit department once each day at about 11:00 A.M. Several clerical employees open the envelopes and key the invoice data and payment amount into your accounts receivable information system. If the payment agrees with the invoice data, the check is separated from the invoice and placed in a stack to be deposited. If the check amount does not reconcile with the invoice data, the check remains with the invoice and another clerical employee begins the reconciliation process. Once the problem is resolved, the check is separated from the invoice and prepared for deposit. By 3:30 P.M., a deposit ticket is made for the growing stack of checks and a deposit is made at a nearby branch of your firm's bank. Although this system has appeared to work well for the past 20 years, you wonder why your competitors have adopted what is referred to as a lockbox collection system and whether this could have any impact on your cash flow.

EXHIBIT 9-1
Cash Flow Timeline Related to Cash Collection Float

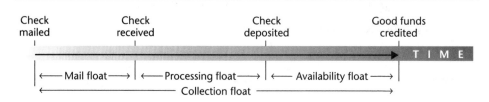

THE CASH FLOW TIMELINE AND CASH COLLECTION

Exhibit 9-1 displays the cash flow timeline detail related to the cash collection problem. As the exhibit shows, there are three types of delays that can occur between the date the check is placed in the mail and the date the deposited check is cleared and cash is actually available in the bank account. Together, the sum of these three types of delays is referred to as **collection float.** Float is the time lag between one result and another result.

The first delay is the mail time it takes for a check to arrive at its destination. This is referred to as **mail float** and the length of the delay is obviously related to the physical distance between the two points. It is also related to holidays, weekends, the efficiency of the postal system, and the weather.

The second delay is **processing float.** Once the check is received, it must be processed. That is, the envelope must be opened, the check prepared for deposit, and then physically deposited in the firm's bank.

The final delay is called **availability float.** The deposited check is not immediately converted into cash. Rather, the depositing bank first estimates the time it will take to deliver the check back to the bank on which the check is written. This is determined by scanning the magnetic ink character recognition (MICR) line printed at the bottom of each check. The MICR line contains the transit routing number that identifies the bank on which the check is written. The depositing bank's computers have a database that is used to assign an availability time to each deposited check. The availability time is the estimated time it takes to clear the check once it is deposited. The depositing bank is obligated to give credit to the deposited checks after the elapse of the availability date, even if it has been unable to clear the check.

The problem confronting the financial manager is the design of a collection system that addresses each of the three component parts of collection float. Mail float can be anywhere from 1 to several days. Processing float can generally range from a few hours to 1 or more days. Availability float can range from immediate availability to as many as 5 days if weekends or holidays are involved. Thus the financial manager is probably dealing with collection float from 1 day, at the very best, to as much as a week or more at the extreme. This may seem trivial until you begin to calculate the opportunity cost of these idle funds. For example, assume a firm has $1 million of daily receipts and these remittances take an average of 7 days from the date they are mailed to clear. If the annual opportunity cost of money is 8 percent, the annual cost is $560,000 = $1,000,000 $\times$ 7 $\times$ .08. This relationship indicates that the firm has an average of $7 million of uncollected funds ($1,000,000 $\times$ 7 days) at any time during the year. Using an 8-percent opportunity cost, the firm is losing $560,000 annually as a result of the collection process.

EXHIBIT 9-2
A Simple Example to Calculate the Cost of Float

Remittances	× Collection float	= Dollar-day float
$ 50,000	× 2	= $ 100,000
$1,200,000	× 5	= $6,000,000
$ 500,000	× 7	= $3,500,000
$ 1,000	× 10	= $ 10,000
$1,751,000		$9,610,000

$$\text{Average dollar-day float} = \text{Dollar-day float/Days in month}$$
$$= \$9,610,000/30$$
$$= \$320,333.33$$
$$\text{Average collection float} = \text{Dollar-day float/Remittances}$$
$$= \$9,610,000/\$1,751,000$$
$$= 5.49 \text{ days}$$
$$\text{Annual cost of float} = \text{Average dollar-day float} \times \text{Rate}$$
$$= \$320,333.33 \times 0.08$$
$$= \$25,626.67$$

THE COST OF FLOAT

Float refers to the time lag between events. Although the time lag is important to the financial manager, the dollar amount of remittances being affected by the time delay is also important. **Dollar-day float** is a measure that incorporates both the time lag and the dollar amount involved. Exhibit 9-2 presents a simple example demonstrating how to calculate the cost of float. In the example, there are four remittances during a given month totaling $1,751,000. The dollar-day float related to each remittance is calculated by multiplying each remittance by its associated collection float. The total dollar-day float for the month is $9,610,000. The total dollar-day float divided by the number of days in a month results in average daily dollar-day float of $320,333.33. The remittances and collection float in the example result in an average of $320,333.33 of idle funds daily throughout the month. If the firm's opportunity investment rate is 8 percent per year, the annual cost of the collection float is $25,626.67, assuming the remittances and collection float are replicated throughout the remaining 11 months.

TYPES OF COLLECTION SYSTEMS

Once a company begins to sell to customers outside of its headquarters city, the problem of collecting payment from geographically dispersed customers becomes an important issue. Should the firm continue to have its customers remit to company headquarters, or should the firm allow its field offices to collect payments? What are the payment collection alternatives and what are the advantages and disadvantages associated with these alternatives? This section discusses the two basic cash collection systems available for collecting customer remittances: company processing centers and lockbox systems. Because the discussion of company processing centers and lockbox systems focus on the collection of checks, the section ends with a brief discussion of two alternative collection systems that do not involve checks.

Collection System Cost Factors

Collection systems incur both a fixed cost and a variable cost. Fixed costs include such items as clerical salaries, account maintenance fees, fees charged to transfer balances from the collection bank to another bank, a deposit notification charge, and a deposit charge. Variable costs include a processing charge per item, a charge for encoding each remittance item, and a deposit charge for each item. A final cost factor is the opportunity cost of float. Equation 9-1 develops a total cost equation for a general cost model for a cash collection system.

$$\text{Total Cost} = N \times ((F \times D \times i) + VC) + FC \qquad \text{(9-1)}$$

In which:

N = the number of remittances processed

F = the average face value of remittances

D = the number of days it takes to clear the check

i = the daily opportunity cost of funds

VC = the variable cost charged for each remittance item

FC = the fixed cost of managing the collection system

Company Processing Center

A company may decide to process and deposit its own checks. Such a system is referred to as a **company processing center.** If company processing is chosen, then management must decide whether to have a **decentralized processing system** or a **centralized processing system.** Deciding which to use depends primarily on the volume of checks processed and the dollar size of the checks.

DECENTRALIZED COLLECTION SYSTEMS. One company processing option available to the corporation is to have its various field offices or stores around the country receive payments from the company's customers. This simple system has two major advantages. First, mail delay is minimal because the customers and the store or field office are in the same location. Second, availability delay is minimal because the check is more than likely drawn on a bank in the same location. It is even possible that the customers' accounts are at the same bank used by the store or field office.

The decentralized processing system also has several disadvantages. First, the store or field office staff may not deposit checks in a timely manner. This offsets some of the mail float and availability float advantages. Second, the funds deposited remain in the field office's or store's local bank account until they are transferred to the bank(s) used by corporate headquarters. Only then will the corporate cash manager have use of the funds.

CENTRALIZED PROCESSING SYSTEM. At the other extreme is the company centralized processing system, in which corporate headquarters receives all customer remittances. The checks with invoices are mailed to one or two major administrative centers for processing. These centers have high speed equipment for processing the remittance information and a staff dedicated to this task. The advantage to a centralized processing system is that the processing time is reduced compared with the field office or decentralized alternative. In addition, the corporate cash manager has more control over the system and bank account balances. The account balances, rather than being spread all over the country, are in only one or two locations. The disadvantages are that mail and availability time generally increase. Because this alternative requires commitments on the part of the firm to maintain costly state-of-the-art processing equipment, most consultants only consider this alternative when the monthly remittance volume exceeds 100,000 items per month.

COST ANALYSIS.   Company processing centers incur both a fixed cost and a variable cost. Fixed costs include clerical salaries, equipment rental fees, account maintenance fees, a fee charged to transfer balances from the collection bank to another bank, a deposit notification charge, and a deposit charge. Variable costs include processing charges per item, a charge for encoding each remittance item, and a deposit charge for each item.

Suppose you have estimated the following cost data for a decentralized and a centralized company processing centers. Note that the number of days it takes to clear a check (D) is less for the centralized system. In this case, the longer processing time taken by the decentralized system does not offset the longer mail time and availability time of the centralized system. The centralized system is able to incur a lower variable processing charge because it uses more competitive banks. Finally, the centralized system incurs a higher fixed charge as a result of equipment costs and salaries for dedicated clerical staff.

	COMMON DATA	DECENTRALIZED	CENTRALIZED
N	1,000		
F	$1500		
D		7	6
i	.10/365		
V		$.25	$.20
FC		$100	$600

$$\text{Total Cost (Decentralized)} = 1,000(\$1,500 \times 7 \times (.10/365) + \$.25) + \$100$$
$$= 1,000(\$2.877 + \$.25) + \$100$$
$$= \$3,127 + \$100$$
$$= \$3,227$$

$$\text{Total Cost (Centralized)} = 1,000(\$1,500 \times 6 \times (.10/365) + \$.20) + \$600$$
$$= 1,000(\$2.466 + \$.20) + \$600$$
$$= \$2,666 + \$600 = \$3,266$$

Thus even though the decentralized system in this example incurs a longer float period and a higher variable processing charge, the lower fixed costs allow for a lower total cost compared with the centralized system.

Lockbox Collection System

A **lockbox collection system** is really a blend of the two company processing systems just discussed with the exception that a bank or third-party does the processing. A lockbox system is similar to the field office collection system in that the lockbox system consists of dispersed collection sites. It is similar to the centralized collection system in that there are a limited number of collection sites and the deposited funds are transferred from the lockbox collection sites to the corporate headquarters bank on a frequent basis.

The first lockbox system was developed by the Radio Corporation of America (RCA) in conjunction with its major bank, First Chicago, in 1947. The primary purpose served by the lockbox system was to allow RCA to reduce its level of bank borrowing.

A lockbox collection system initially consisted of a physical post office box serviced by a bank. The company sent out remittance envelopes with each billing that had the post office box preprinted on the envelope. The bank's employees emptied the contents of the post office box several times daily, delivering the contents to the bank's lockbox processing area. The remittances were opened, the checks proofed and deposited, and the invoice material routed to the company.

Today, most banks have a **unique zip code** for their lockbox operation and instead of a box, the mail sorted to that zip code is bagged and placed in a designated area of the post office. The bank staff makes several trips daily to the post office, 7 days a week, to retrieve the bags of mail. The remittances are then processed in batches as received with the heaviest amount of processing done by 7:00 a.m. because most of the mail sorting is done at night. This early morning processing schedule allows the bank to meet same-day settlement deadlines and other check-clearing deadlines that accelerate availability of the deposited items.

TYPES OF LOCKBOX COLLECTION SYSTEMS.   There are two basic types of lockbox collection systems. The **retail lockbox system** is structured to handle a large volume of standardized invoice materials and the remittance checks have a relatively low average dollar face value. The standardized remittance information is a requirement in this system because it allows the bank to reduce its costs of handling the item. Cost reduction is essential because the average dollar face value per item is low and therefore the value of the float is low. Most consumers receive a standardized monthly invoice for phone bills, gasoline purchases, and credit card purchases. Companies with a large consumer base, such as AT&T, Texaco, or Visa, send a standardized invoice with a machine-readable scan line at the bottom of the remittance ticket.

Even though there is much fanfare over the use of technology to remit payments, a 1998 survey by Treasury Strategies, Inc., found that the use of paper-based payment systems for retail payments is still growing. The survey determined that over 70 percent of recurring consumer payments are made by mailed checks and that volume is growing. Although it is anticipated that electronic and card payment mechanisms will capture a growing percentage of new volume, paper-based processing will continue to grow in absolute terms as paper declines as a percentage of total payments. In addition, remittance processors are investing heavily in technologies that reflect their long term commitment to paper-based payments.

Contrast a retail lockbox system with a **wholesale lockbox system.** The wholesale lockbox system is designed to process large average dollar items with nonstandard remittance information. A retail lockbox system is used by companies receiving large volumes of remittances from consumers, whereas wholesale lockboxes are used for business-to-business trade payables.

COST ANALYSIS.   Lockbox processors charge both a fixed cost and a variable cost. Fixed costs include an account maintenance fee, a fee charged to transfer balances from the collection bank to another bank, a deposit notification charge, and a deposit charge. Variable costs include a lockbox processing charge per item, a charge for encoding each remittance item, and a deposit charge for each item. The other variable cost is not directly bank related. It has to do with the opportunity cost of float.

Suppose you have approached two different lockbox processors, Citibank and Chase, and gathered the following data:

	COMMON DATA	CITIBANK	CHASE
N	1,000		
F	$1500		
D		6	5
i	.10/365		
V		$.45	$.50
FC		$225	$275

$$
\begin{aligned}
\text{Total Cost (Citibank)} &= 1{,}000(\$1{,}500 \times 6 \times (.10/365) + \$.45) + \$225 \\
&= 1{,}000(\$2.465 + \$.45) + \$225 \\
&= \$2{,}915 + \$225 \\
&= \$3{,}140
\end{aligned}
$$

$$
\begin{aligned}
\text{Total Cost (Chase)} &= 1{,}000(\$1{,}500 \times 5 \times (.10/365) + \$.50) + \$275 \\
&= 1{,}000(\$2.055 + \$.50) + \$275 \\
&= \$2{,}555 + \$275 \\
&= \$2{,}830
\end{aligned}
$$

Therefore, even though Chase charges a higher variable processing cost and a higher fixed cost, the shorter check clearing time provides enough opportunity cost savings to generate a lower total cost. The lockbox system offered by Chase is cheaper than the decentralized company processing system alternative analyzed earlier.

Now assume that there are 100,000 checks and a face value of $15 per check (note that the total dollar value is the same).

$$
\begin{aligned}
\text{Total Cost (Citibank)} &= 100{,}000(\$15 \times 6 \times (.10/365) + \$.45) + \$225 \\
&= 100{,}000(\$.0246 + \$.45) + \$225 \\
&= \$47{,}460 + \$225 \\
&= \$47{,}685
\end{aligned}
$$

$$
\begin{aligned}
\text{Total Cost (Chase)} &= 100{,}000(\$15 \times 5 \times (.10/365) + \$.50) + \$275 \\
&= 100{,}000(\$.0205 + \$.50) + \$275 \\
&= \$52{,}050 + \$275 \\
&= \$52{,}325
\end{aligned}
$$

With the increased number of checks and lower face value, Citibank provides the lower total cost because the float savings are less significant when the dollar value of the check is small. In such a case, the processing costs are the more significant factor in determining total cost.

Alternative Collection Systems

Company processing systems and lockbox systems are the two major collection systems used today for the collection of check remittances. However, other forms of payment can be used that alleviate the need to process paper checks.

One alternative collection system uses **pre-authorized payments.** In this situation, the buyer and seller agree to a payment date, such as the twelfth of each month, and the seller initiates a request to the buyer's bank for payment of the predetermined amount. Pre-authorized payments eliminate mail float, processing float, and availability float and improve the cash flow forecasting ability of both the buyer and seller. A limiting factor is that time is needed to set up the system for each customer, so the transactions handled this way are best suited for regularly recurring payments. For example, insurance companies regularly collect monthly premiums using preauthorized payment systems.

FOCUS ON PRACTICE

DATA TRANSMISSION ENHANCES LOCKBOX VALUE Many banks offer electronic transmission of lockbox data. There are many benefits of this service, including:

- No computer input preparation by clerical staff
- Same-day accounts receivable updating
- More efficient credit management
- Reduction of potential credit/collection problems
- Greater flexibility when selecting lockbox banks

One of the most important benefits is the reduction in manual data entry in the corporation's accounts receivable area. When a bank provides a hard-copy report with lockbox remittance information, accounts receivable clerks must manually type the data into their computer system. Electronic transmission allows a company to feed the data automatically into the system. Such electronic data transmission enables a company to update its accounts receivable system faster, which results in increased control and more efficient credit management.

As **electronic corporate trade payments** become more common, wholesale lockboxes, as we know them today, will most likely be phased out. Electronic corporate trade payments involve an arrangement between a buyer, a seller, and the banks of the two parties involved so that payment is effected without a paper check being issued. A seller transmits an electronic invoice to the buyer and payment occurs electronically between the two parties' banks, eliminating the need for wholesale lockboxes. Chapter 19 discusses this payment alternative in more detail as a part of what is commonly referred to as electronic data interchange (EDI). An example of an electronic collection system is an **electronic lockbox.** This collection system is offered by banks to allow companies to receive payments via wire transfer or automated clearing house (ACH) rather than by paper checks.

THE LOCKBOX LOCATION STUDY

How does a corporation decide whether or not to have a lockbox? If a lockbox system is desirable, how does a firm decide how many lockboxes to have, where to locate them, and how to allocate the firm's customers among the chosen lockbox sites? The process by which these decisions are made is called a **lockbox study.** These studies are usually conducted by commercial banks. Money center banks and many of the large regional commercial banks have a cash management consulting group that markets the banks' cash management services. One way to market such services is through a lockbox study.

A lockbox study involves the collection of data that are fed into a computerized model that then determines the optimal number and location of lockbox sites. The data collected consist of a sample of remittance information including the number of checks and the dollar amount, postmark city, postmark date and date received, and the drawee bank's transit routing code for each remittance check. The data sample may include one or more months of remittance information depending on whether seasonal factors are important.

Let's compare the data gathered with the cost equation shown earlier in Equation 9-1 to see how they relate. The number of checks, N, and the face value of each check can be used to determine the average face value, F. The postmark city, postmark date, and date received are necessary to determine mail float, one component of the total number of days it takes to clear a check, D. The other component of D is availability float and it can be determined given the drawee's bank transit routing number. The consultant's database should include some estimated cost data that may be bank specific or may simply be proxies for variable and fixed costs. Once these data are collected, they are fed into a computerized optimization model to determine the number and location of lockbox sites. As with any type of research study, many choices related to the input data must be made based on judgment. We now turn our attention to some of the more complicating factors that exist in the data collection effort for the lockbox location study.

Customer Groups

How should customer groups be determined? One approach is to let each customer represent a unique customer group. If the firm has a relatively small number of customers, this may be the best approach.

What if the firm has tens of thousands of customers? This results in a very large optimization problem. At this point it might make sense to organize the firm's customer base into customer regions based on ZIP code. If additional refinement is required, each ZIP code group can be further grouped by size or even by Federal Reserve District.

Remittance Sample

How large should the remittance sample be? First, the number of items in the sample should reflect the size of the company. Second, consultants usually recommend using a stratified sample technique. The stratified sample technique fully incorporates the largest dollar items. If these items represent about 80 percent of the total dollars being received then the remainder of the sample may be disregarded. If the small items represent a significant dollar amount, then a sample of the items should be included.

Mail and Availability Times

Mail times can be estimated using the postmark date of the remittance envelopes and the date the remittance was received. However, this approach has been found to be prone to errors.

One popular source for mail time data is a database provided by Phoenix-Hecht. This company has developed a standardized technique for measuring mail times between central post offices.

Availability times can be obtained from a variety of sources. One source is Federal Reserve Schedules. As we have seen however, banks may not use the Federal Reserve System for clearing checks. Another source is City Averages, which represent the average of major clearing banks in a particular city. The third and final source of availability data is from published individual bank availability schedules. This source is the most accurate but also the most troublesome to obtain. However, most banks are willing to provide their availability schedules for lockbox study purposes.

FINANCIAL DILEMMA REVISITED

To resolve the financial dilemma mentioned at the beginning of this chapter, suppose the cash manager decides to bring in a consulting group to study the firm's cash collection system. The consultant, after reviewing the remittance information, determines the following remittance characteristics.

CUSTOMER GROUP	NUMBER OF REMITTANCES	AVERAGE FACE VALUE	MAIL AND AVAILABILITY FLOAT	PROCESSING FLOAT
1	25	$75,000	7 days	2 days
2	10	100,000	2 days	2 days
3	5	150,000	8 days	2 days

Variable processing cost per item: $.35

Monthly bank account fixed cost: $125

As the sample shows, there are three geographically dispersed customer groups. As the data are analyzed, the consultants find that customer group 2 is composed of most of the company's original customers and that groups 1 and 3 are customers that have been added more recently as the company has grown and attracted a more geographically dispersed product demand. The consultant determines that remittances take an average of 2 days to process before they are deposited at the company's bank. The consultant further indicates that this processing delay can be substantially reduced, if not eliminated, by allowing a bank to handle the processing. Currently, all customers mail their remittances to corporate headquarters. The total monthly cost of the current collection system using Equation 9-1 is:

$$
\begin{aligned}
\text{Total Cost} = \ & (25 \times \$\ 75{,}000 \times 9 \times (.10/365)) \\
& + (10 \times \$100{,}000 \times 4 \times (.10/365)) \\
& + (5 \times \$150{,}000 \times 10 \times (.10/365)) \\
& + (25 + 10 + 5) \times \$.35 \\
& + \$125 \\
= \ & \$7{,}913
\end{aligned}
$$

The total monthly cost of the float and processing charges amount to $7,913. For 1 year, this equals $94,956 = $7,913 × 12.

In the next section, the consultant estimates the cost of using a lockbox system to collect the company's remittances to see if a lockbox system is cost effective.

THE LOCKBOX MODEL

Once all data have been gathered through the lockbox study, they are entered into a **lockbox optimization model.** Such a model determines the optimal number of lockboxes and their locations. In addition, the model allocates the customers among the selected lockbox sites.

Complete Enumeration

A **complete enumeration model** analyzes all possible lockbox sites to determine the optimal combinations that maximize shareholder wealth. For example, if a firm wanted to find the optimal combination of lockbox sites out of a sample of three potential sites, the complete enumeration model first finds the best one-bank site by comparing the total cost (Equation 9-1) for each of the potential lockbox sites. Then the model finds the best two-bank combination. Finally the model finds the best three-bank combination. In all, given three possible lockbox locations, there are seven comparisons made to determine the site combinations with the lowest total cost. In general, the number of different lockbox combinations is $2^n - 1$, when n is the number of different sites. The possible combinations for n=3 are shown below.

- Best One-Site
  Choose from: Bank 1, Bank 2, or Bank 3
- Best Two-Site Combination
  Choose from: Bank 1-Bank 2, Bank 1-Bank 3, or Bank 2-Bank 3
- Best Three-Site Combination
  Bank 1-Bank 2-Bank 3

The optimal solution is the site combination that provides the lowest total cost. We develop the complete enumeration model through an application of the financial dilemma data collected earlier.

As a part of the lockbox study the consulting group developed, they presented the following remittance data and collection float data for a sample of three banks. Bank A is the current corporate headquarters' bank. Notice that the variable processing costs and fixed costs are higher for Bank A using a lockbox system compared to the company's current system because of the additional costs incurred related to the lockbox processing activity. Also, days of float include only mail and availability float because a lockbox system essentially eliminates processing float.

CUSTOMER GROUP	NUMBER OF REMITTANCES	AVERAGE FACE VALUE	DAYS OF FLOAT		
			BANK A	BANK B	BANK C
1	25	$ 75,000	7	3	1
2	10	100,000	2	5	3
3	5	150,000	8	2	4
Variable processing costs			$.45	$.35	$.75
Fixed costs			$275	$200	$150

The next table shows the total cost matrix for the three customer groups and the three banks. Total cost is calculated using Equation 9-1. The numbers calculated for each combination of customer group and bank represent variable costs computed using the opportunity cost of float and the variable processing costs. The total variable cost for each bank plus the respective bank fixed cost represent the total cost of processing the indicated customer groups for that particular bank. For example, allocating all customers to Bank A generates a monthly total cost of $6,081 compared to the monthly cost of $7,913 computed earlier using corporate headquarters as the collection site and Bank A for deposit services only. The optimal one-lockbox system is Bank C with a monthly cost of only $2,338. This represents a significant savings over the current system.

CUSTOMER GROUP	BANK A	BANK B	BANK C
1	$3,607	$1,550	$532
2	552	1,373	829
3	1,646	413	826
Fixed cost	$275	$200	$150
Total cost	$6,081	$3,536	$2,338

The next step is to compute the total cost for all combinations of two sites. The allocation of customer groups to specific banks is based on the very simple rule of minimization of variable costs. For example, look at combination 1 below. Customer group 1 is assigned to bank B because its variable costs of $1,550 are less than the variable costs of $3,607 that would result if it was assigned to bank A.

CUSTOMER GROUP	COMBINATION 1		COMBINATION 2		COMBINATION 3	
	A	B	A	C	B	C
1		$1,550		$532		$532
2	$552		$552			829
3		413		826	413	
Variable cost	$552	$1,963	$552	$1,358	$413	$1,361
Fixed cost	275	200	275	150	200	150
Total cost		$2,990		$2,335		$2,124

The optimal two-site system is combination 3, which includes bank B and bank C, with a total cost of $2,124. Customer groups 1 and 2 are assigned to bank C and customer group 3 is assigned to bank B. Because the total cost for a two-site system is less than the total cost for a 1-site system, we conclude that a 2-site system is preferred.

We now analyze a three-site system. If the minimum cost for a two-site location exceeded the minimum cost for a one-site location the analysis could end at this point.

CUSTOMER GROUP	COMBINATION 1		
	BANK A	BANK B	BANK C
1			$532
2	$552		
3		$413	
Variable costs	$552	$413	$532
Fixed costs	$275	$200	$150
Total costs			$2,122

A three-site solution offers the minimum monthly total cost of $2,122, which beats the best two-site solution by $2 and the best one-site solution by $215 and the current system by $5,790. It is no wonder that the firm has been losing some competitive advantage as a result of the significantly higher costs related to the centralized company processing cash collection system.

Other Solution Techniques

The problem with the complete enumeration model is the computational requirements for large problems. It is not uncommon for a lockbox problem to analyze a set of 50 different collection sites and possibly hundreds of different customer locations. This has led researchers to develop models that find the best combinations of sites without having to analyze all possible combinations. Lockbox models have gone through significant development since the early 1970s. The most popular model used today is The Collection Model (sometimes referred to as the 5.1 Model or the "Duke" model because of the author's former affiliation with Duke University.) The Collection Model is an optimization model that runs on the Windows platform and represents the most advanced collection modeling technology available.[1] The Collection Model used by Phoenix-Hecht is a proprietary model. To demonstrate the use of an optimization model, the appendix to this chapter develops a linear programming model that can be used to solve the lockbox location problem using the add-in Solver to Microsoft Excel.

---

[1] 1997. *Measuring, modeling & monitoring your lockbox.* Chicago: Phoenix-Hecht, p.19.

LOCKBOX BANK SELECTION

Once the lockbox model has chosen the optimal number of and location for lockbox collection sites, the final decision is to decide which banks to contract with for the actual lockbox services. Although the lockbox database may have included individual bank site mail and availability data and cost data, it is more likely that the database includes mail times between central post office sites and average availability data. Therefore, once the optimal sites are chosen, specific banks must then be chosen at the optimal sites.

The US banking system has historically banned nationwide branching, generally endorsing the unit banking structure or state-branching bounded by state lines. This banking structure has historically caused administrative problems for companies establishing nationwide lockbox systems because a company must establish separate bank accounts with a potentially large number of different banks. However, statewide branching is now common as a result of recent legislation allowing nationwide branching.

To combat these structural inefficiencies, banks have developed several different options from which to choose. Some banks have developed a **lockbox consortium.** This system is composed of several independent banks operating under a contractual agreement to provide lockbox services for each other's customers. A company chooses one bank to act as a lead or concentration bank. Some banks have developed **multiple processing centers.** Processing centers are established around the country to pick up lockbox mail and do the processing while the processed checks are deposited in accounts at correspondent banks in the company's name. Cash is then concentrated in the company's account at the lockbox bank's headquarters.

Because of the difficulties experienced by the banking system during the 1980s, banking laws had to be amended to allow out-of-state banks to absorb failed in-state banks. For example, the Bank One organization, based in Ohio, was allowed to purchase the insolvent Texas-based MBank system. The insolvency of such a high number of large regional banks has accelerated the movement to a regional branch banking system, a prelude to nationwide branching, which will create a much more efficient collection system. This system has advantages such as lower administrative costs, lower internal processing costs, and lower concentration costs. However, there are disadvantages. One disadvantage is that bundled services may make cost comparisons difficult. There also may be some additional risks entailed by having all collection, concentration, and reporting activities performed by one bank.

A LOCKBOX STUDY CASE EXAMPLE

A bank in Dallas, Texas, was asked by the subsidiary of a Dallas-based oil company to evaluate its current cash collection system and to offer suggestions for improvements. The subsidiary did not use a lockbox collection system and at the time had all customers remitting to company headquarters in Dallas. Dollar volume of remittances by state were: Texas (13%), New York (12%), Illinois (10%), California (10%), Pennsylvania (7%), Ohio (6%), and other (42%). Exhibit 9-3 displays the initial remittance data collected for a 2-month period by the bank's consulting group.

For the 2-month period, the company received over $53 million in remittances for an average daily remittance of $858,379. Total number of remittances included 1600 items for an average face value per remittance of $33,262. The current system resulted in 4.97 days of float, including mail and availability float. The number of days of float multiplied by the average daily remittance of $858,379 resulted in dollar-day-float of

EXHIBIT 9-3
Remittance Data

Number of Days in Study	62 (2 months)
Total Dollar Value	$53,219,517
Average Daily Remittance	$858,379
Estimated Number of Remits	1,600
Average Remittance Size	$33,262
Current System Float, days	4.97 days
Current System Float, dollars	$4,266,144

EXHIBIT 9-4
Lockbox System Monthly Costs

SERVICE ITEM	1-BOX	2-BOX	3-BOX
Account Maintenance	$ 15	$ 30	$ 45
Lockbox Processing (800 × $0.28)°	224	224	300
Deposit Notification	50	100	150
Items Deposited (800 × $0.04)	32	32	32
Encoding (800 × $0.025)	20	20	20
Wire Transfer—Incoming (22 × $5)	110	220	330
Wire Transfer—Outgoing (22 × $6)	132	264	396
Deposits Credited, 2/day (50 × $0.60)	30	60	90
Total Cost	$ 613	$ 950	$ 1,363
Estimated Balance Requirement	$111,454	$172,727	$247,818

(**NOTE:** Estimated balance requirement is calculated using an ECR of 7.5 percent, a 12-percent reserve requirement, 30-day months, and a 360-day year. Thus for a 1-box system, the firm can choose to pay a fee of $613 or leave balances of $111,454 to compensate the bank for the services rendered.)

° The lockbox processing fee is different for a three-bank system, assuming that each bank has a $100 minimum per month charge. Dividing the estimated total processing charge of $224 by three banks results in a charge per bank less than the required minimum charge.

$4,266,144. That is, on any given day, the company had over $4 million of idle funds in the remittance/clearing system.

The bank consulting group used the cost data contained in Exhibit 9-4 as an estimate of the total bank charges incurred by different banking systems analyzed. It was estimated that the firm's current cash collection system incurred a banking charge of $100 monthly or a required compensating balance of $18,182, based on an earnings credit rate (ECR) of 7.5 percent, a bank reserve requirement of 12 percent, and 30 days per month in a 360-day year.

Exhibit 9-5 shows the optimal solutions for a one-box, two-box, and three-box system. An optimization routine is used to determine the best bank combinations for a one-, two-, and three-bank system. The cost data, converted to required balances, are then added to the resulting dollar-day float for each system to determine the net improvement so that the optimal number of bank sites can be selected.

Note that the results for the second-best solution for each system are also displayed. If the firm wishes to use the second-best solution because of a desired bank relationship, the cost of suboptimizing can be easily assessed. As previously mentioned, the exhibit takes the resulting dollar-day float and adds the required balances to service the

EXHIBIT 9-5
Comparative System Float and Cost Results

SITE	DAYS	DOLLAR FLOAT	REQUIRED BALANCES	TOTAL IDLE BALANCES	NET IMPROVEMENT	INVESTMENT EARNINGS, 9%
Current System	4.97	$4,266,144	$18,182	$4,284,326		
Optimal One-City Systems:						
Chicago	3.46	$2,969,991	$111,454	$3,081,445	$1,202,881	$108,259
Pittsburgh	3.52	$3,021,494	$111,454	$3,132,948	$1,151,378	$103,624
Optimal Two-City Systems:						
Chicago/Pittsburgh	3.25	$2,789,732	$172,727	$2,962,459	$1,321,867	$118,968
Houston/Pittsburgh	3.33	$2,858,402	$172,727	$3,031,129	$1,253,197	$112,787
Optimal Three-City Systems:						
Chicago/Dallas/Charlotte	3.11	$2,669,559	$247,818	$2,917,377	$1,366,949	$123,025
Chicago/Newark/Charlotte	3.19	$2,738,229	$247,818	$2,986,047	$1,298,279	$116,845

bank system cost for a total idle dollar balance resulting from the banking system. Then the benefit of using each lockbox system relative to the current system is estimated based on an assumed opportunity rate of 9 percent. The optimal system is a three-bank system using banks in Chicago, Dallas, and Charlotte for an annual benefit of $123,025.

SUMMARY

Once the customer has mailed a remittance, the financial manager can significantly affect the amount of time it takes to get that mailed check converted into usable cash. This chapter has focused on the application of a lockbox system to quickly and efficiently convert the remittance check into cash. A lockbox system reduces mail and availability delay by intercepting the check close to the point at which it is mailed, and it reduces processing delay by having a bank process the remittance and make a deposit within a couple of hours. The processing bank uses state-of-the-art equipment and a highly trained and dedicated staff.

The lockbox study is an essential ingredient in determining whether a lockbox system is advantageous for a specific situation. The study process collects the necessary data with which to determine the optimal collection system. The firm's staff must work closely with the consulting group to make a wide variety of decisions in the data collection process to determine the size of the remittance sample and the time frame of the sample. Collected data that are not truly representative of the firm's total remittances will cause a less than optimal system to be created.

This chapter developed the basics of the lockbox model using a complete enumeration approach. The complete enumeration model, although very simple, is not very efficient at solving large scale problems because it analyzes every possible combination. An optimization model is typically used that is based on the same types of cost equations, but is able to find the best solution without evaluating each and every possible site. Appendix 9A provides a linear programming approach to developing a lockbox model.

The chapter concluded by demonstrating many of the principles discussed through the use of a case study. In the case study, a bank consulting group recommended that a company replace its centralized company remittance processing center with a three-bank lockbox system.

Useful Web Sites

A good general site for cash management systems:
Phoenix-Hecht: www.phoenixhecht.com
For information on lockboxes, go to the PNC Bank site and use the search function to explore such terms as retail lockbox, wholesale lockbox, etc.:
www.treasury.pncbank.com/

Questions

1. Explain the role that each of the following play in the cash collection process.
   a. Mail float
   b. Processing float
   c. Availability float
2. What are the advantages and disadvantages of the following cash collection systems?
   a. Decentralized collection
   b. Centralized collection
   c. Lockbox collection
3. How does a lockbox collection system help a firm's liquidity and cash flow situation?
4. Compare and contrast a retail lockbox system with a wholesale lockbox system.
5. What are the major variables in the total cost function for lockbox processing?
6. What are the major points of inquiry in a lockbox study?
7. How does a lockbox collection system reduce mail delay? How does it reduce processing delay? How does it reduce availability delay?
8. As the US financial system moves to nationwide branch banking, how will this impact the collection systems used by corporations?

Problems

1. A company has five remittances for the typical month as listed below. Assume the typical month has 30 days. The days of mail float and availability float for each remittance is also shown. Processing float is negligible.

REMITTANCE	MAIL FLOAT	AVAILABILITY FLOAT
$75,000	5	1
$1,000	7	3
$225,000	1	1
$5,000	1	1
$200,000	4	3

   a. Calculate the total dollar-day float for the month.
   b. Calculate the average dollar-day float.
   c. Calculate the average collection float in days.
   d. If the annual opportunity rate is 8 percent, calculate the annual cost of float.
2. A company has five remittances for the typical month as listed below. Assume the typical month has 30 days. The days of mail, processing, and availability float for each remittance is also shown. Under the firm's current system, remittances of $1 million or more receive expedited processing and all other remittances receive standard processing.

REMITTANCE	MAIL FLOAT	PROCESSING FLOAT	AVAILABILITY FLOAT
$500,000	5	2	3
$100,000	2	2	2
$50,000	5	2	3
$1,000,000	6	0.25	1
$25,000	1	2	2

    a. Calculate the total dollar-day float for the month.

    b. Calculate the average dollar-day float.

    c. Calculate the average collection float in days.

    d. If the annual opportunity rate is 10 percent, calculate the annual cost of float.

3. As cash manager for a sporting goods manufacturer, you are responsible for the firm's cash management activities. One of these activities is the management of the firm's cash collection system. Your firm receives an average of 5,000 remittances per month with an average face value of $10,000.

    Your current collection system consists of your customers remitting to your company headquarters. You estimate the average mail delay is 3 days. The typical remittance remains at headquarters for 2 days. You are informed that the average deposit receives good funds in 2 days.

    a. Based on this information, compute the monthly total cost for your cash collection system if your firm's opportunity investment rate is 8 percent and your bank charges $.35 per item and a monthly fixed cost of $150.

    b. Your bank, interested in selling you a lockbox system, indicates that a lockbox system will reduce mail float by 2 days, processing float by 1 day, and availability float by 1 day. If the system charges a variable cost of $.80 per item and monthly fixed cost of $375, should you change to the lockbox system? You may assume your opportunity investment rate remains at 8 percent.

4. As cash manager for an oil company, you are responsible for the firm's cash management activities. One of these activities is the management of the firm's retail cash collection system. Your firm receives an average of 65,000 remittances per month with an average face value of $375.

    Your current collection system consists of your customers remitting to your company headquarters. You estimate that the average mail delay is 3 days. The typical remittance remains at headquarters for 1 day. You are informed that the average deposit receives good funds in 1.5 days.

    a. Based on this information, compute the monthly total cost for your cash collection system if your firm's opportunity investment rate is 8 percent and your bank charges $.25 per item and a monthly fixed cost of $125.

    b. Your bank, interested in selling you a lockbox system, indicates that a lockbox system would reduce mail float by 2 days, processing float by 1 day, and availability float by .5 days. If the system charges a variable cost of $.75 per item and monthly fixed cost of $425, should you change to the lockbox system? You may assume your opportunity investment rate remains at 8 percent.

5. Your firm sells to wholesalers nationwide. Your bank has just completed a lockbox study of your cash collection system. After a thorough study of your remittance information, they categorized your customers into four groups, as shown below. Your opportunity rate is 11 percent.

	Average monthly remittances		Days of float		
CUSTOMER GROUP	**NUMBER**	**FACE VALUE**	**BANK A**	**BANK B**	**BANK C**
1	2,000	$50,000	5	3	1
2	4,000	30,000	1	6	4
3	1,000	18,000	3	7	5
4	200	20,000	7	1	3
Variable processing costs			$.30	$.60	$.80
Fixed costs			$300	$400	$150

Using the complete enumeration model, determine the optimal number of lockbox sites and the customer allocation among the chosen sites.

6. Your firm sells to retail customers nationwide. Your bank has just completed a lockbox study of your cash collection system. After a thorough study of your remittance information, they categorized your customers into three groups as shown below. Notice that the consultants expressed remittance data on an average daily basis, assuming 30 days in a month. Your opportunity cost of funds is 10 percent.

	Average monthly remittances		Days of float		
CUSTOMER GROUP	**NUMBER**	**FACE VALUE**	**BANK A**	**BANK B**	**BANK C**
1	2,000	$500	6	2	1
2	10,000	900	5	1	3
3	4,000	1,500	1	4	6
Variable processing costs			$.55	$.20	$.70
Fixed costs			$350	$550	$250

Using the complete enumeration model, determine the optimal number of lockbox sites and the customer allocation among the chosen sites.

References

G. Cornuejols, M.L. Fisher, and G.L. Nemhauser. 1977. Location of bank accounts to optimize float: An analytical study of exact and approximate algorithms. *Management Science* 23(8):780–810.

B. D. Fielitz and D.L. White. 1981. A two stage solution procedure for the lockbox problem. *Management Science* 27(8):881–886.

B. D. Fielitz and D. L. White. 1982. An evaluation and linking of alternative solution procedures for the lockbox location problem. *Journal of Bank Research* 17–27.

F. K. Levy. 1966. An application of heuristic problem solving to accounts receivable management. *Management Science* February 12(6):B236–B244.

S. F. Maier and J.A. Vander Wiede. 1976–1977. A unified location model for cash disbursement and lockbox collections. *Journal of Bank Research* 166–172.

S. F. Maier and J. A. Vander Wiede. 1983. What lockbox and disbursement models really do. *Journal of Finance* 38(2):361–371.

Larry A. Marks and Denise A. Arnette. 1986. Data sample key to accurate lockbox analysis. *Cashflow* October:37–38.

R. M. Nauss and R.E. Markland. 1974. Theory and application of an optimizing procedure for lock box location analysis. *Management Science* 27(8):855–865.

R. M. Nauss and R. E. Markland. 1979. Solving the lockbox location problem. *Financial Management* 8(1):21–31.

B. K. Stone. 1981. Design of a receivable collection system. *Management Science* 27(8):866–880.

Appendix 9A

A Linear Programming Formulation of the Lockbox Model

Linear programming (LP) is a mathematical model that optimizes an objective function subject to specified constraints. The objective function and constraints must be linear equations. If a feasible solution exists for the given problem, it can be proven that the LP model will find the optimal answer, the one that maximizes or minimizes the objective function subject to the constraints. One interesting feature of the LP model is that the solution can be found at one of the corner solutions of the constraint region so that not all possible solutions must be examined. Because there are only a finite number of corner solutions in the feasible region, it only takes a computer a relatively small amount of time to find the optimal solution.

There are four general classes of business problems that are well suited for the LP model. Product mix is a problem situation in which the attempt is to combine limited resources to maximize profit. Staff scheduling problems try to meet staffing needs at minimum cost. Optimal routing problems attempt to ship goods from sources to demand points at minimum cost. Lockbox problems fit into this problem classification. Finally, blending mixes of raw materials to meet blending requirements at minimum cost represents the fourth and final general class of business problems that are well suited for the LP model.

The formulation of the objective function for a linear programming application to lockbox application is basically a repeat of the total cost equation developed in the chapter as Equation 9-1. The primary difference here is that the equation is expressed as a total cost function for all customer groups j and for all bank sites k.

$$\text{Minimize } TC = \sum_{j} \sum_{k} [(N_j \times F_j \times D_{jk} \times i)$$
$$+ (N_j \times V_k)] X_{jk} + \sum_{k} FC_k Y_k \quad \text{(9A-1)}$$

In which:

N_j = the number of checks remitted by customer j

F_j = the face value of remittances by customer j

D_{jk} = collection float between customer j and bank k

i = daily interest rate

V_k = variable cost for bank k

X_{jk} = 0,1 variable for customer/bank relationship

FC_k = dollar fixed cost for bank k

Y_k = 0,1 variable for whether or not a bank is active.

The solution or decision variables are X_{jk} and Y_k. The Xs represent the allocation of customers, j, among the banks, k; the Ys indicate which banks are included in the optimal solution.

Another characteristic of a linear or integer programming formulation is that the objective function is optimized with respect to a set of constraints. In the case of a lockbox problem, the constraints are generally structured to ensure that all customer remittances are assigned to some lockbox site and that no customer remittances are assigned to a lockbox site that is not "open," that is, one that is not in the solution. For a lockbox solution, Equation 9A-1 is minimized subject to the following set of constraints.

Subject to:

$$\sum_{k} X_{jk} = 1, j \in J \quad \text{(9A-2)}$$

Constraint set 9A-2 allows customer j to be allocated to only one bank k. There are J constraints, each one summing across K banks.

$$\sum_{k} Y_k \le Z \quad \text{(9A-3)}$$

Constraint 9A-3 sets the maximum number of bank sites chosen to be less than or equal to some arbitrarily chosen maximum of Z. At times, the user may wish to constrain the maximum number of lockbox sites. The model then solves for those sites yielding the minimum cost so that the number of lockbox sites is less than or equal to Z.

$$Y_k \in \{0,1\}, k \in K \qquad \text{(9A-4)}$$

Constraint set 9A-4 specifies that a bank is either in the solution or out of the solution. A bank cannot be partially in the solution. Rather than enter these constraints explicitly in the constraint matrix, the integer constraint is generally handled by special instructions to the optimization model.

$$X_{jk} \in \{0,1\}, j \in J, k \in K \qquad \text{(9A-5)}$$

Constraint set 9A-5 specifies an integer solution for a customer allocation. There are $J \times K$ constraints so that a given customer's remittances are allocated to only one bank. Rather than enter these constraints explicitly in the constraint matrix, the integer constraint is generally handled by special instructions to the optimization model.

$$\sum_j X_{jk} \leq MY_k, k \in K \qquad \text{(9A-6)}$$

Constraint set 9A-6 specifies that a lockbox bank k must be open for customers to be assigned to it. M is some arbitrary large number such as 100.

The format for the objective function and constraint matrix is shown in Exhibit 9A-1. The V coefficients in the objective function represent the total variable costs related to each X. X is a decision variable that has a solution of either zero or 1 and represents the customer allocation among the possible bank sites. The subscripts are the jk subscripts in which j is the index for the customer group and k is the index for the bank site. Y is a decision variable that also has a solution of zero or 1 indicating whether or not a bank site is chosen ($Y = 1$) or not chosen ($Y = 0$). The numbers in the body of the constraint matrix represent the coefficients for the variable in the respective column. Exhibit 9A-2 shows the format for the integer programming format using the data for the financial dilemma problem developed in the chapter.

PROBLEMS

A-1. Develop the data matrix for problem 5 at the end of Chapter 9. This problem has three bank sites and four customer groups. Solve this problem using an integer programming model.

A-2. Solve problem 6 using an integer programming model.

EXHIBIT 9A-1
Format of the Integer Programming Data Matrix

Objective Function
Minimize TC

$$V_{11}X_{11} + V_{12}X_{12} + V_{13}X_{13} + V_{21}X_{21} + V_{22}X_{22} + V_{23}X_{23} + V_{31}X_{31} + V_{32}X_{32} + V_{33}X_{33} + F_1Y_1 + F_2Y_2 + F_3Y_3$$

(**NOTE:** $V_{jk} = N_j \times F_j \times D_{jk} + N_jVC_k$ represents total variable cost for a given combination jk)

SUBJECT TO:

	X_{11}	X_{12}	X_{13}	X_{21}	X_{22}	X_{23}	X_{31}	X_{32}	X_{33}	Y_1	Y_2	Y_3	
9A-2	1	1	1										$= 1$
				1	1	1							$= 1$
							1	1	1				$= 1$
9A-3	0	0	0	0	0	0	0	0	0	1	1	1	$\leq Z$
9A-6	1			1			1			$-M$			≤ 0
		1			1			1			$-M$		≤ 0
			1			1			1			$-M$	≤ 0

EXHIBIT 9A-2

Integer Programming Data Matrix and Solution for the 3 Bank/3 Customer Group Problem

Let $M = 100$
Let $Z = 3$
Objective Function
Minimize TC

$$3607X_{11} + 1550X_{12} + 532X_{13} + 552X_{21} + 1373X_{22} + 829X_{23} + 1646X_{31} + 413X_{32} + 826X_{33} + 275Y_1 + 200Y_2 + 150Y_3$$

SUBJECT TO:

	X_{11}	X_{12}	X_{13}	X_{21}	X_{22}	X_{23}	X_{31}	X_{32}	X_{33}	Y_1	Y_2	Y_3	
9A-2	1	1	1										$= 1$
				1	1	1							$= 1$
							1	1	1				$= 1$
9A-3										1	1	1	≤ 3
9A-6	1			1			1			-100			≤ 0
		1			1			1			-100		≤ 0
			1			1			1			-100	≤ 0

Solution:

$TC = \$2,123$

Customer Allocation: Customer 1 to bank C, $X_{13} = 1$
Customer 2 to bank A, $X_{21} = 1$
Customer 3 to bank B, $X_{32} = 1$

$Y_1 = 1$
$Y_2 = 1$
$Y_3 = 1$

CHAPTER 10

Cash Concentration

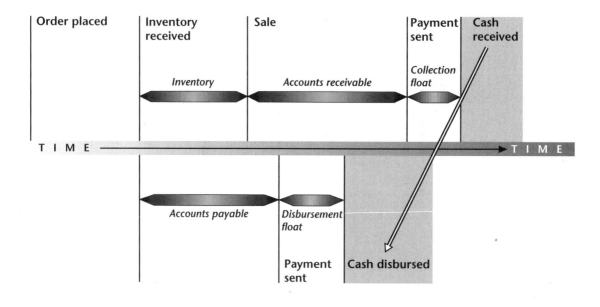

OBJECTIVES

After studying this chapter, you should be able to:

- Understand the need for a cash concentration system.
- Formulate a cash transfer decision model.
- Understand the advantages and disadvantages of the different cash transfer tools.

In the previous chapter, we developed an efficient cash collection system that accomplished three things. First, it reduced mail float. Second, it reduced processing delays. Third, it reduced availability float. Given these benefits, the cash collection system, such as the lockbox system, leaves the cash manager with one problem. There are now multiple deposit accounts spread around the country. To combat this problem, the cash manager must design a system to concentrate these deposit balances into the company's major concentration bank or banks so that the collected balances can be used to fund disbursements or to invest.

Cash concentration is the process of moving dollar balances from deposit banks to concentration banks. A **concentration bank** is a bank that receives balance transfers from several deposit or gathering banks. Although a corporation's cash management system may have many deposit or collection banks, it generally has only a few concentration banks.

FINANCIAL DILEMMA

How to Consolidate Collected Balances

The cash management consulting group from your lead bank has just completed a lockbox study of the cash collection system of Tri-Teck Products, Inc. The report suggested that Tri-Teck develop a lockbox collection system using five different lockbox banks. Tri-Teck historically had all customers remit to corporate headquarters. However, the estimated savings in collection float, which translate into increased interest earnings from the additional invested funds generated by the suggested lockbox system, is significant. The concern in the treasurer's office at Tri-Teck now centers on the lack of control treasury will have over the dispersed collection system. Tri-Teck's cash manager ponders how he will know the dollar amount of daily receipts and how to get the funds out of the deposit banks and into the firm's disbursement and investment accounts. Certainly there are costs and delays in getting the collected balances into usable accounts. Will these costs and delays offset the benefits generated by the lockbox system?

THE BASIC STRUCTURE OF A CASH CONCENTRATION SYSTEM

A visualization of a typical cash concentration system would look very much like the pyramid shown in Exhibit 10-1. At the base of the pyramid are the scores of deposit banks connected with field offices or store outlets. In the middle of the pyramid are the several lockbox collection banks. Finally, at the top of the pyramid are the central or main corporate concentration banks. The funds transferred to these banks are used to fund the firm's disbursement accounts and pay down credit line borrowing with any surplus funds invested. From the base of the pyramid to the top of the pyramid is a continual flow of collected balances and deposit information.

Cash Transfer Tools

There are three basic methods by which cash managers transfer funds from accounts at one bank to accounts at another bank. These three methods are:

- depository transfer check (DTC)
- electronic depository transfer (EDT)
- wire transfer

Each transfer method has its own characteristics regarding cost and performance, and the cash manager must use judgment in selecting the transfer method or combination of methods to properly trade off the benefits and costs of each transfer instrument. Each transfer instrument will be discussed separately.

DEPOSITORY TRANSFER CHECKS (DTC). A **depository transfer check** (DTC) is a non-negotiable, usually unsigned check payable only to a single bank account at a particular

EXHIBIT 10-1
A Typical Cash Concentration System

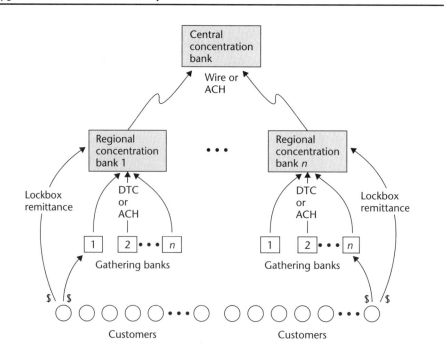

bank. Firms use these checks to transfer balances from one bank to another. Each check costs approximately $1 to use and is especially valuable when the dollar amount of funds to be transferred from one bank to another is relatively small, less than $5,000.

A prime example of an effective use for a DTC is an oil company with retail service stations located in all areas of the country. Each day the service station manager prepares a local deposit of cash and credit card receipts, fills in the deposit amount on a preprinted DTC, and delivers both the deposit and DTC to his or her local bank. In the context of a cash concentration system, these banks are generally referred to as gathering banks. The DTC is forwarded to the concentration bank. At the same time that the DTC is processed via the normal check processing channels, the local checks that were deposited are being cleared locally. By the time the DTC clears, the deposited checks will have cleared and balances are then transferred to the concentration bank.

As an alternative, the station manager could have reported the dollar amount of the deposit via telephone through an operator, touch-tone telephone, a dedicated terminal, or personal computer. When the concentration bank receives this information, it generates a paper-based DTC with the proper magnetic ink character recognition (MICR) line data and places the DTC in the deposit process, or initiates an electronic transfer of the funds. Although the DTC historically was the primary transfer tool for smaller cash balances, the electronic depository transfer has now largely replaced it. Although DTCs still exist, electronic versions of this process are replacing the paper process.

ELECTRONIC DEPOSITORY TRANSFERS (EDT). An **electronic depository transfer** (EDT), also known as an ACH debit, is handled through the automated clearing house (ACH) network. Automated clearing house debit entries are used in place of DTCs and this transfer method has largely replaced the use of DTCs. In this case, the cash manager authorizes the company's concentration bank to originate an ACH debit entry against the company's accounts at various gathering banks for a specified amount. When settlement occurs, 1 day is the norm for the company's account at the concentration bank to be credited and for the local gathering bank account to be debited. The advantage of the EDT is that collected funds are available at the concentration bank the day after the ACH debit is originated regardless of the location of the gathering bank.

WIRE TRANSFERS. A **wire transfer** represents a real-time transfer of account balances. Historically, only bank employees could activate a wire transfer. Today, many treasury workstations allow cash managers to initiate a wire transfer via their own computer terminal. There are two drawbacks related to the use of wire transfers. First, they are relatively expensive. There is generally a charge by the bank being debited as well as by the bank being credited with the transfer balance. The total charge can be as high as $20 for the complete transaction. Thus wire transfers are best for larger balances. Second, because wires represent immediate transfer of funds, the deposited balances being transferred must be collected funds, not just ledger balances. Although DTCs and EDTs may clear more slowly, if the cleared DTC and EDT matches the availability of the deposited checks, then they are far superior to the wire because they are much cheaper and yield transferred funds as quickly as the wire, given the availability constraint.

Initiation of the Cash Transfer

The previous section focused primarily on the transfer tools available for the transfer process. This section presents a more detailed look at the two different approaches to the transfer initiation process.

DECENTRALIZED INITIATION. An example of a **decentralized transfer initiation** process is the field office or store manager who makes a deposit including a paper DTC. In essence, the manager is initiating the transfer and the amount is generally the amount of the deposit.

CENTRALIZED INITIATION. **Centralized transfer initiation** is an alternative system in which the timing and the amount of the transfer are centralized either at the concentration bank or corporate headquarters. In this case, the field manager simply makes the deposit in the local bank and reports the deposit via a third-party information vendor who transmits the data to the concentration bank and corporate headquarters.

More recently, the information retrieval process has become even more advanced. In some cases, the field offices' cash register terminals are scanned by the corporation's computers on a daily basis to determine the dollar amount of receipts. Thus a telephone call by the local manager is not even necessary.

Costs of Running a Concentration System

There are three major cost categories associated with running a cash concentration system. We examine each of these cost categories separately.

OPPORTUNITY COST OF IDLE BALANCES. It is very difficult to always transfer the balance from the deposit bank to the concentration bank exactly when it becomes a collected balance. Deposits may consist of a variety of cash, checks of varying availability, and charge card vouchers. Given this variety of availability it is very common for idle balances to exist at the deposit bank. When idle balances occur, those balances can be used to offset bank service charges, yet this does not outweigh the lost interest.

TRANSFER COSTS. Actual charges for transferring balances vary depending on the transfer instrument chosen. Exhibit 10-2 shows the range of charges that are generally associated with the three major transfer instruments. Wire transfers are the most expensive and EDTs are the cheapest.

ADMINISTRATIVE COSTS. Managing the concentration system is a major cash management responsibility. Receiving and reviewing deposit reports from the gathering banks, third-party information vendors, and concentration banks consume a portion of the cash manager's day. If overdrafts are created or some type of fraud is detected, returned checks are included in the deposit. Another administrative cost is associated with developing and maintaining a cash forecast system if transfer scheduling is based on anticipated deposits.

EXHIBIT 10-2
Service Charges for the Three Basic Transfer Instruments

	COST PER TRANSFER	AVAILABILITY
Wire Transfer	$15–$20	Immediate
EDT	$ .20	1 Business Day
DTC	$1.00	0–2 Business Days

Benefits Derived From the Concentration System

There are significant benefits associated with a well-designed cash concentration system that offset the costs outlined above.

ECONOMIES OF SCALE.   It is not efficient or profitable to leave small balances deposited in several deposit accounts spread around the country. It is much more economical to concentrate those balances into one or only a few concentration accounts so big blocks of funds can be invested at one time. The cash manager, with sizable funds to invest, can find readily available investments in major markets yielding good rates. The field manager in charge of the local deposit account will find only very limited opportunities for short-term investment of balances. So it is much more economical to invest large balances than to make several different investments of small balances.

ENHANCED VISIBILITY AND CONTROL OVER BALANCES.   Control is a major advantage afforded the company's cash manager by the cash concentration system. It is impossible for the company's cash manager to effectively control and manage the firm's cash balances if they are spread around the country in several hundred deposit accounts. A concentration system continually concentrates the geographically dispersed balances to a limited number of concentration accounts that are readily controlled by the cash manager.

POSSIBILITY OF DUAL BALANCES.   A **dual balance** is created when the transfer instrument, such as a paper DTC, is granted availability at the concentration bank before the transfer instrument clears back against the deposit account. When this happens, the same collected balance exists at both banks. Thus the cash manager has use of a balance that is twice the size of the transfer. Funds can be invested from the concentration account and the balance at the original deposit bank remains as a collected balance that can be used to offset bank service charges. However, the increased efficiency of the payment system has significantly reduced the likelihood of dual balances existing and thus they are now of little value to the financial manager because they can't be predicted.

The Future of Cash Concentration Systems

Much of what has been discussed thus far are concerns and issues for the cash manager because of the fragmented banking and payment system that currently exists in the United States. As the banking and payment system evolves toward a nationwide branching system with a relatively small number of national banks, these inefficiencies will begin to disappear. The gathering banks will probably be branches of the national bank chosen by the corporation and rather than incurring the transfer and administrative costs involved in moving balances between separately incorporated banks, there will simply be debits and credits between accounts within the same banking organization. With less time spent on managing the cash-concentration processes between separately incorporated banking institutions, the cash manager's time will more likely be spent managing and improving information flows and forecasting cash flows.

CASH CONCENTRATION AND THE CASH FLOW TIMELINE

Exhibit 10-3 displays on a timeline the major intervals related to cash concentration. Times T3, T5, T6 are critical because these are the periods when cash is actually affected by the

EXHIBIT 10-3

Cash Concentration and the Cash Flow Timeline

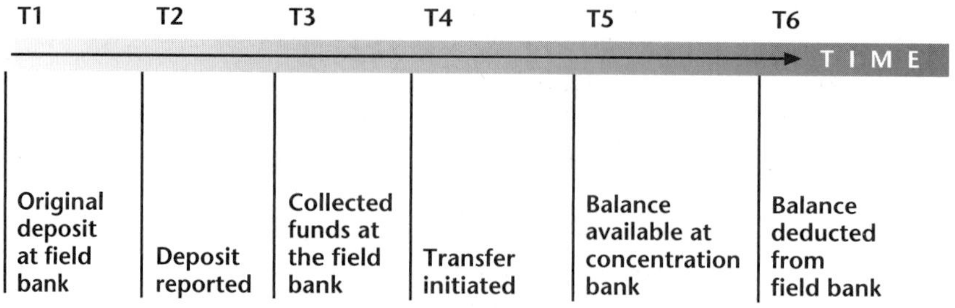

T1 – T3: Availability granted by deposit bank
T1 – T2: Efficiency and structure of concentration system
T2 – T4: Efficiency and structure of concentration system
T4 – T5: Type of transfer mechanism chosen and availability granted by the
          concentration bank
T5 – T6: If the balance is deducted from the gathering bank after the balance is
          available at the concentration bank then a dual balance is created. Dual balances
          are generally created by inefficiencies in the payment system.

concentration system. T3 is the period when collected balances are credited at the deposit bank. This may either be a lockbox bank or a field office deposit or gathering bank. Collected funds are credited at the concentration bank as a result of the cash transfer at T5. Collected funds are debited from the original bank deposit account at T6. T6 can come after T5, contemporaneous with T5, or before T5. The normal situation is for T5 to occur contemporaneous with T6. Dual balances are created when T5 occurs before T6.

CASH TRANSFER SCHEDULING

There are several factors complicating the decision when to transfer balances and how much to transfer at a time. First, daily deposits generally fluctuate. Second, the deposits may consist of a mixture of currency and checks with immediate, 1-, or 2-day availability. The deferred availability on a part of the deposit causes the ledger and collected balance to be different and only collected balances can be transferred. A third complicating factor is the delay in the transfer instrument and matching that delay with the availability schedule of the deposits. Fourth, weekends cause a problem because Friday ending balances are carried over the weekend and deposits made during the weekend are not credited to the account until Monday. Also, weekends cause delays in clearing the transfer instrument. Finally, there are two cost trade-offs, the differences in the cost of each transfer instrument and the differences in the time required to transfer a cash balance, that must be considered. The three types of transfer instruments have very different costs. Wire transfers, which grant immediate availability, are the most expensive, and EDTs, which grant 1-day availability, generally are the least expensive. Paper-based DTCs have a range of availabilities and have a cost higher than EDTs resulting from the inefficiencies of dealing with a paper-based system.

Calculating the Minimum Balance to Transfer

The higher the cost of the transfer instrument, the larger the balance must be to make the transfer cost effective. Any collected balance that remains in the deposit account incurs an opportunity cost. However, these balances can be used to cover bank service charges through the earnings credit rate (ECR). Although the ECR is generally lower than the firm's opportunity investment rate, especially considering the allowance made for the reserve requirement, at least some benefit is derived from collected balances remaining in the deposit accounts.

A simple break-even equation for this aspect of the transfer problem can be developed as shown below in Equation 10-1. This equation is derived from the incremental cost relationship that relates days saved, the difference between the investment rate and the earnings credit rate adjusted by the required reserves, and the balance to be transferred.

$$\text{Incremental Cost} = DS \times (k - ECR \times (1-rr)) \times TBAL$$

In which:

DS = the number of days saved by the transfer instrument

k = the firm's investment opportunity rate

ECR = the bank's earnings credit rate

rr = the required reserve rate, generally 12 percent

$TBAL$ = the balance to be transferred

Solving this equation for TBAL, the minimum balance required to justify the higher cost transfer instrument is:

$$TBAL = \frac{\text{Incremental cost}}{DS \times (k - ECR \times (1-rr))} \qquad \text{(10-1)}$$

Notice that instead of using only the investment opportunity rate, this equation uses the difference between the investment opportunity rate and the reserve adjusted ECR because collected balances at the deposit bank can earn the ECR. Of course, this is only the case once the transferred balances cause the remaining balance to fall below the required balance to compensate the bank for its services. If the balances being transferred are simply excess balances, then the effective ECR is zero and thus irrelevant.

To see how to apply this equation, assume that the financial manager is trying to decide between using a wire transfer and an EDT. The costs of these transfer instruments are shown in Exhibit 10-2. Assume that the firm's opportunity investment rate is 10 percent, the ECR is 8 percent, the EDT takes 1 day longer to clear, and the reserve requirement is 10 percent. Entering these data into Equation 10-1 results in the minimum balance that must be transferred to justify the incremental cost.

$$TBAL = \frac{\$19.80}{1 \times (.10 - .08 \times (1-.10))/365}$$

$$TBAL = \$258,107$$

This balance seems large because the wire transfer only yields a 1-day advantage and the return is only the increment over the reserve adjusted ECR. If the balance is an excess balance and does not earn the ECR, then recalculating Equation 10-1 with ECR = 0 results in a break-even transfer balance of only \$72,270.

$$TBAL = \frac{\$19.80}{1 \times (.10 - 0 \times (1-.10)) /365}$$

$$TBAL = \$72,270$$

The Transfer Scheduling Decision

The objective for the cash transfer scheduling decision is to minimize cash concentration costs while adequately compensating the deposit banks. The cash concentration costs include the cost of the transfer instrument, generally a fixed charge per transfer, and the costs associated with excess collected balances remaining at the deposit bank. The total cost of the transfer scheduling decision can be expressed as Equation 10-2.

$$\text{Total cost} = FEE + (k \times (ACB - ((SC - FEE)/ECR(1 - rr)))) \quad \text{(10-2)}$$
$$= FEE + (k \times (ACB - RCB))$$

In which:

FEE = The amount of the total service charge, SC, that is paid through fees.

SC = The bank service charge related to transfer activity. This is equal to the charge per transfer times the number of transfers.

k = The firm's investment opportunity rate.

ACB = The average collected balance at the gathering bank resulting from the transfer scheduling decision.

RCB = The required collected balance to be maintained at the deposit bank to compensate the bank for those services not paid by fees.
$RCB = (SC - FEE)/ECR(1 - rr)$.

FINANCIAL DILEMMA REVISITED

The application of this total cost equation can now be applied to the Tri-Teck problem mentioned in the Financial Dilemma at the beginning of the chapter. Exhibit 10-4 presents the daily deposits made at each of the firm's lockbox banks. Tri-Teck's cash manager now must transfer those deposited balances to the firm's lead corporate bank where the major disbursement accounts are located. Two different daily deposit structures are shown in Exhibit 10-4. The situation presented as Case 1 assumes that deposits occur evenly throughout the week and Case 2 assumes that daily deposits vary. Note that the total weekly deposits are the same in both cases. Further, assume that the cost of an EDT is $.20 per transfer and that Tri-Teck's investment opportunity rate is 10 percent.

EXHIBIT 10-4
Tri-Teck's Daily Deposits

DAY OF THE WEEK	CASE 1	CASE 2
Monday	$ 5,000	$ 3,000
Tuesday	5,000	2,500
Wednesday	5,000	5,000
Thursday	5,000	7,000
Friday	5,000	5,500
Saturday	5,000	8,000
Sunday	5,000	4,000
Total	$35,000	$35,000
Daily Average	5,000	5,000

To understand the basic complexities of the cash transfer scheduling problem, we apply one of the most basic scheduling rules, transfer daily the dollar amount of the daily deposit, under differing structural assumptions. The **daily transfer rule** is applied to situations involving weekend bank processing and no weekend bank processing, immediate deposit availability and deferred deposit availability, and cash transfers with immediate availability and cash transfers with 1-day availability.

DAILY TRANSFER RULE. This is the simplest and most common transfer rule of the four we review. The rule is to initiate a daily transfer from the deposit bank to the concentration bank in the amount of the daily deposit. Several factors that complicate the transfer of funds include:

- weekend bank processing schedules
- availability schedule for deposit items
- type of transfer instrument and delay in transfer

Exhibit 10-5 applies the daily transfer rule to the case 1 deposit schedule shown in Exhibit 10-4, assuming that banks process items 7 days a week, that the total deposit is immediately available, and that the transfer of funds is accomplished on the same day it is initiated. As a result, the deposit availability matches exactly the transfer schedule leaving zero ledger and zero available balances. This necessitates the compensation of the bank for its banking services through the payment of fees because no balances are maintained.

Exhibit 10-6 applies case 1 deposit data under the same assumptions with the exception that there is no weekend bank processing, which means that the only difference in this situation is that the firm loses interest on the deposits made during the weekend. However, on Monday when the weekend deposits are credited to the account, they are immediately transferred along with Monday's regular deposit.

Exhibit 10-7 applies the case 1 deposit schedule to the daily transfer rule assuming weekend processing and immediately available funds from deposit, but the transfer is delayed 1 day. The result is that a $5,000 balance is maintained in the ledger and collected funds accounts. The firm is losing interest on a perpetual $5,000 balance as a result of the discrepancy between the availability schedule for the deposit items and the availability schedule for the transfer item.

Exhibit 10-8 continues with the assumption of the 1-day delay in the transfer clearing but assumes no weekend bank processing. The major impact is the increase in the collected balance account on Monday from $5,000 to $15,000 resulting in an average weekly collected balance of $6,428 versus $5,000. Daily transfers become costly as deposit availability exceeds transfer clearing time. Lack of weekend processing causes increased opportunity costs as the time discrepancy increases.

Exhibit 10-9 maintains the same transfer schedule and no weekend processing but changes the deposit availability schedule so that only $2,500 (or 50 percent) is immediately available and $2,500 (or 50 percent) has 1-day availability. The impact is to reduce the average collected balance because the availability of the deposit more closely matches the availability of the transfer item. In fact, Exhibit 10-9 demonstrates that if the entire deposit had 1-day availability, then the ledger balance would generally be $5,000 and the collected balance would generally be zero.

The total cost for the daily transfer rule for case 1, based on the assumptions in Exhibit 10-9, is computed below. To compute the total cost, based on Equation 10-2, we further assume that the *ECR* is 8 percent per year and the reserve requirement is 12 percent. The firm compensates the bank with balances and thus pays no fees. This makes sense based on the average collected balances left in the gathering bank. The required

EXHIBIT 10-5
Worksheet for Case 1 Deposit Structure

| DAY OF WEEK | DAILY DEPOSIT | AVAILABILITY | | | TRANSFERS | ENDING BALANCES | |
		Immediate	1-day	2-day		Ledger*	Collected**
Sunday							
Monday	$5,000	$5,000	$0	$0	($5,000)	$0	$0
Tuesday	5,000	5,000	0	0	(5,000)	0	0
Wednesday	5,000	5,000	0	0	(5,000)	0	0
Thursday	5,000	5,000	0	0	(5,000)	0	0
Friday	5,000	5,000	0	0	(5,000)	0	0
Saturday	5,000	5,000	0	0	(5,000)	0	0
Sunday	5,000	5,000	0	0	(5,000)	0	0
Beginning of steady state:							
Monday	5,000	5,000	0	0	(5,000)	0	0
Tuesday	5,000	5,000	0	0	(5,000)	0	0
Wednesday	5,000	5,000	0	0	(5,000)	0	0
Thursday	5,000	5,000	0	0	(5,000)	0	0
Friday	5,000	5,000	0	0	(5,000)	0	0
Saturday	5,000	5,000	0	0	(5,000)	0	0
Sunday	5,000	5,000	0	0	(5,000)	0	0
Average, 2nd week						0	0

EXHIBIT 10-6
Worksheet for Case 1 Deposit Structure: No Weekend Processing

| DAY OF WEEK | DAILY DEPOSIT | AVAILABILITY | | | TRANSFERS | ENDING BALANCES | |
		Immediate	1-day	2-day		Ledger*	Collected**
Sunday							
Monday	$ 5,000	$ 5,000	$0	$0	($ 5,000)	$0	$0
Tuesday	5,000	5,000	0	0	(5,000)	0	0
Wednesday	5,000	5,000	0	0	(5,000)	0	0
Thursday	5,000	5,000	0	0	(5,000)	0	0
Friday	5,000	5,000	0	0	(5,000)	0	0
Saturday	0	0	0	0	0	0	0
Sunday	0	0	0	0	0	0	0
Beginning of steady state:							
Monday	15,000	15,000	0	0	(15,000)	0	0
Tuesday	5,000	5,000	0	0	(5,000)	0	0
Wednesday	5,000	5,000	0	0	(5,000)	0	0
Thursday	5,000	5,000	0	0	(5,000)	0	0
Friday	5,000	5,000	0	0	(5,000)	0	0
Saturday	0	0	0	0	0	0	0
Sunday	0	0	0	0	0	0	0
Average, 2nd week						0	0

*Ending ledger balance equals the previous ledger balance, plus the daily deposit, minus the transfer clearing.

**Ending collected balance equals the previously collected balance, plus immediate availability, minus transfer clearing, plus deferred availability.

EXHIBIT 10-7
Worksheet for Case 1 Deposit Structure: Transfer Clearing Delay

| DAY OF WEEK | DAILY DEPOSIT | AVAILABILITY | | | TRANSFERS | ENDING BALANCES | |
		Immediate	1-day	2-day		Ledger*	Collected**
Sunday							
Monday	$5,000	$5,000	$0	$0	0	$5,000	$5,000
Tuesday	5,000	5,000	0	0	($5,000)	$5,000	$5,000
Wednesday	5,000	5,000	0	0	(5,000)	$5,000	$5,000
Thursday	5,000	5,000	0	0	(5,000)	$5,000	$5,000
Friday	5,000	5,000	0	0	(5,000)	$5,000	$5,000
Saturday	5,000	5,000	0	0	(5,000)	$5,000	$5,000
Sunday	5,000	5,000	0	0	(5,000)	$5,000	$5,000
Beginning of steady state:							
Monday	5,000	5,000	0	0	(5,000)	$5,000	$5,000
Tuesday	5,000	5,000	0	0	(5,000)	$5,000	$5,000
Wednesday	5,000	5,000	0	0	(5,000)	$5,000	$5,000
Thursday	5,000	5,000	0	0	(5,000)	$5,000	$5,000
Friday	5,000	5,000	0	0	(5,000)	$5,000	$5,000
Saturday	5,000	5,000	0	0	(5,000)	$5,000	$5,000
Sunday	5,000	5,000	0	0	(5,000)	$5,000	$5,000
Average, 2nd week						$5,000	$5,000

EXHIBIT 10-8
Worksheet for Case 1 Deposit Structure: No Weekend Processing, Transfer Clearing Delay

| DAY OF WEEK | DAILY DEPOSIT | AVAILABILITY | | | TRANSFERS | ENDING BALANCES | |
		Immediate	1-day	2-day		Ledger*	Collected**
Sunday							
Monday	$ 5,000	$ 5,000	$0	$0	0	$ 5,000	$ 5,000
Tuesday	5,000	5,000	0	0	($5,000)	$ 5,000	$ 5,000
Wednesday	5,000	5,000	0	0	(5,000)	$ 5,000	$ 5,000
Thursday	5,000	5,000	0	0	(5,000)	$ 5,000	$ 5,000
Friday	5,000	5,000	0	0	(5,000)	$ 5,000	$ 5,000
Saturday	0	0	0	0	0	$ 5,000	$ 5,000
Sunday	0	0	0	0	0	$ 5,000	$ 5,000
Beginning of steady state:							
Monday	15,000	15,000	0	0	(5,000)	$15,000	$15,000
Tuesday	5,000	5,000	0	0	(15,000)	$ 5,000	$ 5,000
Wednesday	5,000	5,000	0	0	(5,000)	$ 5,000	$ 5,000
Thursday	5,000	5,000	0	0	(5,000)	$ 5,000	$ 5,000
Friday	5,000	5,000	0	0	(5,000)	$ 5,000	$ 5,000
Saturday	0	0	0	0	0	$ 5,000	$ 5,000
Sunday	0	0	0	0	0	$ 5,000	$ 5,000
Average, 2nd week						$ 6,428	$ 6,428

*Ending ledger balance equals the previous ledger balance, plus the daily deposit, minus the transfer clearing.

**Ending collected balance equals the previously collected balance, plus immediate availability, minus transfer clearing, plus deferred availability.

EXHIBIT 10-9
Worksheet for Case 1 Deposit Structure: No Weekend Processing,
Deposit Availability Delay, Transfer Clearing Delay

		AVAILABILITY				ENDING BALANCES	
DAY OF WEEK	DAILY DEPOSIT	Immediate	1-day	2-day	TRANSFERS	Ledger	Collected
Sunday							
Monday	$ 5,000	$2,500	$ 0	$0	0	$ 5,000	$2,500
Tuesday	5,000	2,500	2,500	0	($5,000)	$ 5,000	$2,500
Wednesday	5,000	2,500	2,500	0	(5,000)	$ 5,000	$2,500
Thursday	5,000	2,500	2,500	0	(5,000)	$ 5,000	$2,500
Friday	5,000	2,500	2,500	0	(5,000)	$ 5,000	$2,500
Saturday	0	0	0	0	0	$ 5,000	$2,500
Sunday	0	0	0	0	0	$ 5,000	$2,500
Beginning of steady state:							
Monday	15,000	7,500	2,500	0	(5,000)	$15,000	$7,500
Tuesday	5,000	2,500	7,500	0	(15,000)	$ 5,000	$2,500
Wednesday	5,000	2,500	2,500	0	(5,000)	$ 5,000	$2,500
Thursday	5,000	2,500	2,500	0	(5,000)	$ 5,000	$2,500
Friday	5,000	2,500	2,500	0	(5,000)	$ 5,000	$2,500
Saturday	0	0	0	0	0	$ 5,000	$2,500
Sunday	0	0	0	0	0	$ 5,000	$2,500
Average, 2nd week						$ 6,428	$3,214

collected balance (RCB) is equal to $\$738.63 = (5 \times \$.20)/((.08/52) \times (1 - .12))$. The total 1-week cost of the cash transfer system is $4.76 as shown in the following equation.

$$\text{Total cost} = (.10/52) \times (\$3,214 - \$738.63)$$
$$= \$4.76$$

The daily transfer rule applied to case 2, shown in Exhibit 10-10, is presented for the situation with no weekend processing and the deposits and transfer instrument receive deferred availability. Note that a low collected balance of $1,250 occurs on Tuesday and a high collected balance of $7,500 occurs on Monday. When daily deposits vary, the cash manager must be careful to make sure that the amount requested to be transferred does not exceed the dollar amount of collected balances at the time the transfer clears.

MANAGING ABOUT A TARGET.   Rather than making daily transfers, the **managing about a target rule** makes only one transfer for several days of deposits. This rule is particularly appropriate when a firm has a target collected balance it is trying to maintain in the deposit bank.

Initially, the firm transfers its balance out of the deposit account, thus beginning with a zero balance. Then it lets the deposits accumulate until the average daily balance hits the target balance. The accumulated balance is then transferred to the concentration account. This transfer rule has two advantages. First, it allows the firm to make a one-time transfer out of the deposit account at the time the rule is initiated. Assuming that an initial balance exists, this money represents a permanent one-time interest earning opportunity for the firm. Second, this rule can reduce the dollar amount of transfer costs because of the reduced number of transfers while maintaining the target balance.

EXHIBIT 10-10
Worksheet for Case 2 Deposit Structure: No Weekend Processing,
Deferred Availability on Deposits and Transfers

		AVAILABILITY				ENDING BALANCES	
DAY OF WEEK	DAILY DEPOSIT	Immediate	1-day	2-day	TRANSFERS	Ledger	Collected
Sunday							
Monday	$ 3,000	$1,500	$0	$0	0	$ 3,000	$1,500
Tuesday	2,500	1,250	1,500	0	($3,000)	$ 2,500	$1,250
Wednesday	5,000	2,500	1,250	0	($2,500)	$ 5,000	$2,500
Thursday	7,000	3,500	2,500	0	(5,000)	$ 7,000	$3,500
Friday	5,500	2,750	3,500	0	(7,000)	$ 5,500	$2,750
Saturday	0	0	0	0	0	$ 5,500	$2,750
Sunday	0	0	0	0	0	$ 5,500	$2,750
Beginning of steady state							
Monday	15,000	7,500	2,750	0	(5,500)	$15,000	$7,500
Tuesday	2,500	1,250	7,500	0	(15,000)	$ 2,500	$1,250
Wednesday	5,000	2,500	1,250	0	(2,500)	$ 5,000	$2,500
Thursday	7,000	3,500	2,500	0	(5,000)	$ 7,000	$3,500
Friday	5,500	2,750	3,500	0	(7,000)	$ 5,500	$2,750
Saturday	0	0	0	0	0	$ 5,500	$2,750
Sunday	0	0	0	0	0	$ 5,500	$2,750
Average, 2nd week						$ 6,571	$3,286

ANTICIPATION.   The **anticipation rule** initiates a transfer before the related deposit is
made. This rule is very helpful for those cases in which the deposits have a shorter availability than the transfer instrument, thus better matching the clearing of the transfer
instrument with the availability of the deposit. As was demonstrated with the daily transfer rule using the case 1 data, the more closely matched the deposit availability is to the
availability of the transfer item the lower the average collected balance that remains in
the deposit account.

   Although anticipatory transfers can reduce balances, there are additional costs to
be considered. First, additional administrative costs are incurred as a result of the forecasting system that is required. Second, this type of transfer system is riskier. The dollar
amount of the transfer is based on a forecast that may be different from the actual
deposit. As a result, the potential for overdrafts is increased. The likelihood of incurring
overdraft costs must be taken into consideration.

WEEKEND TIMING.   As we have seen, the lack of weekend processing by banks causes
a great deal of inefficiency when the cash manager is attempting to minimize the collected balances that remain in the deposit bank. Weekend balances are a critical factor
in deciding which transfer rule to use. Under the current US banking system, closing
balances on Friday are carried over until Monday. In addition, deposits made during the
weekend are not credited to the account until Monday. This means that if Friday's closing balance is expected to be an excess balance, that balance has a 3-day impact. The
transfer rule chosen should consider the impact of Friday balances on the calculated
average balance so that excess compensation is avoided. In addition, if dual balance possibilities exist, the weekend effect is important.

E.F. HUTTON: A SYSTEM THAT LOST CONTROL[1]

E.F. Hutton's basic cash concentration system design was the typical cash concentration system shown earlier in Exhibit 10-1. In the early 1980s, Hutton had approximately 400 branch offices located in all parts of the United States. It was common for these offices to receive payments from customers on a regular basis. Thus the 400 gathering banks were at the bottom of the cash concentration pyramid. In the middle of the pyramid were a smaller number of regional concentration banks, some of which were part of the same bank chain as one of the gathering banks located in a larger city. At the top of the pyramid were two national concentration banks, one located in Los Angeles and the other in New York.

The cashier at the local office would call the regional cashier with the amount of daily deposits adjusted by an approved formula. Because the clearing of checks in the local deposit bank did not always match with the clearing of the concentration instrument, and because some of the daily deposits contained immediately available items, an adjustment was made in the amount to be transferred to reduce or prevent excess compensation. The formula took this into account so that Hutton would be able to draw down these excess balances. The regional cashier would then deposit a DTC in the regional concentration account. Later the same day, the regional cashier would call the national cash desk and another DTC would be created between one of the two national concentration banks and the regional concentration banks. In this way balances were continually being transferred from the 400 deposit banks through the regional concentration banks to one of the two national concentration accounts.

Although the basic system previously described is very typical and legal, some of Hutton's branch managers began to modify the system. Hutton's branch managers received bonuses based on interest earnings. If a branch could generate additional balances, interest earnings would increase, creating a larger bonus for the branch manager. So, during the early 1980s, some of the branch managers began to modify the formula that determined the size of the cash transfer and, in addition, they revised the concentration system design to create multiple transfers to generate dual balances. They began to transfer balances among some of the gathering banks on the way to one of the concentration banks.

In 1985, Hutton pleaded guilty in federal court to two charges: excessive drawdowns and multiple transfers. When the legal charges were made public, many corporate cash managers became concerned that their cash concentration practices might be seen as illegal. Perhaps one of the biggest concerns focused on the creation of a DTC for an amount different than the related deposit. This is a typical type of activity and is the only way that a cash manager can effectively manage the amount of compensation being paid for bank services. Although the basic practice was deemed appropriate as long as the DTC amount is based on the deposit or the excess balances at the bank, the

---

[1]Anthony Bianco, G. David Wallace, Peter Phillips, and Daniel B. Moskowitz. 1985. What did Hutton's managers know—and when did they know it? *Business Week* May 20:110–112.

Vince DiPaolo and Richard Stolz. 1985. When E.F. Hutton's caught, treasurers listen. *Cashflow* July/August:49.

Dexter Hutchins. 1985. Post-Hutton lessons in how to manage corporate cash. *Fortune* November:134.

Editorial. 1985. Learning from the E.F. Hutton experience. *Journal of Cash Management* July/August:12, 80.

Arthur L. Herold, Mary C. Driscoll, and Richard J. Poje. 1985. E.F. Hutton: Reactions and commentary. *Journal of Cash Management* July/August:14–21.

Various issues of the *Leahy Newsletter*.

EXHIBIT 10-11
Code of Conduct for the Association for Financial Professionals

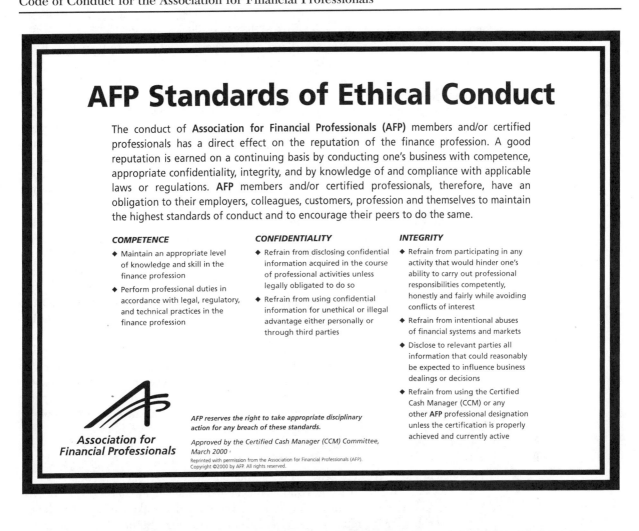

AFP Standards of Ethical Conduct

The conduct of **Association for Financial Professionals (AFP)** members and/or certified professionals has a direct effect on the reputation of the finance profession. A good reputation is earned on a continuing basis by conducting one's business with competence, appropriate confidentiality, integrity, and by knowledge of and compliance with applicable laws or regulations. **AFP** members and/or certified professionals, therefore, have an obligation to their employers, colleagues, customers, profession and themselves to maintain the highest standards of conduct and to encourage their peers to do the same.

COMPETENCE

◆ Maintain an appropriate level of knowledge and skill in the finance profession

◆ Perform professional duties in accordance with legal, regulatory, and technical practices in the finance profession

CONFIDENTIALITY

◆ Refrain from disclosing confidential information acquired in the course of professional activities unless legally obligated to do so

◆ Refrain from using confidential information for unethical or illegal advantage either personally or through third parties

INTEGRITY

◆ Refrain from participating in any activity that would hinder one's ability to carry out professional responsibilities competently, honestly and fairly while avoiding conflicts of interest

◆ Refrain from intentional abuses of financial systems and markets

◆ Disclose to relevant parties all information that could reasonably be expected to influence business dealings or decisions

◆ Refrain from using the Certified Cash Manager (CCM) or any other **AFP** professional designation unless the certification is properly achieved and currently active

Association for Financial Professionals

AFP reserves the right to take appropriate disciplinary action for any breach of these standards.

Approved by the Certified Cash Manager (CCM) Committee, March 2000

Reprinted with permission from the Association for Financial Professionals (AFP).
Copyright ©2000 by AFP. All rights reserved.

---

legal proceedings made it very clear that cash managers should have a written document drawn up with their bank regarding how overdrafts of collected funds will be handled. Many of Hutton's accounts at smaller banks were consistently overdrawn on a collected balance basis and the banks did not have accounting control systems sophisticated enough to monitor the situation. In fact, Hutton admitted to fraudulently obtaining the use of more than $1 billion in interest-free funds through its concentration system over the 2-year period that this activity took place.

This case also prompted the Association for Financial Professionals, then known as the National Corporate Cash Management Association, to draft a code of conduct for its members. The code is shown in Exhibit 10-11. The second bulleted item under the Integrity heading of this code relates directly to the Hutton case by stating that the cash manager should, "Refrain from intentional abuses of financial systems and markets."[2]

---

[2]Code of Ethics for Certified Cash Managers.

CASH CONCENTRATION: THE CANADIAN EXPERIENCE[3]

A review of the Canadian banking structure and the Canadian cash concentration system may give a glimpse into the future of the US banking system.

Until 1980, the Canadian banking system consisted of no more than 12 national banks. Revisions in the Bank Act during the early 1980s relaxed chartering restrictions so that there are now over 60 banks. Many of the new banks are foreign-owned. The original 12 banks, primarily the largest five, dominate the cash concentration effort used by corporations operating in Canada because of their extensive network of branches.

Compared to the current US system, the Canadian payment system is very efficient. Because of the large scale of business done by these five major banks, they have invested in very efficient communications and computer systems that link their branches nationwide. Thus intrabank check clearing and balance transfers are generally handled on an immediate availability basis. Even interbank clearings are handled in a similarly efficient manner. The Bank of Canada, the country's central bank, assumes no float responsibilities.

The Canadian banks and their customers are not encumbered by many of the restrictions common in the US system. For example, there are no interest restrictions on deposits. Thus even small deposit balances held at remote branches can earn interest before they are concentrated. In addition, overdraft privileges are common, reducing the problems of transfers clearing against insufficient collected balances.

Cash concentration systems include a telephone transfer system, which results in immediate availability of funds. In addition, there is an automatic transfer system (ATS) that is used only for branches within the same bank. A company can specify a wide variety of automated decision rules that are time-based, such as once a day, every other day, and so on; or they may be balance-based, such as setting a trigger level so that once it is reached a prespecified balance is transferred. Finally, there is a terminal-based paperless concentration system. A cash concentration order is entered through the computer terminal to the company's bank to transfer a specified balance from a deposit account at a branch to a concentration account located at the company's main branch.

One service that reduces the need for cash concentration is the availability of off-set balances. Off-set balances allow companies to specify a group of accounts at different branches to be treated by the bank's accounting system as a single account.

Currently, the US banking system has over 9000 individually chartered banks. Historically, we have been a country of unit banks, but given the banking crisis in the 1980s, we are slowly evolving into a large regional branch banking system. This evolution has been somewhat by default as the Federal Reserve has sold insolvent banks to stronger out-of-state banks. As the evolution continues, we may keep our eyes on our neighbor to the north for clues to the cash concentration systems that may emerge as the US banking system moves toward a national branching system.

SUMMARY

As a financial manager attempts to reduce collection float through the development of a lockbox collection system, a cash concentration system becomes essential in moving the collected deposit balances to banks where the balances can be better managed. An effective cash concentration system provides deposit information to the corporate cash manager that is critical if the cash manager is going to effectively manage the firm's

---

[3]SOURCE: Mohsen Anvari (1988). Alternative cash concentration systems in Canada: An example of national banking. *Journal of Cash Management* June/July:48–56.

daily liquidity. The improved deposit information allows the cash manager to move the accumulating balances from the original banks of deposit to fewer deposit accounts of greater balances so that the funds can be managed more efficiently.

This chapter discussed the structure of a cash concentration system and the cost components and benefits were emphasized. The chapter developed an objective function for the cash transfer scheduling problem. Three basic transfer scheduling rules were discussed including daily transfer, managing about a target, and anticipation. The problems of weekend timing were also noted.

The chapter concluded by comparing the cash concentration characteristics of the Canadian banking system with those of the US banking system. As the US banking system moves toward a national banking system, the structure of cash concentration systems in the United States will probably take on the major characteristics of their Canadian counterparts.

Useful Web Sites

PNC Bank: www.treasury.pncbank.com/Treasury-Management.html.
Use this site to explore different aspects of cash management services offered by PNC Bank. Click on *AskPNC* and key-in *Cash Concentration*. It will return optional pages for you to explore, showing a description of the services they offer.

Questions

1. What are the three principal cash transfer tools and what are the main differences between them?
2. List the three costs of running a cash concentration system.
3. Identify the benefits derived from a cash concentration system.
4. Briefly discuss the major complicating factors affecting cash transfer scheduling.
5. What advantage does managing about a target have over the simple daily transfer rule?
6. What additional advantages and disadvantages are related to the anticipation rule?

Problems

1. The cash manager of BRONCO, Inc. is contemplating the choice between using a wire transfer and an EDT. She estimates that her investment opportunity rate is 10 percent. The bank's ECR is currently 7 percent and the reserve requirement is 10 percent. Her bank account officer informs her that a wire transfer will cost $20 and will provide collected balances 1 day earlier than the EDT, which costs $.75.
   a. Assume that the balances transferred are above the balances required to compensate the deposit bank for its services. Calculate the minimum transfer balance required to justify the use of a wire transfer.
   b. Assume that the balances transferred are below the balances required to compensate the deposit bank. Calculate the minimum transfer balance required to justify the use of a wire transfer.
   c. Why are the answers in parts *a* and *b* different?
2. The cash manager of VEREMATIC, Inc., is contemplating the choice between using a wire transfer and a paper-based DTC. He estimates that his investment

opportunity rate is 10 percent. The bank's ECR is currently 6 percent and the reserve requirement is 10 percent. His bank account officer informs him that a wire transfer will cost $15 and will provide collected balances 4 days earlier than the DTC, which costs $1.50.

   a. Assume that the balances transferred are above the balances required to compensate the deposit bank for its services. Calculate the minimum transfer balance required to justify the use of a wire transfer.

   b. Assume that the balances transferred are below the balances required to compensate the deposit bank. Calculate the minimum transfer balance required to justify the use of a wire transfer.

   c. Why are the answers to parts *a* and *b* different?

3. You have just been promoted to the cash manager's position at your firm. Your first assignment is to analyze the firm's cash-concentration system. You discover that the firm currently compensates the bank with balances and uses a paper DTC daily (5 days per week) to concentrate collected balances. The weekly DTC transactions cost $7.50. The firm's average collected balances equal $35,000 as a result of the transfers. The bank's ECR is 6 percent and the reserve requirement is 10 percent. Your investment opportunity rate is 12 percent.

   a. Calculate the cost of the current system assuming the bank is completely compensated with balances (no fee is paid).

   b. Now assume that if a wire transfer is used, the average daily collected balance can be reduced to zero. However, the weekly transfer costs will increase to $100. Assuming that fees are paid only as needed, estimate the total cost of the revised cash concentration system.

   c. What is your recommendation and why?

4. As the new cash manager for your firm, your first task is to analyze the firm's cash-concentration system. You discover that the firm currently compensates the bank with balances and uses a paper DTC daily (5 days per week) to concentrate collected balances. The weekly DTC transactions cost $10.00. The firm's average collected balances at the deposit bank equal $15,000 as a result of the transfers. The bank's ECR is 4.5 percent and the reserve requirement is 10 percent. Your investment opportunity rate is 10 percent and you may assume 52 weeks in a year.

   a. Calculate the cost of the current system assuming the bank is completely compensated with balances (no fee is paid).

   b. Now assume that if a wire transfer is used, the average daily collected balance can be reduced to zero. However, the weekly transfer costs will increase to $100. Assuming that fees are paid only as needed, estimate the total cost of the revised cash-concentration system.

   c. What is your recommendation and why?

5. The following data were recently collected by the cash manager at RAYCO Department Stores, Inc.

DAY	DOLLAR DEPOSIT
Monday	$ 1,500
Tuesday	2,000
Wednesday	1,000
Thursday	10,000
Friday	25,000
Saturday	35,000
Sunday	10,000

These daily deposits are typical of RAYCO's ten regional stores. RAYCO is headquartered in Oklahoma City and concentrates cash from the ten local deposit banks to its concentration bank in Oklahoma City. You may assume that RAYCO's opportunity investment rate is 10 percent, the ECR is 8 percent and the reserve requirement is 12 percent. Further assume that RAYCO uses EDTs to concentrate the cash balances and that the EDT is initiated on the day of deposit and clears the next day. Deposits are made before the daily ledger cut-off time. Also half of each deposit is cash and half is in checks with 1-day availability. Finally, assume that no bank-clearing activity is conducted on the weekends and that the beginning ledger and collected balance for the first week are equal to zero.

  a. Assuming that the deposit schedule is typical of each week, create 2 weeks of deposit and transfer clearing activity similar in format to Exhibits 10-5 through 10-10.
  b. Calculate the average collected balance at the typical deposit bank.
  c. Assuming that each EDT costs $1.00, calculate the dollar amount of collected balances required to compensate the deposit bank.
  d. What is the total cost of the cash-concentration system for one bank for 1 week?
  e. Can you suggest any improvements in RAYCO's cash-concentration system?
6. The following data were recently collected by the cash manager at Wonder Burger, Inc.

DAY	DOLLAR DEPOSIT
Monday	$ 5,000
Tuesday	4,000
Wednesday	6,500
Thursday	5,000
Friday	10,000
Saturday	35,000
Sunday	15,000

These daily deposits are typical of Wonder Burger's 150 regional restaurants. Wonder Burger is headquartered in Cleveland, Ohio, and concentrates cash from the 150 different local deposit banks to its concentration bank in Cleveland. You may assume that the opportunity investment rate is 12 percent, the ECR is 7 percent, and the reserve requirement is 10 percent. Further assume that Wonder Burger uses EDTs to concentrate the cash balances and that the EDT is initiated on the day of deposit and clears the next day. Deposits are made before the daily ledger cut-off time. In addition, 80 percent of each deposit is cash and the remaining 20 percent is in checks with 1-day availability. Finally, assume that no bank-clearing activity is conducted on the weekends and the beginning ledger and collected balance for the first week are equal to zero.

  a. Assuming that the deposit schedule is typical of each week, create 2 weeks of deposit and transfer clearing activity similar in format to Exhibits 10-5 through 10-10.
  b. Calculate the average collected balance at the typical deposit bank.
  c. Assuming that each EDT costs $.20, calculate the dollar amount of collected balances required to compensate the deposit bank.
  d. What is the total cost of the cash-concentration system for one bank for 1 week?

e. Can you suggest any improvements in Wonder Burger's cash-concentration system?

7. The cash manager at Curry Office Products, Inc., is contemplating changing the company's current cash-concentration system from a daily transfer of deposited balances using an EDT system to managing the system based on a target balance. Under the proposed plan, only one transfer will be made weekly using an EDT. The transfer will occur on Thursday. Currently, the company experiences an average daily deposit of $3,700. The earnings credit rate is 6 percent, the bank has a 10-percent reserve requirement, and charges $.50 per EDT transaction. Curry's opportunity rate is 12 percent on these balances. The resulting daily collected balances under both plans are shown here:

Current System Daily Collected Balance

MON	TUES	WED	THUR	FRI	SAT	SUN
$3,700	$3,700	$3,700	$3,700	$3,700	$3,700	$3,700

Proposed System Daily Collected Balance

MON	TUES	WED	THUR	FRI	SAT	SUN
$14,800	$18,500	$22,200	$25,900	$3,700	$7,400	$11,100

Daily receipts and deposits equal $3,700. Under the current system, the company transfers the deposit amount each day (deposit and clearing activities occur 7 days a week) using an EDT that clears the next day. Under the proposed system, the accumulated balance of $25,900 is transferred on Thursday of each week using an EDT that clears the next day.

a. Calculate the average daily balance for each system.

b. Calculate the required collected balance for each system for 1 week.

c. Calculate the opportunity cost of any excess balances left by each system for 1 week.

d. Calculate the weekly service charge imposed by the bank under both systems.

e. Which system should the cash manager choose and why?

References

Bernell K. Stone and Ned C. Hill. 1980. Cash transfer scheduling for efficient cash concentration. *Financial Management* Autumn:35–43.

Linda A. Zang. 1990. Cash management at a mid-sized retailer. *Journal of Cash Management* January/February:12–15.

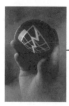

FOCUSED CASE

Gold Star Laundry and Drycleaners, Inc.

Gold Star Laundry and Drycleaners, Inc., is a regional chain of laundry and dry cleaning outlets in the southeast United States. The company is headquartered in Atlanta, Georgia, and has outlets in four states. The company has grown rapidly in the last 5 years and recently created a treasury office.

Historically, Gold Star had the manager of each local outlet establish a bank relationship with a local bank for deposit of daily cash receipts. The corporate controller would then initiate a deposit transfer once each week to move the funds from the local bank accounts to the corporate headquarters bank in Atlanta. The controller relied on depository transfer checks (DTCs) for this purpose and liked the fact that a paper document existed for an audit trail. DTCs cost $1.50 each and seemed quite economical because only one transfer was made each week.

The chief financial officer (CFO) asked the newly hired treasurer to review the company's existing cash management system and put all recommendations in a report to be submitted by the end of the month. The CFO felt that the company was not as efficient as it might be from a cash management perspective but he did not have any hard data to back up this hunch.

THE CURRENT SITUATION

The treasurer began to pull together the pertinent information. There were 50 different outlets in four states. The outlets were located in the major cities of these states and each city was serviced by a number of major banks; some of these were referred to as super regional banks because they had branches in all four states. However, the treasurer discovered that, because of the lack of a corporate bank policy, the managers were free to select their own banks and as a result the corporation had relationships with over 15 separately incorporated banking institutions. The following data were computed from the company's records by the analyst staff and represents the typical outlet's weekly cash receipts.

DAY	CASH RECEIPTS
Monday	$25,000
Tuesday	6,000
Wednesday	8,000
Thursday	15,000
Friday	30,000
Saturday	10,000
Sunday	0

The cash receipts were deposited in the local bank the following day by 9 A.M. and the bank credited the deposit that same day because the receipts consisted of cash and checks drawn on local banks. The outlet manager then sent a DTC on Thursday morning to the corporate headquarters bank in Atlanta in the amount of Thursday's collected balance, which included Wednesday's cash receipts deposited on Thursday morning. The DTC arrived on Friday at the headquarters' bank and is given a 1-business day availability clearing the amount of the DTC out of the depository bank on Monday.

The corporate policy has been to compensate the bank system with balances rather than fees. The treasurer agreed with this policy given the balances maintained at the depository banks, but wondered if this would continue to be a reasonable policy if there was going to be a change in the transfer system in general. In discussions with the headquarters' bank, he learned that the Federal Reserve was currently requiring a 10 percent reserve requirement. The average earnings credit rate among the banks was 4.7 percent and in most cases the overnight investment rate offered by the depository banks was about 3.00 percent. The treasurer estimated that the corporation's overnight opportunity rate was about 4.50 percent.

Scenario One

One option the treasurer easily recognized was to maintain the current transfer system but shift the transfer initiation day from Thursday to Wednesday. If the same DTC system was continued, this 1-day shift would cause the transfer to clear on Friday and would reduce the idle balances carried over the weekend. However, he was not sure how this would impact the average daily collected balance; he did not know if this would be the best solution.

Scenario Two

The treasurer wondered why the company was not using an automated clearing house (ACH) transaction to make transfers, because an electronic depository transfer (EDT) was cheaper and more efficient to use. In most cases, the company's banks charge $.50 for an EDT with 1-business day availability. Several options exist to transmit the collected balance information. At a minimum, the outlet manager could simply call the treasurer's office with the information. A more expensive option would be to install electronic cash registers/terminals at each outlet; the cash register/terminals can be queried daily by the computer at the headquarters to retrieve the daily cash receipts. The treasurer thought that it might be prudent to defer the more technological alternative as a second step to be investigated more thoroughly in a few months. He settled on having the outlet manager call in the previous day's cash receipts the following morning and then corporate headquarters would contact the headquarters' bank to initiate an ACH in the amount of the previous days cash receipts. The ACH would be given 1-business day availability and would clear the next day. His plan was for this to happen on a daily basis and he wondered what impact a daily transfer would have on the collected balances maintained at the bank. He also wondered where this would leave the typical outlet's bank compensation situation and whether there would still be enough balances to compensate the bank.

Other Alternatives

The treasurer's project team came up with two other alternatives for his consideration. The first alternative was to wire transfer the daily collected balance each day and the second alternative was to purchase a daily cash forecasting software package promoted by a cash management consulting firm. This would allow the daily collected balance to be forecasted and an EDT initiated in advance of the deposit so that the collected balance could be transferred the same day it is collected. The wire transfer would cost $20 for the combined incoming and outgoing wire, and the cost of the forecasting package was estimated at $10,000 plus an annual maintenance contract of $500. Although the treasurer realized that both of these alternatives would have the same impact on the level of collected balances, he wasn't sure how to compare the advantages and disadvantages.

Finally, as the treasurer was putting together his report consisting of his analysis of the various scenarios and alternatives, he wondered what the impact would be on the system he recommends when nationwide branch banking is put into place.

Appendix 10A

A Linear Programming Cash Transfer Model

The transfer scheduling problem is set up to minimize the total costs associated with the transfer scheduling decision. The two costs are the dollar amount paid in fees, FEE, and the opportunity cost of leaving average collected balances in excess of required balances, $k \times (ACB - RCB)$, in which k is the investment opportunity rate, ACB is the average collected balance, and RCB is the average required balance. The actual formulation for RCB was developed previously as a part of Equation 10-2. This form of the objective function allows the solution to not only solve the transfer scheduling problem, the dollar amount of the transfer, and the specific days that transfers are initiated, but also solves the fee versus balance problem by directly solving for the dollar amount of fees to be paid considering the collected balances left on account at the bank. The objective function set to be minimized is thus:

$$TC = FEE + k \times (ACB - RCB) \qquad \text{(10A-1)}$$

We next must create the constraint equation set. The constraint equations are developed below.

$$LB_t = LDEP_t - TF_{t-d} + LB_{t-1} \quad t = 1,2,3,4,5 \qquad \text{(10A-2)}$$
$$LB_t - LB_{t-1} + TF_{t-d} = LDEP_t \quad t = 1,2,3,4,5$$

Constraint set 10A-2 defines the daily closing ledger balance. The first equation set establishes the ledger balance relationship logic by setting the ledger balance for day t equal to the day t's ledger deposit ($LDEP$) less the transfer clearing (TF) plus the previous day's ending ledger balance. The d in the previous equation represents the days of delay from the day the transfer is initiated to the day the transfer actually occurs. The second equation set shown previously is the same equation, but is rewritten to be used in a linear programming problem. This formulation puts all the decision variables on the left-hand side of the constraint equation and all constants or fixed values on the right-hand side of the constraint equation.

$$CB_t = CDEP_t - TF_{t-d} + CB_{t-1} \quad t = 1,2,3,4,5 \qquad \text{(10A-3)}$$
$$CB_t - CB_{t-1} + TF_{t-d} = CDEP_t \quad t = 1,2,3,4,5$$

Constraint set 10A-3 defines the daily closing collected balance. The first equation set establishes the collected balance relationship logic by setting the collected balance for day t equal to the day t's collected deposit ($CDEP$) less the transfer clearing plus the previous day's ending collected balance. The second equation set shown previously is the same equation but is rewritten to be used in the linear programming formulation. This formulation puts all the decision variables on the left-hand side of the constraint equation and all constants or fixed values on the right-hand side of the constraint equation.

$$\sum TF_t = \sum CDEP_t \qquad \text{(10A-4)}$$

Constraint set 10A-4 constrains the total transfers in a week or some other fixed time period to be equal to the sum of the collected deposits for the same time.

$$(-M \times TD_t) + TF_t \leq 0 \quad t = 1,2,3,4,5 \qquad \text{(10A-5)}$$

Constraint set 10A-5 constrains the transfer day variable, TD_t, which is a 0,1 variable, to assume the value of 1 for day t if TF is greater than zero on day t. M is some arbitrarily chosen number that is greater than the maximum transfer.

$$\sum \frac{CB_t}{7} - \sum TD_t \left(SC/ECR(1-rr) \right) = EXCESS - DEF \qquad \text{(10A-6)}$$
$$\sum \frac{CB_t}{7} - \left(\left(\sum TD_t \times SC \right) - FEE \right)/ECR(1-rr) - EXCESS + DEF = 0$$

Constraint set 10A-6 establishes the definition of excess and deficit balance by relating the average daily collected balance to the balance required to compensate the bank for the transfer charges.

$$\left(\sum \frac{CB_t}{7} \right) \times ECR \times (1 - rr) + FEE - \left(\sum TD_t \times SC \right) > = 0 \qquad \text{(10A-7)}$$

Constraint set 10A-7 constrains the solution result so that the earnings credits earned on the average collected balance plus the fees paid are at least equal to the total bank service charges incurred by the transfer system.

PROBLEMS

A-1. Using the model formulation presented in this chapter, solve the cash transfer scheduling problem presented in Exhibit 10-9. Solve for the optimal dollar amount of fees, the optimal balance to leave at the deposit bank, and the transfer schedule and amount to be transferred using Microsoft Solver.

A-2. Using the model formulation presented in this chapter, solve the cash transfer scheduling problem 5 at the end of the chapter. Solve for the optimal dollar amount of fees, the optimal balance to leave at the deposit bank, and the transfer schedule and amount to be transferred using Microsoft Solver.

CHAPTER 11

Cash Disbursement Systems

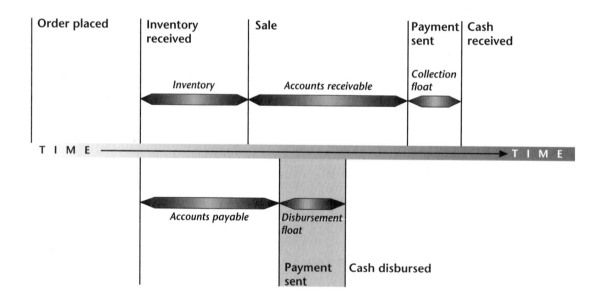

After studying the chapter, you should be able to:

- Identify the environmental variables influencing disbursement decisions.
- Identify the major disbursement mechanisms, relevant institutional aspects, and major implementation variations.
- Specify the major funding alternatives for disbursement accounts.
- Conduct valuation of payment mechanism decisions.
- State the contribution of and steps involved in disbursement location model application.

A company's decision regarding the payment methods and systems it will use in various situations is a major financial decision. The payment methods, disbursement banks, and locations chosen make up a company's **disbursement system.** In this chapter, we show how the payment dollar amounts and the location and type of collection system used by the party being paid influence whether a company opts for checks or electronic transfers. The payment methods offered by a company's banking system or by third-party service providers also constrains the paying company's flexibility. The disbursement system chosen affects value by changing the company's cost structure or by altering the payables cycle and thereby the cash conversion cycle. We already developed major aspects of payables management (Chapter 7), and the payments system and financial institutions (Chapter 8). Using this background, we analyze the major disbursement systems issues, the context of disbursement decisions, the major disbursing alternatives, funding the disbursement accounts, site location of the disbursement account(s), and global disbursing.

FINANCIAL DILEMMA

Is It Time to Go Electronic with Payments and Payment Information?

Many companies are wondering if they should emulate Sears, Roebuck & Company in its implementation of electronic disbursing.[1] After negotiating new payment terms with each of its suppliers, it quickly built up a significant volume of electronic payments: 1000 transactions, 60,000 invoices, and $500 million in payments per month. When evaluating electronic payments, Sears calculated that it would save $0.40 and the payee as much as $1.10 per payment by going through the automated clearing house (ACH). The savings to Sears as payor was based on the difference between the per-check cost and the ACH payment cost:

ACH CORPORATE TRADE PAYMENTS CHECKS

Item	Cost per Transaction	Item	Cost per Transaction
Process tape	$0.01	Check stock	$0.01
Tape delivery	$0.01	Processing	$0.08
Personnel	$0.03	Personnel	$0.14
Bank service fees	$0.02	Postage	$0.22
Tape transmission	$0.05	Bank charges	$0.14
Return items	$0.01		
Lost float	$0.06		
TOTAL	$0.19		$0.59

[1]Cited in The Globecon Group, Ltd. 1988. *Electronic Data Interchange and Corporate Trade Payments.* Morristown, NJ: Financial Executives Research Foundation, 1988.

DISBURSEMENT POLICY

Four guiding principles should drive corporate disbursement system decisions:

1. *Maximize value through payment timing.* Payments should be timed to add the maximum value to the company. Three observations help us see how to implement this principle. First, this is basically equivalent to asking the decision maker to minimize costs—particularly for the cash-poor company that is typically in a net borrowed (illiquid) position—by paying on terms but not before. Second, the principle implies that a company should take cash discounts when preferable, as demonstrated in Chapter 7. Third, within ethical, legal, and practical constraints, a company should take advantage of float offered by strategic location of disbursement banks. You may wish to refer to Exhibit 10-11 for a review of ethical aspects of cash management. The Federal Reserve System has largely eliminated "Fed float," which is the difference between the availability float experienced by the payee and the presentment float experienced by the payor. This implies that the payor's float gains come solely from a bank's or payee's pocket. Increasingly, abuses of float are considered unethical and poor business practice, because the payee and collecting bank(s) are damaged by it.

2. *Optimize the accuracy and timeliness of information.* Accuracy and timeliness of information are key attributes of disbursement systems. Optimizing a company's configuration of disbursement systems means getting accurate information in a timely manner without incurring excessive costs. Accurate funds balance information received early in the day adds value through access to investments with higher interest rates or better credit quality.

3. *Minimize balances in disbursement accounts.* Although some demand deposit balances may be necessary to support disbursements, as a rule these balances should be minimized. There are three possible exceptions to this principle. First, nonprofit organizations, governmental agencies, and sole proprietorships are permitted to have interest-bearing checking accounts and those with low average balances may not lose much interest by leaving funds in the disbursement account. Second, when the company contracts with its bank(s) for a bundled package of services, a global systems approach may negate this principle. The systems approach involves considering the *total* cost and reliability of bank services instead of negotiating the price for each service individually. For banks that have adequate cost accounting systems and will bundle services (sell services as a group), significant cost savings may be possible for the corporate customer. The appropriate focal point is the company's overall banking costs, not the cost of each individual service. Third, compensating balances needed to support a loan may limit how far a company can go in reducing disbursement account balances.

4. *Prevent fraud.* One of the fastest growing crimes in the United States is check fraud. Fraud prevention and detection techniques as well as greater use of electronic payments are disbursement system essentials.

Our central focus in applying these principles is the development of a disbursement policy. A company's **disbursement policy,** whether an informal strategy or a formal written document, specifies which payment mechanism to use for a given disbursement type or vendor, when to pay a given invoice,[2] and sets up guidelines for the disbursement system (including which bank(s) might be involved). The disbursement policy should reflect the

---

[2]We do not deal with the payment timing decision here, because we discussed managing payables and accruals in Chapter 7, including such decisions as whether to take cash discounts or pay at the end of the normal credit period.

application of the four guiding principles. It is important to understand the context within which policy decisions are made as a guide to implementing the principles.

CASH DISBURSEMENTS AND THE CASH FLOW TIMELINE

Six major factors influence a company's disbursement policy. The economy's payment system is the only factor that is external to the company and therefore uncontrollable. The remaining five factors are internal and mostly controllable: the company's philosophy, its organizational structure, its banking system, its information system and computer capabilities, and the predictability and size of its average daily net cash flow. Before examining these factors, we review the disbursement situation in the context of the cash flow timeline.

Disbursement Float and the Cash Flow Timeline

Corporations continue to pay most bills with mailed checks. From the time a check is put in the mail by the buyer, there are three major delays that together compose disbursement float: mail float, processing float, and clearance (availability and clearing slippage) float. The length of these components depends on the locations of the mail initiation and destination points, the time it takes the receiver to process it before depositing it at the bank, and the clearance mechanism used. Exhibit 11-1 shows mail, processing, and clearance float. Mail float varies from 1 to 5 calendar days, processing float varies from 1 to 3 calendar days, and clearance float ranges from 0 (e.g., "on-us" checks) to 3 business days. In the 1970s, companies quite often extended mail float through remote mailing points[3] or clearance float through remote disbursement banks, but pressure from the Federal Reserve (the Fed) and the Justice Department as well as negative publicity received by Merrill Lynch (which was paying East Coast vendors from West Coast sites, and vice versa) has largely curbed these practices. The Fed has greatly reduced the clearing slippage float, or Fed float, which occurs when it grants availability to the depositing bank before debiting the drawee bank (see Chapter 8). Cash managers now place less emphasis on maximizing float and more emphasis on better control and forecasting of disbursements to minimize idle account balances and prevent fraud.

EXHIBIT 11-1
Components of Disbursement Float

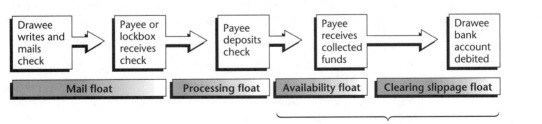

SOURCE: Copyright © 1997 by The Association of Financial Professionals. All rights reserved. Used with permission of the Association of Financial Professionals.

---

[3]Widespread use of the postmark date as the payment date allowed the remote mailing practice to succeed.

Payment System

The payment mechanisms available to a company, their current state of development and relative costs, the available clearing and settlement mechanisms, and the regulatory framework are all important parts of the payment system. Regulatory changes enabling US nationwide banking, European economic integration, and pricing for daylight overdrafts are noted in Chapter 8. At the beginning of 1995, the Federal Reserve implemented **Same-Day Settlement** (SDS), whereby any bank may present a check for payment to any drawee bank, and the check must be paid by the close of the business day. These checks must be presented by 8 A.M. local time at the drawee bank or its designated site (which may be the district's Fed processing center). The checks may be presented using **electronic check presentment** if the depositing and drawee banks participate in this banking industry-developed program. Electronic check presentment involves the bank of first deposit doing a magnetic ink character recognition (MICR) line image capture followed by an electronic transmission of that image to the paying bank (the paper check is forwarded through the usual channels), and if the check is presented after the 8 A.M cutoff, many banks will await physical presentment before paying the check. The Electronic Check Clearing House Organization (ECCHO) and the New York Clearing House Electronic Check Clearing System (CHECCS) are private-sector bank groups that participate in electronic check presentment. For example, about 37 banks in ECCHO participate in bilateral electronic presentments to each other. The three impediments to greater use of electronic check presentment are the following: (1) many banks and customers will not accept check truncation, so the physical checks must be transported and presented; (2) the laws in some states require the return of canceled checks; and (3) a paper check is often necessary to prove a court case.[4]

Ethics and Organizational Policies

Subsequent to the E.F. Hutton check-kiting fiasco, many companies have formulated or revised disbursement guidelines. A survey of 197 cash managers regarding certain practices that were thought to be either unethical or possibly illegal is shown in Exhibit 11-2. A majority of the managers thought that three practices were unethical and/or possibly illegal: altering checks so they have to be manually processed by bank personnel, drawing on uncollected funds when the paying bank has poor float tracking systems (Uncollected funds 1), and drawing on uncollected funds when not covered by an agreement with a bank (Uncollected funds 2). Less than half the managers thought these practices were unethical or illegal: rotating disbursement points (to add float based on the changed locations of their vendors' lockboxes), writing checks in anticipation of adequate balances by the clearing time, sending checks to a company's office instead of the lockbox designated by the vendor, paying East Coast vendors from West Coast banks and/or mailing points, overdrafts, use of systems designed to extend disbursement float, or using uncollected funds at any time (Uncollected funds 3). It is possible some of these practices have come to be accepted because of their prevalence in certain industries or during eras of high interest rates. However, it is difficult to rationalize the obvious detriment that many of these practices create for the payees and disbursement banks.

---

[4]2000. A new twist to the old "checks-to-electronics" question. *AFP Pulse* October:ec1. The Fed has proposed that two-sided images or "substitute checks" be considered legally equivalent to the original checks to get around these issues.

EXHIBIT 11-2
Views on Ethics and Legality of Disbursement Practices

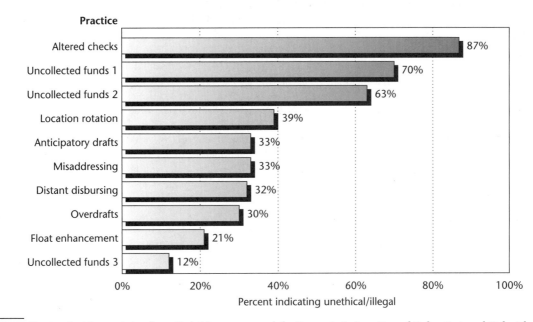

SOURCE: Reprinted with permission from *Cash Management and the Payments System: Ground Rules, Cost, and Risks.* The Globecon Group, 1986, Financial Executives Research Foundation.

Decentralization versus Centralization of Disbursements

We saw in earlier chapters how collection and concentration systems might be centralized or localized, and this distinction also characterizes disbursement systems. **Centralized disbursing** allows the corporate headquarters' staff to oversee each disbursement and possibly also initiate each disbursement. Centralized control is a means to ensure disbursement account balance adequacy because the cash manager at headquarters has a better view of the company's cash position than plant or divisional managers. Centralized data allow a more rapid and accurate reading of disbursement timing and amounts, providing a more accurate forecast and better decisions about such things as whether to take a cash discount and how much to "fund" the disbursement account. Generally, disbursement float is higher with central disbursing than when local operating units pay nearby firms from nearby banks. Elimination of duplicate disbursement accounts also reduces costs and deters fraud. If disbursement services are bundled with credit services, the greater size of centralized balances should enable the manager to negotiate lower total (credit and noncredit service) banking costs. Young, small companies and those operating at a single location are centralized and tend to deal with only one bank.

Decentralized disbursing allows payments to be made by divisional offices or individual stores, usually from accounts held at nearby banks. Companies with operations spread throughout multiple locations or even multinationally tend to be decentralized because of the need to pay wages and local bills or to disburse from an overseas subsidiary. Although decentralization may improve relationships with suppliers, who receive both payment and available funds more rapidly, it can severely hamper the efficiency and control of the disbursement accounts. Narrowed investment opportunities may result. The treasurer of ARMCO, a company that switched from centralized to decentralized disbursing, expresses some of his frustrations in the following example.

> You can never get your controlled disbursements [amount] early enough. If I'm managing anywhere between a $500 million and $1 billion portfolio, I'd like those numbers the night before, but that's not practical. The problem that we have now in our company is that we are decentralizing. I used to have control of the whole position. We worked with one controlled disbursement bank. Now we are setting up three or four divisions, and I'm acting as a short-term lender; an in-house bank, so to speak. Instead of having one system to worry about, I now have three or four. The investment process, which could have started at 9:00 or 9:30 A.M., still starts at 9:00 or 9:15 continues to around 9:45, or maybe a little later, 10:15 or 10:45, until you've got all four of these pieces, and you finally finish that puzzle up at 11:30. And, as you get later and later into the morning, [investment] rates seldom improve. Quality and supply [of attractive investments] diminish as the day goes on.[5]

Between centralized and decentralized disbursing is a mixed approach, which combines some features of each approach. Here, checks are issued and accounts reconciled at field operations, but they are written on a central disbursing account. Headquarters does bank selection and disbursement account funding.

Organizational Structure

Various functional areas within the organization affect a company's disbursement systems. By organizational structure, we are referring to the firm's functional areas and how they are interrelated, chains of command, informational and decision-making flows, and formal and informal groups. Businesses often construct organizational charts to indicate formal chains of command and the functional areas such as purchasing or sales that compose departments within the company. The impact on the disbursements activity comes mainly from treasury, purchasing, production, accounts payable, and personnel. These areas can influence disbursement policies and practices because each has responsibility for some aspect of the resource acquisition process. Exhibit 11-3 indicates some of these responsibilities. Because treasurers or cash managers are in a staff position, they do not have direct authority over any of the other departments.

Improvements in disbursement practices, particularly in switching to electronic ordering and payments, are highly dependent on the purchasing department's cooperation. A major study of selected purchasing tasks in different industries found that in a significant number of manufacturing companies, the purchasing area prepared financial forecasts; very often, the purchasing area coordinated its activities with the manufacturing and material planning areas (and, in a few companies, with the marketing area).[6]

Having other corporate personnel involved with disbursements presents both a problem and an opportunity. The problem arises when the fragmentation in control and oversight causes poor decisions to be made. Assuming equal quality and reliability, the purchasing agent might lean toward selecting the supplier based only on material cost, whereas using a supplier with a slightly higher material cost but who allows electronic ordering and payment might reduce total costs. The opportunity presented is for the

---

[5]1990. Focus on technology. *Journal of Cash Management* September/October:20.

[6]Robert E. Shealy. 1985. The purchasing job in different types of business. *Journal of Purchasing & Materials Management* 21:17–20.

EXHIBIT 11-3
Functional Areas Influencing Disbursements

ORGANIZATIONAL UNIT	PRACTICES/POLICIES INFLUENCED
Treasury Department	• Bank relationships • Bank services • Disbursement policies • Funding policies • Disbursement mechanisms • Account balance oversight
Accounts Payable Departments	• Disbursement records • Disbursement policies • Discount policies • Invoice information • Disbursement scheduling/forecasts
Production Department	• Status of inventory position • Initiation of orders, quantities • Initiation of charge-backs
Purchasing Department	• Negotiation for vendors, prices, terms • Discount policies • Assist in determination of orders, quantities • Vendor relations • Utilization of electronic purchase orders, payment
Personnel Department	• Negotiation of wages, pay periods • Localized payroll policies • Direct deposit policies

treasury area to captain and more heavily influence the overall ordering, invoicing, payment, and crediting process. Put another way, the finance function might gain greater control of the entire cash flow timeline. Given top executive support, the treasury area has the clout to push for implementation of improved systems. Recent changes in many US companies have given treasury departments a bigger voice in the reengineering of business processes.

Banking System

The ability of a company's banks to provide the appropriate services in the right locations at the right prices is a key to efficient disbursing. The starting point for many disbursement decisions is the flexibility and cost of the company's existing disbursement system, which is highly dependent on its disbursing banks' capabilities. The availability of fraud prevention methods such as "positive pay" is also a key consideration. We return to this theme later in the chapter. Many times, the greatest reductions in cost and accompanying increases in value come from modifying the company's use of banking services and/or banks. Just as important in today's payment environment is whether a bank has electronic data interchange capability; in other words, whether it is "EDI-capable." This means that the bank has the capacity to send "dollars and data" together so that the payment and invoice information do not have to be coupled by the payee, and the payee's receivables area can automatically process the cash application. Even companies with extensive experience using financial EDI have only been able to convert about one-third of their total financial transaction volume to EDI, but new browser-based applications promise to change this quickly. However, the Fed is making a low-end financial EDI translation software package available to the many financial institutions that are not EDI-capable. Called Fed°EDI, it is motivated by the Electronics Funds Transfer 1999 initiative to convert all Federal payments, except tax refunds, to electronic mode, and a National Automated Clearing House Association rule change. That rule change requires that on the request of the receiver (corporate customer), a receiving depository financial institution must provide all payment-related information within the addenda record *for corporate payments.*[7]

Treasury Information Systems

The capabilities of the company's management information systems are another limiting factor on a company's disbursement systems. The degree of automation of the accounts payable process varies across companies. Companies are more highly automated in payables than in any other cash management area. Automated systems ensure that bills are paid on time, without manual intervention, achieving substantial cost savings. One foreign subsidiary that had been paying each bill 30 days early estimates that it saves $250,000 annually resulting from implementation of an automated system. Ford Motor Company cut its payables processing staff from 200 to 40 after automation. A chemicals company set up a process in which a computer determines disbursement float for each check by matching issue dates with presentment dates. Some vendors yielding disbursement float as long as 10 days were identified and disbursement accounts were funded later, allowing a substantial reduction in account balances.

Computerization permits the payables area to speed account reconciliation, initiate and track orders electronically, and initiate electronic payments (PC-initiated ACH payments or wire transfers). The same system can be used by the cash manager to access account balances at concentration and field banks and initiate investment of excess balances or borrowing under prearranged credit agreements. Chapter 19 deals almost entirely with this important topic.

Cash Flow Characteristics

The final consideration affecting disbursement systems is the nature of a company's cash flows. Cash management systems create value because cash flows are unsynchronized, uneven, and uncertain. Here, our focus is the predictability of those flows and whether the company typically is in a net-invested or net-borrowed cash position. Relatively small or predictable flows generally moderate the need for establishment of sophisticated disbursement accounts with their higher fees. A company with predictable cash flows that is cash-rich prefers a disbursement system in which surplus balances are easily and inexpensively transferred into interest-bearing investments. The company might select banks having the most attractive sweep accounts, in which amounts above compensating balance requirements (or all positive amounts) are automatically transferred to overnight or other short-term investments. Companies that are typically cash poor, especially those with unpredictable cash flows, prefer banks that link disbursement accounts and services seamlessly to attractive credit facilities. Companies having relatively large cash flows might also bargain for volume-based pricing when negotiating with disbursement banks.

[7]See *The Financial Connection,* July 1998, available at the time of this writing at: http://www.fms.treas.gov/finconn/fcjul98.html.

DISBURSEMENT SYSTEMS

Each of the factors we have mentioned influences the disbursement system that a company establishes. The appropriate disbursement system for a small company with local dealings might be very simple, whereas a large multinational corporation may enhance shareholder value with a complex system. We now investigate simple disbursement systems, complex disbursement systems, and trends in today's environment.

Simple Disbursement Systems

Simple disbursement systems tend to be manual and paper-based. Standard payment services such as demand deposit accounts, payroll services, and drafts are especially attractive to companies that have small daily cash flows, untrained treasury personnel,[8] minimal computer facilities or skills, and localized business dealings.

These companies may also find it advantageous to use **account reconciliation,** a disbursement-related service in which the company provides the bank with a record of checks drawn. The bank essentially helps balance the company's checkbook, providing the company information regarding which checks have been paid. There are three common types of reconciliation from which cash managers may select, based on how much information they wish to pay for, beyond what is already being provided in a monthly statement. **Paid-only reconciliation** reports all paid checks by check number, with check number, dollar amount, and date paid. The latter can be compared with the check issue date to determine individual check's disbursement float. The total number of checks written and their dollar amount, as well as any stopped payments or miscellaneous debits to the account, also are noted. Companies with automated payables systems can receive this information via PC transmission or on floppy disks and use it to automatically update their payables records. Another form of partial reconciliation, **range reconciliation,** provides subtotals of all checks within a range of check serial numbers. This is especially useful for identifying disbursements from the same account but from several locations. **Full reconciliation** provides detailed "checks outstanding" information, along with the "checks paid" data from company-supplied check issue detail. It generally costs $30 to $40 per month per account more than partial reconciliation.

PAYMENT MECHANISMS.   The major paper-based payment mechanisms are checks and drafts.[9] Exhibit 11-4 summarizes the major attributes of each mechanism. Both are considered simple because they are easy to use, do not require a special computer or an advanced information system for payor or payee, do not require special skills to handle, and can be implemented by any financial institution.

Checks have several advantages, including their ability to be cashed or transferred ("negotiability"), their disbursement float, the stop payment feature, and the ability to include extensive remittance detail with mailed checks. Except for recurring, same-dollar payments, they remain the payment method of choice when paying individuals. Negatives include labor and paperwork costs to the issuer and delayed availability to the payee.

---

[8]A study of accountants in small- and medium-sized companies found that next to financial accounting, their largest job responsibility was cash/treasury management—especially in payables and receivables. Bradley M. Roof and Charles R. Baril. 1991. How does your accounting department measure up? *Management Accounting* April:39–42.

[9]The reader may wish to review the discussion in Chapter 8 on paper-based payment systems.

EXHIBIT 11-4
Checks and Drafts

INSTRUMENT	CLEARING PROCESS	USES
Checks (Regular demand deposit account)	Deposited by payee, cleared back to drawee bank when they are paid unless a stop payment has been issued or a forgery detected.	Any payment situation except when immediate transfer of value is required.
Drafts	Deposited by payee, cleared back to agent ("payable through") bank, which presents check to payor; if payor approves payment, bank pays check. Agent bank is charged for draft amount at the time of presentment, and may charge for float from that point until the payor authorizes payment. Alternatively, payor allows all drafts to be paid by agent bank (from demand deposit account), with refused drafts later credited back.	When authorization control is desired over field payments (as in property and casualty insurance, when signature of agent and dollar amount need to be verified) or off-premise purchases by an employee who cannot get the needed second signature on a check. Formerly used by auto manufacturers to get payment from dealers. Deters fraud and misuse of funds.

Despite the need to manually handle drafts, bank charges for drafts are as much as 75 percent lower than those for paying checks, primarily because banks do not need to verify signatures or do account reconciliations. Furthermore, because companies that use drafts usually issue many of them, the bank can process and present them as a batch total instead of individually. The issuing company bears full responsibility for record keeping and reconciling drafts issued, which it accepts because of the greater control and lower bank fees. On the downside, many banks will not cash drafts, making payment to individuals problematic. Drafts primarily are used for business-to-business payments because of consumer complaints about difficulty and delays in getting them cashed. Insurance companies use them for large-dollar field claims disbursements because of the extra control and fraud prevention.

DISBURSEMENTS FUNDING. A simple disbursement system also uses basic methods to fund disbursements. Disbursement account funding is provided by existing demand deposit account balances, deposits of daily cash receipts, or maturing investments. Companies may have an automated sweep account, in which balances in excess of the sum of compensation requirements and an average daily disbursement amount are taken out of the account overnight and invested in one of the bank's money market accounts.[10] Depending on the average balance in the disbursement account, the rate of interest earned might be $\frac{1}{4}$ (one-quarter) to $\frac{1}{2}$ (one-half) percent less than a benchmark rate (usually the Treasury bill or federal funds rate). In low interest rate eras, such as in 1993, some banks were inducing corporate customers to leave balances in the account by

---

[10]This is not actually an overnight investment, but a 24-hour investment made the next business day based on a day's closing balance. What if a wire drawdown is presented against the account or ACH debits are presented against the account the next morning? Many banks do not charge for an intraday overdraft, because they recognize that the necessary funds are coming into the account at the close of the day. In essence, they look at the intraday account balance as (collected balances + incoming sweep funds).

offering an earnings credit rate that was almost as high as the sweep account rate. However, the excess balances left on account are reduced by the Fed's required reserve ratio (presently 10 percent). This leaves only 90 percent of the excess balances to obtain credit.

Cash-poor organizations and organizations that have disbursement accounts at banks that provide their credit lines follow one of two complementary funding approaches. One approach is to leave excess balances in the disbursement account, a buffer that is replenished from daily cash receipts. If this is insufficient, the company draws on its credit line to meet disbursement needs.

COMPANY CHARACTERISTICS.   Companies using a simple disbursement system generally share several characteristics. First, they are often localized smaller businesses selling one or a few products. Second, a significant proportion of their funds transfers are local (e.g., paying employees) or between company units. Third, they often operate with a limited treasury department—with limits on skilled personnel, computers, and information systems. Fourth, their trading partners either have not invested in electronic order and remittance capabilities or have not applied pressure for electronic payments. Taken together, these four properties portray companies whose disbursement systems are characterized by paper-based payments and simple funding approaches.

Complex Disbursement Systems

Complex disbursement systems are characterized by a greater use of electronic payments, specialized disbursement accounts, flexible account funding, and greater control and information capabilities. The additional capabilities come at the expense of higher compensating balances or fees, but the increases in control, information, and net interest income outweigh the costs. Complex systems often are linked to the company's collection and concentration systems to maximize efficiency of funds movement. Finally, these systems often are the product of elaborate disbursement studies that guide bank selection and may recommend establishment of a disbursement network of strategically sited disbursement accounts.

PAPER-BASED PAYMENT MECHANISMS.   Regular checking accounts play a smaller role in complex systems as a result of inadequacies related to control, cost, and funding uncertainty. These problems are especially acute for larger companies. A company with centralized disbursements but dispersed locations that issues paychecks and supplier payments faces a *control dilemma*. Specialized checks called **multiple-drawee checks** have more than one bank listed on the face of the check; one of the banks is located near the disbursing location (for which the check is an on-us item). These are used by companies located in states that require paychecks be drawn on an in-state bank, when the companies use a centralized disbursement system with the primary disbursement bank located in a different state. The *cost dilemma* springs from the large number of small-dollar checks that a company issues. This can be handled by attaching a draft to the purchase order, called a **purchase order with payment voucher attached.** Good only up to a specified dollar amount, the draft (voucher) is filled out for the amount of sale and then detached and deposited by the supplier after the goods are shipped. These drafts save payables processing time and expense for the customer and eliminate supplier invoicing and receivables processing. *Funding uncertainty* arises because banks do not generally provide same-day presentment information on regular checking accounts; this has been addressed through specialized checking accounts called controlled disbursement accounts and zero balance accounts.

A **controlled disbursement account** is a checking account for which the bank provides early morning presentment information via a telephone call, fax, or computer message to the cash manager. The bank is able to ensure the total amount is accurate because it receives only one presentment daily[11] and does not permit same-day availability for electronic or physical presentments (direct sends or over-the-counter presentments) after that time. The major advantage to the disbursing company is the ability to maintain zero or minimal balances in the disbursement account. This means that no disbursement forecast need be made, and otherwise idle balances can be invested on an overnight basis for a greater yield than would have been earned in a sweep account. The company also picks up a small clearing float increase because the controlled disbursement account is generally located near a regional check processing center or at a country bank. For example, Cleveland's National City Bank runs its accounts through its Ashland, Ohio, affiliate. Companies are careful to avoid the appearance of maximizing clearance float, however, because the practice is considered unethical and it is in violation of Justice Department guidelines issued as part of its prosecution of E.F. Hutton.[12]

Controlled disbursement accounts are very popular with mid-sized and larger companies. A 2000 Phoenix-Hecht survey found that almost 90 percent of large corporations and almost 70 percent of mid-sized corporations used these accounts.[13] Greenwich

EXHIBIT 11-5

Use of Disbursement Services as Compared with Collection and Information Services

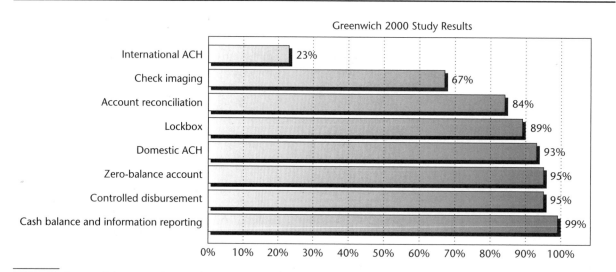

Greenwich 2000 Study Results

Service	Percentage
International ACH	23%
Check imaging	67%
Account reconciliation	84%
Lockbox	89%
Domestic ACH	93%
Zero-balance account	95%
Controlled disbursement	95%
Cash balance and information reporting	99%

SOURCE: Greenwich Associates, Greenwich, CT 06831. Based on Greenwich Associates 2000 study of the cash management practice of large US corporations. Reprinted with permission.

---

[11]Increasingly, as part of the Fed's High Dollar Group Sort program, the bank also receives a late-morning presentment of large checks. The Fed provides the bank with advance warning of this noon presentment by electronic notification of dollar totals so that the bank can pinpoint the day's total presentments and then communicate the figure to the payor while there are still good investment opportunities.

[12]A predecessor of the controlled disbursement account, the remote disbursement account is now used by relatively few companies. It purposefully picks banks in remote areas (hypothetically, "Sneaky Falls," Wyoming), which maximizes clearance float and minimizes prospects of over-the-counter check cashing.

[13]Cited in "Cash Management Trends for a New Century: Quality and Consolidation. A Report from the 2000 Cash Management Monitor Survey," by Phoenix-Hecht, 2000. Published online at http://www.phoenixhecht.com. Used by permission of Phoenix-Hecht, Inc. This survey targets companies of $40 million or better in sales.

Associates data (shown in Exhibit 11-5) shows usage of controlled disbursement accounts by midsize and large companies to be 95 percent, up from 81 percent in 1990, and 73 percent in 1986. Utilization rates are much lower for smaller companies. The economies of scale inherent in use of software for which a bank pays an annual license fee (representing a fixed cost) increasingly make the controlled disbursement account a competitively priced service. This, in turn, may make it cost beneficial for smaller companies to adopt the controlled disbursement account.

If the controlled disbursement account typically maintains a zero balance (which is actually negative by the amount of the day's presentments until the account is funded), it qualifies as one type of **zero balance account** (ZBA). A ZBA maintains a zero dollar balance because another company account, usually the master or concentration account, automatically funds the total presented against it each day.[14] By special arrangement with the bank, the company may have several ZBAs, each of which is funded from another account at the same bank or a correspondent bank at the time checks are presented (a setup with three ZBAs is depicted in Exhibit 11-6). At all other times, the balance is zero, meaning that no idle funds are left in the non-interest-bearing account. If the ZBA also receives deposits, any positive balances will be transferred to the master or concentration account. In total, the company can have lower deposit balances because the cash flow variability can be managed in the master account instead of holding positive balances in each individual account. Because of the risk to the bank that the corporate account holder will not have adequate funds for the automatic transfer into a ZBA, a pseudo-ZBA (perhaps called a target balance account) is sometimes established instead. This type of account has daily balances equal to an average day's disbursements. Some banks require ZBA account holders to also hold money market investment accounts and/or credit lines at the bank. Cash managers should realize that their company will have to pass a credit review to be approved for a controlled disbursement account or ZBA because the bank is exposed to the risk that a company will be unable to fund the account. The bank's exposure lasts from the time of presentment until the time of funding.

Should a company set up ZBAs or controlled disbursement accounts? The answer depends on many of the factors that we have highlighted throughout this chapter:

- Companies with centralized disbursing can set up controlled disbursement accounts or ZBAs at each subsidiary or division, then fund these from a central master account.

EXHIBIT 11-6
Typical Zero Balance Account Configuration

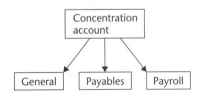

---

[14]Not all ZBAs are controlled disbursement accounts. Banks do not notify the ZBA holder of daily presentments but automatically debit the master or concentration account to cover the sum of ZBA presentments. With a controlled disbursement account, the advance notification gives the cash manager time to arrange a transfer, sale of securities, or credit line drawdown.

- Either type of account is advisable when a company's cash flows are unpredictable; the account should be tied to an investment account or credit line when cash receipts are volatile.
- Neither account makes sense if the company needs only one disbursement account and receives an earnings credit rate roughly equivalent to the rate at which the company could invest excess balances.
- ZBAs that upstream funds to a concentration account might be preferable for the company whose divisional personnel do not have the time or expertise to determine where to invest freed-up funds.
- A controlled disbursement account generally is used instead of a ZBA when the company has no master account at the disbursement bank, its affiliates, or correspondent banks—implying automatic transfers are not as easily accomplished.
- Companies with tight cash positions might prefer the extra control afforded by the controlled disbursement account, which provides extra flexibility by giving early-morning notification of the day's disbursements.

The number of accounts set up might depend on the number of decentralized disbursement locations and the company's desire to gain additional clearance float. Controlled disbursement accounts typically provide about half a day's additional float; Chase obtains this by disbursing from Syracuse instead of from the customer's concentration account location (New York City).

ACCOUNT FUNDING. Funding of disbursement accounts in a complex disbursement system is often based on a choice between several vehicles. ZBAs commonly are funded by intrabank transfers from master accounts or concentration accounts, overnight bank loans paid off by next-day funds transfers,[15] and money market funds. Controlled disbursement accounts might be funded in the same ways, as well as by maturing overnight investments (usually repurchase agreements), wire transfers, paper depository checks (DTCs), or ACH debits to a funding account. Until same-day settlement is available through the ACH system, companies will continue to leave monies equivalent to one day's average disbursements in the disbursement account. ACH funding is preferred over wire transfers because it presently costs $1 or less per transaction, whereas wire transfers involve a total charge of $15 to $17. Most companies use wire transfers or ACH debits for funding controlled disbursement accounts.

ELECTRONIC DISBURSING MECHANISMS. Companies with sophisticated disbursing systems not only use electronic funds transfers to fund disbursement accounts but increasingly pay employees and suppliers electronically via ACH transfers. We discuss the electronic payment alternatives from the decision-maker's perspective and then devote the following sections to the combination of EDI with electronic fund transfers and international disbursing.

Direct deposit of payroll is easily the most popular electronic payment application. Greenwich survey data indicates that two of five companies having sales of $5 to $9 million and four of five companies having sales of at least $250 million use payroll direct deposit.[16] One-half of all ACH transactions in the United States are electronic payroll deposits. The federal government has given a strong impetus to direct deposit by implementing it for a significant proportion of Social Security payments. The company's payroll department

---

[15]When preauthorized loan arrangements are used, the coverage of presentments achieves the same goal as an overdraft disbursement account, which is common in Europe but cannot be offered in the United States.

[16]Cited in "The Best Bank Monitor," Greenwich Associates, 2000.

FOCUS ON PRACTICE

PIZZA FRANCHISES SEND THE DOUGH ELECTRONICALLY   Franchises of a national pizza chain formerly placed their orders for supplies and ingredients with the parent company headquarters and later paid by mailed checks. Now they order and issue payment instructions electronically. They dial up the company's computer system and key in specific payment and invoice information such as the store ID number and payment amount using a touch-tone telephone. The parent company creates debit instructions and transmits them to its bank, which in turn initiates an ACH debit to collect the funds from the franchise's bank. The franchises much prefer the new system.

SOURCE: Presented in Walter C. Repak, "'What Check?'—Innovative Electronic Payments," TMA Journal, November/December 1995, pp 50–53.

provides employees' banks (for employees who have opted for direct deposit) with a computerized listing of employees, their Social Security numbers, bank account numbers, and payment amounts. This is done at least 2 days before payday. When communicating direct deposit information electronically, the company simply transmits the data to the region's ACH for all employees' banks that are members of the ACH.[17] Advantages include reductions in the number of lost and stolen checks; in payroll processing, check printing, and storage costs; and in disbursement bank charges. Personal computer software can automatically format employee payment data in ACH format. Now, direct deposit applications are being extended with increasing frequency to travel and entertainment reimbursement, dividends, pension payments, and interest. The federal government and Missouri, Pennsylvania, and New Jersey are beginning to use electronic benefit transfer as a way to reduce administrative costs and the risk of fraud.

Paying vendors through ACH debits and credits is increasingly attractive to companies. Although some suppliers are very inefficient in processing customers' check payments, mainly because of slow invoicing or slow check processing before deposit, the disbursement float advantage of paying most suppliers by check has been greatly reduced in recent years. The small remaining float must be weighed against the primary electronic payment advantages: reductions in bank charges, internal processing costs, and decreased potential for fraud or error. Paying suppliers electronically is most often accomplished through an ACH transaction. A major impetus to electronic payment is the insistence by the Internal Revenue Service that any corporation having $47 million or more of payroll taxes (withheld employee income taxes, Social Security, and railroad retirement contributions) per year *must* pay those taxes electronically through the Electronic Federal Tax Payment System (EFTPS). Forty states now have voluntary or mandatory electronic remittance of certain business and withholding taxes.

An **ACH debit** is a payment order originated by the payee, based on the prior authorization by the payor, which is routed through the payee's bank (originating depository financial institution [ODFI]). If the payor's bank (receiving depository financial institution [RDFI]) is a member of the same ACH as the originating institution, the bookkeeping entries to make the transfer are made by that ACH's computer. Otherwise, the ACH (now called the **originating ACH**), must transmit the payment order to the receiving institution's ACH (termed the **receiving ACH**). Presently, the major uses of debits are the collection of preauthorized dealer and distributor payments and internal cash concentration transfers. (See the Focus on Practice box.) An **ACH credit** is originated by the payor, so

---

[17]Nonelectronic direct deposit also is possible and is best accomplished by opening zero balance disbursement accounts at all the employees' banks, so that each bank can transfer funds by making on-us bookkeeping transactions.

EXHIBIT 11-7
Corporate ACH Payment Formats

FORMAT	USES	ADVANTAGES/DISADVANTAGES
Prearranged payments and deposits (PPD)	Direct deposit of payroll, automatic utility or loan bill paying services.	Normally settle in 2 business days; generally used only for crediting or debiting consumers' accounts.
Cash concentration or disbursements (CCD)	Movement of funds to concentration accounts or electronic payment of suppliers.	Electronic depository transfer checks (EDTCs or EDTs) created for next-day settlement. Simple data format and almost universal ability of banks to initiate or receive account for increasing utilization.
CCD plus addenda (CCD+)	The federal government uses this format in its Vendor Express payments. This format adds an addendum (up to 80 characters of computer-readable data) to the CDD format, enabling computerized relay of the remittance data into the cash application component of the company's receivables software.	Next-day settlement. Banks may not be able to capture and relay the addenda information, however.
Corporate trade exchange (CTX)	Used for intercorporate payments. As many as 4990 addenda records (an invoice might be one record). A standardized (ANSI X12) format that already is used by numerous companies in dealings with suppliers and customers via EDI.	Next-day settlement and standardized formats. The number of banks that can originate and receive has been an impediment to use, but that number is increasing rapidly. Companies can read and translate ANSI X12 for automatic processing and updating of payments. Encryption and authentication is feasible.

the routing bank (originating institution) in this case is the payor's disbursement bank. Direct deposit of payroll or dividends and payment of trade accounts payable are the most common uses of credits.

Companies initiate ACH payments by putting transaction details into standardized computer formats prescribed by the National Automated Clearing House Association and then transmitting the transactions to the originating institution. The four formats that companies can use, and their advantages and disadvantages, are listed in Exhibit 11-7. One of these formats, corporate trade exchange (CTX), is commonly used along with EDI. We conclude our discussion of electronic disbursement by noting three stages that a company's system might go through[18]: the enhancement systems stage, the substitution systems stage, and the metamorphic systems stage.

In the enhancement systems stage, the objective is convenience; companies are optimizing their disbursement systems based on other companies' proven experiences. There is very little application risk (possibility of this mechanism not working properly) or technology risk (possibility of mechanical failure in using the mechanism). In the subsequent substitution systems stage, companies begin substituting electronics for part of their paper-based systems. Companies entering this stage generally have a higher level of management support for electronic payments and are able to effect cost reductions by switching. There is no application risk and little technology risk. The final metamorphic systems stage entails changing the form or structure of the payments system. More and more companies are entering this stage, which involves changes in the way that a

---

[18]John Somers. 1989. A fail-safe ACH strategy—Beyond costs versus benefits. *Journal of Cash Management* November/December:74–78.

company does business as a result of new electronic capabilities. Examples of Exxon's applications at this final stage are point-of-sale debits and a customer-initiated payment entry system, which has taken the place of a lockbox system. Application risk and technological risk may both be significant at this stage, but the company adopting these applications may gain a competitive advantage in selling its products. The financial manager must assist top management in assessing the risk/reward tradeoffs inherent in advanced electronic disbursing.

Despite the cost advantages experienced by companies such as Sears, as documented in our chapter-opening financial dilemma, companies continue to resist abandonment of simple check-based disbursement systems. A 1998 Treasury Management Association survey[19] found that the despite the federal and state mandates to have tax payments made electronically (implying at least some corporate familiarity with electronic payments), many companies continue to resist electronic payments because of the lack of vendor (trading partner) capability to receive electronic payment with the associated remittance information, lack of systems integration, and costs of additional technology. Other surveys have indicated that renegotiating credit terms to share the float savings may be an issue. Regarding the latter, one midwestern hospital supply company added up to 15 days to its credit terms to induce hospitals to pay electronically. An impediment that was not mentioned, but which may surpass all others in importance, is the loss of flexibility when switching to electronic payments. This is especially true for payee-initiated ACH debits. It is much easier to stretch payables ("the check's in the mail") than to delay electronic disbursements. Then, when the check is actually mailed, the disbursement float further delays value loss. The 1998 TMA survey indicates that average mail float was 3.2 days, equal to the average of bank-clearing times for check disbursements.

ELECTRONIC DATA INTERCHANGE.   Prospects for electronic payments are improving because more companies are using EDI. **Electronic data interchange** (EDI) is the electronic transmission of purchase-related data such as orders, shipping notices, invoices, credits and other adjustments, and payment notices. The data are in standardized computer-readable format.[20] Companies began using EDI for electronic purchase orders and have begun transmitting invoices and shipping receipts electronically. An increasing number of companies were adopting **financial EDI,** which adds electronic disbursing via an ACH transfer to the process, but some of this usage is being replaced by Internet transaction initiation. One estimate of the total cost to payor and payee of handling the exchange of paper documents and making a single payment by check is $8.33 per payment, as compared with $3 for the handling of the same transaction using financial EDI. Phoenix-Hecht 2000 survey data documents 64% large company (sales of at least $500 million) and 50% "upper middle" company (sales of $100 to $499 million) usage of corporate trade payments. Note in Exhibit 11-8 the increased usage rates of direct deposit of payroll and corporate trade payments as company size increases. It is also noteworthy that from 1996 to 2000, usage rates of electronic disbursing products have increased dramatically for companies regardless of size.

In a situation involving product delivery and repeat orders, companies are increasingly paying under **evaluated receipt settlement** (ERS). In this electronic payment process, the buyer triggers payment on receipt of goods, not invoice arrival. Invoices are eliminated, and price and payment terms are determined in advance. Bar codes on

---

[19]Aaron L. Phillips, 1998, cited in chapter references.

[20]Electronic mail and facsimile (fax) transmissions are not considered EDI, because they are not in structured form nor are they computer-readable. They are, however, considered part of electronic commerce.

EXHIBIT 11-8
Trends in ACH Payments

ACH USAGE

	Middle Market		Upper Middle Market			Large Corporate		
	1999	2001	1996	1998	2000	1996	1998	2000
Direct Deposit of Payroll	73.2	83.7	68.0	73.8	91.1	77.5	80.2	96.5
ACH Concentration Debits	51.9	53.9	58.8	61.2	62.6	74.2	74.5	74.1
Corporate Trade Payments	36.4	41.9	34.4	41.5	49.9	53.6	59.9	64.2

SOURCE: Phoenix-Hecht Cash Management Monitor™

merchandise are scanned when received at the loading dock. That information is transmitted to payables to trigger payment. Evaluated receipt settlement is usually tied to EDI but can be used as a separate process. It is used primarily in the auto industry, but use is expanding to other similar industries. As payables management is increasingly automated, EDI and financial EDI or the Internet replacement for it will be more commonly used. We return to these topics in Chapter 19.

Disbursement System Trends

We briefly profile four related trends in domestic disbursement systems: comprehensive payables, purchasing cards, payables security and fraud prevention, and use of the Internet for ordering and payment. The first two are forms of **outsourcing,** or contracting with outside companies to do certain business functions, and are mainly cost-motivated. Security and fraud prevention is largely a response to the advances in technology that make it easier to issue bogus checks and the shorter availability times mandated under Regulation CC. The fourth trend represents a small but explosively growing mode of EDI and financial EDI.

Comprehensive payables, also called integrated payables, involves the outsourcing of part of or all of the accounts payable and/or disbursements functions. Some companies outsource payments, others outsource almost the entire payables function. For example, CoreStates, a large eastern bank, offers a "CorePay" service in which it receives from the company a daily payables file in an agreed-on format, then creates paper checks, ACH, or wire transactions for the company. Remittance information can be delivered with the payment or transmitted directly to the payee via a third-party company. Advanced notification may be optionally provided to the payees. From the company's perspective, this service may reduce the internal and external payables costs while streamlining or enhancing the company's payables system. For example, Thrift Drug estimates that it saves $7,000 per month by having a bank handle its pharmacy payments instead of having its own employees process the payments internally. A company may outsource more of the payables function by providing to its banks more extensive payables information, starting as early in the payment process as the original purchase order initiation. Some companies transmit trade payables, employee reimbursement, and employee benefit payment information. The data are provided to the bank, which develops a database of the company's payees, preferred payment methods, transit routing numbers of payees' banks, and other remittance information. The database is periodically updated with new payees or changes to existing payee profiles. First Union, another large eastern bank, notes four advantages for the paying company:

1. Increased accuracy—elimination of paper documents and manual data entry
2. Improved cash-flow management—the use of EDI and financial EDI, and the certain payment timing that results
3. Reduced administrative costs—computer exchange of data instead of human involvement
4. Proactive control—payables transmitted in EDI format include control totals, or if not in EDI format, the company faxes, mails, or e-mails control totals to the bank, ensuring file accuracy and an improved audit trail

Greenwich survey data indicates that 15 percent of companies having $500 million or more in sales are using payables outsourcing. With the recent emphasis on fraud prevention, and given that 90 percent of check fraud is committed against corporations (St. Goar, 1996), moving the liability to a third party is attractive.

Purchase cards, also called procurement cards, are another form of outsourcing. Because it costs from $25 to $45 to process a purchase order all the way through payment, companies are eliminating the requirement for requisitions and purchase orders and allowing employees to use a credit card to make purchases of small-dollar maintenance, repair, and operating supplies. Although they may not get much purchase detail on the monthly statement, companies appreciate having to only make one payment instead of hundreds or thousands per month for these items. A list of approved vendors may be kept on an internal database, often an "intranet," or the company may allow the employee to buy from any vendor accepting Visa, MasterCard, or American Express credit cards. Phoenix-Hecht survey data in 2000 found that although less than 35 percent of corporations used purchase cards, 49 percent of companies with revenues of $500 million or more (up from 25 percent in 1996) are using them. The main obstacles to further growth, the survey showed, were low management priority, loss of control, time commitment to implement, lack of systems resources, cost, and state sales and use tax issues.

One of the biggest trends in the past decade was the increased attention paid to payables security and fraud prevention. Check fraud has grown exponentially in recent years. Banks absorb much of the loss, but in contested cases, corporations usually end up with the loss liability. Some of the steps being taken to prevent fraud include positive pay, reverse positive pay, internal controls, and greater use of financial EDI. In the case of **positive pay,** a company sends its daily check issue file to its disbursing bank. Before it honors incoming checks, the bank refers to the issue file to see if the payee and check amounts match up. If they do not (e.g., because a check issued later in the day was presented as an "on-us" check), they contact the issuer to see whether the item should be honored. In the case of **reverse positive pay,** the disbursement bank sends the check presentment file to the company to see if all the items should be honored (a system that operates much like payable through-drafts). Internal controls include special check stock (e.g., checks that have the word *VOID* showing diagonally across them when photocopied), restrictions on check stock access (or use of laser-printed checks), and restrictions on the checks issued file. Most banks do not sign up a new controlled disbursement account customer without a positive pay or reverse positive pay agreement. Finally, some companies are moving toward ACH payments as a way of reducing the number of checks issued.

The Internet is probably the single biggest development within the electronic commerce field; most businesses are in the beginning stages of using it for business applications. The Internet may be thought of as a network connecting many computer networks, based on a common communications protocol. An organization known as CommerceNet is bringing a wide range of business services, including financial EDI, to the Internet. This is appealing because most companies already have access to the Internet or can gain access inexpensively, saving the cost of investing in specialized software and of paying a third-party company substantial monthly connect fees. Furthermore, the problems of differing corporate systems and their incompatibilities go away when using the Internet. For example, Lawrence Livermore National Laboratory inserts standard EDI transactions inside secure e-mail envelopes and mails them over the Internet. Digital signatures and encryption are used as security measures (these are discussed further in Chapter 19). Many mid-sized companies use the Internet instead of EDI to get around the message formatting and costs of EDI; Greenwich survey data indicates that 35 percent of mid-sized companies now initiate payments over the Internet. Furthermore, the Financial Services Technology Consortium has developed an enhanced, all-electronic check for use over the Internet. Businesses and consumers can create "digitally signed checks" (with the help of a secure memory card) and deliver them to authorized recipients by "sending" them (much like an e-mail message) over the Internet. Eventually, it is hoped that recipients will be able to authenticate the payments and deposit them immediately and directly into their bank accounts, without any kind of physical movement.

A separate trend that may use Internet delivery and facilitate positive pay is **check imaging.** Phoenix-Hecht survey data indicates that the most important uses of imaging technology are for long-term storage of paid items and on-line approval of positive pay items. Imaging for same-day retrieval of recently paid items is also moderately important. All three services are rated slightly more important for larger companies than mid-sized ones. (Imaging is also used on the collection side, with imaging of return documents and checks slightly more important than imaging for long-term storage of paid items.)

Integrated evaluation of the entire purchasing and payables process, not just the payment mechanism used, offers tremendous profit and value enhancement. Most companies that have reengineered their payment methods have also reengineered their receivables and payables, including using EDI to eliminate paper and manual processing and using purchase cards to eliminate purchase orders on small-dollar maintenance, repair, and operating supplies. After a brief discussion of international disbursing, we can see how to calculate the value effects of disbursement decisions.

GLOBAL DISBURSEMENT STRATEGIES

Our focus in presenting international disbursing is to highlight major elements affecting the international disbursement system: the payment system differences, the additional risks involved, and advanced techniques for handling intracompany funds flows. When appropriate, we distinguish between foreign disbursements that are between countries and those that are within a given country. More detailed information on international cash management is provided in Chapter 18.

Payment System Differences

One very important difference in disbursement systems abroad is the existence of interest-bearing demand deposit accounts, often with an automatic overdraft provision. This makes the minimization of disbursement account balances and careful control of those balances much less important. Not surprisingly, controlled disbursement accounts are rarely available outside the United States. One caution is appropriate: The interest rate on deposit balances may be relatively low, especially relative to the interest rate charged when the account is overdrafted.

A second difference is that disbursement float on checks depends greatly on what currency the check is denominated in and from where it is mailed. Checks must clear back to the country of the currency in which the check is denominated because there is no centralized settlement bank. If Ford Motor Company's West German subsidiary sends a dollar-denominated check to a French supplier, the check must clear back to the US bank on which it is written, even if that bank has a European branch. The clearing time could exceed a week in such a case. Furthermore, when a European customer sends a franc-denominated check to a multinational company in the United States, the mail time from a European city to New York City might also exceed a week. But within a given country, check clearing is usually quite rapid because of the smaller geographic area most countries occupy and the smaller number of banks within most foreign countries.

Third, there are two payment mechanisms that are much more prominent in foreign transactions. We have mentioned the giro system that is popular in Europe, which uses postal system clearing of many payments. This and other direct debit systems are very common abroad. We also noted in Chapter 8 the use of drafts in international purchases. Both mechanisms greatly reduce both the importance of and discretion over disbursement float. Value dating, a European practice in which debits of checking accounts may be back-valued to the date on which checks were issued, may further reduce disbursement float. These payment system differences are reflected in the Focus on Practice.

International Disbursing Risks

Two risks that must be carefully evaluated in administering international disbursements are country risk and foreign exchange risk. **Country risk** refers to the possibility of loss of assets resulting from political, economic, or regulatory instability in the nation in which business is being conducted. Studies of country risk are usually conducted by banks or specialized consultants. **Foreign exchange risk** is the possibility that exchange rates will move adversely, causing results of foreign business activities to have a reduced value when converted into the company's home currency. Various strategies are used to manage this risk. A simple strategy is to expedite outgoing disbursements when it is feared that a local currency will weaken (drop in value) against the dollar. The Brazilian subsidiary anticipating paying a dividend to its US-based parent will accelerate the disbursement if a depreciation of the cruzeiro is anticipated. It is hoped that this payment will be made before the depreciation occurs; if not, less dollars will be received on exchange.

Managing International Intracorporate Payments

There are two advanced mechanisms that companies can adopt to manage intracorporate payments: netting systems and reinvoicing centers. **Bilateral** and **multilateral netting systems** are centralized bookkeeping entries made to eliminate (net out) offsetting amounts owed by divisions or subsidiaries within a company. Only the net amount owed between the entities is actually transferred, and that transfer may only be a bookkeeping transaction, as opposed to an actual funds transfer. These systems greatly reduce the average size and actual number of transfers and simplify the monitoring and control of multinational operations. A bilateral system nets out any two divisions' charges, whereas a multilateral system nets out charges among several entities, with only the net amount owed to (or from) a subsidiary from all other company entities actually being transferred to (or from) that subsidiary. Cash managers should be aware that South American countries may prohibit netting systems as part of their system of foreign exchange controls, and some European countries require that the company establish a

FOCUS ON PRACTICE

POINTERS FOR MAKING INTERNATIONAL PAYMENTS   Disbursements outside one's home country can be tricky. Here are six pointers:

1. When you begin making payments internationally, look for a provider with global knowledge and international capabilities. It is often more efficient to initiate a new relationship with an international payments bank that has operations in the countries in which you anticipate doing business. This is so because using foreign currency checks for small value payments and wire transfers through a correspondent banking network for high value payments must pass through several banks, increasing expense and reducing speed. Furthermore, the global bank may be able to facilitate payables outsourcing as payment volumes grow.

2. Understand the payment mechanisms and the preferred payment method in each country where you conduct your business. Just because a payment mechanism is available in your country does not mean it will be in every country abroad. In Germany checks account for less than 8 percent of all payments made, both retail and wholesale, and in the Scandinavian countries less than 1 percent of payments are by check. Banks can help in this assessment, or you can go to websites such as that offered by the Bank of International Settlements to get this information.

3. Seek alternative ways of providing detailed remittance information. Using in-country local banks for local currency and cross-border payments within a region provides access to less expensive, local clearing systems, but at the price of an inability to move remittance data with the payment through banks and the local clearing systems. The remittance advices may be mailed separately or conveyed via the Internet, or use a provider that automatically produces and mails this detail for you.

4. Centralize your accounts payable and consider outsourcing options for all of your payments within a region. Establish a regional headquarters to centralize and control payables, possibly. Some companies outsource payments through a shared service central managed by a regional network bank that operates in the same countries as the company. The bank essentially acts as the company's regional central for funds disbursement.

5. Automate your payables function. Functions may be duplicated at various local sites. One company doing a treasury review found out that its decentralized disbursement process involved more than 800 locations issuing disbursement checks, and was able to both reduce risk and cut $400,000 in administrative costs annually (McDonough, 1997). When centralizing payments at a regional headquarters, efficiency is gained but the complexity of making payments in many different payment systems within central bank reporting requirements can be overwhelming. The solution is to automate payments, possibly by having a bank accept a single electronic file of both electronic and check disbursements in one format, which is then reformatted into the various formats required by countries' clearing systems. Or the company can use industry standard formats or common EDI message standards for payment instructions.

6. Work toward creating a "global payments factory." A "super center" may be able to handle a company's payments regardless of their destination worldwide in the not-too-distant future. Several regional centers can be tied together as part of the company's enterprise resource planning (ERP) system. A bank with global payments capability and linkages to all major local clearing systems can pave the way for making the necessary country-by-country modifications of payment instructions.

SOURCE: Michael Burn, "Making International Payments—Navigating the Course," *AFP Exchange* Winter 2000:62–64.

formal agreement when setting up a netting system. Netting systems usually are administered in-house but may be operated by one of the company's banks.

Reinvoicing centers include a netting system but also use a centralized foreign exchange monitoring and control capability. A **reinvoicing center** buys raw materials and final products from producing units of the company, then rebills (reinvoices) those items to foreign selling subsidiaries and noncompany customers. The major advantage of reinvoicing is centralized foreign exchange exposure, removing exposure from all subsidiaries. Lesser advantages include better control and monitoring of company cash flows, particularly intracompany payables and receivables, added flexibility of subsidiary-to-subsidiary or subsidiary-to-parent payments, and possible tax advantages if transfer prices are set at a higher level to compensate the reinvoicing center's services.[21] Strategic timing of payables and receivables, illustrated earlier, is greatly facilitated by such an arrangement.

OPTIMIZING THE DISBURSEMENT SYSTEM

We opened the chapter by defining a company's disbursement system as its payment methods and disbursement banks and disbursing locations and suggesting that the disbursement policy should maximize value through payment timing, optimize the accuracy and timeliness of information, and minimize balances in disbursement accounts. Ideally, the optimal disbursement system is assembled by formulating disbursement strategies and goals while considering the company's collection and concentration systems, selecting the appropriate disbursement mechanisms and account structures, selecting the best disbursement banking network that offers those mechanisms and accounts, establishing a disbursement security and control process, and specifying how and when elements of the company's disbursement system will be reevaluated. Profitability assessment and valuation of alternatives enable the manager to carry out the second and third steps by showing the financial impact of various alternatives. We demonstrate the financial analysis applicable to disbursement mechanism and bank selection by detailing four major decisions. Although it would be ideal to simultaneously evaluate all four, it is too complex to do so in practice, and the decisions are treated separately. The four major decisions are:

1. Selection of the optimal disbursing mechanism for a given transaction or transaction type.
2. Establishment of the disbursement network by specifying the number and location(s) of disbursement accounts.
3. Selection of the disbursement bank(s).
4. Selection of the funding mechanism(s) for disbursement accounts.

Selecting Optimal Disbursement Mechanisms

Recall our chapter-opening financial dilemma, in which Sears was used to illustrate the paper check versus ACH disbursing decision. We return to that situation now.

---

[21]Originally, reinvoicing centers were principally motivated by the lower tax rates in particular countries. The US tax code (subpart F) now provides that profits generated by reinvoicing are taxable at the US tax rate whether they are remitted or retained. The US tax code does allow a credit to U S corporate income taxes for taxes paid abroad, however, and a US-based multinational company anticipating foreign tax credits in excess of its US tax liability may benefit from reinvoicing. By charging higher transfer prices to subsidiaries located in countries with high tax rates, the subsidiaries' tax payments (and the associated credit) will be reduced. Although the multinational must pay tax at the US rate on the now-higher reinvoicing center's profits, the company saves on balance because the US rate is less than would have been paid in the high-tax countries.

FINANCIAL DILEMMA REVISITED

In evaluating the choice between paper check disbursement and ACH disbursement, we assume that the payment terms involve roughly equivalent timing of the transfer of value. Although not mentioned in the example, Sears would incur up-front investment costs to enable conversion to ACH disbursing; this initial incremental investment might be $40,000. Based on a perpetuity of 1000 payments per month, per-payment savings of 40 cents, and an assumed annual cost of capital of 10 percent (which we convert to a monthly rate based on simple interest), the net present value (NPV) of switching to ACH disbursing would be $8,000.19, as shown in the following equation.

$$NPV = PV \text{ of net cash flow} - \text{Initial investment}$$

$$= \frac{1,000 \times \$0.40}{(0.10/12)} - \$40,000$$

$$= \frac{\$400}{0.0083333} - \$40,000$$

$$= \$48,000.19 - \$40,000$$

$$= \$8,000.19$$

The present value of the cash flows, excluding the initial investment ($48,000.19 in this case) represents the most Sears is willing to pay to implement the new disbursement system. The ACH savings are warranted on economic grounds.

Our first illustration addressed *company-wide* disbursement practices. A second use of valuation techniques is to determine if electronic payment terms *offered by an individual supplier* are at least as attractive as the present check payment.[22] Here, the objective is to minimize the present value of the outflow. The electronic alternative is preferable if the present value of the outflow, including variable transaction costs, is less than it would be with a check. This hinges on the value transfer date specified in the electronic payment terms. We assume a longer period is given for payment initiation for electronic payments (n_e) than for checks (n_c) to offset the clearing delay (mail plus clearance float) advantage of checks. Relevant variables are defined as follows:

A = average payment amount ($)

n_c = credit period for check payment

n_e = credit period for electronic payment

i = daily cost of capital

c_c = clearing period for check payment

c_e = clearing period for electronic payment

VC_c = variable cost per check

VC_e = variable cost per electronic payment

The present value of the outflow for a check payment, PV_c, is given in Equation 11-1; a simple interest formula provides sufficient accuracy here because we are valuing only one payment:

---

[22]A full discussion of variants of the terms negotiated between supplier and customer is beyond our scope. See the Hill and Ferguson citation in the chapter references for a more complete discussion.

$$PV_c = \frac{A}{[1+i(n_c+c_c)]} + VC_c \qquad \text{(11-1)}$$

The present value of the outflow for an electronic payment, PV_e, is shown in Equation 11-2:

$$PV_e = \frac{A}{[1+i(n_e+c_e)]} + VC_e \qquad \text{(11-2)}$$

Which payment method would be preferable to the payor if the credit period for checks is 30 days and for electronic payments is 32 days, the payor's daily cost of capital is 0.02740 percent (equivalent to 10 percent annually), the clearing period for checks is 3 days and for electronic payments is 1 day, the variable cost per check is $2.10 and per electronic payment is $1.00? The accounts payable area informs us that the average payment is $4,500. Substituting the numbers into Equation 11-1, the present value of the outflow when paying by check is:

$$PV_c = \frac{\$4,500}{[1+0.0002740(30+3)]} + \$2.10$$

$$= \frac{\$4,500}{1.0090420} + \$2.10$$

$$= \$4,459.68 + \$2.10$$

$$= \$4,461.78$$

The present value outflow if payment is made electronically is found using Equation 11-2:

$$PV_e = \frac{\$4,500}{[1+0.0002740(30+1)]} + \$1.00$$

$$= \frac{\$4,500}{1.0090420} + \$1.00$$

$$= \$4,459.68 + \$1.00$$

$$= \$4,460.68$$

Because it involves lower present value costs, the electronic payment is preferable, because $VC_e < VC_c$. This simple model can be extended to include discounts offered by the supplier to induce electronic payment, which in effect is a price change. The relative costs of capital of the customer and supplier are very important in that case; the customer may have a much lower cost of capital than the supplier and be willing to take a lower price but pay immediately. The supplier and customer can negotiate the share of the gains accruing from electronic disbursement in that situation.

Selecting Disbursement Banks and Locations

Disbursement models used by banks and third-party consultants to assist companies in their selection of disbursement banks, and account locations are very similar to lockbox models. Instead of minimizing collection float, the model might maximize disbursement float, or at least specify the float characteristics of various account sites. The disbursement model differs from a lockbox model because it takes into account the location of mailing points as well as of drawee banks. It is usually not advantageous to have disbursement accounts in a very large number of locations because of the cost of the accounts. Disbursement models use as inputs a sample of the company's checks and a proprietary

EXHIBIT 11-9
Optimal Disbursing Locations versus Present Locations

Optimal System   Disbursement Micro Model Version 1.1   Page 3
Solution Summary   Copyright 1993 Phoenix-Hecht   1/08/97
Study File: SAMPLE   Phoenix-Hecht   15:36:38

Disbursement Micro Model
January, 1997
Sample Analysis

CURRENT SYSTEM

DISBURSEMENT LOCATIONS			TOTAL DOLLARS (30-DAY SAMPLE)	CLEARING FLOAT (DAYS)	FLOAT VALUE AT 10.00%
04500	Atlanta	GA	$ 888,450	1.03	$3,061
17500	Columbus	OH	315,913	1.10	1,160
		Total	$1,204,363	1.05	$4,222

OPTIMAL SYSTEM

48100	Newburgh	NY	$ 706,845	2.16	$5,082
64600	Rolla	ND	419,845	2.58	3,608
81500	Walnut Creek	CA	77,673	2.50	649
		Total	$1,204,363	2.33	$9,339

SOURCE: Reprinted with permission of Phoenix-Hecht, a division of UAI Technology, Inc., Research Triangle Park, NC.

database of clearing times. From this, using built-in computer algorithms, the model determines the optimal set of disbursement banks and assigns suppliers to these banks. To avoid the practice of remote disbursing and yet retain some clearance float, the model can assign all suppliers within a particular geographic area to the closest disbursement site.

We illustrate the process by showing computer output from the Phoenix-Hecht Disbursement Micro Model (Phoenix-Hecht is a division of UAI Technology, Inc., Research Triangle Park, NC), which runs on a personal computer. The model works basically the same as the lockbox location model presented in Chapter 9, except that float is now maximized instead of minimized. Relatively few companies strictly follow the model's recommendations because of the ethical issues involved in remote mailing and remote disbursing. Exhibit 11-9 shows a comparison of the model's optimal disbursing locations, as compared with the company's two existing locations. For the 30-day period sampled, the firm is paying $888,450 from its disbursement account in Atlanta, and $315,913 from its disbursement account in Columbus, Ohio. On average, the clearing float is 1.0336 days (the 1.03 days shown is a rounded figure) for the Atlanta account and 1.1016 days for the Columbus account. Although not shown, total dollar days of float can be calculated simply by dividing the number in the Total Dollars column by 30 and then multiplying that number by the number in the Clearing Float column. For Atlanta, this gives total dollar days of ($888,450/30) × (1.0336) = $30,610 dollar-days. The float value given in the rightmost column is calculated by multiplying the total dollar-days by the opportunity interest rate—10 percent in this example. Thus $30,610 × 0.10 = $3,061, as shown in Exhibit 11-9. The same procedure is followed for Columbus, giving total float value of $4,222. After implementation of the proposed three-point disbursement location

EXHIBIT 11-10
Optimal Mailing Sites

Optimal System	Disbursement Micro Model Version 1.1	Page 5
Destinations	Copyright 1993 Phoenix-Hecht	1/08/97
Study File: SAMPLE	Phoenix-Hecht	15:36:46

Disbursement Micro Model
January, 1997
Sample Analysis

ZIP CODE(S)	DRAWN ON		ZIP CODE(S)	DRAWN ON	
004-069	Rolla	ND	640-648	Rolla	ND
070-079	Walnut Creek	CA	650-652	Newburgh	NY
080-084	Rolla	ND	653	Rolla	ND
085-089	Walnut Creek	CA	654-655	Newburgh	NY
100-209	Rolla	ND	656-679	Rolla	ND
210-219	Newburgh	NY	680-681	Newburgh	NY
220-266	Rolla	ND	683-686	Rolla	ND
267-268	Newburgh	NY	687	Newburgh	NY
270-299	Walnut Creek	CA	688-691	Rolla	ND
300-319	Newburgh	NY	692	Newburgh	NY
320-334	Rolla	ND	693-714	Rolla	ND
335-342	Walnut Creek	CA	716-722	Newburgh	NY
344	Rolla	ND	723	Rolla	ND
346	Walnut Creek	CA	724-729	Newburgh	NY
347-427	Rolla	ND	730-758	Rolla	ND
430-433	Walnut Creek	CA	759	Newburgh	NY
434-436	Rolla	ND	760-769	Rolla	ND
437-439	Walnut Creek	CA	770-778	Newburgh	NY
440-455	Rolla	ND	779-847	Rolla	ND
456-458	Walnut Creek	CA	850-865	Newburgh	NY
460-462	Rolla	ND	870-885	Rolla	ND
463-464	Newburgh	NY	889-969	Newburgh	NY
465-497	Rolla	ND	970-999	Rolla	ND
498-639	Newburgh	NY			

SOURCE: Reprinted with permission of Phoenix-Hecht, a division of UAI Technology, Inc., Research Triangle Park, NC.

system, total float value will be $9,339—assuming the numbers used are accurate and no vendor changes collection point locations. The incremental value of the float gain is $5,117 ($9,339 − $4,222). The reason for the improvement is that the company adds 1.67 days (3.67 days proposed, as opposed to 2 days existing) to its average mail and clearance float. If the opportunity cost of funds is 10 percent as assumed, optimal disbursing adds $5,117 ($9,339 − $4,222) profit per year. Exhibit 11-10 shows the optimal mailing sites, should the company wish to use them to extend disbursement float. Exhibit 11-11 shows the savings by vendor areas, which might help the manager anticipate any adverse reactions suppliers would have because of increases in their collection float.

Phoenix-Hecht also has two products for assisting in disbursement bank selection. For any given bank, the TimesPlus™ spreadsheet worksheet gives the disbursement pricing and account analysis information. Combined with the company's disbursement amounts and cost of capital, TimesPlus calculates a cost/benefit report (Exhibit 11-12) for the bank, based on presentment float and annual service charges. The annual value

EXHIBIT 11-11

Float Increases by Vendor Geographic Areas

Optimal System	Disbursement Micro Model Version 1.1	Page 7
Float Comparison	Copyright 1993 Phoenix-Hecht	1/08/97
Study File: SAMPLE	Phoenix-Hecht	15:36:55

Disbursement Micro Model
January, 1997
Sample Analysis

VENDOR AREAS			TOTAL DOLLARS (30-DAY SAMPLE)	FLOAT IN DAYS			SAVINGS VALUE AT 10.00%
				CURRENT	OPTIMAL	SAVINGS	
045	Atlanta	GA	$ 43,217	.00	2.10	2.10	$ 302
060	Baltimore	MD	4,082	1.50	2.70	1.20	16
075	Birmingham	AL	4,669	1.45	3.80	2.35	37
085	Boston	MA	11,349	1.40	2.70	1.30	49
130	Charlotte	NC	50,730	1.00	2.60	1.60	271
150	Chicago	IL	501,449	.85	1.90	1.05	1,755
155	Cincinnati	OH	17,673	1.60	2.70	1.10	65
160	Cleveland	OH	27,726	1.40	2.90	1.50	139
175	Columbus	OH	5,462	1.50	2.05	.55	10
180	Dallas	TX	23,697	.95	2.40	1.45	115
195	Denver	CO	54,500	1.40	2.80	1.40	254
200	Des Moines	IA	7,482	1.40	2.70	1.30	32
205	Detroit	MI	29,922	1.45	2.70	1.25	125
300	Hartford	CT	11,455	1.47	2.90	1.43	55
315	Houston	TX	4,778	1.40	3.30	1.90	30
330	Indianapolis	IN	3,227	1.40	2.80	1.40	15
340	Jacksonville	FL	3,839	1.45	2.60	1.15	15
365	Kansas City	MO	2,693	1.42	1.60	.18	2
391	Little Rock	AR	426	1.50	3.05	1.55	2
395	Los Angeles	CA	14,376	1.50	3.60	2.10	101
405	Louisville	KY	4,309	.90	2.80	1.90	27
430	Memphis	TN	4,863	1.40	1.90	.50	8
440	Miami	FL	2,184	1.45	2.80	1.35	10
450	Milwaukee	WI	33,588	1.40	2.60	1.20	134
460	Minneapolis	MN	16,882	1.40	2.65	1.25	70
475	Nashville	TN	5,808	1.40	2.80	1.40	27
480	Newark	NJ	20,072	1.40	2.35	.95	64
495	New York	NY	33,616	1.40	2.60	1.20	134
525	Oklahoma City	OK	4,461	1.40	2.80	1.40	21
534	Orlando	FL	300	1.40	2.70	1.30	1
555	Philadelphia	PA	24,001	1.45	2.80	1.35	108
563	Phoenix	AZ	5,492	1.65	3.35	1.70	31
565	Pittsburgh	PA	122,507	.80	2.20	1.40	572
585	Portland	OR	697	1.55	3.00	1.45	3
620	Richmond	VA	3,687	1.40	2.80	1.40	17
640	Rochester	NY	4,605	1.70	2.90	1.20	18
670	Saint Louis	MO	59,947	1.43	3.05	1.62	324
682	Salt Lake City	UT	2,396	1.45	2.80	1.35	11
685	San Antonio	TX	6,208	1.45	2.80	1.35	28
695	San Francisco	CA	15,126	1.45	3.15	1.70	86
715	Seattle	WA	5,950	2.60	3.10	.50	10
765	Tampa	FL	1,409	1.45	3.05	1.60	8
800	Washington	DC	3,503	1.45	2.80	1.35	16
	Total		$1,204,363	1.05	2.33	1.27	$5,118

(continued)

EXHIBIT 11-11 (continued)
Float Increases by Vendor Geographic Areas

VENDOR AREAS			TOTAL DOLLARS (30-DAY SAMPLE)	CLEARING FLOAT (DAYS)	FLOAT VALUE AT 10.00%
045	Atlanta	GA	$ 43,217	2.10	$ 303
060	Baltimore	MD	4,082	2.70	37
075	Birmingham	AL	4,669	3.80	59
085	Boston	MA	11,349	2.70	102
130	Charlotte	NC	50,730	2.60	440
150	Chicago	IL	501,449	1.90	3,176
155	Cincinnati	OH	17,673	2.70	159
160	Cleveland	OH	27,726	2.90	268
175	Columbus	OH	5,462	2.05	37
180	Dallas	TX	23,697	2.40	190
195	Denver	CO	54,500	2.80	509
200	Des Moines	IA	7,482	2.70	67
205	Detroit	MI	29,922	2.70	269
300	Hartford	CT	11,455	2.90	111
315	Houston	TX	4,778	3.30	53
330	Indianapolis	IN	3,227	2.80	30
340	Jacksonville	FL	3,839	2.60	33
365	Kansas City	MO	2,693	1.60	14
391	Little Rock	AR	426	3.05	4
395	Los Angeles	CA	14,376	3.60	173
405	Louisville	KY	4,309	2.80	40
430	Memphis	TN	4,863	1.90	31
440	Miami	FL	2,184	2.80	20
450	Milwaukee	WI	33,588	2.60	291
460	Minneapolis	MN	16,882	2.65	149
475	Nashville	TN	5,808	2.80	54
480	Newark	NJ	20,072	2.35	157
495	New York	NY	33,616	2.60	291
525	Oklahoma City	OK	4,461	2.80	42
534	Orlando	FL	300	2.70	3
555	Philadelphia	PA	24,001	2.80	224
563	Phoenix	AZ	5,492	3.35	61
565	Pittsburgh	PA	122,507	2.20	898
585	Portland	OR	697	3.00	7
620	Richmond	VA	3,687	2.80	34
640	Rochester	NY	4,605	2.90	45
670	Saint Louis	MO	59,947	3.05	609
682	Salt Lake City	UT	2,396	2.80	22
685	San Antonio	TX	6,208	2.80	58
695	San Francisco	CA	15,126	3.15	159
715	Seattle	WA	5,950	3.10	61
765	Tampa	FL	1,409	3.05	14
800	Washington	DC	3,503	2.80	33
		Total	$1,204,363	2.33	$9,337

SOURCE: Reprinted with permission of Phoenix-Hecht, a division of UAI Technology, Inc., Research Triangle Park, NC.

of presentment float is calculated the same way as demonstrated in Exhibit 11-11; the service charges are based on the fixed account maintenance fee plus the per-item cost multiplied by the number of disbursements made. Finally, another valuable report is a disbursement profile for the operational and service features of a bank (Exhibit 11-13). All banks subscribing to the Phoenix-Hecht Clearing Study receive the disbursement profiles and can pass them along to actual or potential corporate customers.[23] The Bank

[23]All displays courtesy of Phoenix-Hecht. Phoenix-Hecht is the provider of the most complete clearing times study done in the United States and licenses the illustrated disbursement models to consultants and banks.

EXHIBIT 11-12
Cost/Benefit Report for Disbursement Bank

Total dollars in sample	$6,955,600
Length of sample period	30 days
Opportunity cost	10.00%
Average presentment float	1.74 days
Annual value of presentment float	$40,344
Less annual service charge	27,848
Net annual benefit	$12,496

SOURCE: Reprinted with permission of Phoenix-Hecht, a division of UAI Technology, Inc., Research Triangle Park, NC.

Administration Institute (BAI) has developed a comprehensive questionnaire for getting the appropriate information from potential disbursement banks. Companies have found this BAI disbursement questionnaire very helpful in evaluating qualitative as well as quantitative aspects of disbursement services.

Selecting Disbursement Funding Mechanism

Our final decision area is the choice of funding mechanisms for controlled disbursement accounts and zero balance accounts. This decision is very similar to the decision on how to transfer funds to a concentration account. The valuation analysis for this decision amounts to a simple profitability estimate. Basically, the lowest cost approach to funding the account is chosen, taking into account transfer costs and float. In almost every case, transfers from other accounts or ACH transfers are preferable to wire transfers because of the high cost of wires and the zero float aspect inherent in a wire's immediate value transfer.

Other Factors

In addition to the value considerations we have analyzed, several other factors must be taken into account when optimizing the company's disbursement system. The main considerations are the company's organizational form or structure, the size and frequency of disbursements, and the nature of the company's existing bank relationships. There are also risks inherent in any decision, because the moment a supplier finds out about your company's new disbursement sites, it may "deoptimize" the sites by changing lockbox or mail-to locations.

SUMMARY

In this chapter, we have learned about the major disbursement strategies used by companies. The objective of a company's disbursement system is to pay with the right method, at the right time, in an efficient manner. Efficiency was shown to depend on the company's banking options and characteristics of the company. Some of the most important characteristics are the payment system of the country in which the company is operating, the policies and philosophy of the company, the organizational structure, and the size and predictability of cash flows.

EXHIBIT 11-13
Disbursement Bank Profile

DISBURSEMENT SITE SURVEY™	CONTROLLED DISBURSEMENT REPORT
©2001 Phoenix-Hecht, a division of UAI Technology, Inc.	Survey 01-1: July 2001

Phoenix-Hecht Bank

68 Alexander Drive
Research Triangle Park; NC 27709

David A. Bochnovic

Executive Vice President
(919) 541-9339

S i t e Chapel Hill, North Carolina

Sample Financial Center, N.A.
- This site receives a second cash letter presentment from the Fed.
- The average total controlled disbursement presentment at this site is $88,000,000 per day.
- Routing Transit Number: 0311-0099   Federal Reserve RCPC Point
- *Phoenix-Hecht Bank, Chapel Hill, NC* appears on checks drawn on this site.
- This site is an affiliate or subsidiary of the provider bank.

Notifications

Last Fed cash letter received at 9:30 (EST)
Usual first notification time(s): 7:30 to 8:30 (EST) (89% of total dollars reported)
Usual second notification time(s): 9:30 to 9:50 (EST) (100% of total dollars reported)

Same day notification made by: ☐ NDC   ☐ ADP   ☐ BankLink   ☐ Chase Access Svc
                                ☐ Telephone   ☑ FAX   ☑ Internet   ☐ In-House System

Funding

Same-day funding upon notification (so that the company always has positive collected balances by the end of the day) is required.

Funding options: ☑ Wire Transfer   ☐ DTC   ☑ ACH
                            ☑ Internal Bank Transfer   ☐ Credit Line

Option(s) offered for dealing with the second presentment:

☑ Two notifications - one for each presentment   ☐ Delay funding for second presentment
☐ One notification - after second presentment   ☐ Delay funding for both presentments
☐ Split funding - first and second presentments
    funded separately

Check Images

☑ Same day on-line for exception items (PositivePay)   ☑ On-line archive of checks paid
                                                         ☑ Monthly CD-Rom

Account reconcilement product may be used with the controlled account.
Full account reconciliation statements are available 7 business days after month end.
Safekeeping of checks offered.

Over-the-counter presentments are accepted for same-day credit after the first daily notification cutoff.
This site does not accept correspondent direct sends for same-day credit after the first daily notification cutoff.
Over-the-counter presentments are accepted for same-day credit after the second daily notification cutoff.
This site does not accept correspondent direct sends for same-day credit after the second daily notification cutoff.

SOURCE: Reprinted with permission of Phoenix-Hecht, a division of UAI Technology, Inc., Research Triangle Park, NC.

Simple disbursement systems are paper-based and use basic funding mechanisms. Companies for which simple systems are appropriate are those with one or a few products, local operations and business dealings, and small predictable cash flows. If poorly managed, simple systems can be very costly; some companies' systems are so slow that by the time a check is ready to be disbursed, the company has lost the opportunity to take a cash discount.

Sophisticated disbursement systems are prone to use electronic payments, controlled disbursement accounts and ZBAs, and electronic funding of the disbursement account. Sophisticated systems also are more likely to be tied in with the company's collection and concentration systems and may be developed from a formal disbursements study.

We recommended valuation as the appropriate method for evaluating disbursement alternatives. Payment mechanism, funding mechanism, and account sites are all important aspects of a company's disbursement system, and the options selected have measurable impact on the cash flow timeline. The disbursements manager must also recognize qualitative dimensions of such decisions, however.

Several important differences in international disbursements also were noted. The use of drafts, overdraft checking accounts, and value-dated transactions are key differences. Companies use netting systems and reinvoicing centers to improve their grip on international funds flows.

Disbursement systems should be well coordinated with cash collection and cash concentration systems. The master account used in controlled disbursement is often the concentration account to which surplus cash flows from collections are directed. The entire collection-concentration-disbursement network should be carefully designed to ensure maximum efficiency and value contribution. Managing the financial risks of the company's cash position requires accurate and timely balance information and accurate short-term cash forecasts—the subject of Chapter 12.

Useful Web Sites

Association for Financial Professionals: www.afponline.org
BankOne: www.bankone.com/commercial/managecash/treasury/services/ecommerce
Greenwich and Associates: www.greenwich.com
Global Treasury News: www.gtnew.com
Phoenix-Hecht: www.phoenixhecht.com

Questions

1. What is a company's disbursement system, and why is it an important part of that company's short-term financial management? What principles should guide disbursement system decisions?
2. Remote disbursing was widely practiced in the 1970s because the Federal Reserve granted availability much more quickly than it was able to collect from banks in its clearing practices, leading to significant Fed float. Now that much of this type of float has been eliminated, at whose expense are companies achieving

their float gains when slowing disbursements? How does the first disbursement system guiding principle apply here?

3. Describe the three components of disbursement float, and indicate whether disbursement float on a given check is always the same as the collection float on that check.

4. Apart from questions of legality, do you agree or disagree with the surveyed cash managers' views on the ethics of the various disbursement practices? Use the AFP Standards of Ethical Conduct (Chapter 10) and the payables ethics discussion (Chapter 7) to support your position.

5. What are the advantages achieved by a company switching from decentralized to centralized disbursing?

6. Cash managers generally are part of a company's treasury department. With what other organizational units might cash managers interface to determine disbursement policy and to make day-to-day disbursements?

7. Some observers consider the selection of the company's disbursing bank(s) to be the most important disbursement-related decision. Do you agree or disagree? Support your position.

8. How do a company's cash flow characteristics influence its selection of a disbursement system?

9. What are the major differences between simple and complex disbursement systems? Construct a table showing the important differences.

10. Define a controlled disbursement account, and indicate why it is appealing to companies. How is it different from a ZBA?

11. Indicate the major electronic disbursing mechanisms.

12. How are controlled disbursement accounts and ZBAs funded?

13. What are the obstacles to greater use of electronic payments? Which of these is the single most important obstacle?

14. Summarize the payment system differences, risks, and intracompany techniques used in global disbursing.

15. What are disbursement models? How do they differ from lockbox models?

16. If a company radically changes its disbursement systems following the prescriptions flowing from the use of disbursement models, what would the likely effect on shareholder value be? What caution(s) might you offer regarding that anticipated effect?

Problems

1. Using the data from the chapter-opening financial dilemma, rework the NPV analysis for each of the following situations. For each situation in parts *a–d*, assume all data are the same as that given in the textbook analysis except the one item indicated. In part *e*, assume all four changes indicated in parts *a–d* are applicable. Make a recommendation either for or against the ACH disbursement system in each case. If you have access to spreadsheet software, you can save time by developing a worksheet or by using a preprogrammed worksheet.

   a. The initial investment is $60,000 instead of $40,000.

   b. The company makes 5000 payments per month instead of 1000.

    c. The annual interest rate is 5 percent instead of 10 percent.

    d. The per-payment savings is $1 instead of $0.40.

    e. All the changes in parts *a–d* are applicable.

2. Rework the problem 1 by first using the original data, but using compound interest instead of simple interest. Then rework the analysis for each change listed in part *e* from problem 1, again using monthly compounding instead of a simple interest formula. To what degree does the calculated NPV change? Is there any situation in which your recommendation changes?

3. ACD, Inc., a computer parts company, presently pays its largest supplier by check and is trying to determine whether to switch to electronic payment. Its present credit period is 45 days. Its opportunity cost for funds is a 12 percent annual rate. The disbursement float on its checks averages four days. It estimates the variable cost per check to be $8.35. Its average payment to the supplier is $20,000. Using ACH debits initiated by its supplier would result in per-payment charges of $3.00 and clearance float of 1 day. Its supplier has generously agreed to pay any switch-over costs necessary to make ACD "financial EDI-ready." The credit period for electronic payments would be 48 days.

    a. Should ACD switch to electronic payments?

    b. ACD decides not to go with the switchover. One year later, the supplier approaches ACD again and asks for a reconsideration. What are the present values of check and electronic payments if the annual opportunity rate on funds has dropped to 8 percent? How does this affect the relative attractiveness of electronic payments?

    c. Is there any reasonable opportunity cost of funds (i.e., less than 30%) for which your recommended payment method would change?

4. Consider the sample bank cost/benefit report shown in Exhibit 11-12. Assume that disbursements and clearings occur at a constant daily rate and that the "annual service charge" is a fixed expense.

    a. Develop a formula to indicate how the annual value of presentment float is calculated. *(Hint: Consult Exhibit 11-11.)*

    b. Using a financial spreadsheet program, program your formula into a work-sheet. Print out a copy of the worksheet using the data from Exhibit 11-12. What is the maximum annual service charge the test company is willing to pay to the sample bank?

    c. Using your computer worksheet, conduct a sensitivity analysis on the key input variables. Vary the total dollars in the sample from $3 million to $9 million in $1 million increments, and indicate what happens to the net annual benefit. Do the same for the opportunity cost (vary in 1-percent increments from 5 percent to 15 percent), then the average presentment float (vary in 0.5-day increments from 0.5 days to 3.0 days). Summarize your results. (You may wish to use the Data Table menu sequence in Microsoft Excel, the Data Table function in LOTUS 1-2-3, or Tools/What-if/2 variables function in Quattro Pro to simultaneously vary two of these three variables. Otherwise, vary the three input variables one at a time. (1) For help using the Excel data table, click on Help, then Microsoft Excel Help, then in the Type keywords menu box, type "data_table" without the quotes, then in the "Choose a topic" menu box double-click on "create a two-variable data table.")

    d. Reformulate your equation in part *a* to properly value the daily perpetuity of cash disbursements. (Convert the annual interest rate to an equivalent daily rate using an exact daily interest formula to reflect the compounding of interest earned on float-related savings.) Calculate the NPV of the sample bank. Comment on your findings here as compared with your analysis in part *a*.

References

Association for Financial Professionals. 2001. Study finds apparent paradox in procurement trends. *Finance IT* April:1, 6.

Michael Burn. 2000. Making international payments—Navigating the course. *AFP Exchange* Winter:62–64.

Business International. 1988. *Automating global financial management.* New York: John Wiley & Sons, 1988.

Beth A. Dubyak. 1996. Outsourcing payables at Thrift Drug. *TMA Journal* January/February:40–44.

1990. EDI Automates the Paystream. *Journal of Cash Management* September/October:60.

D.M. Ferguson and S.E Maier. 1984. Reducing the risk in the corporate disbursement system. *The Magazine of Bank Administration* June:28–42; July:66–72.

Richard Gamble. 1998. Breaking up over fraud. *Treasury & Risk Management* November/December:47, 49.

Christine Handt. 1999. Creating a global payments platform. *TMA Journal* May/June:52–54.

Ned C. Hill and Daniel M. Ferguson. 1988. Negotiating payment terms in an electronic environment. In Y.H. Kim, V. Srinivasan (eds): *Advances in Working Capital Management.* Greenwich, CT: JAI Press, pp 131–146. Vicki L. Jones. 1992. Corporate disbursements yesterday, today and tomorrow. *TMA Journal* May/June:41–44.

Steven F. Maier and Jack M. Meckler. 1990. The current state of controlled disbursing. *Journal of Cash Management* November/December:37–38, 40, 42–43.

Steven F. Maier and James H. Vander Weide. 1983. What lockbox and disbursement models really do. *Journal of Finance* 38:361–371.

Stephen G. McDonough. 1997. Internal treasury management reviews. *TMA Journal* July/August:28–31.

Betsy Olson. 1993. Corporate disbursing: A fresh look at strategies and applications. *Journal of Cash Management* March/April:8–12.

Aaron L. Phillips. 1998. Migration of corporate payments from check to electronic format: A report on the current status of payments. *Financial Management* Winter:92-105.

Walter C. Repak. 1995. "What check?"(Innovative electronic payments (1). *TMA Journal* November/December:50–53.

John T. Soma and Michael C. Tierney. 1987. Cash management after E.F. Hutton. *Bankers Magazine* 170:25–28.

Jinny St. Goar. 1996. Positive pay combats check fraud. *Treasury & Risk Management* September:47–48.

Gerald Stephens. 1998. Don't let your check fraud nightmare come true! *TMA Journal* May/June:28, 30–32.

Kathryn J. White and Mary McKenney. 1998. Payment systems that work. *TMA Journal* March/April:32–35, 36.

FOCUSED CASE
Structuring a Payment Decision

Joe Walker just got back from a 1-day conference put on by the regional ACH association in which all of the speakers and some of the audience participants bragged about the benefits of direct deposit. One comparative cost analysis pegged the cost of a payroll check to be $1.90, including $1.25 of lost employee time for those making a trip to the bank on company time, versus a direct deposit per item cost of $0.14. His company, which has only 25 employees, has always paid its employees by check. All employees are presently paid biweekly.

One of the pamphlets passed out at the conference talks about the experience the Social Security Administration (SSA) has had in persuading benefit recipients to accept direct deposit. SSA uses ACH credits to make the payments. Advantages the SSA used to "sell" recipients include:

- No paper check to be lost, stolen, or misplaced.
- No waiting for the check to be delivered.
- Assurance that your money gets to the bank, even if you are sick or traveling at the time the payment is made.
- No special trip to the bank or waiting in line at the bank to cash your check.
- Money is available the same day you would have received a check.

Joe is impressed with the fact that about 60 percent of the 43 million people who get Social Security already receive their benefit by direct deposit. Further, SSA estimates total savings to taxpayers of another $9.6 million a month if the 24 million Social Security *and* Supplemental Security Income recipients who now receive checks switched to direct deposit. Reading further, Joe sees that this estimate is based on an estimate that it costs SSA 42 cents to process and mail each check, as compared to 2 cents for direct deposit.

The combined carrot-and-stick approach SSA is using to enroll additional recipients in the direct deposit program interests Joe. A program recently inaugurated by SSA enables those now receiving paper checks to be automatically enrolled in direct deposit by their bank. The bank sends the recipient's account number directly to Social Security, and the individual does not even have to contact the agency. SSA tells new enrollees that they must be paid by direct deposit. Existing recipients were required to switch to direct deposit by January 1999. If they didn't have a bank account at that time, a special debit-only checking account was made available to them at a designated bank.

Joe finds the idea of mandating direct deposit appealing, but wonders if state law will permit it. He also wonders if his experience will mirror that of the Social Security Administration. Another question crosses his mind: Do all of my employees have bank accounts?

QUESTIONS

1. In what ways is Joe's situation similar to that of the Social Security Administration? Different?
2. What additional financial data does Joe need before reaching a decision? Nonfinancial data?
3. What is the effect of time value of money in this situation, if any?
4. Does Joe's company have to be "EDI-capable" to convert to direct deposit? What about his bank's capabilities? What alternative(s) will his company have for implementing direct deposit in the event that appropriate capabilities are unavailable?

INTEGRATIVE CASE—PART 3
Harker Telecommunications, Inc.

Harker Telecommunications, Inc., is a full-line telecommunications corporation. After graduating from college with a degree in electrical engineering, Ted wanted to join a firm with high-tech products where he could spend his efforts in the research lab generating new products based on the semiconductor. Harker Telecommunications, Inc., seemed to be the ideal employment prospect. It had an immediate opening in their research lab and the company was at the forefront of research.

Julie, Ted's wife, also graduated the same year with a degree in business and was able to join Harker as a treasury analyst. As the company grew, both Ted and Julie's careers took off. Ted is now director of research, and Julie has been promoted from assistant treasurer to treasurer. As treasurer, her main responsibilities are dealing with bank relationships and cash mobilization.

Julie is always trying to find a more efficient way to manage the company's cash receipts and disbursements between its two banks and two administrative financial centers. By December of 2001, Harker had grown into a large corporation with customers and suppliers nationwide. A listing of the typical monthly cash receipt and disbursement activity is shown below:

CHECKS WRITTEN	CHECK VOLUME	FACE VALUE PER CHECK
Vendors	8,000	$400
Payroll	10,000	$550
Deposits		
Customer Group 1	4,000	$1,200
Customer Group 2	7,000	$1,200

Harker is currently using two banks; Bank 1 is used only for a credit line facility related to the company's seasonal financing needs. Julie has learned that Harker has been paying a fee of $10 per month to maintain the account at Bank 1. However, all daily transactions are currently being conducted out of Bank 2. Julie has the following activity charges for both banks in her cash management project file.

ACTIVITY	BANK 1	BANK 2
Vendor checks	$.30	$.50
Payroll checks	$.40	$.60
Deposits	$.30	$.50
Earnings credit rate	8.00%	10.00%
Maximum fee payment	50%	50%
Monthly maintenance fee	$10.00	$20.00

Julie always makes it a practice to analyze the monthly account statements sent to her from the two banks. The basic statement format follows, showing the most recent month's activity provided for Bank 2.

Average ledger balance	$2,308,333
Less: float	$869,667
Average collected balance	$1,438,667
Less: 12% reserves	$172,640
Less compensating balances	$0
Average available balance	$1,266,027

SERVICES RENDERED	PRICE	VOLUME	AMOUNT
Account maintenance	$20.00	1	$20.00
Vendor checks paid	.50	3,367	$1,683.33
Payroll checks paid	.60	9,000	$5,400.00
Deposits posted	.50	10,217	$5,108.33
Cost of bank services			$13,328.33

Average ledger balance: Records all transactions (checks paid and deposits posted). Note that half of deposit and disbursement float is mail float and half is availability float. Also, average ledger balance is an average for the month, which is calculated by taking the total ledger balance and dividing by two.

Float: Float on the bank statement represents receipt or availability float on checks deposited in the bank but not yet cleared.

Collected balance: Average ledger balance less float. This is the average dollar amount of good funds in the bank account.

Average available balance: This is the balance on which the bank pays an earnings credit. It is the average collected balance for the month, less the 12 percent reserve requirement, less any other required balances for other activities such as loan compensating balances.

Julie is frustrated because the past treasurer seems not to have kept Harker's balances invested, leaving rather sizable funds idle. She also is irritated to learn that the company has been paying to maintain the account at Bank 1 but has not been using it. Because the company has no balances at Bank 1, the charge has been paid with a fee, violating the bank's requirement that no more than 50 percent of bank service charges can be paid by fee. In fact, the service agreements with both banks call for bank service charges funded by fees not to exceed 50 percent. She wonders, because no fees are paid to Bank 2 at all, whether the firm's idle balances cover the service charges, and if so, how much in overcompensation is being paid. As can be noted by the most recent account analysis statement, the average collected balance is $1,438,667.

Julie has been a member of the local chapter of the Association for Financial Professionals for about 5 years and she recently passed the Certified Cash Management exam. As she studied for the exam she realized it might be possible to reallocate her bank activity to solve some of her more pressing cash management problems. After all, the main reason she was able to determine that Harker was using Bank 2 was that the loan officer at Bank 2 always let the previous treasurer win at golf. Julie prefers fly fishing, so she feels that the time is long overdue to complete a careful analysis of Harker's cash management system. She requests that her bank provide her the following float data for all of her receipt and disbursement activity for a typical month. The data show the days of float between her two administrative financial centers, her two banks, and the two different types of check activity. In addition, the data reveal the differences in float between her two customer groups and her two banks.

i = Administrative financial center (1 or 2)

j = Type of activity
   $j = 1$, vendor checks
   $j = 2$, payroll checks

k = bank (1 or 2)

m = customer group (1 or 2)

d = disbursement float in days

r = receipt float in days

She readily notices that Bank 1 charges less to clear checks and to deposit checks, but offers a lower earnings credit rate. She wonders how these differences interact with the differences in float days generated by the two banks. At minimum, given the current allocation of activity, Julie decides that she should determine the appropriate balances to leave and invest the difference at her opportunity investment rate, which is 7.5 percent per year. Second, she would like to see if a reallocation of Harker's receipts and disbursements can generate additional investable fund balances while properly compensating the banks. Currently, the responsibility for writing and sending out vendor and payroll checks is divided evenly between the two administrative financial centers.

REQUIRED

1. Determine whether Harker should pay in fees, up to the maximum allowed, or pay by balances.

2. Given Harker's current activity allocation, determine if there are idle balances in Bank 2 that could be invested. If so, how much?

3. After studying the bank cost data, the receipt and disbursement float characteristics, and the relative earnings credit rates, intuitively construct a cash management allocation plan disbursing the required number of checks and depositing the appropriate numbers of check receipts among the two banks and two administrative financial centers. Your objective is to pay the appropriate fee levels, leave the appropriate collected balances in the banks, and to earn as much interest incomes as possible. You may wish to take the firm's current situation and incrementally change it to take advantage of any float variations or relative cost differentials.

4. Discuss the results of your intuitive plan relative to the firm's current cash management system.

Float Characteristics

ijk	d(ijk)	mk	r(mk)
111	4.5	11	6
112	5	12	3
121	6	21	2
122	3	22	5
211	4.5		
212	4.5		
221	4.5		
222	3		

For example, how much additional interest income net of activity charges were you able to generate and why?

5. Now optimize the cash management system using a mathematical optimization program such as Microsoft's Solver. Discuss the results of the optimized plan relative to Harker's current allocation plan and also relative to your intuitive plan. How much improvement did the optimized plan generate? What opportunities for improvement did the optimized plan take advantage of that you failed to recognize in your plan?

TECHNICAL NOTES FOR THE WORKSHEET MODEL LOGIC

Objective function: Maximize net profit

$$(k \times I) - fees - k \times (ACB - RBL - (SC - fees)/ecr(1 - rr))$$

k = monthly opportunity investment rate
I = average daily investment of surplus collected balances
fees = fees paid to the banks
ACB = average collected balance
RBL = required balances for loans
SC = charges for bank services
ecr = monthly earnings credit rate
rr = reserve requirement

Average ledger balance

X = number of checks written
FVC = average face value of checks
Y = number of checks remitted by customers
FVD = average face value of deposits
d = average days of disbursement float
r = average days of receipt float
ALB = average ledger balance
AF = average value of float
$$ALB = ((Y \times FVD \times (1 - .5r/30)) - (X \times FVC \times (1 - d/30)))/2$$

$$AF = Y \times FVD \times (1 - (.5r/30)) \times (.5r/30)$$

Number of checks paid = $X \times (1 - d/30)$
Number of deposits posted = $Y \times (1 - .5r/30)$

The days of receipt float are adjusted by 0.5 assuming that half the float is mail float and half is clearing float. Once the cash management system reaches a steady state, the number of checks paid and deposited will not be adjusted by the float because checks written from the previous month will clear in the current month, offsetting the checks written during the current month but not paid by the bank this month because of float. The changes in float that release cash or soak up cash then reflect the one-shot impact that a change in float causes. For example, an increase in disbursement float allows the payer to conserve a lump sum balance and keep it invested until float characteristics change. If the float characteristics don't change next month, no additional balances are created, but the firm can continue to keep the original balances invested.

The following decision variables are needed for an optimization formulation:

1. X(ijk)
2. Y(mk)
3. FEE(k)
4. Investments(k)

For an optimization formulation, the following constraints are needed:

1. Constraints to ensure that all vendor and payroll checks are written and all remittances are received by one of the banks.
2. Constraints to ensure that the average ledger balance is >= 0.
3. Constraints to ensure that the average collected balance is >= 0.
4. Constraints to ensure that each bank is properly compensated by a combination of fees and balances, and that the payment of fees does not exceed the maximum percentage allowed.

PART IV
Forecasting and Planning

Chapter 12   **Cash Forecasting**
Chapter 13   **Short-Term Financial Planning**

Once Part III is concluded, the financial manager now has a picture of the cash position of the firm based on daily cash collections and daily cash disbursements. The next step is to invest cash surpluses and borrow to cover cash deficiencies. However, before an investment and borrowing strategy can be developed, the financial manager must look to the future to assess the future cash flow scenario. Chapter 12 develops a process for developing cash forecasts. A framework is first developed, followed by a discussion of a variety of techniques to generate cash forecasts. Chapter 13 then introduces a short-term financial planning model that uses forecasts of cash flows to aid the financial manager in developing a short-term investment and financing strategy.

CHAPTER 12

Cash Forecasting

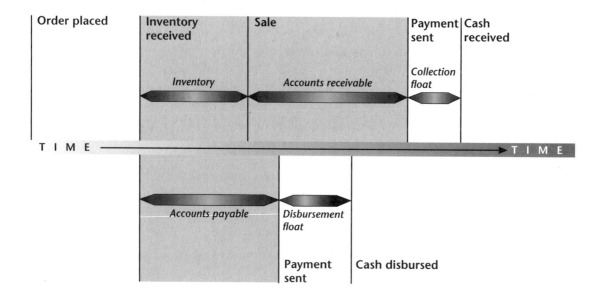

OBJECTIVES

After studying this chapter, you should be able to:

- Explain why companies should emphasize short-term cash forecasts.
- Indicate why the monthly cash budget is important to top management, and specify the two objectives for its development.
- Indicate how the process of daily cash forecasting differs from that used in monthly forecasting.
- Explain the receipts and disbursements, pro forma balance sheet, and distribution methods of cash forecasting.

Online toy retailer eToys missed badly on its sales and cash receipts forecasts in late 2000, estimating double the sales that actually materialized. This led to a revised "out of cash" cash position forecast within 3 months, a hasty plea for a "substantial cash infusion" that went unmet, and a bankruptcy declaration in early 2001. We noted in Chapter 2 that financial flexibility in the form of unused borrowing capacity can be critical, and eToys found itself without that flexibility. One wonders if eToys might have taken more drastic action to stem losses had its forecasting been more accurate. The treasurer of a consumer goods company asserts, "Cash forecasts are the most important tool for monitoring and controlling corporate cash. Without them, good cash management is simply impossible."[1] Furthermore, a 1997 survey of over one thousand treasury professionals found that within the whole realm of domestic cash management, knowledge of mathematical statistical forecasting techniques was the most important quantitative skill.[2] Four factors account for corporate emphasis on short-term cash forecasts.

First, cash forecasts drive the short-term investing and borrowing strategies. Selecting the maturity of a short-term investment, when to repay borrowings, or the size of a credit line to request all depend critically on the forecasted cash position. Alternating cash surpluses and shortages occur because cash receipts and disbursements are not synchronized.

Second, as noted in earlier chapters, the forecast is an important input into short-term financial policy decisions, including disbursement policies, credit terms, and bank selection; *making decisions along the cash flow timeline requires accurate estimation of flow size and timing.* Accurate anticipation of cash balances might be less important if the company has a controlled disbursement account (particularly when funding is automated) or has sufficient balances (e.g., to compensate for credit and/or noncredit services) to absorb uncertainties.

Third, cash forecasts function as a control device. Before the beginning of each year, the forecasting staff develops a cash budget, which is a forecast of cash flows and the cash balance for each month. As the year progresses, deviations of actual cash balances from cash budget projections signal the cash manager to investigate and take corrective action. Sales and marketing managers may use the cash balance variances as an early warning system

---

[1]Quoted in *Business International, Automating Global Financial Management.* New York: John Wiley & Sons, 1988, p 172.

[2]Survey reported in Phillips (1997), cited in chapter references.

when declining cash receipts are found to be the cause of the variance. Accurate forecasts can provide added value when they signal a cash shortage and the need for action before problems emerge, or corrective action as actual data become available. Sagner (2000) estimates that a $15 million portfolio will earn an added 1/5 to 1/4 of 1 percent (equal to $37,500 per year) and save an additional $5,500 in transactions costs when moving from overnight (sweep account) investing to 1-month maturities.

Fourth, effective risk management is impossible with forecasts of the cash-flow effects of interest rate changes, commodity price changes, and foreign exchange rate changes.

FINANCIAL DILEMMA
Which Cash Balance Should We Forecast?

The first issue a manager must face when establishing a cash forecasting system is how to define cash. Should cash be based on the company's accrual-based accounting records or on bank balances? Specifically, should cash as shown in the general ledger be forecasted? Or how about cash and cash equivalents as shown by the ledger? Another set of alternatives arises if, instead, the focus is on the cash balance on deposit at the bank. If bank balances are used, should they be bank ledger balances or collected (or available) balances, and how should compensating balances be incorporated into the forecast, if at all?

In this chapter, you are provided with a cash forecasting framework useful for monthly, weekly, and daily cash forecasting. We develop the techniques and approaches used in monthly and daily forecasting. The chapter concludes with a portrayal of state-of-the-art corporate practice. Material on useful statistical techniques and the main forecasting error measures is provided in the chapter appendixes. An integrated financial modeling approach that builds on this chapter's material is presented in Chapter 13.

THE CASH FORECASTING PROCESS

Even before beginning the forecasting process, the forecaster must give careful consideration to the nature and objectives of the task. In most companies, this work is done by the cash or treasury manager or one of their assistants. Because of the necessity of immediate access to transactions throughout the company that have a cash effect, other corporate personnel in operations, marketing, and purchasing should be consulted in this preliminary stage. Objectives for the cash forecast should be established. An example would be accuracy of ± 3 percent for the 3-month forecast. Other objectives might address ease of generation, speed of updating, flexibility, and documentation of procedures used. Having the forecast available to higher-level financial and administrative managers also might be desirable. Minimal requirements relating to what is to be forecast and how often might be prespecified or developed during the forecasting process. Here is the cash forecasting policy adopted by 3M:

> Accurately forecast cash sources and uses and take whatever actions are deemed appropriate so that adequate cash is on hand at all times and so that daily and long-term liquidity needs are met at the best price.

It is best to view the cash forecasting process as an integrated part of the company's financial management, not simply a separate activity. The forecasting process involves the company in anticipating possible futures and preparing for them. Consequently, the forecasting approaches we now discuss should be developed carefully and communicated to appropriate units within the organization. Carfang[3] lists as his first cash forecasting success factor "endorsement by senior management," which means senior management gives it priority, allocates necessary resources, management is involved in continuous improvement of the process, and can clearly articulate and endorse the cash forecasting process. Affected areas are those that provide input data for the forecast or units that should be alerted to the developing future of cash receipts and disbursements because of their ability to affect the cash flow stream.

Cash managers may be using treasury information systems (see Chapter 19), and real-time transaction data are now available for many financial variables. The Internet has allowed reporting of cash positions and upcoming payments to become faster and therefore forecasts are more accurate (Forster 2000). This allows managers to see their cash positions in (or close to) real time (Webb 2000), but that does not eliminate the need to forecast cash flows. That conclusion holds even for corporations with extensive supply chain interaction with trading partners. Knowing supplier and customer availabilities and needs reduces uncertainty in regard to disbursements and receipts, respectively, but does not eliminate that uncertainty. A good example is the severe shortage of components in the high tech electronics industry in 2000, which significantly affected cash flows for suppliers and customers, and was only partially anticipated.[4]

FORECASTING MONTHLY CASH FLOWS

The most important cash forecast from a top management perspective is the monthly cash forecast. This forecast shows cash receipts and disbursements on a monthly basis for a minimum horizon of one year; when done before the beginning of a new fiscal year, it is called the cash budget. The cash budget is a document showing anticipated cash receipts and disbursements for a future period, usually one year. This cash budget is formulated to be consistent with the company's operating budget, which specifies planned sales and operating expenses. Many companies extend the monthly forecast out to a 5-year horizon to correspond with the company's long-range financial plan. The level of detail and anticipated accuracy diminishes with longer forecast horizons, however. The Focus on Practice box illustrates cash forecasting, or cash planning, in the US Air Force.

We begin our presentation of the monthly cash forecast by arguing for its importance. This is followed by the underlying objectives and cash forecasting philosophy. We then consider the key decisions a forecaster must make, especially regarding the forecasting horizon, interval, and update frequency. The three major approaches to monthly cash forecasts are then developed in the context of numerical examples. Appendix 12B profiles the main statistical tools that can be used to assist the forecaster.

Importance to Top Management

The monthly cash forecast serves as a valuable planning tool for top-level managers. First, the typical billing and payment cycle in most industries is monthly. Second, the

---

[3]A.J. Carfang, "Cash Forecasting," May 20, 1999. Found online at: http://www.treasurystrat.com.

[4]Some analysts have contended that a movement to "sell-one-make-one" supply replenishment would eliminate inventory needs as well as all demand uncertainty, but this is not the case, as noted by Lapide (2000), cited in end-of-chapter references.

FOCUS ON PRACTICE

FUNDAMENTALS OF CASH PLANNING AT THE US AIR FORCE*   Cash budgeting is important in the public and nonprofit sectors as well as in corporate America. The rationale and some of the components of cash budgeting used by the Air Force Working Capital Fund (AFWCF) are presented.

- Actual cash inflows and outflows may vary from forecasted results, with AFWCF activities experiencing differing degrees of variability. To minimize the variance between actual and forecasted inflows and outflows, a cash manager must develop a carefully constructed monthly cash plan. The cash plan should begin with projected sales and the pattern of collections as key elements in estimating future cash flows. In addition, the outlay plan should provide a forecast of purchases, disbursements, capital requirements, and net outlays (disbursements minus collections). The cash manager should base his or her forecasts on a combination of historical experience, known events, expected values, and projected financial performance standards.
- A monthly cash plan should identify which activity groups require additional cash, where excess cash will accumulate, and the length of time either of these conditions may exist. The plan must consider timing differences for obligations, sales, billings, collections, and disbursements. Accurately forecasting cash flows affords management the opportunity to develop and subsequently implement alternative strategies for maintaining an appropriate cash position.
- Development of an effective cash plan requires the involvement of all levels of management. Moreover, effective development and execution of that plan requires integrated functional and financial systems that provide timely, accurate, and complete information throughout the organization. Unfortunately, the host of systems currently in use throughout the AFWCF activity groups and Defense Finance and Accounting Service (DFAS) are neither fully integrated nor use the same standard general ledger. The lack of integrated systems impairs the DFAS' ability to provide the Air Force with timely, accurate financial reports. Thus manual intervention at the technician level (e.g., through manual billings, reconciliation of error reports, and so on) and closer scrutiny of the financial reports are necessary to effectively manage cash.

Because timely, accurate, and complete information is not available, AFWCF managers must be proactive in identifying cash problem areas rapidly, implementing corrective actions, and effectively managing cash. Cash managers must be alert to internal changes (e.g., lower than expected

continued

monthly interval is generally thought to be adequate for anticipating funding requirements. Quarterly forecasts may mask important within-quarter cash receipt and disbursement imbalances, causing the business to underestimate peak funding needs and then arrange too little in external financing. Businesses often assemble the next year's monthly cash budget several months before the start of the year.

Once the budget year begins, two comparisons provide valuable information to management: a comparison of actual cash versus budgeted cash for the most recent month and for the year to date, and an updated cash forecast for the remainder of the year, which includes an explanation of any variance relative to budgeted cash.

The third benefit of the monthly cash forecast is that it alerts management to threats to organizational stability and survival. Particularly for smaller companies and nonprofit organizations that are growing rapidly and cannot tap external credit, the picture of deteriorating liquidity can give warning while adjustments in the selling rate or in the level of asset investment are still possible. However, small companies have organizational attributes that may hinder cash forecasting, as noted in the second Focus on Practice.

FOCUS ON PRACTICE

sales) and external changes (e.g., contingency operations, Department of Defense policy changes) that can affect sales and subsequent collections and disbursements. Proactive cash management can preclude an Anti-Deficiency Act (a law that limits the amount of funds available for obligation and expenditure in an attempt to avoid situations of deficient funding) violation and yield a more efficient and effective AFWCF business.

The cash forecasting requirement is legislated as part of the Department of Defense's Financial Management Regulation, which identifies the requirement to conduct cash outlay planning. Chapter 54 of the regulation identifies the requirement to develop a cash plan to facilitate the cash management process, and states that the plan "Shall consider collections, disbursements, appropriations, and other cash transactions based on Department of Defense component estimates. This annual plan will be initially developed during the budget process and will be an integral part of the budget document. In addition, a monthly phasing of the cash plan is required to monitor execution. A monthly execution review should lead to increased management attention to reduce costs, emphasize timely billing and collection of revenue, and timely disbursement."

Implementation of forecasting and related cash control functions work their way down to the Commander level. Various Commanders are responsible for managing their assigned activity groups, divisions, or subdivisions in a manner consistent with their assigned cash outlay targets. Responsibilities include:

1. Developing a cash plan consistent with approved budget levels for revenues or sales, expenditures or costs, investments, and credit policies;
2. Submitting cash plans for approval/disapproval as part of the budget submission or as required;
3. Distributing cash targets to subordinate operating activities;
4. Reviewing, controlling, and adjusting subordinate level cash outlay targets;
5. Preparing necessary budget schedules and analysis related to cash plans;
6. Monitoring collections, disbursements and other transactions to ensure adherence to approved division cash targets.

*SOURCE: Located online at http://www.afmc.wpafb.af.mil/HQ-AFMC/FM/FMRS/noframes/chap83a.htm Used by permission.

Monthly Cash Forecast Objectives

Two main objectives characterize the monthly cash forecast: accuracy and usefulness. The forecaster wants the forecast to be accurate enough to avert account overdrafts, to determine the amount of short-term credit lines, and to aid in the selection of investment maturities when excess cash is projected. Beyond some point, increased accuracy becomes more expensive, and the forecaster must weigh the improved accuracy against the increased cost. On a year-ahead forecast, +5 percent or +10 percent are common targets. The usefulness of a forecast involves more than its accuracy. A useful forecast allows timely and appropriate managerial responses to foreseen cash surpluses or shortfalls and specifies the variability of the cash flows and cash position. A forecast allows preemptive managerial responses when it is done with sufficient lead time and at an adequate level of detail. If overly aggregated, it may be impossible to ascertain why cash flow is inadequate or the cash position is deteriorating. With proper detail, the manager can alter the amounts of individual elements making up the forecast and observe the effect on liquidity. The forecast template thus doubles as a decision-making model.

ORGANIZATIONAL ASPECTS OF SMALL BUSINESS CASH FORECASTING   Small businesses often rely on an unsophisticated and informal cash forecasting approach. This happens for several reasons:

- Managers may lack the training and experience to appreciate the importance of cash forecasting.
- The limited number of management and employee team members may not allow for formal systems.
- Senior management experience may substitute for formal forecasting and review processes.
- The business may be easily managed by simple controls, lessening the need for forecasting processes.

In many small companies, the cash forecasting and review process is the weakest part of the cash management system, and analysis might be limited to a quarterly review of performance. There is less automation and more subjectivity than is the case with larger companies.

When small companies develop cash forecasts, they typically start with annual financial forecasts (already developed by the chief financial office [CFO] with department manager input). A monthly source and use of cash schedule then becomes part of an annual planning package that includes balance sheet and income statement projections. The package is approved by senior management, the Board of Directors, and all lending institutions. On a weekly basis during the year, departmental cash reports (weekly and year-to-date) may be generated by the controller and distributed to appropriate division heads. Then, perhaps on a semimonthly basis, revised cash projections (with horizons of 30 days, 60 days, 90 days, and 1 year) are developed by the CFO and reviewed with the top management team during staff meetings. To underscore the importance of cash to the organization, each staff meeting might begin with an overview of the company's current cash position. Senior management might proceed to discuss any large variances between forecast and actual, new large cash requirements, and how future cash needs should be prioritized. In smaller companies, managers must collaborate with each other to review and allocate cash.

SOURCE: Andrew R. Jassy; Laurence E. Katz; Kevin Kelly; & Baltej Kochar. 1998. Cash Management Practices in Small Companies. *Harvard Business School Teaching Note 9-699-047,* December 4.

The usefulness of the forecast is further enhanced if the variability of individual elements making up the forecast (or at least the variability of the bottom-line cash position) is specified. From this, management can calculate the probabilities of running short on cash[5] and the need for and potential magnitude of contingency plans. Risk analysis can

---

[5]If the distribution of the cash balance is normal, a "Z score" can be calculated by subtracting the average cash level from zero (or some other minimum cash balance), taking the absolute value of that difference and dividing the absolute difference by the standard deviation of the cash flows. This Z score is then compared with a critical value from a standard normal distribution table to get the probability of the cash position staying above the minimum cash balance. Assuming an average cash position during the year of $1,000,000, a standard deviation of $425,000 for the annual cash position, and a minimum cash balance of zero, the probability of running below zero during the year is calculated as follows:

$$Z = \frac{(\$0 - \$1,000,000)}{\$425,000}$$
$$= 2.35$$

The probability of staying above a $0 cash position based on this Z value is determined by looking up the probability associated with a Z score of 2.35 in the standard normal table. The probability of falling below $0 in cash is the one-tailed probability of (0.50 − the tabled probability of 0.4906), or 0.0094. The chance of running out of cash is then 0.94 percent, or less than 1 percent. Management will have to determine if this is an acceptably low risk; if not, more than $1,000,000 will have to be maintained in the cash account. The reader is cautioned that existing studies of cash distributions document non-normality, implying that this calculation only gives a rough approximation of cash shortage probabilities.

be implemented by formally recognizing that some items are better characterized as probability distributions, not point estimates (Tezel and McManus 1999). Contingency plans are actions that can be taken if and when necessitated by deteriorating liquidity. For example, one ladies wear retailer calls its stores and directs them to run 40 percent-off storewide sales when the chain's cash position is poor. Variability might be communicated by giving a range of anticipated outcomes, or more formally through sensitivity analysis or simulation.

Forecasting Philosophy

A company's forecasting philosophy affects the potential accuracy and usefulness of its cash forecasts and the techniques used in making the forecast. The philosophy refers to management's views on the number and type of cash forecasts made, the amount of money the company is willing to spend developing the forecast, whether the company prefers to develop the forecast internally or to use an external forecaster, and the preference for a quantitative (usually computerized) versus a judgmental approach to forecasting.

NUMBER AND TYPE OF FORECASTS.   Companies may have up to three types of cash forecasts: short term, intermediate term, and long term. These forecasts may range from as short as 1 day ahead to as long as 5 years ahead. Some companies do no daily forecasting because of lack of time, forecasting expertise, or ignorance of the value of the daily forecast. Likewise, some companies see the 5-year financial plan as meaningless because of its questionable accuracy.

EXPENDITURE ON FORECASTS.   Smaller companies or companies with stable or consistently positive cash flow patterns may not be willing to spend very much for the forecasting function. In any business, top management may not see the value of achieving accuracy in the cash forecast and consequently may underfund or understaff the forecasting function.

EXTERNAL VERSUS INTERNAL FORECASTS.   Companies also differ in their willingness to use an outside third party to develop part or all of the forecast. Macroeconomic forecasts and industry forecasts are commonly provided by consulting agencies such as Data Resources, Inc. (DRI), and Wharton Econometrics (WEFA). Even for cash forecasts, outside help is available in the form of customized computer forecasting models, some of which are integrated with the accounting and inventory management system. When done internally, managerial philosophy may dictate who does the forecast. Increasingly, line personnel are doing strategic long-term forecasting; these same personnel might also develop short-term and intermediate-term forecasts. The rationale is that line managers are "close to the action" and are responsible for implementing the plans, whereas a forecasting staff is neither. Even when the cash manager does all of the cash forecast, he or she is wise to check with appropriate operating personnel for up-to-date developments that will affect cash receipts or disbursements.

QUANTITATIVE VERSUS JUDGMENTAL FORECASTING.   Some managers favor judgmental forecasting approaches, whereas others favor quantitative approaches. Also called subjective forecasting, the **judgmental approach** relies heavily on intuition to adjust what is known about upcoming cash flows to arrive at the cash forecast. Quite often, preference for the judgmental approach arises from a very short forecast horizon, a distrust of computers, or an inability to understand the statistics that underlies quantitative models. The **quantitative approach** involves the use of a numerical model to forecast and is usually implemented on a computer.[6] Of course, these two approaches may be used in conjunction with one another, in which case the firm is using a **mixed approach.**

Forecast Parameters

The forecasting philosophies interact with other aspects of the forecasting situation to guide the forecaster in making some of the key decisions regarding the nature and format of the forecast. The four key parameters that we investigate here are the forecast horizon, the forecast interval, the update frequency, and the presentation format. These parameters, in turn, largely determine the forecasting approach used. Before making these key decisions, the forecaster must consider the volatility of the forecast variables and the company's existing planning methods. The inherent uncertainty of the forecast variables indicates whether sensitivity analysis or simulation should be incorporated into the forecast model. Existing planning techniques with which managers already are comfortable are the best candidates for the cash forecast, because managers are reluctant to base decisions on unknown methods. The degree of decentralization in the company also has an affect on the forecast process because of the required aggregation of field or divisional forecasts.

We consider the monthly cash forecast within five steps involved in forecasting: setting the forecast horizon and interval, identifying the variables that need to be forecasted and how they may be measured, formulating a mathematical model, estimating that model, and then validating the model. We expand on the third step, modeling the cash flow sequence, to include the statistical tools from which the forecaster can select. We also highlight practical concerns faced by the forecaster as each step is developed. Because the forecast interval is monthly, our first step reduces to specifying the forecast horizon.

FORECAST HORIZON.   The monthly cash forecast horizon, indicating how far ahead the cash balance is being projected, may range from the next month to the next 5 years. Normally, a forecast is prepared for each month interval within the horizon, but that would change to quarterly forecasts as the horizon moves beyond 2 years. Short-term forecasts might be made for the next 1 to 3 months. Most of the events giving rise to cash flows (sales and purchases, leases and rental contracts, dividend declarations and loan arrangements, and salary and wage amounts) already are known for the month-ahead forecast, making this the easiest monthly forecast. Partially offsetting the ease of this forecast is the level of detail required in that horizon, which we reconsider in our discussion of the variable identification step.

The second horizon for the monthly forecast is the intermediate term, encompassing forecasts for 3 to 18 or 24 months into the future. An example of a cash forecast with a 3-month horizon, without the detail behind the totaled cash receipts and disbursements, appears in Exhibit 12-1. This intermediate-term horizon may have cash flow forecasts tied directly to the organization's budget. One form of intermediate-term

---

[6]A survey conducted by Business International in the mid-1980s found that 13 percent of the responding firms had already implemented highly automated forecasting systems, 45 percent said they would have such systems within a few years, and fully 87 percent of the firms anticipated having some aspect of their forecasting computerized in the foreseeable future.

EXHIBIT 12-1
Simple Cash Forecasting Model

SIMPLE CASH FORECASTING MODEL

ITEM	JAN	FEB	MAR
Cash receipts	$125	$145	$150
− Cash disbursements	$85	$125	$135
= Cash flow	$40	$20	$15
+ Beginning cash	$35	$75	$95
= Ending cash	$75	$95	$110

forecast used by most firms is the cash budget. One survey of businesses indicated that 95 percent of large (Fortune 500) firms project a cash budget. The cash budget shows the anticipated cash receipts and disbursements for the next 12 months. A recommended accuracy target is ±3 percent, achieved 95 percent of the time.[7]

A possible third horizon is the long-term forecast, from 18 or 24 months to 5 years out. Longer horizons imply less forecast accuracy and greater applicability for statistical forecasting techniques. Far fewer companies provide a monthly breakdown for these more-distant horizons. Instead, the year-end cash balances or the quarterly cash flows might be projected. These longer horizon forecasts are mainly used for anticipating financing needs. Correspondingly, companies with substantial intrayear variability in their cash flows find it advantageous to estimate a monthly breakdown because they can identify peak financing needs. The peak needs dictate minimum amounts of short-term or medium-term financing to arrange, because actual needs may exceed anticipations as a result of forecast error.

VARIABLE IDENTIFICATION.   The shorter the horizon, the more detail the cash forecast will show—and therefore the more variables that will be included in the analysis. The company's operating, credit, inventory, capital expenditure, financing, investing, and tax-related decisions give rise to cash flows that must be identified and estimated. Depending on the horizon and the forecasting technique used, some of or all the following cash receipt variables might be included: cash sales, cash collections from credit sales, rent, interest, dividends from stockholdings, royalties, asset sales, and proceeds from new borrowings. Cash disbursements might include supplier cash or payables disbursements, wage and salary payments, pension fundings, utility bills, tax payments, capital expenditures, dividend payments, interest payments, principal repayments, and insurance premiums.[8] The forecaster may wish to order the receipt or payment variables based on whether management has any control over the payment amount and timing. This provides a tool for determining when and how to adjust collecting or paying patterns to alter the company's cash position if the plan is untenable or when the actual figures arrive worse than anticipated.

A related decision to be made here is the format of the forecast. One option is to use the Statement of Cash Flows format (as prescribed in Financial Accounting

---

[7]Target recommended in A.M. Cunningham, "The Accrual Addback Technique for Medium-Term Cash Forecasting," *Journal of Cash Management* September/October 1988, pp 46–50.

[8]An excellent "user-friendly" guide to practical aspects involved with specifying each of these variables is provided in the Loscalzo citation found in the end-of-chapter references.

Standards Board Statement 95).[9] One problem posed by the Statement of Cash Flows format is the proper treatment of compensating balances. It is best to treat these balances as cash and to provide disclosure on withdrawal restrictions.

When setting up the format, the forecaster should remember that the forecast will be used later as a monitoring device. Comparisons can be made more easily by setting up a financial spreadsheet model with separate columns for the actual amount, the forecasted amount, and the difference. The amount by which the actual amount is over or under the forecasted or budgeted amount is termed the **variance.** Large dollar or percentage variances stand out and command management attention and remedial action.

MODELING THE CASH FLOW SEQUENCE.   Once the variables have been defined and the forecaster has determined how each will be measured, he or she is ready to model the cash flow sequence. The present focus is limited to the three major approaches to monthly cash forecasting. Several statistical tools that can assist the implementation of two of these approaches also are developed. The three commonly used cash forecasting approaches are the receipts and disbursements method (sometimes referred to as scheduling), the modified accrual method, and the pro forma balance sheet approach.

The **receipts and disbursements method** involves looking up most of the data variables in company sources and estimating cash effect timing of noncash events. The major noncash events are product sales and material purchases. Usually, receipts are listed separately on a receipts schedule and disbursements on a separate disbursements schedule. The forecaster then combines the receipts and disbursements on a projected schedule (think of it as a projected cash flow timeline) according to anticipated cash flow dates. The layout used may vary from a desk calendar to a fancy computer spreadsheet that is linked to numerous other corporate spreadsheets. Periodic and accurate intracompany communications are critical to the accuracy of the approach. Accuracy suffers when the horizon extends beyond 1 month, however, and earlier inaccuracies compound into large errors for longer horizons.

FORMAT OF THE RECEIPTS AND DISBURSEMENTS FORECAST.   A template that might be used for receipts and disbursements is shown in Exhibit 12-2. Note that this format takes into account beginning and ending cash (both calculated by assuming no short-term investments or borrowings), the period's cash flows, and required minimal cash levels. The ending cash for 1 month serves as the beginning cash for the following month. The minimum cash balance is a function of management policy that a certain emergency cash stock be held and/or a compensating balance be kept at deposit banks. The bottom line, excess cash or required total financing, is a cumulative total. It represents the account balance of the amount invested or borrowed as of the end of the period. The net cash flow indicates how much additional money is invested or paid back (on outstanding loans), if positive, or the dollar figure of investments liquidated or additional lending, if negative.

An alternative format is to use the Statement of Cash Flows format for the receipts and disbursements, thereby classifying sources and uses of cash according to whether they are operating, investing, or financing cash flows. Because businesses must include the cash flow statement as part of their reporting, monitoring forecast accuracy is simple.

---

[9]Refer back to Chapter 2 for a detailed presentation of the Statement of Cash Flows (FASB Statement 95). Under the previous Statement of Changes in Financial Position (sometimes called a funds flow statement), many companies reported sources and uses of funds on a working capital basis, which disguised cash fluctuations and was of little help to the individual managing the cash position.

EXHIBIT 12-2
Template for Receipts and Disbursements Method

WORLD COMMUNICATIONS CORP.
CASH RECEIPTS AND DISBURSEMENTS

	JANUARY 2001	FEBRUARY 2001	MARCH 2001
BEGINNING CASH BALANCE	$ 1,500,000	$ 2,612,050	($ 1,552,238)
CASH RECEIPTS:			
Cash sales	$ 5,600,000	$ 3,500,000	$ 3,125,000
Cash collection of prior month's credit sales	$10,200,000	$ 8,400,000	$ 5,250,000
Cash collection of credit sales made 2 months ago	$ 5,750,000	$ 3,187,500	$ 2,625,000
Interest income received	$ 9,675	$ 2,535	$ 0
Cash dividends received	$ 375	$ 245	$ 165
Cash from asset sales	$ 0	$ 15	$ 0
Cash proceeds from long term borrowings	$ 4,500	$ 0	$ 0
Cash proceeds from equity issuance	$ 0	$ 0	$ 0
TOTAL CASH RECEIPTS:	$21,564,550	$15,090,295	$11,000,165
CASH DISBURSEMENTS:			
Cash purchases	$ 6,750,000	$ 2,720,000	$ 2,500,000
Cash payment for prior month credit purchases	$11,250,000	$ 4,533,333	$ 4,166,667
Cash payment for credit purchases made 2 months ago	$ 0	$ 0	$ 0
Interest payments	$ 250	$ 250	$ 250
Principal repayments	$ 1,000	$ 1,000	$ 1,000
Cash dividends paid	$ 0	$12,000,000	$ 0
Tax payments	$ 1,250	$ 0	$ 0
Asset acquisitions	$ 2,450,000	$ 0	$ 1,250,000
TOTAL CASH DISBURSEMENTS:	$20,452,500	$19,254,583	$ 7,917,917
CASH FLOW (RECEIPTS − DISBURSEMENTS)	$ 1,112,050	($ 4,164,288)	$ 3,082,248
ENDING CASH (BEG CASH + CASH FLOW)	$ 2,612,050	($ 1,552,238)	$ 1,530,010
LESS: Minimum cash balance	$ 1,000,000	$ 1,000,000	$ 1,000,000
CASH SURPLUS (IF POSITIVE)	$ 1,612,050	0	$ 530,010
CASH SHORTFALL (IF NEGATIVE)	0	$ 2,552,238	0

INTERPRETING THE RECEIPTS AND DISBURSEMENTS FORECAST. Take a closer look at Exhibit 12-2 to see how the treasury analyst can use it to make investing and borrowing decisions. The company starts the quarter with $1.5 million in cash and cash equivalents. Everything looks fine after January, with an ending cash position of $2.6 million. Even after subtracting the minimum cash balance of $1 million, there is a large cash surplus. This represents an investable balance, which usually is invested in short-term securities.

The large net cash outflow in February, mainly resulting from the dividend payment, causes the company to liquidate the short-term securities but still run short of cash. Even before considering the required minimum of $1 million, the company is unable to cover the cash outflow. The company will have to borrow more than $1 million to maintain the necessary minimum cash. March brings a net cash inflow, large enough to not only pay off the $1 million-plus credit line borrowing but also to invest in $530,010 of short-term securities.

Notice three uses for the monthly cash forecast. First, we are able to anticipate the need for credit and the amount of borrowing that should be prearranged to cover anticipated deficits. In World Communication's case, the company will likely arrange a credit line of at least $3 million because forecasts are never perfect and there might be a smaller receipt total or larger disbursement total in any given month. Or the company may allow the $1 million minimum liquidity to act as a buffer against unforeseen cash needs and only borrow $1 million. Of course, the analyst looks at least 1 year ahead, not merely the 3 months we show here. Second, we are able to project short-term investment amounts and, based on how long cash surpluses will persist, the allowable maturity of those securities. Normally, longer maturities bring higher yields, and the analyst will study the forecast for 6 or 12 months ahead to see how long projected cash surpluses will last. Third, the analyst might use such projections to help establish the company's target cash balance. The company might arrange more long-term borrowing to increase the year-beginning cash position and avoid short-term borrowing altogether. One caution when using monthly cash budgets: This forecast is giving us anticipated *end-of-month* cash balances. These could well mask larger intramonth receipt and disbursement mismatches, and the analyst will look at the historical pattern of cash flows to determine if these have occurred. This provides further motivation to arrange credit lines larger than the largest cumulative month-end cash shortage recorded in the cash forecast.

DEVELOPING THE RECEIPTS AND DISBURSEMENTS FORECAST.   The steps involved in generating the cash forecast using the receipts and disbursements method are straightforward. First, the analyst must develop or look up the company's sales forecast. Preferably, a range of sales forecasts can be developed, linked to likely scenarios for the horizon period. This enables the forecaster to incorporate the uncertainty inherent in the sales forecast through techniques such as simulation. To aid in the sales projection, the analyst may break down the sales revenue forecast into its components, unit sales and selling prices.

Second, the analyst lays out the incoming cash from cash sales, cash collections, asset sales, and other sources. But what if the company offers credit terms, and a given month's sales generates cash across several subsequent months? The historical or anticipated payment pattern for the company's customers is used to project the cash receipts from sales. Returning to the receipts and disbursement illustration (Exhibit 12-2) helps.

World Communications first projects sales for its product lines, which we show as a memo item at the top of Exhibit 12-3. Next, it studies historical collection patterns, to determine the uncollected balance fractions shown in the second column (these may already be available if the credit department is using them to monitor collection efficiency, as demonstrated in Exhibit 6-5). The key is to determine when cash is received from customers—when does the customer actually make payment? A few months of actual sales will also be included in our data, because of the lag in collections. Here, the analyst is making a projection in early January, so we have actual data from October, November, and December, in case there is a 3-month lag in collections. In World Communications' case, October's sales are not used, because 95 percent of sales are collected within 2 months, and the remaining 5 percent are uncollectible. World receives 32 percent in the month of sale, 48 percent in the next month (lag 1 month), and 15 percent in the second following month (lag 2 months). These proportions add to 100 percent only if World experienced negligible bad debt losses. Here, as noted, World fails to

EXHIBIT 12-3
Cash Receipts from Sales Worksheet

Projecting Cash Collections from Earlier Sales

				MONTH SALES			
ITEM	PROPORTION	OCT 2000	NOV 2000	DEC 2000	JAN 2001	FEB 2001	MAR 2001
MEMO: Actual (Forecast) Sales:		$20,000,000	$38,333,333	$21,250,000	*$17,500,000*	*$10,937,500*	*$9,765,625*
Cash Sales	32%				$ 5,600,000	$ 3,500,000	$3,125,000
Collections of Credit Sales:							
Lagged 1 Month	48%				10,200,000	8,400,000	5,250,000
Lagged 2 Months	15%				5,750,000	3,187,500	2,625,000
Lagged 3 Months°	0%				0	0	0
Total Cash Receipts from Sales					**$21,550,000**	**$15,087,500**	**$11,000,000**

°Bad debt loss rate is 5% (=100%−32%−48%−15%).

collect 5 percent of sales (100%-32%-48%-15%). To calculate January's cash receipts from sales, we take 32 percent of January's projected sales of $17.5 million, plus 48 percent of December's sales of $21.25 million, plus 15 percent of November's sales of 38.33 million. The sum is $21.55 million of cash receipts, which constitutes most of January's total cash receipts in Exhibit 12-2.

Third, cash disbursements, including payments to suppliers, employees, governments, and funds providers are arrayed. The difference in the cash receipts and disbursements gives the period's net cash flow. Many forecasters stop here, but, as shown in Exhibit 12-2, it is valuable to go beyond this to add beginning cash, arriving at ending cash. Financing and investments can be handled in two different ways. They can be treated as a residual: If ending cash is negative, arrange this amount of financing; if positive, plan to invest the surplus amount. Or the financing and investing can be built into the forecast to reflect planned financing and investing. Regardless, asset sales and capital investments should be included as separate categories under receipts and disbursements. Strengths of the receipts and disbursements method include simplicity, accuracy for near-term forecasts, and attractiveness as a monitoring and control tool. Weaknesses include the inaccuracy for forecast horizons greater than 3 months (largely resulting from the cumulation of early errors) and the over-reliance on the forecaster's judgment that typifies real-life applications of the technique.

MODIFIED ACCRUAL METHOD. A second technique useful for monthly forecasts is the **modified accrual method.** Sometimes called the accrual addback technique or adjusted net income technique, the approach begins with accounting reports or the operating budget and then adjusts these numbers to reflect the timing of cash flows related to these transactions. For small businesses and nonprofit organizations doing their income statements on a cash basis, very few adjustments to the operating budget or projected income statement are necessary. The only problem encountered in that case is if the historical tracker used to develop a forecast is invalidated because of faster or slower processing of invoices, checks received, and so on. In its simplest form, the modified accrual forecast is easily determined, as shown in Equation 12-1.

$$CF_t = NI_t + NC_t - CA_t + CL_t \qquad (12\text{-}1)$$

when for period t:

CF_t = cash flow

NI_t = net income

NC_t = noncash charges

CA_t = current asset change

CL_t = current liability change

EXAMPLE OF THE MODIFIED ACCRUAL TECHNIQUE. AMAX Coal has assembled the following pro-forma income statement and parts of its present and pro-forma balance sheets, which are shown in highly condensed form:

PRO-FORMA INCOME STATEMENT ($ MILS.)

Sales	$10,000
− COGS	$6,000
Gross Margin	$4,000
− Operating Exps.	$3,150°
Operating Profit	$850
− Interest Exp.	$25
Pretax Income	$800
− Taxes	$300
Net Income	$500

°Includes depreciation and other noncash charges of $145 million.

	PRESENT BALANCE SHEET ($ MILS.)	PRO-FORMA BALANCE SHEET ($ MILS.)
Current Assets:		
Cash	$10	Uncertain; assume to be unchanged.
Accts. Receivable	$970	$960
Inventories	$835	$820
LONG-TERM ASSETS		
Property, Plant, and Equip.	$12,000	$11,700
CURRENT LIABILITIES:		
Accounts Payable	$745	$730
Notes Payable	$500	$500
Long-Term Debt	$7,000	$8,000

Forecast Solution:

Net income and the noncash charges are taken from the projected income statement. Changes in current assets and current liabilities are calculated as (Projected Balance Sheet Amount − Present Balance Sheet Amount). If AMAX Coal, Inc., projects net income of $500 million, noncash charges of $145 million, decreases in current assets of $25 million (in this case, the change in accounts receivable plus change in inventories), and decreases in current liabilities of $15 million (here, the change in accounts payable), cash flow for the period using our simple equation is:

$$CF_t = \$500 + \$145 - (-\$25) + (-\$15) = \$655 \text{ million}$$

Current asset changes are subtracted because increases in items such as inventories drain cash flow, and current liability changes are added because they represent sources of cash flow. Typical noncash charges are depreciation, amortization of intangibles, and gains or losses on asset sales. Notice that the cash flow formula presented is an operating cash flow forecast. The change, if any, in long-term assets, long-term liabilities, and equity will not affect the forecasted cash flow. If desired, Equation 12-1 easily can be expanded to include anticipated dividends, loan interest or principal payments, acquisitions, and other episodic cash flows. At that point, however, it might be easier to simply change to a projected statement of cash flow format.

The major strength of the modified accrual technique is ease of implementation: The data are already available, in most cases, in the form of a budget or projected income statement. The adjustments to net income to arrive at cash flow are easily made, as shown above. The technique is also relatively accurate for intermediate-term forecasting, when compared with other techniques. However, it suffers from inaccuracy in the short-run horizons and may lack sufficient detail to ensure accuracy.[10]

PRO FORMA BALANCE SHEET METHOD.   The pro forma balance sheet approach to generating a cash forecast involves determination of the amount of cash and marketable securities by computing the difference between projected assets (excluding cash and marketable securities) and the sum of projected liabilities and owner's equity. This approach, very popular for medium-term and long-term forecasting, is illustrated in Exhibit 12-4.

In projecting the balance sheet, current liabilities and noncash assets might be predicted as a percentage of anticipated sales, and the long-term liabilities and common stock assumed to remain constant. The change in retained earnings is based on anticipated net income less planned cash dividends. If we subtract the sum of liabilities and owners' equity from noncash assets, we get a residual amount labeled "cash and marketable securities," which is our cash forecast. If this amount is negative, additional financing will have to be arranged. Then the new financing amount is plugged into the liability section; interest expense, net income, and additions to retained earnings recomputed and a new cash amount calculated. In other cases, the figure may be a large positive amount, in which case some previous borrowings may be paid down, stock repurchased, or greater expansion in fixed assets arranged.[11] The fact that the forecast leads naturally to financial planning demonstrates the value of longer-term cash forecasts. The pro forma balance sheet approach is well suited for these longer-range cash forecasts.

Basically, the pro forma balance sheet represents a crude approximation of sources and uses of funds, with funds defined as cash and marketable securities. Liability and equity accounts represent sources of funds; asset amounts represent uses of funds. The major strength of this forecasting approach is its ease of implementation. The major weakness is the difficulty in making accurate monthly forecasts by using balance sheet projections. For annual totals, the technique is acceptable, but for monthly forecasts, the

---

[10]In response to this weakness, Alan Cunningham has devised a more elaborate modified accrual technique that he terms the *accrual addback technique* (AAT). Adjusting for uncontrollable elements, the technique has achieved impressive accuracy for intermediate-term horizons. The model is documented and an example provided as part of our text's computer supplement.

[11]Another way of approaching this exercise, if the primarily goal is planning short-term borrowing, is to make Notes payable the plug figure and insert some targeted minimum cash & marketable securities amount.

EXHIBIT 12-4
Projected Balance Sheet Method

BALANCE SHEET PROJECTION FORECASTING METHOD
Cash and Marketable Securities Residual of Balance Sheet Projection

MONTH

ACCOUNT	Jan	Feb	Mar
Cash and M.S.°	Plug	Plug	Plug
Accts. receivable	$ 35	$ 36	$ 36
Inventories	$ 65	$ 66	$ 68
Prepaid expenses	$ 15	$ 15	$ 16
Current assets	$115	$117	$120
Prop., plant, equipment	$210	$223	$227
TOTAL ASSETS	$325	$340	$347
Accts. payable	$ 30	$ 31	$ 31
Notes payable	$ 25	$ 26	$ 26
Accrued expenses	$ 10	$ 10	$ 10
Current liabilities	$ 65	$ 67	$ 67
Long-term liabilities	$ 45	$ 46	$ 47
TOTAL LIABILITIES	$110	$113	$114
Stockholders' equity			
Common stock	$ 5	$ 5	$ 5
Paid-in capital	$ 20	$ 20	$ 20
Retained earnings	$205	$220	$235
EQUITY	$230	$245	$260
TOTAL LIABS. and EQUITY	$340	$358	$374

°Calculation of Cash & Marketable Securities Plug Amount
Cash and M.S.
  = (Totals Liabs.
  + Stockholders' Equity)
  − Total Assets: 340 − 325 = 15   358 − 340 = 18   374 − 347 = 27

failure to adjust for differences between accrual-based net income (which drives the retained earnings projection) and cash flows arising from that income stream hurts forecast accuracy.

MODEL ESTIMATION.   Once the variables included in the model have been specified, the forecaster must estimate the model with real data. Model estimation includes the selection of an appropriate forecasting technique and model calibration. Model calibration, in turn, refers to fitting the data to the model so that coefficients can be determined. Illustrating, finding the coefficients for a model in the form $Y = a + b(X)$ involves computation of the numerical values for a and b. It is important to not overlook the fact that forecasts are subject to error, however. To incorporate the uncertainty underlying the cash forecast, the forecaster might supplement the forecast with sensitivity analysis or simulation. **Sensitivity analysis** involves varying the input values for each key assumption, such as the sales level, that bears on the cash forecast. This process reveals which assumption(s) has the greatest impact on cash flow. The forecaster can then restudy those assumptions to ensure they are accurate or at least have contingency plans ready if, during the middle of the year, they turn out to be overly optimistic or pessimistic. The forecaster also can present a range forecast, indicating the likely span of values that the forecast variable will adopt if sales or interest rates vary from their expected values. Another means of incorporating the underlying forecast uncertainty is through **simulation.** Simulation involves simultaneously varying key input variables, using values corresponding to their historical frequency of occurrence, and noting the effect on the cash position.

MODEL VALIDATION.   We have mentioned at several points the difficulty of detecting breakdowns in the modeled behavior of the forecast variable. The model validation (or validity-checking) stage should have a built-in means of detection, such as the occurrence of a forecast error that is more than one standard deviation from the mean or mean-adjusted-for-trend. Such an approach has been successfully used to detect the need for production machine adjustment in the statistical process control used by manufacturing and processing firms such as Frito-Lay.

FORECASTING DAILY CASH FLOWS

Forecasters typically use the receipts and disbursements method for daily cash forecasts, especially for short horizons. Statistical tools can be helpful for the recurrent nonmajor elements in the forecast, however. As noted earlier, many smaller and some medium-sized companies do not even forecast on a daily basis, and are relying on funding from investments or credit lines to cover shortfalls. Mid-sized companies not developing daily cash forecasts manage the uncertainty of check clearing with controlled disbursement accounts. As the opportunity cost for suboptimal investing increases as a result of increasing interest rates, more companies find it profitable to do daily forecasts. Before considering the steps in developing the daily cash forecast, we return to our chapter-opening financial dilemma to consider which cash balance to forecast.

FINANCIAL DILEMMA REVISITED

An analyst developing the daily cash forecast must first determine how best to measure the company's cash position. Generally, it is preferable to measure the company's available cash, which means we wish to forecast the collected bank balance. The level of the bank balance (or balances, in the case of multiple accounts) is what triggers short-term investing or borrowing. For most companies, it is just too cumbersome to adjust the company's ledger cash balance as shown in its accounting records. In fact, for companies using controlled disbursement accounts, that cash balance typically is negative because checks are charged against cash even though they have not yet cleared because of float. The accrual-based balance must reflect sales revenues that have not yet been collected and expenses for which no disbursement has yet been made, as well as prepaid and deferred expenses.

The second decision relates to what inputs will be used to forecast the collected bank balance. The forecasts of cash receipts and disbursements made by various divisional and field personnel might be aggregated, or the forecaster may use the historical relationship of sales volume to cash receipts and disbursements to statistically forecast the cash position. If the company's bank accounts have been structured properly, the forecaster should be able to forecast cash flow by operating units. A very simple approach, which might be appropriate for a small company with only one account, includes the following variables:

VARIABLE	HOW MEASURED
Cash receipts (CR)	Credits to demand deposit account
Cash disbursements (CD)	{Debits to demand deposit account
	{Petty cash disbursements
Cash flow $(CF = CR - CD)$	Difference between cash receipts, disbursements

For example, one US manufacturer has all its subsidiaries forecast each of the following elements: profits before interest, interest, depreciation, inventory, receivables, payables, capital expenditures, dividends, and long-term debt payments. Another company requires each subsidiary to further specify total cash flows by currency.

Horizon

For most companies doing daily forecasting, the immediate day's cash flows are simply gathered from balance-reporting systems. For the next day and up to 2 weeks in the future, historical collection and payment patterns can be used in connection with sales and purchases to project cash flows.

Variable Identification

The shorter the horizon, the more detail is shown in the cash forecast. Ideally, the format includes columns for the forecast, the actual amount (as it materializes), the budgeted amount, and variances. Typically, actual-vs-forecast and actual-vs-budget variances are calculated. Explanations of likely causes and corrective actions accompany the numbers.

With the requirement to present a Statement of Cash Flows, some companies are finding it fruitful to prepare their cash forecasts with separate subtotals for operating, financing, and investing cash flows. Although the Statement of Cash Flows format might be more appropriate for a monthly forecast, it provides a checklist of line items that should be incorporated into daily forecasts as well.

FOCUS ON PRACTICE

HOW CAN A COMPANY MEASURE THE RESULTS AND IMPROVE THE PERFORMANCE OF ITS DAILY CASH FORECASTING SYSTEM? One major industrial company has applied service quality improvement techniques to its treasury department. Comparing actual performance to departmental goals has led to improved intraday forecasts, which have led to smaller and more tightly controlled end-of-day balances.

The service improvement effort began with the establishment of "minimally acceptable performance standards" for daily cash forecast deadlines, bank balance forecasts, and presentment notification from disbursement banks. The daily cash forecast minimum standard was set at 10:00 A.M., with 9:45 A.M. as the goal. Major disbursement banks were graded based on the percentage of the total day's presentments making the first presentment deadline. Because daily investing and borrowing decisions are based on the first presentment and large later presentments might lead to an overdraft situation, larger first-presentment percentages are preferable. After the standards were implemented, a "below standard" bank was identified and forced to improve. In line with the forecasting improvements, the company established a minimally acceptable ending daily cash position of $1 million and a goal of $500,000. Performance tracking and adjustments have enabled managers to approach attainment of that goal. The company's review and improvement of forecasting and other treasury department processes has saved it an estimated $1 million annually.

SOURCE: 1990. Treasury finds a tape to measure quality, improve performance. *Corporate Cashflow* April:24.

Modeling the Cash Flow Sequence

The major differences when it comes to modeling the daily cash-flow sequence are a greater reliance on bank-supplied deposit and clearing data, an emphasis on scheduling the upcoming cash flows via the receipts and disbursements technique, and a lesser reliance on statistical forecasting techniques. Scheduling upcoming cash receipts and disbursements requires close contact with any corporate personnel having responsibility for or knowledge of impending cash flows. Cash managers who have not yet discovered computers have been known to use their desk calendars to keep track of these flows.

Structuring the Daily Cash Forecast

Even the structuring of which inflows and outflows to forecast is different in the daily cash forecast.[12] Typically, there are a few large-dollar items and many small-dollar items. For the major flows, such as taxes, dividends, lease and bond payments, and wages, the amount and timing are usually known in advance, and these can be separately projected 1 to 2 months into the future. Other major flows may be impossible to anticipate, such as payments from financially distressed firms that are in arrears (and have a large balance due) and some international remittances. These are often offset through a financial transaction: When unanticipated monies come in, they are used to pay down a credit line or invest overnight; when amounts are debited, these are offset with a transfer from the short-term investments portfolio or a credit line drawdown. In any case, there may be no sense in trying to pinpoint their timing, as long as contingency plans have been made to handle them. What we *are* interested in is the sum of the many small-dollar flows, and this net cash flow total is amenable to forecasting.

Distribution Method

One area in which statistics has been instrumental in achieving accuracy is for spreading out (distributing) check clearing or receivable cash effects throughout the days of the week and month. Here, regression analysis has been very useful, in that the day-of-the-week and even day-of-the-month effects can be modeled by assigning each a separate regression coefficient. The regression-based distribution method also has been used to model the cash disbursements related to how many business days have elapsed since payroll checks have been issued. In general, distribution simply refers to spreading out the month's cash forecast into daily flows, thereby showing the intramonth cash-flow pattern. Analysts not having an understanding of regression may estimate daily proportions by calculating average values from the past. Notice that this method still relies on the monthly cash budget to provide the total dollar amount that is to be distributed.

USING THE DISTRIBUTION METHOD FOR DISBURSEMENTS. We can illustrate this in the disbursements context by assuming that October's total disbursement is forecast to be $40 million. Equation 12-12 indicates how we can forecast the disbursements for Friday, October 15, which is the 11th work day of the month:

$$CD_{11} = (d_{11} + w_5) \times MDF \qquad \text{(12-2)}$$

[12]The definitive source of this topic, on which much of our discussion is based, is B.K. Stone and R.A. Wood, "Daily Cash Forecasting: A Simple Method for Implementing the Distribution Approach," *Financial Management*, Fall 1977, pp 40–50. See also, T.W. Miller and B.K. Stone, "Daily Cash Forecasting: Alternative Models and Techniques," *Journal of Financial & Quantitative Analysis*, September 1985, pp 335–351.

In which: CD_{11} = cash disbursement forecast for the 11th work day of the month

d_{11} = coefficient for 11th work day (from regression model)

w_5 = coefficient for fifth day of week, Friday (from regression model)

MDF = month's disbursement forecast (from cash budget)

If regression analysis indicates that historically d_{11} is 0.04 and w_5 is 0.015[13] and our best estimate of MDF is $40 million, we have:

$$CD_{11} = (0.04 + 0.015) \times \$40,000,000$$
$$= (0.055) \times \$40,000,000$$
$$= \$2,200,000$$

One can think of the work-day coefficient as the effect of the day-of-the-month effect, holding constant the day-of-the-week, and the day-of-week coefficient as that day's effect holding constant the day-of-the-month.

USING THE DISTRIBUTION METHOD FOR COLLECTIONS.   We can also use the distribution method for collections of credit sales. One month's cash and credit sales can be distributed partially across that month (cash sales and cash discount takers) and the remainder across the next and following months. Or a typical month-end receivables balance can be distributed across the next 60 or 90 days, with some residual amount left uncollected at the end of that period.

EXAMPLE OF DISTRIBUTION METHOD.   We can learn how to develop a 5-day payroll disbursement forecast by looking at an example. This example also illustrates the basics of the distribution method and how proportions can be determined without the help of regression modeling. First, we need to know the total dollar amount of payroll checks being issued. Then we take the proportions clearing 1, 2, 3, 4, and 5 days after the issue date. To keep things simple, we assume the payroll checks are issued after the ledger cutoff time of the local banks, so that at best the depositor can get 1-day availability. In our example, we analyze check clearings based solely on business days after issuance and overlook the day-of-the-week, day-of-the-month, and whether a holiday intervenes. Here is the background data for a US company that issues only monthly payroll checks:

1. Amount of payroll checks issued on Wednesday, June 30: $455,000
2. Historical check clearing data (past five payroll check issuances) and the calculated averages:

Proportion Clearing

DAYS AFTER ISSUANCE	PAYROLL #1	PAYROLL #2	PAYROLL #3	PAYROLL #4	PAYROLL #5	CALCULATED AVERAGE PROPORTION
1	45%	42%	47%	42%	43%	44%
2	32%	33%	31%	35%	33%	33%
3	14%	16%	10%	18%	15%	15%
4	7%	5%	10%	4%	7%	6%°
5+	2%	4%	2%	1%	2%	2%

°Rounded down to force column total to 100 percent.

+Very small amounts for days 6 and following are lumped together with day 5 clearings.

[13]The technique used to estimate the day-of-week or day-of-month effects is regression analysis with dummy variables. See the discussion of the dummy variable technique and seasonal variations in the monthly forecast section in Appendix 12B.

To get the clearing forecast, take the dollar amount of the payroll and multiply it by the calculated proportions:

Next-business-day clearing (Thursday, July 1) $455,000 × 0.44 = $200,200

Second-business-day clearing (Friday, July 2) $455,000 × 0.33 = $150,150

Third-business-day clearing (Tuesday, July 6—banks closed on July 5) $455,000 × 0.15 = $68,250

Fourth-business-day clearing (Wednesday, July 7) $455,000 × 0.06 = $27,300

Fifth-business-day clearing (Thursday, July 8) $455,000 × 0.02 = $9,100

Having the proportions and the total amount of payroll checks issued, the disbursement account clearings are easily obtained. A caution is in order: The simplicity masks some important differences that may alter the historical proportions. In this case, a bank holiday combined with an intervening weekend makes the forecast suspect. Most likely, the day 1 and day 2 clearings will be higher than the historical amounts because of quicker deposits triggered by consumer anticipation of the Independence Day weekend and the correspondingly higher spending.

FINAL COMMENTS ON THE DISTRIBUTION METHOD. The distribution method works well when the intramonth cash flow pattern is stable so that historical patterns persist into the future. Once the distribution proportions have been determined, it is simple and inexpensive to use them to make the cash forecast. It is generally recommended that receipts be broken into several categories of nonmajor flows, and each forecasted separately. Likewise, splitting out categories of nonmajor disbursements and forecasting them separately can help improve disbursement timing accuracy. One layout might be by subsidiary, product group, or product line. Be careful about special events such as bank holidays—when disbursements or deposits do not clear the bank and mail is delayed. Recognize that you may need to gather a large amount of data to estimate the proportions, and then you will have to do it all over again when the pattern changes because of changes in employee or vendor behavior or payment method. Finally, the accuracy of the forecasts obtained is closely linked to the accuracy of the monthly or weekly amount being distributed—an inaccurate total gives inaccurate daily amounts. Thus monthly and daily cash forecasts are necessarily closely tied together when using the distribution method.

Model Estimation

We cannot profile model estimation for a receipts and disbursements forecast, because data are gathered through telephone calls and access to the corporate database. For the distribution method of statistical forecasting, regression analysis with dummy variables is used. Additional detail on regression analysis is provided in Appendix 12B.

Model Validation

Once again, the model validation phase is very similar to the process conducted for monthly forecasting. The primary difference is that the time frame within which the model validation takes place is very compressed. Once inaccuracies are detected, the model must be quickly altered to avoid overdrafts, excess borrowing, or opportunity costs related to very large demand deposit balances. Stone and Wood recommend using a cumulative error measure, in which each receipts or disbursement subtotal and the overall net cash flow forecast errors are cumulated over time. If the monthly forecasts are fairly accurate, the cumulative errors will approach zero. When in error, the cumulative error measure will grow over time. With the daily error cumulative total, if errors grow, a warning flag is provided. This is monitored for each nonmajor component being forecasted. Distribution fractions may be recomputed when it is clear that the pattern (number of elapsed business days, day-of-week, or day-of-month) has changed.

SUMMARY

We started our presentation of cash forecasting with the philosophy and environment within which cash forecasts are made. Forecasts add value primarily by enabling the company to borrow less or extend investment maturities, resulting in higher investment yields. Even the existence of real-time order, shipment, or payment data does not eliminate the need to forecast. The two major cash forecasting intervals, monthly and daily, were then presented. We demonstrated within those intervals the processes of variable identification, modeling the cash flow sequence, model estimation, and model validation.

We intensively developed the monthly cash forecast by first indicating its importance to senior management. Then we worked through the process of developing and validating the forecast. Finally, we briefly discussed daily cash forecasting by highlighting how one's approach for this interval differed from the monthly interval. The distribution method for spreading a month's cash receipts or cash disbursements forecast into daily intervals also was demonstrated.

Useful Web Sites

Association for Financial Professionals: www.afponline.org
Global Treasury News: www.gtnews.com (search in Trends or Cash Management sections for articles by McDonough or Sagner)
Treasury Strategies: www.treasurystrategies.com
Treasury Strategies: www.treasurystrategies.com/tsi/PDF/TSI%20Pres/wc52500a.pdf

Questions

1. Why do corporations put so much emphasis on cash forecasts? What happens if a company continually relies on inaccurate cash forecasts?
2. How can a company's cash position be measured for forecasting purposes? Why do managers generally prefer using the available bank balance?
3. Why does top management focus more on the monthly cash forecast than the daily forecast?
4. "The cash budget is just a glorified name for a cash forecast." Comment on this statement, indicating whether you agree and why you think the statement was made.
5. What constitutes a useful forecast? What does usefulness include beyond forecast accuracy?
6. Why is a company's forecasting philosophy an important ingredient in determining potential forecast accuracy?
7. Define the receipts and disbursements method of forecasting and briefly explain the process of developing a forecast using this method. Why do most forecasters limit its use to very short-term cash forecasts?

8. Briefly summarize differences between daily cash forecasting and monthly forecasting.

Problems

1. Fill in the missing cells in the following simple cash-forecasting template. Explain what the cash flow, beginning cash, and ending cash line items represent. Assume short-term borrowing and investing are not included in any of the cash flow items.

Simple Cash Forecasting Model

ITEM	JUNE	JULY	AUGUST
Cash receipts	$375	$345	$450
− Cash disbursements	$295	$425	$535
= Cash flow	____	____	____
+ Beginning cash	$ 35	____	____
= Ending cash	____	____	____

2. Omega, Inc., has been running short on cash with increasing regularity. The cash manager wishes to know the reason why. She determines that the average cash position over the past 12 months has been $300,000, the standard deviation of that cash position over the same period has been $275,000, and the distribution of day-ending cash positions is approximately normal. The company's minimum cash balance is $0. Can you help her? (Note: Consult Exhibit 2-6 or a standard statistics textbook for any necessary tables using one-tailed probability values.)

3. Below is the sales forecast, in dollars, for the upcoming year for BeachTop Boats, Inc. BeachTop collects 5 percent of each month's sales in cash, 45 percent 1 month later, and 47 percent the second month after the sale. Examination shows that 3 percent of sales are uncollectible. A given month's purchases are 50 percent of the forecasted sales amount for that month and 50 percent of the next month's sales forecast. All purchases are paid on "net 30 terms," so purchases and the associated cash payments on those purchases do not occur within the same month. The other cash flows for the last quarter of the year (October through December) are $15 interest income to be received in November, a principal repayment of $165 in December, interest payment of $20 in December, tax payments of $40 in December, cash proceeds from asset sales of $35 in October, and asset acquisitions of $75 in November. BeachTop policy mandates that a minimum of $100 be kept in cash at all times. Ending cash in September is $165, and the company has no outstanding short-term borrowing or investments at that point in time.

MONTH	SALES FORECAST	MONTH	SALES FORECAST
Jan.	$36	July	$75
Feb.	$38	Aug.	$63
Mar.	$50	Sept.	$57
Apr.	$55	Oct.	$40
May	$59	Nov.	$32
June	$65	Dec.	$45
		Jan.	$40

Based on this information, prepare a cash forecast for October through December using the cash receipts and disbursements method. Interpret your projections for the cash surplus (shortage). Then indicate whether a study of the seasonality of sales should have forewarned the cash manager of potential problems in the fourth quarter.

4. Here are the data from a company's sales for January–June. Use these data to get a forecast for the collection forecast, including cash sales, for June.

MONTH	SALES
January	$220,000
February	$140,000
March	$150,000
April	$140,000
May	$170,000
June	$150,000

Of the sales above, 30 percent are for cash and 70 percent are for credit. Of the credit sales, 55 percent are collected 1 month later, 30 percent are collected 2 months later, and 15 percent are collected 3 months later. What is the collection forecast for June?

5. Here is the background data for a company that issues monthly payroll checks:
   • Amount of payroll checks issued on Monday, April 30: $1,750,000
   • Historical check clearing data (past four payroll check issuances)

Proportion Clearing

DAYS AFTER ISSUANCE	PAYROLL #1	PAYROLL #2	PAYROLL #3	PAYROLL #4	AVERAGE PROPORTION
1	65%	60%	58%	66%	
2	32%	33%	33%	32%	
3	2%	6%	5%	2%	
4	1%	1%	3%	0%	
5+	0%	0%	1%	0%	

Use the distribution method to forecast check clearings for the company.

References

Paul J. Beehler. 1983. *Contemporary cash management: Principles, practices, perspectives.* 2nd ed. New York: John Wiley & Sons.

Michael J. Brennan and Thomas M. Carroll. 1987. *Preface to quantitative economics & econometrics.* Cincinnati, OH: South-Western Publishing.

Alan M. Cunningham, Dennis James Hogan, and Richard Bort. 1996. Medium-term funds flow forecasting. In Richard Bort (ed): *Corporate Cash Management Handbook.* Boston: Warren, Gorham, & Lamont.

William Forster. 2000. Treasury management and the use of the internet. April 6, 2000. Accessed at: http://www.gtnews.com/articles3/2023.html.

James A. Gentry. 1996. Short-run financial management. In Dennis E. Logue (ed): *Handbook of Modern Finance.* Boston: Warren, Gorham, & Lamont.

Clive W. J. Granger and M. Hashem Pesaran. 2000. Economic and statistical measures of forecast accuracy. *Journal of Forecasting* 19:537–560.

John J. Hampton and Cecilia L. Wagner. 1989. Working capital management. New York: John Wiley & Sons.

W. C. F. Hartley and Yale L. Meltzer. 1979. *Cash management: Planning, forecasting, and control.* Englewood Cliffs, NJ: Prentice-Hall.

Monzurul Hoque and James A. Gentry. 1989. *Forecasting daily cash receipts and disbursements.* Paper presented to the Financial Management Association, October 19.

Jarl G. Kallberg and Kenneth L. Parkinson. 1984. *Current asset management: Cash, credit, and inventory.* New York: John Wiley & Sons.

John M. Kelly. 1986. *Cash management.* New York: Franklin Watts.

Richard P. Kramer, 1988. Corporate cash: Why its meaning differs between treasurers and controllers. *Financial Executive* 4:53–55.

Larry Lapide. 2000. New developments in business forecasting. *The Journal of Business Forecasting* Fall:15–16.

Eugene M. Lerner. 1968. Simulating a cash budget. *California Management Review* 9:79–86.

William Loscalzo. 1982. *Cash flow forecasting.* New York: McGraw-Hill.

Stephen Manthey. 1994. Cash forecasting: Fictional facts and factual fiction. *TMA Journal* March/April 1994:24–26.

Thomas W. Miller and Bernell K. Stone. 1985. Daily cash forecasting: Alternative models and techniques. *Journal of Financial & Quantitative Analysis* September:335–351.

Aaron L. Phillips. 1997. Treasury management: Job responsibilities, curricular development, and research opportunities. *Financial Management* Autumn:69–82.

Bennett Quillen. 1993. Effective cash flow forecasting techniques. *Journal of Cash Management* September/October:58–61.

Zinovy Radovilsky and John Ten Eyck. 2000. Forecasting with Excel. *The Journal of Business Forecasting* Fall:22–27.

James Sagner. 2000. Cash forecasting and the behavior of interest rates. January 7. Accessed at: http://www.c-stream.com/www.gtnews.com/articles3/1890.html.

Bernell K. Stone and Robert A. Wood. 1977. Daily cash forecasting: A simple method for implementing the distribution approach. *Financial Management* Fall:40–50.

Bernell K. Stone, Robert A. Wood, and Thomas W. Miller. 1987. Daily cash forecasting with multiplicative models of cash flow patterns. *Financial Management* Winter:45–54.

Ahmet Tezel and Ginette McManus. 1999. Monthly cash budget under sales and collections uncertainty. *Journal of Financial Education* Fall:75–82.

Treasury Management Association. 1997. The practice of treasury management. *TMA Journal* May/June:8–10, 12, 14.

James H. Vander Weide and Steven F. Maier. 1985. *Managing corporate liquidity: An introduction to working capital management.* New York: John Wiley & Sons.

Andy Webb. 2000. All together now. October 11. Accessed at: http://www.gtnews.com/articles4/2377.html.

Appendix 12A

Measuring Forecast Errors

In this appendix we present five measures of forecast error: the mean absolute error, mean square error, root mean square error, coefficient of determination, and error distribution. A forecaster might use only mean absolute error to gauge cash forecasting accuracy, or some combination of these measures.

Let's reconsider a cash forecasting model's validity. The adequacy of a forecasting model usually is assessed by some measure of forecast error. One use of these measures is to evaluate a model's goodness-of-fit when the model is first calibrated. Observations that were not part of the data used to calibrate the model generally are used in the evaluation.

A second use of the forecast error measures is to quickly detect a breakdown in an established model's adequacy. When large errors occur, the forecaster seeks to determine whether the model is no longer valid—perhaps because a new trend has been established—or whether the errors are a result of unusual and nonrecurring factors.

The five forecast error measures that have been found useful for short-term forecasts are mean absolute error, mean squared error, root mean squared error, coefficient of determination, and error distribution. Arguably the best measure, **mean absolute error** (MAE), is developed first, then the others are presented for comparison. MAE involves adding the absolute values of the difference between forecasted and actual values and then dividing by the number of forecasts. Equation 12A-1 provides a symbolic representation of the MAE calculation.

$$MAE = \frac{\sum_{i=1}^{n} |(a_i - f_i)|}{n} \quad (12A\text{-}1)$$

In which: MAE = mean absolute error

n = number of forecasts

a_i = actual value for period i

f_i = forecast value for period i

Exhibit 12A-1 provides a set of forecasted and actual values and illustrates computation of the mean absolute error. Notice that had we simply summed the forecast errors without first taking the absolute values, we would have found the mean error to be $[(-3) + (-1) + 2 + (-1) + 2]/5 = -0.20$. This greatly understates the errors of the model, causing the unwary analyst to have false confidence in it. The mean absolute error measure is not distorted by the averaging of offsetting errors because the absolute value of each forecast error is taken before summing up the errors.

Substituting column 4 values into Equation 12A-1, we arrive at:

EXHIBIT 12A-1
Computation of Mean Absolute Error

(1) FORECAST VALUE	(2) ACTUAL VALUE	(3) DIFFERENCE (2) − (1)	(4) ABSOLUTE VALUE OF DIFFERENCE (3)
15	12	−3	3
17	16	−1	1
19	21	2	2
21	20	−1	1
23	25	2	2
			= 9
			$\Sigma/n = 9/5 = \underline{\underline{1.8}}$

$$\frac{[(3 + 1 + 2 + 1 + 2)]}{5} = \frac{9}{5} = 1.8$$

The analyst can compare forecast accuracy for variables with varying magnitudes by calculating a mean absolute percentage error, which involves dividing each row's column 4 value by the column 2 actual value, summing the resulting percent error, and dividing the sum by n.[1A]

Mean square error (MSE) weights large errors more than small ones and thus favors forecasting models that rarely, if ever, miss by a large amount. The calculation of MSE is shown in Equation 12A-2:

$$MSE = \frac{\sum\limits_{i=1}^{n} |(a_i - f_i)|}{n} \qquad \text{(12A-2)}$$

In which: f_i = forecast value for time period i

a_i = actual value for time period i

n = number of time periods in sample

The MSE shares an advantage of MAE: It handles positive and negative errors in a way that does not bias the model's accuracy. Before averaging, the square of the error is calculated, getting rid of any negative signs. Exhibit 12A-2 illustrates an MSE calculation with the same data used in our earlier MAE computation.

A closely related measure, **root mean square error** (RMSE), has become increasingly popular in business and economic applications. It simply involves taking the square root of the MSE. RMSE has all the advantages of MSE, plus the added advantage that it is expressed in the same units as the original series being forecasted. Expressing the error measure in percentage or dollars certainly communicates the idea better than expressing it as "percentage squared" or "dollars squared." RMSE is formulated as Equation 12A-3.

$$RMSE = \sqrt{\frac{\sum\limits_{i=1}^{n} [(a_i - f_i)]^2}{n}} \qquad \text{(12A-3)}$$

Using the same numbers as earlier, RMSE is calculated exactly like MSE, with the added final step of taking the square root. Thus, in that example, $RMSE = \sqrt{3.8} = 1.9$.

When regression analysis is used in the forecasting model, an additional error measure often is reported. The **coefficient of determination** (r-squared) gives the goodness-of-fit for the fitted regression equation. It indicates the proportion of the total variance of the forecasted variable that is accounted for, or "explained," by the fitted regression equation. Thus r^2 is the regression sum-of-squares (RSS) divided by the total sum-of-squares (TSS); alternatively, it is $(1 - [(\text{error sum-of-squares})/(\text{total sum-of-squares})])$. When forecast errors have already been calculated, the latter formula can be restated as:

$$r^2 = 1 - \frac{Variance\ of\ forecast\ error}{Variance\ of\ series\ being\ forecasted}$$

$$= 1 - \frac{MSE}{\sigma_{a_i}^2}$$

If forecast errors have not already been calculated, use the equivalent expression for r^2 shown in Equation 12A-4, in which $\bar{a}_i$ is the mean of the actual values:

$$r^2 = 1 - \left[\frac{\sum\limits_{i=1}^{n} (a_i - f_i)^2/n}{\sum\limits_{i=1}^{n} (a_i - \bar{a}_i)^2/n} \right] \qquad \text{(12A-4)}$$

$$r^2 = 1 - (3.8/19.76)$$
$$= 0.81$$

Using our example data, the mean of the actual values is $[(12 + 16 + 21 + 20 + 25)/5] = 18.8$. Thus the variance of the actual values (a's) equals $[(12 - 18.8)^2 + (16 - 18.8)^2 + \ldots (25 - 18.8)^2 / 5]$, or 19.76.

Substituting the MSE from an earlier calculation, the computed variance gives us:

EXHIBIT 12A-2
MSE Computation Example

(1) FORE- CASTED VALUE	(2) ACTUAL VALUE	(3) DIFFERENCE [(2) − (1)]	(4) SQUARED DIFFERENCE [(3)²]
15	12	−3	9
17	16	−1	1
19	21	2	4
21	20	−1	1
23	25	2	4
$MSE = 19/5 = 3.8$			$\Sigma = \overline{19}$

[1A]This would give us a mean absolute percentage error (MAPE) of 10.75 percent in our example:

PERIOD	PERCENT ERROR
1	3/12 = .25
2	1/16 = 0.0625
3	2/21 = 0.0952
4	1/20 = 0.05
5	2/25 = 0.08

Sum = 0.5377, or 53.77 percent. Dividing by 5, we get $MAPE$ = 53.77/5 = 10.75%.

EXHIBIT 12A-3
Systematic Forecast Bias in Third Quarter Forecast

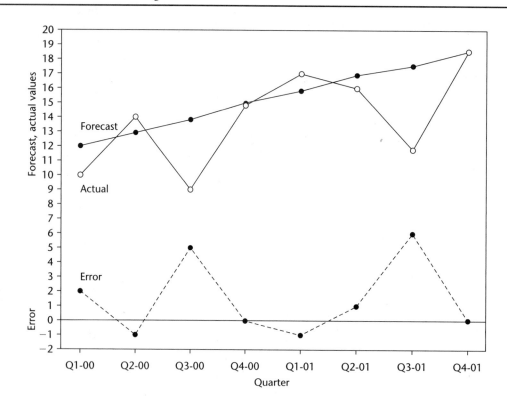

$$r^2 = 1 - (3.8/19.76)$$
$$= 0.81$$

The estimated model, from which the forecasted values were obtained, "explains" 81 percent of the variation in the forecasted variable.[2A]

Our final measure of forecast accuracy is the **error distribution.** The error distribution refers to the shape or pattern of the forecast errors. A graph of forecast errors over time or across values of an important predictor variable sometimes reveals a forecast bias. Bias exists when the model systematically underpredicts or overpredicts the forecasted variable. For example, graphical analysis might reveal a systematic overprediction of third-quarter sales, as depicted in Exhibit 12A-3. Although there is no pattern evident for the first, second, or fourth quarters, clearly the

third-quarter forecast is missing some important influencing factor(s). Another pattern to watch for is shown in Exhibit 12A-4 in which the model is increasingly underpredicting each value, implying that a new trend is being established. A recalibration of the model is the appropriate course of action in such a case. If forecast accuracy is not adequate when the new model is tested, the analyst must search for new predictor variables to add to the forecast model.

Determining why a forecast is in error is not always easy. It helps to know the error distribution that should be expected for a given forecast variable, in addition to the realized error distribution. Vander Weide and Maier[3A] distinguish between three types of error distributions: normal, causal, and stable. A forecasted variable can be characterized by any one of these or a combination. Normal distributions are characteristic of

---

[2A]The reader is cautioned that simply adding an independent variable to the model can increase the coefficient of determination. An adjusted coefficient of determination can be used for cases in which there are multiple independent variables. This is illustrated in the coverage of regression in Appendix 12B.

[3A]See page 128 in the Vander Weide and Maier citation in the end-of-chapter references.

EXHIBIT 12A-4
Increasing Bias Over Time: Increasing Forecast Error

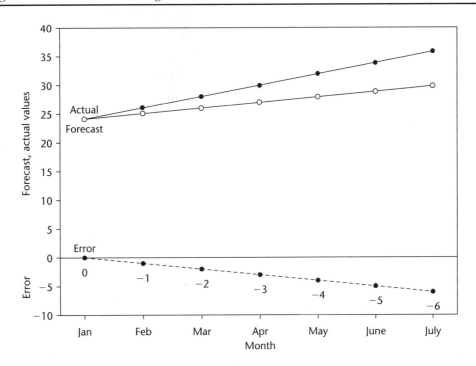

unpredictable errors, which occur in seemingly random fashion above and below forecasted values. Causal distributions characterize situations in which a predictor variable has changed from what was expected, causing the forecasted variable to deviate from what was expected. For example, a key supplier that has always paid promptly on day 30 misses its payment for the first time ever, causing the lockbox cash receipts forecast to be off target. Finally, stable distributions characterize variables with well-defined consistent trend or seasonal components. Until adjusted, forecasting models will tend to under- or overpredict whenever the trend changes or a new season is entered. Exhibit 12A-4 illustrates such an occurrence when the trend changed. Seasonal swings are sometimes hard to anticipate, especially for retail sales, in which seasonal behavior may be delayed as a result of inclement weather or external shocks. Once recognized, such delays are easily handled by the forecaster, because the period's forecast error can be subtracted from the next period's forecast with some assurance that the historically stable patterns will persist.

Advanced thinking on the subject of forecast accuracy, beyond our scope here, may be found in Granger and Pesaran (2000). They argue that financial forecasters should think more like physical scientists, and link the forecast evaluation to the decision situation.

PROBLEMS

A-1. Compute the mean absolute error for the following table. Also, determine the mean of actual values ($\bar{a}_i$), and compare the calculated mean absolute error to the mean error. It may help to graph the actual values to aid you in summarizing the reason behind your findings.

(1) FORECAST VALUE	(2) ACTUAL VALUE	(3) DIFFERENCE [(2) − (1)]	(4) ABSOLUTE VALUE OF DIFFERENCE (|3|)
135	120		
127	86		
139	210		
121	200		
143	125		

A-2. Rework problem A-1 to calculate the following additional error measures:

a. Mean square error

b. Root mean square error

Comment on the meaning of each of these error statistics.

A-3. Locate a data set of at least 30 consecutive observations for a financial or economic variable. Add an independent variable to account for time, with the first observation being assigned a value of 1, the second observation coded as 2, and so on. Conduct regression analysis of the time series using a financial spreadsheet. You may wish to consult Appendix 12B before conducting your regression analysis.

a. What is the fitted equation for your financial time series?

b. What is the coefficient of determination of your fitted equation? What does this tell you about the "goodness-of-fit" and possible forecasting accuracy of your equation?

c. Does a high value for the coefficient of determination necessarily imply that the model will provide accurate forecasts of the financial variable? Explain.

Appendix 12B

Statistical Forecasting Tools

For longer-term forecasts, quantitative modeling can be advantageous. Beehler[1B] cites four advantages to quantitative approaches: The methods can be easily used year after year; variance analysis is facilitated because the forecaster can pinpoint more easily the cause of forecast misses (e.g., the sales forecast was overly optimistic); statistical confidence can be determined based on probability concepts, indicating how much confidence the forecaster can place in the model; and in most cases, the model results provide the basis for decision making. With longer horizons, statistical forecasting is even more valuable because collections and disbursements (and the sales and purchases that give rise to them) are not known but also must be forecasted.

There are two categories of statistical tools: causal and time-series. **Causal techniques** link the forecast values of an effect variable to one or more anticipated causes. Inventory levels should change in response to changes in sales, for example. Two statistical tools that can be used in causal modeling are simple regression and multiple regression. **Time-series techniques** link future movements in the forecast variable to patterns revealed by historical movements in that same variable. The series of historical values over time, therefore, sets the stage for future movements. The moving average, exponential smoothing, time-series regression, statistical decomposition, and Box-Jenkins methods are all time-series tools. Many of these tools can now be implemented without much training or difficulty in Microsoft Excel™ (Radovilsky and Ten Eyck, 2000). We turn now to a brief discussion of these various techniques.

REGRESSION

The most important statistical tool used in causal modeling is regression analysis. Regression analysis is often used in **percent of sales** forecasting models, in which an expense or balance sheet amount is expressed as some percentage of sales. **Simple regression** involves just one predictor (independent) variable, whereas **multiple regression** incorporates two or more predictor variables. Regardless, regression analysis finds an equation for the "line of best fit,"

[1B]Cited in the end-of-chapter references.

EXHIBIT 12B-1
Causal Model Using Simple Regression

Month	Sales (000)	Inventories (000)
1	$295	$100
2	$250	$ 86
3	$225	$ 85
4	$265	$ 95
5	$270	$100
6	$265	$100
7	$275	$100
8	$275	$100
9	$280	$100
10	$310	$125
11	$355	$170
12	$360	$175

EXHIBIT 12B-2
Relationship Between Sales and Inventories

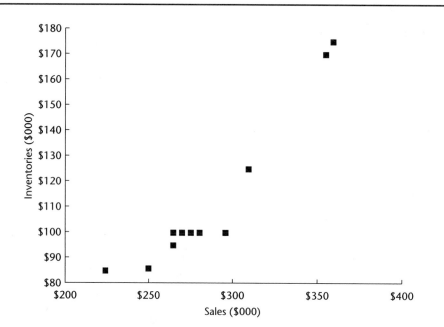

so that as much variation in the forecasted dependent variable is accounted for as possible. The simple regression equation is in the following form (Equation 12B-1):

$$Y = a + b(X) + e \qquad \text{(12B-1)}$$

In which: Y = forecasted variable

   a = intercept

   b = slope

   X = independent predictor variable

   e = unpredictable part of movements in Y

The unpredictable part of movements in Y, symbolized by e, might signal that our model omits an important predictor variable. We can illustrate this with sales (X) being used to forecast inventories (Y). We use the data in Exhibit 12B-1 to calibrate, or fit, the model.

   The forecaster commonly views a graph with the values of Y plotted against values of X, in the form of an XY graph. Exhibit 12B-2 shows us the plot for the sales and inventory relationship. We see the expected relationship: As sales increase on the X axis, we find increasing inventory levels on the Y axis. Each data point represents a month's observed sales and inventory levels.

   Now, conduct a regression analysis to find the equation for the line of best fit. This is easily accom-plished using a computer-based statistical package or financial spreadsheet. The output results from a spreadsheet are shown in Exhibit 12B-3, based on a Microsoft Excel™ fit (using the **T**ools/**D**ata **A**nalysis/**R**egression commands). Spreadsheet regression out-puts label a the constant and b the X coefficient. The fitted equation is thus:

   Inventories $= -95.99 + 0.7264$ (Sales).

Once we have the sales forecast for a future period, we plug that amount into the equation and get the fore-casted inventory amount. Notice that Excel does not give an error term; simply append this to the end of the equation as a reminder that unpredictable aspects of Y cause the forecasted values to differ from the actual values. Plugging the X values back into the fit-ted equation, we get forecasted values that can be compared with those actually observed. Because the coefficient of determination is so high ($r = 0.953$, compared with the highest possible value of 1.0), we see the forecasted values being very close to the actual values (consult graph of fitted points versus actual points for months 1 through 12 in Exhibit 12B-4).

   Now that we know the model's a and b coeffi-cients, we can plug next period's sales forecast in and calculate the forecasted value for inventories. If the Month 13 sales forecast is $375, the inventory forecast is 176.41 [$= -95.99 + 0.7264(375)$].

EXHIBIT 12B-3
Regression Results for Simple Regression of Inventory (Y) on Sales (X)

SUMMARY OUTPUT

Regression Statistics

Multiple R	0.953457533
R Square	0.909081268
Adjusted R Square	0.899989395
Standard Error	9.561158646
Observations	12

ANOVA

	df	SS	MS	F	Significance F
Regression	1	9140.50912	9140.50912	99.98833521	1.5904E-06
Residual	10	914.1575466	91.41575466		
Total	11	10054.66667			

	Coefficients	Standard Error	t Stat	P-value	Lower 95%	Upper 95%	Lower 95.0%	Upper 95.0%
Intercept	−95.99278413	20.91672334	−4.589284018	0.000996343	−142.5981561	−49.38741213	−142.5981561	−49.38741213
X Variable 1	0.726398076	0.072644056	9.999416743	1.5904E-06	0.56453703	0.888259122	0.56453703	0.888259122

EXHIBIT 12B-4
Forecasted Inventory versus Actual Inventory Using Simple Regression

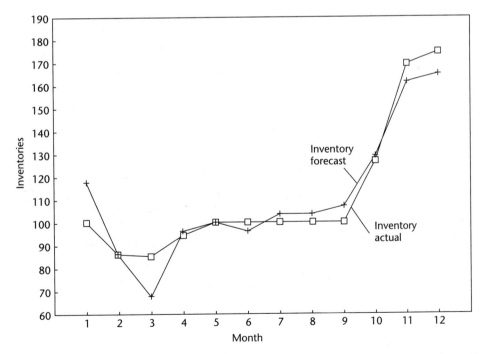

In multiple regression, inventories are modeled as a function of sales and some other variable(s). Possible candidates for predictor variables include the existence of quantity discounts (which increase order size and therefore inventory levels) and interest rates (which represent the opportunity cost of having money invested in inventories). We can revise Equation 12B-1 to include multiple predictor variables:

$$Y = a + b_1(X_1) + b_2(X_2) + \ldots + b_n(X_n) + e \quad \text{(12B-2)}$$

Several cautions are offered to the forecaster using multiple regression. First, a high r^2 value can be attained by simply including more variables—a problem that is especially pertinent in our simplistic example, which includes only 12 data points. A related measure, **adjusted r^2**, compensates for this upward bias in goodness-of-fit. Because we only have one predictor variable in our model, our adjusted r^2 is almost as high as the original r^2 (refer to Exhibit 12B-3).

Second, correlation does not imply causation. Although we are calling ours a causal model, spurious correlation might account for our high coefficient of determination. A predictor variable may simply be associated with another predictor variable, which in turn is the true cause of the dependent variable.

Third, one must ensure that the data approximately meets the assumptions of regression analysis. Two potential problems in our illustration are **multicollinearity**, which is a correlation between predictor variables, and **serial correlation**, which is the existence of correlated errors through time. **Omitted variables** that could have helped us predict inventories may give rise to the serial correlation. At times, the included predictor variables have a joint effect on the dependent variable, in which case the model should include an interaction term (for example, the product X_1X_2). A full discussion of these problems is given in forecasting and econometrics textbooks.

TIME-SERIES METHODS

The noncausal models we address are those that extrapolate past data observations into the future. The historical time path is assumed to persist into the future, although the analyst might override the model-based forecast for known changes. So either the item being forecasted moves upward or downward through time in some consistent pattern, or it is correlated with an unknown or unobserved predictor variable that moves in that consistent pattern over time. Our presentation moves from the simplest method to the most complex: moving average, exponential smoothing, time-series regression, statistical decomposition, and Box-Jenkins (ARIMA) modeling.

A moving average evens out temporary ups and downs by taking the mean of the most recent observations. One might calculate a 3-month, 6-month, or 12-month moving average. The average for the period then becomes the forecasted value for the next month. A key advantage of the technique is that the longer the averaging period, the less a recent observation will change the average—and, therefore, the forecast. Exhibit 12B-5 shows a 3-month moving average that illustrates this situation. It is evident that the average lags behind the original series. This may be a disadvantage at times, because there may be a new trend established that the average is slow to incorporate. The result is inaccurate forecasts.

EXHIBIT 12B-5
Three-Month Moving Average: Sales and Moving Average

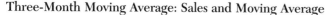

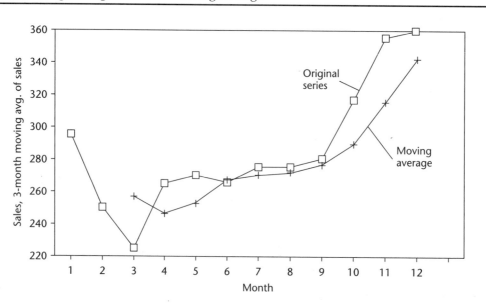

Exponential smoothing overcomes this weakness by allowing a greater weighting for more recent data. Specifically, it starts out with a base forecast for the next period and then adjusts that base by the error from last period's forecast. Think of it as a model that learns from its errors. Mathematically, the exponential smoothing model appears as Equation 12B-3:

$$F_{t+1} = F_t + \alpha(A_t - F_t) \qquad \text{(12B-3)}$$

In which: F_{t+1} = forecasted value for next period $(t+1)$

F_t = forecasted value for present period, made earlier

α = smoothing constant $(0 < \alpha < 1)$

A_t = actual value for present period

The larger the forecast error for the present period, represented by $(A_t - F_t)$, the greater the revision made to the present period's forecast to arrive at the next period's forecast. Also, the larger the smoothing constant a, the larger the revision, given the forecast error. Regardless of the value of α, actual observations in the distant past are weighted less heavily than recent values. Even so, trend changes or new seasons have a lagged effect on the forecast in the exponential smoothing model.[2B]

A cash-flow series with both trend and seasonal components is tabled in Exhibit 12B-6. Notice the effect on forecast accuracy, as measured by mean absolute error (MAE). The graphs of two exponential smoothing models, one with $\alpha = 0.25$ and the other with $\alpha = 0.75$, are shown in Exhibit 12B-7. The data series is both seasonal and trended, and the model with the higher α is somewhat more accurate (has a lower mean absolute error) because it adjusts more rapidly to the recent values. Neither model is very accurate, however. The models are particularly inaccurate in the months when the cash flows reach their seasonal highs. Also, note the greater smoothing accomplished by the model with the lower α, which is not appropriate for the example data.[3B] Perhaps the failure to use modified exponential smoothing to handle seasonal and trend variations accounts for the low

EXHIBIT 12B-6
Exponential Smoothing with Two Values for α

Exponential Smoothing: Two Models Fitting a Data Series
(Series exhibits trend, seasonal factors)
Note: Seed Value for initial forecast is based on moving average.
Forecast errors equal (actual − forecast).

MONTH	ACTUAL	FORECAST #1 $\alpha = 0.25$	FORECAST #1 Error	FORECAST #2 $\alpha = 0.75$	FORECAST #2 Error
Jan	45	40.0	5.0	40.0	5.0
Feb	42	41.3	0.7	43.8	−1.8
Mar	40	41.4	−1.4	42.4	−2.4
Apr	50	41.1	8.9	40.6	9.4
May	55	43.3	11.7	47.7	7.3
Jun	60	46.2	13.8	53.2	6.8
Jul	54	49.7	4.3	58.3	−4.3
Aug	52	50.8	1.2	55.1	−3.1
Sept	64	51.1	12.9	52.8	11.2
Oct	70	54.3	15.7	61.2	8.8
Nov	90	58.2	31.8	67.8	22.2
Dec	100	66.2	33.8	84.4	15.6
Jan	65	74.6	−9.6	96.1	−31.1
Feb	62	72.2	−10.2	72.8	−10.8
Mar	60	69.7	−9.7	64.7	−4.7
Mean Absolute Error:			11.4		9.6

[2B] Extensions to the basic model to handle trends (Holt's Two Parameter Linear Exponential Smoothing Method) and seasonal variations (Winter's Three Parameter Model) are developed in John E. Hanke and Arthur G. Reitsch, *Business Forecasting* (Boston: Allyn & Bacon, Inc., 1981), 254–264.

[3B] For specifics on how to use Microsoft Excel's Solver function to determine the "best" exponential smoothing model, see Radovilsky and Ten Eyck (2000), cited in chapter references.

EXHIBIT 12B-7
Exponential Smoothing of Trended and Seasonal Series

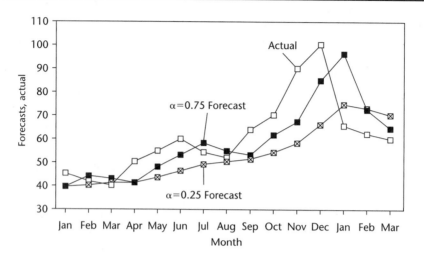

degree of usage for cash forecasting. At a minimum, exponential smoothing can generate naive forecasts, with which users can compare the forecast accuracy of other techniques.

Another extrapolative method is **time-series regression.**[4B] It is a naive modeling approach in the sense that it seems to imply that the mere passage of time causes the forecast variable to change in value. Users of this approach defend it on the grounds that whatever is causally affecting the forecast variable is behaving with a systematic regular effect through time. We reformulate our earlier regression equation to make the time period (t) the independent variable:

$$Y_t = a + b(t) + e_t \qquad \text{(12B-4)}$$

Here, Y_t is the value that the dependent variable takes on in time period t. Coefficients a and b and the error term (e_t) for the time period are defined in the same way as earlier, although the interpretation of b is now the change in Y over each time period. The model extrapolates the historical trend based on the set of observations included when fitting the equation.

Using the data from Exhibit 12B-6, in which the month variable is reassigned an integer value from 1 (earliest) to 15 (most recent), we regress actual cash flow on time. The fitted equation is $Y_t = 41.0286 +$

$2.4464(t)$ and accounts for 51 percent of the variation in cash flow. The forecast for the next period (period 16) is computed by plugging 16 in for t, giving a forecasted cash flow of $80. For a variable with a stable trend, time-series regression is an accurate technique. However, be careful about two issues when using this technique to forecast. First, few financial variables are characterized by stable trends. This implies that the linear regression model that we are using may have to be adjusted to a more complex (an exponential or polynomial) form, and the forecaster may have to use multiple regression incorporating predictor variables other than time. Second, correlated forecast errors violate an important assumption of regression analysis and must be treated with first differencing or another corrective to ensure efficiency and proper statistical testing of the model's coefficients.[5B] **First differencing** is accomplished by subtracting the previous value for Y from the current value and then using the differences as the dependent variable (instead of the original Y values).

A novel approach to time-series regression estimates the compound annual growth rate of an dependent variable growing continuously at an uneven rate. A growth rate formula that involves log-linear regression takes into account all values of the time series. If we have a continuously growing

---

[4B]Although times-series regression can refer to any X-Y relationship through time, we are using it in a more limited sense of trend analysis.

[5B]See the Brennan and Carroll citation in the chapter references for an excellent basic treatment of Durbin-Watson, Cochran Orcutt, and Hildreth Lu correctives and the efficiency and statistical testing ramifications of correlated errors.

series of cash flows (C_t) starting with C_0, the relationship between each cash flow and the beginning cash flow is

$$C_t = C_0\, e^{gt} \qquad \text{(12B-5)}$$

in which e is the natural number (approximately 2.71828), g is the growth rate, and t is the number of time periods over which the series has grown. Taking the natural logarithms of each side of Equation 12B-5 gives us Equation 12B-6:

$$\ln C_t = \ln C_0 + \ln e^{gt} \qquad \text{(12B-6)}$$
$$= \ln C_0 + gt$$

As long as we are careful to later convert predicted Y values from logarithmic units back into dollar cash flows, we can set Y equal to the $\ln C_t$. This gives us the regression equation shown as Equation 12B-7:

$$Y_t = \ln C_0 + gt \qquad \text{(12B-7)}$$

Historical cash flow data can be fitted with ordinary least squares regression because the functional form is "linear in the logarithms"—hence the name log-linear regression. Plugging a new t value into the fitted equation gives a value for the natural logarithm of the predicted cash flow, which is converted to dollars by raising e to that power. We fit the following data using the log-linear model: $2.75 (CF_0)$, $2.48, $2.85, $3.15, $3.55. The coefficients from the regression analysis are 0.926338 for a and 0.074984 for g. The *antilog* of the g coefficient is the percentage compound annual growth rate, in decimal form. Plugging in the number 5 to represent a future time period gives us a Y_t value of 1.3012569; taking $e^{1.3012569}$ (using the spreadsheet EXP function) gives us a cash flow forecast of $3.67 for period 5.

EXHIBIT 12B-8
Seasonal Indices for Statistical Decomposition

Statistical Decomposition Using Centered Moving Average

MONTH	(1) Actual Cash Flow	(2) Rolling 12-Month Cumulative	(3) Rolling 24-Month Cumulative	(4) 12-Month Centered Average	(5) [(1)/(4)] % of 12-Month Centered Average
Jan 2001	45				
Feb	40				
Mar	50				
Apr	55				
May	55				
Jun	60				
Jul	62	772	1549	64.54	96.06%
Aug	65	777	1572	65.50	99.24%
Sep	65	795	1600	66.67	97.50%
Oct	70	805	1625	67.71	103.38%
Nov	95	820	1655	68.96	137.76%
Dec	110	835	1685	70.21	156.68%
Jan 2002	50	850	1714	71.42	70.01%
Feb	58	864	1743	72.63	79.86%
Mar	60	879	1773	73.88	81.22%
Apr	70	894	1808	75.33	92.92%
May	70	914	1838	76.58	91.40%
Jun	75	924	1868	77.83	96.36%
Jul	76	944			
Aug	80				
Sep	80				
Oct	90				
Nov	105				
Dec	130				

Seasonal variations, intrayear movements that tend to occur each year, are easily handled by including **dummy variables.** The number of dummy variables included in the regression equation is one less than the number of seasons.[6B] Each dummy variable that is included as an independent variable takes on a value of 1 only when the season it represents is the season for which the forecast is being made, and 0 at all other times.

The main pitfall plaguing these two time-series regression models is the difficulty of detecting a change in trend. Unfortunately, trend shifts usually are not detected until the incoming actual values reveal very large forecast errors. Even then, the forecaster is at a loss on how to refit the model because there is not enough recent data to conduct a valid regression analysis. Model forecasts will have to be subjectively overridden in this event.

A fourth time-series model, **statistical decomposition**, is more complex. Sometimes called Census X-11 decomposition (after the computer software developed by the Census Bureau), this approach is especially useful for forecasting variables that have trend, seasonal, and cyclical variations. By decomposing the historical observations into trend, seasonal, cyclical, and irregular (unpredictable) components, the separate effect of each is determined. The forecaster can then study each component in arriving at forecasts. The cyclical component, which refers to regular up-and-down phases lasting longer than 1 year, is ignored when doing short-term and most intermediate-term forecasts.

The decision process begins with trend identification, which is usually done by using time-series regression. The purpose is to "de-trend" the data to isolate seasonal and/or cyclical influences. Next, the seasonal component is identified. This is achieved by first developing a moving average. For a daily forecast, five days' values are averaged; for a monthly forecast, values for 12 months are averaged.

Exhibit 12B-8 gives the computation of a 12-month centered moving average (column 4) and the seasonal indices (column 5) for monthly data exhibiting seasonal variation. To get column 4 numbers, we

start with rolling cumulative 12-month numbers in column 2: the first entry, 772, is the sum of January 2001–December 2001 cash flows, the second entry drops January 2001 and picks up January 2002, and so on. Column 3 takes month-beginning (772 for July 2001) and month-ending (777 for July 2001) numbers and adds them, so that the month's average in column 4 (64.54 for July 2001) is centered at midmonth. The actual cash flow (column 1) is then divided by the 12-month centered average (column 4) and the quotient multiplied by 100 to get the percentage seasonal index in column 5. Thus July experiences a very slight seasonal downswing, because the index (96 percent) is slightly less than 100 percent. Notice the pronounced seasonal upswing for this company in November (138 percent) and December (157 percent).

If several years of data are available, the seasonal percentage indices can themselves be averaged to come up with a more reliable estimate. The seasonal indices should sum to 1200 because the 12 values average out to 100 percent each. However, when they are used in arriving at a forecast, they are first converted to decimal form.

Once we have calculated the trend and seasonal indices, we are ready to do our forecast for the next 12 months. Assume the trend is level at a cash flow amount of $75. Our January 2003 cash forecast is made using Equation 12B-8, which includes a subscript for the month for which we are making the forecast.

$$CF_m = T \times S_m \times C \times I \qquad \text{(12B-8)}$$

In words, the cash forecast for month m is the product of the trend forecast, that month's seasonal index, and the cyclical index (if used). The irregular component is included, but generally no forecast is made for it, implying an irregular component value of 100 percent. Other indices can be added to Equation 12B-8 to reflect the effects of other important causal predictor variables, such as interest rates or exchange rates, although this removes the equation from the domain of a purely time-series model. Because we are not concerned about C in the short-term forecast, and by definition we cannot predict I, we are left with the following short-term monthly forecast equation:

$$CF = T \times S \qquad \text{(12B-9)}$$

Using our trend value of 75 and the January seasonal index of 0.7001, we have our January forecast:

$$52.51 = 75 \times 0.7001$$

[6B]The reason for this is to be able to retain the intercept (a) in the equation and still be able to estimate the b coefficients. In technical terms, including one dummy variable for each season leads to a situation in which the X9X matrix does not have an inverse and unique estimators of the regression coefficients cannot be found.

For intermediate-term and long-term forecasts, we want to incorporate a cyclical component to reflect, among other things, the phase of the business cycle.[7B]

Box-Jenkins models are our final class of time-series techniques. Named after two pioneers in the field of time-series modeling, this approach lets the data specify the best model. Multistage development using iterative testing is done to arrive at the final model. Exposition of these models is beyond our scope, but we mention them because forecasts of some items such as interest rates have been best handled by Box-Jenkins models. These models are sometimes called ARIMA models because they combine AutoRegressive,[8B] Integrative, and Moving Average elements into one model. Advanced forecasting sources and econometrics textbooks take up these models in greater detail.

We have completed our statistical technique coverage. These techniques are especially useful for the repetitive, smaller-dollar cash receipts and disbursements. Large and nonrepetitive elements should be handled with the receipts and disbursements method. Many businesses, especially smaller ones, subjectively adjust the statistically generated forecast. Many also rely heavily on field data, collected from field sales representatives and collection banks, to assist in the cash forecast. Field deposit data and information on new orders is especially helpful. These inputs are critical for daily cash forecasts made up to a 2-week horizon. For horizons beyond 2 weeks, statistical tools begin to pay off with greater accuracy. Because of the widespread use of personal computers, the necessary statistical computations involve a minimal expenditure of time and money.

[7B]The effect of the cyclical component is to increase revenues during the recovery phase of the business cycle and to shave revenues during recessions. Different industries experience cycles of varying length. For the mechanics of cyclical index computation, see Hanke and Reitsch or another business forecasting textbook.

[8B]Autoregressive modeling specifically accounts for the nature of the correlation between forecast errors through time. The term *autoregressive* refers to the process of determining the correlations by regressing the data series on itself. An advanced use of ARIMA modeling is as a second step to follow up a single equation regression daily cash flow forecasting model. Gentry (1991) and Hoque and Gentry (1989) use the ARIMA structure to extract information from a previous regression fit to improve the forecast model. Background information on how to integrate both regression and ARIMA components into a more general forecasting model is presented in P. Newbold, and T. Bos, *Introductory Business Forecasting,* Cincinnati, OH: South-Western Publishing, 1990, pp 366–373.

SUMMARY

In this appendix we have reviewed some of the statistical tools that a cash forecaster might use in modeling various cash inflow or outflow elements. We subdivided models into causal and time-series categories. In the causal section, we saw how simple or multiple regression analysis can be used to show the impact of a causal variable on the effect (forecasted) variable. Time-series models included in our presentation were moving averages, exponential smoothing, time-series regression, statistical decomposition, and Box-Jenkins. We noted that one might be forecasting sales, receivables, inventories, payables, or net cash flow as part of the short-term financial management process. Any item that can change the organization's future cash position is a candidate for quantitative or judgmental forecasting.

QUESTIONS

B-1. Contrast causal techniques and time-series techniques. What do the two classes of techniques have in common?

B-2. You have been assigned to develop a cash forecast for Greenlawn, a lawn fertilizing service operating in a medium-sized city. For cash disbursements, you need to develop a sales forecast. Your boss heard somewhere that regression analysis is good for sales forecasting. What causal (predictor) variables might you include in the set of independent variables?

B-3. Joe, one of your old college buddies, just received a pink slip from his first employer. No reason was given for his dismissal, but Joe suspects office politics. He was a sales analyst, responsible for sales forecasts. His last attempt at using regression to predict sales resulted in a reported r^2 value of 0.290. He is on the phone with you wondering whether to include his forecasting prowess on his updated resume. A longtime baseball fan, Joe remarks that "a 0.290 batting average sounds major league to me."

   a. Should Joe brag about his forecasting accuracy?

   b. A month later, Joe is cleaning out his desk, and as he throws out the computer output, he is startled to notice that the r^2 on his forecast was 0.79, not 0.29. Reevaluate his forecasting accuracy.

B-4. Describe a data pattern well suited to moving average forecasting.

B-5. What is the effect of using a larger value for α in an exponential smoothing model?

B-6. How is time-series regression different from other regression models?

B-7. Explain briefly how dummy variables are used to model seasonal effects in a regression model.

PROBLEMS

B-1. The following represent some recent quarterly data available to Freddy Garcia, the credit analyst responsible for reporting the "percent of sales" relationship of accounts receivable to sales. All sales are credit sales. He has a sales forecast for next quarter (quarter 9) and wishes to know what receivables amount he should forecast.

   a. Can you help him out by using regression analysis to determine the relationship? (Hint: Force the constant, or Y-intercept, to zero.)

   b. Is your regression fit a good one?

   c. Graph the receivables data, using the time period as your independent variable. Is there anything that Freddy can do to improve a given quarter's forecast?

QUARTER	SALES	ACCOUNTS RECEIVABLE
1	$255	$125
2	$265	$128
3	$260	$127
4	$290	$140
5	$275	$136
6	$285	$140
7	$278	$138
8	$310	$160

B-2. Using the template below, and a starting forecast of 75, develop the forecasts and evaluate the two exponential smoothing models using mean absolute error (see Appendix 12A). Comment on the effect of the different smoothing constants (*a*'s) used in the two models. For advanced model evaluation, you may wish to compute several of the other error measures presented in Appendix 12A.

Month	Actual	Forecast #1 $\alpha = 0.20$	Forecast #1 Error	Forecast #2 $\alpha = 0.80$	Forecast #2 Error
Jan.	90	75.0		75.0	
Feb.	85				
Mar.	87				
Apr.	90				
May	95				
June	96				
July	98				
Aug.	102				
Sept.	110				
Oct.	122				
Nov.	110				
Dec.	100				
Jan.	110				
Feb.	112				
Mar.	120				

Mean absolute error MAE =   MAE =

B-3. Using the fifteen actual values shown in problem B-2, calibrate a time-series regression model. Include an intercept (a) in your model.

   a. Comment on the goodness-of-fit for your model of the 15 months shown, using only the model's r^2 (consult the discussion of r^2 in the Appendix 12A if necessary).

   b. Is it advisable to measure the goodness-of-fit for the model by using only the sample data from which the model coefficients are determined?

   c. The next 3 months (April, May, and June) need to be forecasted. Based on your regression model, what are your forecast values?

   d. Compute the mean absolute error for the 15 months in the data sample. Use the regression model coefficients to get the forecasted values, then compare those with the actual values presented in the table.

B-4. A company's sales have exhibited the following pattern (all numbers are in thousands): $3,050; $3,250; $3,125; $3,500; $3,975. Apply the log-linear regression model to the data.

    a. Comment on the goodness-of-fit for your model (consult the discussion of r^2 in Appendix 12B if necessary).

    b. What are the forecasts for the next two periods, based on your model?

    c. Plot the data. Do you think a simple linear time-series regression model would do as well in fitting the data?

    d. Test your hypothesis from part *c* by fitting a linear time-series regression model. Comment on the goodness-of-fit, this model with the log-linear model calibrated in part *a*.

B-5. Beginning with July 2002 and ending with June 2003, fill out columns 2 through 5 in the format shown on the right. Indicate the interpretation of the calculated percentages in column 5 and how they would be used in a forecast based on statistical decomposition.

Month	(1) Actual Cash Flow	(2) Rolling 12-Month Cumulative	(3) Rolling 24-Month Cumulative	(4) 12-Month Centered Average	(5) [(1)/(4)] Percentage of 12-Month Centered Average
Jan. 2002	125				
Feb.	140				
Mar.	150				
Apr.	155				
May	175				
June	160				
July	168				
Aug.	175				
Sept.	165				
Oct.	170				
Nov.	190				
Dec.	220				
Jan. 2003	175				
Feb.	185				
Mar.	160				
Apr.	170				
May	190				
June	175				
July	176				
Aug.	200				
Sept.	180				
Oct.	190				
Nov.	195				
Dec.	230				

CHAPTER 13

Short-Term Financial Planning

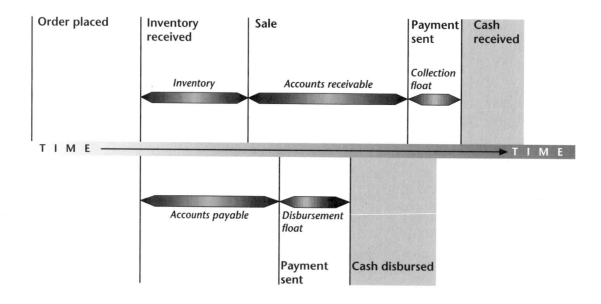

After studying this chapter, you should be able to:

- Implement the six steps involved in the modeling process.
- Differentiate between a long-term financial planning model and a short-term financial planning model.
- Develop a short-term financial planning model so that different short-term investment and financing strategies can be tested.

This chapter demonstrates how to develop a short-term financial planning model so that the financial manager can better ascertain the overall impact that short-term financial management decisions have on the net operating cash flows of the company. With such a forecast in hand, the financial manager can better plan the firm's short-term investment and financing strategies.

Modeling is the process of establishing a relationship between a set of independent variables to produce an estimate of a dependent variable. For example, meteorologists have devised sophisticated computer models to predict weather patterns. Economists estimate econometric models to explain and predict complex relationships dealing with various aspects of the macro economy. As we are all aware, these modeling applications have met with only limited success.

In this chapter, we begin with a general discussion of the modeling process. Then we develop the logic for a relatively complex short-term financial planning model. This model generates financial statement projections, specifically balance sheets, income statements, and cash budgets for a predetermined planning horizon.

FINANCIAL DILEMMA
What Does the Future Hold?

Management at Francine's Attic, Inc., a nationwide specialty retail outlet chain in the southeast, just accepted a recommendation to relax its credit terms to stimulate sales. However, management is concerned about what the new policy might do to its cash flows and wonders what type of funding contingencies should be arranged over the next 6 months. The corporate treasurer wants to try and create a forecast of the firm's cash flow position to anticipate the timing and amount of potential financing needs or investing opportunities.

TYPES OF MODELS

There are two basic model formats. A model may be **deterministic** or a model may be **stochastic.** Data input for a deterministic model are single point estimates, and data input for a stochastic model include probability distributions for one or more of the variables. For example, suppose that we determined that the accounts receivable balance is forecasted to be 20 percent of sales. Thus the receivables balance is the dependent variable and sales is the independent variable. The type of input used for the sales estimate defines whether the model is deterministic or stochastic. If we want to find out the level of receivables if sales are expected to be $50,000, then the model is deterministic. If, instead, we let the sales estimate be drawn from a normal distribution, for example, with a specified mean and standard deviation, then the model is stochastic. For example, the Lotus or Excel add-in product @RISK allows the modeler to convert a deterministic model into a stochastic model with minimal effort. The models discussed and developed in this chapter are deterministic models, but they can easily be adapted to include probability distributions for selected variables.

THE MODELING PROCESS

The first step in designing a model is to determine the question being asked. The modeler must clearly define the objective of the model. For example, a financial manager may wish to create a model to estimate the required level of external financing given a range of sales growth rates. Or the personnel manager may wish to estimate the number of new entry level positions that will need to be filled during the coming year. Clearly defining the problem generally allows the modeler to better determine the appropriate relationships and variables required to model the problem.

Having defined the problem, the next step is to specify the variables to be used in the model. A personnel manager estimating new entry level positions to fill needs to know how many promotions are expected during the period, growth in business activity, and the number of people leaving the firm for various reasons.

Variable specification is also affected by the time period for the forecast. Does the financial manager wish to estimate the required external funding for the next month, quarter, year, or 5 years? Defining the time period for the forecast will generally determine the level of detail necessary to model the problem. Determining the funding requirements for the next month requires detailed data about cash collections and cash disbursements. Estimating funding requirements for the coming year or 5-year period generally requires more aggregate data such as estimating the level of total assets.

The third step in the modeling process is determining the relationship between the selected variables. Suppose that a financial manager wishes to estimate cash collections from credit sales for the coming month. Cash collection is the dependent variable. Current and previous months' credit sales are the independent variables. The relationship between these variables might be expressed as the following:

$$C_t = a_1 CS_t + a_2 CS_{t-1} + a_3 CS_{t-2}$$

This relationship says that cash collection in month t, C_t, is equal to some fraction, a_1, of credit sales during month t, CS_t, plus some fraction, a_2, of credit sales last month, CS_{t-1}, plus some fraction, a_3, of credit sales 2 months previous, CS_{t-2}.

To estimate cash collection, the financial manager must arrive at an estimate of credit sales for the given month, estimates of the collection percentages, and actual historical data on the previous months' credit sales. In addition to these data, an estimate of current month's sales is required. This calls for the development of a sales forecast that can be fed into the cash collection forecast model.

Once the variable relationships have been developed, the fourth step is parameter estimation. The cash collection model requires the financial manager to form estimates of the collection percentages, a_1 through a_3, and the parameters for current and past months' credit sales. There are several ways to do this. One approach is to estimate the collection fractions by calculating a simple average over a historical time. A more sophisticated approach may involve running a lagged regression model with monthly cash collections as the dependent variable and current and lagged credit sales as the independent variables.[1] Alternatively, the financial manager can treat the collection percentages as policy variables and arbitrarily enter "desired" collection percentages.

Once the model has been developed, it must be validated. The financial manager should "run" the model on a variety of data sets and manually check the results. The sixth and final step is to document the model. The model's logic should be documented so that if errors are subsequently found or if model logic might change in the future, it can be more easily edited and modified.

A SIMPLE PERCENT-OF-SALES FORECASTING MODEL

We first apply the modeling principles previously discussed by developing a relatively simple financial forecasting model. The example model estimates the needed external funds required for a given sales growth estimate.

The heart of this relatively simple forecasting technique lies in the assumption that current assets and possibly noncurrent or fixed assets as well as current liabilities fluctuate proportionately with sales. For example, if total assets are currently 45 percent of sales and if it can be assumed that this relationship will remain roughly the same over the next year or two, then for every additional $1,000 of sales over the current sales level, total assets must increase by $450. This increase in assets must be financed by a source of funds, such as an increase in liabilities or an increase in equity.

One readily available financing source, often referred to as a spontaneous source, is current liabilities. Accounts payable and accrued wages vary with the level of sales. If current liabilities traditionally amount to about 25 percent of sales, then for every $1,000 of sales above the current level, current liabilities (a source of funds) will increase by $1,000 \times .25$, or $250.

We still have an excess of uses of funds (an increase in assets) over sources of funds (an increase in liabilities) in the amount of $200 = $450 − $250. The final source of funds considered is retained earnings. This internal source can be calculated by multiplying the firm's net profit margin m by the forecasted sales level S over the planning period multiplied by the fraction 1 minus the dividend payout ratio (dpo). This final figure represents the funds from operations that will be retained for internal investment purposes. Note that depreciation is not added back because the asset figure is net of depreciation. At this point, if uses of funds still exceed sources of funds, new external financing will be required during the planning period. This forecasting model for needed external funds (NEF) can be reduced to the relatively simple formula shown below:

---

[1]J. K. Shim. 1981. Estimating cash collection rates from credit sales: A lagged regression approach. *Financial Management* Winter:28–30.

$$\text{NEF} = (\text{Total assets/Sales}) \times \text{Change in sales}$$
$$- (\text{Current liabilities/Sales}) \times \text{Change in sales}$$
$$- \text{Sales} \times \text{Net profit margin} \times [1 + (\text{Dividends/Net profit})]$$
$$\text{NEF} = (\text{TA/S}) \times \Delta S - (\text{CL/S}) \times \Delta S - [S \times m \times (1 - \text{dpo})]$$

In this equation, ΔS represents the expected change in sales over the planning period.

We now use an example to show how this forecasting model works. Assume the following data are representative of a company's financial position.

BALANCE SHEET FOR 2001

Total Assets	$15,580,000	Current Liabilities	$ 4,261,000
		Long-Term Debt	3,638,000
		Net Worth	7,681,000

INCOME STATEMENT FOR 2001

Net Sales	$12,250,000
Net Profit	692,000
Dividends	429,000

Thus

$$\text{TA/S} = 1.272$$
$$\text{CL/S} = .348$$
$$m = .056$$
$$\text{dpo} = .62$$

Furthermore, assume that management expects sales to increase by $2.75 million during the coming year, 2002. Plugging these values into the forecasting model yields the following estimate of NEF:

$$\text{NEF} = (1.272 \times \$2.75) - (.348 \times \$2.75) - (\$15 \times .056 \times (1 - .62))$$
$$= \$3.498 - \$.957 - \$.319 = \$2.222$$

If sales increase by $2.75 million, then total assets will expand by $3.498 million, current liabilities will expand by $.957 million, and retained profits will expand by $.319 million. The company's 2002 balance sheet will look like the following:

2002 Total Assets	= $19,078,000	= $15,580,000 + $3,498,000
2002 Current Liabilities	= $ 5,218,000	= $ 4,261,000 + $ 957,000
2002 Long-Term Debt	= $ 3,638,000	= Assumed held constant
2002 Net Worth	= $ 8,000,000	= $ 7,681,000 + $ 319,000

Summing up the current liabilities, long-term debt, and net worth, we arrive at a total of $16,856,000. We can see above that total assets are forecasted to be $19,078,000. Thus the financing side of the balance sheet is $2,222,000 short of the funds needed to finance the asset side of the balance sheet as predicted by the NEF equation.

The financial manager now knows that if sales grow as predicted and if the financial and operating policies are such that there should be $1.272 of assets for each dollar of sales, $.348 of current liabilities per dollar of sales, a profit margin of 5.6 percent, and 62 percent of the profits paid as dividends, then the firm must obtain $2.222 million of outside financing. This new financing may be obtained through either new debt or through new equity sources, but that level of funding must be acquired to finance the forecasted growth in assets.

BASICS OF BUILDING A FINANCIAL MODEL

This simple percent of sales forecasting model assigns sales as the **driving variable.** Most financial forecasting models contain a driving variable that is the basis of many of the forecasting relationships. In the simple model presented above, the growth in total assets is driven by the change in sales. In addition, current liabilities and retained profits are driven by the change in sales. The change in total assets, the change in current liabilities, and the retained profit are then linked to the driving variable through relationship variables. The relationship variables, or parameters, in the model are the asset to sales ratio, the current liabilities to sales ratio, the profit margin, and the dividend payout ratio. These parameters may also be called policy variables because they are basically relationships over which the financial manager has some control and can change if necessary or desired. The dependent variable is the dollar amount of NEF.

There is always the temptation to make a model too detailed. Caution should be used to minimize the number of policy variables and to try and find the most basic driving variable, the one to which most relationships can be tied.

Building this simple model into an electronic spreadsheet requires careful organization to maximize efficiency and effectiveness of the modeling process. First, the model must be conceptualized as has been discussed and demonstrated through the percent of sales forecasting model. Then the relationship or policy variables should be entered in a separate area of the worksheet. The layout may be as shown in the following:

ROW	Column A	Column B
1	Assets to Sales	_____
2	Current Liabilities to Sales	_____
3	Net Profit Margin	_____
4	Dividends to Net Profit	_____
5	Change in Sales	_____
6	Current Sales Level	_____

The labels for the relationship and driving variables are entered in Column A and the user can then enter the values for these variables in Column B.

The forecasting model is developed in another part of the worksheet such as Column C on line 50 as shown in the following. Note that the model is developed using cell references for the relationship or policy variables and the driving variable.

ROW	Column C
50	$(B1 \times B5) - (B2 \times B5) - (B3 \times (1-B4) \times (B5 + B6))$

Financial models should always be developed using cell references rather than inputting the actual values for the policy variables into the model itself. If the user wishes to then see how a change in the value of a policy variable or driving variable affects the result, the user simply keys in a different number in the cell labeled for that variable, such as in cells B1-B5, and the model, in cell C50, is automatically updated. Otherwise, the user would have to edit the model itself with the danger of inadvertently changing the logic.

You may wonder why the model logic was placed in Column C and on a row below the policy variables. Basically, this is a good idea because adding or deleting columns in the data entry section could destroy some of the model logic, especially in a model more complex than the one under consideration.

A SHORT-RUN FINANCIAL PLANNING MODEL

The short-run financial planning model we now develop is basically a sophisticated per-cent of sales forecasting model that links a proforma income statement, cash flow state-ment, and balance sheet together for as many months in the future as the user wants to project. The basic driving variable is sales, because the model ties the financial state-ment items not controlled by the user to sales. The policy variables, over which the user has control, are:

Gross profit margin

Level of operating expenses

Receivables collection pattern

Desired ending inventory

Accounts payable payment pattern

Marketable securities maturity structure

Debt maturity structure

Other variables that we take as givens include:

Sales level

Level of fixed assets

Level of depreciation

MODEL LOGIC

The following material describes the basic logic used to forecast each item on the pro-jected income statement, cash budget, and balance sheet. Spend some time reviewing these relationships. The better you understand the relationship logic the better you will understand how each account value on the projected financial statements interrelates with other financial statement accounts.

INCOME STATEMENT

Estimated sales	(S_t). Forecasted sales for any proforma period are a given. The purpose of the model is to develop a financial plan based on an assumed level of operations.
Cost of sales	$(S_t \times (1-gpm_t))$. The user can control the relationship between sales and cost of goods sold by specifying a desired gross profit margin, gpm_t. Cost of goods sold is then Estimated sales $\times (1-gpm)$.
Gross profit	(Estimated sales − Cost of sales).
General and administrative expenses	$(G\&A_t)$. In our simple model, the user enters the expected level of operating expenses for each period.
Depreciation	$(DEPR_t)$. In our simple model, the user enters the expected level of depreciation for each period.
Operating profit	(Gross profit − General and administrative expenses (excluding depreciation) − Depreciation).

Interest income	$(MS_{t-1} \times i)$.
Interest expense	$(STD_{t-1} + LTD_{t-1}) \times i$ Monthly interest income and expense is equal to the previous period's marketable securities balance multiplied by the investment interest rate and the short-term and long-term debt level multiplied by the monthly interest rate, respectively.
Profit before tax	(Operating profit − Interest expense).
Tax liability	$(TL_t = $ Profit before tax $\times T)$.
Profit after tax	(Profit before tax − Tax liability).

CASH FLOW STATEMENT

OPERATING CASH RECEIPTS

Sales collections

$(S_t \times cf_t) + (S_{t-1} \times cf_{t-1}) + (S_{t-2} - \times cf_{t-2})$.
Cash receipts from sales are estimated by taking current period sales and past period sales (S_t) and multiplying the appropriate collection fractions (cf_t) by the appropriate period sales.

It is important to remember that the December base period data including the December receivables balance are based on past period collection fractions. If collection fractions for the planning period are different, the planning model should use the past collection fractions to apply against the historical period sales to properly collect the base period receivables balance during the first month or two of the planning period. If this is not done, then the base period receivables balance will not be properly collected and the balance sheet for the planning period will not generally balance.

Operating cash receipts:

Sum of the above items.

OPERATING CASH DISBURSEMENTS

Payment of payables

$(Pur_t \times pf_t) + (Pur_{t-1} \times pf_{t-1}) + (Pur_{t-2} \times pf_{t-2})$.
Cash disbursement resulting from current and prior period purchases is a function of the dollar amount of purchases in the current and past periods and the payment fractions assumed by management.

The monthly purchase amount is determined by the level of beginning inventory and the firm's policy related to the desired amount of ending inventory in the current period. This basic accounting relationship follows:

Desired ending inventory = Beginning inventory + Purchases − Cost of goods sold.

Solving this accounting relationship for Purchases results in the following equation:

Purchases = Desired ending inventory − Beginning inventory + Cost of goods sold.

The only thing still lacking from making this equation operational is a policy relationship establishing the firm's desired ending inventory. To make this relatively uncomplicated, we express the desired inventory balance as some relationship to cost of goods sold such as assuming that the firm desires to maintain one month's cost of goods sold as ending inventory, or 2 months' cost of goods sold as ending inventory, and so on.

It is important to remember that the December base period data including the December purchase amount are based on past period inventory order policies and the payment of purchases is based on past period payment fractions. If these policies are changed in the planning period, the planning model should use the past payment fractions to apply against the historical period purchases to properly disburse the base period purchases during the first month or two of the planning period. If this is not done, then the base period purchases will not be properly disbursed and the balance sheet for the planning period will not generally balance.

General and administrative expenses

$(G\&A_t)$.
To simplify the model, we assume that all monthly operating expenses, except depreciation, are paid in the month they are incurred. Thus the number in the cash budget is taken directly from the number generated in the income statement.

Taxes disbursed	(TP_t). Taxes disbursed is equal to the balance sheet account, Taxes payable (TP), if the current month is a tax payment month. We assume that Month 3, March; Month 6, June; Month 9, September; and Month 12, December are tax payment months.
Operating cash	The sum of the above items disbursed:
Operating net cash flow	Operating cash receipts − Operating cash disbursed

FINANCIAL STRATEGY SECTION

Marketable securities	Purchase marketable securities (MS) if the ending cash balance exceeds the minimum cash balance.
Notes payable and long-term debt	Borrow notes payable (NP) or long-term debt (LTD) if the cash balance is less than the minimum cash balance.

FINANCIAL SERVICING FLOWS

Interest received	$MS_{t-1} \times i$
Interest paid	$(NP_{t-1} \times i) + (LTD_{t-1} \times i)$
Debt maturing	NP_{t-1} (based on maturity schedule)
Maturing investments	MS_{t-1} (based on maturity schedule)
Beginning cash	CB_{t-1} The beginning cash balance for each month is equal to the previous month's ending cash balance.
Ending cash balance	CB_{t-1} + Operating net cash flow$_t$ + Interest received$_t$ − Interest paid$_t$ − Debt maturing + Maturing investments + New debt − New investments. The month ending cash balance is equal to last month's ending cash balance, plus the current month's operating net cash flow, plus investment interest received, less interest paid, less debt principal due, plus maturing investments, plus new debt acquired, less new investments.

BALANCE SHEETS

ASSETS

Cash (CB_t)	The cash account is estimated by the cash budget in the previous section. It is the monthly ending final cash balance.
Marketable securities	MS_{t-1} − Maturing investments$_t$ + New investments$_t$ The balance for the marketable securities portfolio is taken directly from the financial strategy section of the cash budget.
Accounts receivable	$S_t \times (1 - cf_t) + S_{t-1} \times (1 - cf_t - cf_{t-1}) + S_{t-2} \times (1 - cf_t - cf_{t-1} - cf_{t-2})$. The accounts receivable balance is determined through the assumed accumulated collection fractions for the appropriate current and prior period sales levels. Another approach to estimating the balance of accounts receivable is the following: $$AR_{t-1} + S_t - \text{Cash collections from sales}_t$$ The cash collections from sales is the dollar amount of cash collections from sales estimated in the cash budget.
Inventory	$$INV_{t-1} + PUR_t - COGS_t$$ The inventory balance is controlled through the inventory policy variable discussed earlier and the month ending balance is equal to the ending balance for the prior period plus purchases less the cost of goods sold.
Total current	Sum of the above. Note that we implicitly assume that cash, marketable securities, receivables, and inventory are the only current assets on the balance sheet. A more real-world financial planning model needs to include prepaid assets and other current assets.

Gross fixed assets	GFA_t The ending balance for gross fixed assets is equal to the ending balance for the prior month plus any new purchases of gross fixed assets. To reduce the complexity of the forecasting model we assume that during the planning period no gross fixed assets will be sold or acquired.
Accumulated depreciation	$\text{ADEPR}_{t-1} + \text{DEPR}_t$ The ending balance for accumulated depreciation is equal to the ending balance for the prior month plus the depreciation expense for the current month.
Total assets	Sum of the above components except accumulated depreciation − accumulated depreciation

LIABILITIES AND OWNERS' EQUITY

Accounts payable	$\text{PUR}_t \times (1 - \text{pf}_t) + \text{PUR}_{t-1} \times (1 - \text{pf}_t - \text{pf}_{t-1}) + \text{PUR}_{t-2} \times (1 - \text{pf}_t - \text{pf}_{t-1} - \text{pf}_{t-2})$ The accounts payable balance is controlled through the payables payment fractions. An alternate method to calculate the ending balance for current period payables is the following: $$\text{AP}_t = \text{AP}_{t-1} + \text{PUR}_t - \text{Cash disbursed for purchases}_t$$
Notes payable	$\text{NP}_{t-1} + \text{New notes borrowings}_t - \text{Notes retired}_t$ The ending balance for notes payable is equal to the prior period ending balance plus new borrowings determined by the cash budget and the financing policy variable for long- versus short-term debt and the dollar amount of notes payable retired determined by the maturity of the notes.
Taxes payable	$\text{TP}_{t-1} + \text{TL}_t - \text{Taxes paid}_t$ The ending balance for the taxes payable account is equal to the ending balance for the prior period plus the new tax liability (TL) determined on the current period income statement less any taxes paid based on the tax payment month. This last number comes directly from the cash budget.
Total current	Sum of the above
Long-term debt	$\text{LTD}_{t-1} + \text{New LTD}_t$ The balance of long-term debt outstanding for the current period is equal to the balance for the prior period plus any new long-term debt acquired as a result of cash needs and the firm's assumed financing policy related to short-term versus long-term financing.
Common stock	Assumed constant value
Retained earnings	$\text{Re}_{t-1} + \text{Profit after tax}_t$ Current period retained earnings is equal to the prior period balance plus the profit after tax projected by the income statement. No dividends will be paid.
Total liabilities	Sum of the above components and net worth

UNDERSTANDING THE MODEL

At this point, you may be a little dazed by all the financial relationships developed to create the short-term financial planning model. However, before we apply the model to the financial dilemma presented at the beginning of the chapter, consider what the model does. As a company begins producing and selling a product or service, it generates revenues and expenses represented by the income statement. Our financial planning model then transforms the income statement into a cash flow statement by converting revenues into cash receipts based on collections fractions and converting expenses into cash disbursement based on payment fractions. The projected income statement and resulting cash flow statement then impact the balance sheet by changing the level of current assets (cash, receivables, and inventory), current liabilities (accounts payable), accumulated depreciation, and retained earnings. If spontaneous assets grow faster than spontaneous liabilities and equity, then additional financing is required to improve the company's financial position. The financial manager is then faced with choosing the type, amount, and maturity of financing that enhances the value of the firm. If spontaneous liabilities and equity grow faster than spontaneous assets, then excess liquidity is generated and the financial manager can either retire debt, pay a dividend, or invest in financial assets. Again, the choice made should be the one that enhances the value of the firm. In our simple optimization model, discussed next, firm value will be enhanced by maximizing the net interest income for a given a set of constraints.

FINANCIAL DILEMMA REVISITED

Exhibit 13-1 reviews the base period information, the exogenous/environmental variables, policy variables, and decision variables that will be incorporated into the financial planning model to help solve Francine's Attic, Inc.'s dilemma. This exhibit also displays the assumed data for each of the variables in the financial planning model for the first 6 months of the new operating year for Francine's, Inc., a specialty retail outlet chain dealing in outdoor recreational equipment in the southeast. The exhibit presents the base period financial data for the ending month of the prior year, management's expectations for sales, operating expenses, depreciation, and the future monthly term structure of interest rates. In addition, the exhibit presents environmental parameters such as the tax rate and management's policy variables including collection and payment fractions and the desired gross profit margin. Management is relaxing its credit policy and expects that the collection fractions will slow from 10 percent, 60 percent, and 30 percent to 10 percent, 10 percent, and 80 percent for the month of sale, 1 month after, and 2 months after sale, respectively. Management is concerned about the financial impact of this decision and wants to know what it will cost the firm in terms of additional financing costs. In addition, management wants to determine the optimal investment and financing plan given the future course of interest rates. Exhibit 13-1 presents the investment instrument and financing instrument options available to the firm along with their respective interest rate forecasts for the next 6 months.

The financial strategy designed to support the firm's operating plan presented in Exhibits 13-2 through 13-4 is based on an optimization process, discussed in the next section. The plan results in a net interest earned for the 6-month planning period of −$99.83 (interest expense exceeds interest income). The financial manager should plan to invest in 30-day and 90-day marketable securities in January at 8 percent and 9.50 percent, respectively; 30-day marketable securities in February at 9 percent; and 30-day marketable securities in April at 9.50 percent. The plan also requires the use of 180-day notes payable financing commencing in January at 10 percent, 90-day notes payable financing commencing in February at 10 percent, and 30-day notes payable in the month of May at 9.5 percent. This financing plan allows the firm to meet its desired minimum cash balance of $250 for each month, while maximizing the dollar amount of net interest earned.[2]

---

[2]The financial manager has already determined that under the current policy an optimal financing and investing strategy will result in a net interest earned for the coming 6-month period to be −$64.18.

EXHIBIT 13-1
Data Input for the Short-Run Financial Planning Model

Base Period Information and Sales Forecast

	NOV	DEC	JAN	FEB	MAR	APR	MAY	JUNE	JULY
Sales	$1,400	$1,500	$1,700	$1,800	$2,000	$2,600	$2,400	$1,900	$1,400
Operating expenses			250	250	250	250	250	250	
Depreciation								100	
Cash		250							
S-T investments		0							
Accounts receivable		1,770							
Inventory		1,275							
Gross fixed assets		4,000							
Accum. depreciation		1,200							
Accounts payable		1,275							
Notes payable		0							
Taxes payable		200							
Long-term debt		1,000							
Common stock		1,000							
Retained earnings		2,620							

Exogenous/Environmental Variables

Tax Payment Months, March (3), June (6), September (9), December (12)
Tax Rate, $T = 40\%$; Rate on existing long-term debt $= 10.5\%$

EXPECTED TERM STRUCTURE OF INTEREST

	JAN	FEB	MAR	APR	MAY	JUNE
INVESTMENT INSTRUMENTS						
30-Day Investments	8.00%	9.00%	10.00%	9.50%	9.00%	9.00%
90-Day Investments	9.50%	9.00%	9.50%	9.00%	9.50%	9.50%
FINANCING INSTRUMENTS						
30-Day Notes Payable	9.00%	10.00%	11.50%	11.00%	9.50%	9.50%
90-Day Notes Payable	9.50%	10.00%	11.00%	11.00%	10.00%	10.00%
180-Day Notes Payable	10.00%	10.00%	10.00%	10.00%	10.50%	10.50%
LONG-TERM DEBT	10.50%	10.00%	10.00%	10.00%	11.00%	11.00%

Policy Variables

	Month of Sale	1 Month After	2 Months After
Collection fractions	10%	10%	80%
	Month of Purchase	1 Month After	
Payment fractions	0%	100%	

Inventory policy: Ending inventory equal to next month's COGS
Gross profit margin   25%
Minimum cash balance $250

Decision Variables

Short-term investment amount and maturity, January–June
Short-term borrowing amount and maturity, January–June
Long-term borrowing amount, January

EXHIBIT 13-2

Projected Income Statement Based on Exhibit 13-1 Data

	JAN	FEB	MAR	APR	MAY	JUNE
Sales	$1,700	$1,800	$2,000	$2,600	$2,400	$1,900
Cost of goods sold	1,275	1,350	1,500	1,950	1,800	1,425
Gross profit	425	450	500	650	600	475
General & administrative	250	250	250	250	250	250
depreciation	0	0	0	0	0	100
Operating profit	175	200	250	400	350	125
Interest income	0	8	10	6	4	0
Interest expense	9	18	26	26	26	22
Profit before tax	166	190	233	380	327	103
Taxes	67	76	93	152	131	41
Net income	100	114	140	228	196	62

EXHIBIT 13-3

Projected Cash Budget Based On Exhibit 13-1 and 13-2

CASH RECEIPTS	JAN	FEB	MAR	APR	MAY	JUNE
Month of sale	$ 170	$ 180	$ 200	$ 260	$ 240	$ 190
1 Month after sale	900	170	180	200	260	240
2 Months after sale	420	450	1,360	1,440	1,600	2080
Total cash receipts	1,490	800	1,740	1,900	2,100	2,510
Purchases	1,350	1,500	1,950	1,800	1,425	1,050

CASH DISBURSEMENTS						
Month of purchase	$ 0	$ 0	$ 0	$ 0	$ 0	$ 0
1 Month after purchase	1,275	1,350	1,500	1,950	1,800	1,425
General & administrative	250	250	250	250	250	250
Taxes	0	0	436	0	0	324
Total disbursements	1,525	1,600	2,186	2,200	2,050	1,999
Operating net cash flow	−35	−800	−446	−300	50	511

INVESTMENT/FINANCING STRATEGY (DECISION VARIABLES)*						
MS (30)	$ 298	$ 462	$ 0	$ 458	$ 0	$ 0
MS (90)	778	0	0	0		
N/P (30)	0	0	0	0	489	
N/P (90)	0	975	0	0		
N/P (180)	1,120					
LTD	0					

FINANCIAL FLOWS (RESULTING FROM DECISION VARIABLES)						
Interest received	$ 0	$ 8	$ 10	$ 6	$ 4	$ 0
Interest paid	9	18	26	26	26	22
Debt maturing	0	0	0	0	975	489
Maturing investments	0	298	462	778	458	0
Beginning cash	250	250	250	250	250	250
Ending cash balance	250	250	250	250	250	250

*Note: 90-day MS cannot be purchased in May and June and 90-day notes payable cannot be obtained in May and June. In addition, January is the only month that 180-day notes payable and long-term debt can be obtained. These restrictions are imposed to keep the financing and investment decisions made during the period related to the excess or surplus cash flows during the period. Also, many of the numbers in these exhibits are rounded to integer values to keep the exhibits from becoming too cluttered.

EXHIBIT 13-4
Projected Balance Sheet Based on Exhibits 13-1 through 13-3

	JAN	FEB	MAR	APR	MAY	JUNE
Cash	$ 250	$ 250	$ 250	$ 250	$ 250	$ 250
MS (30)	298	462	0	458	0	0
MS (90)	778	778	778	0	0	0
Accounts receivable	1,980	2,980	3,240	3,940	4,240	3,630
Inventory	1,350	1,500	1,950	1,800	1,425	1,050
Gross fixed assets	4,000	4,000	4,000	4,000	4,000	4,000
(Accum. depreciation)	1,200	1,200	1,200	1,200	1,200	1,300
Total assets	7,456	8,771	9,018	9,248	8,715	7,630
Accounts payable	$1,350	1,500	1,950	1,800	1,425	1,050
Taxes payable	267	343	0	152	283	0
N/P (30)	0	0	0	0	489	0
N/P (90)	0	975	975	975	0	0
N/P (180)	1,120	1,120	1,120	1,120	1,120	1,120
Long-term debt	1,000	1,000	1,000	1,000	1,000	1,000
Equity	3,720	3,834	3,974	4,202	4,398	4,460
Liabilities & NW	7,456	8,771	9,019	9,248	8,715	7,630

FOCUS ON PRACTICE

OPTIMIZING THE FINANCIAL PLAN   TreasuryPoint.com recently went on-line with the "Optimizer." The Optimizer is a state-of-the-art analytical system that can be used to optimize a company's daily short-term borrowing and investing decisions given a company's short-term financial position, cash flow forecasts, and risk guidelines. Each day, the Optimizer's analytical engine goes through a systematic analysis of the company's financial position and the current markets. Then it works within the investment guidelines and borrowing parameters set up by the financial manager to recommend the optimal solution for the company. Based on five case studies of companies with $250 million to $15 billion in sales, the Optimizer generated annualized savings of 10 to 65 basis points versus actual results. In one case study, the Optimizer recommended borrowing from a higher-rate credit line rather than a lower-rate, longer-term borrowing source. It calculated the total cost of borrowing for a few days at the higher rate and compared it to the total cost of borrowing at a lower rate and investing excess borrowings for a longer time. See the list of useful web sites at the end of the chapter.[4]

⁴2000. Optimizing Short-Term Cash. *Treasury and Risk Management* April:20.

OPTIMIZING THE FINANCIAL PLAN

This section presents an optimization formulation of the financial planning model. The optimization focus is on the financial strategy section choosing the investment amount and maturity and the financing amount and maturity with the goal of maximizing the net interest income over the 6-month period.

The decision variables include 10 investment decision variables and 11 financing variables for a total of 21 decision variables. The 10 investment decision variables include six 30-day marketable securities variables, for January through June, and four 90-day marketable securities variables, for January through April. The 11 financing variables include five 30-day notes payable variables for January through May, four 90-day notes payable variables for January through April, one 180-day notes payable variable for January, and one long-term debt variable for January.

The objective function of the optimization model is to maximize the net interest income over the 6-month planning horizon. This is formulated as the sum of the interest received row less the sum of the interest paid row on the cash flow statement.

OBJECTIVE: Maximize Net Interest Income for the Six Month Period

Some of the relevant constraints have already been programmed into the spreadsheet relationships. For example, the decision variable cells are referenced in the financial flow section of the cash flow statement so that new notes payable automatically mature in the appropriate month, creating a new cash disbursement draining cash. Likewise, marketable security investments in a given month are referenced to automatically mature in the appropriate month, providing additional cash receipts.

The only constraint that is not explicitly considered in the financial planning model is the minimum cash balance constraint shown below. This constraint indicates that the ending cash balance for any given month must equal the minimum cash balance for that month. Any cash over the minimum is invested and any cash shortage is borrowed. The optimization program then solves for the combination of financing and investment decision variables that maximize the objective function subject to the restrictions considered in the worksheet relationships and the explicit minimum cash balance constraint. The minimum balance constraint follows:

SUBJECT TO:

$$CB_{t-1} + ONCF_t + \text{Interest Received}_t - \text{Interest Paid}_t - NMS(30)_t + NMS(30)_{t-1}$$
$$- NMS(90)_t + NMS(90)_{t-3} + NNP(30)_t - NNP(30)_{t-1} + NNP(90)_t - NNP(90)_{t-3}$$
$$+ NNP(180)_{Jan} + NLTD_{Jan} = MIN_t \text{ for } t = 1-6$$

In which:

CB = Cash balance

ONCF = Operating net cash flow

NMS = New marketable securities

NNP = New notes payable

NLTD = New long-term debt

MIN = Minimum cash balance

Additional constraints can easily be added to the model. For example, if there are upper limits on the amount of financing outstanding for the various borrowing categories, these can be added, as the following demonstrates:

$$NP(90)_t = 700, \text{ for } t = 1-4.$$

This equation constrains the dollar amount of 90-day notes payable outstanding to be no more than $700 for any of the first 4 months of the planning period. The NP variable is the one on the balance sheet. Thus new 90-day notes payable for any given month is constrained such that the total balance for this loan category does not exceed the $700 maximum. Note that Exhibit 13-3 indicates that without this constraint 90-day notes payable will equal $975 beginning in February. Adding this constraint will cause 90-day notes payable to equal $700 in February and some other source of financing will be increased. The objective function will also be reduced in value because adding additional constraints such as this adds costs. Other possible constraints might include setting minimum levels for ratios such as the current ratio or the level of net working capital. Using a model like the one discussed in this chapter can help the financial manager enhance the value of the firm by choosing those financing and investment alternatives that maximize the net interest earned for a given financial position, operating cash flow forecast, and a given level of risk, however risk may be defined by the financial manager.

SUMMARY

This chapter began by discussing financial modeling in general. Then a simple percent of sales forecasting model was developed and discussed. This type of forecasting model was discussed because its logic is at the heart of many financial planning models. Finally, the chapter developed the logic for a fairly detailed short-run financial planning model. This model forecasts a firm's monthly balance sheet, income statement, and cash flow statement for an assumed 6-month period. The chapter concluded by discussing the basic logic for each item on the forecast income statement, cash budget, and balance sheet, and presenting a financial strategy based on optimizing the financial plan using an optimization program.

Useful Web Sites

Two sites covering short-term financial modeling:
Treasury Point: www.treasurypoint.com
Wisdom Corporation: www.wisdomcorp.com

Problems

1. Summit, Inc., just completed its best year ever. Sales for 2001 were $5.5 million. Its year-end balance sheet follows:

BALANCE SHEET 2001

Current assets	$1,000,000	Current liabilities	$500,000
Net fixed assets	2,000,000	Long-term debt	1,500,000
		Owners' equity	1,000,000
Total	$3,000,000		$3,000,000

INCOME STATEMENT 2001

Sales	$5,500,000
Cost of goods sold	3,500,000
Gross profit	2,000,000
Operating expenses	1,000,000
Interest	170,000
Taxes	350,200
Net profit	$ 479,800
Dividends	$ 400,000

Summit's financial manager wants to forecast the dollar amount of external financing the firm will need in 2002. The financial manager assumes that sales will increase 30 percent and that because the firm is operating at capacity, total assets will stay in the same proportion to sales in 2002 as in 2001. In addition, all current liabilities are assumed to be spontaneous.

a. Forecast the dollar amount of external funds needed in 2002.
b. How might the firm reduce its reliance on external funds?

2. Program the financial planning model developed in this chapter using spreadsheet software such as Lotus 1-2-3 or Microsoft Excel. Exhibits 13-2 through 13-4 present the optimized financial plan given management's assumptions and policy variables. Enter your own financing and investment plan in the financial strategy section of the plan based on your analysis of the operating cash flow needs and management's interest rate scenario. In other words, try to intuitively determine the best plan without using an optimization program. Make sure that your plan meets the minimum cash balance requirement. Compare the resulting net interest income from your revised plan with that occurring from the optimized plan. Interpret the financing plan logic of the optimized plan shown in the exhibits in relation to the logic you used to devise your plan.

3. Program the financial planning model using spreadsheet software such as Lotus 1-2-3 or Excel. Use zeros for the financing and investment variables and use an add-in optimization program such as Solver for Microsoft Excel to determine the optimal solution. Check your answers against those presented in Exhibits 13-2 through 13-4. Change your input for collection fractions to the company's original policy of 10 percent, 60 percent, 30 percent for the month of sale, month after sale, and 2 months after sale, and compare the net interest income with the optimal net interest income for the new terms. Assume that projected sales under the old terms were the following:

January	$1,600	April	$2,500
February	$1,600	May	$2,400
March	$2,000	June	$1,800

How much does the new credit policy cost the company? Is the change in credit policy advantageous to the firm?

4. Using the financial planning model developed in problem 13-2, assume that the bank allows a maximum 180-day note payable of $500. Implement this new constraint into the model and reoptimize the financial plan. What is the resulting net interest earned from the revised plan? Explain the logic of the result.

5. Beginning with the financial planning model as developed in this chapter, discuss how the model can be adjusted to include a line of credit as a financing choice rather than the various maturities of notes payable. The firm will draw down the line as needed on a monthly basis but can also repay the line as surplus funds become available. Assume the line has a monthly fee that needs to be paid the month after it is incurred, the line requires a minimum monthly compensating cash balance of X percent of the amount borrowed, and that interest is paid the month following the borrowing. The required compensating balance is effective the month following the borrowing because it is assumed that borrowing occurs at the end of each month.

References

Alan M. Cunningham and Richard Bort. 1991. Medium-term cash flow forecasting. In *Corporate Cash Management Handbook.* Cumulative Supplement. Boston: Warren, Gorham & Lamont.

B. K. Stone. 1973. Cash planning and credit-line determination with a financial statement simulator: A cash report on short-term financial planning. *Journal of Financial and Quantitative Analysis* 8(5):711–729.

David A. Wismer. 1985. Approaches to cash flow forecasting. Parts I, II, and III. *Journal of Cash Management* (Jan/Feb, Jul/Aug, Nov/Dec).

FOCUSED CASE

Jones Salvage and Recycling, Inc. (Case A)

Jones Salvage and Recycling, Inc., was started by Mr. John Jones in 1985. Mr. Jones was concerned about the industrial impact on the world's environment and felt that it was time to be proactive in attempting to save the world's decreasing natural resources. His company takes scrap metal and compresses it into 4-ton blocks. His company then ships the blocks to steel mills that melt it down to take out the impurities, and recycle it back into bars and pipes for the construction industry. Jones also recycles glass bottles and jars. They crush the glass into fine powder and ship it to a local glass company that recycles the glass powder into new bottles, which saves natural resources as well as energy. Although Mr. Jones is convinced that this type of business is the wave of the future, the business has not prospered and at times he feels he is out in front of the wave rather than riding it.

The financial manager at Jones Salvage and Recycling, Inc. is attempting to estimate the financial needs of the company for the first half of the new year. The company's end-of-year balance sheet is presented below:

ASSETS		LIABILITIES AND NET WORTH	
Cash	$ 1,000	Accounts payable	$65,000
Marketable securities (30-day)	84,000	Taxes payable	0
Accounts receivable	75,000	30-day notes payable	71,000
Inventory	65,000	Mortgage loan	150,000
Gross fixed assets	251,000	Common stock	100,000
Accumulated depreciation	(25,000)	Retained earnings	65,000

All sales are made on credit with terms of net 30 days, which is standard for the industry. However, the following cash collection schedule for the most recent six months is pretty typical:

Month	Credit sales	Cash collections month of sale	Cash collections 1 month after sale	Cash collections 2 months after sale
July	$60,000	0	$15,000	$25,000
August	90,000	0	30,000	15,000
September	75,000	0	45,000	30,000
October	100,000	0	37,500	45,000
November	100,000	0	50,000	37,500
December	25,000	0	50,000	50,000

Jones purchases materials on terms of net 30 days and pays when due. He purchases enough materials in any given month based on a desired inventory policy of ending each month with enough inventory to satisfy next months' sales at cost. His gross profit margin is 35 percent.

General and administrative costs run about $30,000 per month, and taxes are paid quarterly at the end of March, June, September, and December. The tax rate is 40 percent. Depreciation expense runs $1,000 per month. Jones is currently required to leave a minimum of $1,000 in the company's bank account. Jones forecasts sales for the next eight months to be:

MONTH	FORECASTED SALES
January	$80,000
February	180,000
March	300,000
April	200,000
May	160,000
June	120,000
July	100,000
August	90,000

REQUIRED

1. Using the financial planning model provided to you on disk, enter the necessary data from the information presented and forecast Jones' monthly cash flow position for each month of the 6-month period January through June. You should also construct a monthly income statement, cash budget, and balance sheet for the 6-month planning period.
2. Ignoring any interest expense or interest income, what is the total amount of financing that Jones' financial manager must plan for to cover the coming 6 months?

INTEGRATIVE CASE—PART 4
Toy World, Inc.

Grace Jones, the recently hired treasurer of Toy World, Inc., a manufacturer of specialty toys, was summoned to the office of Dan Culbreth, the president and chief executive officer. When she got to Dan's office, Grace found him shuffling through a set of worksheets. He told her that because of a recent tightening of credit by the Federal Reserve, and hence an impending contraction of bank loans, the firm's bank has asked each of its major loan customers for an estimate of their borrowing requirements for the remainder of 1995 and the first half of 1996. Also, Dan informed Grace that the bank planned to continue its practice of charging a commitment fee of 1.5 percent per year (0.1250 percent per month) on any unused committed funds.

Dan had a previously scheduled meeting with the firm's bankers the following Monday, so he asked Grace to produce an estimate of the firm's probable loan requirements that he could submit at that time. Dan was going away on a white-water rafting expedition, a trip that had already been delayed several times, and he would not be back until just before his meeting with the bankers. Therefore, he asked Grace to prepare a cash budget while he was away.

Because of Toy World's rapid growth over the last few years, no one had taken the time to prepare a cash budget recently, so Grace was afraid she would have to start from scratch. From information already available, Grace knew that no loans would be needed from the bank before January, so she decided to restrict her budget to the period of January through June 1996.

As a first step, she obtained the following sales forecast from the marketing department:

1995	November	$800,000
	December	925,000
1996	January	500,000
	February	300,000
	March	280,000
	April	225,000
	May	200,000
	June	250,000
	July	350,000
	August	400,000

Note that the sales figures are before any discounts; that is, they are not net of discounts. Also, the marketing people cautioned Grace to recognize that actual sales could vary substantially from the forecasted levels, because kids are fickle in their choice of toys.

Toy World's credit policy is 2/15, net 30. Hence, a 2 percent discount is allowed if payment is made within 15 days of the sale; otherwise, payment in full is due 30 days after the date of sale. On the basis of a previous study, Grace estimates that, generally, 35 percent of the firm's customers take the discount, 60 percent pay within 30 days, and 5 percent pay late, with the late payments received about 60 days after the invoice date, on average. For monthly budgeting purposes, discount sales are assumed to be collected in the month of the sale, net sales in the month after the sale, and late sales 2 months after the sale. Of course, variances could occur from all of these figures.

Toy World begins production of goods 2 months before the anticipated sale date. Variable production costs are made up entirely of purchased materials and labor, which total 70 percent of forecasted sales—30 percent for materials and 40 percent for labor. Again, these figures could change if operating conditions depart from norms. All materials are purchased just before production begins, or 2 months before the sale of the finished goods. On average, Toy World pays 60 percent of the materials cost in the month when it receives the materials, and the remaining 40 percent the next month, or 1 month before the sale. Half of the labor expenses are paid 2 months before the sale, and the remaining 50 percent is paid 1 month before the sale.

Toy World pays fixed general and administrative expenses of approximately $95,000 a month, and lease obligations amount to $60,000 per month. Both expenditures are expected to continue at the same

Copyright © 1994. The Dryden Press. All rights reserved.

level throughout the forecast period. The firm estimates miscellaneous expenses to be $40,000 monthly, and fixed assets are currently being depreciated at the rate of $47,500 per month. Toy World has $1,600,000 (book value) of bonds outstanding. They carry a 10 percent semi-annual coupon, and interest is paid on January 15 and July 15. Also, the company is planning to replace an old machine in June with a new one expected to cost $100,000. The old machine has both a zero book and a zero market value. Federal and state income taxes are expected to be $90,000 quarterly, and payments must be made on the 15th of December, March, June, and September. Toy World has a target minimum cash balance of $450,000, and this amount will be on hand on January 1, 1996.

Assume that you were recently hired as Grace Jones's assistant, and she has turned the job of preparing the cash budget over to you. You must meet with her and Dan Culbreth on Sunday night to review the budget prior to Dan's meeting with the bankers on Monday. You recall the cash budgeting process from your recently completed finance course, and you plan to use the format shown in Table 1 as a guide to prepare a monthly cash budget for Toy World for January through June 1996. Based on information obtained from the firm's credit department, Grace suggests that the following assumptions be used to prepare the budget. Initially, disregard both interest payments on shortterm bank loans and interest received from investing surplus funds. Also, assume that all cash flows occur on the 15th of each month. Finally, note that collections from sales in November and December of 1995 will not be completed until January and February of 1996, respectively.

Grace is extremely concerned about the peak funds shortfall during the 6-month planning period. She is hoping that a $500,000 line of credit will be sufficient to cover any expected cash shortfall. There has been talk in the industry about changes under which suppliers would bill on terms requiring payments early in each month and, separately, customers would pay toward the end of the month. If these changes are made, competition would force Toy World to adapt to them. Therefore, Grace would also like to know how the cash budget would be affected if Toy World's cash outflows start to cluster at the beginning of the month, while collections become heaviest toward the end of the month.

At the last minute, Grace decided that a daily cash budget for the month of January should also be

developed (Table 2 is provided as a guide). She obtained the following information from Toy World managers for use in developing the daily cash budget:

1. Toy World normally operates 7 days a week.
2. Sales generally occur at a constant rate throughout the month; that is, 1/31 of the January sales are made each day.
3. Daily sales typically follow the 35 percent, 60 percent, 5 percent collection breakdown.
4. Discount purchasers take full advantage of the 15-day discount period before paying, and "on time" purchasers wait the full 30 days to pay. Thus collections during the first 15 days of January will reflect discount sales from the last 15 days of December, plus "regular" sales made in earlier months. Also, on January 31, Toy World will begin collecting January's net sales and December's late sales.
5. The lease payment is made on the first of the month.
6. Fifty percent of both labor costs and general and administrative expenses are paid on the first and 50 percent are paid on the 15th.
7. Materials are assumed to be delivered on the first and paid for on the fifth.
8. Miscellaneous expenses are incurred and paid evenly throughout the month, 1/31 each day.
9. Required interest payments are made on the 15th.
10. The target cash balance is $450,000, and this amount must be in the bank on each day. This balance is higher than the firm would otherwise keep, but it is required as a compensating balance under terms of the firm's bank loan agreement. However, the bank may be willing to renegotiate this provision.

Dan has expressed some concern about the efficient use of his firm's cash resources. Specifically, he has questioned whether or not seasonal variations should be incorporated into the firm's target balance. In other words, during months when cash needs are greatest, the target balance would be somewhat higher, and the target would be set at a lower level during slack months. He asked you to consider this situation and to run some numbers to demonstrate the effect of using different target balances. Of course, this requires a modification to the bank loan agreement.

Grace noted that the only receipts shown in Toy World's cash budget are collections. She notes that

Toy World pays a 7 percent interest rate on the short-term bank loan and would probably earn 5 percent on surplus cash. She wants to know how these new items could be incorporated into the cash budget. Additionally, she would like your views on an investment strategy for Toy World to invest any surplus funds. Toy World's policy has been to invest only in securities that provide liquidity and safety, yet offer a reasonable rate of return. Grace has heard about securities called "derivatives" that are backed by US Treasury bonds yet offer higher returns than T-bonds, and she wonders if they should be used.

Dan Culbreth is an astute businessman, so he realizes that the cash budget is a forecast, and that many of the cash flows shown are expected values rather than amounts known with certainty. If actual sales, hence collections, are different from forecasted levels, the forecasted surpluses and deficits would be incorrect. He is interested in knowing how various changes in the key assumptions would affect the firm's cash surplus or deficit. It would be particularly bad to obtain a $500,000 line of credit and then find that, because of incorrect assumptions, the actual loan requirement is $700,000. Labor costs and many other expenses are set by contract at the start of the 6-month forecast period on the basis of the original expected sales. Therefore, many of the outflows cannot be adjusted downward during the planning period even if sales decline below the forecasted levels. Therefore,

Dan sent Grace a memo requesting that the following three scenarios be specifically considered: (1) What would be the impact on the monthly net cash flows from January to June 1996 if actual sales for November through June were 20 percent below the forecasted amounts? (2) What if actual sales were only 50 percent of the forecasted level? (3) Even if sales are as expected, what would happen if customers changed their payment patterns and began paying more slowly, such as 25 percent in the month of sale, 55 percent in the following month, and 20 percent in the second month versus the old 35-60-5 pattern?

Based on an analysis of the situation, recommend the size of the credit line Toy World should seek. Think about any other related issues that Grace, Dan, or the bankers, might raise concerning the budgets. In particular, be prepared to explain the sources of all the numbers, and the effects on the company's cash requirements if any of the basic assumptions turn out to be incorrect. It would be useful to do some sensitivity analyses, and to be prepared to answer various "what if" questions Dan might ask. Be prepared to discuss the tradeoff between a high credit line with a high commitment fee versus a low credit line with a low commitment fee. Finally, Grace knows that Dan has been thinking about altering the production process to produce at a level rate all year rather than producing 1 month based on sales expected in the next month. How might such a change affect loan requirements?

TABLE 1
Monthly Cash Budget Worksheet

	November	December	January	February	March	April	May	June	July	August
I. Collection and Payments										
Gross Sales (expected)	$800,000						$200,000	$250,000	$350,000	$400,000
Gross Sales (realized)	$800,000						$200,000	$250,000	$350,000	$400,000
Collections										
Month of Sale	$274,000	$317,275			180,000	168,000	68,600	$ 85,750		
1 Month After Sale					25,000	15,000	135,000	120,000		
2 Months After Sale							14,000	11,250		
Total Collections			$766,500	$449,150	$ 60,000	$ 75,000	$105,000	$120,000		
Purchases	$150,000									
Payments:										
2 Months Before Sale	90,000	54,000	50,400	33,600						
1 Month Before Sale		60,000	36,000							
Total Payments			$ 86,400					$114,000		
II. Cash Gain (Loss) For Month										
Collections			$766,500							
Payments										
Purchases								$114,000		
Labor										
2 Months Before Sale			56,000	$ 56,000	$ 45,000	$ 40,000	$ 50,000	80,000		
1 Month Before Sale			60,000					70,000		
General/Admin. Exp.			95,000							
Lease			60,000							
Miscellaneous Exp.			40,000							
Taxes					90,000			90,000		
Interest (on bonds)			80,000				90,000			
New Equipment								100,000		
Total Payments			$477,400							
Net Cash Gain (Loss)			$289,100	$ 79,050						
III. Cash Surplus or Loan Requirement										
Cash at Start (no borrowing)			$450,000	$739,100						
Cumulative Cash			$739,100							
Target Cash Balance			$450,000							
Surplus Cash or Total Loans Outstanding to Maintain Target Cash Balance			$289,100							

TABLE 2
Daily Cash Budget Worksheet

Day:	1	2	•••	5	•••	10	•••	15	16	•••	28	29	30	31
I. Collections and Payments														
Gross Sales	$ 16,129		•••		•••		•••	$16,129	$16,129	•••			$16,129	$16,129
Collections:														
Discount Payers	$ 10,235		•••		•••		•••		$5,532	•••			$5,532	$5,532
Net Payers	17,903		•••		•••		•••		17,903	•••			17,903	9,677
Late Payers	1,333		•••		•••		•••		1,333	•••			1,492	1,492
Total Collections	$ 29,471	$ 29,471	•••	$ 29,471	•••	$ 29,471	•••	$ 29,471	$ 24,768	•••	$ 24,768	$ 24,768	$ 24,927	$16,701
Purchases	$ 84,000													
Payments:														
2 Months Before Sale														
1 Month Before Sale				$ 36,000										
Total Payments		$0	•••	$ 86,400	•••		•••	$0	$0	•••	$0	$0	$0	$0
II. Cash Gain (Loss) For Day														
Collections	$ 29,471	$ 29,471	•••	$ 29,471	•••	$ 29,471	•••	$ 29,471	$ 24,769	•••	$ 24,769	$ 24,769	$ 24,927	$16,702
Payments:														
Purchases				$ 86,400										
Labor														
2 Months Before Sale	$ 28,000							$ 28,000						
1 Month Before Sale	30,000							30,000						
General/Admin. Exp.	47,500							47,500						
Lease														
Miscellaneous Exp.	1,290	1,290	•••	1,290	•••	1,290	•••	1,290	1,290	•••	1,290	1,290	1,290	1,290
Taxes								80,000						
Interest (on bonds)														
Total Payments	$106,790	$ 1,290	•••	$ 87,690	•••	$ 1,290	•••	$186,790	1,290	•••	$ 1,290	$ 1,290	$ 1,290	$1,290
Net Cash Gain (Loss)	($177,319)	$ 28,181	•••	($ 58,219)	•••	$ 28,181	•••	(157,319)	$ 23,479	•••	$ 23,479	$ 23,479	$ 23,637	$15,412
III. Cash Surplus or Loan Repayment														
Cash at Start (no borrowing)	$450,000	$312,681	•••	$397,224	•••	$451,728	•••	$592,633	$435,314	•••	$717,056		$764,013	$787,650
Cumulative Cash	$312,681	340,862	•••	339,005	•••	479,909	•••		$458,792	•••			$787,650	$803,061
Target Cash Balance	450,000	450,000	•••	450,000	•••	450,000	•••		450,000	•••			450,000	450,000
Surplus Cash or														
Total Loans Outstanding to Maintain Target														
Cash Balance	($137,319)	($109,138)	•••	($110,995)	•••	$ 29,909	•••	$ 8,792		•••	$290,534	$314,013	$337,650	$353,061

PART V
Short-Term Investment and Financing

Chapter 14   The Money Market
Chapter 15   Short-Term Investment Management
Chapter 16   Short-Term Financing
Chapter 17   Managing Interest Rate Risk

With a cashflow forecast and a financial planning model, the financial manager is now ready to develop an investment and financial strategy. Chapter 14 introduces the basics of the money market, the financial environment in which investment and financing strategies are developed. Chapter 15 then introduces a portfolio approach to investment decision making. Chapter 16 provides a broad overview of short-term financing and how to compare effective costs of bank financing with direct financing. Finally, in Chapter 17 we indicate how to manage interest rate risk through hedging with a variety of financial derivative securities.

CHAPTER 14

The Money Market

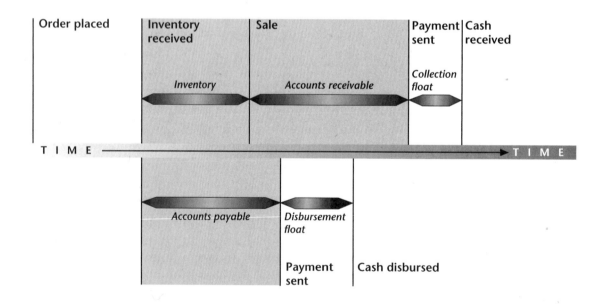

OBJECTIVES

After studying this chapter, you should be able to:

- Specify the important features of money markets.
- Define the various money market instruments by category: bank, corporate, federal government, and state and local government.
- Calculate taxable-equivalent yield, yield from dividend capture, discount yield, coupon-equivalent yield, and effective annual yield.
- Specify types of investment risk and their effects on yields.
- Indicate the importance of yield curves and theories that explain the shape of an empirical yield curve.

Toyota Motors, called Toyota Bank by some, piled up cash and securities surpluses amounting to more than $27 billion in 1996, and in early 2001 still had $8 billion in cash and equivalents and another $9.7 billion in short-term investments. Primarily resulting from a surplus of operating cash flow awaiting long-term reinvestment coupled with a meager 6 percent dividend payout ratio, these funds must be invested carefully. Otherwise, stockholders could justifiably demand that Toyota simply pay large cash dividends and later issue new shares of stock if profitable capital investments became available. General Motors once amassed liquid assets of $9 billion before acquiring Electronic Data Systems (EDS) and Hughes Aircraft for a combined $7.6 billion. Similarly, in the late 1980s, Ford accumulated more than $12 billion, mostly in the form of short-term and very liquid long-term securities. At the time, this was equivalent to approximately $40 per share—40 percent of the market value of Ford's common stock—leading one securities analyst to christen the company Fort Knox. Some of this cash was used to repurchase common stock.[1]

---

[1]For an interesting diagnosis of what Shell should do with its $12.4 billion of cash and short-term securities, see The $12.4 billion problem. *Fortune* August 4, 1997:125.

Knowing the available investment options and how to evaluate them is important for three major reasons. First, the company that has worked hard to improve its cash management and forecasting ability has done so to no avail if it cannot increase interest income or reduce interest expense. It makes no sense to leave freed-up cash idle. Second, even when the company is a net borrower during much of the year, it still needs a liquidity reserve—and not all of this would be in the form of cash or untapped short-term borrowing. Recall that cash flows are unsynchronized, uneven, and uncertain. If cash receipts and disbursements (including capital investments and dividends) were perfectly synchronized and even, there would be a much smaller money market. Third, the corporate treasurer must understand the money markets because each investment represents someone else's borrowing. Learning about potential investments implies understanding when and how each security could be used as a way to borrow funds. We develop the borrowing aspects of the money market instruments in Chapter 16.

Short-term investment and borrowing decisions require a mastery of money market concepts, as the following financial dilemma illustrates.

FINANCIAL DILEMMA

Selecting an Investing Maturity

Dave's workday was just interrupted by a telephone call from his relationship banker recommending that Dave look into longer maturities for his company's investments. Dave has been investing the surplus cash exclusively in overnight repurchase agreements (RPs), but the banker insists that monies the company will not need for 6 months will receive higher interest with certificates of deposit (CDs). The normal "premium" for "extending maturities" in this fashion is about 1.4 percent. In fact, the banker suggested that if the company later needs the money on short notice, it could use the CDs as collateral. Dave cannot understand why 6-month CDs should offer a higher yield than overnight investments and wonders what the banker meant by the expression "riding the yield curve." A thought crosses Dave's mind: "Maybe this banker's just trying to sell some of the bank's CDs."

In this first of two investments chapters, we examine the short-term investment alternatives and the risks that account for different yields on specific investments. These risks are related to differences in maturities, default risk, interest rate risk, and other factors. We also discuss the growing focus on event risk. In Chapter 15, we show how the investments manager puts information about alternatives and their risks together in assembling a securities portfolio.

NATURE OF THE MONEY MARKET

The money market is composed of all securities maturing in 1 year or less. It is not a single unified market, but a collection of markets for various short-term securities. Two words for investment alternatives, security and instrument, are often used interchangeably, but it is useful for our purposes to distinguish between them. We define a security as a specific investment issued by a given issuer.[2] An example is the Student Loan Marketing System's $650 million issue of short term floating rate notes on March 12, 2001, with an interest rate reset each week on the day following the US Treasury bill auction, with the repayment of the notes due (maturing) on September 20, 2001. Each security belongs to a class of similar investments that we define as an instrument. Examples of instruments are agency notes, commercial paper (CP), Treasury bills, CDs, bankers' acceptances (BAs), and RPs. The investment process thus involves selecting an instrument before choosing among all the different issuers' securities for that instrument.

Primary and Secondary Markets

The money market does not exist merely in a single location. Rather, there are several key locations where much of the security issuance occurs. The primary market, or new issue market, is centered in money centers such as New York City, London, Frankfurt, Singapore, and Hong Kong. Investors can access this over-the-counter market from anywhere because the market consists of telephone and computer hookups among all participating dealers and brokers. It is in the primary market that investment bankers arrange for the marketing and pricing of new issues of money market securities.

---

[2]Technically, a security is distinguished by the qualities of marketability and negotiability, but with rare exception, all the money market instruments corporate investors might consider for investment purposes have these qualities.

Sometimes a group of investment banks, called a syndicate, works together on the marketing and shares the risk involved with bringing a new issue to market—which may or may not be acceptable at the predetermined price. Alternately, the investment banker may arrange a private placement, in which a large institution such as a retirement fund or insurance company buys the entire issue. To distinguish the money market from capital markets, only securities with a current maturity of 1 year or less are included. When first issued, a 5-year Treasury note has an *original maturity* of 5 years; 1 year later, it has a *current maturity* of 4 years. Four years after its issue, it has a current maturity of 1 year and changes from a capital market security to a money market security. If traded, it is not considered part of the primary market.

Investors holding the investment to maturity will receive the face value of that investment from the issuer. Not every investor holds the security to maturity, however, necessitating a well-functioning secondary market (in which outstanding issues are traded) for resale. Securities with a current maturity of 1 year or less bought and sold on the secondary market are considered part of the money market. The secondary market, even more so than the primary market, is best thought of as a global network of telecommunication hookups between all potential buyers and sellers. Primary and secondary markets are interrelated because the larger the volume on the resale market, the less risk involved with buying the security on the primary market. Treasury bills and other instruments with smoothly functioning secondary markets can offer a slightly lower interest rate when originally issued, corresponding to this lower risk. Rates on a given instrument with identical maturities and the same issuers can vary depending on whether the quote is on a new issue or a resale. These differences are mainly a result of differences in an instrument's liquidity, which is the ability to sell quickly at or very close to the present market price. An instrument is considered liquid if it has high degrees of *secondary market* breadth, depth, and resiliency. *Market breadth* refers to the number and size of parties that are potential buyers of the instruments. Thus a thin market is one with little participation by buyers and/or sellers. The *depth* of a market is its ability to absorb a large quantity of a security without a major change in the security's price or yield. *Resiliency* exists if many new orders enter the market in response to a temporary imbalance in buy or sell orders that has pushed the price away from its equilibrium level. In a later section of this chapter, we note the instruments whose marketability is compromised by lack of market breadth and depth.

Wholesale and Retail Markets

Another common way of dividing the money market is into wholesale and retail markets. The wholesale market is for large-dollar transactions between large investors. The transaction amount may be large because a group of securities is being sold or because one large denomination security is involved. The denomination of a security refers to its face value. Much of the dollar volume in the money market is characterized by such trades, in which typical "round lots" are $1 million or more. In contrast, individuals might purchase $500 CDs from their local banks as part of the small-dollar retail market. The money market is largely a wholesale market, and we are exclusively interested in that segment because most businesses take part in it. Corporate investors are sometimes labeled institutional investors, along with other large, nonpersonal investors such as pension funds, governments, mutual funds, and insurance companies. Because fixed costs are involved in preparing securities for sale and selling them, the issuer offers a lower yield on retail securities. The growing popularity of money market mutual funds, as an investment both for individuals and businesses, arises from the fact that investors can achieve the higher wholesale market interest rates by pooling their funds with other investors until the fund has large enough sums to invest in large-denomination securities.

Money Market Interest Rates

Interest rates on money market securities typically move in unison. Rates (or yields, when considered from the perspective of the investor) are only partly the results of supply and demand conditions in the instrument's market. The various instruments are close substitutes for one another, particularly for the short-term investor. Thus the major investor(s) and borrower(s) in one instrument's market influence yields in all other markets. The most important common influences arise from the activities of the US Treasury, the Federal Reserve, and daily CD or CP issuers such as Citicorp and General Motors Acceptance Corporation.

The Treasury conducts weekly auctions of Treasury bills, as well as less frequent auctions of notes and bonds, as a means of financing the huge federal debt. These multibillion dollar issues exert tremendous influence on all money markets because of their size and also because Treasury securities constitute an investment alternative for most investors. There is essentially no risk of the Treasury not paying interest and repaying principal on its securities, so risk premiums on corporate or other government securities are priced relative to Treasury securities.

ROLE OF THE FEDERAL RESERVE.   The Federal Reserve (Fed) directly and indirectly influences interest rates as it carries out its monetary policy. The open-market buying of Treasury securities influences demand and supply conditions. The Fed also sets the discount rate and the Fed funds rate. The discount rate is the rate charged depository institutions when they borrow reserves from the Fed to meet their reserve requirements. The Fed funds rate is the rate charged on reserve borrowings, mostly overnight, transacted between banks. Whereas the discount rate is not changed often, the Fed funds rate may vary widely even within one day's trading. Alternate Wednesdays experience the most volatile rate swings, as banks jockey to get their reserves up to required levels for Federal Reserve reporting purposes. Except when affected by these technical conditions, Fed funds rate movements tend to underlie movements in all money market rates.

CORRELATION OF SHORT-TERM INTEREST RATES.   To demonstrate how short-term interest rates move together, we conducted a correlation analysis between US domestic Certificates of Deposit, Treasury bill, Commercial Paper, Eurodollar Certificate of Deposit, and Fed funds rates for the 6-year period in the 1990s. We found a very high correlation between these rates (Exhibit 14-1). Rates on the investments that represent

EXHIBIT 14-1
Correlation Between Short-Term Interest Rates

	TREASURY BILL	CD	CP	EURODOLLAR CDS
CD	0.991			
CP	0.994	0.993		
Eurodollar CD	0.993	0.994	0.997	
Fed funds	0.982	0.985	0.980	0.979

NOTE: Rates cover the period from 5/8/90 to 9/30/96.

close substitutes for the investor—Treasury bills, domestic CDs, CP, and Eurodollar CDs—track very closely with each other, with correlations between these securities all being 0.99 (compared with a perfect positive correlation of 1.00). This does not mean that the rates are identical, but that the differences between them tend to persist as rates move up and down together. Some astute corporate investors will watch for temporary divergences between the rates and buy the attractively priced securities.

Tax Status

Money market instruments can also be divided into taxable and tax-advantaged categories. Taxable instruments include CP, domestic and Eurodollar Certificates of Deposits, Bankers Acceptances, Repurchase Agreements, and money market mutual funds invested in these instruments. Interest is fully taxable, as are capital gains.

Tax-advantaged instruments are those on which part or all of the income is exempted from taxation or on which the tax is deferred. In most states, there is no tax liability for interest income on Treasury securities. Corporations buying another company's stock may exclude 70 percent of the dividends received from taxable income. Municipal obligations, or "munis," pay interest that is not taxable for federal income tax purposes. Additionally, interest on munis is often exempted from tax for residents of the state in which the issuer is located. Capital gains on Treasury bills or munis are fully taxable, however.[3] The differential tax treatment of some securities implies that the investor must adjust both taxable and tax-advantaged yields to a common basis for comparison. We illustrate this adjustment in a later section.

Market Mechanics and Intermediaries

The market microstructure consists of the participants and mechanics involved in making transactions. Other than the buyers and sellers, the key actors in money markets are dealers and brokers. Sales agents and traders also play a role.

Dealers typically "take a position" in the security instrument(s) that they trade, meaning they hold an inventory of securities. Independent securities dealers, investment banks, and large commercial banks commonly have individuals that perform the dealer role. Like car dealers, money market dealers profit from the difference between what they pay for the security and what they sell it for. At any time, a dealer's profit margin is revealed by the spread between his or her quoted bid (buy) and offer (sell) prices. The spread in large CDs is approximately 5 basis points,[4] and on CDs issued frequently in large volumes, the spread may even be lower.

Dealers finance this inventory of securities mainly by borrowing funds on an overnight basis. Dealers are exposed to interest rate risk—the possibility that interest rates will increase, causing the prices of existing fixed-income securities to drop. This motivates dealers to sell off and replenish their inventory as quickly as possible.[5] When dealers have relatively small supplies of securities and customer demand for those securities increases, dealers may drive prices up and interest rates down as they enter the markets to fill demand, as happened in late 1993.

---

[3]An additional complication is posed by the alternative minimum tax, which applies to individuals and corporations claiming an unusually large number of deductions in a given year. Items normally not taxed may be assessed under the alternative minimum tax.

[4]A basis point equates to 1/100 of 1 percent, making 100 basis points equivalent to 1 percent.

[5]Generally, this is the case because of financing costs and interest rate risk. However, sometimes the dealer speculates on interest rate movements in the role of a trader.

FOCUS ON PRACTICE

HOW IMPORTANT IS TRUST IN THE MONEY MARKET?   If power corrupts, and absolute power corrupts absolutely, the classic example is the Salomon Brothers manipulation of Treasury security issues in the early 1990s. Seizing a large proportion of a given issue in the preliminary trading of these securities, Salomon tacked on abnormally large spreads before reselling the securities. Other dealers, among the more than 40 then authorized to deal in government securities, subsequently were squeezed because they had already committed to supply securities to their customers at agreed-on prices. None of this would have created a furor except that Salomon went well beyond the legal maximum amount for which a dealer is permitted to bid, in effect cornering the market. Mostly, this was done through fictitious orders placed on behalf of Salomon's customers. The stir was so great that the government opened Treasury security bidding to all parties, not just approved dealers and commercial banks. Additionally, some of Salomon's biggest customers, including the World Bank, quit doing business with the company for 3 months or more. Possibly, the difference between primary and secondary market yields will decline because of the elimination of fraud and the newly intensified competition.

Trust plays a vital role in transacting business, as most trades are agreed on by telephone, with no written contract. Because the money markets are so dependent on integrity, particularly on the part of dealers, the Salomon Brothers scandal in 1990 and 1991 rocked the markets (see Focus on Practice).

Brokers also are middlemen, but they do not inventory the securities; they arrange transactions. When receiving an order, they check around for the security; when located, the brokers execute the trade. They are paid a commission for their services, which may be as small as $1 per $1 million on Fed funds trades. Dealers often work through brokers when trading with other dealers, to hide their identity.

Dealers function as brokers in their role as sales agents for banks (bank deposit notes and bank notes) and CP issuers. For a commission, the agent locates buyers for the institution's securities; again, this is without risk, because the agent does not have to buy and resell the securities.

In addition to their middleman roles, brokers and dealers sometimes participate as traders, trying to profit on anticipated interest rate or currency movements. Here, they are "positioned" in securities not as intermediaries but as traders for their company's own account. When traders guess right, their trading profits add to the revenues gained from brokerage commissions and bid-ask spreads. However, trading is extremely risky when interest rates are volatile.

In their roles as dealers, brokers, sales agents, and traders, money market intermediaries provide market breadth and depth. The result is greater marketability and smaller bid-ask spreads for investors, reducing securities' liquidity risk.

MONEY MARKET INSTRUMENTS

Treasury professionals invest in a wide array of short-term securities to earn a high yield while preserving the invested capital. Capital preservation guidelines in most companies' investment policies dictate that safety and liquidity be preeminent in investment selection decisions. Security safety implies a very low default risk (or credit risk), the possibility that the issuer will not meet contractual obligations to pay interest or repay principal. It also implies that securities with low interest rate risk be selected.

Liquidity risk is tied to the marketability of a security—the ability to sell quickly at or very near the current market price. Money market securities are generally both safe and liquid, but there is some variation across the spectrum of instruments. We complete our discussion of risk attributes after surveying the major classes of short-term instruments: bank, corporate, federal government, state and local government, and mixed.

Bank Instruments

The most convenient method of investing for corporations is to leave the excess cash at the bank. Although corporations cannot legally be paid interest on demand deposit accounts, surplus funds can be swept into overnight investments or invested in the bank's CDs or the parent bank holding company's CDs, other time deposits, or CP. Large banks also offer for corporate investors part or whole interests in loans, known as loan participations, and securities backed by credit card receivables or auto loans. These forms of asset securitization have become prevalent in the United States because of the need for banks to increase their capital-to-assets ratio. Banks, especially those with sizable problem loan portfolios, have had difficulty selling new capital stock, necessitating asset sales and slowed loan growth.

CERTIFICATES OF DEPOSIT.   Large-dollar CDs were formerly a favorite instrument of corporate investors, but many money-center banks have recently turned to other time deposits to raise additional funds. First offered in 1961 by Citibank, a certificate of deposit (CD) is an interest-bearing account having a specific denomination and a specific maturity. Most CDs impose a substantial penalty for early withdrawal, usually 3 months of interest. To avoid this, a business might invest in a large-dollar negotiable CD, which comes in $100,000 and larger denominations. Negotiability means the security can be legally sold and exchanged between investors, circumventing the early withdrawal penalty charged by the issuing bank. On approximately 40 of the largest money centers and super-regional banks' negotiable CDs, there is very good liquidity because of an active secondary market centered in New York City. Investors buy and sell round lots of $1 million or more. Basic information regarding negotiable CDs and other bank-issued instruments, including typical denominations and maturities and major risk attributes, is presented in Exhibit 14-2. The growth of the large-dollar CD market is evidenced by the amount of large-denomination deposits outstanding, which peaked at more than $440 billion in 1996 and continues to total about $380 billion at the end of 1999.

The Eurodollar CD market has grown rapidly, eclipsing the domestic CD market for institutional investors. Eurodollar securities are dollar-denominated deposits held in banks or bank branches outside the United States or in international banking facilities (which can offer Eurodollar deposits only to non-US residents) within the United States. Most Eurodollar deposits are in London-based branches of US or foreign banks, but volume is increasing in Frankfurt and non-European locations such as Hong Kong and Singapore. Eurodollar CDs and other time deposits range from overnight to 5 years in maturity, but most are 6 months or shorter. They are mainly used to make dollar-denominated loans to US multinational corporations, to foreign corporations and governments wishing to borrow in dollars, and to domestic banks. The banks borrow funds in the Euro market as a substitute for Federal Reserve funds borrowing so that interest rates track fairly closely with the Fed funds rate. Eurodollar deposits are not assessed a Federal Deposit Insurance Corporation (FDIC) premium, nor are they required to

EXHIBIT 14-2
Bank Instruments

INSTRUMENT	PURPOSE ISSUED	DENOMINATION	MATURITY	RISK ASPECTS
Certificates of deposit	Raise funds to make new loans.	Primary market: $100,000+ (mostly $1 million) Secondary market: round lot is $2–$5 million	Range: 7 days to 8 years Typical: 1,2,3,6 months	Default risk: • only first $100,000 guaranteed by FDIC • amount of premium not guaranteed if buying on secondary market at premium
Time deposits	Raise funds to make loans. Interbank deposits for domestic correspondent banks and other banks in Eurodollar market.	Any amount, except when minimum amount set by bank.	Range: 1 day to 3 months when purchased for short-term investments portfolio.	Liquidity risk: • usually non-negotiable • fixed maturity Political risk: • Eurodollar time deposits at branches may be vulnerable to expropriation by government
Bankers' acceptances	Finances import or export by having bank accept a time draft drawn on buyer, usually linked to the bank's letter of credit.	Mostly $500,000 to $1 million.	Range: Up to 270 days Typical: 3 months	Default risk: • negligible because buyer and bank obliged to pay draft Liquidity risk: • active secondary market implies little liquidity risk
Loan participations	Risk sharing strategy of lender; also allows bank to relend part of or all loan principal. Substitutes for commercial paper, which banks are prohibited from underwriting.	Varies	Range: 1 day to 3 months	Default risk: • investor takes part of or all the default risk when buying part of or all the loan participation. Some issuers are not creditworthy enough to issue commercial paper. Most participations have guarantor. Liquidity risk: • not liquid, no secondary market
Securitized assets: Auto loans Credit cards Other	To take existing assets off the books of the bank while retaining servicing fees. Allows banks to reloan the money.	Varies	Range: 1–3 years for securities backed by auto loans and credit card receivables.	Default risk: • depends on credit enhancement. Partly mitigated by the portfolio effect of pooling many loans.

have reserves held against them. The lower costs to issuers imply higher yields than domestic CDs for the investor. Eurodollar CDs yield slightly less than the **London Interbank Offer Rate** (LIBOR), the rate at which banks offer term Eurodollar deposits to each other. Liquidity risk is minimal because of an active secondary market.

OTHER TIME DEPOSITS.   Corporate investors rarely invest in domestic time deposits other than CDs because they are illiquid until the principal is repaid at the end of the fixed term. The flexibility of Eurodollar time deposits, which may be structured for the individual company's specific cash needs, makes these investments appealing. However, three factors make the Eurodollar time deposits less attractive than other alternatives such as domestic CDs. First, there is no FDIC guarantee. Second, the investor bears the risk that the host country where the deposit is issued may seize foreign investors' funds or at least block dollar outflows. Third, if the investor is basing the maturity decision on a flawed cash forecast, illiquidity is problematic. As with non-negotiable CDs, the investor can get around the illiquidity of time deposits by arranging beforehand for the option to make a deposit-collateralized loan.

Two unique time deposits that have recently appeared and grown rapidly in the domestic money market are bank deposit notes and bank notes. **Bank deposit notes** range from 9 months to 30 years in maturity and have an active secondary market. The issuing bank's credit quality is the key for assessing default risk, but the first $100,000 is federally guaranteed. Not so for **bank notes**, which technically are not deposits and therefore avoid FDIC insurance premiums (and also forfeit deposit insurance coverage). Corporate investors invest mainly in top-rated bank deposit notes and bank notes.[6] Suntrust Banks had to pay 8 basis points above the 3-month LIBOR (about 50 basis points above a 3-month Treasury bill) on its 5-year A1 rated floating rate bank notes, issued in the late 1990s.

BANKERS' ACCEPTANCES.   Corporate time drafts that are accepted, or guaranteed, for payment by the issuer's bank are called **bankers' acceptances** (BAs). Acceptances mainly are used to finance international trade but also have been used in domestic transactions. They arise from the difficulty businesses in the exporting country have in assessing the creditworthiness of importers. Having the importer's bank guarantee payment implies two parties are liable for the importer's time draft: the importer and its bank. The creditworthiness of the accepting bank is substituted for that of the importer, leading exporters to request guarantee by a AAA-rated bank.

A BA often is issued consequent to a bank letter of credit (LOC), which states that the bank will pay the amount owed if the buyer defaults. Once the exporter receives the accepted draft from the importer's bank, it can endorse and sell it to receive immediate cash, because acceptances are negotiable instruments. The difference between the discounted price at which the acceptance is sold and its face value paid at maturity is the interest return to the investor. Liquidity is good because of an active secondary market. Since their inception in the 1920s in the United States, there never has been a default on a BA, except when a counterfeit acceptance was executed. Bankers' acceptances yield 0.5 to 2 percent more than Treasury bills of the same maturity. Details regarding denominations, maturities, and default risk are provided in Exhibit 14-2.

LOAN PARTICIPATIONS.   After a bank or syndicate of banks arranges a large loan, part or all of the loan may be sold off in the form of a loan participation. Banks may sell loans to other banks or corporate investors. The bank arranging the loan receives fees from loan

---

[6]See the brief discussion of these securities in Alan Seidner's *1990 Supplement*, cited in the chapter references.

originating (setting up the documentation and payment structure) and servicing (processing interest payments and principal repayment and passing correct proceeds to loan participants). The bank thereby maintains its capital-to-assets ratio while increasing profits. Although the originating bank is charged with ensuring that the borrower adheres to the payment structure, the investor(s) assumes the loan's default risk. Many times, the borrowers are companies that are not creditworthy enough to issue securities directly, suggesting that the corporate investor buying a participation must do an extensive analysis of the borrower's financial statements. Correspondingly, yields are higher than CD or CP yields. Aggressive cash managers, such as those at Chrysler, invest in the 30-day loan participations for the 1/8 percent additional yield they provide above standard overnight investments such as RPs. The lack of marketability makes participations illiquid. On the positive side, studies done by rating agencies such as Moody's and Fitch indicate that *post-default* loan recoveries are much higher (70 percent to 92 percent on secured bank loans) than on subordinated, unsecured corporate bonds (about 34 percent). The recovery rates are highly variable, depending on the quality of collateral and other loan covenants. Other features of participations are included in the bank instrument exhibit.

SECURITIZED ASSETS. Credit card receivables and automobile loans also have become candidates for corporate investors by being transformed into asset-backed securities. Corporate investors may then buy these securities, which are backed by pools consisting of the original loans or other assets. As with loan participations, the effect is to improve capital ratios and enhance bank liquidity because of the transformation of a future stream of cash flows to a lump-sum present receipt. Recently, the captive finance subsidiaries of automobile manufacturers and other manufacturers' leasing subsidiaries also have begun to offer securitized loans, some backed by leases.[7] Additionally, receivables of all types such as insurance and mutual fund receivables and even trade receivables are being securitized: excluding mortgage-backed securities, the amount of asset-backed securitizations grew from $108 billion in 1995 to $204 billion in the third quarter of 2000. These asset-backed securities (ABS) are not held by most short-term investors because of the maturities. The maturities range from 1 to 3 years on automobile loan securities and 1.5 to 2 years on credit card receivables, subjecting the short-term investor to interest rate risk. The securities are quite often overcollateralized in the sense of having more receivables or loans than the aggregate face value of the securities issued. The issuer (if a bank) or a bank (through a LOC) also may guarantee security interest and principal payments. Both credit enhancement measures effectively reduce default risk, allowing AAA-rated securities to be issued for about 30 basis points above Treasury securities with comparable maturities. The inclusion of many loans or credit card accounts in a pool, which in turn backs the individual securities, diversifies the default risk of individual accounts.

Corporate Instruments

Next to bank securities, the most popular securities for corporate investors are instruments issued by other corporations. One reason for this is that CP is now widely available

---

[7]A good summary of many innovative short-term securities is provided in Duen-Li Kao. 1988. Short-term notes: Investment innovations and dangers. *Journal of Cash Management* March/April; Jack W. Aber. 1988. Securitization in the retail banking world. *Journal of Retail Banking* Spring; and Moody's Investor Service. 1996. Securitization and its effect on the credit strength of financial services companies: Moody's special comment. November. In the latter report, Moody's Chief Credit Officer Kenneth J.H. Pinkes and senior analyst Eric Goldstein note that the coupling of securitization and information technology is fundamentally altering the structure and competitive environment of financial services.

for overnight investing. Corporate short-term instruments traditionally have been issued to raise funds to finance seasonal working capital needs, but increasingly they fund permanent current asset and fixed-asset investments. The latter may occur as the borrower awaits lower long-term interest rates, or a higher stock price. When this comes about, the short-term borrowing will be retired as bonds or stock, or both, are issued. Medium-sized and larger corporations commonly issue three securities that appeal to corporate investors: CP,[8] floating-rate notes, and common or preferred stock with high dividend yields.

COMMERCIAL PAPER. Banks have lost much of their prime corporate lending business to the issuers of CP. Total dollar volume outstanding has exploded from $120 billion in 1981 to $1.6 trillion at the beginning of 2001—exceeding every other money market instrument including Treasury bills. Historically almost all CP was unsecured, meaning there was no collateral backing it up in the event of a default. High-quality issuers have always been able to issue CP, but the market now includes medium-quality issuers offering credit enhancement in the form of collateral (over $600 billion asset-backed CP outstanding in 2000) or a backup line of credit from their banks. Often issued in conjunction with a letter of credit, which guarantees the investor of principal repayment, the use of backup bank financing allows the bank's credit rating to be substituted for the issuer's credit rating. Most CP is issued by companies in the financial sector, including bank holding companies, but nonfinancial issuers now account for about one-fifth of outstanding volume. The average maturity of CP issued in the United States as of year-end 1999 was 40 days. Typical denomination, maturity, and risk attributes are provided in Exhibit 14-3. Some paper is issued "direct," in which the borrower sells it to the investor without a dealer being involved. The GE Capital Corporation issues in Exhibit 14-4 illustrate this. Most industrial paper, which can be bought in denominations as small as $1,000, is sold through dealers. Yield calculations and risk ratings are discussed later in the chapter. Commercial paper investment decision-making is illustrated later in the chapter and is covered in greater detail in Chapter 16 because of the importance of this instrument to corporate borrowing.

A hybrid instrument related to CP being issued with increasing frequency is the master note. Master notes are open-ended CP, allowing investors to add or withdraw monies on a daily basis, up to a specified maximum amount. The interest rate paid is tied to the CP rate, and the investor is notified of the newly revised rate daily. Investors determine the dollar amount their companies wish to invest at that rate. Most of the master note arrangements are offered by super-regional bank holding companies, as opposed to nonfinancial companies. Master note arrangements are brokered by firms such as Merrill Lynch; an automated, computer-based program is offered by Shearson Lehman Hutton in a minimum denomination of $250,000. Investors can specify whether they prefer interest to be paid monthly, quarterly, or semiannually.

FLOATING-RATE NOTES. Medium-term notes are unsecured promissory instruments issued by corporations in maturities of 270 days to 10 years. These notes are distinguished by the fact that they are continuously offered to investors. Securities with original maturities greater than 270 days must be registered with the Securities and Exchange Commission (SEC), so issuing corporations must be willing to accept the

---

[8]CP is issued by bank holding companies as well as finance companies and other nonbank issuers.

EXHIBIT 14-3
Corporate Instruments

INSTRUMENTS	PURPOSE ISSUED	DENOMINATION	MATURITY	RISK ASPECTS
Commercial paper	Typically unsecured borrowing to support working capital, especially seasonal needs. Sometimes used as bridge borrowing until long-term rates are more favorable. Issued mainly by finance companies, bank holding companies, and insurance companies but also by large and some mid-sized nonfinancial companies.	Primary market: As low as $25,000 but almost always $100,000+ and commonly $1 million Secondary market: round lot is $5 million	Range: 1 day to 270 days Typical: 5–45 days, 30 days most common	Default risk: • usually low because of credit quality of typical issuers or of bank providing backup letter of credit Liquidity risk: • dependent on quality of issuer, but higher than on Treasuries because individual issues are too dissimilar to assemble into large blocks for secondary market trading • very large issuers such as GMAC are exceptions, offering excellent liquidity
Floating-rate notes	Raise funds to make loans. Mostly issued by finance companies and banks.	Primary market: $1,000–$100,000 Secondary market: $5 million is round lot	Range: 9 months to 30 years 20% are 9 months to 2 years, 60% are 2–5 years, and 20% are more than 5 years. However, interest rate resets may be as often as weekly.	Default risk: • can be high, depending on issuer Event risk: • as with bonds, investor is concerned about subsequent issues of bonds or preferred stock, which imply lower coverage ratios on existing notes Liquidity risk: • depends on dealer's willingness to buy back from investor
Common or preferred stock with high dividend yield OR Adjustable-rate preferred stock	As with all common or preferred stock, issued to raise long-term funds in support of capital projects and permanent working capital. The issues of special interest to corporate investors are those with high dividend yields, including those whose yields adjust to prevailing interest rate conditions. Utilities account for many of these issues.	No typical price	Permanent financing unless later repurchased. Rates on adjustable issues typically reset every 49 days because corporate investors must hold at least 46 days to qualify for 70% dividend exclusion.	Default risk: • varies greatly, depends on issuer. Utilities have negligible default risk, with rare exceptions Risk of declining stock price: • on issue without periodic reset, exposure to stock price decline often hedged with put options. Always a big concern for stock investors, regardless of issue type or issuer Event risk: • can be a major concern on utility issuers or other capital-intensive issuers, because of possibility of subsequent bond and stock issues reducing coverage ratios. On utilities, additional concerns are accidents at nuclear generating plants and the possibility of rate hike proposals being turned down by state energy commissions

EXHIBIT 14-4
Money Rate Table

Monday, March 5, 2001

Money Rates
Published Tuesday, March 6

Data shown are for Monday.

The key U. S. and foreign annual interest rates below are a guide to general levels but don't always represent actual transactions.

PRIME RATE: 8.50% (effective 02/01/01). The base rate on corporate loans posted by at least 75% of the nation's 30 largest banks.

DISCOUNT RATE: 5.00% (effective 01/31/01). The charge on loans to depository institutions by the Federal Reserve Banks.

FEDERAL FUNDS: 5 9/16% high, 5 1/4 % low, 5 % near closing bid, 5 3/8 % offered. Reserves traded among commercial banks for overnight use in amounts of $1 million or more. Source: Prebon Yamane (U.S.A) Inc. FOMC fed funds target rate 5.50% effective 01/31/01.

CALL MONEY: 7.25% (effective 02/01/01). The charge on loans to brokers on stock exchange collateral. Source: Reuters.

COMMERCIAL PAPER: placed directly by General Electric Capital Corp.: 5.20% 30 to 39 days; 5.07% 40 to 50 days; 5.03% 51 to 67 days; 4.93% 68 to 94 days; 4.84% 95 to 131 days; 4.76% 132 to 156 days; 4.69% 157 to 190 days; 4.57% 191 to 270 days.

EURO COMMERCIAL PAPER: placed directly by General Electric Capital Corp.: 4.77% 30 days; 4.75% two months; 4.72% three months; 4.69% four months; 4.64% five months; 4.61% six months.

DEALER COMMERCIAL PAPER: High-grade unsecured notes sold through dealers by major corporations: 5.20% 30 days; 5.03% 60 days; 4.90% 90 days.

CERTIFICATES OF DEPOSIT: Typical rates in the secondary market. 5.24% one month; 5.03% three months; 4.90% six months.

BANKERS ACCEPTANCES: 5.30% 30 days; 5.15% 60 days; 5.04% 90 days; 5.01% 120 days; 4.97% 150 days; 4.93% 180 days. Offered rates of negotiable, bank-backed business credit instruments typically financing an import order. Source: Reuters

LONDON LATE EURODOLLARS: 5.25%–5.13% one month; 5.19%–5.06% two months; 5.13%–5.00% three months; 5.00%–4.88% four months; 5.00%–4.88% five months; 4.94%–4.81% six months.

LONDON INTERBANK OFFERED RATES (LIBOR): 5.2750% one month; 5.0800% three months; 4.9600% six months; 4.9300% one year. British Banker's Association average of interbank offered rates for dollar deposits in the London market based on quotations at 16 major banks. Effective rate for contracts entered into two days from date appearing at top of this column.

EURO LIBOR: 4.80938% one month; 4.75375% three months; 4.65375% six months; 4.57625% one year. British Banker's Association average of interbank offered rates for euro deposits in the London market based on quotations at 16 major banks. Effective rate for contracts entered into two days from date appearing at top of this column.

EURO INTERBANK OFFERED RATES (EURIBOR): 4.807% one month; 4.761% three months; 4.659% six months; 4.585% one year. European Banking Federation-sponsored rate among 57 Euro zone banks.

FOREIGN PRIME RATES: Canada 7.25%; Germany 4.75%; Japan 1.50%; Switzerland 5.375%; Britain 5.75%. These rate indications aren't directly comparable; lending practices vary widely by location.

TREASURY BILLS: Results of the Monday, March 5, 2001, auction of short-term U.S. government bills, sold at a discount from face value in units of $1,000 to $1 million: 4.700% 13 weeks; 4.530% 26 weeks.

OVERNIGHT REPURCHASE RATE: 5.50%. Dealer financing rate for overnight sale and repurchase of Treasury securities. Source: Reuters.

FREDDIE MAC: Posted yields on 30-year mortgage commitments. Delivery within 30 days 6.92%, 60 days 6.98%, standard conventional fixed-rate mortgages: 5.125%, 2% rate capped one-year adjustable rate mortgages. Source: Reuters.

FANNIE MAE: Posted yields on 30 year mortgage commitments (priced at par) for delivery within 30 days 7.07%, 60 days 7.12%, standard conventional fixed-rate mortgages: 6.30%, 6/2 rate capped one-year adjustable rate mortgages. Source: Reuters.

MERRILL LYNCH READY ASSETS TRUST: 5.38%. Annualized average rate of return after expenses for the past 30 days; not a forecast of future returns.

CONSUMER PRICE INDEX: January, 175.1, up 3.7% from a year ago. Bureau of Labor Statistics.

Copyright © Dow Jones & Company, Inc. All Rights Reserved.

delays and costs involved.[9] These notes are generally noncallable, implying that the investor need not worry about the issuer forcing a buyback of the securities if interest rates rise subsequent to issuance.

Short-term investors are most attracted to one form of medium-term notes, the **floating-rate note.** The interest rate on these is reset either daily, weekly, monthly, quarterly, or semiannually. Yields are pegged to either the Treasury bill rate, prime rate, LIBOR, or a composite CP rate. Except during the period between interest rate resetting, the investor is shielded against interest rate risk. An example is the Student Loan Marketing Association ("Sallie Mae") short-term floating rate notes mentioned earlier, which are priced at a spread (some amount above) the 91-day US Treasury bill. The interest rate is reset each week the calendar day following that week's Treasury bill auction. Investors can add to their holdings of these notes each month because of the regularity of Sallie Mae issues of short-term floating rate notes.

HIGH-DIVIDEND-YIELD STOCK.   When money market interest rates drop to historically low levels, as in 1991 when Treasury bills reached the lowest yield since 1972, Treasury professionals look to dividend capture and other strategies to maintain attractive yields. Dividend capture simply means buying a common or preferred stock shortly before it pays its dividend or buying a preferred stock having an adjustable dividend payment.[10] Utilities and some banks pay large dividends relative to their common stock's price, and almost all preferred stock is high in yield. High yields attract income-oriented investors who by choice or necessity cannot wait for capital gains. Corporate treasurers investing surplus funds are willing to take the risk that the stock might drop in price because of the high yield that can be captured. This strategy is enhanced if the investor can invest large dollar amounts, because the 3 to 5 percent commission on a small purchase (and paid again on the subsequent resale) would negate stocks' typical yield advantage over safer investments. The federal income tax deduction of 70 percent of intercorporate dividends (if the stock is held at least 46 days) makes dividend-paying investments even more attractive. Because only 30 percent of the income is taxable, the investor in the 35-percent tax bracket retains 89.5 percent of its income instead of only 65 percent of it (100% − 35%). Put another way, it pays tax on the dividend income of only 10.5 percent if it is in the 35 percent tax bracket. We illustrate the dividend capture yield and the taxable equivalent yield from dividend capture in a later section.

In some market eras, investors earn substantial returns using dividend capture. Illustrating, corporate investors willing to endure the price risk on a diversified portfolio of adjustable-rate preferred stock were rewarded with a 1991 total return of almost 20 percent, even after subtracting transaction costs. By contrast, Treasury bill yields averaged only 5 percent in 1991. The two dividend-capture strategies that can be used are short-term captures of dividends paid on high-yield common or preferred stock and purchase and long-term holding of preferred stock whose dividends are adjusted to prevailing money market interest rates. Some of the largest users of high-yield captures in the 1980s were Japanese insurance companies, which at the time were required to invest

---

[9]Fixed costs associated with SEC registration are reduced somewhat if the company executes a *shelf* registration, whereby it is approved for an ongoing, multiyear issuance program. One estimate places the legal, investment banking, documentation, and SEC registration costs at between 0.8 and 1 percent ($800,000 to $1 million for a typical $100 million medium-term note, issued by a creditworthy issuer). Savings from fewer registrations can therefore be significant. Merrill Lynch underwrites most medium-term notes, and more information on these notes is available in the occasionally issued *Medium-term notes: An investment opportunity.* New York: Merrill Lynch Money Markets.

[10]Dividend yield is computed as the annual dividend per share divided by the current stock price.

most of their premiums in income-producing investments. Japanese regulators relaxed the mandate in 1987, however, and the insurers largely abandoned the practice. We return to this form of dividend capture in Chapter 15, in which we evaluate portfolio strategies, because it represents an important active investing strategy.

Preferred stock on which the dividend is reset quarterly (**adjustable-rate preferred stock [ARPS]**) or every 49 days through an auction bidding process (**auction preferred stock [APS]**) emerged in the early 1980s as vehicles to gain dividend income. Although both types of preferred stock protect against interest rate risk, only the APS has survived as a viable investment. All purchases and sales are made at the original issue price (par), insulating the investor from price fluctuations related to interest rate changes. About 10 percent of outstanding preferred stock is APS, but more noteworthy is the fact that about 60 percent of new issues are of this form. Yields move within range of a maximum of 100 percent and a minimum of 59 percent of the 60-day CP rate but may be higher or lower depending on the issuer. The APS offers some liquidity, because investors can sell their $100,000 units at each auction. Illiquidity can still be a problem, however. If insufficient bids are offered at an auction for the amount of stock present investors wish to sell, the auction is said to have failed, and the issuer must pay a penalty in the form of a higher dividend rate—typically 100 to 120 percent of CP rates. The investor is stuck with an illiquid investment until the next auction. There is a way around this problem, and that is to diversify across issuers by investing in a mutual fund holding APS.

Federal Government Instruments

Because corporate investors wish to preserve their principal when investing surplus cash, securities issued by the US Treasury or by federal government agencies are very attractive. Treasury securities have the lowest default risk of any security available worldwide.

US TREASURY SECURITIES.   Investors seeking the highest degree of safety possible prefer bills, notes, and bonds issued by the Treasury. Backed by the full faith and credit of the federal government, default risk on these securities is considered to be almost nonexistent. Maturing securities can be paid off with tax revenues, money creation (through Fed purchase of the securities, which expands reserves and ultimately the money supply), or by rolling over the borrowing by replacing the maturing securities with newly issued securities. Liquidity of Treasury securities is also unequaled, because the secondary markets experience daily volumes that dwarf the stock market. In addition to the high degree of safety and liquidity, interest income from Treasury securities is exempted from state and local income taxes. Treasury bills are offered in an auction held every Monday for 3-month and 6-month maturities and on the fourth Thursday for 1-year maturities.[11] Notes and bonds are sold on an as-needed basis, with notes having original maturities from 2 to 10 years and bonds having original maturities beyond 10 years. Exhibit 14-5 profiles the typical Treasury auction schedule along with maturities and minimum face values. The treasurer investing for the short-term generally considers notes and bonds when their current maturities are 1 year or less but may extend maturities for the normally higher yield.

There are two types of bids investors may make when buying new issues of Treasury securities in the primary market. Competitive bids are mainly entered by financial institutions, including dealers such as Salomon Brothers. Competitive bidding is preceded

[11]On occasion, the Treasury also sells short-term "cash management bills" that provide interim financing in anticipation of tax collections and have maturities up to 2 months.

EXHIBIT 14-5
US Treasury Auction Schedule

TREASURY SECURITY	MATURITIES	EXPECTED SCHEDULE	MINIMUM FACE VALUE
Treasury bills	3 and 6 months	Weekly	$ 1,000
	1 year	Monthly	$10,000
Treasury notes	2 years	Monthly	$ 5,000
	5 years	Quarterly: Feb, May, Aug, Nov	$ 1,000
	10 years	Quarterly: Feb, May, Aug, Nov	$ 1,000

SOURCE: Fidelity Investments.

by close watching of the secondary market for existing securities, right up to the time of the new issue. Competitive bidders hope to receive a better yield than the average yield for the auction. Investors willing to accept the yield of accepted competitive bids enter a noncompetitive bid.[12] Investors may bid directly through a "tender offer" to the nearest Federal Reserve district bank or through a broker or commercial bank. Investors not wishing to participate in the new issue auction may defer until a short time after the auction and purchase the security in the secondary market. Refer to Exhibit 14-6 for additional details on Treasury securities.

AGENCY INSTRUMENTS.   For a slightly higher default risk and less liquidity, investors can gain higher yields on federal agency securities than on Treasury securities with similar maturities. Agencies are securities issued by governmental agencies and several private financing institutions that have governmental backing. The securities' proceeds are used to support lending to farmers (Farm Credit Administration), savings and loans associations (Federal Home Loan Bank), mortgages (Federal Home Loan Mortgage Corporation, or "Freddie Mac"; Federal National Mortgage Association, or "Fannie Mae"; and the Government National Mortgage Association, known as "Ginnie Mae"), and federally guaranteed student loans (Student Loan Marketing Association, or "Sallie Mae"). Freddie Mac and Ginnie Mae typically buy mortgages from the originating lenders, pool them, and then package them into small-denomination pass-through certificates.

Mortgage-backed securities, although the most prominent of agency securities, are not well suited to the corporate short-term investor because of uneven cash flows, interest rate risk, and prepayment risk. Uneven cash flows result from the fact that part of the principal is returned each month along with interest. Interest rate risk applies because these are mostly fixed-income securities; they are backed by fixed-rate mortgages (although adjustable-rate mortgages also are available). Prepayment risk refers to a return of principal whenever a mortgage in the pool is paid off because of homeowner relocation or a drop in general interest rates, which triggers refinancing.

Discount notes and short-term coupon securities are appropriate for the money market portfolio. Although not exempted from state and local income taxes, they are considered to be very low in default risk because of the belief that they are a moral obligation of the federal government on which Congress and the president would never

[12]Treasury securities are now sold at "single-price auctions." According to the Bureau of Public Debt, " In a single-price auction, all successful competitive bidders and all noncompetitive bidders are awarded securities at the price equivalent to the highest accepted rate or yield of accepted competitive tenders." (http://www.publicdebt.treas.gov/sec/secfaq.htm).

EXHIBIT 14-6
Federal Government Instruments

INSTRUMENTS	PURPOSE ISSUED	DENOMINATION	MATURITY	RISK ASPECTS
Treasury bills	US Treasury raises money to finance US debt.	Primary market: $1,000+, in multiples of $1,000. Secondary market: round lot is $1 million	Range: 3 months 6 months 1 year	Default risk: • none, because of taxing and money creation abilities of the issuer Liquidity risk: • none if have $1 million block for secondary market resale Interest rate risk: • insignificant on 3-month, small on 6-month, of concern on 1-year
Treasury notes and bonds	US Treasury raises money to finance US debt.	Primary market: Notes: • 2-year notes have minimum of $5,000, then multiples of $5,000 • 5-, 7-, 10-year notes have $1,000 minimum, then multiples of $1,000 Bonds: same as longer-term notes Secondary market: $1 million is round lot	Notes: 2–5, 7, 10 years Bonds: >10 years, mainly 20 or 30 years	Default risk: • none, for same reasons as on Treasury bills Liquidity risk: • secondary markets do not have same breadth or depth as Treasury bill market Interest rate risk: • substantial except on seasoned issue with short current maturity
Government agencies: • Discount notes • Coupon securities	US government agency securities issued by the Farm Credit System, Federal Home Loan Banks, and the Federal National Mortgage Association. Provide bridge financing until agency can issue longer-term securities or when the rate on long-term securities is relatively high and agency does not want to lock in that rate.	Primary: $1,000 minimum Secondary: Discount Notes: mainly $5–$10 million but up to $50 million Coupon Securities: mainly $500,000 but up to $10 million	Discount: most < 6 months, with 3 months most common Coupon: range is from overnight to 360 days	Default risk: • low, but difficult to estimate because of uncertainty over whether government will honor in event of default Liquidity risk: • sporadic liquidity, based on dealer's willingness to rebuy Interest rate risk: • low on discount notes and short-term coupon securities. Significant on longer-term agencies, such as those issued by the Government National Mortgage Association ("Ginnie Maes") Event risk: • can be a major concern on mortgage-backed securities because of the prepayment risk involved. On shorter-term notes, the major concern is changing regulation or legislation affecting governmental agencies

allow a default. The liquidity of agency securities can be quite good, but this is predicated on the willingness of the dealer from which they were purchased to buy them back. The combination of these risk factors causes agency yields to rise slightly above comparable-maturity Treasury securities. Consult Exhibit 14-6 for further details on agencies.

State and Local Instruments

Municipal securities (munis) are issued by any governmental authority below the federal level: states, counties, localities, and school districts. They generally fund water treatment, sewage, pollution control, bridges, or turnpikes, but at times will fund projects such as baseball stadiums, dormitories, or even private-purpose projects for nonprofit organizations or businesses. Munis are exempt from federal income tax, except for private-purpose projects. Tax-exempt securities appeal to corporations that are in the higher federal income tax brackets, because the taxable-equivalent yield makes these securities yield more on an after-tax basis than comparable taxable securities. The **taxable-equivalent yield** is the nominal (stated) yield divided by (1 − corporation's marginal tax rate).

Most municipal securities are **general obligation securities,** meaning the backing for the interest and principal payments is simply future general revenues and the issuer's capacity to raise taxes. Examples are tax anticipation notes, revenue anticipation notes, and bond anticipation notes, which provide working capital financing for states and localities as they await anticipated revenues from tax collections, other sources of revenue, or upcoming bond issuance, respectively. Exhibit 14-7 describes the essential features of municipal instruments of interest to corporate short-term investors.

Municipal securities also may be **revenue securities,** which tie security cash flows to pledged revenue from the facilities being financed: for example, rental revenue from a convention center, or tolls from a bridge or toll road.

Longer-term bonds also found in some corporate portfolios because of their periodically reset interest rates are known as **variable-rate demand notes.** If investors do not prefer the reset interest rate, which is a function of supply and demand factors in this specialized market, they can put (sell) the bond back to the issuer at par. Between reset dates, the securities are very illiquid, however, as a result of a thin secondary market. The interest rate reset and put feature imply that 20-year or 30-year maturities do not pose much interest rate risk. These notes are often backstopped by a bank line of credit, which guarantees the securities if the issuer defaults or if put-back securities cannot be resold to new investors. They are often issued to support construction of educational facilities, hospitals, and sewage projects. They will continue to be popular because of the inadequate supply of anticipation notes available to buyers of tax-exempt securities.

States and localities also issue some **tax-exempt CP.** The risks are very similar to those of anticipation notes. These securities are very illiquid because of the absence of a secondary market.

We have covered the major money market instruments offered by banks, corporations, the US government, and state and local governments. We now conclude our discussion of short-term alternatives by looking at some creative hybrids that may invest in a cross section of instruments. The repackaging involved in what we term *mixed instruments* offers tailoring to the specific desires of the investor.

Mixed Instruments

We address three popular mixed instruments: money market mutual funds, RPs, and sweep accounts. One similarity that they share is the ability to invest surplus cash on an overnight (actually 1 day) basis. Basic features are provided in Exhibit 14-8.

EXHIBIT 14-7
State and Local Government Instruments

INSTRUMENTS	PURPOSE ISSUED	DENOMINATION	MATURITY	RISK ASPECTS
Anticipation notes	State and local governments issue securities to get "cash in advance" of anticipated revenues from taxes, bridge or tollroad user fees, or bond issues, for example.	Primary market: $5,000 minimum Secondary market: round lot is $100,000 minimum	Range: few weeks to several years	Default risk: • low, because of taxing and reborrowing abilities of the issuer. Depends on municipality offering—default is possible in certain circumstances Liquidity risk: • depends on lead dealer's willingness and ability to buy back at market prices, which is hard to estimate Interest rate risk: • Insignificant on shorter maturities, of concern on several-year maturity
Variable rate demand notes (VRDNs)	Securities issued by states and localities in long-term maturities, but with "put" feature enabling investor to liquidate if periodically reset interest rate is not acceptable.	Primary market: $5,000–$100,000 Secondary market: $100,000 minimum is round lot	30 years, but with put feature. Interest rate is reset periodically, when period could be 1–90 or 180 days	Default risk: • same as anticipation notes, except for longer maturity, implying greater uncertainty about future tax base and financial condition of issuer Liquidity risk: • same as anticipation notes Interest rate risk: • insubstantial because of periodic reset of coupon
Tax-exempt commercial paper	Same as for anticipation notes, and possibly to finance seasonal needs.	Primary: $50,000–$100,000 Secondary: $100,000 minimum is round lot	Range is from few days to several years, most commonly 30 days	Default risk: • same as anticipation notes Liquidity risk: • same as anticipation notes

EXHIBIT 14-8
Mixed Instruments

INSTRUMENTS	PURPOSE ISSUED	DENOMINATION	MATURITY	RISK ASPECTS
Money market mutual funds (MMMFs)	Fund administrator collects money from investors, pools to enable purchase of diversified large-dollar denominations. Mostly invest in commercial paper; but also in negotiable certificates of deposit, bankers' acceptances, Treasuries, and repurchase agreements (see below).	$10,000 usual minimum for institutional account	Range: 25–60 days for weighted average maturity	Default risk: • unlike MMDAs, no FDIC guarantee. Risk is comparable to commercial paper because of its heavy weighting in most MMMF portfolios. Some MMMFs are insured by third-party, private insurer Liquidity risk: • no risk because of daily access through wire transfers or check-writing privileges Interest rate risk: • on pure money fund, net asset value is kept at $1.00, and short maturities eliminate risk. For new funds that are invested in maturities >65 days, slight risk
Repurchase agreements (RPs)	Bank or security dealer uses to raise money to finance investments or loans. Financing occurs because originator "sells" portfolio of investments with an agreement to repurchase them shortly at a slightly higher price.	Can be under $100,000, but typically $1 million. Term, as opposed to overnight, repurchases may be over $25 million, but are typically $10 million.	Mostly overnight. Term RPs are up to 3 weeks, with some longer	Default risk: • higher when institution initiating RP is an aggressive trader of securities • linked to risks of underlying securities (collateral), whether the securities are, in fact, considered to be collateral and whether the investor's custodian takes possession of the collateral Liquidity risk: • overnight RPs are obviously liquid, but term repos also offer some flexibility for post-agreement alteration of maturity to provide for early resale Event risk: • investor must guard against fraud and valuation mistakes, particularly when dealing with unregistered, nonprimary government securities dealers
Sweep accounts	Deposit account in which excess balances are automatically transferred, on overnight basis, into interest-bearing investment. Sweep may be initiated by bank or broker; if by broker, monies are moved via wire transfer. Offered mainly as customer convenience but may fund loans or investments much like repurchase agreement.	Bank sweep account: amount of surplus balance, above compensating balance. Broker sweep account: amount large enough to make the interest exceed the wire transfer costs.	Overnight	Default risk: • linked to the instrument invested in. Primarily, these are invested in mutual funds offered by the bank's parent bank holding company or the brokerage house. These might be invested in one or more of the following: commercial paper, Treasury bills, Euro time deposits, or tax-exempt securities.

MONEY MARKET MUTUAL FUNDS.   A money market mutual fund is a company that invests in short-term securities with funds pooled from numerous individuals or institutions. A 1999 survey by Treasury Strategies, Inc., found that 8 percent of all liquid funds (demand deposits plus other short-term investments) was placed in money funds (for non-financial companies having revenues in excess of $100 million). Smaller companies find this vehicle relatively more attractive because of the lack of in-house time and expertise. The advantages of pooling monies before investing are:

- *Professional money management.* Professional money managers make the investment decisions and oversee the securities in the funds.
- *Diversification of default risk.* Many issuers' securities, and possibly even securities from issuers in various countries, are included in the pool.
- *Higher yields.* Investment in much larger denominations than would be possible for any single investor increases overall yield.
- *Enhanced liquidity.* As some investors withdraw funds, others are reinvesting; individual securities do not have to be sold to fund withdrawals.
- *Greater flexibility.* Any combination of securities can be assembled—by maturity, issuer type, issuer geographic location, or other mixes investors might desire.

Money funds have parlayed the enhanced liquidity into an even greater feature by allowing investors to write checks (minimum of $100 for institutional funds offered to corporate investors), wire transfer, or telephone transfer among the same provider's funds. Interest rate risk is eliminated because the price[13] of the money fund is kept constant at $1.00, regardless of changes in interest rates. This is possible because the funds' average maturity of 24 to 48 days combined with the practice of buying and holding securities until maturity insulates the funds' values from interest rate movements. Management fees are as low as 0.26 percent, which is achieved by Vanguard's Prime Portfolio Money Market Fund. Business corporations have increased their investments in money market funds markedly in recent years, growing from $142 billion in 1995 to about $436 billion in late 2000. IBC USA data indicates that the average maturity of money funds' portfolios in year-end 1999 is 46 days. In Chapter 15, we weigh the advantages of having an outside entity make almost all the treasurer's short-term investment decisions.

There are several other types of mutual funds that are not technically money funds but may be used in their place. Short-term government bond funds or short-term municipal bond funds, holding portfolios with average maturities of 2 to 3 years, and APS funds are options for the investor willing to take more interest rate risk or even some price risk (on the preferred stock).

The Franklin Corporate Cash Management Fund (since renamed the Franklin Corporate Qualified Dividend Fund; see ad copy in Exhibit 14-9) exemplifies the price appreciation or depreciation that might occur with the additional risks on an APS mutual fund. Although these funds lagged behind income-oriented bond funds in the late 1980s, in 1991 the Franklin Fund's total return was 19.8 percent—about 12 percent of which was linked to increased preferred stock prices. The minimum initial investment is $25,000, and the investor can write checks for $100 or more. Interest is computed daily and paid monthly, and much of the dividend return is not taxed because of the 70 percent federal income tax exclusion for intercorporate dividends.

---

[13]Technically, price is a misnomer, and net asset value is quoted, which equals [(Sum of market values of securities − Liabilities)/Number of shares]. Liabilities would consist of accrued expenses for commissions or management fees.

EXHIBIT 14-9
Franklin Corporate Qualified Dividend Fund

___

**Franklin Corporate Qualified
Dividend Fund**

Franklin Fund Number: 0117   NASDAQ: FCCPX

Objective:
The Fund seeks to have all of its dividends qualify for the Corporate Dividends-Received Deduction through investment in conventional fixed-rate, adjustable-rate and auction-rate preferred stocks and common stocks. At least 75% of assets purchased will be in investment grade issues selected with the goal of producing both high after-tax income and stability of principal.

Key Features:
■ **Tax Advantage:** In 1996, dividends received from common or preferred stocks of a domestic corporation held 46 days or longer qualify for a 70% deduction. Assuming the maximum federal corporate tax rate of 35% for calendar year 1996, the Fund's ordinary dividends will be taxed at an effective tax rate of only 10.5%, and after-tax income will be 89.5% of the dividends received.* The chart below compares the net after-tax yields at the maximum federal corporate income tax rate of 34% for 1989 for investments in taxable money market instruments and the Franklin Corporate Cash Fund.

☐ Fully taxable money market investment ▨ Franklin Corporate Qualified
Dividend Fund

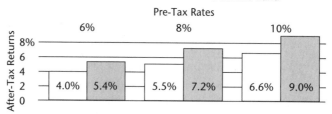

* Assumes that 100% of the Fund's dividends qualify for the 70% deduction.

■ **Ready Accessibility, Easy Liquidity:** Shares of the Fund may be redeemed at any time at the then current NAV on any business day by telephone, wire or mail. There are no redemption charges. Payments may be sent directly to a predesignated corporate bank account by Federal Funds wire the day after a redemption request is received, if the Fund is notified by 1:00 p.m., Pacific Time.

■ **Free Checkwriting:** Shareholders can write an unlimited number of free personalized checks for amounts of $100 or more. For record keeping convenience, cancelled checks will be returned once a month.

Manager:
Franklin Corporate Qualified Dividend Fund, member of the $180 billion Franklin Templeton Group, is managed by Franklin Advisers, Inc. and sponsored by Franklin Templeton Distributors, Inc.

___

SOURCE: © Franklin Distributors, Inc. Reprinted by permission.

REPURCHASE AGREEMENTS.   A **repurchase agreement** (RP, or "repo") is the sale of a portfolio of securities with a prearranged buyback 1 or several days later. The difference in sale price and repurchase price constitutes the interest yield. Banks and securities dealers needing to finance inventories of loans or securities on a short-term basis may do so by engaging in RPs. Until the 1980s, RPs were the only means for most corporate investors to gain a 1-day return on surplus cash, so they were very popular. Although RPs still are widely used (about 11 percent of liquid funds are placed there according to the 1999 Treasury Strategies survey), other instruments such as money funds, overnight CP, muni notes, Eurodollar time deposits, and sweep accounts (our next topic) are replacing them. Repurchase agreements must be structured carefully so that the underlying securities count as collateral. Investors should take the precaution of having a custodian bank take possession of these securities. Borrower defaults are not a serious concern, because the investor can sell the underlying securities, which are generally Treasury bills or government agency notes. Term repos can be arranged for several days up to several weeks for the company having an investment horizon longer than 1 day.

SWEEP ACCOUNTS.   Banks and brokerage firms offer sweep accounts in which excess funds are automatically or at the cash manager's request transferred (swept) from the demand deposit account into an interest-bearing overnight investment. Treasury Strategies did a survey in 1999 and found that the popularity of sweeps continues to grow. Banks offer the convenience of one-stop shopping, automatic transfers of amounts above the compensating balance level, choices of several pooled investments to select from, and perhaps even an optional credit line paydown ("loan sweep") instead of investing the surplus. Brokerage houses have the money wired out into a money fund or some other short-term investment. It is conceivable that future regulations will hamper banks' ability to avoid also wiring funds out of deposit accounts (at present, they simply make a bookkeeping entry to sweep monies) because of Federal Reserve concern that they are circumventing reserve requests by reporting lower transaction account balances because of the sweep accounts.[14] Banks will doubtless contest any proposed change vigorously, because they need to offer sweep accounts to have a competitive product for corporate overnight investments.

Our survey of short-term investment instruments has highlighted key features, including the major risk attributes of the various instruments. We will be prepared to consider security risk-return tradeoffs and all types of investment risk after presenting the essential money market yield calculations.

MONEY MARKET CALCULATIONS

There are several essential calculations that the short-term investor must master, all dealing with various yields. Yield calculations depend on whether the security is a tax-advantaged or fully taxable security. Then, for fully taxable securities, the proper calculation depends on whether the security is a discount security or an interest-bearing, or coupon, security. Calculations of money market yields are based on simple interest—as if interest is paid once a year, at year's end. We go beyond the standard calculations to demonstrate how to calculate an effective annual yield from a nominal yield.

Yields on Tax-Advantaged Securities

Recall from our earlier discussion that municipal securities are usually tax exempt, meaning that investors do not have to pay federal income tax on the interest received.

---

[14]The Fed has prohibited multiple savings accounts, in which one of the accounts is used for incoming transfers from demand deposit accounts, and now requires that banks assess early withdrawal penalties to any withdrawal from a corporate time deposit made within 6 days of the most recent deposit to the account. See Sweep account loopholes closed in federal reserve requirement rule. *The Regulatory Compliance Watch* (American Banker Bond Buyer newsletter) April 12, 1991:1–2.

When comparing munis to fully taxable securities, the investor may calculate a taxable-equivalent yield on the municipal security. This is the yield that a fully taxable security must provide to leave the investor with the same after-tax yield as he or she is getting on the muni.

TAXABLE-EQUIVALENT YIELD ON MUNICIPAL SECURITY.   Assuming the security is selling at par, the taxable-equivalent yield is calculated as shown in Equation 14-1:

$$Taxable\text{-}equivalent\ yield = \frac{Nominal\ Yield}{(1-T)} \qquad \text{(14-1)}$$

Illustrating, a company in the 35-percent tax bracket would have to get 6.15 percent $(4\%/(1 - 0.35))$ from a taxable security to match a municipal security's 4-percent nontaxable yield. The fact that municipal securities are generally exempted from state and local income taxes in the state where issued means the treasurer might want to use an overall combined income tax rate instead of the federal rate.[15]

YIELD ON DIVIDEND CAPTURE.   The annualized yield for the dividend capture, y_{cap}, ignoring commissions and compounding, is given in Equation 14-2:

$$y_{cap} = \frac{D}{P} \times \frac{365}{n} \qquad \text{(14-2)}$$

In which D = dollar amount of dividend

P = price (amount invested)

n = holding period

Illustrating, if you buy a stock for $20 per share, receive a $0.20 dividend, and sell the stock after 47 days, the annualized yield is:

$$y_{cap} = \frac{\$0.20}{\$20} \times \frac{365}{47}$$

$$= 0.07766\ or\ \underline{7.77\%}$$

The federal income tax deduction of 70 percent of intercorporate dividends (if the stock is held at least 46 days) makes dividend-paying investments even more attractive. Because 30 percent of the income is not taxed, the investor in the 35-percent tax bracket retains 89.5 percent $[100\% - (30\% \times 0.35)]$ of its income instead of only 65 percent $(100\% - 35\%)$. Put another way, it pays a tax rate on the dividend income of only 10.5 percent if it is in the 35-percent tax bracket. To compare the yield with fully taxable securities' yields, we need to compute a taxable-equivalent yield from the dividend capture. We can use this relationship to calculate Equation 14-3, $y_{cap\text{-}te}$, the taxable-equivalent yield of the dividend capture:

$$y_{cap\text{-}te} = \frac{y_{cap}[1 - (0.30 \times T)]}{(1 - T)} \qquad \text{(14-3)}$$

---

[15]The taxable-equivalent yield when taking into account state income taxes, assuming the state allows deductibility of the interest and the issuer is located in the same state, involves a change in the denominator of Equation 14-1. Distinguishing between T_F (the corporation's marginal federal tax rate) and T_S (the corporation's marginal rate on the state income tax), the denominator becomes:

$$Taxable\text{-}equivalent\ yield = \frac{Nominal\ Yield}{1-(T_F + T_S\,(1-T_F))]}$$

For details on the adjusted formula, see John R. Walter. 1986. Short-term municipal securities. *Federal Reserve Bank of Richmond Economic Review* November/December:25–34.

In which: y_{cap} = annualized yield for dividend capture

T = investor's marginal tax rate

Continuing with our example, with a dividend capture yield of 7.77 percent and assuming your company is in the 35-percent marginal tax bracket, to do as well with a fully taxable security you would have to find one yielding:

$$y_{cap\text{-}te} = \frac{7.77[1 - (0.30 \times 0.35)]}{(1 - 0.35)}$$

$$= \underline{\underline{10.70\%}}$$

As we cautioned earlier in the chapter, recognize that you are taking the risk that the stock price will drop during the holding period unless some type of hedging is done. Any commissions paid will reduce the dividend capture yield and the taxable-equivalent yield of the dividend capture.

Discount Yield

Treasury bills, CP, BAs, agency discount notes, and some RPs are discount securities, meaning they are bought at a price below their face or par value and the investor receives face value at maturity. The difference is the interest return on the security. We can apply Equation 14-4 to calculate a Treasury bill **discount yield,** y_d:

$$y_d = \frac{FACE - P}{FACE} \times \frac{360}{n} \tag{14-4}$$

In which: y_d = discount yield

$FACE$ = face value (or par)

P = price

n = number of days until maturity

Notice that this is a nominal yield, not an effective annual yield. We illustrate the discount yield calculation with the actual results of a Treasury bill auction, shown in Exhibit 14-10.

The 13-week (3-month) bill had $29.92 billion in bids for the $10.01 billion offered for sale (the Fed's rollover of maturing Treasury bills is in addition to these totals). In late 1998, the Treasury changed all auctions to a single-price format. Starting with the highest price (lowest yield, or cost) bids, it sums up bid dollar amounts until all of the auctioned securities are accounted for. The price (yield) at which the last Treasury bill would have to be sold to complete the amount offered becomes the single price (yield) at which all successful bids are transacted. In Exhibit 14-10, that price (yield) is the "Dollar price" listed: $98.812. The "high discount rate" associated with this price, or the discount yield for this particular auction, is 4.700 percent. We can see how this is calculated on these $1,000 minimum denomination bills by plugging into Equation 14-4 the $1,000 face amount, the Price (found by taking the Dollar Price/$100, or $98.812/$100, times the face amount of $1,000), and a factor to annualize the period rate (360/number of days):

$$y_d = \frac{\$1{,}000 - (0.98812 \times \$1{,}000)}{\$1{,}000} \times \frac{360}{91}$$

$$= 0.0470 \text{ or } 4.70\%$$

As stated, this is the "high discount rate" shown for the auction.

EXHIBIT 14-10
Treasury Auction Information

March 5, 2001

Dow Jones Newswires

US T-Bills: 3Mo 4.700%, High 40%; 6Mo 4.530%, High 45%

Dow Jones Newswires

($ in blns)	3-month	6-month
High discount rate	4.700%	4.530%
Percent at high	40	45
Median discount rate	4.690%	4.510%
Low discount rate	4.670%	4.480%
Applications	$29.92	$23.37
Accepted bids	$10.01	$10.00
Bid-to-cover ratio*	2.99	2.34
Noncompetitives	$ 1.35	$ 1.12
Foreign, Intl Noncomps	$ 0.19	$ 0.03
Coupon equivalent	4.822%	4.700%
Dollar price	98.812	97.710
Fed tenders	$ 5.39	$ 5.38
Fed bids accepted	$ 5.39	$ 5.38
CUSIP numbers	912795GK1	912795HN4

(*Ratio is based on public bidding and does not include bids submitted by the Federal Reserve for its own account or foreign official accounts)

The bid-to-cover ratio, an indication of demand, was 2.99 for the three-month bills and 2.34 for the six-month bills.

The Treasury sold $193 million of the three-month bills and $25 million of the six-month bills to foreign and international monetary authority accounts on a noncompetitive bidding basis. Foreign and international noncompetitive tenders totaled $193 million for the three-month bills and $25 million for the six-month bills.

The Federal Reserve apparently rolled over its holdings of maturing short-term bills by about $10.78 billion. The Fed held $10.99 billion of maturing three- and six-month bills when the auction was announced last Thursday.

The bills awarded to the Federal Reserve are in addition to the public offering amount.

The high discount rates were mixed from last week's auction, when they were 4.710% and 4.495%, respectively.

The rate on the three-month bills was the lowest since the rate of 4.660% at the auction on Sept. 20, 1999. The rate on the six-month bills was the highest since the rate of 4.770% at the auction on Feb. 20, 2001.

Rates prior to Nov. 2, 1998 refer to average discount rates in multiple price auctions, before Treasury changed all auctions to the single-price format.

Both issues are dated March 8, 2001. The 13-week bills mature June 7, 2001, and the 26-week bills mature Sept. 6, 2001.

—By Jonathan Nicholson, Dow Jones Newswires;
202-862-9255;
jonathan.nicholson@dowjones.com

SOURCE: Jonathan Nicholson. 2001. US T-Bills: 3Mo 4.700%, High 40%; 6Mo 4.530, High 45%. *Dow Jones Newswires* March 5.

Coupon-Equivalent Yields

Notice, in the 3-month Treasury auction detail, the coupon-equivalent yield of 4.822 percent. This yield is calculated based on a 365-day year instead of 360 days and assuming that interest owed is based on the actual number of days elapsed. For a discount security maturing within 1 year, the **coupon-equivalent yield** also is adjusted to account for the fee that the price paid is less than the face value, which increases the true yield. The coupon-equivalent yield on a discount security, y_{ce}, would be:

$$y_{ce} = \frac{FACE - P}{P} \times \frac{365}{n} \qquad \text{(14-5)}$$

Substituting the figures for the 13-week Treasury bill, we get the following nominal yield:

$$y_{ce} = \frac{\$1,000 - (0.98812 \times \$1,000)}{(0.98812 \times \$1,000)} \times \frac{365}{91}$$

$$= 0.04822 \text{ or } 4.82\%$$

The coupon-equivalent yield is always higher than the discount yield, with the gap widening at higher interest rates.

On coupon securities, such as Treasury notes and bonds, short-term CDs, muni and corporate notes, Eurodollar CDs and time deposits, and money market mutual funds, the quoted coupon rate is already comparable with the above coupon-equivalent yield. For a 10 percent note, the simple interest calculation implies that every $100 of principal will be paid $10 $(0.10 \times \$100)$ of interest each year.[16]

Annual Effective Yield

Neither of the yields considered up to this point account for the compounding of interest earned on a short-term security. To get an effective annual yield (y_{eff}), we adjust for the fact that the investor has only invested P (the price), a 365-day year, and the ability of the investor to earn compounded interest until year's end. This is shown in Equation 14-6:[17]

$$y_{eff} = \left[1 + \left(\frac{FACE - P}{P}\right)\right]^{365/n} - 1 \qquad \text{(14-6)}$$

Illustrating with the 13-week Treasury bill again, we have:

$$y_{eff} = \left[1 + \left(\frac{\$1,000 - 988.12}{988.12}\right)\right]^{365/91} - 1$$

$$= 0.04910 \text{ or } 4.91\%$$

Because of the compounding of intrayear interest, the equivalent annual yield exceeds the coupon-equivalent yield as well as the discount yield. Assuming we can reinvest

---

[16]The fact that half the interest is paid every 6 months on most coupon securities implies a higher effective yield, however. We note in Chapter 3 that the effective yield is $[(1 + i/2)^n - 1]$. For the 10 percent note, the effective yield is $[(1 + 0.10/2)^2 - 1 = 0.1025$, or 10.25 percent. The effective yield of the Treasury bill can be annualized in a similar fashion if no change in the 91-day yield for the remainder of the year is assumed.

[17]Another way to get to the same result is: $y_{eff} = (FACE/P)^{365/n} - 1$.

interest and principal at the coupon-equivalent rate or higher, this measure gives us a more accurate picture of the increase in portfolio value that occurs over time.

The return calculations have prepared us to take a closer look at how to analyze individual security risks and evaluate the risk-return tradeoff. Portfolio aspects of having numerous securities to evaluate at one time are covered in Chapter 15.

YIELD AND RISK ANALYSIS

The magnitude of securities available to the corporate investor can be overwhelming unless some technique for narrowing candidates is implemented. Comparing yields is helpful, but return is only half the picture. Knowledge of the risks involved and how they affect yield facilitates comparisons. Corporate investors lacking the time or expertise to conduct formal risk analysis may minimize certain of these risks (e.g., diversify away much of the default risk by investing in a large managed portfolio of securities) or delegate risk management (e.g., by assessing default risk through reliance on third-party rating services). However, not all risks can be simultaneously minimized, and lowered risks generally entail lowered returns.

We classify risks in relation to how they determine security yields: risk factors influencing return differences for different maturities, and risk factors that drive yields for securities with identical maturities. Yield relationships in the first category are generally characterized as the term structure of interest rates, and we define the second category as the risk structure of interest rates. We use an additive risk factor model (Equation 14-7) to show the overall yield-risk relationship:

$$k_s = k_{rf} + k_{tm} + k_{rp} \tag{14-7}$$

In which: k_s = interest rate for security s

k_{rf} = risk-free interest rate

k_{tm} = term premium

k_{rp} = risk premium for security s

The risk-free rate is determined primarily by investors' collective time preferences, the rate of inflation expected over the maturity period, and demand-side influences such as economic productivity. It is apparent that there is no default risk or liquidity risk incorporated in the risk-free rate, which explains why Treasury bill or Treasury bond rates are used to proxy for this unobservable rate. If the security being evaluated with the model is a municipal note or bond, the risk-free rate used must be for a tax-exempt security without default risk. The **term spread** (k_{tm}) captures the component of a security's return that is necessary to induce investors to bear risks linked to maturity. The **risk spread** (k_{rp}) is the added yield necessary to compensate for other risk factors such as default risk (which, technically, gives rise to the default spread or credit spread) and liquidity risk that make up the risk structure of interest rates. Inadequate term or risk premiums do not persist in the efficient money market, because investors will sell (or at least not buy) securities with inadequate yields, leading to lower prices and correspondingly higher yields.

Term Structure of Interest Rates

One of the most important determinants of a security's yield is its maturity. Securities issued by the same issuer offer varying yields-to-maturity for different maturities. The

EXHIBIT 14-11
Yield Curve

Early 2001

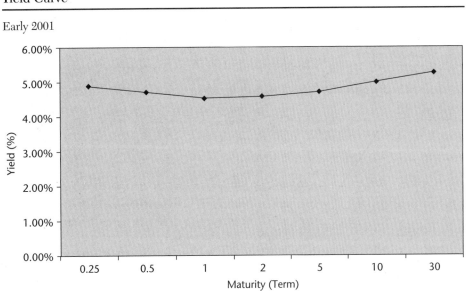

tendency for the maturity-yield relationship to hold across all issuers in a systematic way is called the **term structure of interest rates.** A graph of the term structure, showing current maturities on the horizontal axis and yield-to-maturity on the vertical axis, is known as the **yield curve.** Usually, Treasury securities are plotted to not confuse default risk or liquidity risk effects with maturity effects on yields. Yield comparability is achieved by expressing Treasury bill yields on a coupon-equivalent basis or by using only zero-coupon Treasury notes and bonds. Typically, the curve is upward-sloping, because 30-year Treasury bonds yield more than 3-month bills. Exhibit 14-11 shows the early 2001 yield curve. The normal yield curve is generally upward-sloping, with longer-term maturities yielding more than short-term, for several reasons.

- Liquidity risk may be similar because all Treasury securities have active secondary markets, but Treasury bond investors are committing their principal for a much longer period—especially for the institutional investors that buy and hold to maturity—and some yield inducement is appropriate to cover the possibility that interest or principal payments might be late or missed.
- Longer maturities involve higher probabilities of capital losses because of their greater interest rate risk (the possibility that interest rates will increase, leading to capital losses for existing securities) combined with the fact that investors may have to sell before maturity.
- Purchasing power risk is related to interest rate risk but is distinct: for long-term investors unexpected economy-wide price increases cut into the purchasing power of interest and principal cash flows and tend to drive prevailing interest rates up, feeding back into interest rate risk.
- On foreign securities, another risk that is greater for longer time horizons is the exchange rate risk, in which adverse changes in exchange rates cut into the dollar value of interest and principal returns when converted out of the foreign currency.

The yield curve is also affected by future interest rate expectations, however, leading at times to a flat yield curve and less often to a downward-sloping or inverted yield curve. We require a deeper understanding of what factors lie behind the makeup of a yield curve to explain flat and inverted curves.

TERM STRUCTURE THEORIES.   There are four prominent explanations for the interest rate term structure. Ideally, an explanation for the shape of the yield curve will be able to interpret the interrelationships of a security's issues across the maturity spectrum.

The oldest explanation and first in importance is the **unbiased expectations hypothesis.** This theory posits that the prevailing yield curve is mathematically derived from the present short-term rate and expectations for rates that will exist at various points in time in the future. Existing interest rates in today's markets are called **spot rates;** rates that the market collectively forecasts today for future years are called **forward rates.** Combining the shortest-term spot rates with the forward rates being forecasted by the market, we can derive today's spot rates for medium-term and long-term securities. If we assign the spot rate the symbol $_tR_n$, in which the preceding subscript refers to the point in time when it occurs and the following subscript refers to the maturity, we have the following rather elaborate expression:

$$(1 + {_tR_n}) = [(1 + {_tR_1})(1 + {_{t+1}r_{1,t}}) \times (1 + {_{t+n-1}r_{1,t}})]^{1/n} \tag{14-8}$$

In which: $_tR_n$ = spot rate for one-year security as of time period t

$\qquad$ $_{t+1}r_{1,t}$ = forward rate, the rate the market thinks will exist at period t + 1, for 1-year security, predicted as of period t

$\qquad$ $1/n$ = nth root of entire expression

If we subtract 1 from both sides of Equation 14-8 (after taking the root on the right-hand side) and t is set equal to 0, we have formulated the expression we need for linking today's 1-year rate $(_0R_1)$, to longer-maturity rates. Let's look at an example.

If the 1-year Treasury bill coupon-equivalent yield is 5.50 percent and the 2-year rate is 5.80 percent, what 1-year rate did the money market expect to exist at the end of the first year?

SOLUTION.   First, recognize that the observed current rates are spot rates $_0R_1$ and $_0R_2$, respectively, and the solution that we are seeking is a forward 1-year rate. Here, $t = 0$ and $n = 2$; we plug the values into Equation 14-8 to solve for $_{t+1}r_{1,t}$. Because $t = 0$, we are solving for $_1r_{1,0}$:

$$(1 + 0.0580) = [(1 + .0550)(1 + {_1r_{1,0}})]^{1/2}$$
$$1.0580 = [(1.0550)(1 + {_1r_{1,0}})]^{1/2}$$

Because raising an expression to the $\frac{1}{2}$ power is the same as taking the square root, we must square both sides to get rid of the square root on the right:

$$1.119364 = (1.0550)(1 + {_1r_{1,0}})$$

Dividing by 1.055 and subtracting 1 from both sides, we have

$$0.06101 = {_1r_{1,0}}$$
$$6.10\% = {_1r_{1,0}}$$

Interpreting our example, the expectations theory states that the year-ahead 6.10 percent forward rate for a 1-year security, when combined with the spot 1-year rate

EXHIBIT 14-12
Alternative Classic Yield Curves and Their Explanations

Hypothetical	Actual	Market Segmentation	Unbiased Expectations	Liquidity Premium	Biased Expectations
Normal (Yield vs Maturity)	September 1980 (Yield percent 8–11, Maturity 1–4 years)	Banks have some excess investable funds versus insurance companies	Yields are expected to rise moderately	Liquidity premiums increase with maturity at a decreasing rate	Yields are expected to remain unchanged; liquidity premiums increase with maturity at a decreasing rate
Rising (Yield vs Maturity)	June 1980 (Yield percent 8–11, Maturity 1–4 years)	Banks have substantial excess investment funds versus insurance companies	Yields are expected to rise substantially	Liquidity premiums increase with maturity	Yields are expected to rise substantially; liquidity premiums increase with maturity at a decreasing rate
Falling (Yield vs Maturity)	February 1981 (Yield percent 8–11, Maturity 1–4 years)	Banks are in an extreme investable funds deficit compared to insurance companies	Yields are expected to fall substantially	None	Yields are expected to fall substantially; liquidity premiums increase with maturity at a decreasing rate
Humped (Yield vs Maturity)	March 1980 (Yield percent 8–11, Maturity 1–4 years)	Banks and insurance companies have equivalent investable funds positions; there is a void between their maturity preferences	Yields are expected to first rise and then fall	None	Yields are expected to fall; liquidity premiums increase with maturity at a decreasing rate

Used by permission of Business One Irwin, Homewood, IL. © Richard D. Irwin, Inc., 1983, 1987, 1991.

SOURCE: Adapted from Exhibit 56-7 in Richard W. McEnally and James V. Jordan. 1991. The term structure of interest rates. In Frank J. Fabozzi (ed): *The Handbook of Fixed Income Securities.* 3rd ed. Homewood, IL: Business One Irwin, p 1268.

of 5.50 percent, causes the market to require 5.80 percent (spot rate) from the 2-year security to be in equilibrium. Investors with a 2-year investment horizon are assumed to be indifferent to holding one 2-year security or two consecutive 1-year securities and will engage in arbitrage (a sale of the 2-year security and purchase of the 1-year, or vice versa) until the equilibrium relationship holds. Although we worked backward to reveal the unobservable forward rate (you will not find forward rates in *The Wall Street Journal*), we could just as easily have polled market participants for their year-ahead forecast for a 1-year security, plugged that in, and solved for the theoretical 2-year spot rate, $_0R_2$.[18] Study Exhibit 14-12, in which you will see the unbiased expectations explanation for empirically observed US yield curves (middle column).

The second explanation for a yield curve's shape is the **liquidity preference hypothesis.** Recall our earlier argument about the higher yields necessary to induce

---

[18]We are portraying one of five versions of the expectations hypothesis; see the McEnally and Jordan citation for an exposition of the others.

investors to tie their funds up for long periods (i.e., to be illiquid) in the light of the increasing default probability and interest rate risk. Preference for liquidity is thought to characterize enough investors that the yield curve (in the absence of expectations or other influences on other than the short-term securities) should slope upward from left to right—yielding a "liquidity premium." The longer the maturity, the larger the liquidity premium that must be offered to attract investors. Liquidity preference, as a sole explanation for the yield curve, is unable to explain flat, humped, or inverted yield curves.

The **market segmentation hypothesis** contends that instead of being close substitutes, securities with short, medium, and long maturities are seen by investors (funds suppliers) and issuers (funds demanders) as quite different. The implication is that the term structure for a given issuer or group of similar issuers must be assembled by looking at separate supply and demand conditions in each segment of the maturity spectrum. Proponents point out that banks issue mainly short-term securities and utility companies mainly deal in long-term securities, whereas on the investing-side money funds invest only in short-term securities and insurance companies almost exclusively in long-term securities. Also, recall the role of the Fed in controlling the money supply, which mainly involves open market purchases and sales of Treasury bills as opposed to notes or bonds. The markets are thus separated, or segmented, by the self-limiting behavior of institutions staying within their preferred habitats. Arbitrage across maturities that makes investors indifferent to which maturity they select, as perceived by advocates of the unbiased expectations hypothesis, is thought to be nonexistent by the market segmentation school. This view implies that investors should try to beat the market by searching out attractive risk-return tradeoffs in overlooked maturity segments.

Our fourth hypothesis merges unbiased expectations and liquidity preference in the biased expectations hypothesis. Basically, this hypothesis reflects expectations modified by some degree of liquidity preference (see Exhibit 14-12, right column). Many market observers find the biased expectations hypothesis to be the most plausible of the four explanations. They use the forward rates, which are implied interest rate forecasts, as a tool for discerning the market's collective interest rate forecast. Investors then use that information to decide when to take advantage of the higher yields available on longer-term securities during normal yield curve eras. We develop the mechanics of this "riding the yield curve" strategy in our resolution of the chapter-opening management dilemma after commenting on the empirical evidence supporting the four explanations.

The best-supported explanation for yield curve configurations is the biased expectations hypothesis. Although the market segmentation hypothesis clearly applies to some markets at certain times (e.g., when the Fed is actively increasing or draining credit) and provides a rational explanation for humped yield curves (refer to Exhibit 14-12), studies fail to find consistent support. Yet, there are some puzzles remaining to be solved, such as why Treasury bill rates on recently issued securities behave oddly when a new auction approaches (changing the yield curve from what unbiased expectations would predict). The chapter references provide citations for the major studies that have been conducted on the different theories. We close our survey of the term structure of interest rates by resolving our financial dilemma.

FINANCIAL DILEMMA REVISITED

The banker advising Dave is basing his recommendation to move from overnight investments into 6-month CDs on a normal yield curve. Dave may want to first investigate the reason(s) for the forecasts of higher future rates to better evaluate the interest rate risk he would be facing. Although he anticipates not needing the funds for 6 months, his cash flow forecast may be in error. This would force him to liquidate the CD early and accept the associated penalty. After you explain to Dave about the higher yield for longer maturities, he begins eyeing a 1-year maturity. He decides that he does not want to deal with early withdrawal penalties and insists he will only invest in 6-month CDs with active secondary markets—otherwise, he will stay with overnight investments.

We can help Dave by simulating his total return for the two alternatives in which he is interested: buying a 6-month CD and holding it to maturity or buying a 1-year CD and selling it in the secondary market after 6 months. The first alternative does not subject Dave to any interest rate risk, but the second clearly does. Dave's enthusiasm for riding the yield curve by investing in a maturity longer than his investment horizon may wane if we show him two scenarios: one in which the yield curve remains stable (scenario 1) and the other in which it shifts upward or steepens in slope (scenario 2). Six-month CDs presently yield 6 percent, and 1-year CDs yield 6.5 percent. We will assume a $1 million negotiable CD is to be bought.

SCENARIO 1: STABLE YIELD CURVE.   Labeling the 6-month alternative as option A and the purchase and resale of the 1-year CD as Option B:

Option A: Total return is simply the 6 percent yield received on the 6-month CD. Option B: Total return is the sum of a half-year's interest on the 1-year CD, plus the capital appreciation that will occur as the 1-year CD moves down the yield curve and becomes a lower-yielding 6-month CD. The adjustment process involves an increase in the CD's price, because the coupon is fixed. The interest return received in the first 6 months ($\frac{1}{2}$ year) is $32,500:

$$\text{Interest return} = \frac{1}{2}(0.065) = 0.0325 \times \$1,000,000 = \$32,500$$

The 6.5 percent coupon on the $1 million CD means the dollars of interest per year would be $65,000 ($0.065 \times$ $1 million). Of this, half of the year's interest, or $32,500, has been paid at the end of 6 months, leaving $32,500 to be paid for the last half of the year. That amount will help determine the change in price that occurs during the first 6 months. That change in price provides the second portion of total return, which we label capital gain or loss.

$$\text{Capital gain (loss)} = \text{Sale price} - \text{Buy price}$$

The sale price is based on the CD yielding 6 percent (annualized) after the first 6 months. Because only half the year is remaining, we divide 6 percent by 2:

$$\text{Sale price} = \frac{\$32,500}{0.06/2} = \$1,083,333.30$$

Thus, we have:

$$\text{Capital gain return} = \$1,083,333.30 - \$1,000,000 = \$83,333.30$$

Finally, we add the interest and capital gain returns together to arrive at Option B's total return:

$$\text{Total return for B} = \$32,500 + \$83,333.30 = \$115,833.30$$

On a percentage basis, we find the 6-month total return to be 11.58 percent ($115,833.30/$1 million).

Riding the yield curve is much more profitable if this fairly steep yield curve remains stable. You warn Dave that the reason that he might get this attractive return is because the money market investors anticipate that short-term rates will move sharply higher in the near future. Dave immediately asks what his risk exposure would be, so you show him a second scenario that is predicated on a higher 6-month forward rate.

SCENARIO 2: YIELD CURVE SHIFTS OR TILTS UPWARD.   If the new 6-month rate when Dave sells the CD 6 months from now is higher than 6.5 percent, the price of his 1-year CD would have had to have dropped accordingly. Let's predict the new 6-month CD rate to be 6.75 percent; the same 6-month CD (Option A) return of 6 percent would now be compared with:

Option B: The interest return is still 3.25 percent, or $32,500.

$$\text{Capital gain (loss)} = \text{Sale price} - \text{Buy price}$$

The sale price is now $32,500/(0.0675/2) = $962,962.96.
The capital loss is:

$$\text{Capital loss} = \$962,962.96 - \$1,000,000 = -\$37,037.10$$

This leaves Dave with a 6-month total return of:

$$\text{Total return} = \$32,500 - \$37,037.10 = -\$4,537.20$$

In percentage terms, he would receive -0.45 percent ($-\$4,537.20/\$1$ million). Notice that the higher interest return on the 1-year CD partly offset the capital loss, enabling Dave to almost break even.

So, if the CD market perception of an increase in short-term yields is correct, Dave will lose about 0.5 percent over the 6-month period. Dave looks wistfully at the stable yield curve scenario analysis but shakes his head negatively when you ask him if his company's investment policy permits this kind of risk taking with its temporary cash surpluses.

Risk Structure of Interest Rates

Securities with the same maturity but issued by different issuers and with different issue characteristics are priced to reflect risk differences. The major risk factors accounting for this risk premium are default risk, liquidity risk, reinvestment rate risk, purchasing power risk, and event risk. With foreign securities, the analyst also must consider exchange rate risk and political risk. Even interest rate risk can influence identically termed securities. Differing durations (a measure closely linked to the security's maturity) account for the difference.

Default risk and liquidity risk, defined earlier, obviously vary depending on the creditworthiness of the issuer and the depth and breadth of the security's secondary market, respectively. One other concern, which is specific to the *investor*, is the probability that the security will have to be sold before maturity. When riding the yield curve, by definition the security will be sold prematurely. When the corporate investor is matching the maturity to his or her best estimate of when the proceeds will be needed, the liquidity risk (and interest rate risk) is partly linked to the certainty of the investor's cash flows and the accuracy of the cash forecast. The more certain the company's cash flow and the more accurate its cash forecast, the less of a concern liquidity risk is. Again, if the corporate investor is riding the yield curve—buying maturities in excess of the investment horizon—the company is knowingly exposing itself to liquidity risk. Exhibit 14-13 has been developed to help focus on the primary questions an investment analyst would address when evaluating each type of risk. For example, the worse the outlook for

EXHIBIT 14-13
Risk Structure of Interest Rates

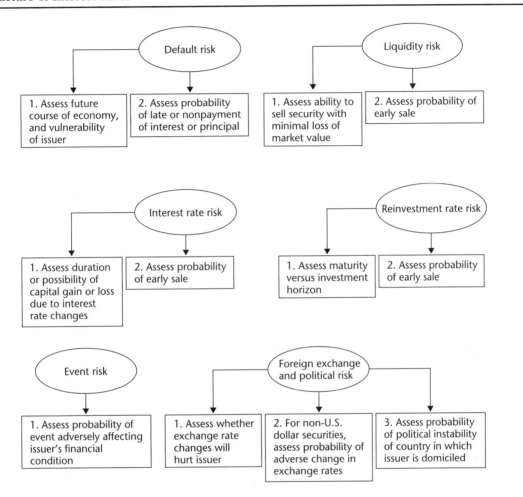

the economy and the higher the probability that a particular issuer's security interest coverage will be inadequate as a result of that company's business and financial risk, the higher the default risk and the larger the required risk premium for that security.

Reinvestment rate risk is the possibility that the investor will have to invest cash proceeds at a lower interest rate for the remainder of the predetermined investment horizon. Reinvestment rate risk is borne when the maturity is less than the investment horizon or the company invests in a coupon security that pays one or more interest payments before the end of the investment horizon. Accrued interest, which is interest earned but not yet paid out in cash, is not a problem because it does not need to be reinvested yet. Recognize that, like interest rate risk, reinvestment rate risk cuts both ways. The treasurer may find rates have gone up, and cash proceeds from maturing investments can be reinvested at higher yields than were achieved earlier.

Event risk includes any security feature or possible event that subjects the investor to a disruption to or reduction in the expected yield. Outstanding RJR-Nabisco bond prices dropped more than 20 percent within 48 hours of an announcement that the company was going to be taken private by using massive amounts of debt. This is a type of **financial restructuring.** Also of concern is **operational restructuring,** in which the company changes its product lines or use of assets with heavy fixed operating costs and alters the company's business risk. Call features, prepayment risk on mortgage-backed securities, problems affecting the guarantor of an issuer's securities, the default of a major issuer in the instrument's market, and unforeseen regulatory changes are other events that hurt investors and should be compensated for in the form of higher yields. The most common event risk in the twenty-first century is litigation.

On foreign securities, such as CP issued by a US manufacturer that is denominated in French francs, the investor should be alerted to foreign exchange risk and political risk. We illustrated foreign exchange risk earlier and merely point out that although the French government might not seize the US company's French operations or block the outflow of investment proceeds, there are other countries that have and will continue to initiate such actions.

Although not a major factor in the US money market during the twentieth or early twenty-first centuries, and therefore not included in our diagram of risk factors, purchasing power risk also can affect yields. Anticipated inflation is built into the risk-free interest rate, but investors still are vulnerable to losses in purchasing power from unanticipated inflation. This risk is especially problematic for investments made in foreign securities issued in countries with high and volatile inflation rates. In fact, this is a major reason for the extreme foreign exchange risk evident in many less-developed countries.

We conclude our analysis of individual money market security risk-return evaluation by providing an analysis of how default risk and liquidity risk can be assessed. These are the main determinants of investment safety, which is consistently ranked as the key attribute for treasurers in their security selection.

Risk-Return Assessment in Practice

How are the safety and risk-return features of an issuer of short-term securities evaluated? We provide the details of CD evaluation to illustrate a process that is similar for all money market securities. Because few CDs are offered with variable interest rates, we only consider fixed-rate CDs. The evaluation of CDs and other bank securities became even more important in the 1990s because the **1991 Banking Act** passed by Congress prohibited the FDIC from voluntarily covering a bank's uninsured depositors (starting in 1995), except when the Department of the Treasury, the Federal Reserve Board, the FDIC, and the President all agree that the financial system would be endangered by the bank's closure. Treasury professionals apply two main approaches to evaluating a bank's safety: yield spread analysis and third-party safety ratings.

YIELD SPREAD ANALYSIS.   Yield spread analysis involves calculating or plotting the differential between CD yields and Treasury bill yields, which might be considered a risk premium. For example, an analyst might infer that the roughly 20 to 50 basis point yield spread between Eurodollar CDs and domestic CDs of the same issuer is due to greater risk, because the $100,000 federal guarantee is absent. The analyst might also compare a bank's CD rate with an identical term Treasury bill, implicitly assuming that the yield difference is due to default risk differences. Although early empirical studies could not detect higher yields for riskier banks, three recent studies all have found higher yields offered by riskier banks.[19] Exhibit 14-14 illustrates this approach with a yield comparison of large-denomination CD rates offered by INB National Bank (now part of First Chicago/NBD) to comparable yields on Treasury bills for the same periods.

---

[19]See Table 3, pp 14–15, of Gilbert (1990), cited in end-of-chapter references.

EXHIBIT 14-14
Yield Spreads for Large CD and Treasury Bills

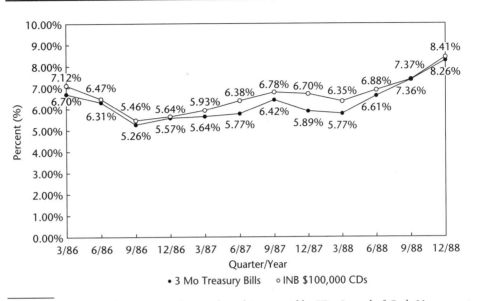

SOURCE: John T. Zietlow. 1990. Evaluating the risk in negotiable CDs. *Journal of Cash Management* September/October:39–46. Copyright by the Treasury Management Association. All rights reserved. Reprinted with permission of the TMA.

Such yield comparisons are inadequate for risk evaluation purposes, however. First, yield premiums are constantly changing. As money market rates move up, bank CD yields may noticeably lag behind Treasury bill rates. Second, there are important risk factors, other than default or marketability risk, that influence yield spreads:

- the supply and demand of loanable funds in a bank's "relevant market"—that area within which the bank generally does business.
- the negative "halo effect" of the concentration of problem banks in a bank's geographic area.
- current money market conditions (especially in the federal funds and CP markets) that affect CD yields differently at various points.

A larger problem is the counterintuitive historical evidence regarding the yield spread. This CD–Treasury bill "default" premium is the highest for 1-month CDs (despite their excellent liquidity) and declines with maturity (apparently as a result of the Treasury's dominant role in the bill market), and longer-maturity expected premiums are lower during recessions than during good times.[20] Finally, trying to implement this approach to risk analysis is complicated. The treasurer must analyze instrument average premiums (CDs versus Treasury bills, CDs versus CP, and so on) as well as issuer characteristic premiums (e.g., money centers versus regional banks), which are very difficult to segregate from the yield figures. Furthermore, some empirical evidence regarding using yield spreads in other sectors of the market indicates that the investor may have to wait at least 6 months before spreads return to normal and the above-average return is earned.[21] In summary, using yield premiums to accurately infer default risk is difficult.

[20]This is documented in Fama's (1986) study of yield behavior. See end-of-chapter references.

[21]This is documented in Fridson and Bersh (1994). See end-of-chapter references.

EXHIBIT 14-15
Standard & Poor's Rating Categories on Long-Term CDs

Long-Term Rating Categories (Grades)

Investment Grades:

AAA   Overwhelming repayment capacity, highest grade.

AA   Very high degree of safety and repayment capacity, differing by only a small degree from AAA.

A   Somewhat more likely to experience effects of adverse economic conditions.

BBB   Satisfactory safety and repayment capacity, but more vulnerability to unfavorable economy or changing circumstances.

Speculative Grades:

BB   Less near-term chance of default than other two grades of speculative CDs, but major ongoing uncertainties or vulnerability to bad economic or financial conditions, posing threat to ability to pay interest and repay principal on timely basis.

B   Still have capacity to pay interest and repay principal but greater chance of default than BB. Likely that adverse business, financial, or economic conditions will impair capacity to continue to make those payments at some future time.

CCC   Currently identifiable vulnerability to default, and strong dependency on continued favorable conditions to maintain payments. Adverse developments would make payments unlikely.

SOURCE: *S&P's Bank Book,* 1989, Volume I, 307. Used by permission of the Standard & Poor's Ratings Group (Standard & Poor's: New York, NY). Plus (+) or minus (−) reflects relative standing within a major rating grade and may be appended to any except the D (already in default) grade.

SAFETY RATINGS.   Another approach to safety assessment is to get help from third-party rating services that have specialized expertise in risk evaluation. Several agencies presently rate banks for performance and creditworthiness: Standard & Poor's (S&P); Keefe Bankwatch, Moody's; and Duff & Phelps are four of the most important[22]. Alternatively, the analyst can use specific CD safety rankings, such as that assigned by S&P ratings, which were first published in 1985. S&P specifically rates bank CD creditworthiness because of the fact that many large corporate and institutional investors are only partly covered by the $100,000 FDIC guarantee and smaller investors would be inconvenienced in the event of bank failure. CD ratings are based on the following:

- fundamental credit analysis of portfolio quality, liquidity, earnings and profitability, and capital adequacy.
- subjective factors such as management depth and quality, risk profile, business aggressiveness, and regulatory sponsorship and support.

---

[22]The corporate investor must consider whether the expense of a separate CD rating is worthwhile. Bank or bank holding company bond ratings are publicly available and might already be part of the treasurer's information database because of their relevance for corporate financing decisions. These debt ratings measure creditworthiness and default risk, but the treasurer must consider whether they adequately incorporate liquidity factors and other financial data, which will also impinge on bank creditworthiness and CD safety. Our study of this issue, using S&P ratings, found that ratings on long-term instruments do not proxy well for short-term CDs or CP ratings, mainly because of the differing importance of financial data going into the various ratings. Of all the long-term and short-term ratings assigned for a given bank, the only ratings that were closely associated and that could proxy for each other were the short-term CD and CP ratings.

With regard to the regulatory support, S&P suggests that it will weight financial strength heavily in ranking a weak bank, regardless of S&P's perception of regulatory support. Moody's, by contrast, attempts to predict regulatory support for uninsured depositors. Exhibit 14-15 gives an abbreviated listing (long-term CDs only, with an original maturity of 1 year or more) of the possible ratings. It is noteworthy that rating downgrades have significantly exceeded rating upgrades during the 1980s.[23]

Be careful not to assume that the rating system useful for one instrument must apply to all other short-term instruments. To help you see the differences, we have included in Exhibit 14-16 part of S&P's CP rating approach. These ratings are not perfect, as investors found out with west-coast utility CP defaults in early 2001.

INVESTMENT USES OF RATINGS. There are two basic ways to incorporate the information in CD or CP ratings into the investment process: generating an "approved list," and developing performance benchmarks against which to evaluate realized returns.

The approved list specifies which banks will be considered for future CD investments and how much (maximum) might be invested in the CDs of each one. Ratings provide an intuitive and easily implemented means of setting a dollar limit for a certain institution. Although yields basically are segmented largely on size alone, the ratings also are a function of other variables—giving the treasurer value added in the risk assessment.

Ratings are especially valuable for considering issuers of "Yankee" CDs, which are issued by foreign banks that are difficult to assess. A joint approach can be used here: $10 million per top-rated institution, $5 million for institutions ranked in the second class, and no investment in any lower class. Or one might invest in only the shortest maturities of lower-rated issuers.

One benchmark, useful in selecting CDs as investments as well as evaluating realized returns from CDs recently held, is to compute risk-adjusted yield premiums. This simply involves subtracting Treasury bill rates from a bank's quoted CD rate and assessing the difference in the light of the bank's CD rating. A novel approach to investment vehicle selection might be suggested here: Assuming the approved list already has been generated, the treasurer might switch from Treasury bills to listed CDs whenever the CD yields exceed the Treasury bills by a certain number of basis points, with the exact spread depending on which rating class the issuing institution is in. To illustrate, INB's top-rated CDs might have been bought in June and December 1987, when yield spreads exceeded 50 basis points (refer back to Exhibit 14-14). Should INB's rating drop one class, the treasurer might shy away from its CDs until the yield spread exceeds 65 or 70 basis points.[24]

CDs and CP issued by bank holding companies are popular investments for corporate treasurers. Corporate investment analysts may decide to do their own financial evaluation of the issuing bank to determine if a risk-return tradeoff is attractive. This can supplement yield spread analysis and a third-party rating or be used as the sole means

---

[23]Confidence in the ability of raters to capture key financial data requires an understanding of what data is most important in determining ratings assignments. To provide further insight into what goes into a bank's CD rating, S&P initial (1985) CD ratings were modeled based on COMPUSTAT bank data using several multivariate statistical techniques (see the Zietlow citation in the chapter references). The financial variables and ratios best able to classify banks into the assigned ratings were statistically selected using 5-year averages of 1981 through 1985 quarterly data. Taken jointly, and judged by the ability to most closely mirror assigned ratings, the best set of classification variables is net income, equity reserves, the debt ratio, the price-to-book ratio, and equity.

[24]Another benchmark, useful for portfolio evaluation, is the average yield of similarly rated banks for the most recent investment period. The treasurer, or someone assessing the performance of an organization's treasury function, can determine if appropriate risk-based yields were obtained. Portfolio risk assessment is covered in greater detail in Chapter 15.

EXHIBIT 14-16
Standard & Poor's Commercial Paper Rating Criteria

Evaluation of an issuer's commercial paper (CP) reflects Standard & Poor's opinion of the issuer's fundamental credit quality. The analytical approach is virtually identical to the approach followed in assigning a long-term rating, and there is a strong link between the short-term and long-term rating systems. In effect, the minimum credit quality associated with the "A-1+" CP rating is the equivalent of an "A+" long-term rating. Similarly, for CP to be rated "A-1," the long-term rating needs to be at least "A−." (In fact, the "A-/A-1" combination is rare. Typically, "A-1" CP ratings are associated with "A+" and "A" long-term ratings.) Conversely, knowing the long-term rating will not determine a CP rating, considering the overlap in rating categories. However, the range of possibilities is always narrow. To the extent that one of two CP ratings might be assigned at a given level of long-term credit quality (e.g., at the "A" level), several criteria apply to make that determination. Overall strength of the credit within the rating category is the first consideration. For example, a marginal "A" credit likely will have its CP rated "A-2"; a solid "A" will almost automatically receive an "A-1." Next come liquidity considerations, which receive greater emphasis in CP ratings than in long-term ratings. The purpose and pattern of commercial paper usage are rating elements. For example, if commercial paper is used only to finance seasonal working capital requirements, that could contribute to a higher rating. The rating benefits because the assets liquidate in a predictable way and enable repayment of the CP. Finally, the CP rating perspective sometimes focuses more intensely on the nearer term. The time horizon for a CP rating extends well beyond the typical 30-day life of a CP note, the 270-day maximum maturity for the most common type of CP, or even the one-year tenor used to distinguish between short-term and long-term ratings. Thus CP ratings are likely to endure over time, rather than change frequently. Nonetheless, occasionally, the near-term outlook is distinct from long-term prospects. For example, there are companies with substantial liquidity, providing protection in the near or intermediate term, but which also have less than stellar profitability, a long-term factor. Similarly, companies with relatively large cash holdings that may be used to fund acquisitions in the future fit in this category. This distinction, in reverse, often applies after an issuer makes a major acquisition. The analyst's confidence that the firm can restore financial health over the long term is factored into its long-term ratings, while financial stress that dominates the near term may lead to a relatively low CP rating. Use of different time horizons as the basis for long- and short-term ratings implies that either one or the other rating will change with time.

Back-up policies
In the past, a key purpose of Standard & Poor's requiring bank-line backup was to assure that an issuer would be able to meet its obligations in the event of a disruption to the financial

continued

of investigation. Whatever approach is used can be applied to evaluation of CDs, CP, government securities, as well as other bank securities such as time deposits.

ASSESSING LIQUIDITY RISK.   The liquidity risk assessment of securities is more problematic than default risk appraisal. The differences in various instruments' liquidity are so intangible that treasury professionals have struggled with liquidity evaluation. Individual security liquidity assessment has been slightly easier, at least for issuers that have issued securities for several years and for which a secondary market activity track record has been established. Alan Seidner of Fiduciary Trust International of California (Los Angeles) has developed a subjective rating system for instrument liquidity, which is adapted in Exhibit 14-17.

SUMMARY

We have surveyed the menu of short-term investment alternatives and indicated popular choices within bank, corporate, US government, state and local, and mixed investment

EXHIBIT 14-16 (*continued*)
Standard & Poor's Commercial Paper Rating Criteria

markets that might inhibit the normal rollover of commercial paper, even while the issuer's own financial condition remained strong. However, the growth of the CP market prompted a reevaluation. It is Standard & Poor's current judgment that the protection afforded by back-up facilities could not be relied on with a high degree of confidence in the event of widespread disruption of the commercial paper markets. A general disruption of commercial paper markets is a highly volatile scenario, under which most bank lines represent unreliable claims on whatever cash is made available through the banking system to support the market. Standard & Poor's neither anticipates that such a scenario is likely to develop nor assumes that it never will.

Standard & Poor's continues to emphasize bank-line availability as an important buttress to liquidity, but only in the context of normal market conditions. The change in Standard & Poor's commercial paper back-up policy shifts the focus away from market disruption, while confirming the utility of bank facilities in supporting operations of any entity that incurs short-term obligations in the normal course of business. A substantial level of liquidity—in the form of bank facilities or readily available liquid resources—is prudent for virtually all issuers and will continue to be necessary to support an investment-grade rating on both commercial paper and long-term debt. From time to time, there will be developments—for example, bad business conditions, a lawsuit, management changes, a rating change—affecting a single company or group of companies, which may make CP investors nervous and unwilling to roll over the issuer's paper, even though the issuer remains creditworthy. Prearranged bank facilities are often essential in protecting against the risk of default under these circumstances.

Industrial and utility issuers typically provide 100 percent backup—excess liquid assets or bank facilities—for paper outstanding. However, companies with the highest credit quality can provide a lower percentage of coverage. Issuers rated "A-1+" need not prearrange 100 percent coverage because they should be able to raise funds quickly even if some adversities develop. The exact amount is determined by the issuer's overall credit strength and its access to capital markets. Some "AAA" issuers may have as little as 50 percent backup.

Importantly, backup must be sufficient to provide the appropriate level of coverage for other maturing short-term debt, not just commercial paper. Backup for 100 percent of rated commercial paper is meaningless if other debt maturities for which there is no backup coincide with those of commercial paper. Thus the scope of backup must extend to Eurocommercial paper, master notes, syndicated bank notes, and other similar confidence-sensitive obligations.

SOURCE: Standard & Poor's Ratings Web site at www.ratings.standardpoor.com

categories. Typical denominations for many of these exclude small businesses and individuals, who must turn to money market mutual funds for the high yields offered to "wholesale quantity" investors. The money market is a global web of telecommunication ports, with dealers and brokers playing a vital role in coordinating investment purchases and sales.

Surveys indicate the major concern of corporate treasury personnel is investment safety, with the related notion of liquidity second and yield third. Sweep accounts and money market funds continue to grow in importance, especially for small and mid-sized organizations. The slight differences in many money market instruments, as far as safety and liquidity are concerned, imply that yield shopping is more frequent than it would seem. Safety particularly means default risk, whereas liquidity translates into marketability. We investigated the safety evaluation of negotiable CDs in detail, noting that creditworthiness of CP and other types of instruments might be similarly appraised.

Safety also relates to interest rate risk, which we analyzed by drawing a yield curve and estimating price changes that occur for given changes in market interest rates. Longer maturities imply larger price swings on existing securities when prevailing

EXHIBIT 14-17
Instrument Liquidity Ratings

INSTRUMENT	LIQUIDITY (0 LOW TO 10 HIGH)
United States Treasury bills	10
United States Treasury notes	9
United States Treasury bonds	8+
Agency discount notes	9
Municipal notes	7
Municipal commercial paper (tax-exempt)	7
Municipal floating-rate notes	9+
Bankers' acceptances	8
CDs issued in United States:	
United States bank	8
Foreign bank	7
Savings and loan	5
Eurodollar CDs:	
United States bank	7
Foreign bank	5
Eurodollar time deposits	0
Commercial paper	8
Corporate notes	6
Preferred stock	5
Term repurchase agreements	0

SOURCE: Reprinted from Alan G. Seidner, *Corporate Investments Manual* (New York: Warren, Gorham, & Lamont) ©1989. Research Institute of America, Inc. Used with permission.

money market interest rates change. We noted the four major explanations for a given yield curve.

In the next chapter, we look at risk and return from the portfolio manager's perspective. Individual security risks are still important in that context, but the manager also must attend to the interrelationships in security risk.

Useful Web Sites

BanxQuote: http://www.banx.com/
Bloomberg: www.bloomberg.com
Fidelity: www.fidelity.com
US Treasury: http://www.publicdebt.treas.gov/of/ofsectable.htm
US Treasury: http://www.publicdebt.treas.gov/sec/secfaq.htm
SEI Investments: http://www2.seic.com/cash/
Standard & Poor's:
    http://www.standardandpoors.com/ResourceCenter/RatingsDefinitions.html
SEI Investments: http://www.treasurypoint.com/
Treasury Strategies, Inc.: www.treasurystrat.com

Questions

1. Why is knowledge of the money market important for carrying out of value-maximizing short-term financial management? What are the opportunity costs of not taking into account the risk-return tradeoffs of the various short-term instruments?

2. What is the difference between a primary and a secondary market? Why does a primary market's functionality depend on the secondary market?
3. "Interest rates moved up today in the money market." Comment on why this statement can be made without detailing the rates on each different type of money market instrument.
4. How do the roles of money market dealers and brokers differ?
5. Define the following:
   a. default risk
   b. liquidity risk
   c. reinvestment rate risk
   d. interest rate risk
   e. prepayment risk
6. Why do Eurodollar CDs generally yield more than domestic negotiable CDs?
7. Given that the major concern of short-term corporate investing is safety of principal, why are corporate investors buying unsecured CP?
8. Why would corporate investors use a dividend capture strategy? What is the major risk involved?
9. Are agency securities as creditworthy as Treasury securities? Explain.
10. Explain the mechanics of interest rate resetting on variable rate demand notes.
11. List and explain briefly the advantages of pooling investors' monies in a money market mutual fund.
12. Explain how an RP works, and distinguish it from a sweep account.
13. Why are sweep accounts done with a company's deposit bank the most convenient method of investing surplus cash balances? Why do large companies not use them as commonly as small companies?
14. Distinguish between discount securities and coupon securities.
15. In Exhibit 14-10, note the coupon-equivalent rates for the 3-month and 6-month Treasury bills. Use the models of term structure from Exhibit 14-12 to explain what might account for the relationship between the two rates.
16. What is the mathematical relationship between the discount yield and the coupon-equivalent yield?
17. Summarize the theories regarding the term structure of interest rates.

Problems

1. Reggie White, a corporate treasurer, is trying to decide which of two 1-year securities to purchase: a negotiable CD with a nominal yield of 6 percent or a municipal security with a nominal yield of 4.25 percent. The issuing municipality is not in the same state as Reggie's company, but he recognizes that the muni's interest is exempt from federal income taxation. His company's marginal federal tax rate is 39 percent. Which security should the treasurer select, assuming the securities have equal default risk?
2. Jacqui Velasquez, a treasury assistant, is considering the purchase of municipal notes but needs to compare its tax-advantaged yield with the yield on taxable securities. The company's marginal federal tax rate is 35 percent.
   a. What advice would you give her about comparing these securities?
   b. If she is considering a muni that is yielding 5 percent, how high must the taxable rate be to provide a higher after-tax yield on the taxable security?

3. Heather Bell, the new cash manager at Centron, a small electronics firm, is excited about the possibilities of investing in high-dividend-yield stocks. She found one, a stable nuclear electrical utility, whose stock is yielding 8 percent. Centron's marginal federal income tax rate is 35 percent.
   a. What would be the dividend capture yield to Centron?
   b. How much would CP have to yield to be equivalent (on an after-tax basis) to the stock's yield?
   c. What types of risk should Heather be made aware of? Are there extra return possibilities to offset this risk?

4. Cash manager Ken Johnson just picked up the financial newspaper and is having trouble understanding the jargon. He notices that at a recent Treasury auction of 13-week Treasury bills, the lowest price bid for $10,000 bills was 97.569 percent of par. Can you help Ken understand the various yield calculations?
   a. What is the discount yield on these securities?
   b. What is the coupon-equivalent yield on the Treasury bills?
   c. What is the annual effective yield on the Treasury bills?
   d. Comment on the relationship between the results you got in problems *a* through *c*.

5. CP is a discount security whose nominal yield is very similar to the coupon-equivalent yield of Treasury bills. The CP nominal yield (CPNY) formula uses a 365-day basis:
   $$\text{CPNY} = (\text{Dollar discount/Purchase price}) \times (365/\text{Days to maturity})$$
   In which: Dollar discount = Face value − Purchase price
   Use this relationship to find the nominal yields of the following securities:
   a. A 45-day, $100,000 CP issue selling at a price of $98,950.
   b. A 30-day, $1 million CP issue selling at a price of $990,450.

6. If the 1-year Treasury bill coupon-equivalent yield is presently 5.25 percent and the 2-year Treasury note is yielding 5.95 percent,
   a. What is the implied 1-year forward rate?
   b. Should a corporate investor buy two consecutive 1-year securities or buy and hold the 2-year security if his or her forecast for the 1-year forward rate is 7 percent (assuming that he or she trusts the reliability of the forecast)?

References

N. Arshadi. 1989. Capital structure, agency theory, and banks. *Financial Review* 24:31–52.

W. Brian Barrett. 1988. Term structure modeling for pension liability discounting. *Financial Analysts Journal* 44:63–67.

W. Brian Barrett, Thomas F. Gosnell, and Andrea J. Heuson. 1995. Yield curve shifts and the selection of immunization strategies. *Journal of Fixed Income* September:53–64.

Brian Belt and Keith V. Smith. 1989. Working capital management in practice: An update. Working Paper 951, West Lafayett, IN: Krannert Graduate School of Management, Purdue University.

John Y. Campbell. 1986. A defense of traditional hypotheses about the term structure. *Journal of Finance* 41:183–193.

Timothy Q. Cook and Timothy D. Rowe, eds. 1993. *Instruments of the money market.* 7th ed. Richmond, VA: Federal Reserve Bank of Richmond.

John Cox, Jonathan E. Ingersoll, Jr., and Stephen A. Ross. 1981. A reexamination of traditional hypotheses about the term structure of interest rates. *Journal of Finance* 36:769–799.

John M. Culbertson. 1957. The term structure of interest rates. *Quarterly Journal of Economics* 71:485–517.

Steven W. Dobson, Richard C. Sutch, and David E. Vanderford. 1976. An evaluation of alternative empirical models of the term structure of interest rates. *Journal of Finance* 31:1035–1065.

Michael E. Echols and J.W. Elliott. 1976. A quantitative yield curve model for estimating the term structure of interest rates. *Journal of Financial and Quantitative Analysis* 11:87–114.

J.W. Elliott and Michael E. Echols. 1976. Market segmentation, speculative behavior and the term structure of interest rates. *Review of Economics and Statistics* 59:40–49.

Frank Fabozzi, ed. 1991. *The handbook of fixed income securities,* 3rd ed. Homewood, IL: Business One Irwin.

Eugene F. Fama. 1984. The information in the term structure. *Journal of Financial Economics* 13:509–528.

Eugene F. Fama. 1986. Term premiums and default premiums in money markets. *Journal of Financial Economics* September:175–196.

Irving Fisher. 1930. *The theory of interest.* New York: Macmillan.

Martin S. Fridson and Jeffrey A. Bersh. 1994. Spread versus treasuries as a market-timing tool for high-yield investors. *Journal of Fixed Income* June:63–69.

R.A. Gilbert. 1990. Market discipline of bank risk: Theory and evidence. *Federal Reserve Bank of St. Louis Review* January/February:3–18.

Michael J. Hamburger and Elliot N. Platt. 1975. The expectations hypothesis and the efficiency of the treasury bill market. *Review of Economics and Statistics* 57:190–199.

M.K. Lewis and K.T. Davis. 1987. *Domestic & international banking.* Cambridge, MA: MIT.

Miles Livingston. 1977. A theory of humpbacked bond yield curves. *Journal of Finance* 32:1747–1751.

Jeff Madura. 1989. *International financial management,* 2nd ed. St. Paul, MN: West.

Burton G. Malkiel. 1966. *The term structure of interest rates.* Princeton, NJ: Princeton University.

J. Huston McCulloch. 1975. An estimate of the liquidity premium. *Journal of Political Economy* 83:95–119.

Richard W. McEnally and James V. Jordan. 1991. The term structure of interest rates. In: Frank J. Fabozzi (ed): *The Handbook of Fixed Income Securities,* 3rd ed. Homewood, IL: Business One Irwin, pp 1245–1295.

David Meiselman. 1962. *The term structure of interest rates.* Englewood Cliffs, NJ: Prentice-Hall.

Charles R. Nelson. 1972. *The term structure of interest rates.* New York: Basic Books.

Mary Jean Rivers and Barbara M. Yates. 1997. City size and geographic segmentation in the municipal bond market. *Quarterly Review of Economics and Finance* 37:633–645.

Richard Roll. 1970. *The behavior of interest rates: An application of the efficient market model to U.S. treasury bills.* New York: Basic Books.

Alan G. Seidner. 1989. *Corporate investments manual: Short- and intermediate-term fixed-income securities.* New York: Warren, Gorham, & Lamont.

Alan G. Seidner. 1990. *Corporate investments manual: Short- and intermediate-term fixed-income securities.* 1990 cumulative supplement. New York: Warren, Gorham, & Lamont.

Andrew F. Siegel and Charles R. Nelson. 1988. Long-term behavior of yield curves. *Journal of Financial and Quantitative Analysis* 23:105–110.

Manoj K. Singh. 1995. Estimation of Multifactor Cox, Ingersoll, and Ross Term structure model: Evidence on volatility structure and parameter stability. *Journal of Fixed Income* 8:10–28.

Venkat Srinivasan, Paul J. Bolster, and Ronald A. Johnson. 1990. Sovereign debt ratings: A judgmental model based on the analytic hierarchy process. *Journal of International Business Studies* 21:95–117.

M.L. Stigum. 1990. *The money market,* 3rd ed. Homewood, IL: Dow Jones-Irwin.

M.L. Stigum and R.O. Branch. 1983. *Managing bank assets and liabilities: Strategies for risk control and profit.* Homewood, IL: Dow Jones-Irwin.

Duane Stock. 1985. Price volatility of municipal discount bonds. *Journal of Financial Research* 8:1–13.

Suresh Sundaresan. 1994. An empirical analysis of U.S. Treasury auctions: Implications for auction and term structure theories. *Journal of Fixed Income* September:35–50.

Susan Woodward. 1983. The liquidity premium and the solidity premium. *American Economic Review* 73:348–361.

Michael Zaretsky. 1995. Generation of a smooth forward curve for U.S. Treasuries. *Journal of Fixed Income* September:65–69.

John T. Zietlow. 1990. Evaluating the risk in negotiable CDs. *Journal of Cash Management* November/December:39–41, 43, 45–46.

CHAPTER 15

Short-Term Investment Management

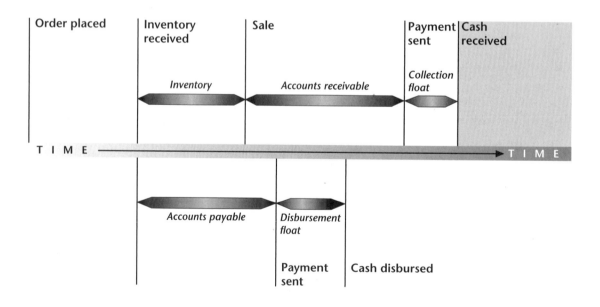

After studying this chapter, you should be able to:

- Define an investment policy and indicate what inputs are used to develop the policy.
- Describe the cash and securities allocation decision.
- Describe the short-term investment decision-making process.
- Calculate portfolio return for the purpose of evaluating portfolio performance.
- Indicate how a portfolio manager might assess risk and return tradeoffs involved with assembling a short-term investment portfolio.

Investments is one of the most exciting areas in finance. Deciding which investments to include in the corporate marketable securities portfolio and in what amounts is an intriguing part of the treasury management process. Shareholder value is enhanced by decisions that properly balance risk and return in the short-term portfolio in light of the liquidity position of the firm and its forecasted cash flows.

In the previous chapter, we presented the major short-term investment alternatives and their chief characteristics. We now turn our attention to how the investments manager can select from among those alternatives to assemble a portfolio that meets the company's investment objectives. We consider the factors driving an investment policy, what that policy might include, and how the company decides on the size of its cash and securities holdings. Additionally, we propose the major advantages and disadvantages of external and internal portfolio management and indicate how the portfolio performance might be monitored and evaluated. Part of our discussion focuses on active management strategies such as investing in securities with longer maturities to attain a higher yield. The financial dilemma illustrates a typical decision facing the investment manager pursuing an active strategy.

FINANCIAL DILEMMA

Evaluating Interest Rate Risk

Margaret Becker, fresh out of B-school, has been started in the cash management area of her company as part of the management development program. The company pursues an active portfolio management strategy that attempts to gain extra yield by taking measured risks. She has $1,000,000 to invest, and it appears from the cash forecast provided to her by the previous analyst that the company will not need the money for 90 days. She notices that the investment policy recommends choosing either 3-month or 1-year Treasury bills for any investment horizon in excess of 30 days. Margaret is more than a little nervous about the prospect of botching her very first assignment, and she does not know how to compare the risks involved with 3-month and 1-year bills.

SHORT-TERM INVESTMENT POLICY

The sheer number of alternative investments, available in varying denominations and maturities—each with slightly different risk-return dimensions—presents a major challenge to the investment manager. Increased complexity results from the manager's own view of risk and his or her desire to reflect shareholders' risk preferences in portfolio decisions. Managers have found that a prerequisite for screening investment alternatives is to formulate an **investment policy.** Unfortunately, the 2000 Liquidity Survey conducted by Treasury Strategies finds that only about 45 percent of companies have an active, up-to-date investment policy. The investment policy defines the company's posture toward risk and return and specifies how it is to be implemented. A common risk perspective is the evaluative criteria of "safety, liquidity, and yield," implying that risk aspects take precedence over return because of the importance of preserving the principal invested. Specific policy directives might address potential investment eligibility standards such as:

- the minimal acceptable security rating
- limits to dollar amounts or percent of portfolio invested in any one issuer's securities, industry, geographic area, or instrument
- whether a "buy and hold" strategy will be used
- absolute or relative portfolio return (yield) targets
- whether the company will invest through investment company brokers, dealers, or bank traders
- maturity limits

EXHIBIT 15-1
Short-Term Investment Process

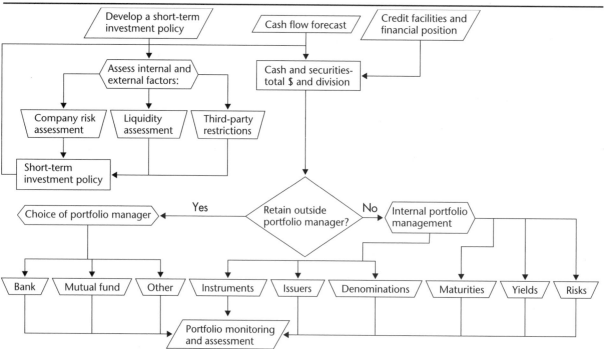

FOCUS ON PRACTICE

State, county, and city treasurers often work within the most restrictive investment policies. State laws in Idaho and Missouri, for example, prohibit public funds from being invested in commercial paper or bankers' acceptances. In many states, federal agency obligations are also off limits, despite their relative safety. One way to increase yield, given these constraints, is to carefully segment the investable funds into an amount that must be available at short notice and another amount that can be tied up for longer periods and therefore invested in longer-term securities that yield more. That is exactly what has been done in Missouri, where the total short-term investment portfolio of $3.6 billion was divided into $2.6 billion "short notice" funds (average maturity of 5 months) and $1 billion in intermediate term investments (average maturity of about 2 years). However, the investment policy group decided to play it safe—the economy might slow down and tax receipts decline—and put only $500 million of that latter amount into the 2-year portfolio. Because Missouri was the only one of nine states with the top AAA credit rating that was not permitted to buy commercial paper (39 states have investment policies allowing commercial paper as an eligible investment), a ballot proposal was put together to liberalize the state's investment policy.

SOURCE: Richard Gamble. 1998. Cash Rich with Few Freedoms. *Treasury & Risk Management Magazine* November/December. Available online at: www.treasuryandrisk.com/html/Articles/TRM/1998/98NOcash.html.

- procedures and controls, including authorized individuals and approvals
- how portfolio performance will be monitored and evaluated

Before the policy can be developed, the treasury department should assess the company's liquidity, its tolerance for risk, and whether any external third-party restrictions limit investment policy. Exhibit 15-1 diagrams these inputs into the policy-making decision, which is one of the first decisions a business must make regarding its investing strategies.

Liquidity assessment can be done using the tools presented in Chapter 2. Dynamic liquidity indicators such as lambda and the net liquid balance can be calculated and evaluated, and the analyst should project both a monthly cash budget for the next 6 to 12 months and a statement of cash flows for each of the next several years. Most important, at a minimum, the pattern of cash flows (including trend, cyclical, and seasonal components) and the variability of cash flows should be identified. Finally, stocks of liquid assets—particularly of cash and securities—and unused short-term borrowing capacity should be incorporated into the comprehensive liquidity analysis.

The risk tolerance of both the management team and the stakeholders also enters into the investment policy formulation, as noted in Focus on Practice. The management team has the best grasp of the overall risk attributes of the company. This includes **business risk,** the possibility that the company will not be able to meet ongoing operating expenditures[1]; and **financial risk,** the possibility that the company will not be able to cover financing-related expenditures such as lease payments, interest, principal repayment, and preferred stock dividends. A different perspective on risk characterizes the company's investors who are well diversified, meaning that they own stock in other companies as well.

[1]The major determinants of a company's business risk are the vulnerability of sales to recession, input price variability, output price variability and flexibility, degree and size of competition, and degree of operating leverage (preponderance of fixed operating costs such as depreciation, taxes, insurance, and utilities). For a lucid discussion of operating leverage measurement, see Thomas J. O'Brien and Paul A. Vanderheiden, "Empirical Measurement of Operating Leverage for Growing Firms," *Financial Management* 6(Summer 1987): 45–53.

SHORT-TERM INVESTMENT MANAGEMENT OUT OF CONTROL. Archer Daniels Midland, better known as ADM, is a large food processing company headquartered in Decatur, Illinois. ADM's monthly purchases of corn and other grains average several hundred million dollars, and it hedges its exposure to higher crop prices by using commodity futures. Somehow, things got out of hand in 1989. Having gained futures market experience through ultraconservative hedging, one or more finance personnel started betting on interest rates by buying financial futures. As sometimes happens to gamblers, they bet wrong. ADM had to take a $6.5 million charge to 1992 fiscal year profits because of large losses that the traders suffered. The treasurer quietly left the company a short while later, primarily because of the trading loss, which was discovered by auditors 2 years after it occurred.

Risk that is relevant to them is **systematic risk,** which is the degree of sensitivity of the company's stock returns to marketwide returns. To the degree that the company's business and financial risk is company-specific, and therefore the overall business and financial risk are in excess of the systematic (market-related) risk, there is a divergence of risk perceptions. This is an example of an **agency problem,** in which the interests of the principals (stockholders) do not coincide with those of the agents (managers). Stockholders may elect to introduce monitoring, incentive, and control mechanisms such as stock option plans to realign managerial and stockholder interests.[2]

Lender, bank, and regulatory restrictions compose the third area of influence on short-term investment policy. Loan covenants may restrict the types or amounts of securities in which companies may invest. Bank compensating balances limit the amount of surplus funds that can be invested, lowering the overall rate of return on cash and securities because of the lower-than-market earnings credit rate that banks apply. Regulators restrict the types of investments that utilities, insurance companies, and banks can make.

Taking the historical liquidity assessment, company risk tolerance, and third-party restrictions into account, company personnel are able to devise an appropriate investment policy. The remainder of this chapter addresses portfolio decision making with the implicit understanding that the investment manager is making decisions consistent with that policy. Although not all organizations have policies and those that do may have ambiguous policies, investment decisions are generally made with greater ease and consistency when guided by such a policy. We conclude this section with an example of what can happen when a company has either not formulated a policy or is careless in implementing its policy (see the Focus on Practice box).

CASH AND SECURITIES ALLOCATION DECISION

The first two investment decisions that a company makes, sometimes unconsciously, are to allocate a portion of total assets to cash and securities and then to allocate funds between cash and securities. The former decision is closely related to the working capital investment decision, and the outcome is usually linked closely to the company's risk posture. The working capital investment decision refers to the proportion of total assets held in current asset accounts. The second decision, determining the proportion of the company's most liquid

---

[2]The classic reference on agency problems and their correctives is Amir Barnea, Robert A. Haugen, and Lemma Senbet, *Agency Problems and Financial Contracting* (Englewood Cliffs, NJ: Prentice-Hall, Inc., 1985).

assets to be held in cash versus short-term investment securities, is usually approached by viewing cash as a necessary evil. Cash is viewed as a stock of liquidity needed to meet upcoming disbursements. Aside from any earning credits applied to demand deposit balances by the company's bank, the cash balance can be seen as an inventoried, nonearning asset, necessary to offset unsynchronized cash receipts and disbursements. The objective of managing cash is to minimize total cost, which is the sum of transaction costs (for funds transfers and brokers' commissions) and the opportunity cost of foregone interest. Cost is minimized just like it would be in the EOQ model for inventories when using the most basic of cash management models. In fact, the early attempts at modeling decisions involving cash and securities were based closely on the EOQ inventory model.

Aggregate Investment in Cash and Securities

The manager may select from three generic strategies when deciding what quantity of total assets to hold in the form of cash and securities: a low-liquidity, moderate-liquidity, or high-liquidity strategy. The lower the liquidity, the riskier the strategy, and the higher the strategy's expected profitability.

The **low-liquidity strategy** entails driving the investment in cash and securities to a minimum. Therefore, cash and securities are a very small proportion of total assets. Assuming that the company does not subsequently overinvest in inventories and receivables, this approach should enhance profitability while also increasing business risk. Lesser amounts invested in cash and securities implies larger amounts invested in receivables, inventories, and higher-return fixed assets.[3] This comes at the expense of greater default and bankruptcy risk, however, because the company has a smaller liquidity cushion with which to weather unexpected and business cycle–related downturns in operating revenues. Obviously, other sources of liquidity—salability of inventories and receivables (or the ability to secure these), available credit lines, and other sources of untapped debt capacity—affect the risk (and therefore the advisability) of the low-liquidity strategy. Companies following the low-liquidity strategy justify it on the basis of untapped credit lines, which we included in the definition of the liquid reserve (see Chapter 2 section on lambda).

The **moderate-liquidity strategy** implies a somewhat greater investment in cash and securities, with correspondingly less risk. This strategy may be premised on a matching philosophy: the higher the level of near-term current liability obligations, the greater the proportion of assets the company should hold in cash and securities. The many defunct savings and loan associations are sober reminders of what can happen to organizations whose assets and liabilities are substantially mismatched.[4]

The **high-liquidity strategy** prescribes a higher proportion of assets to be held in cash and securities. Risk of default on securities and the risk of bankruptcy are reduced because of the greater liquidity cushion, but profitability is lower as well. Companies with significant business risk or financial risk might implement this strategy. Automakers and Microsoft justify their high-liquidity strategies because of unknown future capital investment opportunities, such as newly-developed technologies. Again, the company's posture toward risk and the availability of other potential sources of liquidity should be analyzed before adopting a particular cash and securities strategy.

---

[3]Fixed asset investments are generally property, plant, and equipment expenditures made in support of new products and market expansion, which presumably have positive net present value, thus enhancing shareholder value.

[4]In fact, the best way to gain an appreciation of the importance and mathematics behind maturity matching is to consult sources on bank asset and liability management regarding a measure of the degree of mismatch known as "duration gap." Bank management textbooks provide a formula and discussion of this topic.

The company's present financial situation may lead it to temporarily deviate from its chosen strategy. It may invest either more or less in cash and securities than the chosen strategy indicates. The current cash-flow forecast, in connection with the amount of borrowing, the amount of untapped short-term credit lines, and the financial position of the company, might be taken into consideration. The cash and securities balance might be augmented if the cash forecast shows net cash outflows or increased uncertainty in the cash forecast and a lack of alternate sources of liquidity. The treasurer also may take other precautions, such as engaging in hedging transactions if the cash-flow uncertainty stems from future movements in interest rates or commodity input prices. Finally, the decision maker should consider what fraction of the total will be held in cash and what fraction will be held in securities when determining the company's aggregate investment in cash and securities.

Empirical evidence on the use of the various strategies provides some clues about the effects of the operating and financial motives just mentioned.[5] Although based on the ratio of current assets to total assets, the ten-industry, 10-year study by Weinraub and Visscher (1998) indicates that industry has a very large affect on which strategy is adopted (which we note may link to business risk differences) and low-liquidity strategies are often offset by low-risk current liability postures (relatively more permanent financing). Kim, Mauer, and Sherman, using a large panel of US industrial firms spanning 1975 to 1994, find that more cash and short-term securities are held by firms facing higher costs of external financing, having more volatile earnings (and presumably, more business risk), and having lower returns on physical assets *relative* to returns available on financial securities. They also find companies building liquidity when anticipating profitable future investment opportunities. However, Opler, Pinkowitz, Stulz, and Williamson (1999) find that many firms seem to hold too much cash (moderate-liquidity or high-liquidity strategies, in our framework) and they do so for extended periods. Pinkowitz extended that study and found that, despite the agency problems associated with leaving discretionary cash with managers over long periods, the market for corporate control is unable to exert a monitoring effect on cash (and short-term security) holdings. This is so even for those firms that appear to hold "too much cash" based on several measures of excess cash holdings. This is also true, Pinkowitz finds, for firms with poor capital investment opportunities. Ironically, firms reduce their cash holdings shortly after states pass antitakeover legislation. It appears, then, that agency problems motivate some of the firms opting for moderate- or high-liquidity strategies, and that such strategies are not linked only to business risk or financial concerns. However, the same study does note a negative correlation between the ratio of cash flow to total assets and the ratio of cash and securities to total assets. Reflecting on the current liquidity index and lambda, in our Chapter 2 discussion of "how much liquidity is enough," this is exactly what we would expect for managers targeting some level of liquidity based on their business and financial risks.

Cash and Securities Mix

The proportional breakdown of cash and securities may be termed the **cash and securities mix decision.** This mix decision may or may not be the result of a well-thought-out strategy. When it is not consciously planned, it is simply the end result of the current

---

[5]Excellent background information on the theoretical issues involved in determining optimal and excess liquidity may be found in Tsetsekos (n.d.), Ang (1991), John (1993), and Haubrich and dos Santos (1997), cited in the chapter references.

operating, investing, and financing practices of the company. There is much confusion about this mix decision and the actual or potential use of cash management models in selecting the mix. For clarification, we distinguish between two interrelated decisions: setting the target mix, and managing the cash and securities balances as they deviate from the target mix.

The "target mix" simply refers to the average or ideal mix of cash and securities. The treasurer might set the target mix based on historical averages or on some type of a financial model or simulation.[6] It may be helpful to view this as an equilibrium value that the treasurer strives toward but may not attain—at least not for long. Cash flows are dynamic, pushing the cash position away from the target level as quickly as it has been attained.

When formal cash optimization models are used, they primarily address the management of the cash and securities balances over time. To some degree, this is uncontrollable, because the aggregate position changes in response to outside forces, as mentioned earlier. However, the cash manager wants to maintain control over how much is kept in cash because although cash is the most liquid asset, it incurs opportunity costs in the form of foregone investment interest income or increased interest expense, and there are transactions costs associated with security purchases, sales, and the related funds transfers. If there are no brokerage commissions or other transactions costs, and investments (paying competitive interest rates) that might be easily sold and quickly converted to cash can be found, the decision rule simplifies to cash balance minimization. Practically, this translates into holding the minimal balances in transactions accounts to pay 1 day's disbursements or meet the bank's compensating balance requirements. Money markets are characterized by imperfections such as transactions costs, however, and the manager must determine how large a cash balance to hold to minimize the costs of cash management.

Three cash management models, each with different assumptions, can be used to reallocate the cash and securities mix through time. Each views cash as an inventoried asset, with the transaction motive driving a company's allocation of resources to cash held in the form of transaction account balances.[7] Given the total disbursements for a period, each model can specify the number and timing of securities-cash transfers. The larger the per-transfer cost and the higher the interest rate being earned on securities, the fewer and more delayed the sales of securities. These models are profiled in the chapter appendix.

INVESTMENT DECISION-MAKING PROCESS

Once the total amount of cash and securities has been determined, along with a target amount for each, the investment manager is ready to engage in the most exciting aspect of portfolio management—selecting the investments to be included in the portfolio. Some companies shy away from doing this internally. Many times, the treasury staff is just too small, resulting in a shortage of time or lack of expertise. For smaller companies the company's short-term investments portfolio also may be too small to make internal management economically desirable.

---

[6]An illustrative simulation, based on historical analysis of actual cash flows, is presented in Daellenbach, cited in the end-of-chapter references.

[7]Although the models tend to focus on the transactions motive for holding cash, the addition of a safety stock buffer enables the models to also incorporate the precautionary and speculative motives for holding cash. The precautionary balance is kept to protect against unforeseen shortages in cash flow, perhaps related to unexpected sales declines. See the discussion of the EOQ model and safety stock considerations in Chapter 4.

Outside Management

The decision-making emphasis when portfolio management is delegated to an outside party centers on selection of the manager and performance evaluation. Specific portfolio-related decisions retained internally are how much to invest, allocation among outside parties when using more than one advisor, and perhaps specification of the maturities of securities selected by the outside portfolio manager.

SELECTING THE PORTFOLIO MANAGER.   The company using an outside investment manager must first decide what type of manager to use. Selections can be made from among brokerage houses, banks, and money market mutual funds (refer to Exhibit 15-1 for a schematic representation of this decision).[8] Brokerage houses specialize in investments, and they are really the department stores of financial services. They are the first to offer innovative products such as the master note commercial paper and online commercial paper programs offered by Salomon Smith Barney and Merrill Lynch. Brokers offer slightly higher yields than banks on comparable securities, and they have been more aggressive in introducing customer conveniences such as before- or after-hours order initiation and computerized order transmission and confirmation. An example of a brokerage product is Salomon Smith Barney's Bank Deposit account. Idle balances, awaiting reinvestment, automatically are swept into the account. Clients wishing to invest funds on an overnight basis can contact Salomon Smith Barney with the dollar figure, and Salomon Smith Barney automatically initiates a wire drawdown to transfer the funds from the client's bank account. The balances earn a competitive rate that is revised on a daily basis, and if clients desire, the funds are invested in a tax-free account. Sample rates are provided in Exhibit 15-2.

Banks may offer the corporate investor bank-issued certificates of deposit, money market deposit accounts, or the parent holding company's commercial paper as ways of funding the bank's operations. Security traders in the parent company also compete for corporate clients but trade for their own accounts. As is the case when the customer is buying from a brokerage dealer, there is a potential conflict-of-interest inherent in this latter arrangement. It is difficult to know if the interest rate quoted to the investor is a competitive market rate or if it is artificially low because the trader wants to pocket a slightly larger profit.[9]

Investing through the bank has three main advantages. First, as long as the bank's securities are invested in (other than commercial paper), the customer has deposit insurance coverage up to $100,000 of total balances. Second, the ultimate in convenience is afforded when the bank where the company invests is the same one it disburses from and concentrates to. Either an automated sweep account can be opened, or the bank can open a **custody account,** in which it holds securities, automatically reinvests interest and other investment-related cash receipts, transfers funds per corporate instructions, monitors issuers actions such as calls and refundings, and provides a monthly statement on all account transactions. This is provided by the larger banks for a fee that ranges from two to ten basis points, depending on the size of the account.

---

[8]We identified three major classes of outside advisors in Exhibit 15-1: brokers, banks, and others. Although the most popular other advisor is a money market mutual fund, other options such as insurance company-based advisors are available.

[9]Dealers sell securities from their inventories. They have purchased these at some rate, say, 5 percent, and they profit by reselling them at a lower rate (higher price). The difference in interest rates comprises dealers' total return on the transactions.

EXHIBIT 15-2
Salomon Smith Barney Bank Deposits Interest Rates (5/9/01)

Daily Interest Rate

MUTUAL FUND TYPE	7 Day Effective Average		
Taxable sweep fund	4.45%	Tax-free sweep fund	3.36%

SOURCE: Data provided is for May 9, 2001, from Salomon Smith Barney, Inc., by William R. Kiesel, First Vice President, Indianapolis, IN. Funds are invested overnight in a Citibank deposit account with FDIC insurance (up to statutory limit of coverage, presently $100,000), at a rate of 5 basis points above the prevailing average money market fund interest rates.

If immediate reinvestment saves even 1 day of interest on a 30-day investment yielding 6 percent, this service prevents an annual 20-basis-point reduction in yield. Finally, a third advantage to investing with the bank is that the securities portfolio can serve as collateral for a loan, providing greater liquidity for the corporation. At a minimum, a better rate might be possible for existing credit arrangements if the company can offer a portfolio of securities as collateral.[10]

We have alluded to the rapid growth of money market mutual funds in earlier chapters, and for many smaller or medium-sized companies, this seems to be the way to go. The economies of scale and benefits of specialization that accrue to these mutual funds have enabled them to offer extremely competitive yields. Additionally, the company can write checks for amounts of $500 or more from the fund account, allowing the fund to be used partly for disbursing. Perhaps the major attraction is the ability of the funds to diversify the company's monies by pooling it with other investors' funds and then investing it in many different securities from various issuers. The large dollar amounts of such investments provide an additional bonus to fund investors: higher yields than they would be able to get on their own. The professional management of the money funds allows the corporate cash manager to concentrate on other issues. In response to the market share gains of the money funds, brokerage houses and banks are beginning to offer their own money funds—which, for the banks, is a tacit admission of the eroding attractiveness of money market deposit accounts.

EVALUATING PORTFOLIO PERFORMANCE. A 2000 Liquidity Management survey by Treasury Strategies finds that only about one-third of companies are measuring their short-term investment performance against a benchmark. There are four main benchmarks that can be used to evaluate portfolio performance: US Treasury instruments, other money market instruments, money market mutual funds[11] (particularly when evaluating a bank or brokerage), and a synthetic composite. Because of yield curve relationships, the evaluator must be careful to match the maturities of the benchmark as closely as possible to the average maturity of the company's portfolio. Money market mutual funds publish their average maturities along with their 7-day and 30-day yields. The synthetic composite is an artificial security that is devised to mirror the portfolio's average

---

[10]An excellent discussion of the interface of short-term investing with banking considerations is found in Nuttall on which much of this section is based. See end-of-chapter references for complete citation.

[11]William Donoghue's *Money Fund Report* summarizes the performance of many money market funds, with some information about each. *Pension & Investment Age* now reports on an index of short-term investment yields, the Yanni-Bilkey Cash Universe. Finally, several organizations will do more focused or even customized indices, the Butcher Consulting Group being the main vendor of the latter. See "Cash Benchmark Evolving Slowly," *Pension & Investment Age* (October 3, 1988): 3.

coupon interest rate, maturity, and risk rating.[12] This single composite then serves as a benchmark for an entire portfolio. The composite could be maturity of 63 days, yield of 6.75 percent, and a rating equivalent of A-1/P-1 commercial paper, which represents the safest issuers. This composite cannot only be used to calculate the interest rate risk of the company's portfolio, but its yield can be compared with Treasury bills to see how much of a risk premium should be received on that portfolio. Every time the company's portfolio changes, the evaluator must alter the synthetic composite accordingly. Proactively, the synthetic composite can be used as a target that the manager tries to match with respect to portfolio interest rate, maturity, and risk rating.

Internal Portfolio Management

If the company manages the portfolio itself, many more decisions must be made. As investable funds become available, the investment manager must decide from among options available for each of the following:

- *Instruments*—foreign or domestic, and what category, such as money market securities (and within that category, what type: Treasury bills, commercial paper, etc.), preferred stock, common stock, or bonds (refer to Chapter 14).
- *Issuers*—Treasury, federal agency, municipality, corporate (including sectors within any of these that would be unacceptable in any situation).
- *Denominations*—generally larger denominations (the face value dollar amounts) are chosen when feasible because of their higher yields and the fact that some of these are negotiable.
- *Maturities*—will the time when the face value is repaid by the issuer be matched to the investment horizon, and if not, how will the additional risk be weighed?
- *Yields*—although safety and liquidity often come before yield[13] on short-term investments, the manager must determine when, if ever, the company will be more aggressive and reach for yield.
- *Risks*—the probability of issuer default and bankruptcy, of a capital loss resulting from higher interest rates, and other aspects of overall investment risk must be traded off.

Some of these decisions must be tailor-made to the particulars of an individual situation, and although some of these decision realms are most likely addressed in the company's investment policy, the policy may be purposefully vague to retain latitude for the manager. Blanket statements such as "invest in the largest denomination possible" prevent the manager from selectively making exceptions to take advantage of market situations, such as a very attractive yield on a Eurodollar certificate of deposit sold by Chase Bank in the London market.

Internal portfolio management does not eliminate the need for performance monitoring. The company again might measure itself against an external passive index, a benchmark security, a managed portfolio, or the performance of a peer manager at a

---

[12]The synthetic composite idea was formulated by Lee Epstein in his "Basis Points" column, *Corporate Cashflow* (May 1989): 56–57. For more on all four of the evaluation benchmarks, see the excellent presentation by Richard Bort in *Corporate Cash Management Handbook*, 1991 Cumulative Supplement, Chapter 21.

[13]This ranking has been documented in two surveys: (1) a survey of 46 companies conducted by the National Association of Accountants ("Performance Measurement of Short-Term Investments," *Management Accounting* [August 1983]: 20) and (2) a survey of the Fortune 500 by Keith V. Smith and Brian Belt ("Working Capital Management in Practice: An Update," Krannert Graduate School of Management Working Paper 951, March 1989, Exhibit 19).

similar company (if available). Management accounting principles suggest that the investment manager's area within the company be treated as an "investment center," meaning that he or she must earn an adequate return given the resources allocated to that area.[14] Otherwise, the activity should be outsourced. One additional complication that may be encountered when evaluating internal versus external portfolio performance is the difficulty calculating realized portfolio yield for a period. Although the calculation is straightforward for an individual security with a lump-sum end-of-period payout, it is more complex when considering an account in which monies were added (as with intermediate interest payments) or withdrawn from time to time. The calculation is likewise more complicated when there is a succession of shorter periods making up the period of comparison, which we demonstrate later in the chapter in our discussion of the structure of interest rates. Furthermore, transaction costs and taxes affect the realized yield earned on investments.[15] The following example illustrates portfolio return calculations for the simple case in which the entire amounts invested in each security are left invested throughout the period, and there are no transaction costs or taxes.

Generally, the portfolio rate of return is the weighted average of the individual security returns. Assume that the manager bought (or already held) each of the securities at the beginning of the period. We simply multiply the dollar amounts invested in each by the security return, add the products together, and divide by the total amount invested in the portfolio:

SECURITY	DOLLAR AMOUNT INVESTED	RATE OF RETURN	DOLLAR RETURN
Treasury bill	$100,000	6.05%	$6,050
Commercial paper	$250,000	6.75%	$16,875
Certificates of deposit	$100,000	6.65%	$6,650
TOTAL	$450,000		$29,575

The portfolio return is determined by dividing the total dollar return by the aggregate investment. In this case, the return is 6.57 percent ($29,575/$450,000).

If we already know the ending dollar figure for the portfolio, the process is much simpler. We simply solve for the interest rate that equates the ending portfolio balance with the beginning balance. The $450,000 invested in our example grew to $479,575. Thus $479,575 = $450,000 $(1 + i)^t$, in which t represents the time during which the money was invested. If $t = 1$ year, $i = (\$479,575/\$450,000) - 1 = 6.57$ percent, just as we saw above.

In reality, money is alternately withdrawn and added to the investments account throughout the period. Calculating the portfolio return is more complex in this case. We develop the appropriate formula in the context of the following example.

---

[14]This is not as easy as it might seem. For one thing, a decision must be made about whether resources should be calculated on a direct cost or fully allocated cost basis. The investment area may share resources with other areas in the company, meaning that subcontracting investment services may not reduce costs as much as it would appear. The existence of shared costs suggests the company is enjoying *economies of scope,* which are difficult to estimate. For help with cost allocations, see Letricia Gayle Rayburn, *Principles of Cost Accounting,* 5th ed. (Homewood, IL: Richard D. Irwin, Inc., 1992); investment centers are dealt with in detail in Robert N Anthony, John Dearden, and Vijay Govindarajan, *Management Control Systems,* 7th ed. (Homewood, IL: Richard D. Irwin, 1992).

[15]It is not enough to simply adjust pretax returns by multiplying them by (1 − marginal tax rate). Unlike individuals, corporations are not permitted to use capital losses to offset ordinary income. Instead, they must net capital losses against capital gains. Consequently, if a corporation has a tax loss carryforward, it would prefer to receive investment income in the form of capital gains. Treasury bill income is not taxable in most states and localities. Transaction costs, if explicit, are more easily handled. The cost would be subtracted from the investment income; if it is charged at the beginning of the investment period, it should also be added to the amount invested.

At the beginning of a year, $500,000 is invested. The company pulls out $45,000 at the end of the first quarter, $55,000 at the end of the second quarter, and $35,000 at the end of the fourth quarter. If the company invested an additional $100,000 at the end of the third quarter and has $535,000 still invested at the end of the year, what rate of return did the portfolio earn? Assume that the company earned $20,000 of interest during the first quarter, $15,000 in the second quarter, $20,000 in the third quarter, and $15,000 in the fourth quarter.

SOLUTION.   We need an equation that converts intrayear rates of return to their annual equivalent rate. Equation 15-1 indicates that to do so, we must add 1 to the period rate of return, then take the product of all periods' returns. Finally, 1 is subtracted from the result to get the decimal equivalent of the annualized rate of return:

$$K = \prod_{t=1}^{N} (1+i_t) - 1 \qquad \text{(15-1)}$$

In which: K = annual effective rate of return

$\quad$ t = time period

$\quad$ N = total number of time periods

$\quad$ i_t = interest rate earned during a period

The number of time periods for which i_t must be calculated depends on the frequency with which the manager either invests new money or withdraws new money from the investment account. In our example, this is quarterly, but managers investing varying amounts overnight must do this each day. The formula says to calculate the rate of return for each period, then add 1 to each period return. After this has been done for each period, the product of all $(1 + i)$'s is calculated. Finally, 1 is subtracted from this product to arrive at the decimal equivalent of the annualized return. Note in the table that we used a shortcut (ending value/beginning value) to get $(1 + i)$. The end-of-year withdrawal shown at the bottom of the table is irrelevant for computing the year's return. For the quarterly activity in our example, the annualized return is 15.25 percent:

(1) Quarter	(2) Beginning of Period Investment/(Withdrawal)	(3) Beginning Value	(4) Interest	(5) End of Period Value [(3)+(4)]	(6) 1 + i_t [(5)/(3)]
1	$500,000	$500,000	$20,000	$520,000	1.0400
2	($ 45,000)	$475,000	$15,000	$490,000	1.0316
3	($ 55,000)	$435,000	$20,000	$455,000	1.0460
4	$100,000	$555,000	$15,000	$570,000	1.0270
5	($ 35,000)				

Annual Rate of Return: 0.1525 or 15.25%

We have now worked through the development of the short-term investment policy and how companies can make the aggregate cash and securities allocation. We have briefly developed the nature of the decision about whether to manage the portfolio internally or externally, along with several of the implications of that decision. We now move into a presentation of the principles involved in assembling a portfolio, whether done by an outside advisor or the company's investment manager.

ASSEMBLING THE PORTFOLIO

Three principles govern the portfolio selection process. First, the basic objective is to balance risk and return within the parameters set by the company's investment policy.

Second, unlike stock or bond portfolio management, safety predominates in the short-term portfolio. The securities portfolio represents a vital part of the company's liquidity, so security defaults or capital losses jeopardize the holder's financial health. Third, the investment manager must learn how to make security selection and disposition (abandonment) decisions efficiently. A bewildering array of choices confronts the manager, who must learn to economize on the information processing involved. These three principles can be implemented if the manager understands the underlying factors driving risks and returns, how the individual risk factors fit together in the portfolio context, and several approaches to trading off risk with expected returns.

General Risk-Return Factors

In the money markets, there is a very high degree of correlation between the returns on various instruments. Generally, as the federal funds rate moves up or down, the Treasury bill rate, commercial paper rate, and certificate of deposit rate moves correspondingly (as noted in the previous chapter). Technical factors such as an imbalance of supply and demand, especially in the federal funds market, can cause temporary deviations from the overall pattern. Our present focus, however, is on what common factors cause the rates on all of these instruments to change. Most movements in securities' interest rates can be linked to three common factors: changes in gross national product (GNP), an industry-specific factor, and an underlying interest rate trend factor (which subsumes all other influences on the supply or demand for near-maturity loanable funds). Ideally, the investment manager obtains or conducts forecasts of each of these factors.

GNP.   GNP movements give insight into the present and future demand for credit. Real interest rates are affected by the prospects for making positive net present value investments, which in turn affect GNP and are reflective of GNP trends. Money is said to be "tight" when GNP is increasing, especially as inflation rates begin an upsurge and the Federal Reserve (Fed) curtails money supply growth.

INDUSTRY-SPECIFIC EVENTS.   The industry a company is in may have even more influence on that company's fortunes than overall GNP. Not only does industry membership affect a company's stock returns, it also has an effect on its business risk and therefore the default probability of its borrowings. This translates into changes in the interest rate that investors require for that issuer.

INTEREST RATE TRENDS.   Interest rate trends are best divided into shifts in the yield curve and changes in the slope of an existing yield curve. By looking at a Treasury yield curve, we can eliminate default risk. In this way, we will not confuse changes in default risk with overall interest rate trends.

Any catalyst that changes all interest rates, both short-term and long-term, can be analyzed to arrive at a forecast for yield curve shifts. Either an increased risk aversion on the part of investors or an increase in inflation expectations will shift the entire curve. Although risk aversion is unobservable, there are various surveys of economists and market participants that give insight into inflation expectations. Many of the same techniques used for cash forecasting (in Appendix 12B) can be used to forecast overall interest rate trends.

Shifts in the yield curve relate primarily to Fed policy actions. The Fed's open market operations, in which it buys or sells Treasury bills to achieve reserve targets, greatly influence short-term rates. Adherents to the market segmentation theory also appraise relative supply and demand in each maturity spectrum to arrive at a yield curve forecast. Political or economic instability, whether in the United States or another country, many times leads to a massive inflow of funds into the Treasury bill market, pushing prices up and yields down. Finally, market participants might anticipate an upsurge in inflation that begins at some point in the future, affecting medium-term and long-term securities much more than short-term securities.

Risk Factors Revisited

In the previous chapter, we developed several types of individual security risk: default risk, interest rate risk, reinvestment rate risk, liquidity risk, and event risk. In this section, we further our analysis by noting the interrelationships between two or more of these risk elements. We also indicate why the risk estimates themselves are subject to uncertainty and how to bring that uncertainty into the analysis. Our goal throughout is to enable the investment manager to determine whether the company will be adequately compensated for risk for any given security alternative and what the appropriate level of risk is for the company's short-term portfolio. Although exact answers to these questions sometimes elude the manager, a fundamentally sound approach can at least narrow the menu of choices.

INTERRELATIONSHIPS AMONG RISK TYPES.   We can analyze the important security risks jointly by conceptualizing that portfolio risk is a function of several risk factors, as shown in the following risk model:

$$\text{Portfolio risk} = f(\text{default risk, liquidity risk, interest rate risk,} \qquad \text{(15-2)}$$
$$\text{reinvestment rate risk, event risk)}$$

Portfolio risk, evaluated for a given investment horizon, is seen to be a function of default risk, liquidity risk, interest rate risk, reinvestment rate risk, and event risk. Of these risk determinants, default risk stands out as the most important single factor. Most analyses of portfolio risk, however, do not consider the interactions of these risk factors with one another or with outside variables. No operational approach exists at present to quantify and trade off the interrelationships among these risk factors. Managerial judgment regarding relative importance of each risk as it occurs in the portfolio must be applied instead.

A good example of risk interaction is the decision to match the maturity of the investment to the investment horizon. This strategy greatly reduces interest rate risk and liquidity risk, but at the expense of greater reinvestment rate risk. To see this, recognize that by focusing only on the investment horizon, the decision process is limited to a single period. However, the strategy that is optimal in the long run should be pursued, and the long run is simply a series of short runs. A technical way of saying this is that single-period optimization may result in multiperiod suboptimization. Only if we had perfect certainty about future cash flow needs and were forced into investing in securities equal to a given horizon could we overlook the reinvestment rate implications of our investment strategy—and then only if we invested solely in Treasury bills or other discount securities.

Risk factors also are linked to other company attributes. Liquidity, interest rate, and reinvestment rate risks are inextricably tied to the accuracy of the company's cash flow forecast. If the manager is absolutely certain that the period-beginning excess cash will not be needed until the end of the horizon, then liquidity and interest rate risk take on much less importance, because the vulnerability of the company to premature sale of securities is eliminated. The accuracy of the cash flow forecast, in turn, is a function of the amount expended on developing the forecast and the variability (e.g., standard deviation) of those flows. Ideally, all variables affecting the individual risk factors, as well as their interactions, are incorporated into the portfolio risk assessment.

UNCERTAINTY OF RISK ESTIMATES.   The uncertainty of risk estimates refers to the fact that our risk estimates are subject to error. For example, we do not know exactly how much variability characterizes the return distribution at present. Does the distribution of certificate of deposit rates still have a standard deviation of 4 percent, if that is our most recent estimate? Our estimate may be based on a historical distribution of certificate of deposit returns, but we realize that changes in bank regulation or in the certificate of deposit market may invalidate this sample estimate. Each risk component is likewise estimated subject to error. An estimate of interest rate risk depends on our forecast for the probabilities of rates increasing, staying the same, or decreasing. Our probabilities, and thus the entire probability distribution, again are just estimates, subject to error. Similar difficulties attend default, liquidity, and reinvestment rate estimates. Just as crucial, the importance of liquidity risk or interest rate risk is tied to the future possibility of premature liquidation, signaling the need to bring the cash forecast uncertainty into the portfolio selection process.

There are several ways to incorporate uncertainty into portfolio risk-return evaluations. First, sensitivity analysis can be used. Recall that sensitivity analysis involves varying key inputs, one at a time, and observing the effect on the decision criterion. This can be done with arbitrary ranges of values, such as −15 percent to +15 percent in 5-percent increments, or in conjunction with realistic scenarios (e.g., recession, stable economy, moderately growing economy) guiding the choice of what input values to use. Either way, a judgment call is required of the portfolio manager regarding the cutoff point in the decision criterion that results in one alternative being selected over another.

A second, and preferred, approach to incorporating uncertainty is simulation. Simulation begins with calculation of the expected value and standard deviation of the input variables, then uses iterative draws from each variable's probability distribution to draw up a probability distribution for the decision criterion. Many theoretical distributions, including the normal distribution, can be modeled using computer simulation software such as @RISK or Crystal Ball, add-in software packages for Microsoft Excel. Even before spreadsheet-based packages became available, roughly half of all large companies reported using simulation for uncertainty modeling in financial decisions. Microcomputer-based software makes simulation accessible to even the smallest organization.

PORTFOLIO RISK AND THE RISK-RETURN TRADEOFF.   Modern portfolio theory informs us that when we invest in more than one security, the portfolio's risk is generally lower than the average of the individual securities' risks. Although a detailed explanation is beyond our scope, we point out the lower the correlation between two securities' returns through time, the greater the reduction in risk that is achieved by combining them in a portfolio.[16] Unfortunately, the interest rates of most domestic money market securities are so closely

---

[16]This is especially true if foreign money market securities are included in the portfolio. Salomon Brothers data indicate that the monthly return correlation (in terms of U.S. dollars) between the United States and non-U.S. money markets for the period from January 1985 to June 1990 was only 0.07. Non-U.S. money markets underperformed the U.S. market for the period 1978–1985 but returned 17.9 percent per year from 1985 to mid-1990, versus a U.S. money market return of 7.9 percent per year. The standard deviation for the non-U.S. markets' monthly returns was about twice that of the U.S. market: 1.4 percent versus 0.7 percent. Investing internationally requires a careful analysis of hedging the currency risk, however. See Duen-Li Kao, "Global Short-Term Investments and Currency Hedging Strategies," *Journal of Cash Management* (September/October 1990): 55–57. Also see Ahmad and Sarver, cited in chapter references, who document that international money markets are less interdependent than equity markets, and changes in the U.S. market are less dominant in affecting other markets.

associated that this type of a risk reduction is limited. Two determinants of individual security risk, default risk and event risk, are reducible because of the diversification effects of having multiple securities in a portfolio. Put simply, the more securities one has in the portfolio, the less effect an individual security default will have on overall performance. With equal dollar amounts invested in 100 securities, even if the investor loses his or her entire investment in a given security, 99 percent of the capital is still intact.

ASSESSING THE RISK-RETURN TRADEOFF.   One of the most underexplored areas in treasury management is how to determine when a security or portfolio offers an acceptable return for its risk characteristics. In the absence of an established theoretical framework, for money market securities we offer a three-step approach:

1. Account for the contextual variables affecting the present investment decision.
2. Evaluate the individual security risks for a set of potential investments, sifting out only those that appear ideal (dominant) on an individual basis.
3. Redo the risk analysis while additionally considering the interactions of the securities' risk elements and portfolio effects.

Exhibit 15-3 depicts the three decisions in a flowchart format.

Contextual parameters include the current cash-flow forecast, existing short-term borrowings and investments, the investment horizon, and the investment policy. There are some obvious overlaps here: The cash-flow forecast helps define the investment horizon, for example. Short-term borrowings are relevant because they indicate one of the components of financial risk and because untapped short-term debt capacity can be drawn on (instead of prematurely liquidating securities) if the cash forecast turns out to be overoptimistic. We do not want to overexpose the company to a single type or issuer of securities, implying the need to inspect present security holdings. The horizon also is important. If the horizon is a day or several days, the company will probably want to minimize interest rate and liquidity risk by relying on overnight investments such as commercial paper, repurchase agreements, or sweep accounts (which usually direct investment into either commercial paper or repurchase agreements). Finally, the investment policy may specify risk-oriented limits on instruments, guarantors, issuers, and currencies. It also may specify the management perception of what is appropriate risk taking, which ideally should reflect shareholder preferences.

EXHIBIT 15-3
Risk-Return Evaluation for Short-Term Investments

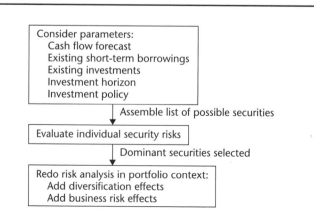

Individual security risk-return tradeoffs can be evaluated statistically or graphically. To assess the variability of a security's returns, vis-à-vis the return itself, the analyst can compute the coefficient of variation. The **coefficient of variation** is the standard deviation of a return distribution divided by the expected return.

Another approach is to plot the risk-return relationships for a manageable list of potential securities on the same graph and to pick those with the best return for a given risk. Those securities that provide a higher expected return for a given amount of risk are said to be dominant.

If the analyst wishes to focus primarily on default risk, a listing of securities' returns by rating class is a workable approach. To get a broader picture of risk, which encompasses default as well as liquidity risks, the analyst can compare the difference between a security's return and the return on a Treasury bill of the same maturity. The difference, expressed as a percentage, is one type of **yield spread.** As we saw in the previous chapter, however, this approach also has some limitations. Probably the best approach for jointly assessing risk and return is to conduct a simulation or sensitivity analysis. We present a sensitivity analysis a bit later when discussing riding the yield curve.

Once the individual security evaluations are complete, the analyst should have a listing of dominant securities based on the criteria the company applies to candidate investments. At this point, the risk analysis is redone, but from a portfolio vantage point. Diversification effects and risk interactions, discussed earlier, are of primary interest. Diversification objectives may address any or all of the following categories:

- instruments
- issuers, both within and across different instruments
- industries
- markets (geographic and currencies)

In addition, the analyst considers management's target values for the size and composition of cash accounts and securities purchases. There may also be ad hoc standards for the company's portfolio, such as "no more than 15 percent of short-term investments may be held in securities rated below A-1/P-1" (the highest rating class for short-term securities, signifying the least default risk). Although it is futile to search for the best possible set of securities, because of the large number that exists from which to choose, selecting from a carefully limited field can bring about near-optimal results. The company's willingness to take risks, the size of its portfolio, and the resources it can dedicate to portfolio management direct the company's decision on whether it will use an active or passive portfolio management strategy.

A very recent development, a comprehensive treasury department risk report card, is being used by companies such as the Federal Home Loan Mortgage Corporation (Freddie Mac) (Smith and Miles, 1997). This approach, although somewhat subjective, gives a global and integrated picture of an organization's financial risks.

Short-Term Investment Strategies

There are many possible investment strategies that can be used. Generically, we divide them into passive strategies and active strategies. A **passive investment strategy** involves a minimal amount of oversight and very few transactions once the portfolio has been selected.

An **active investment strategy** involves more trading and active monitoring of the portfolio and may be motivated by a philosophy that the investor can "beat the market." In the money markets, this generally means earning higher-than-normal yield spreads and/or capital gains as a result of accurate anticipation of interest rate movements.

EXHIBIT 15-4

Historical Average Yield Spreads Instrument versus Treasury Bills (Basis Points)

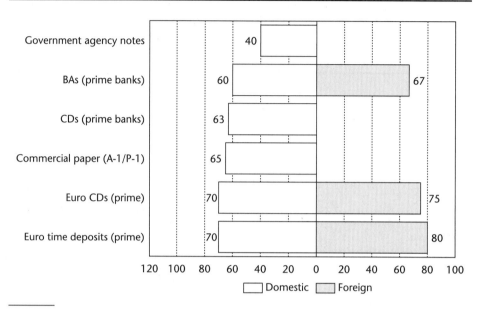

SOURCE: Reprinted from Alan Seidner. *Corporate Investments Manual.* New York: Warren, Gorham & Lamont, 1990. Research Institute of America. Used with permission.

PASSIVE STRATEGIES.   A popular passive strategy is the **buy-and-hold strategy.** Quite often, this is part of a "maturity matching" approach to investing that prescribes investing in a security that will mature at the end of the investment horizon. The horizon is based on how long the company can tie up the investable funds. This eliminates interest rate risk if the company does hold the security to maturity as planned, because it will receive the face value of the security at that time. The buy-and-hold strategy may be implemented by investing part or all of the portfolio in an index fund, which is a managed portfolio assembled to mirror a particular money market composite. The composite serves as an index because it is calculated by averaging the yields of a broadly based basket of securities. A **modified buy-and-hold strategy** might be used when the investor wishes to take advantage of favorable interest rate movements, should they occur. If rates come down and the portfolio report shows a paper capital gain, the investor may sell or swap for another security to capture the gain.

ACTIVE STRATEGIES.   There are numerous active strategies. One strategy is to try to spot inefficiencies in the way securities are priced at present and to buy those that are underpriced (have higher yields than warranted by their level of risk). These are then held to maturity or sold at a capital gain when the market recognizes the mispricing and corrects it by bidding up the price. One way of implementing this strategy is to study yield spreads.

Historical yield spread analysis suggests other profitable trading strategies. For temporarily underpriced securities, the yield offered will be higher than warranted by the underlying risks. Market overreactions to events such as credit rating changes (part of the event risk phenomenon) may open up some attractive yield opportunities. The historical yield spreads, computed as the difference between a given security and short-term Treasury bills on the top-quality securities for each instrument, have been determined by consultant Alan Seidner (Exhibit 15-4). The analyst compares the current yield spread for the instrument type (or given rating class) or for an individual security within that type to see if abnormally large spreads exist.[17] An aggressive investor might research the largest spreads available, seeking to determine why they exist, and if there is no exceptional default, liquidity, or event risk associated to account for the spread, a purchase would be made.

A second, and also a very popular, active strategy is **riding the yield curve.** This involves buying securities with maturities longer than the investment horizon, fully intending to liquidate the position early. If the yield curve is stable, meaning it neither shifts nor changes slope during the holding period, the investor can generally outperform a maturity matching strategy. This occurs because the normal yield curve is upward-sloping, giving higher interest rates for longer-maturity instruments. Domian, Maness, and Reichenstein (1998) document the very attractive return-risk tradeoff available to treasurers willing to stretch 3-month Treasury bill investments out to 6 months, 1 month, or 1 year.

FINANCIAL DILEMMA REVISITED

Returning to our chapter-opening financial dilemma, assume that an investor with a 3-month horizon has available a 3-month Treasury bill yielding 5 percent, a 9-month bill yielding 5.6 percent, and a 1-year bill yielding 6 percent. Not only will the investor gain additional interest for buying the 1-year bill, but he or she also will earn a capital gain as the 1-year bill increases in price until it yields 5.6 percent at the end of the 3-month horizon (the current maturity is then 9 months). To evaluate this strategy, an investor might use sensitivity analysis. Exhibit 15-5 profiles the advantage to the 1-year bill in terms of its yield differential over the 3-month bill. Each entry in the table represents the total return for the 1-year bill (interest +/− capital gain or loss) less the total return for the 3-month bill (interest +/− capital gain or loss). This is calculated while varying two important assumptions: what happens to interest rates over the holding period (each row represents a possible change, with the middle row showing the baseline no-change forecast) and the holding period (starting with liquidation after 1 week, implying 12 weeks left in the period, etc.).[18] Note that the advantage to the 1-year bill increases with general interest rate reductions (the first four rows in the table) and with longer holding periods (as we move rightward in the table). This makes sense because the 1-year bill has a larger interest rate risk than the 3-month bill, implying capital gains when rates fall and capital losses when rates rise.

We can see the break-even situation, in which there is no advantage to riding the yield curve, for any combination of interest rate changes and liquidation dates. Because of the relatively large difference in maturities (1 year versus 3 months) in Exhibit 15-5, an investment manager is better off investing in the 3-month bill for even a 5-basis-point increase in rates (the row corresponding to 0.005), but better off in the 1-year bill if rates are stable or decrease.

---

[17]Yield spread analysis is covered in Irving and Raney, Zietlow, and Khaksari. Full citations appear in end-of-chapter references.

[18]The analysis is performed using a financial spreadsheet (e.g., 2-way Table in Microsoft Excel). The advantage to the longer-term investment is calculated as the difference in yield over the holding period, plus (minus) the capital gain (loss) difference when selling either or both of the securities before their maturity dates.

EXHIBIT 15-5
Sensitivity Analysis: Riding the Yield Curve

Spreadsheet table for evaluating riding the yield curve; relative advantage (in terms of effective yield) to a 1-year Treasury bill. The middle row in the table below is a "no change" interest rate scenario.

INPUTS:

3-Month Rate, Annualized	0.05	Most Likely Change in Rates	0
1-Year Rate	0.06	Horizon (weeks)	13
		Transaction Cost	$2,000

Change in Short-Term Interest Rates	*Number of Weeks Left Within Horizon When Cash Flow Causes Premature Liquidation*						
	12	*10*	*8*	*6*	*4*	*2*	*0*
−0.020000	0.015192	0.015577	0.015962	0.016346	0.016731	0.017115	0.017500
−0.015000	0.011442	0.011827	0.012212	0.012596	0.012981	0.013365	0.013750
−0.010000	0.007692	0.008077	0.008462	0.008846	0.009231	0.009615	0.010000
−0.005000	0.003942	0.004327	0.004712	0.005096	0.005481	0.005865	0.006250
0.000000	0.000192	0.000577	0.000962	0.001346	0.001731	0.002115	0.002500
0.005000	−0.003558	−0.003173	−0.002788	−0.002404	−0.002019	−0.001635	−0.001250
0.010000	−0.007308	−0.006923	−0.006538	−0.006154	−0.005769	−0.005385	−0.005000
0.015000	−0.011058	−0.010673	−0.010288	−0.009904	−0.009519	−0.009135	−0.008750
0.020000	−0.014808	−0.014423	−0.014038	−0.013654	−0.013269	−0.012885	−0.012500

In conjunction with the uncertainty surrounding the cash flow forecast and the short-term borrowing situation, the investment manager can decide whether the risk merits selecting the longer maturity. Empirical evidence about the relative advantage of riding the yield curve is mixed, indicating an advantage to the strategy for periods of generally declining rates, and reduced portfolio performance when the yield curve flattens out or shifts upward.[19] This confirms the finding of our sensitivity analysis in Exhibit 15-5.

Even more explicit in its reliance on interest rate forecasts is an active **trading strategy** based on augmenting yields with capital gains. When the analyst forecasts a change in interest rates, trading strategies can be devised to enhance investment profits. This approach is very risky and is little used for short-term portfolios, as pointed out earlier in our portrayal of ADM.

An active strategy that became popular in the 1980s is the **dividend capture strategy.** Because intercorporate dividends have been largely excludable for income tax purposes (presently, there is a 70-percent exclusion), corporate investors decided to buy a stock with a high dividend yield,[20] hold until just after the record date for payment, and then sell the stock. This strategy is sometimes termed a **dividend roll.** For a company in the 34-percent tax bracket, the tax rate on dividends is reduced to 10.5 percent [34%(1 − 0.70)]. Thus the after-tax yield is 89.5 percent of the pretax yield, whereas on taxable commercial paper or certificates of deposit, it would only be 66 percent of the pretax yield. By law, the company must hold the stock for at least 46 days to qualify for the 70 percent exclusion. The obvious risk of the strategy is the possibility of the stock price declining during the holding period, which might be hedged by buying a put or

---

[19]See Ed A. Dyl and Michael D. Joehnk, "Riding the Yield Curve: Does It Work?" *Journal of Portfolio Management* (Spring 1981): 13–17.

[20]Dividend yield is the year's cash dividend divided by the current stock price.

selling a covered call.[21] The Japanese insurance industry is one of the main investor groups pursuing this strategy because of its unique regulatory and tax situation. The dividend capture strategy has become less popular for US companies because of the availability of the auction rate preferred stock mentioned in Chapter 14.

Active strategy managers also use **swap strategies,** particularly when a position has already been taken but a new, better opportunity arises. There are numerous types of swaps, but we limit our discussion to two popular types: a **maturity extension swap** and a **yield spread swap.** In each swap arrangement, the present holding is sold and replaced with another security that will increase the yield or dollar return while minimally affecting credit risk. The maturity extension swap is executed when the manager wishes to ride the yield curve, but instead of investing a recent cash inflow, he or she must liquidate another security to make the investment. Yield spread swaps are similar, except the motivation is to take advantage of a mispriced security based on historical spread analysis.

STRATEGY IMPLEMENTATION.   Whether a company uses a passive or active strategy, it may implement the strategy itself or rely on an outside advisor or money market mutual fund to carry the strategy out. The company might evaluate these alternatives by conducting a "make versus buy" analysis. The relative costs are more easily estimable than the potential gains of going outside.

SURVEY EVIDENCE ON STRATEGIES.   Evidence regarding short-term investment practices represents most companies as applying many of the principles we have developed in this chapter. One of the most revealing summaries of portfolio management, although somewhat dated, is a *Fortune 1000* survey conducted in the mid-1980s by Frankle and Collins.[22] Although they asked the highest-ranking financial officers about their approach to cash management strategy, not specifically their investment strategy, the concepts should overlap greatly. Aggressive cash managers are more likely to use active strategies, and passive managers probably use the buy-and-hold approach more often. Respondents labeled themselves as aggressive (47 percent), moderate (34 percent), conservative (17 percent), and passive (2 percent). As might be expected, the division of cash and securities was weighted toward investments for the aggressive (74 percent of aggressive managers had 75 percent or more of the excess cash invested, on average) and lowest for the passive (50 percent invested). Rate of return was deemed to be the most important attribute of potential investments to the aggressive strategist, whereas moderate and conservative strategists ranked default risk the highest (the passive strategists did not rank any attribute as very important, possibly because they had less funds invested). Aggressive strategists used the "riding the yield curve" strategy much more often (30 percent usage rate) than moderate (24 percent) or conservative (9 percent) strategists. In the era studied, Eurodollar certificates of deposit and time deposits ranked as the favorite instrument, followed by repurchase agreements (moderate and conservative managers) or commercial paper (aggressive managers).

In the *Fortune 500* survey by Smith and Belt,[23] additional evidence on two of these issues is provided. First, the determination of how much to transfer between cash and

---

[21]For the dynamics and advantages to these risk-reduction strategies, see Krause. An excellent risk-return model for evaluating hedged and unhedged capture strategies is contained in Duen-Li Kao and Mark A. Zurack. Kling and Atchison present a good review of previous simulations and original results of their simulation of the dividend roll strategy. See end-of-chapter references for full citations.

[22]See end-of-chapter references for full citation.

[23]See end-of-chapter references for full citation.

securities was only made with cost balancing models by 10 percent of the respondents (these models are discussed in the chapter appendix); 42 percent used subjective judgment, and 23 percent used established guidelines (the remainder specified "other" as their approach). Second, the buy-and-hold portfolio management strategy was the most popular strategy used by the *Fortune 500* companies.

CRITIQUE OF STRATEGIES.   Active portfolio management strategies, much more than passive strategies, rely on the ability of the investment manager to forecast interest rates. The extensive literature on money market pricing efficiency and interest rate forecasting is conclusive in its findings: Pricing is rapid and mainly unbiased, and most forecasters cannot forecast more accurately than either a naive "no change from last period" forecast or a forecast based on the futures market.[24] Unless the forecaster knows something about the pricing of securities or the future course of interest rates that is not known by other market participants, passive portfolio management strategies should be used.

SUMMARY

Short-term investment management is a challenging and rapidly changing area of financial management. The number of securities from which the investment manager can select and the stream of innovative new securities that must be evaluated present a unique opportunity to conduct risk-return analysis. Not only must individual security risks be appraised, but interdependencies and risk in a portfolio context must also be managed.

The investment manager begins the portfolio selection by considering the cash forecast, the company's financial position, and the investment policy. The investment policy limits the types of securities to be included and perhaps gives guidelines to follow in assembling the portfolio. This information is combined with an understanding of the company's posture on the total amount invested in cash and securities and the cash-securities mix. The Baumol, Miller-Orr, and Stone models covered in the chapter appendix may be consulted for help in determining how and to what extent funds should be reallocated from securities to cash. These models should be used only as part of a more comprehensive analysis of liquidity and current asset investment, so that shareholder wealth is maximized. The financial manager is attempting to maximize the present value of cash flows, not merely to minimize the company's costs.

If the company decides to have an outside investment manager, the next step is selecting the manager(s) to be used. A common choice for such firms is to wire money to a money market mutual fund, which provides daily interest and immediate access to funds. If done internally, corporate personnel are faced with sifting through a set of potential securities to evaluate their risk and risk-return tradeoff. After doing individual security risk analysis, the manager should have a shorter list of potential investments, which are then reevaluated from a portfolio perspective. Regardless of whether decision making is done externally or internally, the results must be monitored and evaluated.

---

[24]A good but somewhat dated review of the literature on interest rate forecasting accuracy is contained in R.W. Hafer and Scott E. Hein, "Comparing Futures and Survey Forecasts of Near-Term Treasury Bill Rates," Federal Reserve Bank of St. Louis *Review* (May/June 1989): 33–42. Investment textbooks generally support money market efficiency; however, some counterevidence is presented in Marcia Stigum, *The Money Market*, 3rd ed. (Homewood, IL: Dow Jones-Irwin, 1990), 511–512, 527–533.

The common benchmarks are Treasury bill rates, money market mutual fund rates, indexes, or synthetic composites.

The chapter concluded with profiles of passive and active investment strategies. Passive strategies, such as the buy-and-hold strategy, typify the approach taken by many companies when investing surplus cash. Active strategies usually imply an interest rate forecast, but the analyst may be wrong more often than right unless the forecaster possesses special analytical ability or more rapid access to critical information. The predominant concerns for most managers are safety and liquidity, not yield. The possibility of yield enhancement may be viewed as too risky for the short-term securities portfolio.

Useful Web Sites

Association for Financial Professionals: www.afponline.org
CFO Magazine: www.cfomagazine.com/printarticle/1,4580,3|17|AD|919,00.html
CFO Magazine: www.cfomagazine.com/tracking/trn_channel_nav_track/1,4830,3|17,00
   .html?channel=bp_treasury
International Treasury Management Benchmarking Consortium: www.itmbc.com/
Product Management Group: www.mcs.com/~tryhardz/tmpages55.html
Treasury Corner: www.treasurycorner.com
Treasury and Risk Management Magazine:
   www.treasuryandrisk.com/issues/May01/01MYhard.html

Questions

1. What is an investment policy? What are the key inputs that a company might use in developing the policy?
2. How can a liquidity assessment be conducted? Why is this an important prerequisite to determining the target mix of cash and marketable securities?
3. Contrast business risk and financial risk. Of what relevance is either to the risk posture a company might take regarding short-term investments?
4. Agency problems occur when managerial interests deviate from those of shareholders. Given that managers may be more interested in business and financial risk than systematic risk,
   a. How might this affect the short-term investments policy?
   b. What effect will this have on the investment returns earned?
5. Compare and contrast the low-liquidity, moderate-liquidity, and high-liquidity strategies. Include the following in your answer:
   a. Regardless of which strategy is used, what specifically is being determined?
   b. The riskiness of each strategy
   c. The likely profitability (or return) effects of each strategy
   d. Which strategy you would recommend to a stable consumer goods company that is not currently facing any strong competition for its market position and is not likely to face strong competition in the near future?
   e. What additional information about the company mentioned in *d* would you collect if you were actually making this decision?
6. What is the difference between the target mix decision and the management of cash and securities balances as they deviate from the target mix?
7. What steps should a portfolio manager follow when selecting individual securities for inclusion in the company's short-term securities portfolio?
8. What are the pros and cons of using outside advisors to manage the company's short-term portfolio?

9. List and define briefly the four major benchmarks that can be used for evaluating portfolio performance.
10. List the decisions the portfolio manager must make when the short-term investments portfolio is managed internally.
11. "The short-term portfolio performance can be assessed by taking the year-end account value and dividing it by the year-beginning value, then subtracting 1 from the quotient." When is this statement invalid for assessing actual performance?
12. Because the returns on most money market instruments are highly correlated, why does it make sense to spread a portfolio's allocation across various instruments and securities?
13. What types of risk are reduced by diversification?
14. "Risk factors are interrelated." Explain.
15. What does it mean to say that risk estimates are uncertain?
16. Summarize the approach given for assessing the portfolio risk-return tradeoff.
17. Contrast passive and active investment strategies, giving an example of each.
18. Summarize the survey evidence given regarding real-life cash balance and investment portfolio management. Do you find any of the findings surprising?

Problems

1. A company invests $1,000,000 at the beginning of the year. It adds another $250,000 at the end of the first quarter, withdraws $350,000 at the end of the second quarter, adds $145,000 at the end of the third quarter, and withdraws $450,000 at the end of the year. It earns $20,000 of interest in the first quarter, $17,000 in the second quarter, $12,000 in the third quarter, and $29,000 in the fourth quarter.

   a. What is the annual effective rate earned on the investments portfolio?
   b. What rate of return would have been calculated if one only looked at the ending portfolio value as compared with the beginning $1,000,000 investment?

2. One way of enhancing short-term investment portfolio returns is to "reach for yield." As a small business owner, with no time or expertise to select or evaluate investments, an alternative to a money market mutual fund is an "ultra short-term bond fund." Such a mutual fund invests primarily in very short-term, investment grade debt obligations, with an average effective maturity on the portfolio of 1 year or less. Here are the starting (time of the fund's inception) and ending portfolio values, assuming reinvestment of all dividends and capital gains, for one such fund and two benchmark indexes.

PORTFOLIO/INDEX	Beg. Value (11/25/88)	End. Value (2/28/97)
Strong Advantage Ultra Short Bond Fund	$10,000	$18,331
Salomon 1-Year Treasury Index	$10,000	$16,842
Lipper Ultra Short Obligation Avg.	$10,000	$16,084

As of 2/28/97, the Strong Advantage bond fund had an average effective maturity of 0.74 years. Its portfolio composition was as follows:

Asset Type	Percent of Net Assets
Corporate Debt Securities	63.8%
Non-Agency Mortgage & Asset-Backed Securities	26.4%
Short-Term Investments	7.5%
Preferred Stocks	1.4%
US Government and Agency Issues	0.9%
Total	100.0%

Most of the corporate debt consisted of subordinated notes and floating rate notes. Almost 83 percent of the net assets were investments in US issuers' securities.

a. What is the annualized rate of return for the bond fund and each index for the 8¼ year period? Should the fund manager be proud of this performance (why or why not)?

b. What risks are taken by the bond fund that might explain some of the performance differences in *a*?

c. Comment on the diversification reflected in the bond fund's portfolio composition. What is the relationship between degree and type of diversification and your evaluations in parts *a* and *b*?

d. Assume that the typical money market fund has an average effective maturity of 1½ months. What is the difference in price change for the bond fund relative to the typical money fund, if interest rates were to immediately increase by 1 percent? (Assume the small business owner considering this investment has $35,000 invested in either of the two types of funds at the time.)

e. Assuming that the bond fund earns an average annual return that is 1.2 percent above the typical money fund, how long will it take before the additional interest earned recouped the incremental price change you calculated in *d*?

References

Syed M. Ahmad and Lee Sarver. 1994. The international transmission of money market fluctuations. *The Financial Review* August:319–344.

James S. Ang. 1991. The corporate-slack controversy. In Yong Kim and Venkat Srinivasan, (eds): *Advances in Working Capital Management,* vol. 2. Greenwich, CT: JAI Press, 1991, pp 3–14.

Michael J. Alderson, Keith C. Brown, and Scott L. Lummer. 1987. Dutch auction rate preferred stock. *Financial Management* Summer:68–73.

Michael D. Atchison and John L. Kling. 1988. How good are preferred dividend capture plans? *Journal of Cash Management* November/December:71–74.

Hans G. Daellenbach. 1974. Are cash management optimization models worthwhile? *Journal of Financial and Quantitative Analysis* September:607–626.

Dale L. Domian, Terry S. Maness, and William Reichenstein. 1998. Rewards to extending maturity. *Journal of Portfolio Management* Spring:77–92.

Alan W. Frankle and J. Markham Collins. 1987. Investment practices of the domestic cash manager. *Journal of Cash Management* May/June:50–53.

Larry Gitman and M.D. Goodwin. 1979. An assessment of marketable securities management practices. *Journal of Financial Research* Fall:161–169.

Larry Gitman, Edwin A. Moses, and I.T. White. 1979. An assessment of corporate cash practices. *Financial Management* Spring:32–41.

Joseph G. Haubrich and Joao Cabral dos Santos. 1997. The dark side of liquidity. *Federal Reserve Bank of Cleveland Economic Commentary* September 15.

Sara A. Irving and Timothy G. Raney. 1991. Use yield spreads to score birdies. *Corporate Cashflow* September:37, 40, 42–44.

Teresa A. John. 1993. Accounting measures of corporate liquidity, leverage, and costs of financial distress. *Financial Management* Autumn:91–100.

Ravi R. Kamath, Shahriar Khaksari, Heidi Hylton Meier, and J. Winklepeck. 1985. Management of excess cash: Practices and developments. *Financial Management* Autumn:70–77.

Duen-Li Kao and Mark A. Zurack. 1988. Investment risks of dividend capture programs. *Journal of Cash Management* January/February:46–49.

Shahriar Khaksari. 1990. Analyzing yield spreads between Eurodollar and domestic rates. *Journal of Cash Management* March/April:50–52.

Chang-Soo Kim, David C. Mauer, and Ann E. Sherman. 1998. The determinants of corporate liquidity: Theory and evidence. *Journal of Financial and Quantitative Analysis* September:335–359.

David S. Krause. 1988. The covered call dividend capture strategy. *Journal of Cash Management* March/April:22–25.

Merton Miller and Daniel Orr. 1966. A model of the demand for money by firms. *The Quarterly Journal of Economics* August:413–435.

Dan Moreau. 2001. Ultrashort bond funds trump money funds. *Investors Business Daily* July:11, B1.

Preston Nuttall. 1991. Keep short-term investments on the right track. *Corporate Cashflow* October:56, 58, 60, 62.

Tim Opler, Lee Pinkowitz, Rene Stulz, and Rohan Williamson. 1999. The determinants and implications of corporate cash holdings. *Journal of Financial Economics* 52:3–46.

Lee Pinkowitz. The market for corporate control and corporate cash holdings. Washington, DC: Georgetown University, Working Paper.

Alan G. Seidner. 1989. *Corporate investments manual.* Boston, MA: Warren, Gorham & Lamont.

Alan G. Seidner. 1990. *Corporate investments manual 1990 supplement.* Boston, MA: Warren, Gorham & Lamont.

Cynthia Smith and Sandra Miles. 1997. The risk report card: A risk management tool at Freddie Mac. *TMA Journal* May/June:26–28, 30.

Keith V. Smith and Brian Belt. Working capital management in practice: An update. West Lafayette, IN: Purdue University—Krannert Graduate School of Management, Working Paper 951.

Bernell K. Stone. 1972. The use of forecasts and smoothing in control-limit models for cash management. *Financial Management* Spring:72–84.

George P. Tsetsekos. Liquidity balances and agency considerations. Washington, D.C.: The American University, Working Paper.

Herbert J. Weinraub and Sue Visscher. 1998. Industry practice relating to aggressive/conservative working capital policies. *Journal of Financial and Strategic Decisions* Fall:11–18.

John T. Zietlow. 1990. Evaluating the risk in negotiable CDs. *Journal of Cash Management* September/October:39–41, 43, 45–46.

Appendix 15

Cash Management Models

We noted in Chapter 15 that when cash optimization models are used, they primarily address the management of the cash and securities balances over time. The cash manager wants to maintain control over how much is kept in cash, because although cash is the most liquid asset, it incurs opportunity costs in the form of foregone investment interest income or increased interest expense, and there are transactions costs associated with security purchases, sales, and the related funds transfers. If there were no brokerage commissions or other transaction costs, and investments (paying competitive interest rates) that might be easily sold and quickly converted to cash could be found, the decision rule would simplify to cash balance minimization. Practically, this translates into holding the minimal balances in transactions accounts to pay 1 day's disbursements or meet the bank's compensating balance requirements. Money markets are characterized by imperfections such as transactions costs, however, and the manager must determine how large a cash balance to hold to minimize the costs of cash management.

Three main cash management models, each with different assumptions, can be used to reallocate the cash and securities mix through time. Each model views cash as an inventoried asset, with the transaction motive driving a company's allocation of resources to cash held in the form of transaction account balances.[25] Given the total disbursements for a period, each model can specify the number and timing of securities-cash transfers. The larger the per-transfer cost and the higher the interest rate being earned on securities, the fewer and more delayed the sales of securities. The models are the Baumol model, the Miller-Orr model, and the Stone model.

---

[25]Although the models tend to focus on the transactions motive for holding cash, the addition of a safety stock buffer enables the models to also incorporate the precautionary and speculative motives for holding cash. The precautionary balance is kept to protect against unforeseen shortages in cash flow, perhaps related to unexpected sales declines. See the discussion of the EOQ model and safety stock considerations in Chapter 4.

THE BAUMOL MODEL

The earliest model, an adaptation by William Baumol of the EOQ model, was developed to explain how companies may minimize the total costs involved with transferring funds out of securities into cash during a given time period. The company is attempting to minimize total costs, composed of transactions costs to replenish cash by selling securities and opportunity costs of foregone interest resulting from holding demand deposit balances. The Baumol model assumes that:

- The company receives funds periodically but must disburse monies at a continuous, steady rate.
- The company's cash needs are anticipated with perfect accuracy (complete certainty).
- When the initial cash balance is drawn down to zero (or to a small "safety stock" level), the balance is replenished by a sale of securities identical in size to the initial cash balance, denoted as Z^*.

Diagrammatically, the cash transfer sequence is identical to that shown in the EOQ presentation in Chapter 4 (see Exhibit 4-2). The model allows the analyst to solve for the optimal number of transactions that should be made to invest in securities or to transfer invested monies into cash (the disbursement account). For example, two transactions are implied by a strategy that invests one-half of the funds received until needed, at which time the other half is sold and the proceeds deposited into the disbursement account.

In symbol form, the total costs incurred over a period of time are summed up as shown in Equation 15-1A:

$$\text{Period cost} = F(TCN/Z) + i(Z/2) \tag{15-1A}$$

In which: F = fixed transaction cost, per security purchase or sale

TCN = total cash needs during period

Z = cash balance starting and return point

i = interest rate, per period, on marketable securities (opportunity cost for holding cash balances)

The first term gives us the aggregate transaction cost, because TCN/Z is the number of transactions made and F is the fixed cost per security purchase or sale.[26]

Commissions charged by brokers are an obvious component of securities transactions costs, but there may be other costs such as the cost of communicating the transactions instructions and clerical time necessary for record keeping. $Z/2$ is the average cash balance, which can be multiplied by the interest rate per period (i) to give us the dollar opportunity cost for having funds tied up in interest-bearing disbursement accounts.

Using the derivative of the period cost, which is a total cost function, we can solve for the cost-minimizing number of transactions and the optimal transactions size, Z^*:

$$Z^* = \sqrt{\frac{2(F)(TCN)}{i}} \qquad \text{(15-2A)}$$

Thus Z^* is the optimal dollar amount of securities that should be sold to replenish cash when the disbursements account has been drawn down. It also can be thought of as the optimal return point for the cash balance. Equation 15-2A should look familiar, because it is simply a restatement of the EOQ formula. Economies of scale in cash management are implied by the model, because a given percentage increase in the total cash needs (TCN) leads to a smaller than proportional increase in Z^*. Based on the cash balance specified, we can further calculate the average cash balance ($Z/2$), the frequency of transactions (TCN/Z, rounded to the nearest integer), and when substituting Z^* into Equation 15-1A for Z, the total cost of following the EOQ-based reallocation rules. The following example illustrates use of the Baumol model.

Joe Nevada, entrepreneur and one-time football great, recently started a business that is enjoying un-expectedly rapid growth. Profits have been adequate, but Joe is concerned about maintaining adequate liquidity so he does not get tackled by his banker. Specifically, he is having trouble deciding how to allocate his transaction liquid assets between cash and marketable securities. He figures that his company has disbursements of $1 million per year. His broker charges $65 each time Joe wants to pass money from securities to his cash disbursement account. Short-term interest rates on potential investments are now approximately 7 percent. Not having skill with numbers (other than calling signals at the line of scrimmage), Joe asks your advice. What should Joe do?

Solution

Applying the Baumol model, we solve for the optimal initial and return level for cash by using Equation 15-2A:

$$Z^* = \sqrt{\frac{2(F)(TCN)}{i}}$$

$$= \sqrt{\frac{2(\$65)(\$1,000,000)}{0.07}}$$

$$= \$43,095$$

The average cash balance, $Z/2$, is $21,548 ($43,095/2). Joe's company would transfer money (TCN/Z) times a year by selling securities, which is 23 transfers in this case ($1,000,000/$43,095).

The major shortcoming of the Baumol model is the unrealistic assumptions that are underlying the equation. It is impossible to know if the model Z^* is really cost minimizing unless it is certain that the assumptions hold. The model's simplicity comes at the expense of oversimplifications such as the following:

- known, certain future disbursements (TCN), that implicitly depend on perfect accuracy in cash forecasting
- transaction costs (F) that do not vary with the dollar size of the securities transaction (an assumption that is obviously violated for companies with money market accounts or sweep accounts that do not charge for transactions on a per-transfer basis)
- lumpy periodic cash receipts but a continuous disbursing rate, which fits mortgage bankers and apartment rental businesses and health care

---

[26]Two strategies may help us understand this process. If the entire beginning-of-period cash receipt is deposited into the cash disbursement account, there are no transactions because no securities would need to be purchased or sold during the period. If one-half of the receipt is put in securities, which are sold halfway through the period to fund remaining disbursements, we have TCN/Z = 2. The two transactions involved are the original purchase of securities and subsequent sale to fund the cash account.

EXHIBIT 15-1A
Period Cost When Varying Level of Cash

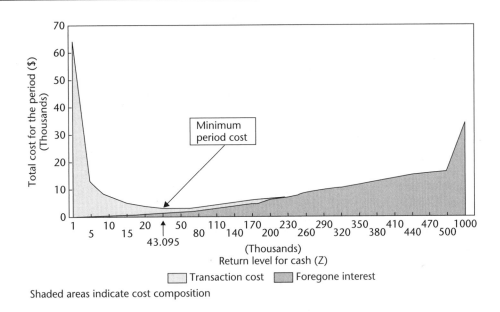

Shaded areas indicate cost composition

providers or governmental agencies receiving lump-sum reimbursements or budget allocations[27]

Despite such oversimplifications, the Baumol model is instructive. First, the model shows the decision maker the extent of suboptimization, in the form of higher cash-related costs, when the initial and return level of cash is set very low or high. Exhibit 15-1A depicts the data used in our earlier example and graphically portrays the cost penalties of extreme cash positions. We can visualize how the company incurs large transaction costs when Z is too low, because of numerous transactions, and loses considerable interest revenue or incurs considerable interest expense when Z is too large. Second, rapid updating, or rerunning the model, is a way to get around the lumpy receipt oversimplification: the period modeled can be shortened to a month or week and rerun as new data become available.

Whether or not a company sets actual transaction cash balances to the model's prescribed Z°, sensitivity analysis using the model can show how to revise the cash replenishment. We can vary the interest rate (i) and the transaction cost (F) up and down 5 to 15 percent from the present levels and calculate the revised values for Z°. This analysis enables the manager to anticipate the revision to the cash balance necessary if and when either of these two critical inputs change and to devote more time and effort to getting accurate data on the cost item that affects the cash balance the most. We hold all other variables constant when changing the value of one input variable. In our example, the interest rate forecast is the most critical variable in the analysis of factors causing an increase in cash balances. The same kind of analysis can be performed for an increase in the interest rate and decrease in the fixed transactions costs. Additionally, as actual interest rates change, cash balances can be rapidly adjusted to the new optimal level prespecified by this sensitivity analysis.

THE MILLER-ORR MODEL

The Miller-Orr model varies from the Baumol model in two ways. First, it allows for unpredictable fluctuations in the cash balance instead of assuming perfect

[27]A model that assumes continuous cash receipts and lumpy disbursements has been developed in William Beranek, *Analysis for Financial Decisions* (Homewood, IL: Richard D. Irwin, 1963), Chapter 11. In situations in which cash accrues and is then paid out in a lump sum (e.g., a quarterly dividend), this model would be appropriate. This model, like the Baumol model, assumes perfect certainty of future cash flows. In companies for which cash receipts are highly predictable, the Beranek model may be used to give guidance on how often to sweep monies from many collection accounts into a concentration account.

EXHIBIT 15-2A
Cash Movements in the Miller-Orr Model

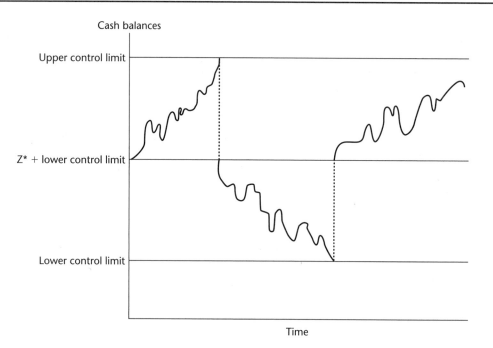

cash forecasting ability. The model accomplishes this by incorporating the variance of the company's daily net cash flows. Second, it permits both upward and downward movements in the cash balance subsequent to replenishment, as opposed to the supposition that the company experiences a one-time cash infusion each period, which is subsequently depleted at a continuous rate. Miller and Orr handled this by including two trigger points instead of one in the model. These trigger points, which signal a purchase or sale of securities, are termed **control limits.** The **upper control limit** (UCL) triggers a purchase of securities large enough to reduce excess cash balances to the return point Z° (Exhibit 15-2A). When the cash balance dips down to the lower control limit (LCL), a sale of securities sufficient to return the cash balance to Z° is initiated. Notice that as long as the cash balance drifts along within the two control limits, no securities trades are triggered. In that case, the stream of cash receipts and disbursements must have been at least moderately synchronized—but the assumption of the model is that cash flows are unpredictable (random), meaning that next period's flows may be totally asynchronous.

The formula underlying the Miller-Orr model is presented as Equation 15-3A:

$$Z° = \sqrt[3]{\frac{3F\sigma^2}{4i}} \qquad \text{(15-3A)}$$

In which: $Z°$ = optimal transfer amount

F = fixed transaction cost

σ^2 = variance of daily net cash flows

i = the daily interest rate

Like the Baumol model, $Z°$ minimizes the sum of transactions and foregone interest costs, except here we are actually balancing the expected value of a probability distribution of costs because of the uncertainty in the future cash flows. Be careful about the interpretation of $Z°$. If the company sets the LCL limit at any value other than zero, then $Z°$ is no longer the return point for cash. Instead, the return point is $Z°$ + LCL. Because we are addressing the disbursement account balance, the company might need to set LCL above zero to meet compensating balance requirements. Or LCL could represent a safety stock of liquidity, with the exact level dependent on management's target for this component of the company's liquidity. While the LCL is set at zero or some arbitrary low value, the optimal value of UCL (derived using stochastic calculus) specified by the model is $3Z° + LCL$. Miller and Orr solved for an average cash balance of $4/3(Z°) + LCL$. The return point is $Z° + LCL$. We can illustrate the computations by returning to our example.

After being presented with your recommendations based on the Baumol model, Joe Nevada asks for some background information about the model and what it is based on. You warn Joe that the model assumes his forecasts of cash needs are perfectly accurate, at which point he becomes visibly uncomfortable. "Our cash flows jump all over the place," he grumbles. "Can we adjust the model?" You reply that there might be a better way, as you think about the less demanding assumptions behind the Miller-Orr model, while hoping Joe will not ask you what variance means. Your thoughts are interrupted by Joe's insistence that you let him know right away how the cash balances will change "if reality is incorporated into the analysis."

Solution

You first analyze the historical net cash flows of Joe's business and compute the variance of the flows to be $1,000,000. Using the example values for F of $65 and converting i to a daily rate of 0.0001917 (0.07/365), you can use Equation 15-3A to compute $Z°$:

$$Z° = \sqrt[3]{\frac{3F\sigma^2}{4i}}$$

$$= \sqrt[3]{\frac{3(65)(\$1,000,000)}{4(0.0001917)}}$$

$$= \$6,336$$

When asked, Joe declares that he would never want the cash balance going below $5,000, because this represents the compensating balance requirement part of his overall bank compensation. Recognizing this value as LCL, we know the return point is:

$$Z° + LCL = \$6,336 + \$5,000$$
$$= \$11,336$$

The UCL is then $3Z° + LCL$:

$$UCL = 3 (\$6,336) + \$5,000$$
$$= \$24,008$$

The average cash balance is $13,448 [4/3($6,336) + $5,000].

You advise Joe that if his company's cash flows are completely unpredictable with the specified variance, he should start with $11,336 in his business checking account. If and when cash builds up to $24,008, he should invest $12,672 ($24,008 − $11,336) in securities. Anytime the cash account is drawn down to $5,000, he should sell $6,336 of securities to return to the $11,336 target.

The Miller-Orr model has two main appeals. First, it presumes that the company's cash flows are random, or entirely unpredictable. Although many disbursements are predictable, for most companies unpredictability of cash flows is closer to reality than the perfect certainty of the Baumol model. Second, it allows the cash manager to manage the cash position between limits of excessive cash and insufficient cash, triggering responses on the manager's part only when the position gets out of bounds. This is intuitively appealing to the manager, and it constitutes an efficient approach because it adheres to a "management by exception" philosophy.

Restrictive assumptions about the statistical nature of cash flows plague this model, however. Cash flows are assumed to be unpredictable, normally distributed with a constant variance, and uncorrelated (independent) across successive time periods. Cash managers recognize that they can predict some elements such as salaries and loan payments. Tests of companies' actual cash flows have revealed nonnormality[28] or shifting cash flow distributions that are correlated through time.[29] There may be some companies with normal distributions of a large number of small receipts, but these are likely to follow some pattern over time—which the Miller-Orr model does not incorporate. The most damaging shortcoming of the Miller-Orr model, however, is the insignificance of the improvement brought about by its use in realistic situations. Because cash managers do have some forecasting ability, they can easily outperform the model-driven strategies.

The main uses of the model's prescriptions, then, might be to provide a starting point for the manager who is deciding where to set the target cash balance and as an after-the-fact benchmark with which to evaluate realized performance. One comparison is the

---

[28]Detected by Miller and Orr in the Union Tank Car data that they modeled and by others who have analyzed actual company cash flows. See full citation in end-of-chapter references.

[29]Gary Emery, "Some Empirical Evidence on the Properties of Daily Cash Flow," *Financial Management* (Spring 1981): 21–28.

cash balances actually held relative to the model's prescription. As opposed to the Baumol model's complete certainty, the Miller-Orr model assumes complete uncertainty, implying larger cash balances if the variance of net cash flows (σ^2) is large relative to the company's total cash needs (TCN). In reality, no company is faced with complete uncertainty (e.g., payroll amounts are easily forecasted), and if the historic cash balances exceed the Miller-Orr recommendation, this signals excessive cash balances and excess costs. A second comparison is to assess the incremental improvements brought about by the cash manager's forecasting and investment abilities. The interest income for a given period, had the model's recommendation been used, would be compared with the actual interest income. Some type of risk adjustment should be made to the realized results to ensure high (low) returns were not simply the product of greater (lesser) risk taking.

Both the Baumol and Miller-Orr models are forms of "automatic pilot" reallocation strategies. But why should an investment manager mindlessly sell securities when the cash balance approaches a lower limit if the company knows it will receive next-day availability on a sizable automated clearing house (ACH) collection initiated today? Bernell Stone has developed a model that allows managerial foresight to change model prescriptions and that operates under much less restrictive assumptions regarding cash flow patterns.

THE STONE MODEL

The Stone model improves on the realism of the Miller-Orr optimization process by allowing the cash manager's knowledge of imminent cash flows to permit him or her to selectively override model directives.[30] This "look-ahead" model promises larger cost savings because there are times that the manager will see a large receipt coming and not have to sell securities, and at other times cash disbursements are large enough to pull the cash balance back within the UCL. Stone's formulation permits cash managers to look ahead up to K (generally 3 to 12) days, with the value

---

[30]Statistically, the Stone model relaxes assumptions about cash flow normality, independence, and variance constancy. Whether or not these assumptions fit a company's cash flows, a manager who is not technically oriented should be more comfortable with the Stone model.

selected for K being larger when company's cash forecasts are relatively accurate. Additionally, the model recognizes that the penalties for being outside the control limits for one or several days are quite small. Therefore, the manager does not need to buy (sell) securities as long as the cash balance will be within the upper (lower) control limit (possibly modified by a safety stock cushion) within K days. A security transaction only occurs when the cash balance is both out of bounds today and will still be out of bounds K days from now. This makes sense because businesses rarely are faced with inviolable minimums (except perhaps zero, which represents an overdraft threshold), and compensating balance requirements are based on month-average balances. A numerical example provides a better understanding of how to apply the Stone model.

Advanced Software, Inc., (ASI) has been unsuccessfully trying to use cash management models for several years. Ed, the cash manager, has just returned from a training seminar at which he heard about the Stone model, and he is excited about applying it. The seminar instructor told Ed to use the same control limits that he has been using but to modify the decision rules. First, transfers between cash and securities will not take place unless the cash position gets very high or low and it looks like it will stay that way for another 3 days. This implies that Ed must make decisions based on the anticipated cash position, which is the sum of today's cash position and the next 3 days' forecasted cash flows ($K = 3$). Second, to adjust partially for forecasting errors, the trigger points will be modified. The control limits will be adjusted by a 3 percent safety stock cushion. This effectively shrinks the range of values the forecasted cash position can move within before a transaction is triggered.

ASI's control limits are $50,000 (LCL) and $125,000 (UCL), and the return point is $75,000. The present cash balance is $105,000. The next 7 days' net cash flows are projected to be:

Day	Cash Flow Forecast
1	$ 45,000
2	(20,000)
3	25,000
4	5,000
5	10,000
6	(35,000)
7	(45,000)

What transactions should Ed make during the next 3 days, if any?

Solution

First add two columns to the problem data to show the new cash position, assuming no transactions are made. The "Cash Balance" shows the daily anticipated balance. "Period Cash" is the anticipated balance K days hence:

Day	Cash Flow Forecast	Cash Balance	Period Cash (Cash Balance + K Days' Cash Flows)
0 (present)	—	$105,000	$155,000
1	$ 45,000	150,000	160,000
2	−20,000	130,000	170,000
3	25,000	155,000	135,000
4	5,000	160,000	90,000
5	10,000	170,000	
6	−35,000	135,000	
7	−45,000	90,000	

Next, we compute modified trigger points for security purchase or sale. The LCL adjusted for the 3 percent safety stock cushion is

$$\$50,000 + (0.03)(\$50,000) = \$51,500$$

The UCL adjusted for the safety cushion is $121,250 (found by subtracting 3 percent from $125,000). Third, we check to see if the cash balance ever gets outside the original control limits of $50,000 and $125,000. If the cash flow balance gets outside the original control limits at any time, an analysis of whether to initiate a transaction is triggered. But no action is taken unless the period cash will be below (above) the modified LCL (UCL) limit *at the end of the look-ahead period.* We notice when visually scanning the cash balances in our table that the UCL is penetrated on day 1. We add the cash balance at that time, $150,000, to the sum of the next 3 days' cash flows—or simply scan to the right in the table—and then compare this figure with the modified control limit. Because the projected period cash of $160,000 3 days hence is obviously greater than the modified UCL, we advise Ed to plan on buying securities on day 1. The dollar amount of the purchase should be sufficient to return the *expected* cash balance in K days to the return point of $75,000. This implies a day 1 transaction of $85,000 ($160,000 − $75,000). One caution: If tomorrow's actual cash flow is $5,000 instead of the forecasted $45,000, the upper limit will not be penetrated during the planning horizon, and Ed can relax instead of worrying about which securities to buy. He will need to redo the table, however, to incorporate the actual cash position in the updated forecast.

Given a choice, this model should be the clear favorite of practicing cash managers. First, it fits well with the decision-making approach used by cash managers. Recall from our discussion of cash forecasting that the scheduling, or receipts and disbursements, method predominates as the preferred forecasting method for daily cash forecasting. This involves laying out cash flows for several days ahead to see if the cash position will be short or in surplus. The Stone approach uses these forecasts as inputs and thus fits extremely well into the operating mode of managers. Second, the Stone model has minimal statistical and data requirements. In our example, we used the Miller-Orr control limits, but there is no need to do this. The cash manager uses his or her own best estimate of what the upper and lower limits or modified limits should be. One alternative approach is to use simulation of the company's cash flows to estimate the probability of running short on cash for any particular limit.

If control limits, modified limits, or the return level are established subjectively, this may reduce the attractiveness of model use, however. For the Miller-Orr model when the assumptions are valid, an optimal cost-minimizing strategy is provided. There is no such assurance with the Stone model. In our view, this is not a major objection. We advocate a three-step approach: using the Miller-Orr limits to get starting values for the permissible cash balance range, lowering them for companies in which the cash flow variability is small, and then managing the cash position using Stone's approach. The cash manager can demonstrate the cost reductions under this approach by conducting a comparative simulation with historical data. The model's recommendations can be back-tested against what was actually done by the cash manager. Relative improvements from model use can be established in this fashion, giving confidence for future use. The key to approaching optimality is having a good understanding of the company's cash forecasting ability. If overly confident, the manager might set K too low or the modified control limits too close to the Miller-Orr control limits. The result(s) would be to undershoot in maintaining compensating balances, overdraft the account, or forego significant interest income.

Recap on Optimization Models

Optimization models are best suited for cash and securities decisions involving very short planning horizons and/or small aggregate cash balances. The net result of either of these situations is to elevate the relative importance of transactions costs such as brokerage commissions. When companies have longer planning horizons (implying the possibility of substantive changes in interest rates during the period), have large investable balances (implying low relative transactions costs and possibly volume discounts on commissions), or are assessed fixed per-year fees to maintain automated investment accounts (implying low or nonexistent per-transaction costs), optimization models are of limited value. The Stone model could still be used, but the limits would have to be set arbitrarily, and the cash manager might do so without the help of the model. The objective switches to yield maximization[31] when transactions costs are low or nonexistent. At a minimum, the philosophy of carefully managing the cash position to avoid having too much or too little of this nonearning asset can be implemented by all organizations.

Cash management models share another common shortcoming: They are partial equilibrium models that address cash management costs but ignore the other current asset accounts. Recall that the target cash balance decision precedes the management of cash balances through time. The former decision should be carefully tied to the company's liquidity objectives, in light of its investment in receivables and inventories. Only in this way can the manager ensure that the limited cash management focus of the models does not interfere with shareholder wealth maximization.

QUESTIONS

A-1. What are the assumptions for each of the three major cash management models? What are some of the characteristics of companies for which each would be most appropriate?

A-2. What are the two components of the total period cost addressed in the Baumol model? Why does one cost component increase as the other decreases?

A-3. The total cash needs of Alpha Grocery is twice that of Beta Grocery. Would Alpha's optimal

cash balance be twice that of Beta, according to the Baumol model?

A-4. How can sensitivity analysis be performed on the results of a Baumol model calculation? How might the results of that sensitivity analysis be used?

A-5. Because no company has completely unpredictable cash flows, why should any cash manager use the Miller-Orr model?

A-6. Why is the Stone model so appealing to practicing cash managers? Are there any weaknesses inherent in the model?

A-7. When does the cash manager take action to sell or buy securities when using the Stone model? How much is bought or sold?

PROBLEMS

A-1. The assistant treasurer of Monroe Tires, Inc., is trying to determine what the appropriate cash return level should be. The company's cash balances have been fluctuating wildly because of unpredictable and wide-ranging receipts and disbursements. The best estimate of annual disbursements is $5,000,000. The investment broker charges $75 per securities transaction. Short-term investment interest rates are 12 percent. The company does not mind a $0 cash balance but does not want the balance to be negative.

   a. What should the cash return level be, according to the Baumol model?

   b. What will the average cash balance be if the company's cash outflows fit the assumptions of the Baumol model?

   c. How many security sales will Monroe have in a year, assuming the model's assumptions are valid?

   d. What will the total period costs be for a year?

   e. Do you recommend that Monroe use the Baumol model? Why or why not?

A-2. Conduct sensitivity analysis on your results from problem 1. What conclusions do you reach based on your analysis? How might Monroe use this information?

A-3. Monroe's assistant treasurer (see problem 1) estimates the variance of daily net cash flows to be $5,000,000. Again, using a LCL of $0:

---

[31]Yield maximization is equivalent to minimizing the foregone investment income of the cash management strategy, within the risk posture stipulated in the investment policy.

a. What should the cash return level be, using the Miller-Orr model?

b. What is your estimate of the average cash balance if the Miller-Orr calculation is used to set the cash return level?

c. How do you explain your finding in part a to the assistant treasurer, who wants to know how to use the information provided by the model?

d. If the variance of daily net cash flows is $10,000,000 instead of $5,000,000, how does this change the answer determined in part *a*? Is the cash return level double your earlier result? How do you interpret this?

e. (Optional) How does your result in part *a* compare with the Baumol model prescriptions found in problem 1?

A-4. Conduct a Miller-Orr analysis using the data in problems 1 and 3 but with a lower cash limit of $5,000.

a. What should the cash return level be, using the Miller-Orr model?

b. What is your estimate of the average cash balance if the Miller-Orr calculation is used to set the cash return level?

c. How do you explain your finding in part a to the assistant treasurer, who wants to know how to use the information provided by the model?

d. If the variance of daily net cash flows is $10,000,000 instead of $5,000,000, how does this change the answer determined in part *a*? Is the cash return level double your earlier result? How do you interpret this?

e. (Optional) How does your result in part *a* compare with the Baumol model prescriptions found in problem 1?

A-5. Megamedia Enterprises wishes to apply the Stone model to its cash position management situation. It has never used a cash management model before. Its control limits are $20,000

(lower) and $75,000 (upper). The company wishes to try the model out with a 2-day look ahead, as well as a 3-day look ahead. In other words, transfers between cash and securities will not take place unless the cash position gets very high or low and it looks like it will stay that way for another 2 days in the first analysis and 3 days in the second analysis. This implies that the cash manager must make decisions based on the anticipated cash position, which is the sum of today's cash position and the next 2 or 3 days' forecasted cash flows ($K = 2$ or $K = 3$). Second, to partially adjust for forecasting errors, the trigger points will be modified. The control limits will be adjusted by a 5 percent safety stock cushion. This effectively shrinks the range of values within which the forecasted cash position can move before a transaction is triggered. The company has been using a return point of $50,000, and the present cash balance is $45,000. The next 7 days' net cash flows are projected to be:

Day	Cash Flow Forecast	Day	Cash Flow Forecast
1	$35,000	5	(10,000)
2	(50,000)	6	25,000
3	(25,000)	7	45,000
4	5,000		

a. What transactions should the cash manager make during the next 2 days, if any, under the 2-day look ahead?

b. What transactions should the cash manager make during the next 3 days, if any, under the 3-day look ahead?

c. What general advice do you have for the cash manager, given what you know about the Stone model and the fact the company has never before used a cash management model?

CHAPTER 16

Short-Term Financing

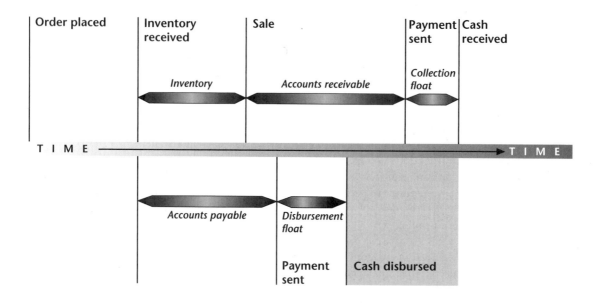

OBJECTIVES

After studying this chapter, you should be able to:

- Formulate a short-term financing strategy.
- Choose the appropriate financing instrument from among the array of financing instruments available.
- Compute the effective cost of short-term financing alternatives when commitment fees and compensating balances are involved.

A business firm in need of additional short-term funds beyond what its spontaneous payables and accrual sources provide can choose among a myriad of alternatives. This chapter introduces the more common short-term discretionary sources of financing. The sum of these sources on any one balance sheet is typically smaller than the funds provided by accounts payable. However, these alternative short-term funding sources are an important part of a firm's liquidity reserve and tend to complement payables and accruals.

Short-term borrowing instruments are different from spontaneous sources in several important respects. First, the firm is actually acquiring the use of dollars directly rather than goods or services as in the case of payables and accruals. Second, these sources are the result of choices made by the financial manager and must be deliberately acquired rather than being spontaneously generated by operations. Third, these funds have an explicit cost as represented by the interest rate and commitment fee charged.

The chapter begins by outlining three strategies that represent the choices that financial managers have in managing the maturity structure, the balance between long-term and short-term financing

sources, of the balance sheet. Then the array of more popular short-term financing instruments is discussed and each financing alternative is reviewed in detail. The chapter concludes with a section discussing the effective cost of short-term financing.

FINANCIAL DILEMMA

When is Prime not Prime?

The treasurer at Beco, Inc., was arranging for a line of credit with its bank for the new 2002 fiscal year. Beco's lending officer indicated that the rate on borrowed funds would be 10 percent, which was the bank's current prime rate, the rate offered to its "best" customers. The treasurer was proud to be labeled a "prime rate borrower." In addition to the 10 percent interest rate, the lending officer went on to say that the line carried a 25 basis point commitment fee to guarantee the availability of funds and that Beco would need to leave a 20 percent compensating balance on funds borrowed. Although the treasurer felt good about getting the prime rate, he was curious as to the impact the commitment fee and compensating balance requirements would have on the overall financing cost of the line.

FINANCING AND THE CASH FLOW TIMELINE

At this point, we have reached a position on the company's cash flow timeline at which cash has been collected and cash has been disbursed, resulting in a daily ending cash position that may be positive or negative. If the daily cash position is positive, then the cash manager faces an investment opportunity discussed in the previous chapter. If the daily cash position is negative, the cash manager faces a dilemma on how to fund the cash deficit.

A deficit cash position may be the result of inefficient or inappropriate working capital policies. As seen in earlier chapters, excess accumulation of inventory, slow collections, and/or quick disbursements may lead to cash being disbursed prior to cash collection. Thus the financial manager should reevaluate the company's working capital policies to ensure the most efficient stream of cash flow resulting from operations.

Even the most efficient working capital policies, however, may result in a deficit cash position at different times during the working capital cycle. This is especially true during periods of rapid growth and during the early phase of the working capital cycle. At this point the manager must have a well-developed plan for financing short-term cash deficit positions.

FINANCING STRATEGIES

Over the course of its operating cycle, a firm's assets tend to fluctuate, rising as operations gear up for seasonal peak sales and then subsiding as sales fall. Exhibit 16-1 demonstrates this trend for a firm that is growing and adding to its fixed asset base. In

EXHIBIT 16-1

The Firm's Fluctuating Assets Over its Operating Cycle

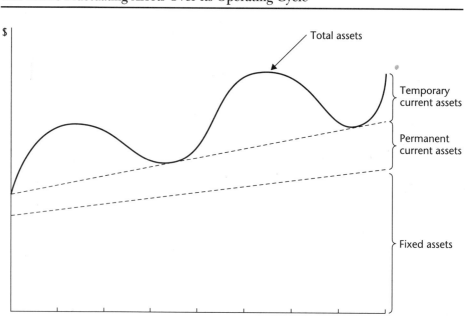

the exhibit, assets begin to grow as time moves from the left to the right with inventory build up in anticipation of future sales. As sales pick up, inventory is maintained for a time by increased production, and receivables begin to accumulate as inventory is sold. As sales level off, production is reduced, resulting in a drop in inventory. Receivables also begin to fall as collections exceed the creation of new receivables. As receivables are collected, the cash received is used to pay off accounts payable and other short-term loans used to finance the earlier accumulation of inventory and receivables. This cycle then repeats itself as the firm approaches a new operating period.

In Exhibit 16-1, you may have noticed the decomposition of total current assets into two parts, a level of **permanent current assets** and a level of **temporary current assets.** It may seem strange to refer to current assets as permanent but a firm always has some minimum or permanent amount of inventory and receivables on its books. Although the products in inventory and the specific accounts held as receivables do turn over, there is always a minimum amount of resources invested in these accounts. This minimum level of ongoing inventory and receivables is what is referred to as permanent current assets.

The temporary component of total current assets, then, represents the accumulation of inventory in anticipation of the peak selling season and the resulting receivables generated by the increasing sales. This bulge in inventory and receivables then subsides as the firm passes through its peak-selling season.

There are three basic strategies from which the financial manager can choose as financing is sought to support the firm's asset needs over its operating cycle. The three strategies include the aggressive strategy, the conservative strategy, and the moderate strategy. These three financing strategies are illustrated in Exhibit 16-2. You may wish to refer to this exhibit as each of the strategies is discussed below.

Aggressive Strategy

The **aggressive financing strategy** is basically a maturity matching strategy. Using this strategy, the financial manager chooses to match the maturity of the source of financing with the duration of the need of cash. In the exhibit, the wavy line represents the total assets of the firm over time. Over the course of the firm's operating activities, total assets rise and fall primarily because of the fluctuations in receivables, inventory, and payables

EXHIBIT 16-2
Financing Strategies

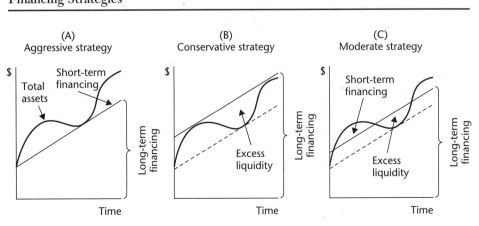

over the working capital cycle. The wavy line will exhibit an upward trend if the firm is growing and adding to its fixed asset base. In Panel A of Exhibit 16-2, The firm is maximizing its reliance on short-term financing and minimizing its reliance on permanent or long-term financing. The corporation's net working capital position, as a result, is minimal because of the heavy reliance on short-term financing, and therefore the solvency position of the firm, as measured by the current ratio, will suffer. This strategy has an advantage in that during normal financial conditions, short-term sources of financing cost less than longer-term sources. For example, on April 14, 2000, 90-day Treasury bills yielded 5.67 percent while 5-year Treasury notes yielded 6.18 percent. Thus there is normally a trade-off of a lower financing cost at the expense of a reduced solvency level.

There is some evidence that firms use a maturity matching strategy as reported by Beranek, Cornwell, and Choi. In their research, they found that firms do not emphasize external short-term sources in the financing of capital expenditures, nor do they use the bulk of long-term external financing in a given period to finance the acquisition of short-lived assets. Thus firms generally act as if they seek to match the maturity of their external financing with the life of their acquired assets.

Conservative Strategy

The **conservative financing strategy** uses only long-term sources to fulfill all the corporation's financing needs as demonstrated in Panel B of Exhibit 16-2. As total assets increase as a result of a build up of inventory and receivables, the firm draws down its excess liquidity stored in short-term investments. Then as inventory is sold and receivables collected, excess cash is reinvested in short-term investments. Thus over a part of its working capital cycle, the corporation has an excess solvency position, as indicated by a relatively high current ratio. Because the corporation uses no short-term financing, it will have substantial financing flexibility in acquiring new short-term sources of financing if it underestimates its actual future cash needs. Under normal financial market conditions, this strategy is relatively expensive because long-term financing sources are generally more expensive than short-term sources. However, the reliance on longer-term sources does provide a greater solvency position as measured by the current ratio.

Moderate Strategy

The **moderate financing strategy,** Panel C of Exhibit 16-2, is a blend of the extreme strategies represented by the aggressive and conservative strategies discussed previously. The exact blend of short- and long-term sources depends on the risk preferences of the corporation as well as the current financial market conditions.

SHORT-TERM FINANCING ALTERNATIVES

Businesses borrow short-term for seasonal working capital to cover abrupt changes in payment patterns or unexpected expenses, and when short-term profitability is not adequate to support continued operations. Banks have traditionally provided most of the short-term and medium-term loans for businesses; however, in more recent times financing alternatives such as commercial paper have eroded this once prominent role played by commercial banks. As of 1999, bank loans supplied approximately 26 percent of total non-mortgage credit market debt for nonfinancial businesses.[1] About half of

---

[1]Statistics based on Federal Reserve data.

short-term bank loans are unsecured (usually in the form of a line-of-credit arrangement) and the other half are secured (meaning that collateral is required to ensure an adequate secondary source of repayment).

Increasingly, banks are moving away from a direct finance role to a risk-sharing role, in which they guarantee the payment of corporations' commercial paper borrowings at maturity. Banks collect fees for providing the guarantee, and the issuer receives a better credit rating with a correspondingly lower interest rate.

The financial manager has a wide assortment of bank and non-bank short-term financing sources from which to choose. Although this section does not attempt to be exhaustive, the primary short-term financing alternatives are discussed.

The Role of the Internet in Obtaining Credit

Internet usage is having a dramatic impact on how financial managers seek information regarding credit alternatives as well as on how they make actual transactions. According to a survey conducted by the Association for Finance Professionals, four of five respondents reported that they are likely to use the Internet to obtain information and communicate with service providers as well as actually transact business.[2] Two years earlier, less than 20 percent of the respondents indicated that they made credit transactions over the Internet. Approximately 70 percent indicated that they currently make credit transactions over the Internet and 90 percent indicated that they anticipate doing this in the coming 2 years. For example, Norwest Bank (now Wells Fargo) was one of the first institutions to offer their customers in the United States and Asia the ability to initiate letters of credit on the Internet. As you will learn in a later section of this chapter, letters of credit are one of the payment vehicles US importers obtain from financial institutions to ensure timely delivery of their overseas purchases.

The International Trade Administration (ITA) recently unveiled a new Web site that enables exporters to find firms that can finance their sales to overseas buyers. Historically, it took days, weeks, and even months for exporters, especially smaller businesses, to find the right financing to support their export business. However, thanks to this new Web site, exporters can find firms that can finance their foreign sales almost instantaneously. Once the application is submitted, the Export Finance Matchmaker (EFM) Web site searches its database for a financial institution that matches the loan needs of the company. On completion of the search, the exporter is provided the contact information for all matches.

Credit Lines

A **line of credit** is a short-term source of funds in that it represents a sum of funds that a bank stands ready to lend a corporate client on demand at any time during a given period, generally a year. Most banks require customers using credit lines to "clean up" any outstanding balances for a period of a few weeks each year to demonstrate the line is used for short-term purposes only. The length of the "clean-up" period is a feature that can be negotiated by the firm.

Banks usually require a **compensating balance** on the line of credit so the firm does not have full use of the line. For example, if a bank required a compensating balance of 20 percent on the amount borrowed, then the corporation could only avail itself of 80 percent of the line of credit. In a later section, we address how such required balances affect the effective cost of credit lines.

---

[2]1999. Survey results: Changes in the short-term credit market. *Association for Financial Professionals* December 21:4–5.

FOCUS ON PRACTICE

HOW CREDIT LINES ARE STRUCTURED   A mid-western utility supplies the electrical power for much of the state of Indiana. The primary purposes of its credit line bank borrowings are to provide funds for periods of cash shortage and as an emergency source of funds. The first need is met by either committed, formal lines of credit (totaling $106 million) or commercial paper—whichever is less expensive at the time funds are required. The utility has established committed lines of credit with 12 banks: six domestic and six foreign. The foreign banks have higher credit ratings from agencies such as Moody's Investor Services and Standard & Poor's, which rate the creditworthiness of banks, indicating greater soundness and that "they'll be there when you need them." Most foreign banks also have fiscal years ending in March instead of December, making them more willing to lend at the end of December when the utility generally needs funds. The utility pays a commitment fee averaging 3/16 of 1 percent on unused portions of these credit lines, and on amounts borrowed, it is charged a floating interest rate that is typically 1 percent or 2 percent below the prime interest rate. These rates are based on the federal funds rate, or the London Interbank Offered Rate (LIBOR). In the past few years it used committed lines of credit rarely, usually around the date of its quarterly dividend payment or when paying for a major coal shipment.

The utility also has established uncommitted, informal credit lines with five banks totaling $123 million. It never has used any of these funds. The rate charged on these lines, if used, are higher than on the committed lines. No fee is paid on unused balances.

Credit lines come in two basic forms, committed lines and uncommitted lines. A **committed line of credit** is a formal, written agreement contractually binding the bank to provide the funds when requested. Such agreements require a **commitment fee** paid to the bank to ensure the availability of the funds. Also, committed lines generally have covenants to ensure that the borrower adhere to certain basic conditions generally specifying limits on a variety of financial ratios.

An **uncommitted line of credit** is technically not binding on the bank, although it is almost always honored.[3] These informal arrangements are appealing to companies who only rarely need to draw down the credit line, who maintain a consistently strong financial position, and who like the fact that uncommitted credit lines do not require a fee on unused balances. The only charges are interest on amounts borrowed. Banks like the flexibility offered by such arrangements, which free the bank from providing funds in the event of deterioration by the borrower or because of capital restrictions being imposed on the bank by regulators.

A noteworthy trend regarding credit lines is the rapid growth of the standby letter of credit, which guarantees that the bank will make funds available if the company cannot or does not wish to meet a major financial obligation. This constitutes one form of guarantee a bank can provide for borrowers.[4]

---

[3]The banks give themselves the flexibility to deny some borrowers credit if many requests are received at the same time. Thus total credit lines for a given bank exceed its ability to finance them simultaneously. Furthermore, material changes in the potential borrower's financial condition might result in the bank's denial of credit for an uncommitted line, although this is rare.

[4]Commitments and contingent claims that banks make include financial guarantees and trade finance instruments. Financial guarantees include standby letters of credit, lines of credit, revolving loan commitments, note issuance facilities, and no recourse securitization. Trade finance services offered by banks include commercial letters of credit and acceptance participations. These are profiled briefly in George Hempel, Alan B. Coleman and Donald G. Simonson. 1990. *Bank Management.* 3d. ed. New York: John Wiley & Sons:46–47, and in some depth in M. K. Lewis and K.T. Davis. 1987. *Domestic and International Banking*. Cambridge, MA: MIT, Chapters 4 and 8.

Letter of Credit

A **letter of credit** (LOC) is a promise, generally by a bank, to make payment to a party on presentation of a draft provided that the party complies with certain documentary requirements as stated in the LOC agreement. The net effect of the LOC is to trade the credit of a well-known bank for that of a perhaps lesser-known corporate borrower. LOCs are generally a required feature of international borrowing.

Banker's Acceptance

A **banker's acceptance** is a time draft drawn against a deposit in a commercial bank but with payment at maturity guaranteed by the bank. The original time draft usually is a result of international transactions between importers and exporters.

For example, a US importer wishing to import goods from abroad may request its bank to issue a letter of credit on its behalf in favor of the foreign seller. If the bank finds the importer's credit standing satisfactory, it will issue such a letter, authorizing the foreign exporter to draw a time draft on it in payment for the goods delivered. Equipped with this authorization, the exporter can discount the time draft with its bank when it ships the goods, thereby receiving payment immediately; the foreign bank then forwards the time draft, along with the shipping documents, to its correspondent bank in the United States. Generally, the US correspondent bank will present the time draft for "acceptance" at the importer's bank, which forwards the shipping documents to the importer, who now may claim the shipment. Once accepted by the importer's bank, the time draft becomes a negotiable money market security, referred to as a bankers acceptance that trades in the money market until the maturity date of the time draft.

Reverse Repurchase Agreement

Repurchase agreements were discussed in Chapter 15 as a short-term investment alternative. In essence, a **reverse repurchase agreement** (a reverse repo) is the other side of the repurchase agreement transaction. In this case, a corporate investment manager may negotiate with its bank to sell to the bank a specific dollar amount of marketable securities currently held in the firm's investment portfolio at a specified price. Thus the party currently holding the securities initiates reverse repos. In addition, the contract stipulates that the selling corporation agrees to repurchase the designated securities at the same price plus a stipulated amount of interest in an agreed on number of days in the future. Most repos or reverse repos are overnight or 1-day contracts.

Such an agreement might be used to obtain a quick infusion of cash to offset the delay of forecasted cash receipts without actually liquidating a portion of the firm's investment portfolio. Such transactions can also be useful for end-of-year financial statement window dressing.

Commercial Paper

Commercial paper is a short-term promissory note issued by a corporation for a fixed maturity at a fixed yield. It is usually issued in bearer form with a minimum denomination of $100,000. Historically, commercial paper was unsecured. However, since the failure of the Penn Central Transportation Company in 1970, firms have had to support new issues of commercial paper through dealer networks with bank lines of credit or letters of credit. Maturities can be tailored to fit the need of the issuing corporation and range from 1 to 270 days. Securities with maturities greater than 270 days must be registered with the Securities and Exchange Commission, a relatively expensive and time-consuming exercise. Most commercial paper issues carry an original maturity of less than 180 days and the average is about 30 days.

Commercial paper can be issued directly by the borrower itself or through a dealer network. Generally, commercial finance companies such as General Motors Acceptance Corporation (GMAC) and bank holding companies directly issue their paper and most nonfinancial firms use commercial paper dealers to facilitate the issue of new commercial paper. Dealers act very much like investment banking underwriters. They not only distribute the paper, they may also advise their clients on terms of the paper regarding price and maturity.

There are two pricing formats for commercial paper. Most commercial paper is sold on a **discount basis,** similar to Treasury bills. The paper is sold at a price less than its face value or maturity value. The interest paid to the investor is thus the difference between the proceeds of the issue and the dollar amount of the face value. Discounted commercial paper is by far the more popular pricing format. An alternative, and less popular pricing format, is commercial paper that is **interest-bearing.** In this case, the paper has a face value and the interest paid is based on a quoted rate based on the face value. At maturity, the issuer repays the face value along with the appropriate amount of interest.

Yields offered by commercial paper exceed those on comparable maturity Treasury bills because of the credit risk associated with the issuer. Although only the most creditworthy firms can issue commercial paper, some credit risk remains. However, the yields on commercial paper are generally less than the effective cost of bank lines of credit, which explains why banks have lost a substantial portion of their short-term lending to firms that can access the commercial paper market.

Exhibit 16-3 shows the dollar volume of financing obtained over a 20-year period through three major sources including commercial paper, bankers acceptances, and commercial loans.

Commercial paper is rated by five different agencies including Standard & Poor's; Moody's; McCarthy, Crisant, Maffei, Inc.; Duff and Phelps, Inc.; and Fitch Investor Services Corporation. Standard & Poor's ratings range from A, for the most creditworthy, to D, the least creditworthy. Within the A category, the agency further refines the rating with a 1, 2, or 3. The A-1 rating, for example, "indicates that the degree of safety regarding timely payment is either overwhelming or strong," with the 2 and 3 designation indicating slightly less strength. Finally, the agency adds a "+" to the A-1 rating for the financially strongest companies. So the highest-rated company would carry a rating of A-1+. Ratings are important because the better the rating, the lower the borrowing cost.

A good example demonstrating the intricacies of commercial paper is the Salomon Brothers situation in 1991. Salomon Brothers, like most other major investment banking firms, used a backup line of credit to support its outstanding commercial paper.

EXHIBIT 16-3
Three Major Financing Sources (billions of $)

Source	1980	1985	1990	1995	2000
Commercial paper	$125.1	$300.8	$561.1	$671.5	$1,428.6
Bankers acceptances	54.7	68.1	54.7	29.8	NA
Commercial and industrial loans	323.1	499.5	648.1	718.3	1,029.1

SOURCE: Federal Reserve Bulletin, various issues.

FOCUS ON PRACTICE[7]

COMMERCIAL PAPER USAGE COMPARED TO BANK CREDIT According to a survey administered December 9 through 16, 1999, by the Association for Financial Professionals, large and mid-sized corporations looking for short-term credit are increasingly turning away from commercial banks and toward the commercial paper market. For these firms, bank credit accounted for approximately 43 percent of their total corporate borrowings. This is expected to drop to 37 percent in the coming 2 years, which is a continuation of a trend that saw bank credit accounting for over 50 percent of corporate borrowings 2 years earlier. During this 4-year period, the use of commercial paper is expected to increase from 13 percent of borrowings to 18 percent. The survey was administered to senior level financial professionals at companies with revenues of $100 million or more.

[7]1999. Survey results: Changes in the Short-term credit market. *Association for Financial Professionals* December 21:3.

During 1991, Salomon had a $2 billion credit line at its disposal for this purpose. The credit line generally covered a quarter of the total paper outstanding with unencumbered securities guaranteeing the balance. For Salomon to have a guarantee of the funds available, it had to pay an annual commitment fee of between 10 and 15 basis points on the credit line and an interest rate of 25 basis points above LIBOR on funds drawn down. Salomon was required to renew $500 million of the $2 billion line every 3 months.

During the fall of 1991, after Salomon's disclosure of its illegal bidding tactics in the government bond auction, Salomon's financial prospects changed dramatically. There were three basic responses to the Salomon situation. First, Salomon began to consider reducing the size of its credit line. This was partly a response to its reduced need for commercial paper because Salomon's business activities were shrinking as a result of its illegal activities. Second, the rating agencies were reevaluating Salomon's liquidity situation and its ability to fund its commercial paper to determine whether or not a rating change was needed. Finally, the banks that held Salomon's credit lines were reassessing the appropriate premium to charge as well as renegotiating the bank syndicate arrangement offering the line.[5]

Many top rated US corporations are taking advantage of placing euro commercial paper. There are many advantages of issuing commercial paper to foreign investors. First, as long as commercial paper is targeted for foreign investors, it is not subject to several Securities and Exchange Commission requirements. This generally results in some cost and paperwork savings. Second, the euro commercial paper (CP) market is name-oriented and it is uncommon for euro commercial paper to be rated. For those companies that have international name recognition, this offers additional cost savings because rating agencies charge for their services. Finally, although domestic issues require a back-up credit facility, euro CP programs generally require no such collateral.

The euro market differs from its US counterpart in that the maturities of euro CP are generally longer than domestic CP maturities. Euro paper generally carries maturities that average in the 60- to 90-day range, and the average maturity for US domestic CP is in the 30-day range. In addition, US companies are effectively limited to issuing euro CP for a maximum of 183-day maturities because of US withholding tax considerations.[6] Thus financial managers at large multinational US corporations can compare effective rates domestically against their euro CP counterparts to trim additional basis points from the cost of their short-term financing strategies.

[5]For additional information on the Salomon credit line see: Steven Lipin. 1991. Salomon reduces bank credit line. *The Wall Street Journal* September 23:C1.

[6]Alan Taylor. 1986. Euro CP. *Cashflow* October:50.

Asset-Based Loans

Asset-based loans represent a source of financing obtained from a bank or commercial finance company secured by accounts receivable or inventory. Two of the more prominent commercial finance companies include CIT Group and GE Capital. Asset-based loans are generally more expensive than unsecured financing as a result of the transactions costs of monitoring the collateral, and the fact that such collateral has been pledged indicates that the loan has some degree of risk of nonrepayment. For example, the company may have already borrowed all of the unsecured funds it can get and is now turning to secured financing sources.

RECEIVABLES FINANCING.   The first asset-based financing source to be discussed is the **pledging of receivables.** This is a situation in which a lender, such as a commercial bank or a commercial finance company, makes a loan protected by a lien placed on a certain portion of the firm's receivables. In those cases in which receivables represent a major portion of financing need, this represents an effective method of financing.

There are three basic drawbacks to this type of financial arrangement. First, a receivable does not represent a tangible piece of property, and the lending institution will rarely lend 100 percent of the book value of the receivables. Indeed the ratio of loan value to collateral value may not be higher than 50 percent depending on the perceived quality of the receivables. Second, the lender requires the borrower to keep detailed records of any change in the status of the pledged receivables. Finally, risk remains with the borrower. If the receivable is not collected, the borrower must still repay the lending institution.

Loans based on pledging receivables are typically obtained from both commercial banks and commercial finance companies. The main difference between these two lending institutions, from the borrower's standpoint, is that commercial finance companies usually allow a greater loan-to-collateral ratio but, in so doing, charge a higher rate of interest on the loan (about 5 percentage points above prime).

The second receivables financing technique is **factoring.** A factor is a corporation that participates as an original party to the sale of a product on credit. The factor makes the decision involving assessment of the buyer's credit-worthiness. In this situation, the seller of the product never becomes the creditor and is not held responsible for any bad debts. In this capacity, the factor acts as a substitute for an internal credit department for the seller. The seller receives its money in a stated number of days after the end of the credit period. This, in itself, is not a financing arrangement in the strict sense of the word. Rather it is a process in which a company can sell on credit without establishing a credit department.

What if the seller needs its money earlier than at the end of the credit period? The seller is basically holding only one receivable called due from factor rather than a multitude of receivables from many different customers. This receivable can effectively be pledged as collateral for a short-term loan from the seller's commercial bank. The bank finds it much easier to evaluate the creditworthiness of a large, nationally known factoring company than a multitude of individual customers spread throughout the nation.

Some factors actually "buy" receivables from companies for cash—usually at a stated discount from face value of the receivables. It is important for the seller to know whether the receivables are sold with or without recourse. If the receivables are sold **with recourse,** then the factor can demand funds returned for uncollected receivables. If the receivables are sold **without recourse** then the seller is not liable for uncollected receivables.

An example of nonrecourse factoring arrangement is the MasterCard and Visa credit card operations. The customer purchases an item from a particular retail outlet but pays the factor, either Visa or MasterCard. These companies provide the credit check for the selling company and an established payment pattern usually for a fee of around 3 percent. The company selling the product receives payment from the credit card company and the credit card company is at risk if the customer defaults on the payment.

INVENTORY FINANCING. **Inventory financing** is an extremely critical component of the total financial plan of most corporations. This is because, historically, inventory has generally represented a significant portion of the corporation's total working capital, and as we have seen, inventory represents a resource commitment that has yet to release cash and will not do so until the item is sold and cash collected. In terms of volume, total business inventory is in the hundreds of billions of dollars. Inventory financing can take several different forms.

Floating Lien. A **floating lien** is very general in nature. Basically, under this type of arrangement the borrower pledges its inventories "in general" without any particular specification. Under this type of arrangement, the lender typically only lends a relatively small fraction of the total value of the inventory.

Trust Receipts. A **trust receipt loan** is just the opposite of a floating lien. In this situation, a serial number or some other readily identifiable mark notes the collateralized inventory items. Thus the lender has a direct lien on a specific inventory item. This type of arrangement is suitable for relatively expensive and low turnover items such as automobiles, consumer durables, and industrial machinery and equipment. Because the inventory is easily identifiable by serial number, the lender allows it to remain on the borrower's premises. As the inventory is sold, the borrower remits payment on the loan along with accrued interest. The lender then releases the lien and the appropriate item.

Commercial banks, commercial finance companies, and captive finance companies issue receipt loans. For example, GMAC, a captive finance company of General Motors Corporation, makes these types of loans to GM's dealers, also known as floor planning.

Warehouse Receipts. From a lending institution's viewpoint, the main inventory-financing problem is securing the collateral—the inventory item.

One method of inventory financing is called field warehousing. This technique results in advances issued against field warehouse receipts. Essentially, a **field warehouse** may be nothing more than a segregated area of the borrower's facility housing the pledged inventory. A third-party firm is responsible for issuing the receipts, which ensures that the pledged items are physically located on the premises. These warehouse receipts are viewed by lending institutions as acceptable collateral for the basis of a loan. In a sense, the pledged inventory items are in the possession of the field warehouse firm—not the borrower.

The problem with this financing technique is that it is rather inflexible. The pledged inventory items must be segregated and stored in a mutually acceptable location. In addition, this type of arrangement is not really feasible for small inventory items that have a frequent turnover. The reason is that before the field-warehousing firm can release the item, it must receive approval to do so from the lending institution.

EXHIBIT 16-4

A Comparison of Average Short-Term Financing Rates for 1994 through 1999

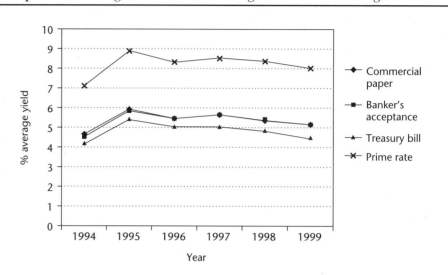

A **terminal warehouse agreement** is similar to a field warehouse agreement except that in this case the inventories pledged as collateral are moved to a public warehouse that is physically separated from the borrower's premises. This agreement gives the lender more security for the pledged inventory items.

SECURITIZATION.   **Securitization** involves issuing debt securities collateralized by a pool of selected financial assets such as mortgages, auto loans, or credit card receivables to name a few. Banks and large finance companies have issued increasingly larger amounts of commercial paper securitized in such a fashion. It is not uncommon for financing rates on such paper to be cheaper than rates obtained on more conventional bank financing.

Trends in Lending Services

Many banks are going after smaller companies as part of their client base. For example, Wells Fargo has begun offering small businesses a credit card that acts as a committed line of credit. For larger corporations, lending services are more extensive. When the loan principal is very large, a group (syndicate) of banks will jointly make the loan, spreading the risk. This adds complexity to attempted restructuring, as in the case of Trans World Airlines' efforts at negotiating with a syndicate of 92 banks during its financial crisis in the late 1990s. Participations involving other nonfinancial corporations also have appeared, offering a substitute for commercial paper borrowings.

Comparing Short-Term Financing Rates

Exhibit 16-4 displays comparative yields on many of the short-term financing alternatives previously discussed. The 3-month Treasury bill rate is also included for comparison purposes.

THE EFFECTIVE COST OF SHORT-TERM FINANCING

Short-term financing arrangements have several features that cause the stated interest rate on the financing to be different from the **effective interest rate.** A very general formula that forms the basis for our discussion is shown in Equation 16-1.

$$\text{Effective Rate} = \frac{\text{Out-of-pocket expenses}}{\text{Usable Funds}} \times \frac{365}{M} \qquad \text{(16-1)}$$

Out-of-pocket expenses include interest expense and fees. Interest expense is based on the stated interest rate and the amount borrowed over the funding period. Fees include commitment fees charged by the bank for the total amount of funds the bank stands ready to lend to the firm through a line of credit or a letter of credit facility, letter of credit fees, or commercial paper dealer fees. **Usable funds** represent the net proceeds the firm receives from the financing vehicle. If funds are received through a credit line, the amount received may be less than the amount borrowed if the bank requires the firm to leave compensating balances as a percent of the amount borrowed. If funds are received through an issue of commercial paper, then the amount received is reduced by the discounted interest paid.

The final part of Equation 16-1 annualizes the length of the borrowing period, M, assuming that it is 1 year or less. The effective rate thus calculated is the annualized effective simple interest rate on the financing arrangement. This equation is applied to commercial paper and a bank credit line facility in the following sections.

Effective Cost of Commercial Paper

The treasurer at Consolidated Trailways, Inc., is preparing a new issue of commercial paper through a dealer network. Commercial paper is a typical source of financing for Consolidated and the firm generally has several million dollars of paper outstanding throughout the year. In discussing the new issue with its commercial paper dealer, Consolidated has learned that new 30-day issues in the range of $1 to $5 million can be priced to sell at a 9-percent discount rate. The dealer's fee will be an annual rate of 1/8 of 1 percent and the commitment fee on a back-up line of credit will be an annual rate of .25 percent. The treasurer wants to know what the effective rate of issuing $3 million of commercial paper will be.

OUT-OF-POCKET COSTS To apply Equation 16-1, the treasurer needs to determine the value of two variables: out-of-pocket costs and usable funds. Let's start with out-of-pocket costs. First, the major component of out-of-pocket costs is the interest that Consolidated will have to pay. The commercial paper will be issued on a discount basis; the difference between the face amount and the discounted price is the interest that the firm pays. The face amount is the $3 million stated earlier. The discounted price is the face amount minus 30 days interest, 30 days being the maturity of the paper. The discount price is $2,977,500 = $3 million − (.09 × (30/360) × $3 million). The interest paid is thus $22,500. Note that the interest computation uses a 360-day year, which is the convention with discount rates. The dealer's fee is .125 percent, which costs the firm $312.50 = $3 million × .00125 × (30/360). The commitment fee for the back-up line of credit is $625 = $3 million × (.0025 × (30/360)). The total out-of-pocket cost is the sum of the interest expense, dealer fee, and bank commitment fee, which totals $23,437.50 = $22,500 + $312.50 + $625.

USABLE FUNDS.   Next, the dollar amount of usable funds must be determined. The treasurer has determined that the discount price of the $3 million issue will result in proceeds of $2,977,500, which is equal to the face value minus the discount interest at the asked rate.

EFFECTIVE INTEREST RATE.   Plugging the values for the out-of-pocket costs and usable funds into Equation 16-1 results in the effective annualized interest rate for the 30-day commercial paper.

$$\text{Effective Rate} = \frac{\$23,437.50}{\$2,977,500} \times \frac{365}{30}$$

$$\text{Effective Rate} = .0958 \text{ or } 9.58\%$$

The effective cost of the paper is 58 basis points above the stated asked discount rate of 9 percent. Note the money market convention that effective rates are based on a 365-day year rather than a 360-day year.

Had Consolidated not been a regular issuer of commercial paper, using a line of credit as a back-up facility might not be appropriate. Credit lines are not generally set up for periods less than 1 year. Therefore the annual cost of the credit line will have to be allocated to the 30-day financing period and then annualized. This will result in an out of pocket cost of $30,312.50 = $22,500 + $312.50 + $7,500. The $7,500 is the annual cost of the credit line commitment fee and must now be allocated in total to the 30-day financing period. Usable funds will remain unchanged. The effective rate then becomes 12.39 percent. In this case, the use of a letter of credit rather than a line of credit as a back-up facility is more appropriate. A letter of credit can be designed to be in effect for any length of period necessary.

FINANCIAL DILEMMA REVISITED

As indicated in the dilemma box presented at the beginning of the chapter, the treasurer at Beco, Inc., arranged for a line of credit with its bank. The line is for $100,000, which can be drawn down at any time during the year, but the line must be fully repaid by the end of the year. The stated rate on funds borrowed was set at 10 percent and the bank assessed a fee of 1/4 of a percent on the unused portion of the line. Beco is required to maintain a compensating balance of 20 percent of the funds borrowed. Beco's cash management system keeps all current balances fully invested so it essentially must borrow the balances required for compensation. Over the course of the year Beco borrows an average of $60,000 for the year. The interest paid is $6,000 = $60,000 × .10 and the commitment fee paid is $100 = ($100,000−$60,000) × .0025. Although Beco borrows an average of $60,000, $12,000 = $60,000 × .20, of that must remain at the bank as a compensating balance leaving $48,000 of usable funds. Applying Equation 16-1, Beco's effective rate of interest for the year is:

$$\text{Effective Rate} = \frac{\$6,000 + \$100}{\$48,000} \times \frac{365}{365}$$

$$\text{Effective Rate} = .1271 \text{ or } 12.71\%$$

Beco is effectively borrowing at a rate of 12.71 percent rather than the stated interest rate of 10 percent. The effective rate is 271 basis points higher than the stated rate because of the fee and more importantly because of the compensating balance requirements reducing the usable amount of funds.

Suppose that Beco had been carrying idle balances at the bank that could be used as compensating balances. Because the firm only received the use of $48,000 we recalculate the effective rate assuming Beco borrows $48,000 and the compensating balances are covered by existing cash balances at the bank. The interest expense is $4,800 = $48,000 × .10 and the fee is $130 = ($100,000−$48,000) × .0025. The dollar amount of usable funds in this case is equal to the $48,000 borrowed. The effective rate is:

$$\text{Effective rate} = \frac{\$4,800 + \$130}{\$48,000} \times \frac{365}{365}$$

$$\text{Effective rate} = .1027 \text{ or } 10.27\%$$

In this case, the effective rate is only 27 basis points above the stated rate of 10 percent solely because of the commitment fee. The commitment fee can be reduced if the firm reduces the size of the credit line to an amount closer to the amount borrowed. However, remember that the $48,000 borrowed is an average and the firm may actually need to borrow as much as $100,000 at some point during the year. The point here is that setting a credit line for an excessive amount is expensive and effective cash forecasting should be used to estimate the maximum borrowings needed.

SUMMARY

The short-term financing alternatives discussed in this chapter differ from spontaneous financing provided through trade credit and accruals as discussed in Chapter 7. The financing sources discussed in this chapter are discretionary, the use of which must be explicitly sought.

The chapter began with a discussion of financial strategy focusing on the maturity decision. The question of managing the maturity structure of the firm's financing sources is difficult, but three different strategies to mitigate this difficulty were discussed: the aggressive strategy, the conservative strategy, and the moderate strategy.

Attention then turned to a discussion of the major forms of short-term financing available. Each of the major short-term sources was described and the basic characteristics outlined.

The chapter concluded with a discussion of calculating the effective rate of interest on two popular forms of short-term financing: a bank credit line and commercial paper. Commercial paper was chosen because it offered a good example of non-bank financing and the inclusion of dealer spreads and commitment fees. The bank credit line financing source was chosen because it includes factors, such as compensating balances, that are not a part of commercial paper issues.

Short-term financing is an important component of maintaining the firm's liquidity. The financial manager should forecast the firm's cash position on a regular basis and then have in place contingency financing sources to handle forecasted as well as unexpected cash needs. Effective financing of the firm's short-term financing position impacts the firm's liquidity position and so ultimately affects its value.

Useful Web Sites

Integral Development Corporation: www.CFOWeb.com
Export Financing Matchmaker: www.ita.doc.gov/td/efm

Commercial Finance Association: www.cfa.com
KPMG LLP: www.kpmginsiders.com

Questions

1. How do cash forecasting and short-term borrowing strategies relate?
2. Compare and contrast the three short-term borrowing strategies. Which strategy generally results in the lowest borrowing cost? The highest borrowing cost? The most solvency? The least solvency?
3. How does the amount of buffer that a treasurer decides to use when establishing a line of credit affect the effective cost of the credit line?
4. What factors cause the nominal rate on a credit line to differ from its effective rate?
5. What factors cause the nominal rate on commercial paper to differ from its effective rate?
6. How does a firm's short-term financing strategy impact its liquidity?

Problems

1. You are provided the following 10 years of asset data for Smacker's Candy Company.

Year	Current	Fixed	Total
2001	$100	$100	$200
2002	130	110	240
2003	150	120	270
2004	140	130	270
2005	170	140	310
2006	190	150	340
2007	180	160	340
2008	210	170	380
2009	230	180	410
2010	220	190	410

   a. Draw a simple graph of the data with assets on the vertical axis and time on the horizontal axis.
   b. Graphically depict what might be considered to be the level of permanent current assets.
   c. Suppose that Smacker uses the aggressive strategy to finance these assets. Indicate this financing strategy on your graph, and discuss the financial implications of using this particular strategy.
   d. Suppose that Smacker employs the conservative strategy to finance its assets. Indicate this financing strategy on your graph and discuss its implication.
   e. Suppose that Smacker decides to employ the moderate strategy to finance its assets. Indicate this strategy on your graph and discuss its implication.
2. Gilmore, Inc., builds recreational equipment. Its sales are very seasonal; most sales occur between February and August. The following data contain some working capital to sales ratios as well as a sales projection for the next four quarters:

$$\frac{\text{Cash} + \text{Mkt Sec.} + \text{A/R} + \text{Inventory}}{\text{Sales}} = .25$$

$$\frac{\text{Accounts Payable}}{\text{Sales}} = .10$$

(in the table below, dollars are in millions)

	Jan-Mar	Apr-Jun	Jul-Sept	Oct-Dec
Sales	$10	$40	$20	$10
Purchases	18	10	5	5

Gilmore's level of net fixed assets is $1,500,000, and its capital structure consists of $1,500,000 of shareholders' equity. Current liabilities consist solely of accounts payable. Net income as a percentage of sales is forecasted to be 5 percent for the coming year. Dividends equal to net income are paid out.

a. Calculate Gilmore's balance sheet for each of the four projected quarters. Use the following form:

Cash+Mkt Sec+A/R+Inventory Net Fixed Assets	Accounts Payable New Loans Shareholders' equity

Force the balance sheets to balance by putting new financing needs in the new loans account.

b. Calculate the current ratio for Gilmore at the end of each quarter for each of the three financing strategies: aggressive, conservative, and moderate (using half long-term and half short-term financing).

c. Discuss your results in part *b* regarding the impact that financing strategy has on Gilmore's solvency.

d. What options are open to Gilmore if it does not want to increase borrowing?

3. Sarah, treasurer for SAFECO Instruments, Inc., updated her firm's short-term cash forecast only to discover that the firm will suffer a cash shortage of $7.5 million for a period of 2 months or 60 days. SAFECO issues commercial paper sporadically and currently has none outstanding. One alternative is to liquidate a portion of her marketable securities portfolio, but with interest rates up, this is not a good alternative. She just learned from one of her commercial paper dealers that paper in the 60-day range is in demand by investors and that the asked discount rates are comparably good at about 7.5 percent. The dealer's annual fee is 15 basis points and the annual commitment fee on a back up line of credit is 25 basis points. Estimate the effective cost of the commercial paper assuming this is the only commercial paper issue she will make during the year.

Sarah was also approached by a bank that wants her company's business. This bank is offering a letter of credit back-up facility with an annual fee of 50 basis points rather than a line of credit. Sarah wonders how this will affect the cost of the commercial paper issue because the fee seemed a little high.

4. Ralph, treasurer for M and M Products, Inc., recently updated his firm's short-term cash forecast only to discover that the firm will suffer a cash shortage of $12 million for a period of 30 days. One alternative is to liquidate a portion of his marketable securities portfolio, but with interest rates up, this is not a good alternative. Ralph just learned from one of his commercial paper dealers that paper in the 30-day range is in demand and that asked discount rates are comparably good at about 9 percent. The dealer's annual fee is 20 basis points and the annual commitment fee on a back up line of credit is 50 basis points.

a. Estimate the effective cost of the commercial paper assuming that this is the only commercial paper issue planned for the year.

b. Estimate the effective cost of the commercial paper assuming that there will be recurring issues of commercial paper all year long.

5. You recently approached your bank about establishing a credit line facility. The terms offered by your bank include a nominal rate of prime +1.5 percent (prime is currently 8 percent) on the amount borrowed, a commitment fee of 25 basis points on the unused portion of the credit line, and a compensating balance of 10 percent on the amount borrowed.

   You decide to establish the line for $65 million. Over the course of a year, you anticipate the average amount borrowed to be $40 million. Your firm keeps no balances at the bank and pays fees for all cash management services.

   a. Estimate the cost of the credit line.

   b. Assume that the firm does have cash balances to cover the required compensating balances resulting from the credit line borrowings. Estimate the effective cost of the credit line.

6. As treasurer of your firm, you wish to establish a credit line facility to cover an expected average annual borrowing of $50 million. You have asked two banks to submit proposals for a credit line. Based on a credit line of $55 million, Bank of the West proposes a nominal rate of 6 percent, a commitment fee of .25 percent on the unused portion of the credit line and a 20 percent compensating balance on the amount borrowed. Bank of the East offers a rate of 5.75 percent if the size of the credit line is $70 million. In addition, the commitment fee on the unused portion of the credit line is 20 basis points and compensating balances of 25 percent will be required on the amount borrowed.

   Calculate the effective cost of both proposals and indicate which proposal should be accepted.

FOCUSED CASE
Jones Salvage and Recycling, Inc. (B)

Note: This is a continuation of the Jones Salvage and Recycling, Inc. (A) case found immediately following Chapter 13. That case concluded with a monthly forecasted income statement, cash budget, and balance sheet for the first 6 months of the new year. Jones (B) will use that information to determine the financing and investment strategy that is best for Jones to use.

Mr. Jones was very impressed with the ability of Carl Malone, the company's financial manager, to forecast the company's cash position for the coming 6 months and felt that this would put the company in a great position to prevent the recurring liquidity crises the company has faced each spring. Historically, although the company has always been able to get the needed financing, it was obvious that "eleventh hour" nature of its loan requests were very frustrating to the company's bank. Armed with the projected financial statements, Jones asked Malone to approach the bank and develop a financing strategy in anticipation of the coming 6 months.

During the discussions with the bank's lending officer, Malone asked for and received the following interest rate projections that the bank uses for its planning purposes. One thing that was painfully obvious to Jones was the dramatic jump in interest rates expected to occur in January. In addition, it appeared that interest rates would continue to rise for the next several months. Mr. Malone confirmed this and observed that the current Fed chairman was a real inflation hawk and was taking a very aggressive approach to controlling inflation by tightening up bank credit. The raw data comes from an economic forecasting service and then the bank adjusts the raw data to arrive at its projected lending rates for loans of various maturities for the local market. A table of the interest rate data follows:

Month	MS (30 day)	MS (90 day)	NP (30 day)	NP (90 day)	NP (180 day)	LTD
January	6.00%	6.75%	8.00%	8.50%	9.50%	10.00%
February	7.00%	7.00%	9.50%	9.50%	9.50%	9.50%
March	8.00%	7.50%	10.50%	10.00%	9.50%	9.00%
April	7.50%	7.50%	12.00%	10.00%	9.50%	9.00%
May	7.00%	7.00%	10.00%	10.50%	10.00%	9.50%
June	6.00%	6.00%	9.00%	10.00%	11.00%	12.00%

The company has limited investment and financing opportunities. Investments can only be made in 30-day and 90-day marketable securities (MS). Mr. Malone's discussions with the bank lending officer centered on 30-day, 90-day, and 180-day loans. Although long-term financing is a possibility, Mr. Malone will only consider it for the month of January, which is also the case for the 6-month loan.

The financial planning model Jones uses assumes that investments and financing are done at the end of the month, which means no interest is earned or paid until the following month. Interest is received and paid on a monthly basis. The current mortgage loan is carrying an interest rate of 8 percent and no principal payments will be made until December. The current 30-day note payable is carrying an interest rate of 6 percent. Note the following restrictions: 180-day and long-term financing can only be taken out in January; 90-day notes cannot be taken out nor can 90-day MS be invested in during May or June; no financing is available during the month of June.

REQUIRED

1. Develop a financing and investment plan that will maximize the sum of net interest income of the 6-month planning period.
2. Develop a financing plan that is consistent with a conservative financing strategy as defined in Chapter 16. You should plan to keep all surplus cash over $1,000 invested.
3. Develop a financing plan that is consistent with the aggressive strategy as defined in Chapter 16. You should plan to keep all surplus cash over $1,000 invested.
4. Compare the month current ratio and net profit margin for each strategy. Discuss the trade-offs that the financial manager must consider when deciding on a strategy.

Appendix 16A

The Effective Cost of Credit Lines

This appendix develops a much more explicit and detailed model, based on the Hill, Sartoris, and Visscher approach, to estimating the effective cost of bank credit lines when compensating balances and commitment fees are present. The advantage of this model is that it can account for the exact timing and amount of borrowing over a year rather than just assuming an average borrowed amount as does the model discussed in Chapter 16.

The effective rate on a bank credit line is impacted by the nominal interest rate charged, the commitment fee, the structure of the compensating balance requirements, the seasonality of borrowing, and the difference between the maximum amount borrowed and the size of the credit line. The critical relationships are presented in Equations 16A-1 through 16A-4.

Equation 16A-1 states that the dollar amount of required compensating balances for month t is equal to the proportion a of the amount borrowed during the month plus the proportion b of the dollar level of the credit line established.

$$CMP_t = aTLOAN_t + bCRLN \qquad \text{(16A-1)}$$

CMP = the dollar amount of compensating balance required during month t

TLOAN = the total loan borrowed during month t

CRLN = the dollar amount of the credit line

    a = the percentage compensating balance required on the total amount borrowed

    b = the percentage compensating balance required on the size of the credit line

Equation 16A-2 states that the total loan during month t is equal to the total cumulative cash needs plus the dollar amount of compensating balances that must also be borrowed. If the firm has enough idle cash balances at the bank to offset the compensating balance requirement, then the total loan for the month will equal just the total cumulative cash needs.

$$TLOAN_t = TCCN_t + aTLOAN_t + bCRLN \qquad \text{(16A-2)}$$
TCCN = total cumulative cash needs

Equation 16A-3 calculates the size of the credit line. The credit line is equal to the maximum cumulative cash needs times one plus the buffer percentage plus the dollar amount compensating balances based on the maximum borrowing level that will equal the size of the credit line.

$$CRLN = (1+B) \max(TCCN_t) + aCRLN + bCRLN$$
$$\text{(16A-3)}$$

The variable B is the percentage amount of desired credit line buffer over the maximum total cumulative cash needs forecasted without consideration of the additional amount borrowed to satisfy compensating balance requirements.

Equation 16A-4 calculates the annual effective rate of interest based on the calculated out of pocket expenses and the dollar amount of usable funds.

$$I = \frac{i_t \times TLOAN_t + f \times CRLN}{TCCN_t/12} \qquad \text{(16A-4)}$$

f = the annual commitment fee rate based on the size of the credit line

i_t = the monthly interest rate for each month t

I = the annual effective rate of interest

The information required to implement the model includes a monthly forecast of the firm's cumulative cash needs, the nominal or stated interest rate on funds borrowed though the credit line, compensating balance parameters, and finally the percentage commitment fee. For demonstration purposes, assume the following forecast of a firm's total cumulative cash needs and credit line parameters provided by its bank.

TOTAL CUMULATIVE CASH NEEDS, TCCN$_t$

January	$50,000	July	$ 0
February	75,000	August	100,0000
March	75,000	September	150,0000
April	25,000	October	75,0000
May	0	November	50,0000
June	0	December	0

a = .05

b = .05

f = .005

i = .10/12

B = .20

The solution begins by solving for the size of the credit line, CRLN, using Equation 16A-3. In this equation, CRLN is substituted for TLOAN with the parameter a because we are solving for the size of the credit line consistent with our maximum borrowing, which is when TLOAN = CRLN. Plugging in the values for the variables in Equation 16A-3 results in a credit line of $200,000 as shown below.

CRLN = (1 + .20)×($150,000) + .05 × CRLN
                          + .05 × CRLN

CRLN = $200,000

Once CRLN is determined, the monthly total loan, TLOAN$_t$, can be solved using Equation 16A-2. This equation is shown below in a form that can directly solve for the dollar amount of the total loan for each month.

$TLOAN_t = TCCN_t + a\ TLOAN_t + b\ CRLN$

$(1-a)TLOAN_t = TCCN_t + bCRLN$

$TLOAN_t = TCCN_t/(1-a) + bCRLN/(1-a)$

MONTH	TCCN	TLOAN
January	$ 50,000	$ 63,158
February	75,000	89,474
March	75,000	89,474
April	25,000	36,842
May	0	10,526
June	0	10,526
July	0	10,526
August	100,000	115,789
September	150,000	168,421
October	75,000	89,474
November	50,000	63,158
December	0	10,526

Finally, having solved for the monthly TLOAN and the size of the credit line, CRLN, we have all the numbers necessary to solve for the annual effective rate of interest using Equation 16A-4. The effective interest rate paid on the credit line is 14.63 percent—a rate that is 463 basis points above the stated 10 percent rate. The additional basis points paid result from the 20 percent buffer, the compensating balance requirements and the commitment fee charged.

The usefulness of such a model can readily be seen when different banks offer different terms and you are trying to determine the terms that are most cost effective. Alternatively, you can perform a sensitivity analysis by varying the terms so that you can offer an alternative set of terms for your bank to consider. In fact, in the article by Hill and associates, they show how to solve for the incremental impact that the compensating balance terms, buffer size, and seasonality have on the effective rate.

Problems

A-1. The treasurer at AFC Videos, Inc., has established a credit line with its bank. AFC's estimated seasonal cumulative borrowing needs are shown below.

January	$100,000	July	$300,000
February	50,000	August	90,000
March	0	September	50,000
April	0	October	10,000
May	50,000	November	50,000
June	200,000	December	100,000

AFC's bank indicates the stated rate on the line will be 8 percent with a .5 percent commitment fee on the unused balance and 15 percent compensating balances on the amount borrowed. AFC's treasurer wants to establish the line with a 20 percent buffer. That is, the size of the credit line will be 20 percent above the maximum estimated amount borrowed. Estimate the effective annual rate of the credit line.

A-2. Repeat A-1, but now assume that the percent buffer is zero rather than the stated 20 percent. How much does the 20 percent buffer contribute to the effective cost of the credit line?

A-3. Repeat A-1, but now assume that AFC maintains average idle cash balances at its bank of $5,000 throughout the year. Reestimate the effective cost of the credit line.

A-4. The treasurer at Fun Corporation of USA, Inc., just established a credit line with its bank for the coming fiscal year. Fun Corporations's estimated seasonal cumulative borrowing needs are shown below.

January	$ 0	July	$200,000
February	0	August	100,000
March	0	September	25,000
April	50,000	October	0
May	100,000	November	0
June	300,000	December	0

Fun Corporation's loan officer indicates the stated rate on the line will be 8 percent with a .15 percent commitment fee on the unused credit line and 25 percent compensating balances on the amount borrowed. The treasurer wants to establish the line with a 10 percent buffer. That is, the size of the credit line would be 10 percent above the maximum estimated amount borrowed. Estimate the effective annual rate of the credit line.

A-5. Repeat A-4, but now assume that the percent buffer is zero rather than the stated 10 percent. How much does the 10 percent buffer contribute to the effective cost of the credit line?

A-6. Repeat A-5, but now assume that the treasurer maintains average idle cash balances at its bank of $40,000 throughout the year. Reestimate the effective cost of the credit line.

References

William Beranek, Christopher Cornwell; and Sunho Choi. 1995. External financing, liquidity, and capital expenditures. *The Journal of Financial Research* 18(2):207–222.

S. H. Griffiths and N.J. Robertson. 1987. Global cash: Short-term investing and borrowing overseas. *Journal of Cash Management* March/April:52–56.

B. W. Harries. 1971. How corporate bonds and commercial paper are rated. *Financial Executive* September:30–36.

N. C. Hill, W. L. Sartoris, and S.L. Visscher. 1983. The components of credit line borrowing cost. *Journal of Cash Management* October:47ff.

J. C. T. Mao. 1968. Application of linear programming to the short term financing decision. *Engineering Economist* Summer:221–241.

K. L. Stock. 1980. Asset-based financing: Borrowing and lender perspectives. *Journal of Commercial Bank Lending* December:31–46.

O. Williamson. 1988. Corporate finance and corporate governance. *Journal of Finance* July:567–592.

J. D. Stowe, C.J. Watson, and T.D. Robertson. 1980. Relationships between the two sides of the balance sheet: A canonical correlation analysis. *Journal of Finance* September:973–980.

CHAPTER 17

Managing Multinational Cash Flows

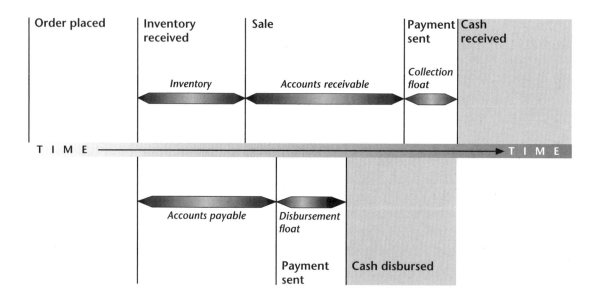

OBJECTIVES

After studying this chapter, you should be able to:

- Have an appreciation of the development of the current exchange rate system.
- Understand the basic driving forces that cause exchange rates to fluctuate.
- Gain a basic understanding of the various means by which firms can create internal structures to manage exchange rate fluctuations.
- Have an appreciation for the differences between the US and foreign banking systems.

Throughout this book, we have attempted to integrate the international aspects of short-term financial management decisions. This chapter presents an overview and synthesis of many of these areas, but, more importantly, the chapter also introduces some of the features that are unique to managing international cash flows, in particular managing the firm's exposure to movements in foreign currency exchange rates. The fact that managing international cash flows is different from managing domestic cash flows is highlighted by the fact that most large corporations have financial managers who specialize in domestic cash management and a different set of financial managers who are responsible for the international dimension of the firm's business.

This chapter focuses on the management of cash flows created through international transactions. For example, suppose an exporting firm sells to various countries and receives foreign currencies at a future date for the products sold. The exporter is exposed to exchange rate movements between the foreign currency received and the exporter's domestic currency. We develop a variety of strategies to manage these types of foreign exchange problems.

FINANCIAL DILEMMA

What Can Be Done About Uncertain Currency Exchange Rates?

A mid-size family-owned business in the pharmaceutical industry is based in Basel, Switzerland. The company's currency structure included 60 percent of sales in Swiss francs, 23 percent of sales invoiced in euros, 15 percent invoiced in US dollars, and the remainder in various other currencies. It had 11 bank accounts in Switzerland, Austria, and Germany, with non-interest bearing checking accounts and high interest line of credit accounts.[1]

[1]Regula Spottl. 2000. Reorganizing cash management and foreign exchange in an industrial company. www.gtnews.com, July 21.

EXCHANGE RATES

When a domestic corporation does business in a foreign country, currency exchange problems occur. For example, a US financial manager may buy products from a German supplier. If the German corporation decides to export, should it demand payment at the end of the stated credit terms in dollars or in euros? If it accepts payment in dollars, the US importer is able to transfer all currency exchange risk to the German supplier because when the German exporter receives dollars, it then must convert them to euros. If, instead, the German exporter demands payment in euros, then it transfers all currency exchange risk to the US importer. The importer must exchange dollars for euros and remit the invoice price in euros.

Exhibit 17-1 displays a comprehensive list of exchange rates for the world's major currencies stated in terms of US dollars per unit of foreign currency and unit of foreign currency per US dollar. A **foreign exchange rate** is the price of one currency stated in relation to the price of another currency. For example, according to Exhibit 17-1, on Thursday, December 14, 2000, one euro was valued at $.8915 or 1.1217 euros were worth 1 US dollar.

Fixed Versus Floating Exchange Rates

The exchange rate quotes shown in Exhibit 17-1 indicate the relative price of the various currencies at a particular time, specifically, December 14, 2000. Currently, exchange rates are free to change on a daily basis depending on the relative supply and demand for the currencies. However, this has not always been the case.

Before World War I, a gold standard existed in which all currencies were priced relative to gold and each country attempted to maintain the price relationships. Because of the disruption caused by the war, the gold standard was abolished and all currencies were allowed to float; that is, their exchange rates were allowed to fluctuate based on the supply and demand conditions for the currency relative to other currencies.

Following the depression and World War II, the major trading countries met in Bretton Woods, New Hampshire, and signed the **Bretton Woods Agreement.** This agreement essentially returned the world economy to a type of gold standard. The

EXHIBIT 17-1
Exchange Rate Quotes for Selected Currencies[2]

Country	Currency	US $ per unit of foreign currency	Unit of foreign currency per US $
Australia	Dollar	.5424	1.8435
Brazil	Real	.5092	1.9640
Britain	Pound	1.4731	.6788
Canada	Dollar	.6584	1.5189
China	Renminbi	.1208	8.2768
Greece	Drachma	.002616	382.26
India	Rupee	.003367	296.99
Israel	Shekel	.2442	4.0955
Japan	Yen	.008920	112.11
Saudi Arabia	Riyal	.2666	3.7509
Switzerland	Franc	.5920	1.6893
Thailand	Baht	.02299	43.500
	Euro	.8915	1.1217

[2]*Quotes for Thursday, December 14, 2000,* from the December 15, 2000 Wall Street Journal.

United States fixed the price of an ounce of gold at $35. Each country then fixed its currency in relation to the dollar. Only the US dollar was convertible into gold at a fixed price of $35 per ounce. Each country agreed to maintain its exchange rate into the dollar within 1 percent of this established price. This agreement essentially returned the world economy to a system of fixed foreign exchange rates.

The foreign exchange system created by the Bretton Woods Agreement worked well initially. However, by the late 1960s, problems were developing as evidenced by a large balance of payment deficits in the United States and other major trading countries. Inflation was increasing, and in the 1970s, the Organization of Petroleum Exporting Countries (OPEC) began to cause serious disruptions in the world economy through oil price shocks and oil embargoes. By this time, the fixed exchange rate system had already evolved into a system of "managed" floating rates in which exchange rates were allowed to float within boundaries wider than the 1 percent band determined at Bretton Woods.

The world economy continued to struggle as a result of rising rates of inflation, continuing balance of payments problems, and shocks created by OPEC. In particular, currency decisions made by the newly rich OPEC countries became a key to the stability of the world's currencies. As a result, the exchange rate boundaries were continually tested, and by 1976 the **Jamaica Agreement** was signed by the major trading nations, which created a system of floating exchange rates and the demonetization of gold.

Since the Jamaica Agreement in 1976, the only major change in the structure of the foreign exchange markets has been the development of **currency blocs** in which major European trading partners, members of the European Economic Community (EEC), have created a subset of controlled exchange rates between the currencies of the partners referred to as the European Monetary System (EMS). The outgrowth of the EMS is the creation of a new currency unit known as the **Euro** that represents a basket of currencies of the participating countries. The whole system, though, is then allowed to float relative to the currencies of those countries not included in the system. Thus the foreign exchange market is evolving into a system of floating currency blocs.

Spot Rates

Spot currency rates are exchange rate quotes based on immediate delivery of the currency being traded. Generally, a corporation that needs to purchase foreign currency contacts its bank. The bank purchases the desired currency through the interbank market; that is, spot exchange rate quotes are received from other banks wishing to sell the currency. Settlement of the interbank market transaction generally takes 1 to 2 days. The settlement date is referred to as the value date.

Forward Rates

A **forward currency rate** is an exchange rate between currencies that is contracted to exist at a future value date. The exchange rate is established at the time the forward contract is created, but payment and delivery do not occur until the maturity date of the forward contract, generally 30, 90, or 180 days in the future.

Exhibit 17-2 shows spot and forward rates that existed on Thursday, December 14, 2000, for selected foreign currencies as reported by *The Wall Street Journal*. According to the exhibit, a financial manager wishing to purchase British pounds sterling on the spot market could buy them at an exchange rate of $1.4731 per pound sterling. However, if the foreign currency was needed in 180 days, it could be purchased at an exchange rate of $1.4767.

EXHIBIT 17-2
Selected Spot and Forward Exchange Rates

COUNTRY (CURRENCY)	US $ EQUIVALENT
Britain (Pound)	1.4731 (Spot)
1-month forward	1.4740
3-month forward	1.4752
6-month forward	1.4767
Japan (Yen)	.008920 (Spot)
1-month forward	.008963
3-month forward	.009050
6-month forward	.009178
Switzerland (Franc)	.5920 (Spot)
1-month forward	.5937
3-month forward	.5967
6-month forward	.6008

Futures Rates

A **futures exchange rate** is similar in concept to a forward rate. It reflects the exchange rate at which currencies can be traded at a future date. Chapter 18 goes into more detail regarding futures contracts. The primary difference between a futures contract and a forward contract is standardization. A **futures contract** is standardized and is traded on a national market and a clearinghouse guarantees each trade. Thus a financial manager can purchase a foreign currency contract on one day and sell it on another day. A **forward contract** is a contract negotiated between the financial manager and a bank. It is not a negotiable instrument.

Another important difference between these two types of contracts is that **margin** must be posted when a futures contract is bought. This margin is generally only a fraction of the total value of the contract, but if the value of the contract falls, additional margin may be requested. A forward contract, on the other hand, requires no margin, and no cash is exchanged until the forward value date.

FACTORS AFFECTING EXCHANGE RATES

If demand for a particular currency exceeds the supply of that currency, then the relative value of that currency increases. Movements in the exchange rate between two currencies basically demonstrate the change in the relative values of the two currencies. For example, suppose the current exchange rate between British pounds and dollars is $1.47 per pound sterling and then increases to $1.60. This indicates that it takes more dollars to equal the value of a pound sterling resulting in a depreciation of the dollar and an appreciation of the pound relative to the dollar.

There are several factors that can cause exchange rates between any two currencies to change. One important factor is the relative level of interest rates that exist between the two countries. A country that has high interest rate levels relative to another country may experience excess demand for its currency as global investors purchase the currency to invest in that country's financial markets to take advantage of the relatively high interest rates. The **interest-rate parity hypothesis** suggests that exchange rates will adjust to offset the interest rate differential.

A second factor is the relative rate of inflation in one country compared with another. The **purchasing parity hypothesis** suggests that exchange rates between two countries will adjust to offset the relative rates of inflation between two countries. As one country experiences inflation at a rate greater than another country, its currency will be devalued relative to the currency of the country with the lower inflation rate.

A third factor affecting exchange rates is the respective governments' central bank reaction to changes in exchange rates caused by economic circumstances such as inflation. Historically, central banks have stepped in to purchase their currency when it begins to lose value relative to other currencies. The central bank's purpose in doing this is to reduce the supply of the currency, because a currency that is being devalued in the currency markets is one in which supply of the currency exceeds the demand for it. On the other hand, a currency's appreciation means that the respective currency is becoming more valuable relative to other currencies. The central bank might begin to sell its currency in the currency markets to increase supply for the purpose of stabilizing the exchange rate. An appreciating exchange rate will make that country's products more expensive overseas and will therefore hurt exports.

Economic and political factors generally change the supply and demand balance of the world's currencies. For example, during the period 1979 to 1986, the United States experienced relatively high interest rates, drawing a large increase of foreign investment to the US financial markets. Foreign investors must obtain the domestic currency before investing in domestic financial markets. Consequently, the US dollar appreciated dramatically compared with most other major currencies.

The impact that politics plays with exchange rates was evident when France shifted to a socialist government in 1981. France's major industries perceived this socialist government as a threat because they feared that the new government would nationalize industry. Consequently, the French franc was devalued dramatically in the currency markets by the flight of capital from francs into other currencies.

FOREIGN EXCHANGE EXPOSURE

Because exchange rates between currencies do change, the multinational corporation faces risks not experienced by a corporation doing all its business domestically. These risks associated with floating exchange rates include economic exposure, transaction exposure, and translation exposure.

Economic Exposure

Economic exposure is the possibility that the long-term net present value of a firm's expected cash flows will change as a result of unexpected changes in exchange rates. For example, a US exporter gains international sales and cash flows when the dollar depreciates against world currencies. This makes US goods cheaper relative to foreign goods, and demand for US goods increases.

Transaction Exposure

Transaction exposure relates to the gains or losses associated with the settlement of business transactions denominated in different currencies. For example, the transaction between the US importer and German exporter discussed earlier is an example of transaction exposure. Suppose the importer entered into a contract to purchase goods denominated in Euros with payment due in 90 days. The US importer faces transaction exposure because it must obtain Euros in 90 days to honor the contract. Although the contract is fixed in terms of Euros, it is not fixed in terms of US dollars, which the importer will use to purchase the Euros.

Translation Exposure

Translation exposure results when the balance sheet and income statement of a foreign subsidiary are translated into the parent company's domestic currency for consolidated financial reporting purposes. If exchange rates have changed during the financial reporting period, then a translation gain or loss occurs that affects the consolidated financial position of the parent company. For example, the assets of a foreign subsidiary of a US multinational corporation will experience a translation loss if the foreign currency depreciates relative to the currency in which the parent company's assets are denominated. Suppose the subsidiary is based in London and the subsidiary's assets are valued at 100 million pounds sterling. Now assume that the exchange rate changes from $1.50 per pound to $1.10 per pound over the accounting period. At the beginning of the accounting period, the 100 million pounds were worth $150 million; but at the end of the accounting period, the assets are only worth $110 million. The subsidiary's assets experienced a translation loss of $40 million.

The currency translation process for consolidating financial statements for a corporation with foreign subsidiaries is governed by the Financial Accounting Standards Board's Statement Number 52 (FAS 52). Under this ruling, translation exposure is based on the dollar value of all assets denominated in a foreign currency less the dollar value of all liabilities denominated in that currency. A translation gain or loss is then posted to a reserve account on the balance sheet rather than running it through the income statement as was done under FAS 8 prior to 1981.

MANAGING FOREIGN EXCHANGE EXPOSURE

A corporation that deals in one or more currencies other than its own domestic currency must be concerned about its exposure to changes in foreign exchange rates. This section addresses several different techniques for managing this risk exposure other than using exchange-traded instruments such as futures, options, and swaps. Most firms implement these internal strategies prior to using the kinds of strategies discussed in Chapter 18.

Avoidance

Perhaps the simplest way to manage the exposure is to avoid it altogether. Invoices can stipulate that only the selling firm's domestic currency will be accepted for payment of goods and services. However, this may cause ill will and loss of international business. In addition, this simply is not realistic for larger firms with multinational subsidiaries.

Leading and Lagging

Because exchange rates do fluctuate, one tool to manage fluctuating exchange rates is to try and take advantage of these changes by leading and lagging cash flows related to collections and payments in foreign currencies. **Leading** is the practice of accelerating collections or payments and **lagging** is the practice of delaying collections or payments.

Why would a firm wish to lag collections or lead payments? This seems to be the opposite of sound financial practice given what we know about the time value of money. However, lagging collections denominated in a foreign currency that is appreciating or accelerating payments of a currency that is expected to depreciate is a very sound financial policy.

An example will help demonstrate this strategy. Suppose a US importer has an invoice for 100,000 British pounds sterling. The payment is due in 60 days. However, the dollar is expected to continue to depreciate from the current $1.45 per pound to $1.55 in 60 days. The US importer can speed up payment by buying pounds sterling in the near future for $1.45 and paying the invoice costing $145,000. Waiting and buying pounds later when the dollar has depreciated results in the US importer paying $155,000 or an increase in cost of $10,000 over the 60-day credit period. Of course, a leading or lagging strategy is only effective if the firm guesses correctly about the direction of exchange rate movements. Thus when a firm anticipates that the domestic currency will appreciate, it should lead collections and lag payments. When it anticipates that the domestic currency will depreciate, it should lag collections and lead payments.

Netting

The first line of defense in managing foreign exchange exposure is to develop an information system that allows the firm to track its current and expected daily cash flows in all currencies in which it does business. This allows the cash manager to net outflows in one currency against inflows of the same currency reducing foreign exchange exposure to only the net difference. For example, payment of an invoice for 10,000 pounds sterling payable in 20 days might be covered by receipt of 10,000 of pounds sterling in 20 days as a result of selling activities in Great Britain. The firm therefore does not need to purchase sterling because that currency will be generated by the firm's multinational operations.

Bilateral netting is a system set up between two subsidiaries of the same company that transact between each other in different currencies. At the end of each month, typically, the transactions are netted against each other and the net difference is transferred.

Firms with more than two subsidiaries dealing in different currencies may use a **multilateral netting system.** Exhibit 17-3 demonstrates the basic structure of a multilateral netting system. Each subsidiary informs the central treasury management center, or in some cases its financial institution that manages its foreign exchange exposure, of all planned cross-border payments. To determine the netting transactions, payments are

EXHIBIT 17-3
A Typical Multilateral Netting System

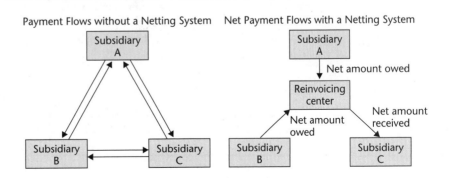

converted into a common reference currency and then payments are combined resulting in fewer and possibly larger currency transactions. Prior to the settlement date, each subsidiary is informed of the net amount to pay or to be received in its own currency.

Re-invoicing

A **re-invoicing center** can be used to centralize the monitoring and collecting of accounts receivable and for managing foreign exchange exposure. It is a company-owned subsidiary that buys goods from an exporting subsidiary in the subsidiary's currency and sells those goods to an importing subsidiary in its own currency. At the center of the system is a re-invoicing center that receives all the invoices from all the firm's subsidiaries. The re-invoicing center re-invoices only the net difference owed to each subsidiary. It is also common for the re-invoicing center to manage the firm's foreign currency exposure that results from the netting process. Although actual delivery of the goods occurs between the exporting and importing subsidiaries, it is common for the title to flow through the re-invoicing center. Both the netting system and the re-invoicing system can be used to implement a leading and lagging cash flow management system that can be effective in managing the liquidity of the organization by timing the cash inflows and outflows within the system.

Hedging

In most cases, some exposure to foreign exchange movements remain after the firm has netted all possible cash flows. The financial manager may wish to consider hedging the remaining exposure through the use of forward, futures, option, or swap contracts. In this section, we discuss the use of forward contracts and hedging through the use of futures, options, and swaps is discussed in Chapter 18.

A forward currency contract represents an agreement to buy or sell a specified amount of a stipulated foreign currency at a specified price on a specified date. The forward contract terms dealing with the amount, currency, and maturity are negotiable. There are, however, standard maturities for these contracts including 30-day, 90-day, and 180-day forward contracts and the forward exchange rates on many of these contracts are reported in *The Wall Street Journal* as was shown in Exhibit 17-2. According to this exhibit, the 90-day forward rate that could be obtained on Thursday, December 14, 2000, for the British pound was shown to be $1.4752 per pound. If a US importer needed British pounds to pay for an invoice in 90 days, the importer could contract today to purchase those pounds 90 days in the future at a rate of $1.4752 per pound.

This forward currency exchange market is primarily an interbank market because most of the volume of these contracts is composed of currency transactions between banks. The corporation wanting to purchase a forward contract must either contact a dealer or deal directly with its bank's foreign exchange department. Additional hedging strategies are developed in Chapter 18.

FINANCIAL DILEMMA REVISITED

The company hired a consultant who offered the following recommendations.

- Institute a "macrohedge" by using a multilateral system netting required foreign currencies to pay for imports against incoming foreign currencies from exports.

- Institute the use of "microhedges" using foreign currency option contracts related to large single transactions of goods for the purpose of securing an exchange rate guarantee.
- For foreign currency purchases and sales, the consultant recommends a time frame no longer than 6 months to avoid locking in prices for export markets that could result in loss of revenues or market share.
- The consultant negotiated new conditions on bank account debit and credit interest rates. The number of US dollar and euro accounts were reduced from 11 down to 4 accounts at banks in Switzerland, one in Austria, and one in Germany. As a result, the daily cash report immediately improved in quality and saved time in executing bank and account transfers.
- As a result, charges on term loans were reduced by up to 30 percent and the interest paid on overdrawn accounts reduced to zero.

FEATURES OF NON-US BANKING SYSTEMS

Non-US banking systems are quite different from their US counterparts. This section presents an overview of some of the more important differences between the US and foreign banking systems.

Check Clearing

It is common practice in non-US banking systems to value-date checks. Checks deposited are granted a **forward value date** that is the date that good funds will be credited to the account (this is actually similar to the availability schedules used in the United States). Cleared checks may be assigned a **back value date,** in essence drawing funds out of the account before the check actually arrives. Back-value dating is not generally done in the United States. Foreign banks value date as a means to enhance the compensation for their clearing services beyond the fees charged.

    Because most non-US banking systems have far fewer banks than in the US, the clearing of domestic checks within a country is more straightforward than in the United States. However, the clearing of checks denominated in one currency drawn on a bank in another country that uses another currency is more complicated because the check generally has to travel between several correspondent banks to finally clear. A check denominated in a foreign currency and deposited in a US bank, for example, must be transported back to the country of origination, the currency converted and exchanged for a dollar denominated check drawn on a US bank. The process can take from a couple of weeks to a month compared with only a few days for the clearing of domestic checks.

Interest on Demand Deposits

To compensate for the uncertainties created by the value-dating system, it is common practice for non-US banks to pay interest on corporate demand deposit balances and to charge interest on overdrafts. The fact that interest is earned on balances and that overdraft facilities exist lessens the need for daily cash balance reporting, which is not always available internationally.

Governmental Policies and Restrictions

There are other problems related to the movement of funds across national borders. For example, some countries tax international funds transfer across their borders. This is why netting systems, discussed earlier, are so important because they reduce the number and amount of transfers. Some countries that stringently control cross-border cash flows, for example, many countries in South America, have gone so far as to make netting systems illegal.

Cash Management Services

The banking system in the United States is relatively unique in that nationwide branching prior to 1997 was illegal. As a result, independent or unit banks dominated the system. The cash management services that are so common in the United States, for example, lock boxes, controlled disbursement systems, concentrations systems, and balance reporting, have developed to provide the financial manager of a company selling nationwide an efficient means of pooling cash resources given the fragmented banking structure.

Such services are not as essential in non-US banking systems, and in some cases not available, because most countries have far fewer independent banks with a multitude of branches. Companies that use the same bank in a foreign country can use the branches of the bank for collection services, obviating lock box and concentration systems because the funds are in the same bank. In fact, it is common to find the banks offering pooling services that allow a firm's excess balances spread across its bank branches to offset corporate deficit balances in other branches of the same bank. In essence, the bank can treat all the accounts for a firm in its branches as one account thereby allowing the firm to avoid interest charges at those branches where deficit balances are occurring.

One collection system for consumer payments that is common in Europe is the giro system, which is similar to the automated clearing house (ACH) system in the United States. The invoice that sellers send to their customers includes a payment stub encoded with the seller's bank account number. The customer signs the stub and then takes it to a giro processor such as the local post office. The processor delivers the stubs to the nearest giro bank, which in turn debits the customer's account and credits the seller's account.

SUMMARY

Although managing cash flows domestically in the United States is somewhat complicated by the number of banks and other regulations that exist, managing international cash flows is even more complex. Some of the factors that contribute to the additional complications in managing multinational cash flows include different banking systems, structures, and regulations that exist in each country; the restrictions imposed on data and funds flows across borders; value-dating systems; and the fluctuating values of currencies.

This chapter began by providing a brief history of the exchange rate system and a description of the different forms of currency quotations including spot rates, forward rates, and futures rates. Given the fluctuating values of exchange rates, managing the firm's foreign currency exposure is one of the more important aspects of managing international cash flows. The reader was introduced to three types of foreign exchange exposure. A variety of techniques for managing foreign currency exposure were described. The chapter concluded with a discussion of the characteristics of non-US banking systems.

Useful Web Site

Futures Magazine, Inc.: www.futuresmag.com/

Questions

1. When should a company get foreign exchange in the spot rate and when should the company use the forward market to get foreign exchange?
2. What is the difference between transaction exposure and translation exposure?
3. How does a multilateral netting system help manage foreign currency exposure?
4. How is transaction exposure different from economic exposure?
5. Identify some of the key differences between the US banking system and the banking systems outside the United States.

Problems

1. Convert the following exchange rates expressed as US dollars per unit of foreign currency into the number of units of foreign currency per US dollar.

COUNTRY	US$ PER UNIT OF FOREIGN CURRENCY	UNIT OF FOREIGN CURRENCY PER US$
Australia	0.44	
Britain	1.67	
Japan	0.010	
Thailand	0.03	

2. A multinational company has three subsidiaries located in the United States, Switzerland, and Great Britain. The company recently set up a multilateral netting center to help manage its foreign exchange exposure. Listed below are the average monthly invoices sent from each country to each of the other subsidiaries with which it does business. Calculate the net flows that will occur as a result of the new netting system. The company uses the US dollar as the common referencing currency.

Existing Exchange Rates:

Swiss franc (SF) = $0.13
Pound sterling (PS) = $1.45

U.S.	To	Switzerland	$	100
	To	GB	$	250
Switzerland	To	US	SF	300
	To	GB	SF	150
GB	To	Switzerland	PS	200
	To	US	PS	100

3. You are concerned about your transaction exposure on a recent purchase from an exporter in Great Britain. The invoice, just received, is for 275,000 pounds sterling payable in 90 days, which will be about mid-June. The current exchange rate is $1.35 per pound sterling and you fear that the dollar will depreciate against the pound as a result of the relatively low interest rates currently prevailing in the United States.

The following forward rate is $1.38.

a. What is the cost of the invoice in dollars at the current spot rate?

    b. If a forward contract is purchased, what will be the cost of the invoice in dollars at the forward rate?

    c. What are the advantages and disadvantages of hedging the transaction with a forward contract?

References

K. Alec Chrystal. 1984. A guide to foreign exchange markets. Review Federal Reserve Bank of St. Louis March:5–17.

William R. Folks, Jr. and Raj Aggarwal. 1988. *International dimensions of financial management.* Boston: PWS-Kent.

Susan Griffiths. 1992. International pooling—Getting the story straight. *Journal of Cash Management* November/December:26–34.

Neil A. Leary. 1993. The basics of doing business overseas: An overview of international treasury management. *The Journal of Cash Management* March/April:33–38.

Cecilia Wagner Ricci and Gail Morrison. 1996. International working capital practices of the Fortune 200. *Financial Practice and Education* Fall/Winter:7–20.

INTEGRATIVE CASE—PART 5
Jones Salvage and Recycling, Inc. (C)

Note: This is a continuation of the Jones Salvage and Recycling, Inc. (A) case found immediately following Chapter 13 and Jones (B) found immediately following Chapter 16. Jones (A) concluded with a monthly forecasted income statement, cash budget, and balance sheet for the first 6 months of the new year. Jones (B) used that information to determine the financing and investment strategy that is best for Jones to use. Jones (C) focuses on solving the company's liquidity needs by changing its working capital policies.

Mr. Jones was impressed with the financial strategy created by the lending officer and the company's financial manager. However, Mr. Jones had heard and read a lot about the reengineering efforts that companies were employing in their working capital management with what seemed to be great successes. In fact he was aware that some companies were striving for zero working capital, a concept foreign to him. He always considered working capital an asset, something that created value on the balance sheet.

In his discussions about this with Carl Malone, his bank's relationship manager, he learned that indeed there was an industry trend toward zero working capital and that this should really be investigated. Zero working capital basically means that the sum of the accounts receivable and inventory equal the sum of accounts payables and operating accruals. In other words, the working capital is self-financed, an intriguing idea, Mr. Jones thought. All of a sudden he realized that this could mean a drastic reduction in the need for bank financing and consequently less interest to be paid. Being a pragmatist, however, he quickly realized that this could not be achieved without some kind of cost involved. He just wasn't sure what those costs might be and immediately asked Bob Jones, his business manager, to study the issues and submit a report in a week.

ACCOUNTS RECEIVABLE

Obviously, one part of the solution would be to tighten up on collections or even change the company's credit terms. Tightening up on the existing credit terms could only be done by spending additional sums of money on credit investigation and collection efforts. Bob estimates that this would not cause any noticeable change in sales but would increase operating expenses by $2,000 per month. The benefit would be that the collection fractions might improve to 20 percent for the month of sale, 70 percent for the month after sales, and 10 percent for 2 months after sale.

Giving shorter credit terms would probably cause a decrease in sales and invoke some type of reaction from the company's competitors and Bob preferred to not touch this approach at this time.

INVENTORY

As discussed earlier, the company's current inventory policy is to end each month with ending inventory equal to the following month's cost of sales. This is a relatively conservative policy and the company has never stocked out in the past, a fact that Mr. Jones was rather proud of. However, Bob used this opportunity to suggest that this policy was simply too conservative and costly for the firm in light of the projected financing needs of the company. Carl felt that with a closer coordination with their commercial suppliers of scrap as well as better information from their commercial customers, the company could afford to turn their inventory over at a faster pace. His estimate is that by incurring an additional $1,000 per month of personnel time and communication costs they could reduce their ending inventory needs to only a quarter of what they were currently.

ACCOUNTS PAYABLE

After calling several suppliers, Bob discovered that they indeed were already getting the best credit terms available and did not see much opportunity to improve in this area. He briefly considered stretching payables by simply not paying within terms but quickly dismissed this idea.

THE PROPOSED PLAN

Bob Jones put the plan together and had it on Mr. Jones' desk at the end of the following week. The plan consisted of the components as discussed above. Mr. Jones was intrigued with the idea but was concerned about the trade-offs and wasn't sure if the reduced inventory and receivables would contribute enough to offset the increased costs. He also wasn't sure how to compare this alternative with the best financing strategy.

REQUIRED

1. Input the suggested working capital management plan into the financing planning model from Jones (A) and discuss the impact it has on the projected cash flow of the company.
2. Given the results in part 1, invest any monthly surplus cash or borrow to fund any deficit so that the minimum cash balance of $1,000 is maintained.
3. Compare the result you arrive at in part 2 with your conclusions drawn from Jones (B). Which strategy would you recommend and why?

PART VI
Special Topics

Chapter 18   Managing Financial Risk with Futures, Options, and Swaps

Chapter 19   Treasury Information Management

Part 6 includes two chapters that offer additional insight and detail into two very important short-term financial management topics. Chapter 18 studies the management of financial risk including interest rate as well as exchange rate risk by hedging with a variety of financial derivative instruments. Another critical area impacting short-term financial management is the area of managing information flows. Although a variety of information management issues were discussed at appropriate places in the text, Chapter 19 cohesively brings together some of the more critical aspects of the problem for a more complete treatment of this emerging and very important topic.

CHAPTER 18

Managing Financial Risk with Futures, Options, and Swaps

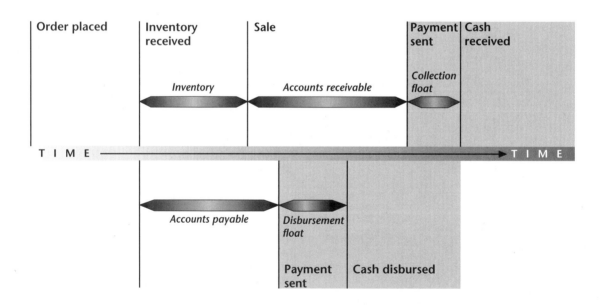

OBJECTIVES

After studying this chapter, you should be able to:

- Understand the basic difference between hedging and speculating.
- Discern between hedging instruments including futures, options, swaps, and products such as interest rate ceilings, floors, and collars.
- Develop appropriate hedging strategies using futures, options, swaps, caps, floors, and collars.

In earlier chapters, various strategies such as balance sheet matching to manage interest rate risk or netting to manage exchange rate risk were discussed. However, even after these strategies are used, some exposure to interest or exchange rate movements may remain. This chapter focuses on using financial derivatives such as futures, options, and swaps to manage uncertain cash flows resulting from movements in market interest rates and exchange rates. We first discuss the characteristics of these three contracts and then develop appropriate strategies for the different types of contracts as they apply to managing the variability of cash flows.

In Chapters 14 and 15 we discussed the various types of money market investment strategies useful for investing short-term funds. The basic purpose of short-term investments is to earn a reasonable rate of return until the funds need to be redeployed back into the operations of the firm. Thus the decision to invest or not and the maturity decision had to weigh transactions costs against the opportunity cost of idle funds. Some of the strategies left the firm exposed to interest rate risk. For example, a "riding the yield curve" strategy forces the firm to sell the security before it matures, exposing the firm to an uncertain selling price, which is dependent on the interest rate structure that exists at the time the security is sold. Chapter 16, dealing with short-term financing decisions, related similar types of problems from the financing or liability management side. Finally, when firms do business with foreign corporations as discussed in Chapter 17, financial risk is created because of the differences in the currencies used by the two firms. This chapter discusses a variety of strategies useful in managing risk associated with uncertain movements in interest and foreign exchange rates.

FINANCIAL DILEMMA

What Can Be Done About Uncertain Interest Rates?

Mark Thompson wondered what he should do. His most recent cash flow forecast indicated that in 30 days he would need to borrow $3 million for approximately 3 months. Although he was currently enjoying a healthy liquid asset balance of marketable securities, those funds would be drawn down in the near term, resulting in needed external financing to fund the firm's seasonal working capital needs.

His concern was over the future direction of interest rates. The current yield curve was relatively flat with short-term borrowing rates at 9.75 percent. He thought that this level represented a reasonable borrowing cost and wished he could "lock-in" that rate today as his financing cost in 30 days. Although rates could go lower, he was more worried about them rising over the next month.

HEDGING COMPARED WITH SPECULATING

The same financial contracts that allow a financial manager to hedge movements in interest rates can also be used to speculate on the future direction of these rates. Although both hedgers and speculators use the same financial contracts, how they are used is quite different.

A **hedger** has a cash position or an anticipated cash position that he or she is trying to protect from adverse interest or exchange rate movements. A **speculator,** on the other hand, has no operating cash flow position to protect and is trying to profit solely from rate movements.

An example may help to differentiate hedging strategies from speculative strategies. Suppose a financial manager forecasts a temporary surplus of funds for a brief period beginning 30 days from today. The plan is to invest these funds in a short-term money market instrument but the future interest rate environment is relatively cloudy. The current level of interest rates is reasonable and the financial manager would not mind getting today's rates 30 days from now. In essence, the financial manager wants to hedge against future movements in interest rates and lock in today's rate if possible.

Contrast this hedging situation with a local floor trader on the Chicago Mercantile Exchange's International Monetary Market where Treasury bill futures are traded. The local floor trader purchased a seat on the exchange some years ago and earns a living by trading interest rate futures contracts. If the trader senses that interest rates are rising, he will sell a futures contract short, buying it back at a lower price after rates have risen.[1] If the trader senses that rates are falling, he will purchase futures contracts and then sell them at a higher price after interest rates have fallen. Thus a speculator trades to profit from changes in interest rates or exchange rates. A hedger trades futures contracts to protect a cash position from changes in interest or currency exchange rates.

Speculators serve a very important function by providing liquidity in the futures markets through their continual trading of contracts. This liquidity provides assurance to hedgers that they can liquidate their hedging contracts whenever they need to.

HEDGING WITH FINANCIAL FUTURES

The first hedging strategy we develop uses a futures contract. The next section provides a background on futures contracts and then develops the basic hedging strategies for managing interest and exchange rate risk for a variety of cash positions.

Introduction to Futures Contracts

A **futures contract** is a standardized contract that carries with it a performance obligation at the expiration of the contract. For example, the buyer of a 90-day Treasury bill futures contract first purchases the futures contract by putting up a margin, a small percentage of the contract price, rather than paying the price of the contract. At expiration, the buyer pays the contract price, less the dollar amount of funds in the margin account, and receives the cash market instrument, which in this case is a Treasury bill with 90 days to maturity.

A unique feature of a futures contract is the **margin account.** The margin account, created as a part of the futures contract transaction, is **marked-to-market**

---

[1]As interest rates rise, the price of a futures contract falls.

EXHIBIT 18-1

Variations in the Margin Account as a Result of Future Contract Price Changes

Day	Contract Price Change	Margin Account
0		$2,000
1	$ 625	2,625
2	100	2,725
3	−900	1,825
4	−1,500	325
5	−500	−175 Margin Call

daily with the positive changes in the market price of the contract credited to the buyer's margin account and debited from the seller's margin account. Negative changes in the price of the contract will have just the opposite transactions with the margin account for the buyer and seller. Margin calls occur if the margin account falls below a predetermined level.

For example, assume that a financial manager purchased a Treasury bill futures contract with an initial margin of $2,000. The treasurer gives her broker $2,000 and as a result owns a Treasury bill futures contract. Assume the contract is initially priced at $950,000. The next day interest rates fall and as a result the contract price increases by $625. The financial manager now owns a contract worth $950,625 and at the close of business that day her margin account is worth $2,625. Exhibit 18-1 carries this example on for several more days, showing how the margin account varies in relation to the change in the price of the futures contract.

On day 5 the financial manager receives a margin call from her broker requesting that the financial manager deposit enough cash that day to bring the margin account back to a level referred to as the **maintenance margin.** The margin call is at least $175, bringing the margin account to zero, in addition to an amount sufficient to return the account to the maintenance level.

The first financial futures contracts began trading in 1972 and were on foreign currencies. In that year, the Chicago Mercantile Exchange organized the International Monetary Market to trade the newly developed financial futures instrument. Exhibit 18-2 shows the more popular exchange rate futures contracts including the Japanese yen, the British pound, and the euro. To better understand the information presented in the exhibit, let's take the British pound quote from Exhibit 18-2 as an example. There are two contract months reported. Contracts expire the third Wednesday of the contract month. The British pound contract is for 62,500 pounds sterling and the March 2001 contract price closed on Thursday, December 14, 2000, at a price of $1.4736 per pound. Thus one contract could have been purchased on that day, and if held to expiration, the buyer of the contract would receive 62,500 pounds sterling in exchange for $92,100 = 62,500 × 1.4736. To purchase the futures contract the buyer would have to post an initial margin of approximately 1 to 2 percent of the contract price and pay the contract price at expiration of the contract.

In 1975, a futures contract on a Government National Mortgage Association (GNMA) pass through security began trading followed by trading in 90-day Treasury bill futures contract in 1976. Since that time, a wide range of futures contracts has been created. Exhibit 18-3 displays the interest rate futures contracts reported by *The Wall Street Journal.*

Because we will use the Treasury bill futures contract in later examples, let's discuss the information about that contract as highlighted in Exhibit 18-3. The Treasury bill

EXHIBIT 18-2

Foreign Currency Futures Contracts

CURRENCY

Japan Yen (CME)-12.5 million yen; $ per yen (.00)

	Open	High	Low	Settle		Change	Lifetime High	Lifetime Low	Open Interest
Dec	.8910	.8923	.8850	.8907	+	.0006	1.0434	.8850	52,580
Mr01	.9039	.9053	.8998	.9037	+	.0004	1.0300	.8998	70,968
Sept	....	....	....	.9290	−	.0002	1.0050	.9360	96

Est vol 34,012; vol Wed 42,344; open int 123,780, −6,267.

Deutschemark (CME)-125,000 marks; $ per mark

Dec	.4490	.4536	.4490	.4546	+	.0067	.5000	.3891	273
Mr01	.4570	.4570	.4570	.4564	+	.0067	.4624	.4225	210

Est vol 20; vol Wed 32; open int 483, −146.

Canadian Dollar (CME)-100,000 dlrs.; $ per Can $

Dec	.6586	.6611	.6572	.6597	+	.0017	.7025	.6403	24,146
Mr01	.6588	.6625	.6583	.6609	+	.0017	.7040	.6415	41,897
June	.6618	.6635	.6597	.6620	+	.0017	.6990	.6425	3,877
Sept	.6633	.6633	.6633	.6630	+	.0017	.6906	.6445	1,201
Dec	.6640	.6645	.6635	.6640	+	.0017	.6825	.6452	519

Est vol 16,201; vol Wed 18,723; open int 71,647, −4,347.

British Pound (CME)-62,500 pds.; $ per pound

Dec	1.4560	1.4730	1.4540	1.4716	+	.0174	1.6500	1.3966	18,523
Mr01	1.4572	1.4750	1.4564	1.4736	+	.0170	1.6050	1.4010	18,417

Est vol 11,977; vol Wed 8,263; open int 36,986, −1,730.

Swiss Franc (CME)-125,000 francs; $ per franc

Dec	.5846	.5910	.5846	.5906	+	.0079	.6687	.5488	31,712
Mr01	.5880	.5958	.5876	.5953	+	.0080	.6309	.5541	31,451

Est vol 11,423; vol Wed 12,076; open int 63,183, −1,003.

Australian Dollar (CME)-100,000 dlrs.; $ per A.$

Dec	.5400	.5425	.5400	.5413	+	.0027	.6704	.5075	11,895
Mr01	.5396	.5439	.5394	.5418	+	.0027	.6390	.5100	17,408

Est vol 3,931; vol Wed 3,135; open int 29,335, −727.

Mexican Peso (CME)-500,000 new Mex. peso, $ per MP

Dec	.10610	.10640	.10595	.10613	−	.00030	.10738	.09200	10,005
Ja01	....	....	....	.10523	−	.00030	.10535	.10035	3,632
Mar	.10340	.10370	.10320	.10328	−	.00035	.10370	.09120	18,506
June	.10130	.10130	.10080	.10073	−	.00030	.10130	.09070	758

Est vol 4,394; vol Wed 9,071; open int 33,299, +1,150.

Euro FX (CME)-Euro 125,000; $ per Euro

Dec	.8762	.8900	.8762	.8892	+	.0132	1.0572	.8305	44,725
Mr01	.8797	.8937	.8791	.8927	+	.0132	.9999	.8333	56,801
June	.8920	.8962	.8920	.8957	+	.0132	.9784	.8358	313
Sept	.8981	.8981	.8981	.8984	+.	.0131	.9002	.8379	391

Est vol 32,736; vol Wed 37,239; open int 102,236, +3,914.

futures contract is for a $1 million face value 90-day US Government Treasury bill. Two contract months are reported in the exhibit: December 2000 and the March 2001 expiration dates. The contracts trade on the International Monetary Market of the Chicago Mercantile Exchange (CME) and the March contract closed or settled on Thursday, December 14, 2000, priced at an annualized discount rate of 5.60 percent. If someone purchased the March contract on this day and held it to expiration, they would receive $1 million face value Treasury bills priced at a 5.60 percent discount rate. Characteristic of all futures contracts, at the time the contract was purchased, only a small margin had to be posted with cash settlement of the contract price at contract expiration. Although not shown in the data reported in *The Wall Street Journal,* the initial margin for Treasury bill futures contracts is approximately $2,000 per contract.

The numbers under the heading of Open, High, Low, and Settle in the body of the table in Exhibit 18-3 for the Treasury bill futures contract represent an index number that is calculated by taking the annual discount rate from 100. Although this index does not represent the price of the contract, it does reflect direction of price movement when interest rates change. For example, if interest rates rise, the dollar price of a futures contract will fall, just like any other fixed price financial contract. The higher the interest rate, the lower the financial futures contract index.

This "price" index was developed when the interest rate futures contracts were first developed in the 1970s. The price index helped futures traders, used to trading commodity contracts based on quoted prices, make a smooth transition to the interest rate futures markets where information is quoted based on interest rates and prices

EXHIBIT 18-3
Interest Rate Futures Contracts

```
                           INTEREST RATE
Treasury Bonds (CBT)-$100,000; pts 32nds of 100%
Dec   104-02 105-00 104-02 104-15  +  14  105-00  88-13   41,298
Mr01  104-03 105-02 104-02 104-17  +  14  105-02  88-06  409,522
June  104-16 104-31 104-10 104-16  +  14  104-31  96-21    1,191
Sept   ....   ....   ....  104-13  +  14  103-07  96-22      244
Est vol 307,000; vol Wed 179,282; open int 452,313, +5,531.
Treasury Notes (CBT)-$100,000; pts 32nds of 100%
Dec   104-00 04-085 103-30 04-025  +  11.5 04-085 96-075   8,104
Mr01  04-025 104-20 04-015 104-12  +  12.5 104-20 98-04  491,374
June   ....   ....   ....  04-115  +  12.5 103-27 99-11    2,490
Est vol 234,000; vol Wed 164,298; open int 501,968, +4,439.
10 Yr Agency Notes (CBT)-$100,000; pts 32nds of 100%
Dec   99-24  99-29  99-16  99-195  +  19.0 99-29  91-17    6,446
Mr01  99-26  99-29  99-165 99-19   +  18.0 99-29  93-25   47,551
Est vol 12,500; vol Wed 6,145; open int 53,997, +651.
5 Yr Treasury Notes (CBT)-$100,000; pts 32nds of 100%
Dec   102-29 02-305 02-235 02-275  +  8.0  02-305 98-13   33,247
Mr01  102-23 02-315 02-215 102-28  +  7.5  02-315 100-11 340,758
Est vol 103,000; vol Wed 92,573; open int 374,010, −2,562.
2 Yr Treasury Notes (CBT)-$200,000; pts 32nds of 100%
Dec   101-00 101-00 00-295 100-30  +  2.0  10-095 99-12      527
Mr01  100-30 01-097 100-30 101-07  +  2.0  01-097 00-075  76,445
Est vol 6,800; vol Wed 5,361; open int 76,973, −921.
30 Day Federal Funds (CBT)-$5 million; pts of 100%
Dec   93.530 93.550 93.530 93.540 + .010 93.590 9.350   19,053
Ja01  93.55  93.58  93.55  93.56  + .02  93.61  93.25   16,560
Feb   93.75  93.79  93.75  93.79  + .04  93.79  92.59   16,638
Mar   93.85  93.86  93.85  93.85  + .04  93.86  93.21    5,444
Apr   94.01  94.03  94.00  94.01  + .04  94.03  93.21    1,479
Est vol 11,000; vol Wed 8,132; open int 59,244, +4,831.
Muni Bond Index (CBT)-$1,000; times Bond Buyer MBI
Dec   102-21 103-05 102-20 102-27  +  11  103-05 91-19    9,056
Mr01  102-09 102-27 102-08 102-14  +  11  102-27 98-03    9,706
Est vol 4,700; vol Wed 2,957; open int 18,762, +89.
Index: Close 102-03; Yield 5.57.
                                                          OPEN
      OPEN   HIGH   LOW  SETTLE CHANGE  YIELD CHANGE      INT.
Treasury Bills (CME)-$1 mil.; pts of 100%
Dec   94.14  94.14  94.14  94.14   ....  5.86   ....      1,143
Mr01  94.43  94.43  94.40  94.40 + .01   5.60  −.01       1,571
Est vol 69; vol Wed 34; open int 2,714, +1.
Libor-1 Mo. (CME)-$3,000,000; pts of 100%
Dec   93.34  93.34  93.30  93.30   ....  6.70   ....     12,489
Ja01  93.57  93.58  93.57  93.57 + .02   6.43  −.02      16,890
Feb   93.68  93.72  93.68  93.70 + .02   6.30  −.02       9,453
Mar   93.86  93.87  93.84  93.84 + .01   6.16  −.01       4,317
Apr   93.93  93.94  93.92  93.91 + .01   6.09  −.01       1,917
May    ....   ....   ....  93.99 + .01   6.01  −.01         392
June   ....   ....   ....  94.14 + .04   5.86  −.04         604
Est vol 5,460; vol Wed 10,234; open int 46,062, +2,858.
Eurodollar (CME)-$1 Million; pts of 100%
Dec   93.46  93.47  93.45  93.45 + .02   6.55  −.02     437,847
Ja01  93.65  93.66  93.64  93.65 + .03   6.35  −.03      14,952
Feb   93.80  93.80  93.78  93.78 + .01   6.22  −.01       6,255
Mar   93.91  93.91  93.87  93.87 + .01   6.13  −.01     564,551
June  94.15  94.17  94.11  94.14 + .05   5.86  −.05     428,987
Sept  94.27  94.30  94.24  94.26 + .06   5.74  −.06     481,265
Dec   94.19  94.22  94.17  94.18 + .06   5.82  −.06     305,508
Mr02  94.25  94.29  94.22  94.24 + .05   5.76  −.05     250,340
June  94.20  94.24  94.18  94.18 + .06   5.82  −.06     165,957
Sept  94.16  94.19  94.13  94.14 + .06   5.86  −.06     127,565
Dec   94.05  94.07  94.02  94.02 + .06   5.98  −.06      99,161
Mr03  94.10  94.11  94.06  94.06 + .06   5.94  −.06      80,796
June  94.06  94.08  94.02  94.03 + .07   5.97  −.07      66,591
Sept  94.05  94.06  94.00  94.00 + .07   6.00  −.07      63,433
Dec   93.96  93.97  93.90  93.91 + .07   6.09  −.07      47,982
Mr04  94.00  94.02  93.95  93.95 + .08   6.05  −.08      50,044
June  93.97  93.99  93.92  93.92 + .08   6.08  −.08      48,433
Sept  93.96  93.96  93.89  93.89 + .08   6.11  −.08      46,858
```

move inversely to interest rates. The exhibit shows the "price" index on December 14 at the opening of trading, the high, the low, and the settlement index. The settlement index is basically the index of the last trade and is the basis by which margin accounts are adjusted at the end of the day.

Finally, Exhibit 18-3 reports the number of outstanding contracts at the close of trading for each day. This is termed open interest. Nearby contracts generally have the

EXHIBIT 18-4

Cash Position and the Corresponding Futures Position

CASH POSITION	FUTURES POSITION
A future investment	Buy Hedge
Retire liability prior to maturity	Buy Hedge
A future issue of a liability	Sell Hedge
Current investment that will be sold prior to its maturity	Sell Hedge

greatest number of contracts outstanding with the amount of contract activity quickly dwindling the further out the contract.

Type of Hedge: Buy Versus Sell

A financial manager can create a hedge by either initially buying a futures contract, referred to as a **buy hedge,** or by issuing a futures contract, referred to as a **sell hedge.** The type of hedge desired depends on the hedger's cash flow position that is being hedged, not on the anticipated direction of interest rates. Generally, the financial manager places a hedge that, in effect, acts as a temporary substitute for the cash transaction that will take place.

Suppose that a financial manager's cash budget indicates a cash surplus to occur in 2 months. The financial manager cannot invest today but will have available funds in the near future. How can the financial manager reduce the uncertainty of the future investment rate? The proper hedge in this situation is a buy hedge. The financial manager could buy an appropriate futures contract now to act as a substitute for the future investment of cash in 2 months. If the contract expires in 2 months, the financial manager can use the futures contract to receive the money market instrument underlying the futures contract. If expiration of the futures contract is beyond 2 months, then the contract will be sold in two months and the gain or loss incurred by the futures contract can be used to offset the opportunity loss or gain incurred in the cash market that results from interest rate movements over the 2-month period.

Whether a hedge is created by issuing a futures contract or by purchasing a futures contract depends on the cash position being hedged. Exhibit 18-4 presents several different cash flow positions and the type of hedge that is appropriate for each. The guiding principle in determining whether to form a buy hedge or a sell hedge is to use the type of hedge that allows the cash instrument to be delivered through the futures contract if it is held to expiration. For example, a sell hedge allows the financial manager to "sell" an investment prior to its maturity at a predetermined price by delivering it through the futures contract.

Choosing the Proper Futures Instrument

As Exhibits 18-2 and 18-3 show, there are a wide variety of futures contracts from which to choose. The basic principle guiding the choice of the type of futures contract is that price movements of the futures contract and the cash market instrument should have a high correlation. A **direct hedge** is a hedge in which the underlying instrument of the futures contract and the cash market instrument being hedged are the same. If the underlying instrument of the futures contract is different from the cash position being hedged, then this is referred to as a **cross hedge.** For example, because there is not an actively traded commercial paper futures contract, investments in and issuance of commercial paper are often hedged with Treasury bill futures contracts or some other closely related contract.

Choosing the Proper Expiration Date

The choice of the proper expiration date is relatively simple. A quick reference to Exhibit 18-3 and the Treasury bill futures quote indicates that there are two possible contracts including the December 2000 and the March 2001 contracts. The contracts generally expire on the third Thursday of the contract expiration month. In fact, up to eight Treasury bill futures contracts are available for trading, that is, six expiration dates beyond those reported in *The Wall Street Journal.*

The guiding rule for the choice of the contract expiration month is to choose the contract expiration month that occurs nearest to, but after, the date of the cash market transaction to be hedged. This contract is referred to as the **nearby contract.** That is, if the cash position to be hedged is to take place in February, then the March contract should be chosen. The closer the price movements of the futures contract follow the price movements of the cash position being hedged, the more effective the hedge. The more distant the contract expiration month is from the date of the cash position, the less correlation will exist between the cash and futures price movements. Because there are only four expiration dates per year for the Treasury bill futures contract, it is unlikely that the expiration date will match up exactly with the cash position date to be hedged. Thus the best that can generally be accomplished is to hedge with the futures contract whose expiration date is nearest to the cash transaction date.

Choosing the Number of Contracts

The choice of the number of futures contracts to use is a function of two variables. The first variable, the denomination of the contract, is fairly obvious. The 90-day Treasury bill futures contract, shown in Exhibit 18-3, has a denomination of $1 million. If the financial manager needs to hedge a $3 million cash position, then three futures contracts are needed based solely on the differences between the hedger's cash position and the dollar size of the futures contract. Contract denomination is the sole variable that determines the number of contracts for currency futures.

Hedging with interest rate futures, however, requires a second variable to determine the number of contracts. This second variable is the maturity of the cash market instrument relative to the maturity of the instrument underlying the futures contract.[2] For example, suppose the financial manager plans to make a future investment in 180-day Treasury bills and wants to hedge the future investment with a 90-day Treasury bill futures contract. The longer the maturity of a financial instrument such as a Treasury bill, the greater the price movement for a given movement in interest rates. For example, the price of a $1 million face value 90-day Treasury bill changes $25 for each basis point change in interest rates.[3] The price change of a $1 million face value 180-day Treasury bill changes $50 for each basis point change in interest rates. Thus for the

---

[2] Actually, the ratio of the maturities of the cash and futures instruments is only an approximation. The actual variable is a sensitivity factor or a type of beta coefficient that measures the degree of sensitivity of the price of the cash instrument and the price of the futures contract to changes in interest rates. The ratio of maturities only approximates this sensitivity factor but is a reasonable approximation for our purposes.

[3] A basis point is 1/100 of 1 percent. Value of 1 basis point is Principal $\times$ (.0001) $\times$ (days/360). For the Treasury bill futures contract, the contract principal is $1 million and days is 90 days. Thus the dollar value of one basis point is $25 = $1,000,000 $\times$ .0001 $\times$ (90/360).

financial futures contract to effectively hedge a cash position, the maturities of the cash and futures instruments should be the same, or the number of futures contracts can be adjusted to equal the dollar price change per basis point. In our example, the cash position is an investment in a 180-day Treasury bill. Because the price movement of a 90-day instrument, which is the futures contract, will only be half that of the cash instrument per basis point change, it will take two contracts to equal the price volatility of the cash instrument. An equation that calculates the proper number, N, of futures contracts based on these two variables is presented in Equation 18-1.[4]

$$N = \frac{\text{Size of Cash Market Position}}{\text{Futures Contract Denomination}} \times \frac{\text{Maturity of Cash Market Instrument}}{\text{Maturity of Futures Contract Instrument}} \qquad \text{(18-1)}$$

Evaluating the Performance of an Interest Rate Hedge

Having discussed all the component parts of a hedge, it is now time to learn how to properly assess the performance of the hedge.

The first part of the performance analysis is to evaluate the change in the cash market instrument from the time the hedge is placed, at time period 0, to the time the hedge is lifted, at time period 1. The spot rates, SR_0 and SR_1, are annual bank discount rates related to the cash market instrument and must be de-annualized using the factor, $MAT_c/360$. MAT_c represents the number of days to maturity for the cash market instrument. Equation 18-2 computes the change in the value of the cash instrument over the hedge period resulting from a change in interest rates and is an estimate of the gain or loss that will occur if a hedge is not placed. Face value cash should be a negative number if investing cash (this is equivalent to disbursing cash) and a positive number if issuing a liability or selling an asset (this is equivalent to receiving cash).

$$\text{Cash Position} = \text{Face Value Cash} \times (SR_0 - SR_1) \times \frac{MAT_c}{360} \qquad \text{(18-2)}$$

Equation 18-3 is an expression for the gain or loss that occurs in the futures contract over the hedge period. Because the futures rates, FR_0 and FR_1, are annualized rates, the factor, $MAT_f/360$, de-annualizes the impact of the change in interest rates so that the value change is just for the hedge period. To make this expression work appropriately, the variable, Face Value of the Futures Contract, should be a positive number for a buy hedge (a buy hedger first buys the futures contract to place the hedge but then sells the contract at the end of the hedge period so the positive number represents the selling aspect of the hedge at the time the hedge is unwound) and a negative number for a sell hedge (a sell hedger first issues a futures contract but then buys it back at the end of the hedge period).

$$\text{Futures Position} = \text{Face Value Futures} \times (FR_0 - FR_1) \times \frac{MAT_f}{360} \qquad \text{(18-3)}$$

In Equation 18-3, MAT_f represents the maturity of the instrument underlying the futures contract.

---

[4]Note that if this equation is used to calculate the number of contracts for a riding the yield curve hedge, the maturity of the cash instrument changes each day. Thus the number of contracts should be adjusted of the duration of the hedge. For simplicity, we will ignore this adjustment process.

Next, there are commission rates for buying and selling financial futures. A ballpark cost figure for the round trip commission charge for one financial futures contract is $60.[5] Equation 18-4 can be used to compute the financial futures commission costs.

$$\text{Commission Cost} = N \times \text{Commission Rate Per Contract} \qquad \text{(18-4)}$$

The final consideration involves the opportunity cost of the initial margin. Margin, MRG, of approximately $2,000 per contract must be used to set up the margin account. The initial margin may differ among different types of futures contracts. However, $2,000 is a reasonable estimate of the initial margin for one 90-day Treasury bill futures contract. These funds do not earn interest while in the margin account and thus incur an opportunity cost. This is computed in Equation 18-5. In this expression, D represents the number of days the hedge is maintained and k is the annual opportunity cost of corporate idle cash balances.

$$\text{Margin Cost} = N \times MRG \times (D \times k/360) \qquad \text{(18-5)}$$

It is now time to put Equations 18-2 through 18-5 together to compute the net gain or loss resulting from the hedge. Equation 18-2 will either be an inflow or an outflow depending on the direction of the interest rate change and the type of cash market transaction that is being made. For example, issuing a liability with interest rates falling results in a gain. Investing with interest rates falling results in a loss. The same is true for Equation 18-3. A buy hedge with interest rates falling results in a gain and a buy hedge with interest rates rising results in a loss. A sell hedge with interest rates falling results in a loss and a sell hedge with interest rates rising results in a gain. Equations 18-4 and 18-5 will always be outflows.

FINANCIAL DILEMMA REVISITED

Let's apply these equations to analyze Mark Thompson's dilemma as given at the outset of the chapter. You may remember that the current short-term borrowing cost was 9.75 percent. Mark plans to issue 3-month commercial paper in 30 days. He plans to hedge the commercial paper issue with a 90-day Treasury bill futures contract given the high degree of liquidity of the contract and its high degree of correlation with commercial paper rates. The interest rates on the spot commercial paper and the Treasury bill futures contract at the time the hedge was created and then lifted are shown below.

	TODAY	30 DAYS FROM NOW
3-month commercial paper rates	9.75%	11.25%
3-month T-bill futures	9.60%	11.00%

Cash Position:	$3,000,000 \times (.0975 - .1125) \times (90/360) =$	$-\$11,250.00$
Futures Position:	$-\$3,000,000 \times (.0960 - .1100) \times (90/360) =$	$10,500.00$
Commission:	$-3 \times \$60 =$	-180.00
Margin:	$-3 \times \$2,000 \times 30 \times (.0975/360) =$	-48.75
Net Position From the Hedge		$-\$\ 978.75$

Had Mark not hedged, the increase in interest rates would have cost him an additional $11,250 of interest on the commercial paper. The hedge resulted in a gain in the

[5]The term roundtrip with respect to hedging reflects the creation and then unwinding of the hedge position.

futures contract of $10,500. However, with costs of $180 in commissions and $48.75 in opportunity cost of the initial margin, a net loss of only $978.75 occurred as a result of the hedge. This represents savings of $10,271.25 on this one transaction. Although the hedge did not perfectly offset the increase in interest rates, it substantially offset the increase.

Evaluating the Performance of a Currency Futures Hedge

Now let's explore how futures contracts can be used to hedge exchange rate risk. The basic principles are the same as hedging interest rate risk presented earlier. A buy hedge is used to hedge the purchase of foreign currency in the future and a sell hedge is used to hedge the selling of foreign currency in the future. To illustrate this, assume a US importer just received invoices to pay a British exporter 62,500 pounds sterling in 2 months. The US importer has several options. First, the importer can do nothing now and then buy pounds sterling in 2 months in the spot market. Or, the importer can buy pounds sterling now and hold them for 2 months. Another option is to buy a futures contract that allows the US importer to receive pounds sterling in the future at an exchange rate determined today.

The four transaction cash flows (cash position, futures position, commission, and margin) related to a foreign exchange futures contract are shown below and are similar in concept to those for an interest rate futures contract developed earlier. CX stands for cash market exchange rate and FX stands for futures market exchange rate. The subscripts 0 and 1 stand for the current period and future period, respectively. In the example below, assume that the cash exchange rate now is $1.73 per pound sterling and will be $1.83 in 60 days. The futures exchange rate now is $1.75 and will be $1.84 in 60 days. One futures contract carries a round-trip commission rate of $60 and each contract requires an initial margin of $1,500. Assume that the current money market interest rate is 9 percent.

Spot Market Position:

$$\text{Pounds Sterling} \times (CX_0 - CX_1) = \text{Gain(Loss) on Spot}$$
$$62{,}500 \times (1.73 - 1.83) = -\$6{,}250.00$$

Futures Market Position:

$$\text{Pounds Sterling} \times (FX_0 - FX_1) = \text{Gain(Loss) on Futures}$$
$$-62{,}500 \times (1.75 - 1.84) = +\$5{,}625.00$$

Commission Cost:

$$\text{Number of contracts} \times \text{Commission} = \text{Commission Cost}$$
$$-1 \times \$60 = -\$\ 60.00$$

Opportunity Cost of Margin:

$$\text{Number of Contracts} \times \text{Margin} \times \text{days} \times \text{rate} = \text{Margin Cost}$$
$$-1 \times \$1{,}500 \times 60 \times (.09/360) = -\$\ 67.50$$

Net Position From the Hedge $-\$752.50$

Some explanation of the positive and negative signs is warranted at this point. In the cash position, the pounds sterling is positive because pounds are received or purchased. Pounds sterling has a negative sign in the futures position line because a pounds sterling futures contract was initially bought and then sold in 60 days thus getting rid of pounds sterling.

In this example, the US importer loses a net $752.50 as a result of the hedge, but would have lost $6,250 if pounds sterling had been purchased in the open market 60 days after receiving the invoice. Thus the hedge saved the importer $5,497.50 = $6,250 − $752.50 relative to waiting to buy pounds sterling in 60 days. Of course, the importer could have purchased pounds sterling at the time the invoice was received but this would have negated the credit terms, allowing 60 days to pay because the importer would have had to use dollars now to buy the pounds sterling. The hedge nearly accomplished the same result without having to commit dollars (with the exception of the margin) immediately.

Why Hedges Are Not Perfect

A perfect hedge is one in which the gain (loss) on the cash position is exactly offset by the loss (gain) related to the futures contract. In Mark Thompson's case, the hedge was imperfect as evidenced by the net loss of $978.75. Several factors can impact the financial result from the hedged position. First, as was the case in Mark Thompson's situation, the interest rates on the cash instrument and on the futures instrument were not 100 percent correlated so the price movements of the two instruments did not exactly match. Second, futures contracts are for only one contract size and they expire on only a very limited number of dates. For example, the 90-day Treasury bill futures contract is for $1 million and expires on only four dates each year (March, June, September, and December). If you wish to hedge a $1.5 million cash market Treasury bill position in February, the hedge will be imperfect because the exact dollar amount cannot be hedged and only a nearby contract expiration date, such as the March contract, can be chosen because there is no February contract. Finally, a hedge may be imperfect because a futures contract for the exact cash market instrument to be hedged may not be available. In this case, the cash market position is cross-hedged with a futures contract that is as similar as possible to the cash instrument.

HEDGING WITH OPTIONS

Options provide an alternative hedging tool to financial futures contracts. This section develops a hedging strategy using option contracts.

Introduction to Option Contracts

An **option contract** gives the option buyer the right but not the obligation to purchase the underlying asset at a specific price, referred to as the **striking price,** over a specific span of time. This type of option is known as a **call option.** The option buyer pays a premium for this right. If the option buyer does not exercise the option by the expiration date, it expires worthless.

A **put option** allows the owner of the option to sell the underlying asset at a specific price during a specific time. The purchaser pays a premium for the right, but not the obligation to sell at a predetermined price. Thus options are fundamentally different from futures contracts because there is no performance obligation. If the option is not exercised by the expiration date it simply expires worthless.

Option contracts were initially developed for common stocks, but now there are option contracts on futures contracts, or, as reported in *The Wall Street Journal,* futures options. These options on futures provide a more palatable alternative to futures contracts because options are purchased by paying a premium rather than purchased on

EXHIBIT 18-5
Exchange Traded Interest Rate Futures Options

INTEREST RATE

T-Bonds (CBT)
$100,000; points – 64ths of 100%

STRIKE	CALLS-SETTLE			PUTS-SETTLE		
PRICE	Jan	Feb	Mar	Jan	Feb	Mar
102	2-34	2-51	3-06	0-01	0-18	0-37
103	1-34	2-02	2-24	0-01	0-32	0-55
104	0-39	1-24	1-49	0-05	0-55	1-15
105	0-07	0-56	1-17	0-37	1-22	1-47
106	0-01	0-34	0-57	1-31	....	2-22
107	0-01	0-20	0-39	2-30	2-49	3-04

Est vol 102,000;
Wd vol 27,035 calls 27,359 puts
Op int Wed 233,580 calls 271,024 puts

T-Notes (CBT)
$100,000; points – 64ths of 100%

STRIKE	CALLS-SETTLE			PUTS-SETTLE		
PRICE	Jan	Feb	Mar	Jan	Feb	Mar
102	2-24	2-31	2-40	0-01	0-07	0-17
103	1-25	1-42	1-56	0-01	0-18	0-33
104	0-28	0-63	1-17	0-04	0-39	0-57
105	0-02	0-34	0-52	....	....	1-28
106	0-01	0-17	0-32	....	....	2-07
107	0-01	0-08	0-19	....	....	....

Est vol 70,000 Wd 23,609 calls 31,683 puts
Op int Wed 265,266 calls 278,471 puts

5 Yr Treas Notes (CBT)
$100,000; points – 64ths of 100%

STRIKE	CALLS-SETTLE			PUTS-SETTLE		
PRICE	Jan	Feb	Mar	Jan	Feb	Mar
10200	0-56	1-05	1-13	0-01	0-13	0-22
10250	0-25	0-47	0-57	0-01	0-23	0-33
10300	0-05	0-30	0-40	0-13	....	0-48
10350	0-01	0-18	0-28	....	....	....
10400	....	0-11	0-18	....	....	....
10450	0-01	....	....	....	....	....

Est vol 23,000 Wd 4,692 calls 4,948 puts
Op int Wed 88,572 calls 103,384 puts

Eurodollar (CME)
$ million; pts of 100%

STRIKE	CALLS-SETTLE			PUTS-SETTLE		
PRICE	Dec	Jan	Feb	Dec	Jan	Feb
9300	4.57	....	....	0.00	....	....
9325	2.07	....	....	0.00	0.00	0.00
9350	0.02	3.75	3.75	0.45	0.05	0.07
9375	0.00	1.50	1.60	2.92	0.30	0.40
9400	0.00	0.35	0.60	5.42	1.65	1.90
9425	0.00	0.07	0.20	7.92	....	....

Est vol 173,913;
Wd vol 102,390 calls 62,408 puts
Op int Wed 1,508,587 calls 1,178,611 puts

margin. Consequently, hedging with options does not incur the potential for margin calls, but still provides interest or exchange rate protection.

Futures options give the holder the right to buy (call option) or sell (put option) a single standardized futures contract for a specified period at a specified striking price. Exhibit 18-5 lists several of the more heavily traded interest rate futures options.

Take the eurodollar futures option in Exhibit 18-5 for example. This contract is based on $1 million 3-month eurodollar deposit and, like the Treasury bill contract, is traded on the International Monetary Market of the CME. The premium for the December call option with a striking price of 9300[6] is reported as 4.57 points of 100 percent or 4.57 basis points.

The biggest difference between the futures option and a futures contract is that the option limits the loss exposure to the option premium. The premium paid for the option is the most that can be lost, whereas the theoretical loss on a futures contract is unlimited. We discuss hedging strategies with futures options in a later section.

------

[6]The 9300 quoted in *The Wall Street Journal* represents the striking price quoted as an index. So 9300 represents an index value of 93 which is related to a 7 percent annualized discount rate.

EXHIBIT 18-6
Cash Positions and Related Futures Options Transactions

CASH POSITION	FUTURES OPTIONS TRANSACTION
A Future Investment	Buy a Call
Retire Liability Prior to Maturity	Buy a Call
A Future Issue of a Liability	Buy a Put
Current Investment That Will Be Sold Prior to its Maturity	Buy a Put

Type of Hedge: Write or Purchase, Call or Put

As we saw with financial futures hedging strategies, a financial manager who will be investing funds in the near future can buy a futures contract as a temporary substitute for the anticipated cash position. As an alternative, a hedger can form a buy hedge with futures options by purchasing a call option on a futures contract. That way, if interest rates fall, the price of the futures will rise and the price of the futures option will likewise rise.[7] A call option used in this way provides protection against falling interest rates, or, put another way, rising prices on the anticipated cash investment instrument. Thus the purchase of a call futures option is used to hedge the future investment of cash or retiring liabilities prior to maturity.

A put option is used to protect against lower prices or correspondingly higher rates. Thus, put options are useful in hedging the future issue of liabilities or the future liquidation of financial assets when the financial manager is afraid that interest rates may rise. Exhibit 18-6 summarizes the four types of cash positions and their related futures options transactions.

Should a hedger ever write option contracts? The primary reason for writing or issuing call and put options is to earn the option premium that is really not related to any hedging motive. Thus hedgers normally either buy a call or buy a put, depending on the cash position they are trying to protect.

Another reason that hedgers don't write options is that writers of futures options contracts are required to post margin. This is required because option writers face similar risks as participants in the futures markets. The exercise of an option is up to the option buyer. Thus the call option writer may have to issue a futures contract that will result in the same financial risk as having originally sold a futures contract. Therefore the option writer is required to post margin to demonstrate the ability to meet potential contract obligations and the option writer's position is marked-to-market daily.

Number of Contracts

The number of options that need to be purchased is based directly on the number of futures contracts needed. For example, we saw earlier that one eurodollar futures option is for $1 million face value futures contract. Thus if a futures hedging program called for 10 futures contracts, an equivalent futures option hedging strategy will require 10 futures options.

---

[7]The price of a call option always increases as the price of the underlying asset of the option increases because the call option gives the holder the right to purchase the underlying asset at a fixed price. Thus as the price of the underlying asset rises, the call option becomes more valuable.

Evaluating the Performance of the Interest Rate Option Hedge

Returning to Mark Thompson's dilemma, suppose that Mark considered using futures option rather than the futures contract as used earlier and the following interest rates exist today along with the expected rates to occur in 30 days.

	TODAY	30 DAYS FROM NOW
Cash Rates	9.75%	11.25%
90-Day Eurodollar Futures Rates	9.60%	11.00%
90-Day Eurodollar, $1 million Contract Futures Option (Put, pts of 100%) Striking Price		
	Points of 100%	
8875	.00009	.0001
8900	.0005	.01
8925	.0009	.25
8950	.003	.50
8975	.007	.75
9000	.009	1.00
9025	.01	1.25
9050	.10	1.50

Mark could have purchased three 90-day Eurodollar put futures options with a striking price of 9050 for $750 = $3,000,000 × (.10/4)/100. Note that the stated premium is based on annualized rates of interest and must be de-annualized by dividing it by the number of periods in a year. Because this is an option contract on a 90-day futures instrument, the premium is divided by 4 because there are four 90-day periods in a 360-day year. In 30 days, according to the data for this example, the 90-day eurodollar futures contract interest rate rises to 11 percent. As a result, the option with a striking price of 9050 will be priced at 1.50 points per 100 percent, according to the example data provided, or three options will be worth $11,250 = $3,000,000 × (1.50/4)/100. The three options can be sold for that amount, netting Mark a gain of $10,500 = $11,250 − $750, which offsets most of the $11,250 loss in cash market position resulting from the rise in interest rates.

A major advantage of this option strategy is that the treasurer established an interest rate ceiling, but not an interest rate floor. Had interest rates fallen, the value of the put option would have fallen and Mark could have let the option simply expire or even sold it and then issued the commercial paper at the new lower rates. The only loss would have been the original premium paid for the three options at a cost of $750. But because rates rose, the option became more valuable as interest rates rose to higher levels. Rising interest rates drive the market price of a futures contract down. Given the fixed striking price, the put option, which allows the owner to sell at the fixed striking price, gains in value offsetting the increasing level of interest rates.

Evaluating the Foreign Currency Option Hedge

There are two types of foreign currency options available. Hedgers can trade options directly on the foreign currency or they can trade options on foreign currency futures contracts. We first explore options on currencies and then options on futures contracts.

FOREIGN EXCHANGE OPTIONS. Exhibit 18-7 reports pricing data for options on a variety of foreign currencies. The data presented, all expressed in cents per unit of foreign currency, includes the various striking prices for which options are being traded in the first column from the left, and the premiums for the various call and put options. For

EXHIBIT 18-7
Foreign Currency Options

PHILADELPHIA EXCHANGE OPTIONS

		CALLS VOL.	CALLS LAST	PUT VOL.	PUT LAST
BPound					147.69
31,250 Brit. Pound-cents per unit.					
145	Jan	10	3.15	50	1.05
BPound					147.69
31,250 Bril. Pounds-European Style.					
158	Dec	...	...	50	11.60
CDollr					66.48
50,000 Canadian Dollars-European Style.					
67^{50}	Mar	...	...	10	1.69
CDollr					66.48
50,000 Canadian Dollars-cents per unit.					
65	Mar	2	1.42	...	...
66	Mar	17	0.94	...	...
JYen					92.53
6,250,000J.Yen-100ths of a cent per unit.					
90	Dec	...	...	20	1.00
91	Dec	...	...	10	2.06
JYen					92.53
6,250,000J.Yen-European Style.					
87	Jan	...	...	10	0.32

		CALLS VOL.	CALLS LAST	PUT VOL.	PUT LAST
89	Jan	10	1.30	...	...
90	Dec	...	...	10	0.99
JYen					92.53
6,250,000J.Yen-EuropeanStyle.					
68	Dec	...	...	10	2.24
Euro					88.15
62,500 Euro-European style					
88	Dec	...	...	8	0.79
Euro					88.15
62,500 Euro-European style.					
96	Dec	...	...	55	7.15
96	Mar	...	...	26	7.05
102	Dec	...	...	6	13.15
Euro					88.15
62,500 Euro-cents per unit.					
82	Dec	2	6.33	...	...
86	Jan	...	...	5	0.40
86	Mar	10	4.06	...	...
88	Dec	20	0.64	...	...
88	Mar	2	2.96	...	...

		CALLS VOL.	CALLS LAST	PUT VOL.	PUT LAST
88	Jun	5	4.15	...	...
90	Dec	107	0.05	10	1.32
92	Jan	10	0.38	...	...
114	Dec	...	...	2	25.35
SFranc					57.83
62,500 Swiss Francs-European Style.					
53	Jan	34	5.94	...	...
54	Jan	6	5.04	...	...
57	Jan	34	2.04	...	...
58	Jan	3	1.44	...	...
59	Jan	34	0.74	...	...
60	Jan	24	0.44	44	1.53
61	Jan	48	0.22	16	2.40
62	Jan	72	0.10	...	...
SFranc					57.83
62,500 Swiss Francs-cents per unit.					
59	Dec	13	0.24	...	...
62	Dec	50	0.01	50	3.13
Call Vol.........601			Open Int.............10,874		
Put Vol.........509			Open Int.............8,543		

example, the January call option on the British pound with a striking price of 145, or $1.45, has a premium of 3.15 cents per pound. The option contract is for 31,250 pounds sterling, so one option will cost $984.375 = 31,250 × $.0315.

Let's now look at an example of using currency options to hedge the future purchase of a foreign currency. Suppose that an American importer will have a cash outflow of British pounds in late January 2002. The importer wants to protect herself against a deteriorating dollar, that is, having to pay more US dollars to purchase the same number of units of pounds sterling in January; she therefore buys one 145 call option at $.0315 per pound.[8] The importer has guaranteed an exchange rate of $1.45 + $.0315 = $1.4815, which is the 145 striking price plus the $.0315 premium. If the dollar weakens (i.e., the dollar price of pound sterling increases), the importer will exercise the option to purchase pounds at an effective cost of $1.4815. If the dollar strengthens (i.e., the dollar price of pound sterling decreases), the importer will simply purchase pounds in the spot market and let the option expire. The cost of the option is $984.375 = 31,250 × $.0315 for the option to acquire 31,250 pounds sterling, which has a dollar value at the striking price of $45,312.50 = 31,250 × $1.45. Thus the option premium represents a little over 2 percent of the dollar price of the contract or .0217 = $984.375/$45,312.50.

FUTURES OPTIONS. Buying call or put options on foreign currency futures contracts is also possible. These contracts are referred to as futures options and Exhibit 18-8 displays quotes for a variety of these contracts. Futures options work the same way that options work; the only difference is that the option is on a futures contract rather than on the foreign currency itself.

For example, in Exhibit 18-8 the March call British pound futures option with a striking price of 1450 or $1.45 can be purchased for a premium of $.0424 per pounds sterling. The contract denomination is 62,500 pounds. The cost of the March call option is therefore $2,650 = 62,500 × $.0424.

The buyer of a call option can exercise the option anytime before it expires in March and receive a futures contract on the pounds sterling. A financial manager wishing to hedge the future purchase of a foreign currency should buy a call and if a foreign currency were to be sold in the future, then buying a put option would be appropriate.

---

[8]These quotes are taken from Exhibit 18-7 for currency options shown earlier.

EXHIBIT 18-8
Foreign Currency Futures Options

FUTURES OPTIONS PRICES

Thursday, December 14, 2000

AGRICULTURAL

Corn (CBT)
5,000 bu.; cents per bu.

STRIKE	CALLS-SETTLE			PUTS-SETTLE		
PRICE	Jan	Feb	Mar	Jan	Feb	Mar
190	....	....	28½	⅛	....	¼
200	10½	....	19	⅛	....	¾
210	1¼	....	11½	¾	1½	3
220	⅛	....	6⅛	9½	5¾	7½
230	⅛	1¾	3⅛	....	....	14¼
240	⅛	½	1⅜	....	....	22¾

Est vol 14,000 Wd 5,355 calls 4,640 puts
Op int Wed 213,427 calls 121,215 puts

Soybeans (CBT)
5,000 bu.; cents per bu.

STRIKE	CALLS-SETTLE			PUTS-SETTLE		
PRICE	Jan	Feb	Mar	Jan	Feb	Mar
460	44¼	....	54	⅛	....	¾
480	24¼	35	37	⅛	....	3¼
500	5¼	19¾	23¼	1¼	6	9½
520	⅛	9½	13½	15⅞	15¾	19½
540	⅛	4	8	35¾	....	34
560	⅛	....	4⅝	55¾	....	50

Est vol 11,000 Wd 6,652 calls 4,187 puts
Op int Wed 108,150 calls 52,524 puts

Soybean Meal (CBT)
100 tons; $ per ton

STRIKE	CALLS-SETTLE			PUTS-SETTLE		
PRICE	Jan	Mar	May	Jan	Mar	May
180	9.30	9.50	9.25	0.05	3.75	7.00
185	4.40	7.00	7.25	0.05	6.00	10.00
190	1.00	5.10	5.50	1.60	9.10	....
195	0.15	3.50	4.75	5.85	....	....
200	0.05	2.65	3.75	....	....	....
205	....	....	....	....	....	....

Est vol 2,400 Wd 1,065 calls 589 puts
Op int Wed 27,825 calls 15,743 puts

Soybean Oil (CBT)
60,000 lbs.; cents per lb.

STRIKE	CALLS-SETTLE			PUTS-SETTLE		
PRICE	Jan	Mar	May	Jan	Mar	May
140	....	....	....	....	....	....
145	.480	1.080	....	.005	.200	.300
150	.060	.750	....	.060	.380	.450
155	.005	.520	....	.520	.640	.680
160	.005	.360	.760	....	.980	.970
165	.005	.260	.600	....	1.370	1.310

Est vol 4,000 Wd 609 calls 765 puts
Op int Wed 29,890 calls 10,037 puts

Wheat (CBT)
5,000 bu.; cents per bu.

STRIKE	CALLS-SETTLE			PUTS-SETTLE		
PRICE	Jan	Mar	May	Jan	Mar	May
250	....	20½	....	....	2⅜	3⅜
260	....	13½	25	....	5½	6¼
270	1	8½	19¼	3	10½	10¼
280	⅛	5½	14½	12	17⅜	15½
290	⅛	3½	11	....	25½	21¾
300	....	2¼	8⅜	....	34	28⅞

Est vol 5,500 Wd 2,825 calls 928 puts
Op int Wed 63,986 calls 37,931 puts

Cotton (NYBOT)
50,000 lbs.; cents per lb.

STRIKE	CALLS-SETTLE			PUTS-SETTLE		
PRICE	Mar	May	Jly	Mar	May	Jly
64	2.66	4.60	....	0.99	1.07	1.13
65	2.06	3.94	5.11	1.38	1.39	1.42
66	1.56	3.34	4.50	1.87	1.77	1.76
67	1.17	2.80	3.91	2.47	2.21	....
68	0.86	2.32	3.38	3.15	2.71	2.58
69	0.63	1.90	2.90	3.91	3.27	3.07

Est vol 3,100 Wd 5,299 calls 2,906 puts
Op int Wed 38,948 calls 43,850 puts

Orange Juice (NYBOT)
15,000 lbs.; cents per lb.

STRIKE	CALLS-SETTLE			PUTS-SETTLE		
PRICE	Jan	Mar	May	Jan	Mar	May
70	11.45	16.00	18.20	0.05	0.80	1.25
75	6.45	12.00	14.30	0.05	2.30	2.25
80	1.65	9.20	12.40	0.45	4.35	4.40
85	0.10	7.25	8.85	3.60	6.90	6.90
90	0.05	5.50	6.45	8.55	....	....
95	0.05	4.25	....	....	....	....

Est vol 1,000 Wd 983 calls 1,072 puts
Op int Wed 41,271 calls 20,502 puts

Coffee (NYBOT)
37,500 lbs.; cents per lb.

STRIKE	CALLS-SETTLE			PUTS-SETTLE		
PRICE	Feb	Mar	May	Feb	Mar	May
60	6.38	7.52	11.01	0.85	2.00	2.50
62.5	4.75	5.93	9.48	1.70	2.90	3.45
65	3.40	4.60	8.16	2.85	4.10	4.60
67.5	2.40	3.70	6.94	4.34	5.64	5.85
70	1.55	2.80	6.00	5.99	7.35	7.38
72.5	1.15	2.25	5.15	8.08	9.16	9.01

Est vol 4,939 Wd 887 calls 939 puts
Op int Wed 38,564 calls 11,655 puts

Sugar-World (NYBOT)
112,000 lbs.; cents per lb.

STRIKE	CALLS-SETTLE			PUTS-SETTLE		
PRICE	Feb	Mar	May	Feb	Mar	May
800	1.25	1.33	1.19	0.05	0.14	0.36
850	0.81	0.96	0.91	0.11	0.26	0.57
900	0.47	0.65	0.67	0.27	0.45	0.83
950	0.25	0.42	0.50	0.55	0.72	1.15
1000	0.12	0.27	0.38	0.92	1.07	1.53
1050	0.06	0.17	0.27	1.36	1.46	1.91

Est vol 1,965 Wd 3,249 calls 1,919 puts
Op int Wed 109,969 calls 90,623 puts

Cocoa (NYBOT)
10 metric tons; $ per ton

STRIKE	CALLS-SETTLE			PUTS-SETTLE		
PRICE	Feb	Mar	May	Feb	Mar	May
650	82	85	106	3	6	12
700	39	50	73	10	21	28
750	14	28	48	35	49	53
800	7	16	36	78	87	90
850	3	11	27	124	131	131
900	1	7	20	172	177	174

Est vol 694 Wd 916 calls 256 puts
Op int Wed 32,419 calls 11,269 puts

Gas Oil (IPE)
100 metric tons; $ per ton

STRIKE	CALLS-SETTLE			PUTS-SETTLE		
PRICE	Jan	Feb	Mar	Jan	Feb	Mar
22500	15.30	16.45	15.45	4.30	9.45	14.70
23000	12.15	13.80	13.20	6.15	11.80	17.45
23500	9.40	11.55	11.20	8.40	14.55	20.45
24000	6.85	9.55	9.45	10.85	17.55	23.70
24500	4.80	7.80	7.95	13.80	20.80	27.20
25000	3.20	6.30	6.80	17.20	24.30	31.05

Est vol 805 Wd 310 calls 0 puts
Op int Wed 5,182 calls 1,907 puts

LIVESTOCK

Cattle-Feeder (CME)
50,000 lbs.; cents per lb.

STRIKE	CALLS-SETTLE			PUTS-SETTLE		
PRICE	Jan	Mar	Apr	Jan	Mar	Apr
9000	1.55	1.65	1.70	0.80	1.95	2.25
9050	....	....	....	....	....	....
9100	0.85	....	....	1.10	....	....
9150	....	....	....	....	....	....
9200	0.47	0.85	0.85	....	....	....
9250	....	....	....	....	....	....

Est vol 468 Wd 178 calls 477 puts
Op int Wed 2,584 calls 14,571 puts

Cattle-Live (CME)
40,000 lbs.; cents per lb.

STRIKE	CALLS-SETTLE			PUTS-SETTLE		
PRICE	Jan	Feb	Apr	Jan	Feb	Apr
75	....	2.52	....	0.15	0.75	1.05
76	....	1.90	3.15	0.35	1.10	1.30
77	0.55	1.30	2.57	0.75	1.15	1.72
78	0.30	0.82	1.92	....	....	2.05
79	....	0.52	1.37	....	....	....
80	....	0.32	0.92	....	....	....

Est vol 5,984 Wd 1,042 calls 1,338 puts
Op int Wed 30,227 calls 51.717 puts

Hogs-Lean (CME)
40,000 lbs.; cents per lb.

STRIKE	CALLS-SETTLE			PUTS-SETTLE		
PRICE	Dec	Feb	Apr	Dec	Feb	Apr
57	1.82	2.57	....	0.00	1.15	....
58	0.82	1.97	2.35	0.00	1.52	2.37
59	0.02	1.45	....	0.20	2.00	....
60	0.00	1.00	1.40	1.17	2.52	3.38
61	....	0.67	....	....	....	....
62	0.00	0.45	0.85	....	....	....

Est vol 474 Wd 609 calls 488 puts
Op int Wed 7,976 calls 10,538 puts

METALS

Copper (CMX)
25,000 lbs.; cents per lb.

STRIKE	CALLS-SETTLE			PUTS-SETTLE		
PRICE	Jan	Feb	Mar	Jan	Feb	Mar
86	3.35	4.20	4.90	0.25	0.90	1.75
88	1.90	2.90	3.70	0.80	1.60	2.55
90	0.90	1.90	2.55	1.80	2.60	3.60
92	0.40	1.30	1.95	3.30	4.00	4.80
94	0.20	0.95	1.15	5.10	5.60	6.15
96	0.10	0.70	0.90	7.00	7.35	7.70

Est vol 150 Wd 37 calls 28 puts
Op int Wed 3,398 calls 1,590 puts

Gold (CMX)
100 troy ounces; $ per troy ounce

STRIKE	CALLS-SETTLE			PUTS-SETTLE		
PRICE	Feb	Mar	Apr	Feb	Mar	Apr
260	12.00	15.20	17.00	0.70	1.40	2.40
265	7.90	11.20	12.70	1.40	2.40	3.40
270	4.30	7.70	8.80	2.80	3.70	5.00
275	2.10	5.20	6.10	5.60	6.30	7.10
280	1.30	3.50	4.90	9.70	9.60	10.80
285	1.00	2.60	3.50	14.50	13.60	14.00

Est vol 6,500 Wd 3,897 calls 1,032 puts
Op int Wed 227,557 calls 63,581 puts

Silver (CMX)
5,000 troy ounces; cts per troy ounces

STRIKE	CALLS-SETTLE			PUTS-SETTLE		
PRICE	Feb	Mar	May	Feb	Mar	May
425	42.5	43.8	48.6	0.8	1.7	3.2
450	19.8	22.6	29.0	2.7	5.4	8.5
475	5.3	8.8	16.0	13.0	16.5	19.6
500	2.1	4.3	9.0	34.8	38.1	38.2
525	1.2	2.8	6.2	59.0	60.0	59.7
550	0.8	2.0	3.9	83.7	84.8	82.2

Est vol 4,200 Wd 1,472 calls 418 puts
Op int Wed 46,671 calls 12,838 puts

INTEREST RATE

T-Bonds (CBT)
$100,000; points – 64ths of 100%

STRIKE	CALLS-SETTLE			PUTS-SETTLE		
PRICE	Jan	Feb	Mar	Jan	Feb	Mar
102	2-34	2-51	3-06	0-01	0-18	0-37
103	1-34	2-02	2-24	0-01	0-32	0-55
104	0-39	1-24	1-49	0-05	0-55	1-15
105	0-07	0-56	1-17	0-37	1-22	1-47
106	0-01	0-34	0-57	1-31	....	2-22
107	0-01	0-20	0-39	2-30	2-49	3-04

Est vol 102,000;
Wd vol 27,035 calls 27,359 puts
Op int Wed 233,580 calls 271,024 puts

T-Notes (CBT)
$100,000; points – 64ths of 100%

STRIKE	CALLS-SETTLE			PUTS-SETTLE		
PRICE	Jan	Feb	Mar	Jan	Feb	Mar
102	2-24	2-31	2-40	0-01	0-07	0-17
103	1-25	1-42	1-56	0-01	0-18	0-33
104	0-28	0-63	1-17	0-04	0-39	0-57
105	0-02	0-34	0-52	....	....	1-28
106	0-01	0-17	0-32	....	....	2-07
107	0-01	0-08	0-19	....	....	....

Est vol 70,000 Wd 23,609 calls 31,683 puts
Op int Wed 265,266 calls 278,471 puts

5 Yr Treas Notes (CBT)
$100,000; points – 64ths of 100%
STRIKE CALLS-SETTLE PUTS-SETTLE

10 Yr. German Euro Gov't Bd (Eurobund) (Eurex)100,000;pts In 100%

STRIKE	CALLS-SETTLE			PUTS-SETTLE		
PRICE	Jan	Feb	Mar	Jan	Feb	Mar
10700	1.04	1.30	1.49	0.01	0.27	0.46
10750	0.60	0.96	1.17	0.07	0.43	0.64
10800	0.26	0.67	0.90	0.23	0.64	0.87
10850	0.08	0.45	0.67	0.55	0.92	1.14
10900	0.02	0.29	0.49	0.99	1.26	1.46
10950	0.01	0.19	0.35	1.47	1.66	1.82

Vol Th 82,461 calls 64,749 puts
Op int Wed 543,091 calls 517,727 puts

CURRENCY

Japanese Yen (CME)
12,500,000 yen; cents per 100 yen

STRIKE	CALLS-SETTLE			PUTS-SETTLE		
PRICE	Jan	Feb	Mar	Jan	Feb	Mar
8800	....	....	3.36	0.24	....	1.02
8850	....	....	....	0.32	....	....
8900	....	....	2.71	0.44	1.00	1.36
8950	....	....	....	0.59	....	1.56
9000	1.15	....	2.14	0.78	1.40	1.78
9050	0.88	....	1.89	1.01	....	2.02

Est vol 5,045 Wd 1,808 calls 2,118 puts
Op int Wed 21,106 calls 20,370 puts

Deutschemark (CME)
125,000 marks; cents per mark

STRIKE	CALLS-SETTLE			PUTS-SETTLE		
PRICE	Jan	Feb	Mar	Jan	Feb	Mar
4450	....	....	....	....	....	....
4500	....	....	1.56	....	....	....
4550	....	....	....	....	....	1.42
4600	....	....	....	....	....	....
4650	....	....	....	....	....	....
4700	....	....	0.70	....	....	....

Est vol 60 Wd 0 calls 0 puts
Op int Wed 4 calls 12 puts

Canadian Dollar (CME)
100,000 Can.$, cents per Can.$

STRIKE	CALLS-SETTLE			PUTS-SETTLE		
PRICE	Jan	Feb	Mar	Jan	Feb	Mar
6500	....	....	1.43	0.11	....	0.36
6550	0.80	....	1.10	0.21	....	0.52
6600	0.49	0.68	0.82	0.40	0.59	0.73
6650	....	....	0.59	....	....	0.99
6700	....	....	0.41	....	....	1.31
6750	....	....	0.29	....	....	1.68

Est vol 135 Wd 19 calls 37 puts
Op int Wed 8,848 calls 2,450 puts

British Pound (CME)
62,500 pounds; cents per pound

STRIKE	CALLS-SETTLE			PUTS-SETTLE		
PRICE	Jan	Feb	Mar	Jan	Feb	Mar
1450	2.86	3.74	4.24	0.50	....	1.90
1460	2.16	....	3.64	0.80	....	2.30
1470	1.56	....	3.10	1.20	....	....
1480	1.10	....	2.58	1.74	....	3.22
1490	0.78	1.66	....	....	....	....
1500	0.54	....	1.76	....	....	4.36

Est vol 762 Wd 125 calls 231 puts
Op int Wed 3,096 calls 3,007 puts

Swiss Franc (CME)
125,000 francs; cents per franc

STRIKE	CALLS-SETTLE			PUTS-SETTLE		
PRICE	Jan	Feb	Mar	Jan	Feb	Mar
5800	1.71	....	2.36	0.19	....	0.85
5850	1.34	....	....	0.31	....	....
5900	1.01	....	1.77	0.48	....	1.25
5950	0.73	....	....	....	....	....
6000	0.54	....	1.30	1.01	....	1.76
6050	0.37	....	....	....	....	....

Est vol 987 Wd 250 calls 43 puts
Op int Wed 4,651 calls 1,023 puts

INDEX

DJ Industrial Avg (CBOT)
$100 times premium

STRIKE	CALLS-SETTLE			PUTS-SETTLE		
PRICE	Dec	Jan	Feb	Dec	Jan	Feb
105	15.00	46.20	....	0.25	18.40	....
106	6.00	39.40	....	1.00	21.50	30.60
107	1.30	33.20	....	6.30	25.30	....
108	0.25	27.50	....	15.25	29.50	38.80
109	0.05	22.40	....	25.00	....	....
110	0.05	17.90	....	35.00	39.80	....

Est vol 850 Wd 266 calls 493 puts
Op int Wed 6,832 calls 10,710 puts

S&P 500 Stock Index (CME)
$250 times premium

STRIKE	CALLS-SETTLE			PUTS-SETTLE		
PRICE	Dec	Jan	Feb	Dec	Jan	Feb
1330	10.00	....	....	1.60	27.70	....
1335	5.90	....	....	2.50	29.40	....
1340	3.00	49.20	....	4.60	31.30	....
1345	1.50	46.10	....	8.10	33.20	....
1350	0.50	43.10	54.50	12.10	35.20	46.60
1355	0.20	40.30	....	16.80	37.30	....

Est vol 12,512 Wd 6,155 calls 10,204 puts
Op int Wed 101,742 calls 214,005 puts

OTHER OPTIONS

Final or settlement prices of selected contracts. Volume and open interest are totals in all contract months.

10 Yr. Agency Note (CBT)
pts 64ths

STRIKE	CALLS-SETTLE			PUTS-SETTLE		
PRICE	Jan	Feb	Mar	Jan	Feb	Mar
99	....	1-12	1-30	....	0-38	0-57

Est vol 300 Wd 6 calls 16 puts
Op int Wed 10,382 calls 5,377 puts

Corn (MCE)
1,000 bu.; cents per bu.

STRIKE	CALLS-SETTLE			PUTS-SETTLE		
PRICE	Jan	Feb	Mar	Jan	Feb	Mar

FOCUS ON PRACTICE

HOW CORPORATIONS USE DERIVATIVES.   Based on survey results presented by Bodnar and associates (1995), there appears to be a reasonably high degree of use of derivatives by nonfinancial firms in an attempt to manage financial risk. Of the 530 firms that responded to the survey, 35 percent indicated that they use derivatives (forwards, futures, options, or swaps). However, when the sample is stratified by size and industry some interesting disparities are discovered. Although 65 percent of the large firms reported using derivatives to manage financial risk, only 30 percent of mid-sized firms and 13 percent of small firms reported doing so. The predominant industry group users were commodity-based industries such as agriculture, refining, and mining, with 50 percent of this group reporting using derivatives as a risk management tool. Manufacturing firms were the second most frequent users of derivatives and services firms were the least frequent users.

Nonfinancial firms use derivatives to manage four general types of exposure including foreign exchange, interest rate, commodity price, and equity price. The survey indicated that swaps were the most prevalent instrument for managing interest rate risk. Forward contracts followed by options and then swaps were used for managing foreign currency risk.

Finally, the survey made it very clear that the predominate use of derivative securities by nonfinancial firms is for hedging purposes and not for speculation. The most common type of hedging was for well-defined exposures arising from firmly committed transactions or anticipated transactions less than a year away. Only 9 percent of the firms reported commonly using derivatives to take position on the direction of market prices or interest rates.

HEDGING WITH SWAPS

A swap is an agreement between two different institutions or firms, generally referred to as **counterparties,** to swap cash flows between themselves. Often there is an intermediary institution acting as a market maker through which the payments flow. In 1982, the combined dollar volume of currency and interest rate swaps was only about $5 billion. By the mid 1990s, the interest rate swap market alone had grown to approximately $3 trillion. Manufacturers, retailers, transportation companies, financial services firms, governmental agencies, and many others now use swaps. The typical swap deal involves $25 to $100 million with maturities ranging from 2 to 10 years.

Introduction to Interest Rate Swaps

In its simplest form, a **financial swap** represents an exchange of periodic cash flows between two parties. The two basic types of financial swaps involve the exchange of different currencies, known as a **currency swap,** and a swap of interest flows, generally referred to as an **interest rate swap.** The swap agreement specifies the currencies to be swapped; the applicable interest rates to be used; an agreed on **notional amount,** which is the agreed on face amount on which exchange rates or interest rates are to be applied to calculate the cash flows; and the timing of the payment of the cash flows.

The most common type of interest rate swap is a **fixed-for-floating rate swap,** as shown in Exhibit 18-9. In it, Party A, with floating rate debt, agrees to pay Party B, who has fixed rate debt, a fixed-rate interest payment based on the notional amount stated in the agreement, in exchange for receipt of a floating-rate interest payment. The receipt of the floating rate payment can be used to cover the cost of the floating rate liability, leaving Party A effectively paying a fixed rate of interest. Party B can apply the receipt of the fixed rate interest payment to the interest due on its fixed rate liabilities, effectively

EXHIBIT 18-9
Fixed-for-Floating Interest Rate Swap

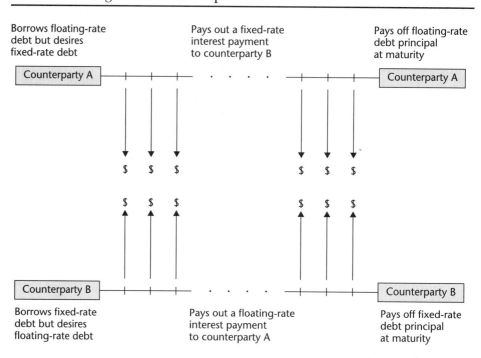

leaving it paying a floating rate of interest. Thus swaps have become a very effective way for firms to manage their interest rate exposure.

One of the main characteristics of an interest rate swap is that the principal amount does not change hands. Rather, only interest payments are swapped and the payments are based on an agreed on notional amount of principal.

Why Swaps Work

Swaps work because of the ability to share the comparative advantage counterparties may have in their own respective market places. The theory of comparative advantage was originally advanced in the international trade area and explains how two countries can both be better off by specializing in those products in which they have a comparative advantage and then trading among themselves to acquire those products they individually did not produce.

The same concept works for corporations in the capital markets. For example, although two companies may both have the same credit rating such a AAA or AA, one may receive a slightly lower borrowing rate in the short-term market because it may tap the short-term market more often and therefore be more familiar to investors, and the other firm may tap the longer-term market more often and thus receive a slightly preferential borrowing rate with longer maturities.

These pricing discrepancies create opportunities for corporations to take advantage of these variations and share the cost savings. Because each firm borrows in the market in which it has a comparative advantage, it can trade a portion of that advantage with a counterparty and both companies can reduce their borrowing costs or enhance their investment returns.

EXHIBIT 18-10
The Basic Structure of an Asset Swap

	Counterparty A	Counterparty B
	ALTERNATIVE INTEREST RATES IN THE HOME MARKET	
Fixed:	9%	8%
Variable:	LIBOR	LIBOR + .5%
ir:	9%	LIBOR + .5%
so:	9%	LIBOR + .5%
si:	LIBOR + .5%	9%
	$k_{swap} = ir - so + si - fee$	
	$k_{swap} = LIBOR + .5\% - fee$	9% − fee

There are two basic categories of interest rate swaps. They are asset or investment swaps and liability or financing swaps. We will discuss each in the following sections.

Interest Rate Asset Swap

Suppose that an institution such as a thrift or savings and loan association has a portfolio of fixed rate investments such as mortgages. Furthermore, assume that the institution's primary source of financing carries a variable rate or has such a short maturity relative to the maturity of the investment portfolio of mortgages that the interest expense is essentially variable. The institution has a problem if interest rates begin to rise because the interest receipts from the mortgage portfolio are fixed but the interest that must be paid on its liabilities increases as market rates rise.

The institution's problem would be solved if it could pay out, or *swap* the fixed rate interest receipts in exchange for a receipt of variable rate interest payments. This type of swap is referred to as a fixed-for-floating swap and was one of the first types of interest rate swaps to be developed. These swaps have three basic cash flows to consider. First the institution has the investment rate, *ir*, that is received from the original investment. Second, there is the swap outflow, *so*, which is the interest rate that the institution agrees to pay to the other party, the counterparty. Finally, there is the swap inflow, *si*, which is the interest rate that is received from the counterparty. If *ir* is fixed, as in our example, the *so* is also fixed because the institution is merely passing the interest received, or some portion of it, on to the counterparty. Further, *si* is a variable rate payment from the counterparty. As a result, the institution is essentially receiving a variable rate of interest.

Exhibit 18-10 presents a summary of these transactions. In this example, Counterparty A has a comparative or relative advantage in fixed rate investments and Counterparty B has a comparative advantage in floating rate investments. Counterparty A takes advantage of its higher fixed rates and passes those rates on to Counterparty B. Counterparty B takes advantage of its higher floating rates and passes that advantage on to Counterparty A.

The effective rate from the swap, k_{swap}, is equal to the original *ir* minus *so* plus *si*. The effective rate from the swap can then be compared to the alternative rate in each institution's respective market to verify that indeed the swap was able to yield a better return than could be obtained otherwise. Note that the swap expression, k_{swap}, also deducts for any fee percentage that the clearing bank or institution may charge for helping to manage the swap flows. In this example, as long as the fee is less than .5 percent per year, the swap is advantageous to both parties.

Interest Rate Liability Swap

A liability swap is similar in structure to the asset swap just discussed except that the counterparties are trying to manage the interest rate risk of their liabilities rather than their assets. To see how a liability swap is structured, assume that Counterparty A can finance at relatively low variable rates compared with Counterparty B, but its fixed rates are relatively higher. Furthermore, assume that Counterparty A desires to finance using fixed rate financing.

The institution's problem will be solved if it issues the relatively cheaper variable rate liabilities and receives variable rate payments from the counterparty in exchange for fixed rate payments. Just like the asset swaps discussed earlier, liability swaps also have three basic cash flows to consider. First there is the financing rate, fr, that is being paid on the original liability. Second, there is the so, which is the interest rate that the institution agrees to pay to the other party, the counterparty. Finally, there is the si, which is the interest rate that will be received from the counterparty. If the fr is variable, as in our example, the si will also be variable because this is the cash flow that the firm will use to pay the interest payment on the original debt, and the so will be fixed because the Counterparty A desires to net out fixed rate financing. As a result, the firm is essentially paying a fixed rate of interest.

Exhibit 18-11 presents these transactions for a liability swap. In this example, Counterparty A has a comparative advantage in floating rate liabilities and Counterparty B has a comparative advantage in fixed rate liabilities. Counterparty A takes advantage of its lower variable rate financing and passes this rate on to Counterparty B. Counterparty B takes advantage of its lower fixed rate financing and passes that advantage on to Counterparty A.

The effective rate from the swap, k_{swap}, is equal to the original fr plus the so minus the si. The effective rate from the swap can then be compared to the alternative rate in each institution's respective market to verify that indeed the swap was able to yield a better financing cost than could be obtained otherwise. Note that k_{swap} also accounts for any fee percentage that the clearing bank or institution may charge for helping to manage the swap flows. In this case, the fee rate represents an addition to the cost of financing.

EXHIBIT 18-11
The Basic Structure of a Liability Swap

	COUNTERPARTY A	COUNTERPARTY B
Alternative Interest Rates in the Home Market		
Fixed:	9%	8%
Variable:	LIBOR	LIBOR + .5%
fr:	LIBOR	8%
so:	8%	LIBOR
si:	LIBOR	8%
	$k_{swap} = fr + so - si + fee$	
	$k_{swap} = 8.5\% + fee$	LIBOR + fee

FINANCIAL DILEMMA

What Can Be Done About Uncertain Currency Exchange Rates?

The Body Shop, LTD., is a retail operation focusing on body care products produced from natural sources. The company was founded in the United Kingdom and found quick success with the consumer public. The company began expansion in the US consumer skin care market during the early 1990s. To fund the expansion, the company should attempt to find dollar-based financing because its earnings will be in dollars, but the company is not well known outside the United Kingdom. If it borrows in the United Kingdom, it will face exchange rate exposure converting its dollar earnings to pound sterling to service its sterling debt. How can the company manage the exchange rate risk of expansion into the US market?

Foreign Currency Swap

A **currency swap** is an agreement between two parties to exchange different currencies and then to re-exchange them at a future date at the same exchange rate. Periodic interest payments are made during the term of the swap.

A currency swap involves three distinct cash flows as shown in Exhibit 18-12. First, there is the initial exchange of principal amounts. Second is the exchange of interest payments over the course of the borrowings. Third is the final exchange, or re-exchange, of principals in their respective currencies.

For example, suppose a UK retailer wants to expand its operations in the US market. It will sell its products in the United States for dollars and thus wants to borrow dollars to fund the expansion. Although it may be a well-known credit in the UK, the firm may be a relative unknown in the US financial markets and thus borrowing may be at relatively high rates. The UK retailer may therefore borrow in pounds sterling in the United Kingdom, where it is a better known credit, and exchange the pounds sterling for US dollars borrowed by a US firm that wants to borrow pounds sterling. The two firms initially swap currencies, generally through an intermediary, at the current

EXHIBIT 18-12
Cash Flows of a Currency Swap

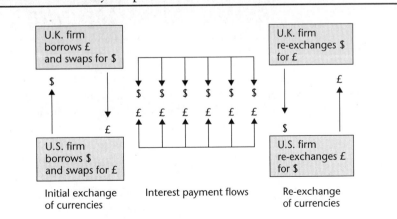

FOCUS ON PRACTICE

HOW DO CORPORATIONS USE FOREIGN EXCHANGE HEDGING STRATEGIES? Aggarwal and Soenen[9] conducted interviews with 30 of the large Fortune 500 companies to ascertain their use of exchange rate hedging strategies. All 30 companies used some type of foreign exchange rate hedging through the use of forwards, futures, or options, primarily to hedge transaction exposure.

Sixty percent of the sample did not perceive any significant difference in the use of futures contracts versus an option contract for hedging purposes and 40 percent rejected the use of futures in favor of options or forwards. Those that did use options, used those written by banks rather than going through the listed options exchange. The respondents felt that the exchange market could not handle the volume needed by the firms without affecting the option price. None of the firms in the sample wrote options. In their view, it was too speculative in nature.

A case in point is Blount, Inc.[10] The company's treasury function attempts to hedge between 50 and 85 percent of its net foreign currency cash flow exposure over $500,000 occurring within a 12-month time frame. The company uses hedging instruments such as forwards, swaps, and options.

More recently, Ricci and Morrison[11] surveyed Fortune 200 firms and discovered that the vast majority of the respondents used only the spot and forward markets often. Put another way, although less than 5 percent of the respondents indicated they never used the spot or forward market, those never using currency options, swaps, and futures contracts averaged almost 30 percent of the respondents. They speculate that the relatively infrequent use of currency options is because currency options are comparatively expensive and the relatively infrequent use of futures may be due to the fact that contracts only exist for seven currencies.

[9]Raj Aggarwal and Luc A. Soenen. 1989. Corporate use of options and futures in foreign exchange management. *Journal of Cash Management* November/December:61–66.

[10]Mark Cook. 1995. Foreign exchange management at Blount, Inc. *TMA Journal* January/February:30–32.

[11]Cecilia Wagner Ricci and Gail Morrison. 1996. International working capital practices of the Fortune 200. *Financial Practice and Education* Fall/Winter:18.

exchange rate. Over the life of the swap agreement, the US firm pays the UK firm's interest payments in pounds sterling, and the UK firm pays the US firm's interest payments in dollars. At the end of the swap agreement period, the two firms re-exchange principals at the original spot exchange rate.

FINANCIAL DILEMMA REVISITED

Recall the Body Shop dilemma described earlier. A currency swap arrangement is an ideal exchange rate risk management vehicle for the firm to consider. First, the financial manager at the Body Shop borrows pounds sterling in the United Kingdom. The pounds sterling can then be swapped for dollars with a counterparty in the United States. The two firms then agree to pay each other's interest payments and finally agree to swap back the principal amounts at the same exchange rate that existed at the time of the swap origination. The Body Shop uses its dollar earnings in the United States to service the dollar interest payment flows.

Let's now put some numbers to this example to better see how it works. Suppose that the Body Shop can borrow pounds at 10 percent and borrow dollars in the United States at 12 percent because of its lack of exposure in the US market. Further assume that its US counterparty can borrow dollars at 11 percent. The current exchange rate is $1.70 per pound sterling. The principal amount involved is $25 million or 14,705,882 pounds sterling. The Body Shop borrows the 14.7 million pounds sterling and swaps it for the $25 million, which is the dollar amount of funding it needs for the US expansion effort. The Body Shop agrees to pay the 11 percent interest in dollars and the US counterparty agrees to pay the 10 percent interest in pounds. At the end of the swap period, the two firms exchange principal; the Body Shop receives 14.7 million pounds sterling and the US counterparty receives $25 million. The advantage to the Body Shop is that it effectively borrowed dollars at 11 percent rather than the 12 percent available to it through the traditional US credit market. In addition, it can now use its dollar earnings to service dollar-denominated debt, thus neutralizing its foreign currency exposure related to its financing needs.

OTHER HEDGING INSTRUMENTS

You probably agree by this time that developing appropriate hedging strategies can be a very complex task. Rather than using futures and options directly, some corporate treasurers take advantage of new products that have been developed from options but are not as complex. Examples of these include interest-rate caps, interest-rate floors, and interest-rate collars.

Interest-Rate Caps

An **interest-rate cap** is marketed by institutions such as commercial banks, which stand ready to buy and sell interest-rate caps. The interest-rate cap contract specifies:

- The reference rate (such as the Treasury bill, LIBOR, Eurodollar, commercial paper or even the certificate of deposit rate)
- The strike rate (the rate level at which payments begin to be made to offset adverse rate movements)
- A notional amount of principal (the dollar amount on which the rate is based)
- The term (generally from 1 to 10 years, but can be as short as 3 months).

The purchaser of a rate cap pays a premium up front, much like an option, and receives cash payments from the rate cap seller whenever the reference rate exceeds the strike rate. The calculation for the cash payment is relatively simple and is shown below in Equation 18-6.

$$\text{Cap Payment} = (\text{ref} - \text{strk}) \times \text{NP} \times \text{L} \qquad \text{(18-6)}$$

In which:

ref = reference rate

strk = strike rate

NP = notional principal

L = length of the payment period

For example, suppose that a bank investment officer wishes to purchase a rate cap that limits the bank's exposure to interest rate increases on its variable rate certificates of deposit (CDs). Assume that the reference rate is an index of CD rates that now stands at 10 percent. Further, assume that the strike rate is 9.50 percent and the notional principal is $10 million. Assuming the payment period is for 6 months (half a year or L = .5), the cash payment received from the rate seller is:

$$\text{Cash Payment} = (.10 - .0950) \times \$10,000,000 \times .5$$
$$\text{Cash Payment} = \$25,000$$

Ocean Spray Cranberries, Inc., traditionally uses short-term financing to finance its seasonal working capital needs. During its peak season in the fall, Ocean Spray finances its expanding working capital with seasonal borrowings until it sells the bulk of its products during the Thanksgiving season. Its receipts are then used to pay off its seasonal financing. However, during the late 1980s the company was hit hard by rising short-term rates. The company decided to protect itself against adverse rate movements by using interest-rate caps. Ocean Spray hedged half of its estimated seasonal borrowing needs by purchasing a two-year interest-rate cap at a 10.5 percent maximum rate, the strike rate in Equation 18-6, to cover a 2-year operating period.[12]

Ocean Spray chose to use a cap rather than an interest-rate floor or collar, which will be discussed in the following sections, because the company simply wanted insurance against upward rate spikes, not an assurance of a specific or set rate.

Interest-Rate Floor

An **interest-rate floor** works in a similar fashion to a rate cap except that it is used to place a lower limit on the selected interest rate. The rate floor purchaser pays a premium for the rate floor contract and then receives from the rate floor seller a cash payment whenever the reference rate falls below the striking rate. The calculation for the cash payment is the same as for the rate cap with the variables ref and strk reversed as shown below in Equation 18-7.

$$\text{Floor Payment} = (\text{strk} - \text{ref}) \times \text{NP} \times \text{L} \qquad (18\text{-}7)$$

Interest-Rate Collar

Rate caps and floors can be combined to form what are called **interest-rate collars.** To create a rate collar, the user purchases a rate cap and sells or issues a rate floor. The premium received from issuing the rate floor is used to offset the cost of the rate cap. If the reference rate exceeds the strike rate on the cap, then a cash payment is received. If the reference rate falls below the strike rate on the floor, a cash payment is made to the purchaser of the floor. Thus the effective interest rate is managed within a narrow bound determined by the strike rate on the cap and floor contracts.

Exhibit 18-13 demonstrates how a collar works over a range of interest rates. Assume that the financial manager of a large financial institution wishes to form an interest-rate collar on its CD cost, essentially forming a maximum borrowing rate of 9.5 percent and a minimum borrowing rate of 9 percent. In the exhibit, the strike rate for the interest-rate cap is 9.5 percent and the strike rate for the interest-rate floor is 9 percent. The notional amount on which the cash payments are based is $1 million and the period is 1 year. If the reference rate is 8 percent, the financial manager makes a cash payment to the floor purchaser of $10,000. No cash payments are made if the reference rate is between 9 percent and 9.5 percent. If the reference rate rises to 10 percent, the financial

[12]For additional details see, Peter D. Hanson. 1990. How Ocean Spray trims the risks of seasonal borrowing. *Corporate Cashflow* May:58.

EXHIBIT 18-13

An Example of the Cash Payments Related to an Interest Rate Collar

Cap Strike Rate = 9.5%
Floor Strike Rate = 9.0%
Notional Amount = $1,000,000
Period = 1 year

REF	Cap Payment	Floor Payment	Effective Rate
.0800	0	$10,000	.090
.0850	0	5,000	.090
.0900	0	0	.090
.0950	0	0	.0950
.1000	$5,000	0	.0950
.1050	10,000	0	.0950
.1100	20,000	0	.0950

Effective Rate = REF + ([Floor Pmt − Cap Pmt]/Notional Amount)

manager receives a $5,000 cash payment from the cap seller. The cash payments received compensate the financial institution for the rates rising above the strike rate and essentially capping the effective cost of its CDs at 9.5 percent. The cash payments paid by the financial institution in essence keep the effective rate of the CDs at a minimum rate of 9 percent.

One example of a business application of an interest rate collar was a transaction involving the business background music company Muzak, Inc. The company decided to take advantage of an interest rate collar to "lock" in or stabilize its borrowing rate over the coming 2 years.[13] The treasury officials at Muzak mainly wanted protection from rising rates but decided to use a collar to reduce the effective cost of the cap. They paid an up-front premium to purchase the cap but received a premium by selling or issuing an interest-rate floor. As a result, Muzak was protected from rate increases over the negotiated strike rate and was willing to forego the benefits if rates declined to reduce the up-front cost of the transaction.

These new interest rate management contracts are gaining in popularity as a result of the reduced complexities they offer the financial manager.

REGULATORY ISSUES

A new reporting policy devised by the Financial Accounting Standards Board, FAS 133 and its amending statement FAS 138, went into effect for all companies with fiscal years beginning after June 15, 2000. These guidelines require hedges to be marked-to-market and recorded at fair value on the hedging companies' financial statements. The problem for corporations, though, is that these changes are recorded without offsetting changes to the value of the currency being hedged unless the transaction can be defined to be a qualifying hedge. For non-qualifying hedges, this exposes the hedging company's financial statements to potential volatility. As a result many financial managers are reassessing their hedging strategies. There are four key rules that form the backbone of FAS 133. These are the following:[14]

---

[13]For additional details on the Muzak transaction see, Lori Kuo-Dillon and Marshall A. Blake. 1990. How Muzak stays in tune with interest rate. *Corporate Cashflow* March:41.

[14]Jeffrey Wallace. 2000. Foreign exchange hedging under FAS 133. *AFP Exchange* Fall:50–59.

- All standalone and qualifying embedded derivatives must be marked-to-market and reported on the balance sheet.
- The gain or loss on changes in the value of the derivative must be reported immediately in earnings unless the derivative is part of a qualifying hedge. To qualify, the hedge must satisfy rigorous criteria regarding its effectiveness.
- If the hedge passes the qualifying test but is not 100 percent perfect, the amount by which it is not perfect must be reported on the income statement.
- Companies must fully describe their derivative and hedging activities in the footnotes to their financial statements.

Prior to FAS 133, accounting for foreign exchange hedging activities was based on a series of accounting standards such as FAS 52 and 80. As a result, there were wide variations in hedge accounting practices and derivative losses could be easily hidden.

Because of the complexity of complying with the FAS 133 guidelines, several software vendors and consulting firms have established Web sites that provide help for corporate treasurers. For example, PricewaterhouseCoopers formed a business in partnership with Gifford Fong Associates. They offer their clients an Application Service Provider tool that gives companies the ability to document hedges, allows one-to-one and many-to-many hedge relationships, archives historic market values and effectiveness, flags hedge types at inception, marks derivatives hedges to market, assesses the prospective effectiveness of derivatives, measures actual effectiveness and prepares compliant FAS 133 reports.[15]

SUMMARY

This chapter discussed several different approaches to managing exposure to changes in interest rates and currency exchange rates. These include futures contracts, options, swaps, caps, floors, and collars. Each of the alternative contracts has their own advantages and disadvantages. Thus the financial manager needs to be aware of all possible alternatives and choose that strategy that best matches the needs and situation of the firm.

Financial risk management is one area that is constantly changing with new strategies and contracts being created continuously. It is imperative that the financial manager stays abreast of the latest developments to best manage the firm's exposure to changes in interest rates and exchange rates.

Useful Web Sites

Futures Magazine, Inc.: www.futuresmag.com
The Publisher of International Treasurer: www.fas133.com

Questions

1. Explain the difference between a speculator and a hedger.
2. Explain in your own words what is meant by hedging.
3. How are futures options different from futures contracts? What are the relative advantages and disadvantages?

---

[15]Steve Bergsman. 2001. 133 help on the web. *Treasury & Risk Management* December/January:15.

4. Why do hedgers not write options on futures?
5. Why should a hedger using futures contracts generally use the nearby contract?
6. What risks are assumed by the counterparties in a swap transaction?
7. Explain the transactions required to create an interest-rate collar. Explain how a collar can stabilize the firm's borrowing rate.
8. Explain how a collar stabilizing an investment rate is different from a collar designed to stabilize a financing rate.
9. How is a forward contract like a futures contract and how is it different?
10. Compare and contrast futures contracts, futures options, and options.

Problems

1. As treasurer of CCM, Inc., part of your job is to invest short-term funds. Your cash budget forecast indicates the firm will generate $10 million of surplus funds in 2 months, which is March 1. The funds can be invested for 90 days. The current cash market 90-day rate on Treasury bills is 5.50 percent and the current futures rate on 90-day Treasury bills is 5.70 percent. Your investment company requires $2,000 of initial margin per $1 million contract and the roundtrip commission rate is $100.
    a. Assume that in 2 months, the 90-day cash rate rises to 6 percent and the 90-day futures rate rises to 6 percent. What is the net position from the hedge?
    b. Assume that in 2 months, the 90-day cash rate falls to 5 percent and the 90-day futures rate falls to 5 percent. What is the net position from the hedge?
    c. Rework parts *a* and *b* assuming that the denomination of the futures contract is $1 million but you plan to invest $10 million and that the only futures contract available is for 180-day Treasury bills. Substitute 180-day futures for 90-day futures in part *a* and *b*, and use the same rates used in parts *a* and *b*.
2. Your firm has been a net borrower of commercial paper for several months. You are preparing a new $20 million issue of 180-day commercial paper and the current cash market rate is 5.5 percent. The futures rate on a comparable instrument is 5.75 percent. You plan to issue the paper in 2 weeks but given the recent volatility in the money market you are uncertain of the rate the paper will be priced at the time of issuance. Assume that margin is $1,500 per futures contract, the contract denomination is $.5 million, and the roundtrip commission rate is $100 per contract.
    a. Assume that cash rates are 6.5 percent at issuance in 2 weeks and the futures contract rate is 6.75 percent. What is the net position of the hedge?
    b. Assume that cash rates are 5 percent at issuance in 2 weeks and the futures contract rate is 5.25 percent. What is the net position of the hedge?
3. You have been pursuing some rather risky money market investment strategies and as result have been burned more than once. You recently came across an article describing hedging techniques using financial futures contracts and wondered how these might apply to a riding the yield curve strategy.
    Suppose that the current cash rate on 180-day Treasury bills is 5.30 percent and 5 percent on 90-day bills. The futures rates on 90-day Treasury bills is

currently 5.20 percent. You invest in 180-day bill today and sell it in 90 days when it becomes a 90-day bill. Rates on 90-day cash bills are 5.25 percent at the time your bill is sold. Assume that the rate on a 90-day Treasury bill futures contract is 5.30 percent in 90 days. If you invest $1 million and the futures contract denomination is $1 million, the commission rate is $100, and the margin is $2,000 per contract, then what is the net position resulting from the hedge? How would this result compare if you had not hedged? How does the original result compare to having invested in a 90-day cash T-bill?

4. The treasurer of ABCO, Inc., is making plans to invest in $12 million, face value, of 90-day Treasury bills on June 1, which is 30 days from today. The current cash rate on 90-day bills is 5.38 percent and the June 90-day futures contract settled at a discount rate of 5.47 percent. She would like to hedge her 30-day exposure until she can make the investment and chooses to use a 90-day Treasury bill futures option. The contract size is $1 million. The striking price she chooses for the June call option is 9400 and the premium is stated as .53 pts per 100%.

   a. Assume that rates on 90-day cash bills increase to 5.70 percent by June 1. At the same time, assume that the futures rate increases to 5.79 percent and the premium on the options contract falls to .21. What is the net result of the hedge?

   b. Assume that rates on 90-cash bills fall to 5 percent by June 1. At the same time assume that the futures rate falls to 5.09 percent and the premium on the options contract rises to 91 basis points. What is the net result of the hedge?

5. The treasurer of COMCO, Inc., is making plans to issue $5 million of 90-day commercial paper on June 1, which is 30 days from today. The current cash rate on 90-day paper is 5.38 percent and the June 90-day futures contract settled at a discount rate of 5.47 percent. She would like to hedge her 30-day exposure until she can make the investment and chooses to use a 90-day Treasury bill futures option. The contract size is $1 million. The striking price she chooses for the June put option is 9500 and the premium is stated as .47 pts per 100%.

   a. Assume that rates on 90-day paper increase to 5.70 percent by June 1. At the same time assume that the futures rate increases to 5.79 percent and the premium on the options contract rises to .79. What is the net result of the hedge?

   b. Assume that rates on 90-day paper fall to 5.3 percent by June 1. At the same time assume that the futures rate falls to 5.39 percent and the premium on the option contract falls to .39. What is the net result of the hedge?

6. OSO, Inc., is concerned about its long-term interest rate exposure. Its bank has just contacted it about entering into a swap arrangement with ESSEX, Inc., which also has an unfavorable exposure to interest rate risk. OSO desires floating rate financing and ESSEX is looking for fixed rate financing. The following table presents the interest rate opportunities available to each company in their own market places.

	OSO, INC.	ESSEX, INC.
Fixed Rate	8%	9%
Floating Rate	LIBOR + 1.5%	LIBOR + 1.75%

The bank recommends that OSO arrange fixed rate financing at the 8 percent rate and that ESSEX arrange floating rate financing at its LIBOR + 1.75%.

Then OSO pays LIBOR + .5% to ESSEX and ESSEX pays 7.5 percent to OSO. Assume the notional amount is for $100 million.

a. What is the effective annual rate from the swap for each company?

b. How much of a fee can the bank charge each party for them to be willing to enter the transaction? (Assume the fee rate must be the same to each firm.)

7. You are currently in the midst of a swap contract negotiation with a counterparty. You need variable rate financing and the counterparty is looking for fixed rate financing.

	YOUR MARKET	COUNTERPARTY'S MARKET
Fixed rates	7%	8%
Floating rates	T-bill + 1%	T-bill + .5%

Please answer the following:

a. What type of financing rate should you lock in at the current time (fixed or floating)? Explain why.

b. What type of swap outflow rate should you agree to (fixed or floating)? Explain why.

c. What type of swap inflow rate should you agree to (fixed or floating)? Explain why.

8. Rail Transport, Inc., is concerned about its interest rate exposure. Its investment bank has just contacted it about entering into a swap arrangement with Agriproducts, Inc., which also has an unfavorable exposure to interest rate risk. Rail Transport desires a floating investment rate and Agriproducts is looking for fixed rate investments. The following table presents the interest rate opportunities available to each company in their own market places.

	RAIL TRANSPORT, INC.	AGRIPRODUCTS, INC.
Fixed Rate	7 %	6.3 %
Floating Rate	T-bill + 1.5%	T-bill + 1.75%

The investment bank recommends that Rail Transport invest in the fixed rate instrument at the 7 percent rate and that Agriproducts invest at its current floating rate of T-bill + 1.75%. Then Rail Transport pays 7 percent to Agriproducts and Agriproducts pays T-bill + 1.75% percent to Rail Transport. Assume the notional amount is for $50 million. What is the effective annual rate resulting from the swap?

9. XYZ, Inc., is concerned about its long-term interest rate exposure to its fixed rate bond portfolio. Current rates are historically low and the firm anticipates that they will rise. XYZ could go liquid by simply selling the bonds. However, the firm's investment banker recently introduced the idea of an interest rate swap. XYZ purchased the 7-year fixed rate bonds as a new issue 3 years ago priced at par with a coupon rate of 12 percent. The current year bid rate on 4-year bonds is 11 percent.

The investment bank has indicated that a swap is possible with an unidentified counterparty for XYZ to pay 11 percent fixed rate to the counterparty and receive a variable interest payment of LIBOR. What is the effective annual rate XYZ will receive from the swap? What benefits are provided by the swap arrangement?

10. TRKY, Inc., is a firm that grows and sells turkeys. The business is highly seasonal, with 80 percent of its revenues generated during the Thanksgiving season. The firm relies heavily on commercial paper to finance its seasonal working capital needs. The financial manager of TRKY, Inc. is considering the use of an interest-rate cap to protect the firm from an increase in borrowing costs. The notional amount is $10 million and the strike rate is set at 10 percent over an effective period of 6 months.

   Estimate the cash payments for reference rates of 9%, 10%, and 11%.

11. The financial manager of Floor-Mart finds the company in a $10 million cash surplus position and wishes to protect its short-term investment portfolio from dropping interest rates. The financial manager wants to create an interest-rate floor on its commercial paper investments. Assume the strike rate is 7.5 percent and the notional amount is $10 million. The protection period is set for 6 months.

   Estimate the cash payments related to the floor for reference rates of 7%, 8%, and 9%.

12. Suppose the financial manager of ACE, Inc. wishes to form an interest-rate collar. Explain the transactions that ACE's financial manager can negotiate with its bank, assuming that she does not want her effective borrowing rate to range outside of a 1-percent band with a high of 9.5 percent and a low of 8.5 percent.

13. You recently sold some goods to an importer in Switzerland and during the negotiations you agreed to invoice the goods in francs knowing that you will need to convert the francs to dollars upon receipt. The current exchange rate is $.60 per franc and the invoice will be for 250,000 francs. Payment is due in 60 days. You decide to hedge your exposure using futures contracts.
   a. How many futures contracts will you need?
   b. Will you create a buy hedge or a sell hedge?
   c. What will your spot market position be if the spot exchange rate is $.70 in 60 days?
   d. What will your futures contract gain or loss be if the futures rate, which is currently $.63, increases to $.71?
   e. Assume that one futures contract has a commission rate of $25 and the margin is $1,000 per contract. The current money market interest rate is 7 percent. What is the net position resulting from the hedge and how does the hedged position compare with an unhedged position?

14. As manager of a US domestic company, you are concerned about the foreign currency exposure of your firm's sales to the United Kingdom. You currently export $10 million of products to the United Kingdom annually and receive payment in pounds sterling. You send two large shipments each year valued at $5 million each. The invoice carries net 90-day terms. Thus your company is exposed to currency exchange risk for 90 days.

   You are considering the possibility of using futures, options, or futures options as possible hedging tools. Your broker recently sent you the following data on the various hedging contracts available for your June 1 invoice with payment due September 1.

   Current exchange rate (June 1): $1.67 per pound

   Assumed spot exchange rate on September 1 is $2.00

90-day Forward rate as of June 1: $1.65

Options (31,250)

STRIKING PRICE	JUNE 1, SEPTEMBER CALL PREMIUM	CALL PREMIUM SEPTEMBER 1
165.0	4.35	35.00
170.0	2.40	30.00
175	1.20	25.00

Futures Options (62,500)

STRIKING PRICE	JUNE 1, SEPTEMBER CALL PREMIUM	CALL PREMIUM SEPTEMBER 1
1650	4.12	33.00
1700	2.20	27.00
1750	1.06	22.00

Futures (62,500)

	JUNE 1 SETTLE	SEPTEMBER 1 SETTLE
September	1.6496	2.055

a. Assume you do not hedge. Calculate the dollar loss occurring from the change in exchange rates from June 1 to September 1.

b. Assume you hedge with an options contract. Calculate the net result from the change in the exchange rate from June 1 to September 1. Assume commission fees equal $60.

c. Assume you hedge with an futures option contract. Calculate the net result from the change in the exchange rate from June 1 to September 1. Assume commission fees equal $60.

d. Assume you hedge with a futures contract. Calculate the net result from the hedge assuming that the margin for one contract is $1,000, roundtrip commission fees equal $60, and your opportunity rate is 6%.

e. Assume you enter into a 90-day forward rate agreement. Calculate the net result from the hedge assuming that the fee for the agreement is $150.

References

Raj Aggarwal. 1991. Assessing risks in interest-rate swaps: The role of legal and institutional uncertainties. *Journal of Cash Management* May/June:15–18.

Raj Aggarwal and Luc A. Soenen. 1989. Corporate use of options and futures in foreign exchange management. *Journal of Cash Management* November/December:61–66.

Robert Baldoni and Gerhard Isele. 1986. A simple guide to choosing between futures and swaps. *Intermarket* October:15–22.

James Bicksler and Andrew H. Chen. 1986. An economic analysis of interest rate swaps. *The Journal of Finance* July:645–655.

Stanley B. Block and Timothy J. Gallagher. 1986. The use of interest rate futures and options by corporate financial managers. *Financial Management* Autumn:73–78.

Theodore Brauch. 1993. An interest rate swap primer. *Journal of Cash Management* July/August:8–14.

Chicago Board of Trade. 1989. *Commodity trading manual.* Chicago, IL: Author.

Mark Cook. 1995. Foreign exchange management at Blount, Inc. *TMA Journal* January/February:30–32.

Richard Filler. 1993. Credit risks and costs in interest rate swaps. *Journal of Cash Management* January/February:38–41.

Brian Genreau. 1986. Interest-rate and currency swaps. *Commercial Lending Review* 4(4):47–54.

Benoit J. Jadoul and Charles M. Seeger. 1994. Hedging currency risk. *TMA Journal* November/December:38–44.

Ira G. Kawaller. 1985. How and why to hedge a short-term portfolio. *Journal of Cash Management* January/February:26–30.

Ira G. Kawaller. 1994. What every treasurer needs to know about interest rate risk. *TMA Journal* September/October:14–20.

Eileen Kleck. 1994. Understanding financial futures. *TMA Journal* July/August:49–53.

John F. Marshall and Kenneth R. Kapner. 1990. *Understanding swap finance.* Cincinnati, OH: South-Western.

A. S. Mello and J.E. Parson. 1995. Maturity structure of a hedge matters: Lessons from the metallgesellshaft debacle. *Journal of Applied Corporate Finance* Spring:106–118.

D. R. Nance, C.W. Smith, and C.W. Smithson. 1993. On the determinants of corporate hedging. *Journal of Finance* March:267–284.

Anita B. Pasmantier. 1993. Hedging foreign exchange exposure. *Journal of Cash Management* November/December:36–43.

A. L. Phillips. 1995. 1995 derivatives practices and instruments survey. *Financial Management* May:115–125.

Robert Richardson. 1994. Developing and implementing corporate foreign exchange policies and procedures. *TMA Journal* July/August:18–21.

Donald J. Smith. 1989. The arithmetic of financial engineering. *Journal of Applied Corporate Finance* Winter:49–58.

Alan L. Tucker. 1991. *Financial futures, options, and swaps.* Minneapolis/St. Paul, MN: West.

Stuart M. Turnbull. 1987. Swaps: A zero sum game? *Financial Management* Spring:15–21.

CHAPTER 19

Treasury Information Management

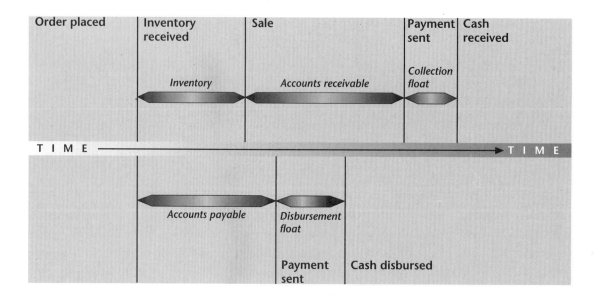

OBJECTIVES

After studying this chapter, you should be able to:

- Appreciate the benefits of e-commerce.
- Understand electronic data interchange (EDI) and the issues involved in its implementation.
- Differentiate between the component parts of EDI.
- Understand the benefits of applying the Internet to e-commerce.
- Understand how treasury managers use information technology to make better financial decisions.

More than anything, this chapter deals with the management of information flows. The previous 18 chapters developed models for making financial decisions in all areas of short-term financial management including inventory, receivables, payables, cash, short-term investing, and short-term financing. Technology advances in information processing impact the management of all of these areas.

This chapter begins by outlining the basic information flows dealing with short-term financial management. We then turn to a discussion of electronic data interchange (EDI) and web-based commerce. The evolution and continued development of information technology promises to have a greater impact on all phases of short-term financial management than did the level and volatility of interest rates from the mid-1970s to the mid-1980s. The impact of information technology will be long-term and process-changing. The chapter concludes with a section providing checklists auditing a company's financial information system.

EXHIBIT 19-1
Three Levels of Information Needs

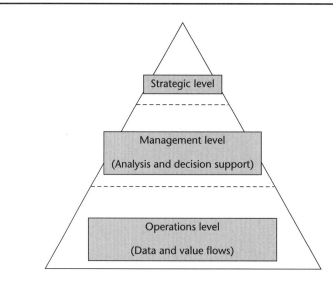

KEY INFORMATION FLOWS

There appear to be three levels of information needs in the financial management of the firm as shown in Exhibit 19-1. The first level is an operations level and deals with routine daily operations and cash management activities. These are daily information flows dealing with sales, receivables, inventory, and payables. In addition, the firm's cash management area processes daily information regarding the discovery and verification of bank balances, cash-concentration activities, developing the daily cash position, reconciliation of outstanding payments and receivables with information received from the bank, bank account analysis, and investment and financing portfolio transaction settlement and accounting.

This level of information flow is extremely important because three critical functions are served, including:

- the updating of the company's general ledger accounts as well as a variety of subledger systems,
- the receipt of timely information from the firm's customers, suppliers and the banking system,
- verification of the information with the company's existing records.

The second information level need is a management level. Rather than being primarily transaction oriented, the management level focuses on analysis and decision support. These information flows include the analysis of working capital accounts (receivables, inventory, and payables), the daily cash position, cash flow and cash balance forecasting, portfolio interest rate sensitivity and development of new portfolio strategies or adjustment of the current portfolio based on the assessed market trends.

Once the company's databases have been updated with new daily information, the firm's forecasting model should be updated so that the current day's forecast can be audited and the variance between actual and forecast can be assessed. Then a new forecast for the future period can be generated. Investment and borrowing strategies can be tested on a what-if basis for different interest rate environments.

The third level of information flows is an executive level. The primary objective here is to provide senior management with timely information regarding the firm's debt/investment management, the firm's relationship with its banks, and its liquidity position.

Although all three levels of information flow are important, this chapter will focus on the evolution of those systems that primarily impact the firm's operations or level 1 information flows. In the past, the majority of level 1 information flows, including payments, were exchanged between companies using paper-based documents. Today, these information and payment flows are more commonly done electronically and this process is referred to as electronic commerce or e-commerce. Electronic data interchange was initially created to apply electronic technology to create efficiencies in the movement of business information and payments. This system initially used proprietary systems of structured data formats to communicate between trading partners and with financial institutions. More recently, the Internet is being used in a more open system to create new and more efficient ways of transmitting information and payments.

ELECTRONIC DATA INTERCHANGE

The much-heralded "checkless" and "paperless" society remains elusive. It was estimated in 1991 that only 1 percent of all corporate trade payments were made electronically. Although the growth rate of such payments is impressive—19 percent growth over 1990s level—about 99 percent of the corporate trade payments remain paper-based. In this section, we explore the whole area of electronic communications between corporations and between corporations and their banks.

Electronic data interchange is the electronic movement of information and funds between buyer and seller for the purpose of facilitating a business transaction.[1] Electronic data interchange comprises **electronic business data interchange (EBDI), financial EDI (FEDI),** and **electronic funds transfer (EFT).** We explore these three major components in the sections that follow.

Electronic Business Data Interchange (EBDI)

The **EBDI** represents those information flows between corporate trading partners. The electronic transmission of purchase orders and invoices are just two examples of EBDI information flows.

EBDI AND THE CURRENT SYSTEM.   To better understand the improvements that EBDI makes in the data interchange between corporations, let's take a look at the traditional product ordering and delivery system. A sales representative visits a customer and an order is consummated. The sales representative may phone in the order to the regional headquarters or field office or may hand deliver a purchase order on return to the field office. The order is processed internally. The customer's credit limit is manually checked and an invoice is created. The order is processed for delivery. Inventory availability is verified and the units ordered are manually tabulated into the firm's inventory control

---

[1]Christopher Skaar, Jr. 1986. Moving toward electronic data interchange. *Journal of Cash Management* July/August:16.

and management system. The order is prioritized and delivery is scheduled. Product shipment is initiated with an enclosed invoice. The customer, on receipt of the shipment, checks for quality and quantity discrepancies. The customer then processes the invoice received, scheduling payment based on the credit terms and the firm's policy regarding payment. A check is then mailed from the administrative office on the date scheduled, dictated by the firm's payment policy. Throughout this process flow, information is manually copied from one source to another source, creating inefficiencies and potential errors.

Contrast this traditional system with a fully implemented EDI system. The customer or sales representative places an order electronically from the customer's location to the supplier's appropriate field or regional office. For example, at Johnson & Johnson's Hospital Services subsidiary, customers can place an order by phone, remote terminal, or computer-to-computer connection. In addition, some field representatives use laptop computers to send and receive real-time reports on shipment status, backorders, and sales volume.[2] The supplier's computers receive the order and feed the information electronically to its inventory and shipping area as well as to the credit department. Without re-keying any additional data, the shipment is confirmed and an invoice is electronically transmitted to the customer at the time of shipment. The supplier then initiates payment instructions to its bank based on a previously agreed-on date. Payment instructions are then transmitted to the customer's bank; the customer's bank account is debited and the supplier's bank account is credited. No paper documents have been transmitted, there is no redundant re-keying of data and, as a result, processing times, transmittal times, and clerical costs are minimized.

BENEFITS AND COSTS OF EBDI.   The EBDI systems such as those described have several advantages. Companies are discovering that past-due receivables can be drastically reduced, effectively reducing days sales outstanding (DSO) and thereby reducing funds invested in receivables. It is not uncommon to experience significant reductions in bad debt write-offs. In addition, banks will often allow for increased credit lines because of the enhanced asset control provided by EDI systems.[3] The reduction in a firm's working capital cycle brought about by the implementation of EBDI systems can be significant and can allow for a competitive advantage in reduced financing costs, effectively enhancing profit margins. The EBDI can also improve forecasts, service quality, and employee productivity.

The major costs associated with EBDI are hardware- and software-related. Companies must invest in the required computer communications systems, including the agreement of data transmission format standards.

Financial EDI

Financial EDI (FEDI) refers to the exchange of electronic business information between a firm and its bank.[4] This is not to be confused with the term electronic funds transfer, or EFT, which refers to payment instructions between banks. Thus FEDI

---

[2]Janet W. Mills and Edward K. Freitas. 1989. EDI at Johnson & Johnson. *Journal of Cash Management* September/October:14–16.

[3]For an example of the impact that EDI has on MicroAge, Inc., see Jeffrey Masich. 1991. Improving cash flow and streamlining operations through EDI. *Journal of Cash Management* January/February:13–16.

[4]N. C. Hill and D. M. Ferguson. 1989. Introduction to EFT and financial EDI. *EDI Forum* EDI Publications, p 26.

encompasses lockbox information reports, daily balance reports, and monthly account analysis reports. Because of the fact that FEDI permits the exchange of extensive information about each payment, companies are able to improve their cash application and account payable processes. Thus buyers and sellers make fewer follow-up calls to complete the payment process and therefore reduce related manual operations.[5]

Treasury workstations were developed during the mid-1980s to facilitate FEDI. A treasury workstation is an automated system of software modules designed to support treasury management operations. Various hardware and software vendors as well as many commercial banks developed systems used by corporate cash managers and treasurers to facilitate the transmission of data and payment requests between the firm and its bank(s). Data transmissions include account balance information from controlled disbursement accounts and lockbox deposit accounts and account analysis statements. Treasury workstations were also designed so that cash managers could initiate wire transfers and automated clearing house (ACH) credits and debits for cash mobilization and payment purposes.

Along with the FEDI systems packaged with the workstations, most treasury workstations also included software to aid in the management of the firm's investment and debt portfolios. Such modules track maturing securities so that the firm's short-term cash forecasting system is regularly updated and even allow the user to initiate and confirm investment transactions. In addition, most systems include the ability to track target required bank balances so that the firm's banks are properly compensated for the services performed.

Electronic Funds Transfer (EFT)

Electronic funds transfer (EFT) primarily deals with the actual electronic transfer of payments, or value, between trading partners involving the partners' financial institutions. Contrast EFT with EBDI, which primarily deals with the electronic transfer of information or data between trading partners, and FEDI, which refers to communications between the firm and its bank. At its inception, EFT was initiated only after paper-based invoices were received. Then EBDI emerged as a replacement for the paper-based information processing activities but not linked with the actual payment system. Today, EBDI, FEDI, and EFT are merging so that the processing of electronic payment requests is linked to order initiation and completion of payment. Although EFT primarily takes care of dollar float, FEDI and EBDI impact information float.

Two decades ago, it appeared imminent that EFT would replace the paper-based payment system. Today, the use of checks by consumers as well as corporations is still growing. The typical routine use of EFT includes consumer bill payment collection through the ACH, cash concentration with wire transfers or the ACH, origination of state tax payments through the ACH, employee expense reimbursements, and direct deposit of payrolls. The two major applications of electronic payments include direct payroll deposit activities and the collection of pre-authorized checks.

The early 1960s witnessed many insurance companies developing the use of pre-authorized checks to collect insurance policy premiums. Originally, this was a paper-based system. The system involved obtaining approval from the company's customers to allow the insurance company to automatically debit the customer's bank account on a particular day each month or some other stipulated payment interval.

---

[5]Susan Rapp. 1993. Successful financial EDI implementation among trading partners. *The Journal of Cash Management* January/February:10.

There are numerous advantages of using EFT over a paper-based system for collecting customer payment, including improved cash forecasting, lower costs per item, and more efficient return item processing.[6] In addition, studies of historical payment trends indicate that policyholders paying with preauthorized payments have a much higher payment rate than policyholders that pay after receiving an invoice for payment.

Another major application of EFT is the direct deposit of payrolls and other payments such as dividends, annuities, and social security checks. The paying corporation collects the payees' bank account information and, prior to the payment date, initiates an ACH transaction that effectively moves funds from the payor's payroll account, or other appropriate expense account, to the payees' accounts. Social security direct deposit represents one of the most successful applications of direct deposit. In 1989, almost half of the eligible recipients received their monthly social security benefits as direct deposits to their bank account through the ACH system. By 1999, over 75 percent did so. The benefits of such a system include substantial processing cost savings and a more predictable cash disbursement for the payor. The negatives include a loss of float for the payor, but the success of the system indicates that the cost savings more than offset the opportunity cost of the float loss.

EDI Communication Formats

A large percentage of one company's output is another company's input. As such, effective EDI can significantly reduce the amount of re-keying of the order, shipping, and invoicing data and instructions. However, such improvements were stymied by the lack of standardized document formats. For some time now, the Accredited Standards Committee (ASC) of the American National Standards Institute has been developing document standards for electronic communication, referred to as ASC X12 Standards. Some of the more common standards, which are referred to as transaction sets, developed so far as to facilitate the electronic communication between trading partners and financial institutions, include the following:

810	Invoice
820	Payment order/remittance advice
821	Financial information reporting
822	Customer account analysis
823	Lockbox information
824	Application advice
828	Debit authorization
832	Price/sales catalog
835	Health care claim payment/advice

These transaction sets are developed for the transmission of data only, not actual payments.

In addition, many countries have developed EDI standards. This process led to the development of United Nations EDI for Administration, Commerce, and Transportation (UN/EDIFACT) rules, which are simply a set of standards for electronic

---

[6]Robert J. DalSanto, A. Post Howland and Sharon Morton. 1991. What's new in EFT? *Journal of Cash Management* May/June:40.

FOCUS ON PRACTICE

HOW TRANSACTION SETS AND PAYMENT FORMATS ARE USED AT GM.   General Motors' divisions transmit remittance instructions using the ASC X12 820 format to their banks. The banks convert the 820 transmission into the CTX format, which includes payment instructions, dollars, and invoice remittance data. If the supplier's bank cannot handle such a format, GM's bank will send the payment instructions in a CCD format and will then route a printed report of the remittance data to the supplier.[7]

The existence of various data formats has led to the creation of value added networks or VANs. A VAN is a third-party service company that receives data transmissions in one format, restructures the data into an alternative format, and then retransmits the data in a revised format to its final destination. Thus subscribing to a VAN service is one alternative to solving the multiple format problem, allowing different trading partners to electronically communicate with each other without having to alter their own systems.

[7]Robert D. Edward and Craig S. Saxer. 1990. EDI payment development: The dollars and data issue. *Journal of Cash Management* January/October:21.

interchange of structured data between computerized information systems in different countries.

Finally, with the popularity of the Internet, developers have created web-based EDI Internet sites using eXtensible Markup Language (XML). With this form of protocol, standard EDI transaction sets are converted either into or from web-based forms to transfer information between large EDI hubs.

Separate from the ASC standards presented above, which have to do with the transmission of information, the National Automated Clearing House Association (NACHA) has developed format options that allow the movement of funds electronically, each with varying amounts of data. These payment formats are presented in Chapter 11, but are repeated below as a quick review.

PPD: Direct deposit of payroll—automatic utility or loan bill-paying services. Settles in 2 days and used for crediting or debiting consumers' accounts.

CCD: Cash concentration and disbursement format—minimal data with payment details submitted separately created for next day settlement. Most banks can process this format.

CCD+: A cash concentration and disbursement format with addendum space for payment details attached. Banks may not be able to capture and relay the addenda information.

TXP: A special provision of the CCD+ for the express purpose of electronic payment of taxes to state and federal governments.

CTX: Corporate trade X12 format—variable data fields as developed by ASC X12. The ability to include variable data fields allows the remittance of information contained in transaction sets such as ASC X12 820, 823, or 835 to move through the ACH network together with the payment rather than having to be separated and sent through a third party.

RCK: Re-presented check entries format—used to transmit ACH debit entries related to paper checks returned for insufficient funds.

Benefits of and Problems With EDI[8]

Several benefits will accrue to firms as the use of EDI proliferates. First, EDI improves quality of services offered to customers. Orders move faster with fewer errors because communication time is reduced and redundant data keying is eliminated. Customer queries about the status of their order or even payment can also be handled more accurately. Second, employee productivity is enhanced because redundant data keying is reduced or eliminated. Paper handling is also reduced and fewer errors are made. Third, operations are streamlined by shortening the processing timeline, controlling and reducing inventory, and improving production forecasting. Fourth, EDI provides a means for more effective asset management. Receivables and inventories can be converted into cash more quickly and payments can be applied more rapidly. Fifth, effective use of EDI can even improve the payables area. In the past, most firms have been reluctant to pay electronically. However, in the mid-1980s, GM realized that the costs of paying by paper were increasing at a high rate as a result of the escalating costs of paper, the costs of employee time, and bank processing and clearing costs. GM contrasted this with declining costs for computer hardware and software and made a strategic decision to move away from paper-based transactions. The sixth benefit is to the firm's cash management area. The costs of cash management will be reduced because the number of bank relationships will generally fall as more payments are processed electronically. Cash flow forecasting is also improved. Finally, as firms move to EDI, banks generally respond by allowing greater credit lines because of the increased asset control provided by the EDI systems.

Most of the improvements that result from EDI implementation affect information float more than dollar float. In fact, the improvements made in the payment system over the last decade have left opportunities for only marginal improvements to be made by improving EFT capabilities. The real opportunities that are open are in the area of process and information flow improvement internally and between trading partners. Thus it should be obvious that many benefits accrue to the firm as paper-based transactions and payments are replaced with their electronic equivalent.

So with all of these benefits favoring EDI, why do we still find ourselves in the infancy of its application? First, is the development and acceptance of standards for data transmission. Second, are concerns about data communication security and authorization. Third, are legal issues dealing with liabilities resulting from failure of various components of the system over which an individual firm has no control. Most of our laws dealing with commercial transactions are based on the premise of paper documents. So new interpretations are needed and in some cases new laws enacted. Finally, some suppliers have been reluctant to negotiate different credit terms for electronic collection of funds owed. The legal issues surrounding changing credit terms based on EDI are not yet clear. The Robinson-Patman Act makes it illegal to offer different credit terms to different customer groups unless justified by the product sold, the quantity sold, or the delivery costs incurred. Because EDI does not neatly fit in any of these categories, suppliers have been slow to offer credit terms for EDI transactions that differ from the credit terms offered to their non-EDI customers.

These are just a few of the many issues that continue to impede progress of EDI implementation. However, each new year witnesses additional support and new applications of EDI.

---

[8]The benefits as outlined in this section were introduced in Victor N. Azar and Tom R. Tabor. 1988. Business justification for electronic data interchange. *Journal of Cash Management* July/August:15–19; and Christopher Skaar, Jr. 1986. Moving toward electronic data interchange. *Journal of Cash Management* July/August:16–20.

E-COMMERCE AND THE INTERNET

"Surfing the net" is no longer an activity reserved for computer "geeks." It seems as though everyone is on the Internet. More and more individuals, firms, interest groups, and associations are creating their own Web pages as a means of communication and, increasingly, as a way to sell products and services and to transact business information. Kathleen Hagen put forth the following vision of how financial managers may "surf the net."

> Working from her "virtual office" at home, Jane Smith begins to prepare the daily cash position for her company. Using a treasury management workstation that provides an automatic Internet link, she clicks on the company logo icon to access the company's internal Web site. Once she has accessed the company's Web site, she downloads all of the investment transactions from the previous business day. The file is stored on her hard drive and the workstation is immediately updated.
>
> To retrieve the details of yesterday's accounts receivable payments, she selects the VAN DOWNLOAD button, which accesses the file transfer protocol (FTP) server of the VAN that processes their EDI transactions. Clicking on an "Update" icon, the receivable information is now copied to the company FTP server and then to the cash position worksheet. Later, the accounts receivable department will access the FTP server to update the receivables system.
>
> To retrieve a list of internal payment requests, Jane clicks the "Today's Payments" button, which automatically accesses the accounts payable information posted on the Web site and downloads the payment requests for the day. The files are "signed" with digital signatures so that Jane can verify that they have been properly authorized. Jane reviews the payment requests and the file automatically updates the daily cash position worksheet. Before finalizing the daily cash position, Jane verifies the target balances calculated by the workstation. She can increase or decrease the amounts with a click of the mouse. She then selects the "Create Payments File" button and a transfer file is created to send the payment instructions to the bank.
>
> Before the file can be sent to the bank, it must first be signed by the treasurer. Jane attaches the file to an e-mail message, which she digitally signs. When the treasurer opens his e-mail, he will review the wire instructions, encrypt the file, and forward it on to the bank by uploading it to the bank's FTP server.[9]

The following sections provide some examples of e-commerce applications that have been developed through the use of the Internet

Information Reporting

In the 2000 Cash Management Services (CMS) Survey,[10] Ernst & Young reported that over 50 percent of the respondent banks offered information reporting services to corporate customers over the Internet. The sample of respondents included virtually all of the nation's largest banks. This compares to only about 5 percent of the responding banks in 1997 and 25 percent in 1999. By 2001, it is expected that over 90 percent of the responding banks will offer information reporting via the Internet.

---

[9]Kathleen A. Hagen. 1996. Banking in cyberspace—A new frontier for treasury professionals. *TMA Journal* March/April:45.

[10]Lawrence Forman and David L. Shafer. 2000. From doubt to adoption . . .Internet delivery of cash management services is changing the marketplace. *AFP Exchange* 20(4):104–107.

Transaction Initiation

In 1997, the CMS survey reported that less than five percent of the respondents offered any form of transaction initiation via the Internet. By 2000, over one-third of the responding banks offered the ability to transfer funds between accounts within the bank and over 30 percent offered ACH initiation. However, less than 20 percent of the respondents offered wire transfer capability over the Internet. The survey did indicate that 80 percent of the respondents plan to offer all three types of transaction initiation by 2001.

Image Access

Although not one respondent to the CMS survey in 1997 offered Internet access to check or associated payment documents images, one-quarter of the respondents offered this service by the year 2000 and almost 70 percent indicated they would be offering the service in 2001.

E-Procurement[11]

Procurement over the Internet offers immediate savings in processing costs and even more significant savings from strategic sourcing. It is estimated that the average cost of generating a paper-based purchase order is $150. However, those companies that automate this function incur an average cost of only $30. In addition, three additional benefits that companies gain include:

- a 5 percent to 10 percent price savings generated by e-procurement,
- an improvement in the purchase and fulfillment cycle that drops from over 7 days to about 2 days, and
- reduction of 25 percent to 50 percent in inventory costs primarily as a result of reduction in inventory.

Perhaps one of the greatest benefits, however, is that purchasing managers no longer are simply executing transactions. They now have time to devote to supplier negotiations and evaluations, which is more strategic with a more direct consequence on company profitability. E-procurement solutions are migrating to supply chain management solutions that enable greater collaboration among trading partners, greater customization of product and service and better management of demand and delivery.

Internet Invoicing and Payment[12]

Although the supplier may gain benefit if the revenue cycle accelerates, the buyer may expect to also gain by taking more trade discounts or better manage its trade credit as a result of more prompt receipt and processing of invoices. Web-based invoicing and payment provide an opportunity for the trading partners to re-negotiate current trade and payment terms. Although there has been almost two decades of EDI experience that indicates significant financial and process benefits, the ubiquitous and non-proprietary nature of the Internet suggests that those benefits may even be more significant. For example, some consultants estimate that there are potential cost savings of up to 50

---

[11]Jane McAllister. 2000. Avoiding online chaos. *AFP Exchange* 20(4):84–87.
[12]Ibid.

percent in the generation, delivery, and processing of invoices and payments when moving from a paper-based system to an electronic system.

Digital Marketplaces[13]

By bringing together buyers and sellers, Internet marketplaces create access to broader markets for sellers and a greater selection for buyers. However, the Federal Trade Commission is taking an active interest in these marketplaces to ensure that business is conducted in an environment of collaboration, not collusion.

Future Role of the Internet

As previously noted, the Internet is providing a less expensive and easier-to-use electronic system, compared with the initial EDI applications. Thus we are witnessing a much more rapid implementation. As web-based systems allow more and more daily processes to be automated, the role of the treasury function continues to evolve. Treasurers will be able to deal with an increasing volume of more complex transactions. This will provide the opportunity for treasurers to focus on more value-adding activities such as for risk management, financial analysis, investing/borrowing strategies, and more effective management of global financial flows.

AUDITING THE STFM INFORMATION SYSTEM

We have and will continue to witness continued improvement in the integration of the management of information flows and dollar flows along the entire path of the cash-flow timeline. Better management of the information flows yields faster cash collections and better control over cash disbursements enhancing the firm's liquidity position. An obvious question is to what extent are firms using electronic information systems as a part of their strategic business plan?

Survey Results

Ahmad W. Salam conducted a survey during 1992 of the Fortune 500 manufacturing firms.[14] A total of 110 completed surveys were tabulated. The survey determined that 94 percent of the respondents have implemented some aspect of EDI for their domestic operations. Only 28 percent have implemented EDI in their international operations and the author suggests that a lack of acceptable worldwide standards is a major factor in this result as well as existing legal issues regarding cross-border EDI transactions.

There were five important reasons that explained why firms implemented EDI. The five stated reasons included being part of an industry group that uses EDI, it was required for implementation of just-in-time (JIT) systems, to reduce inventory, certainty of payment date, and the encouragement of senior management. Each of these implementation reasons was reported by about 30 percent of the respondents.

The survey respondents reported a number of quantifiable benefits derived from the use of EDI. These ranged from the reduction of clerical costs and cost savings of

---

[13]Ibid.

[14]Ahmad W. Salam. 1994. Electronic data interchange and corporate EFT: A survey. *TMA Journal* May/June: 59–61.

reduced paper and forms to resulting reductions in inventory and labor savings through improved scheduling.

The next section highlights the major cash-flow timeline events and the information and dollar variables that are related to those events. We then turn to a more detailed look at the electronic systems available for the cash management function of the firm.

Cash Flow Timeline Events

In this section we are concerned with identifying the major business events along the cash flow timeline, the information required for each event, and some of the relationships involved with each event.[15]

PURCHASING.   The information we are concerned with here is the status of the purchase order. The manager should be concerned with purchase projections and variances from the projection. Discount policies, vendor relations, and bank services expediting the order process are important.

ACCOUNTS PAYABLE.   The firm's cash disbursement ledger is the critical piece of information here, and again, disbursement policy related to cash discounts and the available bank services for finalizing payment are of concern.

A highly computerized disbursement system allows the treasurer to improve cash flow forecasting by having better cash disbursement information. In addition, the use of cash discounts can be optimized and the treasurer can more precisely time the actual disbursement of cash with cash receipts thus optimizing investment opportunities and reducing borrowing costs.

INVENTORY.   Obviously, inventory summaries and shipping schedules are important, as are systems for monitoring inventory. It is critical that inventory and sales systems communicate with each other so that information regarding changing sales patterns translates into appropriate ordering and inventory levels.

SALES.   Sales forecasts and customer billing data are critical pieces of information at this stage in the cash-flow cycle. Proper systems allow the firm to capture sales data, promptly invoice customers, track customer buying patterns and update forecasts.

RECEIVABLES.   At the time that an order is placed on credit, the credit department is immediately notified so that delays related to the credit decision can be minimized. Once credit is granted, credit and collection statistics are maintained and customer profiles established. Payment terms and policies are adhered to and procedures are established for handling overdue accounts.

TREASURY.   The treasury function is extremely important in coordinating cash collection, cash mobilization, and cash disbursements. The treasurer maintains accurate information related to the firm's cash position and constantly updates the daily cash forecast. With this information, the treasurer can make informed decisions regarding investment and financing decisions. The concern here is with managing the proper liquidity level of the firm.

---

[15]The concept of the information requirements for each stage in the cash-flow cycle is from Aviva Rice. 1985. Improving cash flow control throughout the corporation. *Journal of Cash Management* November/December:48–53.

FINANCIAL ADMINISTRATION. Effective financial administration requires the creation of budgets, variance analysis, long-term planning and financial forecasting, and an assessment of long-term capital needs and funding strategies.

Assessment of a Firm's Cash Management Practice

There are four basic cash management areas that need to be assessed: cash positioning/mobilization, bank relationship management, short-term investment/borrowing, and treasury systems management.[16] Each of the four basic cash management areas should be assessed based on six key elements that are listed here.

1. A high level of productivity (efficient use of organizational resources). This includes automation of routine functions; maintenance of a small clerical staff; periodic review of functional techniques, strategies, and systems; and integration with other functions and areas within the company. Obviously, implementation of a complete EDI system ensures easy compliance with this key element.
2. Use of advanced strategies and automation. These include advanced banking/third-party services, advanced cash management techniques, and fully automated and integrated treasury/financial systems. Once again, satisfaction of this key element is evidenced by a well-integrated EDI system.
3. Effective internal controls. This includes regular cash management controls review performed by individuals outside the areas reviewed, adequate backup (both staff and systems), and up-to-date documented policies and procedures.
4. Performance measurement standards. This includes defined performance and/or quality standards, timely tracking of actual performance to performance standards/goals, integration of results with employee performance evaluations, and defined and monitored standards for third-party providers (i.e., banks).
5. Involvement in cash-related decisions companywide. This includes a good working relationship with areas outside the treasury area, a high level of awareness of the importance of effective cash management practices and the involvement and use of cash management personnel as internal consultants in decisions affecting cash.
6. Excellent industry reputation. This includes being known as an innovator to both peer companies and third-party vendors and being used by vendors in evaluating, developing, and implementing new products and services.

Assessing the Treasury Management Workstation

One of the major technological innovations that developed during the 1980s was the Treasury Management Workstation. The following modules and functions are generally provided by a sophisticated workstation.[17] Indeed, this checklist can be used as a basis on which to judge the capabilities of a particular system. By reading through the checklist, you may get a sense of the power and the necessity of such systems if a firm is going to improve its information and dollar flow management.

---

[16]Joseph J. Bonocore and Jeffrey S. Rosengard. 1991. Managing the effectiveness of your cash management function. *Journal of Cash Management* January/February:32–36.

[17]This listing is adapted from Joseph Saturnia, Raymond Houlihan, and Timothy F. Coluccio. 1986. How to evaluate treasury workstations. *Journal of Cash Management* November/December:46–50.

Balance Reporting Module

- Balance reporting
- Target balance
- Exception reporting
- Balance history
- Previous day's credit/debit
- Intraday debit/credit
- Intracompany funds flow analysis

Bank Information

- Account analysis/earnings credit
- Bank relationship manager
- Signature control
- Access to external databases
- Daily events reminder

Cash Mobilization

- Prespecified (line) wires
- Free-form wires
- Automated ACH
- Automated corporate trade payments

Consolidation of Information

- Automated cash ledger update
- General ledger interface
- Cash forecasting & variance analysis

General Investment Module

- Investment portfolio monitoring
- Multiple portfolios
- Position tracking
- Margin reporting and broker status
- Adjusted book versus market analysis
- Track pending trades
- Portfolio performance history

General Debt Module

- Tracking and monitoring
- Swap analysis
- Multiple debt portfolio analysis

Communication & System Features

- Internet access
- Unattended auto-dial
- Parsing of balance report information
- Acceptance of Bank Administration Institute (BAI)-formatted information
- Data backup capabilities
- Communications capability
- Multi-tiered security screen
- Unique preformatted screens
- Electronic mail
- Electronic worksheet capability
- Graphics capability

Word processing
Hardware discounts
Trade-in on old hardware
Trade-in on old software

Vendor Services and Support

Turnkey package
Software customization
Training on-site
Customer references
Nationwide and international coverage
Trial period
System test
Free installation
Published down-time statistics
Date of first system installation
Purchase-to-installation timeframe

A treasury management workstation may be sold by a third-party vendor or by the firm's bank. Although not all treasury management workstations may provide all the modules and services listed above, the list should allow the financial manager to make a comparative assessment of competing systems and choose the system providing the modules and services that the firm needs.

SUMMARY

The major focus of this chapter was twofold. First, the chapter discussed the application of e-commerce through the electronic data interchange format and broke EDI into its component parts of EBDI, FEDI, and EFT. Although EDI impacts the entire business information process system, FEDI and EFT are primarily in the domain of the corporate cash manager. We then brought into the discussion the more recent application of the Internet as a system used to make e-commerce applications.

The chapter concluded with a section providing a variety of checklists for auditing the firm's short-term financial management system. First, a checklist for auditing the firm's cash flow timeline was introduced. One important aspect of this checklist involves the degree of automation used along the cash-flow timeline. Results from a survey were reported indicating the current status of the implementation of EDI. The second checklist focused specifically on the cash management area of the firm. The third and final checklist pertained to the treasury management workstation, an essential tool for the implementation of FEDI.

Effective cash flow management requires an assessment of the firm's cash flow timeline and effective implementation of the appropriate component parts of an electronic data interchange system.

Questions

1. What are the three information level needs in the short-term financial management area?
2. What is electronic data interchange?
3. What are the three component parts of EDI?

4. How does EBDI differ from FEDI? From EFT?
5. How does a VAN fit into an EDI system?
6. Outline the benefits and problems of EDI.
7. Summarize the major activities that a treasury workstation facilitates.

References

Joseph J. Bonocore and Jeffrey S. Rosengard. 1991. Managing the effectiveness of your cash management function. *Journal of Cash Management* January/February:32–36.

Business International. 1988. *Automating global financial management.* New York: John Wiley & Sons.

Lawrence Forman and David L. Shafer. 2000. From doubt to adoption . . . Internet delivery of cash management services is changing the marketplace. AFP Exchange 20(4):104–107.

J. A. Gentry. 1988. Management of information, competitive advantages and short-run financial management systems. In *Advances in Working Capital Management,* edited by Y.H. Kim. Reading, MA: Addison-Wesley.

Jane McAllister. 2000. Avoiding online chaos. *AFP Exchange* 20(4):84–87.

Ahmad W. Salam. 1994. Electronic data interchange and corporate EFT: A survey. *TMA Journal* May/June:59–61.

John F. Wilson and Hugh S. McLaughlin. 1992. Developing an information strategy for treasury operations. *The Journal of Cash Management* January/February:40–44.

INTEGRATIVE CASE—PART 6
General Motors—Europe
The Regional Treasury Center
International Finance

In the fall of 1988, Ellen Stanley transferred to the Regional Treasury Center (RTC) of General Motors–Europe in Belgium after a two-year stint in the Treasury Department of General Motors in Detroit. She was generally well versed in the responsibilities of the treasurer of a large domestic industrial firm, but this assignment was her first in dealing with the international and foreign exchange issues of her firm.

Stanley was spending about four months in the various areas of the RTC in Brussels to familiarize herself with its primary responsibilities. By the time she completed her rotation, she would cover the three areas within the RTC: financing and investment, trading, and accounting.

In the current portion of her training she was trying to quantify the exposure of GM to the currencies of the various countries in which GM operates throughout Western Europe. Second, she needed to assess how the firm had lessened or should attempt to lessen its exposure to these major currencies.

DEVELOPMENT OF GENERAL MOTORS' RTC

During her training, Stanley learned that General Motors was but one of 200 companies that had set up regional coordinating centers within the small Western European country of Belgium. The king of Belgium in 1982 made a conscious decision to provide substantial tax breaks to multinational corporations that set up coordination centers within its country. These tax benefits included exemption from corporate taxes for 10 years. In addition, the centers were exempt from withholding taxes (currently 25 percent) on all payments of dividends, interest, and royalties. Also, the centers were provided a tax credit of 25 percent for interest paid by the centers. The idea behind

SOURCE: *Cases in Financial Management*, © 1992 by Joseph M. Sulock and John S. Dunkelberg, New York: John Wiley & Sons, Inc.

this credit was to enable banks to finance investment projects through the centers at a much lower rate than would be available in other European countries. Likewise, the coordination centers were permitted to receive leasing income free of income taxes.

Other tax benefits included the absence of a registration tax on capital and a tax on real estate owned by the coordination center; exemption from foreign exchange regulations; and tax concessions for expatriate employees. In brief, Belgium created an excellent environment for General Motors, Levi Strauss, Phillips Petroleum, Dow Corning, and many other businesses to carry out the treasury function of their organizations, including their foreign exchange activities.

CURRENT SITUATION FOR GENERAL MOTORS IN EUROPE

Although the General Motors' RTC could be instrumental in helping the firm acquire funds at a reasonable cost as well as managing its foreign exchange exposure, the firm's major task was building automobiles within the highly competitive European market. Volume leaders in Europe were as follows:

MANUFACTURER	HOME COUNTRY
Volkswagen/Audi	Germany
Fiat	Italy
Peugeot/Citroen	France
Ford	U.K.
Opel/Vauxhall (GM)	Germany
Renault	France

The market shares for these six producers ranged from 10.1 percent to 14.6 percent. As the value of each country's currency changed, the competitive position of each manufacturer was helped or hurt. Depreciation in currencies improved the competitiveness of the domestic producer(s) within those countries. Appreciation in currencies impaired competitiveness by raising costs

621

and prices relative to other nondomestic producers. At the present time the Italian lira, the British pound, and the German mark have been relatively strong. Most of General Motors' assembly operations are done in Germany.

In order to cope with the strong currencies in their home countries, both Ford and General Motors adopted a similar strategy. First, to balance their foreign exchange exposure, they diversified their production locations. However, because of economics of scale, the carmakers eventually found it prohibitively expensive to have multiple assembly locations. Instead of multiple assembly plants, the firms relocated the plants that produced such components as brakes, radiators, and transmissions. As Stanley learned, with these relocations the firms were able to benefit from lower wage scales as well as the weaker currency environments. However, it was important for both firms to balance higher shipping costs against gains that might be realized from lower wage rates and weaker currencies than the pound or mark.

A second strategy for both General Motors and Ford was the diversification of their supply bases into weak-currency and low wage countries. This end was accomplished by purchasing tires, plastics, and glass in France and Italy, the home of some of their major competitors. Some of their government-owned competitors, like Volkswagen and Renault, had a difficult time employing this multicountry supplier diversification because of political resistance to foreign purchases by government corporations. The situation provided Ford and General Motors with a significant competitive advantage over Volkswagen and Renault.

THE FOREIGN CURRENCY SITUATION FOR GM—EUROPE

Even with all of General Motors' attempts to balance and diversify its foreign exchange, Stanley was amazed to find that the company still had significant imbalances in its relationship between purchases and sales. Stanley's main assignment for this phase of her training rotation was to identify the magnitude of the firm's exposures in the various key currencies. In addition, since she was new on the job, she was asked to suggest strategies that the firm might use to soften the effect of these exposures, For a veteran in the RTC this

assignment could have been done almost intuitively, but for a rookie there were some serious questions that needed to be answered.

Questions

1. What is the magnitude of the foreign exchange exposure for each of the currencies in Exhibit 1?
2. Does the exposure to the German mark help or hinder the competitive performance of General Motors?
3. How would the parent company in Detroit view the situation if the gross buys and gross sales in Germany were reversed?
4. The data in the case address the currency flows for General Motors—Europe that are tracked by the Regional Treasury Center in Brussels. However, another issue involves the stock of assets that the firm has in Europe. Speculate on what you think might be happening to the value of GM's investment in Europe in light of the various currency appreciations and depreciations, especially the German mark.
5. What techniques and financial instruments might the RTC employ to control its currency exposure? Explain these techniques in light of the French currency situation.
6. What financial benefits, if any, does General Motors have from locating its treasury function in Belgium? What benefits, if any, accrue to Belgium?
7. What parties, if any, might be harmed by the existence of regional treasury functions like GM's?

EXHIBIT 1
Annual Currency Flows ($ millions)

COUNTRY	GROSS BUYS	GROSS SALES
Germany	$ 5,845	$ 2,400
U.K.	440	2,245
Spain	1,395	1,340
France	380	920
Holland	55	750
Belgium	705	560
Italy	180	530
Austria	485	465
Sweden	0	255
U.S.	255	140
Japan	455	0
Australia	195	0
Other	0	785
	$10,390	$10,390

Appendix 19A

Time Value of Money Calculations

Any decision having a quantifiable financial impact lasting beyond the current year should be evaluated using **discounted cash flow** techniques. When companies are making decisions with sizable financial impacts, several alternative proposals typically are considered. Discounted cash flow techniques properly account for the timing of all cash inflows and cash outflows attributable to a given alternative by converting those flows to their value at an identical point in time. In most cases, that point in time is at the time of the initial cash outlay related to that alternative. For example, when evaluating the purchase of a machine, the first cash flow would be the purchase of that machine. Failure to consider the timing of cash flows results in poor decisions, reducing the value of the company's stock.

In this appendix we will first present the necessary discounting and compounding equations. Then we will illustrate a simple discounted cash flow calculation. Almost all of the computations made in the textbook are discounting calculations, so we will conclude with a brief discussion of the appropriate discount rate for determining present values.

In our discussion, we will assume that the annual interest rate is a **nominal rate.** Also called the quoted rate or stated rate, this is best understood by distinguishing it from an **effective annual rate.** The effective annual rate takes into account the frequency of compounding, or how often interest is credited to the account. If **simple interest** is paid, interest is only added one time to the account, at the end of the investment period. For an investment paying simple interest, the nominal rate would be identical to the effective annual rate. For an investment paying **compound interest,** the investor earns "interest on interest." The investment grows in value more quickly because not only is interest paid on the original amount invested (the **principal**), but on intrayear interest as well. The distinction is an important one, because with compound interest the effective annual rate is greater than the nominal rate. In each of the formulas we will demonstrate, we will be working with nominal interest rates, and simple interest, unless we specify otherwise.

DISCOUNTING AND COMPOUNDING

The determination of a present dollar equivalent of a cash flow to be received in the future is called **discounting,** whereas compounding involves determining what a dollar amount invested today would be worth at some specified point in the future. Present value effects of financial decisions are assessed through time value calculations.

Discounting and Compounding Single Sums

The simplest discounted cash flow calculations involve translating a single dollar amount to its value at a different point in time. We begin with the calculation that is used the most throughout this textbook, discounting a future sum to determine its present dollar equivalent. Calculation of the present value is best illustrated by an example.

> Sandy is wondering how much money she needs to invest today to have $10,000 available to pay the first tuition payment for her M.B.A. program, due one year from today. She plans to invest the money in a one-year certificate of deposit, currently yielding 9 percent. To determine the present dollar equivalent of $10,000, she can use Equation A-1:

$$PV = \frac{FV_n}{(1 + k)^n} \tag{A-1}$$

where FV_n = cash flow received in period n

k = interest rate earned

n = number of time periods from now

Substituting the appropriate values into the equation:

$$PV = \frac{\$10,000}{(1 + .09)^1}$$

$$PV = \$9,174.31$$

As illustrated in the example, the cash flow timing is recognized via the number of days or years over which we are discounting.

Finding the future value of a single dollar amount being invested today is accomplished by a technique called **compounding.** The formula for determining the compounded future value of a known present amount is as follows:

$$FV_n = PV (1 + k)^n \qquad \text{(A-2)}$$

where FV_n = future dollar value at end of n years

PV = present dollar amount

k = annual interest rate quoted

n = number of years

The following example shows how this is done. Notice that it is exactly the opposite of discounting.

> Larry has just talked with the trust officer at his bank, who offered him a five-year certificate of deposit paying 12 percent, compounded annually. Larry forgot to ask the officer what his $10,000 would be worth at the end of the five years. Can you help him?

SOLUTION.

Substituting the numbers for Larry, we have

$$FV_5 = \$10,000(1 + .12)^5$$

$$FV_5 = \$17,623.42$$

Compounding and Discounting Periods Other Than Annual

If the time period involves less than one year and compound interest is paid on the account (interest is credited more frequently than once a year), in order to modify Equation A-2 both the k and n must be adjusted. Before showing the future value formula, we'll show how to calculate a period interest rate for a partial year. The general formula we use is shown in Equation A-3:

$$i = \left(1 + \frac{k}{m}\right)^{m \times n} - 1 \qquad \text{(A-3)}$$

where i = interest rate per period

k = nominal interest rate

m = number of times per year compounding occurs

n = number of years

Be careful in selecting the value for n when the compounding occurs over a period less than one year. For example, for daily compounding ($m = 365$) over a period of 270 days, n would be 270/365. Illustrating, if the nominal interest rate is 10%, we would get a period interest rate (i) of 0.0767664:

$$i = \left(1 + \frac{0.10}{365}\right)^{365 \times (270/365)} - 1$$

$$= (1.000273973)^{270} - 1$$

$$= 0.0767664$$

This revised value for i would then be used in the discounting formula to calculate present values. Illustrating, the present value of $1,000 received 270 days from now, assuming daily compounding, is $928.71 [$1,000 / (1 + 0.0767664)].[1]

The future value formula makes use of the same adjustment, as we see in Equation A-4.

$$FV = PV\left(1 + \frac{k}{m}\right)^{m \times n} \qquad \text{(A-4)}$$

Again, if the cash flow is received less than one year later, n would need to reflect that fact. Illustrating, a cash flow received 180 days from now would be handled by using $n = (180/365)$.

Simple Interest

If compound interest is not earned, implying that interest is paid only at the end of the investment period based on the beginning principal, the accountholder is receiving *simple interest*. Simple interest compounding and discounting calculations merely involve multiplying n/365 by the annual interest rate. Equation A-1 would have to be reformulated as shown in Equation A-5.

$$PV = \frac{FV_n}{1 + [k(n/365)]} \qquad \text{(A-5)}$$

---

[1]The keystrokes for a Hewlett-Packard 10B calculator are as follows:

```
365 ■ [P/YR]
1000 [FV]
270 [N]
10 [I/YR]
Press [PV] to get $928.71.
```

Adjustments also would have to be made for partial year interest rate calculations. Returning to our earlier example, with a nominal interest rate of 10 percent and a 270-day period, the 270-day interest rate under compounding, 0.0767664, differs from the rate based on simple interest. With simple interest,

$$i = 0.10 \times (270/365) = 0.0739726.$$

Continuous Compounding

Sometimes you will read an advertisement for a bank account paying interest **continuously compounded.** This means that compounding is done every instant, and the results turn out to be almost the same as with daily compounding. The formula for continuous compounding of a lump sum involves raising e (approximately 2.7183) to the kn power:

$$FV_n = PV(e^{kn}) \tag{A-6}$$

Illustrating, based on an annual interest rate of 6% and 3 years, the future value of $100 would be $119.72 $[(\$100 \ (e^{(0.06)(3)}))]$.

DISCOUNTING CASH FLOW STREAMS: ANNUITIES AND PERPETUITIES

Two other calculations that are especially useful for evaluating financial decisions that will have an ongoing, multiyear or even permanent effect on a corporation's cash flows, are the annuity and perpetuity discounting formulas. To better understand how these work, we must understand the distinction between an annuity and a perpetuity. A constant dollar amount received over a *finite* number of time periods is called an **annuity.** If that cash flow stream will last *indefinitely* into the future, it is termed a **perpetuity.**

Annuity Discounting

We first illustrate how an annuity is discounted. Assuming that the cash flows occur at the *end* of each time period, the formula to be used is as follows:

$$PV = PMT \left(\frac{1 - [1/(1+k)^n]}{k} \right) \tag{A-7}$$

where PV = present dollar equivalent of the series of cash flows

PMT = dollar amount of *each* period's cash flows

k = discount rate per period, in decimal form

n = number of periods

When provided with an annual discount rate, one must be careful to convert that rate to the rate *per period*, expressed in decimal form. The following example illustrates use of the annuity discount formula.

> Concorde Corp. provides electronic check authorization systems to retailers, primarily grocers. If it has been offered a nine-year contract to supply check authorization to a grocery chain, where it figures that the net cash flows arising from the contract would be $350,000 per year, Concorde would have to utilize an annuity present value formula to evaluate the present dollar equivalent of that cash flow series. Assuming the discount rate on similar risk projects is 10%, how much is the contract worth to the company in present dollar terms (ignoring any necessary initial investment outlays)?

SOLUTION.
In terms of the above formula A-7,

$$PMT = \$350,000$$
$$k = 10\%$$
$$n = 9 \text{ years}$$

Substituting these into our formula,[2]

$$PV = \$350,000 \left(\frac{1 - [1/(1 + 0.10)^9]}{0.10} \right)$$

$$= \$2,015,658.34$$

Concorde could compare this present value to the initial investment in order to determine whether the contract offered would be attractive.

The above approach is preferable to the use of financial tables, because most short-term financial management decisions involve time periods of less than one year, and standard tables do not include the necessary values.

To resolve financial decision-making situations such as that provided in the above example, we calculate

---

[2]The keystrokes on a Hewlett-Packard 10B calculator are as follows:

1 ■ [P/YR]
350000 [PMT]
10 [I/YR]
9 [N]
Press the [PV] button.

the difference between the present value revenues and the present value costs. This difference is termed **net present value.** If the net present value is positive, the proposal would add value to the company and should be adopted. If there are several proposals that constitute competing or alternative ways of accomplishing an objective, we call them mutually exclusive projects, and we select the alternative having the highest net present value. In our example problem, the investment represents an independent project, which stands or falls on its own merits. The net present value is determined as follows:

$$NPV = PV_{net\,cash\,flows} - Initial\;investment \qquad \text{(A-8)}$$

Recall the electronic check authorization system that Concorde Computing is considering providing to a grocery chain. Assuming the initial investment for Concorde is $1,500,000, should Concorde proceed with it?

$$NPV = PV_{net\,cash\,flows} - Initial\;investment$$

$$= \$2,015,658.34 - \$1,500,000$$

$$= \$515,658.34$$

From a financial perspective, this is attractive to Concorde.

Perpetuity Discounting

The perpetuity discounting formula is derived in a straightforward fashion from Equation A-7. First, we move the denominator k outside the brackets:

$$PV = \frac{PMT}{k}\left(1 - \left[\frac{1}{(1+k)^n}\right]\right)$$

Second, notice what happens when n goes to infinity: The expression inside the brackets converges on 1. We are left with PMT/k, as shown in the perpetuity formula illustrated below (A-9). It illustrates how the total value effect of a project can be determined when one anticipates a permanent, ongoing stream of cash flows expected to last from the next period on indefinitely. Symbolically, we have $CF_1, CF_2, \ldots CF_\infty$. For annual net cash flows, we can use Equation A-9.

$$PV = \frac{CF}{k} \qquad \text{(A-9)}$$

where k = discount rate
CF = dollar amount of perpetual cash flow stream

Many times we will be working with daily cash flows, however. We can still use Equation A-9, but instead of k we will use the daily discount rate i. How we compute i depends on whether the company receives daily compound interest or simple interest. Where compound interest is received, as in the case where surplus cash balances are swept into overnight investments, we compute i as shown in Equation A-3. Where the company is not paid daily interest (i.e., a daily average balance for the investment period is computed and the interest is posted at the end of the period), simple interest is earned on freed-up cash, and we would compute i by dividing the nominal rate by 365.[3] For example, the present value of a perpetual stream of $100 daily cash receipts, if the nominal rate is 10%, would be $365,000 if we assume simple interest [$100/(0.10/365)].

RISK AND CORPORATE DECISIONS

Risk is brought into the picture by selecting an appropriate discount rate. The rate used should be one that reflects the rate of return that could be earned on another investment of similar risk—where risk refers to the uncertainty of the cash flows. For long-lived capital projects, the company's cost of funds is typically used as the discount rate. Mathematically, discounting at the company's cost of capital enables the analyst to determine whether the project's cash flows are adequate to cover financing costs; when net present value equals 0, the net cash flows just cover the financing costs. For capital projects whose cash flows are more or less risky than the company's typical project, some adjustment must be made to the cost of capital to arrive at an appropriate discount rate. Coming up with the appropriate discount rate is often also a difficult task when evaluating working capital

---

[3]Again, we are assuming k is specified as a nominal or stated interest rate, on an annual basis. If we are presented with an annual effective rate, we would have to use a slightly different formula:

$$i = (1 + k)^{n/365} - 1$$

where k is the annual effective rate and n is the number of days, which for a perpetual stream of daily cash flows would be 1.

decisions. In this appendix, we necessarily limit our focus to the mathematics of time value. In the appendix to Chapter 3 we present the capital asset pricing model, which is one approach which can be used to determine risk-adjusted discount rates.

PROBLEMS

19A-1. Jim is confused about the difference between simple interest and compound interest. He wants to know the daily interest rate equivalent to an 8 percent nominal rate, assuming:

  a. Simple interest is credited to his account.

  b. Compound interest is credited to his account daily.

  c. Compound interest is credited to his account on a continuous basis.

19A-2. How much money would Jim have in his account (see Problem 1) if he starts out with $1,000 and leaves the money in the account for six months, for each of the situations given in *a–c*? Comment on the differences from the results in Problem 1, indicating why they arise.

19A-3. Barbara has inherited a five-year annuity of $2,000 per year. She wishes to know how much this is worth in today's dollars, assuming the discount rate is 11%.

19A-4. How much would Barbara's inheritance (from Problem 3) have been worth if she (and her heirs) had received the $2,000 as a perpetuity instead of an annuity?

19A-5. Diamond Grocers is considering a one-year lease on an automated warehousing system. It estimates the company would save $400,000 from the system, which would have a lease cost of $360,000. Ignoring tax effects, would the system add value for Diamond, if Diamond's cost of capital is 10% per year?

  a. Assume the $400,000 savings occurs at the end of the year.

  b. Assume the savings occurs evenly throughout the year, and with equal amounts realized at the end of each month.

GLOSSARY

account analysis statement monthly listing which banks provide corporate customers indicating the services used and the charges assessed the company. The statement provides in-depth balance information, a 12-month balance history, a detailed listing and pricing of services used, and the degree to which the company's actual balances offset fees charged for the services used.

account parameters and records credit customer identifiers such as name, address, and the customer's bank transit routing number. These items are included in the customer's credit file.

account reconciliation a disbursement-related service in which the bank develops a detailed report of checks paid as well as miscellaneous debits and stopped payments. In a full account reconciliation, the company also provides the bank with a record of checks drawn, and the bank informs the company of which checks remain outstanding.

accounts payable a liability that is generated by purchasing a good or service on credit.

accounts receivable turnover computed by dividing days' sales outstanding into the number of days in the calculation period, which is usually 365. Indicates how many times per year the seller's investment in accounts receivable "turns over" into sales, which is an efficiency measure giving the same signal as days sales outstanding.

accrual a liability account that results from expenses incurred during the operating process that are not yet paid.

ACH credit payment order transmitted through the automated clearing house system and originated by the payor. The routing bank (originating institution) in this case is the payor's disbursement bank.

ACH debit payment order for payment through the automated clearing house system and originated by the payee, based on the prior authorization by the payor. This order is routed through the payee's bank (originating financial depository institution, or OFDI). Another name for an electronic depository transfer.

active investment strategy an approach to investing which involves relatively more trading and active monitoring of the portfolio, and many times is motivated by a philosophy that the investor can "beat the market." Active strategy managers would rarely buy a security with the intention of holding it to maturity. For example, when an analyst forecasts a change in interest rates, trading strategies can be devised to enhance investment profits.

adjustable-rate preferred stock (ARPS) preferred stock on which the dividend is reset quarterly.

adjusted r^2 a measure for a statistical model's goodness of fit which compensates for the upward bias in goodness-of-fit resulting from the inclusion of additional predictor variables.

advised line a standard lending service used abroad, which is very similar to credit lines in the United States. The advised line involves unsecured lending of up to one year maturity, available on short notice to the borrower.

advisory services include all specialized and general financial management consulting banks might provide to corporations.

agencies securities issued by governmental agencies and several private financing institutions that have governmental backing.

agency problem a conflict that arises when the interests of the principals (stockholders) do not coincide with those of the agents (managers).

aging schedule shows a percent breakdown of present receivables, with the categories shown typically as follows: current, 0–30 days past due, 31–60 days past due, and over 90 days past due.

aggressive strategy a strategy that minimizes the amount of long-term financing used. This strategy generally results in a lower current ratio and higher but more volatile profitability during periods of normal yield curves.

ANSI the American National Standards Institute.

annuity a constant dollar amount received over a finite number of time periods.

anticipation this transfer rule initiates a cash transfer before the related deposit is made.

asset based loans   a source of financing obtained from a bank or commercial finance company secured by accounts receivable or inventory.

asset securitization   has become prevalent in the United States because of the need for banks to increase their capital-to-assets ratio.

asset swap   a swap created to hedge cash flows related to assets or investments.

asset-based lending   a form of collateralized lending which has a claim on an asset or group of assets, ordinarily receivables or inventory, which could be easily sold if the borrower defaults on the loan.

auction preferred stock (APS)   preferred stock on which the dividend is reset every 49 days through an auction bidding process.

automated clearing house (ACH)   a quick and relatively inexpensive means of electronically processing large numbers of routine transactions. This system is comprised of a loosely tied network of associations spread across the country. The electronic equivalent of the paper check clearing system.

availability float   the delay from the time a check is deposited and the time when funds are available to be spent. This time lag may not always coincide with the amount of time it takes the check to actually clear, but generally the two are closely linked. Delays in collecting checks caused by delays in the check clearing process after the check has been deposited.

availability schedule   listing of how long after deposit checks will become "good funds" for spending by the depositor. Prior to recording available funds, the bank will credit the depositor's ledger balance, but the portion of the total deposit available as "good funds" ready to be spent varies according to the bank's schedule.

average collection period   how long the typical customer is taking to pay its bills. Alternately, how long, on average, the seller is taking to collect its receivables. It is computed by dividing accounts receivable by daily sales. Also known as days sales outstanding.

avoidance   the pricing of invoices in the seller's currency.

back value date   the date that cleared checks are assigned and may cause funds to be drawn from an account before the check actually arrives at the drawee bank.

balance fractions, inventory   the percent of an inventory purchase order that remains as inventory over succeeding months.

balance fractions, payables   the dollar amount remaining to be paid in succeeding months as a percent of the original accounts payable balance.

balance reporting services   means by which the treasurer may inquire by phone or PC hook-up about the balance positions in many different accounts and about transactions affecting the accounts.

bank deposit notes   short-term debt securities issued by banks, which range from 9 months to 30 years in maturity, and have an active secondary market.

Bank Holding Company Act of 1956   prohibited further acquisitions by bank holding companies unless specifically allowed by state law in the state of the proposed acquisition.

bank notes   technically not deposits, these bank debt obligations thereby avoid FDIC insurance premiums which also forfeits deposit insurance coverage.

bank relationship policy   document which establishes the company's objectives, compensations, and review process for the banks with which it has a relationship.

bank selection process   involves assembling a system of banks to serve all of a company's cash management and related needs.

banker's acceptance (BA)   a corporate time draft drawn on the buyer, whose bank agrees to pay ("accepts") the amount if the buyer does not. Related to this, a short-term acceptance facility allows the selling firm to initiate drafts (called bills of exchange) against the buyer's bank instead of against the buyer, which can be discounted at the bank. A time draft drawn against a deposit in a commercial bank but with payment at maturity guaranteed by the bank.

Banking Act, 1991   prohibited the FDIC from voluntarily covering a bank's uninsured depositors except when the Department of Treasury, the Federal Reserve Board, the FDIC, and the President all agree that the financial system would be endangered by the bank's closure.

biased expectations hypothesis   a theory of the term structure of interest rates in which market expectations are modified by some degree of liquidity preference.

bilateral and multilateral netting systems   are centralized bookkeeping entries made to eliminate ("net out") offsetting amounts owed by divisions or subsidiaries within a company.

Board of Governors   the main Federal Reserve System's policy-making body, which is comprised of seven members. Governors are appointed by the President and confirmed by the U.S. Senate. The Board of Governors supervises the district Federal Reserve banks, limiting to some extent the powers and privileges of their stockholders.

Bond Anticipation Notes   short-term debt instrument which provides working capital financing for states and localities as they await anticipated revenues from upcoming bond issuance.

Box-Jenkins model   a type of time-series forecasting technique. Named after two pioneers in the field of time series modeling, this approach lets the data specify the best model.

breadth   refers to the number and size of parties which are potential buyers of the instruments in a market.

Bretton Woods Agreement   an agreement signed by the major trading countries following World War II which returned the world economy to a type of gold standard. The U.S. dollar was pegged to the dollar at $35 per ounce. Currencies of all other countries were then fixed in price to the dollar and the countries agreed to maintain the established exchange rate within 1 percent.

brokers   middlemen which do not inventory the securities they arrange transactions for.

business risk   the possibility that a company will not be able to meet ongoing operating expenditures.

buy hedge   a hedge created by purchasing a futures contract.

buy-and-hold strategy   an approach to investing which involves holding until maturity securities purchased. Quite often, this is part of a "maturity matching" approach to investing that prescribes investing in a security that will mature at the end of the investment horizon.

call option   a contract that allows the owner to purchase the underlying asset at a specific price over a specific span of time.

capital asset pricing model (CAPM)   a mathematical representation of the relationship between a stock's risk and its expected market return. The CAPM is also used to give the analyst an estimate of the effect of a project's risk on its required rate of return.

captive finance companies   a financing subsidiary of a corporation that facilitates arranging financing for customers of the firm's products.

captive finance subsidiary   separate entity within a company which provides financing for parent company or its customers, and which is thought to provide a marketing advantage or debt capacity advantage.

cash and securities mix decision   the proportional breakdown of cash and securities held by a company as part of its current asset holdings.

cash application   crediting the account upon payment for a credit sale, this process frees up that amount of the credit limit for additional orders from this customer.

cash budget   forecast showing cash receipts and disbursements on a monthly basis for a minimum horizon of one year, typically assembled before the beginning of a new fiscal year.

cash collection system   a management designed system that converts checks to cash and considers mail float, processing float, and availability float.

cash concentration   the process of moving dollar balances from deposit banks to concentration banks.

cash conversion period   a liquidity measure that takes a going-concern approach. It measures the difference in time from when cash is received from credit customers and when cash is paid to suppliers. The length of time from when cash is paid out for purchases and when cash is received from collections on credit sales.

cash cycle   the time that elapses from the purchase of raw materials until cash is received from the sale of the final product.

cash discount   the percentage amount that can be subtracted from the invoice if the customer pays within a stated period of time.

cash flow from operations   one of the most direct measures of liquidity found by subtracting operating cash disbursements from operating cash receipts.

cash flow timeline   the cash cycle displayed along a time dimension.

cash inflows   the cash benefits arising from sources of cash increases.

cash items   deposited checks given immediate, provisional credit by the bank.

cash letter   the accompanying listing of checks that are bundled by the deposit bank for routing through the check clearing process.

cash outflows   cash being disbursed.

causal distributions   a set of outcomes characterized by situations where a predictor variable has changed from what was expected, causing the forecast variable to deviate from what was expected.

causal techniques   forecasting methods linking the forecast values of an effect variable to one or more hypothesized causes.

centralized disbursing   an organizational structure which disburses corporate cash from a central area, allowing the corporate headquarters' staff to check each disbursement and possibly initiate each payment as well.

centralized processing system   a cash collection system where corporate headquarters receives all customer remittances.

centralized transfer initiation   the timing and amount of the transfer is centered either at the concentration bank or corporate headquarters.

certificate of deposit (CD)   an interest-bearing account which evidences (certifies) that a certain amount of money has been deposited at the bank for a pre-specified period of time, and that will be redeemed with interest at the end of that time (maturity).

check processing float   delays in collecting cash caused by delays between the time a check is received and when it is deposited in the banking system.

check truncation   involves expediting clearing by scanning the data on the check's MICR line, and then processing only that data back to the payee's bank.

CHIPS   short for Clearing House Interbank Payment System, the institution which was established in 1970 to handle interbank transactions needed to settle international transactions. CHIPS is a private association of banks that operates through the New York Clearinghouse Association.

clearing agent   often a Federal Reserve bank, branch or RCPC, an entity which uses the information printed at the bottom of the check to process the check.

clearing bank(s)   when checks are deposited, the bank(s) used for processing those checks into the clearing system. Sometimes called deposit bank(s).

clearing float   sometimes called "availability float," the delay in availability incurred after deposit. The length of this component of float is linked to the bank's availability schedule in connection with the location of the payor's bank.

clearing house   a central location where representatives of area banks meet, and each bank settles its balances with one institution (the clearing house) instead of with each bank individually.

coefficient of determination (r^2)   gives the goodness-of-fit for a fitted regression equation. It indicates the proportion of the total variance of the forecasted variable that is accounted for, or "explained," by the fitted regression equation.

coefficient of variation   the standard deviation of a variable divided by the mean or expected value of that variable.

coin & currency services   procedures provided by banks which include receiving of bulk cash deposits sent by armed courier, sorting of deposit items, same day verification of the total deposit if received by the bank's cutoff time, and supply of coins and currency for the company's cash payment needs.

collected balance   sometimes called the available balance, this amount represents how much of a deposit balance is immediately spendable. It may be somewhat less than the ledger balance because of availability delays applied to the checks by the bank.

collection bank   the bank of deposit that encodes the dollar amount of the check in magnetic ink on the bottom right side of the check and then routes the check through the clearing process.

collection float   the sum of the delays in collecting cash from customers caused by mail, process, and availability delays.

collection procedures   detailed statements regarding when and how the company will carry out collection of past due accounts. These policies specify how long the company will wait past the due date to initiate collection efforts, the method(s) of contact with delinquent customers and whether and at what point accounts will be referred to an outside collection agency.

commercial letter of credit   a guarantee of payment by an importer, made by its bank, which becomes binding when the shipping and other documents related to the goods sold are presented to the bank.

commercial paper   an unsecured IOU issued mainly by financial companies such as banks, their parent holding companies, and consumer or commercial finance companies. A short-term promissory note issued by a corporation for a fixed maturity generally in the 30 day range but can be as much as 270 days.

commitment fee   an annual fee of between one-quarter and one-half percent of the size of the credit line a firm pays to a bank to guarantee access to the line.

committed facility   lending arrangement in which the bank charges a fee to compensate it for agreeing to lend upon request for a period of five to seven years.

committed line   a line of credit where the firm pays a commitment fee that obligates the bank to provide funding for the credit line with a formal written agreement.

company processing center   an administrative office or area within the corporation that processes payments received from customers.

compensating balances   amounts held in a deposit account which the company holds to offset bank-provided cash management and/or lending services. When held in support of lending, these balances are not considered to be transaction balances, and are not subject to the Fed's required reserve ratio.

competitive bids   offers to buy securities at a given price or yield. In the Treasury auctions, these are mainly entered by financial institutions, including dealers.

Competitive Equality Banking Act of 1987   allows existing nonbank banks to continue to operate, but prohibits the establishment of new nonbank banks.

complete enumeration   a lockbox model that analyzes all possible lockbox sites to determine the optimal combination that maximizes shareholder wealth.

compound interest   interest paid on interest.

compounding   the future value of a single dollar amount being invested today.

comprehensive payables   is the outsourcing of part or all of the accounts payable and/or disbursement functions.

concentration account   deposit account into which funds are pooled at the endpoint(s) of a company's collection system.

concentration bank   a bank that receives balance transfers from several deposit or gathering banks.

concentration services   closely linked to collection services, these services mobilize and pool collected cash in order to increase interest income and reduce interest expense.

conservative strategy   a strategy that uses a majority of long-term sources to fulfill its financing needs. This strategy results in a higher current ratio but a lower level but more stable level of profitability during periods of normal yield curves.

consignment   an arrangement whereby a retailer obtains an inventory item without obligation. If not sold, the inventory can be returned.

contingency plans   actions that can be taken if and when necessitated by deteriorating conditions.

continuously compounding   when compounding is done every instant.

contracting cost motive   theoretical motive for trade credit extension in which the buyers' sales contracting costs are reduced in that they can inspect the quantity and quality of the goods prior to payment due to the delayed payment offered.

control limits   trigger points, which signal a purchase or sale of securities, and are part of the decision-making apparatus in the Miller-Orr cash management model.

controlled disbursement account (CDA)   a checking account for which the bank provides early morning presentment information via a phone call or computer message to the cash manager. Notification for controlled disbursement accounts involves informing the company of the total dollar amount of checks that will be presented later that day, so that sufficient funds can be transferred into the account. Accounts at banks in small towns that only receive cash letters once a day. The bank can inform the financial manager of the dollar amount of check clears that will be charged against the account early in the day.

corporate agency services   security-related services, some of which are related to short-term borrowing and investing, offered by financial institutions to publicly held corporations.

country risk   the possibility of loss of assets due to political, economic, or regulatory instability in a nation in which business is being conducted.

coupon-equivalent yield   interest return figure calculated based on a 365-day year instead of 360 days. For a discount security maturing within one year, it is also adjusted to account for the fact that the price paid is less than the face value, which increases the true yield.

coupon security   one which pays interest periodically prior to maturity.

credit administration   the establishment of credit policy and planning, organizing, directing and controlling all aspects of the credit function.

credit decision process   sequence beginning with the marketing contact with potential customers and ending with the credit extension decision. Includes credit investigation, customer information contacts, written document preparation, credit file establishment, and financial analysis.

credit extension   the decision to sell on credit to a customer.

credit interchange bureaus   departments of local credit associations that provide information on the credit history of local businesses and individuals.

credit limit   where credit is extended, the maximum dollar amount that cumulative credit purchases can reach for a given customer. Also known as the credit line.

credit period   the length of time allowable for payment of the invoice amount.

credit policy   a company's credit standards, credit limits, approach to credit investigation, credit terms, and collection activity.

credit reporting agencies   sources of business credit information, such as Dun & Bradstreet.

credit scoring models   evaluation approach which weights variables depending on their helpfulness in discriminating between "good" and "bad" applicants, based on past payment histories. These models are developed with the assistance of computerized statistical techniques such as multiple discriminant analysis.

credit standards   the minimally acceptable creditworthy customer, from the perspective of the company extending credit.

credit terms   specification of when invoiced amounts are due and whether a cash discount can be taken for earlier payment.

credit-granting decision   determination of whether and how much credit to give customers, a process which involves four distinct steps: development of credit standards, getting necessary information about customers, application of credit standards, and setting credit limits.

cross hedge   a hedge that uses a futures contract that has a different underlying instrument from the cash market instrument being hedged.

currency swap   an agreement between two parties to exchange different currencies and then to reexchange them at a future date at the same exchange rate. Periodic interest payments are made during the term of the swap.

current liquidity index   a cash coverage ratio found by adding beginning of period balance of cash assets and the cash flow from operations during the period and then dividing this sum by the sum of beginning of period notes payable and current maturing debt.

current maturity   the length of time remaining until a security matures. When first issued a five-year Treasury note has an original maturity of five years; one year later it has a current maturity of four years.

current ratio   the ratio of current assets to current liabilities used to measure the degree of coverage available to short-term lenders.

custody account   specialized account in which financial institution holds securities, automatically reinvests interest and other investment-related cash receipts, transfers funds per corporate instructions, monitors issuers actions such as calls and refundings, and provides a monthly statement on all account transactions.

cutoff time   deposit deadline for receiving a given day's stated availability.

daily NPV   is the difference between the present value of a project's daily inflows and the present value of its daily outflows.

daily transfer rule   the simplest and most common transfer rule that initiates a daily transfer from the deposit bank to the concentration bank in the amount of the daily deposit.

daylight overdrafts   bookkeeping negative account balances which occur when a bank's Federal Reserve account book balance is negative during the day or it sends more funds via Fedwire than it receives, prior to final end-of-day settlements. Many of the overdrafts occur because of international funds transfers of government securities transactions.

days inventory held   the average number of days a firm holds inventory found by dividing average daily cost of goods sold into the balance sheet inventory account.

days of cost of goods sold invested in inventory   an inventory activity measure which indicates the average number of days it takes to sell inventory.

days payables outstanding   the average number of days the firm takes to pay for its purchases found by dividing average daily purchases into the balance sheet accounts payable balance.

days purchases outstanding   the average number of days a firm takes to pay its payables.

days sales outstanding (DSO)   measure of how long a company is taking to collect receivables. Also known as average collection period. It is computed by taking the latest period's accounts receivables and dividing it by daily credit sales. Daily credit sales, in turn, are computed by taking the period's sales and dividing by the number of days in the period—365 when computing DSO over a yearly period. The average number of days credit customers take to pay for their purchases found by dividing average daily sales into the accounts receivable balance.

dealers   market participants which typically "take a position" in the security instrument(s) they trade, meaning they hold an inventory of securities.

debit cards   similar to credit cards except the transaction amount is immediately (or within two business days) charged against the user's checking account balance. These cards allow consumers to pay grocery and other bills through an electronic charge to their bank accounts.

decentralized disbursing   corporate arrangement which allows payments to be made by divisional offices or individual stores, usually from accounts held at nearby banks.

decentralized processing system   a collection system that has the company's various field offices or stores receive payments from the company's customers.

decentralized transfer initiation   the cash transfer decision initiated by the field office manager.

decomposition method   analysis of collection experience which involves segregating the period-to-period changes in receivables into three effects: the collection effect, the sales effect, and the interaction effect.

default risk   the possibility that the issuer will not meet contractual obligations to pay interest or repay principal or will violate a covenant in a debt agreement.

demand deposit account (DDA)   non-interest bearing checking accounts. This account is the foundation for all other cash management services the bank might offer to the corporate client.

demand flow   an inventory system similar to the just-in-time system, but more encompassing.

denomination   refers to a security's dollar amount or face value.

deposit reconciliation   one type of account reconciliation, this service minimizes the number of depository accounts a company must have while offering the added advantage of convenience.

deposit reporting service   information on account balances offered by a bank or third-party vendor, which enables the treasury staff to know when and where the company's operations have deposited money into bank accounts.

Depository Institution Deregulation and Monetary Control Act of 1980   landmark legislation which enabled savings and loans, mutual savings banks, and credit unions to operate more like commercial banks. Also established reserve requirement ranges for various deposit accounts.

depository transfer checks (DTC)   non-negotiable, unsigned checks used by firms to move funds from one account to another. They are often used to move (concentrate) monies collected in many different locations into a pooled account in a "concentration bank," where the money can be invested as a single large amount.

depth   a characteristic of a market in which a very large dollar amount of securities can be easily absorbed without large changes in the market price.

deterministic model data input for deterministic models are single point estimates.

direct deposit service in which the employer's bank automatically deposits employees' wages and salaries. The bank sorts out the on-us checks for employees having checking accounts at that bank, and credits their accounts. Employees banking elsewhere are paid through the local clearing house or ACH-initiated transactions. Direct deposit of payroll is easily the most popular electronic payment application.

direct format one possible format allowed for presenting the Statement of Cash Flows that computes cash inflows and cash outflows directly, showing the major components of operating cash receipts and operating cash disbursements.

direct hedge a hedge using a futures contract that is of the same type as the cash market instrument being hedged.

direct presenting situation in which checks are sent to the drawee bank or its local clearinghouse via courier. Direct presenting is mainly used for large checks.

disbursement float the delay between the time when the company writes the check and the time when its bank charges the checking account for the amount of the check.

disbursement policy whether an informal strategy or a formal written document, specifies which payment mechanism to utilize for a given disbursement, when to pay a given invoice, and the setup of guidelines regarding the disbursement system (including which bank(s) might be involved).

disbursement system a company's payment methods, disbursement banks, and disbursing locations.

disbursing bank bank used to pay from.

discount basis when the selling price of a financial instrument is less than its face value or value at maturity.

discount rate in a capital project evaluation it is the opportunity cost of the use of funds, which is used to determine the present value of cash flows.

discount rate (Fed) the rate charged depository institutions when they borrow reserves from the Fed in order to meet their reserve requirements or meet unusual loan demand.

discount security one which does not pay regular interest payments, but compensates the investor for implied interest by returning at maturity a principal amount greater than the purchase price.

discount yield the difference between the maturity cash flow and the purchase price on a discount (non-interest bearing) security, expressed as a percentage of the purchase price.

discounting the determination of a present dollar equivalent of a cash flow to be received in the future.

distribution method a regression-based cash forecasting approach which spreads, or "distributes," a monthly total across the weeks or days within that month. This method has also been used to model payroll-related cash disbursements by relating cash outflows to how many business days have elapsed since payroll checks have been issued.

dividend capture strategy corporate investment strategy involving buying a common or preferred stock shortly before it pays its dividend, or buying a preferred stock having an adjustable dividend payment. Because intercorporate dividends have been largely excludable for income tax purposes (presently there is a 70% exclusion), corporate investors buy stocks with high dividend yields, hold them at least 49 days (until the record date for payment), and then sell.

dividend roll an investment approach which involves buying stocks with high dividend yields, holding them at least 49 days to collect the dividend, and then selling the stocks.

dollar-day float a measure of delay that considers both the dollar amount and the time lag.

dominant securities which provide a higher expected return for a given amount of risk than other securities.

double counting this can either occur when a bank counts the same balances as compensation for a loan and as compensation for cash management services, or if the company has written a depository check for which it has been granted availability at the concentration bank, but has not had its checking account debited.

draft a written order to make payment to a third party, where the entity ordered to pay the draft is usually a bank. Any party holding a credit balance for the person writing the draft may have a draft drawn on it.

drawee bank   the bank on which a check or draft was written ("drawn").

driving variable   a key variable in most financial planning models to which most relationships are tied. Sales is generally such a variable in many financial planning models.

dual balance   the same dollar balance that is temporarily on deposit at two different banks.

dummy variables   variables included in the regression equation when modeling seasonal or monthly effects. The number included is one less than the number of seasons. Each dummy variable that is included as an independent variable takes on a value of 1 only when the season it represents is the season for which the forecast is being made, and 0 at all other times.

duration   a tool for evaluating the interest rate risk of interest-bearing notes and bonds. It is defined as the weighted average time until the investor receives an investment's discounted cash flows.

earnings credit rate (ECR)   a rate that banks credit collected balances with as compensation for leaving the balances in the account.

economic exposure   refers to the possibility that the long-term net present value of a firm's expected cash flows will change due to unexpected changes in exchange rates.

economic order quantity   the order quantity that minimizes the total cost of managing inventory.

ECU   the outgrowth of the European Monetary System is a new currency, referred to as the ECU, which represents a basket of currencies of the members of the EEC.

EEC   the European Economic Community.

effective annual rate   incorporates the compounding of interest through time to give a more accurate reflection of the increase in wealth gained by holding a security. Whenever the interest is compounded more than once a year, the effective annual rate will exceed the nominal rate. On loan agreements, the effective rate is the annualized effective simple interest rate on the financing arrangement considering all out of pocket costs relative to the dollar amount of usable funds received.

effective interest rate   the rate of interest that is equal to or greater than the stated interest rate because of out-of-pocket expenses and usable funds that are less than the face value of the loan.

efficient markets   where prices change freely and instantly in response to supply and demand, and are not significantly affected by poor information or tax code barriers.

electronic business data interchange (EBDI)   the electronic movement of information such as invoices between corporate trading partners.

electronic check presentment   is an arrangement in which the image of the MICR line of a check is presented to the paying back, instead of presenting the physical check, shortening clearance float.

electronic corporate trade payment   an arrangement between two corporations (a buyer and a seller) and the banks of the two parties so that payment is effected without a paper check being issued.

electronic data interchange (EDI)   the electronic transmission of purchase-related data such as orders, shipping notices, invoices, credits and other adjustments, and payment notices.

electronic depository transfer (EDT)   payment process in which a local or regional account is debited electronically and the amount sent through an automated clearing house to the concentration bank account. Also known as an ACH debit, is an electronic equivalent to the paper DTC. The electronic transaction provides quicker availability in the concentration account for the company.

electronic funds transfer (EFT)   the actual electronic transfer of payments, or value, between trading partners.

electronic lockbox   collection system offered by banks for companies to receive payments, via wire transfers or ACH, from customers.

EMS   members of the EEC created a subset of controlled exchange rates between their respective currencies which is referred to as the European Monetary System.

enterprise resources planning (ERP)   accounting-oriented information systems used for identifying and planning the enterprise-wide resources needed to take, make, ship, and account for customer orders.

error distribution   the shape or pattern of the array of forecast errors.

Euro   a new currency that represents a basket of currencies of the participating countries in the European Monetary System.

euro cp   similar in concept to domestic commercial paper except issued in the Euro-market which has fewer restrictions, is unrated, and generally has a longer maturity averaging from 60 to 90 days.

Eurodollar CDs   dollar-denominated deposits held in banks or bank branches outside the U.S. or in International Banking Facilities (IBFs, which can offer Eurodollar deposits only to non-U.S. residents) located within the United States.

evaluated receipt settlement   an electronic payment process in which receipt of shipment (not receipt of invoice) triggers payment by the purchasing company.

event risk   includes any security feature or possible event that subjects the investor to a disruption to or reduction in the expected yield.

exchange-rate risk   the risk that a firm faces when buying or selling in one or more currencies different from its domestic currency.

expedited check processing   speedier check clearing provided by the clearing bank if the depositor is willing to perform extra tasks or pay the bank the extra charge involved.

Expedited Funds Availability Act of 1987   required that shorter availability schedules be put in place to reduce arbitrarily long holds on deposited checks.

expert systems   computerized decision-making procedure based on a mimicking of what experienced human decision makers have done in many similar situations.

exponential smoothing   statistical forecasting technique similar to a moving average, but overcoming the slowness of adaptation to changing patterns inherent in the moving average by allowing a greater weighting for more recent data.

face value   investors holding an investment to maturity will receive this amount back from the issuer. Also called the investment's principal.

factoring   the process of selling receivables and receiving funds before payment of the receivables is made by the customers.

FASB Statement 95   the accounting standard that created the Statement of Cash Flows.

Fed float   part of the clearing float for a mailed check, it arises because the Fed may grant availability to the clear-ing bank before it presents the check (and debits the account of) the payee's bank. Fed float has been greatly reduced since 1980, because the 1980 Monetary Control Act mandated that the Fed eliminate or charge for Fed float.

Federal Advisory Council   is a group of prominent commercial bankers which gives input into Fed decision making.

Federal Deposit Insurance Corp. Improvement Act of 1991   requires the FDIC to give acquiring banks the choice of whether to bid for all of a failed bank's deposits or just the insured deposits, signaling a reduction in coverage for uninsured deposits.

fed funds rate   the rate charged on reserve borrowings, mostly overnight, transacted between banks.

Federal Open Market Committee (FOMC)   the seven members of the Board of Governors are also members of this group, which makes most of the monetary policy for the U.S. in its eight regularly scheduled meetings per year. The FOMC effects changes in the money supply by buying and selling Treasury securities (open market operations), which affects the reserve position of banks, and ultimately the money supply.

Federal Reserve member banks   see member banks.

Federal Reserve Act (1913)   established the Federal Reserve System to oversee and regulate the national money and credit system.

Federal Reserve System (Fed)   the nation's central bank, this organization oversees the national money and credit system by acting as lender of last resort, lending money to banks through the "discount window," and facilitating the payments mechanism, and is one of several national bodies that supervises and regulates banks.

Fedwire   a linked network of the twelve Fed district banks which transfers funds for banks (and by extension their customers) by debiting or crediting the banks' reserve accounts. It is a major part of the Federal Reserve System's payment system involvement.

field warehouse agreement   inventories pledged as collateral and physically segregated from other inventory generally on the borrower's premises.

Financial Accounting Standards Board (FASB) Statement 95   provides a set of guidelines to help classify cash receipts and disbursement according to type of activity.

financial EDI (FEDI) the exchange of electronic business information such as lockbox information reports, daily balance reports, and monthly account analysis reports between a firm and its bank. In the context of payments, financial EDI refers to electronic data interchange combined with payment instructions. This allows customers to include invoice data and payment instructions in the same payment order.

financial flexibility the ability of the firm to augment its future cash flows to cover any unforeseen needs or to take advantage of any unforeseen opportunities.

Financial Institutions Reform, Recovery and Enforcement Act (1989) allowed bank holding companies to buy healthy savings and loan associations.

financial motive one of the theoretical motives for trade credit extension, applies where the seller has a lower cost of capital than the buyer and is able to pass along some of the difference.

financial restructuring situation in which the company changes it product lines or its relative use of assets with heavy fixed operating costs-altering the company's business risk.

financial risk the possibility that a company will not be able to cover financing related expenditures such as lease payments, interest, principal repayment, and referred stock dividends.

Financial Services Modernization Act of 1999 also known as the Gramm-Leach-Bliley Act, this law repealed the 1933 Glass-Steagall Act's prohibition on bank-investment company affiliations.

financial statement approach utilizes profitability analysis along with a balance sheet evaluation of what the effect of a proposed course of action would have on the company's liquidity and cash position. Approximate timing of financial effects can be seen through the use of pro forma, or projected, financial statements.

financial swap an exchange of periodic cash flows between two parties.

financing activities defined as cash flows resulting from proceeds of issuance of securities, retirement of debt, and payments of dividends or other distributions to shareholders.

finished goods inventory inventory of the finished product ready for sale.

first differencing a means of correcting a data series for autocorrelation, which is accomplished by subtracting the previous value for the dependent variable from the current value, and then using the differences as the dependent variable (in lieu of the original values of the dependent variable).

five C's of credit traditional means of evaluating a corporate credit applicant by investigating character, collateral, capacity, conditions, and capital. Character is thought to be the single most important aspect in this approach.

fixed costs expenses which do not change with changes in activity or sales volume, such as rent or insurance.

fixed-for-floating rate swap in this type of swap, Party A, with floating rate debt, agrees to pay Party B, who has fixed rate debt, a fixed-rate interest payment based on the notional dollar amount stated in the agreement, in exchange for receipt of a floating-rate interest payment.

flat yield curve horizontally shaped graph of the yields to maturity of securities with various maturities, implying a "no change" forecast of future interest rates.

float the delay between the time a payment is initiated and the time when the payment is debited to the payor (disbursement float) or credited to the payee (collection float). Within ethical limits companies try to maximize it on payments or minimize it on collections, and float continues to be an important fact of life that must be coped with.

floating lien a financing arrangement where a borrower's inventory in general is pledged as collateral for a loan.

floating-rate note type of loan in which the interest rate is reset either daily, weekly, monthly, quarterly, or semi-annually.

floor planning the common name used for trust receipt loans made to automobile dealerships.

forecast bias tendency for a forecasting model to systematically over- or under-predict the variable of interest. It can often be detected on a graph of forecast errors over time or across values of an important predictor variable.

forecast horizon how far ahead the cash balance is being projected.

forecast interval the units the horizon is segmented into, such as months in a year-ahead forecast.

foreign exchange rate   the price of one currency stated in relation to the price of another currency.

foreign exchange risk   the possibility that exchange rates will move adversely, causing results of foreign business activities to have a reduced value when converted into the company's home currency.

forward contract   a contract negotiated between a financial manager and a bank for the future delivery of a foreign currency.

forward rates   prices or yields which the market collectively forecasts today for future periods. In foreign exchange markets, forward rates refer to exchange rates between currencies which is contracted to exist at a future value date.

forward value date   the date that good funds will be credited to the account (similar to availability schedules in the US).

full reconciliation   service which provides detailed checks outstanding information along with the checks paid data from company-supplied check issue detail.

futures contract   a standardized contract that obligates the buyer (issuer) to purchase (sell) a specified amount of the item represented by the contract at a set price at the expiration of the contract.

futures option   an option contract that gives the buyer (issuer) the right to purchase (sell) the futures contract underlying the options contract.

futures rates   an exchange rate at which currencies can be traded at a future date. Futures differ from forwards in that the futures contract is standardized and traded on a national exchange.

Garn-St. Germain Depository Institutions Act (1982) enacted alterations allowing: (1) depository institutions to pay interest on money market deposit accounts in order to compete with money market mutual funds; and (2) savings and loans associations to lend to businesses.

general obligation   the banking for the interest principal payments of these securities is simply future general revenues and the issuer's capacity to raise taxes.

giro acceptance   foreign payment method in which computer-processable stub card is signed by the customer, who then takes it to the post office. The bill mailed to the customer has a stub attached to it that includes the seller's bank and account number.

GIRO systems   a collection system for consumer payments that is common place in Europe. Sellers send customers an invoice with a payment stub encoded with the seller's bank account number. The customer signs the stub and then takes it to a GIRO processor. The processor delivers the stubs to the nearest GIRO bank which then debits the customer's account and credits the seller's account.

government warrant   essentially a payable-through-draft issued by a government agency.

hedger   a person who has a cash position or an anticipated cash position that he or she is trying to protect from adverse interest rate movements.

High Dollar Group Sort   a special expediting of large dollar amounts through the clearing system, with the Fed granting the depositing bank immediate credit if it deposits the check early in the morning.

high liquidity strategy   current asset allocation strategy which prescribes a high proportion of assets to be held in cash and securities in order to reduce the chance of running out of cash.

historical yield spread analysis   study of risk-related and maturity-related interest rate differences, motivated by a desire to detect profitable trading strategies.

holding costs   the costs associated with the storage of inventory.

imaging   digitizing documents, such as invoices and checks.

index fund   a managed portfolio assembled to mirror a particular financial market composite.

indirect format   one possible format allowed for presenting the Statement of Cash Flows that begins with net profit and then presents adjustments for items that do not results in current-period cash transactions including depreciation and changes in the various working capital accounts.

initial investment   expenses necessary to implement a capital budgeting proposal must be determined. This may include set-up costs, physical asset acquisition or disposition costs, permanent increases in the company's investment in cash, receivables, and inventories, and other cash outflows incurred at the time the project is initiated.

in-sample validation   involves gauging forecast errors by using the data set on which the model is fitted. This gives an upward bias to forecast accuracy.

instrument   a class of similar investments. Examples are agency notes, commercial paper, Treasury bills, certificates of deposit (CDs), banker's acceptances, and repurchase agreements.

Interdistrict Transportation System   redesign of the Federal Reserve's routing modes and techniques to shorten delays and minimize system-wide float.

interest-bearing   when the interest paid is based on a quoted rate based on the face value of the financial instrument.

interest rate cap   a financial contract which limits the rise in a selected interest rate.

interest rate collar   a financial contract which restricts the movement of a selected interest rate within a narrow band referred to as a collar. It is essentially a combination of an interest rate floor and cap.

interest rate floor   a financial contract which limits the decline in a selected interest rate.

interest rate risk   the possibility that interest rates will increase, causing the prices of existing fixed-income securities to drop.

interest rate swaps   an agreement between two different institutions or firms, generally referred to as counterparties, swapping cash flows between themselves.

Interstate Banking and Branching Efficiency Act (1994)   permitted interstate bank acquisitions, mergers, and branching.

inventory control systems   an information system employed to help control inventory.

inventory financing   a very important component of the total financial plan of most corporations because inventory makes up a significant portion of total working capital.

inventory turnover ratio   a measure of inventory usage that is found by dividing cost of goods sold by either the year-end inventory balance or by the average inventory balance.

inverted yield curve   downward-sloping graph of yields to maturity of securities with different maturities. Given the possibility to engage in arbitrage (simultaneously buy and sell otherwise identical securities having different maturities), this slope implies that the market collectively anticipates future shorter-term interest rates to decline.

investing activities   on the statement of cash flows items that are defined as receipts of cash from loans, sale of property, and cash disbursed for loans to other business entities and payments for property, plant, and equipment.

investment policy   defines the company's posture toward risk and return and specifies how that posture is to be implemented.

Jamaica Agreement   as a result of the inflation and balance of payment problems after World War II, causing many countries great difficulty in maintaining their appropriate exchange rate, the major trading nations signed the Jamaica Agreement in 1976 to demonetize gold and create a system of floating exchange rates.

judgmental approach   relies heavily on intuition to adjust what is known about upcoming cash flows to arrive at the cash forecast.

just-in-time inventory system   an inventory system designed to reduce the levels of inventory kept at the manufacturing site increasing quality in the production process and by shifting the inventory burden to the supplier.

lagged regression analysis   a quick and relatively inexpensive way of determining a company's collection experience by determining a mathematical equation relating cash collections to the sales that gave rise to them.

lagging   the practice of delaying collections or payments.

lambda   a liquidity measure from a function of the likelihood that a firm will exhaust its liquid reserve. The measure's numerator is the sum of the firm's initial liquid reserve and total anticipated net cash flow during the analysis horizon and denominator is the standard deviation of the net cash flow during the analysis horizon.

leading   the practice of accelerating collections or payments

ledger balance　　reflects all credits and debits posted to an account as of a certain time, but this balance may not be entirely spendable.

letter of credit　　a promise by a bank to make payment to a party upon presentation of a draft provided that the party complies with certain documentary requirements. This guarantees the investor of principal repayment, and the use of backup bank financing allows the bank's credit rating to be substituted for the issuer's.

liability swap　　a swap created to hedge cash flows related to liabilities.

LIBOR　　the London Interbank Offer Rate which is commonly used internationally as a reference rate for variable rate loans.

line of credit　　short term lending arrangement which allows the company to borrow up to a pre-arranged dollar amount during the one-year term.

liquidity　　the ability to sell an asset quickly, at or very close to the present market price. For a company the ability of the firm to pay its bills on time.

liquidity preference hypothesis　　theoretical explanation for the term structure of interest rates that hypothesizes that higher yields will be necessary to induce investors to tie their funds up for long time periods (in other words, to be illiquid) in light of the increasing interest rate risk. Preference for liquidity is thought to characterize enough investors that the yield curve (in the absence of expectations or other influences on other than the shortest-term securities) should slope upward from left to right. The longer the maturity, the larger the liquidity premium must be to attract investors.

liquidity risk　　the inability to sell quickly at or very near the current market price, which is tied to the marketability of a security.

loan participation　　after a bank or syndicate of banks arranges a large loan, part or all of the loan may be sold off to corporate or other institutional investors, as well as to other banks.

lockbox　　a special post office box where customers are instructed to mail their remittances.

lockbox collection system　　a cash collection system that intercepts customer remittances close to the sending location and deposits the checks in the banking system prior to the company receiving notification.

lockbox consortium　　a system composed of several independent banks operating under a contractual agreement to provide lockbox services for each other's customers.

lockbox optimization model　　a set of variables, relationships, and rules that determine the optimal number of lockboxes, their locations, and the customer allocations to the selected lockbox sites.

lockbox services　　a collection service offered by banks, with the emphasis being to reduce collection float. Banks receiving one million or more pieces of mail per year can have a unique zip code set up for them, saving one or more sorts by post office personnel.

lockbox study　　a study usually conducted by a bank consulting group to help a corporation decide the structure of its collection system.

log-linear regression　　is an approach to estimating a variable's growth rate, which takes into account all of the variable's observed values.

London Interbank Offer Rate (LIBOR)　　the rate at which banks offer term Eurodollar deposits to each other.

low liquidity strategy　　aggressive current asset allocation strategy which entails driving the company's investment in cash and securities to a minimum.

lower control limit (LCL)　　in the Miller-Orr cash management model, this would be the low point in the cash position, and the point at which a sale of securities sufficient to return the cash balance to the cash return point is initiated.

Magnetic Ink Character Recognition (MICR) line　　the clearing agent, often a Federal Reserve bank, branch or RCPC, uses the information printed at the bottom of the check to process the check. This information can be read by scanning machines and indicates several items about the drawee bank.

mail float　　the time that elapses from the point when the check is written until it is received by the payee. It may range from a day for local checks immediately mailed out to 10 days for a check sent to New York from Rome, Italy.

maintenance margin　　the level that the margin account returns to after a margin call.

managing about a target rule　　rather than make daily transfers, this transfer rule makes only one transfer for several days of deposits and the amount transferred takes into consideration a desired target balance that is to be left at the deposit bank.

manufacturing resource planning systems (MRP II) systems that are made up of a variety of functions that are linked together including business planning, sales and operations planning, production planning, master production scheduling, material requirements planning, capacity requirements planning, and the execution support systems for capacity and materials.

margin a small percentage of the contract price that is put up rather than paying the full price of the contract.

marked-to-market when changes in the market price of the futures contract impact the margin account on a daily basis.

market microstructure consists of the participants and mechanics involved in making transactions.

market segmentation hypothesis a theoretical explanation of the term structure of interest rates which contends that instead of being close substitutes, securities with short, medium, and long maturities are seen by investors (fund suppliers) and issuers (funds demanders) as quite different. Thus interest rates for securities with different maturities are set by diverse supply and demand conditions.

Markov chain analysis an elaborate means of identifying changes in the collection experience. It is related to the uncollected balance percentages.

master note open-ended commercial paper, which allow the investor to add or withdraw monies on a daily basis, up to a specified maximum amount.

material requirements planning (MRP) an inventory planning system that focuses on the amount and timing of finished goods demanded and translates this into the derived demand for raw materials and subassemblies at various stages of production.

maturity extension swap situation where a security is sold and replaced or exchanged with another security which will increase the yield or dollar return, while affecting credit risk minimally. The swap is executed when the manager wishes to ride the yield curve, but to make the investment he must liquidate another security.

McFadden Act (1927) limited branch banking by national banks to the same areas in which state-chartered banks in that state were permitted to branch, effectively prohibiting interstate branching.

mean absolute error (MAE) measure of forecast error calculated by adding up the absolute values of the difference between forecasted and actual values, and then dividing by the number of forecasts.

mean square error weights large errors more than small ones, and thus favors forecasting models that rarely if ever miss by a large amount.

member banks commercial banks which belong to the Federal Reserve System. Being a member of the Federal Reserve System has historically been a requirement of all national banks, and many state-chartered banks joined voluntarily. Subsequent to the 1980 Monetary Control Act membership has been much less important, in that all depository institutions must adhere to reserve requirements and can now borrow from the Fed.

Miller-Orr model cash management model which has two important characteristics: (1) it allows for unpredictable fluctuations in the cash balance instead of assuming perfect cash forecasting ability; and (2) it permits both upward and downward movements in the cash balance subsequent to replenishment, as opposed to the assumption that the company experiences a one-time cash infusion each period, which is subsequently depleted at a continuous rate.

mixed approach when applied to forecasting, involves the use of both quantitative and judgmental approaches.

mixed instruments specialized investment instruments which offer tailoring to the specific desires of the investor.

model audit the monitoring of an existing model to ensure its continued validity.

model estimation includes the selection of an appropriate forecasting technique and model calibration.

modeling the process of establishing a relationship between a set of independent variables in order to produce an estimate of a dependent variable.

moderate liquidity strategy an approach to liquidity management which implies an intermediate concentration of current assets in the form of cash and securities, with corresponding intermediate levels of risk. This strategy falls between and should be contrasted with conservative and aggressive liquidity strategies.

moderate strategy in short-term financing, a strategy that is a blend of the aggressive and conservative financing strategies.

modified accrual technique   sometimes called the "accrual addback technique" or "adjusted net income technique," this cash forecasting approach begins with accounting reports or the operating budget and then adjusts these number to reflect the timing of cash flows related to these transactions.

modified buy-and-hold strategy   an approach to investing in which the investor plans to hold the security to maturity, but will selectively sell securities on which capital gains might be realized. This strategy might be utilized when the investor wishes to take advantage of anticipated favorable interest rate movements.

money market   arena in which buyers and sellers of all securities maturing in one year or less interact; trading does not take place in any one physical location, but mainly by phone and computer communications. To distinguish the money market from capital markets, only securities with an original maturity of one year or less are included.

money market deposit accounts   savings accounts offered by depository institutions which pay interest. These were introduced to give depository institutions an account to compete with money market mutual funds.

money market mutual fund   an investment vehicle which invests in short-term securities with funds pooled from numerous individuals or institutions. The money market mutual fund was first introduced in 1972 and became very popular in the high-interest era of late 1981.

moving average   statistical forecasting technique which evens out temporary ups and downs by taking the mean of the most recent observations.

multicollinearity   presence of moderate or high correlation between predictor variables in a regression equation. This condition is a violation of one of the assumptions of ordinary least squares regression modeling, the most common form of regression analysis.

multilateral netting   a netting system resulting from a corporation having subsidiaries in a number of different countries.

multiple-drawee checks   negotiable payment order having more than one bank listed on the face of the check, with one of the banks being a bank located near the disbursing location, for which the check is an "on us" item.

multiple processing centers   processing centers established around the country to pick up lockbox mail and do the processing while the processed checks are deposited in accounts at correspondent banks in the company's name. Cash is then concentrated in the company's account at the lockbox bank's headquarters.

multiple regression   statistical model incorporating two or more predictor variables to explain the movement in the variable of interest. The form of a multiple regression model having two predictor variables is generally of the form: $Y = a + b_1X_1 + b_2X_2$.

multivariate models   description of the relationship between three or more variables, typically with one of the variables being explained as the influence of two or more predictor variables.

municipal obligations   securities issued by governmental authorities, governments, or government-authorized entities at other than the federal level. These securities, sometimes called "munis," pay interest that is not taxable for federal income tax purposes and usually not taxable for state income tax purposes in the state in which the issuer is located. Examples of issuers would be states, counties, localities, and school districts.

NACHA   the National Automated Clearing House Association. NACHA has been involved in developing five format options that allow the movement of funds electronically, each with varying amounts of data.

nearby contract   the futures contract with a maturity date that occurs nearest to, but after, the date of the cash market transaction that is to be hedged.

negotiable certificate of deposit   bank deposits which come in $100,000 and larger denominations. Negotiability means the security can be legally sold and exchanged between investors, circumventing the early withdrawal penalty charged by the issuing bank. Only the first $100,000 is insured by the Federal Deposit Insurance Corporation, however.

net liquid balance   cash and marketable securities less notes payable and current maturities of long-term debt.

net present value (NPV)   a measure of the present dollar equivalent of all cash inflows and outflows flowing from a capital investment proposal. To compute net present value each cash inflow and outflow must be converted to its dollar value at a standard point in time. Calculation of NPV involves discounting all cash flows to the beginning of the cash flow timeline, then subtracting the present value of the outflows from the present value of the inflows.

net working capital   current assets less current liabilities.

netting   receipts denominated in a currency are netted against expenses due to be paid on the same currency in order to reduce the total volume of foreign currency transactions.

nominal interest rate   the stated interest rate for an investment or borrowing opportunity, ignoring the effect of the frequency of compounding. In order to compare various investments, the nominal rate is usually converted to an effective annual rate.

nonbank banks   make loans or accept deposits, but not both.

noncallable   a feature of a security which stipulates that the investor need not worry about a forced buyback of the security if interest rates fall subsequent to issuance. The absence of a call feature allows the issuer to pay a slightly lower interest rate due to the lower risk to the investor.

noncompetitive bid   bids which are entered directly through a tender offer to the nearest Federal Reserve district bank, or through a broker or commercial bank. Investors willing to accept the average yield of all accepted competitive bids enter a noncompetitive bid.

nonrecourse or without recourse   when a factor buys receivables and the selling firm is not ultimately responsible for final payment.

normal distributions   in forecasting, an array of forecast errors which occur in seemingly random fashion above and below forecasted values and graph as a symmetrical, bell-shaped curve.

normal yield curve   upward-sloping graph of yields to maturity for securities with various maturities, with longer-term maturities yielding more than shorter-term.

notional amount   the agreed upon face amount of the swap contract which exchange rates or interest rates are to be applied to calculate the cash flows which are to be swapped.

number of days of payables outstanding (DPO)   a payables activity measure found by dividing the payables balance by average daily purchases (alternatively, average daily cost of goods sold can be used in the denominator).

omitted variables   independent variables which should have been included in a regression model, and that could have helped the analyst predict the variable of interest. If important, omission may give rise to a violation of ordinary least squares assumption, a condition known as serial correlation.

ongoing validation   involves continually checking a model's forecast accuracy by monitoring each period's forecast error and comparing it to past forecast errors.

on-us   when the payee deposits the check in the bank on which it is drawn.

open account   (or open book account) once approved for credit, a customer can make repeated purchases as long as the total amount owed at any one time is less than some predetermined ceiling.

operating activities   those cash flows that are not classified as either investing or financing activities. Generally operating cash flows are related to cash collected from sales and cash disbursed to supplies, workers, management, and taxes.

operating cycle   the process of funds flowing from inventory to receivables to payables.

operating motive   theoretical motive for trade credit extension in which the seller responds to variable and uncertain demand by altering its trade credit availability.

operational restructuring   when a company changes its product lines or use of assets with heavy fixed operating costs and alters the company's business risk.

opportunity cost   what is given up in order to pursue a course of action. Conceptually, the discount rate chosen in capital budgeting evaluations should reflect the interest rate one could earn on the next best investment opportunity of about equal risk. Correspondingly, the discount rate used for making long-lived capital budgeting decisions is the company's weighted average cost of long-term capital.

order handling   disposition of orders that are within credit limits and handling of orders which violate limits.

ordering costs   costs associated with the inventory ordering process.

original maturity   length of time until principal is repaid, measured at the time the security is first sold.

originating ACH   the automated clearing house contacted by the bank initiating the transaction. The originating ACH must then transmit the payment order to the receiving institution's ACH (termed the receiving ACH).

originating depository financial institution (ODFI) bank which is contacted by the payment initiator.

outsourcing is contracting with outside companies to conduct certain business functions, such as check issuance.

out of pocket expenses financing expenses that include interest and bank commitment fees.

out-of-sample validation using a new data set to assess a forecasting model's forecast accuracy.

overdraft credit lines whether uncommitted or committed, have the added feature of being automatically drawn down whenever the company writes a check for which it does not have the sufficient funds to cover when it clears. Used extensively in foreign countries.

overdraft facility a banking service that allows a firm to overdraw its account. The overdraft is then charged interest as if it were a loan.

paid-only reconciliation bank-provided demand deposit report which indicates all paid checks by check number, with check number, dollar amount, and date paid.

passive investment strategy involves a minimal amount of oversight and very few transactions once the portfolio has been selected.

payable through draft (PTD) gives the payor 24 hours to decide whether to honor or refuse payment after it has been presented to the payor's bank. They are used for claim reimbursement by insurance companies, which use the 24 hour period to verify the signature and endorsements.

payables turnover ratio found by dividing purchases over a given time period by the year-end or average payables balance. Indicates the firm's payment behavior.

paying agent the bank performing this function makes interest and dividend payments to bondholders and shareholders, respectively, and repays the bond principal at maturity.

percent of sales forecasting model in which an expense or balance sheet amount is expressed as some fraction of sales.

permanent current assets the minimum amount of funds that are invested in current assets over the firm's operating cycle.

perpetuity a cash flow stream of equal dollar amounts that will last indefinitely into the future.

piggyback situation in which a bank is permitted to add a check or checks it is clearing and an accompanying listing to whatever checks the local Fed district bank is sending to the distant Fed office. This way the clearing bank can miss the local Fed's cutoff time but still meet the distant Fed's cutoff.

pledging receivables a lender makes a loan protected by a lien placed on a certain portion of the firm's receivables.

pooling a banking service offered by many banking systems outside the U.S. which allows a firm's excess balances spread across its bank branches to offset corporate deficit balances in other branches of the same bank.

positive float the time period between receipt of the goods or services and the date on which cash payment is made.

positive pay a company sends its daily check issue file to its disbursing bank. Before the bank honors incoming checks, it refers to the issue file to see if the payee and check amounts match up.

pre-authorized debits arrangement in which a customer agrees to allow his bank to automatically charge his checking account balance to make a fixed or variable payment each month.

pre-authorized draft payment order initiated by the payee, who has been authorized to draw against the payor's account. Banks sometimes collect mortgage payments this way, and most automobile dealerships now make payments to Ford, GM, and Chrysler by these drafts.

preauthorized payment the seller and buyer agree to a payment date and the seller initiates a request to the buyer's bank for payment of the predetermined amount.

precautionary motive additional inventory held as a cushion for an unexpected increase in demand.

premium the amount paid for purchasing an option or received from writing (selling) an option.

presentment step seven in the check clearing process, when the check is returned to the drawee bank for payment.

pricing motive theoretical motive for trade credit extension in which sellers unable to change prices, perhaps due to market conditions or regulation, alter trade credit instead in order to charge varying amounts to buyers.

pricing market   also called the original issue market, is centered in money centers such as New York City, London, Frankfurt, Singapore, and Hong Kong. Investors can access this "over-the-counter" market from anywhere, as the market consists of phone and computer hook-ups among all participating dealers and brokers.

principal   the original amount invested or borrowed.

private placement   security issuance transaction in which a large institution such as a retirement fund or insurance company buys the entire issue.

pro forma balance sheet approach   method of generating a cash forecast which involves determination of the amount of cash and marketable securities by computing the difference between projected assets (excluding cash and marketable securities) and the sum of projected liabilities and owner's equity.

processing float   the amount of time that transpires from the point of receipt of the check at a post office box or company mail room and the time when the check is deposited at the bank is termed processing float.

prox   payment due on a specific day in the following month.

purchase order with payment voucher attached   a draft coupled with a purchase order, which eliminates the need for a supplier to issue an invoice and for a customer to process the invoice and issue a check.

purchase terms   terms of credit offered by suppliers.

purchasing cards   are credit cards used by businesses to make small dollar purchases of maintenance, repair, and operating supplies. Use of purchasing, or procurement, cards greatly reduces the number of purchase orders and invoices processed and payments made.

purchasing power risk   the possibility that an investment's proceeds will not be worth as much as anticipated due to general price level increases in the economy. Anticipated inflation is built into the risk-free interest rate, but investors are still vulnerable to losses in purchasing power from unanticipated inflation and will require a higher yield when price levels are volatile.

put option   a contract that allows the owners to sell the underlying asset at a specific price over a specific span of time.

quantitative approach   any forecasting technique which involves the use of a numerical model to forecast; the technique is usually implemented on a computer.

quantity discounts   a reduction in the cost per order based on the quantity ordered.

quick ratio   the ratio of current assets less inventory to current liabilities.

range reconciliation   provides subtotals of all checks within a range of check serial numbers. This is especially useful for identifying disbursements from the same account but from several locations.

raw material inventory   inventory of the raw material of production.

receipts and disbursements method   a commonly used cash forecasting approach which involves determining upcoming sources of cash inflows and outflows, then laying these out on a schedule to see the aggregate effect.

receivables control   procedures and methods for following up credit extensions, including monitoring and corrective actions.

receiving depository financial institution (RDFI)   ACH payee's bank in an ACH credit transaction.

recourse   when a factor buys receivables with recourse, the selling firm is ultimately responsible for payment if the customer defaults.

recursive least squares (RLS)   in the context of receivables monitoring, a regression model which allows the estimated receivables collection fractions (the regression coefficients) to change over time.

Regional Check Processing Centers (RCPCs)   eleven Fed offices set up to help clear checks. Together the twelve district banks plus the 25 regional branches and eleven RCPCs gives the Fed a network of 48 offices to clear checks.

registrar   bank which keeps records of the number of shares of stock authorized, issued, and redeemed, and ensures that the number of share issued does not exceed those authorized.

Regulation CC   effective September 1990, this ruling stipulates that from the day of deposit local checks must be given availability within two business days, and nonlocal checks within five days.

Regulation Q   a Federal Reserve regulation that restricts banks from paying interest on demand deposit accounts.

reinvestment rate risk   the possibility that the investor will have to invest cash proceeds at a lower interest rate for the remainder of a predetermined investment horizon.

reinvoicing center   an entity which buys raw materials and final products from producing units of the same company, then rebills ("reinvoices") those items to foreign selling subsidiaries and non-company customers. The center is a separate operation of a corporation where the firm's different subsidiaries dealing in different currencies send their invoices and the center reinvoices only the net difference owed to each subsidiary. As a result, this center is generally responsible for managing the corporation's foreign exchange exposure. The costs of setting up a center are offset by economies of scale in purchasing and centralized exchange rate risk management.

relationship approach   one view of the corporation's link to its banks, in which the corporation chooses its bank services primarily based on pre-existing business dealings. Loyalty to prior arrangements is considered to be more important than price when selecting banks for cash management or lending services. Usually implies that credit and cash management services will both be handled by the same bank or network of banks.

remittance advice   a document which usually accompanies payment, indicating customer, account number, date, and invoice(s) being paid.

reorder point   the inventory level at which an order should be placed.

repurchase agreement (RP)   the sale of a portfolio of securities with a prearranged buyback one or several days later. A repurchase agreement, or "repo" as it is often called, involves the bank "selling" the investor a portfolio of securities, then agreeing to buy the securities back (repurchase) at an agreed-upon future date.

required rate of return   the percent return necessary to compensate investors for the risk borne when holding a company's securities. For a company as a whole, risk is a function of the variability of the average project undertaken. This, in turn, heavily influences the required returns on the company's equity and debt securities. For all capital taken together, the required rate of return translates into the company's cost of capital. For projects of lesser (greater) risk than the company's average capital project, the required return will be lower (higher) than the average cost of capital.

resiliency   condition of a market in which new orders enter when a temporary imbalance of buy or sell orders push the price away from its equilibrium level.

retail lockbox   is set up for a business receiving a large volume of relatively small dollar checks. Processing costs must be considered here along with collection float, and optically scannable invoices are read by machine to minimize human processing.

retail lockbox system   a lockbox system structured to handle a large volume of standardized invoice materials where the remittance checks have a relatively low average dollar face value.

retail market   an exchange situation where the buyers and/or sellers are primarily small entities, especially individuals.

return items   checks that bounce, leading to their return to the bank of first deposit through each bank involved in the forward presentment.

Revenue Anticipation Notes   short-term debt instruments which provide working capital financing for states and localities as they await anticipated revenues from other sources of revenue.

revenue securities   issues which tie cash flows to pledged revenue from the facility(ies) being financed: rental revenue from a convention center, or tolls from a bridge or toll road.

reverse positive pay   the disbursing bank sends the check presentment file to the company to see if all the items should be honored.

reverse repo   the other side of a repurchase agreement. In this case a firm needing a temporary source of cash for a few days can negotiate with its bank to temporarily sell securities with an agreement to repurchase them at the end of the specified period.

revolving credit agreement   allows the borrower to continually borrow and repay amounts up to an agreed-upon limit. The agreement is annually renewable at a variable interest rate during an interim period of anywhere from one to five years.

riding the yield curve   investing strategy which involves buying securities with maturities longer than the investment horizon, fully intending to liquidate the position early.

risk classes   an approach to risk adjusting potential capital projects by developing discount rates based on antic-ipated variability in the projects' cash flows. Proposals with longer time horizons, permanent effects on the firm's cash flows, or those with a short time horizon that might result in a very large range or standard deviation of outcomes would be assigned a higher discount rate.

risk premium   securities with the same maturity but issued by different issuers and with different issue charac-teristics are priced to reflect risk differences. The major risk factors accounting for this are default risk, liquidity risk, reinvestment rate risk, purchasing power risk, event risk. On foreign securities one must also consider exchange rate risk and political risk.

risk spread   the added yield necessary to compensate for risk factors other than maturity differences, such as default risk and liquidity risk.

risk structure of interest rate   set of interest rate dif-ferences between various securities which arise due to any factor other than a different maturity. The main risk factors giving rise to this structure are default risk, reinvestment rate risk, and purchasing power risk.

risk-adjusted discount rate   higher (lower) interest rate used in present value calculations when the project is of greater (lesser) risk than the average capital budgeting proj-ect invested in by the company.

risk-free rate   is determined primarily by investors' collective time preferences, the rate of inflation expected over the maturity period, and demand-side influences such as economic productivity.

root mean square error   has become increasingly popular in business and economic applications. It simply involves taking the square root of the mean square error (MSE).

safety stock   an extra inventory balance that acts as insurance against inventory stock outs.

sales agents   dealers sometimes function as brokers in their role as for banks and other issuers of short-term secu-rities. For a commission the agent will locate buyers for the institution's securities, again without risk because the agent does not have to buy and resell the securities.

Same-Day Settlement   is presentment of a check to the paying bank by 8:00 A.M. local time, with payment of the check required by Fedwire by the close of business day. This Fed initiative was enacted to reduce arbitrary holds or fees used by disbursing banks to slow check clearing.

seasonal dating   allows customers to purchase inven-tory before the peak buying season and defer payment until after the peak season.

secondary market   exchange arena for securities sub-sequent to their original issue. Not every investor holds the security to maturity, necessitating a well-functioning market for resale.

Securitization   involves issuing debt securities collat-eralized by a pool of selected financial assets such a mort-gages, auto loans or credit card receivables.

security   a specific investment offered by a given issuer.

sell hedge   a hedge created by selling a futures con-tract.

sensitivity analysis   means of incorporating risk in financial outcomes which involves varying key inputs, one at a time, and observing the effect on the decision variable(s). For example, the analyst might vary the sales level, and observe the effect on the company's cash forecast.

serial correlation   the existence of correlated errors in a regression model of a time series of data points.

shareholder value maximization   presumed goal of publicly held companies, in which decisions are made which will lead to the greatest anticipated increase in the value of the financial claims on the company. In practice, the com-pany's stock price is utilized as a measure of the value of all financial claims.

sight draft   a formal, written agreement whereby an importer (drawee) contracts to pay a certain amount on demand ("at sight") to the exporter. The bank is not extend-ing credit, but simply helping in the payment process by receiving the draft and presenting it to the drawee. Sight drafts often must have documentation attached to verify that conditions for payment (receipt, or "sight" of goods) have been met.

simple interest   arrangement in which interest is only added to the account at maturity. Because no compounding occurs, the nominal interest rate is also the annual effective rate.

simple interest approximation formula   simple interest formula to approximate the present value effect of a financial decision. the simplicity of this approach makes its use desirable where the effect of ignoring cash flow compounding would not have a significant effect on the valuation of those flows.

simple regression   a statistical model in which the equation used to predict the value of the variable of interest (dependent variable) involves just one predictor (independent) variable.

simulation   statistical technique for modeling uncertainty which begins with calculation of the expected value and standard deviation of the input variables, then uses iterative draws from each variable's probability distribution to draw up a probability distribution for the decision variable. For example, the analyst might simultaneously vary sales and a key input price, and observe the effect on the forecasted cash position.

solvency   a firm is solvent when the dollar level of its assets exceed the dollar level of its liabilities.

speculative motive   additional inventory held to take advantage of unique business opportunities such as future shortages.

speculator   a person who has no operating cash flow position to protect and is trying to profit solely from interest rate movements.

spontaneous financing   those financing sources such as accounts payables and accruals that are generated as a part of the operations of the firm.

spot rates   existing prices or interest rates in today's markets. In foreign exchange, the spot rate is an exchange rate quote based on immediate deliver of the currency being traded.

spurious correlation   chance association between two variables, which the analyst should watch for because it might account for a high coefficient of determination.

stable distribution   pattern of outcomes which characterizes a variable with a well-defined, consistent trend or seasonal component.

standard check processing   when the deposit bank verifies the depositor's cash letter-which lists the checks and their amounts-and then encodes the dollar amount on the MICR line and sends the checks to a correspondent bank or the nearest Federal Reserve facility to be cleared back to the disbursing bank on which the check was written.

standby letter of credit   document which guarantees that the bank will make available necessary funds to meet a financial obligation if the responsible company cannot or does not wish to meet a major financial obligation.

Statement of Cash Flows   a statement created by the Financial Accounting Standards Board, No. 95, showing the change in the cash balance as a result of cash flows from operating activities, cash flows from investing activities, and cash flows from financing activities.

statistical decomposition   a complex forecasting technique which uses the past observations of a variable to forecast future values. Sometimes called Census X-11 decomposition (after the computer software developed by the Census Bureau), this approach is especially useful for forecasting variables which have trend, seasonal, and cyclical variations.

stochastic model   data input for stochastic models represent probability distributions for one or more of the variables.

Stone model   optimization process similar to Miller-Orr but allows the cash manager's knowledge of imminent cash flows to permit him to selectively override model directives.

striking price   the price that an option contract allows the buyer to purchase a security at or a seller to sell a security at.

Super-NOW accounts   while banks continue to set higher minimum balance requirements for NOW accounts, in 1986 regulators removed interest rate distinctions between the accounts by eliminating the maximum NOW rate of 5 1/4%.

supply chain management   the process by which companies move materials and parts from suppliers through the production process and on to the consumers.

sustainable growth   the rate of sales growth that is compatible with a firm's established financial policies including asset turnover, net profit margin, dividend payout, and debt to equity ratio and assumes that new equity is derived only through retained earnings not new common stock.

swap   exchange of securities between two parties, often with the assistance of an intermediary known as a swap dealer. In its simplest form, a company engaging in a swap exchanges a fixed interest rate obligation for one that has a variable, or floating interest rate.

swap strategies   see for example, maturity extension swap and yield spread swap.

sweep accounts   special accounts whereby excess funds are automatically or at the cash manager's request transferred ("swept") from the demand deposit account into an interest-bearing overnight investment.

SWIFT   the Society of Worldwide Interbank Financial Telecommunications, is a communication network for relaying payment instructions for international transactions. It boasts roughly 1,500 member banks in 68 counties, and almost 3,000 banks are connected to the network.

syndicate   sometimes a group of investment banks works together on the marketing and shares the risk involved with bringing a new issue to market-which may or may not be acceptable at the pre-determined price. This grouping is called a syndicate.

synthetic composite   an artificial security which is devised to mirror the portfolio's average coupon interest rate, maturity, and risk rating.

systematic risk   is the degree of sensitivity of the company's stock returns to market-wide returns.

Tax Anticipation Notes   short-term debt instruments which provide working capital financing for states and localities as they await anticipated revenues from tax collections.

tax-advantaged instruments   those on which part or all of the income is exempted from taxation, or where the tax is deferred.

tax-exempt commercial paper   states and localities also issue some of these items. The risks are very similar to those of anticipation notes.

taxable instruments   security types which are not given preferential tax treatment, including commercial paper, domestic and Eurodollar certificates of deposit, banker's acceptances, repurchase agreements, and money market mutual funds invested in these instruments.

taxable-equivalent yield   the yield of a tax-exempt security on an after-tax basis, which facilitates comparison with the yield of taxable securities. The taxable-equivalent yield is the nominal (stated) yield divided by $(1 - \text{corporation's marginal tax rate})$.

temporary current assets   the accumulation of inventory in anticipation of the peak selling season and the resulting receivables generated by the increased sales. This bulge then subsides as the firm passes through its peak selling season.

term loan   a loan made with an initial maturity of more than one year.

term repos   repurchase agreement which is arranged with a maturity of several days to several weeks, making them well-suited for the investor having an investment horizon longer than one day.

term spread   the component of a security's return that is necessary to induce investors to bear risks linked to maturity.

term structure of interest rates   the tendency for the maturity-yield relationship to hold across all issuers in a systematic way. The graph of the term structure existing at a particular point in time is called a yield curve.

terminal warehouse agreement   inventories pledged as collateral are moved to a public warehouse that is physically separated from the borrower's premises.

thin market   one with little participation by buyers and/or sellers.

third-party information vendor   an information service that receives deposit information from field offices and transmits that information to the appropriate concentration banks and to corporate headquarters.

tiered pricing   the Fed has proposed this method where it reduces its charges to banks submitting large volumes of checks. This move to preserve its market share is seen as contradictory to the privatization initiative that the Fed officially espouses.

time draft   involves a credit element, because the payment obligation agreed to by the drawee is designated as due at a specified future date. Time drafts are usually dated after verification of a shipment of goods.

time series regression   a naive modeling approach in the sense that the mere passage of time generally does not cause the variable to change in value.

time-series techniques   forecasting methods which predict future movements in the forecast variable based on patterns revealed in historical movements of that same variable.

trade credit   permission to delay payment which arises when goods are sold under delayed payment terms.

trade discount　　percent reduction to quoted price offered to all customers, and not linked to early payment. This discount is typically offered to all customers, and the seller expects all customers to pay at the discounted price within the agreed-upon period. One example is a quantity discount, a price break given for a large purchase.

traders　　market participants which try to profit on anticipated interest rate or currency movements. They hold securities not as intermediaries, but as investors attempting to gain profits for their company's own account.

transaction approach　　an approach to bank selecting in which there is a decoupling or "unbundling" of services, meaning the company will not necessarily borrow from the bank(s) it utilizes for cash management services. Increasingly prevalent, in this approach the treasurer selects the bank(s) that can best provide a specific service or can provide it at the best price.

transaction exposure　　related to the gains or losses associated with the settlement of business transactions denominated in different currencies.

transaction motive　　inventory held in relation to the level of operating activity expected by the firm.

transaction sets　　a set of standards for EDI information flows developed by the ANSI X12 committee to facilitate the electronic communication between trading patterns.

transfer agent　　the financial institution which takes care of updating the records for the corporation's stock and registered bonds.

transfer items　　checks drawn on banks that do not participate in a bank's local clearing house or exchange; these are sometimes called "out-of-town" checks.

transit items　　are checks drawn on banks that do not participate in a deposit bank's local clearinghouse or exchange.

transit routing number　　also called the FRD/ABA (Federal Reserve District/American Banker's Association) bank ID number, a number imprinted on checks which identifies the payee's bank. This number is used by the deposit bank to determine how best to clear the check.

translation exposure　　this type of exposure occurs when the balance sheet and income statement of a foreign subsidiary are translated into the parent company's domestic currency for consolidated financial reporting purposes.

treasury management workstation　　a computer system that provides a means for the treasury manager to efficiently manage cash concentration, account balances at banks, cash transfers, and the short-term investment and borrowing portfolio. These are sold by banks and some specialized vendors.

trust receipt loans　　a financing arrangement where the collateralized inventory items are noted by serial number or some other readily identifiable mark.

trust services　　safekeeping, record keeping, and perhaps investing of corporate or individual pension or profit-sharing plans. For a corporate pension, the trustee institution receives the payments, invests them, maintains record for each of the employees, and pays the pensioners after they retire.

trustee under indenture　　the third-party financial institution charged by investors with the responsibility of monitoring the issuing corporation to ensure that it abides by all provisions of the bond agreement, called indenture.

unbiased expectations hypothesis　　a theory of interest rate determination which posits that the prevailing yield curve is mathematically derived from the present short-term rate and expectations for rates that will exist at various points in time in the future.

uncollected balance percentages　　a proportional break-down of the present accounts receivable balance, with the proportions based on the month the credit sales originated. The pitfalls of DSO, accounts receivable turnover, and the aging schedule have led to the development of this improved measure, in which the receivables balance is broken down, and the monthly components are divided by the credit sales in the month in which the receivables originated. Sometimes called the "payments pattern approach," the uncollected balance percentages accurately depict a company's collection experience, even when sales are changing.

uncommitted lines of credit　　short-term lending agreements which are not technically binding on the bank, although they are almost always honored. Uncommitted lines are usually renewable annually if both parties are agreeable. A less formal agreement than a committed line and the availability of funds may be in question if the general economic or bank internal liquidity position slips.

unique ZIP code　　used by banks to increase the efficiency of their lockbox operations.

unsecured　　lending arrangement in which there is no collateral backing up the loan in the event of a default.

upper control limit (UCL)   cash balance which triggers a purchase of securities large enough to reduce excess cash balances to a predetermined return point.

usable funds   the net proceeds the firm receives from the financing sources. This represents the amount borrowed less compensating balances, in the case of credit lines, and the bid-ask spread in the case of commercial paper.

usage rate   the daily rate of drawing down the inventory balance. Calculated by dividing the total inventory needs by the number of days in the production planning period.

valuation   the determination of the present dollar value of a series of cash flows.

valuation approach   method of financial decision-making in which the anticipated shareholder value effect determines which alternative is chosen. The present values of cash inflows and outflows are compared for each alternative.

value added network (VAN)   a computer system that receives EDI information from one firm in one format and transmits to another firm or bank in a different format. The system transmits messages and data from point of origination to pre-specified endpoints, and which may offer one or more auxiliary services.

value dating   involves forward movement of the amount of a deposited check and back dating of a presented check. This is a common practice by some European banks.

variable costs   expenses which increase or decrease with the level of production or sales, such as direct labor or raw materials.

variable identification   involves determining what items need to be forecasted and how best to measure those items.

variable rate demand notes   medium-term debt instruments issued by municipalities, which are found in some corporate short-term investments portfolios because their interest rates are periodically reset.

variance   the amount by which the actual amount is over or under the forecasted or budgeted amount.

variance analysis model   receivables control technique which builds on the decomposition model, and compares actual receivables performance to the budgeted amounts. If the budget captures the unique conditions and sales levels a company is experiencing, or is so adjusted after the period is over ("flexible budgeting") then one can discern the true reason(s) for changes in receivables levels.

WCR/S   working capital requirements divided by sales.

weekend effect   a concern in making cash transfers that takes into account weekend balances, since deposit accounts in the U.S. do not earn interest, and also considers weekend deposits that will be credited to the deposit account on Monday.

weighted-average cost of capital   the summed product of the proportion of each type of capital used and the cost of that capital source, this "hurdle rate" for capital investments is usually based on a company's long-term financing sources.

wholesale lockbox system   special arrangement for collecting mailed payments, established for collecting relatively few large dollar remittances. Because the dollar amounts per check are larger (perhaps $1 million or more), the received checks are processed more often and checks are processed for deposit more rapidly by bank than by company personnel.

wholesale market   investment supply and demand interaction for large dollar transactions between large investors (such as the money market).

wire drawdowns   wire transfers which are initiated by the receiving party, instead of the sender or payor.

wire transfers   are bookkeeping entries that simultaneously debit the payor's account and credit the payee's account. The best way to quickly move money from one place to another is with a wire transfer. A real-time transfer of account balances between banks.

with recourse   when the factor can demand funds returned for uncollected receivables.

without recourse   the seller is not liable for uncollected receivables.

work-in-process inventory   inventory of items beyond the raw material stage but not yet at the completed product state.

working capital cycle   the continual flow of resources through the various working capital accounts such as cash, accounts receivables, inventory, and payables.

working capital investment decision   the proportion of total assets held in current asset accounts, with the outcome usually linked closely to the company's risk posture.

working capital requirements   the difference between current operating assets (receivables, inventory, and prepaids) and current operating liabilities (accounts payable and accruals).

yield curve   a graph of the yields to maturity of an issuer's securities having several different maturities, showing current maturities on the horizontal axis and yield-to-maturity on the vertical axis. This curve provides a graphical depiction of the existing term structure of interest rates.

yield spread   the difference between two interest rates, expressed as a percentage difference.

yield spread swaps   exchange of one debt security for another, usually with the motivation of taking advantage of a mispriced security, based on the investor's study of historical interest rate differences.

zero balance account (ZBA)   a corporate bank account which maintains a zero dollar balance because the total presented against it each day is automatically funded by another of the company's accounts, usually the "master" or concentration account.

CREDITS

P. 86   Case 1, "Bernard's New York Deli," by Steven Dawson, *Case Research Journal,* Vol. 19, Issue 1 (Winter 1999). Copyright © 1999 North American Case Research Association. Reprinted by permission.

Exhibit 5-4   Reprinted with permission from the Association for Financial Professionals (AFP)—formerly the Treasury Management Association. Copyright © 1997, 1990, 1999 by AFP. All rights reserved. www.AFPonline.org

Exhibit 5-6   Copyright © 1996 by Dun & Bradstreet, a company of the Dun & Bradstreet Corporation.

Exhibit 5-9   Reprinted from businessweek.com/smallbiz/0005/fi000516.htm of *Business Week* by special permission. Copyright © 2000 by The McGraw-Hill Companies, Inc.

P. 194   Focus on Practice, from "Ten Ways to Get Paid," by Robyn Nissim, *Entrepreneurial Edge,* Summer 1996, pp. 22–23. Copyright © 1996 *Entrepreneurial Edge.*

P. 238   Focus on Practice, from "Bank Consolidation and Interstate Banking: Effect on Treasury Management," by Aaron L. Phillips, *TMA Journal,* March–April 1999, pp. 40–43. Reprinted with permission from the Association for Financial Professionals (AFP)—formerly the Treasury Management Association. Copyright © 1997, 1990, 1999 by AFP. All rights reserved. www.AFPonline.org

Exhibit 8-6   Copyright © 1994 by the American Bankers Association. Reprinted with permission. All rights reserved.

Exhibit 8-8   From "Check it Out: Checks Continue to Increase," by Paul H. Green, *The Green Sheet,* Issue #96: 02:01. Paul Green, www.greensheet.com

Exhibit 8-14   Reprinted with permission from Bank One. All rights reserved.

Appendix 8A   Copyright © 1986 Franklin Watts, Incorporated. Reprinted with permission of Grolier Publishing Company

Exhibit 11-1   Reprinted with permission from the Association of Financial Professionals (AFP)—formerly the Treasury Management Association. Copyright © 1997 by AFP. All rights reserved. www.AFPonline.org

Exhibit 11-2   Reprinted with permission from *Cash Management and the Payments Systems: Ground Rules, Cost, and Risks,* The Globecon Group, 1986. Financial Executives Research Foundation.

Exhibit 11-5   Greenwich Associates, Greenwich, CT 06831. Based on Greenwich Associates *2000 Study of the Cash Management Practices of Large U.S. Companies.* Reprinted with permission.

Exhibit 11-8   Reprinted with permission of Phoenix-Hecht, a division of UAI Technology, Inc., Research Triangle Park, North Carolina.

P. 362   Focus on Practice, from "Making International Payments: Navigating the Course," by Michael Burn, *AFP Exchange* (Winter 2000): pp. 62–64. Copyright © 2000 AFP. Reprinted by permission. All rights reserved. www.AFPonline.org

Exhibit 11-9   Reprinted with permission of Phoenix-Hecht, a division of UAI Technology, Inc., Research Triangle Park, North Carolina.

Exhibit 11-10   Reprinted with permission of Phoenix-Hecht, a division of UAI Technology, Inc., Research Triangle Park, North Carolina.

Exhibit 11-11   Reprinted with permission of Phoenix-Hecht, a division of UAI Technology, Inc., Research Triangle Park, North Carolina.

Exhibit 11-12   Reprinted with permission of Phoenix-Hecht, a division of UAI Technology, Inc., Research Triangle Park, North Carolina.

Exhibit 11-13   Reprinted with permission of Phoenix-Hecht, a division of UAI Technology, Inc., Research Triangle Park, North Carolina.

P. 442   Case 2, "Toy World, Inc.," from *Digital Finance,* by Eugene Brigham. Copyright © 1994 The Dryden Press. Used with permission.

Exhibit 14-4   Money Rates for Tuesday, March 6, 2001, from *The Wall Street Journal.* Copyright © 2001 Dow Jones & Company. Reprinted by permission via Copyright Clearance Center.

Exhibit 14-9   Copyright Franklin Distributors, a division of Franklin Templeton Group.

Exhibit 14-10   From "U.S. T-Bills," by Jonathan Nicholson, *Dow Jones Newswires,* March 5, 2001. Copyright © 2001 Dow Jones & Company. Reprinted by permission via Copyright Clearance Center.

Exhibit 14-12   Adapted from Exhibit 56-7 in "The Term Structure of Interest Rates," by Richard W. McEnally and James V. Jordan, from *The Handbook of Fixed Income Securities,* Third Edition, edited by Frank J. Fabozzi, with the assistance of T. Dessa Fabozzi and Irving M. Pollack. Copyright © 1991. Reprinted by permission of McGraw-Hill Companies, Inc.

Exhibit 14-14   From "Evaluating the Risk in Negotiable CDs," by John T. Zietlow, *Journal of Case Management,* September/October 1990, pp. 39–46. Reprinted with permission from the Association for Financial Professionals (AFP)—formerly the Treasury Management Association. Copyright © 1997, 1990, 1999 by AFP. All rights reserved. www.AFPonline.org

Exhibit 14-17   Reprinted from *Corporate Investments Manual,* by Alan G. Seidner, New York: Warren, Gorham, & Lamont. Copyright © 1989 Research Institute of America. Reprinted by permission.

Exhibit 15-4   Reprinted from *Corporate Investments Manual,* by Alan G. Seidner, New York: Warren, Gorham, & Lamont. Copyright © 1989 Research Institute of America. Reprinted by permission.

Exhibit 18-2   From *The Wall Street Journal,* December 15, 2000. Copyright © 2000. Dow Jones & Company. Reprinted by permission via Copyright Clearance Center.

Exhibit 18-3   From *The Wall Street Journal,* December 15, 2000. Copyright © 2000. Dow Jones & Company. Reprinted by permission via Copyright Clearance Center.

Exhibit 18-5   From *The Wall Street Journal,* December 15, 2000. Copyright © 2000. Dow Jones & Company. Reprinted by permission via Copyright Clearance Center.

Exhibit 18-7   From *The Wall Street Journal,* December 15, 2000. Copyright © 2000. Dow Jones & Company. Reprinted by permission via Copyright Clearance Center.

Exhibit 18-8   From *The Wall Street Journal,* December 15, 2000. Copyright © 2000. Dow Jones & Company. Reprinted by permission via Copyright Clearance Center.

INDEX

A

ABA. *See* American Banker's Association
Ability to pay, 140
ABS. *See* Asset-backed securities
Account analysis statement, 267–270
Account funding, 326
Account management systems, 196
Account reconciliation, 321
Accounts payable, 15–16, 212
    cash flow time line and, 212–218
    balance, 220–221
    information systems and, 219
Accounts receivables
    credit terms and, 225–226
    portfolio monitoring system, 187
    turnover, 184
Accredited Standards Committee (ASC), 610
Accrual-based income statement, 8–9
Accruals, 222
ACH. *See* Automated Clearing House
Acid-test ratio, 26
Active investment strategy, 511
Adjustable-rate preferred stock (ARPS), 461
Adjusted r^2, 388
Administrative costs, 316
Advanced present value analysis, 80–83
    risk considerations, 81–82
Advanced Software, Inc. (ASI), 526
AFP. *See* Association for Financial Professionals
Agency instruments, 462–464
Agency problem, 498
Aggressive financing strategy, 533–534
Aging schedule, 185–186, 190
    development of, 186
Air Force Working Capital Fund (AFWCF), 358–359
Allocation decision, cash and securities, 498–501
Alternative collection systems, 295–296
Amazon.com, 40–41
American Banker's Association (ABA), 242
American National Standards Institute, 610
Annual effective yields, 474
APS. *See* Auction preferred stock
ARIMA. *See* Box-Jenkins modeling
ARPS. *See* Adjustable-rate preferred stock
ASC. *See* Accredited Standards Committee
ASI. *See* Advanced Software, Inc.
Asset-backed securities (ABS), 456
Asset-based loans, 540–542

Assets
    fluctuating, 532
    permanent current, 533
    swap, structure of, 589
Association for Financial Professionals (AFP), 114, 236
    code of conduct, 327
Auction preferred stock (APS), 461
Automated Clearing House (ACH), 153, 240, 335, 526
    advantages and disadvantages, 255
    check payment costs, 313
    credit, 327
    debit, 327
    growth of, 253
    mechanics of, 254–256
    network, 315
    originating, 327
    payment trends, 330
    purpose of, 254
    receiving, 327
    service usage, 257
Availability float, 290
Availability times, 297–298
Average collection period, 184
Avoidance, 560

B

Baan, 109
Back value date, 563
Bad debt loss rate, 176–177
Balance fractions, 105
Balance percentages, uncollected, 188–190
Balances
    enhanced visibility and control of, 317
    vs. fees, 271–272
Balance schedule, uncollected, 188
Balance sheet, projected, 11
Bank check, processing flowchart, 243
Bank consolidation, effect of, 236
Bank credit
    commercial paper and, 539
    vs. trade credit, 119–120
Bank deposits
    interest rates, 503
    notes, 455
Bankers' acceptances (BAs), 448, 454, 537
Bank Holding Company Act (1956), 235
Banking, on internet, 276
Banking Act (1991), 483

Banking evaluation, 284–285
Banking network, 273–274, 286–287
Banking relationships, global, 277
Banking systems, 319–320
   non-US, 563–564
Bank instruments, 453–456
Bank notes, 455
Bank of Canada, 328
Bank One, 267–269
Bank relationships
   managing, 260–261, 266–274
   policy, 266
Banks, 138
   availability schedule, 263–265
   cash management in, 262
   nonbank, 234
   service charges, 270–271
   services of, 261–265
   value to corporate treasurers, 262
Bank selection
   criteria, 265–266
   process, 265
   relationship management, 265–266
BAs. *See* Bankers' acceptances
Basic valuation model, 58–59
Baumol model, 521–523
Beginning inventory (BI), 10
Bell Atlantic, 17
Bernard's New York Deli, 84–87
BI. *See* Beginning inventory
Bilateral netting, 561
   systems, 333
Box-Jenkins (ARIMA) modeling, 388, 393
Bretton Woods Agreement, 556–557
BuildNet, Inc., 219
Business risk, 497
Buy-and-hold strategy, 512
Buy hedge, 576

C
Call option, 581
Campbell Soup, 13
Canadian banking system, 328
Capacity, 130
   to pay, 13
Capital, 13, 130
   allocation decision making, 71–72
   asset pricing model (CAPM), 71, 72
   project evaluation, 72
   resources, 168–169
CAPM. *See* Capital, asset pricing model
CASH/ALPHA, 286
Cash and securities
   aggregate investment in, 499–500
   mix decision, 500–501

Cash application, 125, 127
   importance, 126–127
Cash budget, 11
Cash collections
   cash flow timeline and, 290
   dilemma of, 289
Cash concentration, 313
   basic structures 314–317
Canadian banking, 328
   systems, 317–318
Cash conversion period, 2, 33–36
Cash cycle, 13–15
Cash disbursements, 315–320
Cash discounts, 151, 181–182, 212
Cash flow
   activities, 32
   characteristics, 320
   conversion to, 8–9
   daily forecasting, 371–376
   estimation, 60
   importance of, 357–358
   income statement and, 11–12
   from operations, 33
   managing international, 555
   monthly forecasting, 357–371
   profit and, 7–13
   purpose, 30
   sequence modeling, 364, 373
   statement of, 30–32
   structure, 30–32
   timeline. *See* Cash flow timeline
   vs. profit, 3
   statement, 11–13
Cash flow return-on-investment (CFROI), 71
Cash flow timeline, 4–6, 61, 64, 17–182, 616
   cash collections and, 290
   cash concentration and, 317–318
   cash disbursements and, 315–320
   disbursement float and, 315–316
   for disbursements, 213
   financing, 532
   inventory management and, 100–103
   present credit terms, 63
   proposed credit terms, 62
Cash forecasting. *See also* Cash forecasts
   daily structuring, 373
   horizon, 362–363
   judgmental approach, 361
   methods. *See* Cash forecasting methods
   mixed approach, 362
   model for, 363
   parameters of, 362–371
   performance of, 372
   philosophy of, 361–362
   quantitative approach, 362

of small businesses, 360
  variable indentification, 363–364, 372
Cash forecasting methods
  developing receipts and disbursements,
    366–367
  model estimation, 371
  model validation, 371
  modified accrual, 367–369
  pro forma balance sheet, 369–370
  projected balance sheet, 370
  receipts and disbursements, 364–366
  template for receipts and disbursements, 365
Cash forecasts, 355–356. *See also* Cash forecasting
  expenditure on, 361
  external *vs.* internal, 361
  of monthly cash flows, 357–371
  monthly objectives, 359–361
  number of, 361
  process of, 356–357
  quantitative *vs.* judgmental, 361–362
  type of, 361
Cash items, 248
Cash letter, 244
Cash level, 523
Cash management
  bank selection checklist, 273
  models, 521–528
  non-US services, 564
  practice assessment, 617
Cash Management Services (CMS) Survey, 613
Cash movements, Miller-Orr model, 524
Cash planning, US Air Force, 358–359
Cash position, 576
Cash receipts, 367
Cash transfers
  anticipation, 325
  daily targets, 324
  deferred availability, 325
  initiation of, 315–316
  linear programming model, 336–337
  minimum balance calculation, 318–319
  scheduling, 318–325
  scheduling decision, 320–325
  timing, 325
  tools, 314–315
Causal techniques, 385
CCM. *See* Certified Cash Management
CDs. *See* Certificates of deposit
Centralized disbursing, 317
Centralized processing systems, 292–293
Centralized transfer initiation, 316
Certificates of deposit (CDs), 448, 453
Certified Cash Management (CCM), 114
CFROI. *See* Cash flow return-on-investment
Character, 13, 130

CHECCS. *See* Clearing House Electronic Check Clearing
  System
Check clearing
  mechanics, 240–242
  non-US, 563
  steps in, 240
Check imaging, 332
Checks, 248–249, 322
  clearing mechanisms for, 242–244
  local items, 243
  transit items, 243–244
Chicago Mercantile Exchange (CME), 573
CHIPS. *See* Clearing House Interbank Payment
  System
Chrysler, 17
CIT Group, 540
Citicorp, 450
Clearing float, 245–246
Clearing House Electronic Check Clearing System
  (CHECCS)
Clearing House Interbank Payment System (CHIPS),
  247, 260
Clearing mechanisms, for checks, 242–244
CME. *See* Chicago Mercantile Exchange
CMS. *See* Cash Management Services
Coefficient of determination, 381
Coefficient of variation, 511
COGS. *See* Cost of goods sold
Collateral, 13, 130
Collected balance, 248
Collecting bank, 241
Collection, 153–154
  efficiency, 189
  effort, 191–193
  float, 4, 14, 245, 290
  model, 300
  modifying, 197–198
  monitoring, 183–190
  practices, 192–193
  procedures, 129, 191–193
  systems, 291–296
Commercial paper (CP), 448, 457, 537–539
  bank credit and, 539
  effective cost of, 543–545
  interest-bearing, 538
  rating criteria, 486–487
Commitment fee, 536
Committed line of credit, 536
Company processing centers, 292–293
Compensating balances, 535
  calculating, 270–271
Complete enumeration model, 298–300
Compound interest, 57–58
Comprehensive payables, 330
Concentration bank, 313

Concentration system
  benefits, 317
  costs, 316
Conditions, 13, 130
Conservative financing strategy, 534
Consignment, 212
Contracting cost motive, 121
Control dilemma, 323
Controlled disbursement account, 324
Control limits, 524
Corporate instruments, 456–461
Corporate trade exchange (CTX), 328
Cost analysis
  of company processing centers, 293
  of lockbox collection systems, 294–295
Cost benefit report, 342
Cost dilemma, 323
Cost of goods sold (COGS), 10
Cost results, 303
Costs
  ACH check payment, 313
  administrative, 316
  commercial paper, 543–545
  concentration system, 316
  credit line, 550–552
  EBDI, 608
  fixed, 60
  float, 291
  inventory, 94–95
  lockbox, 294–295, 302
  ordering, 95
  transfer, 316
  variable, 60
  weighted capital, 67–68
Counterparties, 587
Country risk, 333
County Seat, Inc. (CSI), 162–168
  credit agreement, 165–168
Coupon-equivalent yields, 473–474
CP. See Commercial paper
Credit
  administration, 123
  activity, 128
  cash flow timeline, 178
  conditions, 131
  decision making, 123
  department, 193–196
  extension, 125–129, 150
  five Cs of, 130
  function, 123–127
  granting, 123–125, 129–130
  information, 122, 138–139
  information technology and, 123
  in-house cards, 128

  interchange bureaus, 138
  internet role in, 535
  legislation on, 193
  limits, 129, 149–150
  period, 150, 179–180
  regulation of, 193
  reporting agencies, 131
  sales, 176
  scoring models, 122, 140–146
Credit analysis, 138–141
  key financial ratios, 142–145
Credit lines, 533
  effective cost of, 550–552
  structure, 536
Credit management, 113
  benchmarks, 194
  integration of, 196
  international, 196–198
Credit Manual of Commercial Laws, 193
Credit policy, 123, 172–182
  analysis, 197
  components of, 129
  decision variables, 172–173
  establishing, 127–153
  evaluation model, 173–175
  new and existing customers, 177
Credit standards, 129–130, 138–141
  loosening, 177–179
Credit terms, 129, 150–153
  accounts receivables and, 225–226
  change in, 50
  factors affecting, 150
Cross hedge, 576
Crown Corporation, 230
CSI, Inc. See County Seat, Inc.
CTX. See Corporate trade exchange
Currency
  blocs, 557
  futures hedge, 580–581
  swap, 587, 591
Current assets, 533
Current liquidity index, 36
Current maturity, 449
Current ration, 25–26
Custody account, 502
Customers
  characteristics of, 13
  groups of, 297

D
Daily collection
  NPV and, 231–232
  perpetual stream of, 231–232
Daily interest rate, 57

Daily transfer rule, 321–324
Data collection, 114–115
Data Resources, Inc. (DRI), 361
Daylight overdrafts, 272–273
Days inventory held (DIH), 33, 104
Days of payables outstanding (DPO), 33–34, 220
Days sales outstanding (DSO), 33–34, 183–184, 608
    bias in, 187
D&B. *See* Dun & Bradstreet
Debit cards transactions, 257–258
Decentralized disbursing, 317
Decentralized processing systems, 292
Decentralized transfer initiation, 316
Decomposition method, 206
Deli-bucks, 86–87
Dell Computer, 13, 23
    annual balance sheet, 24
    annual income statement, 25
    annual statements of cash flow, 31
Demand deposits
    accounts, 248
    interest on, 563
Demand flow, 14
Denominations, 504
Department of Defence, Financial Management
    Regulation, 359
Depository Institution Deregulation and Monetary Control
    Act (1980), 233
Depository transfer checks (DTCs), 250, 314–315, 334
Deposits
    deferred availability, 325
    structure worksheet, 322
Derivatives, 587
Deterministic model, 424
Digital marketplaces, 615
DigiView, 61
DIH. *See* Days inventory held
Dillard's, 103
Direct hedge, 576
Disbursement banks
    locations of, 337–342
    profile, 343
    selecting, 337–342
Disbursement float, 4, 245
    cash flow timeline and, 315–316
    components of, 315
Disbursements
    cash flow timeline for, 213
    decentralization *vs.* centralization of, 317–318
    distribution method for, 373–374
    ethical practices, 316
    forecasting model, 375–376
    functional areas influences, 318
    funding, 322–323, 342

    global strategies, 332–335
    legal practices, 316
    optimal mechanisms, 335–337
    policy, 314–315
Disbursement services
    collection services and, 324
    information services and, 324
Disbursement systems, 321–332
    company characteristics, 323
    complex, 323–330
    optimizing, 335–342
    simple, 321–323
    trends, 330–332
Disbursing locations, 338
Disbursing risks, international, 333
Discount basis, 538
Discount rate, 67–71
    CAPM-based, 82–83
    market efficiency and, 82
    project life, 67–68, 70
    risk-adjusted, 70
    selection, 67
Discount yield, 471
Distribution methods, 373–376
    for collections, 374–375
Dividend capture
    strategy, 514
    yield on, 470–471
Dividend roll, 514
Dollar-day float, 291
Double-counting, 272
DPO. *See* Days payables outstanding
Drafts, 249–250, 322
Drawee bank, 241
DRI. *See* Data Resources, Inc.
Driving variable, 427
DSO. *See* Days sales outstanding
DTCs. *See* Depository transfer checks
Dual balances, 317
Duke model, 300
Dummy variables, 392
Dun & Bradstreet (D&B), 131
    public filings, 135–136
    rating key, 137
    sample, 132–136

E
Earnings credit rate (ECR), 319
EBDI. *See* Electronic business data interchange
EBS. *See* Evaluated receipt settlement
E-cash transactions, 219
ECCHO. *See* Electronic Check Clearing House
    Organization
e-Commerce, 613–615

Economic exposure, 559
Economic order quantity (EOQ), 95–97
  model extensions, 97–99
Economic value added (EVA), 55–56, 114
  framework, 49
  metrics, 122
Economies of scale, 317
ECR. *See* Earnings credit rate
EDI. *See* Electronic data interchange
EDS. *See* Electronic Data Systems
EDT. *See* Electronic depository transfer
EDTs. *See* Electronic depository transfer checks
EEC. *See* European Economic Community
Effective annual rate, 57
Effective interest rate, 543
E.F. Hutton, 326–327
EFM. *See* Export Finance Matchmaker
EFT. *See* Electronic funds transfer
EFTPS. *See* Federal Tax Payment System
EI. *See* Ending inventory
Electronic-based payments, 250–258
Electronic business data interchange (EBDI)
  benefits and costs, 608
  current system, 607–608
Electronic Check Clearing House Organization (ECCHO), 316
Electronic check presentment, 250, 316
Electronic commerce, 15, 122–123
Electronic corporate trade payments, 296
Electronic data interchange (EDI), 193, 296, 605
  benefits, 607, 612
  collections and, 153–154
  communication formats, 610–611
  financial, 329–330, 608–609
  funds transfer, 609–610
  information flow, 607–608
  problems, 612
  receivables and, 153–154
  survey of, 615–616
Electronic Data Systems (EDS), 445
Electronic depository transfer checks (EDTs), 253
Electronic depository transfers (EDT), 250, 315, 335
Electronic disbursing mechanisms, 326–329
Electronic funds transfer (EFT), 153, 607, 609–610
Electronic lockbox, 296
Electronic marketplaces, 219
Electronic payments, 229–230
Electronic presentment, 246
EMS. *See* European Monetary System
Ending inventory (EI), 10
Enduring projects, 68–69
Enterprise resources planning (ERP), 108, 121
EOQ. *See* Economic order quantity
e-Procurement, 614

Ernst & Young, 613
ERP. *See* Enterprise resource planning
Error distribution, 382
Ethical standards
  conduct, 327
  tiers of, 218
Ethics
  disbursement practices and, 316
  payment decision and, 218–219
  policies and, 317
eToys, 355
Eurodollar CD, 453
European Economic Community (EEC), 557
European Monetary System (EMS), 557
EVA. *See* Economic value added
Evaluated receipt settlement (EBS), 329
Event risk, 482
Exchange debentures, 165, 169
Exchange rates
  currencies quotes, 556
  factors affecting, 558–559
  fixed *vs.* floating, 556–557
Expert systems, 146–147
Expiration date, 577
Exponential smoothing, 389, 390
Export Finance Matchmaker (EFM), 535
eXtensible Markup Language (XML), 611

F
Factoring, 540
Factors, 128
FASB. *See* Financial Accounting Standards Board
FDIC. *See* Federal Deposit Insurance Corporation
Fed. *See* Federal reserve
Federal Deposit Insurance Corporation (FDIC), 235, 453
Federal government instruments, 461–464
Federal Reserve District/American Banker's Association (FRD/ABA), 242
Federal Reserve System (Fed), 232
  Board of Governors, 239
  district boundaries, 238
  organization of, 237–239
  payment system involvement, 239–240
  Regulation CC, 244
  Regulation Q, 233–234
  role of, 450
Federal Tax Payment System (EFTPS), 327
Fed float, 246
FEDI. *See* Financial EDI
Fedwire, 240, 251
Fees, 543
  vs. balances, 271–272
Field warehouse, 541

Financial Accounting Standards Board (FASB), 560
    Statement 95, 31
Financial condition analysis, 167–169
Financial decision making, 50–53
Financial EDI (FEDI), 329, 607, 608–609
Financial Executives Research Foundation, 198
Financial flexibility, 23, 38–40
Financial institutions
    geographic restrictions on, 234–235
    product differences among, 232–234
    safety considerations, 235–237
Financial management practices, 183
Financial model, 427
Financial motive, 120
Financial plan, 435–436
Financial planning model, 428, 433–435
Financial restructuring, 482
Financial risk, 497
    managing, 571
Financial Services Modernization Act (1999), 234
Financial statement approach
    assessment, 53
    project issues, 50–52
Financial strength, 171–172
Financial swap, 587
Financing, 168–169
    short-term, 531
    spontaneous sources, 212
Financing activities, 31
Financing alternatives, 534–542
Financing rates, short-term, 542
Financing sources, 538
Financing strategies, 532–534
Financing system trends, 275–277
First differencing, 390
First National Bank of Panhandle (Texas), 236
Fitch Investors Service, 38
Fixed costs, 60
Fixed-for-floating rate swap, 587–588
Fletcher Company, 113–115
Float
    components, 245–246
    cost calculation, 291
    existence, 230
    increases, 340–341
    system, 303
    value, 230–232
Floating lien, 541
Floating-rate notes, 457–460
Ford Motor, 17, 128
Forecasting
    bias, 380–384
    percent-of-sales model, 425–426
    statistical tools, 385–393

Foreign currency
    futures options, 586
    option hedge evaluation, 584–585
    swap, 591–592
Foreign exchange
    exposure, 559–563
    options, 584–585
    rate, 556
    risk, 333
Forward contract, 557
Forward rates, 475, 557–558
Forward value date, 563
Francine's Attic, 423, 432
Franklin Qualified Dividend Fund, 467–468
FRD/ABA. *See* Federal Reserve District/American
    Banker's Association
Full reconciliation, 321
Funding uncertainty, 323
Futures
    instrument, 576–577
    options, 582–583, 585
    position, 576
    rates, 558
    transactions of, 583
Futures contracts, 558, 572–576
    foreign currency, 574
    interest rates, 575
    number of, 577–578, 583–584

G
Gap, 107
Garn-St. Germain Depository Institutions Act
    (1982), 234
GE Capital, 457, 540
General Electric, 13, 107
General Motors, 93, 128, 611
General Motors Acceptance Corporation (GMAC), 450,
    538
General Motors-Europe
    current situation, 621–622
    development of, 620
    foreign currency, 622
General obligation securities, 464
Gillette, 93
Giro acceptance, 259
Giro system, 258, 562
GMAC. *See* General Motors Acceptance Corporation
GNMA. *See* Government National Mortgage
    Association
Gold Star Laundry, 334–335
Government National Mortgage Association
    (GNMA), 573
Government warrant, 250
Gramm-Leach-Bliley, 234

H

Handling costs, 95
Harker Telecommunications, 339–340
Harley Davidson, 107
Hedger, 572
Hedges
buy *vs.* sell, 576
foreign currency option, 584–585
interest rate option, 584
problems of, 581
regulatory issues, 595–596
type of, 583
Hedging, 562–563
futures, 572–581
instruments, 593–595
with options, 581–586
vs. speculating, 572
strategies using foreign exchange, 592
High-dividend-yield stock, 460–461
High-liquidity strategy, 499
Historical yield spread analysis, 512
Holdover float, 246
House/on-us checks, 242
Hughes Aircraft, 443

I

IBBEA. *See* Interstate Banking and Branching
Efficiency Act
IBF. *See* International banking facilities
Idle balances, 316
Imaging, 275–276
access, 614
Imax Corporation, 171
Income statement
accrual-based, 8–9
annual, 25
cash flow statement and, 11–12
year-end, 157–158
Incremental profits, *vs.* NPV, 173–182
Information flows, 606–607
Information gathering, 127, 128–138
Information needs, 606
Information reporting, 612
Information services, 276
Information systems
accounts payable and, 219
auditing, 615–619
Instruments, 504
agency, 462–464
bank, 456–461
corporation, 456–461
Federal, 461–464
liquidity ratings, 488
local, 464–465

mixed, 464–466
money market, 452–469
state, 464–465
transfer, 316
Integer programming data matrix, 310
problem in, 311
Interest-bearing commercial paper, 538
Interest rates
asset swap, 589–590
bank deposit, 503
caps, 593–594
collars, 594–595
daily, 57
effective, 543
floor, 594
futures, 575
hedge, 578–580, 584
liability swap, 590
money market, 450–451
option hedge, 584
parity hypothesis, 558
portfolio, 507–508
risk structure of, 480–483
short-term, 450–451
swaps, 587–588
term structure of, 475–481
International banking facilities (IBF), 277
International funds transfer, 563–564
International intracorporate payments, 333–335
International Monetary Market, 573–574
International payment systems, 258–260
electronic, 259–260
paper-based payments, 258–259
recommendations, 334
International Trade Administration (ITA), 535
Internet, 613
banking, 276
future role, 615
invoicing and payment, 614–615
Interstate banking, 236
Interstate Banking and Branching Efficiency Act
(IBBEA), 235
Inventory, 15
balance, 94–100, 103–105
cash flow timeline, 100–103
concept, 92–93
control systems, 103
cost, 94–95
financing, 541–542
forecasted *vs.* actual, 387
investment, 105–109
managing, 14, 94–95, 100–103
payables and, 225
purchases and, 225

receivables and, 80
sales and, 386
simple regression of, 387
turnover, 104
Investments
activities, 31
decision-making process, 501–506
maturity of, 448
short-term, 496–498, 511–516
Invoice price, discounted, 216
Issuers, 504
ITA. *See* International Trade Administration

J
Jamaica Agreement (1976), 557
JIT. *See* Just-in-time
Jones Salvage and Recycling, 439, 549
accounts payable, 568
accounts receivable, 567
inventory, 567–568
proposed plan, 568
Just for Feet, 46–47
Just-in-time (JIT), 14, 106–107, 615

K
KBALB. *See* Kimball International
Kimball International (KBALB), 204–205
K-Mart, 151
Kodak, 196

L
Lagged regression analysis, 207
Lagging, 560–561
Lambda, 37–38
Leading, 560–561
Leading Edge, 117
Ledger balance, 248
Lending services trends, 542
Letter of credit (LOC), 537
LIBOR. *See* London Interbank Offer Rate
Linear programming (LP), 308–309
cash transfer model, 336–337
Line of credit, 535
Liquidity, 23, 29–30, 168–169
index, 37
level of, 36–38
measures, 32–36
preference hypothesis, 478
risk, 453, 488–489
Liz Claiborne, Inc., 151
Loan(s)
asset-based, 540–542
participations, 455–456
LOC. *See* Letter of credit

Local instruments, 464–465
Lockbox
bank selection, 301
collection systems. *See* Lockbox collection systems
cost analysis, 294–295
electronic, 296
retail systems, 294
wholesale, 294
Lockbox collection systems, 294–295
consortium, 301
cost analysis of, 294–295
location study, 296–298
model, 298–300
monthly costs, 302
study, 301–303
types of, 293–294
value data transmission enhancement, 296
London Interbank Offer Rate (LIBOR), 455
Long-term CDs, 485
Low-liquidity strategy, 499
LP. *See* Linear programming
Lube-Rite, 91, 102

M
Macy's, 211
MAE. *See* Mean absolute error
Magnetic ink character recognition (MICR), 127, 241, 316
Mail
float, 231, 245, 290
sites, 339
times, 297–298
Maintenance margin, 573
Management
cash, 273, 521–528, 564, 617
CCM, 114
credit, 113, 194–198
financial practices, 183
portfolio, 502–507
relationship, 265–266
supply chain, 92, 108
Manufacturing resource planning (MRP II), 108
Margin, 558
account, 572–573
Marked-to-market, 572
Market efficiency, 82
Market mechanics, 451–452
Markets
primary, 448–449
retail, 449–450
secondary, 448–449
wholesale, 449–450
Market segmentation hypothesis, 479
Markov chain analysis, 206
Materials Requirement Planning (MRP), 108, 196

Maturities, 504
  extension swap, 515
Maximize shareholder value, 49
McFadden Act (1927), 235
Mean absolute error (MAE), 380, 389
Mean square error (MSE), 381
Merrill Lynch, 457
MICR. *See* Magnetic ink character recognition
Miller-Orr model, 523–526
Mixed instruments, 464–466
MMDA. *See* Money market, deposit accounts
Modeling, 423
  process, 424–425
Models
  logic, 428–431
  types, 424
  understanding, 431–435
  variables, 433–434
Moderate financing strategy, 534
Moderate-liquidity strategy, 499
Modified buy-and-hold strategy, 512
Money market. *See also* individual instruments, i.e.,
  Agency instruments; Bank instruments;
  Corporate instruments, etc.
  calculations, 469–474
  deposit accounts (MMDA), 233–234
  instruments, 452–469
  interest rates, 450–451
  intermediaries, 451–452
  mutual funds, 467
  nature, 448–452
  trust, 452
Money rates, comparative table, 459
Monitoring, modifying, 197–198
Moving average, 388
MRP. *See* Material requirements planning
MRP I. *See* Materials requirements systems
MRP II. *See* Manufacturing resource planning
MSE. *See* Mean square error
Mulitple-drawee checks, 323
Multicollinearity, 388
Multilateral netting systems, 333, 561
Multiple processing centers, 301
Multiple regression, 385
Multiyear projects, 69
Municipal securities, 470

N
NACHA. *See* National Automated Clearing House
  Association
NACM. *See* National Association of Credit Management
National Association of Corporate Cash Managers, 327
National Association of Credit Management (NACM),
  138, 193

National Association of Credit Managers, 117–118
National Automated Clearing House Association
  (NACHA), 611
Nearby contract, 577
Needed external funds (NEF), 425–426
NEF. *See* Needed external funds
Negotiated order of withdrawal (NOW), 233
Net interest income, 437–438
Net liquid balance (NLB), 27–28
Net present value (NPV), 49, 53, 172
  analysis difficulties, 54
  calculations, 56–67
  credit policy and, 173–176
  daily, 64
  daily collection, 231–232
  decision making, 66
  extended analysis, 62–65
  vs. incremental profits, 172–182
  investment rate and, 216–217
  model, 61–68, 178, 214–215
  payment decision, 214–215
  valuation, 60–65
Netting, 561–562
  multilateral, 561
Net working capital (NWC), 26–29
New York Cash Exchange (NYCE), 258
NLB. *See* Net liquid balance
Nonbank banks, 234
Notional amount, 587
NOW. *See* Negotiated order of withdrawal
NPV. *See* Net present value
NWC. *See* Net working capital
NYCE. *See* New York Cash Exchange

O
ODFI. *See* Originating depository financial institution
Omitted variables, 388
One-shot projects, 68–69
On-us, 242
OPEC. *See* Organization of Petroleum Exporting
  Countries
Open account, 212
Operating activities, 31, 168–169
Operating cycle, 35
Operating motive, 120–121
Operational restructuring, 482
Operations, 112
  results, 167–168
Optimal cash discount, 152
Optimization models, 527–528
Options
  contracts, 581–583
  hedging with, 581–586
  number of contracts, 583–584

Ordering costs, 95
Order quantity level, optimal, 95–96
Organizational policies, ethics and, 317
Organizational structure, 319
Organization of Petroleum Exporting Countries
(OPEC), 557
Original maturity, 449
Originating ACH, 327
Originating depository financial institution (ODFI), 254
Out-of-pocket expenses, 543
Outsourcing, 330

P
Paid-only reconciliation, 321
Paper-based payments, 246–250
Passive investment strategy, 511
Payables, 113–114
  and inventory purchase, 225
  managing, 14
Payables turnover ration, 220
Payable through draft (PTD), 249
PAYDEX, 131
Payment decision
  ethics and, 218–219
  model principles, 214
  structuring, 349
Payment mechanisms, 321–322
  paper-based, 323
Payments
  ACH trends, 327–330
  electronic-based, 250–258
  formats, 328
  index, 190
  paper-based, 246–250
  US growth types, 247
Payment systems, 316–317
  differences in, 332–333
  international, 258–260, 334
  US, 232–244
Payor identification, 127
PCs. See Personal computers
Penn Central Transportation Company, 537
PeopleSoft, 109
Percent of sales, 385
Permanent current assets, 533
Personal computers (PCs), 117
Phoenix-Hecht Bank, 343
Pledging of receivables, 540
Plus purchases (PUR), 10
Point-of-sale (POS), direct-debit, 258
Portfolio
  assembling, 506–516
  GNP and, 507
  industry-specific events, 507

interest rate trends, 507–508
management, 502–507
manager, 502–503
performance, 503–504
rate of return, 504
risk estimate uncertainty, 509
risk factors, 508
risk-return factors, 508–509
risk-return tradeoff, 509–511
risk type interrelationships, 508–509
short-term investment strategies, 511–516
strategy, 515–516
POS. See Point-of-sale
Positive float, 213
Positive pay, 331
Preauthorized draft, 250
Preauthorized payments, 295
Precautionary motive, 93
Present-value analysis, 53
Pricing motive, 121
Probability values, 37
Processing float, 245, 290
  eliminating, 299
Proctor & Gamble, 108
Profit, 3, 7–13
Proportion clearing, 374
Prox, 212
PTD. See Payable through draft
PUR. See Plus purchases
Purchase
  cards, 331
  order with payment voucher attached, 323
  terms of, 212–213
Put option, 581

Q
Quaker Oats, 13
Quantity discounts, 99
Quick ratio, 26

R
Range reconciliation, 321
Rapid Deposit, 229
Ratings, 487–488
Ratio
  acid-test, 26
  credit analysis, 142–147
  quick, 26
  WCR:S, 29
RAYCO, 330
RDFI. See Receiving depository financial institutions
Receivables, 15–16, 153–154
  as factors, 128
  financing, 540–541

Receivables—cont'd
  inventory and, 80
  investment, 177, 194–196
  managing, 13
  monitoring, 183–188, 206–208
  pledging, 540
  with and without recourse, 540
Receiving ACH, 327
Receiving depository financial institutions
    (RDFI), 254
Recursive least squares (RLS) regression model, 208
Regional Treasury Center (RTC), GM Europe, 621–622
Regression, 385–388
  causal model, 385
  sum-of-squares (RSS), 381
Reinvestment rate risk, 481
Re-invoicing, 562
Relationship approach, 265
Relationship logic, 428–431
Relationship management, 265–266
Remittance, 297
  advice, 127
  data, 302
Repos, 468–469
Repurchase agreements (RPs), 448, 468–469
Retail lockbox systems, 294
Retail spending, 247
Retroactive to opening of business, 272
Return items, 249
Revenue securities, 464
Reverse positive pay, 331
Reverse repurchase agreement, 537
Riding yield curve, 513–514
Risk, 69, 504
  adjusted discount rates, 70–71
  analysis, 147–149, 475–489
  class adjustment, 70–71
  classes, 71
  projects without, 69
  return assessment, 483–489
  spread, 475
  yields, 475–489
RLS. See Recursive least squares regression model
RMSE. See Root mean square error
Root mean square error (RMSE), 381
RPs. See Repurchase agreements
RSS. See Regression, sum-of-squares

S
Safety
  ratings, 484–487
  stock, 98–99
Sales, inventories and, 386
Same-Day Settlement (SDS), 316

SAP, 109
SDS. See Same-Day Settlement
Sears, 151, 313
Seasonal dating, 212
SEC. See Securities and Exchange Commission
Secondary market, 449
Securities and Exchange Commission (SEC), 457, 538
Securitization, 542
Securitized assets, 456
Sell hedge, 576
Selling, general, and administrative expenses
    (SG&A), 168
Senior subordinated notes, 165
Sensitivity analysis, 370
Serial correlation, 388
Service providers, nonbank, 274
SG&A. See Selling, general, and administrative
    expenses
Shane, Michael, 115
Shareholder value, 118–123
  receivable management influence, 119
Shearson Lehman Hutton, 457
Short-term financing, 543–545
Short-term investments, 16–17
Sight drafts, 249
Simple interest, 56–57
  justification for, 58
Simple regression, 385
Simulation, 371
Smyth Appliance, Inc., 225–226
Society for Worldwide Interbank Financial
    Telecommunications (SWIFT), 260
Solvency, 23
S&P. See Standard & Poor
Speculating, vs. hedging, 572
Speculative motive, 93
Speculator, 572
Spot rates, 477, 557
Standard & Poor (S&P), 138
  CD rating categories, 485
  Industrial Index, 71
  rating criteria, 486–487
  Stock Record, 83
State instruments, 464–465
Statistical decomposition, 392
  seasonal indices for, 391
Stochastic model, 424
Stone model, 526–528
Strategies
  active, 511–515
  aggressive, 533–534
  buy-and-hold, 512
  conservative, 534
  dividend capture, 514

liquidity, 499
  moderate, 534
  passive, 511–512
  portfolio, 515–516
  trading, 514
Striking price, 581
Substantial cash infusion, 355
SuperNOW accounts, 234
Supply chain management, 92, 108
Sustainable growth
  parameters, 39
  rate, 38
Swaps
  currency, 587, 591
  hedging with, 587–593
  strategies, 515
Sweep accounts, 469
SWIFT. *See* Society for Worldwide Interbank Financial
    Telecommunications
Systematic risk, 498
System float, 303

T
Taxable-equivalent yield, 464
Tax-advantaged securities, 469–47169
Tax-exempt CP, 464
Tax status, 451
TCN. *See* Total cash needs
Temporary current assets, 533
Terminal warehouse agreement, 542
Term spread, 475
Term structure
  of interest rates, 475
  theories, 476–480
Time
  deposits, 455
  drafts, 249
Time-series
  methods, 388–393
  regression, 390
  techniques, 385
Total cash needs (TCN), 522
Total sum-of-squares (TSS), 381
Toyota, 447
Toys "R" Us, 106
Toy World, 440–442
Trade associations, 138
Trade credit, 15–16, 118–123
  motives for, 120–121
  trends and, 121–123
  vs. bank credit, 119–120
Trading strategy, 514
Transactions
  approach to, 265

exposure to, 559–560
  initiation of, 614
  motive in, 93
Transfer
  clearing delay worksheet, 323–324
  costs, 316
  instrument service charges, 316
Transit
  items, 243–244
  routing number, 242
Translation exposure, 560
Treasury, 114–115
  auction, 472–473
  bills, 448, 450, 484
  information systems, 320
  management workstation, 617–619
  yield spreads instrument, 512
Treasury Management Association, 236
Tri-Teck Products, 313
Trust receipt loan, 541
TSS. *See* Total sum-of-squares

U
UCL. *See* Upper control limit
Unbiased expectations hypothesis, 477
Uncollected balance percentages, 188–189
Uncommitted line of credit, 536
UN/EDIFACT. *See* United Nations EDI for
    Administration, Commerce, and Transportation
Unique zip code, 294
United Nations EDI for Administration, Commerce, and
    Transportation (UN/EDIFACT), 610
Upper control limit (UCL), 524
Usable funds, 543
Usage rate, 96
U.S. Treasury, 450
  auction schedule, 462
  securities, 461–462

V
Valuation, 49, 65–66
  approach, 53–54
  assessment, 54
  compound interest, 57–58
  simple interest, 56–57
  theory, short-term financial decisions and, 80–81
Value
  creation, 51
  dating, 259
  Line, 83
Variable costs, 60
  to sales (VCR), 174–175
Variance analysis model, 206
VCR. *See* Variable costs, to sales

W

Wall Street Journal, The, 562, 573–574
Wal-Mart, 107, 108, 151, 234
WCR. *See* Working capital requirements
WCR:S. *See* Working capital requirements, to sales (S) ratio
Wealth maximization, 152–153
WEFA. *See* Wharton Exonometrics
Weighted average cost of capital, 67–68
Wharton Exonometrics (WEFA), 361
Wholesale lockbox system, 294
Willingness to pay, 140
Wire transfers, 315
    advantages and disadvantages, 252
    mechanics of, 251–253
    uses, 251
Wonder Burger, 331
Working capital, 15–17
Working capital requirements (WCR), 27–29
    to sales (S) ratio (WCR:S), 29

X

Xerox, 107
XML. *See* eXtensible Markup Language

Y

Y. Guess jeans, 162–169
Yield curves, 475–476

shifts upward, 480–481
stable, 480
tilts upward, 480–481
Yields, 504
    annual effective, 474
    coupon-equivalent, 473–474
    curves. *See* Yield curves
    discount, 471
    dividend capture, 470–471
    high, 460–461
    historical, 512
    riding curve, 513–514
    risk analysis and, 475–489
    spreads. *See* Yield spreads
    taxable-equivalent, 464
    treasury instrument, 512
Yield spreads, 511
    analysis of, 483–484
    instrument *vs.* T-bills, 512
    large CDs, 484
    swap, 515
    Treasury bills, 484

Z

ZBA. *See* Zero balance account
Zero balance account (ZBA), 325
Zero net working capital, 122